How to Use the Maps in *The Western Perspective,* Second Edition

Here are some basic map concepts that will help you get the most out of the maps in this textbook.

- Always look at the scale, which allows you to determine the distance in miles or kilometers between locations on the map.
- Examine the legend carefully. It explains the colors and symbols used on the map.
- Note the locations of mountains, rivers, oceans, and other geographic features, and consider how these would affect such human activities as agriculture, commerce, travel, and warfare.
- Read the map caption thoroughly. It provides important information sometimes not covered in the text itself.
- Look for the Web icon next to several of the map captions. This indicates that a similar interactive map is available on this book's Web site at http://info.wadsworth.com/053461065X.

D1511779

The Western Perspective

A History of Civilization in the West

Volume I: Prehistory to the Enlightenment

SECOND EDITION

PHILIP V. CANNISTRARO
Queens College, The City University of New York

JOHN J. REICH
Syracuse University in Florence, Italy

THE WESTERN PERSPECTIVE

A History of Civilization in the West
Volume I: Prehistory to the Enlightenment

SECOND EDITION

THOMSON
WADSWORTH

Australia • Canada • Mexico • Singapore • Spain
United Kingdom • United States

THOMSON

✦ ™

WADSWORTH

Publisher: Clark Baxter
Senior Development Editor: Sue Gleason
Assistant Editor: Stephanie Sandoval
Editorial Assistant: Eno Sarris
Technology Project Manager: Jennifer Ellis
Executive Marketing Manager: Caroline Croley
Marketing Assistant: Mary Ho
Advertising Project Manager: Tami Strang
Project Manager, Editorial Production: Jennie Redwitz
Print/Media Buyer: Barbara Britton
Permissions Editor: Sue Howard
Production Service: Carol O'Connell, Graphic World
    Publishing Services

Text Designer: Garry Harman
Photo Researcher: Sue Howard
Cover Designer: Lisa Devenish
Cover Image: Dioscurides of Samos (1st BCE). "Musicians,
    Street Scene." Mosaic from "Cicero's Villa," Pompeii, 1st
    CE. Museo Archeologico Nazionale, Naples, Italy.
    Copyright Scala/Art Resource, NY.
Compositor: Graphic World, Inc.
Text and Cover Printer: Transcontinental Printing/
    Interglobe

COPYRIGHT © 2004 Wadsworth, a division of Thomson
Learning, Inc. Thomson Learning™ is a trademark used
herein under license.

ALL RIGHTS RESERVED. No part of this work covered
by the copyright hereon may be reproduced or used in any
form or by any means—graphic, electronic, or mechanical,
including but not limited to photocopying, recording, tap-
ing, Web distribution, information networks, or information storage and retrieval systems—without the written permission of the publisher.

Printed in Canada
1 2 3 4 5 6 7 07 06 05 04 03

For more information about our products, contact us at:
Thomson Learning Academic Resource Center
1-800-423-0563
For permission to use material from this text, contact us by:
Phone: 1-800-730-2214
Fax: 1-800-730-2215
Web: http://www.thomsonrights.com

ExamView® and ExamView Pro® are registered trademarks
of FSCreations, Inc. Windows is a registered trademark of
the Microsoft Corporation used herein under license.
Macintosh and Power Macintosh are registered trademarks
of Apple Computer, Inc. Used herein under license.

Library of Congress Control Number: 2003107113

ISBN 0-534-61066-8

Wadsworth/Thomson Learning
10 Davis Drive
Belmont, CA 94002-3098
USA

Asia
Thomson Learning
5 Shenton Way #01-01
UIC Building
Singapore 068808

Australia/New Zealand
Thomson Learning
102 Dodds Street
Southbank, Victoria 3006
Australia

Canada
Nelson
1120 Birchmount Road
Toronto, Ontario M1K 5G4
Canada

Europe/Middle East/Africa
Thomson Learning
High Holborn House
50/51 Bedford Row
London WC1R 4LR
United Kingdom

Latin America
Thomson Learning
Seneca, 53
Colonia Polanco
11560 Mexico D.F.
Mexico

Spain/Portugal
Paraninfo
Calle/Magallanes, 25
28015 Madrid, Spain

DEDICATED TO

Our Students

PHILIP V. CANNISTRARO

Born in New York City, Philip V. Cannistraro is an authority on modern Italian history and the Italian-American experience. He studied in both the undergraduate and graduate programs at New York University and is now Distinguished Professor at Queens College and at the Graduate School, the City University of New York. Professor Cannistraro serves on the boards of several journals and is editor of *The Italian American Review*. He has written or edited a number of books, including *Civilization of the World* (with R. Greaves, R. Murphey, and R. Zaller, Third Edition, 1997), *La Fabbrica del Consenso: Fascismo e Mass Media* (1975), *Fascismo, Chiesa e Emigrazione* (with G. Rosoli, 1979), *Historical Dictionary of Fascist Italy* (1981), and *Il Duce's Other Woman*, a biography of Margherita Sarfatti (with B. Sullivan, 1993).

JOHN J. REICH

A native of England, John J. Reich was trained as a classical archaeologist and did both his undergraduate and graduate work at the University of Manchester. He is an authority on Minoan civilization, pre-Roman Italy, and music. Professor Reich is associated with the Syracuse University study program in Florence, Italy. Reich lectures frequently in Europe and the United States on history, art, and the humanities and is the author of many scholarly articles and several books, including *Italy Before Rome* (1979) and the widely acclaimed *Culture and Values* (with Lawrence S. Cunningham, Wadsworth, Fifth Edition, 2002). He lives in a medieval castle in the hilltop town of Panzano in Chianti, in Italy.

BRIEF CONTENTS

PART I THE ANCIENT WORLD 1
TOPIC 1 People before History 3
TOPIC 2 Mesopotamia and Its Cities 13
TOPIC 3 Egypt of the Pharaohs 23
TOPIC 4 Other Peoples in the Ancient Near East 33
TOPIC 5 Art and Belief in the Ancient World 42
TOPIC 6 The Structure and Economic Life of Ancient Society 53

PART II CLASSICAL ANTIQUITY 64
TOPIC 7 The Emergence of Greece: From Bronze to Iron 67
TOPIC 8 The Greeks in the Archaic Era 78
TOPIC 9 The Greek World in Conflict: The Peloponnesian War and Its Aftermath 88
TOPIC 10 The Classical Vision 97
TOPIC 11 The Life and Commerce of Classical Greece 110
TOPIC 12 Alexander and the Hellenistic Age 119
TOPIC 13 The Rise of Rome 128
TOPIC 14 Romans of the Republic 137
TOPIC 15 The Collapse of the Roman Republic 147
TOPIC 16 The Empire: From Augustus to Marcus Aurelius 157
TOPIC 17 Politics and the Arts: Roman Imperial Culture 168
TOPIC 18 Daily Life in the Roman World 177
TOPIC 19 Christianity and the Crisis of Empire 186

PART III MEDIEVAL EUROPE 198
TOPIC 20 Politics after Rome: The Germanic Kingdoms 201
TOPIC 21 Early Medieval Christianity 210
TOPIC 22 Byzantium: The Eastern Empire 219
TOPIC 23 Europe and Islam 230

TOPIC 24 The First Europe: The West in the Age of Charlemagne 239
TOPIC 25 The Social Order of Medieval Europe 252
TOPIC 26 The Feudal Monarchies 263
TOPIC 27 The Militant Church: Reform and the Papacy 273
TOPIC 28 Scholars, Troubadours, and Builders 287
TOPIC 29 Monarchy and Its Limits: Government in the High Middle Ages 295
TOPIC 30 Art and Ideas in the Gothic Age 305
TOPIC 31 The Fourteenth Century: Stress and Change in European Society 314
TOPIC 32 The Late Middle Ages 326

PART IV THE RENAISSANCE AND REFORMATION 336
TOPIC 33 The Age of the New Monarchs 339
TOPIC 34 Power and Culture in Renaissance Italy 348
TOPIC 35 The Visual Arts of the Italian Renaissance 357
TOPIC 36 Arts and Letters in Renaissance Europe 373
TOPIC 37 Upheaval and Transformation in Eastern Europe 382
TOPIC 38 The Era of Reconnaissance 392
TOPIC 39 The Reformation 405
TOPIC 40 The Social Worlds of the Renaissance and Reformation 415

PART V THE EARLY MODERN WORLD 426
TOPIC 41 Catholic Reform and the Counter-Reformation 429
TOPIC 42 Catholic Spain and the Struggle for Supremacy 438
TOPIC 43 Crown and Parliament in Tudor-Stuart England 446
TOPIC 44 Religious War and the Ascendancy of the French Monarchy 454

TOPIC 45   Patterns of Life in a Time of Upheaval   **465**

TOPIC 46   The European Economy and Overseas Empire   **477**

TOPIC 47   The Baroque Era   **486**

PART VI   THE OLD REGIME   **498**

TOPIC 48   The Scientific Revolution and Western Thought   **501**

TOPIC 49   Southern Europe: Spain, Italy, and the Mediterranean   **509**

TOPIC 50   Absolute Monarchy: Louis XIV and the Divine Right of Kings   **517**

TOPIC 51   England and the Rise of Constitutional Monarchy   **528**

TOPIC 52   Central Europe and the Shifting Balance of Power   **539**

TOPIC 53   The Baltic and Eastern Europe in Transition   **547**

TOPIC 54   The Culture of the Old Regime   **557**

TOPIC 55   Europe and the World Economy   **566**

TOPIC 56   The Global Conflict: Wars for Empire   **577**

TOPIC 57   European Society in the Eighteenth Century   **586**

TOPIC 58   The Age of Reason   **597**

Contents

PART 1   THE ANCIENT WORLD   1

TOPIC 1   PEOPLE BEFORE HISTORY   3
The Planet Earth: Life and the Environment   4
The First People   6
Europe in the Stone Age: Hunters and Artists   7
The Neolithic Revolution: Farming and Technology   8

TOPIC 2   MESOPOTAMIA AND ITS CITIES   13
The Tigris and Euphrates: Rivers and Civilization   14
The Sumerians and the Rise of Cities   15
The Akkadian Conquest and Its Aftermath   17
The Babylonians: The Rule of Law   19
The Assyrians and the Thirst for Empire   19

TOPIC 3   EGYPT OF THE PHARAOHS   23
The Nile and Its Valley   24
The Rise and Fall of the Old Kingdom   27
The Middle Kingdom: The Waning of Stability   27
Empire and Grandeur: The New Kingdom   28
Akhenaton and the Sun God: The Revolution that Failed   30
The Decline of Egypt   30

Across Cultures
Herodotus in Egypt   26

Public Figures and Private Lives
Hatshepsut and Thutmose III   29

TOPIC 4   OTHER PEOPLES IN THE ANCIENT NEAR EAST   33
The Kingdom of the Hittites: Iron, War, and Bureaucracy   34
The Phoenicians: Traders and Sailors   36
Persia: The Tolerant Empire   37
The Hebrews: The People of the Book   38

TOPIC 5   ART AND BELIEF IN THE ANCIENT WORLD   42
Gods, Priests, and Worshipers: Varieties of Religious Experience   43
Religion, Power, and the State   45
Ancient Artists and Their Worlds   46
Faith, Hope, and Despair in Ancient Literature   50

Perspectives from the Past
Aspects of the Divine in the Ancient World   48

TOPIC 6   THE STRUCTURE AND ECONOMIC LIFE OF ANCIENT SOCIETY   53
Class, Status, and Family   54
Women, Power, and Subjugation   54
The Agricultural Economy: Food Production and Consumption   57
Artisans and Traders: The Rise of Commerce   59
Slavery, Human Rights, and the Law   61

Historical Perspectives
The Status of Women in Ancient Mesopotamia   56

PART II CLASSICAL ANTIQUITY 64

TOPIC 7 THE EMERGENCE OF GREECE: FROM BRONZE TO IRON 67
Bronze Age Culture in the Aegean: The Minoans and Mycenaeans 68
The Greeks of the Early Iron Age: The Birth of the City-State 71
Gods, Goddesses, and the World of Homer 73
The Greeks Abroad: Colonies and Markets 74
Greek Ideas and Eastern Art 75

TOPIC 8 THE GREEKS IN THE ARCHAIC ERA 78
City-States in Transition: Aristocracy, Tyranny, and the People 79
Reform at Athens: The Democratic Experiment 80
The Spartan Alternative: Conservatism and the Military Ideal 82
The Persian Challenge and the Victory of the Greeks 83

TOPIC 9 THE GREEK WORLD IN CONFLICT: THE PELOPONNESIAN WAR AND ITS AFTERMATH 88
Pericles and the Primacy of Athens 89
The Greek World Divided: The Peloponnesian War 91
The Defeat of Athens and Its Consequences 93
Philip of Macedon and the End of Greek Independence 95

Public Figures and Private Lives
Aspasia and Pericles 90

Across Cultures
Lord Byron in Athens 100

TOPIC 10 THE CLASSICAL VISION 97
Fate and the Human Condition: The Theater at Athens 98
Perfection and Realism: Classical Painting and Sculpture 99
Architecture and the Triumph of Order 103
History and Philosophy: The Greek Mind 104

Perspectives from the Past
Classical Attitudes to Historical Methods 106

TOPIC 11 THE LIFE AND COMMERCE OF CLASSICAL GREECE 110
Land, Farming, and Food 111
Manufacturing and Trade in the Greek World 112
Sexuality and Family Life in Classical Athens 113
Priestesses, Wives, and Prostitutes: The Roles of Greek Women 116
Freedom and Slavery in Greek Society 117

Historical Perspectives
Marriage in Classical Athens 114

TOPIC 12 ALEXANDER AND THE HELLENISTIC AGE 119
Alexander the Great and His Empire 120
The Successor States: Challenge and Competition 120
Society and Economy in the Hellenistic World 122
Mystics, Stoics, and Epicureans: The Conflicts of Religion and Philosophy 123
The Nature of the Universe: Science, Medicine, and Technology 125

TOPIC 13 THE RISE OF ROME 128
The Etruscans and the Foundation of Rome 129
The Roman Republic: Class and the Politics of Compromise 131
Diplomacy and War: The Romanization of Italy 133
The Punic Wars 134
The Annexation of the Eastern Mediterranean 135

TOPIC 14 ROMANS OF THE REPUBLIC 137
The Trials of Provincial Administration 138
The Roman Economy: Land Tenure, Trade, and Class 139
Women and the Family in a Patriarchal Society 141
Religion and Philosophy: Greek Ideas in Roman Forms 143
The Literature of the Roman Republic 144

TOPIC 15 THE COLLAPSE OF THE ROMAN REPUBLIC 147
The Gracchus Brothers and the Failure of Reform 148
Politics and the Generals: The Struggle for Power 149
Pompey and Caesar: Rivalry and Civil War 151
The Dictatorship and Assassination of Julius Caesar 153
The Triumph of Octavian and the Death of the Republic 154

Public Figures and Private Lives
Antony and Fulvia 154

TOPIC 16 THE EMPIRE: FROM AUGUSTUS TO MARCUS AURELIUS 157
The Augustan Revolution: Appearance and Reality 158
Problems of Imperial Succession: The Julio-Claudians 162
The Army and the Emperors: Vespasian and His Sons 163
The Pax Romana and the "Five Good Emperors" 165

Perspectives from the Past
Political Propaganda in the Roman Empire 160

TOPIC 17 POLITICS AND THE ARTS: ROMAN IMPERIAL CULTURE 168
The World According to Augustus: The Golden Age of Art and Literature
History and Personality in Imperial Sculpture 171
Building the Empire: Architecture in Rome and the Provinces 171
Writers of the Silver Age: Rhetoric, Satire, and History 175

Across Cultures
Mark Twain in Pompeii 174

TOPIC 18 DAILY LIFE IN THE ROMAN WORLD 177
Law, Citizenship, and Bureaucracy 178
The Imperial Economy: Recovery, Stability, and Decline 179
Sexuality and Domestic Life 180
Women in Public Life 181
Slaves, Criminals, and Gladiators 183

TOPIC 19 CHRISTIANITY AND THE CRISIS OF EMPIRE 186
The Jews: A Religious Minority in the Roman World 187
The Rise of Christianity and the Early Church 189
Problems of Empire and the Reforms of Diocletian 192
The Foundation of Constantinople and the Decline of the West 194
Decline and Fall: The Debate 195

Historical Perspectives
The Dead Sea Scrolls 188

PART III MEDIEVAL EUROPE 198

TOPIC 20 POLITICS AFTER ROME: THE GERMANIC KINGDOMS 201
The Germanic Migrations and the West 202
Germanic Society: Warfare, Kinship, and Family 202
Visigoths, Ostrogoths, and Lombards: German Kingdoms in Southern Europe 204
The Franks and Christianity 205

The Making of Anglo-Saxon England   206
German Customs and Roman Traditions: The Formation of Europe   208

TOPIC 21 EARLY MEDIEVAL CHRISTIANITY   210
Christianity and the Classical Heritage   211
The City of God: Augustine and His Vision   212
The Papacy and the Primacy of Rome   213
The Monastic Ideal   215
Women, Christianity, and the Church   216

TOPIC 22 BYZANTIUM: THE EASTERN EMPIRE   219
New Rome in the East: The Successors of Constantine   220
Justinian and the Imperial Quest   221
Byzantium under Stress: Military Threat and Religious Conflict   222
Byzantium in the North: The Slavs   223
Artistic Splendor in the Byzantine World   224
Economic Vitality and Social Inequality   226

Across Cultures
Bishop Liutprand in
Constantinople   226

TOPIC 23 EUROPE AND ISLAM   230
The Arabian Peninsula and Its Peoples   231
Muhammad, the Founder of Islam   231
Islam and the Mediterranean: Conquest, Conversion, and Settlement   233
Spain and Sicily: Muslim Rule in Europe   234
Science and Culture: The Islamic Impact on the West   236

TOPIC 24 THE FIRST EUROPE:
THE WEST IN THE AGE OF CHARLEMAGNE   239
The Carolingians   240
Charlemagne: From Frankish King to Holy Roman Emperor   240
The Carolingian Renaissance   244
Manorialism and the Carolingian Economy   246
The Disintegration of the Carolingian Empire   248

**Perspectives
from the Past**
Charlemagne and His
Government   242

TOPIC 25 THE SOCIAL ORDER OF MEDIEVAL EUROPE   252
The Feudal System: The Search for Security in an Age of Uncertainty   253
Rural Europe: Peasants and Aristocrats   253
The Revival of Trade and Emergence of Cities   256
Jewish Life in the Middle Ages   258
Medieval Women: The Private and Public Spheres   260
The Clergy and Secular Society   261

**Public Figures
and Private Lives**
Matilda of Flanders
and William the
Conqueror   265

TOPIC 26 THE FEUDAL MONARCHIES   263
Norman and Angevin England: The Development
of Royal Administration   264
France and the Capetian Monarchy: Nobles versus the King   267
German Kings and the Lure of Empire:
From Otto I to Frederick Barbarossa   269
The Reconquista and the Kingdoms of Medieval Spain   270

TOPIC 27   THE MILITANT CHURCH: REFORM AND THE PAPACY   273
Reform and Renewal in the Church   274
The Investiture Controversy   275
Schism and the Crisis of Byzantium   277
The Era of the Crusades   278
The Age of Innocent III   281
The Rise of Popular Devotion   285

Historical Perspectives
Francis of Assisi   282

TOPIC 28   SCHOLARS, TROUBADOURS, AND BUILDERS   287
The First Universities   288
Scholasticism: Faith, Reality, and Reason   289
Songs of Love and Battle: Heroic Epics and Troubadour Poetry   291
A New Musical Language: The Polyphonic Style   292
Architects and Sculptors: The Romanesque Cathedral   293

TOPIC 29   MONARCHY AND ITS LIMITS:
GOVERNMENT IN THE HIGH MIDDLE AGES   295
Political Theory and Church-State Relations in the High Middle Ages   296
England: Magna Carta and the Evolution of Parliament   297
The Consolidation of the French Monarchy   298
Stupor Mundi: Frederick of Hohenstaufen and the Imperial Dream   301

TOPIC 30   ART AND IDEAS IN THE GOTHIC AGE   305
Faith versus Reason: The Heirs of Aquinas   306
The Climax of Medieval Literature: Dante's *Divine Comedy*   306
The Gothic Cathedral   307
Sculpture and Painting in the Gothic Age: Art in Transition   309

TOPIC 31   THE FOURTEENTH CENTURY:
STRESS AND CHANGE IN EUROPEAN SOCIETY   314
Overpopulation and Its Consequences   315
The Plague   315
Bad Times and Social Protest: Peasants and Workers in Revolt   317
The Church in Captivity: Schism and the Popes at Avignon   322

Perspectives from the Past
The Black Death   318

TOPIC 32   THE LATE MIDDLE AGES   326
Agriculture, Trade, and Finance   327
European Society Before and After the Black Death   328
The Life of Women   332
Humanism: The Classical Sources of a New Spirit   333

Historical Perspectives
Gender in Medieval Society   330

PART IV   THE RENAISSANCE AND REFORMATION   336

TOPIC 33   THE AGE OF THE NEW MONARCHS   339
The Hundred Years' War and Its Aftermath   340
The Valois Kings and the Revival of France   342
England and the Rise of the Tudors   344
Spain: From Aragon and Castile to Hapsburg Monarchy   345

Public Figures and Private Lives
Margaret of Anjou and Henry VI of England   343

TOPIC 34   POWER AND CULTURE
IN RENAISSANCE ITALY   348
Politics, Class, and Civic Identity: The Italian City-States   349
The Intellectual World of the Early Renaissance   352
Patronage and Statecraft in Renaissance Italy   354
Italy and Europe: Power Politics and the Art of Diplomacy   354

TOPIC 35   THE VISUAL ARTS
OF THE ITALIAN RENAISSANCE   357
The "Modern Style": Donatello, Brunelleschi, and Masaccio   358
Tradition and Experiment: The Later Quattrocento   359
Harmony and Design in the High Renaissance   362
Harmony and Color: The Painting of the Venetian Republic   364

TOPIC 36   ARTS AND LETTERS
IN RENAISSANCE EUROPE   373
The Printing Revolution   374
The Northern Humanists: Education for a Christian Society   375
The Courtier and *The Prince*: Handbooks of Renaissance Strategy   376
The Conquest of Reality: Renaissance Art in the North   377
Music in the High Renaissance   379

TOPIC 37   UPHEAVAL AND TRANSFORMATION IN EASTERN EUROPE   382
The Collapse of Byzantium   383
The Ottomans and the European Response   384
Hungary, Bohemia, and Poland   386
The Growth of the Principality of Moscow   388

TOPIC 38   THE ERA OF RECONNAISSANCE   392
Europeans and the World: The Early Travelers   393
Geography and Technology   395
The Portuguese Initiative   397
Spain, the Americas, and the European Economy   400

TOPIC 39   THE REFORMATION   405
The Roots of Reform: Popular Discontent and the Crisis of the Western Church   406
"Here I Stand": Martin Luther and the German Reformation   407
The Lutheran Movement: Peasant Rebellion and Aristocratic Strife   409
The Advance of Protestantism in Continental Europe   410
The Break with Rome: Henry VIII and the English Church   412

TOPIC 40   THE SOCIAL WORLDS OF THE
RENAISSANCE AND REFORMATION   415
Class, Mobility, and Changing Values   416
Education, Marriage, and the Family   418
The Burdens of Gender: Women in a Changed World   419
Outsiders in Christian Europe: Jews, Muslims, and Blacks   421

Public Figures and Private Lives
Isabella d'Este and Francesco Gonzaga   353

Across Cultures
Charles Dickens on Renaissance Italy   360

Perspectives from the Past
Art and Artists in the Renaissance   366

Perspectives from the Past
The Portuguese in the Wider World   398

Historical Perspectives
The First Africans in Europe   422

PART V   THE EARLY MODERN WORLD   426

TOPIC 41   CATHOLIC REFORM
AND THE COUNTER-REFORMATION   429
The Catholic Church and the Spirit of Renewal   430
Education and Conversion: The Jesuits and the Ursulines   431
The War Against the Heretics: The Sacred Congregation
of the Holy Office   433

*Historical
Perspectives*
The Social Life of
European Jewry   434

TOPIC 42   CATHOLIC SPAIN AND THE STRUGGLE FOR SUPREMACY   438
Religion and Monarchy: The Reign of Philip II   439
Spain and Its Overseas Empire   441
Rebellion in the Netherlands: Religious Freedom and Political Independence   441
Spain versus England: The Armada Disaster   444

TOPIC 43   CROWN AND PARLIAMENT IN TUDOR-STUART ENGLAND   446
Elizabeth I and the Politics of Compromise   447
Toward Confrontation: James I and Parliament   448
Charles I and the Civil War   449
The Protectorate: The Dictatorship of Oliver Cromwell   451

TOPIC 44   RELIGIOUS WAR AND THE ASCENDANCY
OF THE FRENCH MONARCHY   454
Religious Conflict: From the St. Bartholomew's Day
Massacre to the Edict of Nantes   455
The Cardinals and the State: The Administrations
of Richelieu and Mazarin   458
A Scandal in Bohemia: The Protestant Revolt
and the Thirty Years' War   460
From the Swedish Victory to the French Intervention   462

*Public Figures
and Private Lives*
Marie de' Medici
and Henry IV
of France   458

TOPIC 45   PATTERNS OF LIFE IN
A TIME OF UPHEAVAL   465
Health and Medicine   466
Changing Tastes: Food and Diet   467
The Social Pattern of Housing   472
Clothing, Fashion, and Class   474

*Perspectives
from the Past*
Food and the
Columbian
Exchange   470

TOPIC 46   THE EUROPEAN ECONOMY AND OVERSEAS EMPIRE   477
Trade, Finance, and Prices   478
Merchant Capitalists and the State   480
The Heyday of the Dutch Republic   481
Global Competition: The India Companies   482

*Public Figures
and Private Lives*
Anna Magdalena
and Johann Sebastian
Bach   493

TOPIC 47   THE BAROQUE ERA   486
Emotion and Illusionism: The Affirmation of Baroque Art   487
The Making of Baroque Rome: Caravaggio and Bernini   489
Rembrandt and His Contemporaries in Northern Europe   490
Music for a New Public: The Birth of Opera and the Works of Bach   491
The Golden Age of Literature: Shakespeare and Cervantes   493

Across Cultures
Shakespeare
and Posterity   494

PART VI   THE OLD REGIME   498

TOPIC 48   THE SCIENTIFIC REVOLUTION AND WESTERN THOUGHT   501
The Weight of Tradition: God, Nature, and the World   502
Redefining the Universe: From Copernicus to Galileo   502
Medicine and the Human Body   504
The Scientific Method: Bacon, Descartes, and Pascal   505
Newton and the Laws of the Natural Universe   506

TOPIC 49   SOUTHERN EUROPE: SPAIN, ITALY, AND THE MEDITERRANEAN   509
The Eclipse of the Mediterranean   510
From Hapsburg to Bourbon Spain   511
Europe and the Italian States   513

TOPIC 50   ABSOLUTE MONARCHY: LOUIS XIV AND THE DIVINE RIGHT OF KINGS   517
"I Am the State": The Absolutist Government   518
Nobles, Jansenists, and Huguenots: The Domestic Opposition   521
War, Diplomacy, and the Quest for French Hegemony   524

TOPIC 51   ENGLAND AND THE RISE OF CONSTITUTIONAL MONARCHY   528
The Stuart Restoration   529
The Glorious Revolution   530
The Cabinet System and the House of Commons   535

TOPIC 52   CENTRAL EUROPE AND THE SHIFTING BALANCE OF POWER   539
The Fiction of the Holy Roman Empire   540
The Hapsburgs Turn East: The Turkish Defeat   540
The Rise of the Hohenzollerns   542
The Great Elector: Junkers and Army in Prussia   543

TOPIC 53   THE BALTIC AND EASTERN EUROPE IN TRANSITION   547
The Emergence of Russia   548
Peter the Great and the Allure of the West   549
The Great Northern War and the Founding of St. Petersburg   551
The Collapse of the Swedish Empire   554
Poland: The Triumph of the Nobility   554

TOPIC 54   THE CULTURE OF THE OLD REGIME   557
The Arts in Transition   558
Tragedy and Comedy at the Court of Louis XIV   558
Academies and Salons in the Republic of Letters   559
The Popular Press, Novels, and the Circulation of Ideas   561
The Art of the Rococo   562
The Classical Style in Music: Mozart and Haydn   563

Historical Perspectives
Louis XIV: A Bureaucratic King   522

Perspectives from the Past
Resistance and Revolution   532

Across Cultures
Catherine Wilmot in Russia   552

Public Figures and Private Lives
Elizabeth Robinson Montagu and Edward Montagu   560

T O P I C   5 5   EUROPE AND THE WORLD ECONOMY   **566**
Toward a World Economy   **567**
The Slave Trade   **569**
The Speculation Craze: Stock Booms and Crashes   **573**

T O P I C   5 6   THE GLOBAL CONFLICT:
WARS FOR EMPIRE   **577**
Britain versus Spain in the West Indies   **578**
Dynasty and Power Politics: The War of the Austrian Succession   **579**
The Struggle for North America: The Ascendancy of Britain   **580**
The Seven Years' War and the Success of Prussia   **582**

T O P I C   5 7   EUROPEAN SOCIETY IN THE EIGHTEENTH CENTURY   **586**
Society and the Old Regime   **587**
Agriculture and the World of the Peasantry   **589**
Aristocrats, Urban Classes, and the Poor   **591**
Women and the Old Regime   **594**

T O P I C   5 8   THE AGE OF REASON   **597**
The Seeds of the Enlightenment   **598**
The *Philosophes*: The Battle Against Superstition   **598**
"The Infamous Thing": Voltaire and Natural Morality   **600**
Science and Society: Social and Economic Thought   **601**

Glossary   **607**
Credits   **611**
Index   **613**

**Historical
Perspectives**
The Slave Trade
and the European
Economy   **570**

**Public Figures and
Private Lives**
Jeanne Bécu du Barry
and Louis XV   **595**

**Perspectives
from the Past**
The Age
of Reason   **602**

PERSPECTIVES FROM THE PAST

5 ASPECTS OF THE DIVINE
IN THE ANCIENT WORLD   48
The Creation of the World
Differing Human Attitudes to the Divine

10 CLASSICAL ATTITUDES
TO HISTORICAL METHODS   106
Dionysius of Halicarnassus
Herodotus and His Sources
Thucydides and Historical Method

16 POLITICAL PROPAGANDA
IN THE ROMAN EMPIRE   160
An Augustan View of the First Settlement
Differences Between the Germans and the
   Romans
Hadrian Inaugurates His Reign
An Emperor's Advice to Himself

24 CHARLEMAGNE
AND HIS GOVERNMENT   242
Capitularies
The Missi Dominici
The Administration of Justice

31 THE BLACK DEATH   318
Boccaccio's Description of the Plague in
   Florence
Fourteenth-Century Medical Advice
A Universal Plague

35 ART AND ARTISTS
IN THE RENAISSANCE   366
Vasari on Michelangelo
Cellini on the Casting of the Perseus
A Venetian Painer Contracts to Produce an
   Altarpiece

38 THE PORTUGUESE
IN THE WIDER WORLD   398
An Early Account of Slavery in Africa
The Portuguese in India
The First Impressions of China

45 FOOD AND THE
COLUMBIAN EXCHANGE   470
Food of the Amerindians
Food at the Royal Palace
Aztec Markets

51 RESISTANCE AND
REVOLUTION   532
The English Bill of Rights
Locke's Second Treatise on Government
Rosseau on the Social Contract
The Declaration of Independence

58 THE AGE OF REASON   602
On Method
Natural Law
The Principles of Morals
A Call for Toleration
Reflections on Terrorism

37.1 The Ottoman Empire and Collapse of Byzantine Empire, c. 1450   383

37.2 Expansion of the Slavs   384

37.3 Eastern Europe, c. 1450–1500   387

37.4 Growth of the Principality of Moscow   389

38.1 Travels of Marco Polo   394

38.2 The Portuguese Voyages   396

38.3 European Exploration in the Americas   402

39.1 General Religious Divisions in Europe, c. 1560   408

41.1 The Two Major Divisions of European Jewry   436

42.1 The European Empire of Philip II   440

43.1 England in the Civil War   450

44.1 Religious Conflict in France   455

44.2 Europe, c. 1560   456

44.3 The Expansion of Sweden   461

44.4 Europe, 1648   462

46.1 The Dutch Sea Trade, c. 1650   480

46.2 European Possessions Overseas at the End of the 17th Century   484

49.1 Southern Europe, c. 1700   510

50.1 The France of Louis XIV   519

51.1 England and the Low Countries, c. 1688   530

52.1 The Growth of Prussia, 1417–1807   543

53.1 Russian Expansion into Europe, 1589–1796   551

55.1 European Sea Trade, c. 1750   568

56.1 European Possessions Overseas, c. 1780   583

57.1 Growth of European Population, c. 1800–1850   588

57.2 Grain Production in the 18th Century   590

PREFACE

To vary a cliché, each generation rewrites the history textbooks. As a result, there are today well over a dozen books on the market that are suitable for use as texts in college-level Western civilization courses.

Why, then, still another one?

We have each taught Western civilization or similar courses at large universities for more than 30 years and, like countless colleagues, have wished for a book that we felt met the needs of our students as well as our own requirements as teachers. Existing books run the full range, from traditional works that emphasize political, diplomatic, and military history and look at developments largely from the point of view of leaders and elites, to more recent books that emphasize one approach, particularly social history, and try to present historical change as experienced by ordinary people. Traditional treatments reinforce the views of earlier generations but do not stress the trends in more recent scholarship. Another characteristic in recent textbook writing has been the tendency to underrate students and to "unclutter" the picture by omitting the kind of detail that is the guts of history. Such texts can leave students confused about how history changes and civilizations evolve. Conversely, stress on analysis and pattern, rather than on facts, of necessity emphasizes broad economic and social forces to the exclusion of human agency and, yes, even of historical accident.

We believe the best approach is one that conveys the full range of human experience and that considers both the material processes and the spiritual values of historical development. We have sought to achieve a genuine balance between narrative and analysis. The writing of history at its best has always been the ability to tell a story—by which we mean a narrative of the record of human struggle and achievement, of conflict and community, of cultural diversity and social change. It is not always a pleasant or easy story to relate, but it should be told as much as possible as it unfolded rather than as we would have wanted it to. Moreover, history without detail may leave students bored and deprive them of the kind of vivid images that give life and breath to the story. Abstract analysis, while important to critical thinking, is not a substitute for factual knowledge. Both are necessary to our understanding of history and vital to navigating the ever more complex world in which we live.

In this edition, we have updated events on which new light has been shed since the publication of the first edition. We have in general enriched the connections between Western history and developments beyond the West, such as the Roman Empire's contact with Han China. Recent developments, including those in Iraq, the European Union, and, of course, September 11 and terrorism, have been included.

OUR STRUCTURAL DESIGN

A textbook is a learning and teaching tool and should reflect the realities of the classroom. It occurred to us early on that our text should correspond to the needs and interests of today's teachers. A major case in point is the fact that the 30 to 35 chapters into which most books are divided do not conform to the number of class sessions usually available to the instructor. As teachers we must constantly think about how to break up and present material in topics that can be handled in one class period and that students can digest. This means, inevitably, dividing the conventional large textbook chapters into smaller units.

To correct this longstanding pedagogical problem, we have given our book a unique—although not a startlingly different—structure by arranging the story of Western civilization in 95 smaller "topics," corresponding to the approximate number of class sessions in an academic year. Most of our topics are appropriate for a single class period.

In addition, we have renumbered the topics in this edition to run sequentially from 1 through 95, which will allow instructors to refer to them more easily in their syllabi. A correlation guide between the previous part and topic numbers and the new topic numbers is provided in the *Instructor's Manual*.

At first glance, instructors might assume that this structural design artificially separates material that should be presented in an "integrated" manner. But a closer look will reveal that we have simply divided the overly large chapters of conventional texts into logical, teachable units. The result provides the instructor with a great deal more flexibility in terms of assigning student reading, syllabus design, and in-class analysis.

We have also taken pains to provide students with ways to connect these smaller topics to the larger stream of historical narrative, as well as with methods to focus on important themes. Furthermore, we grouped the 95 topics into eight broad chronological parts, corresponding to the traditional divisions of Western history.

Our approach has been to provide full coverage of all major aspects of historical experience. In addition to the political, diplomatic, and military events of the more traditional texts, each part contains topics that deal individually with social, economic, cultural, and intellectual history. Our treatment of cultural history in particular is unusually rich, including a full discussion of art and music. We have also written topics that deal fully with regions that are generally neglected or given only brief mention, such as eastern and southern Europe, and we have included topics that examine economic and technological developments in depth. Our discussion of social trends seeks to offer students an understanding of daily life and the broad patterns of social change, as well as of the status of slaves, Jews, and other ethnic, religious, or sexual minorities. We have, of course, tried to incorporate the most recent findings from the burgeoning world of women's history into our narrative.

It is no accident that the title of our book, *The Western Perspective*, reflects the fact that, while our focus is on the Western experience, we believe it is important to place that experience in the wider context of world history. We therefore discuss developments in Africa, Asia, the Americas, and the Pacific when they had an impact on or were affected by Western history. Indeed, "perspective" has become a stronger theme in this edition, appearing in part openers, chapter overviews, boxed features, and the conclusion to each chapter, now entitled "Putting [Topic] in Perspective."

SPECIAL FEATURES

In addition to the overall structure of our book, we have designed a number of innovative special features that we believe lend both deeper insight and immediacy to the narrative.

Each part is introduced by an essay that puts the broad trends and patterns characterizing the period in perspective. For a further sense of perspective, each part now includes a **new** culturally and topically comparative timeline, which allows students to see at a glance parallel political, social, economic, and cultural developments in different cultures or countries.

Within topics are a number of boxed features.

- **New** *Across Cultures* features explore interactions of individuals with cultures of different times or places. Some depict contemporaries observing the differences of other cultures (such as Bishop Liutprand in Constantinople and Catherine Wilmot in Russia); others deal with those from later times providing their views on older cultures (such as Herodotus visiting the land of ancient Egypt or Lord Byron visiting Athens).

- Many texts print short quotations from primary sources to add flavor to the narrative. Our *Perspectives from the Past* sections are designed with a specific pedagogical purpose in mind. Each of these document sections consists of a variety of readings from primary sources on a selected issue, such as "The Black Death." In this way, students are able to gain a serious, in-depth insight into historical method, analyze conflicting accounts, and engage in genuine class discussion.

- *Historical Perspectives* essays have been written especially for this book by leading experts in the field. These essays furnish students with a sense of the clash of scholarly opinion about particular subjects, such as the French Revolution or Fascism, or shed special light on a particularly interesting or unusual aspect of historical experience, such as the status of women in ancient Mesopotamia or the earliest Africans in Europe.

- Each part also contains boxes entitled *Public Figures and Private Lives*. These are portraits of the private and public lives of couples in which one or both partners played an influential part in culture, politics, or society. Such sketches serve a number of useful purposes: By relating larger trends to individuals, they give students immediate and easily understandable insight into an important era or development; they provide specific examples of the different roles of and the interaction between men and women in various historical periods; and they suggest the impact of gender on social and private lives.

In addition, each of our 95 topics begins with an overview, which provides perspective on the major themes and subjects to be discussed. Where appropriate, the topics contain a box of *Significant Dates* for principal events, as well as boldface key terms, which also appear in a **new** end-of-book Glossary. Each topic ends with a *Putting in Perspective* conclusion, set off from the text; a series of questions for further study; an up-to-date bibliography; and **new** *InfoTrac College Edition*® search terms, which allow students to do further exploration and research on selected topics in the powerful InfoTrac College Edition database made available with this textbook.

Further, all illustrations are now accompanied by expanded captions that point out details of significance to the place and era, which students may not notice on their own. Newly expanded map captions point out much more detail about the movements and places shown on the maps. Web icons next to the captions indicate that similar maps can be found on the book-specific Web site in an interactive format.

FORMATS

To accommodate teachers at institutions with different versions of Western Civilization courses, this book has been produced in seven different formats:

A complete, one-volume edition containing the entire text

An alternate volume, Since the Middle Ages (Parts III–VIII): ISBN 0-534-61068-4

Volume I: Prehistory to the Enlightenment (Parts I–VI): ISBN 0-534-61066-8

Volume II: The Renaissance to the Present (Parts IV–VIII): ISBN 0-534-61067-6

Volume A: Prehistory to the Renaissance (Parts I–IV): ISBN 0-534-61069-2

Volume B: The Middle Ages to World War I (Parts III–VII): ISBN 0-534-61070-6

Volume C: The Old Regime to the Present (Parts VI–VIII): ISBN 0-534-61071-4

ANCILLARY PACKAGE

A wide variety of ancillary materials are available for instructors and students using this textbook.

For Students

Study Guide, Volumes I and II Prepared by Gerald Anderson of North Dakota State University, the *Study Guide* includes a brief overview of each topic, as well as identifications, geographical identifications, map exercises, timeline questions, short-answer exercises, and essay questions.

Map Exercise Workbooks Prepared by Cynthia Kosso of Northern Arizona University, these two volumes include 20 maps and exercises that ask students to identify important cities and countries.

MapTutor This interactive map tutorial helps students learn geography by having them locate geographical features, regions, cities, and sociopolitical movements. Each map exercise is accompanied by questions that test knowledge and promote critical thinking.

Document Exercise Workbook, Volumes I and II Prepared by Donna Van Raaphorst of Cuyahoga Community College, this is a collection of exercises based around primary sources.

Exploring the European Past: Text and Images A new custom reader for Western civilization. Written by leading educators and historians, this fully customizable reader of primary and secondary sources is enhanced with an online module of visual sources, including maps, animations, and interactive exercises. Each reading also comes with an introduction and a series of questions. To learn more, visit http://etep.thomsonlearning.com or call Thomson Learning Custom Publishing at (800) 355–9983.

History: Hits on the Web Hits on the Web (HOW) is an exciting, class-tested product specially designed to help history students utilize the Internet for studying, conducting research, and completing assignments. HOW consists of approximately 80 pages of valuable teaching tools that can be bundled with any Wadsworth textbook at a very affordable price. Available through Thomson Custom Publishing.

The Journey of Civilization CD-ROM This CD-ROM takes the student on 18 interactive journeys through history. Enhanced with QuickTime movies, animations, sound clips, maps, and more, the journeys allow students to engage in history as active participants rather than as readers of past events.

Magellan Atlas of Western Civilization Available with any Western civilization text, this atlas contains 44 four-color historical maps, including "The Conflict in Afghanistan, 2001," and "States of the World, 2001."

Documents of Western Civilization, Volumes I and II This reader, containing a broad selection of carefully chosen documents, can accompany any Western civilization text.

InfoTrac College Edition A Wadsworth exclusive. Students receive 4 months of real-time access to InfoTrac College Edition's online database of continuously updated, full-length articles from more than 900 journals and periodicals. By doing a simple keyword search, users can quickly generate a powerful list of related articles from thousands of possibilities, then select relevant articles to explore or print out for reference or further study. For professors, InfoTrac College Edition articles offer opportunities to ignite discussions or augment their lectures with the latest developments in the discipline. For students, InfoTrac College Edition's virtual library allows Internet access to sources that extend their learning far beyond the pages of a text.

The Western Perspective Web Site The Web site specifically accompanying this text may be found at *http://wadsworth.com/history*. Both instructors and students will enjoy the Wadsworth History Resource Center, which includes access to topic-by-topic resources for *The Western Perspective*, Second Edition. Text-specific content for students includes tutorial quizzes, glossary, Web links, InfoTrac College Edition exercises, Internet activities, interactive maps, and interactive timelines. Instructors also have access to the *Instructor's Manual*, lesson plans, and PowerPoint slides (access code required). From the History home page, instructors and students can access many selections, such as an Internet Guide for History, a career center, the World History image bank, and links to history-related Web sites.

For Instructors

Available to qualified adopters. Please consult your local sales representative for details.

Instructor's Manual Prepared by James T. Baker of Western Kentucky University, this manual includes a summary of each topic, lecture notes, suggested readings, and discussion questions to spark debate among students. The *Instructor's Manual* also includes a correlation guide for topics of the First and Second Editions, as well as a Resource Integration Guide (RIG) featuring grids that link each topic of the text to instructional ideas and corresponding supplemental resources. At a glance, you can see which selections from the text's teaching and learning ancillaries are appropriate for each key topic theme.

Test Bank This test bank, prepared by Marlette Rebhorn of Austin Community College, provides a variety of question styles. In addition to multiple-choice questions, there are identification questions, essay questions, illustration questions, and book report questions.

ExamView® You can create, deliver, and customize tests and study guides (both print and online) in min-

utes with this easy-to-use assessment and tutorial system. ExamView offers both a Quick Test Wizard and an Online Test Wizard, which guide you step by step through the process of creating tests, while its unique WYSIWYG capability allows users to see tests on-screen exactly as they will print or display online. You can build tests of up to 250 questions using up to 12 question types. Using ExamView's complete word-processing capabilities, you can enter an unlimited number of new questions or edit existing questions.

Transparency Acetates for Western Civilization Includes over 100 four-color map images from this and other texts.

Multimedia Manager for Western Civilization: A Microsoft® PowerPoint® Link Tool An advanced PowerPoint presentation tool containing text-specific lecture outlines, figures, and images that allows you to quickly deliver dynamic lectures. In addition, it provides the flexibility to customize each presentation by editing what is provided or by adding a personal collection of slides, videos, and animations. All of the map acetates and selected photos have been incorporated into each of the lectures. In addition, the extensive Map Commentaries for each map slide are available through the Comments feature of PowerPoint.

Lecture Enrichment Slides Prepared by George Strong and Dale Hoak of The College of William and Mary, these 100 slides contain images of famous paintings, statues, architectural achievements, and interest photos. The authors provide commentary for each individual slide.

Listening to Music CD-ROM Set Available to instructors upon request, this CD-ROM includes musical selections to enrich lectures, from Purcell through Ravi Shankar.

ArtStudy Version 1.0 This comprehensive set of fine art images is made up of full images as well as alternate and detail/closeup views, and includes caption information on artists and embedded audio files to assist students with pronunciation.

History Video Library A selection of videos from *Films for the Humanities and Sciences* and other sources, including "Colonialism, Nationalism, and Migration"; "From Workshops to Factory"; "Revolution, Progress: Politics, Technology, and Science"; and many more. Contact your Thomson/Wadsworth representative for additional information on requesting videos. Available to qualified adopters.

CNN Today Video: Western Civilization You can launch lectures with riveting footage from CNN, the world's leading 24-hour global news television network. This video allows you to integrate the news-gathering and programming power of CNN into the classroom to show students the relevance of course topics to their everyday lives. Organized by topics covered in a typical course, these videos are divided into short segments perfect for introducing key concepts. A Thomson/Wadsworth exclusive.

Sights and Sounds of History Video Short, focused video clips, photos, artwork, animations, music, and dramatic readings are used to bring life to historical topics and events that are most difficult for students to appreciate from a textbook alone. For example, students will experience the grandeur of Versailles and the defeat felt by a German soldier at Stalingrad. The video segments average 4 minutes in length and make excellent lecture launchers.

ACKNOWLEDGMENTS

A number of friends and colleagues have contributed to this book over the years in many important ways, and we wish especially to thank the following individuals: Berit Bredahl-Nielsen, Eric D. Brose, Robert S. Browning, H. James Burgwyn, Elisheva Carlebach, Peter Carravetta, Jennifer Cook, Patricia A. Cooper, Alexander DeGrand, Spencer DiScala, Karen Dubno, Monte Finkelstein, Elisabeth Giansiracusa, Charles L. Killinger, Julie Mostov, David Nasaw, Nunzio Pernicone, Alma Reich, Cecil O. Smith, Donald F. Stevens, David Syrett, Elena Frangakis-Syrett, Frank Warren, and M. Hratch Zadoian.

In addition, we are indebted to our colleagues who generously shared with us their wealth of experience and knowledge. Our sincere thanks to the following instructors who advised us on the First Edition: Phillip Adler, East Carolina State University; Gerald Anderson, North Dakota State University; Jay P. Anglin, University of Southern Mississippi; Martin Arbagi, Wright State University; Patrick Armstrong, Jefferson State Community College; Frank Baglione, Tallahassee Community College; Carol Bargeron, Louisiana State University; Ed Beemon, Middle Tennessee State University; Alan Beyerden, Ohio State University; Lawrence Blacklund, Montgomery County Community College; Stephen Blumm, Montgomery County Community College; Melissa Bokovoy, University of New Mexico; Paul Bookbinder, University of Massachusetts at Boston; Darwin Bostick, Old Dominion University; James Brink, Texas Tech University; Daniel P. Brown, Moorpark College; Tom Bryan, Alvin Community College; Gary Burbridge, Grand Rapids Community College; Thomas Burns, Emory University; Elizabeth Carney, Clemson University; Lamar Cecil, University of North Carolina at Chapel Hill; Thomas Christofferson, California State University at Northridge; Orazio Ciccarelli, University of Southern Mississippi; Franz Coetzee, Yale University; Fred Colvin, Middle Tennessee State University; William Connell, Rutgers University; John Contreni, Purdue University; Jessica Coope, University of Nebraska; Marc Cooper, Southwest Missouri State University; Frederick M. Crawford, Middle Tennessee State University; Gary Cross, Pennsylvania State University; Paige Cubbison, Miami Dade Community College; Nancy Curtin, Fordham University; Maribel Dietz, Louisiana State University; Spencer M. Di Scala, University of Massachusetts at Boston; Michael Doyle, Ocean Community College; Charles Endress, Angelo State University; Thomas Fabiano, Monroe Community College; Gery Ferngren, Oregon State University; Monte Finkelstein, Tallahassee Community College; Edward W. Fox, Cornell University; Carl Frasure, University of Alaska; Elizabeth Furdell, University of North Florida; Alan Galpern, University of Pittsburgh; Richard Golden, Clemson University; Seella Gomezdelcampo, Roane State Community College; Karen Gould; David Gross, University of Colorado at Boulder; Alan Grubb, Clemson University; James D. Hardy, Louisiana State University; Jeanne Harrie, California State University at Bakersfield; Stephen Hauser, Marquette University; Peter Hayes, Northwestern University; Neil Hayman, San Diego State University; Susan Holt, Houston Community College; Robert Houston, University of the South; Bill Hughes, Essex Community College; Laura Hunt, University of Dayton; Frances Kelleher, Grand Valley State University; Charles Killinger III, Valencia Community College; Lloyd Kramer, University of North Carolina at Chapel Hill; Thomas Kselman, University of Notre Dame; David Large, Montana State University; Frederick Lauritsen, Eastern Washington University; Ron Lesko, Suffolk Community College; Mary Ann Lizondo, Northern Virginia Community College; Paul Lockhart, Wright State University; Gary Long, Methodist College; Leo Loubere, State University of New York at Buffalo; Gladys Luster, John C. Calhoun College; David MacDonald, Illinois State University; Paul Maier,

Western Michigan University; James Martin, Campbell University; William Matthews, Ohio State University; John Matzko, Bob Jones University; John McFarland, Sierra College; James Mini, Montgomery County Community College; Thomas Mockaitis, DePaul University; Marjorie Morgan, Southern Illinois University; Rex Morrow, Trident Technical College; Pierce Mullens, Missouri State University; Francis J. Murphy, Boston College; Martha Newman, University of Texas at Austin; Bill Olsen, Marist College; Fred Olsen, Northern Virginia Community College; Thomas Ott, University of North Alabama; Neil Pease, University of Wisconsin at Milwaukee; John Pesda, Camden County Community College; Donald Pryce, University of South Dakota; Herman Rebel, University of Arizona; Marlette Rebhorn, Austin Community College—Rio Grand Campus; Larry Rotge, Slippery Rock University; John Rothney, Ohio State University; Jose Sanches, St. Louis University; Lura Scales, Hinds Community College; Robert G. Schafer, University of Michigan at Flint; Ezel Kural Shaw, California State University at Northridge; Susan Shoemaker, University of Delaware; Ronald Smith, Arizona State University; Eileen Soldwedel, Edmonds Community College; William Stiebing, University of New Orleans; David Tait, Oklahoma State University; Maxine Taylor, Northwestern State University; Janet TeBrake, University of Maine; David Tengwall, Anne Arundel Community College; Jack Thacker, Western Kentucky University; Richard Todd, Wichita State University; Spenser Tucker, Texas Christian University; Thomas Turley, Santa Clara University; Jeffry von Arx, Georgetown University; and L. J. Worley, University of Washington.

And for the Second Edition:

Bruce F. Adams, University of Louisville

Lynn Brink, North Lake College

Spencer M. Di Scala, University of Masschusetts at Boston

Lorettann Gascard, Franklin Pierce College

Joanne Klein, Boise State University

William Percy, University of Massachusetts at Boston

Dan Ringrose, Minot State University

Claire A. Sanders, Texas Christian University

Phyllis L. Soybel, College of Lake County

Melanie H. Vansell, Riverside Community College

And a special thanks to Charles L. Killinger of Valencia Community College for all of his contributions to the text and the text's Web site.

Finally, the authors would like to thank each other: Their long friendship over many years has not only survived but actually strengthened since working together on this project. All collaboration should be this good.

THE WESTERN PERSPECTIVE

A History of Civilization in the West

Volume I: Prehistory to the Enlightenment

SECOND EDITION

THE ANCIENT WORLD

The long, slow evolution of modern humans began some 4 million years ago. It took until around 35 thousand years ago for our common ancestor, *Homo sapiens sapiens,* to appear. The first human groups lived on the move, by hunting and gathering, and only with the discovery of farming techniques around 8000 B.C. did the first settled communities begin to develop.

The people of this Neolithic Age invented weaving and the manufacture of pottery. They built houses and lived together in towns. Toward the end of the Neolithic period, around 3500 B.C., the Sumerians of Mesopotamia discovered how to smelt and work with metal, and metal, especially copper, was used extensively in Israel/Palestine before 3500 B.C. Furthermore—a giant step forward in the development of civilization—the Sumerians devised a system of writing. The ability to preserve human thought in permanent form marks the real beginning of recorded history. (At around the same time the ancient Egyptians also began to use writing; it is uncer-

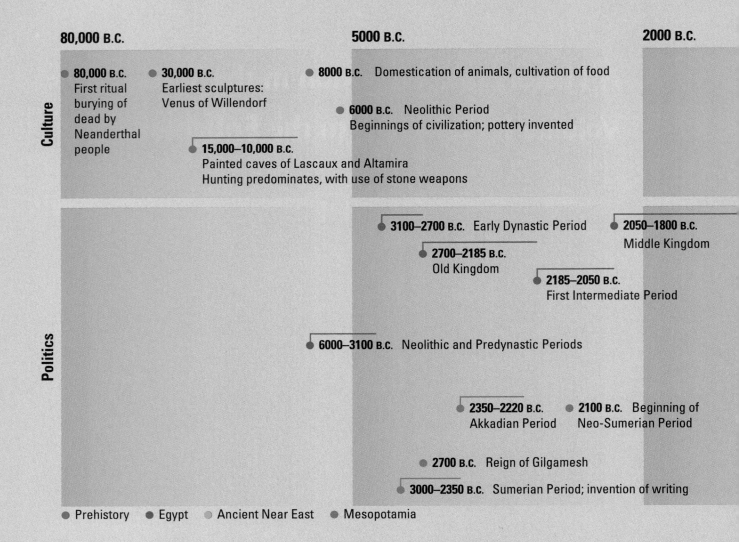

80,000 B.C.

5000 B.C.

2000 B.C.

Culture

● **80,000 B.C.**
First ritual burying of dead by Neanderthal people

● **30,000 B.C.**
Earliest sculptures: Venus of Willendorf

● **8000 B.C.**   Domestication of animals, cultivation of food

● **6000 B.C.**   Neolithic Period
Beginnings of civilization; pottery invented

15,000–10,000 B.C.
Painted caves of Lascaux and Altamira
Hunting predominates, with use of stone weapons

Politics

3100–2700 B.C.   Early Dynastic Period

2050–1800 B.C.
Middle Kingdom

2700–2185 B.C.
Old Kingdom

2185–2050 B.C.
First Intermediate Period

6000–3100 B.C.   Neolithic and Predynastic Periods

2350–2220 B.C.
Akkadian Period

● **2100 B.C.**   Beginning of
Neo-Sumerian Period

● **2700 B.C.**   Reign of Gilgamesh

3000–2350 B.C.   Sumerian Period; invention of writing

● Prehistory   ● Egypt   ○ Ancient Near East   ● Mesopotamia

© bpk, Berlin, Aegyptisches Museum/bpk. Photo: Margarete Buesing

tain whether this was because of Sumerian influence or whether the Egyptians came up with their own discovery.)

River valleys provided the setting for the first flourishing civilizations. Shortly after the Sumerians' inventions, writing and metalworking appeared in the cultures of the Yellow River valley in China and the Indus valley in India. The new skills also spread to Egypt, where the most enduring of all ancient civilizations was developing in the valley of the River Nile.

1500 B.C.

500 B.C.

1570–1070 B.C. New Kingdom

525 B.C. Persians conquer Egypt

1800–1570 B.C. Second Intermediate Period

1070–525 B.C. Late Dynastic Period

1750–1450 B.C.
Hittite Old Kingdom

1400–1200 B.C.
Canaanites flourish

971–931 B.C. Reign of King Solomon

1020–1000 B.C. Reign of Saul, first Hebrew king

1450–1200 B.C. Hittite Empire

1000–971 B.C. Reign of King David

Between 1300 and 1200 B.C. Hebrew Exodus from Egypt

1200–1000 B.C. Rise of Phoenicians

559–530 B.C. Reign of Persian Cyrus the Great

1200 B.C. Migrations of Peoples of the Sea

1800–1600 B.C.
Babylonian Period;
Hammurabi's Law Code

1200–850 B.C.
The rise of the Assyrians

800 B.C. Foundation of Phoenician colony of Carthage

850–612 B.C. The Assyrian Empire

1600–1200 B.C. The Kassites and their successors

612 B.C. Assyrians defeated by Medes and Babylonians

Mesopotamia, the region between the rivers Tigris and Euphrates, saw the rise and fall of successive peoples, among them the Sumerians, the Babylonians, and the Assyrians. The most important cities had their own kings and priests, who divided between them control of the running of the city and worship of its deities. Law codes began to appear, as the ruling classes sought to establish acceptable patterns of human behavior and regulate human relationships.

In Egypt, the pharaohs (or kings) ruled over a more unified society, combining their role as living god with their political and military duties. Over time the authority of the central government slowly eroded, and the stability of the Old Kingdom—the Age of the Pyramids—gave way to the growing disturbances of the First Intermediate Period. The Middle Kingdom saw renewed unification and strong government, but in the New Kingdom, periods of imperialist aggression alternated with waves of anarchy.

Elsewhere in the ancient Near East, other peoples developed their own cultures. The Phoenicians were commercial leaders, trading widely in the Mediterranean world, while the rise of Persia saw the formation of a multiethnic, multicultural empire. Among those ruled for a time by the Persians were the Hebrews (the Jews), over whose long history there developed the belief in a single, universal god.

For all the peoples of the ancient world, religion was fundamental to society, and the conflict between sacred and secular authority became a crucial issue. The arts served as a means of expressing universal human feelings, which ranged from the triumphant grandeur of the New Kingdom temples built for Ramses the Great to the complex world view of the Mesopotamian poem, the *Epic of Gilgamesh*. At the same time, the ruling classes sought solutions to political, economic, and social problems, which continued to trouble most subsequent human societies.

PEOPLE BEFORE HISTORY

The earliest stages in the evolution of the human species go back millions of years. Over millennia a succession of species of **hominids** (the forerunners of modern humans) appeared, slowly developing the use of their forelimbs and walking on their backlimbs. Around a million years ago a creature we call ***Homo erectus*** walked much like modern humans. As brain capacity grew, the species learned to survive by hunting and gathering food, and began to make stone tools—the period from the first use of stone implements to the introduction of farming some 10 thousand years ago is known as the **Paleolithic,** or **Old Stone, Age.** The earliest forms of family and social group began to develop during that time. Some 80 thousand years ago, Neanderthal people invented a system for producing new types of stone tools such as blades and flints. They were also the first living beings to bury their dead.

The species to which we humans all belong, ***Homo sapiens,*** has been in existence for only about 35 thousand years. For the first 25 thousand years of their history, *Homo sapiens* continued to live by scavenging for food and using new and more complex forms of stone tools. They have left us the first works of art in existence, in the form of paintings on the inside walls of caves and small stone sculptures.

Beginning about 10 thousand years ago, humans began to find two fundamental new ways of maintaining their communities: by cultivating crops and domesticating animals. The period that saw the beginnings of farming is called the **Neolithic,** or **New Stone, Age.** This revolutionary break occurred over a prolonged period and was conditioned by major changes in climate and environment.

The shift to agriculture brought many important changes in the patterns of human life. Rather than wandering in search of food, people could settle down in stable villages, where they learned to produce pottery and other manufactured objects. Communities became diversified, as different individuals performed specific functions. Neolithic people developed elaborate cults of the dead and produced works of art that were stylized rather than realistic, as Paleolithic art had been. Economic and social distinctions appeared, as a small minority in each community grew to possess most of the productive land, and thus a greater wealth and authority.

These agricultural villages remained small and self-sufficient. They formed the basis for the growth of city life, which began to develop at the end of the Neolithic Age.

THE PLANET EARTH: LIFE AND THE ENVIRONMENT

The solar system, of which our planet Earth forms a part, came into being around 4.5 billion years ago. As far as we know, Earth is the only one of the nine planets in the system to support life: Scientists have yet failed to find any trace of living things on Mars or Venus, the other two planets whose atmospheres are theoretically capable of maintaining living organisms. Yet our world may not be the only one in existence. Astronomers believe that our galaxy, the Milky Way, composed of about 100 billion stars, contains a billion planets where life could exist. Modern telescopes, furthermore, have identified some 100 million other galaxies. The human perspective, therefore, is inevitably a very narrow one. It is not impossible that other worlds have their own histories of civilization.

THE EARLIEST FORMS OF LIFE

Life began to develop on Earth some time in its first 1.5 billion years of existence. A thin layer of gases on the planet's surface contained the chemical elements necessary for living organisms. Electrical energy caused by the lightning accompanying violent rainstorms, high-energy particles, ultraviolet rays from the sun, and other forms of energy, created the kinds of complex molecules that were to form living things.

The earliest cell-like organisms, fossils of which have been found in rock that solidified more than 3 billion years ago, gradually evolved into photosynthetic cells—with the ability, that is, to convert solar energy into chemical energy. Living off the sun, they produced oxygen, a gas without which higher forms of life could not exist.

These early stages of life occurred in the warm waters that covered much of the earth's surface: The water protected the cells from the sun's ultraviolet rays, which would otherwise have destroyed them. As the oxygen layer around the earth began to build up, it, too, formed a protective barrier against the sun's dangerous rays, and forms of life began to evolve that were capable of existing on the earth's land surface.

In our own time, scientists and ecologists are increasingly preoccupied with the destruction of this protective layer by what is called the "greenhouse effect," the devastating impact of human pollution on the ozone around our planet (ozone is a condensed form of oxygen). From the time of the first photosynthetic cells, living things have changed the natural environment. Modern humans, however, run the risk of destroying the environment and making all life insupportable.

FROM THE DINOSAURS TO THE FIRST MAMMALS

From the earliest water-dwelling organisms there developed the first vertebrates, animals with a central nervous system and an internal skeleton that increases in size along with the animal over time. The earliest of these were fish, and over millions of years some fish species began to evolve with simple forms of lungs. This adaptation in turn led to the appearance of amphibians—modern examples include toads and frogs—that could survive both in water and on land. Some 300 million years ago, a new step in the process saw the appearance of the first reptiles, creatures that reproduced by the internal fertilization of an egg and that could spend their whole lives on land. For the next 200 million years, reptiles were the dominant form of life on earth. These dinosaurs (the word comes from Greek, meaning "terrible lizard") varied in size from that of a small chicken to the gigantic *Diplodocus*, 90 feet long and weighing 30 tons, with a tiny head and long neck and tail. Creatures such as this roamed the surface of the earth, living on the abundant plant life available, although some dinosaurs, including the giant *Tyrannosaurus rex*, were meat eaters. During the same millennia the layers of fossil fuels—coal and oil—slowly formed that were one day to make possible the Industrial Revolution and help shape the modern world.

At the height of the dinosaurs' domination of the earth, the first mammals, warm-blooded and meat eating, began to appear. Birds also evolved around the same time. The earliest mammals were probably a form of shrew: small mouse-like creatures that lived on worms and insects. By comparison with the massive dinosaurs, these tiny creatures—probably nocturnal animals with poor eyesight—must have seemed insignificant. Yet, as in the case of the birds, their warm blood made them capable of a high level of physical activity and a greater sense of mental alertness.

After coexisting with these early mammals, the dinosaurs disappeared around 65 million years ago. No completely satisfactory explanation has been found to account for the sudden extinction—sudden in geological terms, at least—of the giant reptiles, whose period of domination of the planet for millions of years emphasizes the brevity of our own history. Among the causes that have been suggested were changes of climate and environment, to which the dinosaurs could not adapt. These changes may have been produced by the impact of a giant meteor on the earth.

THE FIRST STAGES OF HUMAN EVOLUTION

The theory of human evolution first popularized by the English scientist Charles Darwin in *On the Origin of Species* (1859) and then elaborated in *The Descent of Man* (1871) did not claim, as many of his opponents accused him of doing, that humans are descended from monkeys. Instead, Darwin argued that modern humans and the other primates (the most developed order of mammals, which includes humans, monkeys, and lemurs) share a common ancestral form. About 14 million years ago the evolution of this form split in two directions: One path led to the gorillas and chimpanzees, the other eventually to our own species.

The evidence for the process of human evolution is fragmentary, and new finds provoke constant reinterpretation of earlier discoveries. Nevertheless, despite the many uncertainties and controversies, it is possible to establish some general idea of the process.

MR. BERGH TO THE RESCUE.

THE DEFRAUDED GORILLA. "That *Man* wants to claim my Pedigree. He says he is one of my Descendants."
MR. BERGH. "Now, Mr. DARWIN, how could you insult him so?"

This cartoon by the American illustrator Thomas Nast shows Henry Bergh, the social reformer and founder of The American Society for the Prevention of Cruelty to Animals (ASPCA), reproaching Charles Darwin for his revolutionary theory of evolution. For many 19th-century thinkers, of course, the social and theological consequences of Darwin's ideas about human development were far from laughable. The book under Darwin's arm is *On the Origin of Species,* first published in 1859, in which he first described his theory of evolution.

The creatures whose gradual evolution led over millions of years to the human species are called "hominids." The earliest species of hominid, *Ramapithecus,* is known from fossil fragments discovered in Kenya (east Africa) and in northern India; they date to about 8 to 14 million years ago. Unlike the apes, these creatures do not seem to have used their teeth for stripping and tearing up leaves and other vegetation. They probably used their front limbs for this purpose, perhaps moving around on their back limbs.

The next hominid of which we have evidence is **Australopithecus,** in the form of fossil fragments from sites in eastern and southern Africa. The oldest dates to about 4 million years ago. These creatures, between four and five feet tall, had broad thumbs and the ability to use their hands to grip; also, they walked upright. The species *Homo erectus,* which appeared around a million years ago, is far closer to our own species, but there may well have been other forms of hominid between *Australopithecus* and the development of *Homo erectus.* British and American anthropologists working in Africa have discovered skeletal remains dating to 3 million years ago that show resemblances to modern humans. These finds, along with fossil discover-

ies in China, are beginning to provide a more complex picture of the course of human evolution, which may have occurred over a longer period than was hitherto believed.

Homo erectus had a skeleton and walk closely resembling our own and a brain capacity about half that of ours. The species, which spread from Africa into Europe and Asia, was the first to use fire and invented the earliest tools, made of stone chips. Over time it evolved into *Homo sapiens,* from which our own subspecies, **Homo sapiens sapiens,** developed.

HOMO NEANDERTHALIS

Another variant of *Homo sapiens* is known as **Homo neanderthalis,** the earliest found in Europe. The first examples were discovered in the Neander valley of the river Rhine near Düsseldorf (Germany) in 1856. Neanderthal people flourished from about 40 thousand to 80 thousand years ago. They were muscular and heavy, with a thick skull and a low forehead. Reconstructions based on an early find, the skeleton of an arthritic, did much to shape the popular modern notion of "primitive man," but Neanderthals had brains the same size as those of modern humans, and their period

SIGNIFICANT DATES

Chief Developments of Prehistoric Humans (all dates B.C.)

Before 8,000,000	*Ramapithecus*
4,000,000	*Australopithecus*
1,000,000	*Homo erectus*
500,000	Use of cave shelters
80,000	*Homo neanderthalis*
35,000	*Homo sapiens sapiens*
25,000	Earliest prehistoric art

marks a major development in the history of human thought. Neanderthal people were the first living creatures to bury their dead carefully and place funerary offerings in the graves—the earliest indication of the existence of religious beliefs.

Around 35 thousand years ago, the Neanderthalers became extinct at the same time that our own subspecies, *Homo sapiens sapiens*, appeared (*Homo sapiens sapiens* is sometimes called "Cro-Magnon," after the site in France where remains of the subspecies were first discovered). Skeletal fragments from sites in Europe seem to show large numbers of violent deaths among the last Neanderthal people, who were perhaps attacked and destroyed by the new subspecies. Alternatively, *Homo sapiens sapiens* may have been resistant to a disease that wiped out their predecessors. Whatever the circumstances, with the appearance of *Homo sapiens sapiens* all other forms of hominid died out, and the newcomers began to spread throughout the world. All peoples today, including Europeans, Africans, Amerindians, and Asians, belong to this subspecies.

THE FIRST PEOPLE

Along with physical changes, the immensely long period of human evolution saw the slow growth of social patterns of behavior. Like the other primates, early hominids lived in groups organized according to a system of social hierarchy. Judging from the size of their living areas, bands of *Homo erectus* consisted of around 30 adults and their young. At some sites there is evidence of the butchering and dividing up of food among the various group members, a form of cooperation that distinguished them from other primates. This ability to coexist and collaborate with one another played an important part in the early development of human society.

THE FIRST FAMILIES

Alone among the primates, humans developed societies that were based on the nuclear family, together with the formation of permanent male-female bonds. Some scholars argue that in Paleolithic times women were the dominant force in society, although this theory has not been proven by the evidence. Individual males had exclusive sexual rights to one or more females, and the two sexes worked together to care for and provide for the young. Most groups lived on plants and small game. Men hunted larger animals, while women probably combined childbearing and raising with food gathering. In this way, the group's survival depended equally on both sexes.

It is not clear whether individual family units combined to form groups or whether preexisting bands divided up into families. In any case, two important principles soon came into play. The first was that incest became taboo because interbreeding would have disrupted the formation of nuclear family units (early people did not, of course, realize the genetic dangers of incest). The second increasingly common practice was exogamy, or marriage outside the group. With group membership so small, parents could not always find eligible mates for their offspring. By promoting unions between members of neighboring bands, early humans could "settle" their dependents when they wished and establish friendly relations with their neighbors. Thus they reduced the risk of intergroup fighting while extending their hunting territory. The use of "arranged marriages" of this kind remains common in many parts of the world.

LIVING CONDITIONS AND TECHNOLOGY

Although, like the other primates, early hominids lived on the move, they developed an important difference in living patterns. Many groups formed permanent or semipermanent base camps that were used over several years. The hunters would move out from these camps, leaving behind the children, and return bringing game. The earliest communities, those of the *Australopithecines*, were probably in the open; the sites in southeast Africa are often located near lakes or rivers, useful both for their water and for the animals they would have attracted.

The earliest evidence of the use of caves as habitations dates to about half a million years ago—among the first examples are the Choukoutien caves near Beijing. The move to natural shelters became possible because of a major breakthrough in human development: the discovery of fire.

The Paleolithic burial of a woman aged about 25 to 30 years, an early example of Neanderthal burial methods. The figure has been placed in a crouching position, with a stone placed above to mark the spot. Only the skull and limbs are visible; the softer rib cage has rotted away.

With the protection offered by fire, cave settlers could keep out the bears and other large mammals that also lived in shelters. It also became possible to cook food. Meat was more digestible when cooked, and boiled or roasted grains and seeds—which the human alimentary system cannot digest raw—helped enrich the diet.

According to evidence found in late *Australopithecine* sites in east Africa and early *Homo erectus* sites in China and Southeast Asia, tools seem to have first been used about a million years ago. Known as pebble tools, these implements were smooth stones with flakes split off at the end. Both the pebble and the flake served for chopping, scraping, or cutting.

Over hundreds of thousands of years, successive generations of *Homo erectus* gradually developed a new kind of tool, the so-called hand ax, which was probably an all-purpose instrument. The spread of hand axes—often similar in design—within specific geographical areas, and their absence from other regions, is an early example of cultural diffusion. The technological advances made possible in the areas where the axes were employed were the result of the communication and exchange of ideas, and not the result of physical evolution. This ability of humans to acquire and spread information was a crucial factor in their development.

Neanderthal people continued to use hand axes but also devised a new and far more efficient form of instrument, consisting of sharp flakes of stone struck off from a precut disk. These flints and disks, so characteristic of Neanderthal culture, were in use from 70 thousand years ago to about 32 thousand years ago. The flints would have served to scrape animal hides for the manufacture of simple clothing, another important development that occurred along with organized burial during Neanderthal times.

The tools that *Homo sapiens sapiens* began to produce around 35 thousand years ago were far more refined. At first they still consisted of stone, but the blades were shaped by the use of other stones—a tool to make a tool—into a wide variety of shapes. A tool kit might include instruments for scraping and piercing, chisels, knives, and burins (engraving tools). Our ancestors used these tools to work materials such as ivory and bone into various kinds of sharp points: barbed tips for spears, fish hooks, and needles for domestic use. This advance in turn led to another vast step forward, the use of decoration on some of the instruments and the use of other tools to carve stones and paint on cave walls. Humans had invented art.

EUROPE IN THE STONE AGE: HUNTERS AND ARTISTS

The earliest awareness of aspects of life other than mere survival emerges from some of the Neanderthal cemeteries. These first examples of careful disposal of bodies imply that Neanderthal people developed more complex ideas about the nature of life and death. Some of the dead in the graves were buried with weapons and food—in one case a joint of meat. In another case the body had been covered with spring flowers. Many bodies in Neanderthal graves were colored with a pigment produced from red earth before being buried.

CAVE PAINTING

Finds such as these reveal dawning interest in appearance and, more significantly, the use of images as symbols. Even if we cannot really decipher the meaning of the contents of the graves, those who buried their dead intended the offerings to convey a specific message—whether in this world or in an afterlife. About 20 thousand years ago, this fascination with images suddenly inspired the creation of the first surviving works of art in human history.

Perhaps the most compelling examples of prehistoric art are the painted caves of France and Spain. (Among the most recently discovered ones is the cave of Chauvet, in France.) The scenes of animals depicted there still startle the modern viewer with their keen observation and lifelike vividness. The cave artists incised the outer lines of each image, often using the natural irregularities of the stone surface to suggest, say, the hump of a bull. Then they filled the outline with charcoal and paints made from ground minerals.

From the time of their rediscovery—Lascaux in France, one of the most famous examples, came to light only in 1940—the cave paintings have raised intriguing questions: Why were they created? Are the animals intended as magic symbols for hunting rituals? But, if so, why are the scenes always located in the most remote and inaccessible parts of the caves, far from any source of natural light? A magical function, furthermore, would not explain the paintings' most striking characteristic, their realism, because rituals require only symbolic representation. Some modern observers believe that the herds of animals represent seasonal migrations, while still others have suggested that the various animals were the totems (emblems) of families or clans (human figures appear only rarely in the paintings and are always represented as simple stick figures). What remains certain is that, with great care and under difficult conditions, the cave artists sought to reproduce the animal world they saw around them as vividly as they could.

THE FIRST SCULPTORS

Other artists of the late Paleolithic period turned to bone, horn, and stone. Some of the carvings are of animals, including a magnificent bison from southwestern France, carved out of reindeer horn. As in the paintings, human subjects were shown in a more stylized way. The tiny *Venus of Willendorf* has a featureless face, covered with what look like curls. Clutching her large breasts, she looks down toward her belly (perhaps pregnant). The emphasis on sexual characteristics in this and other female figures may tell us something about prehistoric attitudes toward gender. Perhaps women's practical role as the source of birth and life became symbolic of a more profound feminine life force that sustained the masculine world of the hunt.

The Hall of the Bulls in one of the largest painted caves at Lascaux. The variety of styles suggests that at least two, and maybe more, artists worked in the cave. The large bull to the right is painted in outline, on a natural bump in the rock that suggests the animal's humped back. The other animals have the details of their hair and markings filled in.

THE NEOLITHIC REVOLUTION: FARMING AND TECHNOLOGY

The term *Neolithic* (New Stone Age) was originally coined by 19th-century archeologists to describe the period at the end of the Stone Age when settled and stable human communities had learned to survive by cultivating crops and domesticating animals, but had not discovered metals and still used stone tools and weapons. More recent discoveries tend to show that the development of both agriculture and metalworking took place over a long period and at a different rate in various regions of the world. In some areas people used advanced farming methods along with stone tools, while elsewhere metalworking was combined with less developed agriculture. It is probably best, therefore, to use "Neolithic" to describe the gradual appearance of food production over the period between 7000 and 4000 B.C.

In any case, the gradual discovery of systems of agriculture by Paleolithic people did not in itself immediately lead to a more settled form of living and the appearance of stable communities. Evidence from excavations in Egypt's Nile valley suggests that for thousands of years before the Neolithic period nomadic peoples had planted barley and wheat in the silt left by the river Nile when its floods subsided, without ever settling down as farmers. Hunters and gatherers in other areas as well probably learned to grow crops that served as part of their food supply. The creation of permanent communities came at a relatively late stage in the development of agriculture.

NEOLITHIC FARMERS

The first Neolithic farming communities all began to form around 10 thousand years ago in four parts of the world: the Near East (with important early sites in Syria, including Bouqras), western Africa, northeastern China, and Central and South America. Scholars used to believe that farming techniques were invented in the first of these regions (the Near East) and subsequently spread elsewhere. It now seems more likely that various peoples made the same discoveries at around the same time. The reasons for these discoveries remain uncertain but are perhaps related to the climatic conditions left by the last Ice Age, which ended about 9 thousand years ago.

In northeastern China, a culture known as Yangshao appeared along the middle course of the Yellow River. Its people kept herds of pigs and grew millet, and gradually learned to make pottery. Farmers in western Africa domesticated a wide variety of plants, including yams and sorghum.

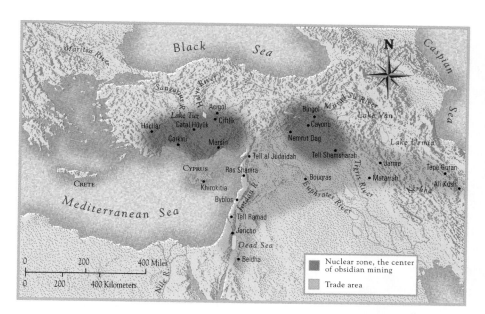

Map 1.1 Near Eastern Obsidian Trade routes in the Neolithic Period.
Obsidian is a natural form of glass found in certain volcanic areas, black and semi-transparent. It was very popular in the Neolithic period for flaking into blades or for grinding into pottery. As this map shows, it was widely traded from its centers of collection, here Southern Asia Minor (modern Turkey) and the Near East.

The Venus of Willendorf (c. 30,000–25,000 B.C.) This tiny figure is only 4¼ inches (11 cm) high. The sculptor has emphasized the sexual characteristics, enlarging the breasts and pregnant belly, and drawing in the pubic triangle. The face, by contrast, is featureless, with a hatched design suggesting hair (or perhaps a woven hat).

history to have survived. Ancient Jericho contained a large columned structure, perhaps a temple, in which archeologists found models of humans and animals. Together with the impressive wall surrounding the settlement—which, with its large round tower, probably served as a defense against both attack and flood—this structure justifies the description of Jericho as the first city in history.

The inhabitants of sites excavated in Iran, Iraq, and Turkey kept herds of sheep and cultivated vegetables, including lentils and peas, and barley and wheat. They located their villages near water, and as the communities prospered they began to expand. The site of Çatal Hüyük in modern Turkey developed between 6400 and 5600 B.C. and eventually covered 32 acres.

European civilization developed more slowly than in the Near East, yet by 3300 B.C. it had clearly begun the transition to the late Neolithic era. In 1991, the virtually intact body of a man was discovered in a melting Alpine glacier on the border between Austria and Italy. This remarkably preserved "Iceman," or *Homo tyrolensis*, who died some 5,300 years ago, was perhaps a herdsman, between 25 and 35 years old. In addition to a cap and leather shoes, he wore a woven grass cape over a fur robe. In his fur quiver were found arrows with flint points and feathers, which show that the bearer was familiar with ballistic principles. Also found along with the body were a wood-handled flint dagger and a copper ax blade. The one decorative object he carried, perhaps a talisman, consisted of a donut-shaped stone disk with a tassel of string.

NEOLITHIC SOCIETY

Once the nomadic ways of hunting and gathering of the Paleolithic period had given way to farming and settled human communities, the way lay open for the growth of civilization. A major factor was the rise in population size and density. Earlier hunting groups, which had a high rate of natural mortality, had probably limited their numbers still

At a slightly later date, Central and South American Indians raised corn, squash, and beans.

The largest Neolithic centers developed in the Near East. Between 8000 and 7000 B.C. at Jericho, in Palestine, a population of some 3,000 lived in round houses made of mud brick set on sturdy stone foundations—the earliest houses in

further by abortion and infanticide. Neolithic communities probably tended to expand to the limits of available food resources, as most modern ones do—farmers can feed a much larger number of people from cultivated land than hunters can from a similar area. The consequence was bigger settlements that were often within reach of one another. Their residents had the opportunity to develop some precious new concepts, among which were leisure and comfort.

Within these communities, individual responsibilities became far more varied. Food production was now in the hands of only a few, and others could develop their own specialized skills, including the making of pottery (which first appeared throughout the ancient Near East in Iran, Syria, and Jordan around 6500 B.C.) and the carving of stone figurines. In Western Europe, perhaps as early as 4000 B.C., local populations began to construct monumental structures using massive stones known as *megaliths*. The most famous of these to survive is Stonehenge, on Salisbury Plain in southern England. Built in several phases, before and after 2000 B.C., this mysterious complex may have served as a solar calendar.

Differences in occupation in turn led to differing economic status. Unlike their predecessors, Neolithic people could accumulate material possessions and own land. Furthermore, the production of goods created possibilities for trade, and some large settlements may have served as much for trading as for food production. Around 6000 B.C., the invention of simple forms of transport such as rafts further encouraged the exchange of goods. In the process, the relative equality of earlier times slowly gave way to far more complex distinctions among various members of the communities. Thus the social divisions that form part of the history of civilization have their roots in the growing stratification of Neolithic life. Objects traded included both finished goods and raw materials, including obsidian, a dark vitreous stone derived from volcanic lava, which was used for cutting softer materials.

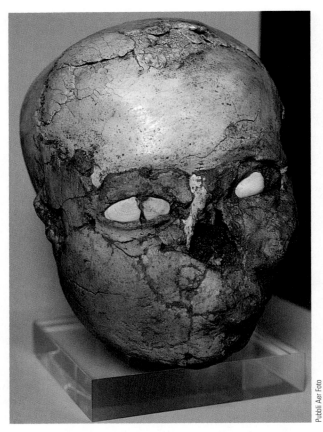

Publii Aer Foto

Neolithic plastered skull from Jericho, c. 7000 B.C. The artist has used an actual human skull as the starting point for this work, filling in the features of the face with plaster. The eyes are made of inlaid seashell, and the hair is painted on. This and other similar skulls were not found with the rest of the body but buried separately.

© 1983 Metropolitan Museum of Art

Aerial view of Stonehenge, Salisbury Plain, Wiltshire, England. c. 2550–1600 B.C. The circle's diameter is c. 97 feet (c. 26.5 m). Constructed of standing vertical stones joined by large horizontal *lintels*, Stonehenge may well have served as a place for astronomical observation.

Putting Prehistory in Perspective

The long, slow material and technological progress of the Neolithic period was to lead to the eventual discovery of metals, the invention of writing, and the growth of cities—all important events in the rise of civilization chronicled in the following pages. Although it is difficult to provide a clear definition of *civilization,* the term usually describes societies with at least the majority, if not all, of the following characteristics:

1. Some form of urban life involving the construction of permanent settlements
2. A system of government that regulates political relations
3. The development of distinct social classes, distinguished from one another by two related factors: wealth and occupation
4. Tools and specialized skills for the production of goods, leading to the rise of manufacturing and trade
5. Some form of written communication, making it possible to share and preserve information
6. A shared system of religious belief, whose officials—or priests—often play a significant part in community affairs

The period between the earliest Neolithic villages and the first real Sumerian cities, which are discussed in the next Topic, spanned some 6 thousand years; during this time, humans learned to dominate and control their environment and to put other creatures at their service.

Along with these material advances, many of the basic social and cultural characteristics listed previously that were to mark civilized life began to appear. (Historically, the term *civilization* is purely descriptive in its significance, with neither positive nor negative connotations.) The importance of commerce, the development of a class system, and the central role played by organized religion all seem to have had their origins in Neolithic communities.

The same may be true of the gender distinctions that characterized Neolithic society. Among earlier hunting and gathering groups, all members played a significant role and enjoyed relative independence. The division of labor made possible for the first time by a sedentary existence may have resulted in women being limited to activities and occupations performed at home. Most of these activities were related to child raising and the practical management of family life, although they probably also included cottage industries such as the manufacture of pottery.

As a result, the rise of civilization saw the appearance of gender inequality. As political and religious structures began to develop within individual communities, creating the need for leaders and organizers, men assumed the chief positions in public life, either excluding women or confining them to private life. This separation became reinforced when conflicts of interest among various communities led to war (another mark of civilization as it developed) because men once again played a dominant role.

To judge from surviving works of art, the worship of a female fertility deity continued. Women remained associated with the natural world, and the Earth Mother or Mistress of the Animals who appears in the religions of the early civilizations seems descended from a Neolithic prototype. Neolithic artists developed a new style. In contrast to the realistic and exuberant depictions of Paleolithic art, Neolithic decoration

Continued next page

is often linear, even abstract. Many of the female figurines are geometric, without the overt sexuality of the earlier period.

The Neolithic Age did more than make possible the rise of civilization by providing stable conditions. For all its apparent remoteness, it established basic patterns of human organization and behavior that were to endure for millennia.

Questions for Further Study

1. What kinds of evidence can historians draw on in the study of prehistory? How do they differ from the information used for studying later periods?
2. What do prehistoric works of art tell us about the people who made them? How far can we use them to reconstruct their ways of thinking?
3. Compare the importance of tool making and farming in the early development of human civilization.

Suggestions for Further Reading

Bahn, Paul. *The Cambridge Illustrated History of Prehistoric Art.* New York, 1998.

Bahn, Paul G., and Jean Vertut. *Journey Through the Ice Age.* Berkeley, 1997.

Beltran, Antonio, ed. *The Cave of Altamira.* New York, 1999.

Chauvet, Jean-Marie, et al. *Dawn of Art: The Chauvet Cave.* New York, 1996.

Chippindale, Christopher. *Stonehenge Complete.* New York, 1994.

Cunliffe, Barry, ed. *The Oxford Illustrated Prehistory of Europe.* New York, 1994.

Leakey, R. *The Origin of Humankind.* New York, 1994.

Price, T. Douglas, ed. *Europe's First Farmers.* New York, 2000.

Scarre, Chris. *Exploring Prehistoric Europe.* New York, 1998.

InfoTrac College Edition

Enter the search term *archaeology* using the Subject Guide.

Enter the search term *antiquities* using the Subject Guide.

MESOPOTAMIA AND ITS CITIES

Mesopotamia (the land between the rivers Tigris and Euphrates), where urban life first developed, is a flat region of the Middle East stretching from eastern Asia Minor to the Persian Gulf. The land presented enormous natural obstacles to the development of agriculture. In addition to the droughts and floods caused by erratic rainfall, the first farmers there had to deal with 8- to 9-foot salt tides from the Persian Gulf, unstable river courses, and the poor protection offered by the nearby Zagros Mountains. To overcome all of these obstacles required unusual reserves of persistence and determination. In order to farm successfully, Mesopotamia's inhabitants needed to build dikes to reduce flooding during the rainy season and dig channels to distribute water throughout the rest of the year. Early settlers discovered that they could more easily construct large-scale projects by combining resources and merging their villages.

By around 3500 B.C., the dominating people in southern Mesopotamia were the Sumerians, who built towns with simple temples. Over the next two millennia, some of these urban centers became larger and more complex as the Sumerians developed many of the innovations that made civilization possible. Among them was writing, which was used to keep records of offerings and inventories in the temples.

About 3300 B.C., cities such as Ur and Uruk—each of them the center of a small city-state—became the bases from which the Sumerians expanded to control the rest of Mesopotamia. Despite internal conflicts between individual Sumerian cities, Sumerian influence over the Semitic peoples of northern Mesopotamia lasted from 2900 to 2331 B.C. (The term "Semitic" originally applied to the language group that included the Hebrews and many of the peoples of the Arabian peninsula.) This period also marked the zenith of Sumerian culture, including the construction of impressive temples and the production of lavish jewelry and gold treasures, together with an amazing sophistication in mathematics.

For the next millennium, a succession of invasions disrupted the entire region. Sumerian rule was ended in 2331 B.C. by Sargon, chieftain of the Akkadians, one of the northern Semitic peoples. His conquest had been preceded by earlier settlement of Akkadians in Sumerian territory, some of whom may have prepared the way for Sargon by holding important political positions. After conquering Sumer, Sargon pushed west to the Mediterranean. The Akkadians maintained Mesopotamia united under their control from 2331 to 2150 B.C. Borrowing many features of Sumerian civilization, including irrigation methods and writing, they used them for large-scale trade and agricultural projects.

When Akkadian rule came to an abrupt and violent end with a severe climate change, accompanied by the invasion of tribes from Iran, the cities of southern Mesopotamia saw a revival of Sumerian culture. About 2000 B.C., this rule too was overthrown, and the whole of Mesopotamia fell into a state of disunity.

A reunited Mesopotamia finally emerged again under the Babylonians, whose most famous king, Hammurabi, ruled from 1792 to 1750 B.C. Equally skilled at warfare and diplomacy, Hammurabi's most lasting achievement was the code of laws he devised. His capital city, Babylon, became a center for the arts and for mathematicians and astronomers.

Around 1530 B.C., new invasions from the east ended Babylonian rule. The Kassites ruled over the former territories of Sumer and Akkad until c. 1200, after which the Assyrians eventually emerged as the ruling power in Mesopotamia. Militant empire builders, they led expeditions of conquest to the north and west, and by 1100 B.C. Assyrian forces had spread as far as the Black Sea and the Mediterranean. After a period of military decline, Assyria rose to new power under a series of warrior kings, notable for the harshness with which they treated the peoples they conquered.

The Assyrian capital, Nineveh, became one of the most magnificent cities of its age, and the clay tablets from its library provide the basis of our knowledge of Mesopotamian literature. In 612 B.C., however, Nineveh fell to an alliance led by the Babylonians and the Medes. Mesopotamia eventually became a province in the Persian Empire, ending its 2,500-year-old independent history.

THE TIGRIS AND EUPHRATES: RIVERS AND CIVILIZATION

All four of the world's first centers of civilization—the Middle East, Egypt, northern China, and northwest India—lie in river valleys, whose abundant water and fertile land attracted early settlers. In the Middle East, the rivers Tigris and Euphrates both have their sources in the rocky peaks of Armenia. (In this account, the term "Middle East" is used to refer to the geographical area. The ancient civilizations in this and subsequent topics are described as those of the Near East.) Flowing southeast, they leave behind the mountains, to cross first barren, flat desert land, and then a 6,000-square-mile expanse of marshes and mudflats. Finally, the two rivers join and enter the Persian Gulf.

In Mesopotamia, a part of the land between these two rivers—often known as the Fertile Crescent, and also including Syria, Lebanon, and Israel/Palestine—the first civilizations in western Eurasia began to develop. Neolithic societies had formed stable communities and improved tools and farming methods. The production of manufactured goods led to the beginnings of trade. The transition from these settlements to cities, with organized government, economy, and religion, occurred in the years between 5000 and 3000 B.C.

THE BIRTH OF CIVILIZATION

The key factor in the rise of civilization was improved farming methods. By growing more food and rearing more animals, communities could enlarge and prosper. Early settlers learned first to irrigate land close to the river and then to divert water by canals to more distant fields. The river waters, with their rich mud, provided a fertile basis for growing crops. At the same time, the rivers not only supplied the developing cities with mud, reeds, and clay for building and pottery making but also contained fish, which played an important part in the Mesopotamian diet.

These great rivers were not always benevolent to those living beside them. In the rainy spring season, unpredictable floods often devastated entire cities as torrents of water poured down from the mountains across the flat desert and marshlands. The biblical story of Noah and the Ark is a reminder of the destructive power unleashed by floodwaters, as is one of the three Sumerian epic accounts of a disastrous flood. (For a discussion of the account of the flood in the *Epic of Gilgamesh*, see Topic 5.)

To avert the danger, the river dwellers sought the protection of their gods. Both the flood described in Genesis and that of the Sumerian tradition were believed to have been sent as divine retribution for human behavior, and the power of the priesthood that developed in the early

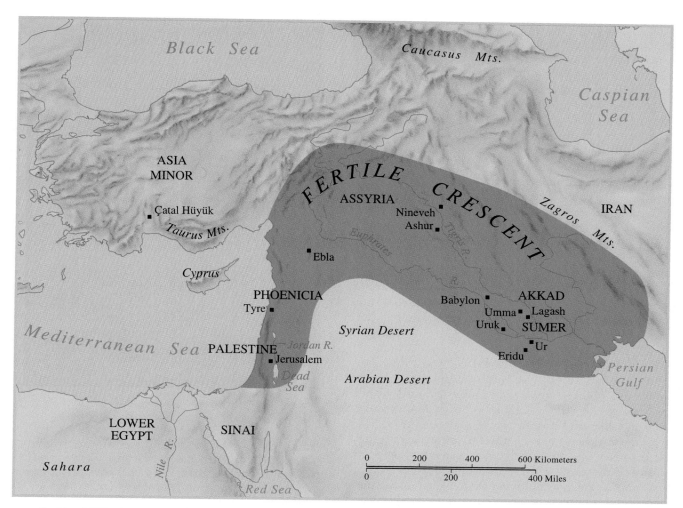

Map 2.1 The Ancient Near East. Note how the line of inhabited settlements falls into the so-called Fertile Crescent between the two main rivers, the Tigris and the Euphrates, which have their source in the lofty Taurus Mountains to the north. The other early sites are also accessible to water, on the east coast of the Mediterranean. Go to http://info.wadsworth.com/053461065X for an interactive version of this map.

cities no doubt depended on its role as intercessor. More practically, communities joined forces to plan and build networks of canals to distribute water and control—or at least reduce—the force of the flooding. Such planning required effective organization and administration, from which there grew the centralized authority necessary for urban life.

THE SUMERIANS AND THE RISE OF CITIES

The land of Sumer lies in the southern part of Mesopotamia, in the fertile valleys separating the desert from the Persian Gulf. By 3000 B.C., its inhabitants had developed political stability and sufficient food supplies to maintain large-scale communities. Cities such as Uruk and Lagash supported populations as large as 20 thousand. In its heyday, Ur and its

surrounding region—the largest Sumerian settlement—perhaps had as many as 400,000 inhabitants.

Each of these cities ruled over its own state. Sharing a common language and religion, the communities nonetheless maintained their autonomy. Conflicts among neighboring cities over land and water rights led to the development of rival alliances and effectively prevented the establishment of a single leading power. The Sumerians managed to achieve their astonishing series of discoveries and inventions in the context of virtually constant warfare against one another. Only around 2400 B.C. did the ruler of Umma briefly unite most of the Sumerian cities under his control. Fifty years later the Sumerians were conquered by the Akkadians.

THE TEMPLE AND THE PALACE
The responsibility for governing each of these city-states fell on two authorities: the priests and the civil governor. At the center of each city stood the chief shrine to the gods. The priests who oversaw the design and construction of the

temples, and performed the divine rituals in them, lived off the land set aside for them by the community. They divided some of the produce among themselves and their staff, used some as offerings for the gods, and sold off the rest to pay for building and maintenance.

Although the priesthood was central to Sumerian life, the priests did not, as scholars used to believe, own all the land and govern the cities by controlling their economies. It is now thought that one-third of the land in each state was owned by the priests, one-third was under royal control, and the remaining third was in private hands.

The chief political authority in each state was a king or governor, who probably achieved power by military prowess. Over time, as the kingship became hereditary, a class of nobles developed. The king and the nobles owned most of the rest of the land. The workers on their estates were either free citizens, who received in return a small piece of land with which to support themselves, or slaves. The Sumerians were among the earliest people to institutionalize slave labor, using prisoners of war and captured foreigners, mainly women.

TECHNOLOGY AND TRADE

Shortly after 3000 B.C., the Sumerians discovered how to combine copper and tin to make bronze and used the new material to cast weapons and tools. They also worked in gold and silver and learned how to solder and rivet. They were the first people to use a wheel to manufacture pottery. At the same time, they devised new methods of transport, inventing the wagon wheel and building sailboats. (One of the Sumerians' minor contributions to civilization was their discovery that by fermenting grain they could produce alcoholic beer.)

Mesopotamia had little in the way of natural resources. Wood, stone, and metal had to be imported from outside the region, and the Sumerians were thus driven to develop an extended trading network. They sent out expeditions and set up overseas trading centers throughout the area from Asia Minor to India; tin came from Asia Minor and Syria, shells from India, lapis lazuli from Afghanistan, and cedar and pinewood from the forests of Syria and Iran.

THE INVENTION OF WRITING

As patterns of administration became ever more complex, the Sumerians found the need for new systems of organization and control. In seeking to create these systems, they invented writing, one of the most crucial tools of civilization. It now seems that around 5000 B.C. earlier peoples of the ancient Near East had devised simple methods of using token signs to record on stone or clay tablets for trade transactions, but the Sumerian cuneiform script was the first fully developed writing system in history. Its signs were based on the shapes of the earlier token signs.

The script's name, *cuneiform,* comes from two Latin words, *cuneus* ("wedge") and *forma* ("shape"). The earliest Sumerian inscriptions used signs that took the form of simplified pictures representing a group of related meanings. A leg, for instance, meant not only the leg itself but also the idea of

The University of Pennsylvania Museum

Ram in a Thicket from Royal Graves at Ur c. 2700 B.C. Height 19 inches (45.7 cm). The goat is rearing up on its hind legs to sniff at the flowers on a bush. The bush is of gold leaf, while the ram's face and legs are of gold leaf, the horns, eyes, and shoulder fleece of lapis lazuli, and the body fleece of white shell. The figure probably served as part of the support for a piece of furniture. The theme of an animal climbing up toward the shoots of a sacred tree is a common one in Sumerian religious art.

walking. The scribes drew or impressed the signs on soft clay tablets, which were then baked hard, either in ovens or more commonly by drying them in the sun. Over time, as the production and circulation of tablets increased, the Sumerians simplified the pictures by using a split reed to press wedge-shaped marks into the wet clay—hence the name cuneiform.

The cuneiform script remained in use for the next three millennia in western Asia, as the Akkadians, Babylonians, Assyrians, and many other peoples adapted versions of the Sumerian system to their own languages. For them, as for the Sumerians themselves, writing proved an essential political and economic tool. It also made possible two other turning points in human culture: the appearance of literature and the setting up of schools. The first schools served as training centers for scribes, but they soon attracted scientists and scholars. Among the subjects taught were mathematics, spelling, and literature. The staff member responsible for discipline was known as "the man in charge of the whip." In a culture with a very low level of general literacy, these schools were of high social status, and the scribes they produced formed an elite class.

For all their creativity and high cultural achievement, the Sumerians' inability to coexist peacefully with one another proved their downfall. When the Akkadians attacked them in

These four tablets show different forms of early writing. The top two are limestone tablets from Kish, dating to c. 3200 B.C., and are among the earliest of all surviving examples of writing. Among the signs are parts of the human body. In the middle is an Egyptian hieroglyphic inscription from a temple at Karnac c. 1940 B.C., using various animals; birds and snakes are clearly visible. The inscription at the bottom is part of the law Code of Hammurabi c. 1760 B.C. The writing is in cuneiform script, the signs in which have lost their resemblance to picture signs.

Hirmer Fotoarchiv

2331 B.C., they were too weak to resist, and Sumerian domination of Mesopotamia came to an end.

THE AKKADIAN CONQUEST AND ITS AFTERMATH

The Akkadian conquest and unification of Mesopotamia formed the cornerstone in the creation of the world's first empire. Sargon (c. 2371–2316 B.C.), who overthrew his overlord to become chieftain of this Semitic-speaking people of central Mesopotamia, was to boast that his power and influence stretched "from the lower sea to the upper sea"—from the Persian Gulf to the Mediterranean. (This was in fact a considerable overstatement; Sargon never ruled Egypt or anywhere south of Ebla in Syria.)

Sargon's success was the result of his combination of military strength with the technology he had learned from his southern neighbors. Akkad, the capital city he founded for his people in 2370 B.C., served as the base for the newly united Mesopotamia. For the first time, the idea of a territorial state replaced that of the city-state and led to a period of imperial expansion.

SIGNIFICANT DATES

**Civilizations in Mesopotamia
(all dates B.C.)**

c. 3000–c. 2350	The Sumerians
c. 2350–c. 2200	The Akkadians
c. 2100–c. 2000	The Third Dynasty of Ur
c. 1800–c. 1600	The Babylonians
c. 1600–c. 1200	The Kassites
c. 2000–c. 850	The rise of the Assyrians
c. 850–612	The Assyrian Empire

© 1984 Metropolitan Museum of Art

Portrait of Gudea, the governor of Lagash, seated in an attitude of devotion before the gods c. 2100 B.C. Height 17½ inches (42 cm). The details of the drapery and headgear contrast with the simplicity of the face, which, like the position of the hands, suggests the humility of this neo-Sumerian ruler.

THE AKKADIANS AND SUMERIAN CULTURE

The culture and technology the Akkadians spread throughout this wide region were basically Sumerian. The chief Akkadian contribution was to use Sumerian ideas and techniques in a broader, more organized way. Irrigation projects no longer fell under the control of the priests but were administered by secular officials. Thus knowledge of agricultural construction methods, which the Sumerian priests had jealously guarded, circulated more widely and made possible large-scale public works programs.

Like the Sumerians, the Akkadians needed to import raw materials for their constructions and were even more inclined than their predecessors to mount military campaigns for the purpose. One of Sargon's most ferocious attacks was on the timber-yielding mountains of the Lebanon. There were tenuous links between Mesopotamia and ancient India, with Indian ivory being exchanged for Mesopotamian oil and textiles.

Only in the past few years have archeologists been discovering the extent to which the Akkadians spread Mesopotamian culture. At the site of Ebla, in northern Syria, excavations have revealed thousands of clay tablets with inscriptions in a version of the Mesopotamian script developed under Sumerian influence, and the works of art produced in Ebla show strong Sumerian influence. The city of Ebla passed under Akkadian rule when it was conquered by Sargon. Other Syrian cities in turn picked up the new culture and spread it farther afield.

THE FALL OF AKKAD AND THE SUMERIAN RENAISSANCE

The unity the Akkadians had imposed on Mesopotamia came to a sudden and violent end around 2150 B.C. Recent discoveries suggest that a major climatic shift occurred then, marked by severe drought. When this drought was accompanied by a wave of invading tribes from the upper valley of the Tigris destroying the Akkadians' central authority, Mesopotamia once again divided into a series of separate kingdoms.

The collapse of the Akkadian empire brought a rebirth of civilization and art in Sumer, which lasted for almost a century. Gudea (c. 2144–2124 B.C.), the ruler of Lagash, was a patron of the arts who commissioned important temple complexes. Several statues of Gudea have survived, showing him in humble and devout prayer. His impact was sufficient for later generations to worship him as a god.

After Gudea's death, Ur replaced Lagash as the principal Sumerian city. Its best-known ruler was Ur-Nammu (c. 2112–2095 B.C.), who introduced a series of laws governing various aspects of society, including the obligations of owners to their slaves. Although Ur-Nammu's laws touched on only a select number of issues and did not form a complete law code, they marked the first time in history that a ruler tried to provide his people with some basis of legal order.

Attacks from east and west put an end to Ur's renaissance around 1950 B.C. For the next century and a half, Mesopotamia lost its importance as a cultural center. Power passed elsewhere as a new people, the Amorites, began to play an increasingly aggressive role in the Fertile Crescent. The third great period in Mesopotamian history began with its conquest shortly after 1800 B.C. by the Amorites' most famous king, Hammurabi of Babylon.

THE BABYLONIANS: THE RULE OF LAW

The Amorites were a Semitic people who migrated from the desert fringes of Arabia about 2000 B.C. Soon after settling in Mesopotamia, they adopted Mesopotamian culture. Their chief city was Babylon, located between Sumerian and Akkadian territory, and thus they were able to control trade in both directions. The Babylonians gradually extended their power throughout Mesopotamia, and at the same time began to establish links further west, with the peoples of Asia Minor. By the time of their definitive conquest of Mesopotamia, their commercial contacts reached as far west as the Mediterranean, while under the dominance of the city of Babylon the trade routes in the region had shifted from the south to the north.

HAMMURABI AND THE UNITY OF MESOPOTAMIA

Babylonian power reached its peak in the reign of Hammurabi (c. 1792–1750 B.C.). Using an adroit blend of diplomacy and aggression, Hammurabi united the whole of Mesopotamia under his rule and made Babylon the region's capital. Among the techniques he used to encourage unity was religious propaganda: The combined deities of Mesopotamia, he claimed, had elected Marduk—the principal Babylonian god—as their king.

The city boasted splendid temples decorated with elaborate sculptures, and the annual New Year festival held there attracted crowds of worshipers. Hammurabi used Babylon's religious prestige to reinforce his own authority, claiming that the gods appointed "me, Hammurabi, the obedient god-fearing prince to cause righteousness to appear in the land, to destroy the evil and the wicked, that the strong harm not the weak."

THE LAW CODE

In order to accomplish these aims, Hammurabi drew up a law code, the first complete one in history to survive. It established procedures for the courts of law, laid down property rights, codified the duties and responsibilities for family members, and fixed penalties for crimes. The system of justice it records was in all probability based on basic legal principles and precedents established by earlier cases. (For a more detailed discussion of the social implications of the law code, see Topic 6.)

Many of Hammurabi's letters and orders have survived, and they provide a vivid picture of an active administrator, who took pride in describing himself at the end of the law code as "the efficient king." Among the issues he deals with in his correspondence are reform of the calendar, the punishment of officials for bribery, and the clearing of a blockage in the Euphrates that was holding up traffic. In one letter he orders a legal hearing to be delayed to let one of the participants, the temple baker, organize the catering for a religious feast at Ur.

THE END OF THE BABYLONIAN EMPIRE

Hammurabi's empire did not long survive his death. Once again Mesopotamia began to fragment, and in c. 1595 B.C. a Hittite army raided Babylon. (For a discussion of the Hittites, see Topic 4.) The resulting confusion left Babylonia wide open to an invasion of Kassites. A nomadic mountain people from the upland region to the northeast of the Mesopotamian plain, the Kassites were able to conquer the region because of their mastery of chariot warfare. They occupied Babylon for some four centuries. The period seems to have been one of relative stability; the Kassites created their own style of art and codified a great deal of Mesopotamian literature. Mesopotamia rose to prominence again only when it came under Assyrian rule around 1150 B.C., when the last great era of Mesopotamian culture began.

THE ASSYRIANS AND THE THIRST FOR EMPIRE

Toward the end of Kassite rule, the Late Bronze Age world of intercultural trade began to fall apart, as the Kassites' northern neighbors, the Assyrians, began their gradual rise to power. This Semitic-speaking people occupied the unprotected plains of the upper valley of the river Tigris, where their most important city was Assur, co-capital together with Nimrud. Forced to defend themselves both from the Babylonians to the south and the fierce nomadic tribes to their north, the Assyrians evolved into one of the most aggressive and grimly militarized societies in history.

With the fall of the Hittites, their chief rivals in western Asia, around 1200 B.C., the Assyrians began to expand rapidly. King Tiglath-Pileser I (c. 1115–1077) grandiloquently took as his title "King of the World, king of Assyria, king of all the four rims of the earth." His boast may have been exaggerated, but his empire building was considerable: He took over much of the Hittite territory to the northwest of Assyria, conquered northern Syria, pushed as far as the Mediterranean coast, and defeated Babylon.

His immediate successors lost some of these gains, but by the time of their period of greatest success, 883–612 B.C., the Assyrians ruled over a mighty empire, stretching at its widest from the river Nile almost to the Caspian Sea, and from northern Syria to the Persian Gulf, and containing virtually all of the earlier centers of power in the ancient Near East.

THE ASSYRIAN MILITARY MACHINE

In order to gain and hold their empire, the Assyrians developed a formidable military force at home and built a reputation as ferocious and bloodthirsty terrorists abroad. All fit Assyrian males were required to serve in their army, the first fighting force to be fully equipped with iron weapons. Assyrian siege artillery was capable of demolishing the city walls of those who were unwise enough to hold out against them.

After the conquest of a city came a campaign of terror. Torture, mass executions, destruction, and plunder were often followed by uprooting the surviving inhabitants of a captured town. Assyrian rulers boasted proudly of their deeds: "Their boys and girls I burnt up in flame . . . pillars of skulls I erected before their town . . . I dyed the mountains with their blood like red wool." Tiglath-Pileser III (744–727 B.C.) proclaimed the forcible transportation of 30,300 people at a time.

The Assyrians undoubtedly encouraged the spread of their reputation for savage cruelty as a means of discouraging resistance and revolt, and the accounts of their deeds in the Old Testament further reinforce their negative posthumous reputation. In practice, they were probably little different from other imperial leaders, and their rule frequently brought benefits to their victims. The imperial administration was the most sophisticated and organized in the history of Mesopotamia. Provincial governors, with their own bureaucracies of scribes and advisers, could collect taxes, decide legal disputes on the basis of a written law code, and raise local armies. They could keep in touch with developments elsewhere thanks to the construction of a road network that linked the chief centers of the empire and to the existence of an efficient postal system.

More important, perhaps, the use of Aramaic as a common language and the wholesale population movements—both of soldiers on duty and civilians—led to the formation of a multinational empire sharing central rule and a common culture, the forerunner of later empires in the ancient Near East: those of the Persians, of Alexander, and eventually the Romans.

ASSYRIAN CULTURE

For all their aggressive political domination, the Assyrians remained under the cultural influence of the Babylonians. Tiglath-Pileser III implicitly acknowledged this point when he added to his title that of "ruler of Babylonia" around 725 B.C. The great library of Ashurbanipal (c. 669–630 B.C.) at Nineveh contained a vast collection of Sumerian and Babylonian literature; some 25 thousand tablets from that collection are now to be found in the British Museum.

The palaces at Nimrud and Nineveh were decorated with intricately carved scenes. Many of them are of war episodes, showing fierce fighting and battlefields littered with the bodies of dead and dying soldiers. The carvings that most clearly evidence an independent Assyrian character are those showing hunting scenes. From as far back as the great Tiglath-Pileser I, Assyrian kings had prided themselves on their hunting prowess, yet surprisingly enough the most striking feature of many of the hunting reliefs is the careful depiction of the animals, together with a sympathetic identification with their suffering.

THE END OF THE ASSYRIAN EMPIRE

The very size of the Assyrian Empire proved in the end to be its undoing. The army, overextended and increasingly dependent on foreign mercenaries, could in the end no longer crush internal revolts or foreign attacks. In 612 B.C. two tribes, the Medes and the Babylonians, joined forces to sack Nineveh, and Assyrian domination was over. By the following century, Mesopotamia had become part of the Persian Empire. The verdict of the Old Testament prophet Nahum was probably heartily echoed by most of

Relief from the Palace of Ashurbanipal at Nineveh c. 668–626 B.C. The scene shows a royal hunt, in which wild asses are attacked by the king's dogs, while his attendants hurl javelins at them. On the lower level a mare turns her head to look for her foal, which is about to be seized by the mastiff behind.

© The British Museum

his contemporaries: "Nineveh is laid waste; who will bemoan her?"

THE NEO-BABYLONIAN EMPIRE

For less than a century following the fall of Nineveh, a part of Babylonia enjoyed a brilliant revival. Chaldean tribes, who had resisted Assyrian rule, set up their kingdom with Babylon as its capital. Under King Nebuchadnezzar (ruled c. 605–562 B.C.), the city became one of the wonders of the ancient world, with its palaces, temples, and the spectacular Hanging Gardens.

In 586 B.C., Nebuchadnezzar's forces crushed the kingdom of Judah, destroyed Jerusalem, and took the Jews back to Babylon in captivity (see Topic 4). An internal power struggle after his death left the Neo-Babylonian Empire fatally weakened, and in 539 B.C. Cyrus the Great, king of the Medes and Persians, captured Babylon and made Babylonia a province of the Persian Empire.

Putting Mesopotamia in Perspective

The earliest settlers of the land between the two rivers, the Sumerians, failed to achieve lasting political or military dominance, but their cultural contribution to Mesopotamian history, and to the growth of civilization, was enormous. All subsequent ruling powers there profited from Sumerian discoveries and advances. The urban skills they developed made possible the ordered society of Hammurabi and the centralized empire of the Assyrians. Sumerian religion and literature continued to influence the ancient Near East for more than a thousand years after their age. Babylonians and Assyrians developed scientific and astronomical research first undertaken by Sumerians.

Yet without the administrative abilities of the Akkadians, and then of the Babylonians and Assyrians, Sumerian ideas would never have had the wide circulation they were to achieve. Each successive conquering power borrowed the culture and, to some extent at least, the religion of its predecessors, and spread them increasingly widely throughout western Asia.

With the absorption of Mesopotamia into the Persian Empire, the direct transmission of accumulated Mesopotamian tradition came to an end. When Alexander the Great conquered Persia, however, Greek scientists inherited from their Mesopotamian predecessors the astrological zodiac and the gleanings of hundreds of years of astronomy. Furthermore, Greeks in Asia Minor had earlier borrowed the Mesopotamian system of time divisions: 24 hours in a day, 60 minutes in an hour, 60 seconds in a minute. Greek art and architecture for a while adopted Mesopotamian and Egyptian styles, but the Greeks were quick to find their own characteristic approach to art.

If anything, the long-term legacy of the history of Mesopotamia, and of the Sumerians in particular, was to implant in the Near East a tradition of small, independent states, capable of surviving the rise and fall of empires. The strong sense of regional diversity outlasted the rise and fall of the Roman Empire, and the rise of Islam, and still dominates the political, religious, and cultural world of the Middle East today.

Questions for Further Study

1. What were the main cultural and political similarities and differences between the Sumerians, Babylonians, and Assyrians? How did these differences affect their history?
2. What part did trade play in the development of Mesopotamia?
3. Among the legacies of the peoples of the ancient Near East were writing and law codes. In what other ways did Mesopotamian culture affect later times?
4. What were the effects of climate and geography on the growth of the first cities? How relevant are these factors to urban life today?

Suggestions for Further Reading

Collon, Dominique. *Ancient Near Eastern Art.* Berkeley, 1995.

Crawford, Harriet. *Sumer and the Sumerians.* New York, 1991.

Frankfort, Henri. *The Art and Architecture of the Ancient Orient,* 5th ed. New Haven, 1996.

Meyers, Eric M., ed. *The Oxford Encyclopedia of Archaeology in the Near East.* New York, 1997.

Porada, Edith, and Robert Dyson. *Man and Images in the Ancient Near East.* Wakefield, 1995.

Postgate, J. Nicholas. *Early Mesopotamia: Society and Economy at the Dawn of History.* London, 1992.

Reade, Julian E. *Assyrian Sculpture.* Cambridge, 1999.

Roaf, M. *Cultural Atlas of Mesopotamia and the Ancient Near East.* New York, 1990.

Saggs, H.W.F. *Babylonians.* London, 1995.

Sasson, Jack M., ed. *Civilizations of the Ancient Near East.* New York, 1995.

Schmandt-Besserat, D. *Before Writing,* 2 vols. Austin, 1992.

Snell, Daniel C. *Life in the Ancient Near East, 3100-332 B.C.* New Haven, 1997.

Visicato, Giuseppe. *The Power and the Writing: The Early Scribes of Mesopotamia.* Bethesda, 2000.

InfoTrac College Edition

Enter the search term *Mesopotamia* using Key Terms.

Enter the search term *Babylonian* using Key Terms.

Enter the search term *Assyrian* using Key Terms.

EGYPT OF THE PHARAOHS

The geography of ancient Egypt played a determining role in the formation of its culture. Lower Egypt lay at the delta of the river Nile, and its access to the Mediterranean facilitated contacts with other neighboring peoples. Upper Egypt to the south, on the other hand, was far more isolated. Because the climate has always been very dry, farmers depended on the river's waters, especially those accumulated in the annual summer flooding.

Egyptian history is divided into four main periods, which were separated from one another by times of upheaval: the Old Kingdom (beginning c. 2700 B.C.), the Middle Kingdom (beginning c. 2050 B.C.), the New Kingdom (beginning c. 1570 B.C.), and the Late Period (beginning c. 1070 B.C.), which ended with Egypt's incorporation into the Persian Empire around 500 B.C.

The unification of Upper and Lower Egypt preceded the Old Kingdom by a little more than a century. Throughout the Old Kingdom a series of powerful *pharaohs*—or kings—ruled over the country. The pharaoh provided strong central government and headed the state religion. He was regarded as a living god and wielded absolute power, although over the centuries the official bureaucracy tended to increase its influence. The grandiose temples and tombs of the Old Kingdom (which include the pyramids) reflect the stability and prosperity of the age.

Around 2185 B.C. political and religious disputes began to undermine the authority of the pharaoh. Order was restored only a century and a half later in 2050 B.C. with the Middle Kingdom. During the first part of this period, Egypt flourished, as improved systems of irrigation raised food production and living standards. The Egyptians began to establish trading contacts abroad and protect their southern borders by military campaigns. By c. 1640 B.C., however, internal rivalries and weakness made it possible for a foreign people, the Hyksos, to invade and conquer the country.

Within less than a century, hatred of their foreign rulers united the Egyptians behind a new dynasty of pharaohs who drove out the Hyksos and established the New Kingdom. For the first time, Egyptian rulers began to wage aggressive empire-building campaigns abroad. Thutmose III even crossed the Euphrates into Mesopotamia. Religion continued to follow the centuries-old traditions. Only the pharaoh Akhenaton rejected much of traditional polytheism and encouraged the worship of the god Aton. After his death, the priests branded Akhenaton a heretic and overthrew his reforms.

Toward the end of the New Kingdom, Hittites, Libyans, and others began to raid Egypt and its empire, and even the mighty Ramses II (1304–1237 B.C.) was forced to conclude a peace treaty. Not long after Ramses' reign, Egypt fell increasingly under foreign control, eventually being conquered first by Assyria and then by Persia.

THE NILE AND ITS VALLEY

Egypt's life is inextricably linked to the Nile. At the beginning of Egyptian history, the earliest Neolithic communities settled in the river's valley, and from then on the Nile inspired and controlled Egypt's political, religious, economic, and social life.

The river divided Egypt into two parts. Lower Egypt consisted of the northern region of the delta—broad, marshy lowlands extending from the modern city of Cairo to the Mediterranean. Upper Egypt was a long, very narrow strip of immensely fertile land stretching some 600 miles along the river, surrounded on both sides by barren desert alternating with cliffs. Farmers were thus virtually dependent on the river waters, augmented by the summer rains and the water of the Nile's six cataracts, for the production of their crops.

THE UNIFICATION OF EGYPT

Although the earliest settlements along the Nile go back to Neolithic times, at first their scattered locations, strung out along the river valley, discouraged them from pooling their

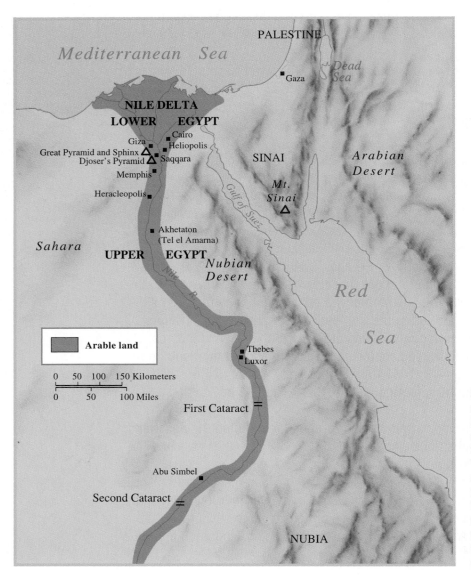

Map 3.1 Ancient Egypt. All of the chief centers of habitation of the ancient Egyptians lay on the Nile River. Its source is to the south of this map, in modern Sudan. At its first great bend lies the ancient capital of Thebes (modern Luxor), where the temple complex of Karnak is located. Directly across the Nile were the Valleys of the Kings and Queens. Farther north was Akhenaton's capital of Akhetaton, while the cluster of settlements around Giza (site of the Pyramids) was to become the location of Egypt's modern capital, Cairo.

resources and joining together. With time, however, communication and commercial exchanges along the river broke the barriers, and the various small communities united to form two states: the kingdoms of Upper and Lower Egypt.

According to tradition, the first ruler to unify the two kingdoms was Menes (ruled c. 3100 B.C.), who also founded the new nation's capital at Memphis and inaugurated the first dynasty of Egyptian pharaohs. Throughout its 3,000-year history, ancient Egypt maintained the tradition of its origins as two states: the official title of the pharaoh was "Lord of the Two Lands."

Menes' original name is lost to us, although most Egyptologists use the name Narmer. The form in which it survived is Greek and comes from the history of Egypt written in Greek by an Egyptian high priest, Manetho (c. 280 B.C.). Manetho's account is also responsible for the traditional division of Egyptian rulers into groups known as dynasties. The period of Egyptian history before Menes is called Predynastic, and from the time of Menes to that of the mid-4th century B.C. there were 30 dynasties.

THE EARLY DYNASTIC PERIOD
(C. 3100–2700 B.C.)

Little is known of Menes and his successors. The royal tombs of the period are known as *mastabas* and were built of mud brick. (The word *mastaba* is the Arabic for "bench," and literally referred to the mudbrick superstructure covering these early tombs, which looked like a bench to the explorers of the 19th century.) In the 3rd Dynasty, the Egyptians turned for the first time to stone, the material that was to characterize their architecture for the rest of Egyptian history. King Zoser (c. 2668–c. 2649 B.C.) commissioned the construction at Saqqara, near Memphis, of a magnificent funeral complex. Its architect was Imhotep (flourished 2630 B.C.), the first known example of a great creative genius. Renowned in his day not only for his buildings, but also as astronomer, priest, and minister to Zoser, Imhotep was revered by later generations for his skills in medicine and worshiped as a god.

Zoser's actual tomb began as a series of stepped *mastabas*, which took the final form of a stepped pyramid, a shape that many of his Old Kingdom successors would modify into true pyramidal form. His reign thus began the tradition of building grandiose funerary monuments to guarantee the immortality of their occupants. Because Egyptian religion taught that physical preservation of the body was necessary for the survival of the soul, the Egyptians developed the art of mummification. Using a complex mixture of oils and spices, they embalmed the corpse and placed it, wrapped in fabric and contained in a series of cases, one within the other, underneath or at the center of the funerary monument.

THE TRADITIONS OF EGYPTIAN RELIGION

The formation of traditional Egyptian religious beliefs and structures also goes back to the Predynastic Period. The pharaoh's role as head of state drew additional strength from

Painted relief from a funerary temple at Abydos, c. 1300 B.C. To the left is the figure of the pharaoh Sethos I, who was buried in a tomb adjoining the temple, dressed as the god Osiris, with his tall crown and holding the divine whisk and crook. Osiris, the deity who presided over the funeral rites, had his chief sanctuary at Abydos. The other figure is Thoth, the ibis-headed god of writing.

his status as living god. Beneath him were the priests, who were jealous guardians of tradition. From the time of Zoser, the chief Egyptian deity was the sun god Re, who had created the world by bringing order from the primeval chaos of the universe. His representative, the pharaoh, similarly ordered the real world.

By the time of the Middle Kingdom, Egyptian religion was based on the belief in life after death. All Egyptians, not only the rich or powerful, could hope for survival in the next world as the reward for a good life. Elaborate funeral rituals recounted the ceremony of the judgment of the dead, who were then pronounced worthy to pass on to the next life. The ruler of the Underworld and judge of the dead was Osiris, who came to symbolize resurrection. Over time, Osiris—together with his wife Isis and son, the falcon god Horus—became the symbol of spiritual, rather than merely material, survival.

In addition to the central cults, Egyptians worshiped an almost infinite number of other deities. The mythology and ritual that developed around these figures came to dominate the daily life of every Egyptian. The sky goddess Nut often appears stretched out on the ceilings of the tombs, swallowing the sun and creating night. Each morning, she would give birth to the sun again. The jackal-headed Anubis was the god of embalming and of the dead.

A C R O S S   C U L T U R E S

HERODOTUS IN EGYPT

In the second book of his *History of the Persian Wars*, the Greek historian Herodotus (for a detailed discussion of Herodotus, see Topic 10) describes his explorations in an Egyptian culture that was already ancient when he visited there in the 5th century B.C. Born in Asia Minor, in the city of Halicarnassus, Herodotus traveled widely in western Asia, visiting

Courtesy of William Duiker

Babylon and the valley of the river Euphrates, and reaching as far north as the land of the Scythians and the Black Sea. We do not know whether his voyages were for the purpose of research for his writings or for business.

While in Egypt Herodotus visited many of the most important monuments and interviewed priests and others to find answers to many of his questions about Egyptian religion, burial methods, and history. He reports his findings with his characteristic tolerance and sympathy for even the strangest of customs. On the Egyptian love of their domestic pets, for example, he writes: "All the inmates of a house where a cat has died a natural death shave their eyebrows, and when a dog has died they shave the whole body, including the head. Cats that have died are taken to Bubastis, where they are embalmed and buried in sacred receptacles; dogs are buried, also in sacred places, in the towns where they belong." On the subject of human mummification, he describes three methods: the best and most expensive, a second one that is less costly, and the cheapest of all, "for those who are not well-off financially."

In describing the building of the pyramids, Herodotus gives the various differing accounts

he heard. The pyramid of Khufu (Cheops) was already some 2,000 years old when he visited it, and memories of its construction were understandably vague. On the raising of the stones to the various levels, he says: "Either there were as many cranes as levels, or they had just one portable crane which they transferred from level to level as the structure rose: I report the alternative versions as I heard them." Like many later visitors, he relied on local guides: "A hieroglyphic inscription on the pyramid records how much radish, garlic, and onion was eaten by the workmen, and, if memory serves, the interpreter who translated the inscription for me said that the expense was 1,600 talents of silver."

Not all subsequent travelers to Egypt were as lucid or as informative. The English explorer Sir Richard Burton wrote in 1855 of his visit to Cairo: "You see nothing but muddy waters, dusty banks, a sand mist, a milky sky, and a blazing sun. . . . The pyramids of Khufa and Khafra (Cheops and Chefren) only suggest of remark that they have been remarkably well-sketched." Herodotus was not only the first known Western tourist in Egypt, but he was also one of the most perceptive.

THE RISE AND FALL OF THE OLD KINGDOM

The 3rd Dynasty inaugurated the Old Kingdom, which lasted from 2700 until 2200 B.C. Three of the 4th Dynasty pharaohs, Khufu (Cheops in Greek), Khafre (Chefren in Greek), and Menkaure (Mycerinus in Greek), were responsible for the famous group of pyramids at Giza, while Khafre also commissioned perhaps the most familiar of all Egyptian images, the colossal human-headed lion known as the Sphinx, which guards his tomb.

THE AGE OF STABILITY

We know practically nothing about the rulers of the 4th and 5th dynasties, apart from their monuments. Later ages recalled Khafre as a good king and Khufu as a tyrant. Certainly the extraordinary size and mathematical precision of Khufu's Great Pyramid suggest a powerfully controlled state, capable of organizing an imposing workforce. Most laborers on the pyramids were peasants working on construction projects when the Nile flooded. The concentration of

General view of the three Great Pyramids of Giza and the Sphinx. The pyramids were constructed by Khufu (c. 2551–2228 B.C.), Khafre (c. 2530–2494 B.C.), and Menkaure (c. 2494–2472 B.C.). Khafre also commissioned the Sphinx, which was carved out of the natural surface of the rock. It has the body of a lion and a human head (perhaps an idealized portrait of Khafre himself) and guards the pharaoh's burial chamber at the heart of his pyramid.

thousands of workers in a single place would have required strong security forces, a constant flow of supplies and food, and massive coordination.

The imposing monuments, together with the superb offerings they contained, mark this period as one of the high points in Egyptian history. The relief carvings of 5th Dynasty tombs provide a detailed description of daily life in pharaonic Egypt, with scenes of goldsmiths, farmers, sandal makers, boat builders, and many others at their work.

All indications suggest that the age was one of stability, in which centralized and efficient government ruled a rigidly stratified society. Contacts with the outside world were limited. There is evidence of some trade with western Asia. Egyptian artifacts of the period have come to light at sites in modern Turkey and Syria. On the whole, however, the 4th and 5th dynasties were a period of internal consolidation.

THE END OF THE OLD KINGDOM

The royal tombs of the 6th Dynasty (c. 2350–c. 2200 B.C.) are far less ambitious than earlier ones, a sign of the diminishing power of the pharaohs. The nobles and high officials in the huge bureaucracies, which ran religious and economic affairs, increasingly challenged the central authority. Meanwhile, several small local principalities sprang up in Egypt whose rulers feuded with one another and ignored the orders of the pharaoh.

With the decline of the Old Kingdom, a century of violence began, exacerbated by the major droughts and climate shifts in the region, which elsewhere contributed to the end of Akkadian domination in Mesopotamia (see Topic 2). One significant factor was the extremely low levels of Nile flooding. Excavation of contemporary cemeteries shows a sharp rise in death rates. With the end of central power and endless fighting among the local rulers, or *nomarchs*, uncertainty replaced the granite solidity of the earlier age.

THE MIDDLE KINGDOM: THE WANING OF STABILITY

The civil wars finally came to an end when Mentuhotep (c. 2061–c. 2010 B.C.) reestablished a central authority and once again united Upper and Lower Egypt. He moved the capital south to Thebes (modern Luxor), which—apart from one brief period—remained the seat of religious influence for the rest of Egypt's independent history. The patron god of Thebes, Amen (whose name means Hidden One), who had earlier been a relatively minor figure, became a dominant force in Egyptian religion.

The Middle Kingdom lasted from c. 2050 until c. 1780 B.C., about two and a half centuries. It began, like the Old Kingdom, with political order, economic stability, and a wave of artistic achievement. Rulers commissioned the building of monuments throughout Egypt, while lavish temples began to adorn the city of Thebes.

SIGNIFICANT DATES

Chief Stages in Egyptian History

(all dates B.C.)

c. 6000	Neolithic and Predynastic Periods
c. 3100	Early Dynastic Period
c. 2700	Old Kingdom
c. 2185	First Intermediate Period
c. 2050	Middle Kingdom
c. 1800	Second Intermediate Period
c. 1570	New Kingdom
c. 1070	Late Dynastic Period (Third Intermediate Period)
c. 525	Persian Conquest

Earlier pharaohs were satisfied to protect Egypt's borders against invasion, the greatest threat having come from hostile Nubians to the south. In the Middle Kingdom, the Egyptians went on the offensive. The powerful pharaoh Senwosret (Sesostris in Greek) III (c. 1878–c. 1844 B.C.) instructed his son: "A valiant man must attack. To retreat is cowardly. Consequently any son of mine who strengthens the frontier which My Majesty has created is truly my son." Senwosret lived up to his words by leading troops against the Nubians on their own territory. He then constructed fortresses along the new border he had created. Other pharaohs preferred to extend Egyptian influence by building trade contacts, and Palestine and the sea ports of the Lebanon became outposts for the Egyptian economy.

THE HYKSOS INVASION

For all the prosperity of the Middle Kingdom, the warning signs of regional squabbles began to appear at the beginning of the 13th Dynasty (c. 1780 B.C.). The rift between Upper and Lower Egypt reopened, and each half further split into warring states.

At this moment of weakness (about 1700 B.C.), Egypt suffered the first invasion in its history. The newcomers were the Hyksos, a group of Semitic immigrants from Palestine. Dominating the Nile valley, they exacted tribute from the Egyptian rulers of Thebes whom they allowed to retain nominal power. In fact, the Hyksos kept the native kings weak by encouraging several rival claimants to the throne at the same time. Although Egyptians of later ages remembered the Hyksos with hatred and fear, their arrival in Egypt brought a host of technological and cultural benefits. Cut off by geography and natural disposition from any real contact with other peoples, the Egyptians had failed to benefit from new ideas and techniques developed in western Asia and by Mediterranean Bronze Age peoples. Under Hyksos influence, they learned to replace their copper tools with bronze ones, which were sharper and lasted longer. Horse-drawn chariots, bronze armor and weapons, and more efficient bows all revolutionized Egyptian warfare. The Hyksos also in-

troduced new kinds of trees and plants, perhaps including the olive and the pomegranate.

After a century of Hyksos influence, Egyptian resentment toward the foreigners drove them to unite behind Ahmose (c. 1570–c. 1546 B.C.). The pharaoh routed the Hyksos in 1550 B.C. and drove them from power. The unified state that he went on to create, with its first capital at Thebes, became during the New Kingdom one of the great international powers of the late Bronze Age.

EMPIRE AND GRANDEUR: THE NEW KINGDOM

For half a millennium, a succession of New Kingdom pharaohs ruled over a powerful and prosperous state. They were absolute monarchs, warrior kings who were also responsible for some of the most enormous buildings ever constructed. The grandeur of their cities and the richness of their treasures were stupefying.

FOREIGN POLICY IN THE NEW KINGDOM

The military and political climate in which these rulers operated was a new one. Before the Hyksos invasion, Egypt's geographical location had protected it from attack. While Mesopotamia endured wave after wave of violence, Egypt was vulnerable only at its borders, in particular to the south where the Nubians continued to threaten. Even aggressive Middle Kingdom pharaohs like Senwosret, who was chiefly concerned with security at home, were not interested in empire building or the military occupation of other countries.

In the New Kingdom, however, the Egyptians began to play a far more active role in international affairs. Relying on a powerful army, consisting largely of mercenaries, the pharaohs used a combination of force and diplomacy to dominate the eastern Mediterranean. Thutmose III (c. 1504–c. 1450 B.C.) waged no fewer than 17 military campaigns, in the course of which he conquered Palestine and Syria and pushed as far east as the river Euphrates. Local governors ruled the occupied territories, and the Egyptians shipped forced laborers back home to work on the monuments and buildings erected to commemorate Egyptian victories.

The policy of empire building continued under Thutmose's successors, his son Amenhotep II (c. 1453–c. 1419 B.C.) and grandson Amenhotep III (c. 1386–c. 1350 B.C.). The latter was one of the few pharaohs to marry a commoner, queen Tiy. The daughter of the commander of the chariotry, she exerted considerable influence during her husband's reign.

Amenhotep III led a successful expedition into Nubia and maintained Egyptian prestige high in western Asia. Under his patronage, the capital city of Thebes became the site of magnificent temples, including that of Luxor. Yet within a few years of his death, the capital was moved elsewhere, and centuries of Egyptian traditions were swept

PUBLIC FIGURES AND PRIVATE LIVES

HATSHEPSUT AND THUTMOSE III

The New Kingdom ruler Queen Hatshepsut (c. 1498–1483 B.C.) was probably the first woman in Egyptian history to become pharaoh. The daughter of Thutmose I, she married his son and heir, her half-brother Thutmose II, and became co-ruler with him—hence, one of her official titles was "Pharaoh's wife and daughter." The royal couple had no male children, and on the death of her husband, the next in line for the throne was Thutmose III, the son of Thutmose II by one of his concubines. Hatshepsut refused to step down, however, and continued to act as regent for the young pharaoh. So far her actions were not unprecedented, for on two earlier occasions queens had reigned for brief periods.

In 1498 B.C. the ambitious Hatshepsut declared herself pharaoh and assumed full power, sending off Thutmose III—by now come of age—to expand Egypt's foreign conquests. In this way she simultaneously disposed of her chief opponents—her resentful stepson and the army that backed him. The queen was astute enough to win over the priesthood, which was still the most influential force in Egyptian society, by claiming divine birth and maintaining traditional customs.

Among the leading figures at her court was the great architect Senmut, who designed her funerary temple at Deir el-Bahri. Some scholars have ex- plained Senmut's preeminence by speculating that he and Hatshepsut were lovers. Although no direct evidence supports this theory, the presence of carved figures of Senmut in a small chapel in the queen's temple complex is highly unusual.

When Hatshepsut died in 1483 B.C., Thutmose became sole pharaoh. During the next 28 years, while he ruled over a period of great prosperity, many of the monuments erected by Hatshepsut were systematically defaced—presumably by royal command. Appearances of Hatshepsut's name in inscriptions were obliterated or covered over, even those in the inner shrines of temples visible only to a handful of priests. In addition, statues and images representing her were destroyed. Even in her funerary temple at Deir el-Bahri, where for once the queen was portrayed alongside her official co-ruler, Thutmose III himself, the vengeful pharaoh hacked out Hatshepsut and cut away most of the statues of Senmut, leaving only his own image. At the great temple complex of Karnak, a wall was built around Hatshepsut's 97-foot-high obelisk.

The careers of Hatshepsut and Thutmose reveal a well-documented power struggle, in which the formidable queen used all the means at her disposal— family, access to power, skill in manipulation—to score a remarkable triumph over a man who was one of the most powerful and determined figures in Egyptian history. She was helped by the fact that according to Egyptian law women and men were equal, and gender discrimination was far less prevalent in Egyptian society than in other cultures of the period. (For a more detailed discussion of the role of women in the ancient world, see Topic 6.) Viewed from the perspective of the past 3,500 years, the fact that Hatshepsut was a woman seems to have played a surprisingly small role in her official life.

© Baldwin H. Ward and Kathryn C. Ward/CORBIS

© 1984 The Metropolitan Museum of Art

away. The old ways were soon to return, but for a brief time the son of Amenhotep and Tiy, whose official title was Amenhotep IV, single-handedly attempted totally to reform Egyptian religious and political life. He is better known to posterity by the name he assumed, Akhenaton.

AKHENATON AND THE SUN GOD: THE REVOLUTION THAT FAILED

The reign of Akhenaton (c. 1350–c. 1334 B.C.) was a brief and dazzling break in the centuries of Egyptian tradition. Rejecting many of the deities of conventional Egyptian religion, Akhenaton promoted the worship of a deity, the *Aton* (the disk of the sun), which symbolized the divine essence; Akhenaton, the name he assumed, means "the servant of Aton." Throughout Egypt, he had the name of Amen, the chief deity of Thebes, erased from inscriptions in temples.

Abandoning the sites that had been sacred for centuries, Akhenaton built a new capital, Akhetaton, 200 miles north of Thebes (the location is generally known by its Arabian name, Tel el-Amarna). From time immemorial, the Egyptians had buried their dead on the west bank of the Nile, the direction of the setting sun. Akhenaton reversed the process, having tombs constructed on the east bank.

The motives for this wholesale revolution in Egyptian religion may have been largely political, as a means of freeing the pharaoh from the powerful and entrenched priests of Amen. The previous 40 years had seen a struggle between the priests of Amen and those of the rival cult of Re, god of the sun. The attempts of the priests of Amen to deemphasize the sun cult led to the rise of the worship of Aton, which Akhenaton promoted. His preoccupation with religious reform dominated his reign, which saw the collapse of Egypt's empire in Asia. At the same time, a new style of art developed at his capital, which proved equally revolutionary.

THE "AMARNA" STYLE

Traditional Egyptian art made use of weighty, massive scale to portray its subjects in an idealized form. For the first time in Egyptian history, the artists of Akhenaton's reign produced naturalistic works, showing Akhenaton and his family in relaxed and even humorous mood. In portraits such as that of his wife, Nefertiti, grace and elegance replace the official solemnity of earlier ages.

Akhenaton's revolution barely survived him. After his death, the priests reintroduced the worship of Amen, and Thebes once again became Egypt's capital. Tel el-Amarna was abandoned and remained uninhabited desert for almost 3,000 years. Many of Akhenaton's statues and buildings were destroyed, and others were thrown down and buried. Later pharaohs branded him a heretic and cut his name out of the monuments of his reign that survived the destruction. References to him in later Egyptian history invariably call him "the criminal Akhenaton."

Relief carving of Akhenaton, his wife Nefertiti, and three of their children, c. 1370–1350 B.C. The height of the limestone slab is 17 inches (43 cm). The royal family sits beneath the rays of the sun, symbolizing the sun god Aton, who was at the center of Akhenaton's religious reforms. The extreme ease and naturalism of the style is typical of the period.

© pbk, Berlin, Aegyptisches Museum/bpk. Photo: Margarete Buesing

THE END OF THE NEW KINGDOM

It is uncertain whether Akhenaton's successor, Tutankhamen (c. 1334–1325 B.C.), was his son or half-brother. His reign, which marked a transitional stage between the worship of Aton and traditional religion, is best known for the treasures of his tomb—the only Egyptian royal grave to have survived nearly intact. Tutankhamen made little impact on Egyptian art or history, but later rulers were more active. The mighty Ramses II (c. 1304–c. 1237 B.C.) built some of the most massive of all Egyptian temples while waging war in Asia. Ramses began his reign with a series of Asian campaigns, leading his troops against the Hittites in Syria and Palestine. In 1283 B.C. he negotiated a lasting peace with the Hittite king, whose daughter he married to cement the treaty, and the rest of his long reign was peaceful, the last peak of Egyptian imperial power. Ramses III (c. 1198–c. 1166 B.C.) successfully defended Egypt against invading Libyans and the mass migrations of a group known as the Peoples of the Sea, who tried to establish themselves in Egypt; he finally drove them out around 1170 B.C. The last years of his reign, however, were marked by internal disturbances, and over the following century Egypt's power began to decline. The central authority of the pharaoh started to crumble as the priests assumed more and more secular control.

THE DECLINE OF EGYPT

By the end of the New Kingdom, a series of powers in Mesopotamia began to chip away Egypt's conquests in Asia and pushed the Egyptians back within their frontiers. Maintaining their traditions, the Egyptians paid the price

Temple of Ramses II, formerly at Abu Simbel, c. 1275–1225 B.C. It was relocated in the 1960s, when the building of the Aswan Dam flooded the valley to create Lake Nasser. The four seated statues of Ramses II are each some 65 feet (20 m) high. Between and near the pharaoh's feet are smaller statues of his mother, wife, and children.

for their unwillingness to adapt to new ways; they were slow to change from bronze to the newly discovered material, iron, which their Mesopotamian enemies used for weapons.

As central authority declined, petty kings, high priests, and usurpers fought for power. In the ensuing chaos, Libyan mercenary soldiers were able to gain the throne. Little new building took place, and the three centuries following 1000 B.C. were marked by stagnation. Only with the reign of the Nubian pharaoh, Shebaka (712–698 B.C.), was Egypt once again unified.

By the time of Shebaka, Egypt had lost any claim to be a major power. For most of the next two centuries following his rule, the Egyptians maintained a precarious independence by a constantly changing series of alliances with the various warring Mesopotamian states. After being invaded by the Assyrians in 667 and 664 B.C., they finally succumbed to the Persians, who invaded Egypt in 525 B.C. The ruthless Persian king, Cambyses (c. 530–522 B.C.), crowned himself king of Egypt and rampaged through the country in a wave of pillaging and destruction. (For a discussion of the Persian Empire, see Topic 4.)

Putting Ancient Egypt in Perspective

Few cultures in human history have preserved their traditional ways as determinedly as the Egyptians. The majestic certainties of the Old Kingdom, with its serene statues and religious ceremonies, remained an inspiration to later Egyptians for almost 3,000 years. Lacking the aggressiveness of their Babylonian or Assyrian contemporaries and the intellectual restlessness of the Greeks, the ancient Egyptians dedicated themselves to an unchanging vision of eternity—the anomaly of the reign of Akhenaton serves only to highlight the astonishing consistency of Egyptian culture.

Continued next page

During the New Kingdom, the cult of Amen continued to rise in importance, and commercial expansion combined with increasing involvement in international affairs to place Egypt on a larger stage. Yet for most pharaohs the conquest of an empire remained secondary to preserving the traditions of Egypt itself; unlike the Akkadians, Babylonians, or Assyrians, the Egyptians were rarely driven by naked territorial expansion.

The Egyptian attitude was partly created by the country's geography. The Nile provided a means of unification and communication, whereas in Mesopotamia the Tigris and Euphrates, with their numberless tributaries, divided the land into isolated areas whose inhabitants were prone to feuding. In addition, the amazing fertility of the Nile valley meant that Egypt was virtually self-sufficient—not for nothing did the Greek historian and traveler Herodotus call Egypt "the gift of the Nile." To the south, the Nubian Desert protected Egypt from invasion; to the north lay the Mediterranean, a barrier for would-be immigrants. Even when foreigners did succeed in penetrating Egypt's defenses, as in the case of the Hyksos, they left little permanent impression. Thus, unlike the various peoples of Mesopotamia, the Egyptians had centuries of undisturbed peace in which to develop their civilization. Once they had formed their culture, they remained faithful to it for 3,000 years.

Questions for Further Study

1. What was the relationship between Egyptian religion and Egyptian political and social development?
2. How did the Egyptians' strong emphasis on tradition affect their history? How does it contrast with their contemporaries?
3. What were the main features of Akhenaton's revolution?

Suggestions for Further Reading

Arnold, Dorothea. *The Royal Women of Amarna.* New York, 1996.

Bard, Kathryn A., ed. *Encyclopedia of the Archaeology of Ancient Egypt.* London, 1999.

Capel, Anne K., and Glenn E. Markoe, eds. *Mistress of the House, Mistress of Heaven: Women in Ancient Egypt.* New York, 1996.

Clayton, P. A. *Chronicle of the Pharaohs.* New York, 1994.

Grimal, Nicholas. *A History of Ancient Egypt.* Oxford, 1992.

Ikram, Salima, and Aidan Dodson. *The Mummy in Ancient Egypt: Equipping the Dead for Eternity.* New York, 1998.

Malek, Jaromir. *Egyptian Art.* London, 1999.

Romer, John. *Valley of the Kings, Exploring the Tombs of the Pharaohs.* New York, 1994.

Shaw, Ian, ed. *The Oxford History of Ancient Egypt.* New York, 2000.

Silverman, David P., ed. *Ancient Egypt.* New York, 1997.

Smith, W. S., revised by W. K. Simpson. *The Art and Architecture of Ancient Egypt.* Rev. ed. New Haven, 1998.

InfoTrac College Edition

Enter the search term *Egypt history* using the Subject Guide.

OTHER PEOPLES IN THE ANCIENT NEAR EAST

The valley peoples of Mesopotamia and Egypt were the earliest to develop urban civilizations in the ancient Near East, but from around 2000 B.C. the gradual rise of other cultures in the mountains and deserts of the region created new forces that often conflicted with the older powers.

Newcomers who spoke an Indo-European language arrived in western Asia (modern Turkey) shortly after 2000 B.C. and combined with the preexisting population to found the Hittite kingdom. By 1600 B.C., the Hittites were strong enough to attempt the conquest of Syria and Babylon. Their empire reached its height in the reign of Suppululiumas (1375–1335 B.C.), only to fall victim around 1200 B.C., like the Egyptian New Kingdom, to the migratory "Peoples of the Sea." Hittite society and culture owed much to Mesopotamian influences but also had their own original aspects. Women achieved a higher social and religious status than in other contemporary societies, while the Hittites made contributions to fields as diverse as architecture and law.

To the south of the land of the Hittites lay Phoenicia (modern Lebanon), where the vital trade routes among Hittite territory, Egypt, and Mesopotamia all intersected. The first important culture to develop there was that of the Canaanites, a collection of small city-states and kingdoms. The southern part of their territory fell to the Philistines around 1200 B.C.; to the north the surviving Canaanites, now known as the Phoenicians, became the leading traders and seafarers of the Mediterranean world. Among their lasting contributions to civilization was the further development of an alphabet that was copied by the Greeks and became the script, as well as the means of transmission, of most of Western culture. Their navy also played a crucial role in military and commercial dealings among Assyrians, Neo-Babylonians, Persians, and Greeks.

The high plateau of ancient Persia (modern Iran) was the home of several important peoples. Both the Medes and the Persians probably migrated there before 1000 B.C. Nomadic tribes, they were famous for their horse breeding and riding exploits. With the vacuum left by the collapse of Egypt and Mesopotamia, their unified forces began the conquest of much of the ancient Near East: Nineveh (the Assyrian capital) in 612 B.C., Babylon in 539 B.C., and all of Egypt by 525 B.C.

Among the peoples living in the Persian Empire were the Jews. Originally a nomadic people in Mesopotamia, according to the Old Testament account the Hebrews migrated to Egypt. After the "Exodus" they settled in Palestine, where Saul established the first monarchy shortly before 1000 B.C. The kingdom eventually split into two: Israel to the north and Judah to the south. The northern half was conquered by the Assyrians in 722 B.C., and its population dispersed; the southern kingdom of Judah fell to Babylon in 586 B.C. When Babylon fell to the Persians a few years later, the Persian ruler Cyrus the Great encouraged the reconstruction of Jerusalem.

THE KINGDOM OF THE HITTITES: IRON, WAR, AND BUREAUCRACY

Before the 20th century, the Hittites were an obscure, little understood people, chiefly known from biblical references. Now, after a century of archaeological excavation and research, they were clearly one of the most powerful and influential forces in the ancient Near East. Furthermore, they played an important role in passing on to their western neighbors, the predecessors of the Greeks, many of Mesopotamia's cultural achievements.

THE INDO-EUROPEANS

Unlike the Semitic-speaking peoples of Mesopotamia or the Egyptians, the Hittites spoke and wrote a language belonging to the Indo-European family. The original speakers of this group of languages probably came from the steppes of Central Asia and may have begun to migrate to Europe, the Near East, Iran, and India around 2000 B.C. As a result, nearly all modern European languages and Sanskrit, the sacred tongue of India, are related.

Recent estimates suggest that almost half the population of the planet at the beginning of the 21st century speaks—and thinks in—a language derived from Indo-European. To take a random example, the English word "three" shares its origins with the Russian *tri*, the Italian *tre*, the Bengali *tri*, and the Welsh *tri*. Yet the origins of the first speakers of Indo-European are remote and confused. As one recent scholar has written, "The Indo-Europeans did not burst into history; they straggled in over a period of 3,500 years." Other experts prefer not even to use the term "Indo-European" for an actual people, but reserve it for a family of languages.

In any case, the presence of the Hittites in the central Turkish region of Anatolia marks the earliest recorded appearance in history of an Indo-European language—recorded on more than 25 thousand clay tablets discovered at their capital, Hattusas (modern Boğhazköy), where the palace archives span the period from 1650 B.C. to 1200 B.C. Because most of their neighbors spoke a Semitic language—or, like the Egyptians, one that was non–Indo-European—the earliest Hittites to settle in Anatolia probably migrated there, perhaps from north of the Black Sea. The first wave

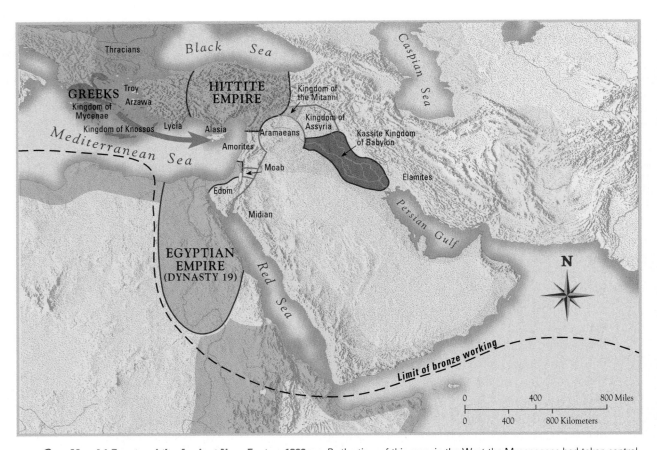

Map 4.1 Egypt and the Ancient Near East, c. 1300 B.C. By the time of this map, in the West the Mycenaeans had taken control of the Minoan Kingdom of Knossos. The two leading international powers were the Egyptians and the Hittites, who had tried to make peace by means of a dynastic marriage—an attempt that ended in failure at the Battle of Kadesh (1276 B.C.). The Kassites in Babylon were on the decline, while the new rising power, destined to dominate the Near East by 1000 B.C., was Assyria. Go to http://info.wadsworth.com/053461065X for an interactive version of this map.

of arrivals probably occurred around 2300–2200 B.C., and the newcomers blended in with the preexisting population.

THE HITTITE OLD KINGDOM
(C. 1750–1450 B.C.)

By 1750, a strong centralized state had emerged, with a king who appointed royal governors for the individual cities. Society was essentially feudal and consisted of three classes: land-owning warrior nobles, artisans, and peasants. Much of the strength of the Hittite Old Kingdom was based on trade. The Hittites mined large quantities of silver, copper, and lead. They also discovered how to smelt iron but jealously guarded the new technology. The technique of iron-working remained their secret until the collapse of the Hittite Empire in 1200.

Hittite scribes developed two writing systems: one based on the Mesopotamian cuneiform and the other their own form of hieroglyphic (picture) script. Using these scripts, the Hittite government officials of Hattusas and other centers organized elaborate and thorough archives that contained copies of a wide variety of documents: trade records, diplomatic negotiations and treaties, and official histories. Surviving literary works retell creation and flood legends, mostly based on traditional Mesopotamian myths.

Although Hittite legal documents were also influenced by Mesopotamian models, they show their own characteristics. The Hittites were clearly enthusiastic bureaucrats who sought to order their society with a seemingly endless series of regulations. The state fixed the prices for manufactured goods, food, and clothing, and an official tariff was levied for services. Land grants were made in return for military service, and strict conditions governed how the land should be farmed.

By contrast with many of their bloodthirsty neighbors, Hittite rulers favored relatively mild punishments. Even premeditated murder received only a financial penalty, and there is no mention of such sentences as impalement or castration, both of which were routinely inflicted by Assyrian law. One of the few crimes to earn the death penalty was stealing property from the royal palace; even a Hittite ruler's clemency had its limits.

THE HITTITE EMPIRE (C. 1450 B.C.–1200 B.C.)

For the most part, Old Kingdom rulers concentrated on internal consolidation, but around 1450 the Hittites felt secure enough to enlarge their borders. By the reign of Suppiluliumas I (c. 1352–c. 1322 B.C.), they had built up a state that stretched from Anatolia to northern Syria and included parts of Phoenicia and Palestine. The Hittites had to deal with the "great power" in the region, Egypt, and the next decades saw an alternation of diplomatic negotiations and skirmishing between the new imperialists and the Egyptians.

The rivalry culminated in 1276 with a pitched battle at Kadesh, in Syria, at which even the mighty pharaoh Ramses II failed to defeat his opponents. The Hittite forces, according to a contemporary inscription, included 2,500 chariots and "the troops of sixteen nations," a formidable coalition. Both Ramses and the Hittite king claimed victory. More to the point, the two leaders negotiated a treaty, preserved in

Relief carving showing a Hittite king and queen worshiping a bull, from the royal palace at Alaja Huyuk, c. 1400–1200 B.C. The stocky figures and the flat style of the carving are very different from the more carefully modeled reliefs of Assyrian art (see the image of the ram in a thicket in Topic 2). The cult of the bull (here seen placed on or behind an altar) was common in the Bronze Age: Among other peoples to revere its strength were those of the Indus Valley civilization and the Minoans of Crete.

Hirmer Fotoarchiv

SIGNIFICANT DATES

Rise and Fall of Empires in the Ancient Near East (all dates B.C.)

c. 1750–1450	Hittite Old Kingdom
c. 1450–1200	Hittite Empire
c. 1400–1200	Canaanites flourish
Between 1300 and 1200	Hebrew exodus from Egypt
c. 1200	Migrations of Peoples of the Sea
c. 1200–1000	Rise of Phoenicians
c. 1020–1000	Reign of Saul, first Hebrew king
c. 1000–971	Reign of King David
c. 971–931	Reign of King Solomon
814	Foundation of Phoenician colony of Carthage

an Egyptian hieroglyphic inscription that is still visible at Karnak in Upper Egypt, which established friendlier relations between the two states.

Within three generations, the Hittite Empire was gone, perhaps swept away by large-scale climatic changes, coupled with the vast migrations of a group of peoples across Anatolia. These wanderers were called by Egyptian scribes the "Peoples of the Sea," whose origins remain obscure. Around 1200, they made a determined effort to settle in Egypt and were only beaten off by massive Egyptian resistance. The result was the weakening and collapse of Egypt's New Kingdom. (See Topic 7 for further discussion of the mysterious "Peoples of the Sea.")

For the Hittites, the turmoil of the times brought the collapse of centralized authority: the long military struggle with Egypt had left the state too weak to resist the new invaders. Some individual Hittite cities in north Syria continued to prosper, but by the end of the 8th century they were annexed by the Assyrians.

THE PHOENICIANS: TRADERS AND SAILORS

Among the Semitic peoples to settle on the Mediterranean coast were the Canaanites, one of whose leading cities, Ugarit, flourished between 1400 B.C. and 1200 B.C. The city's location, together with its splendid natural harbor, made it a center for international trade: Its archives have been found and reveal commercial links with Egypt, the Hittites, and the Mycenaeans of mainland Greece (for a discussion of the Mycenaeans, see Topic 7).

Like the rest of the Near East, the Canaanites were submerged in the chaos brought by the Peoples of the Sea around 1200. Shortly thereafter, the southern half of Canaanite territory was settled by the Philistines, one of the

Peoples of the Sea. To the north, the Canaanite survivors—now known as the Phoenicians—rebuilt their chief cities, Byblos, Tyre, and Sidon, and soon became prominent and successful traders and seafarers in the Mediterranean.

The Phoenicians explored the ancient world, established important colonies, and developed technological innovations in metalworking and shipbuilding. Furthermore, their alphabet was imitated (with some modifications) by the Greeks and became the system of communication for virtually all of Western civilization. Despite these achievements, they are generally not thought of as central to the history of the ancient world.

The reason for the relative neglect of the Phoenicians by later historians probably lies in the fact that they fell foul of the two peoples to whom we owe most of our information about them, the Greeks and the Romans. The Greeks saw them as their implacable—and often superior—rivals in the quest for colonies, while the Romans feared their power in the western Mediterranean. The general feelings of classical antiquity about the Phoenicians were summed up by the Greek historian Plutarch: "A people full of bitterness and surly, submissive to rulers, tyrannical to those they rule, abject in fear, fierce when provoked, unshakable in resolve, and so strict as to dislike all humor and kindness."

It must be admitted that we have little material evidence to offset this unflattering picture. Phoenicia was conquered first by the Assyrians and then by Persia, while the Romans either destroyed or resettled Phoenician centers in the west. As a result, little Phoenician art and practically no Phoenician literature has survived. We have no way of knowing what the Phoenicians thought of the Greeks or Romans, although it is not difficult to guess. Yet discoveries at colonies and trading sites throughout the Mediterranean are beginning to provide a more favorable impression of the nature of Phoenician culture and correct ancient prejudices.

PHOENICIAN TRADERS

The Phoenicians were above all traders and travelers. Phoenician ships transported goods found or made at home, including wine, glass, wood—cedars of Lebanon were used in the construction of Solomon's temple at Jerusalem—and the purple dye for which they were famous. The trading vessels also served as international carriers, shipping products between the eastern and western Mediterranean: Phoenician works of art, mainly small portable objects, have been found throughout the ancient Mediterranean world, from Spain to Greece, and in Assyria.

To facilitate their trading, the Phoenicians established a series of bases throughout the Mediterranean. Moving westward, they founded colonies on the islands of Cyprus, Malta, Sicily, and Sardinia, and in mainland Spain. The traditional date of the foundation of their first North African settlement, Utica, was as early as 1100 B.C. By far the most important of the Phoenician colonies in North Africa was Carthage, founded in 814 B.C. When Phoenicia fell under Assyrian domination, and eventually under Persian rule, Carthage remained the center of Phoenician power and commerce in the west. (For an account of Rome's Punic—i.e., Phoenician—Wars with the Carthaginians, see Topic 13.)

These bases served both as trading posts and for exploration. One Phoenician sailor, Himilco, sailed north by the Atlantic coast of Spain and France to Britain, while the Greek historian Herodotus describes others as having circumnavigated Africa. Overland routes established trade relations with the interior of the Sahara and perhaps even with Nigeria. These Phoenician caravan routes remained in use throughout Roman times, providing gold, ivory, wild beasts, and primarily slaves.

In the absence of much written documentation, it is difficult to gain any real impression of Phoenician politics or society. Although Tyre and Sidon were the richest cities, other communities seem to have maintained a relative degree of independence. The Phoenicians apparently lacked the sense of national identity and taste for empire of the Hittites or the Romans; their various foreign settlements, with the notable exception of Carthage, were commercial bases rather than real towns—another reason we know so little about how they lived.

The names of Phoenician kings are recorded in the Bible and in Assyrian documents, but the system of hereditary monarchy seems to have died out, to be replaced by a council of elders and (according to Aristotle) an assembly of the people. The choice of magistrates and membership of the council depended on wealth rather than birth—an unusual social tolerance in the hierarchical world of the ancient Near East. The same openness applied to their attitude toward their neighbors. Fierce to defend their own self-interests, they seem to have lived peaceably alongside a wide range of other peoples. They shared Sicily with the Greeks for more than 500 years, and only deliberate Roman provocation brought them into open conflict with their eventual conquerors.

PERSIA: THE TOLERANT EMPIRE

Assyrian inscriptions of the 9th century B.C. provide us with the earliest reference to the Medes and Persians. Both peoples spoke Indo-European languages. They probably arrived in what is now Iran as a result of the same extended process of Indo-European migration that had brought the Hittites to Anatolia a thousand years earlier.

The region in which they first settled, to the southeast of the Caspian Sea, is largely composed of arid upland plateau, unsuitable for intensive farming. The Medes and Persians, originally nomadic peoples, devoted their energies to horse breeding, and they soon became famous for the quality of their animals and for their prowess in riding.

At the beginning of the 7th century, the Medes gathered their loose confederation of clans to form a settled society ruled by a king. The Persians followed their example, establishing themselves to the south of the Medes. By the end of the century, the Medes had established themselves as the stronger of the two peoples and made the Persians subject to them. The Persians retained their own king, who was, however, subordinate to the Median ruler. In 612 B.C., the Medes were sufficiently powerful to join with the Babylonians in destroying Nineveh, the capital of the hated Assyrians. The Median Empire they established, the first in Iran, lasted until the charismatic leadership of the Persian king Cyrus the Great enabled Persia to conquer the Medes and turn Media into the first *satrapy* (province) of the Persian Empire.

CYRUS THE GREAT (559–530 B.C.)

Cyrus is one of the few imperial conquerors in history to have been respected, even revered, by the people he governed. The Greeks and the Jews, two peoples who fiercely disagreed about virtually everything else, both regarded him as a model ruler. Much of his popularity was a result of his openness and tolerance: From the beginning he seems to have wanted to create a genuine "world empire," composed of different peoples living side by side while maintaining their own traditions and religions.

After coming to power in 559, Cyrus conquered Media in 550 and moved west. First Anatolia and then the Asia Minor kingdom of Lydia fell to the Persians. The latter conquest brought with it a string of Greek colonies, which had been founded the previous century on the coast of Asia Minor. The inhabitants of these Greek towns were thus the first Europeans to become part of a Near Eastern empire.

Leaving part of his army as a garrison, Cyrus moved east to gain control of a vast swath of land that stretched as far as the Indus Valley in western India. With his eastern borders now secure, and with his army swelled by recruits from the conquered territories, he moved south into Mesopotamia. In 539, Babylon was captured and Babylonia became a Persian province.

Cyrus spent the rest of his life—he was killed in battle in 530—organizing and administrating the empire he had built. He encouraged its various peoples to maintain their own religious and cultural traditions by restoring and rebuilding temples. He made it possible for the Jews, who were brought to Babylon in captivity 50 years earlier, to return to Jerusalem and rebuild their own temple there. Locals were appointed to government positions in their own states, and Medes served as military commanders alongside Persians.

THE PERSIAN EMPIRE UNDER DARIUS

Cyrus was succeeded as Great King of the Persians by his son Cambyses (530–522 B.C.), whose chief achievement was to conquer and add to the empire the only Near Eastern state that was still independent, Egypt. In 525 B.C., with help from Phoenician ships, Cambyses defeated the Egyptians and had himself declared pharaoh.

The long reign of Cambyses' successor Darius (521–486 B.C.), which included a minor conflict with the Greeks (for the viewpoint of the Greeks, who saw the Persian Wars as a crucial turning point in their history, see Topic 8), marked the definitive ordering of their now vast empire. Darius divided it into 20 satrapies, based on local customs, language,

Royal audience hall and stairway, Palace of Darius I and Xerxes I, Persepolis, Iran, c. 521–465 B.C. The sides of the stairway are carved with figures of the royal guards, Persian nobles and dignitaries, and representatives of the 24 peoples under Persian rule. Each group wears national costume and brings an appropriate gift to the Great King of the Persians.

and religion. Each province's administration was in the hands of a *satrap*, a word literally meaning "protector of the Kingdom." The satraps were responsible for both civil and military affairs, and also for collecting taxes. To discourage these local governors from abusing their considerable power, royal inspectors traveled throughout the empire, reporting any irregularities to the central administration in the chief Persian capital, Susa. The inspectors were mockingly dubbed by the Greeks as "the eyes and ears of the Great King."

Crucial to the working of the empire was a quick and efficient communication network. The pride of the Persian road system was the Royal Road, more than 1,600 miles long, which led from Sardis in Asia Minor to Susa, with connecting roads to the empire's chief cities. Another of Darius's innovations that helped promote unity was the introduction of a standardized coinage, an idea first invented by the Lydians before their conquest by Cyrus. It is not certain whether Darius personally introduced Zoroastrianism, the empire's most widespread religion; he certainly favored its spread, without, however, discouraging other religions.

THE HEBREWS: THE PEOPLE OF THE BOOK

The ancestors of the Jews of Cyrus's kingdom were a Semitic people, the Hebrews. The term "Hebrews" describes the 12 original Hebrew tribes; the Jews were two of

SIGNIFICANT DATES

The Hebrew Kingdoms and the Persian Empire (all dates B.C.)

722	Kingdom of Israel destroyed by Assyrians
700–600	Unification of Persians under Achaemenid Dynasty
612	Nineveh destroyed by Medes and Babylonians
586	Fall of Jerusalem and kingdom of Judah; Hebrew exile in Babylon
550	Persians win control over Medes
539	Persian conquest of Babylon
538	Return of Hebrew exiles to Jerusalem
530	Death of Cyrus the Great
521–486	Reign of Persian King Darius

those tribes, citizens of the kingdom of Judah, who survived the Babylonian conquest. The Hebrews were the first people in history to record their own origins and story in a consecutive written account covering many centuries. That narrative is contained in the Old Testament, where it is interspersed with other kinds of writing—poems (the Psalms), proverbs (the Book of Proverbs), and stories (Ruth).

Many parts of the story were written down centuries after they occurred. Many experts agree that the earliest sections date to about 850 B.C., and the contents and arrange-

ment of the work we call the Old Testament were established only in the 2nd century B.C. How reliable is this account, then, in describing the early history of a nomadic
people with a tradition of grazing flocks and herds rather
than settled farming and urban life?

For some 2,000 years, many Jewish and Christian readers
accepted the Bible (the word means "book" in Greek) as the
inspired word of God. In the 19th and early 20th centuries,
however, many Old Testament scholars came to treat it as a
collection of folk tales and legends, valuable for its unconscious revelations about the source of the Judeo-Christian
tradition rather than for serious historical accuracy.

Individual readers will evaluate the Old Testament's spiritual and moral dimensions in their own ways. For scholars, it
is probably safest to regard the historical parts as essentially
reflecting, if oversimplifying, the events they describe.

THE CENTURIES OF MIGRATION

According to tradition, the Hebrews were the descendants
of the patriarch Abraham, who was born in Mesopotamia,
perhaps around 1800 B.C. Abraham and his people migrated
westward to the land of Canaan, later settled by the
Philistines around 1200. At some time after 1600, driven
perhaps by famine, the Hebrews migrated to Egypt and settled down peacefully there. The dates correspond approximately with the Hyksos occupation of Egypt (see Topic 3).
The Hyksos, a Semitic people, might well have been sympathetic to the Hebrew settlers.

Later Egyptian rulers—presumably after the expulsion
of the Hyksos—enslaved the Hebrews. Around 1300 B.C.,
the charismatic figure Moses defied the pharaoh, whom
some scholars identify as Ramses II, freed the Hebrews from
bondage, and perhaps led the "Exodus" toward the
Promised Land. (New archaeological evidence for the period between c. 1200 and 1000 B.C. promises to clarify the
events surrounding the "Exodus.") On the Sinai peninsula,
Moses may have forged what had been so far only a loose
collection of tribes into a more united confederation.

For almost three centuries, the Hebrews battled first
the Canaanites and then the Philistines to win territory in
Palestine. Their division into 12 separate tribes, ruled by
"judges" who were religious rather than military leaders,
proved a serious handicap to organizing coordinated action.
Only when Saul (c. 1025–c. 1000 B.C.) welded the tribes
into a single united monarchy were the foundations of a settled kingdom laid.

THE MONARCHY AND
THE TWO KINGDOMS

Saul seems an enigmatic figure. Although he achieved some
military success against the Philistines, he was eventually driven to suicide by a defeat. His successor—and former rival—
David (c. 1000–c. 971 B.C.) scored a series of overwhelming
victories, driving the Philistines into a narrow strip of land in
the western coastlands.

David's reign marked the Hebrews' final transition from
a nomadic life to a settled urban community. Jerusalem be-

came the capital, where David's son Solomon (c. 971–
c. 931 B.C.) began an elaborate and expensive building program. At the heart of Solomon's new temple stood the Ark
of the Covenant, the chest handed over by Moses as the
supreme symbol of the Invisible God.

Solomon's love of splendor, and his attempts to imitate the power and luxury of other Near Eastern monarchs,
proved unpopular and divisive in the end. At his death,
the 10 tribes in the north established a separate kingdom
of Israel, while the remaining two retained Jerusalem as
the capital of the kingdom of Judah. The northern kingdom soon fell prey to the Assyrians, who imposed the payment of tribute. Finally in 722 B.C. Assyrian forces destroyed the kingdom and Samaria, its capital. The
conquerors deported the Hebrew population to various
parts of their empire, where they disappeared over time,
absorbed by the local population—they are often known
as the "10 lost tribes."

The kingdom of Judah managed to survive for another
century, helped by the fact that Assyrian power was declining. It was the Babylonians, who had finally defeated the
Assyrians a few years earlier, who conquered Judah in 586
B.C. Under their king, Nebuchadnezzar, they plundered and
burned Jerusalem and carried off its leading citizens to captivity in Babylon. Babylon fell in turn to the Persians in 538
B.C., and Cyrus encouraged the Jews—the population of the
kingdom of Judah—to return to Jerusalem and reestablish
the kingdom of Judah as part of the Persian Empire. It remained under Persian control until it was taken by
Alexander the Great in 331 B.C. In 63 B.C. the Romans absorbed the kingdom into their empire.

The Jews remained politically subject to imperial powers for centuries, and their gradual spread throughout many
parts of the world, a process known as the **"diaspora,"** began early: the first Jewish community at Rome was founded
in 139 B.C. Yet unlike the Hebrews of the "10 lost tribes,"
they never lost their sense of identity. Through the
Babylonian captivity, they came to transform the notion of
nationhood as linked with a specific place (or kingdom)
into the sense of a community bound together by shared experience and, above all, religious observance.

GOD, THE COVENANT, AND THE LAW

The survival of the Jews, together with the special role they
played in the Western tradition, is not the result of conquest or political domination, but rather the unique character of their religion. In terms of numbers and material
power, in fact, they were overshadowed by many other ancient Near Eastern peoples. Their legacy consisted not of
monumental sculptures or imperial palaces, but of a concept
of God. This belief evolved over the early centuries of
Hebrew history, until by the 6th century B.C. the Jewish
concept of monotheism was fully established.

According to the Hebrew prophets of the 8th and 7th
centuries B.C., there was only one God for all peoples, in all
times and places. Immortal and invisible, his name,
Yahweh, means "he causes to be." Ruler of the world, God

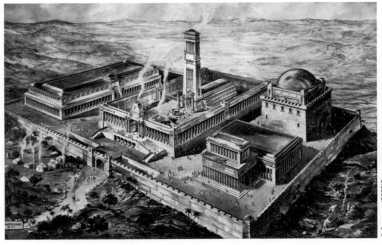

Reconstruction drawing of Solomon's Temple. The Biblical description of this Temple, destroyed by the Romans in A.D. 70, inspired religious architects throughout the Middle Ages. The two bronze columns that flank the entrance may have symbolized the columns of fire and smoke that guided the Israelites through the desert after the "Exodus."

© Bettmann/CORBIS

stands outside the natural world he created: Thus, to worship the sun or stars, as many ancient Near Eastern peoples did, was as idolatrous as to worship statues. (Scholars have noted, however, the similarities between early concepts of Yahweh and Near Eastern "Storm Gods." Certain features of the God described in the Old Testament Psalms resemble Canaanite descriptions of their own gods, El and Ba'al.) A loving father, "slow to anger and rich in love," God would nevertheless punish those who persisted in breaking the ethical principles of divine law.

According to the Hebrew tradition, God first revealed the divine ideals of behavior immediately after the "Exodus." Through the mediation of Moses, God and the tribes of Israel entered into a covenant, whereby the Hebrews promised obedience to God's law as expressed in the Ten Commandments. In return, they came under divine protection as the "chosen people."

Thus, at the very heart of Hebrew monotheism lay the notion of the law of God, which established universal ethical principles by which to live. Many other ancient peoples also ordered their societies by devising law codes. These codes, however, served mostly to maintain a rigid class structure and to protect the power of the rulers. Because the God of the Old Testament was good and loving, his law was one of ethical provisions that apply to all humans: You—that is, everyone—shall not kill, steal, or commit adultery. The moral standards applied to all people—rich and poor, rulers and ruled—and subsequent Hebrew laws made a point of protecting the weak—widows, orphans, and slaves—from the excesses of the powerful.

THE PROPHETS

Moses' encounter with God on Mount Sinai produced the basis for Hebrew law, which subsequently became expanded and extended by the teaching and preaching of the prophets. Many of these figures served as unofficial (and often unwanted) advisers to rulers of the two kingdoms in the times when Assyrian or Babylonian conquest loomed. They drew their authority from the fact that they claimed to speak with God's authority. Rather than try to foresee the future, they sought to call their people back to observance of the covenant and warned of the dire consequences of breaking it.

Prophets such as Amos and Isaiah also concerned themselves with the ethical nature of social justice. Worship in the temple on its own was not enough; it had to be combined with an active life of fairness, generosity, and compassion toward all, especially those most in need of help. The prophets bitterly denounced extravagance and arrogance and mistreatment of the weak. Furthermore, they taught that the Hebrews had been chosen by God to transmit this spirit of universal social justice to the world. Someday they would lead in building a universal human community, bound in peace by its worship of the one true God. In this way, the prophets transformed the separateness of the original covenant into a vision of human unity and the end of war: "Nation will not take up sword against nation, nor will they train for war anymore." Their warnings and gloomy predictions were generally ignored. The consequences, they claimed, were the Assyrian and Babylonian conquests of the two kingdoms, whose citizens were punished in this way for ignoring God's law and breaking the covenant.

Putting the Ancient Near East in Perspective

The first half of the first millennium B.C. saw the final decline of the founders of Western civilization 2,000 years earlier. Egypt became reduced to a province in the

Persian Empire, and the long series of dominant Mesopotamian peoples ended with the Persian victories over the Assyrians and the Babylonians. The Hittites, relative newcomers to the imperial scene, disappeared into obscurity. The Phoenicians lost their homeland in the course of the struggle between the leading powers, although Carthage—their western colony—survived long enough to present a serious challenge to the most successful of all imperialists, the Romans.

All of these cultures developed complex societies and produced significant works of art, which are described and analyzed in the next two topics. Yet their people are long since gone, swallowed up in the course of history. The only survivors from the ancient Near East are the Jews, whose tiny kingdoms, established with difficulty, were conquered by Assyrians, Babylonians, Persians, Alexander's Macedonians, and eventually by Rome. The people who gave Western civilization the source of one of its two great traditions—the Judeo-Christian and the Classical—maintained their own traditions throughout the centuries of the diaspora.

Questions for Further Study

1. How did culture spread in the ancient world? Consider the relative importance of writing, colonization, trade, and technology.
2. What were the chief differences between the Persian Empire and other earlier imperial powers? What were their results?
3. Hebrew culture was, from the beginning, patriarchal. How did this affect its later developments and eventual contribution to Western civilization?

Suggestions for Further Reading

Barnavi, Eli, (ed.). *A Historical Atlas of the Jewish People*. London, 1992.

Bloom, Harold, and David Rosenberg. *The Book of J.* London, 1990.

Bryce, Trevor. *The Kingdom of the Hittites*. New York, 1998.

Curtis, John. *Ancient Persia*. Cambridge, 1990.

Drews, R. *The End of the Bronze Age: Change in War and the Catastrophe ca. 1200 B.C.* Princeton, 1993.

Fox, Robin Lane. *The Unauthorized Version, Truth and Fiction in the Bible*. London, 1991.

Harper, Prudence O., et al. *The Royal City of Susa*. New York, 1992.

Kamm, Antony. *The Israelites: An Introduction*. New York, 1999.

Kung, Hans. *Judaism*. London, 1995.

Markoe, Glenn. *Phoenicians*. Berkeley, 2000.

Matthews, Victor Harold, and Don C. Benjamin. *The Social World of Ancient Israel, 1250-587 B.C.E.* Peabody, 1993.

Oren, Eliezer D., (ed.). *The Sea Peoples and Their World: A Reassessment*. Philadelphia, 2000.

Snell, Daniel C. *Flight and Freedom in the Ancient Near East*. Boston, 2001.

Stiebing, Jr., W. *Out of the Desert? Archaeology and the Exodus/Conquest Narratives*. Buffalo, 1989.

InfoTrac College Edition

Enter the search term *Hittites* using Key Terms.

Enter the search term *Phoenician* using Key Terms.

Enter the search term *Persian* using Key Terms.

ART AND BELIEF IN THE ANCIENT WORLD

For all of their enormous chronological and geographical range and variety, many of the civilizations of the ancient world shared certain common attitudes toward art and religion. The only important exceptions were the Hebrews.

The chief deities of most cultures were inspired by the natural world. The sun god of the Egyptians, the Hittite weather god, and Enlil, the Mesopotamian god of wind, are all examples of forces that could be both life-giving and destructive. The earth was often symbolized as a mother goddess.

The priests in charge of the worship of the various deities often achieved wealth and political power. In Sumerian city-states, the temple formed the center of the community, and the priests played a major role in the city's economic life. Over time, the Egyptian priests of Amen and Re at Thebes became the country's richest landowners. In some cultures, the priests jealously guarded the traditional rites and beliefs: The cult of Amen emerged slowly during the Middle and New Kingdoms, and only one pharaoh sought to make fundamental changes in the established religion. Other peoples were more open to change, which was often inspired by outside influences. The Hittites' religion combined Egyptian and Mesopotamian elements with their own Indo-European gods.

The political leaders of virtually all ancient societies depended on the goodwill of the priestly class for their authority. In some cases—the Egyptian pharaohs, for example—these rulers were worshiped as divinities. Babylonian kings such as Hammurabi, by contrast, thought of themselves as the servants of the gods on earth. The most independent rulers were the Assyrian kings. Although officially the vice-regents of the god Ashur, they acted as absolute monarchs with unlimited powers.

Both political and religious leaders turned to artists to express the beliefs and policies of the state. The great temple constructions of the Nile valley combined architecture and sculpture to proclaim the immortality of their builders. Tombs provided another opportunity for architects, while among the noteworthy palace complexes are the Hittite palace at Boğhazköy and the Assyrian royal palace at Nineveh.

Apart from archives and letters, the writings of the ancient world are generally sacred in inspiration. They range in mood from the weary pessimism of the Sumerian *Epic of Gilgamesh* to the lyric passion of the *Song of Solomon* in the Old Testament: The Old Testament was the Hebrews' major contribution to the cultural achievement of the ancient world.

GODS, PRIESTS, AND WORSHIPERS: VARIETIES OF RELIGIOUS EXPERIENCE

The leading cultures of the ancient world left a rich religious and artistic legacy, much of it still worthy of our attention. The daily life of Westerners at the beginning of the 21st century may seem to have nothing in common with that of the people of Mesopotamia or the wandering Hebrews, yet many of the overriding issues faced by past civilizations are still valid. Do our lives have a meaning, and do they continue in some form after death? Is there a spiritual level of existence, watched over by some form of divinity? On a more mundane level, how should religious issues relate to the secular life of the state?

Perhaps the most powerful link of all between the ancient world and the late 20th century is our shared concern with the world of nature. As we face the ecological crises of the next millennium, the respect of the ancients for the earth—wind and weather, rivers, animals, and vegetation—seems especially relevant. When we can see this sympathy for nature expressed in the form of works of art, the essential unity of human experience becomes even clearer.

Facing such universal problems, it is not surprising that many ancient cultures arrived at similar solutions. Behind the seemingly endless variety of deities and their depictions, and political and social systems of organization, there are often common responses. One people, however, formed an important exception to this tendency: the Hebrews. The belief that they evolved of a single transcendent universal deity has no parallel elsewhere, even in the monotheistic tendencies of Egyptian religion under Akhenaton or in Zoroastrianism, the religion of ancient Persia. As for the visual arts, the Hebrew ban on depicting religious images prevented the development of any significant tradition in painting or sculpture, while the relative poverty of their small kingdoms left little in the way of architecture. The only Hebrew building to achieve fame, Solomon's temple, was essentially designed and built by Phoenicians, and the remains of stone buildings in the large cities of the Northern Kingdom, such as Samaria and Megiddo, probably date to the same period. By contrast, the only surviving Hebrew work of literature, the Old Testament, was a key element in the formation of the Western tradition.

THE EGYPTIANS AND THE DIVINE FORCES OF NATURE

For the Egyptians, the entire world, human and natural, was subject to divine forces. The source of life was the sun, and the sun god Re had created the world by bringing order out of primeval chaos. This sense of a natural order in the world of ancient Egypt owed its origins to the unity of the Nile valley and its ecology. It was further reinforced by the human equivalent of the sun: the Egyptian ruler, the pharaoh, whose title proclaimed him the "Son of Re."

Egypt's survival depended on the annual flood of the Nile, whose waters kept the land fertile, and the river and land deities Isis and Osiris played a central role in Egyptian religion. The god Osiris was killed by his evil brother and then reborn, thanks to the devotion of his wife Isis. His resurrection symbolized the annual rebirth of the earth at flood time.

Over time, the cult of Isis, Osiris, and their son, the falcon god Horus, came to represent the Egyptian belief in human resurrection after death. Osiris presided over elaborate funeral rituals, at which the dead had to account for their lives; the god then judged whether they were deserving of a happy afterlife. These ceremonies were originally reserved for the ruling class, but by the Middle Kingdom, Egyptian religion extended the possibility of life after death to all Egyptians who could afford a tomb, mummification, and proper burial rites—in practice, the upper and middle classes.

Other deities, in the form of animals, symbolized forces of nature. The hawk god Seker was god of the night sun; the cow goddess Hathor symbolized pleasure and love, and was also associated with one of the creation myths. Certain animals, notably the bull and the cat, also had sacred properties. Bastet, the elegant cat goddess, was worshiped at Bubastis; her temple there was begun in the 4th Dynasty, and later pharaohs continued to enrich it over the following 17 centuries. Recent exploration at Bubastis has uncovered a cemetery, whose underground galleries contained thousands of mummified cats.

THE MESOPOTAMIAN UNIVERSE

Like the Egyptians, the Sumerians and later Mesopotamian peoples were at the mercy of their environment. The Egyptians could count on the Nile's regular flooding, but the climate of the land between the two rivers (Tigris and Euphrates) was much less stable, so that springtime melting of winter snows often produced raging and uncontrollable floods. The sense of stress caused by these continual ecological threats permeated Mesopotamian religion and culture, as can be seen in the *Epic of Gilgamesh*.

The deities symbolizing these forces were thus seen as both creative and destructive, with the power to wreak havoc in human lives. Unlike the Egyptians, with their strong sense of order in the universe, the Mesopotamians felt helpless in the face of the inscrutable forces of nature. Their gods were capable of both good and evil, and in any case were unable to control the world. Nor could the Sumerians hope for a happier life after death: They believed that beyond the troubles of this world lay only the dim prospect of eternal gloom.

The three chief gods represented the sky, the earth, and the wind. As sky god and father of the gods, Anu ruled over all, and Sumerian kings served as his agent on earth. Enki, god of the earth, had charge of rivers and canals, which were vital to the irrigation systems of Mesopotamia. The wind god Enlil symbolized force and energy—sometimes positive and creative characteristics, sometimes the cause of violent destruction.

The chief goddess was Ninhursaga, a more beneficent power. Her early connection with mountains and plants

Female head from Uruk, c. 3500–3000 B.C. Height 8 inches (20 cm). The head may represent Inanna, the Sumerian goddess of love and war. The marble from which it is made has been carved with great delicacy to show the planes of the cheeks and the area around the mouth. A wig of hair of gold leaf was perhaps fitted into the central groove at the top, and colored stone inlays probably formed the eyes and eyebrows.

gradually changed emphasis, and she became thought of as a mother goddess figure. The other deities included a goddess of the morning and evening star, Inanna, and gods of the sun and moon, Utu and Nanna.

THE WEATHER GODS OF THE HITTITES

The mountainous territory of the Hittites was a region of clouds and storms, with an ever-changing climate. Not surprisingly, the chief Hittite god was the weather god Taru. On one relief carving he stands threateningly, brandishing what seems to be forked lightning. Unlike the Egyptians and Mesopotamians, the Hittites worshiped a female sun deity, Wurusemu. The sun goddess became the supreme head of the Hittite state, and the king always turned to her first for help in battle or in time of national emergency: "Queen of the land of Hatti, Queen of Heaven and Earth, mistress of the kings and queens of the land of Hatti!"

As the Hittites came into contact with neighboring cultures, they began to incorporate other religious practices into their own. The Mesopotamian gods Anu and Enlil appear in Hittite texts, and the Hittites followed the Babylonian custom of organizing a great New Year festival

The Hittite weather god, armed with thunder (in the form of a hammer) and lightning, c. 1200 B.C. Like virtually all figures carved in relief before the time of the Classical (5th century B.C.) Greeks, the artist has used "twisted" perspective. The body is seen from the front, while the head is shown in profile, although the eye is depicted frontally.

to mark the triumph of spring over winter—life over death or good over evil.

RITUALS, SACRIFICES, AND DIVINATION

Each ancient culture devised its own form of ritual for honoring its deities, but as we have seen in the case of the New Year festival, the holidays and ceremonies of different peoples often resembled one another. The seasons of the year, the consecration of a new temple, a victory over an enemy—all these were marked by processions and sacrifices. Most sacrificial rites involved food, and many included the slaughter of animals. Human sacrifice was rare, but not unknown. After a military defeat, the Hittites sacrificed a man in a ritual of purification, and abundant evidence has come to light of the Phoenician sacrifice of infants. Some Early Dynastic Egyptian kings had their servants buried in buildings alongside their own tombs. The practice was soon abandoned, and later pharaohs' servants and companions were represented symbolically. (The Sumerians also buried servants alongside their masters, as demonstrated by the finds in the tombs of the first dynasty at Ur, c. 2500 B.C.)

In addition to the official state cults, the events in the life of an individual were marked by the appropriate ceremonies. The most obvious example is the funeral ritual. Virtually all the peoples described in these topics inhumed dead bodies (that is, buried them intact). The Hittites sometimes inhumed their dead and sometimes cremated them. The Egyptians were unique in their preservation of the body by an elaborate mummification process and in the complexity of their tombs.

Magic played a large part in much ancient religion. The Babylonians and Assyrians, in particular, developed a wide variety of techniques for trying to read the future by communicating with their gods. The inspection of animal organs, the throwing of dice, a reading of the movements of the stars were all ways to foretell divine intentions. Appropriate prayers could then try to change those intentions if they were undesirable.

One of the regular duties of a Mesopotamian ruler was to spend a night in his state's chief temple, sacrificing, praying, and finally sleeping. The god would then appear to him in his dreams and give him his orders. On one recorded occasion, when the river Tigris failed to rise, Gudea of Lagash went to sleep in the temple to find out the meaning of the drought.

RELIGION, POWER, AND THE STATE

The vast mass of religious materials—prayers, spells, rituals, the interpretation of signs—were all firmly under the control of the priests, who thus wielded power over rulers and ruled alike. The notion of a separation between state and religion would have been unthinkable for any ancient people, but the actual system of government varied from culture to culture.

EGYPTIAN THEOCRACY: THE RULE OF GOD

The Egyptians did not distinguish between the power of the state and that of the gods: They were one and the same. The pharaoh was the link, recreating on earth the role of the sun god in the heaven and bringing order out of anarchy and chaos. The gods had sent him to tend humankind, but he was not human, standing as he did between his subjects and the gods. One Middle Kingdom ruler wearily advised his son and successor: "Do not approach your subordinates in your loneliness. Fill not your heart with a brother, know not a friend, nor create for yourself intimates."

Beneath the ruler were various ranks of priests, some serving state cults, some in the service of local deities. By the end of the Old Kingdom, these religious officials had devised a series of rituals and ceremonies, which remained consistent throughout Egyptian history. In religion, as in everything else, the Egyptian fidelity to tradition is one of their most consistent characteristics. The early rituals prescribe certain kinds and quantities of offerings to the gods. The Egyptians followed the prescriptions, virtually unchanged, for almost 2,000 years.

For all the nominal authority of the pharaoh, so strong a tradition reinforced the power of the priesthood, and over time the Egyptian theocracy depended as much on their rule as on the pharaoh's. Akhenaton, the only ruler to defy the forces of religion and undermine the entrenched position of the priests, was a unique exception, and his reforms collapsed with his death (for a discussion of his reign, see Topic 3).

By the New Kingdom, the chief religious centers of Egypt had accumulated riches and landholdings, and the power of their priests tended to increase. The priests of Amen and Re at Thebes owned even more capital and land than the pharaoh. One of the results of their wealth is a temple whose size is staggering even by Egyptian standards. Legal texts record several cases in which the priests of Thebes, and also those of the god Ptah at Memphis, abused their powers.

Thus the "Rule of God" was really the rule of religion. The priesthood demanded blind obedience to a system that gave the temples power and control, while the remoteness that gave the pharaoh his divine authority eliminated any possibility of change. Every aspect of Egyptian culture worked to maintain its "eternal" character.

KINGS AND PRIESTS IN MESOPOTAMIA

Government in each of the cities of Mesopotamia was in the hands of a civic ruler, who acted in the name of the community's divine protectors. Unlike in Egypt, a Mesopotamian king's subjects did not automatically consider him a god or make him the focus of a cult, although certain rulers became thought of as divine. Instead, acting as the servant of the gods, the king's function was to protect and improve the lives of his citizens by overseeing government projects. Among his responsibilities were economic planning, construction of civic and religious building projects, and maintenance of the laws.

Only the Assyrian rulers, toward the end of the history of an independent Mesopotamia, managed to achieve a consistent degree of secular independence and governed as absolute monarchs sustained by brute force. The militaristic and aggressive nature of Assyrian society meant that successful military leaders could win great power and wealth. Sargon II (721–705 B.C.) probably became king as the result of a military coup. Throughout his reign, his control of the efficient and ruthless Assyrian army enabled him to crush a constant series of rebellions and fend off all challenges to his power.

The Assyrians' almost constant state of warfare meant that their warrior kings were able to maintain superiority over rival religious leaders. Nor could the temple authorities

Seated figure of the Old Kingdom pharaoh Khafre, c. 2575–2525 B.C. About 5 feet 6 inches (1.7 m) high. The sculptor has shown the drapery and anatomy with great realism, while producing an idealized portrait of the god king. His divine power is represented by Horus, the falcon god of the Morning Sun, perched behind his head.

Hirmer Fotoarchiv

take control of other areas of civic life because the lack of a stable peace caused trade and commerce to decline. In any case, the Assyrian ruling class seemed to regard these peacetime occupations as unworthy of fighting men. Thus the only area in which the priests could maintain their influence was that of agriculture because the temples had inherited most of the best farmlands over the preceding centuries.

ANCIENT ARTISTS AND THEIR WORLDS

In societies so dominated by the ruling classes and by religion, in general the visual arts reinforced the official state ideology. The most lasting memorials of ancient culture are temples, tombs, and palaces, and public architecture played a major role in expressing each society's self-image. It is no coincidence that the earliest creative artist whose name is known to history was the Egyptian Imhotep, who worked around 2630 B.C. as the architect and adviser to the pharaoh Zoser.

TEMPLES, TOMBS, AND CITIES

For the Egyptians, a temple was inhabited by the deities to whom it was consecrated and represented a model of the universe seen from the gods' point of view. Around the outside of the buildings making up a temple complex ran a wall of mudbrick, isolating the temple's sacred space from the outside world. This protective barrier symbolized the first stage of creation, the primeval mud produced by uniting heaven and earth. The outer walls of the actual temple

Statuettes of worshipers from a temple at Eshnunna (modern Tell Asmar), Iraq, c. 2700 B.C. The tallest figure is 2 feet 6 inches (80 cm). The wide-open staring eyes suggest intensity of concentration. The two largest figures at the back, a man and a woman, may signify a ritual marriage.

The Oriental Institute, University of Chicago

showed carved scenes of the pharaoh fighting and winning battles against the forces of darkness, both human and divine. Ordinary Egyptians could not pass beyond this point, for only ritually purified priests entered the temple proper.

The colossal temples to Amen, the wind god, at the ancient city of Thebes are the result of successive periods of building extending over hundreds of years. The earliest parts of the temple complex of Karnak date to shortly after 2000 B.C., while the outer gate, begun around 350 B.C., was never finished. At the heart of the constructions at Karnak lies the gigantic Hall of the Columns, begun in 1307 B.C. by Ramses I (1307–1306 B.C.) and finished by his grandson Ramses II (1290–1224 B.C.), the most prodigious of all

builders in the New Kingdom. The Hall contains hundreds of columns (the highest 79 ft. [24.4 m] high) symbolizing a thicket of papyrus plants, springing from the primeval swamp of creation. Outside, the walls bear battle scenes, while the inside surfaces show creation myths. The total space inside the hall is large enough to contain the entire cathedral of Notre Dame in Paris.

Across the Nile from the temple of Karnak, in the Valley of the Kings on the West Bank, are the tombs of successive generations of rulers and high officials. Perhaps the most famous is that of Queen Hatshepsut (1473–1458 B.C.). Its architect, Senmut—a commoner by birth and reputed to be the queen's lover—integrated the tomb's façade into its

© The British Museum

Relief slab from the Palace of Ashurnasirpal II at Nimrud. Late 8th century B.C. The scene shows the king hunting lions from his chariot. The horses' hooves trample over a lion that has already been brought down by the king's arrows, as he turns to shoot over his shoulder at another lion behind, driven up by the royal huntsmen.

PERSPECTIVES FROM THE PAST

ASPECTS OF THE DIVINE IN THE ANCIENT WORLD

One of the functions of religious literature in the ancient world was to explain how the world came into being, and creation myths can be found in many different ancient cultures, often bearing striking similarities. At the same time, since rulers claimed their authority to govern from divine patronage, it was in their interest to emphasize the omnipotence of the gods who had entrusted them with earthly rule.

For ordinary subjects, however, faced with the uncertainties of their daily routine and the mysteries of human existence, the granite certainties of official pronouncements were not always convincing. Documents from both Mesopotamian and Egyptian sources bear witness to a vein of pessimism and scepticism underlying attitudes to sacred and secular authority.

The Creation of the World

Many of the creation myths which circulated in the ancient world have points in common. They emphasize the emergence of order from chaos, the separation of land and sea, the division between heaven and earth, and the creation of humankind in the image of the divine. The first extract below describes the Egyptian creator-god Re-Atum, who existed before the creation of the world. The "primeval hillock" in Hermopolis was one of the "creation mounds" where, the Egyptians believed, the world began. Its shape probably inspired the use of the pyramid as the site of the burial—and subsequent rebirth—of the pharaoh.

The next passage gives the Sumerian version of creation. The benevolent Sumerian god Enlil, "Lord Air," separated the earth from the sky.

Re-Atum

I am Atum when I was alone in Nun (the primordial waters); I am Re in his first appearance, when he began to rule that which he had made. What does that mean? This "Re when he began to rule that which he had made" means that Re began to appear as a king, as one who had existed before the air god Shu had even lifted heaven from earth, when he, Re, was on the primeval hillock which was in Hermopolis.

From H. and H. A. Frankfort, *Before Philosophy.* Copyright © 1949. The University of Chicago Press.

The Sumerian View

Without Enlil, the Great Mountain,
No city would be built, no settlement founded,
No stalls would be built, no sheepfolds established,
No king would be raised, no high priest born. . . .
The rivers—their floodwaters would not bring
    overflow,
The fish in the sea would not lay eggs in the canebrake,
The birds of heaven would not build nests on the
    wild earth,
In heaven the drifting clouds would not yield their
    moisture,
Plants and herbs, the glory of the plain, would fail
    to grow,
In field and meadows the rich grain would fail to
    flower,
The trees planted in the mountain-forest would not
    yield their fruit. . . .

From S. N. Kramer, *History Begins at Sumer.* Copyright © 1959, pp. 93–94. Reprinted with permission of Mrs. Samuel Kramer.

Differing Human Attitudes to the Divine

The three following extracts convey a wide range of responses to traditional religious beliefs. In the first, Hammurabi, the proud king of Babylon, proclaims his achievements, accomplished under divine patronage.

The other two documents are far more somber. In the first, an anonymous Babylonian, echoing the mood of the Sumerian Epic of Gilgamesh, meditates on the brevity and uncertainty of life. The other, the Song of the Harper, dates to Middle-Kingdom Egypt. Like the Mesopotamian writer of the previous passage, its author describes the transitory nature of human achievement, but in the end draws comfort from the idea of living for present pleasure.

Hammurabi's Achievements

(Hammurabi speaks)

I rooted out the enemy above and below;
I made an end of war;
I promoted the welfare of the land;
I made the people rest in friendly habitations;
I did not let them have anyone to terrorize them.
The great gods called me,
So I became the beneficent shepherd whose sceptre
   is righteous;
My benign shadow is spread over my city.
In my bosom I carried the people of the land of
   Sumer and Akkad;
They prospered under my protection;
I have governed them in peace;
I have sheltered them in my strength.

From Pritchard, J. B., *Ancient Near Eastern Texts Relating to the Old Testament.* Copyright © 1995 by Princeton University Press. Reprinted by permission of Princeton University Press.

The Uncertainty of Life

Who came to life yesterday, died today.
In but a moment man is cast into gloom,
   suddenly crushed.
One moment he will sing for joy,
And in an instant he will wail—a mourner.
Between morning and nightfall men's mood may
   change:
When they are hungry they become like corpses,
When they are full they will rival their god,
When things go well they will prate of rising up to
   heaven
And when in trouble, rant about descending into hell.

From Stephen Langdon, *Babylonian Wisdom.* Copyright © 1923, pp. 35–66.

Song of the Harper

One generation passes away
And others remain in its place
Since the time of the ancestors.
The gods that were aforetime
Rest in their pyramids.
They that built houses,
Their places are no more;
What has been done with them?
I have heard the sayings of Imhotep and Djedefhor,
With whose words men still speak so much;
What are their places?
Their walls have crumbled,
Their places are no more,
As if they had never been.
None cometh from thence
That he might tell their circumstances,
That he might tell their needs
And content our heart
Until we have reached the place
Whither they have gone.
May thy heart be cheerful
To permit the heart to forget
The making of funerary services for thee.
Follow thy desire while thou livest!
Put myrrh upon thy head,
Clothe thyself in fine linen,
Anoint thee with the genuine wonders
Which are the god's own.
Increase yet more thy happiness,
And let not thy heart languish;
Follow thy desire and thy good,
Fashion thine affairs on earth
After the command of thy heart.
That day of lamentation will come to thee,
When the Still of Heart does not hear their
   lamentation,
And mourning does not deliver a man from the
   netherworld.
Make holiday!
Do not weary thereof!
Lo, none is allowed to take his goods with him,
Lo, none that has gone has come back!

From Miriam Lichtheim, "The Song of the Harper," *Journal of Near Eastern Studies,* IV, The University of Chicago Press. Copyright © 1945, pp. 192–193.

natural setting, placing it against an immense cliff face towering to a height of 1,000 feet above it. Nothing in Mesopotamia or the ancient Near East matches the grandeur of Egypt's monuments. The existence in Egypt of vast quantities of high-quality granite and other extra-hard stone provided a natural source of construction material that both inspired architects and enabled their buildings to survive the ravages of time. The mudbrick structures of the Sumerians proved less durable.

Toward the end of Mesopotamian history, Assyrian builders created more permanent works by importing stone from the mountains to the north of the rivers Tigris and Euphrates. At the palace at Nineveh built for Asurbanipal (668–626 B.C.), the brick walls and gateways have stone slabs lining them, on which are carved scenes of war and the hunt. The battles show the victorious Assyrians demolishing cities, plundering, and taking away prisoners. In the hunting episodes, the artists seem to depict the suffering of the dying animals with greater sympathy than that of the human victims in the scenes of warfare.

The Hittite capital at Boğhazköy illustrates an earlier tradition of palace sculpture and architecture. The city spread out over 300 acres, within a massive defensive wall of stone and mudbrick. Monumental stone lions and sphinxes flank the gateways, and inside there are four temples, each with its own courtyard.

ART IN MINIATURE

If most artists and craftsmen spent their time on official state projects, others produced jewelry, small sculptures in ivory or other semiprecious materials, and carved sealstones. Many of the most skilled ivory carvers in the ancient world were Phoenician, in part because the Phoenician colony of Carthage in North Africa had its own elephant farms (elephants seem to have become extinct in Mesopotamia during the time of the Assyrians). The animals may have served as fighting beasts in the Carthaginian Army, while their tusks provided the material for Phoenician artists. Phoenician traders sold ivory statuettes, combs, hairpins, and small wooden boxes inlaid with ivory, as well as larger pieces of furniture, throughout the ancient world. The Assyrian rulers were good customers, and their palaces and tombs contained thousands of ivory objects either sold by Phoenician businessmen or paid as tribute. In the west, the Etruscans of Central Italy bought Phoenician ivories, and some pieces even reached Spain.

FAITH, HOPE, AND DESPAIR IN ANCIENT LITERATURE

Much of our understanding of the daily life of the peoples of the ancient world comes from their written records. These range from the trading records of the Babylonians to recipes for love potions found in Egypt, from instructions on how to conduct a Hittite funeral to the law codes of the Mesopotamian states. Little of this material, however, was meant primarily to be read as literature.

Religious texts provide a more universal category of ancient writings, setting out ideas that are often expressed in the form of poetry. Most of them contain the official teachings of the ruling classes, while reflecting the differences among the various cultures of the ancient world. The Egyptian *Book of the Dead*, for example, is a sort of guidebook to the underworld. Its illustrated text describes the judgment of the soul after death and offers to those Egyptians able to afford the appropriate rituals the chance of a happy life in the next world if their lives satisfy the gods. This essentially positive view of death is also borne out in more informal, popular songs:

> Death stands before me today
> Like the fragrance of myrrh,
> Like sitting under the shade on a breezy day.

THE EPIC OF GILGAMESH

The Mesopotamian religious texts convey a very different idea of death and the next life. Beset by the awesome forces of scorching winds and torrential rains, the Mesopotamians viewed existence as a fleeting and harsh struggle against nature, ending in the bleak darkness of death:

> He who came to life yesterday, died today.
> In but a moment man is cast into gloom,
> suddenly crushed.

By far the most impressive Mesopotamian work, perhaps the first in our past that truly can be called literature, is the *Epic of Gilgamesh*. This Akkadian work was first composed around the beginning of the 2nd millennium B.C., although its roots are probably Sumerian. It tells the story of Gilgamesh, ruler of the city of Uruk in southern Babylonia, who is driven by the death of his beloved friend Enkidu to set out on a quest in search of the meaning of life. If death is an evil—the supreme punishment—why are we punished if we have committed no wrong? What role can justice have in a universe where all must die?

Gilgamesh wanders to the mountains of the setting sun and follows it into the darkness of night, despairing of ever seeing light again. All those he meets tell him that the search for meaning is hopeless and advise him to try to make the best of his life: "When the gods created humans, they let death be their share, and withheld life in their own hands. Gilgamesh, fill your belly and wear fresh clothes. Look at the child who is holding your hand, and let your wife delight in your embrace. These things alone are the concern of men."

Yet Gilgamesh refuses to accept his destiny and struggles on. He even crosses the waters of death in search of the plant that can, so he hears, rejuvenate those who eat it. When he finds the sacred plant, he sets off back home in triumph. But exhausted by the heat, he pauses to swim in a cool lake, and a serpent steals the plant: "Then Gilgamesh sat down and wept, tears streaming down his cheeks." The end of the *Epic* sees no hope in sight, no answers to the questions. The weary king returns home and dies.

THE OLD TESTAMENT

The writings described so far help bring remote civilizations to life, but the Bible has been central to the development of our own culture. Whatever our individual beliefs may be, our societies, languages, laws, and systems of values have been shaped by the books of the Old and New Testaments, which together constitute what is often called simply The Book. The standard form of the Hebrew Scriptures, called the Tanach and established in A.D. 90, contains 24 books. The Catholic and Orthodox Old Testaments have 46 books, while the Protestant Old Testament contains 39.

The three traditional divisions of the Hebrew Scriptures are known as the Law, the Prophets, and the Writings. Although the Bible's Hebrew authors occasionally echo themes and ideas that occur elsewhere in ancient religious writings—the Flood found in the book of Genesis has a parallel in the *Epic of Gilgamesh*—its general spirit is profoundly original.

The first five books of the Old Testament are probably compilations of documents going back to the 9th century B.C. The present form of the Old Testament was established by an assembly of rabbis in A.D. 90, although the discovery of the Dead Sea Scrolls, which include large portions of the Hebrew text of the Old Testament, proves that it already existed centuries earlier: The community that produced the Scrolls, perhaps a Jewish sect known as the Essenes, flourished around 200 B.C.

In contrast to the many gods of other religions, Judaism evolved into a monotheistic religion. Its one God is transcendent and cannot be depicted, a fact that explains the absence of a tradition of visual art in Jewish culture. Pure Being, he existed before the world, which he created out of a chaotic ocean—*tehom,* "the Deep." Having created the world with humans as the highest form of living creature, God is involved in the ongoing course of human history as a positive force for good—not, like the gods of many other religions, an impersonal force of nature.

The first part of the Bible sets out the moral code by which, according to its authors, God expects us to live, and describes the "covenant." This is a relationship with the people of Israel, whereby they will spread knowledge of the word of God throughout the world. In the second part, Jewish leaders of the 8th and 7th centuries B.C.—called prophets, although they were concerned with their contemporaries rather than the future—laid great stress on social justice. By contrast with the law codes of the Mesopotamians, or the royal decrees of Egypt, the prophets' teachings are based not on power but on compassion, not on the orders of the state but on a personal code of ethics.

In the Writings of the third part, these ideas are illustrated in a series of stories and poems. Figures such as Job and Daniel, Esther and Ruth, illustrate the consequences of human behavior and divine action. This part also contains the Psalms—150 songs, many of which were traditionally ascribed to King David, that deal with varieties of religious experience. The book known as the Song of Solomon, or the Song of Songs, on the other hand, consists of a series of passionate love songs; both traditional Jewish and Christian commentators have interpreted these songs as symbolic of God's love for his people.

Putting Art and Belief in the Ancient World in Perspective

The teachings of the Old Testament underline the separateness of Jewish culture from their contemporaries, a gulf emphasized by the idea of the Covenant. Elsewhere in the ancient world, artists used images and buildings to express the beliefs and attitudes toward life of their societies. The individual was subordinate to society as a whole, which in turn accepted the rule of its dominant upper class, often perilously split between sacred and secular authorities. The overwhelming importance of religion in all aspects of life gave the priests a distinct advantage in maintaining their power.

Yet despite the often impersonal character of ancient art, the visual artists of the times created works that transcend the remoteness of their cultures. Their sensitivity to the world of Nature, which many ancient peoples believed was even more sacred than their gods, provides a link with our own experience. The writings of the period also continue to be relevant. Few thoughtful persons will be unfamiliar with the kind of questions posed by Gilgamesh in the *Epic,* while the Old Testament provides the basis for a religious tradition that still influences the lives of millions of Jews and Christians.

Questions for Further Study

1. How did the character of the Egyptians' society affect their art? What were the chief subjects depicted by Egyptian artists and why?
2. What was the relationship between state and religion in the ancient Near East, and how did it differ from culture to culture?
3. What are the main features of epic poetry? How many of these can be found in the *Epic of Gilgamesh*?
4. In what ways did the Hebrews' religion and culture differ from those of their neighbors? What were the long-term consequences of these differences?

Suggestions for Further Reading

Alter, Robert. *The World of Biblical Narrative*. New York, 1992.

Collon, Dominique. *First Impressions. Cylinder Seals in the Ancient Near East*, 2nd ed. London, 1993.

Davies, W. Vivian, and Louise Schofield, eds. *Egypt, the Aegean and the Levant. Interconnections in the 2nd Millennium B.C.* London, 1995.

Frankfort, H. *The Art and Architecture of the Ancient Orient*, 5th ed. New Haven, 1996.

Friedman, R. E. *Who Wrote the Bible?* New York, 1987.

Kampen, Natalie B., ed. *Sexuality in Ancient Art*. New York, 1996.

Lichtheim, M. *Ancient Egyptian Literature* (3 vols.). Berkeley, 1973–1980.

Reade, Julian E. *Assyrian Sculpture*. Cambridge, MA, 1999.

Robins, Gay. *Proportion and Style in Ancient Egyptian Art*. Austin, TX, 1994.

Smith, M.S. *The Early History of God: Yahweh and the Other Deities in Ancient Israel*. San Francisco, 1987.

Strouhal, N. *Life of the Ancient Egyptians*. Norman, OK, 1992.

Traunecker, Claude. David Lorton, trans. *The Gods of Egypt*. Ithaca, NY, 2001.

VanderKam, James C. *An Introduction to Early Judaism*. Grand Rapids, MI, 2001.

Wolf, Walther. *The Origins of Western Art: Egypt, Mesopotamia, the Aegean*. New York, 1989.

Zettler, Richard L., and Lee Horne. *Treasures from the Royal Tombs of Ur*. Philadelphia, 1998.

InfoTrac College Edition

Enter the search term *antiquities* using the Subject Guide.

The Structure and Economic Life of Ancient Society

Given the conservative nature of most ancient societies, social mobility was rare. A small ruling class dominated large numbers of workers, peasants, and slaves, whose status was fixed. The most rigid social system of all operated in Egypt. In cultures where commerce and trade were important, such as those of the Sumerians or the Phoenicians, an artisan and trader class developed, offering limited possibility for social advancement.

Laws and traditional patterns of behavior reinforced the family as the basis of society. Mesopotamian law codes illustrate women's rights in their private life and in relation to their family duties. Few women achieved any status in public life, although there were exceptions: The Egyptian queen Hatshepsut and the Hittite queen Puduhepa both played a crucial role in their countries' affairs. The Old Testament also provides examples of influential female figures, who often served as role models.

Agriculture provided the chief source of wealth and work. The ruling classes jealously guarded their possession of the land; laws regulated complicated systems of land tenure and transfer. Fertility in the great estates of Egypt depended on the annual flood of the Nile. Mesopotamian farmers had to deal with a much less predictable climate and learned to develop elaborate irrigation systems and produce abundant crops.

Once communities were self-sufficient in food supplies, they could trade surpluses with neighbors. At the same time, new technologies led to increased manufacture of goods, many of them made for barter or sale abroad. By around 1500 B.C. traders had created a wide network of commercial relations throughout the Mediterranean and the Near East. Each culture had its special products: Egypt was famous for stone dishes and wooden furniture (the wood itself often imported from the Phoenicians) while the Babylonians produced high-quality woolen textiles.

In most ancient societies, cities served originally as religious and administrative centers for the ruling classes. Most of the population lived and worked on the land. Over time, more complex patterns of urban life began to appear in Mesopotamia, reflected in the laws: Hammurabi's Code requires the execution of a builder responsible for a house that collapses and kills the owner.

In each society an individual possessed specific rights and obligations, whether as ruler, farmer, woman, son, or builder. In the rigid hierarchy of ancient life, even slaves had certain established rights, which structured the relationship between them and their owners. In Egypt, these rights were minimal, while elsewhere, as in some periods of Mesopotamian history or among the Hittites, the law provided some variation in the harshness of slavery.

CLASS, STATUS, AND FAMILY

Only with the rise of urban civilization in Egypt and the Near East did a rigid class structure develop that governed all aspects of life. At the top was the ruling class, drawn from a small number of families. This select group, born to power, controlled the economy, state religion, and the armed forces.

ARISTOCRACY IN EGYPT AND MESOPOTAMIA

In the most extreme form of aristocracy, that of Egypt in the Old Kingdom, a single figure was in supreme command of the state. The pharaoh was god-king, head of the state religion, military commander, and owner of all his country's land, large tracts of which he rented out. Powerful and successful pharaohs sought to maintain their family's rule by founding a dynasty, which might last for a hundred years or more.

The three main classes of Egyptian society reinforced this hierarchical pattern. In the first, immediately below the pharaoh, the nobles and priests formed the upper classes and ran the government. Three subgroups made up the middle classes: scribes, merchants, and artisans. Day-to-day administration was in the hands of the scribes, who combined the functions of civil servant, lawyer, and tax collector; popular tales often described them as crooked, greedy, and opportunistic. The merchants organized trade and barter, both internal and international. The artisans produced works of art to decorate the royal palaces, to accompany the upper classes to the next life, and for commercial use.

The overwhelming number of Egyptians belonged to the lowest class. Although most worked the land, some labored on building projects or served in the army or as domestic servants. Over the centuries this rigid system changed somewhat. During the Middle Kingdom, as the economy expanded, the nobles unwillingly made concessions to the middle-class businessmen and manufacturers, while generally retaining most of their privileges. The New Kingdom, with its constant military campaigns and conquests, brought more substantial change. A class of professional soldiers occupied a position below the nobles but above the middle classes. At the very bottom were now the slaves, who had been captured in the wars abroad; their large numbers made possible the grandiose building projects of the 18th and 19th Dynasties.

Mesopotamian society was also based on birth, with the same three general divisions into nobility, middle-class commoners, and workers. It lacked a single supreme ruler, however, corresponding to the Egyptian pharaoh. The resultant conflict between civil and religious authorities and the gradual rise in importance of those engaged in trade and manufacturing meant that traditional social patterns needed some form of codification to set out the official dogma. The Mesopotamian law codes, of which Hammurabi's is the most complete, establish the principle of "an eye for an eye," but at the same time depict a society in which each individual's rights depended on class: "If a nobleman knocks out the tooth of one of the same rank, one of his shall be knocked out. If he knocks out a commoner's tooth, he shall pay a

Limestone figure of a seated scribe, c. 2450–2350 B.C. Height 1 foot 9 inches (56 cm). Scribes, together with merchants and artisans, formed an important element of ancient Egypt's middle class. This figure's sagging breasts and weighty belly show evident signs of prosperity, although the keen gaze suggests a shrewd administrator.

© Réunion des Musées Nationaux/Art Resource, NY

fine." Yet the laws punished nobles more severely than lower-class citizens for some crimes and guaranteed certain rights for the lowest classes.

In both Egyptian and Mesopotamian society, the social rules of public life had their counterpart in private life. Like the state, family life was authoritarian, ruled from the top down. Mesopotamians were constantly reminded: "Listen to the word of your mother as to your god; revere your older brother; do not anger the heart of your older sister." An Egyptian father, advising his son on how to behave to his aging mother, urges him "to carry her as she carried you."

There is some evidence for a less rigid class structure elsewhere in the ancient world. A Hittite royal document, summoning an assembly to advise the king, lists its members as "fighting men, servants, and nobles." Early Phoenician communities were ruled by hereditary kings, but over time, with the growth of a rich merchant class, these were replaced by "councils of elders," whose members owed their status to their success in business rather than to their birth.

WOMEN, POWER, AND SUBJUGATION

The position of women in the ancient world emerges most clearly in the evidence we have about family life. On the whole, ancient society was patriarchal, with men exerting the dominant role, but some traditional patterns were unexpectedly enlightened for so early a period in the history of relations between the sexes.

WOMEN IN ANCIENT EGYPT

On the whole, Egyptian women enjoyed better conditions than most of their counterparts elsewhere in the ancient world. In Egypt most men had only one wife, although they could take another if the first was childless. Even the pharaoh, with his royal harem, distinguished between his Great Wife, the senior one, and the others. Although Egyptian married women were generally subordinate to their husband's authority, they retained control of their own property, with the right to inherit it and pass it on. They, as well as their husbands, could initiate divorce proceedings. Some collections of popular wisdom suggest that they also had emotional rights that were recognized. One such book advises a husband to "make your wife's heart glad as long as you live."

Women confined most of their activities to the home, where they took charge of domestic arrangements and the education of children. Some women, however, operated businesses, and upper-class women could serve as priestesses. During the New Kingdom women worked as authors and scribes. Other areas in which women were employed included music and dance, while countless Egyptian peasant women toiled in the fields. Apart from the very last period of Egyptian history, under the Ptolemies, women played no part officially in the affairs of state, although several royal women wielded political power as co-regents with their young sons or as influential mothers of the heir to the throne. The most powerful of all Egyptian women was Queen Hatshepsut (for a discussion of this remarkable figure, see Topic 3).

WOMEN AND THE LAW: THE HITTITES

Clearly, the legal status of women was not uniform throughout the ancient world. Even in the Near East, legal differences existed. On the whole, Hittite custom seems to have resembled that of the Babylonians. In some respects, however, Hittite women had greater rights. Thus Hittite laws allowed the mother as well as the father to participate in choosing a husband for their daughter, and laid down conditions under which a mother could disinherit her son. Married couples generally lived together, but in some cases a woman had the possibility of continuing to live with her father. This custom also existed among the Assyrians, and presumably applied when a marriage served purely political or financial ends.

A special law governed the welfare of Hittite widows. The nearest male relative on the dead husband's side was obliged to take care of the widow by marrying her and giving any children of this second union the name and inheritance of the dead man. A similar tradition appears in the Old Testament, to preserve the family of the first husband, "that his name be not blotted out of Israel."

The less restrictive conditions of Hittite women may reflect the earliest origins of Hittite society, which were probably matriarchal. By contrast, the Mesopotamian tradition was patriarchal. One result was that a Hittite queen had a much more independent position than her Egyptian or Babylonian counterparts. On the death of a king, his widow became queen mother; the new king's wife had no right to the title of queen until the queen mother's own death. The widow of the great warrior King Suppiluliumas (1380–1346 B.C.) caused so much ill-feeling at the court of the new king, their son Mursilis II (1345–1315 B.C.), that in exasperation he expelled her from the palace.

The most famous of all Hittite queens was Puduhepa, wife of Hattusilis (1289–1265 B.C.). She played an important role in state affairs, and her name appears alongside her husband's in state documents. She even conducted her own correspondence with the Egyptian court: A treaty with Egypt bears a seal impression showing her in the embrace of the sun goddess.

THE WOMEN OF ANCIENT ISRAEL AND JUDAH

The Old Testament reflects the patriarchal tradition of the first Hebrews. As early as the story of Eden in the book of Genesis, Eve is made responsible for listening to the serpent and convincing Adam to eat with her the apple of the tree of knowledge of good and evil—in contravention of God's

Illuminated manuscript page showing four episodes in the Biblical account of Eve: the creation of Eve; the marriage of Adam and Eve; the temptation; and the expulsion from Eden. 6⅝ inches by 4⅞ inches (16.8 by 12.4 cm). The manuscript dates to the mid-13th century.

© The Barnes Foundation, Merion Station, Pennsylvania/CORBIS

HISTORICAL PERSPECTIVES

THE STATUS OF WOMEN IN ANCIENT MESOPOTAMIA

JOANN SCURLOCK   Elmhurst College

It might be supposed that, being more ancient than ancient Greece, Mesopotamian society was comparatively backward in its treatment of women; however, although Mesopotamian women were hardly well-off by modern standards, they managed to exercise more rights and to enjoy more freedoms than their Athenian counterparts.

For most Mesopotamian women, marriage and childbearing were an expected (and desired) part of growing up. Marriages were arranged by parents or by the prospective groom and the adolescent bride's family. Marriages were considered family alliances; if an Assyrian bride or groom died without children, the widow(er) might find him or herself married to one of the late spouse's siblings. This did not invariably result in a young girl being saddled with an old husband. In such marriages, a new husband might be considerably younger than his wife (though at least 10 years old).

Neither was it the case that a woman never had the right to choose. There was a way, if somewhat risky, that "true love" could prevail. Unlike their Athenian counterparts, respectable Mesopotamian girls could be seen in the city streets or out in the countryside and could attend religious festivals with only female friends for company. If a girl allowed a man to deflower her, and if she had clearly done so with marriage in mind, he could

legally be forced to marry her. This was also true if she had been flirting with him and he got carried away. "Playing around" was not, however, an option—a non-virginal bride was damaged goods, facing not only her father's anger but sharply diminished marriage prospects. Girls whose virginity was questioned were cleared by gynecological examination.

A girl who disliked her new husband—if she avoided giving the impression that she had other irons in the fire—could get local authorities to dissolve the marriage. A widow or divorcée with children was free to make her own marital arrangements using her dowry as bait. In Assyria, she could even become a common-law wife, although she lost her property if she moved in with her lover. If, on the other hand, she could persuade him to move in with her, she became owner of his property.

As in ancient Greece, a woman entered marriage with a dowry that was supposed to keep her fed and clothed in the style to which she was accustomed. Unlike the situation in ancient Greece, the Mesopotamian husband was expected to pay her father a bride price for the right to her labor, her undivided sexual attentions, and her children. This was because Mesopotamian wives were not "useless mouths" but essential contributors to the family economy, whether by laboring in the fields or weaving on the family loom.

orders. God decrees that all future women will suffer the consequences of her disobedience: "I will greatly multiply your pain in childbearing."

In the early books of the Old Testament, several patriarchs have two wives or a wife and a concubine—Jacob has two concubines as well as two wives. Women had to be sexually faithful but not men. Husbands could divorce their wives for a series of reasons ranging from forging keys to adultery, but wives could not divorce their husbands. Even the normal processes of menstruation and childbirth were thought to make women ritually "unclean." The birth of a son made a woman "impure" for 7 days, whereas after the birth of a daughter, the mother was "impure" for 14 days.

In contrast to the mainly restrictive picture of women's rights that emerges from the Hebrew tradition, the Old Testament describes several outstanding women who illustrate a wide variety of virtues, and the description of their exploits was clearly intended as inspiration to others. Deborah, a wife and mother, is also a prophet and judge. Together with another woman, Jael, she rallies her people against their enemies. Jael even kills the enemy general by hammering a nail into his head.

Other Hebrew women symbolized less violent heroism. Queen Esther, wife of the Persian king, showed loyalty to her people by preventing the massacre of all Persian Jews. The story of Ruth is an example of steadfastness and loyalty on a more personal level. Widowed during a famine, she fol-

Old Assyrian merchants expected their wives to run the family textile business in Assur while they were off in Anatolia selling cloth and tin. Nuzian husbands gave their wives the right to act as "father and mother" of the household after they died, as long as the widow did not remarry. Even Neo-Babylonian dowry inventories pay silent testimony to a wife's contribution to the family's income: They contain, besides jewelry and house-hold furniture, items of manufacture such as brewing equipment.

There were laws protecting women from assault, particularly when pregnant. An Assyrian man could lose a lip for kissing an unwilling victim and a finger for spanking her. Even husbands were not allowed, when chastising wives, to go beyond beating, hair pulling, and ear boxing or ear piercing. Not that Assyrian women were helpless—stiff penalties were envisaged for women who caused bodily injury to men (crushing their testicles was a particularly dreaded method of assault). Old Babylonian tavern keepers, typically women, were expected to police their male customers vigorously; according to Hammurabi's laws, criminals gathering in their establishments were to be seized and taken to the authorities on pain of death.

A Mesopotamian woman's husband was responsible for *her* debts and, despite the dowry, she was entitled to support throughout the marriage (and after his death unless she remarried). If a virgin priestess or other childless woman wished to choose a second wife for her husband, and if she paid the bride price, the husband could not take a second wife of his own choosing and the second wife (often the first wife's younger sister) could be required by contract to side with the first wife and act as her maidservant. Any children produced from such a marriage belonged to the first wife. A woman who felt neglected could get an injunction for-

bidding her husband from visiting his prostitute mistress. If a husband chose to divorce his wife without her fault, she was entitled to a substantial payment, especially if she had children. Even if the children were adopted, she could keep them upon divorce provided that she, not he, had paid the adoption payment.

Ancient Mesopotamians associated civilized culture with the coming together of men and women and untamed nature with either sex attempting to act alone. Although they would certainly have agreed that a man should be master in his household, the ultra-masculine man without women in the Greek style is presented as at best an "Amorite" and at worst no better than an animal. When the hero Gilgamesh faces the problem of a wild man Enkidu running amuck in the back country of Uruk, he turns him into a civilized human being by sending a prostitute out to seduce him. Similarly, women without men untamed by marriage were regarded as savage, wild, and dangerous.

If a member of either sex died before this civilizing coming together could occur, he or she became a demon doomed to prowl the streets looking for the fulfillment that a cruel fate had denied him or her: "Young girl not fated to be married; young woman who was never impregnated like a woman; young woman who was never deflowered like a woman; young girl who never experienced sexual pleasure in her husband's lap." "Young man who always sits, silent and alone, in the street; young man who cries bitterly in the grip of his death-demon; young man who never married a wife, never raised a child; young man who never experienced sexual pleasure in his wife's lap." For ancient Mesopotamians, it was not rape, but dying without enjoying sexual pleasure in the arms of a man who "loved her like a wife" that was, for a woman, a fate literally worse than death.

lowed her mother-in-law Naomi to Bethlehem, where she survived by gleaning barley from the fields.

THE AGRICULTURAL ECONOMY: FOOD PRODUCTION AND CONSUMPTION

In one important way all ancient societies except the Hebrews and the Persians (both monotheistic) shared a common attitude toward the feminine: They worshiped the earth and the world of nature in the form of a mother god-

dess. The Egyptian "Great Goddess," the Semitic Ishtar, the Hittite sun goddess Arinna, and the Phoenician Astarte or Tanit all represented the cycle of life and growth, which annually renewed itself.

Agriculture had first made possible the birth of civilization, and it remained the economic basis of all ancient societies. Even the Assyrians, with their contempt for trade and business, recognized the need for adequate food production and distribution.

FARMING IN THE ANCIENT WORLD

After marriage and the family, the area that ancient law codes sought to control was land ownership. Early in Egyptian history there had been free farmers, owning their

The Metropolitan Museum of Art, Fletcher Fund, 1957. (57.80.10)

Phoenician ivory carving showing the goddess Isis, c. 700 B.C. Height 6½ inches (17 cm). The figure represented is an Egyptian goddess, wearing a typically Egyptian headdress and hairstyle, but the treatment is Phoenician: An Egyptian artist would never have depicted Isis with wings, and the decorative filling is also non-Egyptian.

own land, but by the end of the Old Kingdom the pharaoh owned all of the farmland and granted or rented estates to the nobles and the religious centers.

In Mesopotamia the laws specified the terms under which tenant farmers could work the land and pay their rent in the form of crops. Another matter of great concern was irrigation, which was vital in a region where the weather was unpredictable. Both owners and tenants were responsible for keeping the water channels in good repair and the water flow efficient. Because one system of irrigation often served several adjoining farms, the failure of one farmer could cause damage to his neighbors. Those whose carelessness caused the destruction of others' crops, and who could not pay for the damage, were liable to be sold into slavery.

Hittite records document similar farming problems, including the danger of fire and stray animals or the theft of a swarm of bees. One land deed also provides a description of the estate of a small landholder called Tiwataparas. His land included one acre of meadow as pasture for his six oxen and 3.5 acres of vineyard, which also contained 40 apple trees and 42 pomegranate trees. His 22 sheep and 18 goats probably grazed in the hills around. With this property, the farmer could support himself, his wife, a son, and two daughters.

FOOD AND DRINK

The Sumerians of Ur used ox-drawn plows to cultivate a wide variety of grains and vegetables: barley, millet, lentils and beans, onions, leeks and garlic, lettuce, and cucumbers. Among their dishes was a round, flat pancake made of ground barley dough garnished with onions and greens, which they baked on a heated stone—a kind of Ur-pizza.

Because most of the beef came from cattle that were old or sick and were of little food value, the ruler of Ur had it distributed to his dogs. The Sumerians bred sheep and goat for their meat, while the domestic pig was introduced into the Near East before 2000 B.C. from Central Asia. Freshwater fish provided another source of protein, and vendors circulated in the streets of cities such as Ur and Lagash

Werner Forman Archive/Art Resource New York

Sumerian seal impression showing peasants farming with their cattle, c. 2700–2400 B.C. This impression is from a cylinder seal, probably used as an owner's mark on clay documents. The animals are long-horned oxen used for ploughing.

with slices of fish fried in sesame oil, along with grilled vegetables and drinks sweetened with honey or dates.

Grapes were cultivated in Mesopotamia as early as 3000 B.C., but by far the most popular alcoholic drink was beer, and half of each year's grain crop was used for brewing. There were at least 19 different types of beer, produced from various combinations of grain. Workers received a daily supply: one liter to each common laborer, five liters to a supervisor—the abstemious could use their allowance as the equivalent of money to barter for other products.

The Egyptian diet was even richer and included fish from the river and the sea, game from the hunt (including deer and antelope), geese, ducks and pigeons, and a wide range of fruits. Among the grains was semolina, known in modern Arabic as "couscous" and still popular in North Africa today. A more simple ancient Egyptian dish consisted of a puree of beans flavored with ground coriander and garnished with almonds.

As in Mesopotamia, food served for bartering. In the time of Ramses III (1186–1155 B.C.), a laborer received four sacks of grain per month, while his overseer's wage was seven and a half sacks. More than a millennium earlier,

even the humble workers employed to build the pyramids could expect a daily allowance of grain, dried fish, garlic, and onion. No wonder that as the Hebrews crossed the Sinai Desert on the way to the Promised Land, they looked back nostalgically to the diet of their exile in Egypt: fish, lamb, eggs, melons, cucumbers, onions, garlic. Many of these foods play a part in the ritual meal, the Seder, with which pious Jews still commemorate the Passover, the departure from Egypt. At the Seder the bread eaten is unleavened, made without the use of yeast, because on the eve of their flight the Hebrews had no time to let their bread rise.

ARTISANS AND TRADERS: THE RISE OF COMMERCE

Once the cultures of the ancient world could count on self-sufficiency in food production, they could move toward the next stage of economic development, manufacturing and trade. The making of works of art and craft began very early,

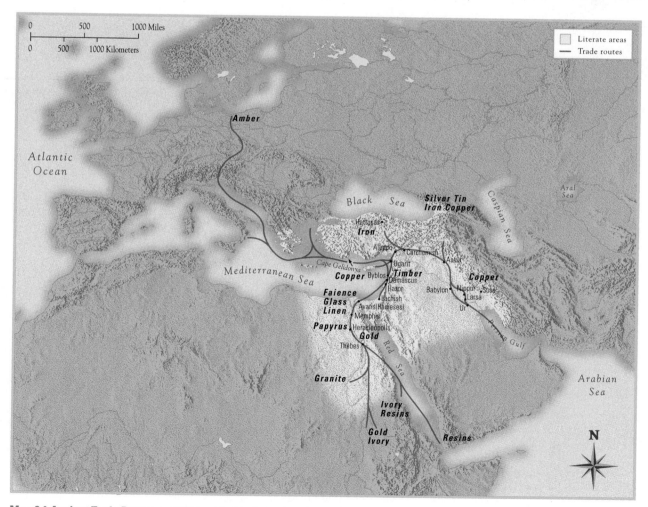

Map 6.1 Ancient Trade Routes, c. 1300 B.C. Most trade involves the two great powers of the age, the Egyptians and the Hittites. For the Hittites, the most important raw material was iron, which only they knew how to smelt. Trade with the north was limited to amber from the Baltic region, while the Arabian Peninsula was still undeveloped.

generally to satisfy the wishes of the ruling class. The miniature ivories of Ur and the monumental sculptures of the Old Kingdom are just two contrasting examples of works commissioned for official use. The artisans who made these artworks acquired the technical proficiency to produce increasing numbers of pieces, and over time merchants began to organize the manufacture and sale of objects.

RAW MATERIALS

In some cases traders used goods to exchange for raw materials lacking in their state, which were then used to produce other objects for export. Thus the Sumerians learned to capitalize on the advantages of their land and to remedy its deficiencies. The river valleys of Mesopotamia were poor in metal deposits and hard wood suitable for furniture. At the same time, sheep farming was common there and grain production high. As a result, the Sumerians made

and exported woolen fabric and grain, bartering it for commodities such as copper and tin. Their craftsmen used the imported metals to produce works of art that served for a further round of trading.

The Egyptians also traded in raw materials, exchanging gold mined in Sudan and high-quality ceramics for silver and ivory. Among their trading partners were merchants from Phoenicia and Syria.

Some peoples managed to maintain a monopoly on a particular commodity. The Phoenicians, for example, were famous for a rich and highly prized purple dye made from a shellfish called murex, large quantities of which swam in the waters off their coast. Phoenician traders imported plain woolen cloth from Mesopotamia and cotton textiles from Egypt, dyed them, and exported the finished product in exchange for grain and livestock, in which Phoenicia was deficient.

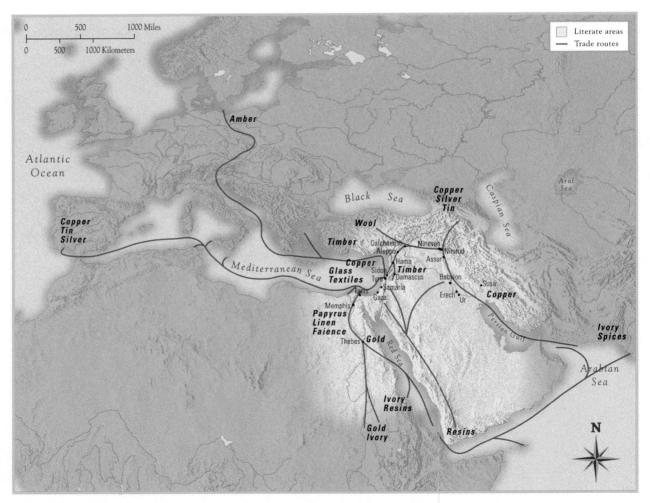

Map 6.2 Ancient Trade Routes, c. 825 B.C. By comparison with Map 6.1, the Hittite Empire has now disappeared, while new contacts have been established in the East and the far West. The Iberian Peninsula (modern Spain and Portugal) was a rich mineral source, while the 1st millennium B.C. saw the opening of one of the trade routes that was to dominate European history for centuries: the spice trade with India and, eventually, Southeast Asia. The growth of settlements in Arabia led to increasing use of the natural resources available around the Caspian Sea.

The great mountain masses of the Hittites' land were rich in minerals, and Hittite merchants traded in copper and silver. Hittite craftsmen even discovered how to smelt iron—a process requiring a very high temperature—and work it. Iron was harder than any other metal known at the time, and iron objects fetched a good price. The Hittite kings were careful, however, to keep the smelting technique secret and to limit the export of iron products. The discovery at Tel el Amarna of an archive of correspondence between the court of Akhenaton and a Hittite king including references to the ban on iron trading provides a vivid illustration of this secrecy, while in a letter to a Mesopotamian ruler (perhaps Assyrian), the Hittite king Hattusilis III refuses a request for "good iron," which, he says, is not available: "I tell you that this is a bad time for producing iron." This may be an early example of an official embargo on vital military supplies, expressed in the language of diplomacy.

PATTERNS OF URBAN LIFE

As manufacturing and trade became increasingly important sectors of the economy, the function of the cities began to change. Urban centers had originally served as bases for administration and important state religious cults. Both nobles and peasants lived on the great land estates, the former in luxurious villas and the latter in mudbrick hovels.

By 2000 B.C. settlements like Ur, Uruk, and Lagash had many of the features of metropolitan life, as excavations at Ur have vividly revealed. Through narrow doors in blank, windowless walls, the visitor could enter the cool central courtyard of a townhouse. The main floor contained the workshop and storeroom, bathroom, and a large oblong room for receiving guests and providing them with a bed for the night. The servants' quarters were also downstairs. The owner and his family lived on the floor above.

Elsewhere along the streets were small shops, either grouped together to form a bazaar or set among the houses.

Each shop had a showroom opening onto the street and a small backroom for storing the merchandise, which might be food, spices, rugs, perfumes, or pots. The dark workshops of the metalworkers, lit with a furnace, alternated with restaurants serving fried fish, cucumbers, and onions. Here and there were little chapels with clay statuettes decorating their façades.

The objects and inscribed tablets found in these buildings make it clear that their residents were neither particularly wealthy nor powerful. Gimil-Sin was the headmaster of a small private school, where he taught writing, mathematics, history, and religion. The bronzesmith's factory contained a Sumerian-Akkadian grammar text, while records found in the copper merchant's house reveal that an unlucky business deal had forced him to sell part of his house to a neighbor. All of these were modest middle-class citizens living in a town that was but one of many similar communities in the area.

SLAVERY, HUMAN RIGHTS, AND THE LAW

The various law codes of the ancient world sought to define the rights and obligations of individual citizens to the overlapping larger groups to which they belonged: their family, their fellow professionals, their city, the state. This complex web of interdependence was the chief means whereby all citizens felt themselves to be members of a single and united community.

The one class that remained relatively uninvolved in this sense of participation was the slaves. Even in their case, however, many ancient peoples had laws that tried to regularize the status of slaves and in some cases provide certain basic rights. In Egypt these laws were minimal. The slaves and land serfs of the Old and Middle Kingdoms had the same

Modern model of a street in Ur, c. 2000 B.C. The flat roofs and enclosed courtyards were characteristic of Sumerian urban architecture. In the background the tip of Ur's principal religious shrine, the ziggurat, is visible.

Ancient Art & Architecture

Copper statuette of a Sumerian slave carrying a basket of bricks to a building site. 3rd millennium B.C. Height 5 inches (14 cm). The inscription on the figure's lower part is in cuneiform and refers to the temple in which the statuette was left as a votive offering, which commemorates the construction of the temple.

possibility of judgment and reward after death as other Egyptians. In life their fate remained grim. The thousands of foreigners captured in the wars of the New Kingdom and sold into slavery worked in the mines and quarries or on building projects. Over time they were allowed to serve as conscripts in the army and could gradually improve their status.

SLAVERY AND THE LAW

The Mesopotamian law codes made a careful attempt to define the relationship between slaves and their owners. This was partly because not all slaves were born as such or captured in foreign wars: Full citizens guilty of certain crimes were punished by being sold into slavery. The offenses included striking an elder brother or kicking one's mother, or defaulting on a loan. Mesopotamian slaves were thus legally entitled to continue to hold property and engage in business, to marry free citizens (their children were free), and to buy their own freedom. Such concessions were clearly for the benefit of citizen slaves and of little consolation to those born or sold into slavery, or who were taken prisoner.

Hebrew law also permitted the enslavement of citizens who could not repay a debt or make good a theft, but only for a period of six years: "in the seventh year he is to go free, without paying anything." Other Hebrew laws encouraged favorable treatment of slaves and punished their abuse: A slave who had been physically injured was set free. On the other hand, a freed slave's wife and children remained the property of his owner. Domestic slaves seem to have been regarded as members of the family with whom they lived. There are cases of slaves even marrying into the family or inheriting its property.

Several Hittite documents serve as a reminder that it is difficult to evaluate the real nature of human relations from law codes, which tried to provide objective "guidelines" for rulers and slaves. Common sense suggests that those living under the same roof must have tried to establish some form of mutual respect. One Hittite text tells us that "if a servant is in any way in trouble, he goes to his master, and his master hears him and is kindly disposed to him, and puts right what was troubling him." Yet the same writer continues: "If ever a servant vexes his master, either they kill him, or they injure his nose, his eyes, or his ears. And if he dies, he does not die alone, but his family is included with him. After all, if anyone vexes the feelings of a god, does the god punish him alone for it? Does he not punish the man's wife and children, his family, his cattle and his harvest?"

Putting the Structure and Economic Life of Ancient Society in Perspective

The birth of civilization in the ancient world saw the emergence of order in the form of urban communities. The regular production of food supplies, the development of large-scale architecture and engineering skills, the growth of manufacturing and trade together with improvements in travel, and the organization of effective systems of government and administration: All of these areas of human experience provided challenges that many ancient societies managed to overcome. In the process, they laid the foundations of later developments.

At the same time the rise of city life created a whole new series of more subtle and complex problems, as people began the often painful process of learning to live together. As the great French historian Fernand Braudel noted of a later age, towns are like electric transformers: "They increase tension, accelerate the rhythm of exchange, and ceaselessly stir up men's lives." All of the ancient cultures examined in these topics tried to deal with and to control issues of human relations in their communities by decree from above, often in the name of the gods. The edicts of Egyptian pharaohs or the law codes of Mesopotamian rulers were the earliest means we have of knowing how people tried to understand themselves and their relations with others. In many cases—the treatment of women, the exploitation of labor—the solutions may seem harsh and arbitrary, even contradictory.

Yet modern observers at the dawn of the third millennium can hardly fail to notice how many of the issues that these earliest civilizations tried to face and resolve remain with us still. If the art of the remote past—the monuments of Egypt or the *Epic of Gilgamesh*—illustrates our shared cultural heritage, the daily problems faced by those past civilizations, and their often faltering solutions, remind us of our own common humanity.

Questions for Further Study

1. What evidence is there for the role of women in the cultures discussed in this chapter? How does it differ in the various societies, and what features remain the same?
2. What was the role of slavery in the ancient world?
3. To what extent did trade and commerce affect political developments in the ancient Near East?
4. What are our main sources of evidence about life in the ancient world? How does their character affect the nature of our impressions of ancient society?

Suggestions for Further Reading

Casson, Lionel. *Everyday Life in Ancient Egypt.* Baltimore, 2001.

Chadwick, Whitney. *Women, Art, and Society.* New York, 1990.

Kozloff, Arielle P., and Betsy M. Bryan. *Egypt's Dazzling Sun: Amenhotep III and his World.* Cleveland, 1992.

Lowenberg, Frank M. *From Charity to Social Justice: The Emergence of Communal Institutions for the Poor in Ancient Judaism.* New Brunswick, 2001.

Mahdy, Christine, ed. *The World of the Pharaohs: A Complete Guide to Ancient Egypt.* London, 1990.

Malek, Jaromir, ed. *Egypt: Ancient Culture, Modern Land.* Norman, OK, 1993.

Oliphant, Margaret. *The Atlas of the Ancient World: Charting the Great Civilizations of the Past.* New York, 1992.

Postgate, J. Nicholas. *Early Mesopotamia: Society and Economy at the Dawn of History.* London, 1992.

Roaf, Michael. *Cultural Atlas of Mesopotamia and the Ancient Near East.* New York, 1990.

Robins, Gay. *Women in Ancient Egypt.* London, 1993.

Snell, Daniel C. *Life in the Ancient Near East.* New Haven, CT, 1997.

Tyldesley, Joyce A. *Judgement of the Pharoah: Crime and Punishment in Ancient Egypt.* London, 2000.

InfoTrac College Edition

Enter the search term *antiquities* using the Subject Guide.

PART II

CLASSICAL ANTIQUITY

I f the developments of the ancient world laid the bases for the growth of civilization, the specific forms that Western culture have taken owe their existence to the two chief peoples of Classical Antiquity, the Greeks and the Romans.

Civilization began to develop in the eastern Mediterranean as early as 3000 B.C., and the first two important cultures to appear were the Minoans of Bronze Age Crete and the Mycenaeans of mainland Greece. The Bronze Age ended around 1100 B.C.

The early stages of the development of Greek civilization saw a pattern that was maintained throughout Greek history: the formation of small, independent city-states. From 1000 B.C. to around 700 B.C., the Greeks laid the foundations of later cultural developments. This period of internal growth led to a century of expansion abroad, throughout the Mediterranean world, during

3000 B.C.   400 B.C.   50 B.C.

Culture

1600 B.C. First Mycenaean palaces constructed; Royal Grave Circle at Mycenae

900–700 B.C. Evolution of Homeric epics

480–323 B.C. Classical period in Greek art

440 B.C. Herodotus begins *History of Persian Wars*

420–399 B.C. Thucydides writes *History of Peloponnesian War*

800–700 B.C. Greeks adapt Phoenician alphabet for their language

600–480 B.C. Archaic art

323–146 B.C. Hellenistic period in Greek art

700 B.C. Beginnings of Etruscan culture

Politics

1550–1100 B.C. Late Minoan period on Crete

510 B.C. Restoration of democracy at Athens

478 B.C. Foundation of the Delian League

91–88 B.C. Social War

82–81 B.C. Sulla dictator at Rome

1950–1550 B.C. Middle Minoan period on Crete; construction of Palace at Knossos

461–429 B.C. Pericles in power at Athens

451 B.C. Promulgation of the Twelve Tables

218–202 B.C. Second Punic War; Roman conquest of Spain

1450 B.C. Fall of Knossos and decline of Minoan civilization

546 B.C. Rule of Pisistratus at Athens

509 B.C. Expulsion of Etruscan kings and foundation of the Roman Republic

146 B.C. Romans sack Carthage and Corinth: Greece becomes a Roman province

1250 B.C. (?) Mycenaean war against Troy

1100 B.C. Final collapse of Mycenaean power

1000 B.C. Beginnings of Iron Age at Athens

264–241 B.C. First Punic War

2800–1950 B.C. Early Minoan period on Crete; growth of Cycladic culture

800–700 B.C. Greek colonizing in East and Italy

431–404 B.C. Peloponnesian War

399 B.C. Trial and execution of Socrates

390 B.C. Rome sacked by Gauls

60 B.C. First Triumvirate: Caesar, Pompey, Crassus

753 B.C. Foundation of Rome (traditional date)

1400–1200 B.C. Mycenaean empire flourishes

594 B.C. Solon reforms Athenian constitution

359–336 B.C. Philip II king of Macedon

336–323 B.C. Alexander the Great king of Macedon

323–281 B.C. Wars of Alexander's successors

490–479 B.C. Persian Wars

● Bronze Age ● The Greeks ● Romans ● The Roman World

Scala/Art Resource

which Greek city-states established colonies from Italy to Egypt to Asia Minor.

During this period, in many cities, individual leaders (known as tyrants) replaced the former aristocratic ruling class. By the time Greece was faced with the threat of invasion by the mighty Persian Empire, shortly after 500 B.C., the two leading Greek cities were Sparta, a conservative military oligarchy, and Athens, which had moved from aristocratic rule to a form of democracy.

A.D. 1

A.D. 300

A.D. 126
Construction of Pantheon at Rome

A.D. 313 Constantine decrees freedom of worship for Christians

A.D. 166–179
Marcus Aurelius writes *Meditations*

46-44 B.C. Caesar rules Rome until assassinated

43 B.C. Second Triumvirate: Antony, Lepidus, Octavian

31 B.C. Battle of Actium won by Octavian

27 B.C.– A.D. 14 Octavian rules under the name of Augustus as first Roman emperor; Vergil, Horace, Livy writing at Rome

A.D. 14–68 Julio-Claudian emperors: Tiberius, Caligula, Claudius, Nero

A.D. 69–96 Flavian emperors: Vespasian, Titus, Domitian

A.D. 70 Capture of Jerusalem by Titus; destruction of Solomon's Temple

A.D. 96–138 Adoptive emperors

A.D. 138–192 Antonine emperors

A.D. 212 Edict of Caracalla

A.D. 284–305 Rule of Diocletian; return of civil order at Rome

A.D. 306–337 Rule of Constantine

A.D. 330 Foundation of Constantinople

A.D. 410 Sack of Rome by Visigoths

A.D. 476
Abdication of last Roman emperor

With the Persians finally repulsed, the 5th century B.C. saw the high point of Classical culture; at the same time, the Athenians and Spartans, together with their respective allies, prepared for confrontation. By the end of the century, the Peloponnesian War was over, leaving Athens defeated, and over the following decades the various city-states fought for leadership before unity finally came, imposed by rule under Philip of Macedon. The brief if spectacular reign of Philip's son, Alexander the Great, carried Greek culture throughout the territories in Asia that he conquered.

The Romans, the Greeks' eventual conquerors and successors in the Classical world, built an empire that spread Classical culture throughout much of Europe and North Africa and large parts of Asia. Founded in the mid-8th century B.C., Rome fell under Etruscan rule, before emerging as an independent republic around 500 B.C. After a period of consolidation, during which the aristocratic patricians and the mass of the population—the plebeians—hammered out a series of political compromises, the Romans began to expand outside Italy.

Their first conquests were in the western Mediterranean, where they faced off against the Carthaginians. Roman power subsequently spread east, absorbing Greece, Egypt, and much of western Asia. External expansion, adding to internal strains, eventually led to the collapse of republican political institutions and to civil war.

After a century of political violence, the republic was replaced by a system of monarchy. Octavian, the adopted son of Julius Caesar, became the first Roman emperor under the name Augustus. The last five centuries of Roman domination brought a renewed period of consolidation, followed by a long, slow decline. By the time Roman power disappeared in the West, a new set of religious and philosophical beliefs had become established: Christianity. The eastern part of the Roman world continued to exist in the form of the Byzantine Empire.

The Greek contribution to the Western tradition laid the foundations for how we think—and talk—about many of the issues that continue to dominate our lives: politics, human relations, the economy, and the arts and sciences. First under Alexander, and then for centuries under the Romans, Greek ideas circulated on three continents. The Romans created a multiethnic empire that brought extended periods of peace to the Mediterranean world, while devising a legal system that remained one of their most durable achievements, and, with the acceptance and spread of Christianity, established the other great tradition of Western culture. From the Western perspective, the world of Classical Antiquity is fundamental in understanding our past.

THE EMERGENCE OF GREECE: FROM BRONZE TO IRON

Throughout the ancient world of the Mediterranean, the period around 1000 B.C. saw a major change in ways of life. Iron replaced bronze as the chief material for the manufacture of tools and weapons, and the new technology revolutionized societies at many different levels. In a small corner of southeastern Europe, the mainland and islands of Greece, the break with the past had special significance for the future of Western history.

In the preceding Bronze Age, the Minoans on the island of Crete and the Mycenaeans of mainland Greece had developed rich and sophisticated cultures and established commercial contacts in many parts of the Mediterranean. With the violent disturbances that brought the Bronze Age to an end around 1000 B.C., their cultures disappeared, only to be rediscovered by archeologists in the 19th and 20th centuries.

Thus the first Greek communities of the Iron Age began afresh to organize their societies and establish an artistic tradition. The development of independent settlements, each known as a ***polis***, or city-state, determined the competitive and often hostile nature of the Greeks' relations with one another.

The first great cultural achievements in the Western tradition—the *Iliad* and the *Odyssey,* two epic poems attributed to Homer and set in the Bronze Age—also date to the beginnings of Greek history and even reflect the earlier Mycenaean period.

The initial growth of Greek culture took place on home territory. By 700 B.C., however, the Greeks were on the move. Greek traders had discovered the rich markets of western Asia and Egypt, and settlers were beginning to establish colonies throughout the Mediterranean. In the process, they spread their ideas and artistic styles and, equally importantly, absorbed the influences of the peoples with whom they came into contact. At the same time, attitudes toward religion and philosophy began to evolve as the Greeks became the first people in the ancient world to ask theoretical questions about the nature of the universe and human existence.

This first period of widespread artistic production and trade saw the development of a style known as Orientalizing, as Greek artists adopted Eastern ideas in their painting and sculpture—and later in their architecture. By the beginning of the following Archaic Age, they had used what they had learned to create a specifically Greek approach to art and ideas that borrowed from other cultures to form the foundation of Western style.

BRONZE AGE CULTURE IN THE AEGEAN: THE MINOANS AND MYCENAEANS

The earliest centers of Bronze Age culture in southeastern Europe were on the Cyclades, a group of islands in the Aegean Sea about halfway between the Greek mainland and the largest Greek island, Crete. Shortly after 3000 B.C.,

Marble idol from the Cyclades, c. 2500 B.C. Height 19¼ inches (50 cm). Like the overwhelming majority of the Cycladic statuettes, this one is of a woman. The form—head back, arms folded—is also standard. Although seen by modern viewers as standing, the figures were probably buried resting on their backs.

small towns began to develop on the Cyclades, whose inhabitants knew how to work stone and metal. Cycladic merchants traded with the peasant communities that were beginning to grow in mainland Greece and Crete, and even went farther afield to sell their pottery and bronze jewelry: Cycladic objects have turned up as far west as Spain.

The most famous and beautiful Cycladic products are the elongated marble statues, or idols, which were made in large numbers and often buried in graves along with the dead. Most of the statues are female and are perhaps related to the Mesopotamian cult of the mother goddess. Certainly a similar reverence for the Earth Mother was central to the people who dominated the following centuries in the eastern Mediterranean, the Minoans of Crete.

THE FIRST CIVILIZATION OF EUROPE: THE MINOANS

Greek myths of the later Iron Age told of the rich and powerful Cretan kingdom of King Minos, who ruled from his palace at Knossos. According to the tales, Knossos was one of many centers on the island. In the *Odyssey*, Homer speaks of "Crete of a hundred cities." Yet the Greeks who retold the story of Minos and the monstrous Minotaur—the creature that was half human and half bull and was kept imprisoned in the labyrinth at Knossos—knew the Crete of their day as only an impoverished backwater. Throughout the Iron Age the island played no part in Greek history, and neither the Classical Greeks nor any later people on the island tried to see if there was any basis for the legends.

In 1894 the English archeologist Arthur Evans first went to the Cretan village of Knossos, to see if anything could be found of the mythical civilization. He returned in 1900, armed with a permit to excavate a small hill to the side of the village. On March 23, his workers "drove a desolate donkey from the hill's slope, and digging began." As Evans' account describes, the donkey had been standing above the site of the throne room of the vast, five-story palace complex he discovered buried in the hill. Evans was to uncover an entire culture, which he named Minoan, dividing its history into three main phases: Early Minoan (c. 2500–1950 B.C.), Middle Minoan (c. 1950–1550 B.C.), and Late Minoan (c. 1550–1100 B.C.). These divisions formed the basis for most subsequent study of Minoan civilization, as other towns and palaces came to light. Scholars have disputed the details of Evans' chronology, but as new excavations continue to produce finds, they confirm his description of the main sequence of events.

The Early Minoan period saw the appearance of small towns in southern and eastern Crete, whose inhabitants began to trade with Egypt and Mesopotamia. After a long, slow growth, this phase ended abruptly shortly after 2000 B.C. Abandoning the scattered communities, the Minoans gathered in large urban centers, such as the one at Knossos. We call these Middle Minoan structures "palaces," but in addition to providing homes for the ruling classes they also fulfilled a wide variety of other functions. They were centers

© The British Museum

The Throne Room, Palace of Knossos, Crete. In its present form, it appears as it did in the last phase of Minoan culture; its decoration—a design of griffins and lilies—dates to c. 1450 B.C. Note the elegant throne, flanked by limestone benches, and the well-paved floor.

of manufacture, trading, and administration, and also contained important religious shrines. Many of these activities required some form of written documentation. Minoan scribes first used a hieroglyphic system of writing, and then a simpler script known as Linear A. Neither of these systems has been deciphered.

Throughout the Middle Minoan period, palace artists produced a wide range of works: superb gold jewelry, decorated stone and ceramic vessels, and the brilliant frescoes that decorated the buildings. Unlike their contemporaries in Egypt and Mesopotamia, they preferred the small, even miniature, to the monumental scale. In depicting nature— dolphins, plants, a cat stalking a bird—Minoan artists aimed for realism and what sometimes seems like humor.

These works document another original aspect of Minoan culture, the importance of women. To judge from the character of Minoan art in the palaces, the aristocratic world gave equal status to women and men. Scenes in the frescoes and on exquisitely carved sealstones show both sexes in elaborate costumes that leave much of the body naked, taking part in palace ceremonies and entertainments. Girls and boys (perhaps slaves who will die in the ritual) share in the various activities, including the ritual "game" of bull-leaping—which may have been at the root of the later legend of the Minotaur.

Bulls played an important part in Minoan religion, but the central figure in Minoan worship was a goddess, whose

chief priestesses were women. Sometimes accompanied by animals, sometimes surrounded by vegetation, depictions of a female figure occur throughout Minoan history. The most famous of all, the terracotta statuette known (incorrectly) as the *Snake Goddess*, shows a priestess grasping a snake in each hand, with a miniature lion sitting on the crown of her hat. Healing cults associated with snakes were one of the aspects of Minoan religion to survive into Greek times; they are similar to Hebrew healing customs involving snakes, as described in the "Exodus."

By the Late Minoan period, Minoan power was on the wane, and around 1450 B.C. invaders attacked Knossos and occupied it. Among the changes they introduced was a revision of the Minoan writing system in the form of a new script known as Linear B. The Linear B tablets contain an early form of Greek, and the invading force probably came from mainland Greece. In any case, shortly after their arrival there is evidence of widespread destruction throughout Crete. Palace life ended abruptly sometime after 1400 B.C., with the few survivors retreating to the remote and rugged mountains in the center of the island.

What caused the collapse of Minoan civilization? Was it an internal revolt against the new rulers of Knossos followed by massive reprisals? A further invasion from outside? Natural causes? A massive volcanic eruption had occurred earlier on the island of Thera, around 1625 B.C., which may

The *Snake Goddess*. Height 13½ inches (36 cm). The figure probably represents a priestess rather than a divinity. The bare breasts are typical of Minoan court dress, but the apron indicates a religious function. The snakes were commonly worshiped as symbols of the Earth Mother.

have created some ecological disaster. The mystery remains unsolved, but one important factor may well have been the rise of a rival power on the mainland, which was perhaps responsible for the invasion of 1450 B.C.: the Mycenaeans.

THE INDUS VALLEY CIVILIZATION

During the height of Minoan culture, there lived in present-day Pakistan a people we call, from the location of their chief settlements in the valley of the river Indus, the Indus valley people. Like the Minoans, they had a form of picture writing that is still undeciphered. Other similarities between the two cultures are the use of small carved sealstones and the importance of the bull in their religion. Two large resident and administrative centers have been excavated, at Harappa and Mohenjo-daro, where archaeologists have discovered large quantities of pottery and stone sculptures. Like Knossos and the other Minoan palaces, the Indus valley sites had elaborate drainage centers.

Around 1700 B.C., the Indus valley region suffered a series of floods and other ecological disasters, and the settle-

ments of the Indus valley people went into a decline that quickly wiped out all traces of their culture. By 1500 B.C. a new people were settled on the Indian subcontinent, known as the Aryans. These newcomers, who had perhaps migrated from the steppes of Central Asia, brought with them two characteristics that were to shape life in India for centuries: a language—Sanskrit—which belongs to the family called Indo-European, and is thus related to European languages including Greek and Latin; and their religion, Hinduism. As in the case of the Minoans, the Indus valley people disappeared from history and were only rediscovered by modern archaeologists. There has been speculation on whether the two cultures were in some way related, but no conclusive evidence has ever been found. At any rate, the origins of the Mycenaeans are far less mysterious than those of the Aryans.

MYCENAE, RICH IN GOLD

The Mycenaeans, the Minoans' successors as dominant power in the eastern Mediterranean, take their name from their most powerful Bronze Age center in mainland Greece, Mycenae. The Homeric epics speak of "Mycenae, rich in gold," and from the first days of his excavations there in 1876, the German archeologist Heinrich Schliemann discovered the truth of Homer's words. Before his explorations, scholars regarded the story of the Mycenaeans and Troy as a fantasy: The wealthy Schliemann believed that the Homeric epics were founded on historical reality, and he had the financial means to prove it by excavation. In the Royal Grave Circle, just inside the palace walls, his team uncovered the tombs of Mycenaean rulers dating to around 1600 B.C., filled with stupendous quantities of gold treasures. In addition to jewelry, weapons, diadems, and goblets, the finds included gold death masks, which allow us to look upon the faces of some of the first rulers in Western history.

Schliemann's first major campaign had taken him in 1870 to the site of Troy itself on the northwest coast of modern Turkey. After uncovering the walls and gate of Homer's city and numerous treasures, he moved to Greece to complete his task by finding the conquerors of Troy, the Mycenaeans. Schliemann was always convinced that the royal family buried in the Grave Circle at Mycenae was that of Agamemnon, the leader of the expedition against the Trojans described in Homer's *Iliad*. Subsequent excavations have revealed that his finds dated to a period toward the beginning of Mycenaean history, long before the Homeric Trojan War.

The earliest stages of construction at Mycenae took place just before 1600 B.C., and Schliemann's discoveries revealed that from its foundation, Mycenaean culture was rich and sophisticated. For their first two centuries, the art and architecture of Mycenaeans was strongly influenced by the leading Aegean power of the time, the Minoans. In addition, the Mycenaean system of writing, Linear B, was based on the Minoan Linear A script. With the fall of Knossos around 1400 B.C., the Mycenaeans asserted their independence and became the dominant force in the re-

The Lion Gate at Mycenae, c. 1300 B.C. Height of relief slab about 10 feet (3.13 m). The post and lintel entrance guards the only public approach to the Palace of Mycenae; there was originally a high tower to the right. The decoration shows two lionesses arranged on either side of a column, which, like all Minoan and Mycenaean columns, has a base narrower than its top.

Erich Lessing/Art Resource New York

gion. One of the most expressive symbols of this later period of Mycenaean power is the massive Lion Gate constructed as the main entrance into the stronghold at Mycenae around 1300 B.C.

Their control lasted for some 200 years, from 1400 to 1200 B.C. During that time, Mycenaean traders traveled east and south to the Near East and Egypt, and westward to Italy, selling their goods and importing raw materials. The successful Mycenaean campaign against Troy, which occurred around 1250 B.C., may well have been the result of a trading dispute or commercial rivalry. Their victory over the Trojans seems to have been complete, yet only a few years later, around 1200 B.C., the Mycenaean territory was in ruins, its chief cities destroyed, and most of them abandoned. As in the case of the fall of Knossos, the cause remains mysterious. Later Greek stories, describing the violent events that followed Agamemnon's triumphant return to Mycenae after the Trojan War, may be based on memories of internal strife caused by dynastic rivalry. Other possibilities include external invasion or natural disaster.

The period following the fall of Mycenae is known, with good reason, as that of the "Dark Ages." Invading forces, some of them Greek-speaking, passed through former Mycenaean territories. Some Mycenaean cultural traditions survived, particularly in Crete and at Athens, but on the whole, when life began to develop again in Greek lands around 1000 B.C., the break with the past was profound. The Greeks of the Iron Age had to discover for themselves the skills of civilization (including writing), how to build, and forms of social and political organization.

Yet despite the gulf that lay between the splendors of the Bronze Age and the simple beginnings of Greek culture proper, some links remained. Many later Greek myths have their roots in Minoan and Mycenaean times, as do the ear-

liest Greek works of literature, the Homeric poems. Perhaps most significant of all, throughout the history of later Greek religion, the cult of the mother goddess—and female creative power in general—echoed Minoan and Mycenaean worship of the Earth Mother and served in the Classical period as a powerful counterbalance to the dominance of Father Zeus. Shrines to the Greek goddesses Hera, Artemis, and others, depictions on vase paintings, and the nature of many myths all attest to the continuity of Bronze Age religious traditions.

THE GREEKS OF THE EARLY IRON AGE: THE BIRTH OF THE CITY-STATE

For the first two and a half centuries of their history, from around 1000 until 750 B.C., the early Iron Age Greeks remained relatively isolated from the outside world. Under the Mycenaeans, the Aegean world had been in close contact with other parts of the Mediterranean, but their Greek successors did not begin to make contact with their neighbors until the beginning of the 8th century B.C. Thus the Greeks' cultural development, at this crucial stage in their history, was slow.

THE SIGNIFICANCE OF THE *POLIS*

Within Greece, the early Iron Age saw the development of a series of separate and independent regions. The mountain ranges of the Greek mainland served as natural dividers, creating geographical areas that were often isolated from one another. Within each zone, an urban community began to develop that served as a base for farming the surrounding

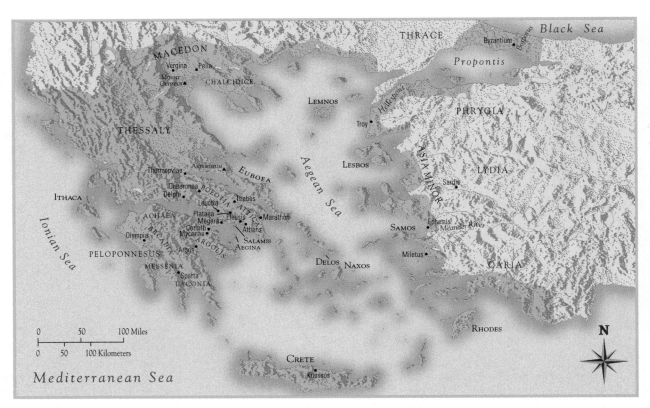

Map 7.1 Ancient Greece. The two chief commercial rivals among the Greek cities, Athens and Corinth, faced one another across the Gulf of Corinth. Athens' main political rival, Sparta, lay to the south, in the Peloponnesus (island of Pelops, the legendary king from whom Agamemnon was descended). This lower part of mainland Greece was known in the medieval period as the Morea, from its resemblance to a mulberry leaf. Note the Greek settlements on the Western coast of Asia Minor (modern Turkey).

countryside. In a similar way, each individual Greek island formed its own urban administrative center. Thus the cities of Athens, Thebes, and Sparta became the dominant forces in, respectively, the mainland regions of Attica, Boeotia, and Laconia, while the capitals of Naxos, Samos, and other islands controlled their island territory.

The name given by later Greeks to these centralized urban communities, originally formed as military fortifications for defense, was *polis*, a Greek word generally translated as "city-state." As the chief form of social and political organization from the beginnings of Greek culture, the polis played a vital role in Greek history, both for good and bad. Each individual city-state generated its own political, social, religious, and artistic developments. The ties of loyalty and obligation that bound its citizens were far more important than any sense of shared identity with the members of other Greek communities. The members of each *polis* were suspicious not only of foreigners but of citizens of other city-states. The sense of competition among the various cities stimulated an astonishing growth in intellectual and cultural achievement, the results of which laid the foundations of Western civilization. At the same time, however, increasingly bitter rivalries led to a constant series of quarrels among cities that developed on occasion into outright war.

GOVERNMENT IN THE CITY-STATES

In the early days of the city-states, the ruling class consisted of the richest, or the "best," people. The Greek word for the "best," the *aristoi*, gives us the term for the system under which they governed: an aristocracy based on birth and inherited land and wealth. These powerful families owned most of the good land, located near enough to the city walls to be easily defended against outside raiders, and could afford the horses and armor necessary to protect the community. In some cities, poorer farmers and workers lived in villages on the outskirts of the *polis*.

The ruling body in most early city-states was a Council of the "Best Men," or "Elders." This Council elected executive officers to carry out its decisions, which were reported to the community at town meetings. The aristocrats also had charge of the chief religious cult of their city. This cult generally focused around a temple dedicated to the state's patron deity, located in a position of prominence. Thus the Acropolis ("high part of the city") at Athens was crowned by the Temple to Athena.

Eventually, as populations grew, popular dissatisfaction with the restricted political system of these early city-states led to important changes in Greek life. Around 800 B.C., increasing numbers of resentful citizens abandoned their communities to form new cities, known as colonies, often on

SIGNIFICANT DATES

From Bronze to Iron in the Greek World
(all dates B.C.)

3000–2500	Culture flourishes in the Cyclades
2500–1950	Early Minoan Period
1950–1550	Middle Minoan Period
1625	Earthquake on Thera
1600	First settlement at Mycenae
1450	Knossos attacked and occupied
1400–1200	Mycenaean power at its height
1250 (??)	Mycenaean campaign against Troy
1200–1100	Destruction and partial reoccupation of Mycenae
1000–750	Early Iron Age in Greece
800	Beginnings of Greek colonization
800–700	Greeks begin to use alphabet

the fringes of the Greek world or even outside it. In other cases, rulers founded colonies and sent members of their families to run them. The Greek "colonizers" of the 8th and 7th centuries B.C. played a vital role in broadening Greek perceptions of the world around them. Meanwhile, back at home, toward the end of the 7th century B.C. broad popular frustration with the conservative rule of the "Best Men," which concentrated power in the hands of a few, produced a wave of revolutions leading to the replacement of aristocratic government by "tyranny"—the rule of a single individual whom the lower classes viewed as a social benefactor.

The early political development of the city-states permitted the slow evolution of the first Greek experiments in the visual arts, the growth of religious speculation, and—most astonishingly—the creation of the first, and still among the greatest, of Western literary masterpieces, the *Iliad* and *Odyssey*.

GODS, GODDESSES, AND THE WORLD OF HOMER

Most of the vast body of Greek religious myth goes back to the time of the early city-states—or, in some cases, even earlier, to the Bronze Age. Later Greeks embellished the stories and sometimes tried to reconcile contradictory versions, but the original character of the Greek attitude toward religion remained consistent.

THE NATURE OF GREEK RELIGION

Despite the enormous influence of Greek culture on our own heritage, Greek religion had little in common with Judaism or Christianity, the chief religious faiths of the Western tradition. In the first place, the Greeks had no sin-gle, divinely inspired text providing a central body of teaching of the kind offered by the Bible to Jews and Christians or the Koran to Muslims. Far from seeking to record a series of objective historical events, Greek myths are often tales that illustrate aspects of human behavior.

Father Zeus, the dispenser of lightning and justice, comes as close as any figure in the Greek pantheon to the Almighty God of the Judeo-Christian tradition, and he often presides over the triumph of right over wrong. Yet the same majestic cloud gatherer became involved in a series of erotic affairs that sometimes degenerate into downright rape (sexual violence is common in Greek myth). The consequences, frequently involving a showdown with his wife Hera, are undignified and sometimes comic.

The explanation of these characteristics is that, unlike Western religions, Greek beliefs tried to understand and illustrate human nature rather than the divine. The Greek gods serve not to illuminate the supernatural, but to symbolize recognizable aspects of human behavior. The goddess Aphrodite epitomizes erotic love; Artemis, the moon goddess, is the guardian of chastity; and Ares is the god of war. No Greek deity represents supreme good, and there is similarly no equivalent of the Christian Satan, or supreme evil. For the Greeks, moral issues could be solved by humans only on an individual basis, without reference to a divinely inspired code of morality.

The various Greek gods reflected the fact that human nature in each of us is often contradictory. Thus the deities Apollo and Dionysus illustrated the duality of reason and emotion. Apollo, the god of light and music, represented order and reason, the power of the mind. Dionysus, god of wine and the theater, represented the casting aside of inhibitions, the power of the emotions. The Greeks, recognizing the duality of human behavior, acknowledged both forces and tried to find a middle way between the two extremes: the "golden mean." One of the few universal statements of Greek religion expresses this search for a prudent balance in the phrase, "Nothing in excess."

Greek writers and artists based their plays, poems, and statues on mythical subjects because the tales illustrated characteristics of practical human experience, albeit often in extreme form. At the same time, the epic plots provided their audiences with the exciting stories that appealed so profoundly to the Greek imagination.

THE HOMERIC EPICS

At the beginning of the Western literary tradition stand two works, the epic poems we know as the *Iliad* and the *Odyssey*. Subsequent ages have regarded their author, Homer, as one of the towering figures of our cultural history. Yet many aspects of his life and achievements still remain mysterious, as indeed they were for the Greeks.

According to later myth, Homer was a blind traveling poet. He seems to have lived toward the end of the five centuries between the late Mycenaean period and the 8th century B.C., when the Homeric works as we know them were in existence. The poems themselves are in any case probably not simply the creation of a single mind but a combination of various folktales, evolving over centuries into their final form.

There are many indications that the process was not an accidental one. The style and language are consistent throughout, and the poems are carefully structured, despite the long time it took for them to crystallize. The earliest versions probably go back to the late Mycenaean period, perhaps describing a Mycenaean raid exaggerated by memory and nostalgia, and then passed down by word of mouth among the traveling professional storytellers of early Greece. The poems first took written form shortly before 500 B.C., when they were put into order and used for the Panathenaic festival at Athens. The works as we have them are in an edition made by a scribe at Alexandria in the 2nd century B.C.

At some stage in this long process, the accumulated mass of material received its definitive form by passing through the imaginative genius of the person we call Homer. Some readers, struck by the different moods of the *Iliad*—grim and violent—and the more romantic, leisurely *Odyssey*, have even suggested that a separate creator was responsible for each. The 19th-century writer Samuel Butler was the first—but by no means the last—to suggest that the author of the *Odyssey* was a woman.

The theme of the *Iliad* is the significance of personal responsibility: We must accept the consequences of our actions, even when they cause harm both for ourselves and for others. Against the background of the bloody conflict between Greeks and Trojans, Homer sets the personal tragedy of Achilles, the proudest and most valiant of Greek heroes. Offended by the behavior of Agamemnon, his commanding officer, Achilles decides to deprive the Greeks of his strength and withdraws from the fighting. It takes the violent death of his dearest friend, Patroclus, at the hands of the Trojan hero Hector, to drive Achilles out of his tent and back to the battlefield. In raging anger he kills Hector and then, driven by guilt at having allowed Patroclus to go to his death, mutilates his opponent's corpse. Only when the dead Trojan's father, Priam, comes to beg for the body of his son does Achilles finally break down and recognize the tragic consequences of his behavior.

Although the gods make numerous appearances in the *Iliad,* and frequently play an important—often crucial—role in determining the actions of the work's characters, the humans themselves decide and think, and hold themselves—not just the gods—responsible for their fates. Achilles and the others must bear the full weight of their conduct. Nor is Achilles guilty of breaking some divine commandment in his refusal to soften his anger. He chooses freely, and he, his slaughtered friend, and the other dead Greeks must bear the consequences. Thus, from the earliest times, the central element in the Greek view of life is not divine order or justice, but individual human conduct. In the eyes of the Greeks, we are all at least partly in control of our destinies.

The world of the *Odyssey* is more relaxed and discursive. It describes the long wanderings of the Greek warrior Odysseus as he makes his way home to Greece after the Trojan War. His adventures bring him into contact with a one-eyed giant, a beautiful if dangerous enchantress, a romantic young princess, and other varied distractions, before he finally returns to the arms of his ever-faithful wife, Penelope.

The period in which the Homeric stories take place purports to be that of late Mycenaean times. Historically, however, the actual conditions described by the poet are a mixture of those of the late Mycenaean period, the Dark Ages, and the very early Archaic period, during which the poems came into existence. The political structures of Homer's world, the councils of elders, resemble those of the early city-states. Even at a more mundane level, the details reveal Homer's daily life. At the funeral games to mark the burial of Patroclus, one of the valuable prizes offered in an athletic competition is a lump of iron: valuable, that is, for Homer's contemporaries, but nonexistent for Achilles and his fellow Mycenaeans of the Bronze Age.

Hirmer Fotoarchiv

A scene from the *Odyssey* decorating a vase from Athens. 7th century B.C. It shows the episode in which Odysseus, taken captive together with his men by the one-eyed giant Polyphemus, escapes by getting the giant drunk and poking out his eye with a heated stick. The giant is seated, as an indication of his size, with a drinking cup in his hand.

THE GREEKS ABROAD: COLONIES AND MARKETS

For the first two centuries of the Iron Age, the city-states prospered under their aristocratic rulers. By the early 8th century B.C., a series of inter-city sacred festivals began to develop that saw the rival communities in peaceful athletic competition. The most famous and venerable of these was at Olympia, a sanctuary sacred to Zeus, where every four years the Olympic Games took place. The first games were held, according to tradition, in 776 B.C., and the last of ancient times more than 1,000 years later in A.D. 394, after which the Byzantine Emperor Theodosius abolished them because of widespread cheating.

As the Greek cities developed, they began increasingly to trade with their neighbors. By 700 B.C., Greek traders had established themselves in markets to the east in Asia Minor and as far north as the Black Sea, where they came into contact with the Scythians, an ancient nomadic people from Central Asia. To the south in Egypt, Greek merchants sold wine and oil in exchange for grain and bartered Greek pottery for Egyptian jewels and carved seals. Most important, other Greeks moved west to Italy, first as traders and increasingly as colonizers; they founded several cities in southern Italy and Sicily.

THE AGE OF COLONIZATION

The motives for the wave of colonization that saw the Greeks establish overseas communities from the southern coast of Russia to the western Mediterranean were twofold. In part they were a result of economic frustration at home, leading to trading abroad: Business contacts with the local populations led to permanent settlements. Food shortages in Greece after 800 B.C. also stimulated overseas migration. At the same time, however, Greek colonizers often left home to escape from political frustration. Despite the growing prosperity of their cities—or in some cases because of it—the entrenched aristocratic rulers continued to retain power. Ambitious citizens either went abroad to find freedom and fortune or, if they seemed to present a threat to the rulers, were sometimes sent abroad. Around 700 B.C., the Spartan leaders eliminated the threat posed by a revolutionary political movement by packing its members off to southern Italy. The exiles founded their new home at Taranto, which grew to become one of the wealthiest of the Greek colonies in Italy. Two important new developments helped facilitate the burst of Greek activity after centuries of relative calm. The first, which occurred some time between 800 and 700 B.C., was that the Greeks began to use an alphabet. They borrowed a system of writing from one of their main trading rivals, the Phoenicians, and adapted it to their own language. The ability to write provided immediate benefits in conducting long-distance business affairs, which was probably the reason for the Greeks' eagerness to become literate. At the same time, it had vast consequences for the development of our culture as well as theirs: The letters in modern Western alphabets are the Roman adaptations of the Etruscan form of the Greek alphabet.

The other significant event was the invention of metal coinage around 700 B.C. in Asia Minor. The Greeks' contacts with the peoples of this region led them to take up the new aid to commerce, and by 600 B.C. most Greek cities,

both in the homeland and abroad, minted their own coinage. In this way, the Greeks simplified their trading and reinforced the identity of their individual cities because each community's currency bore its own individual emblem: the owl of Athens, symbol of the goddess Athene; the head of Dionysus for Naxos, symbolizing the island's chief export, wine.

GREEK IDEAS AND EASTERN ART

The introduction of writing and coinage were only two of the benefits the Greeks derived from their broader contacts. At a more subtle level, their exposure to new ideas radically influenced their intellectual and artistic progress.

GEOMETRIC ART
In the absence of writing, it is difficult to have much notion of Greek thinkers before the Age of Colonization, but in the case of their art, some of the earliest works have survived. They take the form of clay pots painted with a wide

Colorphoto Hans Hinz, Allschwil/Basil

Geometric vase from the Dipylon Cemetery, Athens, c. 750 B.C. Height 4 feet 11 inches (1.24 m). The vase served originally as a grave marker. The main band, between the handles, shows the dead man on his bier. On either side are mourners tearing their hair in grief.

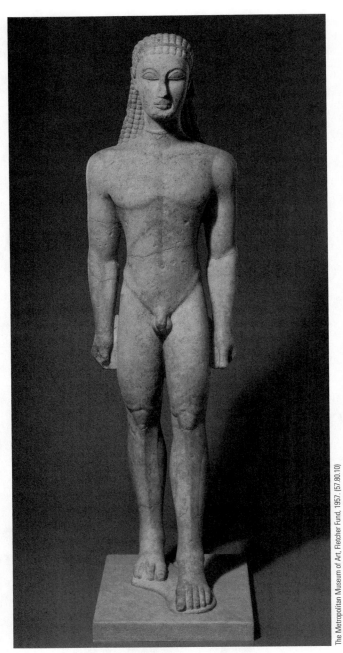

The *New York Kouros*, c. 615 B.C. Height 6 feet, 1½ inches (1.87 m). Note the detailed treatment of the hair, the carefully balanced design of the body, and the absence of a sense of movement—although one foot is forward, there is no displacement of the hips. An early example of Archaic sculpture, the *New York Kouros* is the largest one to survive.

The Metropolitan Museum of Art, Fletcher Fund, 1957. (57.80.10)

range of geometric designs. It may seem strange that a people who relished the exciting narratives of Homer should have limited their visual range to abstract decorations, but the complexity of many of the Geometric vases produced between 900 and 700 B.C. is evidence of the Greek obsession with order and balance. If we are inclined to think of later Greek art as supremely realistic, it is important to remember that Greek artists were always concerned with mathematical relationships. That concern with intellectual clarity is visible even in these earliest pieces.

THE ORIENTALIZING STYLE

First contacts with the long artistic traditions of the Egyptians and the Near Eastern peoples came when the resurgence of the older economies began to stimulate Greek economic growth and trade. The result was a revolution in Greek art. The new style, actually a mixture of various stylistic elements, is known as the Orientalizing, from the strongly Eastern influences (although Egypt is in North Africa, the style of its art during the 1st millennium B.C. had much in common with that of the ancient Near East). In place of the Geometric designs, artists began to decorate their pots with a wide range of motifs borrowed from their Eastern neighbors: sphinxes, papyrus and palm foliage, winged humans, and monsters. Bold colors replaced the black and red of earlier Geometric art. Most important, many painters—especially those working at Athens—began to use their works to tell a story. The narrative tradition in Western art was born in Greece shortly after 700 B.C.

Contacts with Egypt inspired the Greeks' first attempts at stone sculptures. The earliest examples, dating like the narrative paintings to the years following 700 B.C., are stiff and tense, but already they show the beginnings of Greek interest in how human bodies actually work and in proportion. Just as the artists of the Geometric period repeated a few basic designs over and over to perfect them, so the Orientalizing sculptors produced statue after statue of young women (clothed) and young men (nude) to work out the depiction of the human form.

The Greeks of the 7th century B.C. also based their first steps in stone architecture on Egyptian models. Little of the early buildings has survived, but the first stone temples in Greece—those at Corinth and Olympia—used the post and lintel structure of monumental Egyptian architecture. By 600 B.C., Greek architects had evolved the earliest of their own styles, that known as Doric. With the foundations of painting, sculpture, and architecture established, Greek art was ready for the extraordinary developments of the succeeding Archaic Age.

Putting the Emergence of Greece in Perspective

The collapse of Bronze Age culture in Greece saw the disappearance of almost 2,000 years of achievements. The Greeks of the early Iron Age, limited to their own rocky terrain and cut off from the outside world, had to begin to construct a civilization anew. With the momentum of their colonizing movement, driven by economic and social pressures, the Greeks were ready to build on outside influences to create their own unique intellectual and artistic achievement. If the isolation of the first two and a half centuries of their history seems a slow beginning for so dynamic a culture, the speed with which they absorbed a bewildering assortment of outside ideas and influences is equally striking. The 100 years from 700 to 600 B.C. were sufficient for the Greeks to find their own identity.

The following centuries carried Greek political and intellectual experiments and developments further and further from their early Iron Age beginnings. Yet in one respect, at least, they retained a link with their origins and with their Bronze Age predecessors. From childhood, Greeks of later times read and learned by heart the *Iliad* and the *Odyssey.* Through all the hectic and often violent events of their later history, the Greeks never lost their reverence for Homer and his world.

Questions for Further Study

1. What are the differences between the creation of the Homeric epics and other great works of literature? What effect do they have on the character of the *Iliad* and the *Odyssey?*
2. What role has archeology played in the discovery and study of Minoan and Mycenaean civilization? How does its importance—and the absence of other kinds of evidence (literary and others)—influence the picture we have of Bronze Age culture?
3. What evidence is there for the role of women in the Bronze Age?

Suggestions for Further Reading

Boardman, John. *Early Greek Vase Painting. 11th-6th Centuries B.C.* New York, 1998.

Carpenter, Thomas H. *Art and Myth in Early Greece.* New York, 1991.

Dickinson, Oliver P.T.K. *The Aegean Bronze Age.* New York, 1994.

Higgins, Reynold. *Minoan and Mycenaean Art.* Rev. ed. New York, 1997.

McDonald, William A., and Carol G. Thomas. *Progress into the Past: The Rediscovery of Mycenaean Civilization,* 2nd ed. Bloomington, 1990.

Taylour, Lord William. *The Mycenaeans.* London, 1990.

InfoTrac College Edition

Enter the search term *Greek history* using Key Terms.

Enter the search term *Greek mythology* using the Subject Guide.

THE GREEKS IN THE ARCHAIC ERA

The Archaic period (600–480 B.C.) was one of political, economic, and cultural development, which saw the collapse of the old aristocratic order in most of the Greek city-states. Many of the new rulers were disgruntled or ambitious aristocrats and rose to power by playing on the unrest of the middle classes: They were known as tyrants.

At Athens, programs of social and political reform at the beginning and end of the 6th century B.C., introduced respectively by Solon and Cleisthenes, broadened the base of government. In the period between them, midcentury Athens was ruled by the benign tyrant Pisistratus, under whom the city flourished economically and culturally.

By the latter part of the 6th century B.C., the Athenians' chief rivals in the Greek world were the Spartans, who enforced their rigid political conservatism with austere military discipline. Sparta's conquest of the surrounding territory, and enslavement of many of the local inhabitants, enriched the city's citizens, or "Spartiates." By the early 5th century B.C., Sparta had become the symbol of conservatism in Greece and the natural opponent of the progressive Athenians and their allies.

At the end of the Archaic period, in 490 B.C., the threat of open hostility between the two camps temporarily subsided in the face of external danger from the leading power of the day, the mighty Persian Empire. The Persians first came into contact with the Greek cities of the eastern Mediterranean as Persian imperial conquests spread westward in the 6th century B.C. Persian governors absorbed the Greeks into their empire, took over the rule of the Greek cities, and imposed taxes on their citizens.

In 499 B.C. these Greek cities revolted against their Persian overlords. The Persians crushed the rebellion, but not before the Athenians had sent help to their fellow Greeks. Darius, the Persian king, launched an expedition against mainland Greece in 490 B.C. The decisive victory of the Athenians at the Battle of Marathon drove the Persian forces from Greece and at the same time reinforced Athenian prestige as the leading city of Greece.

Ten years later, Athens and Sparta inflicted an even more crushing defeat on the vast military expedition assembled and led by Xerxes, Darius's son and successor. With the end of the Persian threat, and the appearance—at least—of unity among the leading Greek city-states, the following years of the 5th century B.C. inaugurated the high point of Greek culture, the Classical Age.

CITY-STATES IN TRANSITION: ARISTOCRACY, TYRANNY, AND THE PEOPLE

By around the middle of the 7th century B.C., citizens of most Greek city-states fell into one of three distinct levels of social category. At the top were the aristocrats, whose claim to rule depended on both birth and money. The descendants of the original aristocratic founders of their states, they alone controlled political power. They were also the only citizens who could afford the military equipment and horses on which their cities relied for defense, and thereby controlled state security.

At the lower end of the class system were the peasants and land workers, who were disenfranchised and at the mercy of the upper-class rulers. As the cities grew, an increasing population of urban poor added to the numbers of this lower class. Some of its members chose to escape the helplessness of their position in their home city by emigrating and founding colonies abroad (see Topic 7). For others, however, the growth of urban life and commerce brought the possibility of economic betterment and social progress. A middle class of merchants, craftsmen, and successful farmers began to emerge as the Greeks increased their manufacturing and trading activities throughout the Mediterranean world.

Around 650 B.C., an important military development gave these middle-rank citizens a way to exert their influence: Many cities began to use foot soldiers in close formation to supplement the traditional cavalry battalions. The new infantry formation that developed, consisting of rows of eight men, each heavily armed, was known as a **phalanx.** Unlike mounted fighters, who needed to provide their own valuable equipment and horses, foot soldiers could serve at little cost to their families, and sons of middle-income merchant and farming families could now play a role in their city-state's military forces. The demand for a say in political affairs was bound to follow.

THE RISE OF THE TYRANTS

The evolution of the middle class was only one of the factors that destabilized the established aristocratic regimes. In many cities, disputes within the ruling families led to the formation of rival aristocratic clans. Their leaders competed for middle-class support and claimed to champion the interests of the discontented lower classes. Many of the poorest of these people had fallen victim to one of the consequences of economic instability, crushing debt. The result of all this unrest was a rash of political revolutions in the chief trading cities.

The popular leaders who rode to power on the wave of revolt were called **tyrants.** (For the ancient Greeks, the word did not have the modern negative sense and was equivalent to our "boss" or "chief.") Few of the tyrants ruled for more than a few years. Theagenes of Megara (a city near Athens) came to power in 640 B.C. He won the support of poor farmers by ordering the slaughter of cattle straying

Funeral marker of Aristion, a Greek foot soldier, c. 510 B.C. Height 8 feet (2.44 m). The sculptor of this relief was one of the first artists in history to depict the human body in profile. Note the contrast between the leather jacket and the soft folds of the undershirt and the detail of the hair and beard.

Ancient Art & Architecture

onto their land and pleased urban housewives by building an aqueduct to bring running water into town.

The duration of a tyranny depended on the degree to which a ruler could satisfy often conflicting demands. Only a few tyrants tried to hold on to power by deliberate cruelty. The most notorious of these was Phalaris (570–554 B.C.), the tyrant of Akragas—modern Agrigento in Sicily—who roasted his opponents alive inside a hollow bronze bull over open flames. Even so, Phalaris's subjects eventually overthrew him and executed him by his own method.

For all the abuses of a Phalaris, on the whole the tyrants served a useful purpose in the development of their citystates. The tyrants liberated the people from an outdated and inadequate aristocratic system, ended the frequently bloody squabbles of contending aristocratic factions, and provided a period of internal peace. Furthermore, their public works programs—constructions such as Theagenes' aqueduct—stimulated economic growth. At Athens, the ruling tyrant Pisistratus brought even greater benefits to his city, where the 6th century B.C. saw a series of extraordinary political developments.

REFORM AT ATHENS: THE DEMOCRATIC EXPERIMENT

In one important respect, the early history of Athens differs from that of the other chief Greek city-states: The Athenians established no colonies abroad. Political development was slow at Athens, and tyrants—the promoters of colonies in other states—appeared there only relatively late in the Archaic period. Furthermore, although poor in quality, Athenian territory was large enough for its farmers to be able to make a living without going overseas to seek their fortune. Athenian law, however, was extremely harsh and favored the rich and powerful. The law took written form around 620 B.C. under the supervision of Draco, whose name is still synonymous with severity; a later Athenian described the Draconian law code as "written in blood."

In the rest of Greece, tyrants came to power during the late 7th century B.C. to remedy ancient injustices. The Athenians chose a different method of changing the political system. Instead of waiting for someone to seize power, they agreed on a reformer who could command the respect and trust of all classes of citizens: The unusually cooperative spirit that led to this procedure was to lead over time to the growth of democracy. Their choice was Solon (c. 630–560 B.C.). Solon was of aristocratic birth but a merchant of no particular wealth. His chief claim to fame at Athens lay in his poetry, much of it openly patriotic. In 594 B.C. Solon took office as reforming magistrate, with full authority to introduce economic and constitutional changes.

THE REFORMS OF SOLON

When popular support brought Solon to power, many Athenians were suffering from a severe economic crisis. With the increasing circulation of money and the growing custom of interest-bearing loans, poorer citizens fell into debt. Farmers forfeited their land when they were unable to repay their debts, while creditors seized other insolvent debtors and their families as slaves, even selling them abroad.

Those poorer citizens who expected Solon to redistribute landholdings on a fairer basis were disappointed, but his fellow aristocrats would hardly have agreed to his appointment if he had been likely to do so. He did, however, outlaw the enslaving of any Athenian for debt, launched a scheme for finding and buying back those who had been sold abroad, and canceled all existing agricultural debts. Further, he forbade the export of food products (except for olive oil, of which there was a surplus). Wealthy farmers could no longer make profits abroad while poorer

Scene of olive harvesting from an Athenian black-figure vase. 6th century B.C. One of the workers is in the tree, picking olives, while others strike it with sticks to dislodge them and a boy kneels on the ground to collect the harvest.

© The British Museum

Athenians went hungry at home. Other reforms standardized the coinage and introduced a more humane law code.

Solon's constitutional reorganization was equally far-reaching. When he took office, the traditional rulers of Athens were the aristocratic members of a Council of the "Best Men." Before the executive magistrates, the archons, carried out the Council's decisions, an Assembly of the people confirmed them, but this Assembly had no prestige and could take no initiative. Thus the Council of the Best Men, known as the Areopagus (the name of the place in Athens where they met), effectively ran the city.

Under Solon's reforms, the Assembly of the people became central to the government of Athens. All free Athenian males became automatic members, whatever their financial status. Magistrates had to report to this popular Assembly and account for their actions. Solon left the members of the Areopagus with all their ancient prestige as elder statesmen, although wealth rather than birth now served as the qualification for their election. He may have also added a new council, the Boule (the Greek word for council), to take over the Areopagus's role of preparing business for submission to the Assembly of the people. Participation in the Boule was open to all middle-income citizens. Its 400 members, 100 from each of Athens' four chief ethnic groups, or Tribes, were chosen at random by lot in order to give all citizens a chance to serve.

By contrast with the rest of the Greek world, Solon's reforms introduced strong elements of democracy into Athens, and in the process—like many reformers since—he left all sides unhappy. He claimed to have given the people "power enough," and complained at their ingratitude when they accused him of having done too little. The wealthy resented their loss of privileges and the cancellation of the debts owed to them. The weary and disgruntled reformer, tormented "like a wolf among many dogs," left the city in disgust to travel abroad.

If many of his contemporaries bitterly criticized his decisions, later Athenians revered Solon's memory as a great poet and the wisest of all statesmen. Among the remarks attributed to him was his reply to Croesus, the fabulously wealthy king of Lydia, when Croesus asked the sage who was the happiest of all men: "Call no man happy until he is dead." Before Solon's own death, he saw Athens finally under the rule of its first tyrant, but the democratic nature of his reforms left a permanent mark on Athenian history.

ATHENS AFTER SOLON: THE PISTRATIDS

The immediate result of Solon's departure from Athens after 594 B.C. was renewed political instability. By giving new rights to the lower classes, his reforms drew the poorer citizens' attention to their previous mistreatment. The resulting class struggles, combined with rivalries within the aristocratic clans, produced fierce conflict.

The figure who would emerge victorious from the confusion was Pisistratus (605?–527 B.C.), a nobleman and successful general, who became Athens' first tyrant in 546 B.C. Pisistratus was no democrat, making sure that his supporters held the chief positions of power in the state. He left Solon's constitution intact, however, and the stability of his rule made economic recovery possible: One of the contributing factors was his redistribution to the small farmers of the land of aristocrats who had fled to other states. A significant indication of the Athenians' new peace of mind under Pisistratus was the widespread increase in planting olive trees in the first years of his tyranny, encouraged by state subsidies: Olive trees, which produce little fruit for the first 30 years, are a long-term investment.

When Pisistratus died in 527 B.C., rule passed peacefully to his sons, Hippias and Hipparchus. Lacking their father's tact and skill, their government became increasingly repressive and unpopular. In 514 B.C. two young Athenians, Harmodius and Aristogiton, assassinated Hipparchus in an attempt to end their rule (Hippias escaped), and in 511 B.C. Spartan troops took advantage of the increasing unrest at Athens to drive Hippias out, a rare case of interference by a city-state in another city's internal affairs—the Spartan intervention was allegedly in response to the oracle at Delphi, which ordered them to "liberate Athens." (Later Athenians naturally preferred to regard the two tyrannicides, not the Spartans, as the agents of Athenian democracy.) Hippias fled to Persia, seeking refuge at the court of the Persian king.

CLEISTHENES AND ATHENIAN DEMOCRACY

It is a sign of the Athenians' newfound political maturity that Hippias's exile did not plunge the city into a fresh burst of political turmoil. At the first sign of aristocratic rivalry, the popular democratic forces united under Cleisthenes—a member of one of Athens' noblest families—to implement Solon's reforms. The anger of the wealthy landowners induced the Spartans to interfere once again and briefly drive out Cleisthenes, but by 507 B.C. he was back in power.

The new political organization that Cleisthenes devised and put into effect at Athens at the end of the 6th century B.C. continued the growth of participatory democracy in Greece that Solon had initiated. His system aimed to eliminate the basic problem in the Athenian political system, the continued influence of a few wealthy and aristocratic families within the traditional Tribes. In order to dismantle the power of the old guard, he invented a new, purely artificial set of Tribes based on location rather than family.

Each of his 10 new Tribes included some citizens from all three of the geographical regions into which he divided Athenian territory: the city, the coast, and the farmland of the interior. In this way, the members of any one Tribe would be of varied origins, so that sailors would vote alongside farmers and traders and craftsmen from the city. The system seems artificial and improbable, but it worked: It cut through generations of family influence and self-interests and persuaded individual citizens to think of the good of the community as a whole, rather than try to promote their own narrow concerns.

In other reforms, Cleisthenes revised Solon's constitution. The Assembly of the people became the sole legislative body, and magistrates were entirely responsible to it. The Council, or Boule, enlarged from 400 to 500 members, prepared business to present to the Assembly. The 500, each of whom served for a year, were still chosen by Solon's system of random lot drawing, and no man could be on the Boule more than twice in a lifetime. As a result, at any one time in Classical Athens not only were all adult male citizens members of the Assembly of the people, but many thousands of them had served as Boule members, with the experience of participating in the detailed work of government administration.

Cleisthenes' reforms built on those of Solon to eliminate past inequities and prejudices. They created a forward-looking state, modernized and efficient, where the arts could thrive—and did—and in which all voting citizens could feel that they played an active part in running their government. By the end of the Persian Wars, Athens was renowned throughout the Greek world for its political evolution. Those who were suspicious of popular democracy looked elsewhere for inspiration and leadership: to Sparta.

THE SPARTAN ALTERNATIVE: CONSERVATISM AND THE MILITARY IDEAL

Sparta, the leading city in southern Greece—a region known as the Peloponnese—developed a system of government unique in the Greek world: a military aristocracy. The early growth of population there had led the Spartans, like many other inhabitants of Greek cities, to send out colonizers, including those who founded Taranto in southern Italy. In their urge for more territory closer to home, however, toward the end of the 8th century B.C. the Spartans made the highly unusual move of conquering land in their own region, that of their western neighbors, the Messenians. They enslaved the local population, and from then on, alone of the Greek city-states, maintained a permanent army to put down revolts by their subject peoples.

By the Archaic period, Spartan society was rigidly stratified. At the top were the aristocratic Spartiates (Spartan warriors), the only true citizens. Beneath them came the *perioikoi,* or "dwellers around," consisting of conquered neighboring peoples who vastly outnumbered the Spartiates and had no political rights. At the bottom were the **helots,** or serfs, also acquired from Spartan conquests. These serfs were not bought and sold as slaves of individual Spartiates but belonged to the state and mostly worked the land. The threat that a possible helot uprising posed to state security was a constant preoccupation for the Spartiates.

SPARTIATE TRAINING
The way of life of the ruling upper class was intended to maintain this social system: a dominant minority holding down and exploiting a huge population of potentially dan-

gerous subjects. At a time when revolutions elsewhere in Greece—and Solon at Athens—were bringing new rights to the lower classes, the Spartans continually reinforced their conservative military discipline.

The Spartans claimed that their system was the invention of a lawgiver called Lycurgus, who, they believed, had lived in the 9th century B.C. (the later historian Plutarch dated Lycurgus to the period following 669 B.C.). It seems more probable that the system evolved over time because Spartan domination over their captives required increasing severity. The revolt of the Messenians, around 630 B.C., which took the Spartans some 30 years to suppress, seems to have been the final factor in the creation of a state dependent on an efficient fighting machine always ready to swing into action.

Those Spartan babies who appeared sickly were left out to die (infanticide was also practiced in other Greek states, generally as a means of birth control, while the Spartans used it primarily to strengthen the physical condition of their citizens). At the age of seven, male children left their mothers to live and train in camps, where they received scanty clothing and insufficient food. Their elders expected them to survive by stealing from nearby farms, and beat them if they were caught, not for dishonesty, but for their clumsiness in being found out. At 20 years old, the young men stood for election to one of a series of military messes or "clubs." Failure to win unanimous election by the club's members meant utter social disgrace. The young Spartiate warriors were expected to marry by the age of 30, but even then they continued to eat and sleep at their club residence and serve in the military. Spartan men could not farm, trade, or do professional work, all of which fell to the *perioikoi.*

Spartan girls remained with their mothers, living under a regime to promote their physical fitness and prepare them for their chief role in life: motherhood. Domestic activities such as housecleaning and sewing, elsewhere in Greece the normal duties of women of all classes, fell to women of inferior status, and Spartiate young women concentrated on gymnastics, music—an important aspect of education—and studying domestic management and childrearing.

One of the effects of the military system was to emphasize the importance of women to the state, and in general the rest of Greece saw Spartan women as outspoken and immoral. When the Spartan army was abroad for an extended period, the state seems to have encouraged the wives who were left behind to have relations with young and healthy helots, in order to rebuild the population as an insurance against heavy military losses. Even within Spartiate society, according to Athenian writers, wife-sharing was tolerated: The more Spartiates born, the better.

POLITICS AT SPARTA
Young Spartans of both sexes learned to denounce potential troublemakers to the state's ruthless secret police, and the Spartan political constitution betrayed a similar distrust of its citizens. There were two kings. As a further safety measure, the kings fell under the supervision of five *Ephors,* or

"Overseers." Chosen by lot, these overseers served for a year. A Council of Elders, the *Gerousia,* served as the chief executive body. The Spartiate Assembly approved or rejected the executive's proposals, but it could not debate and—to the amused bewilderment of other Greeks—it expressed its opinion not by voting but by shouting: the loudest side won. If the Assembly reached no clear-cut decision, the kings and Ephors could order it suspended.

The same rigidity marked Spartan relations with the rest of the Greek world. The prosperity of the aristocratic upper class depended on agriculture because Sparta discouraged commercial activities and trade with other states. Even though the Athenians and others had developed a controlled currency and banking system, which made commerce abroad possible, the Spartans continued to use antiquated and clumsy iron currency. The very presence of foreigners in Sparta, with their new and unwelcome ideas, was subject to strict control, and from time to time the state would expel those who had managed to obtain admittance.

The cruelty and brutality of many aspects of the Spartans' lives were clear to their Greek contemporaries. If the Spartans kept their subject peoples under the most ruthless control, their own lives were just as grim and austere. One visitor from Greek Italy remarked, after a dinner in an army mess: "Now I understand why the Spartans do not fear death!"

Yet if many Greeks made fun of the Spartans' stubborn conservatism, they were not blind to what they saw as Spartan virtues. They admired the Spartan sense of *eunomia,* of "law and order," and civic discipline. A later writer, Plutarch, tells of an incident at the Olympic games. A feeble old man was wandering around in search of a seat, to the jeers of the crowd. When he came to the Spartan stands, all the young men, and many of the older ones, sprang to their feet to offer him a place. As the old man gratefully sank down, he sighed: "All Greeks *know* what is right, but only the Spartans *do* it."

The Spartan sacrifice of comfort and self-interest in the interests of the state represented an ideal that gave individual lives a meaning and purpose. Developing its characteristic political system before the Athenians had established theirs, Sparta provided a model for other Greek states throughout the 6th century B.C. By the beginning of the 5th century B.C., with the growing threat from Persia, the Greeks' mighty eastern neighbor, the Spartan lifestyle and discipline exerted an increasingly powerful appeal.

THE PERSIAN CHALLENGE AND THE VICTORY OF THE GREEKS

While the Greeks were working out their internal political problems and refashioning their states, the peoples to their east in Western and Central Asia fell with relative ease under the rule of the Persians (see Topic 4). By the middle of the 6th century B.C., the Persian king Cyrus the Great had conquered Babylon and moved westward to capture the territory of the Lydians. The Lydian empire included the Greek colonies of Western Asia (the Greek region along the coast there was known as Ionia), which were under the benevolent rule of the Lydian king Croesus, who a generation earlier had asked Solon to name the happiest of men. With Cyrus's victory over the Lydians in 546 B.C., these Greek cities now became part of the Persian Empire, along with the rest of Lydia.

Thus from the mid-6th century B.C., with the Persians established in Greek Ionia, the mainland Greeks had to face an alarming possibility: A future Persian king might decide to move farther west to add the Greeks' territory to his empire. The best hope of opposing any future Persian aggression lay in a defensive military alliance led by Sparta, the most powerful state in late 6th-century B.C. Greece, but continued squabbling among the various Greek cities made this union an unlikely prospect.

FROM THE IONIAN REVOLT TO MARATHON

In 499 B.C., after half a century of Persian rule, the Ionian Greeks revolted. Burdened with high taxes and the rule of old-fashioned tyrants imposed by the Persians, they looked with enthusiasm to mainland Greece for help.

The Ionian rebels sent messengers to the leading Greek cities to ask for help. Sparta, which was involved in a local war in the Peloponnese, refused. At Athens there was fierce debate between those in favor of sending aid to their fellow Greeks in Western Asia and the pro-peace party who thought resistance to the Persians was useless. As so often happens, compromise won and the Athenians sent a small contingent of 20 ships, which they withdrew a few months later.

It took the Persians six years to beat down the Ionian revolt. A few years after they had finally succeeded, in 490 B.C., Darius—the Persian king (ruled 522–486 B.C.)—led an expedition intended to punish the Athenians for their interference in internal Persian affairs and to discourage any future Greek

SIGNIFICANT DATES

The Archaic Age (all dates B.C.)

650–620	Messenian revolt against Sparta
620	Law code of Draco introduced at Athens
594	Reforms of Solon
546	Pisistratus becomes tyrant of Athens
514	Assassination of Hipparchus
507	Reforms of Cleisthenes
499	Ionians revolt against Persians
490	Darius defeated at Battle of Marathon
480	Xerxes defeated at Battle of Salamis
479	Greek victory at Plataea ends Persian Wars in Greece

meddling. He took the former Athenian tyrant Hippias with him, to install as pro-Persian dictator after the Persians had conquered Athens. The Persian force was relatively small, consisting of some 20,000 men: Darius seems to have counted on internal feuding among Athenian politicians to weaken the city's resistance and place Hippias back in power.

Against all expectations, virtually unaided, the Athenians managed to defeat the Persians at the Battle of Marathon. An urgent plea for assistance had gone out to Sparta, but the Spartans, cautious of fighting alongside their Athenian rivals, refused to send help immediately. Because of a religious festival, they claimed, troops could not march before the next full moon (Spartan forces arrived, in fact, after the battle was over). In the battle on the plain of Marathon, some 25 miles north of Athens, an Athenian force of about half the size of the Persian Army left some 6,400 Persians dead, at the cost of 192 Athenian lives. A further Athenian casualty was the long-distance runner Pheidippides. After running to Athens nonstop to report the Athenian victory, and prevent the garrison there from surrendering prematurely, Pheidippides collapsed and died.

THE INVASION OF XERXES

Few in the Greek world doubted that the Persians would seek a crushing revenge for their humiliating defeat. Fortunately for the Greeks, a revolt in Egypt and the death of Darius created a temporary distraction. Nonetheless the new Persian king, Darius's son Xerxes (ruled 486–465 B.C.), hastened to settle matters in Egypt and began preparations for a massive onslaught on Greece.

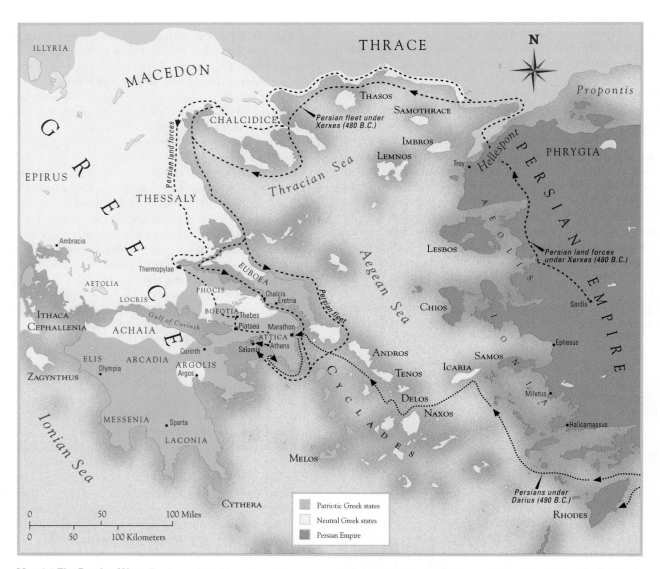

Map 8.1 The Persian Wars. The lower dotted line shows the campaign of Darius, in 490 b.c., which was ended by his defeat at the Battle of Marathon. The upper dotted line traces the much longer route taken by Xerxes in 480 b.c., which involved a far larger number of troops. Note the bridge across the Hellespont, which avoided a much longer overland march, and the canal dug across the most eastern of the three prongs of Chalcidice. Thereafter the Persian forces divided, the land troops continuing south via Thermopylae.

Portrait bust of the Greek statesman Themistocles. This is a Roman copy (1st–2nd century A.D.) of a 5th century B.C. Greek original. The helmet is pushed up to reveal the face (note the eyeholes on the helmet), and the head is turned slightly sideways and downward— a position typical of Athenian sculpture of the period.

For once the Athenians managed to compose their differences and think ahead. In the 10 years between their defeat of Darius at Marathon and Xerxes' invasion of 480 B.C., Athenian miners struck a rich vein of silver in the hills of Attica's hinterland. Following the advice of the statesman Themistocles (c. 525–c. 460 B.C.), the Athenian Assembly voted to spend the money on strengthening the city's fortifications and building up their navy. In the 3 years before the Persian invasion, the Athenian shipyards constructed 200 massive new warships. Their naval strength, which made Athens the greatest maritime power in the Greek world by the end of the Persian Wars, served both for maintaining Athenian domination at sea in their own region and as insurance against possible foreign attack. At the same time, it increased the spread of democracy by empowering the poor who formed the crews of the powerful new warships known as "triremes." Each ship had a crew of 200 men, arranged in three tiers.

Athenian preparations paled, however, in the face of Xerxes' plans. His generals ordered huge cables for building two bridges of boats across the dangerous straits of the Hellespont, which separates Europe from Asia. To avoid the dangerous waters around the cape below Mount Athos, thousands of Persian workers dug a canal through the promontory. In May 480 B.C., after the spring rains, the Persian expedition set out. It took seven days and nights for all of the troops, horses, mules, camels, and wagons to cross the bridge over the Hellespont and begin the journey south toward Greece.

Long before Xerxes began the march, the Greeks had realized what was in store for them. A congress met at Corinth, under the presidency of Sparta, at which several Greek city-states tried to settle on some plan of concerted response, but arguments over who should command any joint forces they might succeed in putting together led to a stalemate. Many of the smaller Greek city-states preferred defeat at the hands of a remote enemy to burying generations of rancor and cooperating with one another. In the end, with the threat of Persian invasion becoming a reality, Athens managed to forge an alliance with the Spartans and their allies. Themistocles even persuaded the Athenians to place their navy under a Spartan admiral.

In the early summer of 480 B.C., the Persian troops moved into northern Greece, and Xerxes sent envoys ahead to demand the surrender of the Greek cities on their route south. Terrified and awed, most of them complied. When the Persian ambassadors arrived in Sparta and issued their king's orders, the Spartans had the envoys killed. Now there was no possibility of truce or negotiation.

As the Athenians and Spartans awaited the wave of Persian invasion, Athens sent to Delphi to ask the advice of the oracle of Apollo. The mysterious message came back that the Athenians should put their trust in their wooden walls. Themistocles, convinced that the Greeks would have to defeat the Persians at sea—their numbers on land were too unequal—persuaded the Assembly that the wooden walls referred to by the oracle were those of the Athenian ships. The Athenian Assembly passed a decree mobilizing the fleet, evacuating women and children, and moving the government and army to the island of Salamis, in the bay to the west of Athens.

Greek strategy was to lure the Persians south to face their naval forces and to hold the land front as best they could. The first major confrontation came at the narrow pass of Thermopylae. In August 480 B.C., a small force of the finest Spartan soldiers and about 1000 other Greeks, under the command of the Spartan king Leonidas, held at bay the vast Persian army—recent estimates put the Persian numbers at around 200,000 men, with around 70,000 horses, mules, and camels. In the fighting the Spartans perished to a man, but their stand had bought time, and their courage became legendary.

The most detailed account of the Persian invasion is that of Herodotus (see Topic 10), who describes the Greeks' growing despair as the Persians continued their inexorable advance south, burning and pillaging. The Athenians evacuated all remaining residents from the city, leaving a volunteer garrison on the Acropolis. Within days, Xerxes reached Athens, captured and burned down the buildings on the Acropolis, and massacred its guards. As the summer ended, Xerxes sent home the news of his "victory."

He still needed to take the Peloponnese, however, and crush the Spartans on their own territory, if possible before winter conditions made feeding his huge expedition problematic. To put an end to the Athenians, meanwhile, the Persian fleet had to defeat the Athenian navy guarding the

Hirmer Fotoarchiv

Scene from a Greek vase showing soldiers marching out to battle. 6th century B.C. They are sent on their way by a musician, who is playing on a double *aulos*—a reeded woodwind instrument that resembles a modern oboe. The soldiers carry a small round shield, probably—to judge from their designs—made from oxhide.

island of Salamis and put to the sword the Athenian population seeking refuge there. Themistocles decided to provoke the Persians into risking a decisive confrontation at sea. He smuggled a message to Xerxes, saying that the Athenian fleet, hopeless and demoralized, was about to break up and flee, and that he wanted to defect to the Persian side. The Persians struck—and Themistocles had the naval battle he had hoped for and planned for a decade.

Trapped in the narrow straits between Salamis and the coast, and facing the experienced Greek crews fighting in their home waters, the Persians were routed. Their ships rammed into one another as the Greeks skillfully encircled them and struck them down one by one, snapping off their oars: "You could not see the water for blood and wreckage" (Herodotus). When night fell, the Athenians still did not realize the completeness of their victory, but at daylight the next morning it became clear that Xerxes had ordered what was left of his fleet to retreat: Not an enemy ship was in sight.

The danger was not yet over because the Persian land forces still presented a threat. The Persians no longer seemed unstoppable, however. The Greeks had the winter to reorganize while Xerxes sent many of his troops home, leaving a moderately sized force in the neighborhood of Thebes to hold what had already been conquered. In the spring of 479 B.C., in the greatest land battle of Greek history, an army led by the Spartans won a shattering victory at Plataea, and the invasion was over. As the remnants of the Persian Army limped home, it remained only for the victorious allies to liberate the Greek cities of Ionia and to ensure that free Greeks would never again have to face the threat of interference from the Great King of Persia.

Putting the Archaic Era in Perspective

As the Greeks well knew, the relative unity with which they had withstood the Persians was the result of the extreme danger the invaders represented. Even then, the unity was incomplete: Among the bravest contingents fighting at Plataea was that sent by the Greek city of Thebes, but the Thebans fought for, not against, the Persians.

By the end of the wars, it was clear that only the desperately forged alliance between Athens and Sparta had guaranteed success. As a result of the hostilities, both cities had built up their armaments and troop numbers, Sparta on land and Athens at sea. Both Athens and Sparta could claim vastly increased prestige in the Greek world and the right to exercise moral leadership. Could they put aside past hostilities and resentments and coexist peacefully? In the immediate celebration of their victories and the outburst of creative ferment at Athens, everything seemed possible, and the optimism of the Greeks' triumph inspired the achievements of the succeeding Classical Age. Yet less than 50 years later, Athens and Sparta were locked in mortal combat, and within a century the conflict between the warring Greek city-states was so violent that the Great King of the Persians was able to step in and impose a peace of his own devising, without fighting a single battle.

Questions for Further Discussion

1. How and why did the political systems developed at Athens differ from those of Sparta? What effect did the differences have on society in the two city-states?
2. What were the strengths and weaknesses of democracy at Athens?
3. What were the main factors in the Greeks' success in the Persian Wars? What were the political consequences of their victory?

Suggestions for Further Reading

Biers, William. *The Archaeology of Greece: An Introduction*, 2nd ed. Ithaca, NY, 1996.

Grant, M. *The Rise of the Greeks*. New York, 1987.

Hanson, V.D. *The Western Way of War: Infantry Battle in Classical Greece*. New York, 1989.

Manville, P.B. *The Origin of Citizenship in Ancient Athens*. Princeton, NJ, 1990.

Morris, Sarah P. *Daidalos and the Origins of Greek Art*. Princeton, NJ, 1992.

Sainte-Croix, G.E.M. de. *The Class Struggle in the Ancient Greek World*. Ithaca, NY, 1982.

Starr, C.G. *The Birth of Athenian Democracy*. New York, 1990.

InfoTrac College Edition

Enter the search term *Greek history* using Key Terms.

THE GREEK WORLD IN CONFLICT: THE PELOPONNESIAN WAR AND ITS AFTERMATH

With the defeat of the Persians in 479 B.C., the victorious alliance between Athens and Sparta began to crumble and the Greek world returned to its divisive ways. Although the Spartans withdrew again into isolation, the Athenians remained diplomatically active. Their arguments convinced several Greek city-states to join with them in a league to defend Greece from any future threat of aggression by Persia. By 454 B.C., when the Athenians moved the league's treasury from its original neutral location on the island of Delos to Athens itself, the free association of independent city-states had turned into an Athenian Empire.

Over the following two decades, under the leadership of their most famous statesman, Pericles, the Athenians reinforced their domination of the Greek world. The sight of the growing power of Athens, made visible in the city's magnificent new buildings, awoke old suspicions and rancors. Fear of Athenian imperialistic designs drove those cities not yet under her control to form an alliance led by Sparta. Outright war, setting the Spartans and their new allies against the Athenian Empire, seemed increasingly inevitable.

It came in 431 B.C. The Peloponnesian War dragged on until 404 B.C., when it ended with the ignominious defeat of Athens. One of the main causes of Athens' eventual collapse was a disastrous campaign the Athenians waged against the Greek city-states of Sicily between 415 and 413 B.C., during a lull in the main fighting. Its utter failure left Athens weakened and demoralized, although the remaining 10 years of war saw some further Athenian victories.

In the generation following the end of the war, the Spartans maintained a brutal if uncertain control over Greek affairs, under the watchful eye of the Great King of Persia. In 371 B.C. Thebes briefly succeeded in challenging Spartan supremacy, but rivalry among Thebes, Sparta, and Athens continued to destabilize the Greek world.

In the end, the ruler of Macedon, a kingdom to the north of Greece, stepped in to fill the vacuum. Philip of Macedon, who became king in 359 B.C., first cajoled and then used open force to take control of Greek affairs. By the time of his death in 336 B.C., he had defeated a combined Theban and Athenian army and united the chief Greek city-states in the League of Corinth. Only the Spartans stubbornly held out.

Alexander, his son and successor, paused only long enough to enforce Macedonian domination in Greece before launching a triumphant campaign eastward against Persia. With their political independence gone, the Greeks became absorbed into the multinational Macedonian Empire that Alexander built. In the process, however, Greek culture and ideas became increasingly influential in the Mediterranean world, as Alexander's conquests spread them abroad.

PERICLES AND THE PRIMACY OF ATHENS

The Persian threat had finally managed to unite the Greeks, but with the wars over and the Persians defeated, the chief Greek city-states reverted to their traditional behavior. The Spartans withdrew into isolation. They had no intention of helping in the future protection of the Greek cities of Ionia or of defending the Aegean against another Persian attack.

THE DELIAN LEAGUE

In 478 B.C., the Athenians, by now the greatest naval power in Greece, willingly took on the role of organizing a defensive association to be ready for any future emergency. To this end, they organized a league, whose members consisted of the chief maritime city-states of the Aegean region. Each member-state could contribute ships, men, or money. The Athenian general, Aristides the Just, assessed the financial payments, which were collected in a treasury on the island of Delos; the association became known as the Delian League.

Delos, a small island in the central Aegean, was the home of the great panhellenic shrine of Apollo—Greek alliances always had a religious basis—and its choice as headquarters was intended to demonstrate the League's neutrality. From the outset, however, it was clear to all the participants—not to mention outside observers such as the Spartans—that Athens was the League's dominating force. Quite apart from the Athenians' enormous political prestige, the 200 ships they contributed to the joint forces gave them an overwhelming military superiority.

The Athenians' willingness to exert their dominance became clear in 469 B.C., when one of the members, Naxos, announced its decision to withdraw from the League. The Athenians blockaded Naxos and forced the islanders to surrender, then compelled them to reenroll. Over the next few years other states wishing to resign their membership received the same treatment, and some of those who had never been members were forced to join.

The transformation of an association of independent partners into an Athenian Empire became plain to all in 454 B.C., when the Athenians moved the headquarters and treasury of the League from Delos to Athens. At the same time, they insisted that all legal disputes among members should be settled in the Athenian courts. The justification for these actions was "administrative convenience," but the effect was to confirm the suspicions of Athens' enemies that the Athenians were aggressively building an empire.

ATHENS UNDER PERICLES

Throughout this crucial period, which was to culminate in 431 B.C. in the outbreak of the Peloponnesian War, the leading political figure at Athens was Pericles (c. 495–429 B.C.). The policy of the dominating politician of the previous generation, the aristocratic Cimon, had been to build up Greek defenses against another Persian attack, while keeping on friendly terms with Sparta. In 461 B.C., however, the popular forces at Athens drove Cimon from power, and Pericles, a moderate, replaced him. From then until his death in 429 B.C., Pericles was by far the most influential and popular politician in the Assembly. Although elected frequently to public office, his chief political role was as speaker at Assembly meetings.

In theory, as Pericles himself pointed out, the humblest Athenian citizen had as much right as he to express opinions on the complex and vital questions of the day, before the Assembly then democratically decided on Athenian policy. In practice, the power of Pericles' oratory and the success of his recommendations when they were followed left him as unchallenged leader for some 30 years.

Certain points remained constant in Pericles' political program. He reversed Cimon's priorities by making peace with Persia and accepting the inevitability of bad feelings between Athens and Sparta. After further skirmishes, the Athenians finally came to an agreement with the Persians, and the two sides reluctantly signed a peace treaty in 449 B.C. Neither party was very proud of the terms, which included unpopular concessions, and at the time the treaty received little publicity.

As for Sparta, the best Athens could do—according to Pericles—was to become so powerful that no other Greek state or alliance would dare to attack her with impunity. The support of the Delian League and the financial contributions of its members were a vital element in this military buildup. In 445 B.C. Sparta and Athens made a halfhearted attempt to block the drift toward war by opening negotiations. Each side yielded a series of relatively minor concessions and signed the Thirty Years Peace. Few were optimistic, however, about the probability of its lasting as long. Pericles observed later: "What I bought was not peace but time."

Pericles used the time he had won not only to build up military forces, but also to provide Athens with a visible splendor that would proclaim the city's cultural supremacy. Ever since, later generations have looked to the artistic achievements of this High Classical period as a golden age.

As the clouds of war began to gather, on the hill of the Acropolis thousands of workers finally cleared the debris of the buildings destroyed by the Persians in 480 B.C. In their place arose the temples that are still visible there today. The crowning glory was the Parthenon, constructed under the supervision of Phidias, the greatest sculptor of his day and a personal friend of Pericles (see Topic 10). The Athenians built it in honor of Athene, their patron goddess, but its real purpose was to provide a monument for all time to the glory of Periclean Athens.

The years of construction on the Acropolis also saw the performance in the Theater of Dionysus, below the Acropolis, of the tragic dramas of Sophocles and others, many of them still ranking among the masterpieces of Western literature. Two other momentous developments occurred in this same period. Herodotus arrived in Athens from one of the Greek cities of Ionia, to continue work on his *Histories*. The earliest surviving Greek historical work written in prose, it has won Herodotus the nickname, "the Father

PUBLIC FIGURES AND PRIVATE LIVES

ASPASIA AND PERICLES

Ancient Art & Architecture

© Scala/Art Resource, NY

Pericles' influence and authority at Athens depended on his popularity. With his public status came the glare of attention. Not only did he oversee Athenian domestic and foreign policy, but he also played an active part in plans for the building program on the Acropolis and other cultural affairs. No wonder his fellow Athenians noted that "Pericles never had time to go to parties." Yet in his private life he kept in touch with the intellectual ideas of the day. Among his close friends was Anaxagoras—the first foreign philosopher to take up residence in Athens and teach there—whom Pericles personally provided with financial support for many years. At the height of Pericles' political activity, he found time to pursue his musical interests, by standing for election in 442 B.C. to the committee organizing a new music festival.

Pericles married early in life. His wife, as often happened in aristocratic families, was a distant relative. She bore him two sons before the couple divorced, apparently by mutual consent. The austere statesman now devoted all of his time to public life. The Athenians nicknamed him "Zeus" and called his speeches to the Assembly "the divine thunder."

In 445 B.C., shortly after negotiating the Thirty Years Peace, Pericles—then around 50 years old—began a relationship with a young woman that lasted until his death and provided Athenian writers and gossips with a never-ending source of material. Aspasia was born around 465 B.C. at Miletus, a Greek town in Ionia. She came to Athens to earn her living as a *hetaira*, a "companion to men." These women, generally freed slaves or non-Athenians, were self-employed prostitutes. The state required them to register and levied a special tax on them.

The highest-paid *hetaira*, in addition to their physical beauty, were often educated and cultured women who could provide their customers with a level of intellectual companionship beyond the reach of most sheltered Athenian housewives (for the social status of the *hetairai*, see Topic 11).

As all of Athens knew, Pericles and Aspasia set up house together. Observers recounted, with a mixture of amusement and disbelief, that "Pericles would kiss her warmly when he left the house for work and when he came home again." The couple had a son, but because Aspasia was not an Athenian citizen, their child was not entitled to citizenship. A few weeks before the great statesman's death in 429 B.C., the Assembly voted to confer citizenship on his and Aspasia's son.

Public opinion was not always so favorably disposed toward the couple. The comic playwright Aristophanes jokingly accused Pericles of starting the Peloponnesian War through Aspasia's influence, and other writers openly called her a whore. These attacks became more serious during the year before the war, when Pericles' political enemies launched an attack on Aspasia as a means of undermining Pericles' own position. They brought her to trial for "impiety," and witnesses at the hearings claimed that, as a foreigner, she was a "security risk." The fact that she was known to be well-educated and politically astute—Socrates often visited her, bringing his pupils—was held against her. Her detractors claimed that she played too strong a part in Pericles' political decisions. With war looming and political tension at its height, Pericles appeared in court at her trial to plead for her. He broke down and wept, and the jury acquitted her.

At a time when respectable Athenian males, especially those in the public eye, rigorously maintained the social rules, Aspasia and Pericles—the most visible of all couples—openly flouted all conventional standards of behavior. It says much for their prestige at Athens that the Athenians continued to reelect Pericles as first citizen, and that—for all the gossip—Aspasia retained their respect. After Pericles' death, Aspasia married a democratic politician and continued to live quietly at Athens.

of History." Meanwhile, Socrates, a stonemason (he may even have worked on the Parthenon), began to debate with those Athenians who would stop and listen to him. Socrates never wrote down his ideas, but a generation later Plato, one of his pupils, wrote dialogues featuring Socrates and in so doing laid down the foundations of Western philosophy. (For the cultural developments of the period, see Topic 10.)

THE GREEK WORLD DIVIDED: THE PELOPONNESIAN WAR

By the outbreak of the Peloponnesian War in 431 B.C., Greece was openly divided. Each of the two sides claimed to be on the side of freedom, although neither really practiced what it preached. The Athenians encouraged, even insisted on, their allies maintaining democratic systems of government in their states, but prevented those states from acting contrary to Athenian wishes—by force, if necessary. The Spartans and their allies accused Athens of ruling its empire as a tyranny, while their own states were antidemocratic oligarchies, in which most residents had no rights. The irony of Athens' or Sparta's claim to be the champion of Greek freedom was not lost on many observers.

THE FIRST 10 YEARS

In the end, war came not because of a fight about political theory but over a matter of money and trade. The Spartans had little interest in business, and Athens' main commercial rival was Corinth. When the Athenians began to interfere in relations between Corinth and the Corinthian colonies in western Greece, the Corinthians persuaded the Spartans that Athens had imperialistic designs on the whole of trade with the western Greeks. If the Spartans and their allies did not act now, it would soon be too late: the Athenians would add the western Mediterranean to their empire. Thus when war finally came, it was the result of Corinthian reaction to Athenian pressure, rather than as a conscious step on the part of Sparta or Athens.

Although hostilities in the Peloponnesian War dragged on for 27 years, from 431 to 404 B.C., they were not continuous. The first 10 years' campaigns led to a stalemate and a temporary peace treaty. Neither side scored a decisive victory. The Spartan Army marched overland to lay waste the countryside around Athens, while Athenian naval forces raided the Peloponnesian coast. The greatest blow to Athens in the early stages of war came, in fact, not from the Spartans but from the terrible plague of 430–427 B.C. In addition to the loss of life and consequent psychological damage caused by the disease, the death of Pericles left the Athenians bereft of firm leadership at the worst possible time.

The events of these years form the subject of the *History of the Peloponnesian War*, written by the Athenian Thucydides (c. 455–c. 399 B.C.). He based his incomparably lucid account on his own experiences, serving in the fight-

ing as a general at one point. Thucydides' Athenian birth and admiration for the achievements of Pericles did not blind him to the growing violence with which Athens waged war after Pericles' death. By the time the weary combatants paused for breath in 421 B.C., the Athenians, upholders of democracy, were as guilty of atrocities as their opponents. When in 422 B.C. their erstwhile ally Skione revolted, the Athenians starved out its citizens, executed all male adolescents and adults, and sold the women and children into slavery. With the signing of the Peace of Nicias (named after Athens' leading general and negotiator) in 421 B.C., neither side could easily assert its moral superiority.

THE SICILIAN DISASTER

In the aftermath of the peace negotiations, Nicias (c. 470–413 B.C.) reinforced his position as spokesman for the political moderates at Athens. The leader of his more radical opponents was Alcibiades (c. 450–404 B.C.), one of the most complex and contradictory figures to emerge in these tumultuous years. Handsome, charming, and extravagantly flamboyant, Alcibiades seemed determined to outrage his fellow aristocrats by supporting the radical democrats in the Assembly. Yet he became one of the closest intimates of Socrates, alongside whom he had served as a young soldier. Plato assigns Alcibiades an important role in the dinner party attended by Socrates, which he describes in *The Symposium*.

As the relief at the coming of peace gave way to planning for the inevitable resumption of war, Alcibiades threw his support behind a foolhardy and dangerous scheme, the conquest and pillage of Sicily. The rich cities of Greek Sicily were centers of trade and prosperity, famous for their cultural and intellectual achievements—the remains of their spectacular buildings are still visible today. The greatest dramatic poet of the mid-5th century B.C., Aeschylus of Athens, visited Syracuse and wrote plays for the theater there. The Syracusans, like many other Sicilian Greeks, lived in a democratic state, with a constitution modeled after the one invented by Cleisthenes for Athens in the late 6th century B.C.

The capture of all this wealth, Alcibiades urged, could fund Athens' renewed war effort and lay the basis for an Athenian Empire in the west. At the same time, Sicily was a major grain producer whose crops supplied many of Sparta's allies. By gaining control of the island, the Athenians could starve out their enemies. The threefold appeal of money, strategic advantage, and military glory proved irresistible, and in 415 B.C. the Athenians prepared their Sicilian Expedition to sail westward. Nicias argued in vain that Athens should concentrate on reconstruction at home rather than taking such an immense leap into the unknown. The members of the Assembly overruled him, although, as Thucydides caustically observes, "most of them had no idea of the size of the island or of its population, or that they were embarking on a war as serious as that against the Peloponnesians."

When it was clear to Nicias that no considerations of caution—to say nothing of morality—would overcome the

Athenians' eagerness for conquest, he successfully urged them at least to send the largest possible force. In the spring of 415 B.C., the huge naval and land force prepared to set out under the joint command of Alcibiades, Nicias, and the general Lamachus.

During the night preceding the expedition's departure, unknown vandals mutilated sacred statues in Athens. The incident caused panic and was taken as the worst of omens for the coming campaign. The culprits were never identified. Alcibiades' enemies accused him of being responsible and pointed to his notorious lack of reverence and love of creating outrage, but it was too late to halt the fleet. It sailed with the hostility between the two chief commanders, already implacable political opponents, further inflamed by the suspicions falling on Alcibiades.

In the event, Alcibiades played little part in the Sicilian debacle. Shortly after the troops arrived in Sicily, the Athenians recalled him to Athens for questioning about his possible involvement in the mutilations. Whether or not he was guilty, Alcibiades had no intention of going home and submitting to investigation. He gave his guards the slip and fled to Sparta. In his absence, the Athenians found their former commander guilty and sentenced him to death.

In the meantime Nicias and Lamachus embarked on the siege of Syracuse. Lamachus fell in the initial skirmishes, leaving Nicias, by now fatally ill, the sole commander of an expedition he had always opposed. When news came that the Spartans, taking the advice of their new friend Alcibiades, were sending troops to help the Syracusans, Nicias's colleagues begged him to order a retreat. The dying commander, fearing the wrath of the Athenians at home, refused.

The result was disaster. The Syracusans blocked the Athenian ships in the bay of Syracuse. The desperate troops on board disembarked to take refuge on land, where the Spartan troops picked them off. The few Athenian survivors were herded into the quarries outside Syracuse, where a few months of winter cold and damp and below-starvation rations soon finished most of them off. Far from

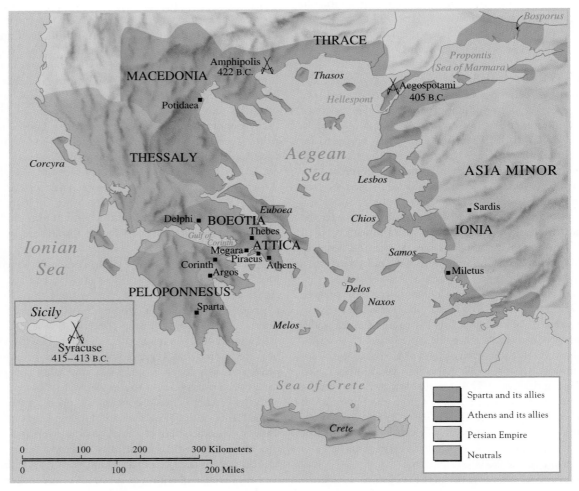

Map 9.1 Greece During the Peloponnesian War. Note that the Spartans enjoyed the solid support of their neighbors, while Athens' main allies were scattered—from Corcyra (modern Corfu) in the west to the eastern islands off the coast of Asia Minor, bordering the Persian Empire.

SIGNIFICANT DATES

Greece in the Classical and Late Classical Periods (all dates B.C.)

478	Formation of Delian League
454	Treasury of Delian League moved to Athens
431–404	Peloponnesian War
430–427	Plague in Athens
429	Death of Pericles
421	Peace of Nicias
415–413	Sicilian Expedition
404	Fall of Athens; rule of "The Thirty"
399	Trial of Socrates
387	The King's Peace
359	Philip becomes king of Macedon
338	Battle of Chaeronea
336	Assassination of Philip and accession of Alexander

enriching Athenian coffers, the calamitous Sicilian Expedition fatally weakened the Athenians' morale and fighting capacity. When fighting in Greece resumed in 412 B.C., the end was only a matter of time.

THE END OF THE PELOPONNESIAN WAR

The last phase of the war began under conditions not very different from those a hundred years earlier, with Athens torn by political rivalry and the Persians preparing to interfere in Greek affairs.

The failure of the Sicilian Expedition helped the conservatives at Athens to discredit the democratic leaders responsible for it. In 411 B.C. a group of oligarchs calling themselves the Council of Four Hundred staged a coup to oust the democratic Boule and seize power. Their plan was to replace the Assembly with a carefully selected Council of Five Thousand, made up of their supporters, and to try to make peace with Sparta.

The scheme was foiled by the reappearance on the scene of Alcibiades. He had outstayed his welcome in Sparta and, living under Persian protection, he urged the Athenians not to give in but to continue to fight the Spartans. With the restoration of democracy at Athens in 410 B.C., the Athenian fleet once again went on the offensive with Alcibiades returning triumphantly as its commander.

Yet the longer the war dragged on, the more hopeless became the Athenians' chances. When Cyrus, the Persian king, decided to intervene and sent help to the Spartans, even Alcibiades' charisma was of no avail. The Athenians called him back to Athens once more. Again he fled into exile, leaving the Athenian navy to face ignominious defeat in 405 B.C. at the Battle of Aigospotamoi. Of the 180 Athenian ships present, only nine escaped. The Spartans executed 4,000 prisoners in cold blood, as reprisal for similar atrocities committed by the Athenians.

Back at Athens, refugees poured into the city. Somehow or other, under siege and with people dying in the streets, the Athenians made it through the winter. By spring 404 B.C., they could take no more. The fight was over. The Athenians offered unconditional surrender.

THE DEFEAT OF ATHENS AND ITS CONSEQUENCES

When the victors convened at Sparta to fix the terms of Athenian surrender, Thebes and Corinth urged that the city should be put to the sword. The Spartans, however, cautious as ever, refused to destroy a city "which had done good service" in the defense of Greece against the Persians. The Athenians could keep 12 ships but lost control of their foreign policy to Sparta and had to demolish the defensive long walls that connected the city to the harbor of Piraeus. The Spartan fleet sailed to Athens to enforce the terms, and "the walls were demolished by eager hands, while the flute girls played, and men thought that day marked the beginning of freedom for Greece." Events were soon to prove them wrong.

REVOLUTION IN POSTWAR ATHENS

For many Athenian voters, the democratic party was responsible for Athens' present lamentable state. The democrats had, under Pericles' leadership, got Athens involved in the war in the first place and had consistently refused to negotiate an end to the fighting with Sparta. To make matters worse, their leaders were implicated in the acts of wanton violence—the killing of hostages and innocent civilians—which had made Athens so hated by her conquerors.

In the weeks following the city's surrender, a group of archconservatives seized power. "The Thirty," as they were styled, acted with the full approval and protection of the Spartan general in command of the garrison still occupying Athens. It soon became clear that rule by The Thirty was becoming a reign of terror, in which any conceivable opponent faced summary arrest and execution. As the number of innocent victims mounted, the democrats summoned the courage and the popular support to fight back.

They banded together during the winter in the hills around Athens, and early in 403 B.C. open opposition to The Thirty, by now dubbed The Thirty Tyrants, broke out in Athens. A burst of violent street fighting at Athens' harbor, Piraeus, left the ringleaders of the oligarchy dead, and within a short time the brutal tyranny was over.

THE DEATH OF SOCRATES

The most controversial event in the early years of renewed democratic government at Athens occurred in 399 B.C.: the trial of Socrates on charges of impiety and corrupting the youth of Athens, and his execution. The conduct of the trial itself, Socrates' subsequent time in prison, and the actual scene of his death are all immortalized in the accounts writ-

© Giraudon/Art Resource, NY

Portrait bust of the philosopher Socrates. This is a Roman Imperial copy of a 4th century B.C. Greek original. The realistic treatment of the wrinkles on the face and untidy hair and beard is characteristic of the last phase of Greek Classical sculpture and very different from the idealizing style of High Classical art of the preceding century.

ten by his pupil Plato. Under the influence of Plato's poignant and dramatic descriptions, posterity has accepted his verdict that the death of Socrates was the end of "the noblest and wisest and most just of men." Plato went on to use Socrates as the mouthpiece for much of his own philosophy (see Topic 10), thereby increasing our sense of outrage at the execution of Socrates by a supposedly democratic regime, especially on charges that even at the time seemed flimsy.

The real reasons for Socrates' trial have far more to do with the psychological state of postwar Athens than with Socrates' religious beliefs. Years of preparation and almost 30 years of brutal war had ended in utter humiliation and the bloodthirsty tyranny of The Thirty. Throughout the whole period, Socrates publicly questioned traditional Athenian standards of belief and morality and pointed out the defects of democracy. Among the young Athenians who flocked to hear and take part in Socrates' discussions, none was better known or more hated by the average Athenian than Alcibiades. To make matters even worse, the chief instigator of The Thirty's reign of terror, Critias, was also Socrates' pupil and friend. Socrates himself had always been loyal to Athens, but popular opinion held that Alcibiades had learned his treachery and Critias his ruthlessness from their teacher.

In the circumstances, the trial produced a verdict of guilty by a majority of 281 votes to 220. The prosecutors

claimed the death penalty, and Socrates had the right to propose an alternative; the jury would then decide between the two choices. After saying that if it were up to him, he would choose to be maintained for life as a public benefactor, Socrates gave way to the pressure of his friends and proposed a fine. The jury, offended, voted for the death penalty by a larger majority than had found him guilty. Socrates could have agreed to face exile rather than execution. Once imprisoned and awaiting death, he could have escaped from jail as his judges encouraged him to do, in order to avoid having to carry out the sentence. Yet Socrates died, as he had lived, according to his principle of consistency and obedience to the laws: "No evil can come to a good man, either living or dead."

SPARTA VERSUS THEBES

The war finally behind them, the Athenians began the long, painful process of adjusting to their new, reduced position in the Greek world. With their military strength gone, and their status as political and moral leaders of Greece a thing of the past, the Athenians could only watch helplessly as the other Greek city-states fought for supremacy.

Of the two chief contenders, Sparta and Thebes, the Spartans were the first to establish themselves as the dominant power in Greece. They had, after all, led the coalition responsible for breaking up the Athenian Empire. Whatever goodwill they may have gained in the eyes of the Greeks, however, they soon lost by their behavior as victors. The boards of military governors that they set up proved to be arrogant and rapacious and speedily alienated the local populations under their jurisdiction.

The result was an extended period of skirmishing between the Spartans and a coalition of other states, led by Thebes, during which the Persians quietly stirred up as much rancor as possible among the various parties. Finally, in 387 B.C., the Persian king dictated the terms of the King's Peace, by which all Greek city-states were to regain their independence: Less than a century after their humiliating defeat, the Persians were openly interfering in Greek affairs.

The Persian intervention was a failure. Even the Great King himself could not stem the tide of Greek violence, much of it caused by a resurgent Athens, and the Spartans once again went on the attack. Their leadership came to a violent end in 372 B.C., when the Thebans and Spartans clashed head-on in the Battle of Leuctra. To the astonishment of all of Greece, the Thebans won. In a move typical of the confusion of the times, the Athenians, who had been enthusiastic backers of Thebes, immediately switched sides and transferred their loyalty to the defeated Spartans.

The last hopes of the Greeks ever setting aside their destructive rivalries came in 362 B.C. at the Battle of Mantinea, where Spartans and Athenians fought side by side against the Thebans. The result was a draw. The historian Xenophon (c. 430–c. 354 B.C.), whose son died on the battlefield, comments: "There was even more chaos and confusion after the battle than there ever had been before in Greece."

PHILIP OF MACEDON AND THE END OF GREEK INDEPENDENCE

For the better part of a century, first the Athenians, then the Spartans, and finally the Thebans had tried to establish their supremacy over the rest of Greece. In the end, it took an outsider to impose unity, and the result was the loss of independence for all of the Greek states.

To the north of mainland Greece was the kingdom of Macedon, rich in farmland, horses, and timber and, in the eyes of the Greeks, populated by barbarians (a term used by the Greeks to describe all foreigners). The Macedonians spoke a rough dialect of Greek, to be sure, but their language was the subject of jokes at Athens. Furthermore, unlike the sophisticated Greeks to the south, the Macedonians were still ruled by kings, under a system of government reminiscent of the primitive world of Homer.

In 359 B.C., rule of Macedon passed to a new king, Philip (ruled 359–336 B.C.). Twenty-two at the time, in his youth Philip had been a hostage in Thebes and was thus educated in Greek culture. Now he was quick to see the possibilities presented by the chaos in Greece and launched a plan of expansion aimed at uniting the Greeks under his rule. The first task was to improve his armed forces. The Macedonians already had fine cavalry troops, and Philip added to them infantry brigades who were trained and disciplined in the Greek way.

DEMOSTHENES AND THE FAILURE OF ATHENS

Over the next 20 years, Philip negotiated, bribed, and when necessary fought his way to controlling most of north and central Greece. The chief obstacle blocking his way to complete conquest was the passionate campaign waged against him—not on the battlefield but before the Athenian Assembly—by the greatest of Greek orators, Demosthenes (384–322 B.C.).

Demosthenes was one of the first in Greece to realize that Philip's growing involvement in Greek affairs represented a dangerous threat. The only way the Greeks could maintain their independence was to form a panhellenic coalition, led by Athens and Thebes—and helped, if possible, by Persia. In the years from 351 to 338 B.C., Demosthenes delivered a series of powerful and increasingly desperate orations against Philip, known as the *Philippics*.

Portrait bust of Demosthenes, the Athenian politician and fiery opponent of Philip of Macedon. Demosthenes, a great orator, overcame a natural stammer by sheer perseverance. The sculptor has tried to show the speaker's intense concentration, with furrowed brow and lips tightly compressed.

By the time Demosthenes had succeeded in convincing the Thebans to fight alongside Athens, it was too late. At the Battle of Chaeronea in 338 B.C., Thebans and Athenians stood together for Greek freedom. They went down fighting, but the battle was lost. The following year Philip assembled a league at Corinth. When the Spartans contemptuously refused to participate, the Macedonians confiscated some of their territory in reprisal.

The supreme commander of the league was Philip himself. At the age of 45, and at the height of his powers, Philip's next goal was to lead his army into Asia and defeat the Persian Empire. In 336 B.C., a young assassin stabbed and killed the king while he was walking in a triumphal procession. Philip never fulfilled his dream of conquering Asia, which fell instead to his son and successor, Alexander (see Topic 12).

Putting the Peloponnesian War in Perspective

The political, economic, and social divisions that beset ancient Greece came to a head in the war between Athens and Sparta. The resulting defeat of Athens was the first step in a process that led to the disintegration of an autonomous Greek civilization at the hands of the Macedonians.

Continued next page

By the end of Philip's reign, the history of an independent Greece was at an end. The Greeks first became subordinate allies of the kingdom of Macedon, and then became part of the vast Macedonian Empire, which Alexander built in the few years before he died. In the course of time, Greece took its place as one of the provinces of the Macedonians' eventual successors, the Romans (see Topic 13). The Greeks never regained complete control over their own affairs or political destiny, yet in one way their influence increased with their defeat. The impact of the Greek intellectual and cultural achievement became diffused throughout the territories of its conquerors, to form the foundation of Western civilization.

Questions for Further Study

1. What were the chief causes of the Peloponnesian War? How—if at all—could collision between Athens and Sparta have been avoided?
2. What effect did the Sicilian Expedition have on the outcome of the war? What role did Alcibiades play in the Sicilian Expedition and in the following decade?
3. What were the underlying factors leading to the trial of Socrates? In what ways did his defense and ultimate execution illustrate his philosophical principles?
4. What were the main stages in Macedon's rise to power? When and how could the Greeks have blocked Philip's advance?

Suggestions for Further Reading

Borza, E.N. *In the Shadow of Olympus: The Emergence of Macedon*. Princeton, NJ, 1990.
Grant, M. *The Classical Greeks*. New York, 1989.
Kagan, D. *Pericles of Athens and the Birth of Democracy*. New York, 1991.
Ober, J. *Mass and Elite in Democratic Athens: Rhetoric, Ideology, and the Power of the People*. Princeton, NJ, 1989.
Pugliesi, Carratelli. *The Greek World*. New York, 1996.
Rhodes, P.J. *The Athenian Empire*. Oxford, 1985.
Starr, Chester G. *The Birth of Athenian Democracy: The Assembly in the 5th Century* B.C. New York, 1990.

InfoTrac College Edition

Enter the search term *Greek history* using Key Terms.

Enter the search term *Peloponnesian War* using Key Terms.

THE CLASSICAL VISION

Alongside the political upheavals of the 5th and 4th centuries B.C., there occurred in Greece a series of artistic and intellectual developments that permanently shaped Western culture. The Greeks' striving for order and balance left its mark on literature and the visual arts, and their pursuit of self-knowledge opened up new ways of thinking about human existence, among them history and philosophy.

At the theater festivals of Athens, tragic dramatists produced cycles of plays that used myths to explore human behavior, both individual and collective. Meanwhile, comic playwrights wrote satires, often bitter ones, on contemporary events, including the Peloponnesian War.

Greek painters and sculptors continued to explore ways of depicting the human form realistically, working along lines already laid out in the preceding Archaic period. By the High Classical period, artists were able to achieve a balance between realism and idealism that has remained "classic" ever since. In the Late Classical 4th century B.C., the heroic calm of High Classical art gave way to a greater interest in the emotional states of individuals.

Pericles' plans to make Athens the cultural center of the Greek world included an ambitious building program to reconstruct the temples on the Athenian Acropolis, which the Persians had destroyed in 480 B.C. The structures built there during the second half of the 5th century include the Parthenon and represent the high point of Greek architectural achievement, and one of the supreme moments in the history of Western art.

Writers and thinkers of the Classical Age laid the foundations for three areas of intellectual inquiry: history, science, and philosophy. The historians Herodotus and Thucydides, in their very different ways, chronicled the chief events of their own age. Even before the 5th century B.C. and the time of Socrates, thinkers had begun to study the physical nature of the world. In doing so, they asked questions that anticipated the inquiries of modern science.

The teachings of Socrates, which he expounded at Athens in the late 5th century B.C., formed the inspiration for the works written by Plato in the 4th century B.C. Plato's dialogues attempted to achieve imaginative insights into the general nature of the universe. Plato's successor, Aristotle, sought not so much to speculate about universals as to order and classify the visible world. Between them, Plato and Aristotle laid the foundations of Western philosophy.

FATE AND THE HUMAN CONDITION: THE THEATER AT ATHENS

The tragic dramas written and performed at Athens during the 5th century B.C. represent some of the most enduring of all Classical masterpieces. The first works in the history of the Western theater, many of them still retain the power to grip and move audiences today, some 2,500 years after their creation.

THE DRAMATIC FESTIVALS OF DIONYSUS

The origins of drama go back to the 6th century B.C., in the form of choral hymns in praise of the god Dionysus. For the Greeks the theater retained its connection with worship, and audiences at the performances of the Classical era regarded them as religious rituals. All of the surviving plays were written for one of the two annual festivals of drama dedicated to Dionysus, the god of the theater and of wine.

Each author competing in the festival—competition always played an important part in the Greek attitude toward life—composed four plays, to be performed on a single day. The first three dramas were tragedies, sometimes forming a *trilogy*—three episodes in a single story—and sometimes three different stories with a common theme. The last work in each author's offering was a more lighthearted "satyr" play. The plots of the tragedies were generally based on myths, with which the spectators would already be familiar. Writers could thus employ "dramatic irony," whereby the audience possessed information that was still hidden from the characters.

SOPHOCLES AND *OEDIPUS THE KING*

The dramatist Sophocles (496–406 B.C.) made especially powerful use of this device in *Oedipus the King*. The fact that at the beginning of the play we, the onlookers, already know the terrible secret of Oedipus's birth—how he was fated to kill his father and marry his mother—only increases the tension as the other characters gradually realize what the proud king refuses to see. When Oedipus finally faces the truth and learns who he is, he blinds himself in horror.

Oedipus the King, like many of the Classical tragedies, deals with the nature of suffering and human destiny. Sophocles seems to be pointing out that we cannot avoid our fate, even if we seem to have done nothing to deserve it. For all the glorious possibilities of human achievement, there are aspects of existence beyond our understanding and control. As the play ends and the wretched figure of Oedipus, self-blinded, leaves Thebes to go into exile, the new king of Thebes, Creon, sends him on his way with the warning: "Do not seek to be in control of all things, for what you control will not follow you through life." Yet by blinding himself, Oedipus has regained control and responsibility for his own life: The individual asserts his independence in the face of fate and divine will.

Sophocles was a young man when the Greeks triumphantly defeated the Persians, yet he lived long enough to see the glories of Periclean Athens shattered by the disastrous Peloponnesian War. The inevitability of the tragic

The ancient theater at Epidaurus, before a modern performance. The original building dates to around 350 B.C. At the foot of a natural hillside, into which the rows of seats were cut out of the rock-face, stood a raised stage on which the actors performed. The chorus moved in the circular area between stage and spectators.

Rhoda Sindey/PhotoEdit

events in many of his plays seems to some degree to reflect the collapse of Athenian glory.

AESCHYLUS AND EURIPIDES

If Sophocles seems to epitomize the contradictions of the Golden Age of Athens, the other two dominant figures of 5th-century drama, Sophocles' predecessor Aeschylus (525–456 B.C.) and his successor Euripides (c. 484–406 B.C.), illustrate the spirit of their own times. Aeschylus was old enough to have fought with the victorious Greek troops at the Battle of Marathon, and died when Athens' prestige was at its height. For all the grim violence of his works, they emphasize that although human suffering is inevitable, in the end justice will guarantee the triumph of right—as the Greek victories in the Persian Wars seemed to demonstrate.

The fullest statement of this principle comes in the *Oresteia*, the only complete trilogy by any Classical author to have survived. Aeschylus uses the myth of Agamemnon, king of Argos, and his family to illustrate the passage from primitive society, based on *vendetta*—blood for blood—to civilization and the rule of law.

By contrast, Euripides' plays, written at the end of the 5th century B.C., express the sense of frustration and disillusionment caused by the disasters of war. Many of his works, including *The Suppliant Women*, are openly antiwar statements, describing the senseless miseries that humans inflict on one another. He drew the stories from traditional mythology, but the situations would have had a terrible relevance for the Athenian audiences of the late 5th century B.C., with news of the calamitous Sicilian Expedition ringing in their ears.

Euripides also broke new ground in his sympathetic understanding of the problems of women in a world dominated by men. Characters such as Medea and Phaedra, depicted with vivid psychological realism, struggle against the conventions of a society that tries to make them conform. This concern with the personality and choices of individuals, rather than broad general principles, foreshadows the spirit of 4th-century B.C. philosophy and art. Nor does Euripides have any belief in divine justice. If the gods exist, they are as cruel and irrational as humans.

GREEK COMEDY

Aristophanes (c. 450–385 B.C.), the greatest of Greek comic playwrights, used satire and ridicule, rather than blood and violence, to hammer home an antiwar message similar to that of Euripides.

One of his best-known plays, *Lysistrata*, was written in 411 B.C., the year in which fighting resumed in the Peloponnesian War. Its chief character, Lysistrata, persuades the women of Athens to seize the Acropolis and refuse to make love with their husbands until the men agree to negotiate a peace settlement. Driven by their frustrations, the husbands give in and summon ambassadors from Sparta. As the play ends, Athenians and Spartans dance together in joy at the return of peace. In the real world, seven years were to pass before—far from negotiating—Athens was reduced to abject surrender.

PERFECTION AND REALISM: CLASSICAL PAINTING AND SCULPTURE

By the mid-5th century B.C., artists were producing works that tried to find a perfect compromise between realism and idealism. The notion of perfection of form in the human body became expressed by a canon of proportion, a series of

Scala/Art Resource New York

The Spearbearer, by Polyclitus. Roman marble copy of a bronze original dating to c. 450–440 B.C. The spiral position of the figure, the downturned gaze, and the dreamy expression of the face are all typical of Early Classical art. The Roman copyist has left the right wrist joined to the body with a short support, in fear that otherwise the arm might snap off—not a problem in the bronze original.

ACROSS CULTURES

LORD BYRON IN ATHENS

For the great Romantic poet, George Gordon, Lord Byron (1788–1824), Greece symbolized both a glorious past and a tragic present. By the beginning of the 19th century, Athens and most of mainland Greece had been under Turkish rule for more than two centuries, and Byron was one of the leaders of the campaign to restore Greek independence. As early as 1809 he wrote: "Fair Greece! Sad relic of departed worth/Immortal, though no more! Though fallen, great!"

Courtesy of William Duiker

The same year Byron made his first visit to Greece and found Athens filled with arguments over the transfer of most of the surviving sculptures from the Parthenon to London. In 1799, Byron's fellow-Scot, Lord Elgin, then the British ambassador to Constantinople, had noticed the appalling condition of the 5th-century B.C. relief carvings and negotiated with the Turkish authorities for their removal and shipping to England. The last consignment left Athens in 1809, only weeks before Byron's arrival there. (Elgin's actions still remain highly controversial, and successive Greek governments have demanded that the "Elgin Marbles"—now in the British Museum—be returned to their homeland.) Early in January 1810, Byron climbed the Acropolis and stood before the ruined temple to Athene, the Parthenon. The moment is recaptured in lines at the beginning of Canto (Part) II of his poem, *Childe Harold's Pilgrimage:*

> Goddess of Wisdom! Here thy temple was,
> And is, despite of war and wasting fire,
> And years, that bade thy worship to expire . . .

mathematical formulas that represented ideal beauty of form. The famous Classical sculptor Polyclitus (active mid-5th century B.C.) even wrote a book, *The Canon*, which described the perfect male body. The book is lost, as is the statue of the *Spearbearer*, which he made in bronze to illustrate his text. Many marble copies of his statue have survived, however, which give us a good impression of Classical notions of ideal beauty.

THE PARTHENON SCULPTURES

For the most part, sculpture was public art, intended for display, and the works of the Athenian High Classical period generally aimed to reinforce the pride and self-confidence of Periclean Athens. The finest examples of this spirit are the sculptural decorations of the Parthenon, produced between 448 and 432 B.C. under the general supervision of Phidias (c. 500–c. 430 B.C.).

Look on its broken arch, its ruin'd wall,
Its chambers desolate, and portals foul:
Yes, this was once Ambition's airy hall,
The dome of Thought, the palace of the
    Soul . . .

Byron admits that contemporary Athenians are as indifferent to their noble heritage as the Turkish oppressors: "Unmov'd the Moslem sits, the light Greek carols by . . ." His full wrath, however, is reserved for the British government and its representative:

worse than steel, and flame, and ages slow
Is the dread sceptre and dominion dire
Of men who never felt the sacred glow . . .

The "last, the worst, dull spoiler" is Elgin himself:

Cold as the crags upon his native coast,
His mind as barren and his heart as hard,
Is he whose head conceiv'd, whose hand
    prepar'd,
Aught to displace Athena's poor remains . . .
Ancient of days! August Athena! where,
Where are thy men of might? Thy grand in
    soul?
Gone—glimmering through the dream of
    things that were.

Over the next few weeks Byron traveled in the countryside around Athens, visiting the ancient quarry on Mount Pentelicon from where the stone for the Parthenon sculptures had

come, and recording his impressions of spring-time in Greece:

Sweet are thy groves, and verdant are thy
    fields,
Thine olive ripe as when Minerva smiled,
And still his honied wealth Hymettus
    yields;
There the blithe bee his fragrant fortress
    builds,
The free-born wanderer of thy mountain air.

Greece, Byron said, had made him a poet. In return he would lead the cause of Greek independence. Nor was this to be merely a poetic conceit. After years of campaigning, as European governments began finally to move to free Greece from Turkish rule, Byron returned there in 1824. One of the leaders of the Greek resistance movement named him as "commander in chief of western Greece," and he began to supervise the training of local forces—at his own expense. At the western Greek town of Missolonghi he was struck down by a fever and died there on April 19. Among the last lines he wrote were these:

If thou regret'st thy youth, why *live?*
The Land of honourable Death
Is here—up to the field! And give
Away thy breath.

He was 36 years old.

The Parthenon has three distinct parts decorated with sculpture. In each place the subject and even the technique are different, but the three themes all illustrate the glory of Athens. The frieze running around the entire building, carved in low relief, shows the Great Panathenaic Festival, a religious celebration held every four years.

The statues decorating the scenes on the east and west pediments are freestanding. Both scenes commemorate Athene, the city's patron and protector. The east end shows her birth, while on the west end she persuades the citizens to accept her patronage by presenting them with the olive tree.

The scenes on the *metopes,* stone slabs around the outside wall of the building, are carved in high relief. They, too, although mythological in subject, relate to Athenian greatness. Most of them show episodes from the battle between the Lapiths, a people in central Greece, and the Centaurs

Himmer Fotoarchiv

One of the carved *metopes* decorating the Parthenon, c. 448–442 B.C. Height 4 feet 4 inches (1.34 m). The scene shows an episode from a battle between the Lapiths (a northern Greek tribe) and the centaurs, a mythological race of creatures half horse and half human. One of the great achievements of High Classical Greek sculpture, the scene depicts rapid, violent movement.

Capitoline Meseums, Rome/Barbara Malter

Pothos (*Desire*), by Scopas. Roman copy after Late Classical original of c. 350 B.C. By contrast with *The Spearbearer*, Scopas's figure is more elongated and slender, with a smaller head and a sense of strain that seeks to convey the emotion for which the statue is named.

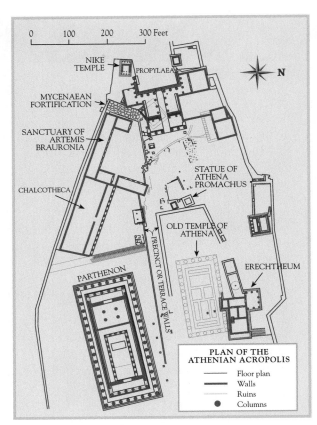

Map 10.1 Plan of the Athenian Acropolis. The Acropolis (high city) had been important in Athenian life since Mycenaean times. After the Persians destroyed the chief buildings there during their occupation of Athens in 480 B.C., Pericles supervised their reconstruction. The Old Temple to Athena was replaced by the Parthenon (447–432 B.C.)—lower left—which occupied (and still occupies) the highest point on the natural rocky hill. The Propylea, at the top of the plan, provided a majestic entrance, while the Ionic Erechtheum (lower right) was built during the second phase of the Peloponnesian War and only finished in 406 B.C.

LATE CLASSICAL ART

By the Late Classical period, with artists using realism to depict emotion, sculptors developed new themes. Praxiteles (active c. 370–330 B.C.) was famous for his statue of Aphrodite nude, one of the first attempts in Western art to depict the sensuality of the female body. The original is lost, but some 50 copies have survived. Another new area for exploration was that of the portrait. Our impressions of Alexander the Great owe much to the works of his official portraitist, Lysippus (active mid-4th century B.C.), known to us through copies.

Perhaps the most renowned of all Late Classical statues, again surviving only in copies, was by Scopas (active mid-4th century B.C.). It was called *Pothos*, or *Desire*, and its intense, yearning pose is in the strongest contrast with the sturdy, stocky *Spearbearer* of a century earlier. The statue dramatically illustrates the Late Classical concern with individual emotional states.

(half men, half horses). This story, which the Greeks used frequently in the years following the Persian Wars, became symbolic of the Greek victory over the Persians: The human Lapiths represent civilization and therefore the Greeks, while the monstrous Centaurs stand for barbarism, in this case that of the Persians.

ARCHITECTURE AND THE TRIUMPH OF ORDER

The Greeks' concern with order and proportion emerges in its most complete form in their architecture. The origins of the Greek architectural orders go back to the period around 650 B.C., when Greek colonizers established their earliest links with Egypt and became familiar with the stone temples there. By 600 B.C., two main styles of Greek temple architecture had developed: the Doric, popular in mainland Greece, and the Ionic, which was widely used in the Asian Greek cities of Ionia.

THE PARTHENON

The Doric order is the simpler and grander of the two. Austere and dignified, with little in the way of superfluous decoration, it reached its climax in the Parthenon. This structure, the crowning monument of Periclean Athens and the largest Doric temple in Greece, stands on the highest point of the Acropolis. Its architects were Ictinus and Callicrates.

The design of the building incorporates several refinements, which give the Parthenon its unique sense of richness. The columns, whose thickest point is not at their base but about one-third of the way up, taper inward. If extended upward, their tops would meet at a single point about two miles above the top of the building. The corner columns are thicker than the others and closer together. The floor, which appears flat, is in fact convex. All of these features correct optical distortions and required the most careful and precise mathematical calculations. Their perfect execution

represents the Classical concern with order and control in its most complete form.

THE IONIC ORDER: THE ERECHTHEUM

The other chief style of Greek architecture, the Ionic, is more decorative and graceful. Unlike the simple, massive Doric columns, Ionic columns are slender and rise from an elaborate base. The ornate carving that decorates an Ionic temple conveys a sense of lightness, by contrast with its more weighty Doric counterpart.

The most important Ionic structure on the Acropolis is the temple known as the Erechtheum, the last building to be completed there. Begun in 421 B.C., after the signing of the Peace of Nicias, it was finished only in 406 B.C., on the eve of Athens' defeat. It commemorates several important religious events in the history of Athens and was the center of the celebration of the Great Panathenaic Festival, illustrated in the sculptures of the Parthenon frieze.

In the South Porch of the Erechtheum, the Ionic love of ornateness reaches its most complete form: The roof rests not on columns but on statues of young women, the famous *caryatids*. They stand quietly with one knee bent, supporting the weight of the building. The Erechtheum, which combines architecture and sculpture, structure and decoration, rejects traditional attitudes and raises new possibilities in a way similar to Euripides' questioning of conventional religious and moral beliefs.

Later Greek architects increasingly preferred the elaborate Ionic order to the more traditional Doric. The greatest building project of the Late Classical Age was the Ionic

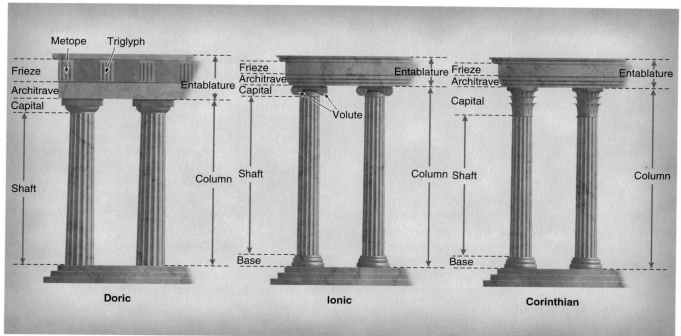

The differences among the Doric, Ionic, and Corinthian orders of Greek architecture. The plain, austere Doric contrasts with the more elaborate, graceful Ionic and Corinthian.

D. Lada/H. Armstrong Roberts

The Porch of the Maidens (*Caryatids*) on the Erechtheum, one of the buildings on the Athenian Acropolis, c. 421–406 B.C. Height of statues 7 feet 9 inches (2.36 m). The graceful figures stand gravely upright, with one knee bent as if to sustain the weight of the building.

Temple of Artemis at Ephesus. An earlier 6th-century B.C. Ionic temple on the same site, built under the Lydian king Croesus, was destroyed by fire in the early years of the 4th century B.C. Work on its reconstruction, one of the Seven Wonders of the Ancient World, began in 356 B.C., the year in which Alexander the Great was born. Worship of the statue of Artemis, which stood in the temple, was still going strong in the 1st century A.D., when St. Paul visited Ephesus.

HISTORY AND PHILOSOPHY: THE GREEK MIND

The Greeks' interest in understanding themselves and their world led them to ask questions that opened up whole areas of human existence for the first time. In fields as diverse as town planning and medicine, government and mathematics, Greek thinkers laid the foundations for later achievements.

THE FIRST HISTORIAN
One of the many results of the Greek victories in the Persian Wars was to inspire the first surviving work of historical writing in the Western tradition. Herodotus of Halicarnassus (484–420 B.C.) migrated from his home in

Greek Ionia to Athens during the time of Pericles. His *History* has as its main subject the Greek victory over the Persians. Herodotus interspersed this chronicle with frequent digressions, including a fascinating account of the Egypt of his times. One tale in the Egyptian section, that of Rhampsinitus and the thief, is the first detective story in our literature.

Like any good scholarly author, Herodotus traveled in order to research his subject; among the places he visited were Babylon, North Africa, and Egypt. Wherever he went, he consulted local archives and questioned experts, and set down in his *History* a faithful record of the information he collected. In cases where his research came up with contradictory explanations, Herodotus did his best to evaluate the relative value of his sources, often including explanations that he did not believe, so that later readers could decide for themselves.

Herodotus's achievement won him the nickname of the "Father of History," but his work was not scientific history in the modern sense. His grasp of military strategy was uncertain, and his geographical information was often confused. He paid little attention to underlying political or economic issues and preferred to interpret events on the basis of personal character. His portrayal of the mad Xerxes is a case in point, with its unforgettable description of the obsessed despot ordering the sea, guilty of wrecking the Persian fleet, to be lashed with chains.

Yet his virtues far outweigh his weaknesses. The *History* dealt with a conflict between Greeks and foreigners, and was written, moreover, at a time of intense national pride, but Herodotus's account always remains impartial and free from racial prejudice. It constantly reveals its author's curiosity about the world around him and the people he meets in it, brought to life by his acute powers of observation. Above all, Herodotus triumphantly vindicates the role of historian as storyteller. His dramatic grasp of the narrative keeps the reader constantly gripped, as the tale reaches its climax in the Greeks' final victories.

THUCYDIDES, THE ANALYTICAL HISTORIAN
The lives of Herodotus and his great successor, Thucydides (c. 460–c. 399 B.C.), overlapped, and both are famous for their accounts of a war. Thucydides' work was his *History of the Peloponnesian War*. Both of them were concerned to establish the accuracy of their accounts, and Thucydides states in his introduction that he conducted careful investigations and questioned eyewitnesses. Furthermore, both writers manage to rise above partisanship and give an impartial account of their subjects.

Yet the spirit of their writings is very different. In part this is the result of the differences between the Persian and Peloponnesian Wars. Herodotus's account emphasizes the belief that the Persians lost because they were morally in the wrong; the Greeks owed their victory to the triumph of right over might. The war that Thucydides described was one in which both sides quickly forfeited any claim to moral ascendancy. Thucydides, although an Athenian and an enthusiastic supporter of Pericles, had no illusions about the corrupting effects of power on his city. His condemnation of the atrocities committed by Athenian forces is unqualified, and he leaves no doubt about the criminal folly of the Sicilian Expedition.

Although Herodotus seemed chiefly motivated by the love of a good story, Thucydides' intentions were more complex. In keeping with the intellectual drive of his times, he used his material to understand human behavior. By analyzing the motives and reactions of those involved in it, he hoped to provide a lesson to posterity based on the behavior and mistakes of his contemporaries. Like the tragic dramatists and Classical artists, Thucydides sought to demonstrate universal principles of human nature.

THE FIRST PHILOSOPHERS: THE PRESOCRATICS

The Western tradition of philosophy was born in the Greek world in the 6th century B.C. For the first time in history, thinkers began to use the power of reason, rather than religion, to ask questions about the universe and human existence. A variety of different schools of thought began to form, which would be known as the "Presocratics." The name refers to the fact that they lived in the century before Socrates, who, together with his pupil Plato, was the first major Western philosopher. The thinkers so described did not belong to a single school of philosophy.

The various Presocratic thinkers are often difficult to understand, largely because their ideas have survived only in fragmentary form. Many of the problems they tried to solve seem scientific, rather than philosophical. How did the world come into being? What is it made of? How does it work? Their answers are varied, but all of them rejected traditional belief in the gods, especially those in human guise. After all, as Xenophanes of Colophon (c. 570–c. 460 B.C.) caustically remarked, "If horses and cattle had hands and could draw, they would draw the gods like horses and cattle."

The ideas of Thales of Miletus (active c. 585 B.C.) were typical of the Materialist school. Thales believed that water is the basic substance of which the universe is made. A later Materialist, Empedocles (active c. 495 B.C.), had a more complicated explanation. There are four basic elements: fire, earth, water, and air. These elements combine through love and separate through strife and war, causing the natural processes of birth, growth, decay, and death. Even if the theories of Thales and Empedocles may seem far-fetched or absurd, the importance of the Materialists is that they were the first people to consider the possibility that the world evolved naturally, rather than having been divinely created.

The most influential Presocratic philosopher was Pythagoras (active c. 550 B.C.), who came from Greek Ionia and settled in southern Italy, where he founded a community. Unlike the Materialists, Pythagoras concerned himself with moral questions. The members of his "commune" had to lead pure and chaste lives, in the spirit of order and harmony for the common good. Basing his theories on the numerical relationship of musical harmonies, Pythagoras claimed that mathematics represented the underlying principle of the universe and of morality—the "harmony of the spheres."

The generation before Socrates saw the last important Presocratic school, that of the Atomists, led by Democritus (active c. 460 B.C.). They believed that the ultimate, unchangeable reality consisted of atoms (tiny invisible particles) and the void, or nothingness. The study—and eventual rejection—of their astonishing insights was to inspire the work of the German physicist Werner Heisenberg in the 1920s on quantum mechanics.

PHILOSOPHY IN ASIA IN THE 6TH CENTURY B.C.

The period of the Presocratics, which laid the foundations for the development of Western philosophy, saw equally crucial innovations in Asia. The traditional religion of the Aryans in India was Hinduism, but in the mid-6th century B.C., a new inspiration appeared in the form of the figure generally known as the Buddha. Born around 563 B.C., his given name was Siddhartha, and his family name Gautama. Leaving his wealthy family, he devoted himself to meditation and self-deprivation, until he eventually devised the principles of living that earned him the name of "the enlightened one," or the Buddha. Basically summarized, Buddhism teaches that life consists of a suffering caused by attachment to worldly things. By meditation and right behavior, humans can eventually overcome the suffering to achieve *nirvana,* or transcendence.

Buddhism was to spread throughout Asia, where it encountered two other world views that were developing during the lifetime of the Buddha himself, as well as Thales and Pythagoras. The two chief schools of Chinese philosophy were founded by Confucius (c. 551–479 B.C.) and Lao-tzu (active c. 570). In contrast to the Buddha, Confucius taught his followers to engage actively with life, serving their families and fellow citizens with love of humanity, altruism, and loyalty. Taoism, the teachings of Lao-tzu, on the other hand, advocated withdrawal and passivity. "The Way" (*tao*) consists of following one's own nature, not distinguishing between good and bad, but accepting both.

THE SOPHISTS

Another approach to philosophical investigation developed during the 5th century B.C., that of the **Sophists**—the "wise men." These were itinerant teachers, who debated the skills of rhetoric and the qualities needed for success in political life. Both Socrates and Plato attacked them for taking fees; teaching skepticism about law, morality, and knowledge; and concentrating on how to win arguments regardless of truth—hence the modern use of "sophistry."

SOCRATES AND PLATO

Toward the end of the 5th century B.C., as the Greek world plunged deeper into war, the search for universal truths took a new direction. At Athens, the teachings of Socrates (c. 469–399 B.C.) questioned traditional values and sought

Perspectives from the Past

Classical Attitudes to Historical Methods

Most of the Greek historians writing before the 5th century B.C. are only names to us, although some fragments of their works have survived. The later historian Dionysius of Halicarnassus (fl. 30–8 B.C.) describes their methods. The most important was probably Hecataeus (fl. c. 500 B.C.), the first Western author to write on history and geography in prose rather than verse.

Hecataeus' works were among those used by Herodotus in preparing his *History of the Persian Wars.* At various points in his narrative, Herodotus refers to the ideas of his predecessors, sometimes with approval, and sometimes to dismiss them. Apart from a general statement of his theme, he sets forth no specific attitude to history, although he makes clear the large amount of "fieldwork" his research involved.

Thucydides, by contrast, sets out his philosophical approach to the writing of history.

Dionysius of Halicarnassus

The best account of early Greek historians comes from the collected writings of Dionysius of Halicarnassus, a Greek scholar of the late 1st century B.C.

Dionysius of Halicarnassus

Before I begin to discuss the work of Thucydides, I want to say a few words about the other historians, his predecessors and contemporaries, which will throw light on the method of the man, thanks to which he was able to excel those who went before him, and his genius. Now of earlier historians before the Peloponnesian War there were a great number in a great many different places. [A list of earlier historians follows.]

These men all adopted a similar method as regards the choice of themes and in talents did not differ very widely from one another, some of them writing Hellenic histories (as they called them), others barbarian histories; but instead of coordinating their accounts with each other, they treated of individual peoples and cities separately and brought out separate accounts of them; they all had the one same object, to bring to the general knowledge of the public the written records that they found preserved in temples or in secular buildings in the form in which they found them, neither adding nor taking away anything; among these records were to be found legends hallowed by the passage of time and melodramatic adventure stories, which to the modern reader seem very naive indeed; the language which they used was for the most part similar (as many of them adopted the same dialect of Greek), clear, simple, unaffected, and concise, appropriate to the subject-matter, and not revealing any elaborate art in composition; there is nevertheless a certain charm and grace which runs through their

to understand the fate of the individual, rather than the community as a whole. When Socrates was executed in 399 B.C. (see Topic 9), his pupil Plato (428–347 B.C.) preserved his memory by writing dialogues in which Socrates appeared as the principal character.

Socrates is a difficult figure to evaluate. He wrote nothing, yet the influence of his teaching and the example of his life are central to Western philosophy. In the difficult years following the death of Pericles, he went around Athens, to public markets and private parties, testing the ideas of anyone who would debate with him—as he put it, "following the argument wherever it led."

Among the enthusiastic band of his youthful disciples was Plato. Sickened by Socrates' death at the hands of the restored Athenian democracy, Plato left Athens in 399 B.C. and devoted the rest of his life to perpetuating the memory

writings, to a greater degree in some than in others, thanks to which their works still survive.

Dionysius of Halicarnassus, *Thucydides*, 5, trans. L. Pearson, in *Early Ionian Historians*, Oxford University Press, U.K. Copyright © 1939.

Herodotus and His Sources

After briefly announcing his subject at the opening of the first book of his History of the Persian Wars, Herodotus provides a leisurely survey of events in the Mediterranean region and the Near East since the time of the Trojan War. He only reaches the Ionian Revolt, which eventually led to the Persian Wars, in the fifth of his nine books. At various points along the way, we learn how he acquired his material.

Why Herodotus Wrote History

In this book, the result of my inquiries into history, I hope to do two things: to preserve the memory of the past by putting on record the astonishing achievements both of our own and of the Asiatic peoples; secondly, and more particularly, to show how the two races came into conflict.

Herodotus, *History*, Book I, 1, trans. A. de Selincourt. Penguin Books Ltd. Copyright © 1954; all translations of Herodotus below are from this source.

Thucydides and Historical Method

Unlike most of his fellow historians, Thucydides was personally involved in many of the events he described in his History of the Peloponnesian War. He served as a general with the Athenian forces, and in 424 B.C. lost the town of Amphipolis to Spartan troops. As a result, "For twenty years I was banished from my country, and associating with both sides, with the Peloponnesians quite as much as with the Athenians, because of my exile, I was thus enabled quietly to watch the course of events."

As the following passage makes clear, Thucydides places high importance on his sense of detached objectivity. He explains his attitude in reporting the many speeches included in the History, few of which he personally heard delivered, and then goes on to describe his general approach to his material.

Thucydides' Historical Method

As to the speeches which were made either before or during the war, it was hard for me, and for others who reported them to me, to recollect the exact words. I have therefore put into the mouth of each speaker the sentiments proper to the occasion, expressed as I thought he would be likely to express them, while at the same time I endeavored, as nearly as I could, to give the general purport of what was actually said.

Of the events of the war I have not ventured to speak from any chance information, nor according to any notion of my own; I have described nothing but what I either saw myself, or learned from others of whom I made the most careful and particular enquiry. The task was a laborious one, because eyewitnesses of the same occurrences gave different accounts of them, as they remembered or were interested in the actions of one side or the other. And very likely the strictly historical character of my narrative may be disappointing to the ear. But if he who desires to have before his eyes a true picture of the events which have happened, and of the like events which may be expected to happen hereafter in the order of human things, shall pronounce what I have written to be useful, then I shall be satisfied. My history is an everlasting possession, not a prize composition which is heard and forgotten.

of his master. Socrates appears in virtually all of Plato's works, which take the form of dialogues between Socrates and a wide variety of other figures. Whether these dialogues literally reproduce Socrates' ideas or are mainly Plato's own inventions has been the subject of endless debate. Modern opinion generally holds that Plato's early works, such as the *Apology*, which purports to be Socrates' defense speech at his trial, probably reflect Socrates' teachings fairly closely.

In his later writings, including the *Republic*, Plato used the figure of Socrates to express his own ideas.

When Plato returned to Athens in 387 B.C., he founded the Academy, forerunner of the modern university, where he spent much of his intellectual life studying the relationship among education, political theory, and government—subjects dealt with in the *Republic* and the *Laws*. In 368 B.C. he had a chance to put his theories into practice, when the young king of Syracuse, Dionysius II, invited the great philosopher to Sicily to create an ideal state. The result was a complete failure, and Plato was soon back teaching in Athens.

The notion of ideals lay behind his most famous idea, the Theory of Forms. According to Plato, in a dimension of existence higher than our own, there are perfect Forms. The objects and phenomena that we perceive in the world around us are pale shadows of the ideal Forms. Thus our notion of justice or beauty reflects the Form of ideal Justice or Beauty. When we recognize these qualities in a person or an action, we are dimly aware of the ideal Form.

ARISTOTLE: PHILOSOPHER AND SCIENTIST

Aristotle (384–322 B.C.), Plato's most gifted pupil, was less interested than his teacher in abstract speculation. He broke with Plato in 335 B.C. and founded a rival institution, the Lyceum. Full-time students came from other parts of Greece to attend Aristotle's morning lecture courses, spending their afternoons doing research in the library, museum, and map collection, which formed part of the Lyceum's facilities. Aristotle gave afternoon lectures to the general public and occasionally took on a private pupil. Among his rare failures was a spell as tutor to the young Alexander the Great: Little of Aristotle's intellectual subtlety seems to have left its mark on the future world conqueror.

In a vast range of works, Aristotle aimed to systematize and classify just about every aspect of human knowledge. In studying the history of animals and describing their parts, he laid the foundation of modern biology, whereas *De Anima (On the Soul)*, which deals with sensation, thought, and imagination, is the first definitive work on psychology. His analyses of literature include the *Rhetoric*, on oratory, and the *Poetics*, the surviving part of which discusses epic and tragedy. The *Physics* is concerned with the elements that compose the universe and the laws by which they operate.

Aristotle laid out his theological ideas in the *Metaphysics*, where he defines God as "thought thinking of itself" and "the Unmoved Mover." He considered the most important human sciences to be ethics and politics. On the latter, he observed: "People came together to live in cities for the sake of life; they continue to do so for the sake of the good life."

The influence of Aristotle's works on later ages was immense. Widely read in Roman times, they were translated into Latin in the Middle Ages and became the basis of Christian theology. St. Thomas's synthesis of Aristotelian philosophy and Christian teachings is still the official philosophical position of the Roman Catholic Church. For much of Western intellectual history, Aristotle has stood, in the words of Dante, as "the master of those who know."

Putting the Classical Vision in Perspective

To some extent the greatness of Classical Greek thinkers and artists lies in the fact that they were often the first in their fields—the first to write history, create naturalistic statues, and invent tragedy and comedy. Yet the Greeks were no mere pioneers, discovering ideas that later figures would perfect. Greek dramas are revived in the modern theater and on television because they provide experiences as intense as any later works in the Western theatrical tradition. The style of Greek architecture continues to influence architects today, in the Post-Modern movement. Furthermore, a resurgence of interest in Classical art—in the form of Neoclassical revivals—has recurred constantly in the history of Western culture, from the Augustan era of 1st-century B.C. Rome to the 19th century in Paris.

The reason for the perpetual appeal of Greek art and ideas is not difficult to understand. The Greeks of the Classical period consciously set out to create works that would transcend the limitations of their own time and make universal statements. Pericles' building plan for the Acropolis, like Thucydides' *History*, was deliberately intended to be a "possession for future generations." It is some measure of the degree to which the Greeks achieved their goal that, 2,500 years later, their works continue to inspire admiration and awe.

Questions for Further Study

1. What contributions did Plato and Aristotle make to the development of philosophy? How did they differ in their approach to the questions they considered?
2. How was sculpture used to decorate the buildings on the Athenian Acropolis? What was the significance of the myths used?
3. How did the works of the chief tragic dramatists reflect the times in which they lived?
4. What were the attitudes of Greek historians to their subject? In which ways—if any—did they differ from those of modern historians?

Suggestions for Further Reading

Barnes, J. *Aristotle*. Oxford, 1982.

Fullerton, Mark D. *Greek Art*. New York, 2000.

Goldhill, S. *Reading Greek Tragedy*. New York, 1986.

Herington, J. *Aeschylus*. New Haven, CT, 1986.

Hurwit, Jeffrey M. *The Athenian Acropolis: History, Mythology and Archaeology from the Neolithic Era to the Present*. New York, 1999.

Lawrence, Arnold W., and R.A. Tomlinson. *Greek Architecture*. Rev ed. New Haven, CT, 1996.

Pollitt, Jerome J. *The Art of Ancient Greece: Sources and Documents*. New York, 1990.

Shapiro, H. *Myth into Art. Poet and Painter in Classical Greece*. New York, 1994.

Stansbury-O'Donnell. *Pictorial Narrative in Ancient Greek Art*. New York, 1999.

InfoTrac College Edition

Enter the search term *classical Greece* using the Subject Guide.

Enter the search term *Aeschylus* using Key Terms.

Enter the search term *Thucydides* using Key Terms.

Enter the search term *Socrates* using Key Terms.

Enter the search term *Plato* using Key Terms.

Enter the search term *Aristotle* using Key Terms.

THE LIFE AND COMMERCE OF CLASSICAL GREECE

For all the urban character of their civilization, the Greek city-states depended for their prosperity on agricultural production. The possession of land was a mark of social status, and farmers learned to cultivate crops suitable for the extremes of summer heat and winter cold. They planted wheat and barley on the plains and cultivated olives and vines on the hillsides.

Although the colonizers of the 8th and 7th centuries B.C. did not leave home with the intention of setting up trading centers, by the time of the Classical period Greek colonies throughout the Mediterranean served as the basis for a complex commercial network. As production increased in mainland Greece, and individual cities began to compete for business at home and abroad, trade rivalry provoked disputes among the leading commercial powers. The long-standing financial competition between Athens and Corinth was the immediate cause of the Peloponnesian War. The effect on trade of this extended conflict between mainland states was to create conditions of extreme economic vulnerability, which led to the undermining of the Classical achievement and—less than a century later—the domination of the Greek city-states by an outside power: Macedon.

In the rich world of Greek mythology and religion, male and female figures—both human and divine—play an equal role. The reality of life in Classical Greece, however, was very different. At Athens, the primary duty of a woman was to marry and produce future citizens. Only men could vote, serve on juries, or hold public office. Women whose family income allowed them the possession of slaves spent most of their lives at home, where they had their own part of the house. Poorer women, who needed to go out to do their shopping or washing, were more likely to spend time socializing with other women as they performed their chores.

Slavery was common at Athens, although only rich citizens owned large numbers of slaves, using them as labor in factories and mines. The average Athenian family had a domestic servant or perhaps an assistant for the workshop or farm. Slaves sometimes rose to become managers of businesses. They were able to acquire personal savings and could win liberation for loyal service. Some who did so had their own slaves, whom in turn they set free.

LAND, FARMING, AND FOOD

Greece is a mountainous country, with little in the way of flat land suitable for farming. Where there are plains, however, as in the region of Thessaly, they are generally very fertile: The limestone folds of rock allow rainwater to seep slowly down the mountainsides and irrigate the flatlands. Each plain of any size contained a city. As Greece emerged from the Bronze Age, most of the good land around these cities was in the hands of the leading families, and its possession distinguished the "best men" from other citizens.

With the revolutions of the Archaic period, ownership of land became more diffused, and by the time of Solon, relatively humble Athenians had their own plots. In a bad year they often had to sell or mortgage their holdings, enabling the newly rich who were not of noble birth to buy them out and build estates for themselves. Solon's reforms were in part an attempt to redress the confusion of debt that had built up (see Topic 8).

By the Classical period the larger cities had developed suburbs, and farmers lived in the country and worked on the land they owned. Thanks to Cleisthenes' constitution (see Topic 8), the Athenian farmers living outside the city could participate fully in the government of their *polis*.

With the exception of Sparta, where the aristocratic Spartiates used their helot serfs to labor on the great estates, most Greeks considered farming an honorable profession, and in many parts of Greece farmers regarded it as their duty to work their own land. As late as the 3rd century B.C., the eminent general and statesman Philopoemen (253–182 B.C.), despite his public responsibilities, insisted on taking part in the harvest on his property. Wealthy Athenian owners of large estates employed slaves or freedmen, whereas small landholders worked their holdings together with their families and perhaps one or two slaves.

Most cities viewed agriculture and its products as of the highest importance to the whole community. Athenian young men, at the age of 18, swore an oath to protect their city's grain, vines, figs, and olives, as well as obey its laws. Furthermore, none but full citizens could own land. Even the richest foreigners and freedmen were not allowed to purchase Athenian farmland.

THE FARMING LIFE

The blazing Greek summers made a winter cycle of cultivation more practical than a summer one. The agricultural year began just before the heavy fall rains. Oxen pulled a wooden plow tipped with iron to break the thin topsoil, while one of the farmer's family members or a slave walked behind to break up the clods, and another worker scattered seed (generally wheat or barley) and covered it with earth.

Throughout the winter and spring farmworkers weeded the fields by hand. The amount of land that one family could cultivate was around 2.5 acres. Harvest time came in May, and all hands labored to gather the grain and carry it to the stone threshing "circles," where oxen were driven round to tread it and separate the wheat from the chaff. The grain harvested had to last until the same time the following year.

Olive trees and vines, with their long roots, could survive the long dry summer, so farmers planted them on the hillsides surrounding the plains. The time for harvesting the fruit was the early fall, and wine made at that time was ready for drinking by the late spring harvesttime. Many farm residents cultivated small plots of beans and peas by their houses and grew fig, apple, and nut trees. Honey, together with figs, provided the most common source of sweetness.

THE GREEK DIET

In general, the average Greek's diet was simple, based chiefly on cereals—a recent study estimates that Greeks of the Classical Age got some 70 percent of their daily caloric

Olive trees on the island of Crete. The mountainous landscape of mainland Greece and the islands is broken by flat plains where it was possible to farm. The extremely dry climate and rocky soil are particularly suitable for the cultivation of olive trees, valuable both for the olives and their oil.

Scene of springtime farming from an Athenian black-figure drinking cup. 6th century B.C. In the center, farmworkers guide a bull with a curved plough attached behind, which is guided by another laborer. Other workers deepen the newly dug furrow and plant seeds in it.

intake from barley, wheat, and millet. In his description of an ideal state, the *Republic,* Plato recommends the "preparation of bread from toasted barley, served on clean vine-leaves." Bread of this kind was unleavened, and often had various herbs and flavorings—thyme, rosemary, olives—mixed in the dough. Sweet loaves contained raisins and dried figs. According to one ancient gourmet, Athenaeus (late 2nd century A.D.?), citizens of Periclean Athens could choose from 72 different kinds of bread.

With starch as the basic filler, the Greeks added a wide variety of accompaniments: beans and lentils (often cooked with pork fat), olives, onions, and cheese, the latter generally of goat milk. Poorer Greeks probably lived mainly on this simple diet, together with anchovies and sardines, washing it all down with water ("the best drink of all," says the poet Pindar), or with *melikraton.* This was a mixture of honey and water, which, when left to ferment, became highly alcoholic.

Prosperous diners had a greater range of possibilities. Athens was famous for its olive oil, which was exported throughout the Mediterranean, while Athenian fruit was known as the sweetest in Greece. Game such as hare and pheasant was popular, but on the whole meat remained a rarity even for the wealthy. Homer's heroic banquets, at which warriors slaughtered whole oxen and roasted them over coals, represented only a dream for most of his audience. Domestic animals were too valuable a part of a farmer's capital to provide more than the occasional treat. Fish was more common. The Greeks caught fresh tuna in their own waters and imported dried tuna from the Black Sea region. Squid, shrimp, and freshwater eels were served for special occasions.

The Greeks always drank their wine diluted and often added honey and spices to it. (The Macedonians did not dilute their wine, which may explain why both Philip and Alexander apparently had problems with alcohol.) They exported it in jars made waterproof by spreading a layer of pine resin on the inside—the origin of the *retsina* (resinated wine) still drunk in Greece today. The chief time to drink wine was at the end of a meal, with the dessert course. The drinking session, or "symposium," often involved singers and musicians, although the most famous of all after-dinner sessions, recorded in Plato's *Symposium,* deals with complex intellectual matters.

MANUFACTURING AND TRADE IN THE GREEK WORLD

Throughout Greek history, cities depended on agriculture to provide the economic basis for their prosperity. Among the most commonly traded commodities in the Greek world were high-quality food products, whose reputation sometimes spread even further afield. In the 3rd century B.C., an Indian king wrote to Athens asking for "some syrup of grapes, some figs, and a philosopher." The Athenians sent

Scene from an Athenian red-figure plate showing a cobbler at work. Late 5th century B.C. The cobbler sits working at his bench, with the tools of his trade (including a hammer and an awl) and other shoes waiting to be repaired hanging above him.

the first two items but not the third, on the grounds that "it is illegal to trade in philosophers."

Trade in manufactured goods increased over time, although it never outweighed the importance of farming. By the Archaic period, individual cities were becoming famous for their products and styles. The Corinthians, for example, manufactured scented oils, which they sold in elegant little flasks. The characteristic decoration and ease of transport of Corinthian perfume flasks made them popular among the Greeks and other neighboring peoples.

By the early 5th century B.C., Athens, Corinth's chief business rival, had captured the market for fine-quality painted pottery and was selling vases and other works of art throughout the Mediterranean. Corinthian resentment at the growing success of Athenian sales in foreign markets, especially those in Italy, was one of the factors that led to the outbreak of the Peloponnesian War in 431 B.C.

Not even the Athenians ever developed any large-scale industry. The two chief categories of goods manufactured for export were pottery and weapons, produced in small numbers by individual craftsmen in their workshops. Assisted by one or two slaves, they filled orders tailored to the requirements of individual customers. The largest production facility we know of in Periclean Athens was a shield factory owned by a resident alien, where the workforce consisted of 120 slaves.

OVERSEAS TRADE

The Greek city-states organized their business dealings by setting up trading posts abroad, competing with one another in the foreign market. Excavators digging at Al Mina, a Greek settlement in northern Syria, have uncovered residential quarters and warehouses. Most of the pottery stored there for sale in the 6th century B.C. consisted of exports from Corinth and the Greek cities of Ionia. The traders of Al Mina enlarged their settlement around the time of the Greek victories in the

Persian Wars, and the bulk of the vases stored in the new warehouses of the 5th century B.C. came from Athens.

The same picture emerges in the western Mediterranean. The Greek cities founded in Italy by the colonists of the 8th and 7th centuries B.C. owed their origins mainly to overcrowding and political disputes in the home communities. By the Classical period, however, the Greek colonies of southern Italy and Sicily formed a complex network of commercial bases. Goods produced in mainland Greece and the islands were exported to these colonies and sold both to the western Greeks and to other peoples in Italy.

Among the Greeks' most enthusiastic customers in Italy were the prosperous Etruscans (see Topic 13). According to the Roman writer Pliny the Elder, a Corinthian aristocrat called Demaratus actually settled in the Etruscan city of Tarquinia shortly before 600 B.C., bringing with him a painter and three clay modelers. Demaratus married a local woman and opened a business, thereby introducing the technique of clay sculpture to central Italy.

The sale of Greek art in Etruria continued to grow in volume during the Classical period. At the time of the Persian Wars, many Greeks fled from the troubles in the Ionian cities of Asia Minor to seek refuge in the West. Some opened shops in the Etruscan cities to supply a market that had learned to appreciate the quality of imported Greek pottery. Others began to trade in reverse, buying raw materials such as iron and minerals from the Etruscans, and even the occasional Etruscan work of art, and taking them back to Greece for sale there. Etruscan bronzes have been found at Olympia and Lindos (Rhodes) and even on the Acropolis at Athens.

MINING
The only economic activity requiring large numbers of workers was mining. The silver mines of Laurion, to the southeast of Athens, were under state ownership. Small operators leased sections from the state and worked them with slave labor, paying royalties on their finds to the Athenian treasury. Several thousand slaves worked 10-hour shifts underground—the time has been calculated from the capacity of their oil lamps.

The mines were a major factor in the Athenian economy. The discovery in 483 B.C. of an extremely rich vein of silver helped fund Themistocles' program to build up the Athenian navy, and thereby defeat the Persians a few years later. Toward the end of the 5th century B.C., as the Peloponnesian War reached its final stages, the slaves of the silver mines took advantage of the desperate conditions at Athens to escape. With their silver supply cut off, the Athenians had to melt down bronze and even gold statues to make coins.

SEXUALITY AND FAMILY LIFE IN CLASSICAL ATHENS

Our picture of private life in Classical times is chiefly based on the evidence from Athens. The aim of the Athenian laws and customs relating to the marriage of Athenian citizens was the production of future citizens. Marriages were the responsibility of the guardian of the bride, who was her nearest male relative (usually her father), and the groom. Women often married two or three times, and a dying husband would sometimes select his soon-to-be widow's next partner.

THE BASIS OF MARRIAGE AND DIVORCE
A responsible father began the search for a suitable husband for his daughter at her birth. If there seemed no prospect of contracting a marriage, a female baby would sometimes be left to die. The natural rate of infant mortality meant that this outcome was generally achieved by neglect, rather than a deliberate act. Some infant females were reared to become slaves, while on occasion prostitutes would bring up girls and train them in their own profession.

The principal factor in arranging a marriage was economic, and the father or other male relative had to provide the groom with a dowry that could guarantee his future wife's maintenance. Poor men often turned to wealthy relatives for help. In certain cases the state provided dowries to the daughters of men in public service. Management of the dowry itself passed directly to the groom on marriage, who used the interest on the money, usually calculated at 18 percent, to maintain his wife. If he died, or the couple divorced, the money returned to the woman's guardian, to be used for any future remarriage.

Divorce was common and easily attained by men and lacked any social stigma for them, as the termination of Pericles' marriage proves (see Topic 9). Pericles and his wife

Clay plaque from one of the Greek cities of Southern Italy. 4th–3rd century B.C. The plaque shows a husband and wife side by side: The husband is looking straight ahead, while the wife turns to catch the viewer's gaze. Their children are shown in miniature standing in front of them, bearing an offering cup. Note the elaborately carved chair.

Marriage in Classical Athens

LOUIS COHN-HAFT   Smith College

Scholars generally agree on these basic facts: Athenians (and Greeks in general) were monogamous. Marriage was between a man and a woman of citizen family. Normally, but not necessarily, marriage was celebrated by a wedding, with family in attendance, with religious ritual, and with feasting and ceremony. Normally a dowry, in the form of a substantial sum of money or of property, accompanied the bride, to be administered by the bridegroom but remaining always the wife's property, eventually to be inherited by her children.

The bride was usually quite young, 14 to 17 years of age, whereas the bridegroom seems generally to have been a man of mature years, from 30 to 35, often considerably older. Marriage was arranged, a contractual agreement between two men, the bridegroom and the father of the bride. The marital couple may not even have laid eyes on each other before their wedding day.

But marriage was viewed as not only setting up a new family and home but also as cementing or creating a relationship between families. Marriage between members of families closely related by friendship or by blood was common. Marriage between first cousins, between uncle and niece, and even between half-siblings was not merely permitted but often enough occurred. Perhaps therefore the depiction of a marriage between strangers may be softened because a prior acquaintance of the couple at family gatherings must not have been unusual.

But what was an Athenian marriage really like? What was the personal relationship between spouses? The privacy of an Athenian home was carefully guarded,

so that we know very little about the daily life that went on behind closed doors, and that little is biased, fragmentary, and often ambiguous.

The scholarly effort to understand the reality of Athenian marital relations is guided by two items, one a fact, the other an attitude. The fact is that wives are after all a particular category of women, and the subordination of women to men in Athenian society is solidly established beyond question. The attitude is that of the modern historian and is a combination of ideology and prejudice and the play of imaginative hunches.

The position of women in Classical Athens is an affront to the modern Western mind. Not only was a woman barred from participation in public life; worse, her legal status was permanently that of a minor, that is, she was under the guardianship of a man all her life—first her father, then a husband, finally often enough a son. She was overprotected to the degree that, in theory at least, she was not able to leave her home unescorted. Her guardian (the Greek word is *kyrios*, literally "lord and master") had legally complete control over her every action. A woman could be accused of crime, tried by a court, found guilty and punished, but she could not defend herself or testify in person in the court.

For some modern historians, these facts settle the matter. For them, the Athenian home is a patriarchal tyranny, in which wife, children, and servants are all heaped together under the absolute rule of a being who regards himself as innately superior. The wife's lot is to

divorced by mutual consent, but in theory the law permitted either party to initiate court proceedings. In practice, however, divorce was much more difficult for women and brought greater stigma, as Euripides' play *Medea* suggests. A man divorcing his wife returned her to her male guardian. Women wanting to divorce their husbands needed a male citizen (generally their father) to bring the case before the courts.

Children born to Athenian couples were the property of their father. When a marriage ended—either in divorce or in the death of the husband—any children remained in the father's house, leaving the woman free to remarry and produce children for her new husband. The evidence of

skeletal remains suggests that the average Athenian woman gave birth to 4.6 infants, with an infant mortality rate of 1.6, leaving 3 survivors per female. Abortion was one of the means used to limit the birthrate: Aristotle distinguished between abortions performed before the fetus felt sensation, which were acceptable, and those performed later in a pregnancy, of which he did not approve.

SEXUALITY IN PERICLEAN ATHENS

The laws regulating sexual behavior in Athens went back to the time of Solon. Because the aim of marriage was to produce legitimate Athenian children, both adultery and rape

be bullied and humiliated, treated with contempt by a worldly, experienced older man who can find no basis for a personal relationship with an ignorant, inexperienced, childish female. The husband can barely bring himself to perform the duty of breeding children with this inferior creature, whom he despises. He spends most of his time with his male friends. He seeks sexual pleasure with prostitutes trained to give pleasure and to be witty and amusing in the bargain, or with young boys. Some historians go so far as to find misogyny, the hatred of women, a fundamental aspect of Athenian male ideology. This is, to be sure, an extreme view, but it is influential. One is probably correct in saying that the general run of current historical opinion is that the daily life of the Athenian wife was empty and miserable, worse even than that of most wives in most societies throughout the centuries of history, in almost all of which women have been regarded as inferior to men.

This writer believes that the true picture is significantly more complex. Such contemporary evidence that has come down to us is found mainly in two very different forms of literature, drama and courtroom oratory. In drama, in tragedy and also in comedy, women are depicted as accepting their statutory inferiority with something less than passive acquiescence. There are despairing, cruelly used, weeping women, but there are also women of strong character who act independently and vigorously—although not always with success. Scholars have for generations used these fictional characters to arrive at very diverse conclusions as to what they tell us about actual Athenian women. Indeed, the very fact that the patron deity of Athens, from whom the city took its name, was a female, the goddess Athene, has served as testimony to support entirely opposing views as to what that tells us about the treatment of Athenian women by their men.

The trial orations, which rank far below dramatic poetry as a literary form, have received—perhaps for that reason—less attention by historians, many of whom are content, if they cite them at all, to observe that women are spoken about but can never speak for themselves. But women, wives too, are spoken about occasionally, and even quoted in the orations. It is noteworthy that if they are women of citizen family they are regularly alluded to with respect, now and then with affection. They are sometimes depicted as competently engaged with their husbands in business and financial matters; occasionally widows ran their own affairs. They are sometimes referred to, even directly quoted, playing a forceful, dynamic role in family affairs.

A most interesting illustration of this attitude occurs in an oration, not in a trial, but in a political debate. The celebrated orator and politician, Demosthenes, accused his rival, Aeschines, while on a diplomatic mission during a war, of having at a drunken party laid indecent hands on a captive woman, a citizen of the enemy city. The speech that Aeschines made in reply happens also to have come down to us. Aeschines says that if even one person among his hearers believed that even drunk he could have done such a thing to a free person or indeed to any human creature, he would not think his life worth living. A grand rhetorical exaggeration, to be sure, but certainly Aeschines did not expect his listeners, who were his male fellow citizens, to laugh at him; he was expressing an attitude that he expected would win their approval and respect.

The probability, then, is that however lacking an Athenian wife was in active rights, and however lordly and masterful her husband may have been in his dealings with her, she may have been at least immune from physical abuse.

To sum up, marriage in Classical Athens appears on balance to have been surely no worse, and in some respects probably less burdensome, for the wife than in most of the male-dominated societies that history records.

---

were held to be crimes against the state, as well as against the father and husband. The husband of a woman who had either been convicted of adultery or raped was required by law to divorce her. The woman could not speak in her own defense but had to persuade her male guardian to represent her. Few women divorced on these grounds had any chance of remarriage. A man responsible for raping another man's wife received a fine, while the punishment for adultery was more severe. The husband was acquitted if he killed his wife's seducer in passion.

Custom required citizen couples to have sexual relations on average no more than three times per month, pre-sumably to maintain a low birthrate. Few women were likely to run the risks inherent in adultery; they were closely watched. There is no evidence for female homosexuality at Athens, although contemporary societies at Sparta and in Mytilene, a town on the island of Lesbos, did not discourage it: hence the term *lesbian*.

Because Athenian men generally did not marry before the age of 30, young Athenian males' sexual activity involved prostitutes and slaves. Married men also made use of prostitutes, and their female slaves were available either for their own use or that of their friends. Greek culture assumed that most men practiced both heterosexual and homosexual relations as a normal aspect of their sexuality. Excess in either was discouraged, but no moral stigma was attached to homosexuality.

PRIESTESSES, WIVES, AND PROSTITUTES: THE ROLES OF GREEK WOMEN

Archeological evidence from Greece in the Bronze Age suggests that the religion of that period may have centered on a mother goddess, whose chief votaries were priestesses. The myths of later times confirm the importance of female deities in Greek religious beliefs.

THE FEMININE AND THE DIVINE

The mother goddess of Minoan Crete (see Topic 7) was probably the ancestor of the Greek earth deities Ge—the name means "earth"—Hera, and Demeter. (Some scholars have disputed the connection between Bronze Age and Classical religion, or even the existence of a prehistoric mother goddess cult, and the question remains open.) All three Greek goddesses symbolized aspects of agricultural fertility, and Hera and Demeter are among the "Twelve Olympians," the chief deities of Greek (and later Roman) religion.

Hera, the wife of Zeus, father of gods and men, was the protectress of marriage, and thus constantly tried by her own husband's infidelity. Zeus, like other gods and heroes, had both heterosexual and homosexual affairs. For all her rank and power, Hera followed conventional Greek custom by remaining faithful to her promiscuous mate. Aphrodite, the only other Olympian goddess to marry, represents a very different attitude toward male-female relations. As the goddess of beauty and sexual passion, Aphrodite seduced a chain of gods and mortals, including no less a figure than Ares, god of war. Her importance as a symbol of sexuality in all its forms made her both sacred to prostitutes and, especially in Hellenistic times, a goddess of marriage.

The other two major female deities are the virgin goddesses Athene and Artemis. Athene is a complex figure, born uniquely from the head of Zeus and combining aspects of male and female. She is the patroness of weaving and other domestic crafts, and her gift of the olive—fertility symbol—to Athens won her the city's name. At the same time, she is a warrior goddess, often portrayed fully armed and famous for her wisdom. As commentators have noted, Athene represents the woman who finds fulfillment in a man's world by sublimating her femininity and acting like a man, and she even appears in some myths in male disguise. Her chastity is thus the denial of her sexuality. Artemis, by contrast, symbolizes purity. At the same time she watches over women's physical welfare, helping them in the moments of shared female experience such as menstruation and childbirth.

WOMEN AND WORSHIP

The worship of these and other deities was practically the only aspect of public life in which women of Classical times could take part. The cults of Athene and Demeter, in particular, had priestesses as their leading figures, and women commonly participated in religious festivals.

The chief priestess of the patron goddess of Athens held one of the city's most prestigious offices. On several occasions, chief priestesses played an important political role in Athenian affairs, as when in 480 B.C. the chief priestess of the day endorsed Themistocles' proposal to evacuate Athens before the Battle of Salamis.

The chief religious festival of the Athenian calendar was the Panathenaea, celebrated annually on Athene's birthday. Every fourth year the Greater Panathenaea saw the replacement of the sacred robe draped around a statue of Athene in the Erechtheum. The task of weaving this robe fell to a group of four young girls known as the *Arrephorai*. Aged between seven and eleven, they were chosen annually from noble families to live and work in the temple of Athene. Other young women carried the "sacred baskets" in the annual processions, as depicted in the sculptured frieze of the Parthenon.

The most important center for the worship of Demeter was at Eleusis, outside Athens, where celebration of the Eleusinian Mysteries drew women, men, children, and Greek-speaking slaves from all parts of the Greek world. The secret nature of the ceremonies—participants had to swear not to "reveal the mysteries"—means that we know little about them. They seem to have involved a fertility cult based on the annual death and rebirth of the crops, with an ear of grain as their central symbol. This illustrated the myth of Demeter's daughter, Persephone, who died every winter, only to be reborn in the spring. At the head of the cult was the chief priestess of Demeter, and women performed many of the most sacred rituals, including dances and a dramatic enactment of Demeter's separation from her daughter, followed by their blissful reunion.

PRIVATE LIVES

With the exception of their participation in religious events, women had no role in public life at Athens. They could not vote, take part in debates, hold office, or sit on juries. Respectable women of the upper and middle classes did not appear in public and spent most of their time at home. Even there, they were confined to the women's quarters, generally located on an upper floor and away from the street (female slaves lived alongside their mistresses). The only men whom they could meet were close relatives. Any man who broke this custom by coming into the presence of a free Athenian woman in the house of another man was tried as a criminal. No women, even upper-class Athenians, could inherit or own property. It was attached to them and ultimately went to their children. Although in general young males had a better chance of receiving an education, some women were educated and many men were illiterate.

Wealthy women supervised the performance of domestic work at home, whereas most Athenian housewives ran

Clay plaque with scene of a woman putting away clothes in a chest. 4th–3rd century B.C. Various domestic objects hang on the wall behind her, including a drinking cup and a long-handled mirror. The two small holes at the top center suggest that this plaque may have been used to decorate a wall.

their own homes. Cooking, cleaning, the care of children, and the nursing of the sick occupied most of their daily lives. The fetching of water was a female task, but because visits to the fountain might lead to casual encounters and gossip, upper- and middle-class women normally sent their female slaves. Poorer women went themselves. The only domestic activity performed by men was shopping, so that women could avoid public markets and strange shopkeepers. Athenian female citizens did not work unless they had no economic choice, and the jobs working women performed were generally extensions of their activities at home, such as washing, spinning, selling food, and nursing.

Athenian males came of age at 18. In legal terms, Athenian females always remained minors. Although women in Classical Athens could inherit property or receive it by gift, all control of their financial affairs was in the hands of their husbands or male guardians. (In Sparta, by contrast, noble Spartiate women managed their own estates.) The gap between Athenian husbands and wives was made even more acute by the lack of female education. When an Athenian male wanted to enjoy the companionship—intellectual, social, or erotic—of a sophisticated, cultured woman, he turned to a prostitute.

COMPANIONS TO MEN
By the Archaic period, prostitution was already established as an institution at Athens, with state-run brothels staffed

by female slaves. In Classical Athens prostitution was by no means confined to slaves, and large numbers of noncitizen women and freed slaves earned a living in this way. Some of them, women whose physical beauty was accompanied by intellectual and artistic gifts, became known as *hetairai*, "companions to men." The most famous of these was Aspasia, Pericles' companion (see Topic 9), and several other *hetairai* had more freedom and greater influence than the wives of Athenian citizens—a commentary on the status of freeborn Athenian women.

In some cases, Athenian men developed long-term relationships with noncitizen women, and couples lived together. The law offered such unions the same protection as regular marriages. Rape or seduction of a female partner brought the same penalties as similar acts committed against a legitimate wife. By the time of Pericles, however, children born to unmarried couples did not have the right to Athenian citizenship.

Successful prostitutes were the only women in Athens who could maintain their financial independence and control their own income, and they could choose whom they met. Furthermore, they were more likely to raise girl children than boys and to save the unwanted infant females of others. They trained these children in their own trade, to support them when they could no longer attract customers. Some of the *hetairai* became famous in their own right. Phryne, one of the most beautiful 4th-century B.C. prostitutes, was the lover of the sculptor Praxiteles and, it was said, inspired his great statue of Aphrodite. She also posed for his friend, the painter Apelles. On the other hand, the lives of many of the prostitutes and courtesans were generally miserable and often brutal.

FREEDOM AND SLAVERY IN GREEK SOCIETY

In the mid-5th century B.C., as the Greeks prepared for war, the overall population of Athens stood at around 250,000. Of these, some 125,000 were citizens—60,000 men and their wives—and 125,000 slaves (all figures are rough estimates). Slightly more than half of the slaves, some 65,000, were engaged in domestic labor. Of the rest, 50,000 worked in shops and factories, and the remaining 10,000 labored in the mines. The remainder of the population consisted of resident aliens.

The treatment of the mineworkers was brutal, but in general the other slaves in domestic employment at Athens shared the living conditions of their employers. The Spartans, whose treatment of their serfs was even more inhumane, scoffed that in the streets of Athens you could not tell a slave from a citizen. Male domestic slaves accompanied their masters on the daily trip to the market, whereas female slaves lived in the women's quarters of the house. By comparison with the grim conditions of ancient Egypt, or the work camps and farm estates of the Roman Empire, or the cotton plantations of the 19th-century American Deep South, even the slaves engaged in agricultural labor seem to have worked alongside their employers and shared their lifestyles.

Yet there still remained a vast difference between the lives of even the poorest citizens and slaves. Employers were under no obligation to treat their slaves humanely. Beating, chaining, and starvation were common ways used to control them. In the mines, many slaves were literally worked to death. If a slave's evidence was required in a law court, it had by law to be given under torture. Nor did slaves have any sexual rights, and the owners of both male and female slaves could make sexual use of their "property" or make them available to others.

Putting the Life and Commerce of Classical Greece in Perspective

Like all ancient cultures—and many modern ones—Greek society in general, and Athenian in particular, was hierarchical. The only residents who enjoyed all the benefits of life at Athens were male citizens. Foreign residents, who were numerous, were given the same legal protection as citizens and shared the same obligations to pay taxes and perform military service. They could not own land or houses, however, but had to rent them. Foreign women often led freer lives than their Athenian counterparts.

The fate of slaves at Athens depended on that of their employers. For many poor citizens, life must have seemed not much more free than for the slaves in domestic employment alongside whom they worked. The only entire category of Athenian resident to suffer from serious underprivilege—and, of course, it was a vast one—was that of female citizens.

Socrates praised the democratic nature of public life at Athens, with its Assembly made up of "laundrymen, shoemakers, carpenters, smiths, peasants, and shopkeepers." When Socrates' wife, Xanthippe, came to visit him in prison before his execution, to see him for the last time, the philosopher told his friends to take her away, before settling down to spend his last hours surrounded by his male friends. The gulf between husband and wife was far greater than that between the aristocratic Pericles and the laundrymen and peasants, sitting and debating together in the Assembly.

Questions for Further Study

1. What were the attitudes in Classical Greece toward gender, marriage, and the status of women? How did they affect Greek society?
2. What role did agriculture play in the development of Greek life?
3. How important was trade in the economies of the Greek city-states? What political impact did it have on political relations among them?

Suggestions for Further Reading

du Bois, P. *Sowing the Body: Psychoanalysis and Ancient Representations of Women*. Chicago, 1988.
Connolly, Peter, and Hazel Dodge. *The Ancient City. Life in Classical Athens and Rome*. New York, 1998.
Frost, F. *Greek Society*, 5th ed. Lexington, MA, 1997.

Garlan, Y. *Slavery in Ancient Greece*. Ithaca, NY, 1988.
Just, R. *Women in Athenian Law and Life*. London, 1990.
Keuls, E.C. *The Reign of the Phallus: Sexual Politics in Ancient Athens*. New York, 1985.
Manville, P.B. *The Origin of Citizenship in Ancient Athens*. Princeton, NJ, 1990.
Reeder, Ellen D., ed. *Pandora: Women in Classical Greece*. Baltimore, 1995.
Stewart, Andrew. *Art, Desire and the Body in Ancient Greece*. New York, 1997.

InfoTrac College Edition

Enter the search term *classical Greece* using the Subject Guide.

ALEXANDER AND THE HELLENISTIC AGE

The century following the accession of Alexander in 336 B.C. marked one of the major turning points in Western history. Within a hectic few years, the young Macedonian king invaded Asia, conquered the most powerful empire of the ancient world—that of the Persians—and put together a kingdom stretching from Greece to India.

With Alexander's premature death, his conquests split into a series of warring successor states, whose rulers—Alexander's former generals—struggled for power. Three ruling dynasties emerged from the conflict: the European Antigonids, the Asian Seleucids, and the Ptolemies of Egypt.

The foundation of the culture that developed in these states, known as Hellenistic, was Greek. Yet although it shared a common language, Greek, and a single basic intellectual tradition, that of 5th-century B.C. Athens, the Hellenistic world was truly international. It was strongly influenced by Achaemenian (Persian) and Egyptian culture and provided the basis for the growth of the Roman Empire in western Asia and the eventual spread of Christianity.

The economic and social basis of the Hellenistic kingdoms remained agriculture, but the city, modeled on the Greek city-state, became of increasing importance. (The term **Hellenistic** is used to refer to the history and culture of the peoples as "Hellenized," that is, brought under Greek influence, by Alexander's conquests.) The growth of urban centers such as Alexandria and Antioch reinforced, in fact, the importance of agriculture and food production while spreading the Greek concept of civilization. At the same time, trade and industry flourished, particularly in Asia.

The impact of non-Greek religious ideas from western Asia and Egypt on traditional Classical patterns of thought stimulated new forms of religious experience. Some of these new forms, like the worship of state rulers, arose for political reasons. Others represented a wide range of philosophical responses to a changing world.

The wealthy capitals of the Hellenistic kingdoms—Alexandria, Pergamum, and others—became centers of research in the pure and applied sciences. There were major breakthroughs in astronomy, medicine, and mathematics, while the search for more efficient weapons and defense systems led to progress in engineering.

In all of these respects, the Hellenistic Age marked the diffusion on three continents of the cultural legacy of Classical Greece, a process that was to continue with the rise of Rome.

ALEXANDER THE GREAT AND HIS EMPIRE

When Alexander succeeded his father Philip as king of Macedon in 336 B.C., his first challenge came from the Greek city-states that Philip had conquered. Taking advantage, as they thought, of the young and inexperienced new ruler—Alexander was 20 at the time of his accession—the Greeks rose in revolt. Alexander's response was immediate. Macedonian troops poured south and stormed Thebes, and Alexander gave orders for the ancient city to be razed to the ground. Only the temples and the house of the 6th-century B.C. poet Pindar were to be spared. The other Greek cities, horrified, abandoned any further notion of opposition.

ALEXANDER BUILDS AN EMPIRE

With Greece secured, Alexander turned his attention east, and in 334 B.C. launched a massive invasion of Asia. By 331 B.C. his forces had crushed the Persian army, driven Darius, the Great King, into flight, and occupied the royal cities of Babylon and Persepolis. The most powerful empire of the ancient world was now in Macedonian hands.

For the next five years Alexander continued his drive east, simultaneously conquering new territory and fighting to hold on to land already won. Finally, in 326 B.C., after barely winning a ferocious combat in the Punjab, the weary

Portrait of Alexander the Great. The sculpture dates to c. 160 B.C. and shows the way in which later ages remembered Alexander, rather than providing a literal portrait. His eyes are turned inward, in deep meditation or concentration, while the furrowed brow and untidy hair, casually thrown back, convey a sense of energy.

Hirmer Fotoarchiv

army refused to go any farther. Alexander's men had been badly scared by the Indians' secret weapon, a herd of 200 trained elephants. Even Alexander's combined glamour and ruthlessness could not drive them on, and the expedition returned to Persia.

Alexander set up his court in Babylon. In 327 B.C., to celebrate his "marriage of East and West," Alexander married Roxana, daughter of a Persian noble. Three years later, in 324 B.C., he assigned noble Persian brides to his officers: Some 9,000 weddings took place on a single day at Susa, as Greek priests and Persian magi prayed together. Only Alexander's death of a fever in 323 B.C. prevented the addition of yet another territory, for he spent his last months planning the conquest of Arabia.

Alexander's empire stretched from western Greece to India, from the Caucasus to the Sahara. He seems to have had no particular plan for its future, except to add more conquests, and never planned how to organize so vast an assortment of peoples and cultures. Long before his death, his Greek and Macedonian followers came to resent the influence of the old Persian aristocracy, many of whom Alexander left in their former positions of power. Nor did they relish the pomp and splendor of court life at Babylon, with Alexander encouraging his subjects to worship him as a god.

News of Alexander's death stunned his contemporaries. One Athenian refused to believe it, remarking bitterly that if it were true the stench would fill the world. Alexander had administered his conquests by improvising as circumstances evolved. The only members of his family left—a mentally limited half-brother and a son born a month or so after his death—were incapable of continuing his work, and it is a measure of his grip on the imagination and the loyalty of his subjects that the overwhelming majority of them remained obedient to his successors. For centuries after his death, the memory of his character and achievements—often exaggerated, to be sure—remained vivid from the central Mediterranean to western India.

THE SUCCESSOR STATES: CHALLENGE AND COMPETITION

Any chance of a united Macedonian Empire surviving its founder soon disappeared, as Alexander's generals killed off his surviving family and began to battle for supremacy and the chance to prove themselves worthy to succeed him. The first two to split off their own territory were Ptolemy (ruled 323–285 B.C.), Alexander's intelligence officer, who won Egypt, and Seleucus (ruled 306–281 B.C.), commander of the footguards, who seized the former Persian possessions in Asia. A succession of generals struggled for control of Macedon, which fell in the end to Antigonus Gonatas (ruled 276–239 B.C.). A generation after Alexander's death, his empire no longer existed.

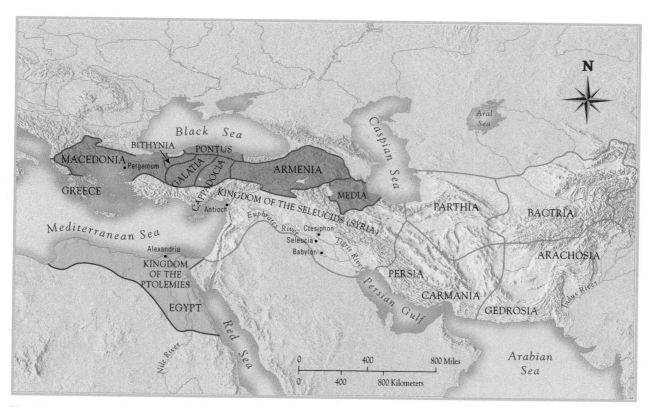

Map 12.1 The Hellenistic World. Note the three chief Kingdoms into which Alexander's conquests were divided, those of the Macedonians (Northern Greece), the Ptolemies (Egypt), and the Seleucids (Asia Minor). Only Ptolemaic Egypt was small enough to remain united. The others soon split into separate states, of which Pergamum (on the west coast of Asia Minor) was to become among the richest. All of these Kingdoms eventually fell under Roman rule.

PTOLEMAIC EGYPT

Ptolemaic Egypt was the most durable of the Hellenistic kingdoms. Under the pharaohs, Egypt had long been ruled by absolute monarchs, and Ptolemy took advantage of the tradition. He established a highly organized bureaucracy at his capital, Alexandria. Alexander had founded the city in 332 B.C., and Ptolemy reinforced his claim to the succession by hijacking the royal body on its journey back to Macedon and had Alexander buried in Alexandria. The lavish tomb that Ptolemy constructed for his late master has never been found.

Ptolemy's other great building project at Alexandria was the "Temple of the Muses," or "Museum," which included the famous library containing copies of everything of note ever written in Greek that had survived. A famous center for research, the library attracted scholars and students from the entire Hellenistic world.

Other foreigners—traders, soldiers, technicians—flocked to Egypt as Ptolemy's efficient administration produced growing prosperity. A complex tax system was in the hands of traveling officials, who were encouraged to be fair in the exaction of revenue.

Within a generation, Ptolemy managed to combine a backward country of poor farming peasants with a small, all-powerful aristocracy. The peasants continued to live in miserable conditions, excluded as they were from many of the benefits of Hellenization. Alexandria remained the only real center of political and cultural life because of all the successor states, Ptolemaic Egypt was the least urbanized. Some of the Greek men who emigrated there married local women, and their children combined the language of their fathers with the religious practices of their mothers. Greek was the official language. The only Ptolemaic ruler ever to speak Egyptian was the last, Cleopatra (ruled 51–30 B.C.; see Part Topic 15). Nonetheless, native Egyptians could rise in the civil service and, from the late 3rd century B.C., serve alongside Greeks in the army.

ASIA UNDER THE SELEUCIDS

Ptolemy's task in Egypt was made easier by the inherent nature of his kingdom, which was relatively small and with a single native ethnic people. The Asiatic parts of Alexander's empire were vast and sprawling, encompassing many different races, while the enormous wealth of many of its regions attracted a succession of rival kings and generals. Largest of all the Hellenistic kingdoms at the death of Alexander, Seleucid Asia shrank during most of its history as the outlying provinces fell to invaders. Furthermore, the Greeks who emigrated and settled there were never able to impose a cultural or even a linguistic unity. Greek was the official language, but a wide variety of local languages continued to flourish, and Seleucid rulers had to make many concessions to differing local traditions.

Its first ruler, Seleucus, died in 280 B.C., assassinated by one of Ptolemy's sons, after founding a new capital at Antioch, named after his son and successor, Antiochus (ruled 280–261 B.C.). Successive rulers tried to construct an artificial sense of unity. As their losses increased, Seleucid kings increased the lavishness of their court, to impress their subjects and enemies alike, and claimed divine status for themselves. In the end, later Seleucid monarchs became trapped in the elaborate ritual and ceremony, buried beneath the masses of attendants and gold ornaments. Symbolically they represented the "living law of the land." In practice, the various regions of their empire increasingly went their own way. By the time the Romans unified Asia under their rule, little was left of the former Seleucid Empire except Syria.

MACEDON AFTER ALEXANDER

The end of its royal family plunged Macedon, the third of the Hellenistic kingdoms, into immediate chaos, from which it eventually emerged under the efficient and organized rule of Antigonus Gonatas. Antigonus resisted the temptation to follow the example of the Seleucids and introduce a cult of king worship. He replied to a poet who obsequiously praised his divinity: "The man who carries my chamber-pot knows better."

Unlike the other Hellenistic kings, Antigonus and his successors made little attempt to expand their territory. They even left the Greeks free to resume the fratricidal intercity feuding that Philip had managed to stop a century earlier. The only area in which Macedonian rulers enforced their authority was control of the Aegean sea routes, which involved facing up to and defeating the Ptolemies of Egypt. By around 200 B.C., Macedon, together with the rest of Greece, began to fall into the orbit of Rome.

SIGNIFICANT DATES

Alexander and the Hellenistic Kingdoms

(all dates B.C.)

336	Accession of Alexander
332	Foundation of Alexandria in Egypt
331	Alexander defeats Persians
326	Alexander reaches India
323	Death of Alexander; Ptolemy becomes ruler in Egypt
306	Seleucus becomes ruler of Seleucid kingdom
276	Antigonus becomes king of Macedon
250	Publication of Septuagint
223–187	Reign of Antiochus the Great

SOCIETY AND ECONOMY IN THE HELLENISTIC WORLD

Although Alexander's legacy of Greek language and culture helped unify the Hellenistic world, there still remained an important social gap between the new Greek cities established in Asia and Egypt and the resident local populations. The new urban centers followed the model of the old Greek city-states, with the citizen-immigrants owning their land and farming it with the help of slave labor. These communities became sophisticated islands of culture surrounded by the great estates of the kings, where peasants continued to live in villages and work the land as they had for centuries.

CITY LIFE

The first three Seleucid kings founded a chain of Greek-style cities running from the Aegean as far east as the Hindu Kush. Many of them were laid out on a rectilinear grid pattern and used the latest engineering techniques to provide public water supplies and toilet facilities. Most of the inhabitants were a mixture of colonists from Greece and Asia Minor and retired veteran soldiers, pensioned off to populate the new settlements.

The political and social organization of these communities followed the model of a Greek *polis*. Thus a form of government invented in the city-states of Archaic Greece over three centuries earlier became transplanted to Central Asia and the borders of India. Each city had its own council and popular assembly, magistrates, and code of law. Many cities acted as if they were free and independent states, although they paid taxes to the king and were subject to his control. In turn the king maintained the political illusion that he "assured the autonomy and democracy of the people."

Unlike the Seleucids, the Ptolemies did not encourage the growth of numerous cities but concentrated their resources in Alexandria. The city's population, made up of Greeks, Macedonians, Jews, and Egyptians, was far more cosmopolitan than the Asian Greek communities. Some lower-class Greeks married Egyptians, but on the whole the Greeks did not mix socially with the other groups. Their centers were the *gymnasia*, clubs where young Greek men went to study literature and mathematics, practice sporting activities, and maintain their "Greekness."

There was more contact in the neighboring countryside, where surviving papyrus records describe racial tension. A camel driver, probably Arab, ascribes the nonpayment of his fees to the fact that "I am a barbarian, and do not know how to behave like a Greek." On other occasions Greeks complain of being discriminated against because of their race.

Ptolemaic Egypt was the scene of the earliest documented anti-Semitic riots. Many Jewish residents adopted Greek ways, speaking Greek rather than Hebrew. One of the results was the earliest translation of the Hebrew Bible into Greek, a work known as the *Septuagint* from the more than 70 scholars who worked on it over a period of some hundred years. The Septuagint was published around 250 B.C. at

Alexandria under the patronage of Ptolemy's son, Ptolemy II. The book of Ecclesiastes, written about the same time, shows the impact of Greek ideas on traditional Jewish beliefs. Not all Jews accepted this Hellenization of their faith, and the book of Ecclesiasticus, composed in Hebrew in 197 B.C. and translated into Greek in 132 B.C., represents an attack on Greek influences. Both the Jewish and Protestant Bibles place the book of Ecclesiasticus in the Apocrypha.

THE HELLENISTIC ECONOMY

The cultural contrast between the sophisticated lifestyle of the cities and the peasant life of the countryside had significant economic consequences. City dwellers of Greek origin were accustomed to using metal coinage, and one of Alexander's most important economic innovations was the introduction of a standard system of money. In the years following his death, large numbers of silver coins bearing his portrait circulated throughout the Hellenistic kingdoms. Both the Antigonids of Macedon and the Seleucids imposed a fixed weight on the money, which became the basis for the first international coinage in Western history.

Local populations living in the villages, on the other hand, were accustomed to an economic system that relied on barter and payment in goods. Bad harvests and grain shortages remained a constant fear, partially alleviated by improvements in agricultural methods. Greater use was made of iron plows, and new forms of dam building and construction of canals helped improve irrigation.

Some cities built highly successful economies based on trade and industry and used their prosperity to introduce social legislation to protect their less-well-off citizens. The Greek writer Strabo (64 or 63 B.C.–after A.D. 21) describes the city of Rhodes, whose rulers "wish to look after their multitude of poor. Accordingly, they supply them with corn, and following an ancient custom the well-to-do support the poor."

Specific cities became famous for their industrial production: Tyre for its dye-works, Tarsus for its linen. Most Hellenistic rulers encouraged the process of industrialization. Antiochus IV (ruled 175–164 B.C.) was famous for escaping from the suffocating life of court ritual to visit the silversmiths and goldsmiths in their workshops, to discuss the technicalities of production with them. As in Classical Greece, the production remained small-scale, with most businesses consisting of the owner and one or two slaves.

MYSTICS, STOICS, AND EPICUREANS: THE CONFLICTS OF RELIGION AND PHILOSOPHY

Belief in the traditional gods was already on the wane in Classical Greece. Socrates and other thinkers had encouraged their contemporaries to take a fresh look at old ideas, and many people continued to perform ancient rituals out of habit rather than conviction. The Hellenistic world brought the Greeks into contact with a whole range of non-Greek peoples and faiths, and the result was a wide variety of new forms of religious experience.

NEW ASPECTS OF ANCIENT BELIEFS

Some aspects of Hellenistic religion were the direct result of political pressures from the ruling class. All of Alexander's

Reconstruction model of the Upper City, Pergamum. Note the abundance of temples and the elaborate public spaces. The Altar to Zeus is in the center foreground, and the theater slopes steeply off to the left.

© bpk, Berlin, Photo: Christa Begall Staatliche Museen zu Berlin

Laocoon and His Sons. Early 1st century B.C. One of the masterpieces of Hellenistic art, carved by three Greek sculptors from the island of Rhodes: Agesander, Athenodorus, and Polydorus. It shows the priest of Apollo and his sons being strangled by sea-serpents, sent by the god Apollo to prevent him from warning the Trojans not to take the giant Wooden Horse (filled with Greek soldiers) within the walls of Troy. Note the difference between the slender young men and the aged Laocoon, and the tight pyramidal composition of the group.

successors came to power by force, and therefore thought that they needed some form of justification for their own rule and that of their descendants. The most common method was for kings to claim descent from the gods and require their subjects to worship them and their families. They also claimed worship on the basis of their own accomplishments, as had been the case with Alexander.

In strong contrast to the official cults were the ways in which ordinary people sought to deal with changing attitudes and new social conditions. One of them was the increase of interest in **mystery religions.** Many of these cults, like the Eleusinian Mysteries, went back to much earlier days (see Topic 11). They offered secret initiation ceremonies and individual salvation and emphasized irrational emotions. One of the most popular mystery religions was

the worship of Asclepius, the god of healing, at the Greek sanctuary of Epidaurus. Pilgrims claimed miraculous cures after spending a night in the temple, as the offerings and inscriptions left there throughout the Hellenistic period demonstrate.

The mystery cults emphasized that the lives of their members had an essential meaning and purpose. Many people, however, faced with the tumultuous events around them, preferred to turn to a very different form of worship. No deity received more attention in the Hellenistic world than Tyche, goddess of Fortune. The power of Tyche was ambiguous, wavering between good and bad, sometimes random and sometimes under the control of a higher force, which operated ambiguously. Many cities tried to win the favor of Fortune by portraying her on their coinage, accompanied by a symbol of abundance, while the historian Polybius (c. 203–120 B.C.) claimed that Fortune played an important role in people's lives—for better or worse—and could not be ignored.

Still other worshipers turned to the greater certainties provided by the ancient gods of Eastern religion. Shrines to the Egyptian resurrection goddess Isis sprang up throughout the Hellenistic world and remained centers of pilgrimage for centuries. Cybele, the mother goddess of Anatolia, the Assyrian Atargatis, and many others had temples built to them in Greece and the Near East. Some of their followers saw them all as incarnations of a single deity, different forms of one god. This process of assimilation, known as *syncretism,* helped pave the way for the spread of Christianity.

STOICS AND EPICUREANS

Athens remained the center of philosophy during Hellenistic times, chiefly because of the prestige of the schools founded there by Plato and Aristotle, the Academy and the Lyceum. The two main systems of philosophical belief to develop after Alexander were Stoicism and Epicureanism. They attracted those in search of intellectually satisfying explanations of life, rather than systems of faith that appealed to the emotions.

Stoicism took its name from the building in which its school was located: the Stoa Poikile, or Painted Hall. The movement's founder, Zeno (335–263 B.C.), taught that the force governing the world was Reason. Through the power of Reason it was possible to learn virtue, which was the supreme good. Those who lived virtuously were under the protection of Divine Providence, which would never allow them to suffer evil.

The other main system, **Epicureanism,** was based on the teachings and writings of Epicurus (341–271 B.C.), whose aim was to free humans from the threat of divine retribution or the fear of the unknown. According to Epicurus, even if the gods exist, they play no part in the world or in human affairs. We are free to live our lives according to principles of moderation and prudence in the pursuit of pleasure. The Epicureans believed that the universe consisted of small particles of matter, or atoms, moving at random in empty space. At death, the atoms separate, and no part of us survives. As a result we should not fear to die because it involves only the complete ending of any sensation.

Both of these schools, first developed at Athens, spread during the Hellenistic period and flourished at Rome (see Topic 14). Another popular movement, that of the Cynics, had a much less intellectual foundation. Its originator, Diogenes (c. 400–c. 325 B.C.), taught that life should be lived with a minimum of material comfort, complete freedom of speech, and shamelessness of action. His behavior won him the nickname of "the Cynic," which in Greek means "the Dog," a label later applied to his followers.

THE NATURE OF THE UNIVERSE: SCIENCE, MEDICINE, AND TECHNOLOGY

While the traditional pursuit of philosophy continued at Athens, the great centers of scientific progress in the Hellenistic world were the new royal capitals, cities like Alexandria and Pergamum, whose monarchs subsidized research projects. The protected life of the scholars working in the museum and library at Alexandria drew the scorn of one contemporary, who described the scientists of his day as "well-propped pedants who quarrel without end in the Muses' bird-cage."

ASTRONOMY AND MEDICINE

The conquests of Alexander had expanded the horizons of immense numbers of people. Perhaps as a consequence, astronomers began to explore new ideas about the world and its place in the cosmos. Aristarchus of Samos (active c. 270 B.C.) was the first person in history to maintain that the earth rotates on its own axis and revolves around the sun. Hipparchus (active c. 146 B.C.) astonished his contemporaries by compiling a catalogue of stars. Two centuries later, the Roman scholar Pliny the Elder observed: "Hipparchus dared to do something that would be rash even for a god. He numbered the stars for his successors and checked off the constellations by name."

Experiments conducted by astronomers in taking measurements led to important geometrical discoveries. Apollonius (c. 262–190 B.C.), known to his age as the "Great Geometer," introduced concepts such as the ellipse and the parabola, and worked on conic sections. Eratosthenes (275–194 B.C.), the chief librarian at Alexandria in the time of Ptolemy III, managed to measure the circumference of the earth, arriving at a figure within 4 percent of the actual one. Eratosthenes also wrote on geology and literary criticism, showing a versatility that led his envious fellow scholars to nickname him "Beta"—"Second-rater"—because there was no single field in which he was first.

While astronomers studied the place of humans in the universe, Alexandria's medical researchers studied humans. Herophilus (c. 335–c. 280 B.C.) founded an institute of anatomy in Ptolemy's capital. One of the first to study the workings of the body by conducting postmortem examinations, Herophilus was able to describe the liver, the genitals, and the ventricles of the brain, to explain the function of the nerves, and to time the pulse.

ADVANCES IN TECHNOLOGY

By around 300 B.C. many important technical devices were already in use, including the lever, pulley, wedge, and windlass. The greatest of all Hellenistic scientists, Archimedes (c. 287–212 B.C.), refined the use of levers, boasting "give me a place to stand and I will move the earth." He also invented another device, a "screw" used for raising water.

The New York Public Library, Astor, Lenox and Tilden Foundations

Reconstruction drawing of the lighthouse, or Pharos, north of the harbor at ancient Alexandria. The original, one of the Seven Wonders of the Ancient World, dated to the early 3rd century B.C. and was 440 feet (134.2 m) high. In the cabin at the top of the building was a lantern, whose beam of light was intensified by a system of reflectors.

After studying in Alexandria, Archimedes returned to his native Syracuse in Sicily, where he became scientific adviser to King Hiero II. Like many of his fellow researchers, he spent much of his time working on projects related to warfare. Hellenistic kings were constantly trying to improve the capability of their weaponry, while strengthening their defense capacities. Among the works designed by Archimedes for Hiero were catapults and grapnels to help defend Syracuse under siege. The grapnel hooks served to tear down mobile siege towers, which formed part of the equipment of a Hellenistic army on the attack.

Toward the end of the Hellenistic period, the drive to invent new technologies began to flag. Nonetheless, Hellenistic scientists and engineers on the whole amply demonstrated two vital methods of research: the use of mathematics to investigate natural phenomena and the importance of practical experimentation to discover the truth.

Putting the Hellenistic World in Perspective

Alexander dreamed of the "unity of empire." Far from becoming unified, the lands and peoples he conquered spent the century after his death in a state of constant tension and rivalry. Hellenistic kings fought offensive and defensive wars against one another, while remaining ever on guard against internal threats. Only the coming of the Romans succeeded in finally imposing unity by absorbing Alexander's conquests into an empire spreading west to the Atlantic.

Yet in other respects the Hellenistic Age did create achievements worthy of Alexander's dream. Greek ideas about politics, economics, and the nature of the universe traveled from a small, isolated country to a stage spanning half the known world. In the process they came into contact with the older, more varied cultures of Asia. The two never really "fused": The Greeks, like later imperialists, were far too certain of their own superiority for that to have been possible. Yet the result was an immense enrichment for both sides, with Greek-style city-states within reach of the borders of India and temples to Asian gods on the islands of Rhodes and Delos.

For the first time in history, an international culture circulated in a multiethnic world. A common language, political system, and currency were shared by a series of independent states, each of which preserved its own special characteristics and ethnic mixture. For all of the inevitable conflict between the Hellenistic kingdoms—in some ways, in fact, *because* of their rivalry—scientists and intellectuals continued to make progress and laid many of the bases of Western civilization. With the rise of Rome, their achievements were to reach an even wider stage.

Questions for Further Study

1. How did Alexander's conquests survive his death? What were the chief differences among the Hellenistic kingdoms?
2. Which aspects of Greek culture were transplanted most successfully to the Hellenistic world? How did they blend with the preexisting cultures of Egypt and western Asia?
3. What are the characteristic features of Hellenistic religious developments?

Suggestions for Further Reading

Barnes, J., et al. *Science and Speculation*. New York, 1982.

Boardman, John, ed. *The Oxford History of Classical Art*. New York, 1997.

Green, P. *Alexander of Macedon, 356–323* B.C.: *A Historical Biography*. Berkeley, 1991.

Jones, H. *The Epicurean Tradition*. London, 1989.

Pollitt, J.J. *Art in the Hellenistic Age*. New York, 1986.

Pomeroy, S. *Women in Hellenistic Egypt: From Alexander to Cleopatra*. New York, 1984.

Ridgway, Brunilde S. *Hellenistic Sculpture I: The Styles of ca. 331-200* B.C. Madison, WI, 1990.

InfoTrac College Edition

Enter the search term *Greek history* using Key Terms.

Enter the search term *Alexander the Great* using Key Terms.

Enter the search term *Archimedes* using Key Terms.

THE RISE OF ROME

In the early centuries of Rome's history, several distinct peoples were established in Italy, of whom the most important were the Etruscans. Technologically advanced and successful in commerce, the Etruscans spread throughout central Italy and conquered Rome at the end of the 7th century B.C. The city of Rome had been founded a century and a half earlier as an amalgamation of several villages on the hills around the river Tiber. The period of Etruscan occupation brought the Romans in contact with a new level of culture.

After a century of Etruscan rule, the Romans were sufficiently advanced to drive out their conquerors and begin their own climb to power. They replaced the system of government by kings, which went back to the foundation of the city, with a republic, based on a careful balance of the two chief social groups: the aristocratic patricians and the plebs, or people. The process of devising a constitution went hand in hand with the creation of a law code.

By the end of the 5th century B.C., the Romans had become the dominant power in their region as leaders of the Latin League and were ready to take on the rest of Italy. In a series of campaigns against the Etruscans and other independent peoples in Italy, they gradually assumed control of the peninsula.

In the mid-3rd century B.C., Rome began to move against the leading power in the western Mediterranean, Carthage (the Phoenician colony in North Africa). The first of the wars between the Romans and the Carthaginians, known as the Punic Wars, left Rome in control of Sicily, Corsica, and Sardinia. The Second Punic War began with the invasion of Italy by a Carthaginian army led by Hannibal, but the attack petered out. The end of the war, in 202 B.C., brought Roman victory and the collapse of Carthaginian power. The Romans' domination now extended throughout the western Mediterranean.

The chief powers of the eastern Mediterranean were the three largest of the Hellenistic kingdoms created after the death of Alexander: Syria, Macedon, and Egypt. The first of these to fall victim to Roman expansion was Macedon, which became a Roman province in 148 B.C. Two years later it was the rest of Greece's turn.

The Roman conquest of the rest of Alexander's former empire was as much by diplomacy as by military force. An alternation of Roman threats and alliances weakened the resistance of the Syrian and Egyptian rulers. Syria fragmented into a series of tiny kingdoms, while Egypt was subservient to Rome long before its "official" conquest in 31 B.C.

By the end of the Republic, the Romans were the masters of the Mediterranean world. At Rome itself, however, the price of success abroad was increasing political turmoil, and the last century of Republican history (133–31 B.C.) brought internal collapse.

THE ETRUSCANS AND THE FOUNDATION OF ROME

Throughout the Bronze Age, Italy remained relatively isolated from events elsewhere in the Mediterranean, cut off to the north by the Alps and reachable from east, west, or south only by long sea voyage. By around 900 B.C., at the dawn of the Iron Age, the population consisted of a series of separate ethnic groups, each with its own culture.

Shortly after 800 B.C., three major developments occurred, which were to prove crucial to the history of Western civilization. The first was the arrival of Greek colonists who began to found trading settlements in southern Italy and Sicily and to transplant their culture into the western Mediterranean region (see Topic 7). Around the same time, Latin herdsmen and farmers living in the valley of the river Tiber—the Latins were a people who had settled in central Italy in the early Iron Age—pooled their resources to form a new community. The future imperial city of Rome began life as a small village; its early Latin founders constructed their huts on the summits of the hills around the valley of the River Tiber, leaving the land below for their animals to graze. Throughout the centuries of their city's growth, the Romans never forgot their origins as a simple farming community. As late as the 5th century A.D., Rome's birthday was celebrated annually on April 21: the festival of the Palilia, in which shepherds and herdsmen purified their land and flocks for the coming year, and the entire population of Rome and the countryside around finished the day with an open-air feast. At the time of the arrival of the Greeks and the birth of Rome, however, central Italy began to fall under the domination of another people who had appeared in Italy around 800 B.C., the Etruscans.

THE ETRUSCANS

Even in ancient times the Etruscans seemed mysterious to their neighbors. The first evidence for their existence dates to the mid-8th century B.C., and by 700 B.C. they were well established in that part of Italy, Tuscany, which still bears their name. The Greeks and Romans believed that the Etruscans were immigrants from the East. According to one story, reported to us by the Greek historian Herodotus, they fled westward from the kingdom of Lydia in Asia Minor at a time of terrible famine.

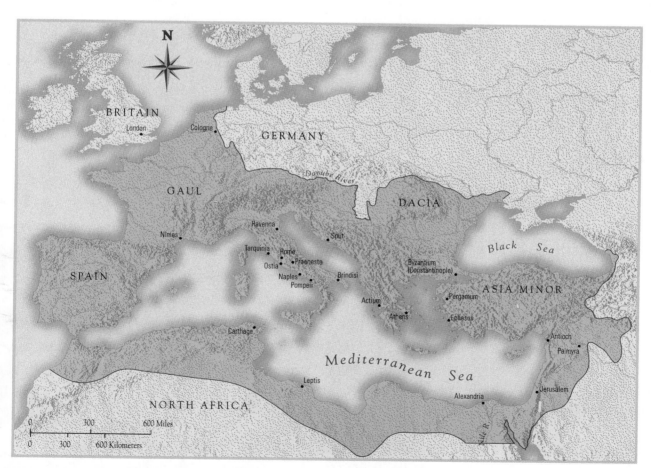

 Map 13.1 The Roman World. The map shows the extent of Roman rule by the time of Augustus (early 1st century A.D.). Britain and southern Scotland (but not northern Scotland or Ireland) and Germany were added in the following century. Roman influence and trading extended far beyond the territory they controlled, reaching eventually to India and China. Go to http://info.wadsworth.com/053461065X for an interactive version of this map.

Both their way of life and art show, in fact, many Eastern characteristics. Etruscan art makes frequent use of Eastern motifs, including the sphinx and palmette. Like many Asian cults, Etruscan religion strongly emphasized foretelling the future and appeasing the gods. The methods used by Etruscan soothsayers to interpret the gods' wishes and intentions—"reading" the entrails of animals and watching the flight of birds and natural phenomena such as lightning flashes—are remarkably similar to Babylonian rituals.

Furthermore, the importance and high social standing of women in Etruscan society had little in common with Greek and Roman custom. Etruscan women could both inherit and pass on possessions and act as the heads of families, legal rights never enjoyed by their Greek or Roman counterparts. The Romans even regarded the Etruscan custom of husbands and wives reclining together to eat as immoral.

Yet, for all its Eastern characteristics, in other ways Etruscan culture seems a natural development of their predecessors in central Italy. Their patterns of settlement also suggest an indigenous origin. New immigrants from an outside culture would either have founded their own centers (as the Greeks did in southern Italy) or fought with the established population for control of their territory (as the Romans were to do over the following centuries). All of the main Etruscan cities developed peacefully where there had been longstanding Iron Age communities before them, and there are no signs of violence in the transition.

Nor does the Etruscan language throw any light on the mystery of their origins because it is related neither to any Italian language nor to any spoken in the East. Although our understanding of how Etruscan works is still far from complete, many of the thousands of surviving inscriptions can be translated.

Whatever their origins, from their earliest appearance the Etruscans were wealthy and technologically adept. The gold treasures buried in their tombs demonstrate a high level of technical skill, as well as their prosperity. Trading widely in the western Mediterranean, the Etruscans also established commercial links with the Phoenicians and other Eastern peoples.

By the 6th century B.C., the chief Etruscan cities were allied with Carthage in a trade war with the western Greeks. A series of painted tombs at Tarquinia, one of the richest of the Etruscan cities, reveals the existence there of an aristocratic society with a high standard of living and extravagant tastes. At the same time, Etruscan forces were in control of most of central Italy, including the city of Rome, founded a little more than a century earlier.

ETRUSCAN RULE IN ROME

Later Romans, with typical precision, dated the foundation of their city to April 21, 753 B.C. Their own account of the city's origins was intended to provide a worthy ancestor to the mighty Rome of the Empire. In reality, however, at the time the Etruscans occupied Rome—the traditional date is 616 B.C.—it was still little more than a small country town. The "kings" who ruled there were probably more like tribal chiefs, the descendants of those early farmers who collected together on the seven hills near the river Tiber in the mid-8th century B.C.

Under the Etruscans, Rome began to grow and develop. Etruscan engineers drained and paved a large marshy area at the foot of the Palatine and Capitoline hills, which was to become the site of the future Roman Forum, center of the city and of the Empire. Etruscan builders constructed roads and temples, including the Temple of Capitoline Jupiter, which was destined to become the most important shrine in the Roman world. Etruscan craftsmen taught the locals how to import and work gold, silver, and ivory.

Husband and wife on the lid of a terracotta Etruscan sarcophagus from Cerveteri, c. 520 B.C. Height 3 feet 9 inches (1.11 m). As often seen in Etruscan art, the faces and upper parts of the body are depicted with realistic detail, while the parts from the waist down are barely indicated. The man's arm is placed affectionately around his wife's shoulder, while she originally held an object in her right hand—probably an egg, symbol of rebirth.

Scala/Art Resource

THE ROMAN REPUBLIC: CLASS AND THE POLITICS OF COMPROMISE

From the early days of Roman history, the population fell into two classes. The kings and ruling class, known as the **patricians,** formed a kind of self-perpetuating aristocracy based on a closed group of families who intermarried among themselves. Most Romans were **plebeians,** with no privileges of birth or rank. In the beginning the patricians controlled the resources of land as well as government, but during the time of Etruscan domination growing numbers of plebeian craftsmen and traders began to acquire money.

With the Etruscans expelled, members of successful and ambitious plebeian families were anxious to play a part in running their city, while poorer plebeians wanted to reduce the economic exploitation under which they lived. The republican political system, which patricians and plebeians hammered out over the following centuries, involved compromise on both sides. The Roman ability to negotiate compromises among conflicting interests made long-term political stability possible.

THE ROMAN REPUBLIC

The choice of a republican government was the result of the Romans' bitter experience of a century of rule by Etruscan kings. In 509 B.C. the new state vowed never again to accept royal rule and drew up a constitution.

In its first form, the system concentrated power in the hands of the patricians. The principal legislative assembly, the Senate, was made up of members of the aristocracy, and the two chief magistrates—the **consuls,** who were elected annually—were also patricians. Each consul had his own army, to prevent the other one from seizing power, and in time of national crisis one stepped down to let the other serve as **dictator,** or supreme commander, for a maximum term of six months. The Senate's powers included control of finance, state security, and relations with foreign governments. In the case of a decision for war or peace, however, the people were also involved.

The plebeians had their own popular assembly, which elected spokesmen known as tribunes; the office of the tribunate was established in 494 B.C. These representatives guarded the plebeians' interests and protected them against injustice on the part of state magistrates. Both assemblies met in the Roman Forum and functioned in the same way. A speaker could address his fellow members only if invited to do so by the presiding magistrate, who at the end of the debate called on those present to vote for or against a proposal under discussion. Blanket acceptance or rejection were the only possibilities.

During the years that followed, the plebeians managed to win an important series of concessions from the aristocracy. The tribunes acquired the right to veto any action by either a magistrate or the Senate, and their person was sacrosanct: Anyone killing a tribune was held guilty of a capital crime. In 343 B.C. a new law made it possible for

Terracotta statue of Apollo from the roof of the Etruscan temple at Veii, c. 510–500 B.C. Height 5 feet 11 inches (1.78 m). The figure, which was originally painted, is striding energetically, the body clearly visible beneath the drapery. Between the legs is a lyre, symbol of the god of music.

© Hirmer Fotoarchiv, Munich

Other Etruscan importations into Rome included the alphabet that is still used today by all Western languages (and many others)—the Etruscans had probably learned it from the Greeks. Some of the customs that became typically Roman, such as public games, chariot racing, and even the wearing of the toga, the most common form of Roman dress, were probably of Etruscan origin.

The greatest of all Etruscan contributions to the Romans, however, was to give them a new and wider outlook on the world. From being villagers living in a small, isolated community, the Romans found that they had become part of an international power with a highly developed culture and connections throughout Italy and the Mediterranean. Within a century, transformed technologically and psychologically, the Romans were ready to repay their conquerors. In 510 B.C. they drove out the Etruscans and began the unrelenting climb to power that was to bring much of the known world under Roman sway.

Scala/Art Resource

Bronze portrait of Brutus (?), one of the leaders of the Roman revolt that drove out the Etruscans and established the Roman Republic in 509 B.C. 3rd–1st century B.C. (?). The head is ancient, inserted into a Renaissance shoulder bust. Note the careful modeling of the expression lines on the face.

plebeians to stand for election to the consulship, while the succeeding decades opened up all remaining state offices to plebeian candidates. The final plebeian victory came in 287 B.C. with the passage of the Hortensian Law. This made the decisions of the plebeian assembly binding on the Senate and Roman people.

The gradual, peaceful process whereby the two classes reached political agreement was in strong contrast to the often bloody class struggles of the Greek city-states. Writing toward the end of the Republic, the Greek historian Polybius (c. 203–c. 120 B.C.) praised the virtues of what he called a "mixed constitution." The popular assembly represented the democratic element and the Senate the aristocratic, while the powers of the consuls were equivalent to those of a king—except that they held office for only a year. This mixture of political types, according to Polybius, gave Rome the stability necessary for winning an empire.

In its final form, the Roman constitution was not the product of philosophical theory but the result of years of tough political experience. In the words of Cato, a distinguished senator of the 2nd century B.C., "Our Republic was not made by the work of one man, but of many, not in a single lifetime, but through many generations and centuries."

THE TWELVE TABLES

If the plebeians' eventual political victory depended on a spirit of compromise, it also required the existence of an impartial code of law. In the first years of the Republic, laws were based on custom and subject to the interpretation of the aristocrats. The plebeians insisted that the state establish a fixed legal code, and a board of 10 commissioners was set up to study the laws of other states. The board visited the chief Greek cities of southern Italy and may even have

A general view of the Roman Forum, seen from the Capitoline Hill. The buildings in the Forum were constructed over a period of more than a thousand years. The small round Temple to Vesta in the bottom left corner dates to shortly after 500 B.C., the columns on the right are part of the Temple of Concord, built in 367 B.C., and the Arch of Titus in the distance was built around A.D. 81. In the background are the remains of the Colosseum (A.D. 69–79).

©1994 Richard T. Nowitz/Photo Researchers, Inc.

gone to Athens. The result of their work was a codification of public, private, criminal, and religious law. The popular assembly, after approving the new code in 451 B.C., had it engraved on 12 bronze tablets known as the Twelve Tables, which were set up in the Forum, in full view of all.

Although Julius Caesar thoroughly overhauled the Law of the Twelve Tables in 46 B.C., he based his new Civil Law on it, and some of its provisions survived into Byzantine times. Over the centuries, the Romans built up a body of legal opinion aimed at being comprehensive and valid for all times and places. The principle governing it was "equity"—fairness for all. Even today millions of people live in countries whose legal systems ultimately derive from the Roman tradition of law based on the Twelve Tables. In the words of one eminent British judge, "There is not a problem of jurisprudence which Roman law does not touch; there is scarcely a corner of political science on which its light has not fallen."

DIPLOMACY AND WAR: THE ROMANIZATION OF ITALY

During the first two centuries of the Republic, while the Romans were refining their political system at home, they also gradually extended their influence in Italy: By mid-3rd century B.C. they were the dominating power from the Gulf of Genoa to the Straits of Messina.

THE ROMANS AND THEIR NEIGHBORS

Even before the end of Etruscan rule at Rome, the Romans had formed an alliance with the other Latin cities of the region, known as the Latin League, in which they played the dominant role. The expulsion of the Etruscans was a clear signal of Roman strength, and Rome's fellow members of the League tried to shake off the alliance with so forceful a partner. The Romans had no intention of giving up their regional dominance, however. They defeated a combined Latin army and in 493 B.C. the two sides signed a treaty, the text of which has survived. The terms seem equitable: "Let there be peace between the Romans and all the Latin cities so long as heaven and earth are still in the same place." Yet clearly Rome maintained its primacy, and the Roman technique of conquering a rival and then making peace as if between equals was to prove useful on many future occasions. Over time, the Romans learned to use the offer of Roman citizenship as an additional way to win over some of its enemies.

With the Latins taken care of, the Romans moved on to deal with their true rivals in Italy, the Etruscans. The Etruscan city closest to Rome was Veii, and in 405 B.C. Roman forces began a siege of Veii that was to last for 10 years. When the Etruscans finally capitulated, the Romans razed the city to the ground. All trace of Veii disappeared. Only in 1916 did archeologists finally recover magnificent Etruscan sculptures buried under the devastation of 2,300 years earlier.

THE GALLIC INVASION

Before Rome could follow up this initial success, disaster struck. In 390 B.C. bands of plundering Gauls moved south down the Italian peninsula, in search of booty. A Roman army moved north to check their advance at the river Allia, and—for the first time in Rome's history—suffered a shattering defeat. For centuries to come, the Romans grimly commemorated "the day of the Allia," July 18, 390 B.C. The victorious Gauls pressed on and took Rome itself. Eight hundred years were to pass before the next enemy occupation of the city. Only the payment of a large, and humiliating, tribute persuaded the Gallic invaders to move back north.

Yet even this setback did little more than postpone Rome's conquest of the chief Etruscan cities of central Italy. Within a few years of the Gallic invasion, the Romans were once again on the offensive. Between 353 and 270 B.C., the Romans attacked and either occupied or destroyed the cities of their former rulers and consolidated their hold on the territory to their north.

THE SAMNITES

To the south, the Romans faced the Samnites, a fierce mountain people who had moved from their homeland in the rugged country of central Italy to occupy Campania, the area around Naples. In a series of hard-fought wars, Roman legionaries, accustomed to fighting on flat land, learned to defeat their enemies on the Samnites' own hilly terrain.

The Samnites proved tougher to subdue than the Etruscans, and in one never-to-be-forgotten battle at the Caudine Forks in 321 B.C., they forced an entire Roman army to surrender. In the end, Roman persistence brought victory. Samnite resistance effectively ended with the signing of a peace treaty in 304 B.C., which—despite its diplomatic wording—signaled the confirmation of Roman supremacy in Italy.

Several factors contributed to Rome's success in winning control of Italy: (1) the speed with which the

SIGNIFICANT DATES

The Rise of Rome (all dates B.C.)

753	Traditional date of foundation of Rome
616–510	Traditional dates of Etruscan rule at Rome
509	Roman Republic inaugurated
493	Treaty with Latin League
451	Law of the Twelve Tables
405–396	Romans besiege Veii
390	Gallic invasion of Italy
304	Romans sign treaty with Samnites
279	Pyrrhus defeats Romans
264–241	First Punic War
218–202	Second Punic War
146	Destruction of Carthage; Roman conquest of Greece

Romans recovered from the Gallic invasion and were able to take advantage of the havoc the Gauls had wrought; (2) continued political stability at Rome itself, which enabled the city to overcome the few serious defeats the Roman army suffered; (3) that same army's fighting efficiency and flexibility; and (4) most important of all, the Romans' policy of being magnanimous in victory. They generally treated their conquered enemies favorably, immediately designating them as "allies" and extending to them the benefits of Rome's growing prosperity. As a result, the victors inspired loyalty in those who, defeated in battle, were then bound to Rome by treaties of friendship and self-interest. The allies were legally independent, but their room for maneuver in foreign affairs was limited, and the Romans generally favored aristocratic local governments where it was possible. Over time, Rome began to play a greater role in the allies' internal affairs. With the essential security at home that this guaranteed, the Romans could face external threats.

THE PUNIC WARS

Rome's chief rival in the western Mediterranean was Carthage, but before that deadly struggle began, the Romans had to deal with a challenge from the east. One of the northern Greek kingdoms to splinter off from Alexander's empire was Epirus. Its king, Pyrrhus (ruled 306–302, 297–272 B.C.), took advantage of an appeal for protection by Taranto, a Greek city in southern Italy, to invade Italy in the hope of taking over Rome's growing empire there. He succeeded in defeating the Romans in 279 B.C., but the battle caused such heavy losses in his own army that the phrase "a pyrrhic victory" became proverbial for one gained at too great a cost. His rueful departure home signaled Rome's first success against an outside invader, while leaving the Romans in control of all the Greek city-states in southern Italy.

THE CARTHAGINIANS AND THE FIRST PUNIC WAR (264–241 B.C.)

The next opponent presented a far more serious challenge. As the Roman poet Lucretius put it 200 years later, the Roman conflict with Carthage was the Great War—"the struggle for universal empire by land and sea."

Carthage was the richest city in the western Mediterranean, founded around 800 B.C. by Phoenician colonists (see Topic 4). The Roman name for the Phoenicians, *Poeni* or *Puni,* came to be used for the wars fought against the Carthaginians. With a superb natural harbor in the Gulf of Tunis, the Carthaginians had control of both the eastern and western Mediterranean. In the east, Carthage's trading partners included Egypt and the cities of Asia Minor, while to the west Carthaginian merchants controlled business in Sardinia and Corsica. Their commercial empire stretched even farther. By 500 B.C., Carthaginian explorers had reached as far south as Sierra Leone, and perhaps

to the mouth of the river Congo, and to the north, beyond the Strait of Gibraltar, the Bay of Biscay was within their reach.

If Rome was to continue its economic expansion, a clash between the leading commercial power of the day and the rising force in Italy was inevitable. The immediate cause was a Carthaginian attempt to head off Roman expansion by gaining control of the Strait of Messina. Lying between the tip of Italy and Sicily, the straits were crucial to communication between the eastern and western Mediterranean. In 264 B.C., with the Senate hesitant whether to risk a conflict, the popular assembly at Rome belligerently voted to send a fleet to Sicily to break the Carthaginian grip there. The First Punic War had begun.

An initial success brought the Romans their first major victory at sea, but Carthage fought back, in a series of naval battles that proved to be among the bloodiest ever fought in the ancient world. In the end, Roman persistence paid off. They besieged the Carthaginians' stronghold in western Sicily, Lilybaeum, by land and sea. The siege lasted eight years and saw the Carthaginian garrison ingeniously countering the Roman blockade. The Roman admiral Claudius rashly attacked a Carthaginian fleet when even the divine omens counseled caution. Hearing that the sacred chickens refused to eat, he retorted, "Then let them drink," and had them thrown into the sea. A later Roman fleet was wrecked on Sicily's rocky southern coast.

After further violent fighting around western Sicily, with the Romans throwing all their resources into strengthening their fleet, an uneasy peace finally came in 241 B.C. Rome was able to dictate the terms. The Carthaginians had to withdraw from Sicily and pay a heavy indemnity. Western Sicily became the first Roman province (Roman territory outside mainland Italy). Neither side was under any illusion, however, that hostilities were over. The Romans' victory, and their seizure of Corsica and Sardinia after Carthage had surrendered, left the Carthaginians weakened and mortified, but thirsting for revenge.

THE SECOND PUNIC WAR (218–202 B.C.)

Sicily had provided the immediate cause for the first round of hostilities; Spain proved the excuse for the second. In the years following their defeat, the Carthaginians strengthened their position in the western Mediterranean by conquering territory in southeastern Spain, gaining access to Spanish copper mines and adding Spanish troops to their already formidable army.

With the Romans on the point of intervening to drive Carthaginian forces out of Spain, Hannibal (247–183/2 B.C.), the brilliant Carthaginian military commander, decided to strike first. The Romans controlled the sea, but they were still vulnerable on land. Furthermore, if the Carthaginians attacked Italy directly, there was a chance that some of Rome's recent Italian "allies" might take the chance to turn on their new masters and throw their support behind Hannibal.

So, in April 218 B.C., Hannibal led his army across to Spain and southern France. Later that summer the Carthaginian forces, which included a herd of elephants—the secret weapons that had so scared Alexander's troops a century earlier—crossed the Alps into northern Italy. The Romans, confident on their home ground, sent forces to block the Carthaginian advance, but they were unprepared for Hannibal's strategic genius in battle. Three times—at the rivers Ticinus and Trebia in 218 B.C., and at Lake Trasimene early in 217 B.C.—Hannibal's army routed the Romans. The last defeat was the worst of all. In the fighting around Trasimene, two Roman legions fell, together with their commanders, and the lake ran red with Roman blood.

Never before had Rome come so close to disaster as Hannibal moved south, bypassing the capital to find fresh supplies in the rich farmland of Campania and hoping to win allies in southern Italy. In the summer of 216 B.C. the two sides faced off again at Cannae in Apulia, and Hannibal scored his greatest triumph yet. Of the 50,000 Roman troops, only 10,000 escaped. Twenty-five thousand died, and the rest were taken prisoner. Centuries later the Romans still remembered the peril of those times, and nursemaids would scare the children in their charge by threatening them that "Hannibal will come and get you."

At this point, with the Romans under heavy pressure, Hannibal avoided further fixed battles and ravaged Italy's agricultural backcountry unchecked. Yet, for all the havoc his troops created over the next 14 years, the worst was over. Two factors worked in the Romans' favor: time and numbers. The longer Hannibal fought so far from home, the weaker his supplies and fewer his men became. In addition, one of Hannibal's gambles failed to pay off, as Rome's allies in central Italy remained loyal. The war ground on, but Rome doggedly resisted the Carthaginians in Italy while fighting their forces in Spain more aggressively. Scipio (236–184 B.C.), the Romans' brilliant young commander, had learned from Hannibal's innovative tactics to avoid pitched battle, but he judged—correctly—that the time had come for a final showdown, and took the fight back onto Carthaginian territory. In the last, terrible battle at Zama in North Africa in 202 B.C., Hannibal, the old lion, led his Carthaginian army to defeat against Scipio. The war was over.

For Carthage, the peace was scarcely less devastating. Fearful of a repeat, the Romans imposed brutal terms. The Carthaginians had to disband their navy and give up all of their foreign possessions, and pay yet another huge indemnity. All that remained of their former greatness was the city of Carthage and the land around it.

Yet even this proved too much for the Romans to tolerate. The so-called Third Punic War of 149–146 B.C. was nothing more than an extended Roman siege of Carthage, its citizens driven by desperation to hopeless resistance. When the end came in 146 B.C., the Romans burned the city, wrecked what remained standing, plowed up the ground, and sowed salt to prevent anything from ever growing there again. They sold into slavery any inhabitants who were unlucky enough to have survived the assault.

The end of the Second Punic War in 202 B.C. left Rome the dominating power in the west, taking over control in North Africa, Spain, and southern France. By the time of the destruction of Carthage in 146 B.C., the Romans were well on the way to extending their empire to Asia.

THE ANNEXATION OF THE EASTERN MEDITERRANEAN

The three great powers of the eastern Mediterranean were the successor kingdoms formed at the death of Alexander: Syria (all that was left of Seleucus's original Asian kingdom), Egypt, and Macedon. A few smaller states had managed to preserve their independence and even play a role in relations among the leading powers. The two most important of these were the maritime republic of Rhodes, leader in the battle against pirates in the eastern Mediterranean, and the kingdom of Pergamum. With its abundant agricultural production and rich mineral resources, Pergamum, in northeastern Asia Minor, was a leading cultural center in the Hellenistic world.

THE ROMANS MOVE EAST

The Romans' first brush with Macedon came in 200 B.C., when they accepted a plea for help from the Greek city-states against the Macedonian king Philip V (ruled 221–179 B.C.). The Roman forces drove Philip out of Greece and then, to everyone's surprise, withdrew back to Italy.

The delay was only temporary. The Macedonians, warned by the example of Carthage, began to strengthen their forces and repair relations with the Greeks, only to be plunged into a full-scale war with Rome in 171 B.C. Roman victory was followed a few years later in 148 B.C. by the conversion of the former kingdom of Macedon into an imperial province under direct rule from Rome.

In 146 B.C.—the same year in which Carthage was destroyed—a turning point occurred in the history of the ancient world. A Roman army under Lucius Mummius attacked Greece and devastated Corinth, the richest city there. As at Carthage, the Romans killed most of the men and sold the rest of the population into slavery. Mummius, whose name was to become a byword for wanton brutality, carried off or sold shiploads of precious masterpieces of art, and Greece

German Archaeological Institute, Rome

Bronze statue of the symbol of Rome, a she-wolf suckling Rome's founders, Romulus and Remus. The she-wolf dates to c. 500–480 B.C.; the twins beneath were added in the Renaissance. The animal's tense pose, with the rib cage clearly visible under its lean flanks, is reminiscent of Etruscan art, and the bronze may, in fact, have been made by an Etruscan artist. Thus, the statue links Rome's early history with subsequent developments in the city's growth.

ended up as part of the province of Macedon. The military triumph was slight, but for Greece's city-states the sack of Corinth ended their hundreds of years of independence.

The message was not lost on the rulers of the remaining Hellenistic kingdoms, who were having trouble enough defending themselves against one another. Attalus III of Pergamum (ruled 138–133 B.C.) made the best of a bad job and bequeathed his kingdom to Rome on his death.

It required no more massive military actions for Rome to become the dominating influence over Syria and Egypt, merely astute diplomacy to keep the two on the defensive. The effect on Syria was to erode its already shaky unity, and by the end of the 2nd century B.C. Seleucus's once formidable kingdom was fragmented into a series of ministates. The Romans let Egypt retain a nominal independence as a threat to any potential troublemakers, but they exploited the abundant Egyptian grain supplies to feed the population back in Rome. Octavian completed Egypt's subjugation in 30 B.C., by officially annexing it as his personal estate.

Putting the Rise of Rome in Perspective

The Romans were right to see Carthage as their most formidable enemy. The struggle to defeat the Carthaginians was by far the toughest in their history, and their victory radically changed the political landscape in the ancient world. Even before the Roman successes in the East, the balance of power between East and West was shifting.

By contrast with their ferocious wars with Carthage, Roman supremacy in the East seems to have come about with comparative ease. One reason was that the Romans, tried by defeat and near disaster, had learned the rewards of dogged persistence. Another was that the naked brutality of the destruction of Carthage and Corinth brought horrified condemnation from Rome's contemporaries, but taught a lesson that was all too obvious. It was suicide to resist Roman determination, and after 146 B.C. no one did.

In 241 B.C., at the end of the First Punic War, Rome was still only the leading state in a relatively obscure part of the Mediterranean. Within a century she was the world's first superpower. The following years were to bring battles of a different kind, as forces within Rome itself clashed, and two bitter civil wars brought the Republic crashing down.

Questions for Further Study

1. What were the chief characteristics of Etruscan culture? Which of them—if any—influenced the development of Roman civilization?
2. How did Rome's political system evolve? Which factors helped make it successful?
3. What were the main stages in Rome's expansion in the western Mediterranean? Which military strategies proved decisive in the defeat of the Carthaginians?

Suggestions for Further Reading

Beard, M., and M. Crawford. *Rome in the Late Republic.* Ithaca, NY, 1985.

Boardman, J., J. Griffin, and O. Murray. *The Roman World.* New York, 1988.

Brendel, Otto. *Etruscan Art*, 2nd ed. New Haven, CT, 1995.

Gruen, E.S. *The Hellenistic World and the Coming of Rome.* Berkeley, 1984.

Keaveny, A. *Rome and the Unification of Italy.* London, 1988.

Richardson, Lawrence, Jr. *A New Topographical Dictionary of Ancient Rome.* Baltimore, MD, 1992.

Spivey, Nigel, and Simon Stoddart. *Etruscan Italy: An Archaeological History.* London, 1990.

InfoTrac College Edition

Enter the search term *Rome history* using Key Terms.

Enter the search term *Roman law* using the Subject Guide.

Enter the search term *Roman republic* using Key Terms.

ROMANS OF THE REPUBLIC

By the mid-2nd century B.C., virtually the entire Mediterranean world was subject to Roman influence to some degree. With the growth of their territory, the Romans devised ways of organizing and administering the subject provinces outside Italy. As in the slow evolution of their own political system, Rome's ruling classes worked out their approaches to provincial governors and their duties—to taxation and the ever-present problems of bribery and corruption—by trial and error.

Meanwhile, at Rome itself, the years following the Punic Wars saw radical changes in economic patterns as large estates, or **latifundia,** replaced small farms, and industry and commerce began to provide the principal source of wealth. As banking, insurance, and investment programs spread, the rise of a new business class changed old established patterns of social relations.

One of the areas affected by shifting class lines was the family. By the late Republic, because money was no longer concentrated in the hands of the patricians, birth was no longer the prime factor in the choice of a marriage partner. With the general improvement in standards of living, girls from the families of businessmen received a better education, and well-to-do women began to lead relatively independent lives, although their progress aroused criticism and mysogyny.

The chief intellectual influence on the late Republic was Greece. Even before the sack of Corinth in 146 B.C., the Romans looked to the Greeks for guidance in art and philosophy. By the 1st century B.C., educated Roman women and men regarded Greek culture as superior to their own. Traditional Roman religion continued to serve the interests of the state, while Hellenistic philosophical systems such as Stoicism and Epicureanism provided more individual enlightenment. Large numbers of the urban masses, impressed neither by philosophy nor by the rituals of power, turned to dramatic and emotional cults introduced from Asia.

The same Greek influences came to dominate Roman literature of the period. Plautus and Terence based their comic plays on Greek originals. The epic poetry of Lucretius set out to expound Epicureanism to a Roman audience. One field in which Roman writers found their own authentic voice was that of intimate, personal love poetry, through which writers like Catullus analyzed the nature of love. At the very end of the Republic, the great orator Cicero, although openly acknowledging the influence of the Greek statesman Demosthenes, composed some of the most powerful and eloquent speeches in the Western tradition.

THE TRIALS OF PROVINCIAL ADMINISTRATION

The Romans continued to describe the peoples they conquered in Italy as "allies," whose independence was limited by their obligations (legal and financial) to Rome. Outside Italy, some territories were called "protectorates," or "client states," theoretically self-ruling but in practice bound to Rome by treaties in which they were the inferior partners. Macedon occupied this status for some 20 years, before becoming a province, and Egypt remained a client kingdom until the time of Julius Caesar. The reigning pharaoh was the nominal head of state but powerless to oppose Roman wishes.

The rest of Rome's overseas territories were provinces, administered directly by a representative of the Senate and Roman people. Roman writers of the Republic regularly described the citizens of the provinces as people who had surrendered to and were therefore at the disposal of the Roman state, with no rights of their own, and with the obligation to pay for the occupying troops who had conquered them. Even as enlightened an observer as Cicero referred to the provinces as "the estates of the Roman people."

THE PROVINCIAL GOVERNOR AND HIS STAFF

The head of each province's administration was the governor. Usually a magistrate sent out from Rome, and receiving no pay, the governor was in charge of the day-to-day running of his province, as well as functioning as its military commander and chief justice. He had the right to introduce new laws when he thought it necessary. As commander-in-chief, he was responsible for internal order as well as defense against outside attack. As chief law enforcer, he was required to hear all cases involving Roman citizens and all other important cases. In order to do this, he traveled on fixed "circuits" within his province, hearing trials in the chief cities.

In theory, governors served for one year and then returned to their duties in Rome, but—as the number of provinces grew—the Senate tended to renew a magistrate's mandate. The acts and decrees of a governor were valid only for his term of office, but his successors rarely undid or revised a predecessor's decisions. Over time, a body of policies, laws, and edicts from the provinces began to accumulate. The material was kept available in the office of the urban magistrate at Rome, and newly appointed governors would consult the files before taking up their post.

Most governors had a chief assistant, who was also appointed annually in Rome (the governor of Sicily had two chief assistants). Known as the *quaestor*, he was in charge of financial matters, accounting for income and expenditures. The quaestor's ability to limit his superior's tendency to exploit the provincials depended on the relationship the two established. Perhaps as a result, governors encouraged their assistants to regard them "as a son does his father."

The Senate chose both the governor and his deputy. The governor could select his aides, or *legati*, although the Senate had to ratify his selections. The aides helped in the administration and could represent the governor in his absence. It was customary for the team also to include some *comites*, "companions," young men from good families in search of experience and adventure, with the added possibility of making some money.

TAXATION IN THE PROVINCES

The original justification for the taxes imposed on the provincials was to cover the cost to Rome of their conquest, but over time the Romans came to look on the funds raised by taxation as income from property that by now belonged to Rome and was being "rented" by its inhabitants. Only under the emperors did administrators claim that taxes actually paid for the running and defense of the provinces.

The tax generally took the form of either a fixed annual sum or a percentage of a province's annual income or agricultural produce. In the case of the former, collection was easy and each community handed over its share to the quaestor. In the latter case, where each year's income fluctuated and therefore had to be assessed to decide how much was due, the state contracted out the collection to tax farmers, or *publicani*. The tax farmers bid against one another for contracts, hoping to bid enough to beat their rivals, but sufficiently little for the sum they actually collected to leave them with a handsome profit.

Over time the system led predictably to abuses. The problem lay not so much in the way the money was collected

Portrait bust of the Roman statesman and lawyer Cicero. 1st century B.C. A characteristic example of late Republican portrait art, this piece aims to convey both Cicero's physical appearance and something of his personality. The thinning hair and lined face are combined with a thoughtful, preoccupied air; the eyes are rapt in deep contemplation.

but in the misuse of office by many of the governors. The internal political structure of Rome depended on a careful series of checks and balances, which permitted control of the acts of individual administrators. By contrast, a provincial governor was the equivalent of a king, unchallenged on his territory and answerable only to the Roman Senate, which was a long way off and in any case more likely to sympathize with "one of their own" than with complaining provincials.

Victims sometimes appealed to Rome, and the Senate established standing juries to hear cases of maladministration, but the juries became as corrupt as the businessmen and politicians involved in the tax scandals. One of the few cases to reach trial in court was Cicero's prosecution of the former governor of Sicily, Gaius Verres (115–43 B.C.) in 70 B.C. The charges were extortion, embezzlement, looting of works of art, bribery and corruption, and general misgovernment over three years. Cicero prepared six speeches, but after the first blasting oration, Verres fled to France, taking most of his loot with him.

On the whole, the justice or injustice of a provincial administration depended on the character of each individual governor. Serving for only a short term, with no adequate control by the central government, irresponsible or corrupt ones could virtually act as they pleased. The opportunity for abuse was very great, and we hear of several who did so.

THE ROMAN ECONOMY: LAND TENURE, TRADE, AND CLASS

Agriculture in Italy during the first three centuries of the Republic was mainly in the hands of farmers living in country villages and working their own small parcels of land. The Punic Wars produced devastating changes to this pattern of rural life. In the first place, many farmers and agricultural laborers ended up in the army and never came home. The level of casualties in battle was frequently staggering: just in Hannibal's first three victories of 218–217 B.C., more than 100,000 Roman soldiers died. Second, those who did live to return to their villages often found them destroyed and abandoned as a result of Hannibal's campaigns in Italy. During the years of travel up and down the peninsula, the Carthaginian army ravaged the communities that refused to collaborate, while Roman troops later took reprisals against those who did provide aid to the invaders.

THE *LATIFUNDIA*

By the time peace returned to Italy, large tracts of land lay abandoned. Many of them were confiscated by the state and sold or rented to those who had made fortunes in trading or selling war supplies and were looking for a way to invest their new income. The farmers of the prewar years, with their small landholdings, cultivated grain, but this approach had little appeal for the new "agri-businessmen." The profit margin was slim, and in any case the newly acquired provinces provided an abundant supply of cheap grain.

The landowners who purchased large estates turned instead to cattle ranching because both meat and dairy products were in great demand at Rome or to the planting of vines and olive trees because good-quality wine and olive oil fetched high prices. Both types of farming required large landholdings and were labor-intensive. The land was already available, and the vast numbers of slaves taken as prisoners in the course of the wars were cheap and expendable. In some cases, the former owners of small landholdings stayed on to work the land as hired help.

Thus, in one generation, the agricultural customs of centuries disappeared, and the working of the *latifundia* went to enrich wealthy politicians and businessmen who

Painting of a garden on a wall in the Villa of Livia and Augustus just outside Rome, at Prima Porta, c. 20 B.C. The peaceful scene, with its abundant fruit and flowers, in which birds fly and perch, reflects the interest in country life that inspired the poetry of Vergil, one of Augustus's leading court poets. Note the use of perspective.

Scala/Art Resource

rarely set foot on their properties and whose only concern was profit. Although northern Italy was less affected by the exploitation, many parts of the south were seriously over-farmed, and massive programs of deforestation caused soil erosion and the formation of malarial swamps. The land exploitation left scars throughout Italy, especially in the south, that were to last for centuries.

Meanwhile, the peasants, having lost their source of work, drifted to the city, attracted by tales of the fortunes to be made there. By the end of the Second Punic War, Rome was drawing rapidly increasing crowds of immigrants: farm-workers from rural Italy, returning veterans whose campaigning abroad had given them a taste for excitement, and tradesmen and craftsmen from other parts of the Empire attracted by the possibilities the market offered. At the same time the numbers of slaves working in the capital rose sharply, many of whom eventually obtained their freedom. The result of all these changes was to produce, for the first time in the ancient world, a huge urban proletariat, which was destined to play an important role in the collapse of the Republic in the 1st century B.C.

MANUFACTURING AND TRADE

Rome's origins were rustic, and even with the city swollen to vast proportions Roman poets and writers looked back nostalgically to the times when their forebears had been farmers and shepherds. Perhaps as a result, manufacturing was never popular in the capital. The Romans preferred to develop regional centers of production. The former

Etruscan lands continued to manufacture bronze and iron objects and cloth. Campania, the center of rich farmland, turned out farm and household implements and rope. The production of weapons remained based in central Italy, within reach of Rome and the politicians.

If Roman businessmen were unwilling to soil their hands with the actual process of manufacture, they were only too happy to put their money to work. Shareholders invested in companies that then put in bids for public contracts: road building, feeding and transport of troops, construction of new law courts. Other companies imported luxury goods from the provinces, for which there was an insatiable demand at Rome. Still others ran transport firms—by land and sea—to deal with the growth in trade. The result of all these developments was to create jobs for the urban poor: stevedores, storehouse keepers, and roadworkers.

As the circulation of money increased, other forms of financial institutions arose to fill the need. Banking became international, as houses established branches in several different countries. Although Roman currency circulated widely, many of the Asian markets preferred to use gold for buying and selling, and some Greek cities chose to keep their own coinage. The result was the appearance of exchange offices to handle currency conversion.

The formation of credit and loan institutions met another need. At first the chief clients were businessmen in need of help with their cash flow, but the lending institutions also provided credit to cities in the provinces that could not pay the annual tribute due to Rome. These loans, made out-

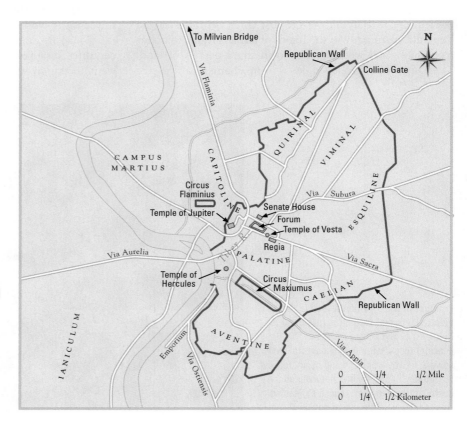

Map 14.1 Republican Rome. The so-called Servian Walls, supposedly built under the early (and probably legendary) king Servius Tullius (6th century B.C.), soon proved too small for the growing city, but they contained Rome's chief monuments for over a thousand years, built on or below the famous seven hills. The Forum, at the center, remained the heart of Roman political and economic life from Etruscan times to the 5th century A.D., while the Palatine Hill became the residence of the Emperors.

side Italy at interest rates that were often shockingly high, provided investors with extremely profitable returns.

THE RISE OF THE BUSINESS CLASSES

The effect of all these rapid economic changes was the gradual but inexorable erosion of Rome's system of political and social balance. In the new postwar climate, the old compromise worked out between patricians and plebeians had to take account of an additional political force, the prosperous business class created by the increase in commerce. As many of the middle-class businessmen saw their fortunes grow even larger, swelled by the commercial boom, they began to lobby for political recognition.

Centuries earlier, one of the ways for a plebeian to rise above his humble origins was to volunteer to provide his own horse (an expensive undertaking) and serve in the cavalry. Such men styled themselves *equites*, or horsemen—the equivalent of the medieval knights. By the 2nd century B.C., many wealthy plebeians could buy and sell horses by the thousands, but the term "equites" remained in use to describe the new class of self-made men and their descendants.

For the old established patrician families, these "new men" at first remained no more than wealthy plebeians, to be excluded from the highest social order. Over time, however, as intermarriage began to blur the lines, the new "equestrian order" played a growing role in factional politics, and both patricians and plebeians vied for their support. Like the urban mob, they too were to play a crucial role in the unraveling of the Republic.

WOMEN AND THE FAMILY IN A PATRIARCHAL SOCIETY

The head of a Roman family was its eldest male—the *pater familias,* "father of the family." The authority of the head of a family extended to all males, of whatever age, and ended only on his death, when the others became emancipated. In the early history of the Republic, custody of females, on the death of their *pater familias,* passed to the nearest male relative, unless the dying man had named a different guardian in his will. Women needed the approval of their guardian when undertaking a business deal, selling land, or freeing a slave.

By the late Republic, as women began to lead far more open lives, many of these provisions were no longer in

Relief sculpture from the Ara Pacis (Altar of Peace) showing Mother Earth with two children, c. 13–9 B.C. Height 5 feet 3 inches (1.61 m). In front of the goddess is a symbol of the sea, riding on a sea-monster, while on the other side a symbol of the air flies down riding on a bird. The background includes plants and animals peacefully grazing. The reliefs underline Rome's agricultural origins, and the importance of the land of Italy, while underplaying the role of commerce in the city's increasing power and prosperity.

Nimatallah/Art Resource

force. When a woman's guardian refused to give his consent, she could appeal to the courts to get his veto waived or to have him replaced. In many cases, serving as guardian gave more trouble to men than to women, and prosperous women of the late Republic often ran large households without ever consulting an adviser.

MARRIAGE AND POWER

Roman marriage customs differed in significant ways from those of Classical Greece. In the first place, both bride and groom were usually around the same age, around 14, and were generally not close relatives, although among the elite, marriage alliances between cousins were fairly common. In early Republican times there were two forms of marriage. The first gave the husband power over his wife. Under the second, which came to be predominant, a wife did not pass under her husband's control at marriage; she remained under the authority of her *pater familias*. The practical effect of this was to give a woman more freedom, answerable as she was not to the man with whom she lived, but to one residing in a different house and sometimes in a different town or country. Furthermore, a woman who could easily return to her father's household was less likely to put up with ill treatment.

A marriage could take place only with the consent of both partners, but the woman had to prove that her prospective husband was "morally unfit" in order for her to escape the match. A father generally, but not always, picked his daughter's husband, generally in consultation with her

Painting from Pompeii showing a couple, perhaps the baker Pacuvius Proclus and his wife, c. A.D. 70–79. Height 1 foot 11 inches (63 cm). The figures are involved in doing their accounts; the man holds a written scroll, while the woman has a folding wax tablet in one hand and presses a "stylus" (a pointed instrument for inscribing on wax) to her lips with the other.

Scala/Art Resource

mother. Cicero found his daughter's first two husbands, but she selected her third herself, with her mother's help, while her father was away—Cicero grumbled, and threatened not to pay the dowry, but in the end gave way.

In the highest ranks of Roman society, both marriage and divorce served as means of financial and political alliance. At the other end of the social scale, lower-class men often married slave women, whom they had to free beforehand. In some cases masters freed their slaves and subsequently married them to make children previously born to the couple free and legitimate. Roman women sometimes freed a male slave to marry him, but this practice was generally frowned upon.

Divorce was common among middle- and upper-class couples and could be initiated by either partner. No legal reason was necessary, but divorce was generally for political or personal motives. One husband of the late Republic recorded in a funerary inscription at his wife's death that years earlier she had offered to divorce him, because she was unable to bear children, and was willing to live with him as his sister while he took a new wife. Forty-three years later, when she died, he affectionately recalled turning down her offer and choosing a life shared with her over marrying another woman and having descendants.

WOMEN IN SOCIETY

The Romans were aware of the differences between the lifestyles of Greek and Roman women. As the late Republican writer Cornelius Nepos (c. 99–c. 24 B.C.) succinctly put it: "Greek women sit secluded in the interior parts of the house, while ours accompany their husbands to dinner parties." Not only did many upper-class Romans regard education as important for both men and women, but successful middle-class families sometimes hired tutors for both sons and daughters, while it was not unusual for the daughters of plebeian fathers to attend elementary school.

For some Romans, education, far from bringing censure, only served to enhance a woman's charms. One writer praised Cornelia, Julius Caesar's wife, because she was well read, could play the lyre, and was well trained in geometry and philosophy, while Quintilian (c. A.D. 30–c. 100), the leading Roman expert on education, recommended that both parents should be as highly educated as possible, for the good of their children.

By the end of the Republic, some of the more sophisticated women-about-town were becoming famous for their love affairs with writers and public figures. Poets such as Catullus, Ovid, and Propertius address their mistresses in their poetry. Propertius's beloved herself wrote verse, he tells us, the equal of the Archaic Greek poet Corinna, and another woman poet of the day, Sulpicia, wrote an elegy in praise of her lover Cerinthus. Some of the glamorous and intellectual women of the age initiated a custom that proved highly important in women's intellectual history: the literary "salon," where men and women could meet and exchange ideas. On the other hand, the increasing prominence of a handful of upper-class women provoked a backlash of considerable criticism and scorn, including predictable bursts of mysogyny, on the part of many Roman males.

Greek women poets, although rare, were not unknown. The notion of a woman orator would probably have horrified an ancient Athenian, but several famous and admired Roman women spoke in public. One of the speeches of Hortensia, the daughter of Cicero's rival Hortensius, which has survived in a Greek translation, was highly praised by Quintilian. These examples, however, were exceptional. In general, those women who rose above an elementary level of education, or distinguished themselves in some area of public life, aroused suspicion and often hostility.

Although there were distinct limits to the freedom of Roman upper-class women, they could influence the society and politics of their times in several ways—and frequently did. They could not vote or hold office, but they could endorse candidates, exercise patronage, be public benefactors, and have buildings and statues erected in their honor. They also played an important role in certain Roman religious cults, particularly those related to marriage, as is illustrated by the fresco cycle in the Villa of the Mysteries at Pompeii. The importance of some women of the elite was such that if their private behavior went too far beyond the accepted norm, they might suffer social ostracism or even, in extreme cases, banishment.

The relative increase in the areas of life open to women by the end of the Republic was almost entirely limited to those from elite families and met with considerable resistance. Yet at least some Roman women had choices. In general, the lives of upper-class women were conditioned as much by their family, income, social status, and physical and intellectual gifts as by their gender. Dining out with their husbands or lovers, going to parties, attending performances in the theater or stadium, taking part in political gatherings—elite women of the late Republic had greater freedom than most women before their times, and many afterward.

RELIGION AND PHILOSOPHY: GREEK IDEAS IN ROMAN FORMS

The early Romans shared the religious beliefs of many of their Italian neighbors. Like the Samnites, the Oscans, and other Italic peoples, they worshiped a series of nature spirits, many of whom were connected with agriculture. With the foundation of the Republic, the state began to adapt traditional religious practices to the needs of official ritual, and throughout Roman history the central government used religion and ceremony to reinforce its authority. As Roman society became increasingly urban, however, the country spirits of its early rural days seemed less and less relevant to the experience and needs of its citizens. As a result, the Romans always remained open to other forms of belief, exploring the cults and philosophical ideas of the peoples with whom they came into contact. At the same time, the official, public forms of religious observance served the political aims of the state, rather than the spiritual needs of its citizens.

Growing awareness of Greek religion led the Romans to identify their own supernatural spirits with the Greek gods and goddesses in human form. The narrative element in Greek mythology appealed to writers and artists, who produced their own versions of the age-old stories of the gods' loves and squabbles. Yet the tales provided entertainment rather than spiritual consolation, and the search for deeper emotional satisfaction led many ordinary Romans to turn to cults imported from Asia.

In 204 B.C., the state officially introduced into Rome the worship of Cybele, a form of the Great Mother Goddess, whose chief shrines had been in Lydia and Phrygia (both now part of modern Turkey). The purpose was to win the help of the goddess in driving Hannibal out of Italy. Once arrived, she stayed. The ecstatic and colorful celebrations in her honor, which often involved orgiastic rites, drew large numbers of enthusiastic devotees among the poorer classes at Rome, seeking distraction from the social upheaval surrounding them. The cult of Cybele retained its grip on the popular imagination for centuries, despite various official attempts to limit its wilder manifestations, including self-castration.

HELLENISTIC PHILOSOPHY AT ROME

Many Roman intellectuals found an explanation of the mysteries of life in Greek philosophy, in particular the schools developed during the Hellenistic Age (see Topic 12). As power in the Mediterranean shifted westward toward Italy, increasing numbers of Greek philosophers and teachers found their way to Rome in search of patrons and students. By the end of the 2nd century B.C., their ideas circulated widely in Roman society.

The two main schools of Hellenistic thought, Stoicism and Epicureanism, each found enthusiastic followers, although Epicureanism's philosophy of seeking active withdrawal from life's battles never really appealed to the practical Roman temperament. The late Republican poet Lucretius (c. 95–c. 55 B.C.) composed a lengthy work, *On the Nature of Things*, aimed at converting his contemporaries to the Epicurean view of the world. On the whole, however, most Romans continued to think of it as an alien system, mainly of interest to intellectuals, whereas some Roman aristocrats used Epicureanism as an excuse for wanton self-indulgence.

Stoicism, with its clarion call to duty, made a broader appeal, especially to soldiers and public servants. Furthermore, the Stoics' belief in the force of reason, which animated all living things, fitted more comfortably with ancient Italian nature cults, while the notion of Stoic behavior—virtuous, grave, impervious to obstacles—reinforced the Romans' sense of their own historical role as world leaders. Moral fortitude and trust in Divine Providence fitted in well with the austerity of the founding fathers of the Republic.

Along with philosophy, Greek literature and art also found a new and enthusiastic audience at Rome. For all the

Wall painting from the Villa of the Mysteries at Pompeii, c. 60–50 B.C. (?) Height 5 feet 4 inches (1.64 m). The scene relates to the cult of the Greek god Dionysus (Roman Bacchus) and his mortal lover Ariadne. At the center, Dionysus—recognizable from his vine-topped staff—is stretched across the body of Ariadne (whose head is missing). The room may have been decorated for a marriage ceremony, but many of the details (the winged figure on the right, for example) are not fully understood.

barbarity of Mummius's looting of Corinth, the conquest of Greece and the shipping home of its treasures brought the Romans into contact with actual Greek bronzes and marbles on a scale hitherto unknown. The first reaction was uncritical admiration. Only with time did Roman artists feel able to make their own contribution to the Classical tradition (see Topic 17).

THE LITERATURE OF THE ROMAN REPUBLIC

Even before their conquests in the East, the Romans were well acquainted with Greek literature. As Roman writers began to lay the foundations of their own literary tradition, they turned to Greek models. Later ages regarded Ennius (239–169 B.C.) as the "father of Roman poetry." Most of his works are lost, but Ennius clearly borrowed his forms from the Greeks, adapting his tragedies from Greek ones and us-

ing Greek meters for his most celebrated work, the *Annals*. This epic chronicle of the early history of Rome aimed at providing his fellow Romans with a Latin equivalent of the heroic tradition of Homer.

For all the awe in which his contemporaries held Ennius, they preferred comedy to tragedy, and the first successful popular writers were the comic dramatists Plautus (c. 254–184 B.C.) and Terence (c. 195–159 B.C.). Of the two, Plautus is the more boisterous, Terence the more sophisticated, but both drew on the same sources—urbane Greek comedies of the Hellenistic Age—and adapted them to Roman taste.

ROMAN LOVE POETRY OF THE LATE REPUBLIC: CATULLUS

By the 1st century B.C., Roman poets were using the forms of Greek love poetry, many of which went back to the 6th century B.C., to relate to their own contemporary world. In lyrics that are at the same time intimate in their revelations and universal in the emotions they express, Roman poets cast an entirely new light on an age of social turmoil.

The poet Catullus (c. 84–c. 54 B.C.) was born at Verona. When he came to Rome around 62 B.C., he was able to see the hectic life of the capital with an outsider's eyes, and he passes on his impressions to us with delighted eagerness: the dinner guests who rob their hosts, the pretty wives who make fools of their pompous husbands, whispered scandals, the white-toothed smiles of a corrupt politician.

When Catullus arrived in Rome, the most famous woman there was Clodia, the central figure in most of the gossip of the day. Her brother (and, it was rumored, lover) Clodius was a notorious gang leader, involved in open warfare with his rival Milo. Meanwhile, with her husband absent on duty in Gaul as governor, Clodia could pursue her own amorous interests with relative freedom. As Catullus began to move in Roman high society, the young provincial's freshness and cynicism were of little defense against her charms—after all, even the staid Cicero was struck by her alluring brown eyes. A series of 25 or so lyrics written by Catullus over the course of the next couple of years charts the course—perhaps based on personal experience—of one of the poet's love affairs.

In addressing his beloved in the poems, Catullus used the name Lesbia, thereby invoking the memory of one of the greatest Greek love poets of the Archaic age, Sappho (who came from Lesbos). At the same time he used verse forms created and popularized at Alexandria in the Hellenistic period, blending the Archaic and Hellenistic traditions to produce his own individual voice.

Catullus's poems describe the various phases of love: blind passion, the dawn of mistrust, disillusion, and final despairing hatred—the moods range from "My darling, let us live and love for ever" to his frantic railing at "Rome's prostitute." Many of the poems of the few years remaining to him after the composition of these earlier works describe his hectic travels in the East in which he sought distraction, but in the end only his secluded villa on Lake Garda, near Verona, brought him peace.

Putting Romans of the Republic in Perspective

In the years following the Punic Wars, the Romans of the Republic lived through external growth and internal upheaval. Social and economic patterns that had lasted for centuries shifted beyond recovery. It took two centuries for Rome to become the dominating power in Italy, a region out of the mainstream of Mediterranean politics and culture. With the passing of only a few more years, the Romans ruled the Mediterranean world, the successors to Alexander the Great.

In developing their system of external rule, Roman administrators had to work out a way of transforming violent conquest into firm and effective rule. In many cases, the Romans' outbursts of arrogant brutality—as at Carthage and Corinth—provoked widespread indignation.

Internally, the acquisition of empire imposed strains on the fabric of life and politics at Rome, which led to violent change. In 133 B.C., the year in which Attalus, the prudent king of Pergamum, willed his kingdom to the Roman people, the first ominous signals appeared of the impending collapse of the Republic.

Questions for Further Study

1. What were the main characteristics of Roman provincial administration, and how did they evolve? How efficient were they?
2. What part did economic development play in Rome's growth? What was its effect on social patterns?
3. How did the role of upper-class women in the late Republic differ from that of women in Classical Athens? What were its limitations?
4. What contribution did Republican writers make to Latin literature? How original was it?

Suggestions for Further Reading

Alfoldy, G. *The Social History of Rome*. Berlin, 1988.

Anderson, James C., Jr. *Roman Architecture and Society*. Baltimore, MD, 1997.

Bradley, K.R. *Discovering the Roman Family*. New York, 1990.

Dixon, S. *The Roman Mother*. Norman, OK, 1988.

Earl, D.C. *The Moral and Political Tradition of Rome*. Ithaca, NY, 1984.

Gardner, J.F. *Women in Roman Law and Society*. Bloomington, IN, 1986.

Hallett, J.P. *Fathers and Daughters in Roman Society: Women and the Elite Family.* Princeton, NJ, 1984.

Kleiner, Diana E.E., and Susan B. Matheson. *I Claudia: Women in Ancient Rome.* New Haven, 1996.

Wacher, J., ed. *The Roman World.* London, 1987.

InfoTrac College Edition

Enter the search terms *Rome history* using Key Terms.

Enter the search terms *Roman republic* using Key Terms.

Enter the search terms *Roman mythology* using the Subject Guide.

THE COLLAPSE OF THE ROMAN REPUBLIC

The first serious attempt to deal with the underlying political and economic problems of late Republican Rome came in the tribunates of the Gracchus brothers. First Tiberius Gracchus, and then Gaius, tried to help the popular cause by introducing land reform measures, while Gaius also moved to establish a political alliance with the middle-class *equites.* Both brothers died violent deaths at the hands of their political opponents.

By the beginning of the 1st century B.C., wars in Africa and Central Europe, a slave revolt in Sicily, and an uprising in Italy brought two rival generals to power at Rome. The first, Marius, claimed to represent the popular interest. His eventually successful rival, the arch-conservative Sulla, reformed the state along archaic lines, before unexpectedly resigning all his powers and retiring to private life.

With the political situation at Rome ever worsening, the stage was set for the disastrous conflict between Pompey, champion of the Senate, and Julius Caesar, backed by the popular party. In 49 B.C., after years of successful campaigning in Gaul, Caesar led his victorious troops in a march on Rome, while Pompey and his supporters fled to Greece. The result was the Civil War, the first in the Republic's 500-year history. The following year Caesar defeated Pompey's forces in pitched battle. After a brief period in Egypt, where his liaison with Cleopatra produced a son, Caesar returned to Rome and became dictator.

When Caesar fell victim to the blows of a band of idealistic republican conspirators in 44 B.C., Rome's internal political order was on the point of collapse. Mark Antony, Caesar's deputy, took immediate command of the situation, but his supremacy came under almost immediate challenge: Octavian, Caesar's young great-nephew and adopted heir, arrived in Rome to claim his inheritance.

Antony and Octavian formed an uneasy alliance to pursue and defeat the conspirators responsible for Caesar's murder. Thereafter, the last 10 years of the Republic saw the return of civil war between the two. Antony's flight to Egypt to seek the help of Cleopatra provided Octavian with a powerful propaganda weapon. In 31 B.C. Octavian's army and navy, fighting for Italy against the "traitor" and his Egyptian queen, decisively overcame their enemies' joint forces at Actium. The Republic was shattered, and the Roman state lay at Octavian's command.

THE GRACCHUS BROTHERS AND THE FAILURE OF REFORM

Throughout the years of the Punic Wars and Rome's successive acquisition of the provinces, the aristocratic Senatorial party retained its supremacy in Roman affairs. Bolstered by the wealth of their great estates, and with their prestige enhanced by Rome's success against Carthage and the defeat of Hannibal, members of the Senate dominated the political scene at Rome and the government of the provinces abroad. By the mid-2nd century B.C., however, demand was growing at a popular level for political reform. When the revolution finally came, its first leaders, the two aristocratic Gracchus brothers, were members of the very social class against which the protest was aimed.

TIBERIUS GRACCHUS AND AGRARIAN REFORM

Tiberius Gracchus (163–133 B.C.) and his younger brother Gaius (153–121 B.C.) were from one of Rome's most distinguished noble families. Their father was widely admired for his governorship of Spain, and Tiberius served in the army there. His experiences on military duty led him to formulate a single overriding reason for Rome's manifold problems. In Tiberius's view, the low morale of the Roman army, urban discontent at Rome, and the constant threat of slave rebellions in the provinces all had the same cause: the excessive growth in power and wealth of the great estate owners.

To remedy this situation, Tiberius proposed a program of agrarian reform that would redistribute public land, limiting the size of farm holdings and settling them with retired veteran soldiers and the urban poor. The aim was to repopulate the countryside with a flourishing peasant class, while reducing the need for massive slave labor.

In 133 B.C., running on his reform program, the aristocratic Tiberius won election as tribune of the people. His campaign speeches gave eloquent voice to the injustices felt by many: "Wild beasts have their lairs, but the men who fight and die for Italy can call nothing their own except the air and the sunshine." Once elected, Tiberius and his supporters in the Senate set up a Land Commission, and its three commissioners began to redistribute public farmland.

The wealthy senators and landowners were outraged, but worse was to come. In the same year, King Attalus of Pergamum died, leaving his kingdom to the Roman state (see Topic 13). Tiberius proposed not only to use the income from Pergamum to underwrite the Commission's work, but also to have the assembly of the people discuss the organization of the new province. At one blow, Tiberius challenged the Senate's authority in the two areas over which it had always maintained control: finance and foreign affairs.

Time was running out, and Tiberius announced that he was standing for reelection as tribune for 132 B.C. Consecutive terms were unusual, although not unconstitutional, and rumors arose—adroitly spread by Senate representatives—that Tiberius intended to make himself tyrant of Rome. On election day, riots broke out, and a band led by a leading Senate conservative surrounded Tiberius and 300 of his supporters and clubbed them to death.

The openness of Tiberius's challenge to the Senate, together with the bloody circumstances of his death, were ominous. His oversimplistic idea of returning to the ways of earlier times, and the speed with which he tried to bring about radical reform, both proved fatal to his cause. Yet these issues highlighted the existence of grave popular resentment and dissatisfaction. The violence used by Tiberius's enemies to suppress political opposition was the prelude to a century of bitter civil strife.

GAIUS, GRAIN, AND THE *EQUITES*

Warned by the brutal ending to his brother's political career, Gaius lay low in the years immediately following Tiberius's death. He served on the Land Commission, which the Senate stripped of its judicial powers while allowing it to con-

Section of the plastic model of Imperial Rome, made in the 1930s. The river Tiber runs through the foreground. The two largest structures visible are the Circus Maximus (the huge stadium where the chariot races were held) and the Colosseum. The complex of buildings between them consists of the Forum and the Emperor's palace on the Palatine Hill.

C.M. Dixon

tinue in operation. Unlike Tiberius, who concentrated all his attention on a single issue, Gaius used the time to prepare a far more general program of reform. To achieve lasting victory, he set about putting together a coalition of support: the urban poor, Rome's Italian allies, and—crucially—the middle-class *equites* with their business interests.

In December 124 B.C., Gaius was ready. He stood for election as tribune, Tiberius's old office, and won triumphantly. The following year he ran again, and again he was elected. He used his two years in power to buttress his support. Contracts in a massive program of public works—roads, harbors, public buildings—went to his business supporters. Better still from their point of view, they secured the contracts to collect taxes in the new province of Asia. Furthermore, Gaius changed the law by which governors accused of misconduct were tried by a jury of senators. From now on, any governor unwise enough to resist pressure from businessmen collecting taxes would be tried before a jury made up of *equites*, the representatives of big business.

Meanwhile, Gaius consolidated his backing among the urban poor by introducing a grain law, giving every Roman the right to a fixed monthly allowance of grain at a specially controlled price. At the same time he strengthened the working of the Land Commission by restoring its judicial powers and planned new colonies where settlers—some from the proletariat, others businessmen of experience—could go to make their fortunes. There was even to be a new colony built on the ruins of Carthage.

For Rome's Italian "allies," Gaius proposed an extension of Roman citizenship to all Latins and Latin rights (including immunity from punishment at the hands of Roman soldiers) to all Italians from the Alps to Sicily.

Such a varied plan of reform was far more threatening to senatorial interests than Tiberius's mere agrarian program of a decade earlier, and the Senate acted accordingly. A Senate proposal outbidding Gaius offered to quadruple the number of colonies to be founded. Even more effectively, Gaius's opponents reminded Roman voters that if they shared their rights with other Italians, they would also have to share their privileges.

As Gaius returned from Carthage to face reelection in December 122 B.C., his coalition fell apart. Amid street riots and frenzied demonstrations by all sides, Gaius lost his bid to be elected for a third term as tribune. Early in the new year, 121 B.C., with the popular leader barely out of office, the senators hastily began repealing Gaius's legislation. In the course of protest rallies, one of the consul's attendants was killed, and the senators lost no time in moving against their enemies. Passing the equivalent of martial law, they instructed the consuls "to provide that the State shall receive no harm." A posse hunted down Gaius's supporters and liquidated 3,000 of them. Gaius himself fell as he tried to escape from the city: He may have committed suicide to avoid finishing in his enemies' hands.

With unconscious irony, a grateful Senate ordered the construction of a new Temple to Concord, to mark the return of harmony to Rome. Yet the result of the lives—and deaths—of the Gracchus brothers was to put the Senate and the popular party on a collision course that could end only with the supremacy of one side and the destruction of the other. Even more ominously, by legalizing the deaths of the brothers, their enemies legitimized the use of political violence and the abrogation of citizen rights. The urban political strife that marked the Gracchus brothers' attempts at reform led in due course to outright civil war.

POLITICS AND THE GENERALS: THE STRUGGLE FOR POWER

With the upper classes back in control, and without a charismatic leader to rally the popular interests, the Senate ensured itself the support, for the moment at least, of the *equites* by making important business concessions to them. It took a long, drawn-out war in Africa to create the next popular leader capable of challenging the newly forged alliance of aristocracy and businessmen.

MARIUS THE POPULIST

Gaius Marius (157–86 B.C.) was born at Arpinum, in the hills to the southeast of Rome. A provincial, he first emerged as a spokesman for the popular interests in 119 B.C., when he won election as tribune. He went on to serve in the provincial administration of Spain.

During the years of Marius's rise, Rome became embroiled in a frustrating conflict in North Africa. Their chief opponent there was the Numidian king Jugurtha (ruled 118–105 B.C.), who cleverly involved the Roman Senate in the internal politics of his kingdom. As the hostilities dragged on, a succession of aristocratic generals led the Roman forces in Africa from one setback to another.

Finally, in 107 B.C., Marius ran for the consulship, campaigning on his promise to put an end to the interminable African conflict. The popular faction, sensing a new champion of their cause, backed him. Marius won and went on to beat Jugurtha by enlisting a fresh, volunteer army from the urban proletariat at Rome and the rural poor, trained by Marius himself—in the past, the Romans had required only citizens with property to undertake military duty, and Marius's recruitment of landless men was, in fact, illegal. All troops carried standardized weapons and learned to march 40 miles a day with their equipment strapped to their backs. Proud of their arduous training, they called themselves "Marius's mules," and their loyalty to their commander meant that for the first time a general representing the popular side had his own military backing.

By 106 B.C. the African war was over and Marius returned to Italy, having transformed the Roman Army into a professional machine. He organized it in regiments, or "legions," with each legion broken down into 10 smaller units called "cohorts." Every legion had its silver eagle, or "standard," with which it marched into battle and to which the men pledged allegiance.

Marius finished his reorganization just in time to fend off a threatened invasion from two northern tribes, the Cimbri and Teutoni. Cutting their way south from Scandinavia to Gaul and Spain, in 102 B.C. they were poised to invade Italy. Marius and his legions were ready for them, however, and routed them in two bloody battles at which, the Romans claimed, 100,000 of the enemy were killed or captured.

Throughout his years of army organization and the subsequent wars with the Cimbri and Teutoni, Marius had repeatedly won election as consul, chiefly as a means of reinforcing his military command. When peace came and he stood for reelection in 100 B.C., he ran as political leader of the popular faction. A brilliant soldier, Marius had poor political judgment and threw his weight behind the extreme fringe of the democratic interests. Faced with their violent behavior, which virtually ended the longstanding alliance between the popular faction and the *equites*, Marius found himself forced to arrest his erstwhile supporters. By the end of the year, his political credit exhausted, he left on a tour of Asia rather than risk certain defeat at the polls.

THE SOCIAL WAR

One of the aims of Gaius Gracchus's program in 123–122 B.C. had been the extension of rights to Rome's Italian allies, or *socii*. With Gaius's death, the scheme held little appeal for politicians at Rome, but the allies continued to press for tax reform and the granting of citizenship. Moderate and liberal Romans recognized the justice of their cause, but both businessmen and the lower classes opposed it. The former feared the competition from Italian manufacturers and traders, while the plebs had no wish to share their power to vote or their supplies of subsidized grain.

Angry and frustrated, the Italians joined forces to throw off Roman rule. The conflict, called the Social War, lasted from 91 to 88 B.C. The combined Italian armies, inspired by their indignation, fought bravely, and only the recall of Marius prevented the rout of the Roman troops in central Italy. In the south, a promising young commander, Lucius Sulla, led the Roman force defending Campania.

In the end, the Romans won not by military action but by making the allies the concessions they were fighting for. The state awarded citizenship first to all those Italian communities that were prepared to lay down their arms and then to all individual Italians who withdrew from the fighting. Within weeks the war was over. By 88 B.C. citizenship rights extended from the Alps to Sicily, and Sulla, by now serving as consul, had mopped up resistance from the rebellious Samnites in the south.

THE TRIUMPH OF SULLA

Lucius Sulla (138–78 B.C.) had first come to prominence under Marius in the war against Jugurtha, and in many ways his career paralleled that of the older man. A successful field commander, worshiped by his men, Sulla, like Marius, nourished political ambitions. The similarities ended there, however, for if Marius's political sympathies lay with the popular cause, Sulla came as close as any Roman figure ever

did to the bloodthirsty dictators of the 20th century. A political and military adventurer, who indulged in repeated urban massacres, Sulla won the backing of the Roman aristocracy only when he was firmly in power.

It was inevitable that Marius and Sulla would become rivals. In 88 B.C. Sulla, then consul, was awarded the prestigious command of the Roman force in Asia for the following year. In a bitterly contested move in the Senate, Sulpicius Rufus, one of the tribunes of 88 B.C., had the command of Asia transferred to Marius in return for his political support. In rage Sulla marched on Rome with his troops—an unprecedented and illegal act that moved Rome one step nearer to military dictatorship—took the city, and had his political enemies declared outlaws. Sulpicius was captured and put to death, Sulla regained his eastern command, and in due course he left for Asia.

With Sulla and his troops gone, it was Marius's turn to march on Rome, ordering the murder of the senators and other figures who had opposed him. Within a month Marius was dead, but his supporters—who claimed to be democratic representatives of the popular interest against the Senate—remained in power.

The war in Asia over and peace negotiated, Sulla, the victorious general, returned to Italy in 82 B.C. Now his time had come, and the relieved Senators, believing him to be their champion, agreed to his demand for appointment as "dictator, to take such steps and issue such laws without veto or appeal as were necessary." Armed with these drastic powers, Sulla was ready for revenge on his political opponents.

The first of his "proscription lists" appeared within days of his entry into Rome. Sulla issued a series of these lists, encouraging informers to supply names of leaders of the popular cause and former supporters of Marius. In all, the lists contained the names of 90 senators, 15 men of consular rank, and some 2,600 *equites*. All of them were to lose their lives, with their property confiscated by the state. Many who provided additional victims did so in pursuit of private feuds, but Sulla did not hesitate to put the names down—later Romans never forgot his cold-blooded casualness.

With (as he thought) the popular faction wiped out forever, Sulla then turned to reform of the state. His aim was to eliminate democracy and strengthen the power of the Senate by returning to the constitution of the 5th century B.C. He abolished the cheap grain allowance and removed many of the powers of the tribunes of the people. He had additional Senators murdered and appointed his own candidates to increase the numbers to 600. Many of his appointees had collaborated in killing their predecessors and were thus liable to Sulla's retaliation whenever he wished. The "reform" was intended as a move to reinforce his authority over the Senate. (Ironically, however, because many of the new senators came from the recently enfranchised Italian municipalities, Sulla's actions introduced new, destabilizing groups into the struggle for power.) He established seven permanent courts for seven types of crime—extortion, murder, treason, and so on—with juries drawn exclusively from the Senate. This legal reform, which took the control of corruption tri-

als away from the *equites,* was the only part of the Sullan reform program to have a lasting effect.

With Rome returned to an archaic and outdated system
of rule, and his own position guaranteed by fear of further
bloodshed, Sulla then bewildered all of his contemporaries
by retiring to private life on his country estate in Campania.
Within a few months he was dead. His constitutional reform fell into ruins, and the battle for supremacy between
the Senate and its opponents, the *equites* and the popular
front, was on again.

The careers of both Marius and Sulla illustrate the danger of successful generals taking up politics, especially in the
extreme form that the two of them espoused. Both of them
used politics—and were used by the politicians—as a means
of achieving personal power. Sulla's epitaph, composed by
himself, claimed that no man had ever done more good to
his friends or harm to his enemies, and Marius might well
have claimed likewise. Both of them caused immense damage to the state.

POMPEY AND CAESAR: RIVALRY AND CIVIL WAR

With Sulla gone, the two groups that had suffered most as a
result of his reforms—the poor and the business class—hastened to challenge the Senate and reclaim their lost rights.
Even if the senators could have presented a united front
against the opposition, and their continued squabbling
made this impossible, events in the provinces provided a series of urgent crises that demanded their attention.

In Asia, Mithridates, king of the small state of Pontus,
went on the offensive, challenging the Roman presence
there. To the west, Sertorius, a former governor of Spain,
led a revolt by the local Spanish population to break away
from Rome. Both Mithridates and Sertorius encouraged the
pirates who were active in the eastern Mediterranean to
play havoc with Roman shipping, and in 70 B.C. the pirates
were emboldened enough to threaten the port of Rome,
Ostia. Meanwhile, the runaway slave Spartacus and an increasing number of fellow deserters moved up and down
Italy for two years, from 73 to 71 B.C., looting the smaller
towns and causing terror among the local population.

POMPEY TAKES CHARGE

As the Senate tried to handle the worsening situation, it
turned increasingly to one of the leading generals of the
day, Gnaeus Pompeius (106–48 B.C.)—the self-styled
Pompey the Great. It was Sulla who first, in ironic reference
to Pompey's arrogance and self-importance, dubbed him
with the nickname, and Pompey—who was not known for
his sense of humor—always used it thereafter.

Pompey's first major assignment was in 76 B.C. to Spain,
where Sertorius managed to hold his own against the
Roman forces until he was assassinated in 72 B.C. by a jeal-

ous subordinate. Without his charismatic leadership the revolt collapsed, with Pompey taking credit for its ending.
Returning to Italy to celebrate a triumph, he took the time
to crush the few rebel slaves still loose (another Roman expedition had already defeated the overwhelming majority of
Spartacus's followers), and claimed when he reached Rome
that he had put down the entire uprising.

By now Pompey was ready, like Marius and Sulla before
him, to aim for the consulship. He ran in 70 B.C. and won
election. His fellow consul was Crassus (c. 112–53 B.C.), a
highly successful businessman and military leader—he had
led the expedition that crushed Spartacus's followers—and
a real-estate magnate reputed to be the richest man in
Rome. Once in power, the two of them finished the job of
dismantling the few remaining traces of Sulla's constitution,
and Pompey received special command over the entire
Mediterranean to eliminate the menace of piracy.

That accomplished, the only serious problem remaining was Mithridates. Between 74 and 67 B.C. the Roman
general Lucullus (c. 117–55 B.C.), later to become famous
for his extravagant tastes, campaigned against Mithridates
with considerable success. The Roman forces drove him out
of his kingdom of Pontus, and Lucullus reorganized the finances of Rome's Asian subjects, bringing welcome relief
from rapacious tax collectors. For Pompey, however, the
Roman world was big enough for only one successful general, and in 66 B.C. the Senate passed a special law transfer-
ring to him the command of Asia. Lucullus bitterly

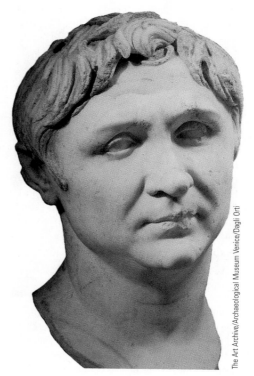

Portrait bust of Pompey the Great, late 1st century B.C. (?). This rather generalized sculpture (note
the stylized hair and lack of facial lines) may be a
later copy of a work dating to Pompey's time.

The Art Archive/Archaeological Museum Venice/Dagli Orti

observed that Pompey was like a vulture, preying on the corpses that others had killed.

THE RISE OF JULIUS CAESAR

With Pompey away in Asia from 66 to 62 B.C., a new figure began to dominate Roman public life: Gaius Julius Caesar (c. 100–44 B.C.). A patrician by birth, in 84 B.C. Caesar married Cornelia, the daughter of the head of the popular faction at Rome, Lucius Cinna. Identifying himself with the popular cause, he was elected quaestor in 69 B.C. and pontifex maximus (chief priest) in 63 B.C. Later that same year he spoke eloquently in the debate about a conspiracy plotted against the state by Catiline, a violent young revolutionary. From the beginning Caesar backed the populist faction, defending the memory of Marius and providing lavish public entertainments during the time he served as magistrate. The cost of winning popular favor was debt, and Caesar turned to Crassus for substantial loans.

When Pompey duly returned to Rome, after having completed Lucullus's work in Asia, he disbanded his army, celebrated a triumph, and settled back to enjoy the Senate's grateful thanks for a decade of hard campaigning. Far from

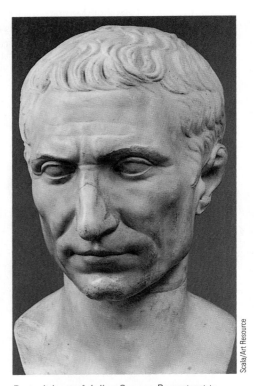

Portrait bust of Julius Caesar. By contrast to the previous figure, a portrait of Pompey, this bust of Caesar, carved around the time of his death in 44 B.C., is far more realistic, with its thinning hair, worried frown, deep-set lines on the cheeks, and tightly pressed lips. These features all convey a sense of the awesome responsibilities facing the ruler of the Roman Republic, which was devastated by a century of civil war.

flattering him, the jealous senators took the chance to cut him down to size, quibbling over his accounts and refusing to provide land for his veteran troops to settle on. Caesar, ever alert, seized the chance to make political capital. He was running for the consulship of 59 B.C. In return for their support, he proposed to Crassus and Pompey the formation of a secret alliance, which became known as the First Triumvirate. As consul, he would get Crassus favorable terms for the contract to collect taxes in Asia and settle Pompey's difficulties with the Senate.

Caesar's plan worked. The "Three-Headed Monster," as its enemies called it, achieved all of its goals. When the three met secretly at Lucca in 56 B.C., they renewed their alliance. This time they agreed that Pompey and Crassus were to be elected consuls for 55 B.C., while Caesar would receive a special term of five years as commander in Gaul. Caesar left to take up his position, returning to Rome only in 49 B.C.

CIVIL WAR

Gaul occupied a crucial position on Italy's northern frontiers and served as a base for driving invading Germans back across the Rhine. It was also rich in fertile farmland. In 55 B.C., under Caesar's command, the Roman troops in Gaul crushed the Germans and over the next two years put down a series of local Gallic rebellions. The uprisings culminated in 52 B.C. in a great national revolt led by the formidable Gallic chieftain Vercingetorix, which brought Caesar his greatest challenge yet. By 51 B.C., he had conquered a vast area and gradually brought the entire region under Roman rule.

Caesar was able to create a united administration for the three separate parts of Gaul that made it one of the most peaceful and loyal provinces in the Roman world. More important for his political future, he led a magnificently trained army that was devoted to its commander and willing to follow him anywhere.

At Rome, Pompey was now the dominant figure. In 53 B.C., Crassus—who was anxious to add yet another military success to his fortune—mounted an expedition against the Parthians on the borders of India (modern Afghanistan). The campaign was a disaster. Crassus was killed in the fighting, and the Parthians captured the standards carried by the Roman soldiers into battle—a fate literally worse than death for a Roman commander.

As the time for Caesar's return approached, it became clear that the headlong collision so long delayed between Pompey and Caesar was looming. In 49 B.C. the Senate ordered Caesar to disband his army and return to Rome. When he refused, they passed a decree naming him an enemy of the state. Caesar continued his march south, crossing the Rubicon (a small river in the Po Valley) and heading for the capital. Pompey, in panic, fled with his supporters to Greece.

There, in sultry summer heat on the plains of central Greece, at Pharsalus, Roman faced Roman in pitched battle. Pompey's men were more numerous, but Caesar's were far better trained and ready to fight. The conclusion was never really in doubt, and by the end of the day half of Pompey's forces surrendered to their opponents. Pompey

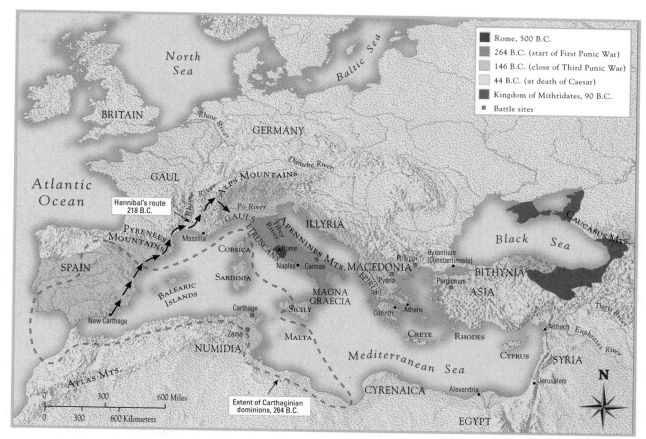

Map 15.1 Growth of the Roman Provinces During the Republic. All of the Carthaginian territory within the red line became Roman after the Punic Wars. Egypt remained nominally independent until the death of Julius Caesar in 44 B.C., but in practice it was a Roman protectorate; it became a Roman province in the early Empire. Other territory subsequently conquered included Britain and southern Scotland, Germany west of the Rhine, and the rest of Asia Minor. Go to http://info.wadsworth.com/053461065X for an interactive version of this map.

fled to Egypt, to seek refuge there at the court of Cleopatra and her brother, Ptolemy XIII. Ptolemy's advisers had Pompey stabbed, decapitated his body, and embalmed the head as a present for Caesar.

THE DICTATORSHIP AND ASSASSINATION OF JULIUS CAESAR

Caesar followed Pompey to Egypt, where he found himself in the middle of a quarrel between the joint rulers, Cleopatra and her brother Ptolemy. Caesar put his forces at the disposal of the queen, and—with Ptolemy disposed of—spent the rest of the summer in Cleopatra's company. By the time he was ready to pay a flying visit to Rome, she was pregnant with their son—she named him Caesarion.

CAESAR'S PROGRAM OF REFORM

By now the Senate had nominated Caesar dictator, and he began to bring under control a century of growing politi-

cal and social chaos. The most immediately pressing problem was the ruinous state of the economy. Many of his supporters, particularly among the lower classes, hoped that he would wipe out all of their debts. To do so, however, would have alienated the business class on whom he depended for a speedy return to financial order. He did cancel interest accumulated during the war and introduced regulations overseeing the valuation of property seized in payment of debt.

At Rome, he brought the urban mob under control by taking a rigorous census of those who claimed the right to the corn allowance. The number was reduced, and many of those whose names were struck from the lists were resettled on land elsewhere in Italy. All estate owners had to hire at least one-third of their workforce from these newcomers, a measure that provided employment for many who had hitherto formed part of Rome's proletariat, while reducing the need for large slave gangs.

Within Italy, Caesar codified city charters and the duties of local officials. (One minor piece of reorganization at this time was his reform of the calendar, which, with the addition

PUBLIC FIGURES AND PRIVATE LIVES

ANTONY AND FULVIA

The status of upper-class women in the late Republic, and the nature of their relationship with their husbands, is epitomized in contemporary views of the three wives of one of the dominating figures of the age, Mark Antony: the manipulative, "masculine" Fulvia, the politically correct and docile Octavia, and Cleopatra, the dangerously seductive Egyptian beauty.

His second wife, Octavian's sister Octavia, provided a political link with Antony's colleague and rival. Newly widowed, Octavia was available in 40

B.C. when, following their defeat of Caesar's murderers, Octavian and Antony needed to cement their unstable political alliance by a dynastic marriage. During the three years they lived together, Octavia fulfilled this role, bearing Antony two children and playing an active role in mediating between her husband and her brother. Even when Antony abandoned Octavia for his third wife, Cleopatra, Octavia remained loyal, disregarding Antony's marriage to the Egyptian queen in 37 B.C. because—by Roman law—marriage to a non-Roman citizen was not valid. She continued to live in Antony's Roman residence, leaving it only in 32 B.C., when her brother Octavian used Antony's formal divorce from Octavia as a justification for declaring war on him.

If Octavia represented the traditional role of woman as peacemaker, Cleopatra became symbolic of woman as seducer and destroyer. Cleopatra had already exercised her charms on Julius Caesar, and in 37 B.C. her political ambitions joined with Antony's

of a minor adjustment in the 16th century, still remains in use.) Elsewhere in the provinces he extended Roman citizenship to parts of Gaul and some towns in Spain. To settle his veteran soldiers and further reduce the numbers of unemployed at Rome, he set up an extensive program of new colonies in Spain, Gaul, Greece, and Africa—including the reoccupation of Carthage, Gaius Gracchus's old dream.

Caesar's plans for constitutional reform are more vague. He certainly permitted none of the settling of old scores typical of Marius's and Sulla's time in power. He strengthened the role of the Senate, increasing its enrollment and including senators from Italy and the provinces. Yet at the same time he concentrated the chief powers of the state in his own hands; he chose the magistrates, controlled the treasury, and commanded all of the armies.

In January 44 B.C., he received the title of dictator for life. Perhaps even Caesar himself did not know whether this was a temporary solution to Rome's crisis or represented the foundation of a system of autocratic rule. Two months later, on March 15, 44 B.C., he was dead, struck down by a band of ideologue conspirators, led by Brutus and Cassius, who saw in his new title and office the death of the Republic.

THE TRIUMPH OF OCTAVIAN AND THE DEATH OF THE REPUBLIC

Even with Caesar gone, his supporters remained, together with the army. In the days of confusion following the assassination, two of Caesar's ablest officers, Mark Antony and Lepidus, took control. The only senior political figure to speak out against them, in favor of the republican cause, was Cicero.

OCTAVIUS BECOMES OCTAVIAN
In his will, Caesar made his nearest male relative, his great-nephew Octavius (ruled as Emperor Augustus 27 B.C.–A.D. 14), his heir, adopting him as his son under the name Gaius Julius Caesar Octavianus—historians conventionally term him Octavian during this period. Caesar may have intended to groom Octavian for a political role. In any case the young man—he was 18 at the time—had the highest of ambitions. Arriving in Rome, he found ready support from those who thought Antony's tactful pardon of Caesar's assassins was too lenient. For many, also, the magic of the name "Caesar," which Octavian immediately began to use, remained potent.

to make them a formidable couple. The intensity of Octavian's propaganda campaign against Cleopatra demonstrates the threat he saw in her. When the future emperor declared war in 32 B.C., he did so against Cleopatra alone. After the defeat of Antony's and Cleopatra's forces at Actium in 31 B.C., Octavian reinforced his attacks on the *fatale monstrum*—the "deadly monster"—and drove her to suicide.

Fulvia, Antony's first wife, provides a far less clear-cut example of the late Republican wife as symbol. Neither the conventional "good" influence, nor the equally conventional "foreign seductress," Fulvia came from a noble Roman family. Her mother, Sempronia, had been implicated in the conspiracy of Catiline in 63 B.C. Famous for her beauty, wit, and charm, Sempronia was described even by her enemies as endowed with considerable intellectual strengths. Even the charge that she had often committed "crimes of masculine daring" seems almost an unwilling tribute to her courage.

Fulvia lacked her mother's charm but not her audacity. Although she had been married twice before she married Antony, and bore children in each of her three marriages, her contemporaries—encouraged by Octavian's propaganda machine—described her as "female in body only," an accusation commonly leveled against politically active women such as her own mother.

Later historians, including Plutarch, credited Fulvia with causing Antony's downfall. By dominating him, she taught him to obey a woman, and thus prepared the way for Cleopatra. Fulvia accompanied her husband on his military expeditions, behavior that was unthinkable for traditional wives. Later, while Antony was away in the East, and beginning his liaison with the Egyptian queen (Cleopatra gave birth to twins fathered by Antony in 41 B.C.), Fulvia instigated a revolt against Octavian in the hope of drawing Antony away from Egypt and her rival. Her death in 40 B.C. conveniently left him free to repair the damage with Octavian and marry Octavia.

Virtually all we know about Fulvia—and about Cleopatra and Octavia, too, for that matter—comes from sources heavily conditioned by Octavian's influence. (No trace has survived of Antony's own attitude toward Fulvia and her family.) Cleopatra's power, her Roman enemies believed, was the result of her exotic charm and the "Oriental debauchery" with which she corrupted her Roman lover. Fulvia presented a more difficult case: a woman of impeccable family and inherited wealth, who managed, at least for a while, to play a significant role in the turbulent history of the collapse of the Republic. The hatred that her "masculinity" provoked is perhaps in the end a tribute to the ability of some women, at least, to make their mark on late Republican political life.

By November 43 B.C., Antony and Lepidus on one side, and Octavian on the other, came to a compromise, known as the Second Triumvirate. The First Triumvirate had been a secret agreement, but this one was public and sanctioned by law. It gave the three men joint rule of the Roman world. (Lepidus's role soon became subordinate to that of the other two.) The new rulers began by eliminating those whom they considered their political opponents—among the victims was Cicero, whose eloquent opposition Antony had never forgiven. The next task was to follow up and defeat the conspirators, and Antony and Octavian led a joint force to victory over them in 42 B.C. at Philippi in northern Greece.

THE END OF THE REPUBLIC

The last 10 years of the Republic saw Antony and Octavian locked in a struggle for supreme power, in which the younger man showed an increasingly brilliant command of the power of propaganda. The first move was to create an appearance of unity, and in 40 B.C. Antony married Octavia, Octavian's sister. The two leaders then divided the Roman world between them, Octavian taking Italy and the west, and Antony the far richer, but less stable, eastern provinces.

Within three years Octavia was back in Italy with her brother, and Antony had fallen under the spell of Cleopatra. He settled in Alexandria, which the two intended to make the capital of a new universal kingdom, because Cleopatra had long cherished dreams of reviving the glories of Ptolemaic Egypt. When Antony made the fatal error of going through a form of marriage with "that Eastern Queen," Octavian portrayed himself as the defender of noble Roman traditions and the gods of Italy against the corruption of the mysterious East.

Once again, the end came in Greece, as it had for Pompey and for the conspirators. In September 31 B.C., Octavian routed the combined forces of Antony and Cleopatra at Actium. The two fled back to Egypt. Octavian followed and easily defeated their few remaining troops. Antony, returning at the end to the old Roman ways, committed suicide, but the queen was less hasty, waiting for an interview with Octavian. Whatever her hopes, it became clear quickly that he was keeping her alive only so she could march in his triumphal procession, and she, too, killed herself.

Putting the Collapse of the Roman Republic in Perspective

Thus, at the age of 32, Octavian was the ruler of a world numbed by a century of conflict and three bloody civil wars. The conspirators had been right that the Republic was in its death throes, but fatally wrong in thinking that the removal of Julius Caesar could prevent the inevitable. Those who killed Caesar and those who avenged his death were all members of the Roman elite locked in a struggle for supreme power.

The rise of the business classes, the stubborn refusal of the Senate to recognize that conditions were changed, the growing role of the urban mob—all of these were factors in making Rome no longer governable by the alternation of rival aristocratic politicians. Caesar was the only statesman who might have been able to break the cycle of political rivalry and bloodletting, but he died before he could devise a solution. Octavian's task was a formidable one: to create a system of authoritarian rule capable of being faithful to Rome's past while guaranteeing future stability.

Questions for Further Study

1. What basic issues were the reforms of the Gracchus brothers intended to address? What did they actually achieve?
2. How far was self-interest the chief motivation for the political leaders of the last century of the Republic? Was it the only one?
3. What were the decisive stages in Julius Caesar's rise to power? Once in control, how did he set about dealing with the problems Rome faced?
4. What part did civil war play in the collapse of the Republic? What does its role indicate about the nature of Rome's political crisis?

Suggestions for Further Reading

Grant, M. *From Alexander to Cleopatra*. New York, 1982.
Greenhalgh, P. *Pompey: The Roman Alexander*. New York, 1980.
Keaveny, A. *Sulla: The Last Republican*. London, 1987.
Leach, J. *Pompey the Great*. London, 1987.
Nicolet, C. *The World of the Citizen in Republican Rome*. London, 1980.
Scullard, H.H. *Roman Politics, 220–150* B.C. Westport, CT, 1982.
Seager, R. *Pompey: A Political Biography*. Berkeley, CA, 1980.

InfoTrac College Edition

Enter the search terms *Rome history* using Key Terms.

Enter the search terms *Roman republic* using Key Terms.

THE EMPIRE: FROM AUGUSTUS TO MARCUS AURELIUS

Having taken control of the state in 31 B.C., Octavian claimed that he was restoring the Republic in 27 B.C., when the Senate granted him the name Augustus. In fact, however, he consolidated his hold on the Roman world and reinforced the rule of one man, governing through his control of the civil service and official appointments.

Augustus's revolution affected virtually all aspects of Roman life: political, economic, social, and cultural. By the time of his death, the Empire was at peace and the authority of its ruler unchallenged. One of the problems that Augustus left unsolved—one that was to cause constantly recurring conflict during the following centuries of imperial rule—was that of the succession. Augustus finally left the government of the Empire to Tiberius, his stepson.

When, after a generally constructive but unpopular reign, Tiberius died in A.D. 37, he left no successor, and the Senate stepped in to appoint Caligula, who was a young relative of Augustus. At the end of Caligula's disastrous rule, it fell to the imperial guard to impose their choice by force: Claudius, Caligula's uncle. Despite Claudius's extensive achievements, the principle of succession according to membership in Augustus's Julio-Claudian family finally collapsed with the reign of Caligula's nephew, the deservedly notorious Nero.

With Nero's downfall in A.D. 68, the power to create new emperors passed to the strongest force available, in this case the army. In the space of a few months—the Year of the Four Emperors—successive military contingents imposed their candidates. The figure who eventually emerged was Vespasian, whose 10 years in office marked a welcome respite from the confusion and violence of the preceding generation. Once again, however, for all the positive achievements of his reign, Vespasian failed to resolve the crucial constitutional problem inherent in the imperial system. If his elder son, Titus, proved the merits of family succession, his younger son, Domitian, confirmed its dangers in a long and turbulent reign.

Domitian had no son, and the Senate chose his successor, Nerva, on merit. Nerva, who was also childless, nominated his own successor and legitimized his choice by adopting him. His four successors, none of whom produced a son, followed the same system. This led to a century of peace and stability in which the Empire reached its maximum size and general prosperity was widespread. The arts, which had enjoyed a Golden Age under Augustus, flourished again in a period known as the Silver Age.

THE AUGUSTAN REVOLUTION: APPEARANCE AND REALITY

Augustus's achievement was to take on an Empire lacking a coherent political system and paralyzed by decades of conflict, and to leave it at his death with a smoothly running political machine, capable of absorbing the wilder excesses of many of his successors. In some ways the total degree of devastation he found helped his task because by 31 B.C. virtually all Romans of whatever party shared a single overriding desire for peace. Another factor contributing to his success was the sheer length of his reign: 45 years of continuity provided time to lay solid foundations for the transformation of the state. Of his own gifts, perhaps that which helped him most was the one that had served him in the struggle with Antony: his masterly use of propaganda. Time after time, Augustus concealed his real intentions under an outward appearance meant for public consumption.

The *Augustus of Prima Porta*, c. 20 B.C. Height 6 feet 8 inches (2.03 m). Found in the Imperial villa at Prima Porta, the statue shows Augustus about to deliver a speech. He wears a mixture of military and civilian dress, and his head and feet are bare. The little Cupid at his feet connects the emperor to the first (legendary) founder of Rome, Aeneas, who, like Cupid, was a child of the goddess Venus.

THE NEW ORDER

In the immediate aftermath of his victory at Actium, Octavian (the future Augustus) renounced his position as triumvir and ran for election as consul. His long-term aim was to retain an autocratic grip on all aspects of power, while appearing to restore the institutions of the Republic—thus avoiding the tactical error of Julius Caesar, who had accepted the title of dictator for life.

The first step came in 27 B.C., when, as he later claimed in his autobiography, "I handed back the state from my own power to that of the Senate and Roman People." He continued to go through the fiction of running for the consulship, but resigned all other special powers to the republican magistrates of the old constitution. The only honor he would agree to accept was Augustus, "the revered one," the name by which he was thereafter known.

For all the apparent restoration of the old ways, however, the reality was very different. After Augustus's thorough revision of the Senate's list of members, it consisted almost exclusively of his supporters. The magistrates—although going through the appearance of popular election—were first chosen by Augustus himself, who also kept control of the treasury and the army.

This arrangement, known as the First Settlement, was perhaps intended as a trial solution. A second one followed in 23 B.C., when finally, after holding the consulship for an unprecedented 11 times, Augustus gave it up. He took instead the ancient power of a tribune, historically the defender of the people, and a vague *imperium* (power) over all officers of the state. His real source of authority, however, lay in the loyalty of the army and, over time, the immense prestige—the Latin word is *auctoritas*—with which a grateful world came to regard him. From now on, his official title was *Princeps*, or First Citizen of the state.

THE ECONOMICS OF PEACE

The belief that an era of peace had finally dawned was one of the prime causes for the immense increase in investment after the Battle of Actium, with interest rates dropping by a third. As a result, there was a boom in trade and industry, which created an even wider circulation of capital.

Augustus encouraged small-scale local industry as a counterbalance to the wealthy nobles of Rome. Pottery and glass remained important sectors, with exportation of high-class ceramics throughout the Empire, from Britain to India. The metal industry developed specialized production systems, with iron mined on the island of Elba and transported to foundries on the Bay of Naples for smelting. The flourishing construction industry, repairing the damage of a century of civil wars, needed supplies of building materials such as bricks and tiles, lead pipes, and cement. During Augustus's reign, the spread of economic prosperity produced a hard-working industrial middle class, loyal to the central government.

With the Mediterranean once again at peace, commerce became truly international. Raw materials and manufactured goods passed between the provinces and reached the marketplaces of Rome. Trade in fine linen from Egypt, Syrian dates and wine, asphalt from the Dead Sea, Spanish gold and silver, and many other products soared as a result of a stable currency. Other factors in the trade boom included good, safe roads, and the revival of leading centers of international commerce like Corinth, Carthage, and—above all—Alexandria, which soon became the second city of the Empire. Nor was business limited to the Mediterranean world. By the late 1st century B.C., Roman traders were importing ivory, incense, and spices from India and silk from China.

The economic boom that marked Augustus's reign was reinforced by a general improvement in the administration of the provinces. During the last centuries of the Republic, the worst excesses in financial corruption on the part of provincial governors and their staffs had paid the bills of political leaders and their supporters at Rome. With power now concentrated in the hands of the emperor, the ruinous expenses typical of the career of Marius or Caesar no longer formed part of the political process.

THE AUGUSTAN IMAGE

Just as Augustus aimed to restore Rome's ancient political institutions—at least in appearance—so his social legislation, aimed chiefly at the upper classes, was intended to return his subjects to traditional family values. Laws provided tax breaks for large families and penalized childlessness and the unmarried. Adultery became a crime against the state. In a revival of ancient religious practices aimed at providing the new laws with moral support, Augustus carried out an ambitious program of restoration for Rome's temples and encouraged the return to ancient deities and ceremonies.

One important aspect of Rome's traditional image was the central role of agriculture and the land. Farming underwent the same expansion as other economic activities during Augustus's rule, but the imperial economy became far more diversified than that of republican times, while increasing numbers of Romans, both in Italy and the provinces, lived in cities. To remind them of Rome's peasant origins, Augustus encouraged artists and writers to portray the joys of the countryside in works such as Vergil's *Georgics*, a lengthy poem on farming (for art and literature under Augustus, see Topic 17).

Despite the success of the Augustan political revolution, it is doubtful if his moral reforming zeal met with more than polite attention. His own daughter and granddaughter, both named Julia, were notorious for the scandals they were involved in. To make matters worse, one of his daughter Julia's lovers was a son of Mark Antony, her father's old enemy. Duty forced Augustus to banish Julia to a remote Mediterranean island. A few years later he had to find another distant location for the banishment of his granddaughter. He hushed up the details of both of the affairs, but there was much gossip.

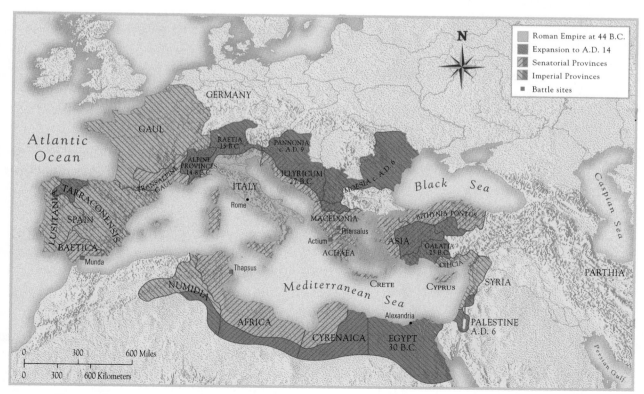

 Map 16.1 The Roman Empire in A.D. 14, at the Death of Augustus. From an economic point of view, Augustus's most important additions were Egypt and the wealthy kingdoms of Asia Minor. Note that, in keeping with Augustus's (false) claim to have "restored the Republic," the provinces are divided into Senatorial and Imperial ones. In practice, of course, Augustus controlled them all, and later emperors did not bother to maintain the fiction. Go to http://info.wadsworth.com/053461065X for an interactive version of this map.

Perspectives from the Past

Political Propaganda in the Roman Empire

From the earliest days of the reign of Augustus, the state carefully controlled all comments on public policy. Virtually no criticism of Augustus's rule was permitted. Few portraits of his opponents, Antony and Cleopatra, have survived, and Augustus even had coins bearing their images melted down. Any challenge to the imperial policy brought at the least permanent exile. Among those banished were Augustus's daughter and granddaughter, and the distinguished poet Ovid.

Later emperors, without Augustus's moral authority, were less able to repress all criticisms, but as in the extract from Tacitus opponents of the regime had to be indirect, and let their readers deduce for themselves the implicit message of condemnation.

The last two passages date to the reigns of Hadrian and Marcus Aurelius. The first, an inscription which claims to represent popular enthusiasm for the Emperor Hadrian, illustrates how simple "official" statements often conceal more complex issues. The other one is an extract from the meditations of Marcus Aurelius, which offers an insider's view of the job of being a Roman emperor.

An Augustan View of the First Settlement

The year before his death, Augustus approved an official description of his achievements, the Deeds of the Deified Augustus. In his will he instructed that inscribed copies should be set up in every province of the Empire. The following extract gives his highly misleading account of the First Settlement of 27 B.C. (see above). Far from handing over power to the Senate and people, he concentrated it further in his own hands.

The First Settlement

In my sixth and seventh consulships (28 and 27 B.C.) after I had put an end to the civil wars and had acquired, by unanimous vote, supreme control, I transferred the Republic from my power over to the authority of the Senate and the Roman People. In return for this service of mine, I acquired the title of Augustus in accordance with a decree of the Senate, and the doorposts of my house were publicly wreathed with laurel and a civic crown was fastened above the entrance. A golden shield was placed in the Julian Senate house which, as the inscription on it bears witness, the Senate and the Roman People gave to me because of my virtue, clemency, justice, and piety. At this time I exceeded all in prestige, but I had no more power than those who were my colleagues in each magistracy.

From MacKendrick, Paul, and Herbert M. Howe, eds. *Classics in Translation, Volume II: Latin Literature.* Copyright © 1952. Reprinted by permission of The University of Wisconsin Press.

Differences Between the Germans and the Romans

The great historian Tacitus lived through the reigns of Nero and Domitian, a period notorious for its moral and political corruption. His monograph Germania, published in A.D. 98, provides a unique insight into the social customs of the ancient Germans. At the same time, sophisticated readers at Rome would make inevitable—and intended—comparisons between the noble "barbarians" to the north, and the decadent ways of the city. The reference in the last sentence is to the continuing decline in the birthrate in Italy during the 1st century A.D., in spite of the passing of laws in favor of large families, and the economic damage this provoked (see below).

Only a decade later, around A.D. 107, did Tacitus feel able to begin the publication of his unvarnished accounts of the Julio-Claudian and Flavian eras.

The Superiority of German Morals

The chastity (of German women) is well protected and there are no allurements of shows, no attractions of parties to corrupt them. Secret love notes are unknown to men and women alike. In so populous a nation there are very few cases of adultery and for these the punishment is immediate and left to the husbands. The adulteress' husband cuts off her hair, strips her naked, and in the presence of the kinsmen expels her from his house and drives her with a whip through the entire village. If a woman surrenders her chastity, she can receive no pardon. Not beauty nor youth nor wealth will find her a husband. Vice is no laughing matter there, and seducing or being seduced is not called the modern fashion. Even higher is the moral standard of those states where only virgins get married and so the wife's hopes and expectations are settled once for all. Thus they receive just one husband, as they receive one body and one life, so that they may have no thought beyond, no further desire, and love their husband not so much as an individual but as representing the state of marriage. To practice birth control or destroy any of the later-born offspring is regarded as criminal, and good morals are more effective there than good laws elsewhere.

From MacKendrick, Paul, and Herbert M. Howe, eds. *Classics in Translation, Volume II. Latin Literature.* Copyright © 1952. Reprinted by permission of The University of Wisconsin Press.

Hadrian Inaugurates His Reign

The issue of how each emperor's successor should be chosen continued to create problems for the Julio-Claudian and Flavian dynasties. In the end, the solution was that of the adoptive emperors. Even this had its problems, however. When Hadrian came to power in A.D. 118, he faced an immediate challenge from the "Conspiracy of the Four Senators." In order to win popular support, Hadrian immediately issued a proclamation announcing the cancellation of 900 million sesterces of back taxes. The following inscription supposedly records the gratitude of Senate and people at Hadrian's generosity, and tactfully makes no reference to the reason for the emperor's openhandedness.

A relief sculpture showing the public burning of records of tax arrears, in the presence of Hadrian

himself, was set up in the Forum (the sculpture is now in the Senate House there). Clearly the emperor intended to make the maximum propaganda use of his gesture.

Rome Expresses Gratitude to Hadrian

To the emperor Hadrian [there follows a catalogue of his titles], who, first and alone of emperors, remitted nine hundred million sesterces owed to the imperial treasury, and who by this generosity freed from anxiety not only the Roman citizens of his own day, but also their posterity, the Senate and People of Rome [dedicated this inscription].

Text copyright Donald R. Dudley in the book *Urbs Roma.* Published by Phaidon Press 1967.

An Emperor's Advice to Himself

Toward the end of the 2nd century A.D. *the philosopher emperor Marcus Aurelius tried to apply Stoic ideals to the administration of a vast state bureaucracy. His Meditations form a kind of journal or diary, recording his successes and—more often—failures in living up to his beliefs. The following passage seems a particularly poignant attempt on his part to adjust to the realities of empire.*

The Moral Burden of Power

Say to yourself in the morning: I shall meet people who are interfering, ungracious, insolent, full of guile, deceitful and antisocial; they have all become like that because they have no understanding of good and evil. But I, who have contemplated the essential beauty of good and the essential ugliness of evil, who know that the nature of the wrongdoer is of one kin with mine—not indeed of the same blood or seed but sharing the same mind, the same portion of the divine—I cannot be harmed by any one of them, and no one can involve me in shame. I cannot feel anger against him who is of my kin, nor hate him. We were born to labor together, like the feet, the hands, the eyes, and the rows of upper and lower teeth. To work against one another is therefore contrary to nature, and to be angry against a man or turn one's back on him is to work against him.

From Marcus Aurelius, *The Meditations* (No. 1), Book II, trans. G. M. A. Grube. Copyright © 1963. Macmillan.

Yet for all the gulf that often existed between appearance and reality in his rule, by the end of his life Augustus was the living symbol of Rome's renewed greatness. As early as 42 B.C., the young Octavian decreed divine honors for the late Julius Caesar. Worship of Augustus as divine began while he was still alive, not in Italy—where public opinion would not tolerate worship of a living man—but in many parts of the Empire. The veneration and simple gratitude with which his fellow countrymen regarded him seem to have transcended a formal cult, and they deified him soon after his death.

The restoration of order that his reign brought came at a price. In all the fulsome tributes his contemporaries paid to his greatness, scarcely a single dissenting voice is ever heard. Whatever the many virtues and achievements of the Augustan Age, freedom of expression was not among them. In life, Augustus aimed to exemplify by his own personal behavior the ancient Roman virtues of frugality and morality, while retaining the absolute power of an Eastern potentate. Perhaps the dying emperor meant to express the complexity of his role when he turned to the attendants surrounding his deathbed and asked: "Tell me, have I played well my part in this comedy of life? If so, applaud me and send me on my way."

PROBLEMS OF IMPERIAL SUCCESSION: THE JULIO-CLAUDIANS

Augustus, the "father of his native land," died leaving no son or other direct male heir. Thus, from the beginning of the history of the Empire, the problem of the succession became crucial. In order to avert the danger of rival ambitions leading to renewed civil war, Augustus's plan was to keep rule of the Empire in his own family, that of the Julio-Claudians, by naming his successor. To that end, he organized a bewildering series of marriages and divorces involving various branches of the family, but as a result of the length of his reign—and sheer accident—he outlived all of the candidates he chose.

TIBERIUS, SUCCESSOR TO AUGUSTUS

In the end Augustus turned to Tiberius (ruled A.D. 14–37), his stepson by his wife Livia's first marriage. The emperor had earlier forced Tiberius to divorce his wife to marry Julia, Augustus's daughter, but then passed him over for the succession at the time of Julia's disgrace and banishment. When no alternative remained open to Augustus, he recalled the embittered Tiberius from self-imposed exile.

When Tiberius finally became emperor at the age of 55, he was already disillusioned. A solitary and unpopular figure, he suffered the further disadvantage of having to follow one of the best-loved leaders in Roman history. He spent as much time as he could in seclusion at his villa on the island of Capri, and Roman gossips outdid themselves in speculating on the vices he practiced there.

Tiberius's successful administration of the Empire was a result of his careful choice of officials and prompt dismissal of those who proved inefficient or corrupt. Under his watchful control, the bureaucratic machinery of government ran smoothly both at home and in the provinces. His fiscal conservatism made it possible to invest public funds in important road construction projects in Gaul and Spain and for an urgently needed overhaul of Rome's water system. The public, used to Augustus's lavish displays and games, grumbled at Tiberius's tight-fistedness.

At the time of his death, there was general peace throughout the Empire, the authority of the Senate was even higher than under Augustus, and the treasury contained a surplus. Yet his contemporaries rejoiced at his demise, and later Roman historians painted him as a bloodthirsty tyrant. Lacking the charisma and sense of public relations of his great predecessor, by his positive achievements Tiberius maintained the stability and prosperity of the Augustan years.

CALIGULA THE DIVINE

In naming a successor, Tiberius had been ordered by Augustus to choose Augustus's great-nephew Germanicus. When Germanicus died in A.D. 19, Tiberius turned to the dead man's son Gaius (ruled A.D. 37–41). The results were catastrophic.

Gaius spent much of his childhood with his father on the Rhine frontier, where Germanicus held command. The troops dressed the child in miniature military costume, and his nickname Caligula (by which he is best-known) means "little boots." Already a favorite of the soldiers, and coming to power after the remote and gloomy old Tiberius, Caligula appeared to offer new promise. The frequent games and festivals he organized at Rome during the early months of his reign aroused wildly popular enthusiasm.

Yet nothing had prepared him for the responsibilities of office, and the absolute power he wielded went to his head. He seems to have spent his mercifully brief reign testing the extent of that power—limitless, he claimed, because of his divine descent from Julius Caesar and Augustus. Among his schemes was the construction of a bridge connecting the Palatine Hill (residence of the emperor) with the Temple of Jupiter on the Capitoline Hill, to make it easier for him to visit his brother god. To fund this project and other extravagances, he appointed professional informers to accuse wealthy citizens of treason. The emperor would then have them executed and confiscate their estates.

His "marriage" to his sister, the naming of his favorite horse to the consulship, an expedition to conquer Britain that took the army up to the northern coast of France, only to have them collect seashells and return to Rome again—the result of all these actions was that the army, which had idolized him as a child, killed him in response to the widespread hatred he had aroused. The feeling was mutual. Caligula once expressed regret that the Roman people did not have just one neck, so that he could sever it with a single blow.

CLAUDIUS THE BUREAUCRAT

Whatever the impact of Caligula's reign at Rome, the administration of the provinces continued to run smoothly—a tribute to Tiberius's organizational skills. With the accession of Claudius (ruled A.D. 41–54) came the restoration of order at Rome.

There is no evidence that Caligula ever gave a moment's thought to naming his successor. In the confusion following his assassination, the palace guard picked the dead ruler's old uncle, Claudius, whose physical disabilities (they included a stammer and a limp) meant that hitherto he had played little part in public life. A professional writer and historian, Claudius brought to his duties a learning and sense of perspective greater than any of his predecessors—and most of his successors.

The soldiers may have chosen Claudius because they considered him weak and therefore easy to manipulate, but Claudius's administration of the state was firm and, above all, efficient. His reorganization of the complex maze of bureaucracy at Rome divided it into a series of departments, whose bureau chiefs reported directly to the emperor. The senators complained that these department heads, often former imperial slaves of Greek origin, had more power and easier access to the emperor than the Senate itself, but Claudius's reforms proved fundamental to stable government over the next two centuries.

Unlike Caligula, Claudius mounted a serious expedition to conquer Britain and add it to the imperial territory. In A.D. 43, Claudius, the scholar emperor, led the forces that won control of most of southern England and made it into a Roman province. Like Caesar in Gaul, Claudius treated provincial citizens in Britain and elsewhere with liberality, extending to them Latin rights or citizenship.

For his contemporaries and immediate successors, Claudius's significant contributions to the welfare of the Empire were far less interesting than the scandalous behavior of his last two wives (he had a total of four). Gossip had it that when the emperor died suddenly in A.D. 54, apparently from eating poisoned mushrooms, Agrippina, his last wife, was responsible for the incident. Whatever the truth of the stories (and there seems little reason to doubt them), Agrippina seized her chance and maneuvered her 16-year-old son by a previous marriage into succeeding Claudius as emperor. His name, Nero (ruled A.D. 54–68), has become a byword for wanton brutality.

NERO THE ARTIST

The first five years of Nero's reign passed relatively uneventfully. Agrippina, his mother, governed on Nero's behalf, together with his tutor Seneca (4 B.C.?–A.D. 65) and Burrus, head of the palace guard. The two men had little patience with Agrippina's autocratic ways and tried to restore elements of a republican system. All three made the mistake of encouraging Nero to distract himself with his stage performances (he sang and played the lyre), and with a series of violent sexual escapades.

The result was to create a monster. On coming of age in A.D. 59, Nero demonstrated his new independence by having his formidable mother murdered. This was the first in a chain of killings, to be followed by his wife and then his mistress Poppaea, whom Nero kicked to death when she was pregnant. In a series of fake treason trials, he adopted Caligula's method of obtaining funds from rich citizens by having them condemned and their fortunes confiscated.

In A.D. 64 a great fire swept through Rome. Many suspected Nero of starting it, although the emperor tried to deflect the accusations by blaming the Christians, a sect that had recently appeared at Rome (see Topic 19). Nero took advantage of the damage caused to the buildings of central Rome to have a large area cleared for the construction of a new imperial residence, the *Domus Aurea*, or Golden House. Many of its buildings were torn down by angry crowds after Nero's fall, while one part of it—Nero's private lake—was cleared to provide the foundations of the most famous of all Roman structures, the Colosseum.

Growing discontent at Rome led to two conspiracies, in A.D. 65 and 66, which were put down with predictable ferocity. In A.D. 68 further revolts broke out in Gaul and Spain, which were actually led by the two provinces' Roman governors. As the situation precipitated, the Senate in desperation declared Nero a public enemy. The emperor, by now abandoned by all, lamented that so great an artist as he should have to die, and then called on a slave to cut his throat. The Julio-Claudian dynasty was over.

At the beginning of Augustus's reign, the founder of the Empire did everything possible to hide the fact that the emperor was all-powerful. By the death of Nero the possible consequences of unlimited power were clear to all. Part of the cause lies in the personal characters of Caligula and Nero, but in part the responsibility also lay with the Senate and—to a lesser extent—the people. Neither class made any real attempt to use the powers that first Augustus and then Tiberius and Claudius tried to share with them. First fawning respect and then simple fear kept the authority of the emperor unchallenged until the situation reached a point of crisis.

The one force that did increase its influence was the army. The last two Julio-Claudian emperors owed their position to military backing or connivance, and when crisis came under Nero, rival military commanders struggled for control.

THE ARMY AND THE EMPERORS: VESPASIAN AND HIS SONS

From April A.D. 68 to December A.D. 69, four successive generals seized imperial power, in a period known as the "Year of the Four Emperors." The last of them, Vespasian (ruled A.D. 69–79), used Roman troops from his command in Jerusalem to march on Italy and win control of Rome. Once again, the army played the chief role in deciding the succession. As the Roman historian Tacitus put it, the secret of empire was that its control depended on the legions.

Aerial view of the Colosseum, Rome. A.D. 69–79. Originally the floor of the Colosseum was covered with sand. Modern excavators have removed this ground level to reveal the passages beneath, which were used to contain the animals for the gladiators to kill; the beasts were housed in cages that could be mechanically raised to the surface for their slaughter. The building held more than 50,000 spectators.

The Image Bank/Guido Ross

SIGNIFICANT DATES

The Julio-Claudian Emperors

31 B.C.	Octavian wins Battle of Actium
27 B.C.	Octavian takes name of Augustus
23 B.C.–A.D. 14	Establishment of Principate and reign of Augustus
A.D. 14–37	Reign of Tiberius
A.D. 37–41	Reign of Caligula
A.D. 41–54	Reign of Claudius
A.D. 54–68	Reign of Nero
A.D. 69	Year of the Four Emperors

VESPASIAN, SECOND FOUNDER OF THE EMPIRE

When Vespasian came to power, the situation he faced was the same as the one Augustus had tried to resolve 100 years earlier: the aftermath of bitter civil conflict combined with financial crisis. Vespasian lacked some of Augustus's advantages. The founder of the Empire came to power at a young age and benefited from the charisma that came from having Julius Caesar in the family. Even more seriously, by Vespasian's time the Romans' faith in the Augustan system was badly shaken. It was clearly flawed and could be capable of spectacular failure.

In one crucial respect, however, Vespasian had an advantage of his own: two sons. From the beginning of his reign he declared them his heirs and set about training them for their future role (the reigns of father and the two sons formed the Flavian dynasty, their family name). He shared the consulship with Titus, his elder son (ruled A.D. 79–81), on seven occasions, and appointed him to most of the highest offices of state. Domitian (ruled A.D. 81–96) held the title of Prince of the Youth. Some Cynic and Stoic philosophers grumbled that a man's sons were not necessarily the best candidates to succeed him, but on the whole Vespasian's subjects greeted his scheme with relief.

In a deliberate attempt to summon up memories of Augustus, the new emperor opened his reign by adding two new buildings to the heart of Rome: a Temple of Peace and a Forum of Peace. At the same time, in constructing the Colosseum as a place of mass entertainment in the ruins of Nero's Golden House, he underlined the contrast between his concern for the public interest and his predecessor's monstrous megalomania: the private playground of one man became a stadium holding some 50,000 spectators.

Unlike Augustus, Vespasian made no pretense that the Senate still ran the government, but used it principally to draw on as a pool of administrative talent. By the time of his death, the emperor was firmly established as the head of a vast centralized bureaucracy, which the imperial staff ran on a day-to-day basis, but in which the final decision was the emperor's alone.

A conscientious worker, Vespasian maintained a grueling schedule and led a modest personal life, sharing the sacrifices of his fellow citizens. During the extensive rebuilding program at Rome, in an adroit public relations gesture, he helped the workmen to cart away baskets full of rubble still remaining from the fire of Nero's reign. His subjects mourned his passing, and after the funeral they made him a god.

FLAVIAN SUCCESSORS

Had he lived longer, Titus might have been one of Rome's greatest emperors. None came so well prepared to power. Experienced in warfare and a proven administrator, in his brief reign Titus became legendary for his generosity. Posterity credits him with remembering one evening at dinner that he had performed no kindness since morning, and remarking: "Friends, I have wasted a day." When he died suddenly, a grieving Senate and people sent him to join his father in heaven.

The Romans had cause to grieve. Domitian, Vespasian's younger son, made it clear from the first that he intended to rule as an autocrat. He held the office of censor permanently, giving him control of membership of the Senate. His own personal behavior recalled the worst excesses of Caligula and Nero. One of his mistresses was his niece, and he required his aides to address him as "master and god."

On the other hand, unlike the worst of his predecessors, Domitian was an efficient and painstaking administrator. He chose provincial governors who proved honest, maintained the support of the legionaries by raising their pay, and won popularity in Italy by giving farmers who were working public land the right to own it. In the end, Domitian's undoing was his own growing paranoia. Fearing plots against his life, he ordered the arrest of anyone whom he suspected, basing his acts on information received from a band of spies who worked for the state. The conspiracy that finally led to his assassination had among its members not only many of his palace staff members, but even his own wife.

Unlike the reigns of Caligula and Nero, Domitian's rule left most Romans better off. The Flavian dynasty as a whole provided the longest period of ordered, methodical government since Augustus. Yet the same problem remained: how should the next emperor be chosen? Domitian died without leaving an heir, and in any case his example showed that passing power down in the family was not without its disadvantages. This time, however, the conspirators—with the cooperation of the Senate—addressed the problem of the succession before eliminating Domitian, rather than waiting until he was dead to find a replacement.

THE PAX ROMANA AND THE "FIVE GOOD EMPERORS"

The Senate and conspirators picked a distinguished elderly senator to provide a period of transition and then Domitian was duly assassinated. The chosen replacement was Nerva (ruled A.D. 96–98). One of the few lasting legislative acts of his brief reign was a scheme to provide food and education for poor Italian children. Known as the "alimentary institution," over the next century it developed into an elaborate welfare system, designed to protect the less-well-off citizens. Realizing the possibility of a military challenge from army forces loyal to Domitian, Nerva hastened to choose and adopt a popular general as his successor (he was childless, as were his four successors), and then died three months later.

THE SPANISH SUCCESSION

Trajan (ruled A.D. 98–117), whose family was from Italica in Spain, was the first provincial to achieve imperial power. A successful general, Trajan was governor of Upper Germany at the time of Nerva's death.

Trajan based his administration on meticulous organization and care for detail. The correspondence has survived between the emperor and one of the provincial governors, Pliny the Younger, governor of Bithynia (in modern central Turkey), and it documents the emperor's operating procedures. Pliny's letters contained many queries and requests for instructions on matters ranging from collapsing buildings to the new sect of Christians. A secretarial staff at Rome consulted the imperial archives to see if there had been a similar problem in the past and passed on any precedent to Pliny. Where a matter broke new ground, Trajan provided carefully considered advice that was generally practical and humane.

Trajan's ambitious building plans at Rome included a Forum commemorating his chief foreign success, the conquest of Dacia (modern Romania)—the last piece of new territory in Europe to be added to the Empire. His last foreign adventure was more ambitious: the defeat of Rome's old enemies, the Parthians. Although weary from years of campaigning and weakened by his heavy consumption of alcohol, Trajan personally led the expedition to the East. Initial victories turned to disappointment as the Parthians fought back, and the emperor—who had suffered a stroke—finally decided to make for home. He died on the way, in the middle of Asia, in the blazing heat of August A.D. 117.

At the end of his life, Trajan finally made official what had long seemed his intention by adopting as his son and successor a distant Spanish relative, Hadrian (ruled A.D. 117–138). Most of Hadrian's life in the years before he became emperor was spent in preparation, holding offices and acquiring experience at home and abroad. When he finally achieved power, therefore, he had a definite program. His economic policy was one of generosity. One of his first acts was to cancel the debts of all citizens to the state. During his reign he reduced taxes and established

Portrait of the emperor Hadrian, c. A.D. 117–138. Hadrian's reign saw a revival of the style of Classical Greek art. Unlike the portraits of the Republican period (see Topic 15's busts of Pompey and Caesar), Hadrian is shown here in an idealized form. Both hair and beard are carefully designed, and the emperor's expression has the lofty remoteness of Greek 5th century B.C. sculpture.

© Werner Forman Archive/Art Resource, NY

SIGNIFICANT DATES

The Flavians and Their Successors
(all dates A.D.)

69–79	Reign of Vespasian
79–81	Reign of Titus
81–96	Reign of Domitian
96–98	Reign of Nerva
98–117	Reign of Trajan
117–138	Reign of Hadrian
138–161	Reign of Antoninus Pius
161–180	Reign of Marcus Aurelius
180–192	Reign of Commodus

volt of the Jews in Jerusalem (A.D. 132–134). Hadrian ordered it crushed with the utmost ferocity.

THE ANTONINES

Hadrian's successor, Antoninus Pius (ruled A.D. 138–161), continued the general lines of his policy, but without the personal supervision that was one of the main factors in Hadrian's success—Antoninus spent the whole of his reign in Italy. At his death, wars broke out in many parts of the empire.

Marcus Aurelius (ruled A.D. 161–180), the last of the "five good emperors," had to deal with trouble in Parthia and the invasion of German tribes across the northern frontiers. A Stoic philosopher, Marcus spent most of his reign in incessant military campaigning. No sooner did he achieve temporary peace in one region than he rushed with his troops to the next crisis spot. He died before reestablishing a strong northern frontier.

The first emperor since Vespasian to produce a son, Marcus Aurelius nominated him as his successor. Commodus (ruled A.D. 180–192) was an incompetent coward who was devoted to the pursuit of pleasure. The result of his father's bad judgment was to place Rome in the hands of a series of military despots. As early as A.D. 193, the palace guards auctioned off the Empire to the highest bidder, and throughout the following century the army and its warring leaders presided over a state that was in increasing decline.

fair maximum prices in years of bad harvests, and extended Nerva's welfare schemes.

In foreign policy, Hadrian reversed Trajan's plans for yet more conquest. The new policy was to maintain and guarantee the peace of the Empire as it was by strengthening its defenses. He had troops stationed on the frontiers, building walls and reinforcing preexisting defense systems. To keep his soldiers' morale high, Hadrian spent much of his reign traveling to virtually every part of the Empire, inspecting their conditions. His peace policy succeeded. The only serious uprising against Rome during his time was a re-

Putting the Empire from Augustus to Marcus Aurelius in Perspective

The 18th-century English historian Edward Gibbon, in an oft-cited passage, described the years from the death of Domitian to the accession of Commodus as "the period in the history of the world during which the condition of the human race was most happy and prosperous." So sweeping a claim is difficult to justify. For all the welfare legislation and building projects, increasing prosperity, and generally efficient provincial government, widespread poverty existed in many parts of the Empire—not least in the urban slums of Rome.

Yet on the whole the adoptive emperors did provide an extended period of tranquillity. Their own sense of duty to the state inspired wealthy citizens to spend money on public projects. It is not simply by chance that the 2nd century A.D. saw the construction of libraries in many provincial cities, accompanied by the spread of education. Rome probably remained free of epidemic disease until the end of the 2nd century A.D. and produced enough food to avoid major famines until the last two decades of the century.

The emperor remained an autocratic ruler. For all the polite gestures that Trajan or Hadrian made toward the Senate, the rulers made their own decisions. Yet by comparison with the repressive regimes of many of the later emperors, these rulers shine as dedicated servants of the state. Gibbon's judgment may be exaggerated, but it contains a germ of truth.

Questions for Further Study

1. What were the fundamental reforms whereby Augustus changed the Roman political system from Republic to monarchy? What, if anything, made them necessary, and how successful were they?
2. What were the chief elements in Roman political life in the first two centuries of the Empire? What part did the army play?
3. What were the effects of imperial rule on life in the provinces? How did it vary under Augustus's successors?
4. How did Augustus and his successors use propaganda?

Suggestions for Further Reading

Barrett, A. *Caligula, the Corruption of Power*. New Haven, CT, 1990.
Campbell, J.B. *The Emperor and the Roman Army*. New York, 1984.
Clarke, John R. *The Houses of Roman Italy, 100* B.C.-A.D. *250*. Berkeley, CA, 1991.
Isaac, B. *The Limits of Empire: The Roman Army in the East*. New York, 1990.
Levick, B. *Tiberius the Politician*. London, 1986.
Millar, F. *The Roman Empire and Its Neighbors*. New York, 1981.
Millar, F., and E. Segal, eds. *Caesar Augustus*. Oxford, 1984.
Perowne, S. *Hadrian*. London, 1987.

InfoTrac College Edition

Enter the search term *Roman Empire* using Key Terms.

Enter the search term *Roman law* using the Subject Guide.

POLITICS AND THE ARTS: ROMAN IMPERIAL CULTURE

The cultural program of the Augustan age played a central role in conveying the political significance of the emperor's reforms. Augustus used the visual arts and literature to spell out his main themes: the return of peace, the importance of Rome's agricultural origins, the Romans' sense of destiny as world rulers.

The historian Livy provided an official account of Rome's early history. The chief poets of the regime, including above all Vergil and Horace, composed works expressing a sense of renewal in keeping with the spirit of the times, while the sculptors of the great Altar of Peace combined myth and historical reality to provide visible proof of the Augustan achievement. The effect of such sustained cultural energy was to produce a Golden Age in the arts.

The art of the portrait bust was first developed in the late Republic, but it became an important element in the official art of the Empire. Augustus maintained an iron control over the use of imperial images. Under his successors, sculptors often succeeded in conveying more complex statements about the ruling classes. In the 2nd century A.D., Hadrian used the style of High Classical Greek art to recreate—in stone at least—a return to the idealizing world of Periclean Athens.

Hadrian also made an important impact on Roman architecture, an artistic field in which the Roman genius for adaptation and control found its highest expression. At Rome, and throughout the Empire, architects produced buildings to satisfy the needs of large sectors of the population, not just a ruling elite. Theaters, stadiums, public baths, forum complexes—each type of structure took the same basic form throughout the Empire.

In this way urban planning and design reinforced the sense of a supranational Roman identity, transcending the enormous differences among the Roman provinces of Europe, Asia, and Africa. At the same time, domestic architects provided comfortable houses in styles suitable to local climates.

The literature of the late 1st and the 2nd centuries A.D., a period known as the Silver Age, is less elevated but more varied than that of the Augustan period. Pliny the Elder combined a wide range of topics in his *Natural History*. Growing interest in theories of education finds its reflection in the writings of Quintilian. Many writers turned to satire to express their anger at the confusion of the times.

Above all, the Silver Age produced one of the greatest historians of antiquity, Tacitus. In his own inimitable style—biting, ironic, and pessimistic—he provides unforgettable portraits of the figures dominating the tumultuous years he lived through.

THE WORLD ACCORDING TO AUGUSTUS: THE GOLDEN AGE OF ART AND LITERATURE

In the last two centuries of the Republic, the Romans looked to Greece for artistic inspiration. They imported Greek statues and based their works of literature on Greek models (see Topic 14). The cultural renewal under Augustus thus served two distinct purposes. It spelled out clearly the chief lines of Augustus's political and social reforms, while also giving the Romans an artistic legacy that was specifically their own.

Augustus entrusted the day-to-day administration of his cultural program to Maecenas (c. 70–8 B.C.), a diplomat and the emperor's personal friend. Maecenas was famous for his wealth, and he used it to provide subsidies for the leading poets of the day, many of whom he personally discovered and encouraged. Enlisting them in the service of the regime, he offered them the support and respect their talents needed—to this day his name is synonymous with enlightened and generous patronage.

THE ACHIEVEMENTS OF LATIN LITERATURE

The hectic years of the late Republic left little time for leisurely contemplation and study of the past. When Augustus came to power, one of his first acts was therefore to commission an official history of Rome from legendary times to his own day, the first complete history of Rome ever written. His chosen author was Livy (59 B.C.–A.D. 17), who came to Rome from Padua as a young man and spent the rest of his life on the project.

Livy's *History of Rome* was in 142 books, of which only 35 survive intact. He began with the (mythical) arrival of Aeneas in Italy and took his narrative up to 9 B.C. Central to his vision of Rome's past—as to Augustus's—is the belief in Rome's destiny to rule the world. Without ever falsifying evidence or wilfully distorting facts, Livy paints a picture that glorifies Rome's origins and emphasizes the heroism of the Roman conquest of the Mediterranean. The battles of the Punic Wars take on an almost cosmic significance.

Even in his day, some of the literary lions at court criticized Livy for his "provincialism," but in general his contemporaries greeted the *History* with enthusiasm. It was just the type of picture of their past for which many Romans had been waiting, one that stressed the nobility of their climb to power and underplayed the bitterness of the last century of the Republic. His rich style—contemporaries called it "creamy"—and the vividness of his descriptions won him instant popularity as the leading prose writer of the Augustan age.

The greatest poet of the times—and one of the towering figures in Western literature—was Vergil (70–19 B.C.), a far more complex figure than Livy. Vergil's origins made him an ideal candidate for official patronage. His parents were farmers near Mantua who lost their estate in the chaos of the civil wars. A personal intervention by Augustus (or

Octavian, as he still was known then) seems to have resulted in the restoration of his land, and Vergil, who had come to Rome to appeal to Rome's new ruler, stayed on in gratitude to his benefactor.

The political context of his first two works was Augustus's plan to revive Italian agriculture. The *Eclogues* (or *Bucolics*) are short pastoral poems describing the lives of shepherds and farmers, with their feuds and rival loves, set against a landscape blending northern Italy and Sicily. His second work, the *Georgics*, is more serious. Composed while Vergil was living in a house near Naples lent to him by Maecenas, the *Georgics* offers a poetic guide to farming in Italy: how to cultivate vines and olives, the breeding of horses and cattle, and beekeeping. The leading character is Italy herself, "mighty mother of crops and men."

So great was the success of the young poet's work that Augustus entrusted to him the most ambitious literary project of the age. At the head of Greek literature stood the epic poems of Homer, the *Iliad* and the *Odyssey*. Now Rome was to have its own epic poem, the *Aeneid*, describing its heroic foundation, and Augustus commissioned Vergil to write it. The poet spent the last 10 years of his life on the *Aeneid*, and when he died the work was still incomplete. In his will, Vergil asked his friends to destroy the manuscript, but Augustus ordered them to disregard his wishes.

The *Aeneid* tells the story of the flight of the Trojan prince Aeneas from the wreckage of burning Troy. In response to a divine command, Aeneas and a small band of Trojan survivors sail westward to build a new Troy in Italy. The first six of the *Aeneid*'s twelve books describe Aeneas's wanderings—a Latin version of the wanderings of Odysseus described in Homer's *Odyssey*. The latter half of the *Aeneid* recounts Aeneas's struggles and eventual success in laying the foundations of his Italian kingdom—the ancestor of Rome. This provides a reverse equivalent of the *Iliad*. Homer's epic deals with the Greek siege of Troy leading to the city's destruction, while in the second part of the *Aeneid*, Aeneas constructs the future of Rome.

The entire *Aeneid* is permeated with Augustan echoes. Aeneas himself—loyal, responsible, and aware of the burden of destiny—seems an idealized portrait of Augustus, the man engaged in refounding Rome's greatness. The importance of family, the function of leadership, and above all Rome's divine mission to govern are all fundamental aspects of the *Aeneid* and of Augustus's program. There is even an Eastern queen to foreshadow the danger of Cleopatra: Queen Dido of Carthage, whose love affair with Aeneas almost distracts him from fulfilling his destiny.

Yet for all the brazen fanfares with which Vergil foretells the future glory of Rome and the mighty achievements of Augustus, the *Aeneid* is not a happy work. Some of its most profound moments deal with loss and sacrifice: "The world has tears, and mortal affairs touch the heart." For all his public heroics, Aeneas is filled with self-doubt, and his break with Dido causes them both deep suffering. Vergil seems to be asking if the sacrifices involved in a revolution on the Augustan scale are worth the price paid in human grief. His instructions to destroy the *Aeneid* may indicate his doubts about the emperor's achievement.

The poetry of Horace (65–8 B.C.) provides a more wholehearted appreciation of Augustus's restoration of peace and prosperity. A more personal poet than Vergil, Horace responds to the mood of the moment, to the warmth of friendship, and to the slow death of the fires of love. His acute sense of time passing increases his delight in the present. Some of his *Odes* are openly political, but they mainly express the return of civilization to Roman life, Augustus's greatest gift to his subjects.

THE AUGUSTAN ALTAR OF PEACE

Augustus claimed in his autobiography: "I found Rome a city of brick, and left it a city of marble." His massive architectural reconstruction at Rome involved the restoration of old temples and the building of new ones, including the Temple of Mars the Avenger.

The most complete artistic statement of the Augustan world view was the Altar of Peace (Ara Pacis), begun in 13 B.C., on Augustus's return to Rome from a tour of the Empire. The dedication ceremony took place on January 30, 9 B.C., his wife Livia's birthday. The four sides of the screen surrounding the altar combine historical and mythological events. The two side panels show the procession making its way to the inauguration in 9 B.C. Preceded by attendants, Augustus leads the priests of Romulus and Remus—legendary founders of Rome—while the imperial family brings up the rear and, on the opposite side, senators and magistrates walk in separate procession.

The front and back panels display myths referring to Rome's past and present greatness. On the front, to left and right of the steps leading to the altar, are scenes referring to Rome's two foundation myths: the birth of Romulus and Remus, and the arrival in Italy of Aeneas. The rear shows on the left Mother Earth, with the bounty of nature that peace makes possible, and on the right the goddess Rome, seated quietly but fully armed—signifying that the only way to guarantee a lasting peace is to be prepared to go to war.

Beneath it all, running around the entire altar, is a richly carved band of vegetation, with fruits, flowers, and birds intertwined, to indicate that both history and myth rest symbolically on the secure foundation of the land. Finally, Augustus's deliberate evocation of a Golden Age is reflected in the style of the altar's sculptures, based on that of Periclean Athens, the Golden Age of Greece.

Entrance to the Ara Pacis (Altar of Peace), c. 13–9 B.C. 36 by 33 feet (11 by 10 m). The center doorway, through which the altar is just visible, is flanked by scenes showing the two stories of the foundation of Rome: on the left Romulus and Remus, on the right Aeneas. Note the elaborate lower decoration, which consists of fruit and flowers—another reminder of Augustus's policy of basing Rome's prosperity on its agriculture.

HISTORY AND PERSONALITY IN IMPERIAL SCULPTURE

By the late Republic, sculptors were producing portraits that combined physical realism with psychological insight. For once Roman art was not based on Greek models because Classical Greek sculpture aimed for idealizing beauty. The Romans derived their interest in realism from the Etruscans and developed it to express individual character. Late Republican images of leading statesmen such as Caesar and Cicero reveal much about their subjects' personalities.

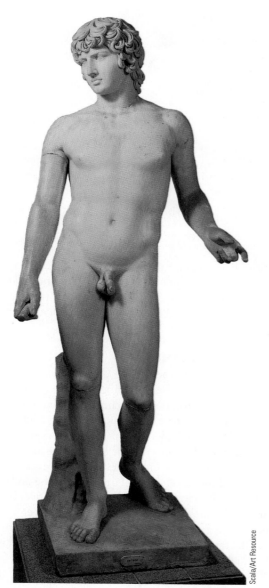

Statue of Antinous, c. A.D. 130. Height 5 feet 6 inches (1.65 m). Antinous was the favorite of Hadrian. When the young man died under mysterious circumstances in A.D. 130, the emperor had statues of him placed throughout the Empire. The style shows a return to 5th century B.C. Classical Greek models, with its nudity, elaborate hairstyle, and dreamy expression.

Augustus, seeing the possibilities offered by the medium, commissioned official portraits that presented the emperor in the way he wanted to be seen. The most famous, the *Augustus of Prima Porta*, dates to A.D. 13, when the emperor was in his mid-seventies. The figure, wearing a combination of civic and military dress, retains all the quiet command and ageless vigor of Augustus's portraits of 40 years earlier.

PORTRAITURE UNDER AUGUSTUS'S SUCCESSORS

Under later emperors, artists tempered the idealism of Augustan art with realism. Official portraits of both Caligula and Nero leave little doubt as to their inherent brutality. Vespasian emerges as capable and considerate, but his image remains unglamorized, with the scanty hair and lined face revealing the years of hard campaigning.

The ideal beauty of High Classical art returned in the sculpture of the reign of Hadrian, which marked a shift in Roman culture from the west (Hadrian was Spanish) to the world of Greece and the eastern Mediterranean. From his youth, Hadrian was infatuated with Greek culture; he received a Greek education, and one of his first acts as emperor was to visit Athens, where he commissioned the building of a library. Hadrian left Greece in A.D. 121 for the Roman province of Asia (modern Turkey), where he met a young man, Antinous, who was thereafter to be his constant companion and lover. In A.D. 130 Antinous died under mysterious circumstances, and Hadrian, heartbroken at his death, commissioned statue after statue to preserve Antinous's memory. Many of them show Antinous as a Greek god—now Apollo, now Dionysus—and all of them try to recapture the youthful perfection of the art of Classical Athens.

BUILDING THE EMPIRE: ARCHITECTURE IN ROME AND THE PROVINCES

Hadrian was an imaginative working architect, whose masterpiece, the Pantheon in Rome, dates to A.D. 125–126, and of all the arts, architecture was the one in which the Romans made their most original and influential contribution to Western culture. Over time, Roman architects produced a series of standard forms of building, ranging from baths to law courts. This standardization of design served a political purpose: The existence of similar types of building in cities throughout the Empire imposed a single, instantly recognizable Roman influence on very different cultures. Wherever Romans went, they could find a familiar urban setting.

Roman temples and other building forms first developed as a response to the fact that Roman culture was predominantly urban. Although most Roman subjects continued to live in rural areas, Rome and the other big cities of the Empire contained millions of citizens whose daily needs be-

Map 17.1 Imperial Rome. By contrast with Map 14.1, Rome has now spread well beyond the Servian Walls. Most of the structures shown can still be seen in Rome today. The Baths of Agrippa (upper center left) were destroyed by fire and became the site of Hadrian's Pantheon (A.D. 125–6). Vespasian built the Colosseum between A.D. 69 and 79. The heart of the city, however, remained the original Forum. Note that the Romans never really built on the other side of the river Tiber, which explains why the early Christians did: The first Basilica of St. Peter and today's Vatican City stand on ground never built on by "pagans."

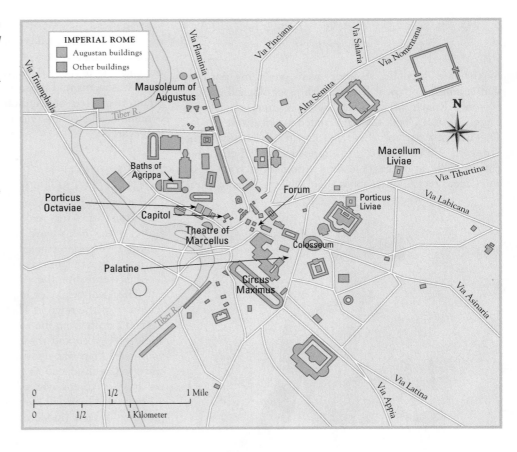

came crucial to the survival of the Empire. For the first time in Western history, administrators had to worry about mass water supplies, efficient transport systems, and the manifold problems of city life. They introduced building codes, devised a postal system, and set up police and fire services.

PLACES OF ENTERTAINMENT

One of the ways in which many of the emperors tried to gain the support of the urban proletariat was by the provision of mass entertainment. The origins of Roman theater and sports and games went back to Etruscan times. Drama was popular by the 2nd century B.C., and theaters built for the performance of Roman plays were a typical Roman adaptation of Greek theater design to an urban Roman setting. Unlike the Greek theaters, with their splendid natural locations offering breathtaking views over the surrounding countryside, Roman ones were completely enclosed.

The growing popularity of events such as gladiatorial contests required the invention of a special kind of structure, the amphitheater. The most famous example, Vespasian's Colosseum (see Topic 16), is only one of hundreds of similar stadiums in every part of the Empire. Nor is its capacity—around 50,000 spectators—exceptional. The most popular of all sports at Rome was chariot racing, and the racetrack where events took place, the Circus Maximus, could contain crowds of 250,000.

The use of architectural facilities for public activities was not limited to spectator sports. One of the most popular Roman pastimes was attendance at the public baths.

Wealthy Romans had their own bath structures at home, but huge public complexes formed an essential part of the urban landscape. The Baths of Caracalla, built at Rome around A.D. 215, could contain 3,000 people at one time in its largest hall.

THE USE OF CONCRETE

One of the chief factors in the construction of these immense buildings was the Roman invention of concrete and its use in the construction of arches, vaults, and domes—all making it possible to build structures that could contain large numbers of people. Before the Romans, problems of stone cutting and balance meant that architects could build only small-scale arches and domes, and the Greeks never really explored the possibilities of the arch. By the 2nd century B.C., Roman builders had discovered how to dissolve stone fragments in quicklime and pour the cement over a wooden frame into the shape of vaults and other curved structures. When hardened, the forms were free of any internal stresses and virtually indestructible.

The new method was cheap and tidy because it used up all of the stone fragments left over from other parts of the building. It avoided the need to cut stones of irregular shape and created huge interiors that were incomparably strong. By the time of Domitian, the use of concrete was widespread in great urban building projects throughout the Empire. Hadrian employed concrete for the dome of his Pantheon and experimented with different kinds of arch and vault in his private villa at Tivoli, outside Rome.

Arial view of the Pantheon, Rome, built c. A.D. 125–126. The huge concrete dome that crowns the Pantheon is open at the top to the sky—the opening is called the "oculus," or "eye." As the sun moves through the heavens, its beam moves around the inner wall of the building, making the whole structure a symbol of the world; the five rows of coffers in the dome originally contained bronze stars.

THE ROMAN HOUSE

Roman building ingenuity was by no means limited to great public constructions. Domestic comfort was also important, and architects adapted their plans to local climates. Most residents of Rome in Augustan times lived in apartment blocks limited to four floors and a total height of 70 Roman feet (68 modern feet). A century later, as crowded conditions at Rome led to hasty and careless construction, Trajan reduced the legal height permitted to 60 Roman feet (58 modern). The apartments were built in rows, with narrow alleys between them, and staircases in the entrances led to the upper floors.

The ground floor almost always contained shops or warehouses. Pipes generally carried water up to the first floor, but residents of the upper-floor apartments had to fetch their own water from public fountains on the street level. Some complexes had an inner courtyard with its own fountain. The most luxurious dwellings were on the lower floors, but rooms in the poorer accommodations above often had elegant mosaic decorations on the floor.

The mild Roman climate meant that houses could be heated with portable stoves. Residences in northern Italy, France, and Britain often had under-floor central heating. Architects in Roman Syria, where summer brings intense heat, built dwellings with thick stone walls and narrow windows, some of which are still lived in today.

THE EVIDENCE OF POMPEII

Our most complete picture of urban life in Roman times comes from the excavations at Pompeii and Herculaneum, cities on the Bay of Naples, which were buried by the eruption of the volcano Vesuvius on August 24, A.D. 79. The slow work of exploring the ruins began in the mid-18th cen-

An aerial view of the excavated city of Pompeii as it appears today. The long, open rectangular space in the lower center is the forum. Although work has been carried out at Pompeii for the past 200 years, two-fifths of the city remain unexcavated.

ACROSS CULTURES

Mark Twain in Pompeii

The American novelist and humorist Mark Twain (1835–1910), whose real name was Samuel Langhorne Clemens, traveled widely throughout the United States and Europe, giving lectures and writing about his experiences. In 1869, he published *The Innocents Abroad*, based on a recent European trip, in the course of which he had visited the excavations at Pompeii.

By the mid-19th century, Pompeii had become an obligatory stop on the itinerary of any serious traveler. After the first discovery in 1711 of the Roman cities on the Bay of Naples that were buried by the eruption of the volcano Vesuvius in A.D. 79, work began at Pompeii in 1748. Among the first distinguished visitors was the great German writer Johann Wolfgang Goethe, who commented, after inspecting the remains in 1787: "There have been many disasters in this world, but few which have given so much delight to posterity, and I have seldom seen anything so interesting"—high praise indeed from such a powerful intellectual. Other writers, poets, and painters followed, among them the English Romantic poet Percy Bysshe Shelley:

> I stood within the City disinterred;
> And heard the autumnal leaves like light footfalls
> Of spirits passing through the streets; and heard
> The mountain's slumberous voice at intervals
> Thrill through those roofless halls.

Twain, the arch skeptic, could hardly endorse such fulsome tributes, and instead of praising the houses or the frescoes, he chose to concentrate his attention on the deep ruts worn by carriage wheels in the soft volcanic stone of the streets—ruts "worn into the thick flagstones by the chariot-wheels of generations of swindled tax-payers." "And," he continues, "do I not know by these signs that street commissioners of Pompeii never attended to their business? And besides, is it not the inborn nature of street commissioners to avoid their duty whenever they get a chance? I wish I knew the name of the last one that held office in Pompeii so that I could give him a blast. I speak with feeling on this subject because I caught my foot in one of those ruts, and the sadness that came over me when I saw the first poor skeleton, with ashes and lava sticking to it, was tempered by the reflection that may be that party was the street commissioner."

Twain's writerly instinct was far more inspired by his climbing Vesuvius and making his way through the lava piled up by past eruptions: "A black ocean which was tumbled into a thousand fantastic shapes—a wild chaos of ruin, desolation and barrenness—a wilderness of billowy upheavals, of furious whirlpools, of miniature mountains rent asunder—of gnarled and knotted, wrinkled and twisted masses of blackness that mimicked branching roots, great vines, trunks of trees, all interlaced and mingled together; and all these weird shapes, all this turbulent panorama, all this stormy, far-reaching waste of blackness, with its thrilling suggestiveness of life, of action, of boiling, surging, furious motion, was petrified!"

---

tury and still goes on. By the early 21st century just over three-fifths of Pompeii are once more visible.

Pompeii was a small, prosperous market town with a population of around 20,000. The main industry was the production and dying of fabric. There were three sets of baths and three places of public entertainment: a theater seating 5,000, a concert hall seating 1,000, and an amphitheater with room for 20,000. Other facilities included sidewalk bars and cafés and several brothels.

The private houses were generally open-plan, with rooms grouped around a central hall, or atrium, and with a pleasant, enclosed garden in the rear. Some houses had a summer and a winter dining area, to take advantage of the sun, while the largest of all, the House of the Faun, had four dining rooms, one for each season. Frescoes decorated the walls, and the furniture included bronze candlesticks, wooden beds, and iron safes for holding money and family treasures such as silver tableware.

To a modern visitor, familiar with the squalor of early 21st-century urban life, a stroll in Pompeii suggests a level of comfort unimaginable for many people today. Yet Pompeii and Herculaneum were small, provincial centers, inhabited by hard-working lower-middle-class and lower-class citizens. One of the most elaborate houses was probably that of the baker, Pacuvius Proclus. The streets of Pompeii offer only the most distant glimmer of the quality of life in the elegant quarters of Rome, Alexandria, or many other centers of Roman culture.

WRITERS OF THE SILVER AGE: RHETORIC, SATIRE, AND HISTORY

The Silver Age of Latin literature extended from the death of Augustus to the end of Hadrian's reign. Although it produced no single writer of the calibre of Vergil, the Silver Age saw a broader range of literary topics and genres. The very grandeur of Augustan literature, in fact, inhibited later writers. Who, after Vergil, would dare to compose an epic, and who, after Livy, could imagine writing a universal history?

In general, therefore, writers of the Silver Age sought to impress their audience with style rather than content, and rhetoric became an end in itself. Learned references, obscure allusions, and clever epigrams were some of the ways in which authors of the period aimed to make their mark. One of the rare exceptions was the *Natural History* of Pliny the Elder (A.D. 23–79), an extraordinary collection of information that was intended for reference rather than entertainment. The subjects covered include animals, insects, trees and plants, medicines, and metals. Influential in medieval Europe, Pliny's work has been described by a modern commentator as "a compendium of all the errors of the ancient world."

RHETORIC IN THE EARLY EMPIRE

The leading authority on education in the Silver Age was Quintilian (c. A.D. 35–c. 95). In the reign of Vespasian, his preeminence in the field earned him an official position and salary as head of the teaching profession, awarded to him by the emperor. Among his pupils were Pliny the Younger—Trajan's correspondent from Bithynia—and Domitian's great-nephews. In addition to teaching, he also practiced as a lawyer.

Quintilian's *Education of an Orator*, published at the end of his life, combined his two main interests: educational theory and rhetoric. Most of the work consists of a rigorous analysis of various kinds of oratorical subject, style, and delivery—"much wormwood and too little honey," as the author disarmingly says of his own dry style. The first part, however, offers a surprisingly enlightened discussion of the education of children. The teacher, he believed, should be the pupil's friend, inspiring by enthusiasm and fundamental human decency and wisdom. Unlike many later theoreticians, Quintilian discouraged the use of corporal punishment, which he believed had only a negative effect.

THE SATIRISTS: PETRONIUS AND JUVENAL

If Pliny and Quintilian represent the serious side of the literature of their age, Petronius (?–A.D. 66) shows us the bizarre

and comic aspects of life during Nero's reign. A favorite at Nero's court, Petronius became the "Arbiter of Taste" there, only to fall foul of the commander of the palace guard. In A.D. 66 he committed suicide, but not before smashing a precious vase, which he knew the emperor coveted.

His novel, the *Satyricon,* of which only parts survive, describes the adventures of three disreputable young men in the bars and brothels of southern Italy. The climax comes with an account of a dinner party given by a vulgar multi-millionaire social climber, Trimalchio. Petronius makes fun of the host's absurd costume, pretentious behavior, and tasteless menu. Later scenes alternate graphically erotic episodes with an ironic plan to fleece legacy hunters—hanging around rich men in the hope of being left something in their wills was a notorious practice in imperial Rome.

Petronius piles on ridiculous details to comic effect. The greatest of all Roman satirists, Juvenal (A.D. ?60–?130), tries to evoke a very different emotion: outrage at the corruption and decadence of his day. Born in central Italy, he came to Rome to make a career as a magistrate, but fell foul of Domitian. After a period of exile he returned to Rome to live in poverty, before ending his days in modest comfort, apparently thanks to help from Hadrian.

Juvenal's 16 *Satires* purport to deal with the age of Domitian and attack only the dead, but his rage against his own time remains blazing. In the Third Satire, he takes on Rome, the center of vice and corruption, filled with extremes of poverty and extravagance, where foreigners—Greeks and Easterners—are among the worst offenders. The Sixth Satire is directed against women. Chastity, says Juvenal, left the earth centuries ago, and he describes in vivid detail what replaced it. All types of women fall victim to his hatred: quarrelsome and bickering ones, gossips, women who procure abortions and drive their husbands insane with drugs, and—in the same breath—learned women who spout Greek quotations.

Juvenal aims his fire at so many targets, and allows rhetoric to carry him to such extremes, that his anger sometimes seems counterproductive. Yet there is no denying the brilliance of his character-drawing or the power of his flashing epigrams, while the picture he paints of imperial Rome provides a dramatic corrective to official propaganda.

TACITUS THE HISTORIAN

Tacitus (A.D. c. 56–120), the greatest historian of his age—and many other ages, too—was also, like Juvenal, concerned to set the record straight. Unlike Juvenal, however, Tacitus was an insider. Vespasian made him a senator, he was consul in A.D. 97, and he served as governor of Asia in A.D. 112–113. His two chief works were the *Histories* and the *Annals.* Written in the reigns of Trajan and Hadrian, they tell the story of the period from the death of Augustus to the assassination of Domitian—an age he describes as "rich in catastrophe, fearful in its battles, fertile in mutinies—bloody even in peace."

Tacitus recounts his terrible tale in a style that combines irony and biting scorn, wit and dignified pessimism.

The first of his targets is Tiberius, and other unforgettable figures to emerge include Nero and his mother Agrippina. Unlike Juvenal, Tacitus sought to express a serious historical judgment: However bad the Republic was at its worst, it was better than the imperial system at its best. In order to make his point, he is not free from bias, and his belief that those in power determine the course of history would not be shared by all historians. Yet the drama of his narration and the eloquence of his language make him one of the highest masters of Latin literature.

Putting Roman Imperial Culture in Perspective

The comedy of Petronius, the savage indignation of Juvenal, and the profundity of Tacitus's moral judgments reveal the darker side of the splendor of the Empire, one very distant from the self-conscious pride of the art and literature of the Augustan age. Both viewpoints are complementary. As Vergil hints, the peace that Augustus brought came at a price. It was inevitable that the sense of relief that permeates the art of the Golden Age would turn to restlessness as the defects of Augustus's political reforms became increasingly glaring after his death.

Both the official character of Augustan art and the growing hostility of tone in sculpture and Silver Age literature have in common one important factor. From the beginning of the Empire, artists were politically "engaged," using their art either in support of or against the regime. Even in the art of ancient Greece, few creative figures dealt with the events of their own times in so direct and down-to-earth a way. For the dramatists, sculptors, and painters of Classical Athens, art was a means of exploring the universal questions of human existence. With the exception of one or two plays by Aristophanes, their works referred to contemporary events only indirectly.

For better or worse, the links binding art and politics in imperial Rome were unbreakable. With the decline and eventual fall of the Empire, the arts shifted to safer, more solid ground at the service of church and state. Only centuries later, at the end of the 18th century, on the eve of the French Revolution, did artists once again take up an active political and social role.

Questions for Further Study

1. In what ways does the *Aeneid* fulfill its aim to provide the Romans with a national epic? How does it compare in this respect with the Greeks' *Iliad* and *Odyssey*?
2. What was the impact of urban life on Roman architecture and planning? In what ways, if any, were the Romans faced with problems similar to those of modern urban existence, and how did they try to solve them?
3. How did Augustus use the visual arts as a means of propaganda? To what extent did his successors follow his example?

Suggestions for Further Reading

Christ, K. *The Romans: An Introduction to Their History and Civilization*. Berkeley, CA, 1987.

D'Ambra, Eve. *Roman Art*. New York, 1998.

Jones, Mark Wilson. *Principles of Roman Architecture*. New Haven, CT, 1999.

Ogilvie, R.M. *Roman Literature and Society*. New York, 1980.

Ramage, Nancy H., and Andrew Ramage. *Roman Art: Romulus to Constantine*. Englewood Cliffs, NJ, 1996.

West, D.A., and A. J. Woodman. *Poetry and Politics in the Age of Augustus*. New York, 1984.

Yegul, Fikrez. *Baths and Bathing in Classical Antiquity*. Cambridge, MA, 1992.

Zanker, P. *Pompeii: Public and Private Life*. Cambridge, MA, 1998.

InfoTrac College Edition

Enter the search term *Roman Empire* using Key Terms.

Daily Life in the Roman World

The aim of the Roman state was to strengthen the sense of Roman unity throughout the Empire by promoting its way of life. A single universal legal system was in operation. The law functioned by the use of past decisions to create precedents, in the light of which new cases were tried. The prime source of law was the emperor, who ratified earlier decisions and served as the final court of appeal. Other factors in encouraging trust in the central authority included efficient municipal government and the role of the army.

The day-to-day running of the state was in the hands of the imperial bureaucracy. Under the Julio-Claudians, many of the most powerful administrators were not Roman citizens but freedmen. By the reign of Trajan, as resentment grew at the influence wielded by these freedmen, members of the class of *equites* began to serve as bureau chiefs, both at Rome and in the provinces.

The first century of the Empire saw the rise of commerce at the expense of agriculture, especially in Italy, where farming continued to decline. Trade became decentralized, with the great cities of Asia and North Africa offering stiff competition to Italian manufacturers. By the 3rd century A.D., with imperial rule in a state of military anarchy, and Germanic raids on many of the chief trade routes, the economy went into serious decline.

The family remained the basis of social life. From the time of Augustus, successive emperors tried in vain to produce a rise in the birthrate. Despite incentives to encourage large families and penalties for the childless, Roman men and women of the upper classes continued to use contraception to avoid pregnancies, and families remained small, especially in Italy.

The chief family of the state was that of the emperor, "father of his native land." The women in the imperial family also received honors. Livia, wife of Augustus, was worshiped as divine during her lifetime, and cities in Asia raised temples to her. After Augustus's death she received the title "Augusta." Women continued to enjoy far more personal freedom than in the Republic, although they still played little visible part in politics. The empresses of the Flavian dynasty maintained an influential salon at court, while in the early 3rd century A.D. the women of the Severan family exercised considerable political power.

One of the functions of the state was to protect the interests of citizens, freedmen, and freedwomen. Slaves and gladiators, two underclasses that played an important role in Roman life, received varying treatment. Slaves could win their freedom and then integrate fully into society. Gladiators, who were often condemned criminals, were expendable once they had provided entertainment in the stadium.

LAW, CITIZENSHIP, AND BUREAUCRACY

Augustus believed that one of the responsibilities of imperial rule was to spread Roman civilization throughout the Empire. Under his successors, the Romanization of the provinces imposed order on a wide variety of different cultures. One of the chief tools for the diffusion of Roman ways was education, and both public schools and private endowments became increasingly common. Vespasian endowed chairs in the universities of the great cities, while Hadrian introduced a tax-exempt status for teachers.

UNIVERSAL LAW

The single most effective force for establishing a standard way of life was the law. In the Republic, the source of legal authority was a body of written statutes, which needed regular updating and was available for public consultation. By the time of the early emperors, the old system was hopelessly out of date, and a new one came into operation.

The law was based on the word of the emperor. Its chief sources were his edicts, his written instructions to officials, and official correspondence. The legal office of the civil service catalogued all of this material and used it to provide precedents for future cases in all parts of the Empire. Augustus defended the concentration of legal power in the hands of the emperor by claiming that in nominating him, the Senate and people had delegated him to exercise their power for them. The same principle justified the emperor's functioning as the final court of appeal, a role originally played by an ancient assembly of the people.

By the time of Hadrian, the legal affairs of the Empire were under the control of a board of professional jurists directly under the supervision of the emperor and his staff. The criminal courts, with their juries of ordinary citizens, which Sulla had introduced (see Topic 9), were replaced by special courts run by the emperor's delegates. In the mid-2nd century A.D., the jurist Gaius (fl. A.D. 130–180) published a textbook, *The Institutes of Roman Law*, which set out the principles of civil law (law affecting private rights). This book remained a bestseller for more than three centuries and served as the basis for Justinian's reforms in the 6th century (see Topic 22).

CITIZENSHIP: CIVILIANS AND SOLDIERS

In the late Republic, the Senate used the grant of citizenship rights as a peaceful means of resolving conflicts (as at the end of the Social War in 88 B.C.; see Topic 9), and to raise the number of people who were eligible to pay taxes. By the time of the adoptive emperors, citizenship grants provided another means of creating a universal state, all of whose members had the same rights.

The emperors used two other methods to unite the Empire's subjects. The first was the standardization of local government. The administration of towns throughout the provinces continued to follow the lines of Julius Caesar's municipal constitution (see Topic 9). The free citizens of each town elected the magistrates, who were in charge of financial affairs and public services. The local government had specific responsibility for ensuring a regular supply of oil and flour at fixed prices and for maintaining reasonable quantities of other provisions, even in times of shortage. The planning of public entertainments was another of the magistrates' duties. Many towns ran municipal shops, baths, and hotels, and used the profits to fund public activities.

The other means of promoting unity, the settlement of Italians in remote parts of the Empire, was less successful. The early emperors encouraged Italians to spread Roman culture and the Latin language and religious tradition by establishing Italian colonies throughout the eastern and western provinces. In many cases the reverse occurred. Italians in Asia or Egypt became converted to local cults and introduced them back into Italy, as in the case of Mithraism and the worship of Isis. A more serious problem was the rapidly declining birthrate in Italy, caused in part by economic deterioration, which severely limited the numbers of Italians who could be sent abroad without depleting the workforce at home.

The military played a more active role in nation building. All legionaries were Roman citizens, but noncitizens could serve as "auxiliaries," and they and their descendants became citizens on discharge. Because Latin was the official language of the army, the auxiliary troops—Gauls, Cappadocians, and others—who learned it became a means of spreading Roman culture.

The armed forces also had an important influence on the regions in which they were posted. For many provincial citizens, nominally Roman but living hundreds or even thousands of miles from Rome, the army was the only state institution with which they had any regular contact. In some cases, army camps evolved into towns and cities. Because the soldiers built many of the canals, baths, theaters, and other public structures and acted as police force, protecting citizens from robbers and highwaymen, the army often came to represent the positive aspect of state interference in local affairs.

THE IMPERIAL BUREAUCRACY

The other arm of state power, the civil service, far from spreading Roman culture, provided non-Romans with a means of winning influence and wealth. The reforms of Claudius strengthened the role of the imperial bureaucracy in the running of government, and many of his former slaves rose to high civil service positions. Unlike the Roman middle-class *equites,* who despised the notion of office work or bookkeeping, these imperial freedmen were efficient and experienced. Some of the best civil servants came from Greek families in Asia, and their level of education was higher than that of many Roman senators.

Standing between the emperor and the reports, petitions, and requests that poured in from all over the Empire, the freedmen prepared answers and submitted them to the emperor for his approval. The mass of paperwork fell into a

Roman relief sculpture showing tax collectors receiving payments. A.D. 2nd–3rd century. The officer on the left holds a scroll containing the accounts, while his colleagues count the money collected. The use of varying degrees of relief—the two chief figures are shown in high relief (almost detached from the stone), whereas the two rear figures are in very low relief—is characteristic of the period.

R. Sheridan/Ancient Art & Architecture

series of categories, each of which had its own department with an imperial freedman attached as permanent secretary. One office handled correspondence from the provinces, another provincial revenues, and another legal cases in which the emperor was interested or involved. Other freedmen occupied positions in the palace that were far below the dignity of Roman citizens but that brought considerable power with them. None was closer to the emperor and his family than the chamberlain, or *cubicularius*. This official controlled access to the emperor, and unscrupulous ones auctioned the chance of an audience to the highest bidder. Some even sold reports on the emperor's mood or state of health—a practice the Romans called "selling smoke."

By the 3rd century A.D., with rule passing chaotically from one military despot to another, the civil service was gradually taken over by the military. Its organization came to resemble the army's, with a chain of command passing from the lowest bureaucrats through the various levels up to the emperor and his chief-of-staff at the top. In the process, the bureaucracy was weighed down with massive increases in the amount of paperwork, while ex-centurions did not always make the most efficient or flexible administrators. Nonetheless, the continued presence of freedmen and imperial slaves as accountants, paymasters, and other office personnel allowed the civil service to continue to function even in time of civil war.

THE IMPERIAL ECONOMY: RECOVERY, STABILITY, AND DECLINE

The reign of Augustus brought an extended period of peace and the conditions for economic recovery. Manufacturing and trade flourished throughout the Empire, with production centers springing up to satisfy local needs. Factories in Gaul made pottery and metal goods for the northern market, while Carthage produced oil lamps for sale in North Africa.

THE SPREAD OF TRADE

As economic stability spread, so did commerce. One of the factors favoring trade was Roman control of the Mediterranean. The Roman Navy, one of the chief forces in Rome's rise to power, had little fighting to do once the Empire was won. From the reign of Augustus to the late 3rd century A.D., there were no real naval wars. The fleet's main duties were to accompany convoys of goods and keep the seas free of pirates. Ease of shipping brought greater prosperity, leading to improved harbors and canal systems, and extended road networks.

Another factor in the growth of commerce in all parts of the Empire was an international banking system, which facilitated currency exchange. Banks accepted deposits, on which they paid interest. Merchants transferred credit from one country to another to pay for goods without having to move cash. The use of Roman currency remained widespread, but in certain periods its value began to fluctuate. Nero was the first ruler to save money by debasing the standard coinage (using less valuable metals), and several of his successors followed his example. As a result, many local mints continued to produce coins that local banks exchanged at rates fixed by the state.

TRADE BEYOND THE MEDITERRANEAN

The Augustan age saw the expansion of Roman trading outside its traditional bases. Roman pottery and bronze objects have been found in many parts of northern Europe, including Poland and Norway, as well as in Britain. In return, the Romans imported British tin, while northern Europe provided furs, skins, dried fish, and amber.

Small quantities of ivory, tortoise shell, and spices were shipped up the east coast of Africa, together with slaves. The most important new areas to be opened up, though, were India and China. Toward the beginning of Augustus's reign, the Romans discovered that monsoon winds could carry Roman ships from ports in southeastern Egypt across the Indian Ocean to the west coast of India. The trip took around 40 days, and soon some 120 ships made the journey each year. The merchants then continued their journeys overland. The huge quantities of Roman pottery and coins discovered on India's east coast, near Pondicherry, may even suggest that traders opened a factory there. In exchange, they shipped ivory, incense, pearls, and spices back to Rome. The most popular of the spices was pepper, for which the Romans developed great enthusiasm, opening large storage facilities along the river Tiber.

Fresco scene from Pompeii showing a busy harbor on the Bay of Naples. A.D. 70–79. The long pier extending from the right creates a sheltered harbor in which various craft are moored. The sense of strong sunlight, created by the use of contrasts between the deep shadows of the foreground and the brilliantly lit rear, gives a vivid impression of the heat of Southern Italy.

Scala/Art Resource

Moving north up the river Indus and through Afghanistan, Roman traders arrived in China, which was then enjoying relatively peaceful rule under the Han emperors (202 B.C.–220 A.D.). Chinese silk became one of the most prized possessions of Early Imperial Rome and far more desirable than the silks produced locally on Cos and other Greek islands. Even though merchants had to take gold, wine, copper, and coral to exchange for the precious fabrics, successful traders could bring back enough silk to cover the cost of the expedition and still multiply their original investment a hundred times over.

TRADE AND AGRICULTURE IN ITALY

There was a price to pay for the spread of stable trading conditions throughout the Empire and expansion outside: recession in Italy. Under Augustus, the factories of central and southern Italy produced goods for sale abroad without much competition. As prosperity spread, the provinces no longer needed to import goods because it was cheaper to make them or to buy them locally. Even the state often saved money on transport by feeding and equipping troops on duty in the East with supplies bought on the spot, rather than shipped from Italy.

It was easy for provincial factories to turn out pottery or metal goods of the same quality as those manufactured in Italy at highly competitive prices. Italian factories, however, could not fight back by manufacturing the kinds of goods produced in the provinces because Italy lacked the raw materials. Egypt maintained its monopoly on papyrus, Spain on steel, and Asia on glass. Thus the richer the Roman Empire grew, the more trade and industry in Italy declined. The gradual shift of economic weight from Italy to the provinces, particularly the wealthy eastern ones, was to have enormous consequences for later imperial history and continued to affect the West after the Empire's fall.

Nor was Italian agriculture in much better shape. For all Augustus's insistence on the fundamental role of agriculture in Italian life, by the early Empire farming in Italy was in decline. One cause was competition from farmers in Spain and Greece, whose olive oil and wine were often of better quality than those produced in Italy.

In the late 1st century A.D., many owners of medium-sized Italian estates gave up trying to make ends meet and sold their land, which was bought up by wealthy absentee landlords. One of the consequences was the decline of country towns, whose income came from the small farmers of their region. *Latifundia* (large estates) continued to take up most of the arable land in other parts of the Empire as well as in Italy, but the negative effects of the concentration of land in a few hands were most marked in Italian agriculture.

SEXUALITY AND DOMESTIC LIFE

One of the key factors in the increasing economic decline of Italy was the continual fall in the birthrate. Augustus's attempt to restore traditional views of marriage and the family was partly inspired by moral considerations, but it also tried to address a growing economic problem: the reduction in the size of the average Italian family.

AUGUSTAN FAMILY LEGISLATION

Under the legislation introduced by Augustus, women who were unmarried and childless at the age of 20 suffered penalties. The equivalent age for men was 25. Couples could divorce, provided that each of them remarried and continued to produce children. The law treated men more favorably than women. Males could marry an underage female and still enjoy the tax benefits of married status, while women could not marry prepubescent males. These legal provisions were applied consistently only to the upper classes.

Despite the Augustan legislation, which Domitian confirmed, and later emperors in the 2nd and 3rd centuries A.D. reinforced, Italian families—particularly those of the upper classes—continued to remain small. When parents did decide to rear a child, they were more likely to allow a male child to survive than a female. The usual ratio of female to male births is 105 to 100. Census figures for the Roman Empire in the 2nd century A.D., however, show the survival rate in Roman Egypt to be 100 females to 105 males. At Rome the rate was 100 females to 131 males, and in Roman Italy 100 females to 140 males.

An additional cause of this imbalance was the impact of a grain-based diet, short of protein and iron, which was a greater problem for women than for men. From the time of menarche, females require twice as much iron as men of a similar age, while pregnant women need three times the quantity. Lack of iron led to anemia and the possibility of premature death caused by complications of respiratory and circulatory diseases—a problem that continued to exist for women of the poorer classes in Europe until the late Middle Ages.

CONTRACEPTION AND ABORTION

One important reason for the striking reduction in the size of Italian families, in contrast with those elsewhere in the Empire, was the general knowledge of contraceptive techniques at Rome.

Many of the contraceptive methods commonly used by upper-class Romans were predictably based on superstition. Thus ancient authors recommended the power of magic amulets or talismans to prevent fertility. Among the more bizarre methods were the liver of a cat, worn in a tube on the left foot, and part of a lioness's womb kept in an ivory container.

Other techniques had a greater chance of working. One was the use of various ointments, both by women and by men, to block the entry to the uterus. The ingredients included oils and honey, and the cream was smeared on the genitals. The Romans also developed a form of condom made of animal bladder and practiced the rhythm method. The most common of all forms of birth control was probably withdrawal.

Opinion on the use of abortion to prevent births was mixed. The rate of death in pregnancy remained high enough for most women to prefer contraception, if they did not intend to carry the pregnancy to term. The Hippocratic Oath forbade the administration of medicines to induce abortion, but not all doctors followed its instructions. The physician Soranus (active 2nd century A.D.), who practiced at Alexandria and later at Rome, wrote an important treatise entitled *On Midwifery and the Diseases of Women*, which remained influential for centuries. He does not forbid the use of abortion-inducing drugs, but recommends contraception as a better means of preventing unwanted pregnancies. For Soranus, the welfare of the mother took precedence over that of the child, and he describes various methods of relieving labor pains.

THE ALIMENTARY INSTITUTION

Despite successive attempts to slow down the decline in population, by the end of the 1st century A.D. the problem continued to present a threat to the economy of Italy and hindered schemes to spread Roman culture by encouraging Italian colonization in the provinces. Attempts to penalize childlessness were clearly not working, and the introduction of the alimentary institution by Nerva (see Topic 16) was an attempt to find a different solution.

If well-to-do couples refused to produce large families, the children of poor parents would have to serve as a substitute. Nerva had Italy divided into a series of regions and appointed a program director in each. These officials had the job of identifying how many children there were in their region who needed financial aid for their support and education. The central government then invested money in local estates—thereby providing much-needed assistance to farmers—and the interest from the loans went to support the needy children. Officials on the spot administered the scheme once it was set up, to avoid involving Rome in unnecessary paperwork.

Government intervention inspired similar programs in the private sector. Businessmen set up funds whose income went to pay for the rearing and education of poor children, and to provide them with a small sum of money when they came of age. Many of the private schools operating in Italy were similarly dependent on grants from private individuals. Pliny the Younger, who had no children, wanted his hometown, Como, to have a teacher of literature and rhetoric. He offered to pay one-third of the salary of a suitably qualified person, if his fellow citizens would contribute the remainder.

WOMEN IN PUBLIC LIFE

Women in the Empire continued to increase their degree of freedom from restrictions, although some areas remained inaccessible, especially active participation in politics. Women did engage in business, however. At Pompeii, the

Alinari/Art Resource

Statue of Eumachia, a wealthy benefactress at Pompeii. A.D. 62–79. As an inscription on the front entrance explains, Eumachia paid for the construction of one of the chief buildings in the forum at Pompeii, the Basilica of Eumachia, which served as the meeting place and storage center for the traders in cloth (e.g., manufacturers, dyers, and laundrymen). She is seen here in her role as priestess (with her head covered) of the cult of the empress Livia, wife of Augustus.

moneylender Faustilla signed loan notes, charging 45 percent interest per year, and Julia Felix owned a building in which she rented out rooms and shops. Eumachia, an important and successful Pompeian businesswoman, paid for a building complex on the Forum, Pompeii's main square.

Some professional fields were open to women. Midwifery was, of course, exclusively a female occupation, and there were also some woman doctors—often the wife or daughter of a medical man. The same applied to woman artists, many of whom studied with their fathers. Those who became adept competed on equal terms in the market. One writer observed of Iaia of Cyzicus, a portrait painter who was active at Rome around 100 B.C., that "her talent was so great that her prices far exceeded those of the most famous painters of the day."

WOMEN OF THE IMPERIAL FAMILY

Augustus's insistence on the importance of the family led to the inclusion of the female members of the family in the distribution of imperial honors. In 27 B.C., at the beginning of his reign, he named an important building in the center of Rome the Portico of Octavia, in honor of his sister, and over the following years he dedicated buildings to his wife Livia. When Octavia died in 11 B.C., the emperor declared public mourning and personally delivered the eulogy in her memory.

Livia became the object of a cult. Within her lifetime several cities in Asia declared her divine and raised temples to her. On the death of Augustus, the Senate voted her the title of Augusta, and Claudius conferred the same honor on his wife Agrippina while he was still alive. Imperial women also often appeared on coinage minted either to mark the birth of a child to them or to commemorate their deaths.

Agrippina, Claudius's wife, was the first imperial woman to wield power openly. For the first five years of her son Nero's reign, she acted as co-regent with his tutor Seneca and Burrus, captain of the palace guard (see Topic 16). Her portrait appeared on coins next to Nero's, and she received visitors on official business—although from behind a curtain. When Nero ordered her assassination in A.D. 59, she is said to have pointed to her womb and told her murderers to "Strike here!"

Agrippina's example seems to have taught most subsequent empresses the danger of overt political involvement. Trajan's wife Plotina provided advice to her husband and even went with him on his last military campaign, against the Parthians, but her contemporaries noted her fidelity and praised her piety rather than her contribution to politics.

The most active and independent of all empresses was probably Julia Domna (A.D. ?167–217), wife of Septimius Severus (ruled A.D. 193–211). She took part in her husband's political decisions and maintained a high-powered salon, which attracted the leading intellectuals of the day. Julia's sister, Julia Maesa (?–A.D. 226), went even further. After the murder of her nephew Caracalla (ruled A.D. 211–217), she managed to get her grandson, the eccentric Elagabalus (ruled A.D. 218–222), proclaimed emperor. While Elagabalus entertained and mystified the crowds at

Rome with bizarre religious ceremonies in honor of his god Elagabal (imported from Syria), Julia Maesa ran the Empire.

On her death, her daughter, Julia Soaemias (?–A.D. 235), assumed the same role for Elagabalus's successor, her own son Alexander Severus (ruled A.D. 222–235). Alexander was 14 years old when Julia installed him as emperor and took control into her own hands. Wielding power openly, the third of these redoubtable Syrian Julias had herself voted the title "Augusta, Mother of Augustus, Mother of the Army and the Senate, Mother of the Fatherland." A Senate and people worn out by the reigns of Caracalla and Elagabalus wearily let her have her way, until mother and son went campaigning against the Germans. Julia persuaded her son to offer the German troops money in exchange for peace, and the disgusted Roman forces under their command killed them both.

SLAVES, CRIMINALS, AND GLADIATORS

Roman society, for all its written and unwritten rules, could be surprisingly flexible, as the attitude toward slaves demonstrates. The example of the gladiators, however, demonstrates that the treatment of the underclasses could also be brutal and dehumanizing.

Roman relief sculpture depicting building operations, late Imperial period (A.D. 3rd–4th century). The workers are installing sculptural decorations on the upper part of a temple. In order to reach the top, they are using a crane that is powered by slaves, who can be seen in the lower right-hand corner as they walk on a treadmill that turns the wheel.

SLAVERY IN THE ROMAN WORLD

By the time of the Empire, the large slave gangs used in Republican days for farm and other labor were far less commonly employed because the security risk was far too high, as Spartacus's revolt demonstrated. Most slaves worked either alongside their owners or in the home, and many achieved social mobility. Any Roman citizen could bestow freedom on a slave, who then became a freedman. Freedmen were barred from certain political positions, but all children born to them after the grant of freedom had the full rights of Roman citizenship.

Most slaves at Rome came from the Greek-speaking East, captured as prisoners of war, or bought from slave traders. Some were sold into slavery by their families. In many cases the slaves were better educated than their masters and were qualified to do skilled professional and commercial work. In a town like Pompeii, most businesses were run by slaves or freedmen. Some of the latter operated as agents of their former masters, whereas others were independent and worked for themselves.

By the end of the 1st century A.D., in Rome and throughout the rest of Italy, slaves, ex-slaves, or the descendants of slaves held a virtual monopoly of professions such as teaching, medicine, accounting, and architecture, as well as providing most barbers, cooks, and office workers. As election posters at Pompeii and elsewhere demonstrate, freedmen often ran for local political office.

LIFE IN THE AMPHITHEATER: THE GLADIATORS

The growth of an urban proletariat in Rome, Alexandria, and the other large cities of the Empire created many of the problems of city life familiar to the early 21st century: urban ghettoes, pollution, and violent crime. Those at the lowest end of the social scale could expect no mercy if they were caught for committing a serious offense, for which the penalty was death. The state executioner, always a slave, executed Roman citizens by strangling them with a leather strap in the state jail across from the Roman Forum, the Tullianum, which dated back to the time of the early kings. In order to prevent their burial, the bodies of criminals were thrown through a hole in the basement of the prison into the great drain, which emptied into the river Tiber.

Non-Roman citizens might expect to die more publicly, as a form of spectacle. The most frequent method of execution for common criminals and political agitators was crucifixion. In other cases offenders were sentenced to provide a different type of public entertainment by taking part in the gladiatorial combats of the arena. In Republican times no Roman citizen could fight in the games. Under the Empire, it was not unknown for a citizen to volunteer to fight as a gladiator, which was sometimes the last refuge for a ruined man.

As the taste for these contests grew, and emperors and magistrates vied for popular favor by staging larger and larger games, specially trained gladiators began to take part in the action. Most of them were slaves or prisoners of war, but there were also some tough professionals.

Ancient Art & Architecture

Wall mosaic from a Roman villa in Sicily. Late Imperial period (A.D. 4th century). The villa at Piazza Armerina, which was perhaps an Imperial hunting lodge, shows scenes from gladiatorial combats. In this one, the fighter on the right is armed with a large shield and a short knife. His opponent fights with a three-pronged weapon, or trident. The imbalance between the equipment of the two men formed part of the "sport" for the spectators.

They trained in schools, most of which were under state control—the four gladiatorial schools at Rome dated to the time of Domitian—where they were put on a special muscle-building diet.

Each gladiator had special training in a specific skill. Some fought with heavy arms, others with only helmet, sword, and shield, and still others with a net, a fisherman's trident, and a dagger—the last type was called the *retiarius* or net-thrower. Other forms of contest involved wild animals or gladiators on horseback. One particularly brutal (and popular) type of battle was between two mounted fighters armed with shield and spear, and wearing helmets without eyeholes. The two charged each other blindly on horseback in the dark. Posters for the shows advertised the specialties of the gladiators taking part, the training school from which they came, and their previous record of successes. In this way the spectators would know what to expect and how to lay their bets.

The games began with a procession of the contestants, after which the trumpet sounded for the first fight, which might be between two individuals or involve two teams of fighters. A wounded gladiator could beg for mercy, appealing either to the organizer of the occasion or—at Rome—to the emperor when he was present. In most cases a wise organizer would follow the wishes of the audience, giving the sign of "thumbs up" for mercy and "thumbs down" to indicate that the contest should be fought to the death. Condemned criminals had no chance of mercy. Professional fighters who were spared lived to fight another day.

The winner of a contest received a palm branch and sometimes money. A gladiator who, by frequently winning or by showing special courage, won popular favor became free from the obligation to fight again. Some retired to private life. Those who chose to continue in the profession could command high fees.

Putting Daily Life in the Roman World in Perspective

In the earliest period of its history Rome was a monarchy, ruled by kings, and in the following centuries the great aristocratic families tracing their origins back to those of the city acquired immense prestige. Yet even in the last two centuries of the Republic, self-made men and their descendants were among the leading players in Roman politics and society. The noble birth of the brothers Gracchus was a handicap rather than an advantage in their attempt to promote reform. By the time of the Empire, social origins were by no means the only conditioning factor in a Roman's life.

One important factor in this change was the growing importance of personal wealth. The businessmen who made fortunes in Rome's various wars could buy, generally for their sons and daughters, the respectability that their birth denied them. Under the Empire, few cared about having exclusive origins except those who had nothing else to care about. A vulgar nouveau riche like Trimalchio would cause some raised eyebrows and sniggers, but guests would still go to his banquets.

Yet perhaps the most significant of all Roman attitudes toward social status and behavior was their sense of practicality. The Romans claimed to be doers rather than thinkers, and the best architects or generals or emperors were not necessarily the highest born. The essentially pragmatic quality of Roman attitudes toward birth emerged in the invention of the system of adoptive emperors: The first requirement was talent, then adoption could take care of the family connections. It also determined the status of women and slaves in Roman society. Both categories operated under significant restrictions, many of which, in practice, they could work around. For many Romans, ability could often carry its owners far beyond their official standing.

Questions for Further Study

1. How did the status of women evolve during the later Empire? To what extent were changes limited to the upper classes?
2. What was the Roman attitude toward slaves? How did it compare with the treatment of slaves in other ancient societies?
3. What were the chief factors that promoted the unity of the Roman Empire?
4. What were the main economic developments in the later history of the Empire? How far were they responsible for the decline of the central authority?

Suggestions for Further Reading

Boren, H.C. *Roman Society: A Social, Economic, and Cultural History,* 2nd ed. Lexington, MA, 1992.
Bradley, K.R. *Discovering the Roman Family.* New York, 1990.
Gardner, J.F. *Women in Roman Law and Society.* Bloomington, IN, 1986.
Garnsey, P., and R. Saller. *The Roman Empire: Economy, Society, and Culture.* Berkeley, CA, 1987.
Kebric, R.B. *Roman People.* Mountain View, CA, 1993.
Kleiner, Diana E.E. *I Claudia II: Women in Roman Art and Society.* New Haven, CT, 2000.
Thompson, L. *Romans and Blacks.* Norman, OK, 1989.
Wiedemann, T. *Greek and Roman Slavery.* London, 1989.

InfoTrac College Edition

Enter the search term *Roman Empire* using Key Terms.

Enter the search term *Roman law* using the Subject Guide.

CHRISTIANITY AND THE CRISIS OF EMPIRE

With the spread of Christianity in the later centuries of the Roman Empire, the history of the ancient world entered its final stages. Christian teachings originated in Palestine, among the Jews living there under Roman rule. The Romans' contact with the Jews extended back into Republican times: The first Jewish community at Rome dated to the 2nd century B.C. The Roman Republic's benevolent policy toward the Jews in Italy was confirmed by Julius Caesar.

Christianity was born in Jerusalem, capital of a Roman province. The Roman community became the Western center of the new religion. The first Christians spoke Aramaic, and many of the early converts were Greek-speaking, the language of the New Testament, but after A.D. 200 the number of Latin converts began to rise. Despite periods of persecution by the state, the church continued to grow in influence, and in A.D. 313 the emperor Constantine legalized the practice of Christianity.

The period marked by the rise of Christianity saw the Roman world slipping into serious decline, as a series of military emperor-despots did little to halt increasing economic collapse. Only the successful military campaigns of Aurelian and the sweeping reforms of Diocletian at the end of the 3rd century A.D., followed by Constantine's reign in the 4th century A.D., managed to bring temporary relief.

When Constantine founded a new Eastern capital for the Empire at Byzantium, thereafter known as Constantinople, he intended it to be a Christian city. He accepted baptism only on his deathbed, but by the end of the 4th century A.D., Christianity was the official religion of the state.

With the shift of power to the eastern Mediterranean, western Europe became vulnerable to a century-long wave of invasions by Germanic tribes on the move from the steppe lands of Eurasia. First the Visigoths under Alaric, then the Vandals and Huns overran Italy, Gaul, and Spain. The effect of the Germanic victories was to complete the long process of decline in the West.

The debate on the reasons for the decline and fall of the Roman Empire began with the writings of St. Augustine, active at the beginning of the 5th century A.D. Among the factors cited by his many successors have been climate changes, illness, errors of individual rulers, and the triumph of Christianity. Most modern observers would probably hold that no single cause or set of causes can explain a process that took centuries to work to a conclusion. A pattern of civilization that had lasted more than 1,000 years slowly broke down.

THE JEWS: A RELIGIOUS MINORITY IN THE ROMAN WORLD

The Jewish community in Rome has a continuous history from the 2nd century B.C. to the present. The first settlers came shortly after 161 B.C., the year in which the Jewish leader Judas Maccabaeus (died 160 B.C.) sent an embassy to the Roman Senate. The ambassadors, Jason (Joshua) ben Eleazar and Eupolemos (Ephraim?) ben Johanan, were the first Jews known to have visited the West. The Senate gave them written assurances of friendship and protection.

In 63 B.C., Pompey the Great conquered Palestine, which under the Empire became the Roman province of Judaea, and a fresh influx of Jewish traders and professionals arrived in Italy. Among the reforms introduced by Julius Caesar in his brief dictatorship of 46–44 B.C. were several involving the Italian Jews. The reforms included exemption from military service and establishing special courts where Jews could try cases according to their own law. Augustus and Tiberius renewed these privileges. When St. Paul visited Rome in A.D. 61, he found active Jewish communities both there and in southern Italy.

THE JEWS UNDER THE EMPIRE

In Palestine there was constant friction between Roman officials, who found Jewish customs unfamiliar and grotesque, and the Jews for whom Roman rule was intolerable. Among

Arch of Titus in the Roman Forum c. A.D. 81. Height 47 feet 4 inches (14.43 m). Roman arches commemorated victories by successful generals. This one celebrates the victory of Titus, the son of the reigning emperor, Vespasian, over the Jews in A.D. 70, and the destruction of Solomon's Temple in Jerusalem. Early Imperial arches like this one had a single span; later monuments often had a large central arch flanked by two smaller ones.

the Jews there were divisions within the upper classes, who tended to adopt Greek ways and had come to terms with the Romans, and the Pharisees and other orthodox groups who maintained strict adherence to traditional Jewish law. Rioting broke out in A.D. 66 and spread to many of the cities, including Caesarea and Jerusalem. In A.D. 70, Titus put down a Jewish revolt in Judaea by sacking Jerusalem and destroying the Temple, and took back to Rome large numbers of Jewish slaves. Some were put to work on the Colosseum and other public building projects. Jews throughout the Empire, who had contributed money each year for the upkeep of the Temple in Jerusalem, were now ordered to send the same sum to the Roman treasury, a tax known as the "Fiscus Judaicus," or "Jewish Tax."

Hadrian's brutal suppression of the Jewish revolt of A.D. 132–135 in Palestine led to the introduction of repressive measures elsewhere in the Empire, but apart from this brief period—Hadrian's immediate successor Antoninus Pius revoked the anti-Jewish legislation—the Jews living outside Palestine enjoyed relative freedom. In A.D. 212, Caracalla passed an edict giving Roman citizenship to almost all free residents of the Empire, including the Jews and other minorities.

THE JEWISH COMMUNITY AT ROME

The size of the Jewish community in Rome during the Empire was around 30,000, although the various revolts in Palestine, which were brutally suppressed, swelled the numbers with prisoners and exiles. Tombstones provide an interesting source of information on Jewish activities at Rome. Among the dead they commemorate are Jewish painters and poets and a Jewish physician. Other more humble Jews were butchers, tentmakers, and cobblers. Jewish women of the lower classes had a reputation as fortune-tellers.

The center of Jewish life was the synagogue, and Rome had 12, each with its own congregation. The dead were buried in catacombs, underground galleries, the oldest of which dates back to late Republican times. The richer tombs often combine typical Jewish symbols—the palm branch, the seven-branched candelabrum used in the temple services—with pagan images, suggesting a fair degree of assimilation.

Their Roman neighbors seem to have had some notion of Jewish traditions, although often in a garbled form. For the Romans, "wasting" one day in every seven—the Sabbath—seemed inexplicable. The poet Juvenal, no lover of "Orientals" or other foreigners (see Topic 17), describes with contempt a Roman father who followed Jewish custom and observed the Sabbath. The man's son became a fully fledged Jew who spent all of his time in prayer, and someone who meets him in the street scornfully asks, "What synagogue can I find you in?" Jewish missionary activity among the Romans was, in fact, unusual.

Anti-Semitism was common in the Roman Empire, especially in Egypt, where the Greeks of Alexandria were in constant friction with their Jewish neighbors. Elsewhere, too, popular opinion was hostile to traditional Jewish

HISTORICAL PERSPECTIVES

THE DEAD SEA SCROLLS

FREDERICK M. LAURITSEN   Eastern Washington University

When a young Arab teenager squeezed into a cave above the Dead Sea in early 1947, he was looking for treasure. He found, instead, something far more important and valuable—the ancient manuscripts known as the Dead Sea Scrolls. These 2,000-year-old manuscripts from the cliffs above the Dead Sea are among the most significant archeological discoveries of the 20th century. This discovery, like another famous find, the tomb of King Tutankhamen, was embroiled in controversy from the start. There were personality rivalries, political intrigue, exaggerated claims, and wild speculation, to say nothing of wishful thinking.

According to the nomads, seven scrolls were found in large pottery jars in cave one. These first scrolls contained both religious and sectarian writings, including a complete book of Isaiah, a Commentary on Habakkuk, and a Manual of Discipline. Eventually 11 caves yielded hundreds of complete scrolls and fragments of leather, papyrus, and a few of metal. (Scrolls, which preceded the codex or book form we now use, were common until late in the Roman Empire. Perhaps Christianity and the need for cross-referencing scriptures had something to do with the change.) Most of the scrolls were written in Hebrew or Aramaic (a Semitic language close to Hebrew and widely used in the first centuries B.C. and A.D.), and a few in Greek.

Many discoveries were made by the nomads or Bedouins from the Ta'amira tribe before the archeologists had a chance to examine the area. These nomads became quite adept at finding and exploring caves. Some of the caves were either in inaccessible regions or virtually impossible to reach. Understandably, the nomads were reluctant to provide complete information. They were able to cross the boundary between Israel and Jordan with a skill that embarrassed the security forces on both sides, and once they found out how much the scrolls were worth it was in their self-interest to maximize their value. Fifty years after their discovery, controversy still surrounds many details.

In the 1960s, the Bedouins moved into eastern Galilee, an area north of the Dead Sea. There, using their cave-finding skills, they found papyrus manuscripts belonging to the Samaritan sect and dating from the time of Alexander the Great. The Bedouins also continued their explorations south along the western shores of the Dead Sea and made additional finds. Israeli archeologists also found manuscripts, the most famous from the Cave of Letters, which contained let-

customs, sometimes violently so. On the whole, however, and certainly in comparison with many later periods, the official state treatment of the Jews' life under the Empire was tolerant. They alone of all Roman citizens were not required to take part in the state religious rituals or to hold municipal offices because both activities conflicted with their faith. A Roman jurist of the 3rd century A.D. described Judaism as "a highly distinguished religion, of indubitable legality."

THE JEWS AND THE COMING OF CHRISTIANITY

With Constantine's edict of A.D. 313 legalizing Christianity, the status of Jews under Roman rule changed abruptly. The "highly distinguished religion" of a few years earlier became a "nefarious sect" or a "sacrilegious gathering." In A.D. 315, Constantine threatened to burn any Jew who tried to "per-

secute" former Jews who had converted to Christianity, "the faith of the True God." Intermarriage between Jews and Christians became a capital offense, unless the Jewish partner became a Christian. Six years later, in A.D. 321, the emperor cancelled the Jewish exemption from public and religious obligations to the state.

From A.D. 339, Jews were forbidden to have slaves or to employ non-Jews. In practice this meant their exclusion from most professional activities, including industry and agriculture. The first destruction of a synagogue took place in A.D. 350, when Bishop Innocentius of Tortona (near Genoa) destroyed the temple there, replaced it with a chapel, and offered the Jews the choice of exile or baptism. At the end of the 4th century A.D., with Christianity installed as the official state religion, St. Ambrose of Milan observed in a letter that he regretted that through laziness he had failed to burn down his city's synagogue.

ters from Bar Kosiba, better known as bar Kokhba, who led a revolt against Rome in A.D. 133. These finds lie, however, beyond the scope of our essay, which is restricted to the original 11 caves.

There are many more caves in the vicinity of the first that did not contain manuscripts but did have archeological remains of the same era as the scrolls. Pottery found in these caves matched the jars found in cave one, showing that they were contemporary with each other. There is no certain count of the number of scrolls found, but of the original 11 caves it is safe to say they numbered in the hundreds. In one cave fragments of hundreds of documents were found, some of which are still being identified and joined to other pieces. Private collectors may also have bought some of the manuscripts or pieces.

The documents raise questions as to how close to the original is the Bible (Old Testament) we use today as well as about our understanding of early Jewish–Christian relations and Judaism. Other controversies include Jewish religious beliefs around the time of Jesus, the background of Christian belief, and who buried the scrolls.

Although there were challenges at first from some who said the documents came only from the Middle Ages, scientific tests such as carbon 14 dating have placed the scrolls between 200 B.C. and A.D. 60. These scrolls are the earliest known examples of biblical writings, and as with all texts, the closer we can come to the original, the better and more complete our understanding will be. It is important to both Jews and Christians to know that the Bible of today has been accurately copied. The scrolls include at least portions of every book in the Old Testament except the book of Esther (perhaps because Esther is the only book that does not mention God). In the case of the Great Isaiah Scroll, it turns out that the copy found in the caves and today's text are virtually the same except that the Great Isaiah Scroll included a verse not in the current version (although this verse is now being restored to modern Bibles). On the other hand, other scrolls are quite different from the current versions, and the scrolls point to the fact that the text of the Old Testament was still fluid until the end of the first century.

Who wrote the scrolls and who buried them? If the scrolls were written over a period of 250 or 300 years, they were of course written by many hands. One name that continues to be repeated is the Essenes. The Essenes were one of several Jewish sects active around the time of Jesus. They had withdrawn from participation in mainstream Judaism and are thought to have established a community at Qumran on the northwest corner of the Dead Sea—the immediate area where the scrolls were found. Though there are other views, a majority of scholars believes that the scrolls represent a library of Essene beliefs and practices. Perhaps some of the caves surrounding Qumran were used by members of the community as living quarters, and when the Roman Army attacked in A.D. 66 the caves were used to hide the manuscripts from the Roman soldiers. This does not account for the condition of some of the manuscripts that were torn, mutilated, and disfigured. Or perhaps the caves are where the library was stored. In this case it seems the Dead Sea Scrolls have raised more questions than answers.

Over the next century the Jewish population of Italy shrank drastically. With the formal division of the Empire into east and west, in A.D. 395 (see Topic 22), the Jews of Palestine and those in Europe were no longer under a single benevolent rule, and the long years of hardship began.

THE RISE OF CHRISTIANITY AND THE EARLY CHURCH

According to the Hebrew prophets, one day their God would send the Messiah (the Hebrew word means "anointed one") to restore Israel and begin a glorious age of peace. In the 1st century B.C., following Pompey's conquest of Palestine, some Jews living there believed that a Messiah would come to bring political liberation. By contrast, the Jewish sect known as the Essenes (active c. 200 B.C.–A.D. 68) withdrew into monastic communities to practice their ascetic lifestyle. Some of their writings are still preserved in the Dead Sea Scrolls, discovered shortly after World War II. (See Historical Perspectives in this chapter.)

THE ORIGINS OF CHRISTIANITY

The historical Jesus (c. 6 B.C.–c. A.D. 30) was born in Palestine in the reign of Augustus. He taught that the Messiah would not be an earthly ruler but would come as spiritual judge to usher in the Last Judgment. The virtues Jesus extolled were humility, charity, and love of others. His teachings offended both conservative and radical Jewish leaders, while the Romans saw his ideas as potentially subversive to Roman rule. As a result, the Roman governor Pontius Pilate ordered his execution.

After the crucifixion of Jesus, his followers continued to spread his ideas, claiming that he had been resurrected and was the Messiah, calling him Christ, the Greek word for "the anointed one." Paul of Tarsus (died c. A.D. 65), one of the earliest converts to Christianity, was a Jewish Roman citizen who traveled in Asia Minor after his conversion, setting up small Christian communities.

Eventually Paul, together with Peter (died c. A.D. 64)—one of Jesus's original 12 Apostles—reached Rome, where, according to tradition, they were both martyred. Before he died, Peter probably founded at Rome the church regarded by later Christians as central to Christianity, in fulfillment of Jesus's prophecy: "Thou art Peter, and upon this rock I will build my Church." (The name "Peter" is a form of the Greek word for "rock.") This traditional belief served to justify the importance of the Roman Church.

By the early 2nd century A.D., most large cities in the Empire had communities of Christians. They met in private to celebrate the Eucharist, or Holy Communion, a ritual enactment of the Last Supper. Most of the early Christians were Greek speakers, and the New Testament (the account of the life and death of Jesus and the beginnings of Christianity) was written in Greek. It is made up of the four Gospels, named after their traditional authors—Matthew, Mark, Luke, and John—the Epistles, or letters written by early church leaders to local churches or individuals, and the book of Revelation. The earliest fragments surviving date to the beginning of the 2nd century A.D., and the text was first standardized in the 4th century A.D., by which time there were increasing numbers of Latin converts.

For most pagan Romans, the Christians were just one more of the many sects flourishing in various parts of the Empire. Yet in important ways Christianity was different from other cults. In the first place Christians claimed that their way was the only true way. No pagan cult ever laid claim to exclusivity. Only the Jews believed that there was no true God but theirs, and even the Jews did not try to persuade others to follow their example. The Christians not only encouraged conversion to their faith, but they actively sought it through missionary work.

Second, the early Christians believed in firm organization. Around each church was a community, and the various communities throughout the Empire maintained links that bound them together. Christians could travel to most countries under Roman rule and find fellow Christians who would provide help and comfort to them.

Scala/Art Resource New York

Mosaic of Christ as the Good Shepherd from the entrance hall of the Mausoleum of Galla Placidia at Ravenna c. A.D. 425. The elongated and elegant figure of Christ is wearing a Roman toga draped with the Imperial purple, an improbable presence in this rustic scene. The rich ceiling pattern is based on Oriental, mainly Persian, motifs.

During its first two centuries, Christianity enjoyed the same theoretical tolerance on the part of the state as the Jews, but from the beginning public opinion was generally hostile; popular dislike and suspicion drove early Christians to be discreet in practicing their faith. Two waves of persecutions in the 3rd century A.D., on the grounds that the Christians refused to worship the official state gods, were followed in A.D. 313 by the decision of Constantine and Licinius, promulgated in the Edict of Milan, to allow universal tolerance of all religions in the Empire. Because around one-third of the Empire was Christian by the beginning of the 4th cen-

tury A.D., Constantine's policy was an attempt to reinforce unity in the Roman world.

According to the account of a contemporary writer, Constantine's inspiration was a dream he had the previous year, on the eve of the crucial Battle of the Milvian Bridge against his rival Maxentius. A voice told him to mark "the sign of God" on the shields of his soldiers, in the form of the Greek letter *Chi* (X) turned and with a loop on top—this would produce the *Chi-Rho* monogram, spelling the first two letters of the word *Christ* in Greek. Constantine won the battle, and with it control of Italy. Whatever the significance of the dream in Constantine's decision, an-

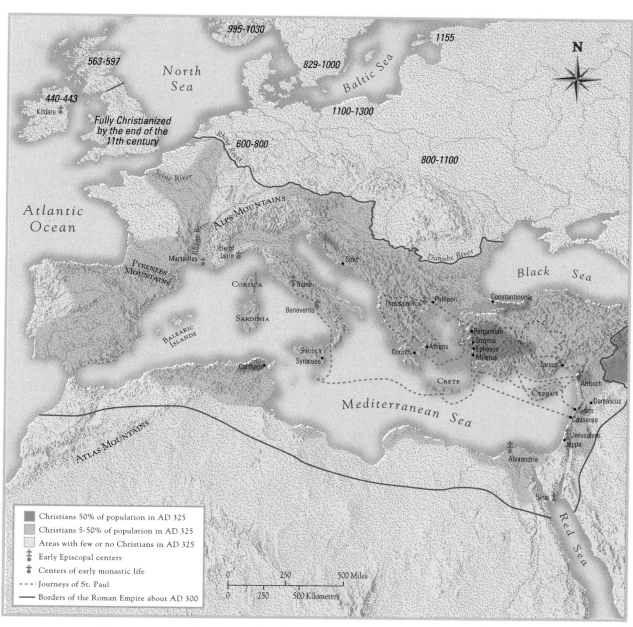

 Map 19.1 The Spread of Christianity. Most of the major Christian centers are in the eastern part of the Empire, a process that intensified when Constantine moved the capital from Rome to Constantinople in A.D. 330. The chief episcopal centers (seats of bishops) and monasteries are on or near the Mediterranean coast, with the outstanding exception of Kildare in Ireland, which was one of the first parts of northwest Europe to be Christianized. Go to http://info.wadsworth.com/053461065X for an interactive version of this map.

SIGNIFICANT DATES

The End of the Roman Empire (all dates A.D.)

c. 30	Crucifixion of Jesus
70	Titus sacks Jerusalem
132–135	Jewish Revolt
270–275	Reign of Aurelian
284–305	Reign of Diocletian
306–337	Reign of Constantine
312	Battle of Milvian Bridge
313	Edict of Milan
325	Council of Nicaea
330	Inauguration of Constantinople
410	Sack of Rome by Visigoths
451	Defeat of Attila
476	Last Western emperor deposed

other reason for his sympathy toward Christianity was the influence of his mother Helena (c. A.D. 248–328). A missionary to her native Britain converted her to Christianity in her youth, and she remained active in promoting her faith throughout her life.

THE ORGANIZATION OF THE EARLY CHURCH

Jerusalem was the birthplace of Christianity, but over time each major city developed its own church. In theory, all of them shared a common creed. In practice, however, beliefs varied widely, as did local forms of organization. The most important Christian communities included those of Antioch, Alexandria, and Carthage. Rome occupied a special position because its church was founded by Peter, but before the Council of Nicaea in A.D. 325 the other centers did not treat the Roman Church as entitled to automatic obedience. Even after the Council, the eastern churches never accepted the final authority of Rome, a disagreement that became an important factor in the eventual split between Catholic and Orthodox Christianity.

The head of each local church was known as the bishop. According to the doctrine of Apostolic Succession, the powers that Jesus's disciples received at his hands were passed down from bishop to bishop, giving them the right to ordain new priests and bishops who could conduct the sacraments. These included baptism into the faith and Holy Communion, whereby the wine and wafer of the Communion ceremony became the blood and body of Christ.

In order to provide a general overall structure for the church, bishops began to meet regularly with their fellow bishops to coordinate belief and policy. The structural system they devised was modeled after the Roman Empire, with its carefully ordered hierarchy. In this way the organization of the church was comprehensible to Christian and non-Christian Romans alike. By the early 3rd century A.D., church councils began to assemble in major provincial centers, in order to distinguish between *orthodox* (literally "right-thinking") doctrines and heresies, or wrong opinions. The first Empire-wide church council took place at Nicaea in A.D. 325, under the patronage of Constantine, to discuss definitions of the Trinity (for a discussion of the controversies of the early church, see Topic 21).

PROBLEMS OF EMPIRE AND THE REFORMS OF DIOCLETIAN

By the time Constantine issued his epoch-making edict, the Roman Empire was emerging from a century of decline. Successive emperors after Alexander Severus (see Topic 18) came to power with army backing, only to fall at the hands of those who had placed them on the throne. In the 50 years

Relief carved in the rock at Bishapur, Iran, showing the victory of the Persian king, Shapur I, over the Roman emperor Valerian and his army c. A.D. 260. The defeated army is represented by a Roman soldier trampled beneath the hooves of the victorious monarch. Roman art is full of scenes of conquered enemies kneeling before triumphant generals, but this time the roles are reversed.

Courtesy Herzfeld Archives, Freer Gallery of Art

from A.D. 235 to A.D. 284, the Senate recognized 25 legitimate emperors, while more than twice as many failed to establish their "legitimacy." In the reign of Gallienus (ruled A.D. 253–268), there were no fewer than 18 unsuccessful claimants to the throne.

The effects of such chronic instability were economic collapse and social disorder, as the bankruptcy of many middle-class citizens left Roman society polarized into upper and lower classes. Matters abroad fared little better. On the eastern limits of the Empire, the Sassanians replaced the Romans' old enemies the Parthians, and in A.D. 259 a Sassanian army captured the Roman emperor Valerian (ruled A.D. 253–260). The only Roman emperor ever taken prisoner, Valerian died in captivity.

Military relief came with the reign of Aurelian (ruled A.D. 270–275), whose energetic campaigns reversed a century of territorial decline. Although he failed to displace the Goths from Central Europe, Aurelian reestablished Roman authority in Britain, Gaul, Spain, and Syria (for Aurelian in the East, see Topic 23).

DIOCLETIAN AND THE LATE ROMAN EMPIRE

The restorer of political order in the Roman state was the emperor Diocletian (ruled A.D. 284–305), whose reorganization of government made possible another century of unified Roman rule of the Mediterranean. The main thrust of his reforms was to restore the authority of central rule, abolishing the rights of the provinces to local self-government.

To reinforce his status, Diocletian changed the emperor's title from *Princeps*, or "First Citizen," to *Dominus*—"Lord"—and ruled as a living god. Elaborate court ceremony underlined the gulf between the figure of the emperor and his mortal subjects, who were not even permitted to set eyes on their divine ruler. A complex bureaucracy stretched downward from the emperor through various levels to the provincial administrations, which were responsible for collecting taxes, recruiting for the army, and imposing orders handed down from above.

Diocletian's reforms required a sound economic base, and to achieve this he restored the full value of the currency and reorganized the tax system. One of his edicts sets out the principle by which he operated: "No man shall possess any property that is tax-exempt." Every year the emperor and his advisers established the state's budget and then calculated the tax rate accordingly. A general review took place every five years. Members of the provincial governments had to collect the revenues and make up any shortages from their own property.

One of the effects of Diocletian's reform of the coinage was rampant inflation, as people tried to get rid of their old coins. To offset this situation, in A.D. 301 the emperor introduced an edict setting maximum prices for goods and

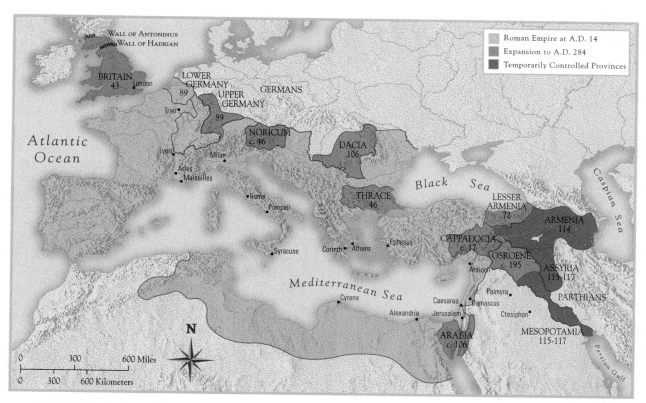

 Map 19.2 The Roman Empire in the Time of Diocletian. For all its size, the Empire was becoming seriously unbalanced: Note how far Rome lies from its geographical center. Furthermore, its eastern provinces were only nominally ruled from Rome. Twenty years after Diocletian's abdication in A.D. 305, Constantine had begun work at a new Imperial capital, the future Constantinople (modern Istanbul), and the Western provinces—Britain, Spain—began to split off. Go to http://info.wadsworth.com/053461065x for an interactive version of this map.

services. The penalty for overcharging was death. The price list casts interesting light on life in the last century of the Empire. A pound of cheese and a pint of ordinary wine both cost eight denarii. Meat varied from eight denarii per pound for beef and mutton to twenty for ham. A haircut cost two denarii. Farm laborers and camel drivers earned 25 denarii a day, elementary teachers 50 denarii per student per month, and lawyers were paid 1,000 denarii for pleading a case.

To help carry out his ambitious program, Diocletian introduced important political changes. In A.D. 286 he nominated a co-emperor, Maximian (ruled A.D. 286–305, 306–308), and in A.D. 293 appointed two deputies, one for himself and one for his co-ruler, to train them as successors. Under this new system, the tetrarchy (rule of four), Diocletian and his deputy Galerius (ruled A.D. 305–311) took charge of the East and Maximian and his deputy Constantius Chlorus (ruled A.D. 305–306) of the West.

In A.D. 304 Diocletian suffered a serious illness, perhaps a stroke, and the following year he abdicated and retired to Spalato (modern Split)—one of the very few reigning monarchs in history to give up power voluntarily. He spent the last 10 years of his life working in his garden. In the chaos that followed his resignation, Maximian, the co-emperor—

whom Diocletian had also persuaded to retire—begged him to come back to Rome and take up the reins of government again. Calmly but firmly, Diocletian refused. If he could only show Maximian the cabbages, he said, which he planted with his own hands in the garden, his former colleague would not try to persuade him to give up the enjoyment of happiness for the pursuit of power.

THE CIVIL WARS OF DIOCLETIAN'S SUCCESSORS

When the two emperors retired, they promoted their assistants to the rank of emperor and named two new deputies, passing over Constantine (ruled A.D. 306–337), the son of Constantius, and Maxentius (ruled A.D. 306–312), the son of Maximian. With the sudden death of Constantius in A.D. 306, the Roman world plunged once more into confusion, as the two sons battled for supremacy and Diocletian steadfastly refused to return to the fray. The decisive confrontation came in A.D. 312 at the Milvian Bridge. With, as he believed, the God of the Christians fighting on his side, Constantine defeated Maxentius and took control of the Empire. Despite the edict of the following year, which legitimized Christianity, Constantine refused baptism until he was on the point of death, believing that he could best retain the support of his subjects—most of whom were pagan—by continuing as head of the state religion. He had his sons brought up as Christians, however, and maintained an iron control over church policy and dogma for the rest of his life.

THE FOUNDATION OF CONSTANTINOPLE AND THE DECLINE OF THE WEST

The crowning achievement of Constantine's reign was to be the creation of the Empire's new Christian capital, which was unsullied by pagan temples. Between A.D. 324 and 330, Constantinople, the city of Constantine, arose on the magnificent harbor of the Bosphorus (see Topic 22). In his last years Constantine ruled with ever greater pomp, reflecting in his life as emperor his vision of the Christians' king of heaven—a long way from Christian ideals of charity and love for others. In A.D. 326 he ordered the execution of his wife, eldest son, and nephew, whom he believed to be more popular than he was.

Constantine had held together an Empire on the point of collapse, and it survived for barely 50 years after his death. When Theodosius divided the Empire between his sons in A.D. 395 (see Topic 22), the split became permanent. The Eastern half continued in the form of the Byzantine Empire, while the West sank into decline.

THE GERMAN INVASIONS

Contact between Roman frontier troops stationed on the Rhine and the Danube and German invaders went back to

Head from the colossal statue of Constantine, which sat in the Basilica of Constantine, Rome, c. A.D. 324–330. Height of head 8 feet 6 inches (2.59 m). The air of majestic simplicity, suggesting the emperor's belief that he represented God's regent on earth, is very different from the earlier tradition in Roman portrait sculpture of depicting realistic hair and expression marks.

Scala/Art Resource

the time of Julius Caesar, half a millennium before the fall of the Roman Empire. Over the years following, Roman culture left its mark on the nomadic tribesmen to the north, as Roman businessmen traded with them and carried German slaves back to Rome, and German families moved across the borders to live on Roman territory. The Roman acceptance of Christianity quickly spread among the Germanic peoples.

The push came at the end of the 4th century A.D., when the Germanic peoples came under pressure. Invaders from the great steppe lands of Eurasia to the east began moving westward into Germanic territory. In A.D. 374, the Huns, a nomadic steppe people, stormed into the land of the Ostrogoths. The Visigoths, neighbors of the Ostrogoths, feared it was their turn next and moved into Roman territory in the Balkans, defeating a Roman army that had been sent to subdue them. When the Romans refused to grant them more land, the Visigothic king Alaric (ruled A.D. 395–410) led his troops to Rome, and in A.D. 410 the Visigoths sacked the city.

The lesson was not lost on the other Germanic peoples. The Vandals took Spain in A.D. 408, and then drove on to North Africa. By the middle of the 5th century A.D., the Franks held most of north and central Gaul. Britain, abandoned by its Roman legions in A.D. 407, fell under Saxons, Angles, and Jutes.

Rome's last stand came in A.D. 451, when Roman and Visigothic troops united against a common enemy and defeated the army of the Huns led by their king, Attila (ruled A.D. 434–453), who had invaded Italy. With Germanic commanders in charge of Roman forces, the Roman government lost its last claim to independence. In A.D. 476 a Germanic general deposed the last emperor of the West, Romulus Augustulus (ruled A.D. 475–476). A century of continual decline reached its symbolic end.

THE HUNS IN THE EAST:
THE FALL OF INDIA'S GUPTA EMPIRE

The same population movements in Eurasia that caused the collapse of the Roman Empire had a similar effect on India's Gupta Empire. In 320 A.D., Chandra Gupta I had united a series of independent small kingdoms into a single united state, which reached its zenith under his grandson, Chandra Gupta II (ruled A.D. 380–415). The Gupta Empire was famous for its economic stability and religious tolerance. Its cultural and scientific achievements were outstanding; the concept of zero may well have been invented by Gupta mathematicians.

Between A.D. 480 and 500, around the time peoples from Central Asia were moving west, a group known as the White Huns invaded the Gupta Empire in a series of waves. They never managed to establish a secure power base in India, but they effectively ended the unity of Gupta rule. Over the following centuries, India split once again into innumerable small kingdoms, which fought constantly with one another and with foreign invaders, and only under Muslim rulers in the 15th and 16th centuries did a new united Indian Empire begin to develop.

DECLINE AND FALL: THE DEBATE

The fall of Rome moved even the most devout of Christians. When Alaric's Visigoths sacked the city in A.D. 410, St. Jerome wrote: "The whole world has perished in one city." A few years later, St. Augustine (A.D. 354–430) began to write *The City of God,* in which he contrasted the earthly city, built on pride and home to materialism and imperialism, with the eternal city of God, the realm of faith. For Augustine, the collapse of Rome was one more stage on the journey toward the Last Judgment and salvation in the kingdom of heaven (see Topic 21).

Over the centuries since Augustine, students of the history of human affairs have often debated the cause of an event that was apparently so cataclysmic. Some have pointed to the fundamental economic difference between the eastern and western provinces. In the East, commerce flourished and prosperity was measured in terms of money and profits. In Italy, the most valuable asset was land, and the old Roman aristocracy never really abandoned its disdain for trade and manufacturing.

Another factor was the continual decline in population in the West. As living standards increased in the period after Augustus, the Italians were unwilling to give up their newly acquired comforts to raise children. The reduction in population had serious effects on agriculture and industry. At the same time, traditional Roman culture and values began to lose their dominating status in the Empire.

In addition, the imperial system of government, which was protective and paternalistic, discouraged the kind of personal initiative that had helped to build the Republic. At the same time, the army became increasingly alienated from the welfare of the state and became embroiled in power struggles among its various leaders. With the drop in civilian population in Italy, more and more soldiers were recruited on the fringes of the Empire, where the austere moral virtues of the ancient Roman Republic were virtually unknown.

Some observers have pointed to external factors. These include a devastating plague in the reign of Marcus Aurelius, the gradual spread of malaria, and possible climate changes, which might have produced less fertile farmland. Other scholars isolate specific moments when a wrong decision proved fatal. Marcus Aurelius's choice of his son Commodus as his successor led to the disastrous dynasty of the Severans. Many people, particularly in the Middle Ages, would simply have echoed Augustine's judgment that the fall of Rome was another stage in God's plan for human redemption.

Many of these factors played their part to some degree or another, but the process of decline extended over centuries, and to look for a single overriding cause is to oversimplify the issue. When the fall came, the exact moment of collapse was arbitrary, and for many purely symbolic. There is no reason to think that the exile of Romulus Augustulus had the faintest significance in the daily lives of the overwhelming majority of Western Europeans who were then living.

The most important feature of the last phase of the Roman Empire was the rise of Christianity to the status of a world religion, yet the victory of the Church Triumphant came at a price for Christians. Freedom from persecution set loose three centuries of theological debate, which led to Christian persecution of pagan and heretic alike. Once in power, church leaders used force rather than persuasion to convert the mass of the population. Furthermore, the church adopted a structure based on the authoritarian government of Diocletian, by which its leaders acquired vast worldly power at the expense of the spiritual domain.

Putting Christianity and the Crisis of Empire in Perspective

The final collapse of Rome left a triple legacy. In the East, for 1,000 years the Byzantine Empire continued to operate under Constantine's system. The emperor controlled the secular policy of the state while maintaining supreme religious authority. In the West, the former Roman provinces fragmented into a series of kingdoms that still form the basis of the states of modern Europe. In the southern region of the Mediterranean, a century after the fall of Rome, Muhammad was born. The religion he founded, Islam, helped create an empire stretching from Spain to India by the 8th century A.D. The fall of the Roman Empire was a transition, not an end.

Questions for Further Study

1. What were the most important stages in the rise of Christianity? How did they relate to the later history of the Roman Empire?
2. What role did women play in the early development of Christianity?
3. What methods did Diocletian use to halt the erosion of the Empire? How far was he successful?
4. What were the long-term causes of the end of the Roman Empire in the West? What effect did the foundation of Constantinople have on its decline?

Suggestions for Further Reading

Benko, S. *Pagan Rome and the Early Christians*. Bloomington, IN, 1986.

Elsner, Jas. *Imperial Rome and Christian Triumph*. New York, 1998.

Jones, A.H.M. *The Later Roman Empire, 284–602: A Social, Economic and Administrative Survey*. Baltimore, 1986.

MacMullen, R. *Christianizing the Roman Empire (100–400)*. New Haven, CT, 1984.

McNamara, J.A. *A New Song: Celibate Women in the First Three Christian Centuries*. New York, 1983.

Morrison, K.E., ed. *The Church in the Roman Empire*. Chicago, 1986.

Wise, M., M. Abegg, and E. Cook. *The Dead Sea Scrolls: A New Translation*. San Francisco, 1996.

Witherington, B., III. *Women in the Earliest Churches*. Cambridge, 1988.

Witherington, B., III. *The Jesus Quest: The Third Search for the Jew of Nazareth*. Downers Grove, IL, 1995.

InfoTrac College Edition

Enter the search term *Roman Empire* using Key Terms.

Enter the search term *Constantine* using the Subject Guide.

Enter the search term *early Christianity* using Key Terms.

PART III

MEDIEVAL EUROPE

Between the collapse of the Roman Empire around A.D. 400 and the beginning of the Renaissance about 1350 or 1400 lay a thousand years of Western experience, the "Middle Ages," or the "medieval" period.

For many scholars of an earlier generation, the Middle Ages was seen as the "Dark Ages," for in contrasting the political grandeur of Rome and the cultural glory of the Renaissance, they found medieval civilization lacking. Historians saw in the medieval period the failure of efforts to recreate political unity, the embroilment of the church in political conflicts and internal dissen-

sion, and unoriginal cultural movements that did little more than attempt to revive a world of art and ideas that had long since disappeared.

Yet despite this long-held prejudice against the Middle Ages, these were centuries of crucial historical development that saw the formation of a unique and vigorous civilization. Today we know that the Middle Ages was a period of great creativity and experimentation, and of growth and expansion, in which many fundamental institutions and practices of the modern world were born. Based on a melding of elements from Roman and Germanic cultures, as well as from

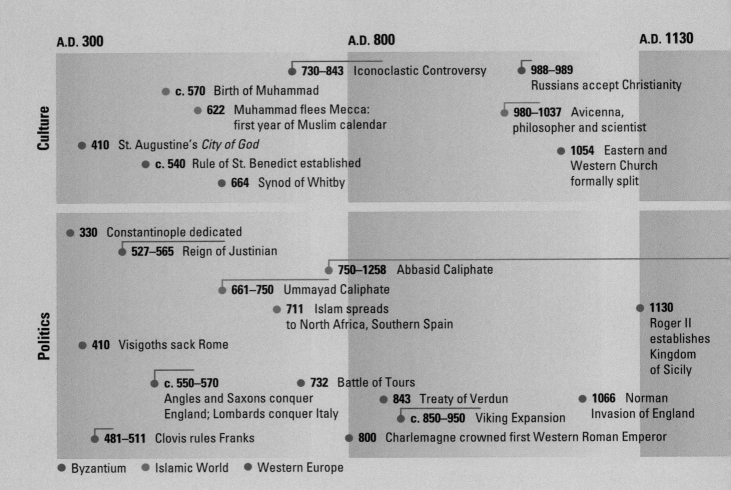

A.D. **300**   A.D. **800**   A.D. **1130**

Culture

- 730–843 Iconoclastic Controversy
- c. 570 Birth of Muhammad
- 622 Muhammad flees Mecca: first year of Muslim calendar
- 410 St. Augustine's *City of God*
- c. 540 Rule of St. Benedict established
- 664 Synod of Whitby
- 988–989 Russians accept Christianity
- 980–1037 Avicenna, philosopher and scientist
- 1054 Eastern and Western Church formally split

Politics

- 330 Constantinople dedicated
- 527–565 Reign of Justinian
- 750–1258 Abbasid Caliphate
- 661–750 Ummayad Caliphate
- 711 Islam spreads to North Africa, Southern Spain
- 410 Visigoths sack Rome
- c. 550–570 Angles and Saxons conquer England; Lombards conquer Italy
- 732 Battle of Tours
- 843 Treaty of Verdun
- c. 850–950 Viking Expansion
- 800 Charlemagne crowned first Western Roman Emperor
- 481–511 Clovis rules Franks
- 1130 Roger II establishes Kingdom of Sicily
- 1066 Norman Invasion of England

- Byzantium   - Islamic World   - Western Europe

© Giraudon/Art Resource, NY

Christianity, the Middle Ages was in effect the first European civilization.

The expansion of Islam under the Arabs that began in the 7th century A.D. disrupted trade and broke the unity of the Mediterranean world, yet it introduced new cultural elements that blended with European civilization, especially in North Africa, Spain, and in Sicily.

Medieval people thirsted for a sense of community, which some scholars refer to as the "medieval commonwealth." The Christian struggle against Islam in part provided Europeans with a common enemy and a single cause. The desire

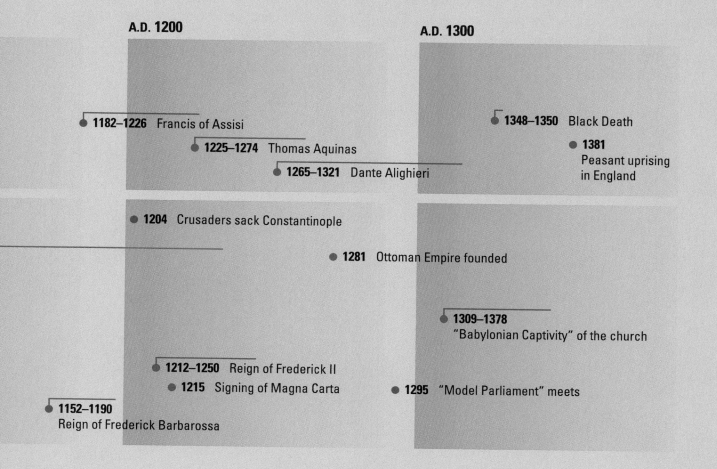

A.D. **1200**

A.D. **1300**

1182–1226 Francis of Assisi

1225–1274 Thomas Aquinas

1265–1321 Dante Alighieri

1348–1350 Black Death

1381
Peasant uprising
in England

1204 Crusaders sack Constantinople

1281 Ottoman Empire founded

1309–1378
"Babylonian Captivity" of the church

1212–1250 Reign of Frederick II

1215 Signing of Magna Carta

1295 "Model Parliament" meets

1152–1190
Reign of Frederick Barbarossa

for unity was supplemented by two ideas and two institutions—the mythology of a universal empire in the form of what came to be called the Holy Roman Empire, and the spirit of Christianity as embodied in the Roman Church and the papacy. While often at odds with each other, the Empire and the papacy provided an important degree of leadership in what had otherwise become a system of localized political and legal power known as *feudalism* and a system of economic self-sufficiency known as *manorialism*.

It is difficult to exaggerate the importance of Christianity and the church to medieval civilization, for religious faith permeated all aspects of daily life and all levels of society. Members of the clergy were deeply involved in the feudal system, in land tenure, and in government, and popes fought with kings and emperors to maintain papal authority. Many of the most critical intellectual and artistic achievements of the period were either inspired by Christian faith or executed in the service of the church. Monasteries and cathedral schools, priests and missionaries, preserved knowledge and shared learning. The first great example of European expansion, the series of expeditions to the Near East known as the Crusades, took place under papal sponsorship and in the name of religion.

POLITICS AFTER ROME: THE GERMANIC KINGDOMS

Of the three fundamental elements that constituted the basis of European civilization, the migration and settlement of the Germanic peoples wrought the most dramatic changes. The Germans, like all of the "barbarians"—as the Romans had called the peoples living beyond the Empire—had their own social institutions, legal systems, and political cultures. In the West, the barbarians included the Celtic Picts (Scotland), Gaels (Ireland), Britons (England), and Gauls (France), while the Slavic tribes inhabited Russia and eastern Europe. The Germans occupied Scandinavia and the coast of northern Germany. These groups all spoke Indo-European dialects but developed distinct cultures.

During the first centuries of the Roman Empire, the Germans had established communities along its fringes and absorbed some Roman values and ideas through trade and other forms of contact. In the 4th century A.D., however, sudden pressure from the Huns, nomadic tribes of central Asia, drove the barbarians to move forcibly across the frontiers and settle among the Roman populations of the Empire. The Germanic invasions did not destroy the political unity of the Roman Empire so much as take advantage of and perhaps hasten the gradual disintegration that was already underway in the West. In time, the resulting German settlements gave way to several "successor states." Foremost among these were the kingdoms of the Visigoths in Spain, the Ostrogoths in Italy, the Anglo-Saxons in England, and the Franks in what is today France, Germany, Belgium, and Holland.

Although they eventually mixed with the Roman populations, the Germanic peoples left their distinctive mark on the emerging civilization of western Europe. The Germanic tribes assimilated much of the Classical tradition handed down from Greece and Rome, while adapting their social and military customs to the evolving societies. Christianity acted as the cohesive element that helped blend the two traditions and forge a new civilization.

THE GERMANIC MIGRATIONS AND THE WEST

The Germans of North and Central Europe consisted of several tribal confederations organized for military purposes, chief among them the Goths, Vandals, Lombards, Alemanni, Burgundians, Angles, and Saxons. In the 4th century A.D., they began to spread out in great migrations westward, south, and southeastward, displacing Celtic and Slavic settlements and coming up against the Rhine and Danube frontiers of the Roman Empire. Their contact with the Romans was first as slaves or prisoners, but later many became peasants under Roman rule. Occasionally the Romans settled a whole tribe as *foederati*, or allies, and assigned them the task of guarding the frontiers against their fellow Germans. Eventually they were able to serve in the imperial military and even gain Roman citizenship. Around 350 A.D. they began to absorb the Arian form of Christianity (for a discussion on Arianism, see Topic 21) as a result of the missionary efforts of Bishop Ulfilas (c. 311–383), who translated the Bible into their language and preached among the Germans.

GERMANIC SOCIETY: WARFARE, KINSHIP, AND FAMILY

Long before the process of Romanization, the Germanic peoples had a well-established culture described by the historian Cornelius Tacitus (c. 55–c. 117) in his treatise *Germania*. Tacitus, bitter and out of favor at the Roman court, presented an admiring picture of a "simple, virtuous, and rugged" German civilization in stark contrast to what he believed was a decadent Roman society. Perhaps less admirable for Tacitus was the male bonding that took the form of rituals, during which large quantities of beer were consumed. Such practices did, however, reinforce tribal unity.

Some three centuries following Tacitus, the numerous German tribes—each tribe consisting of clans of related

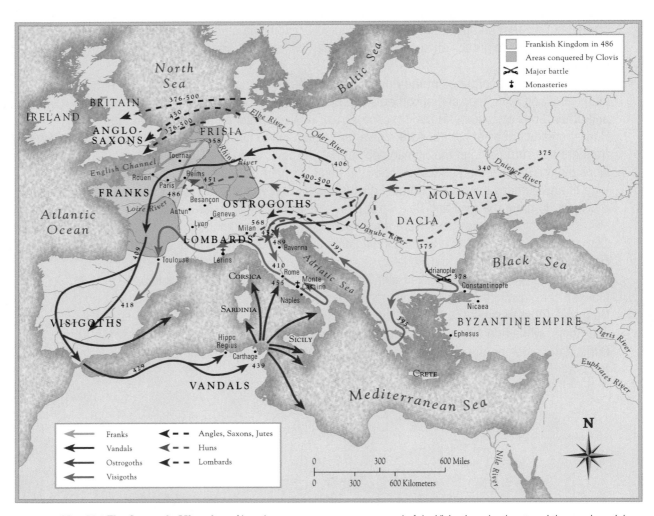

 Map 20.1 The Germanic Migrations. Note the extreme movement eastward of the Visigoths, who threatened the new Imperial capital of Constantinople, and the arrival of the Ostrogoths in Italy, where they took over Italy's Byzantine capital of Ravenna. The region around Milan is still called Lombardy. Go to http://info.wadsworth.com/053461065X for an interactive version of this map.

families—had begun to consolidate into a series of large military confederations. The Germanic peoples continued, however, to maintain a social structure centered in villages and around the patriarchal family, a unit consisting of husbands, wives, children, grandparents, and cousins. Clans generally governed themselves, with little interference from the central tribal authorities. Slavery was widely practiced in Germanic society.

In addition to crop farming, the Germans had two other principal occupations: cattle raising and warfare. The women engaged in agriculture and household chores, while the men were the warriors. Their status generally depended on their valor on the battlefield, the size of their herds, and the number of wives they had. Warfare was an important part of a male's social existence, and strict rules determined how he should conduct it. One of these traditions was that fighting within a clan was prohibited. Within a given tribe, however, clan often fought against clan. Warfare was also common between tribes, whose reputation and status grew with each conquest.

Because German society emphasized kinship rather than citizenship, German law, as opposed to Roman, dealt with individual rights rather than social structures. Thus family honor required kinsmen to defend and protect each other and to seek vengeance for crimes committed against a family member. Because the mutual destruction resulting from kin feuding was so widespread, the tribes developed a system of payments, called the *wergeld*, that took the place of clan vengeance by the spilling of blood.

Warfare sometimes provided a means of creating intertribal connections. Warrior bands, which the Romans called *comitati*, linked brave young fighters to outstanding leaders through personal bonds. In return for their loyalty, the young warriors received a share of booty. Over time, the military basis of society produced large tribal confederations, such as that of the Alemanni and the Franks, which formed around a charismatic warrior leader. The Goths, on the other hand, were consolidated under the leadership of a royal dynasty that passed on military and governing authority within the same family.

HUNS AND GERMANS

In the last third of the 4th century, the Germans were assaulted by waves of ferocious warriors known as the Huns, a people of Tartar or Mongolian ancestry from the steppes and deserts of Central Asia and Russia. Because they had inhabited the region between the Ural and the Altai mountains, the languages of the Huns are called Ural-Altaic. The Huns spread terror as they drove into the Black Sea region and eastern Europe, driving the Visigoths (western Goths) and Ostrogoths (eastern Goths) before them. In 375, after suffering defeat by the Huns, the Goths moved west and south across the Danube and into the Empire, where the Eastern emperor Valens allowed them to settle as *foederati*. Three years later, the desperate Visigoths rebelled against the shoddy treatment they received from the Romans, using their strength in cavalry to wipe out the imperial army at Adrianople. Valens died in the fighting. The Visigoths were now able to settle within the Empire along the Danube frontier, where they maintained a degree of autonomy.

In the 430s, the Huns invaded western Europe under their chieftain Attila (c. 406–453), whom terrorized Westerners called "the scourge of God." Pushing into Gaul, Attila's forces were defeated in 451 at Châlons by a Germanic army under the command of a Roman general, Flavius Aetius. The Huns then turned back and invaded Italy, reaching Rome that same year. In 452, however, near Mantua in northern Italy, Attila met with Pope Leo I (ruled 440–461), who persuaded the Huns to leave Italy. Leo's intervention greatly enhanced the prestige of the bishops of Rome as the protector of the imperial city and

A mosaic showing a Vandal lord hunting outside his villa in North Africa. Early 6th century. The technique of mosaic is based on that of Roman work, although without the realism of Roman art. Note the elongated proportion of the rider. The sparse vegetation and the palm tree indicate the location of the scene.

Michael Holford

helped establish the temporal power of the papacy. With Attila's death in 453, the threat of the Huns to western Europe collapsed, and his followers returned to Asia.

In addition to the Visigoths and the Huns, the rapidly declining Roman Empire was also overrun by the Vandals, who had penetrated the imperial defenses along the Rhine in 406. After marching through Gaul and Spain, the Vandals crossed over to North Africa and conquered it. Establishing a kingdom there in 429 under Gaiseric, they built a fleet, seized Sardinia and Corsica, and harassed the Empire and its commercial shipping in the Mediterranean. In 455 Vandal troops sailed to the mainland of Italy and reached Rome, which they sacked with great violence, leaving devastation in their wake. The survival of the word *vandal* in the English language reflects the Roman view that the Vandals committed senseless acts of destruction against what had once been a well-ordered society.

On the heels of the Vandals came the Burgundians, who also invaded Gaul around 410–411, founding a king-dom known as Burgundy along the reaches of the upper Rhône River. Northeast of Burgundy, along the Rhine River, the Alemanni also established a kingdom of their own, bequeathing to the French language the word *Allemagne*, their name for Germany.

VISIGOTHS, OSTROGOTHS, AND LOMBARDS: GERMAN KINGDOMS IN SOUTHERN EUROPE

The repeated Germanic invasions of the 5th century revealed the degree to which the effective rule of the Roman Empire in the West had deteriorated. In 476, Romulus Augustulus, the last Roman emperor, was overthrown by the Germanic warrior Odoacer, and all Roman claims to rule the western half of the Empire came to an end.

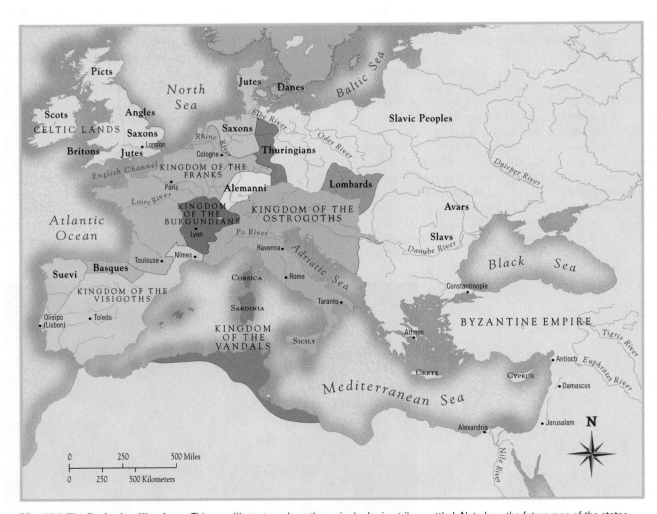

Map 20.2 The Barbarian Kingdoms. This map illustrates where the major barbarian tribes settled. Note how the future map of the states of Europe is vaguely beginning to appear. The medieval kingdoms of France and Spain descended from the territories of the Franks and the Visigoths. The Basques, a people of mysterious origin, whose language is unrelated to any other European one, are already established in the region between modern France and Spain. Apart from the loss of its territories in Italy, the Byzantine Empire is not yet under threat.

THE KINGDOM OF THE VISIGOTHS

In Constantinople, imperial government remained intact, but in the West it disappeared. In place of the political unity of the western empire, the Germans created a series of independent kingdoms that blended their customs and institutions with those of their former Roman rulers. The earliest of these successor states was the Visigothic kingdom in Gaul and Spain, the first autonomous Germanic kingdom in the Empire. Ataulf (d. 415), Alaric's successor, was a typical German leader in his desire to enjoy the benefits of imperial glory rather than destroy it. In 414 he married Galla Placidia (c. 388–c. 450), the daughter of Emperor Theodosius I, and established a government at Bordeaux. Ataulf's successors arranged a treaty with the eastern emperor that recognized the Visigothic state, known as the Kingdom of Toulouse.

The Visigoths tried to unify the peoples of their kingdoms through a combination of military power, law, and religion. Roman law became a model for Visigothic law codes, but the efforts of the new rulers to convert the Gallo-Roman population to Arianism produced local unrest. In 507, the Gallic nobles joined with Clovis, king of the Franks, in conquering the Kingdom of Toulouse. The Visigoths then moved into Spain, where they eventually created another kingdom that endured for more than two centuries. The Spanish state, utilizing Roman administrative practices and the imperial tax system, proved to be a prosperous kingdom. Late in the 6th century, one of its rulers, Recared (ruled 586–601), converted to Roman Catholicism, thus ending the religious conflict that had long divided the Visigoths from the local population and securing the church as an important ally for the Gothic monarchy. At the same time, Recared began a systematic persecution of the large Jewish population of Spain.

Although the Romans did not always observe the principle of hereditary succession, the Visigoths rejected the practice entirely. As a result, rival contenders struggled constantly for the throne, producing political instability. In 711, a Muslim invasion from North Africa conquered the kingdom and ended the Visigothic experiment in government.

THE OSTROGOTHS IN ITALY AND THEIR SUCCESSORS

Roman traditions were preserved most fully in the Ostrogothic (eastern Gothic) kingdom of Italy under the rule of Theodoric the Great (493–526). Theodoric had been educated at Constantinople and had an abiding respect for the civic culture of the Romans. In 493, the Emperor Zeno sent Theodoric to Italy to reconquer it for the Empire, but after murdering Odoacer at a banquet, he established his own kingdom in the peninsula, with its capital at Ravenna. Although the eastern emperors never accepted the legitimacy of Theodoric's reign, they did recognize him as their theoretical representative in the West.

Theodoric, the most powerful of the Germanic kings, sought to create a system in which Romans and Goths could live side by side in peace. While the Ostrogoths were ruled by their laws and officials, the Italian population was governed

S I G N I F I C A N T D A T E S	
The Germanic Kingdoms	
378	Visigoths defeat Emperor Valens at Adrianople
410	Alaric's Visigothic forces sack Rome
429	Vandals invade North Africa
c. 435–453	Huns under Attila invade Europe
455	Vandals sack Rome
476	Odoacer deposes last Roman emperor
481–511	Clovis rules Franks
493	Ostrogothic kingdom established
550s	Angles and Saxons complete conquest of England
560s	Lombards conquer Italy

according to Roman law by Roman officials. Theodoric maintained the structure of the imperial government and administration, including the consuls and magistrates, although the Goths dominated the army. He repaired the old Roman roads, aqueducts, and public buildings. As in the Visigothic kingdom, religious disputes divided the Ostrogoths from the local population and were the cause of some unrest. Unlike Recared, Theodoric never abandoned his Arian beliefs, although he did not seek to force his subjects to abandon their Roman Catholicism. A ruler of practical outlook, he declared that "no one can be forced to believe against his will."

After Theodoric's death, the Byzantine emperor Justinian (see Topic 22) reconquered Italy, laying waste to much of the peninsula. In 568, however, the Lombards, a Germanic tribe from the Danube region, took advantage of the chaos and invaded Italy, seizing control of the northern and central portions of Theodoric's former kingdom. Resistance against the Lombards was organized by Pope Gregory the Great (590–604), but the Byzantines were able to keep control only of a strip of territory from Ravenna to Rome and portions of Italy's eastern coast. The Lombards were even more violent than the Ostrogoths and showed little interest in preserving Roman civilization. Establishing the seat of government at Pavia, they divided their realm into military districts governed by dukes, who replaced the old Roman administrators. Despite their lack of interest in the Roman heritage, by the 7th century the Lombards had converted to Catholicism and merged into the basic elements of Roman culture that continued to characterize Italian life, including law and language.

THE FRANKS AND CHRISTIANITY

In terms of the long-range impact of their achievement, the most important of the Germanic kingdoms on the Continent was that of the Franks. Founded in the early 5th century, the principal Frankish dynasty, known as the Merovingian, eventually gave rise to the 8th-century empire of Charlemagne, the greatest political and cultural achievement of the Early Middle Ages.

The Franks emerged as a distinct unit some time in the 4th century, when they appeared as a confederation of tribes along the Rhine. The Franks eventually separated into two main groups—the Salian ("salty") Franks who settled along the coast, and the Ripuarian ("river") Franks on the Rhine. Defeated by the Romans, the Salians resettled in what is today Belgium and the Netherlands, where they coalesced and grew in importance around the leadership of Merovech, probably a powerful tribal chieftain, from whom the Merovingian dynasty took its name.

CLOVIS, KING OF THE FRANKS

The first ruler of the Franks to exercise real power was Merovech's grandson, Clovis (ruled 481–511). After becoming sole leader of the Salians through the force of his personality—and by murdering several of his relatives—Clovis had himself elected king of the Ripuarians. Then began his policy of trying to unite all of Gaul under his rule. This dream came close to reality in 486, when he defeated the Roman legions at Soissons, followed by victories over the Alemanni and the Visigoths. Other Germanic groups had migrated from one region to another, but the Franks expanded, maintaining the core of their homeland.

Important to Clovis's success as ruler was his conversion to orthodox Christianity. Clovis's wife, the Burgundian princess Clotilda, urged his conversion from the Arian heresy, and the couple had their children baptized. During his battle against the Alemanni, Clovis had vowed to become a Christian if he gained victory. Thereafter he became a champion of Orthodox Christianity against the Arians.

By the time of his death, Clovis had forged the largest kingdom in Europe, ruled from his capital at Paris and reaching from east of the Rhine to the Pyrenees. He ruled this vast domain partly with the cooperation of the Catholic bishops and partly through Frankish counts stationed in the provincial cities. His role as defender of the Western church gained him the support of the Gallo-Roman clergy in his efforts to build a strong royal government. Several factors, however, worked against this trend: A new noble class had begun to develop, which steadily increased its power and wealth through the accumulation of land. These nobles exercised extensive rights through the law of custom—as opposed to royal legislation—over the peasants who lived and worked on their estates, and they held a virtual monopoly over the bishoprics of the realm. Royal authority was also diminished by the emergence of a royal official known as the *major domus,* or mayor of the palace, as the principal figure in the royal household. As administrators of the royal estates, these officers often distributed land to the nobles in return for securing pledges of loyalty. After Clovis died, the *major domus* accumulated significant power in his own right, eventually replacing the king in all but name.

The conversion of the Franks to Christianity helped the fusion of the old Gallic population and the Frankish elite into a cohesive society. As Frankish nobles intermarried with Gallo-Roman families, a new ruling class emerged. This successful synthesis was an enduring legacy of the kingdom of the Franks, for although the kingdoms of the Huns and the Ostrogoths quickly faded after the deaths of their leaders, the dynasty founded by Clovis persisted in one form or another for centuries. Frankish society was not a recreated Roman world but the beginning of a new, European civilization.

THE MAKING OF ANGLO-SAXON ENGLAND

Britain had come into the Roman Empire in the 1st century A.D., when it was annexed by the Emperor Claudius. During the reign of Hadrian, the Romans built a 50-mile-long de-

Fresco painting of the baptism of the Frankish king Clovis. 7th century (?). To emphasize the divine origins of royal power, a bird—symbol of the Holy Spirit—descends bearing the baptismal oil. The attendants at the ceremony represent the two chief groups of the kingdom: bishops on one side and nobles (who wielded secular power) on the other.

© Cliché Bibliothèque Nationale de France, Paris

fensive wall that separated Scotland from Britain, making the line one of the principal defense borders between Germanic territories and the *Pax Romana*. With the abandonment of Britain in the early 5th century, the island was open to invasion by federated Germanic troops, especially the Angles, Saxons, Jutes, and Frisians. Without Roman legions to protect them, the resistance of the Celtic Britons rapidly collapsed. Later legends developed in Welsh and Irish folklore of a King Arthur whose knights fought the invaders, but by 550 Germans had begun to complete their conquest of Britain.

The impact of these Germans, who had been raiding the coast for years, was far different from that of the Goths on the Continent, for these German invaders did not try to blend with the Roman population. Instead, they either eradicated or enslaved the Britons or pushed them westward into Wales and Cornwall. Some Britons even fled across the Channel to northwestern Gaul, which became known as Brittany, or "little Britain."

Because these Germanic groups, unlike the Goths, had had little direct contact with the Romans, they imported their culture and pagan beliefs to Britain. Most of the Angles and Saxons were farmers rather than warriors, and as they settled on the land they replaced the language and customs of the Britons with their own. Urban life and commerce all but ceased as the Germans developed farming communities according to their own traditions. Nor did the conquerors consolidate their rule into a centralized monarchy. Rather, prominent warriors each established small kingdoms, although they recognized the symbolic authority of the strongest of their kings, known as the "wide ruler," who settled disputes among the others. Gradually, Roman Britain became Anglo-Saxon "England"—the land of the Angles.

CHRISTIANITY AND ANGLO-SAXON CULTURE

Because the Anglo-Saxons were pagans, Christianity came to England as a result of conversion efforts from two places—Ireland and Rome. In Ireland, which had remained outside the Roman Empire, Celtic traditions remained largely unchanged until the 5th century, when missionaries and traders began to spread Christianity. The most important of these early missionaries to Ireland was St. Patrick (c. 390–461). As a young man Patrick was kidnapped by Irish raiders and sent to Ireland as a slave. Later, after his escape, he became a monk and returned to Ireland to convert the population to Christianity. Although the form of Christian doctrine introduced was fully orthodox, it stressed the monastic tradition, and its early converts maintained close contact with tribal traditions. As a result, unlike the practice that developed elsewhere in Europe, where bishops became the most important authorities in the church, the Irish church was in the hands of the abbots of monasteries. Followers of the Irish monk Columba (521–597) began the conversion of Scotland and northern England.

In 596, the second effort to convert the Anglo-Saxons began when Pope Gregory the Great sent an Italian mis-

Page from *The Book of Kells.* Late 8th–early 9th century. 1 foot 1 inch by 9½ inches (36 by 28 cm). The *Book of Kells* is an Irish illuminated manuscript, perhaps made by monks from an Irish monastery started by Columba on the island of Iona (off the west coast of Scotland). This opening page of the Gospel of St. Mark shows a blend of traditional Western medieval elements with Celtic motifs.

Board of Trinity College, Dublin

sionary, known as Augustine of Canterbury (d. c. 605), to England to head a group of some 40 monks. Augustine was first allowed to preach by the rulers of Kent, the pagan Ethelbert and his Christian wife Bertha. Ethelbert became the first Christian king of Anglo-Saxon England, and in 601 Augustine became the first bishop of Canterbury. A few years later he established another bishopric in London, then a town of some 30,000 inhabitants.

The Christianity introduced by Augustine followed the Roman pattern in which bishops were the central authority in the church. Tensions developed between Augustine's converts and the more ascetic followers of Columba, who followed the decentralized Celtic model revolving around abbots. Although both were orthodox in their beliefs, they observed different rituals and religious holidays. To resolve these differences, a meeting of bishops, known as a *synod,* met in 663 at Whitby, after which the "wide ruler," King Oswy (d. 670), settled the controversy by siding with the Roman Church.

Once Roman Catholicism became the dominant religion on the island, greater contact with the Continent diminished the cultural isolation of Anglo-Saxon England. Within a generation of the Synod of Whitby, England produced the most prominent scholar of the age, the Venerable Bede (c. 673–735). Bede, an Anglo-Saxon monk who

Kunsthistorisches Museum, Wien oder KHM, Wien

Manuscript painting of the Venerable Bede, c. 9th century (?). One of the first great medieval scholars, Bede is shown here in his study, writing one of his *Histories*. Note the absence of any background setting and the highly stylized architecture, characteristic of the art of the period.

followed the rule of Benedict (see Topic 21), wrote about theological, historical, and scientific subjects. His *Ecclesiastical History of the English Nation*, written in Latin, was based on an analysis of many documents and gives the most reliable account of the growth of Anglo-Saxon culture and the political events of the period from 597 to 731. Bede's works not only represent a great achievement in early medieval scholarship, but reflect the fact that by the 8th century Anglo-Saxon England had become an important center of European culture.

GERMAN CUSTOMS AND ROMAN TRADITIONS: THE FORMATION OF EUROPE

The transformation of the western part of the Roman Empire was virtually complete. During a period that lasted some two centuries, this vast region had been overrun by barbarians. But although the Germanic kingdoms replaced Roman provincial administration everywhere, Roman law,

language, and institutions remained sufficiently strong to influence the new conquerors. For one thing, the Germans were relatively few in number compared with the much larger Roman population—perhaps as few as 5 percent of the total—while a millennium of Roman tradition was a lure too powerful for the Germans to resist.

The new societies of the West represented a gradual blending of Roman institutions, Germanic customs, and Christian ideals. In the 6th century, Gregory of Tours (538–594), a Gallo-Roman historian and bishop, wrote *The Histories*. This work, although handed down to us in the form of badly copied versions from later centuries, nevertheless presents an original portrait of Gregory's time. It is important to remember that the Germanic society he described bore only partial resemblance to that recorded by Tacitus five centuries earlier. The customs and experiences of the different German peoples reveal considerable variation in the degree of Romanization. All of them, however, eventually found their societies and cultures transformed by the Roman legacy, especially as later Germanic rulers absorbed a respect for Roman government and law.

GERMANIC GOVERNMENT AND LAW

Most of the Germanic states developed monarchies that were elective in theory and adopted the notion of dynastic succession. In imitation of the Roman imperial court, German kings like Clovis and Theodoric wore purple robes on state occasions and maintained courts in which officials with Latin titles advised them. There were important differences as well. The Romans conceived of the state as *res publica*, a public matter, whereas the German kings thought of state territory as private estates and royal authority as a personal prerogative. Hence the royal court was the home of the king and moved with him as he traveled throughout his domains. The courts were attended by powerful nobles but were not permanent seats of civil administration. On the local level, Roman bureaucratic machinery continued to operate much as before because the Germans had developed no permanent administrative system. They did, however, institute a system of trusted representatives called counts, who exercised military and judicial powers in the name of the king. Most kings also retained the Roman financial apparatus.

As we have seen, the personal nature of Germanic law differed from the public basis of Roman law. The Roman population continued to live under Roman law, and under German law the *wergeld* was higher for an injured German than for a Roman. Some of the kingdoms eventually adopted the Roman practice of codifying their laws, and the Visigoths, Franks, Saxons, and Lombards drew up their law codes in Latin. The *Lex Salica* (Salic Law), compiled under Clovis, reflected ancient German customs and the values of a more pastoral civilization. The customs of the past, not the will of the king, were regarded as the source of Germanic law.

Germanic law allowed for the determination of guilt or innocence through trial by ordeal. The theory was that divine intervention would prevent the accused from experiencing permanent physical harm during such painful tests as plunging an arm or leg into boiling water or grasping a red-hot iron with bare hands. The Germans also practiced ordeal by battle, believing that God would protect the innocent. Compurgation, on the other hand, involved obtaining a sufficient number of people who would swear that the accused was either innocent or was telling the truth. Compurgation, which was often used in cases involving nobles, required no real hard evidence.

Putting the Germanic Kingdoms in Perspective

In the West, beginning in the 4th century, the Roman Empire effectively came to an end as waves of Germanic migrations moved across Europe. Within a short time, these peoples had established the bases for new governments that replaced the centralized Roman authority with regional kingdoms. Slowly, the new population merged with the old, and by the end of the 7th century many of those elements that had kept the Romans and Germans separated had disappeared. With the decline of Arianism and the conversion of Germans to Catholicism, religious differences faded. In the 5th century the Visigoths abandoned the ban on intermarriage, which was in any case already becoming widespread. In practical terms, the inability of the Byzantine emperors to exercise real influence in the West eventually led the old Roman population to recognize the sovereignty of the Germanic kings and to accept the new situation as permanent.

As popular customs and administrative systems changed, the separate legal systems blended. Thus the Visigoths in 654 issued a new law code that applied to Romans and Germans. Language both reflected and influenced the fusion of the two peoples. Among the new German states Latin remained the official language, and the Romance languages of France, Spain, and Italy evolved from the Latin spoken by the inhabitants of those regions, to which some German words were added. By the 8th century a new, original society had begun to emerge in Europe, a society that was deeply changed by the German migrations but that still retained much of its Roman character. The process of assimilation was encouraged by the church, which had emerged as the real inheritor of universal authority in the West.

Questions for Further Study

1. How did the Romans view "outsiders"? How did the Germans view the Romans?
2. How would you describe the differing patterns of settlement of the Germanic tribes in the Roman Empire?
3. In what ways did the Germans contribute to the formation of a new "European" civilization?

Suggestions for Further Reading

Burns, Thomas S. *A History of the Ostrogoths.* Bloomington, IN, 1984.

Christie, Neil. *The Lombards: The Ancient Longobards.* Oxford, 1995.

Geary, Patrick J. *Before France and Germany: The Creation and Transformation of the Merovingian World.* Oxford, 1988.

Goffart, Walter. *Barbarians and Romans,* A.D. *418–554.* Princeton, NJ, 1980.

Heather, Peter J. *The Goths.* Cambridge, MA, 1996.

James, Edward. *The Franks.* Oxford, 1988.

Murray, Alexander. *Germanic Kingship Structure.* Toronto, 1983.

Schultz, Herbert. *The Germanic Realms in Pre-Carolingian Central Europe, 400-750.* New York, 2000.

Webster, Leslie, and Michelle Brown. *The Transformation of the Roman World AD 400-900.* Berkeley, CA, 1997.

Wolfram, Herwig. *History of the Goths,* rev. ed. T.J. Dunlap, trans. Berkeley, CA, 1988.

InfoTrac Search Terms

Enter the search term *early Christianity* using Key Terms.

EARLY MEDIEVAL CHRISTIANITY

As the political and economic influence of the Roman Empire disintegrated, the Christian Church emerged as the only institution capable of providing continuity and leadership in the West. During the period of relative peace that stretched from 325 to the Germanic invasions a hundred years later, the church spread throughout the Empire, grew in prestige, and strengthened its authority as Christianity became the bedrock of the medieval civilization that was to emerge.

The early Christian intellectuals reconciled the Classical heritage of the Greco-Roman world with the ideals of Christianity. The synthesis of pagan and Christian culture achieved by these Fathers of the Church contributed to the transition from Roman to European civilization. They also established the moral justification for preserving Classical learning for future generations. At the same time, St. Augustine's *City of God,* the most important work of these early church intellectuals, laid the foundation for the Christian worldview that would eventually prevail throughout most of the Middle Ages.

Christianity developed two institutions—the papacy and the monastic orders—that shaped medieval life in significant ways. The growth and centralization of papal authority began under Pope Leo I, who established the basis for papal claims to lead the church, at least in the West. The doctrine of papal primacy had a profound impact on both the theological unity of the church and relations between the Roman Church and secular authority. Monasticism provided an environment in which Christian men and women could devote themselves to the worship of God while experimenting with a new form of communal living that met the economic needs of the age. Monasteries also served as the chief institutional setting for the preservation and transmission of learning. Christianity deeply influenced life in the Middle Ages, for women as well as men of all social classes.

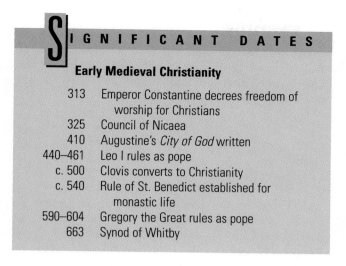

SIGNIFICANT DATES

Early Medieval Christianity

313	Emperor Constantine decrees freedom of worship for Christians
325	Council of Nicaea
410	Augustine's *City of God* written
440–461	Leo I rules as pope
c. 500	Clovis converts to Christianity
c. 540	Rule of St. Benedict established for monastic life
590–604	Gregory the Great rules as pope
663	Synod of Whitby

CHRISTIANITY AND THE CLASSICAL HERITAGE

The Emperor Constantine had legalized Christianity in 313. Nevertheless, by the beginning of the 5th century, most Christians remained removed and alien from what was still a predominantly Classical and pagan world. Many Christians even expressed hostility toward Greco-Roman culture that went beyond the memory of the early persecutions. The Christian belief in the end of the world and the second coming of Christ meant that they attributed little importance to secular knowledge and learning. Roman culture was perceived as the embodiment of spiritual sin and material corruption, of sexual desire and excess. "We have no need for speculation after Jesus Christ," proclaimed the Christian writer Tertullian (c. 160–c. 225), "nor any need for inquiry after the Gospel."

THE LATIN FATHERS OF THE CHURCH

Some Christian intellectuals, however, urged appreciation for and accommodation with the world of Classical learning. Origen (c. 185–254), an early Christian scholar born in Egypt, wrote extensively in an effort to synthesize the fundamental principles of Greek philosophy with Christianity. A stern ascetic, he castrated himself and devoted his life to teaching. The blending of pagan and Christian values that Origen and others helped achieve was to be a principal ingredient in the emerging new "European" civilization. Among the early Christian thinkers, the most influential were four men known as the Fathers of the Latin Church: Ambrose, Jerome, Augustine, and Gregory. (There are also Four Fathers of the Greek Church: Basil, Gregory Nazianzen, John Chrysostom, and Athanasius.) Collectively, these eight figures are known as the Doctors of the Church.

The life of St. Ambrose of Milan (c. 339–397) bridged the gulf between the Roman and the Christian worlds. The son of an imperial official, Ambrose was educated in the Roman tradition and entered the state administration,

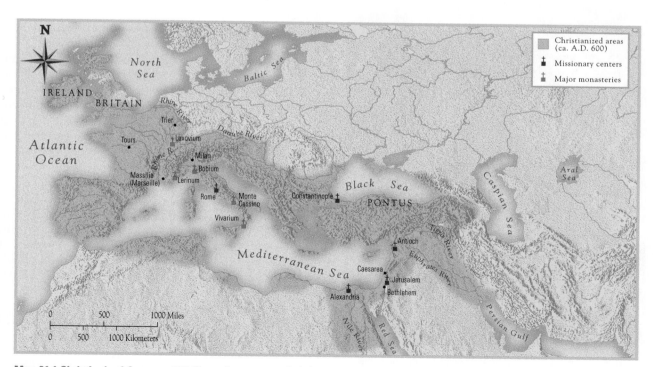

Map 21.1 Christianized Areas, c. 600. The main centers are in Italy and the eastern Mediterranean, regions closely involved with the early stages of Christianity. Southeast England remains unconverted, while Christianity was only brought to Eastern Europe and Russia by Byzantine missionaries, some three centuries later. For all the hostility between Christians and "pagans," Christian territory still generally remains that of the former Roman Empire.

eventually becoming governor of Milan. The people of the city then chose him as bishop.

According to Ambrose, the choice for Christians was not between learning and belief but between the church and the state; accordingly, he defined his duty as a bishop as the protection of the church's independence from the authority of the emperor. When the Emperor Theodosius slaughtered civilians in Thessalonica and Ambrose severely criticized him, Theodosius tried to force Ambrose to give up his church seat. The bishop responded, however, by arguing that "It is written, God's to God and Caesar's to Caesar. The palace is the emperor's, the churches are the Bishop's." Ambrose refused to celebrate Mass in the presence of the emperor and finally forced Theodosius to do public penance. The independence of the church from the state that Ambrose insisted on would become a major ecclesiastical and political doctrine of medieval civilization.

St. Jerome (c. 347–c. 420) was born in the Balkans but received training in Rome as a Latin writer. In Antioch he experienced a vision in which Christ reproved him for his love of pagan culture. He then fled into the desert to live as an ascetic and devote himself to scriptural studies, becoming a distinguished scholar, often called on to settle doctrinal disputes. Jerome never gave up his love for the Classical authors, however, arguing that the ancients should be examined in the context of Christian principles. His facility with both Hebrew and Greek equipped him to compile the letters and writings that formed the basis for the Bible. In

Bethlehem, where he lived from 386 until his death, Jerome worked on a translation of the Old and New Testaments into vernacular Latin. This so-called Vulgate, or common text, became the standard Catholic version of the Scriptures for more than 1,000 years.

THE CITY OF GOD: AUGUSTINE AND HIS VISION

The greatest of the Latin Fathers was St. Augustine (354–430), whose intellect fashioned a blending of Classical and Christian thought that profoundly influenced subsequent generations. Born in North Africa of a pagan father and a Christian mother, he enjoyed an indulgent youth but showed promise as a student and received a limited education in grammar, rhetoric, and law in local schools. At the age of 17, he went to Carthage for further study, where he met a woman with whom he lived for many years and who bore him an illegitimate son.

Augustine underwent a long period of spiritual doubt, during which he experimented with alternative Christian doctrines and Eastern philosophies. After an unsuccessful teaching stint in Rome, in 384 Augustine went to Milan. Further study and the influence of Bishop Ambrose, with whom he corresponded for many years, eventually led him to be baptized as a Christian. Armed with his newfound faith, Augustine returned to North Africa to establish a monastery. In 396, the population of Hippo made him their bishop.

In later life Augustine's conversion led him to preach strict moral teachings, especially on sexual behavior, which he saw as the triumph of passion over reason. For the unmarried, sex should be banned altogether, and married couples should have sex only to procreate. Arguing, however, that the world's population had grown large enough, he insisted that procreation was no longer necessary and that all Christians should practice celibacy. The argument that celibacy was superior to married life stemmed from Paul of Tarsus, a Hellenized Jew whose writings in the 1st century A.D. helped define many basic Christian beliefs.

THE CONFESSIONS OF AUGUSTINE

Around 400, Augustine began work on an autobiography, *The Confessions*, a literary gem as well as a classic of Christian mysticism. Remarkably frank in the details of his wild youth in Carthage, *The Confessions* offers an explanation of his inner struggle between the spirit and the flesh and his conversion to Christianity.

Written as an extended prayer in beautifully crafted Latin, the work is a moving chronicle of a classically trained scholar engaged on a spiritual journey to faith. One result of that journey was that Augustine came to reject the Greco-Roman notion that human virtue was an outgrowth of knowledge. His own wayward youth taught him that knowledge of what is right does not by itself lead a person to act

Manuscript illustration showing St. Boniface, Apostle to the Germans, baptizing a convert, c. 9th century (?). The simplified style is in marked contrast to the *Book of Kells* (see p. 207). The manuscript is in the collection of the Abbey of Fulda, in central Germany.

Staatsbibliotek, Bamberg

in a righteous or rational manner. He concluded, therefore, that human will—even the will of a scholar—is by nature weak and subject to corruption. Augustine hoped that the story of his own experience would guide others.

In addition to his autobiography, Augustine also wrote numerous learned theological works on heresies and doctrinal disputes. His *On the Trinity* offered a systematic assessment of Christian doctrine, while *On the Work of Monks* was widely used by men and women living in monastic communities. Much of his energy, however, was taken up with efforts to counter a heretical movement known as Donatism, named after Donatus, the bishop of Carthage in the early 4th century. Donatus argued that sacraments were valid only if administered by a priest who was free of sin. His followers saw themselves as a specially chosen Christian elite that kept their purity in an evil world and believed that only those living a blameless life belonged in the church. Condemned by a synod and by the Emperor Constantine, Donatism nevertheless spread rapidly, especially in North Africa. Augustine began to write treatises against Donatism, insisting that God's action gave the church its authority, which was the guarantee of the Christian faith, and proclaiming the permanent validity of the sacraments. Augustine said that true Christians should strive for holiness while living in and transforming the world.

THE CITY OF GOD

Augustine's most important work is his monumental *The City of God,* written in 410 in the aftermath of the sack of Rome by the Visigoths that same year. Pagan philosophers attributed the catastrophe to the recognition of Christianity by the Roman state and the Romans' abandonment of the pagan gods. In his attempt to refute this argument, Augustine's *City of God* presents an interpretation of Roman experience in the light of a Christian philosophy of history, in which divine providence affects all earthly events. This philosophy stems in part from Augustine's distinction between God as creator and God as redeemer. He argued that original sin made human beings incapable of their own salvation. Only through God's grace, earned through the sacrifice of Jesus, could salvation be achieved. Even before the creation, however, God had decided which human beings were to receive or to be denied divine grace. Each person, therefore, is predestined to heaven or hell.

Augustine declared that there are two planes of existence, the earthly and the heavenly (the City of God). The earthly city is not the true home of those Christians who, because of the grace of God, will have eternal happiness in the kingdom of heaven. Augustine urged his fellow Christians to focus their energies on the divine rather than on the earthly world. Yet he also taught that the latter was not entirely evil. Because humans are inclined to sin, governments—the cities of earthly society—are needed to preserve peace and order. But, Augustine concluded—along with Ambrose—the church is superior even to Christian rulers.

THE PAPACY AND THE PRIMACY OF ROME

The ability of the church to provide spiritual and secular guidance after the collapse of the Empire was largely the result of the intelligence and will of two men, Pope Leo I (ruled 440–461) and Pope Gregory I (ruled 590–604), who provided vigorous leadership as the early bishops of Rome. They succeeded not only in imposing doctrinal unity and building the administrative structure of the church, but also in asserting the powers and independence of the papacy over the secular rulers of Europe.

THE SEARCH FOR DOCTRINAL UNITY

Several heresies—or conflicting interpretations of doctrine—plagued early Christianity. The Emperor Constantine had attempted to end the problem of heresy by convening a group of bishops and prelates in the Council of Nicaea in A.D. 325. The council was to settle questions regarding the nature of the Trinity raised by Arianism, the principal heresy. Named after Arius, a priest from the Egyptian city of Alexandria, Arianism argued that Jesus Christ was human and therefore of a lower order than God the Father. The Nicene Creed reaffirmed the view that Christ coexisted eternally with and was equal to God. Despite the condemnation of Arianism, however, the heresy persisted and was later adopted by many of the German Goths.

The idea of using ecclesiastical councils to settle doctrinal disputes actually increased the authority of the church, which assumed control over dealing with heresy. Moreover, although held in the East under imperial auspices, two prelates attended the meeting at Nicaea as representatives of the bishop of Rome. In 431, the practice continued with the Council of Ephesus, which was convened to deal with the teachings of Nestorius, who argued that the divine and the human natures of Christ were two separate personalities and that the Virgin Mary was the mother of his human persona only. The council upheld the orthodox doctrine against Nestorianism and described Mary as "Mother of God," thus establishing the basis for the veneration of the Virgin Mary as the most important of the saints.

Twenty years later, the Council of Chalcedon addressed the heresy professed by the Monophysites, who went to the opposite extreme by asserting that Christ possessed a single, combined nature in which his divinity was emphasized over his humanity. When the bishops assembled at Chalcedon failed to agree on this heresy, Leo I settled the argument by issuing a letter condemning the Monophysites. Like the Arians, they continued to attract adherents, especially in eastern regions of the Empire such as Syria, Egypt, and Palestine.

PAPAL PRIMACY

Leo I's initiative at Chalcedon strengthened his position as bishop of Rome, whose powers he believed took precedence in ecclesiastical matters over those of all other cities. The claim of the Roman bishops to supremacy went back to the Scriptures, according to which Christ had given the keys to the kingdom of heaven to St. Peter, his chief apostle. Peter had then founded the Christian Church in Rome and had been its first bishop. Later bishops of Rome therefore thought of themselves as Peter's heirs. At Chalcedon, Leo's declaration was received by the attending bishops with the words, "Peter speaks through Leo."

Once the capital of the Empire was moved to Constantinople, the lack of an emperor in the West allowed the bishops of Rome to assume the prestige identified with the former imperial city for themselves. By the 5th century, the bishops of Rome had adopted the word *pope* (from the ecclesiastical Latin word *papa*, or father) for themselves and referred to other bishops as "sons."

FROM LEO TO GREGORY

The pontificate of Leo I firmly established the doctrine of papal primacy, under which the pope became the leader of the Roman Church. Leo, a member of a Roman aristocratic family, was well educated. He deliberately identified himself as the successor of Peter, a claim that was eventually recognized in the West but not in the East, and assumed the title of *pontifex maximus*, or highest priest. He saw himself as the shepherd of all Christians and the representative (vicar) of Christ on earth. Leo's vision for the church was that of a highly centralized institution, with power focused in the hands of the pope at the top and a host of learned, dedicated priests at the bottom.

Early in Leo's pontificate, he reconfirmed his authority as pope over his bishops in a confrontation with Hilary (d. 449), archbishop of Arles and head of the church in Gaul. Hilary deposed two bishops, who thereupon appealed to Rome. Leo, supported by a letter from the emperor, deprived Hilary of his authority over the Gallic bishops and declared the sovereignty of Rome over all bishops. The prestige of the pope was further enhanced when Leo negotiated with the Hun leader Attila in 452 and with the Vandal leader Gaiseric in 455, thus preventing the destruction of Rome. These actions established the pope's temporal leadership, which he joined to his spiritual authority.

Gregory I, like Leo, was also of noble origins. He began his career in local politics and became, at the age of 30, prefect of Rome, the city's highest civil office. Within several years, however, Gregory felt the need for religious seclusion and, giving up his considerable wealth, converted his home into a monastery. In 578, he became archdeacon of Rome, a position of great importance in the papal administration, and for about six years he resided at Constantinople as a papal representative. He was elected pope by acclamation in 590, much against his will.

Gregory followed Leo's program by insisting vigorously on papal supremacy in religious matters and worked to extend the authority of Rome over the entire Western church. He intervened in ecclesiastical disputes in Italy and Gaul, kept in contact with secular rulers, and began the missionary activities that converted England and parts of the

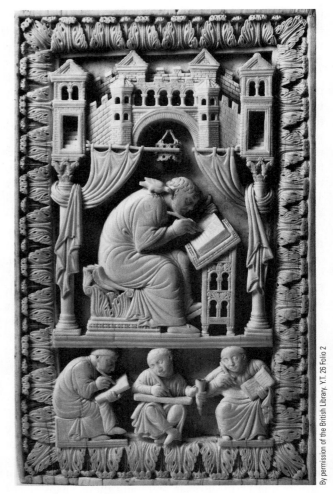

By permission of the British Library. Y.T. 26 Folio 2

Ivory carving showing Pope Gregory at his desk. Early 9th century (?). 9½ inches by 6½ inches (25 by 16 cm). High-quality works such as this one were often used as covers for the Gospels and other liturgical works. Beneath Gregory, as he sits writing, are three scribes, who would make copies of his texts for distribution to a wider audience.

Continent to Christianity (see Topic 20). The pope also insisted that the clergy were exempt from trial in civil courts, a precedent that was to have important repercussions later in the Middle Ages.

Gregory was personally responsible for producing a series of written works that, while not representing original scholarship, were nevertheless useful in the day-to-day functioning of the church. His *Pastoral Care* gave practical guidance to bishops and priests in carrying out their duties, while his *Dialogues* recorded the lives of saints and the miracles attributed to them. Although tradition holds that his interest in the liturgy led to the adoption of official church music that included the official prayers sung during the Mass (see Topic 28), this is now recognized as a legend.

Gregory's pontificate was distinguished above all by the establishment of the papacy's temporal position. The emperors in Constantinople refused to act in the face of continued disorders and war in Italy, particularly the invasion of the

Lombards. The emperor's representative in the West was the exarch of Ravenna, who claimed secular jurisdiction over the city of Rome. Nevertheless, when Rome was threatened by a Lombard attack in 592, the exarch did nothing, and Gregory negotiated his own peace with the Lombards. In this way, he made the papacy independent of the Byzantine emperor in matters concerning the jurisdiction of Rome and the surrounding region, laying the foundation for what would later be called the Papal States. Inside the city, Gregory organized the defense of the city and provided food and water to the population during emergencies.

THE MONASTIC IDEAL

Monasticism was just as important as the papacy to the development of Christianity and medieval civilization. The general concept of the monastic ideal is common to many religions, and the followers of many faiths have sought to withdraw from the ordinary world and the corruption of society in order to devote themselves completely to worship and prayer. In Europe of the Middle Ages the monk (from the Greek word *monos*, meaning alone) became an exceptionally important figure who helped shape the values and norms of everyday life and exercised enormous social, cultural, and economic influence.

HERMITS AND THE FLIGHT FROM WORLDLINESS

Monasticism had its origins in the desire of particularly devout men and women to escape from what they perceived as the immorality of the cities. They chose instead to live alone high up on mountains or deep in deserts—the term *hermit* comes from the Greek *eremos*, or desert. Removed from civilization, hermits could practice asceticism, rejecting bodily pleasures and indulging in fasting and self-mortification as they gave themselves totally to God. The ascetics included women—and although nuns, abbesses, and other official members of the church were not yet part of the hierarchy, many virgins and widows subjected themselves to the same deprivations in their efforts to purify their bodies and come closer to God. Such individuals became mythic figures for the common people and were sought out by rulers for advice and counsel.

One of the earliest persons to make the transition from the life of the hermit to that of the monk was Anthony (c. 250–355). Anthony gave up all of his worldly possessions and fled into the Egyptian desert, where he engaged in self-mortification and constant prayer. But Anthony's reputation began to attract devout Christians, who regarded him as their spiritual leader and formed a religious community around him as their abbot (from the Semitic *abba*, meaning father). This form of eremitical monasticism, centered around the hermit, was particularly widespread in the East, where local conditions enabled it to persist for many years. In the desert of Syria, for example, the climate was milder,

and both water and food were more easily available than in the Egyptian desert. The best known of these Syrian hermits was Simeon Stylites (c. 390–459), who lived for more than 30 years in a basket on top of a 60-foot-high pillar.

Figures such as Simeon were less common in the West, where bishops rather than hermits remained the focus of religious and ecclesiastical authority. In Italy, Gaul, and elsewhere, conditions favored cenobitic monasticism, in which monks lived in organized communities according to established rules. Yet the founding of cenobitic monasticism is usually attributed to another Eastern figure, Pachomius (c. 290–346), who wrote the first rule for such communal living and emphasized chastity, poverty, physical labor, and obedience to the abbot. Later, Basil (329–379) established a monastic community in what is now Turkey and wrote commentaries for the spiritual advice of his followers.

One of the early monastic communities in the West was founded in Marseilles in the early 5th century by John Cassian (360–435), who rejected the model of the solitary hermit. His *Institutes* had considerable influence on the idea of structured communal living. In the following century, Cassiodorus (c. 485–c. 585), a Roman senator, founded two monasteries in Italy, where he gathered learned monks who devoted themselves to scholarship and copying old manuscripts. Monasticism was particularly strong in Ireland, and beginning in the 6th century Irish monks became missionaries, founding monasteries on the Continent.

THE RULE OF BENEDICT

The form of monasticism that came to characterize Western Christianity was principally the work of an Italian monk, Benedict of Nursia (c. 480–c. 543). Benedict was from a noble family and had enjoyed a first-rate education, but his religious faith drove him to seek the isolation of the eremitic life in southern Italy. Soon, however, he attracted numerous followers and founded a monastic community in Subiaco. In 529, after a local priest forced him out of Subiaco, he built a monastery on top of the mountain at Monte Cassino and later wrote the most famous and important rule of monastic life.

The principles behind Benedict's rule contrasted with the extreme intensity of eastern Mediterranean asceticism. Although Benedict envisioned a highly structured world for his monks, including vows of chastity and poverty, the underlying notion was that of balance and moderation. Damaging acts of self-mortification, as practiced by some Byzantine hermits, were prohibited. The Benedictine rule was a practical document designed to make a community economically self-sufficient and enable a group of people to live and work together in harmony. Monks who entered a Benedictine monastery underwent a trial period of one year to determine whether they were suited to monastic existence. They then took a vow of stability, promising to remain in the monastery of their choice and not wander from one community to another. Each monastery was ruled by an abbot who was elected for life, and to whom absolute obedience was to be given. In return, the monks expected the

INDEX/Firenze

Detail of a manuscript illumination showing St. Benedict holding the Rule he devised for monastic life. Late 9th–10th century (?). Although the figures are stylized, the detail and perspective effect of the saint's throne suggest that the manuscript dates to several centuries after Benedict's death.

abbot to demonstrate wisdom and understanding. After the Council of Chalcedon, abbots became subject to the authority of their local bishops, thus integrating the monasteries into the overall life of the church. The distinction was soon made between the secular clergy, who performed church services in the temporal world (*saeculum*), and the regular clergy, who lived away from the world according to a monastic rule (*regula*).

Monks devoted themselves not only to worship but also to study or physical labor and were encouraged not to be idle. Every day was carefully divided into hours consisting of designated tasks and duties, from farming, winemaking, crafts, and copying manuscripts to the celebration of Mass, communal prayer, and the chanting of psalms. Monks ate and worked together, with a social equality unknown in secular society. The number of monks in the larger monasteries ranged from 70 to 150, although a few more imposing houses counted as many as 300 monks.

Monasteries were important economic units in the early Middle Ages. Self-sufficiency meant that each monastery grew and produced whatever was necessary to sustain the community. Although the individual monks followed a vow of poverty, the monastery usually owned considerable land donated to it by devout patrons. The monks knew and practiced the best farming methods of the age, including crop rotation, and managed their estates with great efficiency. They also cleared forests and drained swampy lands, contributing to the agricultural advancement of Europe. Monasteries often provided food and supplies to the local population during periods of shortage or military cri-

sis. In more normal times, products like honey or wine made on the monastic estates were traded to townspeople.

Monasteries sometimes functioned as schools, libraries, and centers of learning, not only for the monks s but also for laychildren from the local community. Many monasteries maintained writing units, called *scriptoria*, where religious and secular manuscripts were copied, and where the practice of illumination—the painting of illustrations and decorative motifs—became an important art form.

The Benedictine rule had great appeal in western Europe, where within a century of Benedict's death hundreds of monasteries followed its regulations. For many Christians, monasteries were a refuge both from the temptations of material life and from an age characterized by the breakdown of government. The creation of self-sufficient communities based on agricultural estates was a practical response to the broad trends in European civilization, especially the decline of cities and trade and the collapse of centralized authority. The monastic ideal represented another important way in which Christianity profoundly affected medieval civilization.

WOMEN, CHRISTIANITY, AND THE CHURCH

Christian doctrine acted as a liberating force because the teachings of Jesus did not make any real distinction between men and women and found flaws in both men's and women's natures. Jesus preached equality and equal access to the kingdom of heaven. Nevertheless, the church had a contradictory impact on the lives of early medieval women.

CHRISTIANITY AND THE STATUS OF WOMEN

The Christian view of women was first presented in detail by Paul the Apostle, who argued the equality of women with regard to salvation but not within the institution of the church. Women helped spread the faith, functioned as deaconesses, and helped the poor through charities. Many of the martyrs to Roman persecution were women, and some early Christian sects permitted women to act as priests. As late as the early 6th century women officiated with priests in churches in Ireland and some areas of Gaul.

On the other hand, Paul also instructed women not to teach or to exercise authority over men. As a result, canon law (the law of the Roman Church) prevented Christian women from taking the priestly sacrament or preaching. Paul also maintained that in marriage women should be clearly subordinate to their husbands. "Let your women keep silence in the churches," he admonished, "for it is not permitted unto them to speak; but they are commanded to be under obedience, as also saith the law. And if they will learn any thing, let them ask their husbands at home" (I Corinthians 14:34–36). In prohibiting women from serving as priests, Paul reflected the Judaic tradition, which barred women from religious service and segregated them in the temple.

The Judeo-Christian tradition provided the rationale for excluding women from the priesthood through the story of the role of Eve in Original Sin. Augustine viewed women as the descendants of Eve, who had seduced Adam when the devil could not. Hence, her subjugation to man is the result of her sin. This view of women as inferior and the mothers of all sin came to be widely accepted by the Church Fathers and is repeated throughout medieval literature. Moreover, the eating of the forbidden fruit in the story of Original Sin became symbolic of women's sexual seduction of men, so that women who led an active sexual life were regarded as unclean. The Church Fathers condemned all women for the lust they inspired in men, and older traditions regarding women's physiology and the reproductive process soon became part of Christian attitudes. As early as the 4th century, women were not permitted to enter the sanctuary because of their menstruation. Virgins were regarded as the only ideal brides for Christ, and Christian writers advocated the exclusive roles of wife and mother for women who rejected celibacy.

THE FEMALE MONASTIC ORDERS

Although Christianity reinforced the inferior status of women, the church did provide women with an opportunity for a life beyond marriage and the family. The first monks were men, but monasteries for women quickly developed in parallel fashion. The communities founded by Pachomius had convents for women, but the laymen who did the physical labor for the convents lived and slept apart. A rule for a female order was written as early as the 5th century in Gaul, but the Benedictine rule proved the most popular among communities for women.

Double monasteries arose almost from the beginning. In these arrangements, monks and nuns lived in separate houses in the same monastery and under a single head. A few were actually headed by an abbess who ruled over both monks and nuns, although many male ecclesiastics opposed this practice. Hilda (614–680) of Whitby Abbey in England was the most famous abbess of a double monastery. In addition to running Whitby, she supervised two other houses. A princess from Northumbria, Hilda became a leading figure in the church and hosted the Synod of Whitby (663) that settled differences between the Roman and Celtic rites (see Topic 20).

To what degree was Hilda the exception? Double monasteries were certainly not the norm, and like their male counterparts, abbesses were under the jurisdiction of the local bishop. In theory, abbesses could not preach to nuns in public or attend high councils of the order to which they belonged, nor were they supposed to receive the vows of nuns or hear their confessions, as did priests. In some double monasteries, males had to pledge obedience to the abbess, although she was forbidden by canon law to exercise judicial authority over them. Moreover, abbesses, like abbots, ruled over the peasants who worked the monastic lands, and managed the order's estates.

Like men, most women entered religious houses out of devotion, but some did so for other reasons. The overwhelming majority were daughters of the nobility or the upper middle class because almost all girls wanting to enter a monastery were expected to bring a dowry with them, although the amount was lower than was expected for marriage. Those daughters for whom a family could not provide a sufficiently large bridal dowry often took the veil. In addition, the nunnery was often an alternative to marriage for illegitimate daughters or those who were physically handicapped or learning impaired. Rulers, husbands, or male relatives sometimes sent girls to nunneries as punishment or to

Sketch showing Hilda of Whitby receiving a copy of the treatise *In Praise of Holy Virgins* from Aldheim, its author. 8th century (?). This extremely rare surviving drawing is now in the library of the Archbishop of Canterbury.

His Grace the Archbishop of Canterbury and the Trustees of Lambeth Palace Library

gain control over their inheritances. Some women went into religious orders simply to escape male authority or an unwanted marriage.

Women in monasteries lived according to the rules of their orders, with their days divided between prayer and work. In the wealthier nunneries, servants generally did the physical labor, but nuns engaged in a variety of activities that included sewing and crafts, studying, and copying manuscripts. Abbesses were among the few medieval women who could act as organizers and administrators, and women had more opportunity for education in the nunneries than in secular society.

Putting Early Medieval Christianity in Perspective

From its position as a persecuted religious sect in the late Roman Empire, Christianity had become by the 5th century one of the essential elements of the new civilization developing in western Europe. The early Christian philosophers and theologians laid the basis for orthodox doctrine and reconciled their beliefs with the Classical heritage of the pagan world. During the centuries from 400 to 700—a period of instability and change as Europe adjusted to the Germanic invasions and the collapse of imperial authority in the West—the church also built an institutional structure that proved remarkably enduring. The bishops of Rome evolved into popes who wielded great power and influence and established the claim to papal supremacy that was to shape much of medieval political thought. The monastic ideal not only gave expression to the deep religious beliefs of early Christians, but also had a considerable impact on secular society. The medieval period was an age of faith, and the church its most important institution.

Questions for Further Study

1. What were the principal doctrinal concerns of the Fathers of the Latin Church?
2. What factors led to the growth of papal power and prestige in the early Middle Ages?
3. What contributions did monasticism make to medieval civilization?
4. In what ways were women excluded from the Christian Church? How did they define roles for themselves within the church?

Suggestions for Further Reading

Brown, Peter. *The Body and Society: Men, Women, and Sexual Renunciation in Early Christianity*. New York, 1988.
Chadwick, Owen. *The Making of the Benedictine Ideal*. London, 1981.
Collins, Roger. *Early Medieval Europe, 300-1000*. New York, 1991.
Herrin, Judith. *The Formation of Christendom*. London, 1989.
Hinson, E. Glenn. *The Early Church: Origins of the Dawn of the Middle Ages*. Nashville, TN, 1996.
Hyldahl, Niels. *The History of Early Christianity*. New York, 1997.
Kelley, Joseph F. *The World of the Early Christians*. Collegeville, MI, 1997.
Lawrence, Clifford H. *Medieval Monasticism*. London, 1984.
Leyser, Conrad. *Authority and Asceticism from Augustine to Gregory the Great*. Oxford, 2000.
MacMullen, Ramsay. *Christianity and Paganism in the Fourth to Eighth Centuries*. New Haven, CT, 1997.
McNamara, Jo Ann Kay. *Sisters in Arms*. Cambridge, MA, 1996.
Ward, Benedicta, trans. *The Sayings of the Desert Fathers*, rev. ed. Kalamazoo, MI, 1984.

InfoTrac College Edition

Enter the search term early *Christianity* using Key Terms.

BYZANTIUM: THE EASTERN EMPIRE

Constantine intended his city on the Bosphorus to be a second Rome. Constantinople was to serve as the Empire's new capital, where church and state would jointly govern in the name of Christ. Its location on the site of the ancient Greek city of Byzantium also gave Constantinople access to the culture of the Greek world. Thus from the beginning three forces dominated the Byzantine Empire: Roman imperial tradition, Christianity (in the Orthodox form defined under Constantine), and Greek culture.

Under Constantine's successors, the Eastern Roman Empire became increasingly detached from the West. Religious disputes split the two halves. While the Western Empire began to crumble as waves of Central Asian peoples invaded the Western provinces, Constantinople provided strong centralized government for the increasingly prosperous cities of Asia Minor, Egypt, and Syria.

In the 6th century, the Emperor Justinian tried to restore the unity of the old Roman Empire. Byzantine forces reconquered Italy and southern Spain and dominated shipping in the Mediterranean. Justinian had the frontiers protected with a vast new system of fortifications and reorganized provincial administration.

His successors faced enemies from the east and north. After a triumphant victory over the Persians in 627, Byzantium failed to prevent the Arab conquest of Syria and Egypt. At the same time Asian peoples like the Bulgars combined with Slavic tribes to push south and overrun the Balkans. An unending series of wars with Arab and Bulgar forces dominated the next three centuries of Byzantine foreign policy.

One of the long-term consequences of Byzantine contacts with the Balkans and other peoples of Eastern Europe was to be the spread there of Orthodox Christianity; Byzantine missionaries converted first the Bulgars and then the Russians. Two of the first missionaries, Cyril and Methodius, invented the Cyrillic alphabet for writing Slavic languages.

At Constantinople the iconoclast controversy (726–843) caused bitter religious conflict. This movement, which sought to ban the use of images in religious art, brought a temporary break in the development of Byzantine art. The artistic achievements of Justinian's reign had marked the First Golden Age. After the defeat of the iconoclasts, the 10th and 11th centuries saw a second wave of artistic creation, marked by the Byzantine love of rich display and magnificent color.

Constantinople's geographical position ensured it a central role in international trade; Byzantine merchants bought goods from Russia, India, and Arabia, and sold them to Western buyers. Its business community was active and prosperous. Both economic and social life were regulated by a complex and rigid state bureaucracy. The tax system was hard on the urban lower classes, but farmworkers on the large monastic and aristocratic estates were reduced to the status of serfs.

NEW ROME IN THE EAST: THE SUCCESSORS OF CONSTANTINE

The foundation of Constantine's new capital in 330 marked one of the great turning points in the history of the Mediterranean. The emperor transferred many features of Roman civilization to the former site of the Greek city of Byzantium. He established a senate there and recreated the structure of the Roman bureaucracy. He encouraged aristocratic Roman families to build villas on the Bosphorus and ordered the construction of a great racetrack to duplicate the chariot races that had provided popular entertainment in his former capital.

More important, he intended to renew and revitalize the centuries-old traditions of Roman government by establishing and maintaining religious unity. The Council of Nicaea of 325 had laid down the tenets of Orthodox Christianity by banning Arianism as heresy (see Topic 21). The Nicene creed, promulgated by the council, declared that God the Father and God the Son were of the same substance. Now the patriarch of Constantinople and the emperor, representing church and state, were to promote these Orthodox teachings and, in their name, preserve the Empire, freed from its pagan associations. Throughout all of the tumultuous struggles of the following centuries, Byzantine rulers maintained their conviction that the Empire was based on the will of the Christian God, as whose representatives they ruled.

If this renewed Empire drew its inspiration from Christianity, and its political and administrative strength from ancient Rome, its cultural foundation was Greek. In its language, literature, and intellectual tradition, the Byzantine Empire followed the Hellenistic reverence for the Classical Greeks and the Golden Age of Periclean Athens. The task for Constantine and his successors was to fuse these three forces—Classical Greece, Rome, and Christianity—into a single civilization and defend them from barbarian attack.

THE BEGINNINGS OF THE BYZANTINE STATE

For all his emphasis on orthodoxy, Constantine had stopped short of making Christianity the official religion of the Roman state. His son and successor, Constantius II (ruled 337–361), maintained his father's caution, while passing edicts against pagan sacrifices and "superstitions."

The Emperor Julian (ruled 361–363) made an attempt to revive the pagan traditions that his predecessor had sought to eliminate. Inspired by the teachings of Neoplatonist philosophers, Julian publicly proclaimed his adherence to paganism and the gods of Homer. He prohibited Christians from teaching literature, but otherwise left them free to practice their religion. The revival did not outlast Julian's reign, and his successors dubbed him Julian the Apostate—he who turns from his own religion.

Toward the end of the century Theodosius the Great (ruled 379–395) proclaimed Orthodox Christianity as established at Nicaea to be the only state religion. His edict banned both paganism and Arianism. Theodosius was the last emperor to rule over a united Empire. Under his two sons, Arcadius and Honorius, the Eastern and Western halves split apart, and within a generation of his death the former Roman territories of Britain, France, Spain, and North Africa had fallen to barbarian conquest.

The break between the two halves was exacerbated by a series of religious controversies that pitted the authority of the pope in Rome against that of the patriarch of Constantinople; furthermore, any chance for the two parts of the Empire to negotiate on equal terms vanished in the course of the 5th century, as the Roman Empire collapsed and the Western church saw its territories conquered.

The geographical position of Constantinople and the rest of the Eastern Empire provided protection from the worst of these invasions. In 400, and again in 471, the capital successfully resisted attack, while wealthy cities like Alexandria and Damascus remained virtually untouched. Trade and commerce continued to flourish. More important, government throughout the Byzantine East remained

The *Barberini Ivory*. Mid-6th century. 1 foot 1½ inches by 10 inches (36 by 30 cm). This famous carving shows a Byzantine Emperor, probably Justinian, riding forward over his victims. To the side of the horse's head, a winged figure descends bearing the symbol of victory, while the soldier on the left also holds a statue of victory. The ultimate source of his triumph is above: a figure of Christ, holding a cross in one hand and blessing the emperor with the other.

©Erich Lessing/Art Resource, NY

under central rule. Constantinople continued to control the army, to collect taxes, and to govern the provinces by appointing local governors.

JUSTINIAN AND THE IMPERIAL QUEST

The extraordinary reign of Justinian the Great (ruled 527–565), the nephew of a Macedonian peasant, dominated the history of 6th-century Byzantium and left its mark on many of the following centuries. In his attempt to recreate the Roman Empire in the East, Justinian waged war on two fronts: abroad, he aimed to recapture imperial territory in the West lost to the barbarians; at home, he used his imperial authority to exert absolute control over church affairs. Both campaigns succeeded in the short term but produced disastrous long-term effects. His most significant permanent contributions to Byzantine civilization were codifying Roman law and building the Church of Hagia Sophia (Holy Wisdom).

THE WARS OF JUSTINIAN

Our knowledge of Justinian as man and emperor owes much to the writings of a contemporary historian, Procopius (born c. 500). *A History of the Wars of Justinian*—his official account of the campaigns of Belisarius, Justinian's leading general—describes the reconquest of Roman Africa from the Vandals (533–534) and Belisarius's brilliant series of triumphs over the Ostrogoths in Italy (536–540). Procopius served on Belisarius's staff as adviser and clearly admired his master, about whom he writes with affection.

In the descriptions of events back in Constantinople that intersperse the military narrative, Procopius's attitude toward Justinian and Theodora, the emperor's powerful wife, is much more ambiguous. His implicit criticism of the imperial couple becomes open hostility in the notorious *Secret History*, which retraces the events covered in the official account, this time in the form of a virulent and sustained attack on them. The character and early career of Theodora—an actress famous for her beauty—are described in scurrilous detail, while Justinian emerges as vicious and vacillating, responsible for every kind of disaster, from bankruptcy to earthquakes.

Whatever the emperor's personal failings, his policies aimed to reinforce the newly reconquered territories. Byzantine fleets patrolled the Mediterranean, protecting trade routes. In Europe, Asia, and Africa, imposing fortifications guarded the Empire's borders, with their reorganized and strengthened garrisons. The imperial staff tightened up provincial administration.

In the capital, Justinian reorganized the mass of Roman law to simplify the machinery of government. The result, the

Church of Hagia Sophia, Constantinople (modern Istanbul), designed for Justinian by Anthemius of Tralles and Isidore of Miletus between 532 and 537. Height 184 feet (55.2 m). The minarets were added after Constantinople fell to the Ottoman Turks in 1453, in order to convert the church into a mosque. The many windows allow light to flood into the building, symbolizing the "Holy Wisdom" that gives the church its name.

© Alan Oddie/PhotoEdit

Corpus Juris Civilis (Corpus of Civil Law), still forms the foundation of actual law in most of continental Europe today.

JUSTINIAN AND THE CHURCH

Military and political supremacy was not enough, however: Justinian was determined to establish his spiritual superiority as God's representative on Earth. This assertion of complete authority is sometimes called "Caesaropapism." One tangible way to achieve it was to give Constantinople (now Istanbul) the foremost church in Christendom as the center of Orthodoxy. To this end, the emperor commissioned the building of the Church of Hagia Sophia, the architectural masterpiece of the First Golden Age of Byzantine art. Justinian's words on first entering the completed church at its grand dedication reflect his intentions: "O Solomon, I have surpassed you!"

In other respects, imperial policy on religious matters created lasting problems. Among the seemingly interminable dogmatic disputes in the Orthodox Church was the question of Monophysitism (see Topic 21). An earlier church council had branded the Monophysite position as heretical, and Justinian set out to eliminate its followers. Wholesale and bloody persecution of those in Syria and Egypt was only lessened by the intervention of Theodora, a Monophysite sympathizer. Popular anger and resentment at the imperial interference remained high. Fed by its memory, the local populations welcomed the Persian and Arab invaders of a few decades later.

Nor were the effects of Justinian's Western conquests destined to last. The imperial administration sought to make good the devastating financial drain of expensive military campaigns by raising taxes, in particular those of the newly reacquired Western provinces. As in the East, the embittered locals subsequently did little to resist the invading enemies of Byzantium, in this case the Germanic Lombards. By the end of the century, Justinian's gains were swept away.

More disasters followed. By concentrating on winning territory in the West, Justinian had been unable to take any significant action against his chief Eastern rivals, the Persians. Only low-key defensive wars and expensive alliances with local enemies of the Persians held back their advance. As the Western conquests disappeared, the threat of first Persian and then Arab invaders cast foreboding shadows over Justinian's legacy.

BYZANTIUM UNDER STRESS: MILITARY THREAT AND RELIGIOUS CONFLICT

The reign of Heraclius (ruled 610–641), son of the Byzantine governor of Africa, began with a string of disastrous losses to the Persians. The Byzantine-held cities of Antioch, Damascus, Jerusalem, and Alexandria all fell to

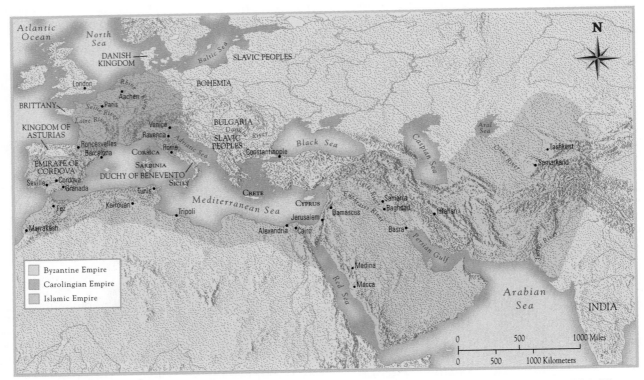

Map 22.1 The Byzantine, Islamic, and Carolingian Empires, c. 800. The Byzantine Empire has shrunk to the western part of Asia Minor—subject to increasing pressure from Islamic forces—the region around Constantinople, and the Italian islands of Sicily and Sardinia. Carolingian forces control northern Italy, while Islam, in a little more than a century, has conquered territory on three continents.

SIGNIFICANT DATES

Byzantine Achievements and Crises

330	Constantinople established
527–565	Reign of Justinian the Great
610–641	Wars of Heraclius against the Persians
642	Muslims take Alexandria
726–787, 813–843	The use of icons banned
811	Bulgars defeat Byzantine army and besiege Constantinople

Persian troops between 611 and 619. To make matters worse, the Avars, another Asian nomadic tribe, moved through Central Europe to threaten the capital.

The turning point came in 626. In that year the heroic efforts of Constantinople's united population defeated an attack on it by the combined forces of Avars, Slavs, and Bulgars. By the end of the century, the latter were to pose a fresh threat, but Heraclius won time to concentrate on defeating the Persians, who in 614 had taken Jerusalem and carried off the wood of the True Cross, Christianity's most sacred relic. In 627 Heraclius moved on the offensive and invaded Persia. In a lightning series of attacks, his troops recaptured all of the lost provinces and forced the Persian king to sue for peace. As Christ's representative on earth, the emperor secured the relic and returned it to Jerusalem. In 629 Heraclius reentered Constantinople in a blaze of glory, the supremacy of his Empire reasserted.

BYZANTIUM AND THE RISE OF ISLAM

Heraclius's triumph was brief. By the end of his reign a new, far more formidable rival appeared on the scene to challenge Byzantine power. Both the Byzantine and Persian empires were weary from centuries of struggle. The rise of Islam and the spread of Arab forces throughout the Mediterranean brought fresh, energetic warrior bands, inspired by their new religion (see Topic 23).

The result was to reverse Heraclius's victories. By the last year of his life, Palestine and Syria were in Muslim hands. In 642 the Muslims took Alexandria and began the conquest of North Africa that would in turn lead them to Spain. Between 673 and 677, Arab forces besieged Constantinople. A further, even more devastating attack came in 717, and only the use of "Greek Fire," the Byzantine secret weapon, saved it from being taken by an Arab fleet ("Greek Fire" was a liquid of unknown composition—probably petroleum-based—thrown in grenades, which caught on fire when wet and burned under water).

THE ICONOCLASTIC CONTROVERSY

No sooner were the Arab forces repulsed than the Byzantine world plunged into a century of religious conflict. The immediate cause was the widespread use of religious

images, or icons—both painted and sculpted—as objects of reverence. The Old Testament prohibited the use of "graven images," but over time icons had become central to Orthodox faith. (The Western church also encouraged the veneration, although not the worship, of sacred images.) The pretext for the ensuing battles over the use of icons was theological, but the bitterness of the conflict reflected the political and social stresses of the times within the Byzantine ruling classes. While the **iconoclastic controversy,** as it became known, took place, another religious revolution was occurring to the south and east of the Byzantine world: the rise of Islam.

In 726 the Emperor Leo III issued an edict against the use of icons and declared that those in existence should be destroyed—the word *iconoclasm* literally means the "breaking of images." Icon worship was reintroduced only in 843. The iconoclastic controversy was more than a learned dispute about theological practice. Echoing Justinian's moves of two centuries earlier, it pitted the authority of the emperor against that of the church. The chief centers of icon veneration were the monasteries, where Byzantine monks jealously guarded sacred images handed down over centuries. Many of these monasteries were the focus of popular religious cults. The iconoclastic emperors were thus challenging church leadership and asserting their own supremacy. At the same time, they also underlined their differences with the Western church because the pope condemned the iconoclastic decrees.

The final triumph of the icon defenders reinforced the power of the monasteries, which were to play an increasingly important part in the later centuries of Byzantine history. At the same time, it was a victory for popular religion and underlined the importance of tradition.

BYZANTIUM IN THE NORTH: THE SLAVS

The most permanent legacy of Byzantine culture was its influence on the Slavs. The origins of these peoples are obscure. Their original homeland seems to have been deep in the forests of western Russia, from where they spread east into the heart of Russia and south into the Balkan peninsula.

It was here, to the north of Greece, that conflicts developed between the Byzantine Empire and the Slavic Bulgars. As early as the reign of Heraclius, Byzantine forces had used the double weapon of military conquest and enforced conversion to Christianity. By the late 7th century, however, the Bulgars were once again on the offensive, and in 716 the Emperor Theodosius III (ruled 715–717) made peace with them and was forced to agree to an annual payment of silks and gold in tribute.

Distracted by the threat of Arab invasions and the iconoclastic controversy at home, successive emperors failed to take decisive action against the buildup of Slavic power. In 811, in one of the most disastrous defeats in Byzantine history, the Bulgarian king Krum (ruled 802–814) destroyed the entire army and its generals and laid siege to Constantinople. The city survived, but the Bulgars continued to threaten the Empire until their final defeat 200 years later, in 1014, by the troops of Basil II (ruled 976–1025), whose grateful subjects dubbed him Basil the Bulgar Slayer.

THE CONVERSION OF RUSSIA

In the mid-9th century, two Byzantine missionaries, Cyril (827–869) and his brother Methodius (825–884), traveled to Moravia (now part of the Czech Republic) to convert the Slavic inhabitants to Orthodox Christianity. As part of their campaign they devised the Glagolitic alphabet, a version of the Greek alphabet, in order to write down the Slavic language. This alphabet, in a modified form known as the Cyrillic, is still used by the Russians and Bulgarians today. Under the counterinfluence of German missionaries, the Moravians eventually rejected Byzantium in favor of Rome, but at the end of the 9th century their Bulgar neighbors and rivals accepted Orthodox Christianity and adopted the new alphabet.

Even more significant in its long-term consequences was the Byzantine impact on Russia. In the course of the 9th century, Scandinavian nomads—they are known as the Rus—overran the steppes of European Russia, to rule over the Slavonic peoples living there. In 862, the Viking Rurik (died c. 879) founded a state at the old Slavonic capital of Novgorod. His dynasty was to rule Russia for the following 700 years. Rurik's successor, Oleg (died c. 912), conquered Kiev in 882 and made it the new capital of the state. Oleg went on to defeat Constantinople in 907. The treaty he negotiated was the basis for trade relations between Byzantium and Kievan Rus, which continued under successive grand princes of Kiev.

Byzantine missionaries, armed with the Cyrillic alphabet, were soon at work at the court of Kiev. In 954 they acquired an eminent new convert in the Dowager Grand Duchess Olga (890–969), who traveled to Constantinople for her formal baptism. Olga eventually became the first Russian saint of the Orthodox Church. Her grandson, Vladimir (ruled 980–1015), after consolidating his rule over a kingdom that stretched from the Baltic to the Ukraine, made a pact in 987 with the Byzantine Emperor Basil II. Converting to Christianity, he was baptized and in return received Basil's sister in marriage. Vladimir's subsequent forcible conversion of his subjects to the Orthodox faith did much to reinforce the authority and prestige of Kiev.

The Orthodox Church soon became a major force in the state. Its clergy established landowning monasteries, on the pattern of those in the Byzantine Empire. Many of the monasteries served as centers of education, where the earliest works of Russian literature were written; most of them were religious in subject. In the visual arts, too, Russian painters and architects followed Byzantine models. The effects on the subsequent development of Russian culture were to last for centuries. Only in the 19th century did Russian intellectuals and artists begin to look to Western Europe for inspiration.

Church of St. Basil, Moscow. The present form of the building dates to the 16th–18th centuries. The various spires and "onion" domes are ultimately derived from the inspiration of Byzantine decoration, although the variety and the use of color are typical of Russian architecture.

© John Lamb/Getty Images

ARTISTIC SPLENDOR IN THE BYZANTINE WORLD

The years following the foundation of Constantinople saw the gradual development of a distinct style of Byzantine art. As successive emperors sought to establish their control over church and state, they used the visual arts as a means of reinforcing their authority. The artistic style that resulted was on the whole static and conservative, emphasizing the glory of God and the splendor of the emperor and his court.

THE FIRST GOLDEN AGE

By the time of Justinian, in the First Golden Age of Byzantine art, architects and mosaic artists had evolved styles capable of expressing the emperor's combined political and spiritual authority. In the great series of mosaics at Ravenna, Justinian's Italian capital, the emperor and his wife Theodora appear as the equivalents of Christ and the Virgin. Justinian is accompanied by 12 companions, corresponding to the 12 apostles, while the embroidery on Theodora's robe shows the three Magi carrying their gifts to Mary and the infant Jesus.

The major monument of Justinian's reign, the Church of Hagia Sophia, combines the basilica plan of Western Christian churches with a vast central dome. Beneath this

Wall mosaic, Church of San Vitale, Ravenna, showing the empress Theodora, wife of Justinian, c. 547. As the empress prepares to enter the sanctuary, its curtain drawn aside by an attendant, she stands beneath the imperial canopy. On the lower border of her robe, an embroidery shows the Three Magi (Kings) who visited the infant Jesus, placing Theodora in their exalted company.

floating dome—described by one of its first viewers as "like the radiant heavens"—the inside space glitters with gold mosaics illuminated by beams of light from the hundreds of windows. Even today the effect is dramatic. Justinian's contemporaries, overwhelmed by the sweep of heavily embroidered vestments and the pungent smell of incense, might well have believed themselves to be in the presence of the divine.

THE SECOND GOLDEN AGE

The two centuries following Justinian produced nothing to equal his achievement. Constant warfare abroad diverted funds for other, less exalted purposes, while the iconoclastic controversy effectively blocked artistic production at home. The Second Golden Age of Byzantine art, which lasted from the late 9th to the 11th centuries, followed the defeat of the iconoclasts.

Many of the greatest achievements of the Second Golden Age show an emotional, suffering quality that was new to Byzantine art. Artists of the First Golden Age had depicted the wisdom and power of Christ and either avoided the Crucifixion as a subject or showed the crucified Christ as triumphant. Perhaps as a result of the victory of popular religion over the iconoclasts, Crucifixion scenes in the Second Golden Age depict Christ in more human terms. The ex-

pression of intense emotion reaches its extreme in a cycle of paintings dating from the early 14th century, which decorate a chapel in the former Church of St. Saviour in Chora at Istanbul. The dynamic and energetic figure of Christ who sweeps down to limbo to raise the dead seems a far cry from the static images of earlier Byzantine art.

THE ART OF ICONS

The earliest Christian sacred images, according to a tradition often cited by the defenders of icons, were the portraits of Christ painted by St. Luke. We know little about the development of icon painting before the end of the iconoclastic controversy because the iconoclasts destroyed the existing ones. With the renewal of their production in the 9th century, a standard type began to circulate, with fixed patterns of composition and decoration repeated on countless examples—the Orthodox Church required that these images be only two-dimensional.

The veneration of icons spread to the newly converted state of Kiev, and they remained popular in Russia over the following centuries. Russian painters continued to develop their own styles after the fall of Constantinople, thereby continuing the evolution of Byzantine art even after the end of the Byzantine Empire.

A C R O S S   C U L T U R E S

BISHOP LIUTPRAND IN CONSTANTINOPLE

Liutprand of Cremona (920–972) was the son of prosperous Lombard parents, whose father had served as Italian ambassador to Constantinople. Liutprand became private secretary to the Italian king, Berengar of Ivrea, and went on diplomatic missions to the Byzantine court in 949 and again in 968. The chronicles of his trips there provide a rare and precious Western perspective on the ritual and ceremony of a 10th-century Byzantine court, as well as court politics.

Courtesy of William Duiker

In 949, traveling with a representative of the Holy Roman Emperor, Liutprand arrived in Constantinople after a journey of six weeks by ship from Venice. Soon after their arrival, both men were each led by two eunuchs into the presence of the reigning Emperor, Constantine Porphyrogenitus. Liutprand describes in some detail the gilded bronze throne and mechanical birds, all singing different songs. The throne "was of immense size, made either of wood or bronze (for I cannot be sure), and guarded by gilded lions who beat the ground with their tails and emitted dreadful roars, their mouths open and their tongues quivering." It sat on a moving platform: "After I had three times made my

ECONOMIC VITALITY AND SOCIAL INEQUALITY

The ability of the Byzantine Empire to survive depended on its financial stability. During the centuries of decline in the West, trade and commerce continued to flourish in the Eastern Empire. City life remained active, not only at Constantinople but also at other centers such as Antioch, Thessalonika, and Trebizond. Production of silk and of gold embroidery, and the maintenance of a stable gold and silver currency, enriched the economy.

With the slow revival of Western Europe that began in the 9th century, Byzantium served as the link for trade between East and West. Constantinople's central position in the Mediterranean made it a natural marketplace, and traders from Italy and farther west came there to buy precious stones and spices from Arabia and India, skins and furs from Russia, and slaves from Africa and the Caucasus.

Although individual merchants and craftsmen profited from their work, trade remained under state control. Official guilds were in charge of manufacturing, and sales took place at state salerooms. The taxes levied on these transactions enriched the imperial treasury, which also collected revenues from state-owned farms, mines, and quarries.

BYZANTINE LAND TENURE

For all the importance of domestic and foreign trade, the chief and continuing economic basis of the Empire's prosperity was agriculture. Both landowners and those who worked it paid taxes. Originally Byzantine farmers were small land-

obeisance, I raised my head and lo! He whom I had seen only a moment before on a throne scarcely elevated from the ground was now clad in different robes and sitting on a level with the roof. How this was achieved I cannot tell, unless it was by a device similar to that we employ for lifting the timbers of a wine press."

Discovering to his embarrassment that the Holy Roman Emperor's ambassador had brought valuable gifts from his master, while he had been sent empty-handed, Luitprand presented Constantine with some gifts that he had brought and was duly rewarded with an invitation to a banquet. As his account makes clear, the occasion was a splendid one, with the food served on dishes of gold, and followed by more mechanical wonders: "After the meal, fruit is brought on in three golden bowls, too heavy for men to lift. Through openings in the ceiling there hang three ropes, covered with gilded leather, with gold rings at their ends. To these rings are attached the handles projecting from the bowls and, with the help of four or five men standing below, the huge vessels are swung on to the table and removed again in the same fashion."

Nineteen years later Liutprand returned to Constantinople, this time as the representative of the Holy Roman Emperor, to receive much less friendly treatment: "The palace in which we were confined was so far from the residence of the Emperor that when we walked there—for we were not permitted to ride—we arrived exhausted. To make matters worse, the Greek wine was quite undrinkable, having been mixed with pitch, resin and plaster."

The Emperor then reigning, Nicephoros Phocas, was outraged at Liutprand's claim to represent a fellow Emperor—after all, the Roman Empire was one and indivisible, and its only ruler occupied the Byzantine throne, as Leo, Nicephoras's brother pointed out: "He called you not Emperor but—most insultingly—King." After an unfriendly audience with Nicephoras, even the food tasted "perfectly disgusting, washed down with oil after the manner of drunkards." His mission a failure, Liutprand left Constantinople, a city that he had earlier found so overwhelming, but that now seemed "a city full of lies, tricks, perjury and greed."

Liutprand's vivid accounts of his missions succeed, in fact, in conveying two aspects of the Byzantine world: the richness and elaborate character of court life and the kind of complex political scheming that has given a special meaning to the word *Byzantine*.

holders, working their own plots of land. Over time, however, individual private landowners began to build large estates, on which the peasants became reduced to the level of serfs, bound to the land and unable to alter their status.

The earliest of these estates belonged to the wealthy aristocratic families of the capital, but with the rise of the monasteries much of the richest land passed into the control of the church. Some small private farmers managed to survive, but by the later history of the Empire most of the state's agricultural revenues came from the large tenant farms.

SOCIETY AND CLASS

From the beginning Byzantine society was based on a rigid system of class hierarchy, with the emperor at the head of both church and state. His chief rivals for power were the wealthy aristocratic families and, increasingly, the monks of the richer monasteries.

Some rulers made an effort to protect the rights of the poorer citizens, while extending the power of the central government. Basil the Bulgar Slayer, for example, confiscated the estates of owners who had acquired them over the previous 70 years and forced more established owners to pay the tax arrears of their peasant laborers. On the whole, though, the wealthy landowners continued to expand at the expense of both the central authority and the workers. The same process occurred in the cities, where the urban lower classes bore an increasing share of the tax burden.

Middle-class Byzantine citizens benefited from a higher level of education than their equivalents in the West or in the Islamic world. Literacy was encouraged, and devotion to

Fresco from the Church of Christ in Chora (now the Kariye Museum), Istanbul, c. 1310–1320. The scene is that of the *Anastasis,* in which Christ descends to Hell to destroy Satan and his works, and, helping Adam and Eve rise from their tombs, begin the Resurrection. The energetic, striding figure of Christ, contained in an almond-shaped *mandorla,* is typical of Late Byzantine art.

Ara Guler, Istanbul

Christian texts did not mean that Classical Greek literature was neglected. Most of the Classical texts we possess, in fact, owe their survival to the Byzantine scribes who continued to copy them. Byzantine exiles, fleeing from the Ottoman Turks in the last days of the Empire, brought many Greek manuscripts with them to the West.

Nor was education exclusively a male preserve. Although young women of upper-class families did not attend school, they had private tutors and on occasion developed careers. Some became physicians, while others established themselves as literary figures. The most famous was the princess Anna Comnena (1083–c. 1153), whose history of the reign of her father, the Emperor Alexius (ruled 1081–1118), shows a profound knowledge of ancient literature and philosophy. Violently anti-Western—in condemning the First Crusade, she apologizes for sullying her pages with the names of Norman barbarians—she paints a fascinating picture of her childhood and early political career, and at one point she apparently took part in a plot to assassinate her brother.

THE BUREAUCRACY

The Byzantine Empire survived for a millennium in the face of continual external threats and internal feudings largely because of the efficiency of its bureaucracy. The education of the middle and upper classes provided a substantial body of citizens on whom to draw for the state government. Whereas in the West only the clergy were literate, lay literacy provided the Byzantine world with an effective civil service.

This bureaucracy, under the supervision of imperial officials, regulated just about all aspects of Byzantine life and society. State bureaucrats controlled prices, issued licenses, regulated wages, and supervised exports and imports. Other offices dealt with education and religion, enforcing such matters as the observance of the sabbath. The law courts, the army and navy, and the diplomatic service all had their own civil service departments to run and control them. The efficiency of this administrative system allowed the Empire to survive many of its most severe crises.

Putting Byzantium in Perspective

In many ways the world of Byzantium seems remote and exotic. The obsession with religion and the finer points of theological dogma, the tumultuous nature of Byzantine politics, with its labyrinthine palace intrigues (which give the word *Byzantine* its modern sense), the glittering, fairytale qualities of Byzantine art—all of these aspects seem more alien to the early 21st century than the workaday world of Byzantium's predecessors, the Romans.

Yet behind the gilded façade lay practical and solid achievements. In political and military terms, Byzantine actions preserved Western Europe for almost 1,000 years from a bewildering range of enemies. Constantinople sustained the economy of the eastern Mediterranean region over the centuries that preceded the revival of the West. Culturally, Byzantium provided the link with the world of Classical Antiquity.

The later stages of Byzantine history (see Topic 27) were clouded by hostility between Eastern and Western Christians. The schism of 1054 and the Crusades fed a mutual hatred, which eventually left Constantinople helpless in the face of its Turkish conquerors of 1453. If for the West the Byzantines were "the dregs of the dregs," the Byzantines saw their Western rivals as "the children of darkness." Yet without the stubborn and often heroic survival of civilization in the East, most of the cultural legacy of ancient Greece would have been lost, and the Renaissance, one of the highest points of Western history and culture, would have been unimaginable.

Questions for Further Study

1. What are the main similarities and differences between the former Roman Empire and the Byzantine Empire? How did the function of the emperor differ in the two institutions?
2. What can we learn about Byzantine society and culture from a study of Byzantine art?
3. What lasting effect did Byzantine civilization produce on the development of Western culture?
4. How successful was Justinian in his attempt to recreate the Roman Empire in the East? What were the main problems he faced?

Suggestions for Further Reading

Borsook, Eve. *Messages in Mosaic: The Royal Programmes of Norman Sicily*. Oxford, 1990.

Cormack, Robin. *Painting the Soul: Icons, Death Masks and Shrouds*. London, 1997.

Evans, Helen C., and William D. Wixom, eds. *The Glory of Byzantium: Art and Culture of the Middle Byzantine Era* A.D. *843-1261*. New York, 1997.

Herrin, Judith. *Women in Purple: Rulers of Medieval Byzantium*. London, 2001.

Kazhdan, Alexander, ed. *The Oxford Dictionary of Byzantium*. Oxford, 1991.

Maguire, Henry. *The Icons of Their Bodies: Saints and Their Images in Byzantium*. Princeton, NJ, 1996.

Mathews, Thomas F. *Byzantium from Antiquity to the Renaissance*. New York, 1998.

Ousterhout, Robert. *Master Builders of Byzantium*. Princeton, NJ, 2000.

Treadgold, Warren T. *A Concise History of Byzantium*. New York, 2001.

Williams, Stephen, and Gerard Friell. *The Rome That Did Not Fall: The Survival of the East in the Fifth Century*. New York, 1999.

InfoTrac College Edition

Enter the search term *Byzantium* using the Subject Guide.

Enter the search term *early Christianity* using Key Terms.

EUROPE AND ISLAM

The history of Islam begins with the birth of Muhammad, around 570. At that time, the Arabian peninsula was inhabited by tribes of Arab nomads, whose way of life had been untouched by the rise and fall of the Roman Empire. Muhammad's early career as a merchant ended around 610, when he experienced the spiritual revelation that forms the basis of Islam. He regarded the new religion that he founded as the highest and final stage in the spiritual development that had led first to Judaism and then to Christianity. Islam's chief teachings are expounded in the Koran, the sacred text put together by the time of the Prophet's death in 632.

Muhammad regarded Islam as a universal faith, which would serve to unite the world. To this end his immediate successors began a series of military actions against their Arab neighbors. In 636 Arab forces defeated the Byzantine army in Syria; 10 years later they added Egypt to their conquests. At the same time the Persian Empire quickly disintegrated under Arab invasion, falling under their control by 651. Early in the 8th century an Arab army crossed from North Africa to conquer southern Spain.

Both Islam and the Arabic language served as unifying forces over this vast range of territories. Islamic culture flourished in great urban centers linked by long-distance trade routes stretching as far as equatorial Africa and China by the 10th century.

The two regions of Europe to fall under direct Muslim rule were Spain and Sicily. Muslim troops conquered Spain in the early 8th century, establishing Cordova as its capital. A later Muslim kingdom was founded by the Nasrid dynasty at Granada. The rise of the Christian kingdoms of northern Spain in the 13th century presented a growing challenge to the Muslims, who were finally driven from the Spanish peninsula in 1492. Arab forces made their first important conquests in Sicily in 831, and they retained control over the island until 1060. Their Norman conquerors maintained many aspects of Muslim culture, diffusing them in due course throughout Europe.

The overall Islamic influence on Western culture was vast. It ranged from new systems of irrigation to paper making. Islamic scholars preserved ancient Greek scientific texts and used them as the basis of their own studies. When Arab discoveries eventually reached the West, they revolutionized fields such as medicine, mathematics, and astronomy. In the arts, Muslim poetry and music inspired the troubadours of medieval France, while the Western intellectual tradition owes an enormous debt to the Muslim world's preservation of the works of Aristotle.

THE ARABIAN PENINSULA AND ITS PEOPLES

Islam, the religion today of around 600 million Muslims, was born in the Arabian peninsula (the word *Muslim* literally means "one who submits"). The land is mainly desert, with some fertile areas in the south where monsoon rains swell the mountain rivers. To the north only a few oases offer meager vegetation for the nomads and their flocks. As early as the 3rd millennium B.C., people from Arabia fled north from their inhospitable territory. The ancestors of the Babylonians who settled in Mesopotamia and those of the Hebrews who finally arrived in Palestine were all Arabian in origin; their languages belonged to the family known as Semitic (the two principal Semitic languages spoken today are Arabic and Hebrew).

In the 4th century B.C., the kingdom of Nabataea formed a center of the caravan route from Arabia to the Mediterranean. As the Roman Empire expanded southward, the Romans allowed the Nabataeans the status of independent allies. In A.D. 106, however, in the reign of Trajan, Nabataea fell to Roman forces. Around the middle of the 3rd century A.D., the Arab Queen Zenobia (ruled 267–272) ruled over the independent state of Palmyra. Famous for her beauty and ruthlessness—she may have arranged the murder of her husband, as the result of which she came to power—she was eventually defeated by a Roman army led by the Emperor Aurelian. Her conqueror brought the formidable Zenobia back to Italy to march in his triumphal procession and then pensioned her off in a villa outside Rome.

The nomadic tribes of Arabia who maintained their ancient lifestyle over the centuries lived on the meat and milk of their flocks and on the fruit produced in the desert oases. They worshiped the forces of nature and natural objects: trees, caves, springs, and large stones. At the city of Mecca, in the building called the Ka'bah, there still stands a black stone that was the object of pilgrimages long before the time of Muhammad.

MUHAMMAD, THE FOUNDER OF ISLAM

Mecca, the Prophet's birthplace, lies in the stony, barren valley of the Hijaz. The city was subject to the Kuraish tribe. Its prosperity depended on pilgrims to the Ka'bah and on its position on the caravan route between southern Arabia and Syria. The traditional date of Muhammad's birth is 570.

Muhammad's father, a merchant, and his mother both died shortly after his birth, leaving him in the care of relatives. As a young man he worked for a rich merchant's widow, 15 years his senior, whom he subsequently married. He seems to have devoted himself enthusiastically to her business interests, and trade forms a frequent metaphor in his later teachings. In the course of his travels he met both

The Sanctuary at Mecca, the chief focus of pilgrims making the *haj*, or pilgrimage. At its center stands the Ka'bah, or Black Stone, marked according to tradition with the footprints of Abraham. The Black Stone thus dated to long before the time of Muhammad, who reconsecrated it in 632, the year of his death.

Mehmet Biber/Photo Researchers, Inc.

Jews and Christians and began to feel unsatisfied with the Arabian pagan tradition in which he had grown up.

In 610 Muhammad experienced a spiritual revelation when a voice from heaven told him that there was but one god, Allah. In later visions he received further illuminations, which formed the basis for the new religion of Islam that he began to preach. His fellow citizens were hostile, so in 622 he and his few followers were forced to move to a nearby city to which they gave the name of Medina ("the City of the Prophet"). This move, known as the "Hegira," became the symbolic inauguration of Islam: 622 is the first year of the Muslim era.

By the time of his triumphant return to Mecca in 630, Muhammad had established the notion of a *jihad,* a holy war to convert unbelievers, in which those who die fighting for the cause win salvation. (This doctrine became less important over time, however, because it was softened by the requirement to "strive in God's Way." It was revived by some modern Muslim fundamentalist groups.)

Muhammad's own death in 632 saw the new faith well established in Arabia. Within a century Muslim forces were on the offensive against the Byzantine Empire and in Western Europe, and the teachings of Islam had arrived in India.

THE DOCTRINES OF ISLAM

Muhammad conceived of Islam as the final stage, the spiritual fulfillment, of the Jewish and Christian tradition. Like the two earlier religions, Islam is monotheistic, emphasizes personal responsibility and morality, and is based on a written, sacred text. Muslims regard the Koran, the collection of teachings written down during the Prophet's life, as the com-

pletion of the Old and New Testaments and think of themselves, like Jews and Christians, as "people of the Book."

At the heart of Islam are the beliefs that Allah is omnipotent, that Muhammad is his last and greatest prophet, and that humans will be judged on the basis of their actions. On Judgment Day, Allah will reward the good with eternal life in paradise and condemn the wicked to everlasting torture.

Islam requires its followers to pray five times a day, facing in the direction of Mecca, to fast during the daylight hours of the sacred month of Ramadan, to give alms to the poor, and if possible to make a pilgrimage—or "haj"—to the holy city of Mecca at least once in their lives. The consumption of alcohol and of certain foods is prohibited. Traditionally, men can marry four wives (although only a minority do) and can divorce by pronouncing a series of formulas.

THE SUCCESSORS OF THE PROPHET

Upon Muhammad's death, his followers named Abu-Bakr, his father-in-law, **caliph.** The term, meaning "deputy of the Prophet," was used for the next 300 years for the supreme head of all Muslims. When Abu-Bakr's successor, the caliph Umar, died in 644, the naming of his replacement caused a split in the Muslim world that still exists today. The majority supported Uthman, a member of the powerful Umayyad family of Mecca, which had earlier opposed Muhammad; others rallied around Ali, the Prophet's cousin and son-in-law.

When Ali was murdered, the Umayyad family took control of the caliphate and held it until 750. Ali's followers broke off from their fellow Muslims to form a minority sect known as Shi'ites: to this day, Shi'ites—who form about one-tenth of the world's Muslim population—believe

A page from the Koran. 8th century. 8 inches by 13 inches (23.6 by32.5 cm). The highly stylized form of writing, known as *Kufic,* is one of the earliest Arabic calligraphic styles. The decoration is provided by gold leaf.

© bpk, Berlin, Kulturbesitz, Berlin

that only a descendant of Ali has any authority over Muslims. Mainstream Muslim believers are called Sunnites.

Muhammad's immediate successors defeated the Byzantine forces occupying Syria in 636 and occupied their principal cities: Antioch, Damascus, and Jerusalem. The following year it was the Persians' turn: Ctesiphon, the Persian capital, fell to Arab forces, who were in control of the entire Persian Empire by 651. The conquests continued under the Umayyad Dynasty (who made Damascus their capital in 661), with the first Arab moves into Europe. In 711, using North Africa as a base (Egypt had fallen in 646), Muslim troops occupied southern Spain.

The only significant failure in the Arab offensive was its inability to take Constantinople, despite a massive attack launched there in 717. The defeat seriously weakened the prestige of the Umayyad Dynasty. In 750 a new family, the Abbasids, took over the caliphate and moved the capital from Damascus to Baghdad.

ISLAM AND THE MEDITERRANEAN: CONQUEST, CONVERSION, AND SETTLEMENT

With their conquest of territory in the Mediterranean and the Middle East, the Arabs spread their religion and culture in re-gions that were once governed by the Romans. The Umayyad caliphs followed the example of the Roman and Byzantine empires in seeking to construct a centralized state. Their capital of Damascus became the seat of a government bureaucracy from which officials administered this new Arab empire. Many of the new bureaucrats were Christian Egyptians and Syrians. The Umayyad caliphate did not particularly encourage conversion to Islam among their Christian or Jewish subjects, whom they accepted as fellow "peoples of the Book." This policy was successful in Syria, where there were many Christians. Farther east, particularly in the former Persian Empire, it caused resentment among new converts and pious Muslims. As a result, many of the local population there became Shi'ite Muslims, supporting the cause of Ali, the Umayyads' opponent. Most Muslims in modern Iran (the name for Persia since 1935) are still Shi'ites.

SOCIETY UNDER MUSLIM RULE
Islamic society was cosmopolitan and based on trade. The chief cities occupied strategic positions on the major commercial routes between the western Mediterranean and the East. By the 10th century, Muslim traders were active south of the Sahara and as far east as China.

Because the Koran claimed that all Muslims were equal, social equality for males was also the norm—by contrast with the far more hierarchic society of the Byzantine Empire. At the Abbasid court of Baghdad, few bureaucratic

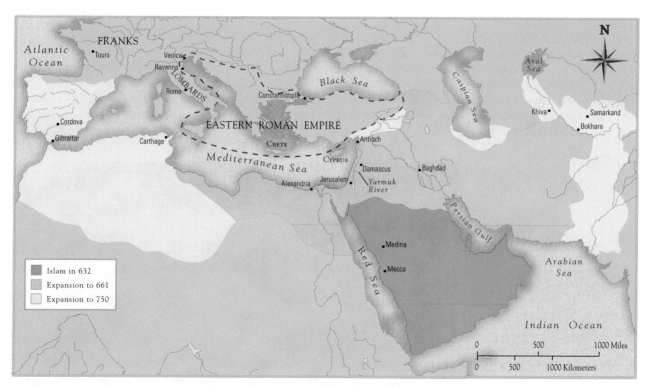

 Map 23.1 The Growth of the Islamic Caliphate, 632–750. The period between the death of Muhammad in 632 and the transfer of the Caliphate from Damascus to Baghdad in 750 saw the spread of Islamic rule in all directions: from Spain in the west to Samarkand (in modern Uzbekistan) in the east; from the Sahara in the south to the Aral Sea in the north. The only rival power in the Mediterranean was the Eastern Roman Empire of Byzantium. Go to http://info.wadsworth.com/053461065X for an interactive version of this map.

SIGNIFICANT DATES

The Spread of Islam

c. 570	Birth of Muhammad
622	The Hegira: Muhammad flees Mecca
632	Death of Muhammad
636	Syria under Muslim control
646	Muslim conquest of Egypt
651	Persia under Muslim control
661–750	Umayyad caliphate in Damascus
710–711	Muslim invasion of Spain
732	Muslims defeated near Tours
750–1258	Abbasid caliphate in Baghdad

positions were hereditary, and talent rather than birth was the way to achieve a career in public life. Education was encouraged. Estimates place the rate of literacy in the Arab world around 1000 at 20 percent of Muslim males, a level that Western European society was not to achieve for centuries. Furthermore, both the Umayyad and Abbasid courts placed a high value on learning and science, commissioning translations into Arabic of important works in Persian and Greek.

WOMEN IN THE MUSLIM WORLD

One of the consequences of the mobility of social status was that a man's position could be improved or damaged by his treatment of his possessions. This led to a curious double standard in the treatment of women. On the one hand, a man's wives were sacrosanct; in the case of wealthy families, they lived in seclusion, cut off from other males. On the other hand, the possession of large numbers of female servants and concubines was a sign of prosperity. Living in the harem, a private part of the house, and guarded by eunuchs (castrated men), elite Muslim wives had little to do other than to promote their own interests and those of their children by complex intrigues. Such complicated and restrictive lifestyles did not, of course, apply to peasant or nomad families.

It must be added that the position of Islam with regard to family life was—and is—complex. The Koran claims a superior right for both fathers and husbands, legalizes polygamy, and permits both husbands and wives to initiate divorce proceedings, although the process is more complicated for women. At the same time it regulates the terms by which men should behave toward women and children under their protection and forbids killing female infants. By comparison with the treatment of women in the pre-Islamic Arab world, these laws seem comparatively humane. Some later interpreters of the Koran, however, took the laws to harsh extremes, while in many modern Muslim countries moves have been made to liberalize them.

SPAIN AND SICILY: MUSLIM RULE IN EUROPE

The first thrust of Muslim conquest had been north and east, toward Syria and Persia. Then, with Egypt won in 642, the Arabs could turn their attention to the western Mediterranean. The former Roman provinces along the coast of North Africa were at that time under Byzantine rule, reconquered by the Emperor Justinian from the Vandals. Justinian's heavy taxation of the provincials, and the persecution of local Monophysite "heretics" (see Topic 22), had created a climate of bitter resentment against Constantinople. When the Arabs moved westward from Egypt, the local population of Berbers (North African tribespeople) resisted as well as they could but refused to cooperate with their Byzantine rulers.

Aerial view of the Great Mosque, Kairouan, Tunisia, c. 836–875. Built under Abbasid rule, the mosque is at the end of a huge courtyard, the entrance to which is crowned by a tower. The entire complex, surrounded by an outer wall, is said to be based on the plan of Muhammad's house at Medina.

© Roger Wood/CORBIS

By 708 the entire region was under Arab control. With the remnants of the Byzantine population dead or in exile, the Berbers put up no more resistance. Many of them converted to Islam (virtually all present-day Berbers are Muslims), and their numbers swelled the ranks of the Arab army, which was now ready for its final push into Christian Europe.

THE MUSLIMS IN SPAIN

On July 25, 711, a Muslim force consisting largely of Berber soldiers crossed the Straits of Gibraltar and landed on the southern coast of Spain. Gibraltar, the mountain on which the troops assembled, takes its name from their leader Tariq: "Jabal Tariq" means "the hill of Tariq." The expedition was intended as a reconnoitering mission, but Tariq pushed on and defeated a Visigothic army the following day. (For the earlier history of the Germanic kingdoms of Southern Europe, see Topic 20.) Roderick, the last Visigothic king, was killed in the fighting.

Quick to follow Tariq and jealous of his success, Tariq's superiors sent reinforcements, mainly Arab soldiers. The combined Muslim forces soon overran the whole of Spain, establishing Cordova as its capital in 725. Flushed by their victories, the Arab commanders drove on north across the Pyrenees, into the Kingdom of the Franks. Here they were

Court of the Lions, the Alhambra, Granada, c. 1391. The palace of the Alhambra was the last great work of Muslim rule in Spain. The use of water—fountains and a waterway decorate the court—and the slender columns and rich decorations are characteristic of Arabic architecture of the period; the English word *arabesque* is derived from the style.

finally brought to a halt by a Frankish army led by Charles Martel, who checked the Muslim forces at the Battle of Tours in 732. This was to be the farthest north the Muslims reached, but they retained control of some towns in southern France for the next three decades. Muslim rule in Spain was to last for more than three centuries.

By around 850, Cordova had a population of more than 1 million, and the Great Mosque there became a center of pilgrimage rivaling Mecca—the building could hold 200,000 people at one time. Cordova's university attracted the finest Islamic and Jewish scholars of the time, and its libraries were the most complete in the world. There were 12 royal palaces in Cordova, each with its own name: "the Flower," "the Diadem," "the Joyful." A thousand mosques, hundreds of public baths, and botanical gardens filled with exotic plants adorned the city. Today only the Great Mosque survives, covered over by a later church.

Around 1100 the Christian kingdoms of the north began to drive back the forces of Islam (for an account of the "Reconquista," see Topic 26). Even when the rest of Spain had been reconquered, the state of Granada remained under the Muslim rule of the Nasrid Dynasty, a center of art and learning, until the expulsion of the Muslims from Spain in 1492. The Royal Palace of the Alhambra, with its gardens and fountains, and forests of slender columns supporting tiled and honeycombed walls, still survives; one visitor described its beauty as "a dream petrified by the wand of a magician."

SICILY AND THE MUSLIMS

Only one city in Europe rivaled the splendor of Cordova in the Middle Ages: Palermo, in western Sicily. The Arabs first arrived in Sicily in 827; by 831 they were in control of Palermo. Muslim rule brought vast numbers of North African and Spanish settlers and was marked by a spirit of tolerance.

By 900, Palermo was one of the great centers of art and scholarship. Surpassed in size in the Christian world only by Constantinople and Cordova, its population at the time is estimated at 300,000. The island's agriculture flourished, and cotton, oranges, and sugar cane were cultivated in Europe for the first time.

Muslim influence in Sicily was so strong that when, in 1091, the island fell into the hands of the Norman Count Roger de Hautville (1031–1101), its culture remained markedly Muslim. Norman knights took up the flowing robes of Arab dress and built their own alhambras in which they installed harems. Roger's court was the wealthiest and most brilliant in Europe.

The spirit of tolerance lasted into the reign of Frederick II in the 13th century (for a full discussion of Frederick Hohenstaufen, see Topic 29). Frederick's court, where Islamic, Christian, and Jewish cultures combined, was famous throughout Europe for its luxury and learning. Under Frederick's influence, Muslim scientific and intellectual achievements spread throughout Europe and profoundly influenced Western culture.

SCIENCE AND CULTURE: THE ISLAMIC IMPACT ON THE WEST

The impact of the Islamic world on Europe was threefold. Practically, Islamic science, industry, and technology developed or passed on new ideas and methods that eventually greatly affected European social and economic life. Intellectually, Muslim thinkers and writers preserved and interpreted the tradition of Classical and Hellenistic Greece. In the arts, Muslim poetry and architecture inspired creative movements in the West.

Industrial production of goods for trading provided the basis of Islamic commerce. Individual cities had their specialties, such as woven figured silk—or damask—in Damascus and fine swords in the Spanish city of Toledo. Techniques of manufacture became refined, and the secrets of Muslim craftsmen in due course helped European workers improve their products. Muslim traders brought back the art of papermaking from China. When the technology finally reached Europe, it provided a whole new industry that revolutionized European cultural life.

Western farmers benefited from improved techniques, devised for the extreme climates of many Arab lands and first introduced into Europe in Sicily and Spain; they included improved irrigation. Among the new plants cultivated was coffee, which is indigenous to tropical Africa. Arab settlers in Ethiopia first began making a hot drink from pulverized coffee beans around 1000. The new drink caught on, and soon enterprising dealers were opening coffee houses in Mecca, Damascus, and Constantinople. The Italians learned how to make marzipan, a mixture of ground almonds and fine sugar, from their Muslim rulers—marzipan candies are still popular in Sicily.

MUSLIM SCIENCE AND MEDICINE

In physics, Arabs invented the science of optics and used magnifying lenses to perform experiments involving the transmission, speed, and refraction of light. Arab chemists discovered or created new substances and compounds, including carbonate of soda, nitrate of silver, and sulfuric acid.

Perhaps the most overarching Arab contribution to the world of science—and to many other fields—was in mathematics. Borrowing a method of numbering (which became known as "Arabic numerals") from the Hindus, together with the concept of zero, they developed a decimal system and devised plane and spherical trigonometry, besides making progress in algebra.

Advances in medicine were equally remarkable. The greatest physician of the Muslim world was Razi (c. 865–c. 930), known in the West as Rhazes. Head of the hospital of Baghdad, he wrote treatises on smallpox and measles (he was the first to discover the difference between them), as well as a compendium of medical knowledge. Latin translations of his works had an immense influence on the later development of medical science in the West. Other discoveries included the diagnosis of stomach cancer, improved

treatment of eye diseases, and an understanding of the nature and spread of infectious diseases.

Equally impressive was the hospital system, which reached a level attained in most European countries only in the 19th century. Hospitals had separate wards for the various fields of medicine, a dispensary for the preparation of medicine, and a library. Medical students attended lectures and demonstrations by the leading physicians and surgeons, who also conducted the students' examinations and issued licenses to practice.

MUSLIM PHILOSOPHY AND THE GREEKS

The texts of Plato, Aristotle, and the Neoplatonist philosophers, translated into Arabic, formed the basis of much Muslim speculation. The great scientist and philosopher known in the West as Avicenna (980–1037) was one of the leading interpreters of Aristotle, and translations of his works into Latin rekindled knowledge of Aristotle's ideas in the West.

Not all scholars accepted the rational approach of the Greek thinkers, and the split between those Muslim scholars who translated and used the Greco-Roman classics and those who rejected them was to become a lasting division in Muslim culture. The mystical philosopher al-Ghazali (1059–1111) wrote *The Incoherence of the Philosophers* to attack all philosophical systems, including those of Plato and Aristotle. A generation later the doctor and philosopher Averroes (1126–1198) answered him in *The Incoherence of the Incoherence*. Averroes was the leading Aristotelian of his day, seeking to reconcile Greek philosophy and Muslim teachings. Within half a century of his death, Latin translations of his books were influencing Jewish and Christian thinkers in Western Europe.

ISLAM AND THE ARTS

For most cultured Muslims, the highest form of art was poetry. One of the earliest and most attractive of Arab poets, Abu Nuwas (762–815) established the popularity of lyrical love poetry, drinking songs, and satirical verse. A favorite at the court of Harun al-Rashid, he appears as one of the characters in the most famous of all Arabic works of literature, *The Arabian Nights*. This celebrated collection of stories is told by the ingenious Scheherazade night after night to her royal husband, to deter him from having her put to death: The cynical and embittered king, after his experience of his previous wives' infidelity, has decided to take a new wife each night and execute her the next morning. Scheherazade's fascinating and exciting tales, needless to say, save her life.

The best-known Islamic poet for most Western readers is Omar Khayyam (d. ?1122), if only through the "translation"—rewriting, rather—of his work the *Rubaiyat* by the Victorian poet Edward Fitzgerald. Omar's skeptical irony and blend of enjoyment and regret in the poem represent only one side of his output. He also wrote treatises on algebra and physics.

The love songs of the Muslim poets of Spain had a special influence on European literature. The traveling poets,

Yoram Lehmann, Jerusalem

The Dome of the Rock, Jerusalem. Late 7th century. After Mecca, this is the second most holy site in the Muslim world. A late medieval tradition connects the site of the building with Muhammad's flight to heaven, and other versions claim it as the spot where Abraham prepared to sacrifice his son. The blue decorations on the upper part of the walls are made of tiles.

or troubadours, of southwestern France picked up the Muslim approach to "courtly" or idealized love, whereby the submissive lover seeks his reward in devotion to his lady, rather than in the fulfillment of his passion. Thus ideas and conceits devised to entertain the courts of Damascus or Baghdad circulated in the aristocratic world of 12th- and 13th-century France. From there they spread to Germany in the work of the German lyric poets known as the Minnesingers.

Islam's ban on the representation of the human form in painting or sculpture—ignored in the later Islamic art of Persia and Moghul India—meant that Arab artists often worked in fields that Western traditions regard as "minor": carpets, tapestry, and bookbinding. The range of design, often using the Arabic script, and richness of detail are frequently breathtaking. Even more impressive are the achievements of Muslim architecture. At a time when most Western building projects were limited to churches, palaces, and defensive walls, Muslim architects were designing and building schools, libraries, and hospitals. The level of domestic architecture was also high, as can be seen from some of the Muslim private houses that still survive in southern Spain.

Putting Europe and Islam in Perspective

The variety and depth of Western culture's debt to the world of Islam emerge in a simple list of some of the Arabic words—and concepts—adopted by our language. Traffic and tariff; orange, lemon, sugar, saffron, syrup; alcohol; zenith and nadir; and cipher, too. The Arabs invented chewing gum and introduced the windmill and the profession of breadmaking to Europe. Above all, they demonstrated that it was possible to build a multinational and multiracial society that spanned

Continued next page

three continents and a bewildering variety of peoples, united by a common language, religion, and institutions.

Of the three parts into which the Roman Empire split in Late Antiquity, the Muslim world was by far the richest and most cosmopolitan; its trade linked Atlantic Spain and Portugal with India and China. By comparison the Byzantine Empire was conservative and unadventurous and in its last centuries mainly confined to Constantinople and the surrounding territories. As for Western Europe, poverty-stricken and divided into warring kingdoms, it was to take centuries before life there could approach the stability or level of comfort and culture of the great cities of Islam.

Questions for Further Study

1. What are the main features of Islam? How do they resemble or differ from the Judeo-Christian tradition?
2. What impact have art and culture made in the growth of Islamic life? How have they influenced Western ideas?
3. What role does Islam play in the modern world? How far does this relate to its historical foundation and development?

Suggestions for Further Reading

Armstrong, K. *Muhammed: A Western Attempt to Understand Islam*. San Francisco, 1992.

Bloom, Jonathan, and Sheila S. Blair. *Islamic Arts*. London, 1997.

Daftary, Farhad. *Intellectual Traditions in Islam*. New York, 2000.

Endress, G. *Islam: A Historical Introduction*. New York, 1987.

Esposito, J.L. *Women in Muslim Family Law*. Syracuse, NY, 1982.

Frishman, Martin, and Hasan-Uddin Khan. *The Mosque: History, Architectural Development and Regional Diversity*. New York, 1994.

Inamdar, Subash C. *Muhammed and the Rise of Islam: The Creation of Group Identity*. Madison, CT, 2001.

Irwin, Robert. *Islamic Art in Context: Art, Architecture and the Literary World*. New York, 1997.

Kennedy, Hugh. *Muslim Spain and Portugal: A Political History of al-Andalus*. London, 1996.

Lapidus, I.M. *A History of Islamic Societies*. Cambridge, MA, 1988.

Lewis, B. *The Muslim Discovery of Europe*. New York, 1985.

Mottadeh, R.P. *The Mantle of the Prophet*. New York, 1985.

Roded, Ruth. *Women in Islam and the Middle East: A Reader*. New York, 1999.

InfoTrac College Edition

Enter the search term *Islam* using the Subject Guide.

THE FIRST EUROPE: THE WEST IN THE AGE OF CHARLEMAGNE

The synthesis of Classical, Christian, and Germanic elements making up medieval civilization first appeared in the early Germanic kingdoms of the Ostrogoths, Visigoths, and Anglo-Saxons, founded between the 5th and 7th centuries. It was, however, in the Frankish kingdom forged by the Carolingian dynasty in the late 8th century that this fusion resulted for the first time since the Romans in a truly impressive European civilization. The empire created by Charlemagne was the first large governing unit to appear in the West since the collapse of the Roman Empire; after it broke apart following Charlemagne's death, no empire would cover as huge an expanse of territory for another 1,000 years.

The age of Charlemagne also saw the revival and preservation of the learning of the Classical world. Although this was an accidental byproduct of Charlemagne's drive to reform his society and establish a biblically centered culture, the Carolingian cultural achievement had important implications for the future. The decentralized agricultural economy of the era was less successful because it was incapable of sustaining the enormous military and political requirements of a centralized empire. New invasions by Vikings and Magyars in the 9th and 10th centuries hastened the disintegration of the Carolingian empire.

THE CAROLINGIANS

In the years after the death of Clovis in 511, the Frankish kingdom was divided into three major units: Neustria, Austrasia, and Burgundy (see Topic 20). A series of weak Merovingian kings sat on the thrones of these realms, but real power was wielded by the *major domus*, or mayor of the palace. By the 7th century, Pepin of Landen (died c. 639), the *major domus* of Austrasia, had reunited parts of the kingdom. His great-grandson, Charles Martel (c. 688–741) subdued unruly nobles and began the reconquest of Burgundy. Charles's greatest achievement, however, came at the Battle of Tours in 732, when he crushed the Muslim advance into Gaul. For this victory he earned the name "Martel," or hammer, as well as the status of defender of Christendom.

PEPIN THE SHORT AND THE CAROLINGIAN REVOLUTION

Charles Martel's son, Pepin III (ruled 751–768), better known as Pepin the Short, finally ended the fiction of Merovingian rule. Determined to seize power in name as well as in fact, but knowing that his assumption of the throne would not be legitimate, Pepin sent two personal envoys to Rome to seek recognition from Pope Zacharias (ruled 741–752). The pope responded that "he who actually had the power should be called king." In 751 Pepin deposed the last Merovingian, Childeric—who was "shaved and thrust into the cloister"—and made himself king of the Franks.

Pepin's appeal to Pope Zacharias rekindled the relationship of mutual support between the papacy and the Franks. When the Lombards invaded Italy and were poised to descend on Rome, the new pope, Stephen II (ruled 752–757), asked the Byzantine emperor for help. After Constantinople refused the appeal, Stephen turned to the Franks. In 754, he crowned Pepin king of the Franks in the Cathedral of St. Denis, Paris, establishing a tradition for future Frankish rulers. Pepin not only defeated the Lombards in 756 but later ceded to the papacy the Italian territory that he conquered, which technically belonged to the Byzantine emperor. Known as the Donation of Pepin, this grant of territory eventually stretched southwest from Ravenna across the peninsula to Rome, forming the basis for what later became the Papal States. The pope exercised temporal authority over these lands for more than 1,000 years.

CHARLEMAGNE: FROM FRANKISH KING TO HOLY ROMAN EMPEROR

The greatest of the Carolingian rulers was Charles (king 771–814; emperor 800–814), Pepin the Short's son, known to history as Charlemagne (from the Latin *Carolus magnus*, or Charles the Great). We have a great deal of information about his personal life thanks to a biography written by Einhard, a Saxon scholar who served as Charlemagne's sec-retary. Einhard, who wrote in Latin, described Charlemagne this way:

> Charles was large and strong, and of lofty stature . . . (his height is well known to have been seven times the length of his foot); the upper part of his head was round, his eyes very large and animated, nose a little long, hair fair, and face laughing and merry. Thus his appearance was always stately and dignified . . . ; although his neck was thick and somewhat short, and his belly rather prominent; but the symmetry of the rest of his body concealed these defects. His gait was firm, his whole carriage manly, and his voice clear. . . .[1]

Charlemagne was an energetic and lusty man, possibly able to read but not to write his own name. For relaxation he enjoyed hunting, horseback riding, swimming, and taking the cure at natural springs—as well as overeating. In addition to marrying four times, he spent much time in the company of concubines and fathered children when well into his sixties. Charlemagne was more complicated than an ordinary Germanic warlord, for he also enjoyed listening to reading, especially Augustine's *City of God*, and debating with scholars. He had a great respect for culture and the arts

[1] Einhard, *Life of Charlemagne*, Samuel Epes Turner, trans. (Ann Arbor: University of Michigan Press, 1960), p. 50.

Bronze equestrian statue of Charlemagne (originally gilded). Early 9th century. Height 9½ feet (c. 3 m). Charlemagne is shown as larger than the horse, in order to appear dominant. He wears imperial robes and a crown and holds a globe in his left hand to symbolize his rule of the world.

Copyright Réunion des Musées Nationaux/Art Resource, NY

and knew Latin and some Greek. He was a hardworking and conscientious ruler who wanted to fashion an administrative structure inspired by the traditions of ancient Rome.

MILITARY CONQUESTS

Charlemagne was first and foremost a warrior king. His army, although small by modern standards, was powerful and disciplined and consisted mainly of foot soldiers. Cavalry were limited in number and effectiveness until the 8th century, when the introduction of the stirrup changed the character of warfare. The stirrup enabled a mounted soldier to strike at the enemy with a lance or sword without falling off his horse. This innovation not only made cavalry the predominant instrument of warfare but had social consequences as well. The high cost of horses and arms meant that fighting was increasingly limited to nobles, who became the full-time warriors, whereas ordinary freemen were now limited to farming.

After stabilizing his rule, Charlemagne fought military campaigns that greatly extended the borders of his kingdom. In 774, he, too, answered a call from the papacy and brought his army into northern Italy to deal with the Lombards, who had seized part of the papal lands. Charlemagne defeated the Lombards and made himself their king, and then visited Rome, where he reconfirmed the donation of territory made by his father.

Four years later, taking advantage of the division among Muslim forces, Charlemagne invaded Spain. He had limited success against the Muslims, and on his way back across the Pyrenees his forces were attacked from behind by the Basques. One of his commanders, Roland, fell in this assault, an event that gave rise to the first great epic poem of the Middle Ages, *The Song of Roland*. Written in an early form of French sometime about 1100, the epic changed the Basques, who were Christians, into Muslims and Charlemagne's soldiers into French knights. *The Song of Roland* portrayed Charlemagne as a devout crusader against the Muslims (see Topic 28).

Another series of military efforts was directed against the last two remaining independent tribes in Germany, the Saxons and the Bavarians. These were long, harsh campaigns made especially fierce by the resistance from the Saxons, who refused to bow to Charlemagne's orders that they convert to Christianity. Once the Saxons were defeated, he forcefully removed much of the population and imposed rigid measures on those who remained in order to stamp out paganism. In 788 he annexed Bavaria, but that victory led to further wars. In the Danube region on Germany's southeastern border were two groups, the Slavs and the Avars, the latter Asiatic nomads. It took a half dozen expeditions to crush the Avars, after which Charlemagne established a military district known as the East Mark, later called Austria.

Map 24.1 The Carolingian Empire. Charlemagne's most important conquests were in what are now Germany and Italy; in Northern Italy he defeated the Lombards. He failed to make any serious inroads on Muslim Spain, and Sicily and Sardinia remained under Byzantine rule until around 830, when Sicily fell under Muslim control. Nevertheless, by unifying the various Frankish kingdoms of Western Europe, he laid the foundations of the later nation state of France. Go to http://info.wadsworth.com/053461065X for an interactive version of this map.

Perspectives from the Past

Charlemagne and His Government

The "government" Charlemagne designed to administer his far-flung empire should not be thought of in the modern sense—or, for that matter, in the Roman sense—of a centralized state with a permanent and professional bureaucracy. Instead, he saw the question of imperial government very much in the Frankish tradition as a personal matter. He relied heavily on the loyalty of the local nobility and the clergy, who acted as royal officials, and the seat of government shifted constantly as he and his retinue traveled around the realm. That the administration of his empire was effective at all was due largely to the fear that Charlemagne instilled in his subjects and to his determination to govern the West, to the conscientious attitude of his officials, and perhaps to the persistence of the memory of the Roman Empire.

Capitularies

Among the devices used by Charlemagne to ensure control over local affairs and extend royal commands to the provinces were the capitularies, instructions prepared by clerics working in the royal court. These documents reveal fascinating details about Charlemagne's interest in all aspects of daily life, from church matters and price controls to coinage and crime. The following are representative selections from a capitulary of 794:

Administering the Realm

4. Our most pious lord the king, with the consent of the holy synod, gave instructions that no man, whether cleric or layman, should ever sell corn [grain] in time of abundance or in time of scarcity at a greater price than the public level recently decided upon, that is, a modius of oats one penny, a modius of barley two pennies, a modius of rye three pennies, a modius of wheat four pennies. If he should wish to sell it in the form of bread, he should give 12 loaves of wheat bread, each weighing two pounds, for one penny, . . . Anyone who holds a benefice of us should take the greatest possible care that, if God but provide, none of the slaves of the benefice should die of hunger; and anything that remains above what is necessary for the household he may freely sell in the manner laid down.

5. Concerning the pennies [royal coinage], you should be fully aware of our edict, that in every place, in every city and in every market these new pennies must be current and must be accepted by everyone. Provided they bear the imprint of our name and are of pure silver and of full weight, if anyone should refuse to allow them in any place, in any transaction of buying or selling, he shall, if he is a free man, pay 15 shillings to the king, and, if he is of servile status and the transaction is his own, shall lose the transaction or be flogged naked at the stake in the presence of the people. . . .

16. We have heard that certain abbots, led on by greed, require a payment on behalf of those entering their monastery. . . . under no circumstances shall money be required for receiving brothers into a holy order, but that they should be received in accordance with the rule of St Benedict.

18. That whatever sin is committed by the monks, we do not allow the abbots under any circumstances to blind them or inflict the mutilation of members upon them, unless the discipline of the rule provides it.

19. That priests, deacons, monks and clerks should not go into taverns to drink.

24. Concerning clerks and monks, that they should remain steadfast in their chosen way of life.

31. Concerning plots and conspiracies, that they should not occur; and where they are discovered they are to be crushed.

39. If a priest is caught in a criminal act, he should be brought before his bishop and be dealt with according to the ruling of the canons.

41. That no bishop should abandon his proper see by spending his time elsewhere, nor

dare to stay on his own property for more than three weeks. . . .

Copyright © H. R. Loyn and John Percival from *The Reign of Charlemagne* by H. R. Loyn and John Percival. Reprinted with permission of Palgrave.

The Missi Dominici

As Charlemagne visited parts of his realm, he took with him his family, servants, and a host of officials, relying on noble hospitality for food and shelter. But travel was slow, and efficient administration required personal visits from royal administrators as well as by the king himself. He therefore appointed officials known as missi dominici, or envoys of the lord, who traveled in pairs (usually one bishop and one lay aristocrat), inspecting secular and ecclesiastical conditions, investigating local officials, and reporting to the imperial court. The missi were given precise instructions and informed of the most recent decrees and laws. Charlemagne transferred them regularly and broke up the teams each year to prevent corruption. The following document, dating from the year 802, describes the missi.

1. Concerning the commission despatched by our lord the emperor. Our most serene and most Christian lord and emperor, Charles, has selected the most prudent and wise from among his leading men, archbishops and bishops, together with venerable abbots and devout laymen, and has sent them out into all his kingdom, and bestowed through them on all his subjects the right to live in accordance with a right rule of law. Wherever there is any provision in the law that is other than right or just he has ordered them to inquire most diligently into it and bring it to his notice, it being his desire, with God's help, to rectify it. . . . And the missi themselves, as they wish to have the favour of Almighty God and to preserve it through the loyalty they have promised, are to make diligent inquiry wherever a man claims that someone has done him an injustice. . . . And if there be anything which they themselves, together with the counts of the provinces, cannot correct or bring to a just settlement, they should refer it without any hesitation to the emperor's judgement along with their reports.

28. The counts and the centenarii should, as they are desirous of the favour of our lord the emperor, provide for the missi who are sent upon them with all possible attention, that they may go about their duties without any delay. . . .

36. That all men should contribute to the full administration of justice by giving their agreement to our missi.

From H. R. Loyn and John Percival, *The Reign of Charlemagne: Documents on Carolingian Government and Administration.* Copyright © 1976. Reprinted with permission of St. Martin's Press, Incorporated.

The Administration of Justice

The observance of law and procedure in the realm was vital to effective imperial government. Charlemagne exercised his power in administering the law in a number of different ways—he could settle disputes himself directly, through his missi, or by delegating authority to a noble. The following extract from a notitia, or notice of judgment, dated 781, describes how he delegated judicial authority to the Duke of Spoleto and how the case was settled.

At the time when our lord Charles, most excellent king of the Franks and Lombards, was returning from Rome and from the churches of the blessed apostles St Peter and St Paul, and had come to Vadum Medianum in the territory of Florence, and when the lord and most glorious duke Hildebrand was present there with him to do him service, Paul, the son of Pando of Rieti, made a complaint to the lord king concerning the monastery of San Angelo which is situated near the town of Rieti, saying that it had belonged to his parents. 'And yet,' he said, 'our duke has unlawfully taken the monastery from us and has given it to bishop Guigpertus.' . . . The lord king therefore instructed him [the duke] that when he returned to Spoleto he should with his justices inquire carefully into the case and settle it. . . . [After testimony of witnesses who swore that the document giving the monastery to the bishop had been burned, the duke found in favor of the bishop]. . . . Wherefore, to put an end to the dispute, this brief notice of the judgement, on the order of the above-mentioned authority and at the dictation of Dagarinus the gastaldius, was written by me Totemannus the notary, in the month of July of the fourth indiction.

From H. R. Loyn and John Percival, *The Reign of Charlemagne: Documents on Carolingian Government and Administration.* Copyright © 1976. Reprinted with permission of St. Martin's Press, Incorporated.

THE CAROLINGIAN BUREAUCRACY

During one of his later campaigns, the most famous event in the reign of Charlemagne took place. In 800, he made a trip to Rome at the request of Pope Leo III (795–816), whose papacy was being threatened by supporters of a rival family. On Christmas Day, while Charlemagne was kneeling before the altar of St. Peter, the grateful Leo placed a crown on his head and, according to Einhard, proclaimed him "Emperor and Augustus."

Whether Charlemagne knew ahead of time of Leo's intention is much disputed, as is the meaning of the imperial coronation. The ceremony marked the permanent division of Western Europe from the Byzantine Empire. Moreover, in bestowing the imperial title on Charlemagne, the pope had underscored the reality that power in the West had passed to the Frankish monarchy. Charles's motto, "Revival of the Roman Empire," suggested that he was very much conscious of the historical significance of his new title and wished to see himself in the tradition of the Christian Roman emperors—on important state occasions, he even wore the imperial purple robe. Charlemagne saw his empire as the reestablishment of the political unity that had once been the pride of Rome. It was equally clear that Charlemagne considered himself a Christian ruler and that

Mosaic showing the seated figure of St. Peter, who is investing Leo III (on his right) with religious power and Charlemagne (on his left) with secular power. 9th century. All three figures are named in Latin inscriptions, and underneath the Latin text repeats the meaning of the scene, which illustrates Charlemagne's political program.

Leo had granted him the imperial crown by virtue of the pope's role as the vicar of Christ on earth, thus asserting the superiority of papal authority over temporal rulers. Nevertheless, it is also true that during the coronation ceremony, Leo knelt at Charlemagne's feet and kissed the hem of his garment. These issues would resurface over the course of the Middle Ages.

Charlemagne's administration was far less sophisticated than the ancient Roman state that he wanted to emulate. In geographical extent the Frankish empire was smaller than the Roman Empire; in Europe alone it lacked control of southern Italy, most of Spain, and Britain. Nevertheless, its government would be without equal for more than 400 years. On the other hand, the empire consisted largely of sparsely populated stretches of rural areas inhabited by peasants who lived in isolated villages or on landed estates. Disease and famine had combined to reduce the population, and it appears that little more than 10 percent of the arable land was under cultivation.

Governing this huge empire in a time of frequent violence and extremely poor communications was difficult. No bureaucratic institutions such as those found in Roman government—law courts, a permanent civil service, a finance ministry—existed. Instead, the emperor relied heavily on the loyalty of the local nobility, who lived on fortified estates and commanded strong armies. Clerics working in the royal court prepared instructions known as *capitularies* for local officials. Charlemagne's predecessors had begun the custom of rewarding these aristocrats with grants of land—generally only for use during their lifetime—in return for service to the crown. Gradually, however, these holdings had become hereditary. From the ranks of the nobility came the counts (*Grafen*), who administered the 300 units into which the imperial lands were divided. Each of the seven marches was under the jurisdiction of a *markgraf*. The *graf* was appointed for life and wielded extensive judicial, fiscal, and military power.

Charlemagne traveled constantly, moving his court and retinue with him, and relying on the noble estates for food and supplies. Such personal visits, however, on which the emperor was accompanied by the aristocrats who ran his administration, were not enough. The emperor appointed officials known as *missi dominici*, or envoys of the lord, who traveled in pairs (usually one bishop and one lay aristocrat), inspecting secular and ecclesiastical conditions, investigating local officials, and reporting to the imperial court. The *missi* were transferred regularly and the teams broken up each year to prevent corruption.

THE CAROLINGIAN RENAISSANCE

Charlemagne's demand for efficient government led him to seek educated men to serve as officials in the state bureaucracy, while his desire to regenerate the spiritual life of his realm required an educated clergy. Although he was with-

Biblical manuscript illustration showing Moses receiving the Ten Commandments. Late 9th century. A fine example of the quality of artistic achievement during the Carolingian Renaissance, the lower part of the painting adds a scene from the imperial court, at which the emperor hands down his own laws, to underline his divine precedent.

© Cliché Bibliothèque Nationale de France, Paris

out formal education, Charlemagne had a genuine intellectual curiosity that led him to value knowledge and to encourage a revival of learning in his realm. This development is sometimes described as a cultural "renaissance," or rebirth, and in the narrow sense of that word the description is correct, but the Carolingian period produced few new or original ideas. Instead, a revival of study in Classical works took place, and a great effort was made to preserve the intellectual legacy of the ancient world as it was then known. It was in the arts that the Carolingian era produced a measure of originality.

THE REVIVAL OF LEARNING

The program of educational reform was carried out under the aegis of the Anglo-Saxon scholar Alcuin of York

(c. 732–804). Alcuin advised Charlemagne on ecclesiastical matters and directed the palace school that was established for the education of ecclesiastical and lay aristocrats. Alcuin emphasized the study of Classical Latin and the ancient texts. Adopting the ideas of Cassiodorus (see Topic 21), a Roman scholar who worked in Italy under the Emperor Theodoric, Alcuin classified all secular knowledge into two groups of seven "liberal arts": the *trivium* (logic, grammar, and rhetoric) and the *quadrivium* (arithmetic, astronomy, geometry, and music). These categories became the foundations of education for the next 700 years. Alcuin combed Italy, England, Ireland, and Spain for scholars and persuaded Charlemagne to establish schools in many of the monasteries of his realm. Later, royal support was substituted by annual donations, known as the *tithe*, of one-tenth

AKG London

The Palatine Chapel of Charlemagne, 792–805. Designed by Odo of Metz, the first architect north of the Alps whose name is known. This view, looking east, shows the emperor's throne on the upper level, above the main altar. The design of the chapel may have been based on that of the church of San Vitale at Ravenna, with its portraits of the Byzantine Emperor and his wife Theodora (see Topic 22).

S I G N I F I C A N T   D A T E S

The Age of Charlemagne

687	Pepin II major domus of Austrasia and Neustria
732	Charles Martel defeats Muslims at Tours
751	Pepin III becomes king of Franks
771–814	Reign of Charlemagne
843	Treaty of Verdun divides Carolingian Empire
c. 850–950	Viking expansion

poses. The Palatine Chapel was built in a three-tiered octagonal form modeled after a church in Ravenna, which had been the capital of Theodoric's empire. Charlemagne's throne sat on the middle level, above the altar, and worshipers below could look up to the emperor's exalted station between heaven and earth.

MANORIALISM AND THE CAROLINGIAN ECONOMY

The fundamentally agrarian economy of early medieval Europe was centered on the large estates, or **manors,** which originated in the Roman *latifundia* (see Topic 18). Many of the old Roman estates had continued to exist during and after the barbarian invasions, although in the Germanic kingdoms much of the land came into the hands of the new German aristocracy and the church. The ecclesiastical or lay lords who owned the estates—and they often owned more than one—provided protection to the dependent peasant class that lived on and worked the land. In an era marked by the breakdown of trade, poor communications, and the devolution of authority from central government to local aristocrats, the manors grew in importance and became increasingly self-sufficient. *Manorialism* is therefore the term used to describe the economic system of the early Middle Ages. By the 9th century, manorialism was well established in northern France, western Germany, the Low Countries, and northern Italy. Eventually it spread to England, Spain, and Central and Eastern Europe.

AGRICULTURE AND THE MANOR

The population of Carolingian Europe was relatively small, and most people lived in isolated rural centers that were heavily forested. Perhaps as much as 90 percent of the population worked the land. Nevertheless, hunting and fishing remained important sources of food because farming took place on perhaps as little as 10 percent of the land. Moreover, the crop yield was low because laborers relied on primitive tools and an inefficient "two-field" planting system that left half of the farm land fallow every other year.

of all harvests, which would be used to sustain church programs and buildings.

The palace school and the monasteries began the systematic collection of texts by the Classical Latin and early Christian authors. Monks working in special writing rooms, known as *scriptoria*, corrected and copied the old texts and evolved innovative techniques for making books. Manuscript production also led to the development of a new artistic style used for illustrations, or "illuminations." This style combined abstract decorative motifs inherited from Germanic tradition with naturalistic representations of figures adopted from Mediterranean artists. The books were often bound in richly decorated covers encrusted with precious stones. This salvage operation by Carolingian monks was responsible for preserving most of the Classical Latin texts that are available today and contributed directly to the revival of Classical learning that took place centuries later in the West.

The palace school, as well as the seat of government in later years, was located in Charlemagne's palace at Aachen (later known as Aix-la-Chapelle). The palace was built between 792 and 805 on the site of natural hot springs, where the emperor enjoyed relaxing. His architects and builders gathered ancient marbles, columns, and decorative pieces from Roman sites in Europe and developed an ensemble of rooms that combined the private quarters of the imperial family and court officials with public rooms for state pur-

Plan of a typical medieval manor, showing the village, manor house, and field system.

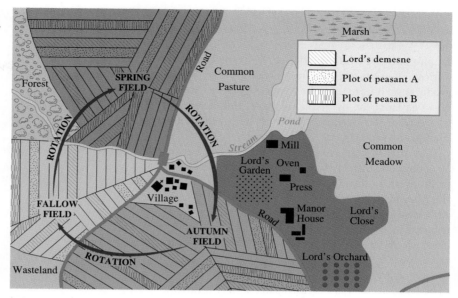

During periods of bad weather and crop failure, starvation was widespread and the death rate high.

The manors varied enormously in size, anywhere from a 300-acre estate supporting a dozen families to one consisting of 4,000 to 5,000 acres inhabited by 50 families; however, each estate was organized roughly in the same way. The peasants lived in cottages in a village, usually located near a stream, while the lord and his family resided in a castle or manor house. Part of the arable land, called the **demesne,** was reserved for the lord's use and was farmed for him by the peasants. The peasants held and cultivated the rest of the land for their use in the open field system, whereby scattered strips of land of about an acre from different sections of the manor were allotted to each villager. Because not all land was equally fertile, the open field system allowed for the distribution of plots of roughly similar quality to each peasant.

The use of slaves to work the large estates had declined during the Merovingian era because landowners found slave labor less economical; moreover, the church had endorsed the freeing of slaves, although it did not prohibit slavery, which continued to operate within wealthy households. Instead, two classes of peasants evolved during the early Middle Ages: freemen and serfs. Freemen were peasants who paid rent for their land, were not required to work in the demesne, and were free to leave the manor by finding other tenants to take their place. The number of free peasants on a manor declined as deteriorating conditions forced them to give up their rights in return for protection and food.

More than half the population of Charlemagne's realm consisted of **serfs**—peasants attached by heredity to the land who could not leave the manor without the lord's permission. Serfs owed certain services and dues to the lord, such as obligatory labor on the demesne for two or three days each week and the payment of a yearly tax known as the *taille*. On the other hand, serfs could not be bought or sold like a slave and could not be evicted from their land. Serfs also had the right to appeal to the manor court for redress against a fellow serf, although they could not do so against a noble or a freeman. The lords obtained additional services or fees from both serfs and freemen by charging for the use of the grinding mills, ovens, and oil and wine presses on their estates.

The manors were administered by a series of officials appointed by the lord. The steward, for example, acted as general supervisor of the manor, including the manorial court, while the bailiff collected rents and fees for the lord and supervised the farming of the demesne. Villagers elected their own foreman, known in Anglo-Saxon communities as the *reeve*, who represented them in dealings with the lord's officials.

THE WIDER ECONOMY

As a result of the breakdown of central government, the disintegration of the road system, and the capture of Mediterranean routes by the Muslims, trade declined during the early medieval period, although it did not disappear entirely. By the start of the Carolingian era, gold coinage had virtually disappeared in the West. The Merovingians had minted gold coins, but these were probably part of a gift-giving economy rather than a real exchange economy. Charlemagne struck a new silver coin, called the *denarius*, but in general fewer coins were available and those in existence were often hoarded, so that local trade generally took the form of barter in surplus agricultural and artisan products. Local markets were usually held every eight days in towns and larger villages, whereas bigger markets usually took place around feast days.

In the early 8th century, the emperor issued professional merchants a charter granting them special rights and protections. Aristocrats demanded rare goods that were not locally available, such as spices, jewelry, and silk, and a luxury trade for these items continued with the Byzantine Empire and the Muslim cities of Western Asia and North Africa. Western and Northern Europe supplied natural products such as furs, timber, and iron, which were moved by river barge or overland by mule and horse caravans. Slaves from Eastern Europe—the modern word *slave* comes from *Slav*—were also in great demand.

In the West, traders were often Jews, but by 900, Venetians and other Italian merchants were establishing port facilities and outfitting ships to trade with the Byzantines and the Muslims. Nevertheless, the Viking and Magyar invaders who struck Europe in the 10th and 11th centuries contributed to the further decline of trade. In the East, Arabs acted as middlemen for items coming from as far away as India and China.

Contrary to what scholars once believed, the early medieval economy was by no means static. Innovations in planting methods and technology eventually enabled farmers to open new areas to cultivation and to increase the crop yield. Although the volume of trade was light, it would begin to revive substantially by the 11th century, at the same time that towns began to grow in size and number. Nevertheless, the Western European economy could not match the vibrancy and strength of the older Roman imperial economy or of the contemporary Byzantine Empire.

THE DISINTEGRATION OF THE CAROLINGIAN EMPIRE

The Carolingian Empire did not long survive the death of Charlemagne in 814. The kind of genuine unity achieved by ancient Rome had never been forged by the Franks. Nor had Christianity prevented the dissension and competition that divided the Frankish nobles. Charlemagne's empire had been held together mainly by the force of his personality. Moreover, the Franks persisted in the notion of the state as a personal possession and followed the practice of dividing royal lands among the king's sons. Aristocrats followed the same custom, so that estates were constantly subdivided. Because Charlemagne's successors found it increasingly necessary to purchase support from one faction of nobles by exchanging grants of land for military service, the royal estates were further diminished.

THE BREAKUP OF THE EMPIRE

On the emperor's death, his only surviving son, Louis the Pious (ruled 814–840), inherited the empire. Louis proved unable to control the unruly aristocrats or the rivalries that divided his three sons. After Louis's death, Charles the Bald (ruled 843–877) joined forces with Louis the German (ruled 843–876) against their older brother Lothair (ruled 840–855), who had inherited the imperial crown. In 842, the two brothers cemented their alliance with the "Strasbourg Oaths," writ-

Map 24.2 The Division of the Carolingian Empire, 843. For all Charlemagne's successes, his Empire did not survive his death. Family divisions and disputes, and aristocratic feuding, succeeded in splitting his conquests into separate kingdoms. The part of the border between the kingdoms of Lothair and Louis that lies along the River Rhine—today the border region known as Alsace-Lorraine, between modern France and Germany—has been the cause of war ever since. The Germans took it from the French in 1871, lost it after World War I, took it back in World War II, only to yield it back to France in 1945. Go to http://info.wadsworth.com/053461065X for an interactive version of this map.

ten in early forms of French and German, and the next year they defeated Lothair and concluded the Treaty of Verdun with him. One of the most crucial treaties of the medieval period, the Verdun agreement provided the basis for all future subdivisions of the empire. Three kingdoms were defined: Charles took possession of the area west of a line running from the Scheldt to the Rhône rivers and to the Atlantic, approximating the region of modern France; Louis ruled over most of the territory east of the Rhine that is today Germany; and Lothair was left the imperial title and an unwieldy realm known as the middle kingdom. It stretched from the North Sea, including the Netherlands and the Rhineland, to Rome.

Lothair's middle kingdom remained the source of frequent conflict. In his will, he followed Frankish practice by dividing his realm among his three sons; one of these sons, Lothair II, received a northern portion that came to be called Lotharingia, or Lorraine. Charles and Louis then seized Lorraine and by the treaty of Mersen in 870 divided it among themselves, thus establishing a contiguous border between France and Germany and a constant cause of trouble between the two countries. The southern portion of

Lothair's kingdom was divided into Burgundy and the kingdom of Italy. One section of the Carolingian family vied with another over the years for control of the imperial title, and by 887, when Charlemagne's great-grandson was deposed by the nobles, the dynasty had all but come to an end.

MUSLIMS, BULGARS, AND MAGYARS

Ever since the Germanic migrations of the 5th century crossed the frontiers of Rome, Europe had been the target of successive waves of invasions. The most disturbing of these assaults had been the Muslim expansion of the 8th century, which had broken the Christian unity of the Mediterranean world (see Topic 23). In the 9th and 10th centuries, as the Carolingian empire disintegrated from within, a new series of invasions by non-Christian peoples occurred: Muslims from the south, Bulgars and Magyars from the east, and Vikings from the north.

From their bases on the coasts of North Africa, Gaul, and Spain, the Muslims launched the conquest of Sicily in 827. Raiding the Italian peninsula, they sacked Rome in 846. In response, Pope Leo IV had a wall built to protect St. Peter's and the Vatican palace, defining an area that today approximates Vatican City. The Muslims swept across Sardinia and Corsica, seized the Carolingian defense positions in northern Spain, and menaced the Alpine passes. Muslim navies virtually cleared the western half of the Mediterranean of European trade. Yet, although the Muslims forged a civilization capable of rivaling Carolingian Europe in power and vitality, their European conquests did not survive the next century.

While Muslims were threatening the Mediterranean frontier, Slavs from Poland and Bohemia periodically attacked northeastern Germany but were repulsed. Both Germans and Slavs were in turn threatened by two new Asiatic peoples, the Bulgars and the Magyars. The Bulgars, distantly related to the Huns, had driven into the Balkans and laid siege to Constantinople, but they soon adopted the civilized customs they came in contact with there. The Bulgar king took the title of tsar (Caesar) and eventually accepted Greek Orthodox Christianity. The Magyars moved from the Black Sea area into Carpathia and Moravia, driving a permanent wedge between the southern, or Yugo, Slavs of the Balkans and the western Slavs of Bohemia, Moravia, and Poland. The Magyars, who came to be called Hungarians because they were mistakenly thought to resemble the Huns, assaulted eastern Germany and penetrated as far west as Lorraine. Only after their defeat at Lechfeld by the German king Otto I in 955 did the Magyars settle into a stable kingdom in east-central Europe and adopt Christianity.

THE VIKINGS

The most widespread and devastating of the new invasions were those of the Norsemen, or Vikings, a Germanic people from Scandinavia. The Vikings had sporadically raided the

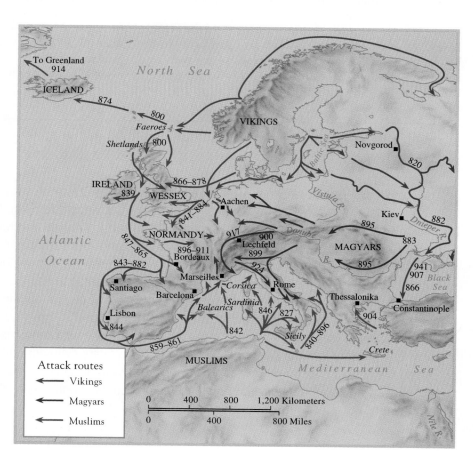

Map 24.3 The Invasions of the 9th Century. The most widespread of these invasions were those of the Vikings, or Norsemen, who reached from Lisbon (in modern Portugal) to Constantinople, where they besieged the Byzantine capital. On the way, they established commercial contacts with cities in Russia, including Kiev. Closer to home, they took over a region still called after them: Normandy, in northwestern France. Go to http://info.wadsworth.com/053461065X for an interactive version of this map.

coasts of Ireland and England in the 8th century, but a growing population, together with the limited resources of the forests of Denmark and the rocky land of Norway and Sweden, drove them to undertake more systematic and powerful invasions in the 9th century.

The Norsemen were consummate shipbuilders and sailors with unparalleled knowledge of winds, currents, and navigation techniques. Their ships were elegant affairs, long and narrow with double ends adorned by tall prows that were often carved in the form of dragonheads. The shallow draft of these ships enabled the Vikings to sail or row up rivers to inland cities of Europe—their sudden appearance and dragon prows striking terror in the inhabitants of European towns.

The Vikings were pagans and fierce fighters. Danish raids on Ireland had destroyed numerous monasteries and had terrorized the coasts of Germany and France. In England, however, they made their most important conquest and eventually accommodated themselves to the Christian civilization they encountered. In 878, after repeated assaults on the east coast of England, the Saxon King Alfred the Great (ruled 871–899) of Wessex ceded a large area of northeastern England to the Danes. Those who settled in Danelaw, as this area was called, became Christians and pledged allegiance to Alfred but remained nominally independent until the region was reconquered in the following century and united with the rest of the kingdom. Another group of Danes settled around the mouth of the Seine River in northern France, where some 40,000 Vikings besieged the city of Paris. In 911 the French king ceded their chieftain Rollo an area that came to be known as Normandy, in return for pledging fealty to the king and becoming Christian.

Farther afield, Swedish sailors gained control of the Baltic Sea and moved east into northern Russia. Eventually they sailed down the Russian rivers as far south as Novgorod and Kiev, and from there to the Black Sea, establishing commercial contact with the Byzantine Empire. Because these Norsemen were called Varangians, their trade path from northern Russia to Constantinople was known as the Varangian route. Farther east, they encountered Arab traders on the Sea of Azov. Bands of Viking warriors sometimes hired themselves to local Slavic rulers and established their own settlements in Russia. Rurik, the leader of one such group, became the prince of Novgorod in 862 (see Topic 22).

The Norwegians generally took a western route, crossing the north Atlantic in the second half of the 9th century as far as Iceland. From this outpost they sailed still farther west. Erik the Red reached Greenland in 975 and established a settlement there. Erik's son, Leif Erikson, is thought to have reached North America because possible evidence of Norsemen landings has been found in Newfoundland.

The impact of the Viking invasions was considerable. They extended their influence from the Atlantic to Russia and from the Baltic to the Mediterranean. They encouraged trade and advanced western sailing techniques, and their adoption of Christianity expanded the strength of the medieval church. But despite the positive features of the Viking expansion, the destruction and chaos of the combined invasions were devastating. Moreover, the failure of royal governments to combat the invaders led Europeans to turn increasingly to local magnates for protection, thus maintaining the trend toward political decentralization that had been in force since the 3rd century. Nevertheless, with the exception of the Muslims, all the invaders of the 9th and 10th centuries were eventually absorbed into European civilization.

Putting the Age of Charlemagne in Perspective

The core of Western European civilization evolved around the Frankish settlements in what is today modern France and Germany. There, the Carolingians emerged as the leaders of an important and far-reaching political and cultural revival that reached its most fully developed form during the reign of Charlemagne. The Carolingian period saw the melding of Roman and Germanic cultures into a new and vigorous European civilization. Using early Christian Rome as his model, Charlemagne applied much energy as a warrior to reestablishing an impressive measure of central authority and was responsible for preserving much of the written culture of the Roman world. Yet the achievement was limited by the constraints of new economic conditions and was short lived. Within less than a century, the Carolingian Empire disintegrated and Europe fell prey to a series of powerful invasions. Out of these circumstances, a pattern of evolving social relationships now became predominant and was to characterize the European experience for centuries.

Questions for Further Study

1. Explain the political success of the Franks in building a state.
2. To what degree was Charlemagne a new kind of "European" ruler rather than a Roman emperor?
3. To what extent was the Carolingian Renaissance an original cultural achievement?
4. Describe how manorialism functioned. To what extent was this a new feature of the European economy?
5. What factors explain the collapse of the Carolingian Empire?

Suggestions for Further Reading

Brown, Peter. *The Body and Society*. New York, 1988.

Bullough, Donald. *The Age of Charlemagne*. New York, 1996.

Collins, Roger. *Charlemagne*. London, 1998.

Folz, Robert. *The Coronation of Charlemagne: 25 December 800*. London, 1974.

Jones, Gwyn. *The Carolingians: The Family Who Forged Europe*. Philadelphia, 1993.

Jones, Gwyn. *A History of the Vikings*, rev. ed. Oxford, 1984.

Loyn, Henry R., and J. Percival. *The Reign of Charlemagne*. New York, 1976.

McKitterick, Rosamond, ed. *The Uses of Literacy in Early Mediaeval Europe*. Cambridge, 1990.

McKitterick, Rosamond, ed. *Carolingian Culture: Innovation and Emulation*. London, 1989.

McNamara, Joann. *Sainted Women of the Dark Ages*. Durham, NC, 1992.

Nelson, Janet L. *The Frankish World, 750-900*. London, 1996.

InfoTrac College Edition

Enter the search term *Carolingian* using Key Terms.

Enter the search term *Charlemagne* using Key Terms.

Enter the search term *Vikings* using Key Terms.

Enter the search terms *feudalism* and *feudal* using the Subject Guide.

THE SOCIAL ORDER OF MEDIEVAL EUROPE

Social structure during the early Middle Ages was governed by a network of personal and legal relationships that we call feudalism. Although limited technically to the aristocracy, the feudal system permeated all dimensions of medieval life. It provided security and local governance for society as a whole during a time when central authority had all but collapsed. The social and political relationships of the aristocracy in the feudal system rested on the revenues of the agricultural economy and the manorial system, in which the bulk of society participated as agrarian workers. The chief social function of the aristocrats was to act as warriors in a military system dependent on personal loyalties and land tenure. As feudal society matured, the code of chivalry developed that reflected the values and mores of this military caste.

For centuries the peasantry and the aristocracy were the two principal social classes of the early Middle Ages. Medieval society was marked by constant recovery and change, and its dynamic nature was demonstrated by the emergence of a new social group, the bourgeoisie. This "urban middle class" developed and grew in importance as trade revived and cities expanded. The lives of women and of Europe's Jewish population, while legally outside the feudal system, also changed and expanded as medieval society became increasingly sophisticated. Throughout the entire period, the clergy—who represented a third, distinct social category—and the Catholic Church were fully enmeshed in the feudal system and thus reflected the social order of Europe.

THE FEUDAL SYSTEM: THE SEARCH FOR SECURITY IN AN AGE OF UNCERTAINTY

The practice of feudalism developed as a response to the disintegration of centralized authority. Its early roots can be traced back to Roman and Germanic customs, but it became more common during the Frankish era, especially after the breakdown of Charlemagne's government.

FEUDAL PRACTICES AND INSTITUTIONS

As officials proved unable to protect people and property from the invaders of the 9th century, the local nobility assumed that task. The collapse of Charlemagne's state administration also necessitated that the nobles take on governmental as well as military functions. These responsibilities required economic support, which in the Carolingian era came largely from the manorial system of land tenure (see Topic 24).

Feudalism covered a variety of political experiences. On the most general level, **feudalism** can be defined as a set of contractual arrangements among free men; it was, however, restricted to noble landowners. These feudal relationships involved two elements. The first was vassalage, a personal bond established between two men based on military service. A **vassal** was a soldier who served a man of greater authority. On the highest level this system involved a relationship between the king and powerful magnates, such as counts and dukes, who served him as "faithful men." The king could and often did also establish lord-vassal relationships with men of lesser rank, including barons and bishops.

The second element involved a military agreement. Feudalism developed because the king, or the lord, needed fighting men, particularly in the form of mounted knights. Because cavalry service was expensive, the early Carolingian rulers developed the practice of making a special grant of land, called a **benefice,** to the vassal in return for such service. The vassals could use the benefice to defray the expenses incurred in providing their horses, armor, and weapons. Over time, complicated feudal relationships developed, known as **subinfeudation,** whereby the same individual could be both a lord to one man and a vassal to another. Moreover, a noble could become the vassal to more than one lord, thereby raising the problem of divided loyalties. In this situation, the vassal usually designated one of his lords as his *liege* lord, to whom he owed primary allegiance.

The feudal relationship carried with it mutual duties and responsibilities. The vassal was required to attend the lord's court, advising him on policy, serving as a juror in cases involving other vassals, and helping to carry out decisions. Vassals also made certain financial contributions to the lord known as the feudal *aids*—the payment of ransom if the lord was captured or gifts on the marriage of the lord's daughter and on the occasion of the knighting of the lord's oldest son. When the lord traveled through a vassal's land, the latter was also expected to provide the lord with lodging and food. In providing military service, the vassal served his lord personally as a mounted knight (usually for a maximum of 40 days) and supplied a certain number of other knights. In turn, the vassal also had several important rights. These included the lord's duty to protect the vassal and grant him access to a trial by his peers. In theory, the authority of a feudal lord—including that of the king—was limited rather than absolute, and a vassal whose lord violated the feudal contract could seek formal redress. Most lords were, however, generally careful not to antagonize their vassals, on whose military service they depended.

RURAL EUROPE: PEASANTS AND ARISTOCRATS

Medieval life was focused primarily, although not exclusively, in the countryside. There agriculture and the cycle of seasons, along with the requirements of manorialism, determined the way most people lived. The bulk of Europe's population, therefore, fell into one of two categories: peasants and aristocrats.

POPULATION GROWTH AND AGRICULTURAL CHANGE

Rural patterns, like other aspects of medieval life, began to undergo significant change in the 10th and 11th centuries. A significant population growth was the most visible sign of the new era. Between roughly 1000 and 1300, the population of western and central Europe may have increased almost three times; in southern Europe it seems to have almost doubled, while in eastern Europe it may have increased by as little as only 50 percent. By 1300, the entire population probably amounted to 75 million. A variety of factors may explain this dramatic population growth. Although mortality rates were high in medieval society—perhaps as many as one of three people died before reaching the age of 20—fertility rates increased. Moreover, although the age was still a violent one, the end of the invasions and the greater security afforded by the feudal system combined to produce a more peaceful society. Most important, however, seems to have been the impact of the changes wrought in agriculture.

The amount of land available for farming expanded greatly after 1000 as peasants cut down forests and drained swamps, especially in Germany and north-central Europe. This process was encouraged by a growing labor shortage, which led landlords to offer special arrangements to groups of peasants who were willing to clear new land. Beginning around 1000, gradually improving weather patterns, marked by slight increases in temperature, made the growing season longer. Finally, technological changes led to major improvements in farming and productivity.

Most important perhaps was the development of a new kind of plow. In southern Europe and the Near East, peasants had long used a light wooden plow without wheels,

Trinity College Library, Cambridge

Manuscript illumination of a scene of plowing. 12th–13th century. The wheelless plow of the late Middle Ages had a sharp blade that cut the soil while the moldboard lifted and turned it. The words above read: "God speed the plough and send us corn enough."

which dug into the topsoil and was easily pulled by one animal. Each family generally owned such a plow, which avoided the need for communal farming. In northern Europe, however, the thick rocky and clay soils made such light plows ineffective. But a new wheeled plow made of iron, developed in the 10th century, enabled farmers to break up the heavy soils, although its increased weight required teams of oxen to pull it. Over the next century, horses soon replaced the slow-moving oxen as a new horse collar and iron horseshoes came into widespread use. Finally, more crop yield was achieved by replacing the two-field system of planting with the three-field system, which kept less land fallow and reduced soil exhaustion. Even with this increased productivity, however, medieval yields never reached those achieved by the ancient Romans.

PEASANT LIFE

Rural dwellers living in villages on lay or ecclesiastical manors constituted about four-fifths of the population of Europe. Legal experts in the Carolingian era divided the population into free and nonfree people, and peasants could fall into either category. Moreover, some peasants owned their own land and were quite well off, although these were a small minority. Most peasants worked on lands owned by others and lived a harsh and crude existence, often surviving on the edge of subsistence. To the long hours of labor on the soil were added the threats of famine, war, and natural disasters. Much of what we know about the daily life of the peasantry comes from surveys and records kept by the monasteries, which controlled a large portion of the manorial lands.

Peasant life reflected the agricultural seasons. The spring was occupied with working the grapevines and putting the cattle out to pasture. In the summer they plowed the fields, hayed, and harvested. Generally, both men and women worked the land during harvest. In the fall, grapes were gathered, the grain milled, and the wine fermented in barrels. If the peasants had pigs, they allowed them to fatten in the forests in preparation for slaughtering. The barren winter saw the peasants gather around their hearths and subsist on what they had saved from the harvest.

The typical peasant home was a crude, one- or two-room mud cottage with dirt or clay floors and thatched roofs. The window openings in the walls were sealed in winter with straw. Heating and cooking facilities consisted of a flat stone in the center of the cottage, while a hole in the roof allowed the smoke to escape. The entire family generally slept in the same bed, consisting of a pile of straw, and domestic animals either lived with the family or were stabled in an adjoining area under the roof. Most of these houses were built in proximity to each other, either in villages or on manors.

The drudgery of peasants' lives was reflected in their diet, which was based on bread. The dark, coarse-textured bread was a source of important nutrients because, in addition to whole wheat, it usually contained rye, barley, and oats. In the place of bread, peasants often ate gruel made of barley and oats, and varied their diet with onions, peas, turnips, garlic, beans, and other vegetables. Occasionally, cheese from cow or goat milk was produced, and in northern Europe butter took the place of olive oil, which was so

Manuscript illumination from the Salzburg *Astronomical Notices.* 13th century. The subject is the months of the year, each of which has its specific agricultural task. Thus January is the time for cleaning and sowing, April for pruning, August for harvesting, and November for hunting.

Oesterreichische Nationalbibliothek, Vienna

prevalent in the south, for cooking. The forests provided berries and nuts as well as fruits. Although they sometimes were able to hunt and fish, peasants seldom ate meat. Cattle were used primarily for dairy products and chickens for eggs. For drink, peasants had water and made beer, which they consumed in large quantities.

Peasant life, for all its hardship, had its moments of relief. Religious holidays, including saints' days and Sundays, were frequent, and on these occasions the church demanded that workers be granted a rest from their labor. Games, including forms of ball playing and wrestling, and dances provided other forms of amusement, as did the celebration of traditional festivals associated with regional markets and seasonal changes.

THE ARISTOCRACY

Medieval society was controlled by the aristocracy, and especially by that elite group of male warriors known as knights. Originally knights were not necessarily of noble origin, but by the 12th century they had risen in social status and eventually merged into a single noble caste marked by their function as warriors and their adherence to a code of behavior known as **chivalry** (the French word for knight is *chevalier*, derived

from the word for horse, *cheval*). Nevertheless, differences in wealth and rank in the feudal system distinguished one knight from another, so that a knight could be a lord, such as a count or a duke, or a lowly vassal.

Knights were bound by the ideals of loyalty, honor, and pride that characterized chivalry. Never a precisely defined institution, chivalry is beyond easy description. Most of what we know about it comes from epic poems such as the *Song of Roland* and courtly romances that recounted brave deeds such as those of British King Arthur and his court. By the 13th century, when Christian ideals had permeated society more fully, notions such as courteous treatment of women and protection of the weak were added to the code. During the era of the Crusades, chivalry also embodied the notion of the Christian knight defending the faith against Muslims and other infidels. Military valor required courage to the death if necessary, while honor demanded both faithfulness to the lord and the willingness to accept any challenge. Yet the true knight had to observe a code of uprightness even in dealing with an enemy and in return expected honorable treatment if captured in battle. So completely did military values permeate medieval society that knights were prone to fight one another as easily as a common enemy, and in 1179 the church felt it necessary to prohibit the jousts and tournaments that were fought for amusement.

Becoming a knight required long and dedicated training. Aristocratic boys were generally "apprenticed" at the court of a friendly lord or relative, where they served as pages and learned the basic skills of horsemanship and fighting. Later, they became "squires" and followed their lord to battle, although they did not actually take part in the fighting and many never became knights. Some time in their late teens, the boys were knighted in a ceremony during which they received their own sword, thus entering the exclusive ranks of young knights who fought for their lords.

Fighting on horseback was the virtual monopoly of the aristocrats, who generally scorned the commoners who made up the ranks of the infantry. The mounted knight, who dressed in chain mail—later replaced by steel plate armor—and a steel helmet, could be wounded but not often killed in battle. Protection against military assault was afforded by castles, which were usually resistant to besiegers. In early days, these castles consisted of square towers of wood known as *keeps*, commonly built on elevated mounds and surrounded by stockades or moats. The round stone towers that dot much of the European countryside today were a later design, whereas more sophisticated structures with concentric circles of walls connecting a series of towers were built after Europeans became familiar with Byzantine and Muslim military architecture.

THE REVIVAL OF TRADE AND EMERGENCE OF CITIES

Nowhere was the changing tempo of the medieval age more evident than in the growth of cities. Commerce was a major factor in the urban development of the 11th and 12th centuries. An increasingly sophisticated aristocratic society demanded luxury goods that could be provided by merchants based in cities, while nobles and kings both required money and credit that only urban moneylenders were able to lend. The stimulation of trade was a major cause of the revival of older towns that had not experienced significant growth since the Roman Empire.

As the population of Europe grew because of increased food production and the end of the invasions, town populations swelled. To the urban merchant class and accompanying service industries of the expanding cities were added numerous peasants, who began moving to the cities to find refuge from the drudgery of their lives in the countryside. Cities increasingly obtained special rights and privileges in the form of charters from kings and lords, and the new air of freedom identified with the towns attracted the feudal underclass.

THE EXPANSION OF TRADE

In the centuries immediately following the Carolingian era, Western European trade—by contrast with that of the Byzantine Empire—was mostly local. A limited number of necessities such as iron, salt, and fish came into the manors from outside, together with luxuries like Oriental goods, especially silk, ivory, spices, and pepper. Nevertheless, most inland regions of the Continent were relatively isolated because overland transportation was difficult and dangerous. The exception to this pattern was to be found along the coasts, especially in the Mediterranean and along the North and the Baltic seas.

The more settled conditions achieved by the feudal system in the West eventually encouraged commercial expansion. Merchants in Venice, Pisa, and Genoa, together with the Norman conquests in southern Italy, had destroyed the Muslim hold on Mediterranean trade. As early as the 11th century, Venetian traders grew so wealthy and powerful that they were able to forge an independent republic that emerged as a great sea power. The Crusades (see Topic 27) not only stimulated trade by making initial contact with Muslims but also enhanced the growing power of European merchants because Western traders who transported and supplied the Christian armies gained control of crucial ports in the eastern Mediterranean. Improvements in ship design, port facilities, and navigation—including the wide use of the magnetized needle (for direction finding) by the 13th century—further stimulated maritime commerce.

In the North, the Low Countries remained the most important commercial area. Cloth manufacturing using raw wool imported from England thrived in Bruges, Ghent, Lille, and Arras, and Flemish cloth was sold throughout Europe. German and Scandinavian merchants joined with Italian, French, and Spanish shippers in securing and transporting Northern finished goods. By 1230, the native cities of the German merchants operating in foreign ports formed a commercial association eventually known as the Hanseatic League, embracing more than 70 cities. Just as Venice and Genoa came to dominate much of the Mediterranean trade, so the Hanseatic League controlled the commerce of northern Europe.

Progress in overland trade came more slowly. Merchants organized to improve roads, bridges, and inland security. As the volume of trade grew, regional markets developed at designated locations into trade fairs (from the Latin *feria*, meaning feast day, because fairs usually opened on a saint's day or a holy day). Fairs usually developed at places along established trade routes and generally in spots that were convenient to merchants from several countries or regions. Kings or feudal lords granted special protection to merchants to promote fairs. Perhaps the most famous were the fairs in Champagne, in northern France, located at the crossroads of inland commerce; these fairs drew merchants principally from France, Flanders, and Germany, as well as from Italy and Switzerland.

The manufacture of goods for sale to regional rather than exclusively local markets developed apace with the expansion of trade. Florentines and Venetians began to purchase Flemish woolens for "finishing" with special dyes imported from the Middle East, after which they were resold. The manufacturing of glassware grew more sophisticated at

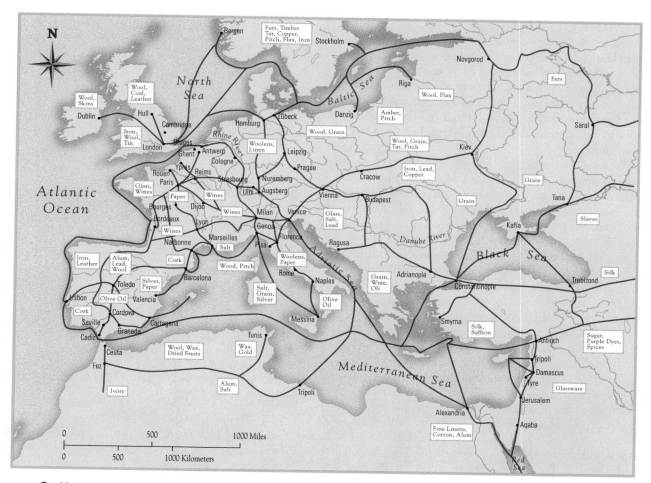

Map 25.1 Trade Routes and Commercial Products of Europe, 800–1300. Note that all of the major cities are either river ports (Prague, Vienna, Budapest), sea ports (Cadiz, Jerusalem, Stockholm), or both (Lisbon, London, Hamburg). It was both cheaper and easier to transport goods by water. The location of Venice made it a crucial link in all four directions, serving Western and Eastern Europe, Africa, and Asia. Go to http://info.wadsworth.com/053461065X for an interactive version of this map.

Limoges and in Venice, while ore production developed in Bohemia, Sweden, Spain, Lombardy, and England. In the North, trade was mainly in raw products such as furs, lumber, salt, beer, and metals that included iron, tin, and copper.

Commercial expansion necessitated more efficient methods of exchange and business practice. New coins with a more stable value were minted in Venice (the silver groat) in 1192 and in Florence (the gold florin) in 1252, although the Middle Ages produced no monetary system that was universally accepted throughout Europe. But better systems of credit and borrowing of money did evolve despite church strictures against the practice of usury—charging interest on borrowed money. In theory only non-Christians, especially Jews, were able to engage in moneylending for profit, although the practice was spreading among Christians by the 13th century.

THE RISE OF CITIES

Unlike other parts of Europe, cities in Italy had continued to flourish because of the peninsula's strong urban traditions and commercial links to the Mediterranean. Northern

Italian cities, especially Venice, Genoa, and Pisa, were at the center of the commercial revival in the Mediterranean region, where they acted as middlemen between Europe and the Middle East. Florence and other manufacturing cities also participated early in the new economic growth based on finished textiles. In the 13th century, merchant firms in Venice, Pisa, and Florence had begun to pioneer new techniques in banking and business, including insurance, double-entry bookkeeping, and limited liability partnerships, and had established branches as far west as the Atlantic coast of Morocco, east as far as the Black Sea and Persia, and north as far as London and Scandinavia. In northern Europe, the towns of Flanders expanded and prospered in similar fashion.

The capitalist ethic first developed in the Italian towns hand in hand with new class distinctions based on economic status. In place of the old feudal orders, there now arose differences between the "popular" citizens and the elite "magnates," whether merchants or landowning aristocrats. In the cities, feudal values were undermined as Italians abandoned noble prejudices against business activity and experienced a new form of social mobility based on commercial profits. Many of these cities achieved the status of self-governing centers known as **communes** as they either rebelled against their overlords or purchased charters from them. The communes developed distinctive forms of self-government that stimulated patriotism and civic pride and controlled all aspects of economic activity. In addition, serfs who escaped to such towns could gain their freedom if they lived there for a year and one day.

Magnates in these cities banded together and established cooperative associations known as **guilds,** which maintained a monopoly of trade in a region, settled disputes, insisted on quality control, and established fair weights and measures. The merchant guilds also acted as charitable institutions and protected the families of members who fell into hard times. As early as the 11th century, the skilled artisans of the towns also established their own craft guilds, which were open only to those engaged in the same craft, to protect and regulate their interests. These guilds functioned much the same as the merchant guilds, regulating production, quality, and prices, and setting standards for artisan training.

In general, the merchant-artisan inhabitants of these towns, who were neither peasant nor noble, evolved into a new social and economic class of *burghers* (from the German word for town), who came to be known as the **bourgeoisie.** These city dwellers, who represented a new culture that was opposed to the ideals and values of the feudal system, became influential allies of the kings in their struggles to resist the power of the traditional lords. As the manorial system, serfdom, and chivalry declined, the bourgeoisie symbolized the new society evolving under the impetus of Western capitalism.

The bourgeoisie grew more independent and powerful with time, electing their own officials to councils in communal government and participating directly in assemblies and civic life. Executive power was generally placed in the hands of councils, although partisan disputes often made them incapable of managing the cities effectively. In the face of growing factional strife, some towns resorted to importing officials, known as the *podestà*, from other towns. These *podestà* ran the communal governments on salary for specified periods and were supposed to remain aloof from the local partisan disputes.

JEWISH LIFE IN THE MIDDLE AGES

Ever since the Diaspora—the dispersion of the Jews out of Palestine—Jews lived mainly in cities, both in Muslim and in Christian territories. In the Roman era, they had settled in Ravenna, Pavia, and Rome and migrated as far west as Spain and France. After the collapse of the Roman Empire, Jewish communities were to be found in Visigothic towns of Spain such as Burgos and Toledo, as well as in French cities such as Arles, Marseilles, Lyon, and Narbonne. Jews of this

Map 25.2 Jewish Communities of Europe in the Middle Ages. The concentration of Jews in Eastern Europe, especially Poland, was to survive until the deportations and killings of World War II. The only Jewish communities in Spain are in the territory under Muslim rule. France's Jewish population is mainly limited to the northeast, bordering the Low Countries.

era were closely integrated into the general communities and stood out neither in language, dress, nor occupation. Although some Jews owned land and engaged in agriculture, most tended to live in towns, where they engaged in the entire range of professions and trades. This pattern was reinforced in North Africa, Spain, and other regions that were overrun by the Muslims, whose tolerant policies enabled Jews to thrive economically and culturally.

During Charlemagne's reign, Jews also settled under imperial charters in Aix-la-Chapelle and Soissons, and during the 9th century Jewish migrants moved from Champagne and the south into the Rhine basin, expanding from there farther eastward into Germany and northward into Flanders. Cities sometimes even competed to attract Jews, as when in 1084 the bishop of Speyer succeeded in drawing Jews to his community from Mainz. In 1066, immediately after the Norman Conquest, French Jews established a community in England.

Throughout this era, Jews lived under either Christianity or Islam, monotheistic religions that claimed that Jews had misunderstood the concepts of their own religious experience. The Jews condemned the worship of a son of God within a Trinity as idolatry and the Christian rejection of the Commandments as prescribed in the Scriptures. The Christians, on the other hand, charged that the Jews rejected their Jewish Messiah and had crucified the son of God. There was no real dispute with the Muslims about the nature of God, only the argument that the Jews had refused to recognize Muhammad as his prophet. Nevertheless, both faiths called on Jews to convert and in the face of Jewish resistance often enacted policies of persecution and suppression against the Jews. On the whole, however, the Muslims seem to have treated the Jews with greater tolerance. Medieval Jews therefore developed in circumstances of both conflict and contact with the dominant cultures in whose midst they lived.

ECONOMIC LIFE

Jewish economic life varied widely, with Jews found in practically every trade and profession, from medicine and banking to more lowly occupations that included shopkeeping and skilled craftsmanship. Jewish doctors were particularly prized by Christians for their skill and learning, and many served as physicians at royal courts. In the early Middle Ages, Jews had engaged extensively in long-distance trade, chiefly because Christians had shown little interest in commercial activities and because Jews in Western Europe maintained contact with those in Western Asia and North Africa as well as good relations with the Muslims. Jews

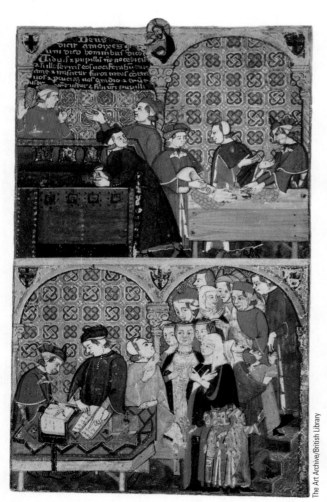

Manuscript illumination from *Book of Vices*. 14th century. The two scenes show Jews performing functions frowned on by the Christian society of the time. The upper episode depicts Jewish moneylenders counting at a table (the Italian word for "table" or "bench"—*banco*—gives us the English word "bank," while below Jewish merchants display their goods.

The Art Archive/British Library

therefore became the international merchants of Western Europe, supplying spices and other luxuries. As early as the 6th century, Gregory of Tours mentions the presence of prosperous and respected Jewish traders among the Franks. By the 9th century, Christian accounts record Jewish merchants in the West whose trade networks reached as far as India and China.

By the late 10th century, Jewish merchants began to engage increasingly in local trade, including buying and selling cattle and other local products, and to conduct financial business on behalf of the feudal lords. Jewish merchants on occasion lent money to local nobles. In the 11th century, Jews were already engaged extensively in credit transactions.

Many of those Jews involved in large-scale trade achieved living standards comparable with the most successful Christians or Muslims. The best Jewish homes even kept slaves, which was permitted by special charter, and employed Christian domestic help. During periods distinguished by famine and economic dislocation, the Jewish chronicles often make no reference to such hardships. Most Jewish families no doubt lived more modestly, but the degree of prosperity recorded among Jewish merchants speaks to the considerable success they had achieved.

The general revival of trade after the 11th century and the high levels of profit to be earned from it attracted more and more Christians to commercial activity. As a result, Jews began to be pushed out of the field. The guilds that came to dominate city life were, after all, Christian associations that excluded nonbelievers from their ranks. The Jews eventually depended on moneylending, one of the few fields still open to them. As the church intensified its regulations against usury, Jewish lenders became more plentiful— although the Torah prohibited interest loans, they believed such rules applied to loans to other Jews, not to Christians. Such transactions were risky but highly profitable, with interest rates sometimes as high as 33 percent.

By the middle of the 12th century, lending money for interest became the principal Jewish business activity in the cities of western and central Europe. For purposes of taxation, careful records of Jewish loans were kept by royal governments in England, France, and elsewhere. During the second half of the 12th century, one such lender, Aaron of Lincoln, granted loans in 25 English counties to clients that included monasteries and cathedrals. Nevertheless, after 1230, the church promoted initiatives to limit Jewish moneylending. French laws against Jewish usury were followed in 1275 by similar measures in England and later in Spain. Such measures had a devastating impact on the prosperity of many Jewish businessmen.

THE GROWTH OF INTOLERANCE

The prominence of Jews in moneylending, together with Christian charges that they had murdered Christ, made Jews easy targets of social prejudice and religious hatred. Persecutions against them mounted in the 11th century in France and Germany. The First Crusade in 1096 stimulated an intensity of feeling against them. The religious fervor of the times, aroused by fanatical sermons preached against all nonbelievers, provoked devastating massacres of the Jewish population in the Rhineland and elsewhere. The Jews defended themselves as best they could, but thousands were killed in cities from Mainz to Prague and as far away as Jerusalem. Although the violence eventually subsided, such incidents recurred with frightening regularity.

Secular and ecclesiastical authorities continued to inflame anti-Semitism. In 1182, King Philip II of France expelled the Jews from his realm, and eight years later, following riots that spread to the countryside from London, Jews were besieged in the town of York and committed mass suicide to avoid death at the hands of Christians. A series of church councils, especially the Third Lateran (1179) and the Fourth Lateran (1215) Councils, adopted increasingly severe regulations that forced Jews to wear identifying symbols on their clothing, to live in segregated sections of cities, and to endure Christian sermons designed to convert them. In 1290, Edward I expelled the Jews from England, forcing thousands to emigrate abroad, and further banishments were enacted in France and the German states. Jews began fleeing to Poland and eastern Europe, creating a growing population there of *Ashkenazi* Jews, as opposed to the *Sephardic* Jews of Spain.

MEDIEVAL WOMEN: THE PRIVATE AND PUBLIC SPHERES

The position of women in medieval society was at best ambiguous. Among peasant families, the typical household was a family consisting of husband, wife, and several children, along with extended relatives such as grandparents and widowed female relations. Harvesting saw men and women working together, but the medieval peasant family generally observed a clear division of labor: Men worked in the fields while women held responsibility for household tasks that included baking and cooking, caring for domestic animals and the vegetable garden, and spinning and weaving. In addition to these duties, women were expected to raise the children. The nuclear family, consisting of parents and children, actually replaced the extended family. Although husbands continued to dominate their wives, in the smaller family units the wife rather than female elders had greater control over household matters and the raising of children.

Bourgeois women in the towns generally had wider opportunities, and in many cases were active in the guild system and in a wide variety of crafts. A growing number of women took employment as domestic servants in the homes of wealthier merchants and also ran retail shops.

Manuscript illumination from Peter the Eater's *Scholastic History.* Late 12th century. The scene illustrates the separate spheres to which men and women were relegated, although the activities in the upper right-hand window suggest that not all attempts were successful. Note the architectural frames within which the figures are set.

© Cliché Bibliothèque Nationale de France, Paris

The position of women in the chivalric society of the aristocrats was less restricted. In noble families, the chief function of daughters was to marry the sons (generally 15 years older) of other noble families by prearrangement and to bear children. In the castles, young girls were trained to assume some responsibility over castle and estate management, particularly because the men were often away fighting for long periods. Young women generally married at age 16 and, because of the high death rate for babies, were expected to have as many children as possible. In turn, women often died giving birth, although poor nutrition seems to have taken an even greater toll on women and children. In a society in which warfare was the central concern, the status of women suffered.

Women were generally excluded from public functions and often could not inherit property, although some, especially widows, did act as property managers and control estates through their infant sons. The feudal order did allow women to inherit fiefs, but generally on condition that the lord would arrange a marriage to a suitable vassal. Gradually, however, the principle of primogeniture took hold, whereby property could be inherited only by the oldest son whenever possible. In the later Middle Ages, women played an important role as hosts in manor houses and castles, while courtly literature and chivalric codes elevated women to an ideal pedestal. Medieval clergy often regarded women as temptresses who used sexuality and cunning to corrupt men.

Beginning in the late 11th century, leadership in the church became exclusively a male domain. The Gregorian reforms (see Topic 27) weakened the role of women in church affairs by insisting on clerical celibacy. Moreover, the increased prominence of bishops further limited the influence of women, who could not have positions in the church similar to those they occupied as heads of abbeys. The development of cathedral schools and universities created a chasm in the world of learning between men and women—the latter being excluded from the new institutions.

The Clergy and Secular Society

The role of the clergy in the feudal system rested on the land tenure system, as did that of all social groups. Abbots and bishops, who managed properties in the name of the church, supervised the lives of peasants in the same way as did lay landlords and were often both feudal vassals and lords. Moreover, in the face of the decline of civil authority, ecclesiastical figures assumed a wide range of functions and duties outside the church, often acting as advisers to noble lords and as representatives of kings, and fulfilled a myriad of administrative responsibilities.

CORRUPTION AND ABUSE IN THE FEUDAL CHURCH

Apart from its spiritual mission and the monastic thrust of early medieval Christianity, the Catholic Church became fully enmeshed in secular society. As it became involved in worldly matters, the church experienced a variety of problems that undermined its spiritual functions. High officials often conducted themselves more like political leaders than religious figures and engaged in practices that weakened the church's stature. Simony, the sale of church offices, became widespread, and many priests ignored the rule against marriage.

One of the most serious problems surrounded the election of bishops. Because success in the feudal system made it essential that secular leaders be able to control their vassals, the king or feudal nobles often selected the candidates, who were then actually elected by canons of cathedral churches. Bishoprics were highly desirable offices, especially for the younger noble sons who did not inherit property. After being rushed through Holy Orders without proper training or religious zeal, these young men entered into their duties with no real interest and continued to lead the lives of feudal knights. An even more explosive issue eventually arose over what came to be known as **lay investiture.** In feudalism, investiture was the ceremony whereby a lord transferred a fief to his vassal, whereas in the church it was the ceremony in which the cleric, once elected, received the pastoral ring and staff that were symbols of his spiritual office. The problem arose when laymen began investing bishops not only with symbols of their fiefs but with these spiritual symbols as well. Did this mean that laymen could control ecclesiastical as well as temporal matters? By the end of the 11th century, this controversy would explode in a struggle for power between the papacy and the rulers of Germany.

Putting the Social Order of Medieval Europe in Perspective

From the 10th to the 12th centuries, European society generally reflected the values and the socioeconomic conditions of feudalism. The Carolingians deliberately used feudalism as part of a management strategy for their vast empire, consciously encouraging and spreading feudal practices. After the collapse of Charlemagne's empire

Continued next page

and the disappearance of central government, feudalism assumed even greater importance. During the height of the feudal age, three social groups, or "estates," constituted the feudal order: The clergy, or first estate, and the nobility, or second estate, were the dominant orders; and the rest of the population, ranging from serfs and rural peasants to servants and wealthy urban merchants, made up the third estate.

Although this arrangement was supposed to be a fixed and permanent one in an unchanging social system ordained by God, medieval society was in fact a dynamic system that saw significant long-range change. Just as feudalism was inevitably if slowly transformed by the new economic forces of urban capitalism and the burgher class, so too it was undermined by the growth of centralized monarchies throughout Europe.

Questions for Further Study

1. What were the main features of feudalism?
2. What was the relationship between trade and cities?
3. In what ways did women and Jews have similar experiences in medieval society?
4. How were the clergy involved in secular society?

Suggestions for Further Reading

Bynum, C.W. *Holy Feast and Holy Fast: The Religious Significance of Food to Medieval Women*. Berkeley, CA, 1987.

Duby, Georges. *A History of Private Life, Vol ii: Revelations of the Medieval World Century*. Cambridge, MA, 1988.

Duggan, Anne J., ed. *Nobles and Nobility in Medieval Europe: Concepts, Origins, Transformations*. Rochester, NY, 2000.

Fossier, Robert. *Peasant Life in the Medieval West*. New York, 1988.

Kaeuper, Richard W., ed. *Violence in Medieval Society*. Rochester, NY, 2000.

Katz, Jacob. *Tradition and Crisis: Jewish Society at the End of the Middle Ages*. New York, 1993.

Miskimin, Harry A., D. Herlihy, and A.L. Udovich, eds. *The Medieval City*. New Haven, CT, 1977.

Newman, Paul B. *Daily Life in the Middle Ages*. Jefferson, NC, 2001.

Reuter, Timothy A., ed. *The Medieval Nobility*. Amsterdam and Oxford, 1978.

Sirat, Colette. *A History of Jewish Philosophy in the Middle Ages*. Cambridge, 1990.

Stow, Kenneth. *Alienated Minority: The Jews of Medieval Latin Europe*. Cambridge, MA, 1992.

Van Houts, E. *Memory and Gender in Medieval Europe*. London, 1999.

Wemple, Suzanne F. *Women in Frankish Society: Marriage and the Cloister, 500–900*. Philadelphia, 1981.

InfoTrac College Edition

Enter the search term *peasantry* using the Subject Guide.

Enter the search term *cities and towns, medieval*, using the Subject Guide.

Enter the search term *Middle Ages* using the Subject Guide.

THE FEUDAL MONARCHIES

After the disintegration of the Carolingian Empire in the 9th century, Western and Central Europe underwent a period of great difficulty. The collapse of political authority was accompanied by new invasions and the subsequent breakdown of communications, trade, and centralized economy. Yet by the 10th century, patterns of recovery began to appear. Despite the emergence of the great lords of the feudal era, the foundations of a new political system were established by the early kings who stood at the apex of the feudal hierarchy.

In the feudal era, kings were in theory the supreme rulers of their realms, who led all of their subjects in war. Nevertheless, the realities of feudalism limited the real power of the kings. Some of the great feudal lords of the age held larger tracts of land and were far wealthier than their kings, and as a result they could control more vassal warriors. The nature of feudal relationships was such that kings were obliged to respect the privileges of their vassals, and any transgressions against the legitimate rights of vassals could and often did result in rebellions against royal authority.

Yet the feudal kings did have some significant advantages over the lords and vassals of their kingdoms. The institution of liege homage clarified the sometimes contradictory feudal relationships that evolved among lords and vassals, giving kings the primary loyalty of some of the nobles. The authority of kings was, moreover, sanctified by divine grace because they were anointed during coronation ceremonies with holy oil. Kings shrewdly extended their realms and their prestige by arranging strategic marriages for their children with powerful noble families. Victory in war often meant that they could distribute to their loyal vassals fiefs that had been taken from vanquished enemies. Finally, monarchs slowly built up the administrative and legal institutions of royal governments in ways that undermined the power of the lords and built a centralized authority on a national level.

During the 11th and 12th centuries, the feudal kings so effectively extended their authority that the monarchies formed the basis for powerful kingdoms that shaped European history for centuries to come. The institution of feudal monarchy flourished in England under the kings who reigned following the Norman Conquest of 1066, and in France under the reign of the Capetian kings from the 10th century. In Germany, the development of monarchy was complicated by the position of the imperial crown, but central authority grew there under the Salian kings and then especially during the reign of the great Hohenstaufen emperor Frederick I. In Spain, the small Christian kingdoms began the reconquest of the territory from the Muslims in the 11th century and established the basis of royal power there.

Norman and Angevin England: The Development of Royal Administration

In the 10th century, the descendants of Alfred the Great (see Topic 24) had produced a united kingdom and an effective royal government in England. The monarchy became for all practical purposes hereditary, as kings were elected from members of Alfred's family. The basic administrative unit of the kingdom became the shire, or county, where the sheriff (*shire-reeve*) supervised local affairs in the name of the king, who communicated with his sheriffs through written letters, known as writs, issued by the chancery office. Despite such administrative advances, however, by the late 10th century, the efficiency of the royal government deteriorated, and the great earls asserted their power. In 1016, the Danes successfully overran England again, although the victorious King Canute of Denmark (ruled 1016–1035) retained English institutions and accepted the Catholic Church. On Canute's death, the throne passed to Ethelred's son, Edward the Confessor (ruled 1042–1066), a devout but weak ruler whose prerogatives were taken over by the nobles.

THE NORMAN CONQUEST

Edward died without children, and the throne was given to Harold Godwinson, an important English earl. Harold's claim was quickly challenged by Edward's cousin, William, Duke of Normandy (ruled 1066–1087). William claimed that during an earlier visit to England, Edward had promised him the throne. In Normandy, a region of northern France, William had used the feudal system to build a centralized feudal state. Technically, William was a vassal of the king of France, but he achieved more power than his sovereign. After subduing the rebellious nobles of his duchy, William established a network of loyal vassals that provided him with the most powerful army in Western Europe.

In the fall of 1066, William and an army of some 6,000 to 7,000 men, including several thousand mounted

Map 26.1 The Norman Conquest. Hastings, the site of the decisive battle at which the Normans were victorious, is the nearest point on English soil to Normandy. Wessex, in which Hastings is located, had been an independent kingdom—its most famous ruler was Alfred the Great—but in 927, more than a century before the Norman Conquest, it had been integrated into the kingdom of England.

knights, crossed the Channel to secure the English throne. On October 14, the Norman knights defeated the English infantry at the Battle of Hastings, where Harold died. Two months later William was crowned king of England, while retaining his position as Duke of Normandy.

The Norman system of feudalism that William had used so successfully in France replaced Anglo-Saxon rule in England, although he needed another five years to pacify the country fully. William claimed all English land by right of conquest. Keeping about one-fifth of national territory for his own royal *demesne*, he distributed the rest in the form of fiefs to royal vassals (mostly French-speaking Normans),

SIGNIFICANT DATES

The Feudal Monarchies

936–973	Otto the Great rules Germany
987–996	Hugh Capet rules as French king
1066	Norman Invasion of England
11th century	Reconquista of Spain begins
1095	Start of First Crusade
1130	Roger II establishes Kingdom of Sicily
1154–1189	Henry II rules England
1166	Assizes of Clarendon establishes jury system
1152–1190	Reign of Frederick Barbarossa as German emperor

Scene from *Bayeux Tapestry*. 1070–1080. Height 1 foot, 8 inches (49 cm). The entire tapestry, more than 200 feet (26 m) long, describes the events associated with the Norman Conquest of England and provides much valuable information about life in these times. In the center of this detail, Halley's Comet passes by overhead.

PUBLIC FIGURES AND PRIVATE LIVES

MATILDA OF FLANDERS AND WILLIAM THE CONQUEROR

William the Conqueror was born illegitimate in 1027 and had to fight repeatedly to secure his rule in Normandy. Unable to shake off the shame of his birth, William seems to have been a temperate man with a deep distaste for sexual promiscuity. Just under six feet tall and rugged, he was described by contemporary chroniclers as "robust" and "burly." Uneducated and crude, and known for bouts of cruelty and harshness, William was an ambitious man of considerable military and administrative ability. William and Matilda of Flanders began courting when he was in his early twenties and she presumably younger. Matilda was descended from Alfred the Great, and her father was the count of Flanders. The political advantages of a marriage to Matilda could not fail to capture William's attention, but he seems also to have become captivated by her personality and intelligence. We have no accurate description of her appearance, but we do know that she was only 4 feet tall. William seems genuinely to have fallen deeply in love with her.

William proposed marriage in 1049. One story, perhaps apocryphal, recorded that at first Matilda refused William's proposal, declaring that she would never marry a bastard. An enraged William rode furiously to Bruges, where he beat and kicked her, after which she took to her bed and declared that she would marry none but William. Pope Leo IX forbade the marriage, perhaps because Matilda and William were distantly related but possibly for political reasons. Nonetheless, in 1053, while Pope Leo was a prisoner of the Normans in Italy, William and Matilda married. As a result, the pope placed Normandy under an interdict, which prohibited most public church ceremonies, including Christian burial. In 1059, Pope Nicholas II granted the couple a dispensation in return for a pledge that each would build

monasteries, Matilda later endowing the Abbey of the Holy Trinity at Caen and making rich gifts to the Cluniac order. They eventually had 10 children.

During William's preparations for the invasion of England, Matilda, who had considerable financial resources of her own, presented him with a ship called the *Mora,* which had on its prow a golden boy with his left hand holding an ivory horn to his lips and his right hand pointing toward England. Legend had it that after Hastings, the devoted Matilda dedicated herself to embroidering the famous Bayeux Tapestry, which recorded the Norman victory. In fact, however, the tapestry was commissioned by William's half brother Odo, the bishop of Bayeux. William left the affairs of Normandy in Matilda's hands, who acted as regent for their oldest son, Robert Curthose. Assisted by a council of nobles, she proved a capable and vigorous administrator.

William thought it best not to delay his coronation until Matilda could join him in England, but in 1068 she crossed the Channel and was crowned Queen of England in an elaborate ceremony at Westminster Abbey. Parts of the royal demesne were placed in her name. A year later Matilda returned to Normandy, resuming her regency, together with Robert, her favorite son. In 1074, after William had subdued England, he was faced with a difficult situation when Robert, anxious to assume his own rule over Normandy, joined a rebellion against his father with discontented local nobles. Robert soon found himself in exile. In 1079, while her destitute son wandered in France and Flanders, Matilda sent him gold and silver without William's knowledge. When William learned of Matilda's gifts to their son, he became furious, proclaiming that "a faithless woman is her husband's bane." Matilda's defense was that of a mother's love for her son, and this event seems to have been the only known quarrel between husband and wife. William eventually forgave Robert and bequeathed him the duchy of Normandy. Matilda died in November 1083. A saddened William mourned her the rest of his life. When he died four years later, William was buried in St. Stephen's Church in Caen, not far from Matilda's tomb in the Church of the Holy Trinity.

Roger-Viollet

Roger-Viollet

including bishops and abbots. In return, the vassals provided William with specified numbers of soldiers. In 1086, every fiefholder in this system, whether one of William's great vassals or a lesser holder, pledged liege loyalty directly to William by swearing the so-called Salisbury Oath. That same year, William commissioned the Domesday Book, a kind of survey of all property throughout the realm. He used this information as a basis for collecting taxes and feudal aids from landholders.

William built a strong, centralized monarchy that blended Anglo-Saxon and Norman institutions and practices. Gradually, the French-speaking nobles intermarried with the English families, creating a ruling class that spoke a new form of English. He continued to use the former system of local administration through the sheriffs, although he replaced the Anglo-Saxon sheriffs with Normans and extended the practice of using royal courts and the tax system to increase the wealth and authority of the king. He replaced the former English advisory body known as the *Witan* with the Great Council (later called the *curia regis*, or royal council), the ancestor of the English Parliament.

HENRY II AND COMMON LAW
William was succeeded in turn by two of his sons. Thereafter, and for almost 20 years, a civil war disturbed England until the succession of Henry II (ruled 1154–1189), founder of the Plantagenet, or Angevin, dynasty. The new king had an impressive if complicated inheritance. Through his mother, wife of Geoffrey Plantagenet, he inherited the French provinces of Anjou and Normandy. Moreover, through his marriage to Eleanor of Aquitaine (1122?–1204), Henry also became Duke of Aquitaine, a territory that stretched through southwestern France to the Pyrenees.

A man of great energy, Henry rapidly restored the power of the monarchy in England. In matters of administration, he made the collecting and recording of taxes more efficient and regular through the office of the "exchequer," or treasury, so named after the checkered tabletop on which his officials counted the royal receipts. Perhaps his greatest achievement lay in extending the authority of the royal courts. In 1166, Henry armed his itinerant justices with a series of instructions known as the Assizes of Clarendon, which established a jury in each shire consisting of 12 important men sworn to report all crimes of which they had knowledge. This method, which was also used to decide civil cases, is the origin of the present-day grand jury. These legal reforms formed the basis for the development of the English common law, which differed from Roman law in that it reflected not the will of the ruler but the principles established by judges in deciding cases.

THE MURDER OF THOMAS BECKET
If Henry was able to build the royal judicial administration while undermining the legal authority of baronial courts, he was less successful in dealing with the church, whose system of canon law operated independently of the state. In 1162, Henry appointed Thomas Becket (c. 1118–1170), his former chancellor, archbishop of Canterbury, making him the highest cleric in the English Church. The king mistakenly

Recumbent effigy of Eleanor of Acquitaine, in Fontevrault Abbey, Normandy, France. 13th century. Eleanor, the daughter of the Duke of Acquitaine, was famous for her intellectual interests; she is depicted here reading as she reclines. Note the sculptor's interest in the drapery, rather than the anatomical details of the body. A century or so later, at the time of the Renaissance, artists were to rediscover how to depict the human form.

Map 26.2 England and France in the Age of Henry II. Note how small the actual territory is that is subject to direct rule by the French king. Bouvines, in the part of northeastern France just across the English Channel, was the site of the battle in 1214 at which Philip Augustus defeated the English forces of King John and took direct control of the land to the east of the Royal domains: Normandy, Maine, and Anjou (see Topic 29).

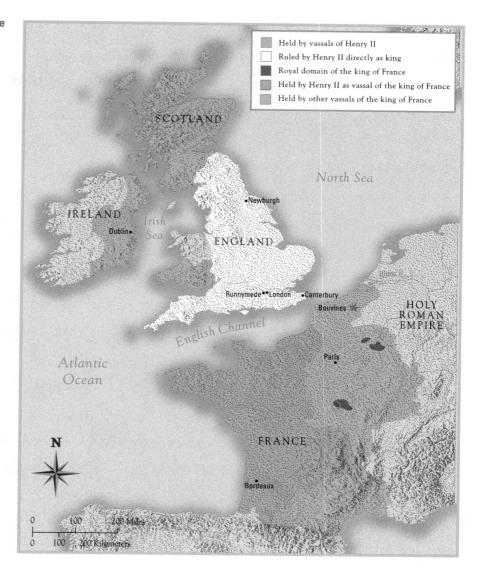

believed that their friendship would guarantee a smooth relationship with the church, but Becket proved to be fiercely independent. The issue came to a head in 1164 when Henry decreed that clergymen found guilty of serious civil crimes, such as larceny or murder, should be tried in royal rather than in ecclesiastical courts. Becket stubbornly opposed Henry's decree, going into exile in France. Although Becket returned to England, all efforts at compromise failed, and Becket excommunicated the English bishops who supported the king.

In a moment of exasperation, Henry is supposed to have lamented that none of his retainers was courageous enough to "rid me of this troublesome priest." On December 29, 1170, four knights took Henry's reckless words at face value and killed Becket before the altar of Canterbury Cathedral. Public outrage was so intense that Henry had to do public penance and compromise with the church by permitting the right of appeal from English church courts to the papal court in Rome, bypassing the royal courts alto-

gether. Becket was instantly a popular hero and became a saint. His tomb at Canterbury was the site of pilgrimages and the symbol of church resistance to royal pride.

FRANCE AND THE CAPETIAN MONARCHY: NOBLES VERSUS THE KING

The descendants of Charlemagne who ruled the West Frankish kingdom, which came to be known as France, were ineffective monarchs who proved unable to defend the realm against invasion. In place of the king, therefore, the great feudal nobles assumed absolute powers on a local level and provided their subjects with military protection and political authority. In 987, when the last Carolingian king, Louis the Sluggard, died, the lords elected Hugh Capet (ruled 987–996), count of Paris, to the throne. Hugh was by no means the strongest of the feudal princes of France, personally controlling only a small area around Paris known as the Île de France, which was surrounded by the lands of other nobles who were wealthier and more powerful. But Hugh was determined to extend his domains and rebuild the royal government.

BUILDING THE CAPETIAN MONARCHY

No one expected that the Capetian dynasty would rule France for very long. Hugh cleverly arranged to have his son crowned as "associate" ruler during his lifetime, a practice that Hugh's successors followed regularly. Hugh strengthened his hold on the monarchy by securing the support of the church. Furthermore, every Capetian king for several centuries had a male heir, thus securing their hold on the throne. By the 13th century, the principle of hereditary rule had become a fixed tradition.

The beginning of the growth of the Capetian monarchy came with the reign of Louis VI (ruled 1108–1137), called Louis the Fat. Louis broke the resistance of the rebellious nobles in the Île de France, where he destroyed their castles and pacified the countryside. He also capitalized on his alliance with the church, which defended his prerogatives against the claims of the feudal barons. One of Louis's most able advisers was the Abbot Suger (1081–1151), from the monastery of Saint-Denis. Suger was responsible for instituting enlightened economic policies in the royal domain, where he established villages, colonized forests, and supported the growth of towns.

Louis the Fat's success in laying the foundations of royal authority increased the status of the dynasty, but his son, Louis VII (1137–1180), was less skillful. Suger arranged for Louis VII to marry Eleanor, the daughter of the duke of Aquitaine and heiress to her father's large holdings, which

Map 26.3 Germany and Central Europe, 12th century. The conquest by Otto the Great of most of northern and central Italy made his kingdom the largest since Charlemagne's. His control of the Po River in Italy and stretches of the Danube in Swabia, and the Rhine and Elbe to the north, provided a sound economic base for German trade. Southern Italy spent most of the 11th century being fought over by Muslim and Byzantine forces, before it was conquered at the beginning of the 12th century by the Normans. Go to http://info.wadsworth.com/053461065X for an interactive version of this map.

would have doubled the size of the royal domain. But the hapless Louis and the brilliant Eleanor were ill-matched, and when Eleanor failed to produce a son for the king, Louis had the marriage annulled. Two months later, in 1152, Eleanor married Henry II of England. The loss of Aquitaine, which now became an English possession, was a crucial blow to Capetian ambitions, and Philip, Louis's son by a second marriage, was determined to regain the lost province.

GERMAN KINGS AND THE LURE OF EMPIRE: FROM OTTO I TO FREDERICK BARBAROSSA

The same pattern of the usurpation of royal authority by ambitious nobles that characterized France was repeated in Germany, the land of the East Franks. On the demise of the last of Charlemagne's successors in 911, the dukes of Bavaria, Saxony, Swabia, and other important states elected as their king Conrad of Franconia, the weakest of their fellow nobles. Conrad ruled only eight years and before his death endorsed the election of Henry the Fowler, duke of Saxony, who took the throne as Henry I (ruled 919–936). Henry proved to be an effective military leader who fought off incursions by the Danes in the north and the Slavs to the east, but he was otherwise unable to build a strong royal government.

OTTO THE GREAT AND IMPERIAL AUTHORITY

Henry's successor, Otto I (ruled 936–973), was the greatest of the Saxon kings. He expanded royal authority by appointing loyal counts to supervise his domains and maneuvering relatives and associates into positions of power in the other duchies. Otto also forged a close alliance with the church, and, as in France, church officials served as royal advisers and administrators. Otto regularly appointed bishops and abbots to their posts and received from their estates monetary gifts and even soldiers. The king's insistence on his right to nominate the high prelates of Germany contained the seeds of future discord.

Otto's prestige grew with his defeat of the pagan Magyars at the Battle of Lechfeld (955), ending the threat they had posed to the West. By the end of the 10th century, they had converted to Christianity. To secure Germany's eastern frontiers, he established military provinces along the eastern borders and supported the Christianization of the Slavs. Otto's ambitions extended beyond his role as German king, for he saw himself in the tradition of the Romans and the Carolingians as the emperor of the West. He already claimed for himself the provinces of Burgundy and Lorraine on the southeastern border of France and Lombardy in northern Italy, all of which had once been part of the middle kingdom ruled by Lothair, Charlemagne's grandson and one of the last Carolingians to hold the title of emperor.

In 951, Otto led his army across the Alps in order to preempt a German noble with designs on northern Italy. By making himself king of Italy, Otto established a link between Germany and Italy that would be a distinguishing feature of medieval politics. Eleven years later, during a second expedition to Italy to protect the papacy, the pope rewarded Otto by crowning him emperor. Without adding any real powers to his position, Otto had become the most prestigious figure in the West since Charlemagne. At his death, Otto's empire—soon to be known as the Holy Roman Empire—was the largest and most powerful in Europe, and he was known as Otto the Great.

With the death of the last Saxon king in 1024, the Salian dynasty assumed control of German affairs for the next century. The Salian kings continued to follow with varying degrees of success the goal of strengthening the powers of the monarchy in Germany against the feudal lords, while pursuing the Italian policy begun by Otto I. But serious obstacles stood in the way of royal ambitions, and no effective centralized monarchy emerged in Germany as it did in England and France. Most significant was the power of the great German nobles, known as the *electors*, to control the selection of the kings. When in time it became customary for the German kings to seek the imperial title, matters were further complicated because the popes claimed the exclusive right to designate the emperors. The experience of Henry IV (ruled 1056–1106) demonstrated the burdens under which the German kings labored. When Henry attempted to appoint church officials as his predecessors had done, a reformed papacy under Pope Gregory VII opposed him. The German nobles seized the occasion of this "Investiture Controversy" to rebel against royal power, and Henry was forced to submit to the pope in a humiliating act of penitence (see Topic 27).

ITALY AND THE IMPERIAL DREAM

In the wake of the Investiture Controversy, which had weakened the prestige of the monarchy, many German nobles began to side with the popes in their struggles against the imperial aspirations of the German kings. Moreover, the unstable conditions prevailing in Italy made the military adventures of the German emperors still more dangerous. In the north of Italy, the city-states that had become wealthy with the revived Mediterranean trade jealously guarded their independence against the encroachments of the German rulers by siding with the papacy. In central Italy, the popes ruled the Papal States as absolute monarchs from their capital at Rome, often playing one city-state against another.

In the south, where the Byzantines and the Muslims had posed a constant threat to the papacy, a new civilization was taking form. In the 11th century, armies of Norman knights under the sons of Tancred de Hauteville invaded southern Italy, fighting the Byzantines, the Muslims, and the popes. In 1059, Pope Nicholas II invested one of Tancred's sons, Robert Guiscard, with the duchies of Calabria and Apulia, while his brother Roger undertook the conquest of Sicily from the Muslims. Robert's death in 1085 left the Norman

Manuscript illumination showing the imperial court at Palermo. 12th century. The picture illustrated the racial diversity of life in Sicily under the Normans. Each separate space contains its own group, labeled (from left to right) Greeks, Saracens, Latins (i.e., Normans), and Byzantines, each in its own distinctive costume (note the Saracens' turbans, for example).

possessions in Roger's hands, and in 1130 his son, Roger II (ruled 1130–1154), established the Kingdom of Sicily, which included the island as well as the Norman possessions on the mainland. Roger II also conquered most of the North African coast from Tunis to Tripoli. The Norman kingdom was administered through a strong central government and fused the Muslim, Christian, Norman, and even Jewish influences into a brilliant civilization in which the arts and sciences flourished (see Topic 23).

No German king was more caught up in the imperial dream and in the desire to extend the empire into Italy than Frederick I (ruled 1152–1190) of the Hohenstaufen family of Swabia. Frederick became king of Germany in 1152, while Roger II still ruled Sicily. Known to the Italians as Barbarossa, or Redbeard, Frederick was a big, handsome man of courage and ambition. Determined to impose his authority over the German nobles, he used diplomacy, military force, and religion to forge the first effective feudal monarchy in Germany. His constant need for financial resources made him turn to Italy, where he hoped to secure revenue by taxing the prosperous cities of the North. Unlike previous kings, who saw Germany as the center of the realm, Frederick focused his attention on Italy, demanding from the German princes only that they acknowledge his overlordship.

Frederick's Italian campaign centered in Lombardy, but papal opposition made his efforts difficult and costly. The pope encouraged the Lombard communes to organize into a defensive alliance known as the Lombard League, which defeated Frederick's forces at the Battle of Legnano in 1176. Through the Peace of Constance (1183), Frederick reached a compromise with the Lombard cities: In return for recognizing Frederick's supreme authority and his control over the Italian countryside, he acknowledged the right of the towns to full control over their internal affairs. Eventually he extracted from the cities an annual payment that gave him the financial resources he had wanted. The coming of peace, after more than two decades of fighting, allowed Frederick to return to Germany, where he emerged as the most powerful ruler since Charlemagne. The emperor died in Asia Minor in 1190 while on the Third Crusade, but before his death he had cemented the connection between Hohenstaufen ambitions and Italy by marrying off his son, Henry VI (ruled 1191–1197), to Constance, the daughter and heiress of Roger II of Sicily. In the next century, Frederick's grandson and namesake, Frederick II, would revive the imperial dream.

THE RECONQUISTA AND THE KINGDOMS OF MEDIEVAL SPAIN

Islamic civilization in Europe had centered in Spain, where the Muslims had established a flourishing economy and culture since the 8th century. Islamic architects erected bril-

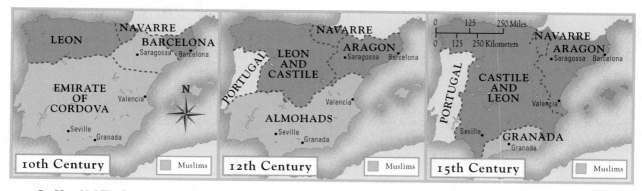

 Map 26.4 The Reconquista. The three maps show the inexorable growth of the Spanish kingdoms at the expense of Muslim rule in the south. The creation of Portugal as an independent kingdom under Alfonso I, in 1143, added to the destabilization of the Muslim state. It finally became reduced to Granada and its territory, which remained under the rule of the Nasrid dynasty until 1492. Go to http://info.wadsworth.com/053461065X for an interactive version of this map.

liant monuments such as the mosque at Cordova, one of the largest cities in Europe, while Islamic scholars advanced knowledge and Islamic tolerance enabled Jewish communities in Spain to prosper (see Topic 23).

THE CHRISTIAN OFFENSIVE

Islamic control began to weaken in the late 10th century as disunity among the Muslims enabled a series of minor Christian states such as Aragon, Castile, León, and Navarre to emerge in northern Spain. By 1100, the Christians, fired by fanatical religious zeal and a growing sense of patriotism, had reconquered most of Portugal and central Spain from the Atlantic to the Mediterranean. Popular enthusiasm for the Reconquista was focused in the late 11th century on the figure of Rodrigo Díaz de Vivar (d. 1099), popularly known as El Cid, a soldier of fortune whose exploits were the basis for the 12th-century epic *Song of the Cid* (see Topic 28). El Cid fought against the Muslims in Castile before being banished by the king, who distrusted his motives, and then fought for the Moors of Saragossa. In 1094 he conquered the kingdom of Valencia, which he ruled until his death. As the Christians pushed the Muslims farther south, they recruited settlers to occupy the reconquered territories. In 1212, a Christian army defeated a Muslim invasion from North Africa, and this victory was followed by the taking of Cordova and Seville. Only Granada was still in Muslim hands.

During the intervening centuries, the Christian rulers consolidated their hold over their kingdoms, which now included Portugal as well as Aragon and Castile. As the price for popular support of the reconquest, the kings had extended considerable autonomy and local rights to their subjects, whether Christian, Muslim, or Jewish. Many of the noble landowners held their properties outright, not as feudal fiefs, so that the kings were forced to recognize the necessity of ruling with the consent of the great nobles. By the late 12th century, the magnates were often represented in institutions known as *Cortes*, which exercised powerful influence in the kingdoms.

Some of the kings followed the example of the English monarchs in attempting to extend their authority by codifying laws and developing royal systems of justice. In Castile and León, for example, Alfonso X (ruled 1252–1284), known as "the Wise," issued the Siete Partidas legal code that established royal law as the principal source of justice. Alfonso, whose wife Beatriz was a Swabian princess, vainly sought to become Holy Roman Emperor. By the following century, Spanish rulers were extending their sway into the Mediterranean, where they seized the Balearic Islands and Sicily and even occupied Athens for a time. The completion of the reconquest and the unification of the Spanish monarchy into a single state would have to wait until the 15th century, when Spain emerged as one of the most powerful states in Europe.

Putting the Feudal Monarchies in Perspective

By the 13th century, an entirely new political configuration had emerged in Europe, as the decentralized feudal system was replaced by a series of fledgling monarchies. These new states, although still in their infancy, had established efficient royal administrations, which increasingly centralized authority, especially through the exten-

Continued next page

sion of royal law. In England, the Normans had led the way in using the principles of feudalism to forge an effective monarchy, while in France the Capetian kings took longer to subdue the feudal nobles by slowly building and extending the royal domain. In Germany, the lure of imperial power both added to the prestige and moral authority of the kings and sapped their resources as they sought to extend their control into Italy. The Spanish kings, faced with a powerful noble opposition, used the moral fervor of the Christian reconquest to strengthen their position. Everywhere, the overall pattern of growing royal authority was similar, and over the following centuries the centralizing efforts of the kings would triumph over the feudal lords.

Questions for Further Study

1. In what ways did feudal kings strengthen their power over the nobility?
2. What does the relationship between Matilda and William tell us about relations between aristocratic men and women in feudal society?
3. What special political conditions existed in feudal Germany that made it different from France and England?

Suggestions for Further Reading

Barlow, Frank. *The Feudal Kingdom of England, 1042–1216*, 3rd ed. New York, 1972.

Bartlett, Robert. *England under the Norman and Angevin Kings, 1074-1225*. New York, 2000.

Brooke, Christopher N.L. *Europe in the Central Middle Ages, 962–1154*, rev. ed. New York, 1988.

Dunbabin, J. *France in the Making, 843–1180*. Oxford, 1985.

Fuhrmann, Helmut. *Germany in the High Middle Ages, 1050–1250*. Cambridge, MA, 1986.

Grape, Wolfgang. *The Bayeux Tapestry: Monument to a Norman Triumph*. New York, 1994.

Hallam, Elizabeth M. *Capetian France, 987–1328*. London, 1980.

Jordan, William C. *Ideology and Royal Power in Medieval France: Kingship, Crusades and the Jews*. Burlington, VT, 2001.

InfoTrac College Edition

Enter the search term *medieval Germany* using Key Terms.

Enter the search term *medieval England* using Key Terms.

THE MILITANT CHURCH: REFORM AND THE PAPACY

By the 10th century, the Catholic Church and the papacy were both in deep crisis. The problems of the church were largely the result of its involvement in the feudal system and deteriorating political conditions in the Italian peninsula. A major problem was the fact that in the 11th century the Eastern Christian Church broke away from the authority of Rome.

Nevertheless, the church also demonstrated a remarkable capacity for reform and spiritual renewal, especially during the period from the 11th to the 13th century. Reform began on the local level, through the establishment of several new monastic orders. From the monastic movement, the reforming impulse spread to the papacy in the 11th century under the leadership first of Pope Leo IX and then of Gregory VII. Under Gregory the Investiture Controversy with the German emperors culminated in the submission of Henry IV to papal authority at Canossa. The renewed vigor of the church and the spiritual influence of Christianity in secular society were reflected in the militant expansion of Western Christendom, as in 1095 the first of a series of Crusades was launched against the Muslims. During the reign of Pope Innocent III in the early 13th century, the papacy successfully asserted its supremacy not only in ecclesiastical matters, but in secular affairs as well. Along with the highly efficient papal administration that evolved with canon law, new religious orders of mendicant friars were formed that brought a fresh measure of spiritual devotion and proselytizing fervor to medieval civilization.

REFORM AND RENEWAL IN THE CHURCH

The principal cause of the breakdown of discipline within the church in the 9th and 10th centuries was that the land tenure system of feudalism tied religious leaders closely to feudal politics. One result of this relationship was that the clergy came increasingly under lay influence. High ecclesiastical officials, especially bishops and abbots, controlled huge estates that were held as fiefs, thereby making them vassals of secular nobles and kings, who wanted to control the selection and appointment of these important prelates. Bishops and abbots chosen in this manner, generally from noble families, often had little concern for the spiritual well-being of the church or its members. The sale of church offices—the practice known as *simony*—and the growing number of married priests were signs of the decline in ecclesiastical discipline.

THE REFORMING IMPULSE

The first serious move toward reform came in 910, when Duke William of Aquitaine established the abbey of Cluny in the Burgundy region of France. In the charter granted to the monastery, William insisted that the order be entirely independent in running its own affairs and in electing its officials. The monks of Cluny strictly observed the Benedictine rule, which had fallen into widespread disuse. The order also adopted the principle of centralization, whereby each branch monastery that was started—and eventually there were more than 1,000, spread from Western Europe to Palestine—was headed by a prior who remained under the authority of the abbot at Cluny.

The centralized organization enabled the order to resist the temptations of secular interference that the feudal system embodied. The abbot of Cluny regularly visited dependent monasteries to ensure spiritual ideals and adherence to the reforming principles of Cluny: the elimination of secular influence and abuses such as simony, the practice of clerical celibacy, and obedience to the supremacy of the pope, who assumed direct authority over the order. Inside the monasteries, monks rededicated themselves to the work ethic and to the spirit of community participation in religious worship.

By the following century, the spirit of reform began to affect both the imperial office and, by extension, the papacy. In 1046, the Emperor Henry III (ruled 1039–1056) faced an embarrassing situation in which three men each claimed to be the legitimate pope. Henry responded by deposing all three rivals and appointing a new pope, Leo IX (ruled 1049–1054). Leo, the last pope to be appointed by an emperor, was dedicated to the reforming ideal and began a series of institutional changes designed to free the church of secular interference. Leo sent papal legates throughout Christendom to inspect and reform local conditions and often summoned corrupt bishops to Rome for disciplining. He also relied increasingly

Map 27.1 The Investiture Controversy: Germany and Italy. The two crucial events in the Investiture Controversy occurred first at the synod of 1075 in Rome and, finally, at the meeting of pope and Emperor at Worms in 1122, at which agreement was finally reached. Between these events, the papacy enjoyed the triumph of an Imperial humiliation at Canossa and suffered the disastrous sack of Rome in 1081.

Manuscript illumination of Henry IV at Canossa. 12th century. In the foreground the emperor kneels in humility, with the figure of Abbot Hugh of Cluny behind him. Within the building (represented by a simple arch) is Countess Matilda of Tuscany. As the inscription below explains, Henry is begging the other two to intercede on his behalf with Pope Gregory VII.

on "cardinals," an honorary title he granted to priests and bishops who were committed to reform, to act as papal administrators. In 1059, a church council issued a decree stipulating that only the cardinals of Rome, who formed the College of Cardinals, had the power to elect popes, a tradition that continues to be followed in modified form to this day. Other reforms, including insistence on clerical celibacy and the prohibition of simony, eventually followed.

THE INVESTITURE CONTROVERSY

The most vigorous of the reforming popes was Gregory VII (ruled 1073–1085), a monk of peasant origin named Hildebrand whom Leo had brought to Rome. Gregory was a true ascetic and a zealous reformer who insisted on the absolute authority of the pope within the church and the spiritual supremacy of the pope over secular rulers, including kings and emperors. Although humble in manner, Gregory did not shrink from taking bold action when he believed it was necessary for the church's welfare.

THE ROAD TO CANOSSA

Gregory furthered the centralization of papal authority, using cardinals armed with full papal authority as legates to impose discipline, and making wide use of ecclesiastical councils, known as *synods,* to reform institutions and practices. In Rome, a *curia,* or papal court, was established and a system of canon law elaborated. Most challenging of all, Gregory decided to eliminate the most important cause of corruption, lay investiture. As with many of his predecessors, Henry IV

(ruled 1056–1105) had continued the practice of investing bishops with the ring and staff, symbols of their spiritual authority. Gregory's policy now meant direct confrontation with the emperor.

The confrontation came to a head in 1075, when a synod held in Rome issued the first direct decree prohibiting lay investiture, a measure that Henry disregarded. Gregory then directly challenged Henry by threatening to excommunicate him (in which case he would be unable to receive the sacraments and would in theory be unable to associate with any good Christians) and depose him as emperor. Henry countered by convening a council of loyal German bishops who voted in turn to depose the pope. In response to such blatant defiance of papal authority, Gregory excommunicated Henry—the first time an emperor had ever been placed under the ban of the church—and declared him deposed. All German bishops who refused to submit to the papal order were also excommunicated. The pope then followed this action by declaring that all of the emperor's subjects were free of their oaths of fealty to him. This action, as expected, resulted in many German nobles using the excommunication as an excuse to rebel against the imperial authority. After meeting with the legates in Germany, the nobles demanded that Henry obtain papal absolution in order to regain their loyalty and invited Gregory to Germany to hold a synod that would discuss Henry's case.

Henry, realizing that his authority could not survive attack from both his nobles and the papacy, decided to resolve the issue before Gregory could convene the proposed synod. In January 1077, the emperor crossed the Alps with a small group of followers and determined to meet Gregory at Canossa, where the pope had stopped en route to Germany.

Manuscript drawings showing episodes from the Investiture Controversy. 12th century. In the upper left drawing, Henry IV, enthroned, presides over the installation of Bishop Guibert, while to the right a soldier in chain mail pushes Gregory out of the door. The ensuing confusion is depicted below, while on the lower right mourners attend the body of Gregory as he lies dead in exile.

There Henry shrewdly asked Gregory for forgiveness. Although Gregory suspected Henry's motives were political rather than spiritual, he could not as a priest refuse the pleas of a penitent sinner for absolution. This maneuver gave rise to one of the most famous legends of the High Middle Ages: that Henry, barefoot and wearing peasant garb, had stood in the snows before the castle for three days, begging for papal forgiveness.

Henry's supposed act of humiliation was seen as evidence of the supreme authority of the church over secular rulers. The truth is more complex. Henry had successfully restored his position, depriving his unruly nobles of their justification for rebellion. On the other hand, in the long run the emperors may have lost more than they achieved, for imperial prestige was never the same again, and this weakness paved the way for a long period of German decline and disunity.

THE CONCORDAT OF WORMS

Gregory was correct in doubting Henry's motives, for the emperor soon returned to his former habits, and in 1080 the pope once again excommunicated him. This time Henry was determined not to give in. He arranged to have an antipope elected in Gregory's place and invaded Italy in 1081, occupying Rome and besieging Gregory in the Castel Sant' Angelo. Gregory called on his Norman vassals in southern Italy for assistance, but was forced to flee Rome and died in Salerno in 1085, depressed and broken.

The Investiture Controversy was finally resolved in 1122, when Pope Calixtus II and Emperor Henry V concluded the Concordat of Worms. By this agreement, the emperor was allowed to invest a new bishop only with the temporal symbols of his rule, whereas he could no longer bestow the ring and staff, which symbolized spiritual authority. Election of bishops was to be held by church officials but in the presence of the emperor, who could resolve the election in the event of a tie. The compromise did not grant a full victory to either side, but it ensured that thenceforth bishops would have to be acceptable to both church and state. Moreover, although the concordat did not eliminate imperial interference in ecclesiastical matters, it did effectively end the practice of lay investiture.

The reform impulse continued apace in the 12th century as new monastic orders were founded. The most significant effort was the establishment of the Cistercians (named after their first monastery, located at Citeaux in Burgundy) in 1098. The purpose of the Cistercian order was to restore the vigor and purity of the Benedictine and Cluniac monasteries, in which discipline had lapsed. The Cistercians adopted an organizational principle that was more hierarchical than the original Benedictine system but less centralized than the Cluniac order: Each monastery was ruled independently by its own abbot, but every year a meeting of all the abbots was held to ensure uniformity of discipline and procedures.

The Cistercians were fortunate in having as one of their abbots St. Bernard of Clairvaux (1090–1153), who combined ascetic spiritualism with a practical bent for action. Bernard insisted on a severe and disciplined life within the monasteries, which were generally located in isolated spots. The Cistercian orders cleared forests and contributed

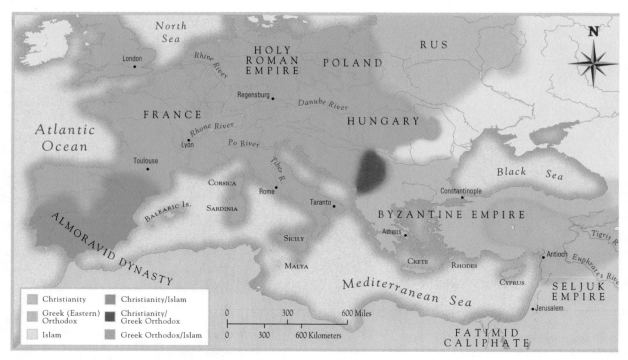

Map 27.2 Major European Religions, c. 1100. Note the spread of Islam from the East into the Byzantine Empire (modern Turkey). Orthodox Christianity has by now spread northward to become firmly established in Russia, without gaining any influence in Eastern Europe. Poland and Hungary have remained bastions of Catholicism to this day.

to the reclamation of unproductive land. Monks observed a strict regimen of manual labor, fasts, and worship, while the monastic buildings were devoid of stained glass, statues, and other ornamentation. Bernard's preaching inspired thousands of pious Christians and launched a crusade against the Muslims. He advised temporal rulers on ecclesiastical affairs and supported the papacy against its secular enemies.

SCHISM AND THE CRISIS OF BYZANTIUM

The religious policies of the Byzantine Emperor Leo III, who had launched the iconoclastic campaign against the veneration of images by Christians (see Topic 22), had created tensions between the Eastern and Western churches. Even though the use of images was eventually restored, the issue added another dimension to the divisions between Rome and Constantinople. The popes had responded in part by sponsoring the Frankish kings and bestowing the imperial title on Charlemagne in 800.

TOWARD THE SCHISM

The Eastern emperor was a sacred figure who fulfilled a religious and a secular mission. Although he was not a priest, the Eastern emperor exercised considerable influence over the church. This tradition was contrary to the experience in the West, where the popes and bishops had assumed political responsibilities as secular authority disintegrated. None of the ecclesiastical leaders in the Byzantine Empire, including the patriarch of Constantinople, ever developed the authority over the Eastern Church that the pope did over the church in the West. Differences did emerge in religious belief and practice, including the Eastern tradition of allowing married men to become priests and the Western belief in purgatory as a stage between heaven and hell. In liturgical matters, the Western Church insisted on Latin as the language of the church, whereas the Eastern Church permitted the use of vernacular languages, including Greek, Slavonic, and Coptic. The only major doctrinal dispute, however, had to do with the Trinity, for Eastern clerics believed that the Holy Spirit derived from the Father, not, as the Roman Church argued, from both the Father and the Son.

The growing chasm between the Eastern and Western churches came to a head in 1054, when Michael Cerularius, the patriarch of Constantinople, declared the independence of the Byzantine Church from Rome. Cerularius had been angered by the haughty behavior of a Roman cardinal who had come to Constantinople to extract concessions from the patriarch. But the notion of papal supremacy, together with papal support for the universal claims of the Western emperors, were the real causes of the break. Although the schism initially had little popular support, the separation of the two churches gradually widened, and the Slavic populations of Russia and the Balkans eventually followed the authority and spiritual leadership of the Byzantine Church.

THE CRISIS OF BYZANTIUM

Byzantine leaders had refused to abandon the idea that there was only one true empire that ruled over all of Christendom. From the 9th to the end of the 11th century, the Byzantine emperors managed partially to restore the military position of the empire. They had waged campaigns against the Bulgars, who had invaded the Balkans, and against the Muslims in southern Italy. In the Middle East, they had recaptured Antioch in 969 and forced the Muslims to retreat into Syria. But as the old military system of *themes*, which supported an army of peasant soldiers, disintegrated in the 11th century, the number of imperial troops declined and the landed aristocracy increased their power. Mercenary armies were hired to make up for the shortage in soldiers. In the place of a once highly centralized imperial government, a feudal system evolved as a series of weak emperors began to give away imperial estates to ensure the loyalty of the nobles. Commercial concessions to Venice and other Italian cities led to a decline in badly needed revenues and weakened the economic position of Byzantium.

Military setbacks began to accumulate. During the course of the 11th century, the Normans under Robert Guiscard wrested Sicily and southern Italy from Muslim control. This loss was followed by the expansion of the Seljuk Turks, a nomadic people from Turkestan in Central Asia who invaded Persia, Syria, and Palestine. The Seljuks embraced the Sunni Muslim faith and eventually took over the Abbasid empire. In 1055 they seized Baghdad, and in 1071 they defeated the Byzantines at the Battle of Manzikert and began to overrun Asia Minor. Some time before 1095, a desperate Byzantine Emperor Alexius Comnenus I (ruled 1081–1118) appealed to Pope Urban II (ruled 1088–1099) for help.

SIGNIFICANT DATES

The Militant Church

910	Cluny monastery founded
1054	Schism between Roman and Eastern churches
1059	College of Cardinals begins to elect popes
1077	Henry IV and Gregory VII at Canossa
1096	First Crusade begins
1122	Concordat of Worms
1147	Second Crusade launched
1187	Saladin seizes Jerusalem
1189	Third Crusade begins
1198–1216	Innocent III reigns as pope
1204	Fourth Crusade sacks Constantinople
1212	Children's Crusade
1215	Fourth Lateran Council; Dominican order established
1182–1226	Life of Francis of Assisi

The appeal was religious and political. One of the most popular forms of religious devotion had long been the practice of visiting shrines that were sacred to Christians, especially the sites that contained relics of Christ or the saints. The most important of such pilgrimages had been to the Holy Land, where the towns of Jerusalem, Nazareth, and Bethlehem had been particular goals. The Turkish conquests now threatened access to the holiest of Christian shrines.

Urban was a Frenchman and a Cluniac monk who saw the danger posed by the Turks to Western Christendom. In 1095, at the French town of Clermont, Urban preached a remarkable sermon in which he called on Christians to take arms against the Turks. With the growth of religious zeal in the 11th century, the idea of waging a holy war against the Muslim "infidel"—as had been done in Spain—gained popularity. Urban appealed to a sense of solidarity with the Eastern Christians but also pictured the Holy Land as a region of untold riches. As an added inducement, the pope also offered a plenary indulgence—meaning the remission of all earthly punishment for sins—for those who died in the effort. Out of these circumstances developed the Crusades, military expeditions through which several generations of European leaders attempted to recapture the Holy Land from the Muslims.

THE ERA OF THE CRUSADES

The Crusades had their origins partly in the reforms within the church, which strengthened the position of the papacy and began to infuse medieval society with a renewed religious fervor. Although the Crusades were a sign of the expanded authority of the church, they were also a sign of the expansion of economic and social life that accompanied the revival of trade and the growth of European cities. In the period from 1095 to 1248, seven official Crusades struck out toward the Middle East, and although in the end they failed to achieve their major objective, they had a significant impact on the religious, economic, and political life of the High Middle Ages.

THE FIRST CRUSADE

Urban's appeal in 1095 received a zealous and unexpectedly broad response. He appointed a bishop to organize the expedition and proclaimed the church's protection for the families and property of volunteers. Women were forbidden to join without the permission of their husbands, but many nonprofessional fighters followed the leadership of two fanatical preachers, Peter the Hermit and Walter the Penniless. Both groups were wiped out by the Turks in Asia Minor. The first real soldiers, mostly French, left Western Europe in the summer of 1096. In all, they probably numbered fewer than 10,000 men, although some sources give larger numbers. When they reached Constantinople, trouble immediately arose, for while the Emperor Alexius had wanted assistance in recovering the Holy Lands, the French warriors were determined to keep whatever land they conquered for themselves. Although they eventually swore an oath of allegiance to the Byzantine emperor, the tensions between the Byzantines and the crusaders were never overcome. The crusading armies also were divided among themselves and often proved less effective as fighters because of their rivalries.

The Peasants' Crusade. This is a later, Renaissance evocation of the First Crusade; no artist of the period (late 11th century) would have painted either architecture or landscape as they appear here. The episode is given an idealized treatment. The peasants, led by the giant figure of Peter the Hermit, are still dressed in spotless white clothes, despite their long journey, while their Turkish slaughterers are shown as a faceless mass of bodies and weapons.

© Cliché Bibliothèque Nationale de France, Paris

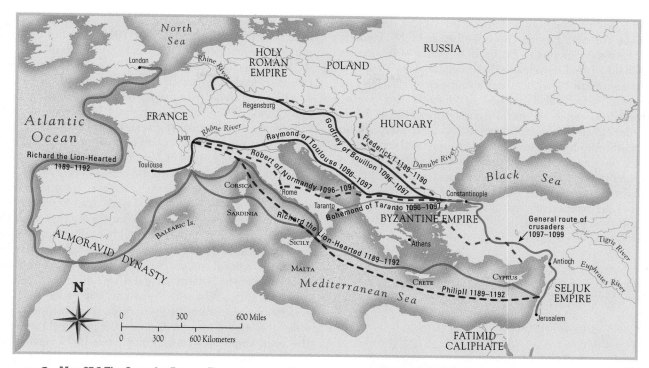

Map 27.3 The Crusader Routes. The convergence of the various routes at Constantinople (modern Istanbul) was to prove a constant nightmare to the Byzantine authorities, theoretically as faithfully Christian as the Western armies, but in practice bitterly hostile to the Western Church, which had supported the Crusades. The outcome was the Crusaders' sack of Constantinople in 1204, fatally weakening the Byzantine Empire. The only ones to profit were the Muslim Ottoman Turks. Go to http://info.wadsworth.com/053461065X for an interactive version of this map.

The crusaders fought their way successfully across Asia Minor, and in 1098, having been reinforced with equipment and supplies by Italian shippers, they took the city of Antioch in Syria. The Italian merchants became indispensable to the crusaders and reaped huge profits for their assistance, eventually establishing important port facilities in the Middle East. In July 1099, the crusaders captured Jerusalem after a six-week siege and massacred most of the Muslim population of the city.

Having achieved the chief purpose of their expedition, many crusaders remained in the Middle East, where they created a group of four independent Christian states: Edessa, Antioch, Tripoli, and Jerusalem, the latter stretching south from Beirut to Egypt. Each of these states was ruled by a Western crusader in the feudal manner, with vassals and fiefs. The landed estates were taken from their former Muslim owners and divided among the Christian knights, although in other respects Muslims were tolerated and were permitted to carry on business activities in the cities. Although the Christian states were surrounded by Muslim and Turkish territory, they survived for almost 200 years.

The Roman Church quickly reestablished jurisdiction over the hierarchy in the Holy Land and exercised authority principally through the patriarchs of Antioch and Jerusalem. Most of the Western monastic orders established houses in the crusader kingdoms, and a new kind of religious organization made its appearance in the form of orders of military monks. The two most famous and powerful, both headquartered in Jerusalem, were the Knights of the Temple, known as the Templars, and the Knights of St. John of Jerusalem, known as the Hospitalers. Their members were devoted to protecting pilgrims and providing care for the sick, but were also dedicated to keeping up a holy war against the infidel. They eventually received papal recognition and through repeated bequests became the owners of extensive estates in the Middle East and in Europe.

THE CRUSADES AND THE DECLINE OF BYZANTIUM

The Second Crusade began as a result of the efforts by the Turks to recapture the Holy Land. In 1144, when news arrived in the West that the Turks had taken back Edessa, the northernmost of the Latin kingdoms, St. Bernard of Clairvaux persuaded King Louis VII of France and Emperor Conrad III of Germany to lead another campaign against them. After two years of futile effort (1147–1149), however, their inability to cooperate either with each other or with the Byzantine generals led them to defeat.

The Third Crusade came after a lull of 40 years. Between 1169 and 1187, the Muslim leader Saladin (1137?–1193), a warrior of Kurdish descent, swept across Syria and Egypt, surrounding the Kingdom of Jerusalem. In 1187, Saladin took Jerusalem. Saladin was an enlightened ruler who rebuilt cities, restored agriculture, and exhibited tolerance toward the Christians he conquered, but his victory sent shock-waves through Europe. In response, in 1189 Frederick Barbarossa of Germany, Philip II Augustus of France, and Richard I (the Lion-Hearted) of England all personally led armies toward Palestine after raising money through a tax known as the "Saladin tithe." But disaster also overtook this effort. After moving overland through Asia Minor, Frederick died of a drowning accident. The French and English, who had traveled by sea, encountered repeated defeats once they began fighting on land. After Philip returned to France in frustration, Richard and Saladin, each of whom respected the other's bravery and chivalry, negotiated an agreement that gave free access to Christians wanting to visit Jerusalem.

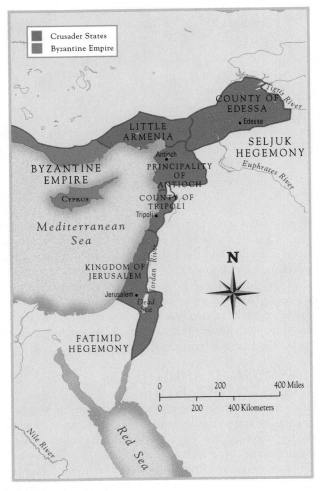

Map 27.4 The Crusader States. These small Western outposts had very little long-term influence in the region but helped establish commercial relations between Western Europe and the Muslim world. Their most famous legacy was the creation of the Order of the Knights of St. John, founded in 1113 to tend sick pilgrims in the Holy Land. After the fall of Jerusalem, the Hospitalers (as they became known) moved first to Cyprus, then to Rhodes, and finally settled in Malta in 1530. Napoleon expelled them in 1798, and they now work in Rome; their "territory"—a palace near the Spanish Steps—is the smallest independent state in the world.

If the Second and Third Crusades were military failures, the Fourth Crusade (1202–1204) proved to be a failure in quite another way. After Saladin's death in 1193 and the collapse of his empire, Pope Innocent III encouraged Christian leaders to launch still another attack against the Muslims. But in order to pay for their transportation to the Holy Land, the nobles who answered Innocent's call were induced by the Venetian shippers to seize Zara, a Christian port city on the Dalmatian coast across from Italy. This gave Venice complete control of Adriatic commerce but put into doubt the real motivations of the crusaders.

Then, as if to confirm their real reason for their campaign, in 1204 events diverted the crusaders to Constantinople, where a struggle for the succession to the Byzantine throne was under way. One of the claimants had promised the knights a large payment for their help, but when the agreed amount was not forthcoming, the crusaders sacked the Byzantine capital, stealing precious metals and holy relics. While the Venetians imposed a trade monopoly on the eastern Mediterranean, the Latin nobles divided the empire into small states, the principal one being the Latin Empire of Constantinople ruled by a Flemish noble. Pope Innocent, who mildly condemned the attack on Constantinople, attempted to force the reunification of the Eastern and Western churches and appointed a Venetian patriarch to Constantinople.

One of the most intriguing episodes of the era of the Crusades was the so-called Children's Crusade of 1212. Led by a visionary French boy, Stephen of Cloyes, and fired by a belief that the innocence of children could achieve what corrupt adults could not, the children embarked at Marseilles but were sold into slavery by unscrupulous ship captains. A group of German children who set out overland made it to Italy before perishing of hunger and disease. However irrational or impractical the Children's Crusade may seem to modern minds, the phenomenon suggests the range of experiences characteristic of medieval Christian faith.

In the face of constant fighting among themselves, the Latin states in Asia Minor did not survive very long. In 1261, the Byzantine leader Michael VIII Paleologus reconquered Constantinople, and Innocent's efforts to reunite the two churches collapsed. Michael's dynasty ruled for another two centuries, but the Byzantine Empire had been shattered beyond repair. Moreover, the Fourth Crusade had so embittered relations between East and West that no unity of Christian forces was again possible.

During the 13th century three other Crusades struck out from Europe toward the Middle East. Despite temporary achievements, none resulted in permanent Christian victories. Yet in other ways the impact of the Crusades was considerable. The Crusades, encouraged by the economic revival of Europe, further stimulated trade and increased the prosperity of some Italian maritime cities. The cost of the Crusades, which was considerable, resulted in more currency and precious metals being put into circulation as well as the development of new methods of raising revenues. The need to construct castles and develop siege and defensive techniques influenced both Western and Muslim methods of warfare. The departure of so many warrior knights, who might otherwise have been involved in repeated conflicts at home, may have helped bring a measure of peace to European society. Furthermore, it is likely that the Western kings and the popes both gained prestige and authority as a result of the leadership they exhibited in the Crusades. On the other hand, the effect of so much aggression and interference on the local Muslim populations, organized and perpetuated by the leaders—both secular and religious—of the West, left deep and lasting hostility in the Middle East. Centuries later, Arab bitterness continued to influence the course of historical events.

THE AGE OF INNOCENT III

The greatest pope of the High Middle Ages was Innocent III (ruled 1198–1216). Innocent's reign was best known for two policies: He developed the instruments of papal government to their fullest extent and insisted on the supremacy of the papacy not only within the church but over secular rulers as well.

THE PAPAL GOVERNMENT

Gregory VII and most of the other reforming popes had been priests who came out of the monastic tradition. Innocent and the other popes of the 13th century, on the other hand, were canon lawyers and professional administrators who viewed the church as a secular and a spiritual institution. Innocent, who was 38 when he succeeded to the papal throne, was an energetic and ambitious ruler. Although the papal conflicts with secular rulers absorbed much public attention, most of the time and energy of popes such as Innocent was devoted to the day-to-day routine of building what was rapidly becoming a highly complex and efficient bureaucracy.

When the pope wanted to deal with important doctrinal or policy issues for the church, he often called special church councils of high prelates. The earlier Third Lateran Council of 1179 was followed by the Fourth Lateran Council in 1215, a gathering of more than 1,200 bishops and abbots that issued important decisions that helped improve standards of priestly behavior. The latter council also concerned itself with clarifying matters of dogma, especially the question of "transubstantiation," the belief that the bread and wine of the Eucharist were changed into the body and blood of Christ. The council declared that although the

Fresco painting of Pope Innocent III. 13th century. Although Innocent is wearing the papal headdress, he is shown as a young man. The Latin inscription beneath records the chief events of his reign.

HISTORICAL PERSPECTIVES

FRANCIS OF ASSISI

LAWRENCE CUNNINGHAM   University of Notre Dame

The fact that one can find cast concrete statues of Francis of Assisi with a bird perched on his shoulder in almost every American suburban garden center is testimony to the persistent fame of this son of a 12th-century Umbrian cloth merchant who went on to become one of the most celebrated saints in the Christian church.

In many ways Francis was a revolutionary, although he did not think of himself as one. In a rare autobiographical moment he described himself as "unlettered and subject to every one." He was also a child of his own time in that there were others who wanted to live a poor life as a quiet protest against the wealth of the medieval church or to be itinerant preachers to serve the swelling urban populations of the day. It was given to Francis, however, to crystallize these impulses and, in the process, to become so famous that he was immortalized less than a century after his death in Dante's *Paradiso* as the exemplar of the Christian gospel.

Francis taught a way of life that was an alternative to the monasteries that had been so crucial in earlier times. He did not want his followers to live in rural settings in a stable environment of prayer and work. He wanted his friars (the word means "brothers") to move from place to place, working with their hands or begging like the other poor when there was no work, while preaching in the city squares. In the wonderful apho-rism of the English writer Gilbert Keith Chesterton, "What Benedict [i.e., the founder of Western monasticism] stored, Francis scattered."

This was a contagious idea. Francis began with a handful of followers, but before 1220 there were nearly 3,000 "little brothers" who were spread all over western Europe and into North Africa. His friendship with Clare Offreduccio (1193–1253) resulted in a "second order" of women who lived a life of poverty in a stable community. This growth inevitably led to a certain institutionalization of his simple ideals, but the plain fact is that his friars were active in every major European city before Francis's death in 1226.

Francis emphasized in his life and preaching a fundamental belief in the capacity of the natural world to teach people about the presence of God. He was not a pantheist or, in the modern sense of the term, a "nature lover." He did very much believe and teach in the natural world as a visible sign of the reality of God. Toward the end of his life he wrote a poem called the "Canticle of the Creatures"—it was one of the very first poems written in Italian—expressing this idea. Here is a sample from that poem:

Praised be You, My Lord, for Brother Fire
Through whom You light the night

outer appearance of the bread and wine remained the same, the inner reality of them was transformed.

PAPAL SUPREMACY AND CHURCH-STATE RELATIONS

As canon law developed, the pope's authority in ecclesiastical affairs was defined and broadened. Innocent III was fond of describing the pope as the "vicar of Christ," a divinely sanctioned role derived as the successor of St. Peter. In this capacity, however, Innocent believed that the notion of papal authority included supremacy over temporal rulers. "The Lord Jesus Christ," wrote Innocent, "has set up one ruler over all things as His universal vicar," and some of the most powerful princes of the age were forced to bow to his will. For example, between 1205 and 1213, Innocent fought a particularly relentless campaign against King John of England (see Topic 29). The dispute arose when Innocent intervened in a contested election for a new archbishop of Canterbury, appointing Stephen Langton as his candidate. John, who maintained it was his right to nominate English bishops, refused to recognize Langton. The pope responded by excommunicating John and placing England under an interdict, which banned all public worship in the kingdom and prohibited all sacraments except baptism and extreme unction. When Innocent learned that the barons were plotting against John, he announced that the king had been deposed and released all of his subjects from their loyalty to him. As in the case of Henry IV and Pope Gregory VII, John now saw the wisdom of submitting to papal authority. In 1213, John accepted Langton's appointment and, in a

He is beautiful and playful, robust and strong.
Praised be You, My Lord, for our sister Mother Earth,
Who sustains and governs us,
Who produces varied fruits, colored flowers and
herbs. . . .

Some scholars, as early as the last century, have argued that this Franciscan emphasis on love for the natural world and respect for animal life (stories tell of Francis preaching to the birds and taming a wild wolf) had a profound impact on the European artistic imagination of the 14th century and may have influenced the Renaissance turn to the natural world in the visual arts. To say it another way, the shift away from the rather "otherworldly" air of Italian and Byzantine painting to a more naturalistic setting may have been hastened by the Franciscan concern for seeing the divine in the natural world.

Francis introduced a new kind of spirituality into Western Christian religiousness. He had a deep conviction that it was possible in life to imitate Christ in a literal and fundamental fashion. Francis sold his possessions and lived without material goods because Jesus had said in the gospels that this was the perfect way to follow Him. He attempted literally to give away everything to the poor. In 1223 he decided to observe Christmas in the town of Greccio in a stable in order to experience the poverty into which Jesus was born. From that event derived the later custom of building a Christmas crèche as a sign of the Christmas season. Francis found the supreme expression of poverty in the passion of Christ on the cross. It is that link between poverty and the cross that most impressed Dante when he speaks of the saint in Canto XI of the *Paradiso*.

Francis' deep meditation on the Passion of Christ in the fall of 1224 triggered a phenomenon called the *stigmata* (i.e., Francis showed signs of the wounds of Christ on his own hands, feet, and side). As far as we know, this was the first time that this phenomenon had been reported in the history of Christianity.

One result of the stigmata was, especially after the death of Francis, an intensified emphasis on the human sufferings of Christ which showed up in everything from more realistic depictions of Christ's wounds in art to new forms of religious devotion which focused on the cross or the crown of thorns or other such incidents in the Passion narratives.

Although Francis always remained a popular saint within the Catholic tradition, he faded from popular view after the Reformation in Protestant Christianity and was severely criticized by nonbelievers like Voltaire in the Enlightenment era. It is noteworthy that the German poet Goethe showed no interest in either Francis or the art inspired by him when he visited Assisi in the late 18th century; according to his *Italian Journey* (written in 1816), Goethe observed the Roman temple in Assisi's main square, got back in his carriage, and headed south to Rome. Of Francis, he recorded not a word.

It was the Romantics, late in the 19th century, who rediscovered Francis of Assisi for the world outside of Catholic piety. They admired his feel for beauty, the simplicity of his poverty, the free wandering of his life, and his capacity for love. In religious circles, Francis is now seen as an ecumenical figure and his city of Assisi is often visited by both Christians and non-Christians.

move designed to secure papal support in his struggle with the barons, acknowledged his kingdom to be a papal fief.

Innocent secured similar recognition from the rulers of Portugal and the kingdom of Aragon, and applied papal sanctions against King Philip II Augustus of France, who had arranged to have his marriage to Ingeborg of Denmark annulled immediately after receipt of her 10,000-mark dowry. Innocent demanded that Philip take Ingeborg back as his legitimate wife and placed France under an interdict, although the king bowed to papal will only after many years. The pope also intervened in German affairs. After the death of King Henry VI, the German nobles quarreled over a successor. Henry's son, Frederick, was only 3 years old at the time, but the boy's mother, acting as regent, made Frederick's royal inheritance in Sicily a fief of the papacy. When his mother

died in 1198, Frederick automatically became the pope's ward (see Topic 29 for details of Frederick's reign). Innocent's policy toward secular rulers was controversial, but he did substantially enhance the power of the papacy.

HERESY AND THE INQUISITION

Beginning in the 11th century, the West was increasingly troubled by the appearance of heresies, which may be simply defined as doctrinal beliefs that differed from those officially accepted by the church. The roots of heresy are varied. No doubt many followers of heresies were disturbed by the decline in moral standards among the clergy. Heresy was particularly popular in the new towns, where social and economic change created a large population of urban poor who resented ecclesiastical privileges and the wealth of the merchant class.

Disenfranchised elements of society, especially young men without careers and women who lacked dowry money to marry or enter convents, were also attracted to heresies.

The sect known as the Waldensians was founded in the 12th century by a pious merchant named Peter Waldo of Lyons. He established a lay order, known as the Poor Men of Lyons, who preached and gave charity to the poor. Although his order received papal approval, his ideas soon ran into trouble, especially the notion that the sacraments were not effective unless given by priests who observed high standards of morality and the belief that laymen could preach the Gospels. The Waldensian heresy, which spread to Spain, Germany, and northern Italy, was officially condemned by the Fourth Vatican Council in 1215 and was virtually wiped out in most places.

The Albigensian movement, which attracted wider support, posed a more serious challenge to the church. Named after the southern French town of Albi, where it had many followers, the movement was also called Catharism, after the Greek for "purity." This heresy seems to have originated in the pre-Christian Manichean move-ment of the Middle East, from where it spread to the Balkans, Italy, and then to France. The belief hinged on the notion of the struggle between good and evil, and the doctrine that everything associated with the material world was evil. The human soul, the Albigensians argued, was good but was imprisoned in the body, which was evil. The Albigensians preached against marriage and sexual intercourse because these acts furthered procreation of the material world, and denied that Christ had ever assumed flesh and blood. They also rejected the sacraments and the notion of priests, holding that pure believers led lives of asceticism in the service of good.

The church fought the Albigensians in several ways. About 1205, a Spanish priest named Dominic de Guzmán (1170–1221) began to preach among the Albigensians in order to reconvert them. Dominic and his followers observed vows of poverty and lived by begging. Ten years later, Pope Innocent III officially approved the Dominican order, formally known as the Order of Preachers. It soon became obvious, however, that reconversion alone was not sufficient to deal with the heresies. The secular ruler of Toulouse refused

Panel from the *St. Francis Altarpiece* by Bonaventura Berlinghieri. 1235. 5 feet by 3½ feet (1.25 by .99 m). Painted shortly after the death of the saint, this work shows him wearing the monastic dress he invented for his followers. His hands and feet bear the *stigmata,* the wounds that marked the nailing of Christ to the cross. The episodes on the sides illustrate scenes from his life, including (middle left) the famous occasion of his preaching to the birds.

© Scala/Art Resource, NY

to work with the church in suppressing the Albigensians, causing Innocent to excommunicate him and call for a crusade against the heresy. The campaign unleashed a wave of terrible violence resulting in the deaths of thousands and the twisting of the holy war into an excuse by leaders from other regions to seize the property of local nobles.

In 1233, one of Innocent's successors, Pope Gregory IX (1227–1241), created a papal tribunal known as the Inquisition to cope with the threat of heresies (not to be confused with the later Spanish Inquisition of the 16th century). The papal Inquisition operated according to established procedures of canon and Roman law, the latter permitting the use of torture to force confessions. Accused heretics who refused to confess and repent could be punished and executed by the secular authorities.

The Albigensian heresy was eventually wiped out, but at such a high price that even Innocent was shocked at the violence. Moreover, the atmosphere of fear and hatred aroused by the war against the heretics was often responsible for persecutions against other kinds of minorities, including Jews and Muslims, and spilled over into intolerance and legislation against homosexuality.

THE RISE OF POPULAR DEVOTION

Papal recognition of the Dominican order in 1215 occurred not only as a response to heresy but in recognition of the need for the church to engage more directly in the lives of Christians and the social realities of the day. Rather than closing themselves off from the secular world in isolated monasteries, these new mendicant (begging) orders lived and worked among the people of the cities, preaching and doing good works.

THE FRANCISCAN RENEWAL

The most famous and popular saint of the Middle Ages was Francis of Assisi (1182?–1226), the son of a prosperous Italian family. At first he led an unruly and dissolute life typical of many young men of his class, but at the age of 22 he underwent a profound religious experience that caused him to abandon all worldly comforts and devote himself to God. Rather than adopting the severe asceticism that drove some Christians into religious melancholy, Francis embraced the challenge before him with joyous fervor.

In 1206, with the approval of the bishop of Assisi, Francis went on a pilgrimage to Rome and began preaching the lessons of love and joy that God bestowed on all creatures of the earth. Soon he had gathered a following of disciples around him who lived in crude huts, which they built themselves, and went from house to house begging and preaching. In 1208, Francis received approval from Innocent III to found a new religious order of mendicant friars, known as the Order of Friars Minor, better known as the Franciscans. Eventually he drew up a simple but persuasive rule based on biblical inspiration.

Francis sent his followers abroad and traveled widely. He visited Spain, France, and Dalmatia, and in 1219 went to Palestine. When he returned he found his growing order riddled with dissension and gave up its leadership to devote himself to preaching. Francis wrote a testament stressing the need to observe simplicity and poverty and was made a saint two years after his death.

Francis inspired many followers, and the order grew rapidly throughout Europe. The orders founded by Francis and Clare attracted members because the 13th century was an age of great religious enthusiasm among all classes. The veneration of saints, and especially the Virgin Mary, and the thousands of people who went on pilgrimages to their shrines, attested to the strength of popular devotion.

Putting the Militant Church in Perspective

Religion was a real and significant part of everyday life in medieval society, and the church was undoubtedly the most important institution of the Middle Ages. Despite setbacks, it demonstrated remarkable powers of regeneration. Out of the criticism of its worldliness and corruption, the church renewed itself through a strenuous movement of reform that reached from the ascetic monks of remote monasteries to the popes of Rome. The reforming popes built an elaborate and effective institution that played a critical and ever-expanding role in the spiritual and secular lives of millions of people. Popes such as Gregory VII and Innocent III undermined secular control of the church, successfully challenged the temporal rulers of the day, and launched a series of dramatic Crusades against unbelievers. Although the rise of heresies suggests that not all believers were satisfied with the spiritual standards of the age, the orders of mendicant friars that arose in the 13th century reveal the profound commitment that many felt to the spiritual and moral ideals of the church.

Questions for Further Study

1. What were the sources of spiritual reform in the church?
2. Over what issues did the papacy and the Holy Roman Empire clash?
3. What factors explain the Crusades? What caused their failure?
4. Describe the nature of Franciscan spirituality.

Suggestions for Further Reading

Boswell, John. *Christianity, Social Tolerance, and Homosexuality.* Chicago, 1980.

Brooke, Rosalind. *Popular Religion in the Middle Ages.* London, 1984.

Constable, Giles. *The Reformation of the Twelfth Century.* New York, 1996.

Cunningham, Lawrence S. *Saint Francis of Assisi.* Boston, 1976.

Gurevich, Avon. *Medieval Popular Culture: Problems of Belief and Perception.* Cambridge, MA, 1988.

Hamilton, Bernard. *The Crusades.* Stroude, 1998.

House, Adrian. *Francis of Assisi.* New York, 2001.

James, Liz, ed. *Desire and Denial in Byzantium.* Aldershot, 1990.

Kedar, Benjamin Z. *Crusade and Mission: European Approaches Towards the Muslim.* Princeton, NJ, 1984.

Lawrence, Clifford H. *Medieval Monasticism.* London, 1984.

Maguire, Henry, ed. *Byzantine Court Culture from 829 to 1204.* Washington, DC, 1997.

Mulder-Bakker, A., and J. Wogan-Browne, eds. *Household, Family and Christian Tradition.* Turnhout, 2002.

Rosenwein, Barbara. *Rhinoceros Bound: Cluny in the Tenth Century.* Philadelphia, 1982.

Tillmann, Helene. *Innocent III.* Amsterdam, 1980.

InfoTrac College Edition

Enter the search term *Saint Francis* using Key Terms.

Enter the search term *Crusades* using the Subject Guide.

SCHOLARS, TROUBADOURS, AND BUILDERS

In the 11th and 12th centuries, Western European society made a series of cultural advances that were to prove central to its intellectual and artistic growth. The foundation of the first universities marked a crucial development in Western thought. With the revival of town life, in addition to the cathedral schools—training institutions for priests—secular institutions began to appear that took lay pupils. During the 12th century, universities evolved first at Paris and Bologna and then in England. For all the differences between the study programs at a medieval university and a present-day one, the degree system and the organizational structure of a modern university have much in common with the earliest institutions, as do many aspects of student life.

Medieval professors used a systematic approach to teaching called *scholasticism*. By this method they sought to reconcile the rational views of the Greeks with the requirements of Christian faith. The development of scholasticism reached its highest point in the two great *Summaries* of St. Thomas Aquinas. In them Aquinas uses philosophical methods to analyze theological questions, while admitting the existence of "mysteries of the faith," which resist rational explanation.

With the rise of lay education, writers began to use their own vernacular languages instead of Latin. Two literary traditions gradually appeared: heroic epics such as the *Song of Roland* and shorter love lyrics, first composed and sung by the troubadours at the courts of southern France.

The history of music took a giant step forward with the beginnings of the polyphonic style, which, unlike earlier Gregorian plainsong, combined several different melodic lines. The result was the first stage in the foundation of modern harmony and counterpoint. Modern methods of musical notation owe their origins to the work of Guido of Arezzo, who in the 11th century invented a way to record the pitch of notes by means of a "staff" of horizontal lines.

The architectural style of the age of Guido and the *Song of Roland* was the Romanesque. Romanesque churches are massive and robust, and many of them have immense towers. Sculptured figures often appear both inside and on the exterior façade. For the first time since the Romans, sculptors began to explore the expressive possibilities of the human body, producing works of striking emotional power.

The result of all these developments was the formation of a cultural movement common to all of Western Europe. The provincialism of feudal life gave way to a broader-based, more dynamic approach to the arts and the world of the mind. The Romanesque age combined veneration for centuries-old religious beliefs with a search for new secular approaches.

THE FIRST UNIVERSITIES

The idea of places of higher learning, where students could hear lectures and scholars could conduct research, was not a medieval invention. Organized schools existed in the ancient world. Both Plato and Aristotle gave formal courses of lectures, and the School of Alexandria was famous in Greek and Roman times for its library and other research facilities. The main contributions of the medieval university system to the history of Western education were three: fixed curricula (courses of study), organized bodies of professors, and the awarding of degrees.

FROM SCHOOL TO UNIVERSITY

With the fall of the Roman Empire, the general level of education in Western Europe collapsed. Even the efforts of Charlemagne to improve the culture of his day by founding primary schools attached to bishoprics and monasteries did little to produce any real change. Several factors combined around 1100 to alter this situation. The growth of towns, the stabilization of the economy, and the development of effective civic government all created an urban society with a demand for better education. Before then, the few people who could read had learned at monasteries, which mainly operated to teach monks.

By 1100 the cathedrals in the towns began to replace the more remote monastic schools with their own urban centers for education. Over the following century, the curriculum, which was originally designed to train priests, began to broaden. The new civic communities required trained lawyers. Furthermore, as economic improvements brought increased travel and trade, Latin—the language of the Catholic Church—began to serve both legal and commercial needs. With the renewed study of Latin grammar and composition came a revival of interest in the Roman classics.

Although the cathedral schools continued to devote themselves primarily to training clerics, alternate institutions began to spring up for the children of upper-class citizens and merchants. Both teachers and pupils in these schools were laymen, while women generally learned to read at home under the instruction of private tutors. As a result, for the first time for centuries the church no longer controlled education.

The rise in literacy was enormous. Around 1100, less than 1 percent of Western Europeans could read, and most of those were clerics. By 1340 perhaps 40 percent of Florentine women and men were literate. The consequence was the development of a class of educated laypeople, who were able to question—or to ignore—the teachings of the church.

The earliest universities came into being to provide more specialized training for those who had received a standard elementary education at a cathedral or secular school. The University of Bologna, the oldest in Italy, specialized in law. The University of Paris actually started as a cathedral school. As it attracted increasingly eminent teachers, its level of instruction rose; by shortly after 1200 it had become the intellectual center of Europe.

Illuminated manuscript from *Lecture of Henricus de Alemania,* by Laurencius de Voltolina, showing a university lecture. Second half of 14th century. The professor lectures from his raised seat (cathedra), while the students sit and take notes. Those in the front row are reasonably attentive, but those farther back are either chatting among themselves or dozing.

© bpk, Berlin, Kupferstichkabinett/bpk. Photo: Joerg P. Andres

THE UNIVERSITY OF PARIS

The transition from school to university at Paris began when its teachers formed a corporation to control the level of instruction and to supervise student admissions. The Latin word for a guild or corporation is *universitas*. The new institution served to protect its members because both students and teachers were at first looked on with suspicion by medieval society. The university also had a legal status that permitted it to raise money and to issue official documents. When students completed a course of studies and satisfied the examiners, they received a certificate that entitled them in turn to teach. The Latin term for teacher, *magister*, gave its name to the rank, or degree, of Master of Arts. Further training was necessary to earn the degree of Doctor (Latin *doctus* means "learned").

The arts curriculum at Paris increasingly emphasized secular learning rather than theology. In 1210 the tension this development caused between arts and theology professors led to a split. The masters and students of arts moved their operations to the Left Bank of the river Seine. To this day that district of Paris, which is still associated with student and intellectual life, retains a name reminiscent of the first university classes taught there: the Latin Quarter.

STUDENT LIFE IN A MEDIEVAL UNIVERSITY

By 1250 there were around 7,000 students at the University of Paris—an astonishing number for a medieval city, and higher than the entire population of many towns. During the same period the University of Oxford, founded shortly after Paris, had about 2,000 students enrolled.

Students could turn to a range of sources for financial support, including family members, civic grants, and charitable individuals. Some generous benefactors paid for the construction of student housing. The most famous of these was Robert de Sorbon, who founded the Sorbonne in 1257. The college became part of the university in the 19th century, and its name now generally refers to the University of Paris as a whole.

Student complaints about their housing included the poor quality of the food and inadequate heating. Books, which were handwritten on expensive parchment, and writing materials were in short supply. Days were long. Most arts students attended their first lectures at 5 A.M., following it with attendance at Mass and then breakfast. More lectures followed for most of the morning, and the hour before lunch was set aside for formal debates, which provided training in clear thinking and public speaking. In the afternoon, tutorial sessions reworked the material of the morning's lessons. After supper at 6 P.M., students could study until bedtime, at 9 P.M.

If this seems an improbably austere description of student life, we receive a far more lively picture of the undergraduates of medieval days from the student poetry that has survived. One of the most interesting collections, the *Carmina Burana (Songs of Beuren)* turned up in a Bavarian monastery (Benediktbeuren) in the 19th century. The poems, dating to the late 12th and 13th centuries, are in Latin, French, and German.

The subjects of these student verses are the perennial ones of student life: drinking songs, love songs (some romantic, some lamenting lost loves, some simply obscene), and satires on pompous professors or lousy housing. The patron saint of college life was the mythical St. Golias, in whose honor students composed Goliardic poems and songs. These works illustrate the exhilaration and sense of freedom that the new educational opportunities opened up for increasing numbers of people.

SCHOLASTICISM: FAITH, REALITY, AND REASON

Professors in the expanding universities of the 12th century drew their ideas from three sources. The first, that of traditional church teachings, had remained authoritative for a millennium. The second source consisted of the advances of ancient Greek thinkers. Knowledge of these had been lost to the West with the disappearance of an understanding of the Greek language. They reentered the Western tradition by means of the third source, medieval Arabic philosophy and science. Muslim scholars had translated many of the most important Greek scientific texts and many of the works of Aristotle into Arabic and used them as the basis of their own inquiries. For Western readers, however, Arabic was as remote as Greek.

The vital key that unlocked the accumulated wisdom of the Greeks and their Muslim commentators for Western culture was the appearance at the end of the 12th century of a flood of Latin translations. Many of these emerged from the Muslim communities in Spain and Sicily (see Topic 23), where Christians could have contact with Arabic speakers or with Jews who spoke both Arabic and Latin. By around 1260, Western scholars could read Latin versions of virtually all of Aristotle's surviving works and writings by major Greek scientists such as Euclid and Ptolemy. At the same time they became acquainted with the ideas of their Muslim contemporaries, including the philosophers Avicenna and Averroes.

THE SCHOLASTIC SYSTEM

Scholasticism represented the attempt to reconcile the sacred teachings of the church with the knowledge acquired by human reason and experience. Its practitioners sought to apply Greek philosophical ideas—principally those of Aristotle—to Christian doctrine. They believed that reason, although always subordinate to faith, increased the faithful's understanding of their beliefs. At the same time, they sought to reclaim the high ground of the intellectual world from the increasing prominence of the secular universities.

The most important, and certainly the most controversial, forerunner of scholasticism was the French philosopher Peter Abelard (1079–1142), one of the few figures in the history of Western intellectual development whose love life is as well-known as his theology.

A brilliant student under William of Champeaux in Paris, Abelard alienated his fellow students and professors alike by his arrogant superiority in public debates. In 1113, after a nervous breakdown caused by the strain of founding and running a series of schools, he began teaching at the University of Paris. Handsome and eloquent, he soon became the most popular instructor there. His courses at the university drew foreign pupils from many countries, including two future popes and some 20 students who later became cardinals.

His most famous student, however, lived within closer reach. Héloise (c. 1098–1164) was the niece of a canon at the Church of Notre Dame, who was famous for her learning and her beauty. Attracted by Héloise's reputation, Abelard took lodgings in the canon's house to act as her tutor. He was 35 at the time and she was 15. In his later autobiography, *The Story of My Calamities*, Abelard describes what happened next: "Under the pretext of work we made ourselves entirely free for love, and the pursuit of her studies provided the secrecy which love desired."

To the fury of her uncle, Héloise became pregnant and gave birth to a son. Abelard proposed marriage, but Héloise at first refused: "What could be in common between scholars and cradles? Who is there bent on philosophical reflection who could bear the wailing of babies?" Abelard insisted, and the two were married secretly in Paris. Thereafter events are confused. Héloise's uncle, although present at the marriage, seems to have plotted revenge for the loss of his niece's "honor." A gang of his servants attacked and castrated Abelard, and Héloise sought refuge in a convent.

Abelard retreated to a monastery but soon returned to teaching in Paris, driven by student demand and his own restless intellect. His autobiography reveals nostalgia for his former life as well as remorse: "I ought to groan for the sins I have perpetrated yet I sigh for those which now I am unable to commit." He continued to teach and to write for the rest of his life.

So controversial were Abelard's philosophical writings that in 1141, the year before his death, a church council condemned him for heresy. One of his works that aroused particular anger was *Sic et Non (Yes and No)*, setting out a series of quotations from the Bible and the early Fathers of the Church, which apparently take contradictory points of view on various theological points. His contemporaries saw this as an attempt to embarrass and confuse the authority of the church, but Abelard's intention was to apply the tools of logic and reason to theology and to reconcile religion and reason—the very method that scholastic thinkers were to develop.

Fresco in the Spanish Chapel of the Church of Santa Maria Novella, Florence, by Andrea di Bonaiuto, c. 1355. The scene is of *The Triumph of Saint Thomas Aquinas*. The saint is enthroned at the top. Heretics crouch at his feet, including the great Muslim philosopher, Averroes. On either side of the throne are the doctors of the Church; beneath there are personifications of the sciences and the liberal arts, with a practitioner of each below the respective discipline.

THOMAS AQUINAS

The most famous of all medieval scholastic philosophers, and by far the most influential, was St. Thomas Aquinas (c. 1225–1274). Born in southern Italy, he studied in Naples, where he became a Dominican, as well as in Cologne and Paris. He was the leading theologian at the University of Paris and also taught at the universities of Bologna and Rome—a measure of the international spirit of the age.

The constant theme of Aquinas's writings was the reconciliation of faith and experience: "nature complements grace." Although only trust in the truths of the Bible could reinforce the highest mysteries of religion, human reason and the natural world confirmed these revelations, and thus enabled humans to accomplish their own salvation. The foundation of his teachings was the philosophy of Aristotle, translated from the Arabic and interpreted according to Christian principles.

Aquinas's most important work was the *Summa Theologica* (*Summary of Theology*), in which he used Aristotelian logic to demonstrate the existence of God. God is the uncaused cause, the prime reason for order in the universe. Humans are rational social animals, whose morality is based on harmony with others and with God. The emphasis on human experience and reason as a guide to faith came as a revelation to his contem-

poraries; it was also to become a basic tenet of subsequent Roman Catholic philosophy.

SONGS OF LOVE AND BATTLE: HEROIC EPICS AND TROUBADOUR POETRY

Before the rise of education and the growth in literacy, the composition of works of literature in the *vernacular* (everyday, spoken languages, as opposed to Latin) was unsurprisingly rare. The only outstanding achievement of the early medieval period was the Anglo-Saxon epic poem *Beowulf*. Although there are elements of Christianity in *Beowulf*, the society it depicts is pagan. The story tells of the triumph of the Scandinavian hero, Beowulf, over the monster Grendel, and is replete with gory feuds and black magic.

THE EPIC TRADITION

In the century between 1050 and 1150, the three chief continental European languages, French, German, and Spanish, acquired their first major works of vernacular literature.

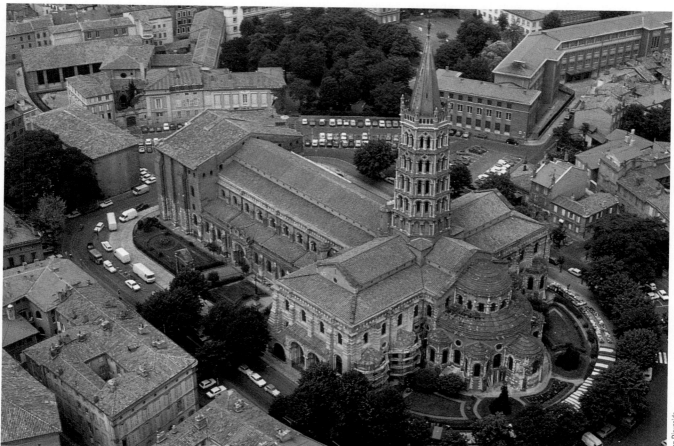

Aerial view (from the southeast) of Saint-Senin, Toulouse, France, c. 1070–1120. Toulouse was an important stopping point for pilgrims on their way through southwest France to the major pilgrimage center of Santiago de Compostela in northwest Spain, and this church, with its very long central nave, was built to house large congregations.

Italian took longer to split off from Latin, and thus developed into a modern language a little later. Its first great writer, Dante, wrote in the early 14th century (see Topic 30). All three are epic poems belonging to the tradition of the **chansons de geste**, or "song of deeds," in which a minstrel recounted heroic deeds.

The French *Chanson de Roland* (*Song of Roland*) was first written down around 1100, probably just before the First Crusade, although it was composed shortly after the event it describes—Charlemagne's invasion of Spain in 778—and passed down by word of mouth. The epic combines two main themes, one public and the other private: Charlemagne's struggle against the Muslim rulers of Spain, to defend the honor of his knights, of France, and of Christendom; and the personal relationships between the hero Roland and his fellow warriors.

Roland's deadly enemy is his stepfather Ganelon, who plots treachery against the hero with the help of the crafty Muslim king. Tempted into rash action and beset by overwhelming enemy forces, Roland manages to summon Charlemagne's troops with a magic ivory horn before falling to his attackers. Ganelon subsequently suffers trial and execution for his betrayal of Roland.

The hero is rather more fortunate in his relationship with Oliver, his beloved friend. The two summarize medieval notions of heroism: Roland is fearless and ambitious for glory, while Oliver, prudent and moderate, tries in vain to restrain his companion from running the risk that eventually proves fatal.

The Spanish *Song of the Cid*, less bloody than the French epic, describes the career of the Spanish knight known as El Cid (his name derives from the Arabic word *Sidi*, "my lord"). The hero appears not only as an exemplary warrior, fighting in the cause of honor, but also as an ideal husband and father, and a devout Christian. If the *Song of the Cid* lacks the energy and concentration of the *Song of Roland*, its characterization is more subtle.

The spirit of the German *Nibelungenlied* (*Song of the Nibelungs*) is very different from the chivalric world of Roland and the Cid. Set in dark forests, with a plot involving stolen treasure, trickery and assassination, a race of dwarfs and a bloodthirsty dragon, it was to inspire the 19th-century German composer Richard Wagner to create an epic cycle of music-dramas (see Topic 79).

THE TROUBADOURS

The other literary form of the age, troubadour love poetry, was a far cry from the heroic, often violent world of the *chansons de geste*. The troubadour poets first appeared at the courts of southern France around 1100, where their verses reflected a new attitude toward love and lovers. Inspired by Platonic notions in the writings of Muslim and Christian philosophers, and by the works of contemporary Muslim poets in neighboring Spain (see Topic 23), the troubadours developed a "code" of "Courtly Love."

The quest for true love was, for the troubadours, like a knight's mission. The submissive lover dedicated himself to the service of his lady, and the roles were never reversed. He fulfilled his love by the intensity of his devotion, neither hoping for nor achieving any actual consummation. The reward was the reputation for "spiritual valor" he acquired in the eyes of his peers. Modern readers are generally struck by the artificial quality of troubadour love poetry, but for medieval society it represented an attitude toward women in advance of that depicted in the *chansons de geste*. In one French heroic epic that reflects traditional misogynist attitudes, a queen, trying to convince her husband to change his mind, receives a blow to the nose that draws blood. For the troubadours and their audience, far from being battered, the beloved was idealized as superior to her devoted servant.

A NEW MUSICAL LANGUAGE: THE POLYPHONIC STYLE

The earliest surviving music of the medieval world is **plainsong.** This consists of a single or "monophonic" musical line to which one voice (either a solo or a group in unison) chants the words of a religious text, generally without any form of accompaniment. The tradition of Christian plainsong developed out of Jewish synagogue rituals. By the 4th century, several distinct schools of chant were in use, some in Eastern Church ceremonies, others in the West.

As part of his campaign to unify his empire and its religious practices, Charlemagne allowed the use in the Western liturgy of only one school of plainsong, that of Gregorian chant, and banned the others. Another tradition, that of Ambrosian chant, continued to survive in and around Milan. Scholars used to believe that Gregorian chant originated at Rome in the time of Pope Gregory (590–604)—hence its name. It is now thought to have come into being around 800, at the court of Charlemagne, created to become the "universal" form of church music.

THE RISE OF POLYPHONY

The musical content of plainsong was essentially limited to melody. The elements of harmony and rhythm, fundamental to Western music since the late medieval period, were not yet present. A move in the direction of harmony (i.e., the simultaneous sounding of more than one note) came in the 10th century, with the invention of "organum" or "consonant music," whereby the musical line of the chant was accompanied by another line, or "voice."

Over the next two centuries, musicians began slowly to develop a more complex style of music, which consisted of several different strands of melody sounding together and making up a harmonic whole. The first important works to use the new technique, known as polyphonic ("many voices"), date to the Gothic age of the 13th century (see Topic 30).

GUIDO OF AREZZO

As music grew in complexity, it became necessary to find a form of notation for writing down the pitches of the notes. The composers of plainsong had developed a series of signs that they added to the words to indicate the relative musical patterns to which the text was sung, but these did not convey the actual notes. With the rise of polyphonic music, in which individual performers needed an objective written "part," setting out their musical line and that of the other participants, some form of written musical "score" became necessary.

The essential breakthrough came shortly after 1000. Guido of Arezzo (c. 991–after 1033), while working in the city of Arezzo in central Italy as a trainer of singers for the cathedral, devised a system of notation. It used a series of parallel horizontal lines, with the lines and the spaces between them representing precise notes or pitches—the forerunner of the modern musical "staff." Guido also gave names to the notes, based on the melody and text of a hymn to St. John: *Ut* (later changed to *Do*) for the note "c," *Re* for "d," *Mi* for "e," and so on.

In 1028 the pope called Guido to Rome to expound his new system, which was to become the basis for all further musical notation in the West. His treatise *Micrologus* set out the Guidonian method and included a discussion of the new polyphonic musical style. The work was the most copied and read musical handbook of the Middle Ages.

ARCHITECTS AND SCULPTORS: THE ROMANESQUE CATHEDRAL

The uncertainties of the early medieval period, beset by conflict and political unrest, had discouraged the construction of new buildings. With the gradual return of stability in the 11th century, towns and monasteries began to commission churches. The growing popularity of pilgrimages to holy sites along "pilgrimage routes" throughout Europe provided an additional stimulus to build pilgrimage churches as well as facilities for the thousands of pilgrims who were on the move each year.

The architects responsible for the first major building programs since Roman times turned to the style of Roman architecture for their inspiration. The new architectural style they created is known as **Romanesque** or "Roman-like." Its characteristics are partly the result of the need for large buildings capable of containing crowds of people. Heavy stone walls could support Roman-style stone arches and barrel-vaulted stone roofs, providing a structure that, unlike the early Christian basilicas, was fireproof.

Romanesque churches are massive, with dark, simple interiors, many of them with lofty towers supported by round arches. There was ample space for the movement of large numbers of people, but little light. As a result, the most important decorations were placed not inside the building but on the exterior. Because paintings would have been subject

Tympanum (semicircular space over a doorway) at the abbey church of La Madeleine, Vezelay, c. 1120–1132. The sculptures show the Ascension of Christ and his Mission to the apostles, depicted around him. Their task is to convert the heathens, who appear above and below the central scene. Placed over the main entrance of the church, the vast and energetic figure of Christ would remind those entering of their own insignificance in the face of divine power.

© Réunion des Musées Nationaux/Art Resource, NY

to damage in the open air, artists turned for the first time since the fall of Rome to stone sculpture to portray the human figure. The scenes and figures decorating Romanesque churches represent a revival of the art of sculpture in stone that was to lead in time to developments in Renaissance art.

One of the chief areas of a Romanesque church to be filled with sculpture was that around the main doorway, where the pilgrims would see the biblical stories or figures as they entered. The semicircular space above the door was especially important; known as the *tympanum*, it often contained an elaborate "program" or message for the devout.

One of the most elaborate is the tympanum above the west door of the Benedictine abbey church of Vézelay in France, dating to around 1120. The central figure of Christ inspires the apostles around him and the assorted peoples of the world below, while healing the lepers and cripples depicted in the scenes above. The whole complex ensemble is surrounded with an abstract decorative pattern perhaps derived from Islamic art of a kind produced by Muslim artists in nearby Spain.

Thus, at the time when contact with the Muslim world was reintroducing the West to Greek and Roman literature, Western artists were rediscovering the most important—and lasting—of Greek and Roman artistic genres, stone statues of the human form. Something of the excitement of Romanesque sculptors is visible in the emotional power of the figures they carved. Elongated, grave, often dramatic, Romanesque statues and relief carvings are an appropriate complement to the massive buildings they decorate.

Architects and builders throughout Western Europe employed the Romanesque style. There are regional variations, of course, but pilgrims traveling, say, from the North through France to the shrine of St. James of Compostela in Spain would see familiar buildings and artworks along their route. The more learned ones who visited the monastic libraries could find there manuscripts illustrated in the same style. Some of the sculpted scenes in Romanesque church decorations were probably based on illuminated manuscripts.

Putting Scholars, Troubadours, and Builders in Perspective

The gradual development of a common European culture owed much to the increasing ease of travel. The pilgrims moving from northern Europe to Italy and Spain—and eventually, after the Crusades, to the Holy Land—the troubadours passing from one aristocratic court to another, university professors traveling to lecture in the major centers of learning—all of these travels led to the circulation of ideas and a shared artistic culture. With its renewed interest in education, and rediscovery of the Greeks and their philosophy, the Romanesque age provided a solid foundation for the international cultural achievements of the succeeding Gothic period.

Questions for Further Study

1. How far do the organization and function of a modern university reflect those of its medieval ancestors?
2. What are the general principles underlying the philosophy of Thomas Aquinas? To what extent do they reflect the intellectual climate of his age?
3. In what ways did the spread of literacy change medieval society? Did it have a significant effect on the status of women?
4. What are the main features of the Romanesque style?

Suggestions for Further Reading

Barral i Alter, Xavier. *The Romanesque: Towns, Cathedrals and Monasteries*. New York, 1998.

Artz, F.B. *The Mind of the Middle Ages*, A.D. *200–1500*. Chicago, 1980.

Bogin, M. *The Women Troubadours*. New York, 1976.

Bumke, Joachim. Thomas Dunlap, trans. *Courtley Culture: Literature and Society in the High Middle Ages*. Woodstock, NY, 2000.

Collins, Roger. *Early Medieval Europe, 300-1000*. New York, 1991.

Diebold, William J. *Word and Image. An Introduction to Early Medieval Art*. Boulder, CO, 2000.

Duby, Georges. *The Knight, the Lady, and the Priest*. New York, 1984.

Keen, M. *Chivalry*. New Haven, CT, 1984.

Stalley, Roger. *Early Medieval Architecture*. New York, 1999.

Torrell, Jean-Pierre. *Saint Thomas Aquinas*. Washington, DC, 1996.

MONARCHY AND ITS LIMITS: GOVERNMENT IN THE HIGH MIDDLE AGES

The territorial and bureaucratic foundations of the European monarchies became established during the 11th and 12th centuries. Decentralized feudal arrangements, in which vassal nobles were generally more powerful than kings, gradually gave way to centralized royal authority, especially in England after the Norman Conquest and in France under the reign of the Capetian kings. On the other hand, in Germany, the development of a strong monarchy was complicated by the imperial aspirations of the German kings. Although central authority grew even in the Holy Roman Empire, especially during the reign of the great Hohenstaufen emperor Frederick I, the claim to universal power began to decline in the wake of the Empire's struggle with the other contender for universal authority, the papacy.

As royal government evolved in practical ways on a day-to-day basis, political theory also reinforced the position of the new monarchs. The medieval political debate essentially revolved around one crucial question: the nature of the relationship between church and state. Despite the repeated claims of the popes, the overall direction of philosophical opinion pressed for the separation of the two spheres of authority, a trend that strengthened the sovereignty of national kings.

In the 13th century, the monarchies continued to grow in power as centralized government was extended in a variety of ways. The development and application of royal law were perhaps the most important means by which the kings built their authority, a policy they pursued both in England and France. Especially in England, the expansion of the royal judicial system and its merger with common law proved to have important implications for the growth of constitutionalism. The notion of the protection of certain basic rights under the law was the basis for the Magna Carta, through which the English barons forced John in 1215 to recognize the limits of his power.

The elaboration of administrative machinery for royal government enabled kings to exercise real power on a regular basis through established procedures of public policy. This was especially true in the collection of taxes and the expenditure of royal funds. Here, too, however, there were unexpected results, as concern over the king's power to impose taxes was combined with the growth of legal procedure to produce representative institutions, such as the Parliament of England, that further limited the king's power.

SIGNIFICANT DATES

Government in the High Middle Ages

1073	Pope Gregory VII publishes *Dictatus Papae*
1215	Magna Carta
1198–1216	Reign of Innocent III as pope
1199–1216	Reign of John as king of England
1180–1223	Reign of Philip II Augustus as king of France
1212–1250	Reign of Frederick II as Holy Roman Emperor
1295	"Model Parliament" meets
1302	Boniface issues *Unam Sanctam*
1324	Marsilio of Padua publishes *Defensor Pacis*
1356	Charles IV issues Golden Bull

POLITICAL THEORY AND CHURCH-STATE RELATIONS IN THE HIGH MIDDLE AGES

In the Middle Ages the two "universal" states, the Holy Roman Empire and the papacy, competed for recognition as the supreme sources of authority in western Christendom. The Empire, which drew Germany and Italy into the same political orbit, claimed a special role as the successor to Charlemagne's vast state. Medieval theorists and millions of people also recognized the temporal government of the popes, which ruled directly over the Papal States of central Italy, while claiming theoretical supremacy over all secular governments.

THE NATURE OF ROYAL POWER

Papal power remained strong well into the late Middle Ages, but by the opening of the 13th century England and France, as well as Spain and Hungary, were expanding the power and influence of their national monarchies. The new kings there could look back to an earlier theory that saw secular rulers not as separate from the church but as integral to the universal church and to Western Christendom. When the pope recognized the right of Pepin III in 751 to take the Merovingian throne, St. Boniface anointed the new king with holy oil, thus beginning the tradition of theocratic monarchy, or monarchy with divine sanction.

The great reform movement that began to sweep the church in the 11th century complicated the relationship between royal and spiritual authority. In 1073, Pope Gregory VII published *Dictatus Papae,* an essay claiming that papal power was supreme over all authority of this world, including emperors and kings. This was a new and startling challenge to secular government that undermined the idea of theocratic kingship prevalent in the early Middle Ages. Gregory revived the principle of St. Augustine's *City of God,*

Panel painting of St. Thomas Aquinas. Late 13th–early 14th century. The saint is enthroned in the presence of Christ, who appears at the top. Earlier thinkers of the Church lean over Thomas, who is flanked by the two greatest philosophers of the ancient world, Plato and Aristotle. At his feet crouches Averroes, Thomas's leading Muslim contemporary, who symbolizes the defeat of heresy.

Scala/Art Resource

claiming that the secular state derived moral strength only from its position as a servant of the church. Hence, the only legitimate power resided in the priesthood.

The first serious clash between kings and popes had come over the question of lay investiture, but the concordat of 1122 settled the issue through a compromise in which neither side won a decisive victory. Strong popes, such as Innocent III, would continue to challenge secular rulers, especially in the case of King John of England and Frederick II of the Holy Roman Empire. Yet the struggle with the papacy strengthened the monarchs as defenders of national sovereignty and the church's position was slowly eroded, a process that culminated two centuries later in the period of the Reformation. Kings, moreover, were becoming increasingly popular as the benefits of orderly and efficient government were appreciated by all social classes. By the end of the 13th century, citizens accepted royal authority in such matters as law, finance, and military policy as routine. National governments had become secular bureaucratic states.

The development of legal studies and the rise of universities contributed to this trend by training the first cadres of professional administrators for royal government: University professors also strengthened the authority of the king by arguing for the separation of church and state. Early medieval theorists had proclaimed that political power was an expression of divine will, and in the 13th century the philosopher Thomas Aquinas continued to argue that a basic harmony existed between the temporal state and divine will. Later in the century, however, the Italian poet Dante Alighieri (see Topic 30) maintained in *De Monarchia* that government was a secular institution that should be dominated by kings and independent of spiritual authority.

The most powerful theoretical defense of secular authority was made by another Italian, Marsilio of Padua (d. 1342?), who studied and taught at the University of Paris. In *Defensor Pacis* (1324), Marsilio strongly opposed ecclesiastical claims of supremacy in temporal matters. Reaching back to Aristotle, he argued that the purpose of the state, which was the creation of human will, was to provide peace and security for its citizens. Although he insisted that only the king was the legitimate ruler of the state, Marsilio also held that all secular power is derived from popular will and that the ruler is the servant of the people. It was no wonder that Pope Clement VI (1342–1352) called Marsilio "the greatest heretic of the age."

ENGLAND: MAGNA CARTA AND THE EVOLUTION OF PARLIAMENT

The foundations of royal government in England had been established by Henry II in the 12th century. Henry created the office of the exchequer to collect taxes and manage finances, and enlarged the jurisdiction of royal justice through the jury system, measures that met with popular approval. He established common law, as opposed to the customary law used in feudal courts, as the legal system of the entire realm. By the time of the king's death in 1189, royal authority had increased significantly at the expense of the power of the feudal barons.

THE KING AND THE BARONS

Henry recognized no limits to his royal power, nor created any institutions through which the barons could participate in public affairs. As royal government evolved, these issues became increasingly important in English politics. Henry's two sons, Richard and John, were unable to increase their power without resistance and eventually were forced to accept limits on their authority.

The talents of Richard I, the Lion-Hearted (ruled 1189–1199), were those of a feudal warrior rather than of a bureaucratic king. Although brave and dashing, he lacked the interest or skill to develop his government. During a decade-long reign, he was actually in England less than a year, spending most of his time attacking Muslims in the Holy Land or fighting the Capetians in France. Nevertheless,

Great Seal of King John of England. This was fixed to the Magna Carta in 1215 at Runnymede, where the king was forced by his barons to accept conditions that limited royal power. The seal, together with the document, is now in the British Museum, London.

©The British Museum

despite his long absence, the government developed by his father operated with great efficiency.

Richard's brother, John (ruled 1199–1216), was a man of a much less appealing personality and ability, and the contrast between the two has given John a much maligned reputation, in the eyes of his contemporaries and of historians. John's unsuccessful attempts to control the English Church resulted in a conflict with Pope Innocent III over the selection of Stephen Langton as archbishop of Canterbury (see Topic 27). John's position further deteriorated in 1204 when Philip Augustus, the French king, took Normandy from him. When John tried to reconquer his lost provinces, he was defeated at the Battle of Bouvines (1214). The feudal barons, from whom John had tried to extort monies to help pay for the French wars, seized their chance to resist the king.

In June 1215, John faced the defiant barons at Runnymede, where they insisted that he endorse and set his seal to the Magna Carta (Great Charter), a document that may have been drafted in its original form by Stephen Langton. The Magna Carta was not a radical departure from tradition because English kings had always sworn to uphold the rights of their subjects as part of their coronation ceremonies. But the Magna Carta was so detailed and direct—it contained more than 60 provisions—and the circumstances surrounding its adoption were so unusual, that its influence grew far beyond its immediate implications.

Magna Carta was a feudal document that restated the rights and obligations of king and vassals "for the reform of our realm." Henceforth, John could not force the payment of special levies from the barons to support his wars. Similarly, the English Church was declared "free" with "its rights undiminished and its liberties unimpaired." The king now recognized the clergy's right to select bishops and to appeal under canon law to papal courts. At a time when towns and their burgher class were growing, John also agreed to recognize the freedoms of the cities, to guarantee the right of travel to all merchants, and to adopt uniform weights and measures in order to streamline commercial transactions.

With respect to the development of English constitutionalism, the Magna Carta contained several general statements that were especially important. "No free man," it commanded, "shall be arrested or imprisoned or seized or outlawed or exiled or in any way victimized, neither will we attack him or send anyone to attack him, except by the lawful judgment of his peers or by the law of the land." The last clause stated that the king and the barons had taken an oath to the effect that "the men in our kingdom shall have and hold all the aforesaid liberties, rights and concessions well and peacefully, freely and quietly, fully and completely, for themselves and their heirs from us and our heirs, in all matters and in all places for ever."*

Later generations see the Magna Carta as a source of English constitutionalism, but the barons merely wanted to protect their own feudal rights against the encroachments of royal government. The barons were not concerned about the great majority of English subjects, who were not free to enjoy the liberties guaranteed in Magna Carta. Only subsequent interpretations extended to the entire English population the notions of due process and trial by jury, and broadened the meaning of the Magna Carta to include the idea that royal power should be limited by law and the consent of the governed.

John's son Henry III (ruled 1216–1272) was also unable to control the barons, who continued to protest royal efforts to tax them and the king's right to appoint officials. These protests came to a head in 1258, when the barons imposed on Henry the Provisions of Oxford, which established councils of barons to assist him in governing the country. When Henry and the barons could not agree on how to put the provisions into practice, they decided in 1264 to accept the arbitration of John's feudal overlord, Louis IX of France, who ruled that Henry should not be forced to accept the provisions. The following year, the steady erosion of royal authority was halted when Henry's son and successor Edward defeated a group of rebellious barons led by Simon de Montfort.

THE EVOLUTION OF PARLIAMENT

Edward I (ruled 1272–1307), one of the most important kings of medieval England, was responsible for the first effort to unite the entire island. He conquered Wales in 1284, extending English law and administration there and giving his eldest son the title of Prince of Wales. But similar efforts to bring Scotland into the realm failed, and in 1314 Scottish nationalists under Robert Bruce defeated the English and reasserted Scottish independence. The two kingdoms were united only in 1603.

*Quoted in Harry Rothwell, ed., *English Historical Documents, 1189–1327*, III (London: Eyre & Spottiswoode, 1975).

Edward, known as the "English Justinian," brought a measure of organization to the common law that had been evolving over the centuries. He began publishing new laws in the *Statutes of the Realm,* which continues to be issued to this day, took special interest in systematizing laws regulating land ownership, and further reduced the jurisdiction of baronial courts.

The most important development during Edward's reign was the emergence of Parliament. The first meeting of this body had already taken place in 1265, when Simon de Montfort called it into session during his revolt against Henry III. In order to obtain the widest possible support, de Montfort increased Parliament's membership by adding two knights from each shire and two burghers from every town. The tradition was followed by Edward when he summoned what is known as the "Model Parliament" in 1295.

Some time in the early years of the 14th century, the knights and burghers began meeting together separately from the barons as the "Commons," thus creating a division between the House of Commons and the House of Lords. In the early days, the king used Parliament mainly to obtain endorsement of royal decisions and to secure additional taxes. Because new taxation demanded popular consent, Edward ordered the shires and towns to elect representatives who would meet in Parliament to discuss and grant the needed taxes. Parliament also functioned as a kind of supreme court to which members would bring petitions or appeals from lower court decisions.

Although institutions similar to the Parliament developed in other countries, it was in England that it became a body of government that represented the authority of the people over that of the king. Moreover, the king's power was further limited by the observance of uniform laws derived from custom and tradition.

THE CONSOLIDATION OF THE FRENCH MONARCHY

The creation of France, which had long been divided by significant regional differences in culture, language, and history, was the work of the Capetian monarchs of the High Middle Ages. The three kings who ruled between 1180 and 1314—Philip II Augustus, Louis IX, and Philip IV the Fair—strengthened royal government and reinforced national identity on foundations already established during the long reign of Louis VII. The result was that France eventually became the most powerful state in Europe.

PHILIP AUGUSTUS

The essential institutions of the French monarchy had been established in the 12th century. The great lords had each become so powerful that the peaceful resolution of conflicts now became more appealing than the destructive feudal wars that had once brought havoc to the French countryside. The legal developments sponsored by the monarchy

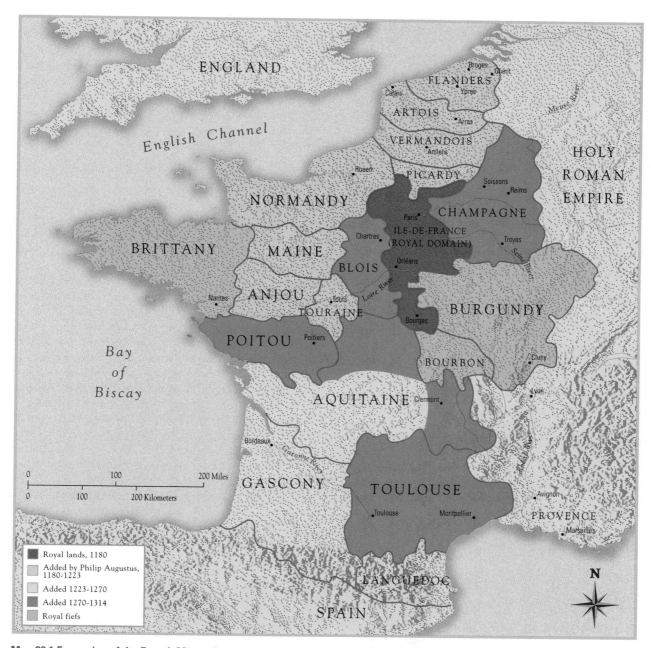

Map 29.1 Expansion of the French Monarchy, 1180–1314. Most of the added territory was taken from the indirect rule of the English king, during the reigns of Philip Augustus and Philip IV. Note that Brittany and Burgundy, although theoretically subject to French control, still maintained their independent status (Burgundy until 1477 and Brittany until 1532).

offered an alternative to fighting. Like his contemporary Henry II in England, Louis VII had greatly expanded the royal judicial system, and by the end of his reign some of the vassals of France were bringing legal disputes before royal courts for impartial settlement.

Louis VII's great failure came as a result of the annulment of his marriage to Eleanor of Aquitaine because her subsequent marriage to Henry II of England transferred her vast lands to the English monarchy. Perhaps to soothe his sensitivity over the loss, Louis had lectured the English envoy to Paris that "Your master, the King of England, wants

for nothing. He has experienced soldiers, horses, gold, silks, jewels, choice of fruits, game worth hunting, and everything the heart could wish. . . . In France things are different. We have only our bread, our wine, and our simple pleasures." Yet already a growing sense of national identity was beginning to separate the French outlook from their English neighbors across the Channel.

Philip Augustus (ruled 1180–1223) reinforced this tendency in real ways. Philip lacked the kind of personal glamour that made Frederick Barbarossa and Henry II so appealing to contemporaries. He was instead shrewd and calculating and excelled in deviousness. Yet he was determined to restore the territories now held by the English Plantagenets in France—Aquitaine, Anjou, Maine, and Normandy. To achieve this goal, he exploited Henry's quarrels with Eleanor and encouraged his sons, Richard and John, to revolt against their father. Using a dispute between John and a French noble as the excuse, Philip invaded the English lands in France. In 1214, Philip crushed the forces of John and his allies at Bouvines and took Anjou, Maine, and Normandy, greatly increasing the size of the French royal domain and its revenues.

ST. LOUIS

Philip's successor, Louis VIII (ruled 1223–1226), reigned for only a few years, but his campaigns against the Albigensian heretics in southern France established the basis for the incorporation of that region into the royal domain. He was succeeded in turn by Louis IX (ruled 1226–1270), a devoutly religious man who ministered to the poor and sick and was later made a saint. His religious convictions also caused him to lead two crusades against the Muslims in North Africa, both of which were failures. Nevertheless, Louis was one of the dominant personalities of the age. Despite his asceticism, he embellished the kingship with elaborate ceremonies and symbolic ritual designed to enhance royal prestige.

Louis extended royal authority over the feudal lords of France in several ways. He imposed a king's peace on the country by forbidding wars among his vassals and began hearing legal appeals and petitions from nobles and commoners alike. He also established the *Parlement* of Paris (a legal tribunal not to be confused with the English Parliament) as the supreme court of France. The king's legal experts, who were trained in universities, began to codify French laws and ordinances.

Louis pursued a policy of peace with his neighbors that resulted in better-defined borders for France. In 1258, he negotiated a treaty with the king of Aragon that established the frontier between Spain and France along the Pyrenees. The next year, he also signed a treaty with the English monarch Henry III, who agreed to recognize the loss of all the lands taken from John in exchange for accepting the area of Gascony in southwestern France, which he still held, as a fief from Louis.

PHILIP THE FAIR

The success of the Capetian kings in building a powerful monarchy capable of molding France into a single state reached its high point in the reign of Philip IV (ruled 1285–1314). Philip IV lacked a strong personality and was not especially popular. He did, however, have the good sense to rely heavily on talented ministers, who sought to increase his authority and strengthen the monarchy in general. Philip's advisers were usually salaried laymen who formed a professional bureaucracy and made the institutions of royal government more efficient. These officials, many of whom were trained in Roman law, separated the offices of the royal household from the king's council, thus initiating a break between the long-established custom of regarding the state as a private possession of the king. Thenceforth, royal authority became more impersonal as a more modern notion of the state developed.

As the English kings did in England, Philip began to expand the idea of a royal council by including in it members of the bourgeoisie from the towns. In England, the nobles and clergy first met together in the early years of Parliament, but eventually the clergy withdrew and gathered in their own ecclesiastical assemblies, leaving Parliament an entirely lay affair. In France, the nobles, clergy, and bourgeoisie formed the three principal "estates" of the realm, each meeting in separate halls but as part of a

Manuscript illumination showing Pope Boniface VIII presiding over his cardinals. 14th century. The pope is wearing his tiara (triple crown), while the cardinals are recognizable from the wide-brimmed red hats they wear. In the foreground, bishops and monks take notes.

British Library/Bridgeman Art Library

single institution known as the Estates General. This body performed the same function as the Parliament, namely to endorse the king's decisions and approve new taxes.

The need for revenue for the royal government became a major theme of Philip's reign. He needed money principally for two reasons: the payment of salaries for a growing bureaucracy and the defraying of military expenses for the war that he launched to drive the English out of Gascony in 1294. Desperate to raise revenue, Philip resorted to underhanded methods. He extorted payments from foreign merchants in France, whom he threatened with imprisonment, and in 1306 he expelled the Jews from the country in order to confiscate their property.

Philip also found himself in open conflict with the papacy, thus breaking with a long tradition of close cooperation between the church and the French monarchy. The conflict with the church developed when Philip had a bishop who served as a papal legate arrested on charges of treason. Tensions worsened when Boniface reprimanded Philip for his actions and the king responded by defaming Boniface's reputation. In 1302, Boniface rose to the challenge by issuing the papal bull *Unam Sanctam*, which declared that Philip had to submit to papal authority or risk damnation of his soul. Philip retaliated by sending agents to Italy to kidnap Boniface and bring him to France to be tried by a church council. Boniface was taken prisoner but was then rescued by supporters; the deeply distressed pope died soon after. Philip's triumph over the papacy seemed to be confirmed when in 1305 a French prelate who took the name of Clement V was elected pope and made the fateful decision to establish his pontificate in France rather than in Rome.

STUPOR MUNDI: FREDERICK OF HOHENSTAUFEN AND THE IMPERIAL DREAM

During the reign of Frederick Barbarossa, the Holy Roman Empire had grown to include both Germany and Italy, much as it had after the coronation of Charlemagne in 800. Yet even at the height of Frederick's power, the Empire remained more an idea than a reality. In his effort to secure his hold over northern Italy, Barbarossa had been forced to grant concessions to the feudal nobles of Germany. Thus while France and England moved toward consolidated national states, Germany continued to be held in the grip of feudal vassals.

On his death in 1190, Barbarossa was succeeded by his son, Henry VI (ruled 1191–1197). Henry reigned for only seven years, however, and it was Frederick, his son, who revived the Hohenstaufen dream of creating a Western empire that would once again dazzle the world. Frederick II (ruled 1212–1250), one of the principal figures of the High Middle Ages, was a brilliant ruler called by some "terror of

the earth" and by others *stupor mundi*, or "wonder of the world." Unlike his grandfather Barbarossa, who was a German prince captivated by the vision of a grander empire south of the Alps, Frederick was an Italian, born in Sicily and steeped in the multicultural traditions of the Mediterranean. His closest advisers included Muslims and Jews as well as Christians, he spoke and read numerous languages, and he commissioned treatises on falconry as well as on political theory. His capital at Palermo was host to a dazzling court that boasted mosques and cathedrals, monasteries and harems.

GERMANY AND THE KINGDOM OF SICILY

From his mother Constance, heiress of Roger II, Frederick inherited the Norman Kingdom of the Two Sicilies, which included the southern half of the peninsula from Naples to the Straits of Messina as well as the island of Sicily. From his father, Frederick inherited a claim to the German throne. This dual legacy threatened the papacy and the Lombard cities of northern Italy more directly than had Barbarossa's military expeditions, both of whom

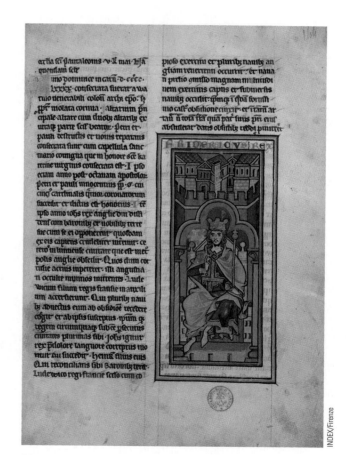

Manuscript illumination with a portrait of Frederick II, the powerful Hohenstaufen ruler. 13th century. In the upper part of the portrait panel there are a series of magnificent buildings, representing Frederick's capital, Palermo, in Sicily. The emperor, who was famous for the luxury of his court, is richly dressed.

feared encirclement by the Hohenstaufen lands. Frederick was thus faced with powerful enemies from the moment of his birth.

Because he was a child when his father died, several German nobles fought over the German kingship while Frederick remained a ward of the papacy. In 1212, when one faction of German princes finally chose the teenage Frederick as their king, Pope Innocent III approved the appointment but extracted from Frederick a promise to remain loyal to the papacy. In 1219 Pope Honorius III (ruled 1216–1227) crowned Frederick emperor on the two conditions that he led a crusade to the Holy Land and never unite Germany and Italy under one crown. Frederick's unwillingness to meet this second condition so incurred the pope's wrath that he was repeatedly excommunicated. After long delays, Frederick at last pretended to start on his crusade in 1226 but fell ill and abandoned the journey; he started out again the next year without first receiving absolution from the papal ban. In Jerusalem, instead of fighting,

Map 29.2 The Hohenstaufen Empire under Frederick II. The hostility between the Holy Roman Emperor and the Papacy—the latter visible as a small island virtually surrounded by enemy territory on this map—dominated much of the 13th and 14th centuries. Two parties developed, one pro-Imperial, the Ghibellines, the other supporting the pope, the Guelphs. Their rivalries spilled over into Italy, where the new city-states were quick to take sides: Florence, for example was Guelph, Siena Ghibelline.

Frederick negotiated an arrangement with Muslim leaders that permitted freedom of worship for Christians and Muslims alike, while returning control of the city to the crusaders. Only in 1230 was the excommunication lifted after Frederick promised to respect the church and protect the lands of the papacy.

Despite his promise to the contrary, Frederick's policy was based on the idea of union between Germany and Italy. He traveled to Germany, however, only to deal with pressing questions. He set up an order of religious warriors known as the Teutonic Knights to guard the eastern frontiers, and recognized Bohemia as a hereditary kingdom within the Empire. Like his grandfather before him, he made concessions to the German princes: In return for control over the Empire's foreign and military policies and the right to settle disputes among the nobles, Frederick recognized the complete authority of the princes within their own territories.

The German settlement allowed Frederick to focus on Italy, where he established an efficient and highly centralized government. Frederick portrayed himself as the supreme representative of divine will and justice and the state as the creation of rulers inspired by divine reason. If the church's mission was the salvation of souls, the purpose of the state, which was ordained by God, was to establish a reign of law and order in the temporal world. These ideas he explained in a code of laws known as the Constitutions of Melfi issued in 1231, which Frederick liked to call in more grandiose terms the *Liber Augustalis*.

In an effort to complete his domination of Italy, Frederick demanded that the Lombard cities of the north submit to his will, but they formed a second Lombard League to resist him. He defeated the League in 1237 at the Battle of Cartenuova and proceeded to conquer all of northern Italy, appointing an imperial official known as the *podestà* in each of the cities that he conquered. Because the pope had encouraged the League, Frederick then invaded the Papal States themselves. In 1245, Pope Innocent IV (ruled 1243–1254) fled to France, where the Council of Lyons excommunicated and deposed Frederick and declared a crusade against him.

Despite the defiant resistance of the church, however, only Frederick's death in 1250 brought an end to the imperial dreams of the Hohenstaufens. Frederick's heirs were unable to regain the momentum, and the pope invited Charles of Anjou, the brother of Louis IX of France, to rule the Kingdom of the Two Sicilies and wipe out the Hohenstaufen "viper breed."

Frederick's demise did not mean peace for Italy because the new Angevin kings were almost as ambitious as the Hohenstaufens and threatened the papacy's control over central Italy. In 1282 a rebellion known as the "Sicilian Vespers" drove the French out of Sicily, which was subsequently taken by the king of Aragon. This disintegration of the former Norman kingdom was clearly a victory for the papacy, which had prevented a unified kingdom from encircling its lands. Nor was the Hohenstaufen dream of binding Italy and Germany together in the Holy

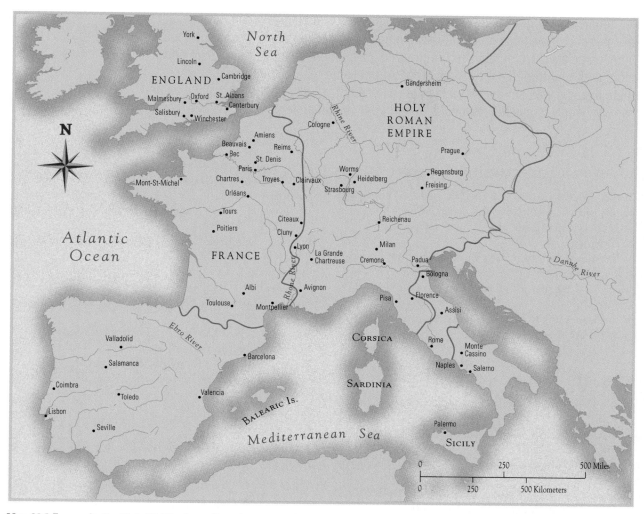

Map 29.3 Europe in the High Middle Ages. Note that most major settlements continue to depend on access to water—even monastic or religious sites such as Clairvaux and Cluny, as well as trading centers like Lyon and Florence. Among the major modern European capitals not present on the map (because they had not yet been founded) are Madrid and Berlin.

Roman Empire ever again seriously revived. German emperors henceforth abandoned Italian affairs and refused even to go to Rome for the imperial coronation. Germany disintegrated further into a conglomeration of independent principalities that prevented the kind of political unity that the rulers of France and England achieved. In 1356, the Emperor Charles IV (1347–1378) issued a document known as the Golden Bull, reinforcing the sovereignty of the great princes and regularizing the election of emperors by recognizing seven official electors. The Golden Bull made no mention of any role for the papacy in selecting the emperor.

Putting Government in the High Middle Ages in Perspective

The end of real power for the emperors in German affairs confirmed the political trend away from the universalism of the Middle Ages and toward an era of national states ruled by secular monarchs. Medieval theorists argued increasingly for the

Continued next page

legitimate power of secular rulers and the separation of church and state. Through the creation of systems of royal justice, regular legal procedures, and professional bureaucracies, kings established centralized governments that removed more and more authority from the old feudal order. At the same time, although the power of the monarchs was limited by the rise of representative institutions, kingship was becoming deeply imbedded in popular imagination and in emerging national identities.

Questions for Further Study

1. What patterns can be discerned in medieval political theory with regard to church-state relations?
2. Was the Magna Carta a feudal or a democratic document?
3. What methods did the early French kings use to consolidate their power over the feudal nobility? In what ways did these methods differ from those used in England?
4. What were Frederick Hohenstaufen's imperial ambitions? Were they realistic?

Suggestions for Further Reading

Abulafia, David. *Frederick II: A Medieval Emperor*. London, 1988.

Baldwin, John W. *The Government of Philip Augustus*. Berkeley, CA, 1986.

Bradbury, Jim. *Philip Augustus: King of France, 1180-1223*. New York, 1998.

Gillingham, John. *The Angevin Empire*. New York, 2001.

Holt, James Clarke. *Magna Carta*. New York, 1992.

More, John C., Brenda Bolton, and James M. Powell, eds. *Pope Innocent III and His World*. London, 1999.

Nicholsen, Helen J. *Love, War, and the Grail: Templars, Hospitallers and Teutonic Knights 1150-1500*. Leiden, 2000.

Prestwich, Michael. *Edward I (Yale English Monarchs)*. New Haven, CT, 1997.

Sayers, Jane E. *Innocent III: Leader of Europe, 1198-1216*. London, 1994.

Strayer, Joseph R. *The Reign of Philip the Fair*. Princeton, NJ, 1980.

Van Cleve, T.C. *The Emperor Frederick the Second of Hohenstaufen*. Oxford, 1973.

Warren, William L. *King John*. Berkeley, CA, 1978.

Weir, Alison. *Eleanor of Aquitaine: A Life*. New York, 2001.

InfoTrac College Edition

Enter the search term *medieval Germany* using Key Terms.

Enter the search term *medieval England* using Key Terms.

ART AND IDEAS IN THE GOTHIC AGE

The later part of the medieval period was marked, intellectually and artistically, by a series of major and lasting developments. In addition to their intrinsic interest, they also helped prepare the way for the watershed of the Italian Renaissance.

The leading scholastic theologian Thomas Aquinas had proclaimed the reconciliation of faith and reason. His immediate successors were less certain of the powers of the human mind. The doubts of thinkers such as Duns Scotus and William of Ockham produced important effects on the course of Western philosophy.

The literature of the age reflected the same concern with naturalism. Writers rejected Latin in favor of their own languages. New forms included long narrative poems called *romances* and short fables in verse. Dante's *Divine Comedy,* the colossal inauguration of Italian literature, provides a majestic synthesis of Scholastic theology, Classical learning, and personal experience. It stands as one of the supreme achievements of the Medieval Age. Dante's successors—Boccaccio in Italy and Chaucer in England—used the naturalistic story to describe the life and characters of their own day.

The last great achievement in medieval art, the counterpart in stone of Dante's literary edifice, was the creation of the Gothic style of architecture. The 13th-century architects and stone carvers of Gothic cathedrals adapted the construction principles of Romanesque style to produce light and airy structures decorated with glowing stained-glass windows and naturalistic sculptures. The achievement of an entire community of workers, a Gothic cathedral represented at the same time the summation of centuries of medieval knowledge and the new spirit of community pride.

Late medieval painters and sculptors, like their counterparts in the other arts, were attracted by the possibilities of realism. The art of naturalistic portraiture and the careful depiction of plants and animals appear in the repertory of late 14th-century painters and illuminators. Although art in northern Europe still remained connected to medieval traditions, Italian artists used naturalism to move beyond and foreshadow Renaissance humanism.

Thus, against a background of turmoil and human suffering, the thinkers and creative artists of the 13th and 14th centuries continued to explore the concerns of the medieval world and push them to their limits, while in Italy the link with the next great turning point in Western culture was already being forged.

FAITH VERSUS REASON: THE HEIRS OF AQUINAS

By the mid-13th century, St. Thomas Aquinas had expressed in his *Summa Theologica* complete confidence in the reconciliation of human reason, as understood by the Greeks, and Christian faith (see Topic 28). Toward the end of the medieval period, thinkers became less convinced of the certainty of the scholastic vision. Perhaps they were inevitably influenced by the natural disasters and political strife that beset western Europe in the course of the 14th century. In the face of the apparently arbitrary blows of destiny—war, famine, plague—it was increasingly difficult to believe that human understanding could grasp God's purpose. Faith in God remained constant; reason, however, seemed unable to explain why or how the divine scheme of things operated as it did.

One of the earliest critics of Aquinas's speculative method was the Scottish Franciscan John Duns Scotus (1265?–1308), whose analytical approach to philosophy marked a break with the medieval synthetic tradition of Aquinas. So dense and difficult was the reasoning of Scotus and his followers that uncomprehending critics labeled them "dunces."

Duns claimed that love and faith were more important than reason and personal experience in understanding God. Reason was capable of only imagining the existence of God because faith had already accepted it. Thus, instead of trying to deduce the concept of the divine by observing the way in which the natural world worked, as Aquinas had, Scotus held that purely intellectual analysis proved that God necessarily exists.

WILLIAM OF OCKHAM

At the very end of the medieval age, William of Ockham (c. 1285–1349) stressed the inability of human reason to understand God's unlimited freedom and power. Surrounded by the uncertainties of the times—Ockham probably died of the plague—it was easier to accept an incomprehensible deity than to count on an ordered, knowable natural world.

In any case, in observing the world around him, Ockham looked for truth in individual things, not in universal principles. It was not possible to know what a table was by simply thinking of the idea, but only by actually seeing one and touching it. Ockham summarized his search for specific concrete examples rather than universal theories in a methodological principle that came to be known as "Ockham's razor." According to this principle, when there are alternate explanations for the same phenomenon, the simpler is always preferable.

Philosophers following this method were called **nominalists.** With their distrust for the more abstruse speculations of their predecessors, and their emphasis on method and solid fact—they claimed that knowledge should rest on direct experience and not on abstract reason—they helped lay the intellectual foundation for the rise of the modern scientific method. At the same time, Ockham's belief in God's absolute autonomy and power became one of the chief tenets of the Protestant Reformation in the 16th century.

THE CLIMAX OF MEDIEVAL LITERATURE: DANTE'S *DIVINE COMEDY*

With the rise of vernacular literature in the Romanesque period, new literary genres appeared that reflected a growing interest in individual human behavior and emotions rather than heroic stereotypes. One of the earliest forms to develop was the *romance*; these were long narrative poems whose interest in plot and character prefigures the modern novel. The first great writer of romances was the French Chrétien de Troyes (c. 1135–1183), many of whose works have an Arthurian setting and describe the quest of his knightly heroes for self-knowledge.

Very different in spirit were the French verse *fabliaux,* short stories written during the 13th and 14th centuries. Satirical, coarse, and sometimes obscene, they are often anti-clerical and seem to have been aimed at a new urban public, as much as for literature's traditional aristocratic readership.

DANTE ALIGHIERI

At the pinnacle of medieval literature and culture stands the work of Dante Alighieri (1265–1321), whose *Divine Comedy* ranges over the religion, politics, and intellectual concerns of the Middle Ages to offer a synthesis of Christian and pagan values, the same combination of faith and reason extolled by Aquinas. Furthermore, Dante brings to the intellectual vision of the scholastic philosopher a richness of poetic language that ranges from gross and violent realism to the heights of spiritual ecstasy.

Dante was born in Florence, the son of a minor noble Guelph family. In his youth, he tells us, he fell in love with a young woman he calls Beatrice, but concealed his devotion. He took an active part in the government of Florence and served as an ambassador for the city. In 1301, during Dante's absence in Rome on a diplomatic mission, political rivals came to power and pronounced a sentence of banishment on him. He never saw Florence again. He died in exile in Ravenna, where—despite later Florentine efforts to recover the body—he is still buried.

The *Divine Comedy* traces the poet's passage from Hell to Purgatory to Paradise. The journey takes place on two levels: In one sense it is Dante's own quest, begun on a specific day and time (the dawn of Good Friday, 1300), which occurred at the symbolic midpoint of Dante's life—his 35th year. At the same time the journey takes on universal significance as a comprehensive view of the destiny of all humans, in this world and the next.

His guide to Hell and Purgatory is the Roman poet Vergil, symbol of human reason and the wisdom of antiq-

Colorphoto Hans Hinz, Allschwil/Basel

Dante, painted by Sandro Botticelli, c. 1480–1485. 24½ by 18½ inches (54 by 47 cm). Painted almost 200 years after the poet's death, this image reproduces the traditional memory of Dante's appearance. Like many other painters, Botticelli depicts him wearing a laurel wreath symbolizing poetry.

uity. They begin by descending into Hell and passing through its circles, peopled by those men and women who have rejected the love of God in favor of worldly sins and temptations: riches, power, greed, fraud, and treachery. At the lowest point is the monstrous Satan, frozen in a lake of ice. Climbing out through the Antipodes (the opposite side of the world), the two poets ascend the mount of Purgatory.

For the final stage of the journey, Vergil, the voice of human reason, can no longer serve as guide. Beatrice herself, symbol of divine grace and revelation, leads Dante through Paradise to the supreme bliss, the contemplation of God.

Several features characteristic of High Medieval culture permeate the work. One is the way in which Dante combines references to Classical myth and Christian tradition. Thus the ferryman of the dead in Hell is Charon, of Greek and Roman myth. Then, numbers play an important symbolic role. The poem is in 100 sections, or *cantos:* an introductory one, and then 33 in each of the stages of the journey. The rhyme scheme mirrors the significance of the number three, symbolic of the Trinity, and is called *terza*

rima; it consists of verses of three lines with the rhyming pattern *aba, bcb, cdc,* and so on. Hell and Purgatory are both divided into an entrance and nine regions, while Paradise has nine heavens (based on the ancient Ptolemaic system—another reference to the pagan tradition) and the Empyrean, the supreme heaven.

Perhaps the most important symbol in the *Divine Comedy* is light, an important element of much medieval allegory. Dante begins in the "dark forest" of doubt and despair, and darkness engulfs the regions of Hell. When Dante and Vergil climb out of the last of the regions, they see the stars above them. Their passage through Purgatory is marked by the daylight of divine light but ends with the sunset of Vergil's exclusion from Christian revelation. At the climax of Paradise, Dante sees God as the "Light Supreme."

If the overall subject of the *Divine Comedy* is the destiny of humanity and the ultimate meaning of history and nature, the poet finds time within his cosmic vision to create a host of memorable characters—some mythological, some historical, some Dante's own acquaintances. Among them are the doomed lovers Paolo and Francesca and the glutton Ciacco the Hog in Hell, and, in Paradise, the young St. Francis, who is presented to Dante by St. Thomas Aquinas.

LATE MEDIEVAL LITERATURE

At the very end of the medieval period, the growing number of readers inspired writers to produce works aimed at an ever broader public. The *Decameron* of Giovanni Boccaccio (1313–1375) is the first major piece of prose fiction in the Western tradition. A collection of 100 short stories, the *Decameron* seeks neither to elevate nor to enlighten, but simply to entertain.

Boccaccio's slightly later contemporary, Geoffrey Chaucer (1340–1400), created a similar collection of narratives in his *Canterbury Tales.* Both writers are among the first in Western literature to make their women characters as lively, witty, and sexually sophisticated as the men.

THE GOTHIC CATHEDRAL

In the last lines of the *Divine Comedy,* Dante tells us that God's Radiance is the light that moves the sun and the other stars. The architectural style of his age, the **Gothic,** similarly uses light to illuminate the divine presence. Furthermore, just as Aquinas's theological synthesis and Dante's metaphorical journey reconciled faith and reason to present a unity of vision, so the builders and sculptors responsible for the great Gothic cathedrals sought to represent the unity of human knowledge and the divine.

The practical Romanesque style of a century earlier produced buildings that were sturdy, fireproof, and capable of containing large numbers of people. With their small windows, however, they were so dark inside that most of the sculpture decorating them was on the outside.

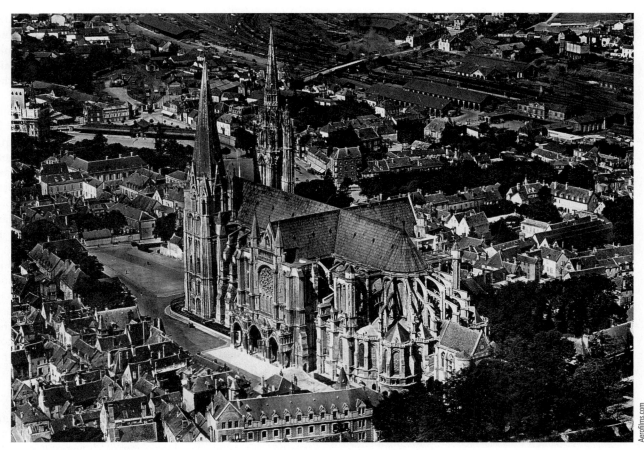

Aerial view of Chartres Cathedral, Chartres, France. Begun 1154; rebuilt after 1194. The large doorway on the building's side, the so-called Royal Portal, is all that is left of the construction begun in 1154; its style is early Gothic. This building was destroyed by fire in 1194, and the rest of the cathedral was built thereafter in the High Gothic style.

Gothic architects took the two most characteristic features of the Romanesque—barrel vaults and stone supporting ribs—and combined them to form high, pointed rib vaults: The ribs provided support for the slender vaults. The results were lofty, light, and airy structures, with the spaces between the vaults cut away and filled with stained-glass windows. To ensure that the buildings were stable, architects added outside supports called "flying buttresses" that shored up the walls. Occasionally the desire to construct buildings that reached to the heavens proved counterproductive, and the structures collapsed before being completed, or shortly thereafter.

The sense of lightness and grace, contrasting with the weightiness of Romanesque architecture, was enhanced by the decorations. The stained-glass windows consisted of multicolored panels placed in a setting of delicate stone framework, or tracery. The shapes of the windows varied. Among the most complex was the great round or "rose" window, which often decorated the main façade of a church. By careful use of the shape, position, and color scheme of the windows, architects could achieve their own control over the light of God.

Outside, the buildings are decorated with a profusion of sculpture combining Christian and pagan stories, fabulous monsters and scientific discoveries, portraits of nobles and merchants, and gutter spouts with grotesque heads, or gargoyles. Other elements include plants and animals as manifestations of the natural world. The total effect has been described as "an encyclopedia of medieval knowledge for those who cannot read." At the same time, the statues and stained-glass windows provided a permanent record of historical events as well as biblical stories, as in the case of the window at Chartres commemorating Charlemagne.

The earliest Gothic church to be built was that of the Abbey of Saint-Denis near Paris, finished in 1144 under the Abbot Suger. Most of the Gothic churches, however, were built over the following century for cities rather than for monasteries. The Gothic style, in fact, was invented for an urban context. Like the universities, it arose as a consequence of the rise of city life. The immense spires signaled to travelers throughout the countryside that they were approaching their destination, and the houses of many a medieval city clustered around its cathedral.

The primary purpose for the construction of a cathedral was religious, but the building projects of the Gothic Age served a variety of other needs. They helped provide employment for large numbers of people, from the permanent

Interior of the upper chapel of La Sainte Chapelle, Paris. 1243–1248. An overwhelming example of the way in which Gothic buildings used light, the chapel was built to house relics of Christ's Passion. Its emphasis on the vertical line and the weightless, transparent character of the construction are both characteristic of the finest Gothic architecture.

© Sonia Halliday

building staff to the specialized craftsmen responsible for stained glass and other decorations to the traveling sculptors who moved from one building site to another. Because they served so wide a variety of community interests, none of the major Gothic building projects was ever completely finished, but continued to provide work as long as funds and workers were available. Only the devastation of the Black Death brought construction to a halt.

At the same time, the cathedrals gave a sense of pride and identity to the communities responsible for their construction. Nor did they serve only religious purposes. Inside there was space for public occasions such as town meetings, concerts, or lectures, and outside minstrels and jugglers provided popular entertainment against the background of the ornate façade.

MUSIC IN THE GOTHIC AGE
It is no coincidence that the most important musical developments of the Gothic Age occurred in Paris, the center of Gothic architecture and of European intellectual life. The musicians of the 12th-century School of Notre Dame in

Paris took the earlier Romanesque form of polyphony known as *organum* and developed it further.

Around 1200 one of the leading composers of the School, Pérotin (d. 1238?), moved from the improvisational style of his predecessors toward a greater sense of musical structure. By simultaneously combining three and even four musical lines in his compositions, Pérotin anticipated developments a century later in harmony, counterpoint, and rhythm.

SCULPTURE AND PAINTING IN THE GOTHIC AGE: ART IN TRANSITION

Throughout the 13th century, the most advanced centers of western European art were in the North, in Paris and the leading cities of England and Germany where major building programs were underway. One of the inspirations for Gothic sculptors working there was ancient Roman art, under the influence of which their statues had increasingly realistic anatomy and drapery.

Yet in Italy, once the center of Roman art, artists remained conservative and isolated from developments to the north of the Alps. The style of their frescoes and mosaics, known as Italo-Byzantine, was still rooted in a medieval tradition of centuries earlier.

Early in the 14th century, this situation abruptly reversed. The Italian painter Giotto and his followers revolutionized the history of painting with their new approaches to realism and emotional expression. Renaissance art was a direct consequence of their breakthrough. Meanwhile, throughout the rest of Europe, artists continued to work in a late medieval version of the Gothic style called the International Style. By 1400, with the early phases of Renaissance art emerging in central Italy, northern European artists were still producing Gothic works.

LATE GOTHIC ART IN THE NORTH

The chief feature of the International Style is its choice of realistic subjects and love of naturalistic detail. Its appearance throughout Europe—from which comes its name—was the result of growing cultural contacts among European countries and the increasing spread of ideas among the leading aristocratic courts.

The most attractive and complete picture of life in the late Gothic period emerges from the *Très Riches Heures du Duc de Berry* (*The Book of Hours of the Duke of Berry*). This prayer book, which includes 12 illuminated calendar pages, is the work of the three Flemish Limbourg brothers—Pol, Hennequin, and Herman—and dates to 1416. The calendar scenes illustrate the months of the year and are filled with realistic observation and the depiction of details from nature.

May page from the *Très Riches Heures du Duc de Berry*. Illuminated manuscript by the Limbourg brothers. 1413–1416. c. 8½ by 5¼ inches (22 by 14 cm). The manuscript includes a page for each month of the year. In this springtime scene, a group of lords and ladies rides out on a hunting expedition, against a background of the fresh spring green, with the turrets of a great castle behind.

© Giraudon/Art Resource, NY

The February page contrasts the farm laborers thawing themselves out in front of the fireplace with the sheep outside in their icy pen huddled together for warmth. In May, behind the verdant spring leaves of forest trees, we can see the spires and turrets of a castle, while in the foreground a procession of medieval courtiers rides out to the sound of music. The world portrayed in these pages is the same as that found in Dante's great poem.

The world of the Limbourg brothers and their Burgundian patrons is that of courtly love and the romances. It comes as something of a shock to realize that, by the time they painted their masterpiece, south of the Alps Giotto had already laid the foundations for the early Renaissance, and some of its greatest artists—Ghiberti, Donatello, Fra Angelico—were already at work in Florence developing the ideas of Renaissance humanism.

GIOTTO'S PREDECESSORS

For all its break with the past, Giotto's revolutionary art has its roots in the style of his immediate predecessors. The most important, Cimabue (1240?–1302?), may even have been Giotto's teacher. Little of Cimabue's work survives, and what there is has been badly damaged—most recently in the disastrous Florence flood of 1966 and the Assisi earthquake of 1997. Judging from what is left, his painting seems to have had a concern with anatomy and an emotional quality lacking in earlier Italo-Byzantine painting.

The same sense of dramatic and emotional involvement emerges in the painting of Cimabue's Sienese contemporary Duccio (1255/1256–1318/1319). Many of the scenes from the lives of Christ and the Virgin, painted on his vast altarpiece for the high altar of Siena's cathedral between 1308 and 1311, the *Maestà*, achieve a sense of vividness by their convincing use of architecture. For the first time in the history of painting, an artist had succeeded in showing figures that appear to be inside an architectural setting. Before Duccio, no painter had conveyed so great a sense of space. Yet Duccio's art remained rooted in a past that continued to be influenced by Byzantine traditions, increasingly imported into Italy by refugees from the Byzantine world to the east.

THE ART OF GIOTTO

The career of the Florentine painter and architect Giotto di Bondone (c. 1266–1337) symbolizes the transition from medieval to Renaissance art. His contemporaries were quick to recognize his originality and the profound importance of his work for the future development of painting. One of the figures whom Dante meets in Purgatory describes Giotto as the most renowned artist of the age, and a character in Boccaccio's *Decameron* remarks that Giotto "brought back to light the art of painting."

For Renaissance critics, Giotto's most important innovation was his realism. Vasari, the 16th-century painter and writer, summed up reactions when he wrote that Giotto "deserves to be called the pupil of Nature and no other." By the careful use of light and dark, he created a sense of depth and volume that made the figures in his paintings seem as solid as sculptures, as lifelike as real people.

Later ages came to appreciate his genius for using this technique to dramatic and emotional effect and giving his apparently real figures a convincing emotional life. Time and time again Giotto manages to touch us by conveying

The Annunciation, by the Sienese painter, Duccio, c. 1308–1311. Height 6 feet 10½ inches (2.1 m). Duccio was one of the first artists since Classical Antiquity to create a convincing architectural space around his figures. Note the simple pilasters at the archways, without any elaborate Gothic decoration.

Scala/Art Resource

Lamentation over the Dead Christ, by Giotto. Scrovegni (Arena) Chapel, Padua, Italy. 1305. Giotto's realism and the powerful emotion of his scenes inspired much Early Renaissance art. Here, as angels wheel overhead, screaming in grief, Mary raises the body of her dead son and stares wildly into his face, while behind her Saint John throws out his arms in anguish. Note the barren landscape.

©Cameraphoto Arte, Venice/Art Resource, NY

the most complete expression of human feelings—and the range of emotions he can summon is almost inexhaustible.

Rather than confine himself to individual paintings, Giotto preferred to work on a more monumental scale. His greatest surviving work is the cycle of frescoes painted around 1305 to 1306 in the Arena Chapel in Padua, a building also known as the Scrovegni Chapel, the name of Giotto's patron. The panels illustrate the lives of the Virgin and of Christ.

In the scene of the *Pietà* (Lament over the dead body of Christ), the mood is of cosmic grief. Angels circle above, howling their sorrow, while Mary stares with disbelief into the face of her dead son and John flings out his arms in despair. Nor does Giotto always use dramatic poses to express extreme emotions. The silent hunched figures in the foreground add their own poignancy. So, too, does the bare tree behind. The painting not only conveys a religious image, but the emotions of the living are as important to the viewer as the identity of the dead figure. Humans and their feelings, hopes and fears, have become the subject of art.

Putting Gothic Art and Ideas in Perspective

Artists and thinkers in the Gothic Age were driven by their urge to find unity in an increasingly complex and threatening universe. Dante's mighty masterpiece and the towering Gothic spires of the cathedrals of Europe looked heavenward for a demonstration of the essential meaning of human life. The Scholastic theologians, led by

St. Thomas Aquinas, combined human knowledge with divine law to reinforce the message of religious faith.

Toward the end of the medieval period, some philosophers began to lose confidence in the capacity of humans to understand such cosmic questions. They chose to concentrate on matters that were capable of being tested by practical examination. At the same time, writers such as Boccaccio and Chaucer turned from the great issues of life, death, and eternity to portray the daily lives and emotions of people with whom they and their readers could identify.

Then came the terror of the Black Death. As the 14th century drew to its painful close, waves of the plague continued to wash over much of Europe, and the later stages of the Hundred Years' War added their own grim confusion to the general political and economic chaos. Artists like the Limbourg brothers tried to turn back the clock and recapture the charm and elegance of a courtly era that a century of trouble had virtually destroyed.

Across the Alps in Italy, the process of intellectual and artistic recovery had already begun. The work of Giotto is the first sign of a cultural revolution that was to remake the Western tradition by going back to the beginnings of Western culture: the Greeks. Just as for the Greeks, so, too, for Renaissance artists, at the heart of their vision of the world was neither God nor nature, but humans. In the slow and painful rebuilding of European society during the 15th century, that vision was to pass northward across the Alps and transform Western life and art.

Questions for Further Study

1. What are the chief features of Dante's style, and to what extent do they reflect the political and intellectual climate of the High Middle Ages?
2. In what ways did the art of Pisano and Giotto break with the past?
3. How does the Gothic style of architecture differ from the Romanesque?
4. What were the reactions of Thomas Aquinas's successors to his ideas, and how did they justify their criticisms?

Suggestions for Further Reading

Camille, Michael. *Gothic Art: Glorious Visions*. New York, 1996.

Courtenay, Lunn T., ed. *The Engineering of Medieval Cathedrals*. Aldershot, 1997.

Grodecki, L., and C. Brisac. *Gothic Stained Glass, 1200–1300*. Ithaca, NY, 1985.

Hollander, Robert. *Dante: A Life in Works*. New Haven, CT, 2001.

Larner, J. *Italy in the Age of Dante and Petrarch, 1216–1380*. New York, 1980.

Lewis, R.W.B. *Dante*. New York, 2001.

Norman, Diana, ed. *Siena, Florence, and Padua: Art, Society, and Religion*. New Haven, CT, 1995.

Radding, Charles M., and William W. Clark. *Medieval Architecture, Medieval Learning*. New Haven, CT, 1992.

Toman, Rolf, ed. *The Art of Gothic: Architecture, Sculpture, Painting*. Cologne, 1999.

West, Richard. *Chaucer 1340-1400: The Life and Times of the First English Poet*. New York, 2000.

White, John. *Art and Architecture in Italy 1250-1400*, 3rd ed. New Haven, CT, 1993.

THE FOURTEENTH CENTURY: STRESS AND CHANGE IN EUROPEAN SOCIETY

Between 1312 and 1314, while in political exile from his home in Florence, the Italian poet Dante Alighieri wrote the *Inferno,* the first part of his great epic the *Divine Comedy.* Dante's vision of the horrors of Hell might well serve as a metaphor for the world of violence, fear, and upheaval that characterized the 14th century. The period that opened around 1300 marked the end of what had been a long era of sustained growth for European civilization, a material and spiritual expansion that had begun centuries earlier with the reform of the church and the Crusades, the revival of learning, and the rebirth of towns and commerce. Moreover, the political stability experienced by Europe with the development of royal government was shattered as a result of a long and destructive war between France and England that stretched into the following century.

By the middle of the 14th century, a difficult era of famine and plague began that decimated Europe's population and caused a more depressed outlook on life. The frenzy of fear that struck millions gave rise to terrible incidents of reprisal against innocent victims who were blamed for the disasters, including the Jews. The fall in population that resulted from the plague and famine led to a severe labor shortage, which at first stimulated living conditions for workers, but then enabled landowners and manufacturers to reduce wages while governments increased taxes. The subsequent economic pressures began a series of violent peasant and worker revolts throughout Europe. The era ended with a schism that split a papacy already "captured" by a hostile French monarchy and the rise of new forms of religious heresy that challenged the hold of the church over the faithful.

S IGNIFICANT DATES

The Fourteenth Century

1309–1378	Babylonian Captivity of the church
1315–1317	Famine strikes throughout Europe
1337	Hundred Years' War begins
1347–1350	Black Death
1357	Peasant disturbances in France
1378	Ciompi revolt in Florence
1381	Peasant uprising in England

OVERPOPULATION AND ITS CONSEQUENCES

By the end of the 13th century, Europe's population had swelled to unprecedented size after a long period of sustained growth. The rising number of inhabitants in cities and countryside had prompted landowners to bring even the most marginal land under cultivation in order to meet the demand for food. The population growth had also increased the labor force, which caused wages—and therefore living standards—to decline.

THE GREAT FAMINE

By the early decades of the new century, serious food shortages began to appear. The scarcity of food seems to have resulted from not only the larger number of people but also a cycle of crop failures caused by changes in Europe's weather pattern. The continent entered what is known as the "little ice age," in which temperatures dropped and winters lasted longer. These climate changes reduced the size of harvests, and hoarding in rural areas became common, causing severe hunger in the cities. The incessant wars of the period, especially the Hundred Years' War between England and France (see Topic 33), added to the dislocation and made the already difficult transportation of grain and other foodstuffs worse. On top of these setbacks, disastrous floods destroyed crops throughout northwestern Europe.

Conditions were made worse by the fact that on the farms people consumed even the seed that normally was saved for the next season's planting, producing even more devastating shortages the following year. People resorted to eating domestic animals and pets and, when these were gone, even mice and rats. The result was that the most extensive and severe famine in centuries struck, killing hundreds of thousands. Famines had not been unknown in Europe, but those of the 14th century were both recurrent and more severe.

The famine, combined with the colder, more humid climate of the period, took its toll on Europe's people, and especially on the poor and working-class population. Medieval sanitation and health conditions were at best poor, especially in the cities, where overcrowding meant that people lived close to each other and sewage flowed in open gutters in the streets. The result was that a population already suffering from malnutrition became more susceptible than usual to disease.

THE PLAGUE

From 1347 to 1348, a pandemic of infectious disease known as the **Black Death** swept across Europe, decimating the population with unparalleled ferocity. This was not the first time that a massive plague had afflicted Europe. In the 5th century B.C., Athens was overcome for several years by a virulent plague that originated in Ethiopia, wiping out large segments of the city's population; in 547, the so-called Plague of Justinian reached Europe from Byzantium and annihilated millions.

THE BLACK DEATH

The plague appeared in 1346, this time near the Caspian Sea, having spread from central Asia. In October 1347, a galley of ships from the Crimea carried the plague, presumably through fleas from infected rats, to the port of Messina, Sicily, where it caused an epidemic. It then spread quickly, mainly along trade routes, to Italy, France, Spain, and Portugal. Eventually the disease spread north, reaching Germany, England, and Scandinavia, and then moved back east to Russia.

The Black Death seems to have been of two basic kinds, bubonic and pneumonic. Bubonic plague was caused by a bacterium transmitted by the bite of fleas infected from humans or rats; the more virulent pneumonic variety, spread by airborne bacteria that attacked the lungs, was probably the disease that killed most Europeans in the 14th century.

Medieval physicians did not, of course, know what caused the plague, although they understood that it was spread by infection. In the cities, where the impact was worse, victims fell by the thousands in streets or were left to die in their homes, family members often fleeing in panic. Ships were prevented from entering ports—the word *quarantine* comes from the 40-day period of isolation required of all incoming ships—and rural villages and larger towns tried to keep strangers away. The wealthier classes took refuge in the countryside, a circumstance that provided the setting for the *Decameron* of Giovanni Boccaccio. The fear that the plague engendered sometimes caused desperate and appalling reactions. In some cities of Germany, the Low Countries, and Switzerland, the Christian population took out their fears on the Jews, accusing them of poisoning the wells.

There is no way to know how many people the Black Death killed. The Italian city-states, which had the best public health systems of the day, provide an appalling illustration of its impact. The peninsula lost about 2 million people. In the central Italian town of Pistoia some 70 percent of the inhabitants died. Many physicians refused to

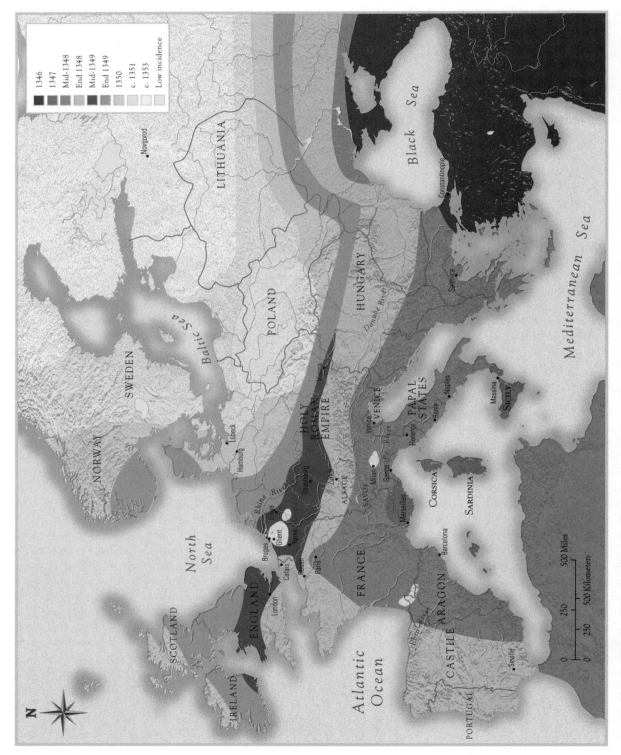

Map 31.1 The Black Death, 1346–1350. The rapid spread is all the more remarkable for a period in which travel and communication was so difficult. The only regions to be relatively little affected are the most remote parts of Europe: the mountains of northwestern Ireland and Scotland, and the rugged fjords of northern Norway. Go to http://info.wadsworth.com/053461065x for an interactive version of this map.

Manuscript illumination showing the burning of Jews. 14th century. Jews were among those accused of causing the plague of the Black Death in 1348. In many parts of Europe they were burned alive. The crowd here looking on includes men and women, soldiers and civilians.

Ms. 13076-77, f. 12v, Bibliotheque Royale Albert 1er, Brussels

treat victims, so that the clergy had to attend to the sick, with the result that large numbers of priests and monks were carried off by the disease. In Florence, Boccaccio explains that the cemeteries soon ran out of space:

> Each hour of the day there was such a rush to remove the huge number of bodies that there was not enough sacred burial ground, especially as the custom was to give every body its own spot. When, therefore, the ground was full, they dug large trenches in all the churchyards and stacked hundreds of bodies in them in layers, like cargo in the hold of a ship, covering them with a little dirt until the bodies reached to the top.

SOCIAL AND ECONOMIC CONSEQUENCES

In all, the plague killed as many as one-third of the overall European population—perhaps 35 million people. Like famine, it returned periodically throughout the 14th century and into the next. In the 17th century, plague hit Venice and other Italian towns—between 1630 and 1631, officials in Venice counted more than 50,000 victims—and as late as the late 18th century it killed even more people in Russia. As a result of the combined effect of plague, famine, and war, Europe suffered tremendous demographic losses. Conservative estimates suggest that between 1300 and 1450 the population declined by half, whereas others put the figure at two-thirds.

The plague destabilized European society. To many pious Christians the Black Death seemed to spell the coming of the Four Horsemen of the Apocalypse, and they responded with both fear and guilt. Fanatical men and women known as _flagellants_, obsessed by feelings of remorse, traveled together in groups from one village and town to another, chanting and whipping themselves in public to demonstrate their thirst for divine forgiveness. Artists of the period revealed the popular obsession with death by making the Last Judgment a recurrent motif in painting and sculpture. Poetry and folk stories recount the Dance of Death, a bizarre ritual in which corpses danced before stunned observers, and peasants acted out the drama in popular festivals.

In addition to the psychological impact of the disasters, a host of more tangible consequences followed. The drastic decline in population dislocated the economy, interrupting production in craft shops, cloth manufacturing centers, and in the fields. Initially, many of the laborers who survived the plague were neither temperamentally nor physically able to return to work. When they did, the shortage of labor meant that they were generally able to command higher wages, while scarcity also drove up the price of goods. Some governments tried to control the situation by placing limits on wages and prices. Food costs, on the other hand, went down as the demand for cereal crops was no longer fed by population pressures, thus causing a slump in agricultural profits for landowners. In the countryside, bands of mercenary soldiers roamed freely, stealing from peasants and merchants and plundering local villages.

BAD TIMES AND SOCIAL PROTEST: PEASANTS AND WORKERS IN REVOLT

The demographic and economic impact of the years of plague and famine had troublesome social consequences. The period from 1350 to 1450 saw waves of peasant and worker upheavals against the propertied classes. Most of these protests were serious and bloody and beyond anything Europe had ever experienced.

Popular unrest manifested itself both in the countryside and in the towns as tensions rose over the hard times. Faced with lower profit margins because of the rise in

PERSPECTIVES FROM THE PAST

THE BLACK DEATH

The devastating impact of the Black Death on 14th-century Europe was echoed in numerous chronicles and contemporary accounts, including fictional stories, poems, and religious chants. The Italian writer Petrarch lost his famous lover Laura to the plague in 1348, and Boccaccio made flight from the plague the setting for his stories in the *Decameron*. The contemporary sources tell us not only how people reacted to the plague—the fear, horror, and panic that struck millions. They also provide historians with valuable information about the disease itself, about efforts, both scientific and spiritual, to combat it, and its social consequences. The items that follow are a few of the many sources that document the Black Death and suggest the possibilities and range of material scholars use.

Boccaccio's Description of the Plague in Florence

In the introduction to the Decameron, the Florentine writer Giovanni Boccaccio gives an eye-witness description of the symptoms and the terrible scenes in the city.

It did not act as it had done in the East, where bleeding from the nose was a manifest sign of inevitable death, but it began in both men and women with certain swellings either in the groin or under the armpits, some of which grew to the size of a normal apple and others to the size of an egg (more or less), and the people called them *gavoccioli* [buboes]. And from the two parts of the body already mentioned, within a brief space of time, the said deadly *gavoccioli* began to spread indiscriminately over every part of the body; and after this, the symptoms of the illness changed to black or livid spots appearing on the arms and thighs, and on every part of the body, some large ones and sometimes many little ones scattered all around. . . .

Many ended their lives in the public streets, during the day or at night, while many others who died in their homes were discovered dead by their neighbors only by the smell of their decomposing bodies. The city was full of corpses. . . . they would drag the corpse out of the home and place it in front of the doorstep where, usually in the morning, quantities of dead bodies could be seen by any passerby. . . .

From "The Decameron" by Giovanni Boccaccio, translated by Mark Musa and Peter Bondanella. Copyright © 1982 by Mark Musa and Peter Bondanella. Used by permission of W. W. Norton & Company, Inc.

Fourteenth-Century Medical Advice

The first case of the Black Death in Paris was noted in May or June 1348. In October, the medical faculty of the University of Paris conducted an investigation of the plague on instructions from King Philip VI. The report they issued

wages, rural landowners tried to reimpose tight controls over the serfs and lower wages to earlier levels. Kings and municipal governments, on the other hand, sought to collect higher taxes from the workers who were earning more in order to pay for the wars and increasing costs of government services. The plague was even more destructive in the towns, where the demand for manufactured goods dropped with the decline in population, resulting in widespread unemployment. Guild members tried to protect their businesses through laws limiting membership and advancement.

REVOLTS IN THE COUNTRYSIDE

One of the first and most disturbing peasant revolts took place in 1358 in northern France, an area that had been devastated by the outbreak of war between England and

explained that the conjunction of three planets—Saturn, Jupiter, and Mars—had caused the disaster. Among the measures they recommended for prevention were the following:

No poultry should be eaten, no waterfowl, no sucking pig, no old beef, altogether no fat meat. The meat of animals of a warm, dry constitution should be eaten, but no heating or irritating meat. We recommend broths with ground pepper, cinnamon, and spices, particularly to such people who eat little but choice food. It is injurious to sleep during the daytime. Sleep should not be extended beyond dawn or very little beyond it. Very little should be drunk at breakfast, lunch should be taken at 11 o'clock, and a little more wine may be drunk than at breakfast and the drink should be a clear, light wine mixed with one-sixth water. Dried or fresh fruit is innoxious if eaten together with wine. Without wine it may be dangerous. Beetroot and other fresh or preserved vegetables may prove injurious; spicy herbs such as sage and rosemary are, on the other hand, wholesome. Cold, moist, and watery foods are generally harmful. It is dangerous to go out at night till three in the morning on account of the dew. Fish should not be eaten, too much exercise may be injurious; the clothing should be warm, giving protection from cold, damp and rain, and nothing should be cooked in rain-water. With the meals a little treacle (*theriaca*) should be taken; olive oil with food is mortal. Fat people should expose themselves to the sun. Excess of abstinence, excitement, anger, and drunkenness are dangerous. Diarrhoea is serious. Bathing dangerous. The bowels should be kept open by a clyster. Intercourse with women is mortal; there should be no coition nor should one sleep in any women's bed.

A Universal Plague

The plague had been a recurrent problem since ancient times and in all parts of the world. The Black Death of the mid-14th century had equally disastrous consequences in the Near East as in Europe. In the account that follows, taken from his universal history, the famed 14th-century Muslim historian and geographer Ibn Khaldun summarizes the international significance of the disease.

Civilization both in the East and the West was visited by a destructive plague which devastated nations and caused populations to vanish. It swallowed up many of the good things of civilization and wiped them out. It overtook the dynasties at the time of their senility, when they had reached the limit of their duration. It lessened their power and curtailed their influence. It weakened their authority. Their situation approached the point of annihilation and dissolution. Civilization decreased with the decrease of mankind. Cities and buildings were laid waste, roads and way signs were obliterated, settlements and mansions became empty, dynasties and tribes grew weak. The entire inhabited world changed. The East, it seems, was similarly visited, though in accordance with and in proportion to [the East's more affluent] civilization. It was as if the voice of existence in the world had called out for oblivion and restriction, and the world responded to its call. God inherits the earth and whomever is upon it.

Quoted in Michael W. Dols, *The Black Death in the Middle East* (Princeton: Princeton University Press, 1977), 67.

France. Known as the *Jacquerie*, this insurrection took its name from Jacques Bonnehomme, the nickname that French landlords commonly used for their peasants. After the French defeat in 1356 and the capture of their king, John (1350–1364), the government had tried to make the peasants pay for the king's ransom. Protesting the deprivations and fearing further oppression, the peasants rose up against the nobles. With no leaders or specific goals, they murdered landowners and their families with great brutality, and burned manor houses, churches, and local archives containing tax records. The rebels took heart from the fact that the king was in captivity and the government in disarray, and a disheveled band of peasants even tried to march on Paris. But within a month the aristocrats had marshaled their forces, striking back with equal ferocity. They massacred those peasants they caught and hunted down the ones

Walters Art Gallery, Baltimore

Painting showing the effects of the Black Death. 14th century. The man writhing on the ground, alongside a corpse already wrapped for burial, points to the swellings on his neck, a typical symptom of the plague. As the priests sprinkle holy water, in the sky above St. Sebastian kneels to plead for God's mercy.

who escaped, drowning some in rivers and burning others alive to set an example for those who managed to survive.

The Jacquerie was followed by similar outbreaks of social violence elsewhere in Europe, including southern France, Spain, Germany, and Sweden. One of the most fa-

mous erupted in England in 1381. This Great Rebellion was a protest against government measures to control wages and workers. Peasant anger increased when royal officials levied a poll tax of equal worth on every inhabitant, rather than a proportional tax based on wealth. The landlords made mat-

Painting of the crushing of a peasant uprising. Late 14th–early 15th century. Peasant revolts such as the *Jacquerie* were punished with great ferocity by the landlords and nobles. The bodies of those executed were either placed on display or—as here—thrown into the river, to provide a warning for other potential rebels.

© Cliché Bibliothèque Nationale de France, Paris

ters worse by trying to restore some of the feudal dues that had been abandoned during good times. After a third poll tax was imposed in 1381, the enraged peasants rebelled under the leadership of several men, including one Wat Tyler. The peasants destroyed local records and noble residences and then marched on London, where the 15-year-old Richard II (ruled 1377–1399) persuaded them to disperse with promises to abolish serfdom and lower rents. Tyler was killed and the king, abandoning his promises, wiped out the peasants and their ringleaders.

DISTURBANCES IN THE CITIES

European cities also saw serious social uprisings in the 14th century. Some of these urban revolts were reactions against taxation or the result of struggles between urban political factions. Others were sparked by the frustrations of exploited workers who felt the impact of the economic depression that followed the Black Death. The most important of these worker rebellions was the Ciompi uprising in Florence. The Ciompi were clothworkers in the Florentine wool industry, which employed tens of thousands of them as

Manuscript illumination showing Wat Tyler's rebellion of 1381. Early 15th century. The peasant army, led by Wat Tyler and John Ball, marches from the right to face a mass of troops. Both sides carry a flag showing the red Cross of St. George, symbol of England, because each claims to represent the interests of the nation.

British Library, London, UK/Bridgeton Art Library

dyers, weavers, and other semiskilled laborers. The wool industry was one of the hardest hit manufacturing sectors in the post-plague slump. As demand fell, the manufacturers created massive unemployment by cutting production to about one-third of pre-plague levels. They also passed legislation that controlled wages and shifted the tax burden away from themselves.

In 1378, the Ciompi revolted and forced several reforms that included increased production levels, the establishment of their own guild, and representation in Florentine government. Without leaders, however, the Ciompi could not control the situation, and the ruling classes soon reestablished their control over the city. Like the other social upheavals of the period, the Ciompi revolt proved to be short lived. Its significance lies in the fact that it was one of the earliest examples of class conflict in an environment of urban capitalism in which workers suffering from economic hardship seized the initiative.

Most of these movements of social protest did not have lasting effect, but they did serve as a warning to the ruling elites that economic conditions could produce serious social upheaval. Yet most of those involved in the revolts were not from the poorest ranks of society. Rather, in the countryside they tended to be relatively prosperous peasants whose condition was threatened by government measures or by the efforts of landlords to increase their profits. The Ciompi, on the other hand, were an exception in that they represented the poorest of the urban workers in Florence. In all cases, it seems clear that the extraordinary circumstances created by the famines, plagues, and war of the period created new social and psychological tensions and further undermined the traditions that had upheld authority in Christian society.

Ironically, by the end of the century the condition of both peasants and workers had improved as Europe began to recover from the disasters and dislocations of the midcentury crisis. Moreover, in western Europe at least, serfdom had practically disappeared and population began to expand once again. Signs of recovery soon obscured the frightening experience of class warfare that had suddenly disrupted the social peace of medieval Europe.

The Church in Captivity: Schism and the Popes at Avignon

If economic and social conditions began to improve in the last quarter of the 14th century, the authority and grandeur of the papacy underwent a wrenching experience that seriously weakened the prestige of the medieval church. Two circumstances, the "capture" of the pope by the French monarchy and a serious division in the leadership of the papacy, paved the way for the later and more serious upheaval that rocked the church in the Reformation of the 16th century.

Map 31.2 The Schism and Religious Divisions. Note the two regions of Europe under Islamic influence: Granada in southern Spain (to be Christianized in 1492) and the territory surrounding Constantinople, which, as part of modern Turkey, is still Muslim today. A little more than a century later than the period of the divisions illustrated by this map, the Western Church was to face a far greater split: the Reformation.

THE BABYLONIAN CAPTIVITY

The crisis of the late medieval church had begun in the struggle for supremacy between Pope Boniface VIII and King Philip IV of France. In 1302 Boniface issued a bull that demanded Philip's submission to papal authority. Although Philip's attempt to abduct Boniface to France to stand trial before a church council failed, the king did manage to secure the election in 1305 of a French pope, Clement V (ruled 1305–1314). Rather than move to the traditional papal palace in Rome, however, the new pope established his court in the city of Avignon in southern France; Avignon was situated within lands belonging to the Holy Roman Empire but in fact lay across the Rhône River from lands of the French monarch. Clement repeatedly said that he planned to go to Rome when local conditions there were more settled, but politics and circumstances kept the papacy at Avignon for 75 years.

Clement's successors built a huge palace at Avignon, which became the official seat of the papacy until 1377. The popes of Avignon lived in great luxury, claiming that the city was safer and better located than Rome, but many were scandalized by what the Italian poet Petrarch (1304–1374) called the **"Babylonian Captivity."** Much to the chagrin of other rulers, the French kings did exercise great influence over papal policies, and all of the popes and

Palace of the Popes, Avignon. 14th century. This huge structure, built after the death of Clement V in 1314, combined elements of a secular palace, a monastery, and a fortress. Its architecture combines the decorative style of High Gothic with a new simplicity that foreshadows Renaissance style.

most of the cardinals appointed during the 75 years at Avignon were French, a fact that reinforced the popular feeling that the church was being held captive. Certainly the papacy was weakened as a result of the Avignon experience. An urgent need for revenue led the papacy into several practices that contributed to the decline in ecclesiastical standards. The popes at Avignon continued the process of making their government a more efficient and specialized bureaucracy, and this was especially true of fiscal administration. They divided all of Christendom into tax districts and appointed collectors and administrators for each district. Within each area, the popes used their authority to appoint clergy to benefices in order to raise papal income. *Benefices* were the ecclesiastical equivalent of a secular fief—that is, a church office that provided the person who held the position with an annual income.

The popes at Avignon included in this category the highest, and theoretically elected, positions in the hierarchy, such as bishops and abbots, as well as a variety of less important offices. Under the new fiscal arrangements, the holders of papal benefices had to pay one-third of their revenue (above a minimum amount) back to the papacy; under that amount, the benefice holders paid an *annate*, equal to the total revenue for the first year in office. In order to pay the required dues, the holders of benefices pressured the lower clergy under their jurisdiction to increase their contributions, a practice that was especially hard on the poor parish priests. Popes also resorted to the simple sale of benefices for prearranged prices.

In addition to the use of benefices to raise revenue, the Avignonese popes increasingly sold *indulgences*, which granted remission from temporal punishment (such as prayers or fasting) for sins; in addition to purchasing indulgences for themselves, family members could actually buy

them for dead relatives, who would then be required to spend less time in purgatory. The papacy also sold *dispensations*, whereby a holder of church office was excused from following certain requirements of church law.

One sign of the weakened power of the popes was to be found in their dealings with the Holy Roman Empire. When Pope John XXII (ruled 1316–1334) tried to stop the election of a Bavarian king as emperor, the German electors simply announced that the emperor did not need papal approval because God had bestowed the position on him. By the end of the 14th century, popes had virtually no real power to intervene in the domestic policies of the European monarchs.

SCHISM: THE CHURCH DIVIDED

Pope Gregory XI (ruled 1370–1378) ended the Babylonian Captivity in 1377 by returning to Rome. His death the following year gave rise to another crisis that only furthered the decline in papal prestige. When the College of Cardinals assembled for the papal election, the people of Rome feared that another French pope would be elected by the French majority of cardinals. The crowds threatened the cardinals unless they chose an Italian pope, and they elected as pope an Italian archbishop, who took the name Urban VI (ruled 1378–1389). Urban announced that he would appoint a large number of new Italian cardinals and embark on a serious reform program.

A crisis arose when the French cardinals reassembled after leaving Rome and declared the election of Urban void. They then elected another pope, this time a Frenchman who called himself Clement VII, and immediately left for Avignon. The existence of two popes, one in Rome and one in Avignon, began what has been called the **Great Schism.** The division within the church also divided Europe along political lines: France and its allies—the Spanish kingdoms of Aragon and Castile, and Scotland—threw their support behind Clement; most of the rest of Europe, including England and Germany, recognized Urban as the legitimate pope. For almost 40 years, pious Christians watched in horror and confusion as rival claimants to the throne of St. Peter attacked and denounced each other as the false pope and the anti-Christ. Nor did the crisis end with the death of the two popes, for their supporters among the cardinals then elected a new Italian and a new French pope. The credibility and authority of the papacy were seriously undermined by this steadily deteriorating situation.

Some leaders began to believe that the schism could only be resolved by a general council of the clergy, and in 1409 a group of cardinals from both the Rome and Avignon sides of the controversy organized an assembly in Pisa. Hoping to settle the division, the council deposed both popes and elected a third, John XXIII. When, however, both Clement and Urban refused to step down, the confusion only worsened. Three popes now claimed the leadership of the church. In 1414, however, the Council of Constance met to bring order back to the church. High ecclesiastical officials from every region of Europe gathered in an assembly organized along national lines. Urban abdicated, but the council had to depose the other two before electing an Italian cardinal from the powerful Colonna family, who took the name Martin V (ruled 1417–1431). The Great Schism was finally over.

POPULAR RELIGION

The calamities that beset Europe in the 14th century created a powerful need among many Christians for a new source of spiritual and emotional comfort, a thirst for a more personal and immediate understanding of God's love and grace. The growth in popular devotion that resulted was especially strong in view of the crisis in faith caused by the Babylonian Captivity and the Great Schism. More and more laypeople began to turn away from the formal religious practices of the church and seek comfort in new forms of piety and in mysticism.

The religious practices of the day included numerous forms of devotion designed to elicit divine grace and salvation, especially pilgrimages, processions, and special masses for the dead. Laypeople joined special branches of the mendicant orders founded by St. Dominic and St. Francis, and established religious guilds called *confraternities* that did charity work while enriching their spiritual values. By far the most important expression of the new piety was mysticism. Mystics contended that believers experience God not through formal dogma or sterile institutional rituals but rather through love and emotional availability, by means of establishing a sense of union with God achieved through spiritual exercises and contemplation.

The Rhine Valley of western Germany was an important center of the 14th-century mystics, and Meister Eckhart (1260–1327) developed a large following there through his impassioned preaching. Although a learned scholar and the author of important theological treatises,

Eckhart denied the importance of traditional dogma and institutional piety, stressing instead the cultivation of a "divine spark" that would achieve oneness with God. Even more influential was the Dutch mystic Gerhard Groote (1340–1384), whose lay followers founded the Brethren of the Common Life. Groote advocated a new form of piety that came to be known as Modern Devotion (*devotio moderna*). Groote maintained that communion with God could best be achieved by imitating Christ and devoting oneself to good works. Groote's followers in the Brethren, and in similar female organizations known as the Sisters of the Common Life, established schools and lived according to self-imposed rules of simplicity and humility. One of the most prominent of the Brethren was Thomas à Kempis, who in 1425 wrote a kind of manual entitled *The Imitation of Christ* that stressed ethical behavior and the attainment of internal peace and tranquillity.

Lay piety revealed that popular religious devotion was still very much alive in late medieval Europe. Moreover, rather than the otherworldliness of an earlier age, it spoke to the desire for more meaningful spiritual experience in everyday life.

THE PROBLEM OF HERESY

Along with the rise of lay piety, the 14th century also saw the rise of new forms of **heresy.** These heresies had widespread appeal because of the church's need to adjust to the changed circumstances of European civilization. The church had developed institutions and procedures to deal with heresy, but on opposite ends of Europe, in England and in Bohemia, new challenges faced the church and its doctrines.

The most famous heretic of the period was John Wycliffe (c. 1330–1384), an Oxford theologian who was influenced by the Babylonian Captivity and the new spirit of nationalism generated by the Hundred Years' War. Wycliffe denounced the corruption that he saw in the church and in the papal curia and demanded an end to the payment made every year by England to the papacy. Like others before him, he argued that there was no scriptural justification for papal supremacy in temporal matters, but went further in rejecting the miracle of transubstantiation, according to which during Mass priests change bread and wine into the body and blood of Christ. The Bible, he asserted, was the only true source of authority. He began but never completed an English translation of the Bible in order to make it available to as many ordinary people as possible. In the theological tradition of St. Augustine, he believed that some humans were predestined to salvation, and that these people should live simple lives governed by high ethical standards.

At first Wycliffe had many supporters among the aristocracy, but his increasingly radical ideas soon limited his followers to the lower classes. The latter, called Lollards (possibly from the word *lollar*, meaning idler), were attracted to his denunciations of church corruption and property. The popularity of the Lollards diminished after the death penalty for heresy was passed in 1399, and when a Lollard uprising in 1414 was put down, the movement went underground. Nevertheless, the Reformation of the 16th century was clearly influenced by Wycliffe's ideas.

In Bohemia, another significant heresy was the work of Jan Hus (1373–1415). A Czech priest who studied at Oxford and was much influenced by Wycliffe's teachings, Hus brought the criticisms of the church and the papacy back to Prague, where they were popular. For a time the king of Bohemia, influenced by the politics of the Babylonian Captivity, protected Hus, and his preachings about social justice gained him a large following. In 1415, however, Hus was summoned to the Council of Constance in order to explain and defend his position on theological matters. Although he was granted safe conduct to attend the council, Hus was put on trial for heresy and burned at the stake.

For the immediate future, the impact of Hus's teachings was greater on Bohemia than on Christendom in general. In Bohemia, disagreements among his adherents led to a civil war between 1421 and 1436. At first the movement was headed by lower-class radicals who wanted to realize Hus's preachings about purifying the church, although eventually leadership shifted into the hands of more conservative elements led by aristocrats. Neither faction, however, was willing to return to orthodox Christianity and the supremacy of Rome. As with Wycliffe in England, the Hussite movement generated considerable support among Bohemian nationalists, who opposed the interference of both the papacy and of the Holy Roman emperor in local affairs. Hussite armies led by a Bohemian general defeated several German efforts to wipe out the heresy. By the mid-15th century, the Catholic Church faced the prospect of dealing with serious challenges to its hold on the faithful as well as to its authority within the increasingly hostile boundaries of national states.

Putting the Fourteenth Century in Perspective

The 14th century proved to be an age of unparalleled disaster that shattered the conservative outlook of the medieval mind and initiated profound changes in the social, economic, religious, and political development of Europe. The disasters that struck the era with such heavy blows—famine, plague, economic dislocation, and social rebellion—were compounded by the crisis that beset the church and the century-long war that broke out between France and England. Yet all of these calamities should be regarded not as the tragic end of the spirit and fabric of life as it was known in the High Middle Ages but as the beginning of a complex transition to a new and challenging world.

Questions for Further Study

1. What was the relationship between population growth, agriculture, and the plague?
2. What conditions in European society contributed to the spread and devastation of the plague?
3. What goals did peasant and worker rebels have? What was the outcome of these revolts?
4. What impact did the residence of the popes in Avignon have on the medieval church?

Suggestions for Further Reading

Barnie, John. *War in Medieval English Society*. Ithaca, NY, 1974.

Cantor, Norman F. *In the Wake of the Plague: The Black Death and the World It Made*. New York, 2001.

Cohn, Sam. *The Black Death: Disease and Culture in Past Time*. London, 2001.

Gottfried, Robert S. *The Black Death: Natural and Human Disaster in Medieval Europe*. New York, 1983.

Hilton, R.H., and T.H. Aston. *The English Rising of 1381*. New York, 1984.

Holmes, George, ed. *The Oxford History of Medieval Europe*. New York, 1992.

McNeill, William H. *Plagues and People*. New York, 1976.

Meiss, Millard. *Painting in Florence and Sienna After the Black Death*. New York, 1964.

Menache, Sophia. *Clement V*. New York, 1998.

Rydzeski, Justine. *Radical Nostalgia in the Age of Piers Plowman: Economics, Apocalypticism, and Discontent*. New York, 1999.

InfoTrac College Edition

Enter the search term *Middle Ages* using the Subject Guide.

Enter the search term *Black Death* using Key Terms.

THE LATE MIDDLE AGES

The centuries between 1300 and 1450 saw the transformation of the European economy and social order from the late medieval world to the era of the Renaissance. After the economic depression associated with the disasters of the mid-14th century, conditions began to improve. Agriculture recovered but changed as new crops and cultivation methods were needed to respond to the decline in agricultural prices. Commerce was not only restored but assumed more modern dimensions as trade zones and cooperative efforts such as the Hanseatic League of northern Germany were developed to deal with increasing competition. Banking became more sophisticated with the growth of accounting procedures, branch-banking concepts, and credit techniques.

Social conditions also underwent transformation. The tempo of urban life accelerated as cities increased their economic and cultural importance. Family structure and the position of women in society reflected these changes. Gender roles were reinforced, marriage patterns altered as people married younger, and parents lavished more energy and resources in rearing children.

The cultural life of the 14th century saw two seemingly contradictory trends in European society. In the North, a late flowering of chivalry and courtly romance reflected preoccupations with an idealized world of the past. The persistence of an exaggerated cult of knightly values has been seen by some historians as the autumn of medieval culture. South of the Alps, however, a new spirit called **humanism** was emerging in Italy, a spirit conditioned by a rebirth of interest in Classical culture and its values and a new emphasis on human beings as the center of the world. In the political and social life of Italy, this preoccupation with classical virtues gave rise to civic humanism, which encouraged a more active role in public affairs and in the welfare of the community. Out of these sources was born the era of the Renaissance. Above all then, the 14th and 15th centuries were an era of transition for European civilization.

AGRICULTURE, TRADE, AND FINANCE

After centuries of economic growth and expansion, European agriculture and commerce experienced severe problems of readjustment in the second half of the 14th century. The Black Death had been the most serious aspect of a crisis in the medieval economy that involved many other causes. In its aftermath, prices, wages, and employment practices changed.

THE AGRICULTURAL SECTOR

As population and urbanization moved forward in the late 13th century, agricultural prices had generally gone up while farm wages fell, and landlords found it more profitable to use hired help rather than serf labor to cultivate their fields. As a result, most peasants found themselves worse off as this trend accelerated, especially because they were also subjected to higher taxes from royal governments. The Black Death reversed this relationship between prices and wages because as the decline in urban population reduced the demand for food, agrarian prices fell sharply. At the same time, wages rose as a result of the labor shortage. Employers and landowners tried to reduce wages and reimpose controls over their laborers. The result was rural and urban rebellion.

Despite the failure of most of these revolts, the ruling classes were unable to maintain their social and economic authority over workers. Most peasants in western Europe were not only freed from serfdom—in England such liberated peasants were called *yeomen*—but steadily improved their standard of living, especially through wage-paying jobs. By the 15th century, agricultural workers in England experienced a "golden age" in which real wages reached the highest levels yet known. Many landowners turned to sheep raising, which required a relatively small labor force of shepherds and yielded a variety of products, including wool and skins as well as cheese and lamb. On the Continent, landowners and free peasants turned increasingly to new crops that could command better prices. They moved away from extensive cereal production to more intensive planting of root crops, the cultivation of vines and the production of wine, and the raising of livestock for milk, butter, and cheese. In this way, different areas of Europe began to specialize in those products that they could produce more cheaply and more easily.

Conditions in Eastern Europe were different. There a smaller population spread over large areas had meant less urbanization and trade. The Black Death left cities decimated and declining, while most inhabitants lived on a level of subsistence lower than anything known in the West for centuries. Without the effective political leadership of centralized royal government to temper the noble landowners, peasants were forced deeper still into serfdom.

THE REBIRTH OF TRADE AND FINANCE

Towns were hit hard by the plague, and the recovery was slow. By the start of the 15th century, the volume of manufacturing and trade was lower than it had been 100 years earlier. By the 16th century, however, the total had reached new highs. As manufacturing and trade began to expand once again, cities grew in population, although an overall regional shift occurred as northern European cities grew more important and Mediterranean towns steadily lost their formerly unchallenged dominance. Nonetheless, Venice still controlled the spice trade from the East. Its galleys, which linked Italian ports with northern Europe, continued to sail, but at a steadily decreasing rate. The Italians retained a profitable commercial empire until the 16th century, when the development of routes around Africa and across the Atlantic shifted the advantage to European Atlantic states such as Spain and Portugal. For now, however, the real change came as control of trade in the North Sea and the Baltic moved into the hands of German cities.

In 1367, Lübeck, Bremen, and Hamburg organized several German trading towns into the Hanseatic League (from the German word *Hansa,* meaning "company") with the aim of keeping foreigners out of northern commerce in favor of their merchants. The League eventually included more than 80 cities and controlled a large fleet and impressive resources, giving it a virtual monopoly over trade in northern Europe. Although the League continued to exist

Map 32.1 Cities of the Hanseatic League. The League's capital was at Lubeck. Note that members included cities along the Baltic Sea in territory that is now Polish and Latvian. The League established commercial centers in numerous foreign towns, including Bergen in Norway, and London. For most of the 14th century, it exercised wide commercial powers, backed by monopoly and boycott, and had strong political influence.

© Scala/Art Resource, NY

Manuscript illumination of the Drapers' Market, Bologna.
15th century. The production and sale of cloth was an important
source of wealth for Italy's city states. In this scene showing one
of the leading fabric markets of central Italy—that at Bologna—
in the center a merchant, dressed in red, measures a customer
who has stripped to his white underclothes. At the counters
ranged around, buyers inspect merchandise.

The depressed economic climate of the late 14th century drove businesses and banks to become more efficient. The invention of double-entry bookkeeping in the mid-14th century was accompanied by the introduction of insurance and book transfer procedures, and all of these advances made business practices more sophisticated. In banking the Italians led the way toward new forms of organization, with the Medici of Florence dominating the field (see Topic 34). Beginning as textile manufacturers, the Medici expanded into banking and had as their clients the papacy and several European monarchs. The Medici bank developed a series of autonomous branches based on partnerships in Rome, Florence, Venice, Bruges, London, and other cities. Although central management remained in the hands of Medici family members, each branch functioned as a separate entity, so that the collapse of one branch did not threaten the others. The Medici empire collapsed at the end of the 15th century when several major borrowers defaulted on their loans and the French seized the Medici property after invading Italy.

By 1500, Europe had achieved a remarkable recovery from the disasters of the previous century. New agricultural and manufacturing products and better production techniques, combined with rationalized and diversified business organization, all contributed to building a reinvigorated and more prosperous economy.

EUROPEAN SOCIETY BEFORE AND AFTER THE BLACK DEATH

The impact of the Black Death on social conditions was profound and long-lasting. Just as the economy adjusted to changed conditions and new stresses, so urban life, marriage and the family, and the condition of women in late medieval society all were transformed by the disasters of the age.

LIFE IN THE CITIES

In the 14th century only a few Europeans lived in cities, at the most 10 percent. Some regions had higher concentrations of urban population, especially northern Italy, where perhaps as many as one of four people lived in towns. By modern standards, however, cities were rather small, with only a handful—among them, London, Paris, Florence, and Venice—boasting around 100,000 people. Yet city life exercised an influence on Europe's cultural and economic life out of all proportion to the size of the urban population.

The plague made the social differences among urban dwellers more stark, so that cities after 1350 tended to have greater contrasts of wealth and poverty. In most medieval cities land was limited to defined areas within the town walls. As a result, whereas the wealthy occupied ever larger and more luxurious homes, often protected against unruly townspeople by thick walls and high windows, the poor continued to live in even more crowded and unsanitary tenements. In the aftermath of the plague, many cities began to

for some 300 years, it began to decline by the end of the 15th century in the face of the growing commercial power of the Dutch.

In manufacturing, textile production remained the dominant industry. By the end of the 14th century, Florence had recovered its former preeminent position in woolmaking and, along with Milan and Venice, added silk and fine linen manufacturing to its industrial base. In the 15th century new industries developed that were increasingly important in Europe's economy. Metalworking, especially armor, became a major industry in Milan, while mining expanded as new technology allowed mine shafts to be sunk hundreds of feet below the surface. The new digging and draining methods opened up rich new mines in central Europe. The discovery of a way to extract silver from lead alloy led to a plentiful supply of silver for making coins, which in turn increased the money supply and economic growth.

provide medical and health services for their inhabitants. Special boards were established to enforce new health and sanitation laws. Given the lack of medical knowledge, however, such measures had limited value in preventing a recurrence of plague and disease.

Public assistance to the poor increasingly took the place of what had once been almost exclusively religious and private charity. Cities created new institutions and used tax revenues to support charity initiatives such as hospitals, food distribution networks, orphanages, and prenatal care centers. Along with aid to the poor, municipal governments sought to curtail the most unpleasant manifestations of poverty and the mounting level of violence that afflicted late medieval cities. Some towns limited begging to particular neighborhoods and times, while some prohibited it altogether and others allowed the unemployed and homeless to remain within the city walls only for a specified number of days.

As urban crime grew, cities adopted harsher methods of punishment in an effort to repress antisocial activity. The use of torture and execution increasingly replaced the payment of fines, exile, or prison terms even for a crime such as robbery; in places where the death penalty was practiced, hanging was replaced by more horrible methods of execution, including mutilation, breaking on the wheel, and burning at the stake. In an age when violence was common, public executions were often occasions for popular festivities.

Many poor girls and young women from the country who were unable to marry or find employment in the cities resorted to prostitution to survive. As the incidence of prostitution increased after the Black Death, many cities tried to regulate it by issuing licenses, conducting health inspections, and controlling prices. The church, on the other hand, tried to reform prostitutes by providing them with housing and religious instruction.

By 1450, after a century of decline, the overall population of Europe started to increase again, although the estimated population of 45 to 50 million people was still only about two-thirds of what it had been before the plague. The Black Death severely affected mortality rates, lowering life expectancy among the affluent merchant class from a pre-plague level of perhaps 40 years to about 30 years in the 15th century. The infant mortality rate was high, most people died young, and extreme old age was rare.

MARRIAGE AND THE FAMILY

It is difficult to generalize about marriage and family life for most Europeans in the Middle Ages, principally because written records about poor peasants and the working class are scant. A few sources do exist, such as tax rolls, court records, and folk stories, which tell us something about the lives of better-off peasants and the merchant or noble classes.

We know, for example, that young peasants courted each other actively and often resisted the prearranged marriages that were more common among the nobility. Court records reveal that premarital pregnancy was not uncommon. Fifteenth-century poems called "How the Wise Man

Painting showing a street scene in a Late Medieval French town. 14th–15th century. The shops include a grocer, tailor, barber, and furrier. The half-timbered style of architecture is characteristic of the rebuilding after the Black Death.

© Cliché Bibliothèque Nationale de France, Paris

Taught His Son" and "How the Good Wife Taught Her Daughter" stress the importance of family tranquillity. Marriages without public ceremonies or the announcements made in church known as *banns*—which the Fourth Lateran Council had required in 1215—were frequent. The dissolution of marriages was extremely rare. Bigamy provided one of the few legitimate reasons, and if the marriage was not consummated it could be annulled after the wife and husband were examined. The wording and dispositions of wills indicate the degree of affection in which most husbands held their wives and children. Among peasant and worker families, training for work came early, and the lives of children were austere.

Most of our knowledge about the private lives of medieval people is limited to the literate men and women of the middle classes and aristocracy. Parental choice and economic factors still tended to determine whom a person married in the upper classes, although emotional affection between spouses and toward children was by no means unusual. Gender relations and functions in these wealthier families more closely resembled modern behavior. Wives, for example, assumed greater responsibility for managing family finances and estates.

One effect of the plague was to alter the age at which marriages took place. Most young men had generally been forced to put off marriage until after their fathers died in order to have sufficient land or resources to raise a family. As a consequence, husbands were often in their late twenties or thirties before marrying; women, on the other hand, seem to have married younger, while still in their teens. The improved economic conditions after the Black Death led to earlier marriages, especially for men.

GENDER IN MEDIEVAL SOCIETY

LISA M. BITEL   University of Kansas

In 585 the bishops of what is now France gathered at Mâcon to discuss policy for the churches under their leadership. Their job was to keep Christian rituals in order, rule on contested points of theology, and set up guidelines for the behavior of priests, deacons, and ordinary believers. One of the council's specific duties was to debate a question with far-reaching effects: were women human? In fact, the clergy at Mâcon were indulging in a grammatical discussion over the wording of the book of Genesis: the Bible said that man (Latin homo) was created in God's image, but could the meaning of that word be extended to include women? The bishops decided that the Latin of the Vulgate was flexible enough to include women among the humans.[1]

The Mâcon debate was only one episode in a long Western history of literate men's discussion of women which has lasted since the days of St. Paul. No single view has predominated, now or during the Christian Middle Ages; indeed, Jewish and Muslim scholars in Medieval Europe carried on their own debates about women and gender relations. What is more, never have the ideas of the scholarly elite fully represented the attitudes or behavior of most people in everyday life. Women never held a single status in any given society, nor did men and women interact in the same way in every situation. Yet the writings of scholars have always influenced as well as reflected the acts and thoughts of other men and women. Thus, the Medieval textual debate about

women reveals that European Christian societies were deeply divided about whether women were good or bad; whether they were like or unlike men; and whether they were to be loved or shunned by men.

In the Middle Ages this debate had two phases. Until about the year 1000, the argument was left mostly to churchmen. Only priests, monks, and bishops knew how to read and write. If other men and women thought about the nature of women, they rarely had the chance to record their ideas. Even the secular poems, stories, and sagas left to us were usually recorded by churchmen, hence subject to their opinions. In the second phase of the Medieval debate over women, a more diverse group of literate men—and a few women—had a chance to express their views to a wider audience in a greater variety of literary forms, including romances, satires, poetry, and even housekeeping guides. Nonetheless, certain themes and ideas about women pervaded all the texts throughout the European Middle Ages. In particular, questions of women's nature and character—by which writers often meant how women measured up to the free adult male norm—came up time and again.

Christian theologians and missionaries articulated an ambivalent theory of women derived from gospel and St. Paul, which admitted the equality of all souls but blamed women for sinning and for tempting men to do the same. One 6th-century Irish saint, for instance, fled whenever he heard the bleating of sheep, reasoning that where there were sheep there were shepherdesses, where women sex, where sex sin, and where sin damna-

[1] Gregory of Tours, Historia francorum, 8.20.

The population increase registered in the decades after the Black Death reflected the accelerated pace of marriages and the fact that improved conditions extended the mortality rate. Those children who survived were reared with more parental attention and care than had been the case in earlier centuries. Educational opportunities were increasingly available for middle-class children—principally for sons—in the cities, where municipal governments often provided schools for preteen children. Both parents seem to have regarded

their children with more affection. Generally, when a wife died, the husband remarried and had additional children with his new and usually younger wife. Despite the new concern for children observed by late medieval parents, the practice of eliminating unwanted infants through exposure was still widespread; because daughters required dowries in order to marry, they were more likely to be killed.

The basic household unit continued to be the nuclear rather than the extended family, with perhaps a widowed

tion. In the centuries after Paul, Christian writers elaborated on the gospel's ambivalence toward women, although they often weighted their discussions on the negative side. Tertullian, 3rd-century bishop of Carthage, who had called women "the devil's gateway," and St. Jerome, who warned women against marriage and motherhood, influenced almost all later discussions of women. But the most persuasive was St. Augustine who, like many of his Medieval successors, conceived of women as both sinful, like Eve, and saintly, like the Virgin Mary: "through women death," he wrote, "through women life."

With all the social, economic, and political changes of the period after 1000, attitudes toward women changed too, but not always for the better. Some of the same old themes continued to appear in theological tracts and other religious literature, and to influence people's behavior. Abelard, the 11th-century philosopher (d. 1142) who initiated a new tradition in logical thought, was enlightened enough to take a brilliant female pupil named Héloise (d. 1163). He also became her lover. But when their affair ended disastrously—a secret marriage, the abandonment of their child to relatives, her forcible claustration, and his castration—he blamed her, or rather, her womanliness. He who had once sung his own love lyrics to Héloise in the streets, complained bitterly that it was Adam's love for Eve that had led all of mankind down the garden path to sin: "from the very beginning of the human race, women had cast down even the noblest men to utter ruin."[2] Despite his personal *calamitas*, Abelard was merely participating in an established tradition when blaming the Fall on women.

The sedate and virtuous lady of 12th-century romance was part of the same world as the careless deceiving wives of fabliaux. They were mirror images, as well as descendants of their ambivalent ancestresses of

[2] Abelard, *Historia Calamitatum* (St. Paul, 1922), 21.

earlier Medieval texts. They sprang from minds who knew what St. Paul, the early Church Fathers, Bede, Aquinas, and all the rest had said about women. Yet these writers also knew the whole variety of real women who surrounded them day by day—the girl next door, the wife, Jeanne d'Arc, famous mystics such as Margery Kempe, queens, servants, good bourgeoises, and a thousand other females encountered briefly or at length. No single text could convey a comprehensive Medieval attitude toward women. Indeed, the ambivalence of the texts suggests the actual diversity of gender relations in Medieval Europe.

Medieval Europeans did not seek systematically to repress women nor to denigrate them. Yet the ambivalence toward women, wrought by native traditions and Christian theologians, persisted throughout the Medieval centuries. It had led the bishops of Mâcon to wonder about the very humanity of women; almost a thousand years later, in 1486, this long tradition of doubt about the female sex caused two Dominican monks to write a tract called *Malleus Maleficarum*, or the *Hammer of Witches*. Women, they claimed, were more prone to desire and lust than men; hence women were more vulnerable to sin and likely to sin sexually with the devil, who would convince them to become witches and attack men. The Dominicans were merely repeating, in exaggerated form, many of the accusations and doubts about women leveled for centuries by respected theologians, philosophers, and poets, as well as joking writers of fabliaux. Not many Europeans in the 15th century read the *Malleus Maleficarum*, and surely not everyone agreed with its claim that women were likely to become witches. Yet this vicious little treatise became the justification for the worst persecution of women ever launched in Europe: the witch-hunts of the 16th and 17th centuries, which resulted in the trials and executions of thousands of women and men—but mostly women—from Eastern Europe to the Western Hemisphere.

mother or aunt living with the husband, wife, and children. Because few people lived to an old age, it was unusual in peasant or worker families for more than two generations to live under one roof. The basic late medieval family consisted of four to six people. Various birth control methods—*coitus interruptus*, douches and purges, and abortion—were practiced in efforts to limit family size. Wealthier families could afford to maintain extended families as well as servants in the household.

THE LIFE OF WOMEN

Despite the powerful social and economic transformations of the 14th century, the lives of most women in the late Middle Ages remained fundamentally focused on marriage and the family. As young girls, women of all classes were trained to be wives and mothers, to manage households, and to bear and raise children. Yet late medieval women faced a peculiar situation. The prominent theologians of the age defined an increasingly circumscribed role for women, while the changing economic and social circumstances following the Black Death made more opportunities for women, especially in the towns. Here, too, generalizations are difficult, for the condition and role of women depended greatly on the class to which they belonged.

WOMEN AND THE SCHOLARS

During the feudal era, women had acquired a significant degree of power that had much to do with the constant warfare that often kept men fighting away from home for long periods. In their absence, women not only saw to the raising of the children and the care of the household but also took on the additional responsibilities for overseeing the family estates and, if their husbands were monarchs, caring for the interests of the dynasty and the realm. In addition, courtly literature placed women at the center of a society in which they were venerated and protected by their men. Even in the church, women could and did achieve considerable prominence and authority.

But the intellectual developments of the 12th and 13th centuries undermined women's status by using the prestige of earlier authorities to define gender roles in ways that limited female participation in society. Thomas Aquinas, the most influential of the scholastics, reached back to Aristotle for guidance on the matter of the proper role of men and women, arguing that it was in the "natural" order for men to be active and women passive, so that while men tended to dominate, women were by nature submissive. The nature of women, he believed, was different from that of men, and it was a difference that Aquinas and other scholastics believed made women inferior.

Such ideas were widely held and discussed in the cathedral schools and in the universities to which they gave rise. As the educational system trained more and more lawyers, priests, and scholars, these misogynist ideas gained more currency in the intellectual community. Women were expressly excluded from the new universities and the renewal of learning—and, by extension, from the new professions that the universities trained men to fill. The intellectual and religious authority of the scholastics established the theoretical basis on which women were expected to give up any active role in society. Instead, a new and sharper division of roles developed, which relegated women to the circumscribed life of household and childrearing.

The economic hardships of the 14th century reinforced these trends by limiting women's opportunities for employment. Even when women worked, a division of labor evolved, which dictated that women and men performed different kinds of tasks. In the early and high Middle Ages, for example, weaving was a task that women performed regularly, both in the home and in the craft shops. By the late Middle Ages weaving became an almost exclusively male preserve. Instead of weaving, women were increasingly limited to spinning. Moreover, even when women did the same kind of work as men for the same employer, they almost always received lower wages than their male counterparts—women were paid from one-third to one-half the wages paid to men for the same tasks.

WOMEN IN CITIES AND THE CHURCH

The economic impact of the Black Death temporarily altered this pattern of inequality. The labor shortage that followed the plague increased the need for women workers, both in manufacturing and in the fields, and had the effect of equalizing wages. Moreover, the growth of towns had a liberating effect on women, as it did on men. Women serfs who escaped their bondage on a master's land could, after one year in a free city, become permanently free. In the cities, working women could marry and find jobs. More than one-half of all working women in towns were employed as domestic servants, but other opportunities were abundant. Although most guilds, for example, limited their membership to men, some allowed women to become apprentices and masters, especially in the textile crafts. Women could gain and control property in cities and live independent lives—in 15th-century Florence, the tax rolls reveal that more than 15 percent of all households were headed by women. The attraction for women of a freer life in the towns is reflected in the fact that most urban populations revealed a disproportionate ratio of women to men.

In late medieval times, some women continued to make a life outside the family by taking advantage of opportunities in the church. The 12th-century abbess Hildegard of Bingen, who founded the convent at Rupertsberg and wrote several learned treatises, wielded considerable power in her day. By the 14th century, the era of the great abbesses was fast fading as the convents came under the authority of male prelates and the papacy limited the powers of women in the church. In 1293, Pope Boniface VIII issued a bull that defined women's roles in the church narrowly and insisted that they be cut off from the outside world: "all and sundry nuns, present and future, to whatever order they belong . . . shall henceforth remain perpetually enclosed . . . ; so that no nun . . . shall henceforth have or be able to have the power of going out of those monasteries for whatever reason or excuse. . . . "* Nevertheless, many women found fulfillment in a world of their own choosing in which they could pursue scholarly interests and work as well as religious devotion.

HUMANISM: THE CLASSICAL SOURCES OF A NEW SPIRIT

The Hundred Years' War that raged between England and France in the 14th and 15th centuries (see Topic 33) was to

*Quoted in Bonnie S. Anderson and Judith P. Zinsser, *A History of Their Own: Women in Europe from Prehistory to the Present,* I (New York, 1988), 193.

be the last gasp of the world of knights and lords and the warrior class that had dominated the feudal order. During the first half of that struggle, a Flemish historian and poet named Jean Froissart (c. 1337–1410?) wrote his elegant and sweeping *Chronicles,* praising the exploits of the brave fighters but arrogantly dismissing the concerns of the common people.

Froissart's aristocratic viewpoint reflected the persistence in northern Europe of interest in courtly life and manners and a preoccupation with an outmoded cult of chivalry. Although feudal warfare was rapidly becoming out of date, the northern aristocracy seemed to want to avoid the reality of changing times by pretending that the virtues of chivalry still determined social and political affairs. Perhaps because of their growing insecurity in the face of rapidly changing conditions—in which a new capitalist merchant class was increasingly dominating society—nobles indulged in deliberately extravagant lives of luxury. They formed exclusive new chivalric orders, such as the Knights of the Golden Fleece and the Knights of the Garter, which they hoped would preserve knightly virtues, and engaged in excesses of courtly ceremony and romantic love.

ITALY AND THE HUMANIST SPIRIT

In contrast, south of the Alps a genuine cultural revolution was taking place. People there began to abandon the other-worldly Medieval outlook and embraced a new, human-centered attitude that emphasized things of this world.

The values that attracted the Italian "humanists"—a word of much later origin that derived from the Latin term for one who is educated, *humanus*—formed part of the heritage of Greek and Roman civilization. The period saw a marked rebirth of interest in the study of Classical texts of the ancient world. In Italian cities such as Florence and Bologna in the 14th century, numerous scholars turned to Classical authors for inspiration and called for a new kind of education. The conviction grew that humanist learning, as opposed to the scholastic learning of the 12th and 13th centuries, would perfect and elevate the individual and prepare a new breed of citizens, who would lead lives marked by wisdom and civic responsibility.

PETRARCH

Fourteenth-century Italy had already seen two major literary geniuses in Dante and Boccaccio, whose works reflected the tension between medieval and humanist ideals. Another pivotal figure in the emergence of the culture of Italian humanism was Petrarch (1304–1374), a Tuscan writer from the town of Arezzo. After having studied law at the University of Bologna at the insistence of his father, Petrarch embarked on a career as a writer. He lived for a time in Avignon, where his talent attracted the attention of several popes. Petrarch spent most of his life wandering across southern Europe, searching for and copying long-forgotten ancient manuscripts. He corresponded with writers and rulers throughout Europe and wrote numerous works of poetry and prose. His learning won him the prestigious title of poet laureate of Rome, an award once famous in ancient Rome.

Although he was profoundly religious, Petrarch's vision did not, like Dante, emphasize the afterlife; instead, Petrarch sought to balance his religious convictions with the more earthly goals of fame and success. In a self-revealing book entitled *My Secret* (1343), he confesses his shortcomings and the ambivalence that led him to seek affirmation in this world as well as salvation in the next. In *Letter to Posterity* (1373?), Petrarch gives us the first important example of autobiography since the time of Augustine and reveals the focus on his life that is an important feature of early Renaissance thought. His interest in individual human personality is also revealed in his letters concerning the great writers of the past such as Cicero and Vergil.

Although Petrarch believed his Latin works would be his lasting contribution to learning, it was the work he wrote in Italian that comes down to us today as some of the finest vernacular literature of all time. In the *Canzoniere,* Petrarch collected hundreds of moving and elegant sonnets and songs, which revolve around his love for a woman named Laura, whom he first saw in Avignon in 1327 and to whom he dedicated his poetry. After Laura died in the plague in 1348, Petrarch poured out his mourning in his beautiful sonnets. Although he says that his love for Laura was never consummated, he viewed her as a real flesh and blood woman rather than as an abstraction. Petrarch established a new standard of elegance and grace in Western writing as well as a fresh appreciation for the human-centered concerns of this world. More than any of his contemporaries, Petrarch defined the attitudes and values of the emerging world of the Renaissance.

Putting the Late Middle Ages in Perspective

Between 1300 and 1450, Europe experienced the transformation from the late medieval world to the early stirrings of the Renaissance. The calamities of the 14th century deeply affected economic and social conditions and altered the character of

Continued next page

everyday life, freeing millions from the bonds of serfdom and accelerating the transition from the manorial to the capitalist era. But such profound economic and social shifts were often slow and subtle in manifesting themselves. Life for most Europeans continued to revolve around the family and religion, although with some changes, and a new conservatism among the scholars and prelates of the age conditioned women to increasingly rigid roles in society. The cultural life of Europe was marked by great diversity that in some regions saw the persistence of outmoded values and preoccupations. But in Italy and elsewhere, the humanist spirit was rapidly shaping a new consciousness and a new culture.

Questions for Further Study

1. What were the causes of social and economic change in rural Europe in the 14th and 15th centuries?
2. What impact did the plague have on European society?
3. How did medieval writers and scholars view women?
4. What were the principal intellectual concerns of the early humanists?

Suggestions for Further Reading

Bois, Guy. *The Crisis of Feudalism: Economy and Society in Eastern Normandy, c. 1300–1550.* New York, 1984.

Cameron, Rondo. *A Concise Economic History of the World.* New York, 1989.

Dahl, Gunnar. *Trade, Trust, and Networks: Commercial Culture in Late Medieval Italy.* Lund, 1998.

Duby, Georges. *A History of Private Life: II, Revelations of the Medieval World*. Cambridge, MA, 1988.

Huizinga, Johan. *The Waning of the Middle Ages*. New York, 1988.

Larner, John. *Italy in the Age of Dante and Petrarch, 1216–1380*. London, 1980.

Nicholas, David. *The Transformationj of Europe 1300-1600*. New York, 1999.

Ozment, Steven. *The Age of Reform, 1250–1550*. New Haven, CT, 1980.

Shahar, Shulamith. *The Fourth Estate: A History of Women in the Middle Ages*. New Haven, CT, 1986.

Swabey, Ffiona. *Medieval Gentlewoman: Life in a Gentry Household in the Later Middle Ages*. New York, 1999.

InfoTrac College Edition

Enter the search term *Middle Ages* using the Subject Guide.

Enter the search term *Black Death* using Key Terms.

Enter the search term *humanism* using the Subject Guide.

PART IV

THE RENAISSANCE AND REFORMATION

The Renaissance and Reformation represent a turning point in history—that is, a series of developments that together produce fundamental change in the human experience.

In its most immediate sense, the Renaissance was a rebirth of interest in Classical civilization and its underlying values that began some time in the 14th and 15th centuries. In a broader sense, however, it represented a revolution in how human beings thought about themselves and their place in the universe. Renaissance ideas, which first appeared in the sophisticated urban environment of the Italian city-states but soon spread northward, placed people at the center of human concerns, emphasizing both the importance of the human condition and a more secular, worldly approach to culture and society.

In politics, the growth of royal government at the expense of feudal nobility and the church accelerated. Increasingly efficient, centralized states evolved under the leadership of several so-called new monarchs in places like England, France, and Spain. The really innovative political development, however, came in Italy, where divisive conditions led to the invention of new methods through which states dealt with each other, methods known collectively as "diplomacy."

Closely related to the intellectual and cultural innovations of the Renaissance was the religious upheaval produced by the Protestant and Catholic reformations. The Protestant revolt against the Roman Church and the papacy provided people with new attitudes toward their relationship to God and questions of sin and salvation. In addition, for millions of people, religious

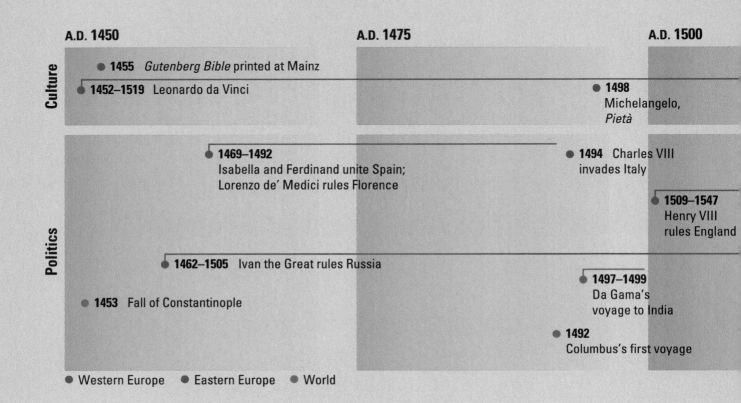

A.D. 1450 **A.D. 1475** **A.D. 1500**

Culture

● **1455** *Gutenberg Bible* printed at Mainz

● **1452–1519** Leonardo da Vinci

● **1498** Michelangelo, *Pietà*

Politics

● **1469–1492** Isabella and Ferdinand unite Spain; Lorenzo de' Medici rules Florence

● **1494** Charles VIII invades Italy

● **1509–1547** Henry VIII rules England

● **1462–1505** Ivan the Great rules Russia

● **1453** Fall of Constantinople

● **1497–1499** Da Gama's voyage to India

● **1492** Columbus's first voyage

● Western Europe ● Eastern Europe ● World

By courtesy of the Trustees of the National Gallery, London

reformers like Luther, Calvin, and Knox helped establish regional and "national" religious identities. The Reformation, then, shattered a millennium of religious unity in the West, while producing a far-reaching impact on the political and social life of Europe. For a variety of reasons that often had little to do with matters of faith, monarchs took sides in the religious struggles of the age, further dividing the Christian commonwealth by making new demands for popular allegiance and state control. At the same time, the Protestant Reformation was an important step in releasing the Western mind from the constraints of religious and political authority that had been so pervasive in the Middle Ages.

The Renaissance and the Reformation both contributed significantly to the intellectual and technical preparation that lay behind the great

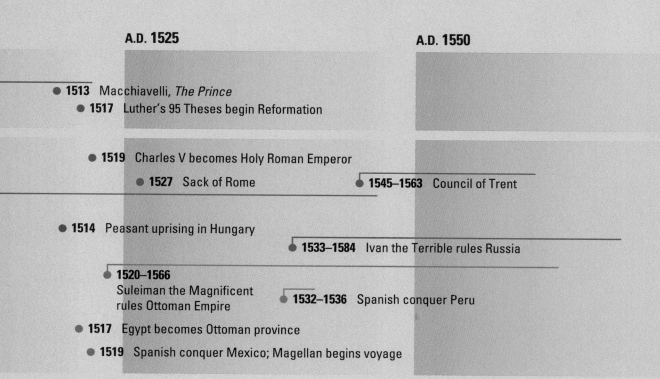

A.D. 1525

A.D. 1550

● **1513** Macchiavelli, *The Prince*

● **1517** Luther's 95 Theses begin Reformation

● **1519** Charles V becomes Holy Roman Emperor

● **1527** Sack of Rome

● **1545–1563** Council of Trent

● **1514** Peasant uprising in Hungary

● **1533–1584** Ivan the Terrible rules Russia

● **1520–1566** Suleiman the Magnificent rules Ottoman Empire

● **1532–1536** Spanish conquer Peru

● **1517** Egypt becomes Ottoman province

● **1519** Spanish conquer Mexico; Magellan begins voyage

epoch of exploration and conquest known as the European Reconnaissance. In less than a century, between roughly 1450 and 1550, Europeans broke their geographic boundaries and sailed literally around the globe. They claimed dominance over the lands and peoples they encountered, establishing overseas territorial and economic empires while embracing a world of rich cultural diversity, with far-reaching consequences.

Out of the vast upheavals wrought by the Renaissance and Reformation came profound, long-range changes that reshaped Europe and the rest of the globe. The long centuries of transition from the Middle Ages established the foundations for the early modern world.

THE AGE OF THE NEW MONARCHS

The great political transformation of the 14th and 15th centuries was the emergence of modern states in Western Europe. At the same time that distinctive national cultures were being consolidated there in the late 15th century, a group of rulers known as the "new monarchs" forged powerful, centralized states that controlled large national territories in England, France, and Spain.

In the case of France and Spain, the new monarchs completed the territorial unity of their nation-states. All of them, however, were determined to reinforce their power over the nobility and extend their control over the church within their borders. They also demanded complete loyalty from their subjects and engaged in deliberate efforts to forge a national spirit designed to create popular consensus. To the degree that these monarchs used all of the techniques available to increase their power, they were typical princes of the Renaissance.

In France, the Valois dynasty fought a long and devastating war with England for mastery of France, and in the aftermath shaped an increasingly powerful national monarchy. The English experienced not only the war with France but also a divisive civil war between two competing noble families, the Yorks and the Lancasters. By the time the domestic conflict was over, Henry Tudor had seized power and became the first of England's new monarchs, laying the foundation for a powerful new dynasty. In Spain, centralization began to take place in Castile and in Aragon, the two kingdoms ruled jointly by Ferdinand and Isabella in the latter part of the 15th century. The process of royal centralization was completed in the next century under the reign of their grandson, Charles V. By then, Spain had become merely one part of a much wider Hapsburg empire.

THE HUNDRED YEARS' WAR AND ITS AFTERMATH

In England and especially in France, the new monarchies emerged against the background of the greatest military conflict of the 14th century, the so-called Hundred Years' War. Rather than a single continuous war, however, the Hundred Years' War was really a series of conflicts between the two states interrupted by periods of peace.

THE ORIGINS OF THE WAR

A complicated series of factors lay behind the conflict. The emergence of France as a centralized monarchy was difficult because its territory had long been divided by strong regional differences in culture, language, and history. Complicating the situation was the fact that the English kings were vassals of the French monarch and controlled significant parts of French territory. Henry II (ruled 1154–1189), founder of the Plantagenet, or Angevin, dynasty, had inherited the French provinces of Anjou and Normandy. Moreover, through his marriage to Eleanor of Aquitaine (1122?–1204), Henry also acquired Aquitaine, a territory that stretched through southwestern France to the Pyrenees (see Topics 26 and 29).

In addition to the territorial problem, economic conflicts disturbed relations between the two monarchies. Flanders, to the northeast of France, was the major market for English wool, but serious conflicts between the artisans

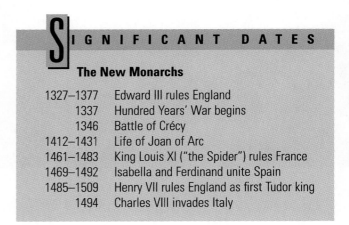

SIGNIFICANT DATES

The New Monarchs

1327–1377	Edward III rules England
1337	Hundred Years' War begins
1346	Battle of Crécy
1412–1431	Life of Joan of Arc
1461–1483	King Louis XI ("the Spider") rules France
1469–1492	Isabella and Ferdinand unite Spain
1485–1509	Henry VII rules England as first Tudor king
1494	Charles VIII invades Italy

and the wealthy merchants there threatened to disrupt a lucrative source of revenue for the English kings. Accordingly, when the French monarchy began supporting the merchants, the English gave their support to the artisans.

English and French relations reached another crisis point in 1328, when the Capetian dynasty came to an end with the death of the French king, who had no sons. Because the Salic Law recognized royal inheritance only through the male line, a Capetian cousin, Philip of Valois, claimed the throne as Philip VI (ruled 1328–1350). But Edward III (ruled 1327–1377) of England, the son of the dead king's sister, challenged the Valois by claiming the throne for himself. When Philip VI invaded Gascony in 1337, Edward declared war.

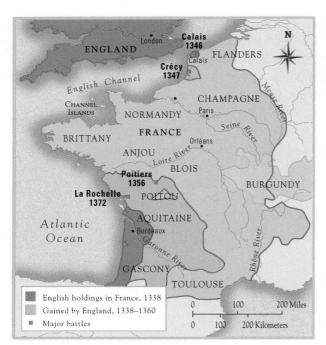

Map 33.1 The Hundred Years' War. The two maps illustrate the extent of English gains and losses in France between 1338 and 1453. After that the English held only Calais, until 1558, and the Channel Islands. (This group of islands has been a dependency of the British Crown since 1066. They are still under British sovereignty, but each island is locally governed, under its own constitution.) Go to http://info.wadsworth.com/053461065X for an interactive version of this map.

THE EARLY PHASE OF THE CONFLICT

The war changed the nature of warfare and undermined the old feudal system that was based on knightly combat. Both sides still relied on heavily armed aristocratic cavalry to do most of the fighting, and the French knights dismissed the importance of the peasant infantry and crossbow soldiers. The English, on the other hand, already employed large numbers of paid infantry, many of whom carried the much superior longbow, which had greater firing speed and range than the crossbow. This difference would determine the outcome of the early fighting.

In an effort to break the pattern of costly failures that marked the first English campaigns in France, Edward III invaded Normandy in 1346. Here, too, he encountered setbacks. When the French forces cut off the English while they were attempting to retreat into Flanders, a major battle took place at Crécy. There the English longbows decimated the larger French army. Edward then pressed his advantage by seizing the port of Calais, which the English held for 200 years and used for later landings. Despite the victory at Crécy, the war dragged on indecisively because the English, with less than half the population of France, were unable to muster sufficient troops or resources to achieve total victory. Under the leadership of Edward, the prince of Wales—known as the Black Prince—the English wreaked havoc and destruction on the French countryside. Rather than risking all on head-to-head battles, the Black Prince attacked unfortified towns, burned crops, and spread terror among the peasantry. Finally, at the Battle of Poitiers in 1356, the French forces were again defeated and their king captured. A peace treaty was signed three years later at Brétigny, but the peace of Brétigny never went into effect

because the war began again under the leadership of a new French king. Using mercenary soldiers to strengthen their position, the French eventually recovered the territory lost to the English. This time, a truce negotiated in 1396 lasted 20 years.

JOAN OF ARC AND THE END OF THE WAR

The war erupted again in 1415, when the English invaded France. After a smashing victory at Agincourt in which some 1,500 French knights were killed, the English conquered Normandy and persuaded the duke of Burgundy to join forces with them. The French monarchy, now led by the weak and indecisive *dauphin* (or royal heir), Charles (ruled 1422–1461 as Charles VII), controlled only the southern two-thirds of the country. When the English pushed south toward the Loire Valley and the heart of France, the moment was unexpectedly saved by a young French peasant girl, Joan of Arc (c. 1412–1431).

The daughter of a comfortable peasant family from the Champagne region, Joan was a devout Catholic who claimed to have experienced divinely inspired visions. In 1429, believing that she was charged by saints to save France from the English, she convinced Charles to allow her to accompany the French army. Inspired by Joan's sincerity and bravery, the French fought with renewed energy and routed the English, driving them from the Loire Valley. Joan's purpose was realized later that year, when the dauphin was crowned as King

Miniature painting of the Battle of Crécy, 1347. 14th century. Note the English soldiers, on the right, armed with their superior longbows; the first French casualty has already fallen. The English troops fight in armor decorated with the red Cross of St. George. The battle proved an important turning point in the first phase of the Hundred Years' War.

© Cliché Bibliothèque Nationale de France, Paris

© Giraudon/Art Resource, NY

Manuscript illumination showing a portrait of Joan of Arc, bareheaded and wearing a full suit of armor. 15th century. The scroll behind her head refers to the divine visions that inspired her to rally the French forces against the English.

Charles VII at Reims, thereby confirming the legitimacy of the Valois line. In 1430, however, the Burgundian allies of the English captured Joan. In a calculated effort to destroy a powerful symbol of a new French patriotism, the English accused her of witchcraft and turned her over to the Inquisition. Although the trial was not conducted by normal Inquisitorial procedures, Joan was condemned as a heretic and burned at the stake in 1431—five centuries later, the Catholic Church made her a saint.

Despite Joan's lamentable end, the French people rallied around Charles as the war continued for another 20 years. Both sides were exhausted, and after a series of English defeats that drove them from Normandy and Aquitaine, the fighting finally stopped in 1453, although no peace treaty was ever signed. England, left only with Calais on the French coast, withdrew from the continent. A devastated France began the slow and difficult process of recovering and solidifying its newly found national unity.

THE VALOIS KINGS AND THE REVIVAL OF FRANCE

The destruction that the Hundred Years' War had caused in France made it difficult for the monarchy to reimpose its authority on the country. Yet the war had enabled Charles VII to strengthen royal power, a trend that continued into the following century.

The three principal "estates" of French society—the clergy, the nobles, and the bourgeoisie—composed the institution known as the Estates General (see Topic 29), a body that endorsed the king's decisions and approved new taxes. During the war crisis, the Estates General had given Charles permission to raise a professional royal army and to pay for it by levying an annual property tax, the *taille*. During the last years of the war, Charles drew strength from the advice of his powerful mistress, Agnes Sorel (c. 1422–1450), whose influence so angered the nobility that they are said to have poisoned her to death.

LOUIS THE SPIDER

The power of the French state was advanced by Charles's successor, King Louis XI (ruled 1461–1483), whose devious and crafty personality earned him the nickname of Louis the Spider. To restore the prosperity of France in the wake of the economic impact of the war, Louis developed new industries, including the manufacture of silk in Lyons, and stimulated trade. Although the *taille* was designed as a temporary war measure, Louis continued to impose it as a regular source of royal income.

Louis strengthened the state by keeping in place the standing army of professional soldiers that the *taille* tax had enabled his father to create. Military expenditures absorbed half of all royal revenues because modern armies were increasingly more expensive and only the royal government

Portrait of Louis XI, king of France, known as the "Spider." 15th century. The chain around his shoulders is a string of cockle-shells, symbol of the Order of St. James of Compostela. Louis was responsible for creating a firm basis for absolute monarchy in France.

© Giraudon/Art Resource, NY

could afford them. Once gunpowder was introduced, new weapons required even more revenue. The invention of the cannon required costly manufacturing and logistical supplies, while a kind of handgun known as the *arquebus* called for large numbers of additional soldiers carrying pikes to protect those armed with guns. Although it was expensive to maintain, the importance of an army that was loyal to the monarchy could not be overlooked.

The royal courts increased their power, and the king's use of Roman law gave him the authority to issue edicts and decrees. Nevertheless, the judicial system reflected the fact that the provinces remained important centers of local privilege: while the crown appointed judges of a central court known as the Parlement of Paris, it also granted important provinces their own parlements. Moreover, the Parlement was expected to register all edicts issued by the king. Louis never succeeded in completely destroying the power of the local nobility, but his reign established the monarchy on a solid footing.

THE CONSOLIDATION OF THE MONARCHY

Charles VIII (ruled 1483–1498), like his father Louis, proved to be an ambitious ruler. His marriage to the heiress of Brittany brought him control of that important province, the last independent region in France. Charles

PUBLIC FIGURES AND PRIVATE LIVES

MARGARET OF ANJOU AND HENRY VI OF ENGLAND

By Courtesy of the National Portrait Gallery, London

Hulton Getty Collection

In 1445, a temporary truce in the Hundred Years' War was sealed by Henry's marriage to Margaret of Anjou (1430–1482), the 15-year-old daughter of the count of Anjou. The women in Margaret's family provided her with important role models because both her grandmother and mother ruled their own lands and had frequently acted for the men in the family.

For many years, Henry and Margaret did not have children. Furthermore, by the time the war ended, Henry had begun to exhibit clear signs of mental instability. His hold on the crown was further weakened by economic unrest that beset England in the aftermath of the war. The discontent coalesced around the figure of Richard, duke of York, who had gained recognition as Henry's heir; Margaret played a central role in the Lancastrian circle opposed to Richard. In 1453, the situation became suddenly unsettled when Margaret produced a son, who now replaced Richard as heir to the throne. Richard took up arms against Henry, and the conflict raged for several years, until in 1460 the Yorkists captured Henry and a compromise was reached by which Henry remained on the throne but Richard was declared his legal heir.

Furious that her son had been disinherited, Margaret formed an army and fought for 16 years in defense of his claim to the throne. She raised money and organized support in her husband's name, acting with courage and determination. The queen's followers defeated the Yorkists and killed Richard on the battlefield. In 1461, Margaret rescued her husband from captivity and together they fled to Scotland, while Richard's son Edward seized the throne, taking the name Edward IV (ruled 1461–1470, 1471–1483). In 1465, Henry was captured a second time by the Yorkists and held in the Tower of London.

With help from King Louis XI of France, Margaret invaded England and restored Henry to the throne in 1470, although the Yorkists quickly recovered and captured the entire royal family. Margaret and Henry's son died, and Henry was murdered in the Tower of London, most likely on Edward's orders. In 1476, Louis XI secured Margaret's release by paying Edward a ransom, although on condition that Margaret gave up all claims to French territory. The former queen of England returned to France, where she spent her last years in obscurity and poverty.

---

invaded Italy in 1494 at the invitation of Lodovico Sforza of Milan. The Italian campaign eventually went against Charles, who struggled for decades against the Hapsburg rulers of the Holy Roman Empire for hegemony over the Italian peninsula.

The Italian wars further expanded the size and powers of the royal government in France. The cost of the campaigns forced the monarchy to increase its revenues, but the wealthiest groups—the nobles, the clergy, and the royal towns—were traditionally exempt from taxes. In a desperate effort to raise money, Charles and his successors began the practice of selling government offices in the bureaucracy and the courts to buyers interested in the tax exemptions and titles that generally went with such positions.

King Francis I (ruled 1515–1547) continued the policy of expanding the bureaucracy by selling positions. He also focused on the Catholic Church, which was a major landowner and a source of revenue for the papacy. In 1516, following military successes in Italy, he secured from the papacy the right to appoint all French bishops and abbots, and this new power gave him access to a tremendous patronage system. Francis increased royal authority in a variety of other administrative ways and embarked on a program of overseas exploration (see Topic 38). By the death of Francis in the mid-16th century, the power that had been accumulated by the French monarchy was considerable, although the subsequent outbreak of religious unrest was to undermine the royal achievement.

ENGLAND AND THE RISE OF THE TUDORS

Even while England was engaged in the costly and draining experience of the Hundred Years' War, the kingdom was thrown into social and political turmoil. Two branches of the royal family, the House of York, which sported a white rose as its symbol, and the House of Lancaster, whose symbol was a red rose, began a struggle for power. Known as the War of the Roses, this conflict eventually pulled other families and England itself into a 30-year civil war. When it was over, a new dynasty, the House of Tudor, ascended to the throne.

THE WAR OF THE ROSES

Although the constant state of warfare between England and France had been the result of intermarriage and disputed inheritances, family links between the two monarchies continued to be forged. In 1420, Henry V of England, head of the House of Lancaster, married Catherine of Valois, the daughter of the French king. The following year, Catherine gave birth to a son, who came to the throne as Henry VI (ruled 1422–1471) when he was still an infant. For some years, an uncle ran the affairs of state for Henry. This hapless monarch was the pawn in the bitter War of the Roses that engulfed his realm.

THE FIRST TUDOR KING

At Edward IV's death in 1483, his eldest son ruled for only three months before the boy's uncle, Richard, duke of Gloucester, sent him and his younger brother to the Tower of London, where they died mysteriously. Richard then assumed the throne as Richard III (ruled 1483–1485). Two

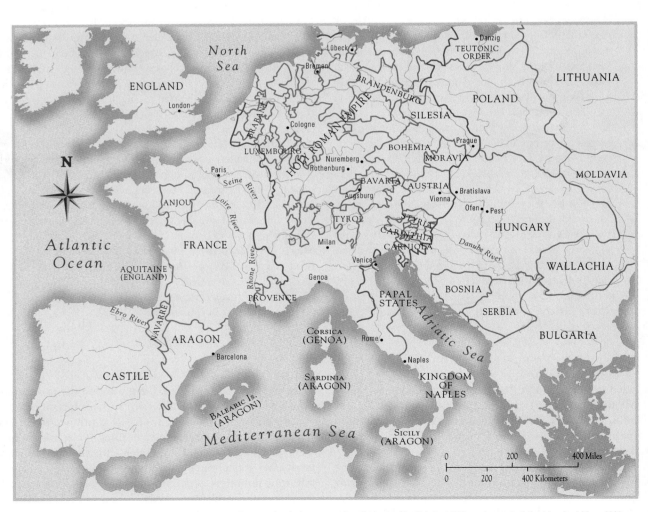

 Map 33.2 Europe, c. 1400. In southwest France, Aquitaine was taken from the English in 1453, at the end of the Hundred Years' War. Navarre caused a century of conflict between France and Spain. During the 16th century, the southern part became conquered by Spain while the king of Navarre became king of France, and the two thus became joined. Anjou remained a powerful independent Duchy until 1480, when it was incorporated into France. Go to http://info.wadsworth.com/053461065X for an interactive version of this map.

years later, Henry Tudor defeated Richard at Bosworth Field and founded the Tudor dynasty.

Henry VII (ruled 1485–1509) was an energetic king who wanted to build an autocratic monarchy that could put an end to domestic discord and govern effectively. To accomplish this purpose, Henry prohibited nobles from maintaining private armies, a practice that had been common because the crown did not yet have a standing army. When recalcitrant nobles refused to comply with the king's demand for internal peace, he had them hauled before a new tribunal, the Court of the Star Chamber, which was presided over by royal judges.

These methods were balanced, however, by the fact that Henry did not arouse noble resistance by seeking to extract special taxes from them. Instead, he increased revenues from royal estates and made the collection of traditional taxes more efficient. Henry not only paid off the royal debt but also accumulated a vast private fortune. To overcome the economic distress that the disruptions of war had produced, Henry refused to engage in costly military adventures and tried instead to promote trade and manufacturing. He relied increasingly on the landed gentry to staff the administrative offices of his government. After almost 25 years on the throne, Henry—England's first new monarch—left a stable and increasingly prosperous kingdom in which the monarchy had once again become a respected institution with much popular support.

SPAIN: FROM ARAGON AND CASTILE TO HAPSBURG MONARCHY

At the time that the new monarchs were forging single nation-states in other parts of Europe, the Iberian peninsula was still divided into separate units. On the western coast, Portugal was a small kingdom with an ambitious monarchy that was leading the way in overseas exploration. On the southern Mediterranean coast lay Granada, the last real stronghold of Muslim power (see Topic 26). The vast central portion of the peninsula consisted of the kingdom of Castile, whose unruly nobles controlled much of the countryside and still waged the war against the Muslims that had begun centuries earlier. The eastern part of the peninsula was dominated by the kingdom of Aragon, which contained three distinct areas: Valencia, a fishing and farming region on the Mediterranean; Aragon, an interior region of unproductive land; and Catalonia, the commercial center of the kingdom containing the important port of Barcelona.

THE KINGDOM OF SPAIN

Although Portugal remained an independent state, the kingdom of Spain was formed in the late 15th century as a result of the union of Castile and Aragon. In 1469, Isabella (ruled 1474–1504), the heir to the throne of Castile, married Ferdinand (ruled 1479–1516), future ruler of Aragon.

Ferdinand was already king of Sicily, and his marriage to Isabella promised to create a kingdom of great influence and wealth. After a decade-long civil war against the nobles of Castile, who feared the power of a centralized monarchy, Ferdinand and Isabella were at last able to create the Kingdom of Spain.

Ferdinand and Isabella continued to recognize the deep-rooted local traditions that had long characterized Aragon. The region remained a collection of autonomous provinces, each with a viceroy and a parliamentary assembly known as the *Cortes*. Separate coinage systems, customs, and dialects continued to prevail even after unification. In Castile, however, the unstable conditions produced by the civil war had caused the spread of banditry in the countryside.

In response, the monarchs began to build a more highly centralized administration. Using the Cortes of Castile as a special tribunal to bring criminals to justice, Ferdinand and Isabella pacified the region. They reduced the power of the nobility in the royal government and relied increasingly on the lesser aristocrats known as *hidalgos*, who were more loyal to the crown.

The monarchs of Spain used religious policy as a force for cohesion. After the end of the civil war, Ferdinand and Isabella launched a renewed crusade against the Muslims in southern Spain, making themselves the symbols of Catholic unity and popular fervor. In 1478, they obtained permission from the pope to create a Spanish Inquisition, an institution that was used to uncover *Marranos*—Jews who pretended to convert to Christianity—and *Moriscos*—converted Muslims. Headed by the infamous Tomas de Torquemada, the Spanish Inquisitors often abused their authority and were fanatical in their efforts to uncover heretics and other nonconformists, including homosexuals and practitioners of magic. When Granada fell in 1492, Ferdinand and Isabella redirected their attack against the Jews, some 150,000 being expelled that same year. Religious policy, with its emphasis on uniformity and loyalty, became an important weapon in the growing arsenal of royal power.

Unlike the case of England, where Parliament restricted the power of the monarchy, royal authority in Spain was not seriously challenged by the Cortes. The rulers could raise taxes without approval of the Cortes and presided directly over the administration of justice. A royal compendium of law codes made the legal system uniform for the entire realm. In addition, Ferdinand and Isabella strengthened the state by replacing the old feudal armies, which relied so heavily on the loyalty of nobles, with a professional royal army. The collection of taxes became more efficient, and as royal revenues increased, so did the strength of the central government.

SPAIN AND THE HAPSBURGS

Ferdinand took an active role in foreign affairs, conquest, and overseas exploration (see Topic 38). With both Granada in the south and Navarre in the north now annexed to Spain, Ferdinand began to look beyond the peninsula.

Portrait of Maximilian I, by Albrecht Dürer. 16th century. Maximilian was a member of the Hapsburg family, Holy Roman Emperors after 1438. The family symbol of the double eagle is visible in the top left-hand corner, while Maximilian holds a pomegranate, whose many seeds represent abundance.

Kunsthistorisches Museum, Wien oder KHM, Wien

In 1495, he sent an army into Italy to prevent Charles VIII of France from bringing all of the Italian city-states under his control, and some nine years later he succeeded in conquering Naples. Spain had become a significant power, and by the end of the era of Ferdinand and Isabella, they had arranged marriages for their five children into prominent European dynasties. It was through one such marriage alliance with the Hapsburgs of Austria that the fate of Spain became enmeshed with that of the Holy Roman Empire.

Over the centuries, the Hapsburg family had gained control of Austria, a series of possessions along the Danube River in central Europe, and ruled a growing empire from their capital at Vienna. In 1438, the Hapsburgs secured the imperial crown of the Holy Roman Empire, and when Maximilian (ruled 1493–1519) married the daughter of the ruler of Burgundy, he expanded Hapsburg rule over the Low Countries, Luxembourg, and into eastern France. Maximilian continued the Hapsburg policy of carefully arranging marriages to further the family's dynastic interests. The link with Spain came in 1496, when Maximilian's son, Philip of Burgundy, married Joanna, the daughter of Ferdinand and Isabella.

Twenty years later, when Ferdinand died, Aragon and Castile finally came together under the rule of one sovereign, Charles I (ruled 1516–1556), the grandson of both the Hapsburg emperor and the Spanish monarchs. Because Charles had been raised in Flanders, the Spanish nobility resented him. His election as Holy Roman Emperor in 1519 (he took the imperial title as Charles V) aroused even further hostility from his Spanish subjects, who felt that Charles's imperial interests had little to do with them. When he left Spain in 1520, a vague sense of Spanish nationalism was already beginning to stir.

Although Charles returned to Spain periodically, his attention was now focused on the immense possessions that he ruled—an empire that, with the exception of France, encompassed virtually all of continental Europe west of Poland and Hungary. Charles V was to be at the center of most of the major political and religious events of the first half of the 16th century (see Topic 39).

Putting the Age of the New Monarchs in Perspective

The development of the modern European nation-state was the work of the new monarchs, ambitious rulers who shaped powerful central governments controlling large national territories. The new Tudor dynasty in England, the Valois kings in France, and the joint reigns of Ferdinand and Isabella in Spain all began the process. The monarchs eliminated or at least reduced the power of the old nobility and extended their control over the church. They also created a bureaucratic structure designed to make the workings of royal government more effective and used several instruments of royal power to advance their program, including the extension of royal justice and the efficient collection of taxes.

In the process, they insisted on complete loyalty from their subjects and encouraged a national spirit designed to create popular support for their centralizing policies. The power and influence of the new monarchs and their centralizing states proved to be irresistible. The trends begun in the 15th century accelerated with time, and the centralized nation-state provided a model for rulers in other parts of Europe.

Questions for Further Study

1. What were the causes of the Hundred Years' War?
2. What was "new" about the new monarchs?
3. What issues led to the War of the Roses? Why were the Tudors successful in establishing their dynasty?
4. How did Ferdinand and Isabella unite Spain?

Suggestions for Further Reading

Allmand, C. *The Hundred Years' War: England and France, c. 1300–c. 1450*. Cambridge, MA, 1988.

Faur, Jose. *In the Shadow of History: Jews and Conversos at the Dawn of Modernity*. Albany, NY, 1992.

Gillingham, John. *The War of the Roses: Peace and Conflict in Fifteenth Century England*. London, 1981.

Hay, Denys. *Europe in the Fourteenth and Fifteenth Centuries*, 2nd ed. New York, 1989.

Hicks, M.A. *Richard III*. Stroude, 2000.

Hillgarth, J.N. *The Spanish Kingdoms, 1250–1516*, vol. II, *Castilian Hegemony*. New York, 1978.

Kadourie, Elie, ed. *Spain and the Jews: The Sephardi Experience 1492 and After*. New York, 1992.

Pernoud, Regine, and Marie-Veronique Clin. Jeremy du Quesnay Adams, trans. Bonnie Wheeler, ed. *Joan of Arc: Her Story*. London, 2000.

Potter, David. *A History of France, 1460-1560*. New York, 1995.

Wood, Charles T. *Joan of Arc and Richard III: Sex, Saints, and Government in the Middle Ages*. New York, 1988.

Wright, Nicholas. *Knights and Peasants: The Hundred Years War in the French Countryside*. Rochester, NY, 1998.

InfoTrac College Edition

Enter the search term *Hundred Years' War* using Key Terms.

Enter the search term *Joan of Arc* using Key Terms.

Enter the search term *Edward III* using Key Terms.

POWER AND CULTURE IN RENAISSANCE ITALY

The period in Western history known as the **Renaissance** (1300–1550) saw a remarkable flowering of artistic and literary genius. It was accompanied by the rise of a new world view that placed a concern for the human condition at the center of intellectual life. The Renaissance began in Italy, the product of its unique social and economic development. Renaissance culture, urban and increasingly secular, flourished in a land that had largely escaped feudalism. Moreover, the rebirth of Classical values was tied closely both to the long tradition of secular learning in Italy and to the memory of ancient Roman civilization, the physical remains of which were scattered throughout the peninsula.

Born in the Italian cities of the 14th century, humanism was a literary movement that stressed the study of Classical texts, new philosophical approaches inspired by Platonic ideas, and the historical sciences. These humanist values gave rise to a new kind of intellectual who participated actively in a political culture inspired by ancient ideals. Humanists regarded themselves as active citizens of their city-states and immersed themselves in the material affairs of their urban settings; they were not ivory tower intellectuals removed from the everyday world. Precisely because they were an educated elite, they believed they had responsibilities to their fellow citizens. This spirit of civic humanism was one of the outstanding characteristics of the Renaissance.

The visual arts played a central role in the public life of the city-states of Renaissance Italy, where political power and culture were inextricably linked. The princes of Florence and Milan, the aristocratic families of Venice, and the popes of Rome all were active and enthusiastic patrons of painting, sculpture, and architecture. Political leaders recognized the powerful role that the arts could have in forging popular consensus behind authority and instilling civic pride in citizens.

Although Renaissance culture represented a community of shared values, standards, and ideals, the political experience of Italy was far less unified. Because the peninsula was divided among several highly competitive and often warring states, it fell prey to more powerful foreign states. In response to their political divisiveness, Italians developed the concept of balance-of-power politics and the new art of diplomacy. By the 16th century, the Florentine writer Machiavelli drew on his Classical training as well as on the bitter political events of his times to fashion a new vision of power removed from the moral codes of Christianity and rooted directly in the gritty realities of everyday experience.

SIGNIFICANT DATES

Renaissance Italy

1311–1447	Viscontis rule Milan
1454	Peace of Lodi
1407–1457	Life of Lorenzo Valla
1450–1494	Sforzas rule Milan
1463–1494	Life of Pico della Mirandola
1494	Charles VIII invades Italy
1433–1499	Life of Marsilio Ficino
1484–1519	Francesco Gonzaga rules Mantua
1434–1494	Medici rule Florence

POLITICS, CLASS, AND CIVIC IDENTITY: THE ITALIAN CITY-STATES

The political and social development of Italian Renaissance cities followed a similar pattern. The remarkable economic expansion that had occurred in Medieval Italy had caused the rise of northern and central Italian cities such as Venice, Genoa, Milan, and Florence. The merchants and bankers who controlled this commercial revival accumulated great wealth. By the 11th century, they allied themselves with the local nobles in the countryside in order to secure independence from the bishops who ruled their cities. The communes came into being as a result of the oaths that the burghers and the nobles took to fight for their common rights. Once independence from the bishops was achieved, the communes took over the municipal governments, often creating new institutions, and soon came to control the hinterland around the cities. On this basis the city-states of the Renaissance eventually emerged.

FROM COMMUNES TO THE SIGNORIE

Political institutions in the cities reflected evolving social arrangements. Many of the rural nobles, attracted to the possibilities of wealth to be gained in trade or by marriage to rich burghers, moved into the cities, forming a new kind of urban nobility connected to the merchants through economic and family ties. This ruling elite strictly limited power and the rights of citizenship in the communes to people like themselves, who owned property and enjoyed high social status. Most of the inhabitants, including males of the middle and lower classes and all women, were excluded from holding office.

The members of the middle class, the *popolo*, particularly resented their second-class status. In the 13th century these alienated groups organized violent seizures of power and replaced communes with republican governments in such important cities as Florence, Siena, and Genoa.

Republican institutions were popular both because of their connection to Roman tradition and because they allowed for access to power by new elites. Once in power the *popolo* sought to exclude the working classes below them—the *popolo minuto,* or little people—from power. As a result, the republican governments never achieved popular consensus and found it difficult to maintain public order. In the early 1300s, republican governments collapsed and were replaced by one of two kinds of new regimes: either group rule by wealthy merchants (oligarchies) or individual despotisms (*signorie*).

THE STATES OF RENAISSANCE ITALY

By the opening of the 15th century, five major states had so expanded their territorial base that they exercised virtual hegemony over the Italian peninsula: Venice and Milan in the north, Florence in north-central Italy, the Papal States in the center, and the Kingdom of Naples in the south. Venice, at the head of the Adriatic Sea, had dominated the commercial revival of the High Middle Ages. Tremendous wealth poured into the city from its galleys and its overseas outposts. The Venetians had also conquered a mainland empire in Italy in order to have steady access to food and to protect themselves from the ambitious Milanese. Behind its long-established republican institutions, some 200 of Venice's merchant nobles ruled one of the most powerful states in Europe.

In Milan, the principal city of the region known as Lombardy, the Visconti family had ruled as tyrants since 1311. In 1395 Gian Galeazzo Visconti (ruled 1395–1402) transformed his rule into a hereditary duchy. By the time of his death, his armies had overrun all of Lombardy and were at the gates of Florence. In 1447, when the last of the Visconti died, Francesco Sforza (ruled 1450–1466), a soldier of fortune in the pay of the Milanese, turned against his masters and conquered the city. The Sforza family governed Milan with a strong hand and dominated the lesser cities of northern Italy.

The republic of Florence had long been controlled by representatives of the trade guilds, and from 1434 to 1494 the Medici, one of the most powerful and wealthy of the guild families, controlled the city. The Medici, who first made their money in banking, ruled behind the city's republican façade for more than half a century, turning Florence into a center of international power and cultural brilliance. Cosimo de' Medici (ruled 1434–1464), the great patron of civic humanists and artists, was a cultivated man of letters. On Cosimo's death, his son Piero (ruled 1464–1469) assumed the position of de facto ruler of Florence. Piero's era was marked by continuing artistic achievement and much political turmoil. He died after only five years in power and was succeeded in turn by his son Lorenzo de' Medici (ruled 1469–1492). Known as Lorenzo the Magnificent, he was the most distinguished of the Medici rulers of Florence. In his youth he was tutored by the humanist scholar Marsilio Ficino, who instilled in him a great love for learning and poetry. He continued the family's

Painting of Venice. 18th century. The main building, center-right, is the Doges' Palace, built 1345–1438, during the city's first great commercial expansion. The open arches on the lower level and the pink stone used for the upper half give the huge building a sense of lightness. To the left is visible the Basilica of St. Mark's, with its tall bell-tower, and to the right the Palace is connected to the Prison of Venice by the "Bridge of Sighs."

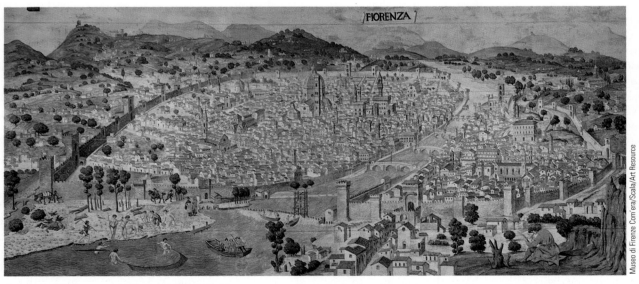

Painting of Florence, c. 1490. The city is divided into two unequal parts by the river Arno and surrounded by a wall with watchtowers, most of which was demolished in the 19th century. In the center of the left-hand section are the *Duomo* (Cathedral) and towered Palazzo Vecchio (Old Palace), which is still the center of city government. The main building across the river is the Pitti Palace, residence of the Medici.

tradition of patronage for the scholars and artists who worked in Florence during Cosimo's day.

Lorenzo's reign was challenged in 1478 when the so-called Pazzi Conspiracy erupted. This complicated plot was fomented by the prominent Pazzi family, who resented Medici rule. Lorenzo succeeded in foiling the conspiracy and imposing an even more firm control on the city. The last years of Lorenzo's life were again marked by turmoil, this time surrounding the career of the Dominican preacher Fra Girolamo Savonarola (1452–1498). Savonarola in-

Map 34.1 Italy, c. 1450. Italy refers at this time to a geographic area and not a political entity. It remained divided into separate states until the 19th century. The leading economic centers were Milan, Venice, and Florence; Siena, soon to pass under Florentine control, had lost its commercial supremacy at the time of the Black Death (1348). Rome had recently regained the prestige of housing the papacy but had little in the way of commerce. Go to http://info.wadsworth.com/053461065X for an interactive version of this map.

veighed against what he saw as the degeneration of life and culture in Florence and gathered a large and enthusiastic following, including some of the most talented artists of the city. He wanted a restoration of the Florentine republic based on Christian morality. In 1496 he staged a huge bonfire in the city in which gambling paraphernalia, cosmetics, and other symbols of decadence were burned. Savonarola eventually came into conflict with the papacy, which had him executed for heresy.

The Papal States, stretching across the peninsula from the Adriatic to the Tyrrhenian seas, were ruled by the popes

from Rome. During the papal residency at Avignon, however, several noble families had grown influential in Rome. Moreover, in the course of the 14th century, secular lords had achieved independence in Ferrara, Urbino, and other cities of the Papal States. With the return of the pope to Rome in 1417, the papacy became increasingly more secular and involved in Italian politics. Some of the most famous Renaissance popes illustrated the temporal attitudes of the papacy: Pope Sixtus IV (ruled 1471–1484) became embroiled in the Pazzi Conspiracy; Alexander VI (ruled 1492–1503) and his sinister son Cesare Borgia schemed in the diplomatic intrigues of the day; and Julius II (ruled 1503–1513), the "warrior pope," personally led his armies in battle.

South of the Papal States lay the Kingdom of Naples, including the island of Sicily. After the death of Frederick of Hohenstaufen in the 13th century, the kingdom had fallen prey to the competing ambitions of the rulers of Aragon and France. In 1435, Naples and Sicily came under Aragonese domination and in 1504 were annexed to the Spanish crown.

The Italian cities were able to develop into sovereign territorial states primarily because Italy, like Germany, possessed no powerful central monarchy such as those that emerged in France and England. In this world of small Italian Renaissance states, ruled by despots and oligarchies, the elite learned to derive significant power from the sponsorship of culture. Out of this age of Renaissance humanism, when one neighbor was pitted against another in endless cycles of wars and alliances, a new conception of power politics was born.

THE INTELLECTUAL WORLD OF THE EARLY RENAISSANCE

In the 14th century, Petrarch introduced the notion of the self-conscious artist in search of personal fame (see Topic 32). The following generation of scholars advanced the notion of humanism further, with the arrival of Byzantine intellectuals who fled westward after the fall of Constantinople in 1453. Under constant external danger from other city-states, especially Milan, Florentine intellectuals turned to the Classical past to find inspiration. Among their models was Marcus Tullius Cicero, the ancient Roman statesman and writer, whose orations, letters, and essays stressed that the educated upper classes should provide leadership for society (see Topic 14). In 15th-century Florence, the civic humanist Leonardo Bruni (1370–1444) wrote a biography of Cicero that portrayed him as the model of the Renaissance ideal of the scholar-activist. Bruni was part of a circle of scholars around Coluccio Salutati who collected and studied ancient manuscripts; the greatest collector of ancient manuscripts was Poggio Bracciolini (1380–1459), a longtime papal secretary. These and other scholars perceived civic activism not only as a duty but also as a stimulant to intellectual creativity.

HUMANISTS AND NEOPLATONISTS

Lorenzo Valla (1407–1457) was the epitome of the civic humanist. Raised and educated in Rome, Valla studied both the Latin and the Greek classics, as Bruni had done. Humanists admired virtually all Latin writers before the 7th century, but Valla's studies—especially his *Elegances of the Latin Language*—revealed distinct periods in the development of Latin. He most admired the style of the late Republic and early Empire (1st century B.C.–1st century A.D.). Valla devoted much of his energy to close textual analysis of ancient manuscripts. His discovery that the document known as the Donation of Constantine was a fake, actually written in the 8th century, brought him much attention; the Donation, which claimed that the Emperor Constantine had actually given political authority over the West to the church in 313, had long been used by popes to assert their temporal rule.

By the middle of the 15th century, humanism had become widely diffused; its basic tenets and methods were accepted; and many of the key Classical texts were known. Humanists now shifted their attention to philosophy, especially as it was influenced by the Greek philosophers, chief among them Plato. The Florentine humanists flourished under the patronage of the city's de facto ruler, the highly cultivated banker Cosimo de' Medici. Cosimo invested much of his wealth in the search for and copying of Classical manuscripts and in supporting the discussion group that came to be known as the Platonic Academy. Marsilio Ficino (1433–1499), one of the circle's most gifted intellectuals, was taken under Cosimo's protection as a child. Ficino received a regular income and access to the library at the Medici villa, and the Neoplatonists gathered here for their discussions.

Ficino's numerous translations from Greek into Latin included the *Corpus Hermeticum*, a series of Hermetic essays prepared at Cosimo's request. Among the subjects covered in the *Corpus* were the supposed secrets of the pagan world, including alchemy, astrology, and magic. The Hermeticists held that although human beings had been created as divine creatures, they had elected to be part of the material world. According to this view, humans could reattain their divine state by becoming sages. These magi, as they were known in the Renaissance, were endowed with knowledge of God and of the powers of nature, which they could use to help humans.

KNOWLEDGE AND EDUCATION

Among the best-known of those regarded as magi in the 15th century was Pico della Mirandola (1463–1494), a churchman who had studied with Ficino and was perhaps the most brilliant of the Florentine humanists—he once boasted that he had read every book in Italy. Believing that it was possible to organize human learning to reveal basic truth, Pico set out to master all knowledge. He learned Latin, Greek, Hebrew, Aramaic, and Arabic, as well as philosophy. When he was 20 years old he claimed to have summed up knowledge in 900 theses, which he described in a treatise called *Oration on the Dignity of Man*.

To the Renaissance mind, education was crucial to the intelligent and proper conduct of public affairs because humanism placed humans at the center of historical development. The authors of medieval chronicles had attributed events in human affairs to divine inspiration or direct intervention by God. The humanists, so taken with the search for texts and the analysis of sources, looked to documents rather than miracles for explanations of historical

PUBLIC FIGURES AND PRIVATE LIVES

ISABELLA D'ESTE AND FRANCESCO GONZAGA

Along with the Medici in Florence and the Sforza in Milan, Italy's smaller city-states were also centers of art and learning. Among the most brilliant of these smaller Renaissance courts was that of Francesco Gonzaga (ruled 1484–1519) of Mantua and his wife, Isabella d'Este (1474–1539).

Like many of his contemporaries, Francesco Gonzaga was first and foremost a warrior-prince. A short, ugly man without serious education, he seems not to have inherited the cultural interests that had long been a tradition at Mantua; while courting his future wife, he sent her poems that he had commissioned but pretended were his own. In 1490, he married Isabella, the 16-year-old daughter of Ercole d'Este, ruler of Ferrara, and Eleonora of Aragon. From that moment, Isabella overshadowed her husband in virtually all matters of domestic state policy and made Mantua a major center of Renaissance culture.

Isabella and her sister, Beatrice, two of the most remarkable women of the Renaissance, grew up in the rarified atmosphere of the Este court at Ferrara. The sisters were both competitive and different, for while Beatrice enjoyed a luxurious lifestyle, Isabella was more serious and mastered both Greek and Latin. Their arranged marriages resulted in major political alliances: While Isabella went to Mantua, Beatrice married Ludovico Sforza of Milan.

Because Francesco spent much time away from Mantua, the self-assured Isabella, who exhibited considerable skill at diplomacy and matters of state, often assumed the reins of government. Isabella's fame, however, rests on her role as an astute and sophisticated patron of arts and letters. Her cultural tastes were broad, ranging from painting, music, and architecture to philosophy, literature, and astrology. She competed for the talents of some of the greatest artists and writers of the era. Titian and Leonardo da Vinci painted portraits of her; Mantegna decorated her private rooms in the ducal palace; and Correggio called her "the first lady of the world."

Francesco Gonzaga's fame rests on his victory at the Battle of Fornovo in 1495, where he led the military forces of the Italian League (including Venice, Milan, and the Papal States) against the invading army of Charles VIII of France. Later, however, he continuously switched sides, and in 1509 he was captured and held prisoner for a year by the Venetians. During that time, Isabella not only made important military decisions and directed the defenses of Mantua but also founded the city's lucrative cloth industry. When he was finally liberated, a humiliated Francesco felt resentful of his talented consort's achievements. "We are ashamed," he wrote to her, "that it is our fate to have as a wife a woman who is always ruled by her head." Increasingly estranged from Francesco because of his repeated infidelities, she spent many of her last years at the papal court in Rome. After her husband died in 1519, Isabella acted as regent and adviser to her son Federigo II and was able to have her younger son, Ercole, made a cardinal. She died a much revered and respected figure, and very much a woman of the Renaissance.

events. Similarly, they saw individual motives behind political developments. The most accomplished of the new secular historians of the Renaissance was Francesco Guicciardini (1483–1540), who had considerable experience as a diplomat and government official. His *History of Italy,* the first work of history since antiquity based on original documents, provided detailed comparative analysis of political affairs in the city-states and decried the lack of unity in Italy. Most of all, Guicciardini saw the need for wise rulers endowed with learning and experience. These and other humanist values remained the core of upper-class education in the West for centuries.

PATRONAGE AND STATECRAFT IN RENAISSANCE ITALY

It was no accident that the cities of the Italian Renaissance were centers of both political power and culture because art served as a medium of education and as propaganda. The church, of course, had always been a great patron of the arts, using architecture, painting, and sculpture to promote worship and respect for religious institutions. In the Renaissance, just as artistic themes became increasingly secular, so laymen emerged as active and generous patrons of the arts.

THE NATURE OF RENAISSANCE PATRONAGE

Following in the tradition of the Middle Ages, guilds and religious organizations commissioned artists to create works of sculpture and paintings that reflected their wealth and influence. In Florence, the cloth merchants hired Filippo Brunelleschi to design and erect the stunning dome of the city's *duomo* (cathedral).

Individual rulers and nobles also came to recognize the power of culture and patronized art and scholarship to show off their wealth and status. Many tried to trace their ancestry back to Roman times and deliberately imitated the lifestyles of the ancient patricians. In their zeal to identify with Classical civilization, princes poured money into excavating archaeological sites and locating lost manuscripts. Wealthy families spent lavishly to build and decorate tombs and chapels in the principal churches of their cities.

Princes used the creative talents they supported to strengthen and legitimize their rule. They brought poets and essayists to their palaces, and hired architects and artists to plan and decorate their public rooms and erect statues and monuments to their achievements. As the social status of the artists grew during the Renaissance, patrons competed to hire the best-known painters and sculptors because the fame of the artist enhanced the prestige of the patron.

ITALY AND EUROPE: POWER POLITICS AND THE ART OF DIPLOMACY

In 1454, the Italian states established a precarious balance of power through the Peace of Lodi. The agreement between Venice and Milan, which conceded Milan to Francesco Sforza and restored Venetian holdings in northern Italy, brought peace to Italy for many years. The Italian states were exhausted by the continuous warfare and agreed to observe the terms of the peace and to join an Italian League for mutual defense.

The Peace of Lodi collapsed in 1494, when Lodovico Sforza of Milan asked for the military support of Charles VIII of France in the midst of rising tensions with Florence and Naples. The French invasion of Italy began a long series of disastrous wars that revealed the inability of relatively weak city-states to withstand the power of centralized nation-states. Italy became a battleground of larger European dynastic interests as the houses of Hapsburg, Valois, and Aragon jockeyed for hegemony. Charles pushed the Medici out of Florence (they returned in 1512), the Hapsburg Emperor Charles V seized Milan, and Ferdinand of Aragon took Naples. When the wars finally ended in 1559, the Hapsburgs were masters of the peninsula, with only Venice and the Papal States remaining independent. Although the memory of Italy's great cultural legacy lingered, its political subservience to foreign powers would not end for three centuries.

DIPLOMACY AND POWER POLITICS

As political life in Europe grew more complex, states began to develop new and more formal ways of relating to each other. The advantages of economic and cultural cooperation, as well as of finding alternatives to war, became increasingly evident to the great powers. Nowhere was the need for organized international relations greater than in Italy, where in the process of creating a balance of power the Italians had invented the art of diplomacy. During the Italian wars that erupted at the end of the 15th century, the Italian style of managing foreign policy was copied by other European states.

The most important novelty devised by Italian diplomats was the use of resident ambassadors. In the place of roving envoys who traveled to accomplish specific missions, states now maintained permanent ambassadors in foreign capitals. The advantages were obvious: Resident ambassadors could not only collect intelligence about conditions and attitudes in their host country, but they also developed personal relationships that could be used to represent the interests of their sovereign more quickly and efficiently. Resident ambassadors gave rise to elaborate embassies staffed by military and commercial experts and using sophisticated reporting procedures. Diplomatic staffs lived in foreign countries with immunity from local laws and adopted both fixed procedures and formal styles of protocol to govern diplomatic relations. These procedures evolved under the impact of the Italian wars because rulers throughout Europe were drawn into the intricate dynastic struggles that marked the struggles for power there. It gradually became clear that the general interests of all states required a balance in which no one power dominated the others.

The collapse of the independence of the Italian city-states, together with the emergence of centralized monarchies elsewhere in Europe, attracted the attention of political analysts, who now began to study diplomacy, politics, and the nature of power from a more practical and secular point of view. The Italians, anxious to understand why their independence had disappeared so completely, were in the

The Departure of the Ambassadors, painting by Carpaccio, c. 1496–1498. 9 feet 2 inches by 8 feet 8 inches (2.80 by 2.53 m). The painting comes from a cycle depicting the Legend of St. Ursula and shows the king of Brittany receiving ambassadors from England. In fact, however, it represents Italian diplomatic practice of the Early Renaissance, and the interior walls decorated with colored stone are typical of Venetian architecture.

Scala/Art Resource

forefront of this new approach to the study of political power. The historian Guicciardini, for example, had examined the histories of the Italian states comparatively and concluded that the lack of unity in the peninsula had enabled foreign powers to crush them. It was, however, the Florentine Niccolò Machiavelli (1469–1527) who epitomized the new politics of the age (see Topic 36).

Many contemporaries were shocked by Machiavelli's advocacy of the amoral manipulation of power, and the term "Machiavellian" became a label for unscrupulousness and evil. The 16th century was perhaps not yet ready to accept this new approach to the use of state power, but the realities of the day pointed to a different direction in political affairs.

Putting Renaissance Italy in Perspective

The Renaissance was the product of Europe's cultural and social vitality, and it set the tone for the modern age. The humanist concerns with Classical virtues and learning, the strength and beauty of Michelangelo's *David,* the raw pragmatism of Machiavelli's advice to the prince, all bespoke a new viewpoint freed from superstition and focused on the human condition. The secular and urban values of Renaissance culture emerged first in Italy, where a combination of history, social development, and economic factors encouraged its flowering. Conditions there first stimulated the growth of humanism,

Continued next page

which in turn nurtured the sense of civic virtue and responsibility that marked the public life of the Renaissance city-states.

As in earlier epochs, rulers of the Renaissance period appreciated and used painting, sculpture, and architecture to enhance their prestige and legitimize their power. Political leaders recognized the powerful role that the arts could have in forging popular consensus behind authority and instilling civic pride in citizens. The experience of numerous city-states vying with each other to control the peninsula had resulted in the invention of important political techniques, although Machiavelli, the most jarringly objective observer of his times, recognized in that lesson that the realities of power were working against the Italians. For all their wisdom and skill in developing effective political systems, Italian rulers were unable to forge unity or to maintain the integrity of their own states against the military power of the newly emerging national monarchies. The Italians, it seemed, had chosen culture over power.

Questions for Further Study

1. What forms did "civic identity" take in Renaissance Italy?
2. With what issues were early Renaissance intellectuals concerned?
3. Why did Italian Renaissance rulers and merchants act as patrons of the arts?
4. What conditions in Italy led to the invention of "diplomacy" in the modern sense?

Suggestions for Further Reading

Brucker, Gene A. *Renaissance Florence*, rev. ed. New York, 1983.

Burke, Peter. *The Italian Renaissance: Culture and Society in Italy*, rev ed. Princeton, NJ, 1999.

D'Amico, John F. *Renaissance Humanism in Papal Rome*. Baltimore, 1983.

Godman, Peter. *From Poliziano to Machiavelli: Florentine Humanism in the High Renaissance*. Princeton, NJ, 1998.

Hale, J.R. *The Civilization of Europe in the Renaissance*. New York, 1995.

Hay, Denys, and J. Law. *Italy in the Age of the Renaissance*. London, 1989.

Holmes, George. *Florence, Rome and the Origins of the Renaissance*. Oxford, 1986.

Johnson, P. *The Renaissance*. New York, 2000.

King, Margaret L. *Venetian Humanism in an Age of Patrician Dominance*. Princeton, NJ, 1986.

Rubinstein, Nicolai. *The Government of Florence under the Medici (1434-1494)*. New York, 1997.

Stephens, J. *The Italian Renaissance: The Origins of Intellectual and Artistic Change Before the Reformation*. New York, 1990.

Trinkaus, Charles E. *The Scope of Renaissance Humanism*. Ann Arbor, MI, 1983.

InfoTrac College Edition

Enter the search term *Renaissance* using the Subject Guide.

Enter the search term *Machiavelli* using Key Terms.

THE VISUAL ARTS OF THE ITALIAN RENAISSANCE

The rise of the Medici in Florence, together with the city's increasing prosperity, culminated in an artistic explosion there. Painters, sculptors, and architects vied to produce works in the "modern style," commissioned by their patrons, which influenced the arts throughout Europe.

Although the Renaissance style was a natural development of the late medieval interest in the expression of powerful feelings, Renaissance artists felt that in turning back to ancient models they were making a decisive break with their immediate past. The greatest sculptor of the Early Renaissance, Donatello, combined a rediscovery of Classical forms with a strong sense of drama.

Brunelleschi, the leading architect of the period, used techniques learned from his study of ancient Roman buildings to create structures dominated by logic and order. Many of his buildings are centrally planned, and the design of details expresses the Renaissance belief in reason. The paintings of Masaccio show a similar concern with order and proportion, combining them with physical realism. Botticelli, one of the leading painters at the Medici court, reflected his patrons' interest in Neoplatonic humanism, while in northern Italy the frescoes of Mantegna continued to experiment with perspective.

The three towering figures of the High Renaissance were Leonardo da Vinci, Raphael, and Michelangelo. Leonardo is known as much for the incredible breadth of his ideas and interests as for his few surviving works. Raphael's paintings express the High Renaissance love of ideal beauty based on Classical standards. Michelangelo's vision was more complex. Recognized in his own day as the greatest artist of the Renaissance, he has been regarded ever since as the archetype of the supreme creative genius.

The masterpieces produced in Florence in the Early Renaissance and at Rome in the High Renaissance emphasized order, form, and line. Venetian painters were more interested in color and light, and their works are often mellower and more relaxed than those produced elsewhere in Italy. Bellini and Titian both used Classical themes. Titian was also a master of portraiture, while his reclining female nudes are among the most sensual in Western art.

The artistic movement of the late *Cinquecento* (16th century), Mannerism, took the main features of Renaissance style to extremes, with the drama becoming artificial, and technical virtuosity an end in itself. By the end of the 16th century, artists and critics were already looking back with awe at the "old masters" of the High Renaissance.

THE "MODERN STYLE": DONATELLO, BRUNELLESCHI, AND MASACCIO

With the rediscovery of Classical Antiquity, artists began to develop new styles based on ancient models. Turning to Roman sculptures, the remains of ancient Roman buildings, and Classical texts on art, they aimed for a "modern style" that would express Classical ideals of order and balance for their own times. Behind their use of perspective and realism to achieve dramatic effect lay the late medieval emotionalism seen in the works of Giovanni Pisano (see Topic 30), but the powerful directness of Early Renaissance art represents a revolutionary break with the past.

SCULPTURE IN THE EARLY RENAISSANCE: DONATELLO

One of the most profoundly original of all Renaissance artists, the sculptor Donatello (1386?–1466) used Classical principles to achieve startling dramatic effects. His statues of *St. Mark* and *St. George*, carved between 1413 and 1417 to decorate the façade of the Florentine church of Orsanmichele, show a sense of the shifting weight of the bodies. This depiction of movement, which was characteristic of ancient Greek sculpture, disappeared with the end of Classical Antiquity, to be reborn in the Early Renaissance. At the same time, Donatello avoids the generalized idealism of Greek art. The two saints emerge as distinct individuals: the venerable St. Mark brooding and intense, St. George youthfully proud and determined.

In his small bronze relief panel of *The Feast of Herod* (c. 1425), which decorates the baptismal font of Siena Cathedral, Donatello's sense of the theatrical makes powerful use of the newly discovered technique of linear perspective. To create the illusion of depth on a flat surface, Early Renaissance artists devised a mathematical system whereby all lines met at a single point on the horizon—an example of the important new relationship in the Early Renaissance between the arts and scholarly learning.

Donatello's panel combines several separate incidents in the story of Salome's dance and the execution of John the Baptist. Herod recoils in terror as the executioner presents the saint's head to him on a dish, and a variety of other figures in the three interconnected rooms express their horror with violent gestures, while Salome continues the sinuous movements of her dance. The remarkable sense of depth represents a break with the generally flat backgrounds of most medieval sculpture. Like ancient Roman artists, Donatello aimed to create the illusion of space, but for the first time in Western art he used the scientific principle of linear perspective to do so.

BRUNELLESCHI AND THE CLASSICAL TRADITION OF ARCHITECTURE

The inventor of linear perspective was the architect and sculptor Filippo Brunelleschi (1377–1446). One of his earliest works was a bronze panel of *The Sacrifice of Isaac*

Donatello, statue of *St. George*. 1415–1417. Height c. 6 feet 10 inches (2.08 m). The work was originally made to stand in a niche on the façade of the Florentine Church of Orsanmichele, and thus only visible from the front. The figure is one of Donatello's earlier statues, with its Classical severity, taut pose, and tense expression.

(1401–1402), made as an entry into the competition organized in Florence to choose an artist for the north doors of the baptistery there. The winner was the sculptor and goldsmith Lorenzo Ghiberti (c. 1378–1455), whose style blended naturalism and classicism to create realistic figures. In disappointment, Brunelleschi devoted most of his remaining career to architecture and went on to become the greatest architect of the Early Renaissance.

One of the key events in the formation of Brunelleschi's style was his journey to Rome in 1402, perhaps in the company of his friend Donatello. After several more visits to study the construction principles used by ancient Roman builders there, he returned to Florence, where he managed to solve an engineering problem that baffled his contemporaries: how to construct a dome for the city's huge unfinished cathedral. The vast octagonal-shaped structure, with its inner and outer shells, still dominates the Florence skyline.

Masaccio, *Expulsion of Adam and Eve from Eden,* c. 1425. 7 feet by 2 feet 11 inches (2.14 by .90 m). The scene combines poignant emotion with a realistic portrayal of human anatomy. A fig leaf added to cover Adam's genitals in the late 15th century was only removed—amid considerable controversy—in the 1980s.

THE REVOLUTIONARY PAINTING OF MASACCIO

The first painter to adopt Brunelleschi's linear perspective was the young Masaccio (1401–1428), whose brief career—he died at the age of 27, probably of the plague—catapulted painting forward into the "modern style." Breaking completely with the elaborate and crowded style of International Gothic artists (see Topic 30), Masaccio used principles of mathematical organization to produce startling effects of realism.

In the frescoes he painted for the Brancacci Chapel in the Church of Santa Maria del Carmine, Florence, at the very end of his short life, Masaccio added an unforgettable emotional impact to his ability to create the illusion of volume. The figures of Adam and Eve, in *The Expulsion from the Garden of Eden,* stumble out of Eden into an inexorably harsh light—Adam unable to face the future and Eve crying piercingly aloud. The weight of their limbs and their leaden footsteps combine with the hazy background to present one of the most poignant images in Western art.

TRADITION AND EXPERIMENT: THE LATER QUATTROCENTO

The most important of Brunelleschi's successors was the architect and art theorist Leone Battista Alberti (1404–1472), whose writings on architecture and painting profoundly influenced later Renaissance artists. In accordance with the humanist ideas of the period, Alberti believed that beauty—whether of a figure or a building—depended on an ideal balance and order, creating a perfect harmony.

PAINTING IN THE LATER QUATTROCENTO

Toward the end of the Quattrocento, some painters continued to work within the mainstream of earlier developments, whereas others broke new ground. Among the traditionalists was Domenico Ghirlandaio (1449–1494), who placed his depictions of scenes drawn from the Bible within the rich Florentine palaces and aristocratic life of his day.

The art of Piero della Francesca (c. 1420–1492) is far more intellectual. Like Alberti, with whom he worked at Rimini, Piero continued to experiment with mathematical and geometrical structures. Many of his paintings use light as one of the elements of composition. *The Resurrection* is based on a triangular arrangement, with the sleeping soldiers forming the base and the head of the risen Christ, set on its strong, column-like body, the apex. The cold light of dawn in the background emphasizes Christ's triumphant stance.

If Piero was inspired by the clarity of mathematical proportion, his younger contemporary Sandro Botticelli (1445–1510) began his career under the influence of the Neoplatonist ideas circulating at the Medici court. The Neoplatonists combined elements of Classical mythology and Christianity in elaborate allegories. Thus the Christian

Canali Photobank, Milan

A C R O S S   C U L T U R E S

CHARLES DICKENS ON RENAISSANCE ITALY

In July 1844, the eminent Victorian novelist, Charles Dickens (1812–1870), set off with his family to spend a year in Italy. As many earlier travelers had done, he intended to turn his experiences into a book. First published as a series of letters to a newspaper, the *Daily News*, his account of the year appeared in the form of a book, *Pictures From Italy*, in 1846.

Many of the events he narrates offer an incomparably vivid impression of life in 19th century Italy—he includes, for example, a characteristically sensitive description of a public execution—but, like most visitors to Italy, then and now, he made a point of visiting as many of the most important works of art as he could see. His comments unwittingly provide an impression of the tastes of the mid-19th century.

In Florence, Dickens admired the architecture: "Magnificently stern and sombre are the streets of beautiful Florence; and the strong old piles of building make such heaps of shadow, on the ground and in the river, that there is another and a different city of rich forms and fancies, always lying at our feet." Among the artists whose work he saw in "these rugged Palaces of Florence," he especially picks out "Michael Angelo, Canova, Titian, Rembrandt, Raphael." Few art historians today would place the sculptor Canova in such exalted company. Meditating on the transience of life and the permanence of art, he cites a painting so well known to his readers that he needed to name neither title or artist: "The nameless Florentine Lady, preserved from oblivion by a Painter's hand, yet lives on, in enduring grace and youth." (Leonardo's *Mona Lisa* is now in Paris, in the Louvre.)

Visiting the Vatican while in Rome, Dickens was struck once again by "the exquisite grace and beauty of Canova's statues," and works by Titian and Tintoretto, but was less impressed by Michelangelo's achievement: "I cannot imagine how the man who is truly sensible

of the beauty of Tintoretto's great pictures can discern in Michael Angelo's Last Judgement, in the Sistine chapel, any general idea, or one pervading thought, in harmony with the stupendous subject." Similarly, the interior of St. Peter's did not appeal to his Anglican tastes: "It is not religiously impressive or affecting. It is an immense edifice, with no one point for the mind to rest on; and it tires itself with wandering round and round. A large space behind the altar was fitted up with boxes, shaped like those at the Italian Opera in England, but in their decoration much more gaudy."

The one city to win unqualified approval is described in a chapter called "An Italian Dream."

> We advanced into this ghostly city, continuing to hold our course through narrow streets and lanes, all filled and flowing with water. . . . Going down upon the margin of the green sea, rolling on before the door, and filling all the streets, I came upon a place of such surpassing beauty, and such grandeur, that all the rest was poor and faded in comparison with its absorbing loveliness.
>
> It was a great Piazza, as I thought; anchored like all the rest in the deep ocean. On its broad bosom was a Palace, more majestic and magnificent in its old age than all the buildings of the earth, in the high prime and fullness of their youth. Cloisters and galleries: so light they might have been the work of fairy hands: so strong that centuries had battered them in vain: wound round and round this palace, and enfolded it with a Cathedral, gorgeous in the wild luxuriant fancies of the East.

The author remains spellbound, "until I awoke in the old market place at Verona. I have many and many a time, thought since of this strange Dream upon the water; half wondering if it lies there yet, and if its name be Venice."

Piero della Francesca, *The Resurrection,* c. 1463. 7 feet 5 inches by 6 feet 6 inches (2.26 by 2 m). The upturned faces of the two soldiers flanking the figure of the risen Christ lead the viewer's eye toward Christ, and the contrast between his light flesh and the dark costumes of all the sleeping figures emphasizes the triangular composition.

Botticelli, *The Birth of Venus,* c. 1482. 5 feet 8 inches by 9 feet 1 inch (1.72 by 2.77 m). The Venus figure, based on statues from Classical Antiquity, represents a synthesis of Classical naturalism and Christian mysticism. At the same time, Botticelli aims to express the Platonic ideal of feminine beauty, rather than the literal appearance of a particular woman.

teaching that "God is love" becomes personified in the form of the Roman Venus, goddess of love.

At first sight, Botticelli's *Birth of Venus* seems a purely pagan image, with the nude goddess—one of the earliest female nudes since Classical Antiquity—borne forward by the winds. Yet not only is the beauty of Venus symbolic of Christian love, but the idea of the birth of Venus corresponds also to Christ's baptism, itself a form of rebirth.

By the end of the 15th century, the overthrow of the Medici and the preaching of Savonarola (see Topic 34) reduced the dominant role of Florentine artists, but the main features of Florentine Renaissance art had already spread to other parts of Italy.

HARMONY AND DESIGN IN THE HIGH RENAISSANCE

For a few brief years, from the French invasion of Italy in 1494 to the death of Raphael in 1520, the Renaissance reached a new peak. Lavish papal patronage made Rome the center of High Renaissance art, although Leonardo da Vinci, one of the three leading figures of the age—the others were Raphael and Michelangelo—worked mainly in Milan and died in France.

RENAISSANCE MAN: LEONARDO DA VINCI
No figure of the Renaissance has evoked greater admiration for the breadth of his mind than Leonardo (1452–1519), the illegitimate son of a notary at Vinci, a small town to the west of Florence. He studied painting in Florence and

worked at the court of the Sforza family, rulers of Milan, as architect, military engineer, inventor, scientist, musician, and painter. He set down many of his ideas in thousands of pages of notes and sketches, exploring the human and natural worlds.

Leonardo's fresco of *The Last Supper*, painted for the Milanese Church of Santa Maria delle Grazie, is the first great work of the High Renaissance. Despite severe damage caused by flaking paint, the work remains a powerful illustration of Renaissance ideals of clarity and harmony. The central figure of Jesus, his head outlined against the open window behind, is flanked by six apostles to each side. Jesus remains still, while shockwaves pass through the others in response to his words to them: "One of you will betray me." The dramatic range of emotions the apostles convey, the careful balance of the composition, and the absence of irrelevant details all combine to produce one of the high points of Western art.

If *The Last Supper* is the most famous of Renaissance religious scenes, Leonardo's portrait of *Mona Lisa*, wife of the merchant Giocondo (the painting is often known as *La Gioconda*—a pun on her husband's name that refers to her smile), is no less celebrated. The sitter's ambiguous smile and the hazy background are made possible by the artist's use of a technique called *sfumato* or "smoky."

THE CLASSICAL HARMONY OF RAPHAEL
Born in Urbino, the painter Raphael (1483–1520) studied in Florence before moving to Rome in 1508, where he received important papal commissions. His Classical balance and order are visible in the series of frescoes with which he decorated a suite of rooms in the Vatican palace, known as

Leonardo da Vinci, *The Last Supper*. 1495–1498. 14 feet 5 inches by 28 feet (4.4 by 7.9 m). The careful, mathematical precision behind the composition of this famous fresco does not detract from its emotional impact on the viewer. The doorway visible below the figure of Christ was cut by soldiers using the monastery where Leonardo painted the fresco as a military headquarters, and the room was also hit by a bomb in World War II.

Raphael, *The School of Athens.* 1509-1511. 26 feet by 18 feet (7.92 by 5.48 m). The Vatican fresco sets the great philosophers of antiquity in a vast illusionistic architectural framework inspired by the ruins of Roman baths and basilicas, and perhaps also by construction on the new Basilica of St. Peter's, which was then in progress.

the *Vatican Stanze*. The most famous, *The School of Athens*, depicts the most renowned ancient Greek and Roman philosophers engaged in earnest discussion.

Like Leonardo's *Last Supper*, the scene shows the figures arranged in groups. The two greatest minds of antiquity, Plato and Aristotle, stand at the center under the receding arches. Plato points upward, to indicate abstract thought, while Aristotle gestures to the ground, symbol of practical and down-to-earth experiment. The round arches and coffered ceilings of the background provide a Classical setting.

For his contemporaries, Raphael's most popular works were his many depictions of the Madonna and Child. Among the best-known is the *Madonna of the Meadows*, which provides another Renaissance example of pyramidal composition. Unlike Leonardo, with his love of mysterious haze, Raphael bathed his figures in a glowing clarity, which emphasizes their High Renaissance blend of Christian devotion and pagan beauty. In the background, the details of the feathery trees are all rendered with loving precision.

THE SUBLIME MICHELANGELO

Even in an age of giants, Michelangelo Buonarroti (1475–1564) inspired awe mixed with fear in his contemporaries, who spoke of his *terribilità*—a combination of the terrible and the sublime. For posterity he has become the

symbol of creative genius, fighting with his patrons and rivals in the pursuit of his titanic visions.

Architect, painter, poet, and engineer, Michelangelo always regarded himself as first and foremost a sculptor because sculptors possessed the almost divine power to "make man." Wrestling with the stone, he strove to release the image, the Idea, locked within it. The basis for Michelangelo's artistic philosophy was Plato's theory of Forms, or Ideas (see Topic 10), and he held that by imitating Nature an artist could reveal the highest eternal truths. Unlike other Renaissance artists, he rejected Classical notions of balance and proportion, claiming that only the inspired judgment of the individual artist could create the rules for his art. His stubborn independence, coupled with his irascible and impulsive manner, won him few friends—the popular and worldly Raphael described him as "lonely as the hangman."

One of the early works to win him fame was the *Pietà*, which shows Mary holding the body of the dead Christ. The contrast between the youthful grace of the grieving mother and the leaden weight of the body, legs dangling, already looks forward to the emotional extremes of later versions of the same subject.

Another figure from the same period, the *David*, has become one of the icons of the Florentine Renaissance. After finishing the *Pietà*, Michelangelo returned from

Raphael, *Madonna of the Meadows.* 1508. 44½ inches by 34 inches (113 by 87 cm). This is one of a series of scenes showing the Virgin with the Christ Child and the infant St. John the Baptist (identified by the cross he carries) for which Raphael used a pyramidal composition.

Erich Lessing/Art Resource, New York

Rome to Florence, drawn by the chance to "release" from a gigantic block of stone—on which other sculptors had worked in vain—the "Idea" within it. The result was the stern, tense image of David, a young man poised between thought and action.

The climax of the first part of Michelangelo's career was the colossal decoration of the ceiling of the Sistine Chapel in the Vatican. Michelangelo painted the entire ceiling, some 5,800 square feet in area, in the four years between 1508 and 1512. In glowing, luminous colors (revealed by their recent cleaning), the paintings depict no less a theme than the Creation, Fall, and Redemption of Man. On the sides, Classical and Hebrew figures foretell the coming of Christ, while in the very center Michelangelo shows *The Creation of Adam* (see p. 370). The hand of God reaches out to awaken the first man by endowing him with the divine spark of life. Adam's body represents not only natural beauty but also the manifestation of the soul itself.

Toward the end of his long artistic odyssey, Michelangelo's style became increasingly complex and tormented. The terrifying scene of *The Last Judgment,* painted on the end wall of the Sistine Chapel 25 years after the ceiling frescoes, echoes to the blaring of trumpets. All creation seems to cower before the gigantic figure of Christ, as the dead arise and the damned hurtle down to eternal torment. Gone is the idealizing Neoplatonic beauty and calm order of the earlier works. The swirling forms and distorted proportions foreshadow the Baroque art of the 17th century, which they directly inspired.

HARMONY AND COLOR: THE PAINTING OF THE VENETIAN REPUBLIC

While many of the leading Renaissance artists and their styles moved between Florence, Rome, and the cities of northern Italy, the Republic of Venice maintained its cultural independence. Venetian artists used ideas developed elsewhere in Italy, but in distinct ways. The main interest of Florentine Renaissance artists was design, and drawing was regarded as crucial in achieving a sense of intellectual order. For the Venetians, color was the primary means of expression. The light of the lagoon that surrounds the city, soft and warm in summer, pearly grey with mist in winter, glows in the paintings of the painters of the *Serenissima*—most serene of cities.

Venice's detachment from the mainstream of Renaissance cultural movements in part reflected the strength of earlier Byzantine influence there, but a more important cause was the city's geographic position and economic ties. As gateway to the East, the Venetian Republic found itself increasingly involved in a protracted struggle with the Ottoman

Michelangelo, *David*. 1501–1504. Height 18 feet (5.49 m). As the figure leans back, most of the weight is borne by the right leg (supported by a tree trunk), in a position called in Italian *contraposto.* The statue was intended to be seen from below—hence the slightly elongated neck.

Erich Lessing/Art Resource

PERSPECTIVES FROM THE PAST

ART AND ARTISTS IN THE RENAISSANCE

Our knowledge of art, artists, and patrons in Renaissance Italy owes much to the *The Lives of the Artists* of Giorgio Vasari (1511–1574), himself a painter and architect. *The Lives* first appeared in 1550, and Vasari published an enlarged version in 1568. His account includes descriptions of more than 100 artists working over a period of some three centuries and combines comments on their works with information about their patrons and the world around them—in the case of the most recent artists, including Michelangelo, based on Vasari's personal observations and inquiries.

Another artist who also wrote was the sculptor Benvenuto Cellini (1500–1571), although his *Autobiography* is devoted to recording, in suitably embroidered form, his own glories rather than the achievements of others. His account of the casting of the *Perseus* describes the artist's triumph in the face of the technical problems of casting a lifesize bronze statue, as well as over the knaves, fools, and doubters who surrounded him.

The production of art objects was, of course, a matter of business in Renaissance Italy. The portion from Cellini's *Autobiography* is followed by a rather more prosaic document, a contract drawn up by the Venetian painter Cima da Conegliano (c. 1459–1518) for the payment for one of his altarpieces.

Vasari on Michelangelo

Behind Vasari's Lives of the Artists, *there is a not-so-hidden agenda: After the empty years under Byzantine influence, Italian art was brought back to life by Giotto, and proceeded to develop until it reached its highest point in the work of the divinely inspired Michelangelo. The fact that this thesis may seem familiar is a tribute to the enormous influence of Vasari on subsequent art historians.*

Michelangelo: Cosmic Genius

While the artists who came after Giotto were doing their best to imitate and to understand nature, bending every faculty to increase that high comprehension sometimes called intelligence, the Almighty took pity on their often fruitless labor. He resolved to send to earth a spirit capable of supreme expression in all the arts, one able to give form to painting, perfection to sculpture, and grandeur to architecture. The Almighty Creator also graciously endowed this chosen one with an understanding of philosophy and with the grace of poetry. And because he had observed that in Tuscany men

were more zealous in study and more diligent in labor than in the rest of Italy, He decreed that Florence should be the birthplace of this divinely endowed spirit.

In the Casentino, therefore, in 1475, a son was born to Signor Lodovico di Leonardo di Buonarotti Simoni. . . .

[The painting of the Sistine Chapel.] Michelangelo returned to Rome and was asked by Pope Julius II to paint the ceiling of the [Sistine] chapel, a great and difficult labor. Our artist, aware of his own inexperience, excused himself from the undertaking. He proposed that the work be given to Raphael. The more he refused, the more the impetuous Pope insisted. A quarrel threatened. Michelangelo saw that the Pope was determined, so he resolved to accept the task. His Holiness ordered Bramante to prepare the scaffolding. This he did by suspending the ropes through perforations in the ceiling. Michelangelo asked how the holes were going to be filled in when the painting was done. Bramante replied that they could think about it when the time came.

Michelangelo saw that the architect was either incapable or unfriendly, and he went straight to the Pope to say that the scaffolding would not do and that Bramante did not know how to construct one. Julius, in the presence of Bramante, replied that Michelangelo might make it his own way. This he did by the use of a method that did not injure the walls, and which has since been pursued by Bramante and others. Michelangelo gave the ropes that were taken from Bramante's scaffolding to a poor carpenter, who sold them for a sum that made up his daughter's dowry.

For this work Michelangelo was paid three thousand crowns by the Pope. He may have spent twenty-five for colors. He worked under great personal inconvenience, constantly looking upward, so that he seriously injured his eyes. For months afterward he could read a letter only when he held it above his head. I can vouch for the pain of this kind of labor. When I painted the ceiling of the palace of Duke Cosimo [Palazzo Vecchio in Florence], I never could have finished the work without a special support for my head. As it is, I still feel the effects of it, and I wonder that Michelangelo endured it so well. But, as the work progressed, his zeal for his art increased daily, and he grudged no labor and was insensible to all fatigue.

Down the center of the ceiling is the History of the World, from the Creation to the Deluge. The Prophets and the Sibyls, five on each side and one at each end, are painted on the corbels. The lunettes portray the genealogy of Christ. Michelangelo used no perspective, nor any one fixed point of sight, but was satisfied to paint each division with perfection of design. Truly this chapel has been, and is, the very light of our art. Everyone capable of judging stands amazed at the excellence of his work, at the grace and flexibility, the beautiful truth of proportion of the exquisite nude forms. These are varied in every way in expression and form. Some of the figures are seated, some are in motion, while others hold up festoons of oak leaves and acorns, the device of Pope Julius. . . .

Michelangelo's powers were so great that his sublime ideas were often inexpressible. He spoiled many works because of this. Shortly before his death he burned a large number of designs, sketches, and cartoons so that none might see the labors he endured in his resolution to achieve perfection. None will marvel that Michelangelo was a lover of solitude, devoted as he was to art, and, therefore, never alone or without food for contemplation. . . . Those who say he would not teach others are wrong. I have been present many times when he assisted his intimates or any who asked his counsels . . . he was an ardent admirer of beauty for art, and knew how to select the most beautiful, but he was not liable to the undue influence of beauty. This his whole life has proved. In all things he was most moderate. He ate frugally at the close of the day's work. Though rich, he lived like a poor man and rarely had a guest at his table. He would accept no gifts for fear of being under an obligation.

This master, as I said at the beginning, was certainly sent by God as an example of what an artist could be. I, who can thank God for unusual happiness, count it among the greatest of my blessings that I was born while Michelangelo still lived, was found worthy to have him for my master, and was accepted as his trusted friend.

From Vasari, G., trans. A. B. Hinds. *Lives of the Painters, Sculptors and Architects.* Copyright © 1900.

Cellini on the Casting of the Perseus

By contrast to the unworldly and reclusive Michelangelo, the Florentine goldsmith and sculptor Benvenuto Cellini led a violent and adventurous life. He fought for the pope in Rome and for Francis I in Paris, and spent time in prison on a charge of theft brought by the bastard son of Pope Paul III. Toward the end of his life, he dictated to an apprentice in his workshop his autobiography, from which the following passage comes.

Continued

All his stories feature himself as the hero, generally triumphing against the plots of his enemies and overcoming the most insuperable difficulties. The casting of the lifesize bronze statue of Perseus with the Head of Medusa, a work still standing in Florence's Piazza Signoria, presented him with his greatest artistic challenge, and his account of it is justly famous.

As his workshop prepares the mold and lights the furnace, Cellini himself is overcome with a fever—probably brought on by nervous strain—and takes to his bed in despair: "I feel more ill than I ever did in all my life and verily believe that it will kill me before a few hours are over." When one of his assistants, however, brings him the news that the statue is ruined, he rushes back to take charge.

Casting the Perseus: The Final Stages

When I had got my clothes on, I strode with soul bent on mischief toward the workshop; there I beheld the men, whom I had left erewhile in such high spirits, standing stupefied and downcast. I began at once and spoke: "Up with you! Attend to me! Since you have not been able or willing to obey the directions I gave you, obey me now that I am with you to conduct my work in person. Let no one contradict me, for in cases like this we need the aid of hand and hearing, not advice." When I had uttered these words, a certain Maestro Alessandro Lastricati broke silence and said: "Look you, Benvenuto, you are going to attempt an enterprise which the laws of art do not sanction, and which cannot succeed." I turned on him with such fury and so full of mischief, that he and all the rest of them exclaimed with one voice: "On then! Give orders! We will obey your least commands, so long as life is left

in us." I believe they spoke thus feelingly because they thought I must fall shortly dead on the ground. I went immediately to inspect the furnace, and found that the metal was all curdled; an accident which we call "being caked." I told two of the hands to cross the road, and fetch from the house of the butcher Capretta a load of young oak-wood, which had lain dry for above a year; this wood had previously been offered me by Madama Ginevra, wife of the said Capretta. So soon as the first armfuls arrived, I began to fill the grate beneath the furnace. Now oak-wood of that kind heats more powerfully than any other sort of tree; and for this reason, where a slow fire is wanted, as in the case of gun-foundry, alder or pine is preferred. Accordingly, when the logs took fire, oh! how the cake began to stir beneath that awful heat, to glow and sparkle in a blaze! At the same time I kept stirring up the channels, and sent men upon the roof to stop the conflagration, which had gathered force from the increased combustion in the furnace; also, I caused boards, carpets, and other hangings to be set up against the garden, in order to protect us from the violence of the rain of sparks.

All of a sudden an explosion took place, attended by a tremendous flash of flame, as though a thunderbolt had formed and been discharged amongst us. Unwonted and appalling terror astonished every one, and me more even than the rest. When the din was over and the dazzling light extinguished, we began to look each other in the face. Then I discovered that the cap of the furnace had blown up, and the bronze was bubbling up from its source beneath. So I had the mouths of my mold immediately opened, and at the same time drove in the two

---

Turks in the century following the Turkish conquest of Constantinople (Istanbul) in 1453. The French and Spanish invasions that shook Florence and Rome in the years of the High Renaissance (see Topic 34) had no significant effect on Venetian politics. On the only important occasion when the other Italian and European powers did intervene in Venetian affairs, it was to fight at the Battle of Lepanto, in 1571, on the side of the Venetians against the Turks.

One of the factors that helped Venetian painters to develop their love of color was the arrival in Venice in 1475 of Antonello da Messina (c. 1430–1479), the only major artist of the Quattrocento born south of Rome. Either in Flanders, or, more probably, through contact with a Flemish artist working in northern Italy, Antonello had learned to work with oil paint, and he introduced the new technique to the Venetians. Oil paint permitted a far greater range of colors than the tempera (egg-based paint) or fresco used by artists elsewhere in Italy, and Venetian artists quickly took advantage of its possibilities. As for style, there is little in Venetian art of the intellectual rigor of Leonardo, let alone the *terribilità* of Michelangelo. Instead, Venetian painters concentrated on more gentle, poetic themes.

plugs which kept back the molten metal. But I noticed that it did not flow as rapidly as usual, the reason being probably that the fierce heat of the fire we kindled had consumed its base alloy. Accordingly I sent for all my pewter platters, bowls, and dishes, to the number of some two hundred pieces, and had a portion of them cast one by one into the channels, the rest into the furnace. This expedient succeeded, and every one could now perceive that my bronze was in most perfect liquefaction, and my mold was filling; whereupon they all with heartiness and happy cheer assisted and obeyed my bidding, while I, now here, now there, gave orders, helped with my own hands, and cried aloud: "O God! Thou that by Thy immeasurable power didst rise from the dead, and in Thy glory didst ascend to heaven!" . . . even thus in a moment my mold was filled; and seeing my work finished, I fell upon my knees, and with all my heart gave thanks to God.

From Cellini, B., trans. J. A. Symonds. *The Life of Benvenuto Cellini Written by Himself.* Copyright © 1906.

A Venetian Painter Contracts to Produce an Altarpiece

Many of the most important Renaissance works of art were made on commission for churches or monasteries. The following document was written in his own hand by the Venetian painter Cima da Conegliano for a work he painted in 1513.

Contract Between Cima da Conegliano and the Fathers of St. Anna

In the name of Jesus Christ and Mary. 18 April 1513, in Venice. Memorandum of agreement between me, Giovanni Battista da Conegliano, painter, living in the parish of San Luca in Venice, and Messer Alvise Grisoni, citizen of Capodistria, and procurator of the reverend fathers of S. Anna, Observants of the order of St. Francis. That I shall make for the said church a painted altarpiece and gild its frame, using good quality colors, all at my own expense, and with the figures represented as they appear in the drawing made by the frame-carver. All this shall be for a fee of seventy ducats, on the condition that when the work is complete, the said Messer Alvise, acting in the name of the afore-mentioned fathers, shall be at liberty to seek professional advice from experts chosen by him and by myself, Giovanni Battista, regarding the value of the work. And I promise to have the work ready for him by next Christmas. I acknowledge receipt of a first payment of ten ducats now, and I understand that I will receive thirty ducats when the work is complete, and the final thirty when it is delivered. As a sign of my good faith, this agreement is written in my own hand, and it is witnessed by master Vettor da Feltre, woodcarver, and my pupil Marco Luciani, both of whose signatures are appended below.

From Humfrey, Peter, *The Altarpiece in Renaissance Venice.* Yale University Press. Copyright © 1993.

THE HIGH RENAISSANCE IN VENICE: TITIAN

Titian (c. 1490–1576) was the dominating figure in Venetian art for more than 50 years and one of the supreme masters of Western painting. He was the first to use oil paint on canvas, rather than on wooden panels, the technique followed by most painters ever since. His ability to use color to depict texture—rich satin, glossy skin, thick rich hair—seems limitless. His subjects ranged from frankly sensual nudes to psychologically acute portraits to the deep spirituality of his later religious paintings.

One of his most influential works was *The Venus of Urbino* (see p. 370), painted when Titian was at the height of his powers for the duke of that city. The nude goddess reclines diagonally on crumpled sheets, in a pose imitated countless times by later artists. In the background two servants search in a chest, perhaps for a gown. The warm flesh, the fluffy little dog dozing at the foot of the couch, the deep red tones in the skirt of the standing servant behind—all play their part in building the composition by means of color.

No other Venetian artist after Titian equaled his breadth of vision. In the works of Tintoretto (1518–1594),

Michelangelo, *The Creation of Adam*. 1508–1512. 8 feet by 9 feet 2 inches (2.44 by 2.8 m). The scene forms part of a complex symbolic meaning behind the ceiling frescoes of the Sistine Chapel. Behind God's left arm, Michelangelo has placed a woman and child, representing both Eve with her children and the "New Eve," the Virgin and Child of the New Testament. Michelangelo signed the fresco—perhaps the summit of Renaissance painting—as "Michelangelo, sculptor."

Titian, *The Venus of Urbino*. 1536. 3 feet 11 inches by 5 feet 5 inches (1.19 by 1.62 m). Titian here shows a characteristic Venetian interest in richness of color and texture, rather than the Florentine preoccupation with mathematical precision of line and composition. Note the emphasis on luxury: the rich brocade, the bouquet of flowers, and the small, fluffy pet dog.

Titian's mystery becomes theatrical, with twisting figures combined in dynamic compositions. Tintoretto's emphatic style had much in common with similar developments elsewhere in Italy in the latter part of the Cinquecento. Following the extremes of Michelangelo's *Last Judgment*, artists developed a style called **Mannerism,** in which the figures were deliberately distorted and exaggerated. Mannerists such as the Florentine Bronzino (1503–1572) replaced the calm, Classical balance of Renaissance art with sophisticated elegance and intricate fantasy. The artificiality of the Mannerist conventions soon proved stilted and repetitive, and by the end of the century Mannerism was a spent force.

Putting the Visual Arts of the Italian Renaissance in Perspective

The Renaissance in Italy represented the rebirth of Classical culture, and, like the artists of Periclean Athens, the artists of the Renaissance knew that theirs was a unique moment in Western civilization. Like the builders of the Parthenon, Michelangelo intended his work in the Sistine Chapel as a "monument for all time."

In the past, sculptors and painters built on the achievements of their immediate predecessors to create new styles. The artists of the Renaissance, beginning with Brunelleschi and Donatello, deliberately and decisively broke with their traditions, to rediscover truth and beauty by following the aesthetic and philosophical ideals of antiquity. They invented more than they rediscovered, and by looking back they thrust art forward. The rapid speed with which Renaissance artists found new ways of describing human life and the world of nature gives their work a special excitement.

At the same time, Renaissance art represented just one aspect of a more general change of outlook in Western society. The career of a Michelangelo exemplified the growing development of civic identity, coupled with a new awareness of individual possibilities. The new learning, the birth of science, and the art of diplomacy are all other ways in which Renaissance culture and society reflected the sense of a fresh beginning.

The Early Renaissance in Florence was the product of several historical forces: the rise of the city-state and the economic developments that made possible the accumulation of personal fortunes such as that of the Medici. Other events also played their part: The precipitous decline of the Byzantine Empire and the fall of Constantinople in 1453 drove Byzantine scholars and intellectuals to take refuge in the West, bringing with them precious manuscripts of Classical works.

The remarkable achievement of Renaissance artists was to forge from these varied historical conditions a "modern style," which changed the way we look at the world. Their works remain relevant still and central to the Western intellectual tradition.

Questions for Further Study

1. How did Renaissance artists break with traditions? To what extent did they return to Classical styles?
2. What were the main developments in Renaissance architecture?
3. What role did private patronage play in the artistic life of the Renaissance? In what ways did it change the status of the artist?
4. Which characteristics of Michelangelo's art led his contemporaries to regard him as exceptional even by Renaissance standards? How far have later generations echoed their judgment?

Suggestions for Further Reading

Adams, Laurie Schneider. *Key Monuments of the Italian Renaissance.* Denver, CO, 1999.

Brown, Patricia. *Art and Life in Renaissance Venice.* New York, 1997.

Carmen, Charles H. *Images of Humanist Ideals in Italian Rennaissance Art.* Lewiston, NY, 2000.

Cole, Alison. *Virtue and Magnificence: Art of the Italian Renaissance Courts.* New York, 1995.

Gilbert, Creighton, ed. *Italian Art 1400-1500. Sources and Documents.* Evanston, IL, 1992.

Hollingsworth, Mary. *Patronage in Renaissance Italy: From 1400 to the Early Sixteenth Century.* Baltimore, 1994.

Humfrey, Peter. *Painting in Renaissance Venice.* New Haven, CT, 1995.

Kemp, Martin. *Behind the Picture: Art and Evidence in the Italian Renaissance.* New Haven, CT, 1997.

Nuland, Sherwin B. *Leonardo da Vinci.* New York, 2000.

Partridge, Loren. *The Art of Renaissance Rome.* New York, 1996.

Turner, A. Richard. *Renaissance Florence: The Invention of a New Art.* New York, 1997.

Welch, Evelyn. *Art and Society in Italy, 1350-1500.* Oxford, 1997.

InfoTrac College Edition

Enter the search term *Renaissance* using the Subject Guide.

Enter the search term *humanism* using the Subject Guide.

Enter the search term *Leonardo da Vinci* using Key Terms.

Enter the search term *Michelangelo* using Key Terms.

ARTS AND LETTERS IN RENAISSANCE EUROPE

As the effects of the Italian Renaissance began to diffuse throughout the rest of Europe, they produced vast and rapid cultural changes. The most powerful new force was printing, which was first invented in the mid-15th century. By 1500, books and pamphlets were circulating in increasing numbers, spreading ideas as the rate of literacy rose. One of the most important long-term consequences was the rise of vernacular literature.

In northern Europe, the humanistic learning developed in Italy took on new forms, as Christian humanists like the Dutch Erasmus combined Classical ideas with traditional Christian attitudes. Both Erasmus and his English friend Thomas More wrote books attacking the religious and social attitudes of their times, in an attempt to define the nature of a truly Christian society. Erasmus's attacks on corruption in the church foreshadowed many of the criticisms of Martin Luther.

In Italy, the leading humanists of the High Renaissance continued to develop themes taken from Classical literature and learning. Castiglione's book, *The Courtier*, discussed the nature of virtue and the ideals of Platonic love. Machiavelli drew on the history of Republican Rome as background for his book, *The Prince*, a study of political power.

As the artistic advances made in Italy began to cross the Alps, Northern artists adapted their styles accordingly. Van Eyck and his Flemish school, working in oils, soon established a market throughout Europe—including Italy—for their finely detailed panel paintings. The Flemish painters retained stylistic links with their Late Medieval past. The great German painter Albrecht Dürer, by contrast, drew on the High Renaissance to forge his own personal style.

The art of Renaissance music often transcended national boundaries. The musical traditions of northern Europe influenced composers in both Rome and Venice, where two musicians from the Low Countries, Josquin des Pres and Adrian Willaert, held important posts.

Toward the middle of the 16th century, the Reformation began to exert a growing influence on the arts in northern Europe. Protestant denunciations of the use of paintings and statues in churches caused a rapid decline in the production of sacred visual art. Literature and music, however, met with the reformers' approval. The results laid the foundations for the flourishing of sacred music and secular painting in 17th-century northern Europe.

THE PRINTING REVOLUTION

The invention of printing with movable type revolutionized Western civilization. The earliest known manufacture of individual characters that could be combined and reused occurred in China as early as the 11th century, but a similar technique developed in Europe only in the mid-15th century. Its introduction is generally credited to the German Johann Gutenberg (c. 1397–1468). The first printed Bible, the so-called Gutenberg Bible, appeared in 1455. Twenty years later, William Caxton (c. 1422–1491) published the first book printed in English, and in 1501 Aldus Manutius (1450–1515) began to sell inexpensive editions of the classics, printed by his Aldine Press in Venice.

THE IMPLICATIONS OF PRINTING

Probably no technological development before the 19th century created such profound changes in Western culture as the invention of printing. The implications of the communications revolution it inaugurated are still with us at the dawn of the 21st century. Among its consequences were the standardization of texts, the acceleration of science, the spread of education—including, increasingly, that of women—and the rapid diffusion of new ideas. Martin Luther's Protestant Reformation was one of the first movements to benefit from the circulation of books and pamphlets (see Topic 39).

Before the mid-15th century, books were extremely expensive, and the supply never equalled the demand. Handwritten copies were produced by stationers—so-called because they worked in a settled, or stationary, place of business—and sold or rented out by booksellers. Most dealers in books worked for the universities. University officials kept a stringent control on the trade and fixed the prices for the benefit of their students, who often hired a book for use during a university session and then returned it to the bookshop. The only people who received no financial benefit from the circulation of books were the authors.

With the introduction of printing technology, the publishers took over the production and distribution of books. The figures attest to the astonishing growth in the publishing industry. By 1500, European presses had distributed between 6 and 9 million books in 13,000 different editions. One of the most popular works of Erasmus, *In Praise of Folly*, went through 27 editions in his own lifetime. Many of these were pirated, generally from the printers to whom authors customarily sold their rights. Unless authors published their own works, they continued to make little profit from their "intellectual property." The first international copyright agreement was signed only in 1886, and the United States did not subscribe until 1929.

PRINTING AND THE VERNACULAR

Most educated Europeans before the Renaissance used two languages: their own native tongue—the vernacular—and Latin. Some popular literature in the vernacular appeared in France, Germany, and England (see Topic 28), but in many countries the first literary works in their own languages were printed ones, often translations of the Bible into the vernacular. In Finland, the Finnish language appeared in written form for the first time as late as the 16th century, in the first printed Bible in Finnish.

In preparing their translations, scholars did not restrict themselves to the standard Latin version of the Bible. Erasmus used three separate Greek manuscripts to compile an edition of the New Testament in Latin. Martin Luther used Erasmus's work in making his great translation of the Bible into German, while for the Psalms he turned to the original Hebrew edition, which had been published in 1516.

When, a century later, the so-called King James Version of the Bible appeared in England, its translators claimed to have consulted editions and commentaries in Hebrew, Chaldean, Syriac, Greek, and Latin, as well as modern versions in Spanish, French, Italian, and Dutch. The consequences for the development of literary culture were profound. In England, the wide diffusion of both the King James Bible and the Anglican *Book of Common Prayer* shaped the future history of the language.

By no means were all printed works in the vernacular of a religious nature. Scholars continued to use Latin for learned communications, but authors who wanted to reach the wider, less academic audience made possible by printing increasingly wrote in their own languages. Castiglione and Machiavelli both published in Italian, and Sir Thomas More in English. Montaigne wrote his essays, inspired by a study of the Classics, in French.

Molite ergo aſſimilari eis. Scit enim pater veſter quid opus ſit vobis : antequã petatis eum. Sic ergo vos orabitis. Pater noſter qui es in celis ſanctificetur nomē tuũ. Adueniat regnũ tuũ. Fiat volũtas tua : ſicut in celo et in terra. Panē noſtrũ ſupſubſtãtialē da nobis hodie. Et dimitte nobis debita noſtra : ſicut et nos dimittimus debitoribus noſtris. Et ne nos inducas in temptationē : ſed libera nos a malo. Si enim dimiſeritis hominibʒ peccata eoꝝ : dimittet et vobis pater veſter celeſtis delicta veſtra. Si autem non dimiſeritis hominibus : nec pa

Portion of a page from the Gutenberg Bible. 1455. The Latin text of the Lord's Prayer (Matthew 6, 9–13) begins on the fourth line with "Pater noster." The first edition of this Bible, printed at Mainz, probably consisted of no more than 150 copies.

Rare Books and Manuscript Division, New York Public Library, Astor, Lenox and Tilden Foundations

The printing revolution was not limited to literary texts. The publication of music led to the wide circulation of Lutheran hymns and secular Italian madrigals. Dürer and other contemporary artists were quick to exploit the possibilities of the print, first in the form of relatively easily produced woodcuts and then in the more difficult medium of line engravings on copper plates. Book publishers began to include visual material in the form of illustrations or diagrams in their printed volumes. No less important in an era of exploration was the printing and circulation of maps and charts (see Topic 38).

The long-term consequence of all these innovations was to undermine the authority of the established institutions of medieval culture and society. People who could read for themselves had independent access to the ideas of others and had less need to turn to the church, the monasteries, or the universities for guidance and instruction. The invention of printing was a key factor in the evolution of the secular state.

THE NORTHERN HUMANISTS: EDUCATION FOR A CHRISTIAN SOCIETY

As humanism began to spread in northern Europe, thinkers there tried to reconcile humanist principles with Christianity. These northern Christian humanists accepted many of the values of Classical Antiquity—idealism, the power of reason, the importance of ancient texts—but used them as a basis for reforming the Christianity of their day, rather than as an end in themselves.

In part, Christian humanism in northern Europe drew its strength from resentment at the corruption of the church in Rome. In Germany, in particular, hostility toward Italian religious leaders combined with nationalism to create a wish to throw off Roman domination and return Christianity to its simple origins. Elsewhere, northern humanists directed their fire against social inequities as well as religious abuses. The English statesman and writer Sir Thomas More (1478–1535) published a satire called *Utopia* (1516–1517). It describes an ideal state, Utopia (his invented name means "no place" in Greek), on an island in the New World. The citizens of Utopia live in a social and political paradise, and when one of them visits England, he contrasts his own society with the social injustices he finds there. The title of More's book added a new word to the English language.

ERASMUS, PRINCE OF HUMANISTS

One of More's closest friends was the man recognized by his contemporaries as the "Prince of Humanists," the Dutch priest and intellectual Desiderius Erasmus (1466–1536). A truly international figure, Erasmus studied and taught in Italy, at Oxford and Cambridge, and at Paris.

Metropolitan Museum of Art (Fletcher Fund, 1919/19.73.120), all rights reserved

Albrecht Dürer, *Portrait of Erasmus of Rotterdam*. 1526. 9¼ inches by 7½ inches (25 by 19 cm). The inscribed panel in the upper left corner is, in characteristic Renaissance style, written in both Latin and Greek. The Latin lines tell us that Erasmus posed for Dürer's portrait, while the Greek refers to the power of the written word. The artist's monogram below appears on almost all of his work.

The writings of Erasmus were the most comprehensive humanist attempt to reconcile Classical learning and simple Christianity. He revered the Classical emphasis on the personal dignity of the individual and on the importance of education. He steeped himself in the works of ancient literature available to him. At the same time, as a Christian, he tried to return to the original "philosophy of Christ," as it was expressed in the Sermon on the Mount, claiming that pure faith was more important than formal religious ceremony. He also attacked the complexity of Medieval Catholic theology, claiming that some issues could never be known: He felt that Christians needed to believe only such basic aspects of their faith as the Creed.

Erasmus wrote his most successful book in 1509 while staying in England as a house guest of Sir Thomas More. The original Latin form of its title, *In Praise of Folly*, was a pun in honor of his distinguished host: The Latin words *Encomium Moriae* can mean "praise of folly" or "praise of More." The tone is lighthearted, but Erasmus is unsparing in his denunciations of social and religious corruption. Among his targets are hypocritical priests and cardinals, fraudulent scholars, and venal lawyers.

For all the force of his criticism, Erasmus was a true moderate. Unlike Martin Luther, he believed that it was possible to reform the church from within. When Luther's

Reformation split the Christian world, Erasmus remained a Catholic. Both sides denounced him: the Catholics for his criticisms of the church and the Protestants because he would not throw his considerable weight behind the Reform movement. The final break between Erasmus and Luther came in 1524, when Erasmus published a pamphlet asserting that humans had free will. Luther's reply came in a tract published the following year. Human will, he claimed, was fatally flawed, and only the grace of God could rescue an individual from the fires of hell. The two men never spoke again.

THE *COURTIER* AND *THE PRINCE:* HANDBOOKS OF RENAISSANCE STRATEGY

While Christian humanists in northern Europe hotly debated the best way to achieve religious reform, humanist writers in Italy occupied themselves with more worldly affairs.

CASTIGLIONE THE COURTIER
Baldassare Castiglione (1478–1529), born into an ancient aristocratic family, received a thorough humanistic educa-

Raphael, *Portrait of Baldassare Castiglione,* c. 1514. 2 feet 6 inches by 2 feet 2 inches (76 by 66 cm). The expert on good manners turns gravely toward us, dressed in rich but not ostentatious clothes. The neutral background and sober gaze reflect Castiglione's views on how the ideal courtier should behave.

Copyright Réunion des Musées Nationaux/Art Resource, NY

tion before serving in the diplomatic corps of Milan, Mantua, and eventually Urbino, where he settled for several years. The duke of Urbino was one of the leading artistic patrons of the day, and his court was a center for writers and intellectuals.

Early in his stay at Urbino, Castiglione conceived the idea of writing a book about life at an ideal court. The result, *The Courtier,* appeared in an edition published by the Aldine Press in 1528, the year before its author's death. Castiglione's work takes the form of a series of imaginary discussions between members of the court on the qualities of the ideal courtier. Drawing on the works of a host of ancient authors, from Plato to Cicero, Castiglione's characters discuss a wide range of topics: Classical views of virtue, the notion of chivalry, Platonic (that is, ideal) love, and above all the nature of the true courtier.

The most important quality in an ideal courtier—and human being—is versatility. Humanistic learning is important, as is a knowledge of Greek and Latin, but so are horsemanship and skills with a sword. The ideal courtier should write both prose and verse, appreciate music and painting, and also hunt, wrestle, and play tennis. Impeccable morals must be combined with exquisite manners and the ability to make fascinating conversation. In love, the true gentleman should worship his beloved's beauty of mind as much as that of her body.

None of these attributes should be so marked that it dominates the others—Castiglione's ideal is the *uomo universale,* the well-rounded person. Equally important is the cultivation of *sprezzatura,* an almost untranslatable Italian word, which suggests an air of casual ease. None of the courtier's accomplishments must seem an effort or draw attention to itself.

The imaginary participants in Castiglione's dialogues also discuss the ideal court lady. With the exception of athletics and warfare, she should cultivate the same skills as men, adding to them charm, grace, and physical attractiveness. She should wear little makeup and avoid calling attention to herself in dress, conduct, or reputation. Above all, she should be feminine, for women exert a civilizing influence on the rough male world. Castiglione argues that women should be the educated equals of men because they make an equally important contribution to society. The emphasis on education and the worth of the individual, whether male or female, is the product of Castiglione's humanistic training, and in strong contrast with the medieval tradition whereby women were excluded from universities.

It is easy to criticize Castiglione for his excessive concern with refinement and the details of courtly decorum, but his description of the ideals of Italian Renaissance court society at the moment of its greatest splendor is deeply felt and elegantly expressed.

MACHIAVELLI THE REALIST
Castiglione's essentially optimistic view of human nature is certainly in the strongest contrast with the opinions of Niccolò Machiavelli (1469–1527), whose writings on political theory drew on his practical experience as statesman. In

1498, when the Florentines drove out their Medici rulers and set up a republic, Machiavelli served his city as diplomat. In the course of his missions, he met many of the leading figures of the day. Among those to make a mark on the observant ambassador were the ruthless Cesare Borgia (1476–1507) and his notorious sister Lucrezia Borgia (1480–1519).

In 1512, with the fall of the Republic and the return of the Medici, the new rulers dismissed Machiavelli from his post, imprisoned and tortured him, and eventually banished him to his family's country estate just outside Florence. Living in exile there, within a year he had completed his most influential work, *The Prince*, a practical guide to the use of political power. It circulated in manuscript during Machiavelli's lifetime, but was published only in 1532, after his death.

Reactions to its apparently cynical endorsement of tyranny and treachery were predictably mixed. The Catholic Church denounced it and listed it on the *Index of Prohibited Books*. The very word *Machiavellian* soon came to mean scheming and unscrupulous, and in England "Old Nick" became synonymous with the devil. On the other hand, many rulers turned to *The Prince* for practical guidance in running a state. Among Machiavelli's later readers and admirers were Catherine the Great of Russia and Napoleon.

Machiavelli's attitude toward political power grew out of the specific historical context of his times. He saw the Italian states of the 16th century as helpless and at the mercy of the rivalries of France and Spain. Italy was "without head, without order, beaten, despoiled, lacerated." When the republic that the Florentines had set up to regain control over their own destiny ended in abject failure, Machiavelli believed that only the creation of a powerful and stable Florentine state could protect Italy against constant foreign intervention. The Medici seemed to offer the promise of strong government, and the Medici pope then ruling in Rome, Leo X, could provide support.

For Florence's new rulers to be effective, however, they needed to set aside moral scruples and take firm charge. Machiavelli's ideal of good government was that of the ancient Roman Republic (509–31 B.C.): He saw its citizens as virtuous and considered the volunteer citizen legions of ancient Rome infinitely preferable to the mercenary armies of his own day. The first crucial step for a modern ruler, he believed, was to reduce the political power of the church. Christianity's role in government had proved disastrous, and the church should limit itself to purely spiritual matters.

The head of state, the Prince of the book's title, should rule by using power wisely and ruthlessly. No moral consideration should deter the Prince from performing this task. Thus cruelty, sensibly used, consolidates power and discourages revolution. Nor was honesty a factor: "A prince must not keep faith when by doing so it would be against his self-interest." In short, because his subjects lack virtue, the Prince must do whatever is necessary to keep the state intact. Nor should he overestimate his subjects: "They are ungrateful, changeable, runaways in danger, eager for gain; while you do well by them, they are all yours; when you are in need, they turn away."

THE CONQUEST OF REALITY: RENAISSANCE ART IN THE NORTH

As in the other arts, developments in Italian Renaissance painting took a while to circulate north of the Alps. When, in the mid-15th century, Florentine merchants began to expand their trade with Flanders, they found a brilliant school of painters already flourishing there.

JAN VAN EYCK AND THE FLEMISH SCHOOL

The greatest of all Flemish painters was Jan van Eyck (before 1395–1441), whose art, according to the father of Raphael, "challenges nature itself." His fame was based on his remarkable use of color, his extraordinary ability to render details realistically, and his technical innovations in the use of oil paint. When Antonello da Messina introduced the use of oil paint into Italy in 1475 (see Topic 35), he was using methods developed earlier in the century by Jan van Eyck.

One of Van Eyck's most celebrated works is a further illustration of the growing links between Italy and northern Europe. Another of the Medici agents in Flanders, Giovanni Arnolfini, who came from Lucca in Tuscany, was a counselor of the ruler of Flanders, the duke of Burgundy.

By Courtesy of the Trustees of the National Gallery, London

Jan van Eyck, *Giovanni Arnolfini and His Bride*. 1434. 32 by 23 inches (81 by 59.7 cm). One of the figures reflected in the mirror is perhaps the artist, as he stands in the doorway. The Latin words on the wall read: "Jan van Eyck was here."

The duke was patron of Van Eyck, and it was probably through this connection that Arnolfini commissioned Van Eyck to paint *The Marriage of Giovanni Arnolfini and Giovanna Cenami*. The artist signed the work and dated it, 1434, on the back wall visible in the painting.

Van Eyck's mastery is apparent in his naturalistic depictions of the various textures: fur, wood, metal, cloth. The sense of space is realistically conveyed, with the cool light coming in from the window illuminating bride and groom in the foreground, while the inner recesses of the room are in shadow. On the back wall, below the artist's signature, there hangs a mirror in which two figures (perhaps witnesses to the marriage) are reflected.

The literal, almost photographic, quality of the scene is the equivalent in three dimensions of the pages from the *Très Riches Heures* (see Topic 30), and typical of the finest Flemish art of the period. So is the abundant use of symbolism. The dog at the couple's feet perhaps represents fidelity. The apples by the window symbolize Adam and Eve, and thereby original sin, and the broom leaning on the wall outside stands for domestic care. Giovanna's hand is over her womb, and the tiny carved statue atop the chair in the background is of Margaret, patron saint of child-bearing.

BOSCH AND BRUEGHEL

If many of Van Eyck's contemporaries and immediate successors imitated his style, although without his superlative technique, two other Flemish artists of the period fit into no general category.

The first of them, Hieronymus Bosch (c. 1450–1516), is one of the great originals in the history of painting. His bizarre scenes depict a fantasy world of demons and monsters, in which the human activities seem as inexplicable as the creatures surrounding them. His most elaborate work, *The Garden of Earthly Delights*, illustrates Bosch's belief that the pleasures of the flesh lead to damnation. The journey from the Creation of Adam and Eve in the left-hand panel to the horrors of hell in the right-hand panel involves frantic scenes of erotic activity. Bosch's message seems to be that even if sinners have the possibility of seeking redemption through Christ, most people are too foolish and depraved to do so.

The other great Flemish painter of the 16th century, Pieter Brueghel (1525–1569), shared Bosch's pessimism, and many of his scenes show the violent consequences of human folly. For Brueghel, however, the transcendent power and beauty of Nature compensate for human sin. In paintings such as *Hunters in the Snow*, the figures shrink to mere specks, dwarfed by the majesty of the mountain landscape—perhaps a memory of the Alps, brought back from a trip the artist made to Italy.

DÜRER AND THE
RENAISSANCE IN GERMANY

No northern painter was more influenced by Italian Renaissance ideas than the great German artist Albrecht Dürer (1471–1528). He visited Italy in 1494 and again in 1505–1507, when he spent most of his time in Venice, discussing art with Bellini and other Venetian painters. The

Hieronymus Bosch, *The Garden of Earthly Delights,* c. 1505–1510. 7 feet 2 inches by 6 feet 5 inches (2.2 by .97 m). Perhaps surprisingly, this catalog of the sins of the flesh was one of the favorite works of the gloomy Spanish king, Philip II. Its three panels represent a journey from Eden, where God nervously contemplates his new creations, Adam and Eve, to the diabolical scenes on the right-hand panel.

Albrecht Dürer, *The Fall of Man (Adam and Eve)*. 1504. 10 by 7½ inches (25 by 19 cm). The animals symbolize the sins and diseases resulting from Adam and Eve's eating the apple from the Tree of Knowledge: The cat stands for pride and cruelty, the ox gluttony and sloth. The detailed anatomy of the human figures is an attempt to return to Classical models.

Photograph © 2003 Museum of Fine Arts, Boston

splendor of the Venetians' use of color made a deep impression on Dürer, and many of his works at this time imitate Venetian color techniques.

A true student of the Renaissance interest in Classical art, Dürer worked out a careful system of proportion based on his readings of Classical authors. In his engraving of *Adam and Eve*, the anatomy and proportions of the figures are based on Classical sculptures—an example of Christian humanism in visible form.

Toward the end of his life, Dürer abandoned painting and devoted himself to engraving and the writing of theoretical works on art. At the time of his death he was preparing *Four Books on Human Proportions*, a work that combined two of the basic concerns of the Renaissance: a return to Classical ideals of beauty, and the quest for scientific precision.

MUSIC IN THE HIGH RENAISSANCE

With the invention of printing and the circulation of printed music, the barriers between musical life in northern and southern Europe became less severe, and by the end of the 15th century, musicians were beginning to travel from one region to the other. The main musical centers in the High Renaissance were Rome and Venice in Italy; and France, Flanders, and England in the North.

MUSIC AT THE PAPAL COURT

The leading choir in Italy, that of the Sistine Chapel, was founded by Pope Sixtus IV in 1473. Its members were all male, with adolescent boys, their voices still unbroken, singing the soprano parts. Between 1486 and 1494, the director of music in the Sistine Chapel was the Flemish composer Josquin des Pres (c. 1440–1521), the greatest musician of his day. His works, many of them written especially for the Sistine choir, have a strong sense of formal structure and balance, and show careful attention to the word-setting—all characteristics likely to appeal to the Italian humanists.

Toward the mid-16th century, the dominant musical figure at Rome was Giovanni Pierluigi da Palestrina (1525–1594). After working his way up directing the choirs of various Roman basilicas, in 1571 he took charge of all music at the Vatican. Palestrina's period at the Vatican coincided with the reforms introduced at the Council of Trent, in response to the Protestant Reformation (see Topic 41). His music is generally traditional in style and preserves the roots of church music in Gregorian chant.

VENICE: MUSIC AT ST. MARK'S

By contrast with the essentially traditional style favored at Rome, Venetian composers were more experimental. In 1527 a Dutchman, Adrian Willaert (c. 1490–1562), became director of music at St. Mark's. Among his pupils were Andrea Gabrieli (c. 1520–1586) and Gabrieli's nephew Giovanni (c. 1556–1612). The latter became the most important Venetian composer of the day, and one of the most remarkable in Europe.

Many of the works written for performance in St. Mark's took advantage of the building's design, with two galleries, one on each side of the church. Giovanni Gabrieli frequently stationed a choir on either side, often reinforced with instruments, generally organ, but sometimes trumpets and even drums. The effect of the sounds coming from left and right—a kind of Renaissance stereophony—is often thrilling, as the massed voices and brass instruments echo and overlap in the interior of the church, which glittered with mosaics. If Roman composers such as Palestrina sought to find the equivalent of Raphael's ideal Classical beauty, the music of Gabrieli glows with the rich colors of Titian.

MUSIC IN NORTHERN EUROPE

Just as northern composers carried their styles south to Italy, so Italian musical forms worked their way to the North. The Italian madrigal, a setting of secular verse for three or more voices, became especially popular with northern composers.

One of the leading French composers of *chansons*, as madrigals were called in France, was Clément Janequin

(c. 1485–c. 1560). Janequin was famous for writing songs that told a story by imitating specific sounds—a form of early "program music." One of his best-known pieces was "*La Guerre*"—"The War"—in which the voices reproduce the noises of rattling guns, fanfares, and the shouts of soldiers. These French *chansons* lack the calm beauty and rich harmonies of the best Italian madrigals, but they have a striking rhythmic vitality and sense of fun to compensate.

In England the leading composer of the 16th century was Thomas Tallis (c. 1505–1585). A master of counterpoint, Tallis developed the art of combining different vocal lines to new heights of complexity. In his great setting of the text *Spem in Alium* ("Hope in Another"), he used no less than 40 separate individual voices, each winding independently around the others. The effect is of extraordinary emotional complexity coupled with the highest intellectual control.

Putting Arts and Letters in Renaissance Europe in Perspective

While writers and artists in Italy continued in the 16th century to work through many of the implications of the 15th-century Renaissance developments, those in northern Europe had a more complex task. In the first place, the break in the North between medieval culture and the new Renaissance ideas was less abrupt than in Italy. Painters like Bosch and composers like Tallis retained their links with the long medieval religious and cultural tradition of their art.

Then, too, Italians had the material remains of ancient culture around them. Raphael could study actual Roman sculptures as they emerged from the excavations he supervised in Rome, while Dürer had to develop his theories of ideal proportion from reading ancient texts.

The greatest difference of all was the religious split caused by the Reformation. There is scarcely a northern creative figure of note whose work was not influenced in one way or another by the upheavals of faith that marked the 16th century. Even Erasmus, who rejected Luther's break with the Catholic Church, reflected the uncertainty of the times in his writings.

Protestant attitudes toward the arts had long-term consequences for future cultural developments in northern Europe. Their rejection of the use of painting and sculpture in sacred buildings meant that, by the end of the 16th century, religious art had virtually died out there, to be replaced by secular themes such as the portrait and still life. Luther's encouragement of music, on the other hand, stimulated a wave of creative energy, which was to reach its highest point a century later in the works of Johann Sebastian Bach.

Questions for Further Study

1. How did Renaissance cultural developments differ in Italy and northern Europe? Were the differences consistent in all of the arts?
2. What was the effect of printing on Renaissance culture?
3. In what ways did Castiglione and Machiavelli, for all their differences, both express the spirit of their times?

Suggestions for Further Reading

Brown, Howard Mayer, and Louise K. Stein. *Music in the Renaissance*. Upper Saddle River, NJ, 1999.

Campbell, Lorne. *The Fifteenth Century Netherlandish Schools*. London, 1998.

Eisenstein, E. *The Printing Revolution in Early Modern Europe*. Cambridge, MA, 1983.

Harbison, Craig. *The Mirror of the Artist: Northern Renaissance Art in its Historical Context*. New York, 1995.

Landau, David, and Peter Parshall. *The Renaissance Print:* New Haven, CT, 1994.

Marius, R. *Thomas More*. New York, 1984.

McGrath, A.E. *The Intellectual Origins of the European Reformation*. Oxford, 1987.

Rabil, A., ed. *Renaissance Humanism*. Philadelphia, 1988.

Skinner, Q. *Machiavelli*. Oxford, 1981.

Snyder, J. *Northern Renaissance Art*. Englewood Cliffs, NJ, 1985.

Viroli, Maurizio. Antony Shugaar, trans. *Niccolo's Smile: A Biography of Machiavelli*. New York, 2000.

InfoTrac College Edition

Enter the search term *Renaissance* using the Subject Guide.

Enter the search term *humanism* using the Subject Guide.

Enter the search term *Machiavelli* using Key Terms.

UPHEAVAL AND TRANSFORMATION IN EASTERN EUROPE

During the 15th and 16th centuries, Western Europe underwent important political changes as centralized states emerged in the place of feudal localism. In the East, the same period saw a similar transformation, although often in quite different circumstances. The venerable Byzantine Empire, which had held sway over the eastern half of the Mediterranean world since the 4th century, experienced a severe decline under the impact of the Western crusading armies and the Mongol invasions. The Paleologus restoration in the 13th century tried to halt the decline, but two centuries later the Empire finally collapsed in the face of the rising power of the Ottoman Turks. The Ottomans built their own state on the foundations of Byzantium, extending the rule of Islam throughout the Balkans, Asia Minor, the Middle East, and North Africa.

The process of state formation in eastern Europe was complicated by the fact that portions of the Slavic peoples who inhabited the Balkan region had come under the influence of Eastern Orthodox Christianity, while other Slavs living in areas of central Europe had been converted to Roman Christianity. Despite this religious division, however, centralized monarchies developed in Hungary, Bohemia, and Poland, along with distinctive national cultures. Further east, in Russia, which the Mongols dominated for two centuries, a centralized state also emerged, first at Kiev, and then at Moscow.

SIGNIFICANT DATES

Eastern Europe

997–1038	Stephen rules Magyars
c. 1162–1227	Genghis Khan rules Mongols
1253–1278	Ottokar II rules Bohemia
1331–1355	Stephen Dushan rules as king of Serbs
1333–1370	Casimir III "the Great" rules Poland
1374–1415	Life of Jan Hus
1453	Ottoman Turks seize Constantinople
1458–1490	Matthias Corvinus rules as king of Hungary
1462–1505	Ivan III the Great rules Muscovy
1520–1566	Suleiman I "the Magnificent" rules Ottoman Empire
1571	Battle of Lepanto

THE COLLAPSE OF BYZANTIUM

Ever since the 11th century, when the Seljuk Turks began to overrun Asia Minor, the Byzantine Empire had suffered one crippling disaster after another. The Western crusaders who moved east in response to the appeal of the Emperor Alexius Comnenus in 1095 had sacked Constantinople in 1204 and divided the empire into feudal states. When Michael VIII Paleologus managed to retake the throne in 1261, (see Topic 27), the reestablished Empire was a remnant of its former greatness. Nevertheless, it persisted for almost another two centuries until its final collapse in 1453.

THE PALEOLOGUS RESTORATION

The Paleologus dynasty was the last of the Byzantine families to rule the Eastern Empire. Michael and his descendants, under whom the Greeks took back control of the state apparatus as well as of the church, tried to restore the earlier glory of Constantinople. But with their power and wealth reduced, they were increasingly subject to domestic challenges and to the political and military ambitions of their neighbors.

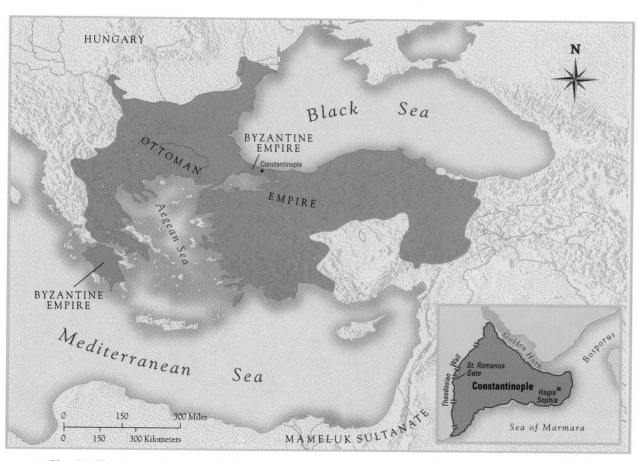

Map 37.1 The Ottoman Empire and Collapse of the Byzantine Empire, c. 1450. The inexorable spread of the Ottoman Turks, and the fratricidal feuding of the Crusaders, had reduced the Byzantine Empire to the land within the walls of Constantinople and a few fiefdoms in southern Greece. All that protected the city were the Theodosian Walls, built a millennium earlier. The final Turkish assault came in the early hours of Tuesday, May 29, 1453 (see p. 385). In the late afternoon, Mehmed II (afterwards known as Mehmed the Conqueror) entered Justinian's Church of Hagia Sophia (Holy Wisdom) and ordered it converted into a mosque. He was 21 years old. Go to http://info.wadsworth.com/053461065X for an interactive version of this map.

The Byzantine nobles successfully ignored imperial authority and ruled their own estates as independent feudal lords, pressing the peasantry on their lands into archaic forms of serfdom. With the dominance of Venice, Genoa, and other Italian trading empires in the Mediterranean, the Byzantine economy steadily declined, and even its once solid coinage began to be debased as inflation spread. The Eastern Orthodox Church, which had provided the emperors with divine blessing and had played an important role in maintaining imperial authority, was mired in doctrinal disagreements that weakened its hold over the people.

BYZANTIUM AND THE MONGOLS

Added to these difficulties was the fact that within its own borders Byzantium experienced growing unrest and resistance from its Slavic populations (see Topic 22), while from the outside came a sudden and shocking danger from the Mongols.

The Mongols were nomadic Asiatic tribes from the area of north-central China where Mongolia is located today. Although they were wild and unruly, one of their chieftains, Genghis Khan (c. 1162–1227) succeeded in uniting them and forging a powerful army. From his capital at Karakorum, Genghis Khan's army, known as the Golden Horde, quickly overran large tracts of China before moving westward through Russia and into Persia. The Mongols killed and conquered with great ferocity and struck terror in their enemies.

Under the successors of Genghis Khan, one Mongol force captured Baghdad and destroyed the 500-year-old Abbasid caliphate in 1258. Meanwhile, another group moved north into Europe, conquering Russia, invading Poland and Hungary, and subduing the Bulgarians and other Slavic peoples of the region. In 1242, however, as they stood on the plains of Hungary, the Mongols suddenly stopped their westward expansion and began to withdraw, racked by divisions over the question of succession. Although they established their dominance over a vast region that stretched from Russia to the Pacific, the Mongols bequeathed no significant cultural legacy. They did, however, leave the Byzantine Empire seriously weakened and unable to resist the last great external threat that arrived in the form of the Ottoman Turks.

THE OTTOMANS AND THE EUROPEAN RESPONSE

The Ottoman (or Osmanli) Turks had settled in northwestern Asia Minor in the 13th century, where they became vassals of the Seljuks. They began to emerge as an autonomous state as the Seljuk empire disintegrated and subsequently expanded into the Balkans, where they overran the Bulgarians and the Serbs. Like the Bulgarians, the Serbs had converted to Orthodox Christianity and founded their own state under King Stephen Dushan (ruled 1331–1355). The Serbs copied the legal structures and courtly practices of the Byzantines, and Stephen laid claim to rule over other peoples in the area, including the Bulgarians, Albanians, and Greeks. The Ottomans crossed the Straits into the

Map 37.2 Expansion of the Slavs. Note the three main divisions into East, West, and South Slavs. These labels describe their eventual destinations, not their origins: Yugoslavia, created in 1919 out of parts of the fallen Austrian and Ottoman Empires, means literally "Land of the South Slavs." All of the Slavs spoke (and still speak) related languages. The language of Romania, which was never settled by Slavs, belongs to the Romance family (i.e., like French and Italian, it derives from Latin). Go to http://info.wadsworth.com/053461065X for an interactive version of this map.

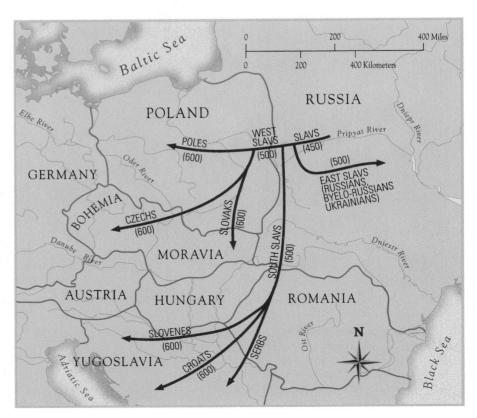

Balkans in 1354, defeating the Serbs at the Battle of Kosovo in 1389 and establishing their capital at Adrianople.

THE FALL OF CONSTANTINOPLE

When the Ottomans proceeded to lay siege to Constantinople, the West gathered a crusade to turn them back. The crusade was poorly organized, and at Nicopolis in 1396 the Turks defeated the knights and killed or captured some 10,000 Europeans. Six years later Tamerlane (c. 1336–1405), a Mongol tribal leader who claimed descent from Genghis Khan, defeated the Turks and relieved the siege of Constantinople. But Tamerlane's victory only delayed the inevitable.

In May 1453, some 160,000 Turkish soldiers under Sultan Mehmed (or Muhammad) II (ruled 1451–1481) smashed a tiny force of 9,000 Byzantines and Genoese troops led by Constantine XI (ruled 1449–1453). Mehmed personally commanded the attack on the walls of the city, which were breached with specially designed cannons of immense size, and Constantine, the last Byzantine emperor, died defending one of the city's gates. The fall of Constantinople—renamed Istanbul by its conquerors—after only 50 days of fighting came as a great demoralizing shock to the rest of Europe.

Ara Güler, Istanbul

Portrait of Mehmed II, who personally led the Ottoman forces that took Constantinople—thereafter Istanbul—in 1453. The Sultan, known as "the Conquerer," is shown sniffing a flower. The Ottoman Turks were enthusiastic cultivators of plants and gardens, and many of the designs that appear on Turkish painted tiles show flowers; the most popular was the tulip.

Mehmed, known as the Conqueror, must be considered the true founder of the Ottoman Empire, and his policies set the pattern for centuries to come. Moving his capital from Adrianople to Istanbul, he began to restore the city to its former glory, repopulating it with Muslim, Christian, and Jewish immigrants. Mehmed personally embraced the Sunni version of Islam (see Topic 23), and although he permitted his Christian and Jewish subjects to practice their religion freely, he converted the Church of Hagia Sophia to a mosque. A patron of learning and the arts, he brought skilled craftsmen and the most talented artists to work on his new capital.

THE OTTOMAN EMPIRE

The Ottomans became famous for their excellent military and political organization. Their empire, which reached its peak in the 16th century, extended deep into Persia and Arabia. Selim I "the Grim" (ruled 1512–1520) defeated the Mamelukes of Egypt and Syria, seizing Cairo in 1517. Under the Turks, Egypt became a province ruled by a *pasha*, or viceroy, appointed from Istanbul. The next year, when the Ottomans took Algiers, they created an empire that stretched across North Africa into the Middle East and up into Asia Minor and the Balkans.

In the hinterland of North Africa, known as the Maghreb, the Ottomans ruled several separate provinces through the same kind of local administrations as they had established in Egypt. Tripoli, Algiers, and Tunis were quasi-independent of Istanbul and controlled by governors and the famous slave corps of troops known as the Janissaries, originally Christians from the Balkans who were converted to Islam. These cities, especially Algiers, were the headquarters for the Turkish *corsairs*, or pirates, who raided European shipping off the coast.

Morocco held a unique place in the Ottoman Empire. In the mid-16th century, an Arab family, the Sa'dids—who claimed descent from Muhammad—united Morocco and ruled the region until 1659. The Sa'dids extended their control south, beyond the Sahara, where they conquered the kingdom of Songhay in 1591 and sacked Timbuktu. In the hinterland and the Atlas Mountains, the nomads were sometimes forced to pay tribute but otherwise remained independent.

Ottoman achievements reached their zenith under Selim's son, Suleiman I, "the Magnificent" (ruled 1520–1566). The golden age of Ottoman culture began after the conquest of Istanbul. Poets began writing in original forms rather than copying from the Persians, as they had done in the past, and court writers produced magnificent plays and short stories. Turkish literature, architecture, and art also flourished. Mehmed built a great Seraglio Palace, whose formidable walls surrounded courtyards and fountains, while Suleiman achieved even more splendid results in the Suleimanye, a complex containing a mosque and his own mausoleum.

TURKS AND EUROPEANS

The Ottoman conquest unleashed a struggle between the Turks and the Christian monarchs of Europe. Suleiman's

Painting of the Battle of Lepanto, which took place in 1571. Early 17th century. The painting, with its bird's-eye view, is an idealized impression of the event, rather than a literal piece of reporting. In the foreground, the artist has placed one of the large European ships, the superiority of which helped defeat the Turks.

© National Maritime Museum, London

military campaigns won him Rhodes and other Mediterranean islands and the city of Belgrade. In 1526, he won a major victory at Mohacs and took Buda in 1541, absorbing most of Hungary. His armies reached as far west as Vienna, the Hapsburg capital, which he besieged, but logistical problems eventually forced him to withdraw. A shrewd diplomat as well as a warrior, Suleiman forged an alliance with the Valois dynasty of France against the Hapsburgs.

The Ottoman Empire had begun to decline by the time of Suleiman's death. The Ottomans had long vied with European rulers for control of the sea lanes of the western Mediterranean. The important port cities, such as Tangier, Algiers, and Tripoli, changed hands several times as first Christians and then Muslims seized them. In the end, however, the Christians gained mastery of the sea lanes following the seizure of Malta in 1565 and the naval battle of Lepanto, off western Greece, in 1571. The Europeans also reconquered lost territory. The Hapsburgs retook Hungary, and by the early 18th century the sultans were forced to surrender Serbia and Dalmatia to the Christians. Moreover, in Istanbul, court intrigue and bribery had become rampant and the Janissaries, once the sultan's loyal soldiers, now began to manipulate their former overlords. Over the course of the next two centuries, the once great Turkish empire gradually shrank.

HUNGARY, BOHEMIA, AND POLAND

Although Serbs, Bulgarians, and Bosnians followed Orthodox Christianity, much of Eastern Europe lay in the cultural and religious sphere of the Roman Catholic Church. The Catholic populations, including Hungarians, Czechs, and Poles, achieved a vibrant cultural life during the 13th century through prestigious universities in Prague, Cracow, and elsewhere. Scholars from the region took part in the great humanist revival of the Renaissance.

THE KINGDOM OF HUNGARY

The Hungarians were a group of nomadic tribes from Asia who spoke a language distantly related to Finnish. Under Arpad (d. 907), the Magyars—the largest of the tribes—crossed the Carpathian Mountains into the plains of Hungary along the middle Danube and expanded steadily until 955, when the Holy Roman Emperor Otto the Great defeated them at Augsburg. By then they had established the basis of a state ruled by the king with the help of a royal council consisting of nobles and clergymen. Under King Stephen (ruled 977–1038), Hungary adopted Western Christianity. Stephen acknowledged the supremacy of the papacy in Rome when he received a royal crown sent by Pope Sylvester II for his coronation in the year 1000. Stephen became a zealous Catholic who bestowed land and abbeys on the church and tried to stamp out both Eastern Christianity and heresy in his kingdom. After his death, Stephen was made a saint.

Stephen's reign proved to be the early high point of Hungarian achievement because over the following century the kingdom was overrun by Germans and Poles and divided by internal strife. In 1046, an uprising of tribal chieftains, who still professed to follow paganism, resulted in the massacre of Christians and the destruction of many churches. The powerful feudal nobles of the realm, known as magnates, ruled their private lands as virtual sovereign lords, a condition reflected in the autonomy of the provinces and the elective nature of the Hungarian monarchy. The kings relied, instead, on the lesser nobility, who filled positions in the royal administration.

Despite the centrifugal force of feudalism, the state founded by Stephen endured. King Ladislas I (ruled 1077–1095) began to restore royal authority and supported the papacy in its struggles against the Holy Roman Empire. In the 12th century, King Bela III (ruled 1173–1196), who had been educated at Constantinople, brought great prestige to the Hungarian crown by marrying the sister of Philip Augustus of France. In 1222, the

Map 37.3 Eastern Europe, c. 1450–1500. By 1500, the Ottomans had conquered not only the former Byzantine territory of Greece and the islands, but also a large part of southern Europe, known as the Balkans. Turkish rule finally ended there with the Balkan Wars of 1912–1913. The Ottomans, however, were to find themselves under pressure from the Mongols, whose power increased around 1500 under the rule of Babur.

lesser nobility forced the king to accept a charter of feudal privilege, similar to the Magna Carta, known as the Golden Bull. Unlike the Magna Carta, this document did exempt the clergy and the nobility from taxation, guaranteed them against arbitrary arrest and imprisonment, and established an annual assembly, or diet, in which they could present grievances to the king. The Golden Bull also prohibited foreigners and Jews from receiving offices or land in the realm.

The Mongols invaded Hungary in 1241 and defeated the king's armies. Although the Mongols soon retreated, they left the country in a state of great devastation, of which the nobles took advantage to strengthen their own position. In the 14th century, various foreign princes vied with each other for control of the crown, and Hungary came under the rule of Charles Robert of Anjou (ruled 1308–1342). Charles established a vibrant dynasty that strengthened royal authority and brought Hungary into closer contact with the West.

The new dynasty expanded Hungarian power south into the northern Balkans and defeated the Ottomans in 1365. Nevertheless, the magnates took back much of their power, and the crown eventually came into the hands of a great frontier nobleman, John Hunyadi, whose son Matthias Corvinus (ruled 1458–1490) succeeded him. Matthias was a skilled ruler and soldier who also brought to his court in the city of Buda famous scholars from France and Italy and who was a great patron of Magyar literature and art. With a powerful standing army of mercenaries, Hungary had become the strongest kingdom in eastern Europe at the time of Matthias's death.

Matthias's successors surrendered his conquests in exchange for recognition from the Hapsburgs and gave up royal power to the magnates. More troubles soon struck the country. In 1514, a great peasant uprising erupted against the exploitation of the magnates, who crushed the revolt with much bloodshed. That same year, the diet passed a constitution, known as the *Tripartitum*, which imposed a permanent system of serfdom on the peasantry. A few years later, the Turks began their invasion of Hungary, which culminated in Suleiman's great victory at Mohacs in 1526 and the occupation of Buda in 1541. The Ottomans occupied the great plain of Hungary and divided it into administrative districts, while the western portion of the country was seized by the Hapsburgs, and Transylvania remained a vassal state of the Turks.

JAN HUS AND THE CZECHS

Sandwiched between southeastern Germany, northern Austria, and western Hungary lay the land of the Czechs, the name used for the Moravians and the Bohemians. When the Magyars invaded central Europe in the early 10th century, they destroyed the empire known as Great Moravia, a Bohemian state with its capital at Prague on the Danube. Given their location, the Czechs maintained close economic ties with the Germans and developed a thriving merchant class. Although they had been first converted to Eastern Christianity, the Czechs eventually became Catholics. A native dynasty known as the Přemyslide attempted to restore an effective Czech state and established royal authority over the nobles. In the 12th century, Frederick Barbarossa awarded the Přemyslide a hereditary crown. Under Ottokar II (ruled 1253–1278) the Bohemian state reached the furthest limits of its power in the region. Ottokar was defeated and killed in 1278 by Rudolf of Hapsburg. Early in the next century John of Luxembourg (ruled 1310–1346), son of Emperor Henry VII, who had married the last Přemyslide's daughter, came to the throne. It was John's son, Charles IV (ruled 1347–1378), who made Prague a great European capital with its own university and a rich cultural life. By the Golden Bull of 1356, the king of Bohemia became the principal member of the seven electors of the Holy Roman Empire.

At the University of Prague in the 15th century, a professor of philosophy named Jan Hus (1374–1415) unleashed a powerful movement of religious reform that soon swept across Bohemia. Hus was greatly influenced by the works of an English scholar of theology, John Wycliffe (c. 1330–1384), who attacked papal authority and the institutions of the church and looked to the Bible as the only source of doctrine. Hus began to preach sermons in the Czech language, calling for church reforms and a simpler religion based on reading the Bible. In 1415, Hus was called under safe conduct before a church council at Constance, which condemned his doctrines and burned him at the stake.

Hus was also the center of a growing nativist movement of Czech patriots who opposed German influence in the kingdom. The condemnation of Hus at Constance led to the outbreak of a revolt in Bohemia, where nobles and burghers joined with peasants in fighting the Hussite Wars against the Germans.

THE POLISH STATE

In their migrations across central Europe, the Slavs settled in the region of the Vistula basin in the 7th century. There in the 10th century the Polish state emerged as a result of the unification of six tribes under the Piast dynasty, whose first ruler was Mieszko I (ruled 960–992). The early Poles found themselves constantly at war, whether against the Germans to the east, the Prussians to the north, or the Bohemians and the Hungarians to the south.

Mieszko was converted to Latin Christianity by Bohemian missionaries. Thereafter, Poland became an outpost of crusading Christianity on the northeastern frontiers of Europe. For centuries the church maintained an alliance with the Polish nobles that worked to undermine royal authority. As in Hungary, the Polish nobility remained a powerful and autonomous force in the country.

An early exception to the rule of weak kings, however, was Boleslav I (ruled 992–1025), generally considered the real founder of the Polish state. An ambitious and unscrupulous king, he created an administrative system, endowed the church, and seems to have aimed at bringing all Slavs under his rule. Nevertheless, when the Piast dynasty ended and the Jagiellonian family came to power in 1386, noble power increased even more.

In the 14th century, the history of Poland consisted largely of the struggle by the new dynasty to reestablish royal authority, while the nobility managed to extract numerous privileges and maintain considerable control over the state. Under the reign of Casimir III the Great (ruled 1333–1370), Poland thrived as the king sought to create an efficient administration, encourage trade, and stimulate cultural developments. In 1364, Casimir established a school at Cracow that soon became a full-fledged university. As early as 1474, a printing press operated in Cracow.

Despite his success in domestic and foreign policy, Casimir left a considerably weakened monarchy at his death. Because he had no direct heir, he promised that on his death the crown would pass to Louis of Hungary, but on condition that he respect the rights of the nobles. This declaration gave rise to the practice of electing the king, who generally felt the need to buy off the magnates with concessions. In 1367, the magnates formed the first diet, and under Louis they extracted further privileges.

In 1384, Princess Jadwiga (ruled 1384–1399) was elected queen after making significant concessions to the magnates, and this was followed two years later by the granting of still further rights to the nobles. In return, they permitted Jadwiga to marry Jagiello, grand duke of Lithuania. Jagiello, a pagan, converted to Christianity and joined his territory, which was three times the size of Poland, to the Polish state.

In 1466, after a war against the Teutonic Knights, the Polish monarchy realized the goal of extending its reach to the Baltic Sea by securing a corridor through Prussian territory to the port of Danzig. Members of the Jagiellonian family also ruled in Bohemia and in Hungary. In Poland, however, the power of the nobility had grown so extensive that the monarchy was unable to put together sufficient force to stop the Ottoman invasion of central Europe in the 16th century. Effective centralized government in Poland ceased in fact with the end of the Jagiellonian dynasty.

THE GROWTH OF THE PRINCIPALITY OF MOSCOW

The Russian Empire that straddled the great Eurasian plain in modern times had its origins in two earlier states, the principalities of Kiev and Moscow. The East Slavs who settled this huge region in the early Middle Ages had ex-

Map 37.4 Growth of the Principality of Moscow. Like the Ottomans (see previous map), the rulers of the growing territory of Moscow had to deal with the Mongols. Successive Grand Princes drove the Mongol forces eastward, tripling the size of their holdings. By making Moscow the center of Russian Orthodox Christianity, Ivan I gave the city great symbolic prestige and turned the wars with the Mongols into a struggle between Christians and "heathens." Go to http://info.wadsworth.com/053461065X for an interactive version of this map.

panded as far as the Volga River, while other Slavic tribes went north almost as far as the Baltic Sea. During the 9th century, Vikings from Scandinavia had pushed into the lands of the East Slavs, where they laid the foundations of the principality of Kiev.

THE GREATNESS AND DECLINE OF KIEV

In the late 10th century, Vladimir (ruled 980–1015), who ruled a kingdom that stretched from the Baltic to the Ukraine, converted to Orthodox Christianity (on the early history of Kiev, see Topic 22). The Principality of Kiev experienced its greatest period during the reign of Vladimir's son, Yaroslav the Wise (ruled 1015–1054).

Yaroslav was both a ruthless military commander and a skilled administrator. After extending his realm to the border of Finland and clearing the area south of Kiev of nomads known as the Pechenegs, he secured religious autonomy for the principality from the patriarch of Constantinople in 1037, establishing an independent "metropolitan" as the head of the East Slavic Church. Yaroslav encouraged cultural development and contact with the West. Known as a great builder, he imported Byzantine architects and artists to construct and decorate important churches, including the great St. Sophia Cathedral in Kiev, inspired by Hagia Sophia in Constantinople. Following Justinian's example in Byzantium, Yaroslav ordered the codification of East Slavic law.

After Yaroslav's death, Kiev was racked by incessant feuds and struggles to secure the succession to the throne. These internal troubles rendered the principality unable to resist the constant incursions of nomadic peoples from the steppes. In the 11th century, the Cumans blocked Kiev from the Black Sea, thus breaking a longstanding and profitable trade connection with the Byzantine Empire. Eventually the nomads pushed the southern frontier of Kiev farther and farther north, isolating the Rus, or Russians, around the forests and the city of Moscow. Kiev fell to attack from the north in 1169.

The Mongol invasions of the 13th century completed the destruction of Kievan civilization. Because the Mongols were relatively few in number, they could do little more than control southern Russia along the Caspian and Black seas as tributary rulers and asserted even less direct authority over northern regions. In the 1240s, a prince of Novgorod, Alexander Nevsky (c. 1220–1263), began cooperating with the Mongols and defeated invading German forces.

Novgorod was a prosperous commercial city that traded with the Hanseatic League of northern German cities. Unlike their treatment of most of the other Russian cities, the Mongols left Novgorod untouched, and for his cooperation the Mongol Khan bestowed on Nevsky the title of Grand Prince. From that basis, Nevsky's descendants built a dynasty that would eventually rule most of Russia.

Manuscript illustration showing Ivan III the Great. 16th century. The stylized treatment of the hair and beard suggests that this is an "icon" of the Russian ruler rather than a realistic portrait. Note the fur collar on his robe; the export of furs was one of the chief economic resources of Ivan's state.

THE ORIGINS OF MOSCOW

By the 15th century, the centuries-old traditions of autonomy that the citizens of Novgorod had enjoyed came to an end. Weakened by strife among the citizens of different classes, and with its economy devastated by the decline of Baltic trade, in 1478 Novgorod fell under the aegis of Moscow.

Moscow had been little more than a frontier fortress on the Moskva River protected by surrounding marshes and forests. Its name first appeared in the chronicles only in 1147. Moscow had been established by a son of Nevsky, who skillfully expanded his powers in the service of the Mongols. The princes of Moscow adopted the policy of primogeniture, whereby the lands and possessions of the ruler passed to the oldest son; this ensured the continuation of power from one generation to another.

The city's rulers pursued a policy of steady expansion as they brought more and more Russian cities into its orbit. In 1328 the Mongols gave Ivan I (ruled 1328–1341), like Nevsky, the title of Grand Prince, with the right to collect all Russian tribute for the Khan—a function that brought him the contemporary nickname "money bags." Ivan also made Moscow the center of the Russian Orthodox Church. In 1380, Dmitri (ruled 1359–1389) greatly enhanced the prestige of his family when he won a victory over the Mongols at Kulikovo, on the Don, in 1380, earning him the title "Donskoi."

The greatest of the early princes of Moscow was Ivan III the Great (ruled 1462–1505). In 1478 Ivan the Great acquired control of Novgorod by incorporating its lands into the state of Moscow. Several years later, at the Oka River, he faced down the Mongol armies, who finally withdrew from Russia. Under Ivan and his successors, the Muscovite principality continued to expand, almost tripling the size of its territory by the mid-16th century. In a deliberate move to enhance his status so as to realize his great ambitions, Ivan married Sophia Paleologus, daughter of the last emperor of Byzantium. Ivan transformed Moscow into the core of a powerful empire and himself into the first tsar of all Russia (see Topic 53).

Putting Upheaval and Transformation in Eastern Europe in Perspective

The formation of national monarchies in Hungary, Bohemia, Poland, and Russia, together with the conquests and expansion of the Ottoman Turks, established the pattern of development for the eastern Mediterranean world for the next four centuries. This process was accompanied by equally fundamental social transformations as the system of serfdom that had developed in earlier periods in Western societies now was imposed by deliberate decision in eastern lands. Although separated from the Western European experience by ethnic, cultural, and religious differences, the entire region gradually established links with the dominant states of the West. As a result, as major political and religious upheavals unfolded in the West in the 16th century, Eastern Europe could not remain isolated from their impact.

Questions for Further Study

1. What effect did Ottoman expansion have on Europe?
2. What common social and economic conditions prevailed throughout eastern and central Europe?
3. How would you describe the Mongols and their impact on Russia?
4. What obstacles stood in the way of building a centralized state in Russia?

Suggestions for Further Reading

Allsen, Thomas T. *Mongol Imperialism*. Berkeley, CA, 1987.

Atil, Esin. *The Age of Sultan Suleyman the Magnificent*. Washington, DC, 1987.

Crummey, Robert O. *The Formation of Muscovy, 1304–1613*. New York, 1987.

Engel, Pal. Tamas Palosfalvi, trans. *The Realm of St Stephen: A History of Medieval Hungary, 895-1526*. New York, 2001.

Franklin, S., and J. Shepard. *The Emergence of Rus*. London, 1996.

Goodwin, Jason. *Lords of the Horizons: A History of the Ottoman Empire*. London, 1998.

Halperin, Charles J. *Russia and the Golden Horde*. Bloomington, IN, 1985.

Kazhdan, A.P., and others, eds. *The Oxford Dictionary of Byzantium*. New York, 1991.

Manz, Beatrice Forbes. *The Rise and Rule of Tamerlane*. Cambridge, 1989.

Morgan, D.O. *The Mongols*. Oxford, 1986.

Norwich, John Julius. *Byzantium: The Decline and Fall*. New York, 1995.

Taylor, J. *Imperial Istanbul*. London, 1989.

Wheatcroft, Andrew. *The Ottomans, Dissolving Images*. New York, 1993.

InfoTrac College Edition

Enter the search term *Ottoman Turks* using the Subject Guide.

Enter the search term *Jan Hus* using Key Terms.

THE ERA OF RECONNAISSANCE

Although the 16th and 17th centuries were a time of great religious upheaval in Europe, the period also saw serious economic and political crisis compounded by war and revolution. Yet, despite these difficulties, European civilization embarked on an unprecedented era of energetic and often ruthless overseas expansion. This age of "reconnaissance" dramatically changed Europe's relationship with the rest of the world, ushering in another fundamental revolution in modern history. The remarkable experience altered the nature of Europe's economy, had important social and cultural repercussions, and broadened the European imagination.

The age of exploration and expansion actually began in the 15th century with the first forays and technical discoveries of the Portuguese sailors. By the end of the 15th century, several Portuguese sailors, especially Bartholomeu Dias and Vasco da Gama, had rounded the Cape of Good Hope and explored the eastern coast of Africa along the Indian Ocean, opening great trade routes to India. These early Portuguese adventurers were followed by the Spanish. In 1492, Christopher Columbus reached the Americas, and within less than a generation Ferdinand Magellan circumnavigated the entire globe.

The immediate result of these early voyages was the establishment of vast overseas empires ruled by the Portuguese and the Spanish. This early experience in political and economic imperialism had tremendous, and often devastating, consequences for the native populations of the Western Hemisphere. For Europe, it laid the basis for the future commercial—and, eventually, for the industrial—development of the modern age.

S**IGNIFICANT   DATES**

The Era of Reconnaissance

1271	Marco Polo begins voyages to Far East
1430s	Portuguese begin exploration of African coast
1487	Dias rounds Cape of Good Hope
1492	First voyage of Columbus
1494	Treaty of Tordesillas
1497–1499	Da Gama's voyage to India
1519	Spanish conquer Mexico; Magellan begins voyage
1532–1536	Spanish conquer Peru
1568	Mercator makes first projection map

EUROPEANS AND THE WORLD: THE EARLY TRAVELERS

The great explorations of the 16th century did not, of course, represent the first expansion beyond Europe's borders. In the 9th and 10th centuries, the Vikings may have crossed the Atlantic and had penetrated into Russia from the north. The waves of successive crusades that invaded the Muslim-controlled Middle East starting in the 11th century revealed aggressive tendencies in the European psyche that presaged later movements beyond the frontiers of Christian society, and conditioned relations between Europeans and non-Europeans for centuries.

EUROPE AND THE LUXURY TRADE

Europeans had long been fascinated by Africa, India, and East Asia. In the Middle Ages, examples of the fabulous products to be found in these regions had trickled back to Europe. Europe's elite grew thirsty for leopard and zebra skins, ivories, rare silks, and precious gems, to say nothing of the wonderful spices that could transform the bland and boring European diet—indeed, nothing was so coveted by those who could afford it as plain, ordinary black pepper, a product that came principally from India and Indonesia.

Since Roman times, a lucrative trade had supplied Europe with the luxurious products of Africa and Asia. Many silks, spices, and other exotic products had flowed through Constantinople and the Byzantine Empire. After the 7th century, however, when the Arabs began to conquer North Africa and the Middle East, Europeans had to buy such goods mainly from the Muslims, who positioned themselves as middlemen between the European market and the source of most of these items. Muslim traders plied the waters of the Indian Ocean between India and Africa as well as up the Red Sea, and caravans snaked their way into the African and Asian interiors.

The Mongol conquests that began in the 13th century established a broad area of stability in the Asian heartland and opened a line of communication between Europe and central Asia. This situation prompted the Polo family of Venetian merchants to make the long and hazardous journey to the Mongol court of Kublai Khan (ruled 1259–1294), a grandson of the fierce Genghis Khan. Kublai controlled most of China, which he ruled from his capital at Tatu, the site of present-day Beijing. A man of broad, sophisticated tastes

Manuscript illumination showing Marco Polo arriving at the port of Hormuz, on the Persian Gulf. 14th–15th century. The picture, which shows Marco Polo's arrival from India with exotic animals, is based on his account dictated while in prison. The original written version was probably—like the text above and below this illustration—in French.

Bibliotheque Nationale/Bridgeman Art Library

who patronized artists and scholars, Kublai also encouraged contact with outsiders. In the 13th century, Pope Innocent IV sent monks to visit the Mongol court, but the Polos were Kublai's most famous Western visitors.

Between 1253 and 1260, Niccolò Polo and his brother Maffeo made several trading expeditions to Constantinople. From there, they went eastward into Kublai's kingdom, returning to Venice in 1269. Two years later, the brothers set out once again for Kublai's court, this time with Niccolò's son, Marco (c. 1254–c. 1324), and two Catholic missionaries. The group reached the capital in 1275, and the young Marco soon became a favorite of the khan, who sent him on trading missions throughout China, as far south as India and as far west as Japan. He apparently even ruled one Chinese city, Hangchow, for three years in the khan's name, describing his own city of Venice as a poor provincial village when compared with what he called the greatest city in the world.

Marco Polo is remembered today mainly for his famous account of his travels, which he wrote while he was a prisoner of the Genoese. His book tells of the customs and peoples he encountered, including those in the Arab world, Persia, East Africa, and Asia; he also described strange products such as paper currency, coal, and other things unknown in the West. He is said to have brought back to Venice a kind of wheat noodle that later became popular throughout Italy as pasta.

Most of all, Marco's account gave Europeans a sense of how he was awestruck by the fabulous splendors and wealth he had seen. These tales made his readers somewhat incredulous, especially because he repeated several mythical stories about things he had been told by others. Nevertheless, Marco Polo's account of his experiences did keep alive the appetites of Europeans for knowledge about Asia, as well as for its rare and exotic products.

The invasions of the Ottoman Turks and the collapse of the Mongol Empire eventually cut off the routes to Asia for Europeans. Nevertheless, an occasional brave traveler from the West, fed by stories such as Marco's or by religious missionary zeal, continued to penetrate beyond Europe's now relatively closed borders. The legend of a Christian

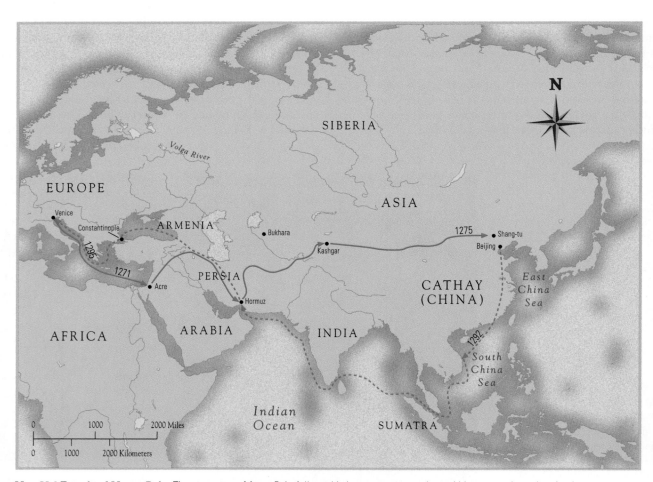

Map 38.1 Travels of Marco Polo. The exact route Marco Polo followed is by no means certain, and his account is unclear in places; some modern experts have cast doubt on the truth of his tales, which were in any case dictated and written down many years later. Whatever the facts, the wide circulation of his stories throughout Europe greatly stimulated European curiosity about the rest of the world. Christopher Columbus's journeys were originally undertaken in search of a sea passage to the East, which Polo described.

king known as Prester John beyond the Muslim world prompted the Portuguese to sail along the western African coast as late as the 15th century.

A THIRST FOR DISCOVERY

The motives that lay behind the growing European interest in the world beyond their borders were complex. Certainly the opportunities for profit in the luxury trade were tremendous, so that the lure of wealth was important. On the other hand, the crusading zeal that European Christians had demonstrated over the centuries also prompted much of the early efforts to reach foreign lands. Nor should we overlook the genuine interest that some of the early explorers and their sponsors had in expanding their knowledge of the world— the first voyages of discovery, it should not be forgotten, took place while Europe was at the height of the Renaissance, when interest in worldly matters was paramount.

The economic motives must surely have been the most powerful and pressing. Some merchants and rulers speculated about the possibility of finding vast deposits of gold and other precious metals. At the time, the Europeans had to pay for most of the luxury goods they imported from Asia with bullion, so that a supply of precious metals was the only real way for the new monarchs of Europe to bring the trade imbalance under control.

Most Europeans, however, thought of the incredible riches that could be made if only they could discover direct sea routes to India and East Asia. In this way, they would be able to bypass both the Muslim middlemen and the Venetians, who dominated the trade of the eastern Mediterranean. Moreover, the price of spices was incredibly inflated, not only because of their scarcity but also as a result of the Muslims' marking them up even higher. Spices dominated the trade with Asia and still captured most of the traders' attention. They served to enhance the flavor of foods and preserve them, as well as for a variety of other purposes, from the manufacture of perfumes and incense to medicinal potions. In addition to pepper, the principal items of the luxury trade were cinnamon, nutmeg, and cloves. Although the risks of the long-distance spice route were great, the return was enormous.

In the case of Portugal and Spain, the two countries that took the early lead in overseas exploration, the religious factor was also a strong motivation. The popes had sent missionary expeditions to Asia in the Middle Ages. It was, after all, on the Iberian peninsula where the Christians had fought the Muslims for centuries, finally conquering them or driving them out. The Spanish conquerors who overran Mexico and Central America were accompanied by missionaries and spoke constantly of the goal of converting the inhabitants of the New World to Christianity. This was especially true after the Reformation and the launching by Rome of the Counter-Reformation, which the church undertook with a renewed zeal.

One final reason explains why Europeans seemed so taken with the spirit of adventure and the desire to explore new regions of the world. The Muslims and the Chinese had been plying the waters of the Indian Ocean and southeast Asia for centuries, but neither had sailed much beyond the regions with which they were familiar. European society had matured to the point where its people simply could no longer remain prisoners of such restricted regions of the globe; perhaps, too, the development of the nation-states of the era had aroused a spirit of competition that drove the explorers to strike out in new directions.

GEOGRAPHY AND TECHNOLOGY

The Europeans had been limited by geopolitical factors to fairly well-defined sea basins—the Baltic and North Seas, and the Mediterranean—since the fall of the Roman Empire. As a result, in 1450 their knowledge of the world's geography was still essentially what it had been at the time of the ancient Romans. European travelers acquired the information necessary to make possible the "age of reconnaissance" only in the latter half of the 15th century, but within 100 years they had circled the entire globe. In addition to geographic knowledge, Westerners had to make certain technological advances, especially in ship design and navigational instruments, before they could set out to explore distant seas.

MAPS AND GEOGRAPHY

Most geographers of the Renaissance were still wedded to the notion put forth by Ptolemy (c. 90–c. 168) that the globe was a large mass of connected land made up of the continents of Europe, Africa, and Asia. Ptolemy also thought the circumference of the globe to be much smaller than it actually is, so that some explorers—like Columbus— thought they could reach Asia easily by sailing westward.

The most up-to-date geographic information available to Europeans came from the *portolani*, which were marine charts drawn on the basis of personal observation by sailors. The *portolani* mainly showed coastlines along the Mediterranean, the Atlantic coast, and eventually the coast of western Africa. Often drawn by sailors working with mathematicians, they contained detailed practical information needed for sailing, including distances, compass directions, and the depth of channels and ports. Mapmakers of the 14th century also prepared charts based on the information contained in the journals of Marco Polo, and Arab and Indian sailors who came to western ports on European ships provided specific knowledge of distant waterways.

Around 1500, mapmakers began to make important advances. The rediscovery of Ptolemy's *Geographia* at about this time, together with the invention of printing and engraving, made great strides possible. In 1538, by which time the information gathered by the early Portuguese and Spanish sailors was available, Gerardus Mercator (1512–1594), a Flemish cartographer, published his earliest map of the world. In 1568, Mercator made his first projection maps, which became widely used for navigational charts.

SHIPBUILDING AND NAVIGATION

Two developments were necessary in order to establish the practical basis for the age of discovery: a new kind of ship capable of traversing the open seas or the oceans, and new navigational instruments to guide the ships in uncharted regions. In the Mediterranean Sea, ships operated mainly along the coast, which navigators had mapped in great detail over the centuries. These ships were galleys rowed by teams of 50 or more slaves or sailors pressed into service from prisons. Because the oar-propelled ships were difficult to operate in rough, open waters, they traveled away from the coast only when the distance to the next island or land mass was relatively short.

Ships that hoped to sail in larger bodies of water, such as the Indian and Atlantic Oceans, had to use sails rather than oars to move them. In addition, instead of the long, narrow shapes of the galleys, which were designed for slicing through calmer waters with the least amount of resistance, oceangoing vessels needed wider hulls that could carry enough provisions to feed crews on long ocean voyages and hold the precious cargoes carried on return trips.

The first ships capable of making the months-long ocean voyages were known as *caravels* and were the work of Portuguese shipbuilders. In the 15th century, the Portuguese, whose ports lay on the Atlantic coast, were pushing carefully along the North African coastal waters. The caravel design innovation drew from both European and Muslim sailing experience. Two of its masts carried large square sails, which used strong winds to move the ship. A third mast supported a more narrow triangular-shaped sail; these were used to give the ship more maneuverability. The large hulls solved the problem of carrying provisions and cargo.

The navigational instruments that medieval European sailors had at their disposal were of limited value. The astrolabe, which may have been available as far back as Roman times, was widely used by the 11th century to determine the height of the sun and stars in order to calculate latitude (measured along imaginary lines around the earth in the form of circles running parallel to the equator). As early as the 13th century, Europeans had developed the compass, which sailors could use to determine direction, especially in bad weather that obscured the stars and the sun. Not until the 18th century, however, were sailors able to calculate longitude (imaginary lines in the form of circles running from pole to pole) with any degree of precision.

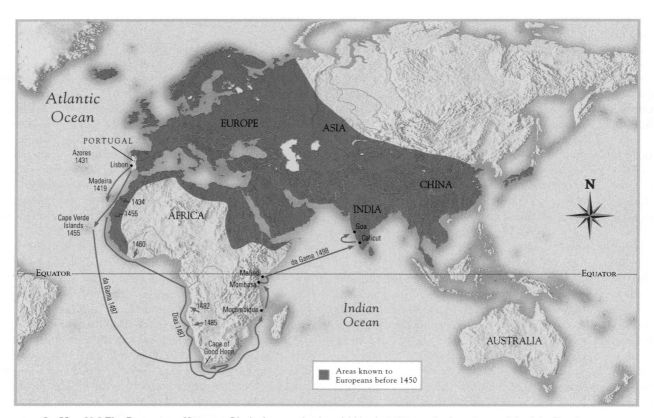

 Map 38.2 The Portuguese Voyages. Dias's circumnavigation of Africa in 1487 was the first great exploit of the Era of Reconnaissance, opening up India and China to commercial exploitation. The Portuguese retained the colony Goa in India until 1961, and their territory of Macao, in southeast China, only passed under Chinese rule in 1999. Mozambique, one of the stops on the east coast of Africa, became a center for the slave trade. The Portuguese colony there became independent in 1975. Go to http://info.wadsworth.com/053461065X for an interactive version of this map.

THE PORTUGUESE INITIATIVE

Once the Portuguese had pioneered the new caravel ship design, they set out on their first voyages of discovery. These early explorations were the work of the remarkable Prince Henry, who sponsored a navigational school and supplied the funds for the trips. After his death, the voyages continued to ever-greater distances around the globe.

PRINCE HENRY THE NAVIGATOR

Henry (1394–1460) was the younger son of King John I of Portugal (ruled 1385–1433). With little prospect of inheriting the throne, Henry devoted himself to geography and navigation. He built a school and observatory at Sagres, situated on the Atlantic at the southwesternmost point of Portugal. He brought sailors, captains, scientists, and mapmakers there and sent out annual expeditions to explore the northwestern coast of Africa.

A stimulus to this interest in Africa came in Henry's youth when the Portuguese captured the Muslim city of Ceuta on the coast of Morocco. Consumed with a passion for knowledge, as well as with the practical ambition of discovering a source of gold that would enrich the kingdom, he eventually sent a fleet as far as Guinea and the Gold Coast (in the vicinity of modern-day Ghana). The hope was that the sea route would circumvent the trans-Saharan caravan routes that the Arabs had used to control the gold supply to the Mediterranean.

THE BIRTH OF PORTUGUESE IMPERIALISM

In the years following Henry's death in 1460, the Portuguese expeditions declined for a time, although they did discover the Azores and the Madeiras, two small island groups hundreds of miles out in the Atlantic that would later serve as stopping places for transoceanic voyages. King John II (ruled 1481–1495) eventually organized new expeditions, this time with the specific goal of tracing a sea route to reach the spices of India. John established trading posts on the Guinea coast and was able to send a Portuguese group inland as far as Timbuktu.

In 1487, Bartholomeu Dias discovered and rounded the Cape of Good Hope on the southern tip of Africa, although bad weather, combined with the threat of a mutiny, made him turn back to Portugal. A decade later, Vasco da Gama retraced the Dias trip and actually crossed the Indian Ocean to the port of Calicut on the coast of India. When da Gama returned to Portugal with a cargo of goods from India, the king sent out a fleet of 13 ships under Pedro Alvares Cabral, who sighted Brazil in April 1500 and claimed it for the king.

From there, Cabral crossed the southern Atlantic, rounded Africa, and arrived in India. Once there, Cabral, assisted by da Gama, set up Portuguese trading posts. Although half his fleet sank before he arrived back in Lisbon, the profit from his cargo of spices was huge. Soon the Portuguese had established regular fleets that sailed to India each year, giving Lisbon a virtual monopoly on the Asian trade with Europe.

To secure their control of that trade, the Portuguese attempted to clear the Indian Ocean of Muslim presence. Under the command of Alfonso de Albuquerque, the Portuguese forces had already taken many of the most strategic ports on the east African coast. Albuquerque, who served as governor of India from 1509 to 1515, now bombarded and seized the Muslim forts along the Indian coast—including Goa and Calicut—and converted them to military and trading facilities.

These assaults on the Indian ports gave Portugal control over the spice trade and established Portuguese imperialism in Asia. They reached as far as Macao, situated at the mouth of the Pearl River in China. Despite the early successes of Portugal, however, the country simply did not have the economic or military strength needed to establish a truly global empire or to colonize the regions under their control. Spain eventually took Portugal's place as Europe's leading colonial power.

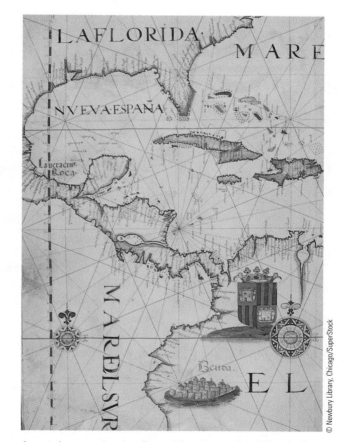

A *portolan* map showing Central America and the West Indies. Late 16th century. The *portolani* were based on information supplied by sailors and enabled early explorers to plan their voyages. Note the use of Spanish and the naming of the region now called the Gulf of Mexico as "New Spain."

© Newbury Library, Chicago/SuperStock

Perspectives from the Past

The Portuguese in the Wider World

Portugal, a small country that hugged the southernmost corner of Europe's Atlantic coast, had not played a major role in European or in global affairs. Beginning in the 15th century, however, the sailors, explorers, and traders of the kingdom suddenly pushed Portugal to the forefront of overseas expansion. A century later, the Portuguese had circled the globe and brought back to Europe the first accounts of the world beyond the West.

The spirit of enterprise and courage that drove Portugal's global expansion was matched, however, by a cultural arrogance and a thirst for conquest that made them the spearhead of a more general Western colonialism. These conflicting attitudes and values are revealed in the documents that follow.

An Early Account of Slavery in Africa

In 1455 and 1456, Alvise da Ca' da Mosto, a Venetian merchant, made two separate voyages to West Africa under a license granted to him by Prince Henry. A hardheaded businessman with a good eye for detail, Cadamosto provides one of the earliest European descriptions of the Guinea coast and the slave trade that had developed there. Along this region of the coast of western Sudan lay Arguim, a small island in the gulf where the Portuguese built a fort in 1448 for the protection of merchants. Arguim was a principal trade site where the Portuguese met caravans coming north from Timbuktu and west from the Sahara.

These Arabs [of the western Sudan] also have many Berber horses, which they trade, and take to the Land of the Blacks, exchanging them with the rulers for slaves. Ten or fifteen slaves are given for one of these horses, according to their quality. The Arabs likewise take articles of Moorish silk, made in Granada and in Tunis for Barbary, silver, and other goods, obtaining in exchange any number of these slaves, and some gold. These slaves are brought to the market and town of Hoden [Wadan, a desert market some 350 miles east of Arguim]; there they are divided: some go to the mountains of Barcha [in Libya], and thence to Sicily, [others to the said town of Tunis and to all the coasts of Barbary], and others again are taken to this place, Argin, and sold to the Portuguese leaseholders. As a result every year

the Portuguese carry away from Argin a thousand slaves. Note that before this traffic was organized, the Portuguese caravels, sometimes four, sometimes more, were wont to come armed to the Golfo d'Argin, and descending on the land by night, would assail the fisher villages, and so ravage the land. Thus they took of these Arabs both men and women, and carried them to Portugal for sale; behaving in a like manner along all the rest of the coast, which stretches from Cauo Bianco to the Rio di Senega and even beyond. This is a great river, dividing a race which is called Azanaghi from the first Kingdom of the Blacks. These Azanaghi are brownish, rather dark brown than light, and live in places along this coast beyond Cauo Bianco, and many of them are spread over this desert inland. They are neighbors of the above mentioned Arabs of Hoden.

They live on dates, barley, and camel's milk: but as they are very near the first land of the Blacks, they trade with them, obtaining from this land of the Blacks millet and certain vegetables, such as beans, upon which they support themselves. They are men who require little food and can withstand hunger, so that they sustain themselves throughout the day upon a mess of barley porridge. They are obliged to do this because of the want of victuals they experience. These, as I have said, are taken by the Portuguese as before mentioned and are the best slaves of all the Blacks. But, however, for some time all have been at peace and engaged in trade. The said Lord Infante will not permit further hurt to be done to any, because he hopes that, mixing with Christians, they may without difficulty be converted to our faith, not yet being firmly attached to the tenets of Muhammad, save from what they know by hearsay.

From *The Voyages of Cadamosto*, trans. and ed. G. R. Crone (London: The Hakluyt Society. Copyright © 1937). Reprinted with permission.

The Portuguese in India

In May 1498, after crossing the Indian Ocean, da Gama sailed into the harbor of Calicut Road on the western coast of India. Other Portuguese sailors followed da Gama's path and explored the cities of the Malabar coast, including Goa and Cochin. In 1510 Alfonso de Albuquerque, who served as governor of India, seized Goa from its Muslim ruler. In Cochin, which Duarte Barbosa described in the following account, the Portuguese found great storehouses of valuable spices.

Further in advance along the coast is the Kingdom of Cochin, in which there is much pepper which grows throughout the land on trees like unto ivy, and it climbs on other trees and on palms, also on trellises to a great extent. The pepper grows on these trees in bunches. . . . This Kingdom possesses a very large and excellent river, which here comes forth to the sea by which come in great ships of Moors and Christians, who trade with this Kingdom. On the banks of this river is a city of the Moors natives of the land, wherein also dwell Heathen Chatims, and great merchants. They have many ships and trade with Charamandel, the great Kingdom of Cambaia, Dabul, and Chaul, in areca, cocos, pepper, jagara, and palm sugar. At the mouth of the river the King our Lord possesses a very fine fortress, which is a large settlement of Portuguese and Christians, natives of the land, who became Christians after the establishment of our fortress. And every day also other Christian Indians who have remained from the teaching of the Blessed Saint Thomas come there also from Coilam and other places. In this fort and settlement of Cochin the King our Lord carries out the repairs of his ships, and other new ships are built, both galleys and caravels in as great perfection as on the Lisbon

strand. Great store of pepper is here taken on board, also many other kinds of spices, and drugs which come from Malacca, and are taken hence every year to Portugal. The King of Cochin has a very small country and was not a King before the Portuguese discovered India, for all the Kings who had of late reigned in Calicut had held it for their practice and rule to invade Cochin and drive the King out of his estate, . . . thereafter, according as their pleasure was, they would give it back to him or not. The king of Cochin gave him every year a certain number of elephants, but he might not strike coins, nor roof his palace with tiles under pain of losing his land. Now that the King our Lord has discovered India he has made the King independent and powerful in his own land, so that none can interfere with it, and he strikes whatsoever money he will.

From *The Book of Duarte Barbosa*, trans. and ed. Mansel Longworth Dames, 2 vols. (The Hakluyt Society. Copyright © 1921). Reprinted with permission.

The First Impressions of China

Since the 1430s, China had been essentially closed to the outside world. The so-called Ming Code had forbidden subjects to travel outside the country, and despite the interest of local merchants in south China in expanding trade, foreign travelers had been discouraged from visiting China. The first Portuguese traders arrived in China in 1514, and three years later Tomé Pires set out as official Portuguese envoy to China. After having been kept in Canton for three years on orders of the emperor, Pires was allowed to proceed to Beijing but never saw the emperor. Instead, in 1521 an imperial decree prohibited trade with foreigners and Pires and his followers were imprisoned in Canton. The letter that follows, written by Cristavao Vieira and smuggled back to Portugal, was the first account of conditions in China to arrive in Europe.

The country of China is divided into fifteen provinces. . . . All these fifteen provinces are under one king. The advantage of this country lies in its rivers all of which descend to the sea. No one sails the sea from north to south; it is prohibited by the king, in order that the coun-

Continued

try may not become known. Where we went was all rivers. They have boats and ships broad below without number. . . . I must have seen thirty thousand including great and small. . . .

No province in China has trade with strangers except this of Cantao: that which others may have on the borders is a small affair, because foreign folk do not enter the country of

China, nor do any go out of China. The sea trade has made this province of great importance, and without trade it would remain dependent on the agriculturalists like the others. . . .

The custom of this country of China is, that every man who administers justice cannot belong to that province; for instance, a person of Cantao cannot hold an office of justice in

SPAIN, THE AMERICAS, AND THE EUROPEAN ECONOMY

The Kingdom of Spain, once it had been united under the joint rule of Ferdinand and Isabella, and the Muslims had been driven out, proved capable of mustering the resources to build a world empire. Moreover, whereas the Portuguese had required a century in order to extend their reach around Africa and across the Indian Ocean, the Spanish sponsored a single expedition that suddenly discovered a vast new continent.

Sebastiano del Piombo, *Portrait of a Man Called Christopher Columbus.* 1519. The identity of the subject is not certain. Columbus, whose voyages to the Western Hemisphere opened the way for colonization of the Americas, has become the object of controversy for those who see him as the symbol of European imperialism.

The Metropolitan Museum of Art, Gift of J. Pierpont Morgan, 1900. (00.18.2) Photograph ©1979 The Metropolitan Museum of Art

COLUMBUS AND THE NEW WORLD

In 1484, even before Dias had rounded the tip of Southern Africa, Christopher Columbus (Cristoforo Colombo, 1451–1506), an Italian sailor from Genoa, attempted to convince the Portuguese to fund a voyage westward across the Atlantic. From studying the geography of Ptolemy and the findings of earlier Portuguese expeditions, Columbus was certain that he could reach Japan and China in a much shorter time by sailing due west. When King John II of Portugal turned down his request, Columbus went to Spain, where Queen Isabella agreed to back his voyage. With three ships under his command, Columbus actually reached landfall in the Bahamas in October 1492. Thinking he had reached Asia, Columbus explored Cuba and Haiti before returning to Spain with news of his discovery. Despite three later expeditions between 1493 and 1502, during which he sailed the Caribbean as far north as Honduras, Columbus would not abandon his conviction that he had reached Asia; therefore, he called the people inhabiting the islands "Indians."

The explorers who came after Columbus were the first to understand that he had in fact discovered an entirely "New World," a term coined by another Italian, Amerigo Vespucci. A banker who was obsessed by exploration fever, Vespucci sailed on several voyages to the Americas—the name that cartographers gave to the two continents after Vespucci described the regions that he explored. Still a third Italian sailor, John Cabot (Giovanni Caboto), was the first European to reach the North American mainland. Commissioned by the English monarch to find a western route to Asia, Cabot sailed along the coast of Nova Scotia and Newfoundland. His son, Sebastian Cabot, sailed to South America on behalf of the Spanish.

The early Spanish and Portuguese explorers were in open competition with each other, and the two states appealed to Pope Alexander VI to divide the world into respective spheres of exploration. In 1493, Alexander, a Spaniard, allocated the New World to Spain and granted Africa and India to Portugal. The Portuguese were not, however, very pleased by this distribution because it removed Brazil, which they had discovered and claimed, from their jurisdiction. In order to avoid war, Spain and Portugal settled

Cantao . . . This is vested in the literates; and every literate when he obtains a degree begins in petty posts, and thence goes on rising to higher ones, without their knowing when they are to be moved; . . . These changes are made in Pequim. . . . Hence it comes that no judge in China does equity, because he does not think of the good of the district. . . . they do noth-ing but rob, kill, whip and put to torture the people. The people are worse treated by these mandarins than is the devil in hell: hence it comes that the people have no love for the king and for the mandarins, and every day they go on rising and becoming robbers. . . .

From "Letters from Portuguese Captives in Canton," trans. and ed. by D. Ferguson, *The Indian Antiquary*, XXXI (January 1902).

the dispute by the Treaty of Tordesillas (1494), which moved the line westward to include Brazil in the Portuguese zone.

By proving that it was possible to sail westward without incident, Columbus had enticed a generation of explorers to try to find the elusive passage to Asia. In 1513, the Spanish explorer Vasco de Balboa crossed Central America, where he became the first European to look on the Pacific Ocean. During the early 16th century, when voyages to the Western Hemisphere became almost commonplace, a Portuguese navigator named Ferdinand Magellan became the first European to circle the globe. Magellan had served in India before joining the service of the Emperor Charles V. In September 1519, he sailed from Spain with five ships, and a year later he discovered the strait now named for him at the southern end of South America. With three of his ships, he sailed north along the coast and then headed west across the Pacific, reaching Guam in March 1521. Magellan was killed in a clash with the local inhabitants in the Philippines, but eventually one of his ships made it back to Spain. Magellan's expedition finally put to rest the question about whether the earth was round, and it demonstrated that Ptolemy had indeed underestimated the size of Earth.

SPANISH EMPIRE IN THE NEW WORLD

The region that Columbus explored on his four voyages embraced the major islands of the Caribbean. These so-called West Indies islands included Cuba, Jamaica, Puerto Rico, Trinidad, San Salvador, and the island the Spanish called Hispaniola (Haiti). For the Spanish, the chief aims of their travels lay in converting the Indians to Christianity and searching for gold and silver. In a short time, the population of the region, which is estimated to have been about as high

Drawing of Amerindians as cannibals. Around 1500. The illustration appeared in an early account of travels in the Americas and was intended as propaganda to justify the forcible conquest of the indigenous population, here portrayed as breaking the taboo against cannibalism and living without government or shame.

The Granger Collection

as 100,000, had been decimated by the oppressive conditions under which the Indians were forced to work and the impact of European diseases, such as smallpox, to which the Indians had never been exposed.

The thirst for gold and silver led the Spanish to transfer their attentions from the Caribbean islands to the mainland. Although the American cultures were advanced, their weapons were no match for European military power. In 1519, a *conquistador* named Hernán Cortés (1485–1547) invaded Mexico with an army of 600 heavily armed soldiers. Cortés captured the Aztec emperor Montezuma and conquered his wealthy empire. Mexico yielded large quantities of precious metals and provided missionaries with another large population to convert.

In the 1530s, Francisco Pizarro (1470–1541) invaded northern South America and destroyed the Inca empire, on

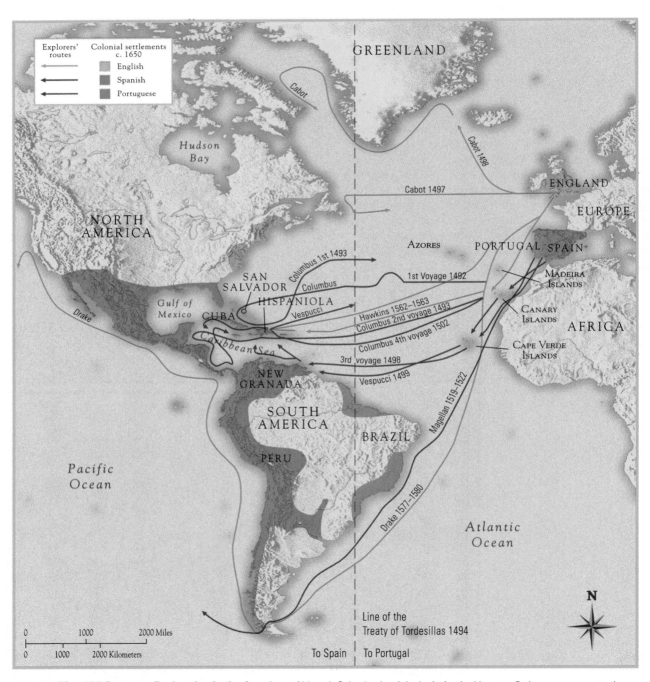

 Map 38.3 European Exploration in the Americas. Although Columbus's original mission had been to find a sea passage to the East, the early Spanish and Portuguese explorers soon realized that the Americas' natural resources could bring rich rewards, and transferred the struggle between Spain and Portugal to distant shores. Go to http://info.wadsworth.com/053461065X for an interactive version of this map.

whose territory he created the viceroyalty of Peru. Rich silver mines were later discovered in both Mexico and Peru. In the second half of the 16th century, up to 60 ships per year sailed for Spain laden with silver bullion.

Gold and silver were only part of the return that the Europeans got from their explorations in the New World. Settlers who migrated from Spain to the New World established huge landed estates that they ran with forced labor. When it was found that the Indian population had high mortality rates from working the sugar fields, the settlers began to import African slaves to take their place. Smallpox, typhus, and other diseases ravaged those whom forced labor failed to kill.

The European diet, as well as that of much of the rest of the world, was dramatically changed as vegetables and plants indigenous to the region were introduced to other cultures: Tomatoes, chili peppers, potatoes, and corn—and especially tobacco—were some of the important products brought to Europe and Asia. On the other hand, the Spanish introduced goats, sheep, and cattle to the New World, with major ecological results, because as they roamed the ranges they destroyed the roots of plants as well as ate the leaves. The impact of the European invasion was as devastating to South and Central America as it was in the Caribbean. By 1650, the Indian population of Mexico was reduced to about 5 percent of its original size of 25 million. A few Europeans, like the Spanish Dominican friar Bartolomé de Las Casas, tried to secure better treatment for the Indians. Las Casas argued that, once they were converted, the Indians should be thought of as fellow Christians. Spanish scholars and clergy debated the question of whether the Indians were fully human and deserved to be treated as such. As the Spanish administrators applied confused policies wavering between paternal dominance and ruthless enslavement, the toll on both sides was heavy: Vast loss of life among the Indian population was accompanied by the moral corruption of the conquerors.

A WIDENING WORLD ECONOMY

One crucial result of the age of discovery was that Europe placed itself at the center of an ever-widening global economy. On the commercial level, European powers, which before 1500 had traded almost entirely along the northern and southern shores of the continent and within Europe, now began to establish trade routes that reached around the world. The implications of this change were felt both in Europe and elsewhere. The first major impact was to be seen in the shifting fortunes of the Italian trading states that had dominated Mediterranean commerce and Europe's supply of spices and other Asian luxury goods for centuries. By 1600, Venice and Genoa were in sharp decline as the nations facing the Atlantic, principally Spain and Portugal, became the new trading powers of Europe. Gradually, the dominant position of the Iberian states was replaced by the Dutch Republic, England, and France.

As in the case of the indigenous American cultures, the spread of Europe's trading network around the globe had equally important consequences for non-European civilizations. In the Indian Ocean, Arab commerce was largely swept away as the Portuguese established their primacy along the East African and Indian coasts. The same was true, although perhaps to a lesser degree, in the trading waters of the Spice Islands and southeast Asia. Profits that had once remained in the hands of Muslim or Chinese merchants now began to flow to Europe, with important results for the decline of prosperity in the regional economy.

The establishment of Portugal's and Spain's overseas empires brought with it both problems and opportunities. The problems of communication and supply made close control from Europe extremely difficult. The principal purpose of these empires had, of course, been to produce revenues for the monarchs, who claimed them as personal property of the crown. At first, the Portuguese kings had allowed for a rather decentralized, almost feudal system of administration. By 1548, however, this cumbersome system was replaced with a more direct royal control over Brazil and the other colonies, and in 1580 the king established municipal councils that governed in his name. To help administer the Spanish colonies and ensure the steady supply of bullion, Spain's

Manuscript page showing a European mistreating indigenous Amerindians. 16th century. The European is wearing typical Spanish dress—broad-brimmed hat, leather jerkin, high boots—as he strips the clothes from his two victims.

The Ancient Art & Architecture Collection Ltd.

kings established a system of viceroys, who ruled the colonies with the assistance of local governors as well as through advisory councils known as *audiencias*. Because of their obsession with supplying the home country in Europe with revenues, Spain and Portugal strictly limited the commercial opportunities of their colonies. Local trade within the Americas, or between them and other parts of the world, was discouraged.

Despite such problems, by 1600 the basis for a truly global economy had been established. The effects of this widening system of trade and production would have important implications for Europe (see Topic 46).

Putting the Era of Reconnaissance in Perspective

The long-range results of the European "discovery" of the Western Hemisphere were incalculable. The flow of gold and silver bullion to Europe not only enriched the coffers of the national states but also seriously affected the economy by impacting prices. Moreover, the increase in trade had a major impact on the development of commercial capitalism and a global economy. The fact, too, that the Europeans assumed an attitude of moral and cultural superiority over the indigenous populations they encountered, and simply claimed these vast regions as their own by right of discovery, reflected an attitude of dominance that was to characterize Europe's relationship with the rest of the globe for centuries to come.

Questions for Further Study

1. What conditions in Europe led to the increase in geographic knowledge and overseas discovery?
2. What technical advances were necessary before the age of discovery could take place?
3. What policies characterized Spanish rule in the Americas?

Suggestions for Further Reading

Braudel, Fernand. S. Reynolds, trans. *Civilization and Capitalism,* 3 vols. New York, 1979–1984.

Curtain, Philip D. *Cross-cultural Trade in World History.* Cambridge, MA, 1984.

Kriedte, Peter. *Peasants, Landlords and Merchant Capitalists: Europe and the World Economy, 1500–1800.* Leamington, Great Britain, 1983.

McAlister, Lyle N. *Spain and Portugal in the New World, 1492–1700.* Minneapolis, MN, 1984.

Tracy, James E., ed. *The Rise of Merchant Empires.* Cambridge, MA, 1990.

Waldman, Carl, and Alan Wexler. *Who Was Who in World Exploration.* New York, 1992.

Whitfield, Peter. *New Found Lands: Maps in the History of Exploration.* New York, 1998.

Wilford, J.N. *The Mysterious History of Columbus: An Exploration of the Man, the Myth, the Legacy.* New York, 1991.

Wood, Frances. *Did Marco Polo Go to China?* Boulder, CO, 1996.

InfoTrac College Edition

Enter the search term *Vasco da Gama* using Key Terms.

Enter the search term *Ferdinand Magellan* using Key Terms.

Enter the search term *Christopher Columbus* using the Subject Guide.

THE REFORMATION

In the early 16th century, the foundations of Western Christianity were severely shaken by the movement of spiritual and institutional reform known as the **Reformation.** What began as an effort to bring about change and improvement in spiritual life became a genuinely revolutionary wave that broke the thousand-year religious unity of western and central Europe by giving rise to a series of new Protestant churches that rejected the authority of Rome. (The word *Protestant* came from a "protest" that a minority group of German reforming princes issued in 1529 against the Catholic majority at an assembly of the Holy Roman Empire.)

The Reformation, which was the culmination of a long tradition of religious questioning and doubt, first took shape through the ideas and work of a German monk, Martin Luther. Soon, however, Luther's ideas spread beyond the borders of Germany. By the middle of the 16th century, northern Scandinavia, England, Scotland, and several cities in Switzerland had all broken from the Roman Catholic Church and embraced new Protestant doctrines. In the next generation after Luther were several other religious reformers, including Huldrych Zwingli and John Calvin, who founded new faiths and new churches.

Because European civilization was intimately tied to the spiritual climate of the times, the Reformation had a profound impact on the society and politics of the age. Luther's doctrines attracted broad strata of the population, especially the middle classes and peasantry, and popular response sometimes resulted in widespread unrest. On the political level, Luther appealed directly to the German princes and to the spirit of nationalism in his struggle against the authority of Rome. Monarchs and rulers took sides in the religious controversies of the period, some of them adopting the new faith not only for themselves but for their entire realm as well. Thus while Emperor Charles V championed the cause of Catholicism, the monarchy in France did not. The long and disastrous wars of religion that disrupted Germany and Europe for decades had complex origins that were sometimes tied to the political ambitions of Catholic and Protestant monarchs.

THE ROOTS OF REFORM: POPULAR DISCONTENT AND THE CRISIS OF THE WESTERN CHURCH

The Reformation had its roots in many of the broad political, social, and economic transformations taking place in Europe in the Early Renaissance. The growing urbanization of Europe's population had created an ever-expanding urban middle class, a social group without traditional close ties to the church and the rural nobility. These middle-class city dwellers were increasingly literate and provided an audience for the circulation of ideas. The very fact that the invention of the printing press made possible the spread of unorthodox teachings to millions of people explains much of the popular success of Protestant thought. By 1520, more than a quarter of a million copies of Luther's works alone were in circulation.

One result of the changing social circumstances was the rise of popular religion and Christian mysticism, which had its most important manifestation in the Modern Devotion movement and its related lay orders known as the Brothers and Sisters of the Common Life. Thomas à Kempis (see Topic 31), the author of the work *The Imitation of Christ*, had urged Christians to follow the pious example of Christ instead of intellectual discourse and official dogma, although he did stress the importance of the sacrament of communion.

Political change provided another source of support for the Reformation. As the national states emerged and grew stronger in this period, conflict inevitably resulted between the powerful new monarchs, who wanted to control all aspects of national life, and the church, which still owned large amounts of land and demanded complete independence from state control. In eastern Europe, where serfdom and the authority of the feudal princes was still strong, the church held a dominant position. But in western and central Europe, where changing economic and social conditions had undermined noble authority, monarchs had long attempted to free themselves from the control of Rome. In Spain and France, rulers secured autonomy through *concordats,* or treaties, with the papacy, while others, such as Henry VIII of England, adopted one of the new Protestant faiths as a means of achieving the same end. Charles V, the Hapsburg monarch who ruled over the Holy Roman Empire as well as over Spain, Austria, Bohemia, Hungary, the Netherlands, and other regions, assumed the role of protector of the faith, an alliance that alienated lesser rulers and nobles (on the background of Charles V, see Topic 33).

INSTITUTIONAL AND DOCTRINAL ORIGINS

Ever since the High Middle Ages, the church had often followed practices that hurt its prestige and called its leaders into question. During the Renaissance, many popes, for example, had widely practiced *nepotism*—the employment of relatives—and some had even fathered children and kept mistresses in the papal court. High ecclesiastical officials, such as bishops and cardinals, lived luxurious lives that clashed with their spiritual positions.

Moreover, the clergy had long engaged in unseemly practices that had doctrinal as well as practical consequences. For example, *simony*, or the sale of church offices, was widespread, as was the profitable traffic in sacred relics, including the bones and body parts of saints. The papacy also sold dispensations, whereby a holder of church office was excused from following certain requirements of church law. Most serious perhaps was the sale of indulgences, which granted pardon from temporal punishment for sins. Indulgences were in effect extra sources of grace accumulated by Christ and the saints, and the penitent who received one had been given credit as if he or she had actually performed a penance. People could purchase indulgences for themselves as well as for dead relatives, who would then be required to spend less time in purgatory. Papal representatives in the indulgences business eventually began touting indulgences as guarantees of entry into heaven, although that was not an accurate description of their function.

Other causes of the Reformation included the spread of humanism out of Italy into northern Europe (see Topic 36). Christian humanism in the North had been inspired by the possibility that the legacies of morality and ethical behavior inherited from Classical works could influence Christian ethics. Erasmus and other Northern humanists urged the translation of the Bible into vernacular languages and the positive impact of popular education on society. Moreover, they severely criticized the abuses in the church.

Several theological issues also attracted the criticism of 16th-century reformers, particularly the excessive influence of rationalist medieval theologians such as Thomas Aquinas, whose teaching was used to support the notion that the clergy and their institutional functions, rather than faith, provided the path to salvation. During the 14th and early 15th centuries, John Wycliffe in England and Jan Hus in Bohemia turned to the Bible as the only legitimate source of spiritual truth. Later, the proponents of the

---

S IGNIFICANT DATES

The Reformation

1517	Luther's Ninety-Five Theses; Reformation begins
1520	Huldrych Zwingli breaks with Catholic Church
1527	Sack of Rome
1541	John Calvin moves to Geneva
1509–1547	Henry VIII rules England
1555	Peace of Augsburg
1529–1558	Charles V rules Holy Roman Empire
1545–1563	Council of Trent

Conciliar movement, who argued for the supremacy of church councils in matters of doctrine and ecclesiastical law, questioned papal authority.

"HERE I STAND": MARTIN LUTHER AND THE GERMAN REFORMATION

Although the Reformation had complicated roots, its immediate source is to be found in the preachings and ideas of Martin Luther (1483–1546) about salvation. As a friar of the Augustinian order, Luther believed that human sinners could be saved only by repentance and faith in divine mercy, not by the good works and indulgences offered by

Lucas Cranach the Younger, *Martin Luther and the Wittenberg Reformers.* Mid-16th century. Painted about a generation after Luther's break with the Catholic Church, this scene shows Luther on the left, hands clasped defiantly in front of him, his fellow-reformer Philip Melanchthon on the right, and between them the Elector (Prince) of Saxony, John Frederick.

the church. That his ideas were so widely and so quickly accepted reveals the deep sense of spiritual dissatisfaction that prevailed in Christian society. On the other hand, it should be remembered that most Europeans remained Catholic.

THE NINETY-FIVE THESES

Luther was the son of a peasant who had risen into the ranks of the lower middle class by becoming a miner. Luther was raised in a strict Christian household and was extremely well educated according to the standards of the time. In 1502, he earned a bachelor's degree from the University of Erfurt and began to study law. Already, however, he demonstrated signs of deep religious faith, and in 1505 he underwent what he believed was a miraculous experience when he was saved from the effects of a terrible thunderstorm. Vowing to become a monk, he joined an Augustinian monastery in Erfurt, disappointing his father, who had wanted his son to become a lawyer.

Luther, who had always been convinced that he was unworthy of God's grace, became seriously troubled by the issue of salvation. Catholics obtained divine grace principally through the sacraments, with confession as the means of securing forgiveness for sins. Plagued by disturbing doubts of his own adequacy, he began to study theology, taking a doctorate in 1512 and becoming a professor at the University of Wittenberg. It was there that he found the answer to his dilemma while reading the Epistle of St. Paul to the Romans, which showed him that a believer received the justification of God—and therefore salvation—through faith alone. God, he concluded, freely bestowed his grace on sinners, not because of their good works but as a result of the sacrifice of Christ. The revelation, he said, made him feel reborn. Having discovered the answer to his quest for salvation in the Bible, Luther henceforth argued that it—not the church or the pope—represented the only source of religious authority, although the Church Fathers had to be used to understand Scripture.

After having arrived at these conclusions, Luther became embroiled in conflict with the church over the issue of indulgences. In 1517, Pope Leo X commissioned a Dominican monk named John Tetzel to sell a special indulgence that would be used to help finance the completion of St. Peter's Cathedral in Rome. To sell his indulgence, Tetzel allegedly chanted to his audiences the catchy refrain, "As soon as the coin in the coffer rings, the soul from purgatory springs." Complicating the matter further was the fact that part of the funds secured from the indulgence would go to pay off a debt that a German archbishop had incurred in order to buy another ecclesiastical office from the pope. Luther was outraged by the crass commercialization of the matter.

In October 1517, he issued the so-called Ninety-Five Theses, a powerful attack against the abusive sale of indulgences in which he denied the power of the pope to secure salvation. The theses were translated from Latin into German and rapidly disseminated, while Luther was hailed as a champion of popular religious belief. The simplicity and clarity of his position, combined with the resentment that many Germans felt against the church hierarchy in Rome, made the people immediately sympathetic to his doctrines.

THE ESTABLISHMENT OF THE LUTHERAN CHURCH

Although at first Luther moved carefully as a good Catholic who wanted only to reform the church, he was bound to clash with the papacy. Accused of heresy by the Dominicans, he responded by debating a well-known theologian, Johann Eck, in Leipzig in 1519. Challenging the idea of the infallibility of the pope or of church councils, he insisted that the Bible represented the sole authority in matters of religious doctrine.

He followed the debate by issuing several powerful pamphlets that set forth his views on important matters. In *On the Freedom of a Christian Man*, Luther repeated his ideas about salvation, arguing for faith rather than good works as the means to grace. Those who had been saved performed good works out of a spirit of thanks to God. The Christian is at once absolutely free and the servant of humanity. Luther took the occasion also to urge the right of clergy to marry. His ideas reflected a belief in the equality of partnership in a Christian marriage and encouraged opportunities for women,

although he later drew back from the view that women and men were equal in all things. In a more political vein, Luther's *Address to the Christian Nobility of the German Nation*, written in German, was a frontal assault on the papacy. Attacking the papacy as the persistent source of all resistance to reform, and denying the pope's sole authority to interpret the Scriptures, he appealed to the nobles to found an independent German church free of the authority of Rome.

In December 1520, Luther defiantly burned the papal bull condemning his doctrines. Within a month, he was excommunicated. The Emperor Charles V summoned Luther to appear before the Imperial Diet of the Holy Roman Empire at Worms. Instead of recanting his heretical ideas, however, Luther infuriated the emperor by remaining firm in his convictions. His courageous response, in which he flatly rejected the authority of the pope and of church councils, ended with the ringing words, "I cannot and will not recant anything, for to go against conscience is neither right nor safe." By some accounts, he added: "Here I stand, I cannot do otherwise."

In response to Luther's defiance, Charles issued the Edict of Worms that ordered Luther's arrest and the burning of his books. Frederick III, the elector of Saxony, placed Luther un-

Map 39.1 General Religious Divisions in Europe, c. 1560. The divisions that appear here generally still apply to Christians in Europe today. There are fewer Protestant communities in France, largely as a result of the St. Bartholomew's Day Massacre of 1572 (see Topic 44). Munich and its province of Bavaria has remained Catholic, unlike most of the rest of the former Holy Roman Empire, which is now Germany. Go to http://info.wadsworth.com/053461065X for an interactive version of this map.

der his protection, and the outcast monk took up residence in Wartburg Castle. Luther eventually returned to Wittenberg, where he translated the Bible into German and began teaching at the university, spreading his ideas about the Scriptures to thousands of students. In 1525, he married Katherine von Bora, who remained his lifelong companion and aid.

Luther laid the foundations of a reformed church, which was independent from Rome and based on his teachings but which nevertheless kept many Catholic practices. Stressing the fundamental importance of faith rather than rituals and good works, Luther preserved only baptism and the Eucharist among the sacraments. He replaced the traditional Mass with a communion ceremony in which priests were not necessary to achieve the miracle of transubstantiation, whereby the wine and wafer were transformed into the blood and body of Christ. Instead, Luther spoke of all believers functioning as a new kind of communal priesthood and maintained that Christians were responsible for their own salvation. He also abandoned Latin in favor of German in services and emphasized the importance of music in teaching the Gospel.

THE LUTHERAN MOVEMENT: PEASANT REBELLION AND ARISTOCRATIC STRIFE

Lutheranism spread rapidly throughout the states of northern and central Germany and became especially popular among the middle classes of the free cities. Among Luther's earliest disciples was Philip Melanchthon (1497–1560), a Christian humanist who wrote some of the first rigorous theological statements on the new faith. Erasmus and other humanists, however, eventually rejected Lutheranism both on theological grounds and because they were dismayed at the prospect of a divided Christendom.

Other problems of a political nature also affected the early Lutheran movement in Germany. As a former Augustinian, Luther believed in the notion of two spheres of existence: the kingdom of God and the kingdom of the material world. Unlike the popes, who had argued for their supremacy over secular rulers, Luther's ideas gave support and strength to the growing power of secular government, which he saw as the protectors of his church. Luther, whose political and social views were generally quite conservative, supported the position of rulers and state power.

THE PEASANT REBELLIONS

If he lent his prestige and that of his new church to the princes of Germany, Luther was, on the other hand, fearful that his appeal for Christian freedom would be used to justify challenges to established authority. This attitude was fully revealed in 1522, when a rebellion broke out among lesser knights who sought to make common cause with the emperor against the more powerful princes, the free cities,

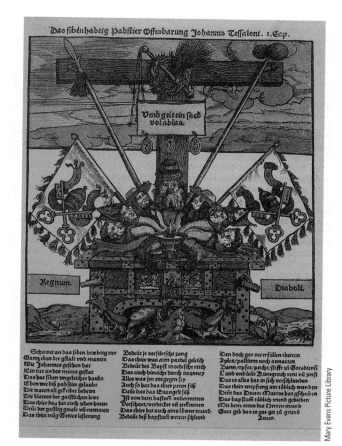

Satirical German print. 16th century. Part of the propaganda war against the Catholic Church, this print compares the "Papist" (i.e., Catholic) sellers of indulgences to the seven-headed beast of the Book of Revelations. One of the chief features of the Reformation movement was its use of the vernacular, in this case German, to reach the widest possible readership.

and the Catholic Church. Although they declared themselves Lutherans, Luther, who was scandalized by their breach of discipline, gave the rebellious knights no support, and the uprising was put down.

More revealing of Luther's conservative social views was the so-called Peasant War that erupted a few years later. The event actually began as a series of revolts among discontented peasants who protested the oppressive treatment that many landowners still meted out to their peasants. Supported by burghers in many cities, and under the leadership of a former follower of Luther, Thomas Muntzer, the peasants presented petitions demanding an end to serfdom and onerous taxes, and claiming religious autonomy.

When violence erupted in 1524, Luther immediately reacted by condemning the peasants in a vicious pamphlet called *Against the Thieving and Murderous Gangs of Peasants*, in which he called on the princes to wipe out the rebels without mercy. Luther believed it was the responsibility of subjects to obey their rulers, who were divinely chosen, and identified social revolution as a great evil. Luther applauded the massacre of peasants in 1525 by the princes, whom he had identified as the mainstay of his church. His reaction to the rebellions cost him support among the lower classes.

THE HAPSBURG-VALOIS WARS

One reason Lutheranism spread with relative ease throughout Germany was because the Emperor Charles V was so preoccupied with holding together his far-flung Hapsburg possessions that he could not focus his attention on stamping out Lutheranism in Germany. The emperor felt that his political aspirations were endangered by the policies of his chief enemy, Francis I (ruled 1515–1547), the Valois king of France. At home, Francis was a vigorous ruler who suppressed the nobles and struck against Protestantism. In the international arena, Francis, whose kingdom was encircled by Hapsburg lands, fought a long and costly series of military engagements—known as the Hapsburg-Valois Wars—against Charles throughout the Continent.

Besides having to contend with Francis, Charles frequently disagreed with the papacy. Pope Clement VII (ruled 1523–1534), who saw Hapsburg dominance in Italy as a danger to the Papal States, sided with Francis. In retaliation, in 1527, Charles's army sacked Rome, an event that shocked Catholic opinion in Europe but that strengthened the emperor's position in Italy. It was perhaps a measure of the times that, instead of joining forces with Charles in the struggle against Lutheranism, the papacy had opted to fight its most powerful ally.

Only after the emperor had repelled the Ottoman Turks from the walls of Vienna in 1529 did he try to deal with the German crisis. The next year, Charles convened the Diet of Augsburg, where he presented the Lutherans with an ultimatum that they return to the church by April 1531. Before the deadline, however, a group of Lutheran princes and free cities formed the Schmalkaldic League to protect themselves from the emperor. Renewal of war with the Turks and then with Francis diverted Charles's attention once again, and only in 1546, after finally having made peace with both enemies, did he act. That year, with a huge army drawn from his various possessions, Charles launched a war against the Schmalkaldic League. By then, Luther was dead and military victory seemed to presage the end of the Lutheran heresy. In 1552, the League joined forces with Henry II (ruled 1547–1559), the new king of France, and forced Charles to make peace. Dispirited by his efforts and broken in health, Charles abdicated in 1556 and retired to Spain, where he died two years later.

With Charles removed from the scene, in 1555 the religious conflict in Germany ended with the Peace of Augsburg. According to the agreement, Lutheranism was legally recognized and the rulers of the German states were free to choose between Lutheranism and Catholicism, although prince-bishops had to either remain Catholic or resign. The existence of the hundreds of independent territorial states in Germany was thereby accepted as an established principle, while the permanent religious division of Europe had become an unavoidable fact.

THE ADVANCE OF PROTESTANTISM IN CONTINENTAL EUROPE

By the time of the Peace of Augsburg, Scandinavia and part of northern Germany had separated from Roman Catholicism and joined the Protestant Reformation. Not only had Luther shattered more than a millennium of religious unity, but in each area of Europe a different variety of Protestantism evolved. In the countries of Scandinavia—Denmark, Norway, and Sweden—official Lutheran churches were established by the monarchies.

JOHN CALVIN AND THE SWISS REFORMATION

It was in Switzerland rather than in Scandinavia that some of the most important reform developments took place. A former part of the Holy Roman Empire until it won independence in 1499, Switzerland was a prosperous region of hard-working merchants and craftsmen. When the stirrings of reform came, many Swiss reacted favorably to another opportunity of distancing the country from papal Rome.

The first reformer in Switzerland was Huldrych Zwingli (1484–1531), a priest and humanist scholar who lived in Zurich. Zwingli always claimed that he arrived at his ideas about the superiority of biblical over papal authority and about justification by faith alone independently of Luther.

© Snark/Art Resource, NY

Woodcut of John Calvin. 1574. The upper inscription describes Calvin as resident in Geneva, and the lower one links him to Luther and Huss, other leading reformers. As in the previous illustration, the text is in German rather than Latin, a sign of the growing importance of literacy in the battle for Reform.

He and Luther differed on several doctrinal issues, including the meaning of baptism and the Eucharist, which Zwingli thought had only symbolic importance. A practical man with a keen sense of political realities, Zwingli convinced the Zurich town council to authorize an assembly of magistrates and clergymen to oversee religious and secular life in the city. As more cities were influenced by Protestantism, a brief but intense civil war erupted, during which Zwingli was killed. A settlement based on freedom of religious choice for each canton restored peace to Switzerland.

John Calvin (1509–1564) represented a later generation of Reformation leadership and spearheaded a more radical form of Protestantism. Born in France, he studied law until, in 1533, he underwent a religious awakening that led him to convert to Protestantism. Accused of heresy by the church, he fled to Basel, where he published a treatise entitled *Institutes of the Christian Religion*, in which he tried to make Lutheran principles into a systematic system of belief.

Calvin, like Zwingli, agreed with Luther's insistence on the importance of faith rather than good works. He also shared with his German predecessor the notion that Christians were constantly engaged in a struggle between good and evil. Humans, they both believed, were depraved sinners, but Calvin was convinced that God's purpose was beyond any human understanding. Before an omnipotent and supreme God, Calvin believed, humans were weak and lacked the necessary free will to bring about their own salvation. Instead, Calvin—like Luther and Zwingli, who were more circumspect in professing the belief—taught the doctrine of predestination, according to which God had decided before the Creation who would be saved and who would be damned. Because humans cannot know who has been chosen and who rejected, good Christians should focus on doing good works—which Calvin thought were a sign of having been selected for salvation—and leading a moral life. Above all, humans should devote themselves to the worship of God.

GENEVA AND THE SOCIAL VISION OF CALVINISM

A man of strong views and determination, Calvin is often thought of as the organizer of Protestantism. When in 1541 he was invited to come to Geneva, he built a Christian society to which reformers of the 16th century looked with pride and where religious refugees found sanctuary. Calvin's most powerful popular attraction was his sermons, and through them he preached his faith and set the tone for the life of morality and seriousness to which he wanted all citizens to aspire.

Calvin hoped to organize Geneva along religious lines, although a civilian magistracy continued to run the city government. On the other hand, Calvin presided over a Consistory made up of laymen and pastors, which established detailed rules by which citizens were to live. Personal conduct, including the manner of dress and the hours during which people could be outside their homes, was strictly controlled. Drunkenness, gambling, and frivolity were prohibited, and religious dissent was harshly punished.

Calvinism represented the most activist and compelling Protestant faith of the period, and his church provided an example that inspired reformers in other countries, from France and Scotland to North America.

THE ANABAPTISTS

As we have seen, Zwingli believed that baptism had symbolic rather than real meaning for Christians. Other reformers, known as **Anabaptists** ("baptized again"), made concern over the idea of baptism a central aspect of their doctrine. Rejecting the idea of predestination, the Anabaptists based their doctrine on the belief that adults alone, not children, were able to choose to enter a religious faith. Although opposed to baptizing children, they insisted that adults should be baptized.

The Anabaptists were considered radicals who thought that Luther had not gone far enough in his reforms. Although the Anabaptists accepted Luther's teachings, they insisted on a literal interpretation of the Scriptures and engaged in only those practices they believed were followed in the early church. Moreover, they saw the true church as

Illustration of an Anabaptist leader being tortured in a cage. 16th century. Popular prints such as this circulated widely as weapons in the Reformers' campaigns, and were intended to stimulate popular resentment against the authorities. The Anabaptists believed in adult baptism and rejected government control.

a voluntary community of equal believers, much like the early Christian church as described in the New Testament. This spirit of democracy may have reflected the fact that most of their members were peasants, artisans, and other laborers linked by social and economic dissatisfaction. Their advocacy of communal property and their prohibition of interest reflected the class base of the movement and partly explains the ferocity of persecution against them. Their radicalism extended to politics as well. Anabaptists, contrary to most other Christians, wanted a total separation of church and state, refusing to serve in government positions or fight in the army.

Anabaptists established groups in Switzerland, Germany, and Austria, and later still in eastern Europe. In Zurich, Zwingli exiled them, and in Germany they were viciously persecuted because their ideas challenged both religious and secular power. In Münster, Germany, the Anabaptists at first were officially recognized in the early 1530s, and the city became a refuge for fellow believers from elsewhere. Here they instituted the practice of polygamy, and women were permitted to become priests.

A less radical Anabaptist group under the leadership of Menno Simons (1496–1561) established a movement that came to be known as the Mennonites, who wanted to withdraw from the world to live a pure Christian existence. Yet Simons too introduced severe discipline among his followers.

THE BREAK WITH ROME: HENRY VIII AND THE ENGLISH CHURCH

In England, where the monarchy and the papacy had often struggled for supremacy, Protestantism was established for reasons that often had little to do with the desire for religious reform. Here, the Reformation was led—unlike the experiences in Germany or Switzerland—by a monarch rather than a priest: King Henry VIII dominated the religious controversies of his age and lent his weight to the drive to separate the English church from Rome.

THE TUDOR SUCCESSION

The Tudor dynasty had been founded in the 15th century by Henry VII, England's first "new monarch" (see Topic 33). His son, Henry VIII (ruled 1509–1547), solidified the Tudor monarchy and proved to be one of the most important kings in English history.

An ambitious, ruthless man of strong appetites, Henry's concern for the future of the dynasty accounted for his decision to break with Rome. A long marriage to Catherine of Aragon (1485–1536) failed to produce a male heir to ensure the Tudor succession, and in 1527 he appealed to the pope for an annulment so that he could take a new queen. Henry had already gone on record in opposition to Luther, and under ordinary circumstances his request would no doubt have been approved in Rome. But two factors worked against

him. First, Catherine had originally been married to Henry's brother, and only a special papal dispensation had allowed him to marry his dead brother's wife. Henry was now convinced that God's punishment had prevented him from having a son, but an annulment now would have suggested that the first papal dispensation had been a mistake. Perhaps more important, Catherine, who refused to accept an annulment, was the aunt of the Emperor Charles V, whose soldiers had already sacked Rome and who had an obvious influence on the pope's decision.

Henry, who had contemplated divorce from Catherine, had already begun an affair with Anne Boleyn (c. 1507–1536), a lady in waiting at the court, who was now pregnant with the king's child. In January 1533, Henry and Anne secretly married. Thomas Cranmer (1489–1556), whom Henry had made archbishop of Canterbury, annulled the marriage to Catherine without waiting for the pope to act and then approved the marriage to Anne. When Anne did give birth, it was to a daughter, whom they named Elizabeth. When the pope finally moved, it was to excommunicate Henry.

THE FOUNDATIONS OF THE ANGLICAN CHURCH

These actions were taken only after a special act of Parliament had prohibited English ecclesiastical courts from appealing cases to Rome. Moreover, in 1534 Parliament passed the Act of Supremacy, which made Henry the supreme head of the English—or Anglican—church. Thomas Cromwell (1485–1540), the king's secretary, then devised plans that ended payments to the papacy and closed hundreds of monasteries, whose confiscated lands were sold to pay off Henry's debts. Sir Thomas More, the humanist scholar who had served as the king's chancellor, was beheaded when he refused to accept Henry's triumph over the church.

Henry's confrontation with the papacy received wide support in England, where Protestantism was spreading, both from Parliament and from the public. But Henry moved cautiously in matters of doctrine, securing passage in 1539 of the Six Articles Act that endorsed important aspects of Catholic doctrine, including celibacy for priests and the miracle of transubstantiation, and rejected only the idea of papal supremacy. Henry's refusal to make substantial changes in religious doctrine or practice was part of a shrewd policy for gaining popular consensus behind the break with Rome.

THE ENGLISH REFORMATION

Despite these major transformations made to secure Henry's marriage to Anne Boleyn, the irony was that Henry eventually had four other wives, two of whom, Anne Boleyn and Catherine Howard, were accused of adultery and beheaded. The successor he so desperately wanted was produced by his third wife, Jane Seymour, whose son eventually took the throne as Edward VI (ruled 1547–1553). During the minority of Edward's reign, religious reformers such as Cranmer were free to establish Protestantism more firmly in England. Through further acts of Parliament, the clergy were eventually permitted to marry, and a new liturgy, contained in the *Book of Common Prayer,* was adopted in 1549.

After Edward's early death, the throne passed to Mary (ruled 1553–1558), Henry's daughter with Catherine. Mary tried to restore Catholicism, a policy that produced widespread hostility and resistance, and the burning of some 300 Protestants earned her the nickname "Bloody Mary." The queen then made herself even more unpopular by marrying Philip II of Spain, the son of Charles V. By the time of her death in 1558, Protestantism had been even more firmly established in England.

In Ireland, which was dominated by the English landlords, the parliament passed measures endorsing the separation from Rome and establishing the Church of Ireland modeled on the Anglican Church, with the king as its head. When the majority of Irish people remained Catholic, no doubt partly to express their opposition to the English, the Catholic monasteries and the churches were ordered closed.

In Scotland, where King James V (ruled 1528–1542) and his daughter, Mary, Queen of Scots (ruled 1542–1567), were both strong supporters of the Catholic Church, the state fought the reform movement. The Scottish Reformation was led by John Knox (c. 1505–1572). Knox, a former priest and a fiery preacher, had studied with John Calvin in Geneva. In 1560, he encouraged the parliament in Scotland to pass laws abolishing the Catholic Mass and paving the way for Knox to establish the Presbyterian Church, which took its name from the *presbyters,* or ministers, who controlled it. In 1564, Knox wrote *The Book of Common Order,* which determined the liturgy for the Church of Scotland.

Putting the Reformation in Perspective

The movement for reform within the Catholic Church started by Martin Luther in the early 16th century destroyed the religious unity that western Europe had enjoyed since the late Roman Empire. The establishment of the Protestant churches and the rapid spread of their doctrines revealed deep popular discontent in spiritual affairs. Its reverberations, however, spilled over from religious issues into the secular realm.

The Reformation profoundly influenced the political and social realities of the day. The broad appeal of many reform doctrines especially touched the lower classes, sometimes unleashing popular unrest. The upper classes responded to the Reformation in different ways. In some regions of Europe, rulers and nobles supported reform as a means of undermining papal authority within their own borders, while others remained attached to Roman Catholicism. In defense, the Church of Rome would soon embark on a vigorous program of internal change and counter-reformation that would aim at pushing back the tide of Protestantism. The religious controversies kept Europe in turmoil for centuries to come.

Questions for Further Study

1. What were the origins of the Protestant Reformation?
2. What were Luther's principal ideas, and how did they differ from conventional Christianity?
3. In what ways did religious reformation reflect and affect social and political conditions in Germany?
4. How did the ideas of the other major reformers differ from those of Luther?

Suggestions for Further Reading

Ackroyd, Peter. *The Life of Thomas More.* New York, 1998.

Bouwsma, William J. *John Calvin: A Sixteenth Century Portrait.* New York, 1987.

Edwards, Mark. *Luther's Last Battles.* Ithaca, NY, 1983.

Galer, U.R. Gritsch, trans. *Huldrych Zwingli: His Life and Work.* Philadelphia, 1986.

Haigh, Christopher. *English Reformations: Religion, Politics and Society under the Tudors.* Oxford, 1993.

Jensen, De Lamar. *Reformation Europe: Age of Reform and Revolution.* Lexington, KY, 1981.

Marius, Richard. *Martin Luther: The Christian Between God and Death.* Cambridge, MA, 1999.

McGrath, Alister E. *The Intellectual Origins of the European Reformation.* Oxford, 1987.

Oberman, Heiko. E. Walliser-Schwarzbart, trans. *Luther: Man Between God and the Devil*. New Haven, CT, 1989.

Pettegree, Andrew, ed. *The Reformation World*. New York, 2000.

Scarisbrick, J.J. *The Reformation and the English People*. Oxford, 1984.

Spitz, Lewis W. *The Protestant Reformation, 1517–1559*. New York, 1985.

Tracy, James D. *Europe's Reformations, 1450-1650*. Lanham, MA, 1999.

InfoTrac College Edition

Enter the search term *Reformation* using the Subject Guide.

Enter the search term *Martin and Luther not King* using the Subject Guide.

Enter the search term *John Calvin* using the Subject Guide.

THE SOCIAL WORLDS OF THE RENAISSANCE AND REFORMATION

The sweeping changes that the Renaissance and Reformation produced in cultural and political life in Europe also profoundly affected social patterns. Despite their long-term significance, however, the immediate repercussions of these developments did not have a consistent impact on all sectors of society, although the rate of change was more intense than at any time since the early Middle Ages.

European society was becoming increasingly urbanized, and a new and more complex class structure began to develop in the growing cities. Although rural life remained comparatively static, the urban setting allowed for significantly more social mobility. Foremost among the new social groups of the cities to emerge in this period was a rapidly expanding middle class. This category included the wealthier merchants who arose as a result of the commercial revolution, as well as the less affluent burghers who operated shops and small businesses. Other factors in stimulating social change included the spread of education among urban dwellers and the growing tendency of urban women of the poorer classes to work. This change, in turn, affected patterns of marriage and family life.

The broad changes in society had both positive and negative effects on women, depending on their status. Aristocratic women lost some of the authority and equality they had enjoyed during the High Middle Ages as the values attached to the concept of chivalry were replaced by the more rigid and confining notions associated with formal court life. One of the consequences of the new code of conduct for these women was a double standard of sexual behavior for men and women. For women of the non-noble classes, on the other hand, new employment opportunities, especially in commerce, arose in the walled cities, allowing them the possibility of greater social mobility than ever before.

While Western society remained overwhelmingly Christian and white, urban life contained small but significant minorities, including Jews and Muslims. With the expansion of Europe overseas as a result of the era of reconnaissance, the growth of the slave trade produced a new minority in ever-greater numbers: black slaves, some of whom eventually won their freedom.

The net result of all these developments was to speed up the transformation of European life from its medieval patterns to a society on the eve of the modern world.

CLASS, MOBILITY, AND CHANGING VALUES

During the 16th century, the three most important long-term forces determining social patterns were demographic change, status, and wealth.

POPULATION TRENDS

During the 16th century, Europe began to recover fully from the destructive effects of the Black Death. Before the 19th century, when governments began to collect the first accurate statistics, all calculations of population can be at best very rough estimates. It seems clear, however, that in the course of the 16th century, population increased significantly, perhaps by as much as one-third. By 1600, Europe may have had more than 100 million inhabitants. The growth pattern was neither constant in time nor geographically even throughout the continent, and a sometimes wildly fluctuating death rate—determined largely by famine, disease, and war—helped keep growth in check.

The repercussions of population growth were varied. For one thing, the supply of labor increased significantly. At first, a larger agrarian workforce resulted in an increase in the amount of food available, while rising wages created a demand for manufactured products.

This expansion in turn stimulated economic activity in the towns, which began to attract ever larger numbers of people. By today's standards, towns in the 16th century were quite small. In 1500, Cologne, situated on the Rhine River, was the largest urban center in Germany with a mere 20,000 inhabitants. In that same year, few European cities had populations of more than 100,000. A century later, however, Paris counted a half-million people, Naples 300,000, and London 250,000.

As the urban population of Europe increased, a surplus labor force was created. This drove down real wages, a setback accompanied by a startling rise in prices in the later 16th century known as the "price revolution" (see Topic 46). The inflation in commodity prices, especially for basic necessities such as bread and wheat, was immense—by 1600, prices had risen to four times their level of a century earlier. Wages did not, however, keep up with prices, and the standard of living for the poorer classes declined.

By the 17th century, therefore, population and economic growth began to slow down and in some cases to reverse themselves. Yet if the rise and decline in population was a volatile aspect of social reality, status remained constant as a determining feature of life for every member of European society. A person's status was fixed in a social hierarchy that determined not only how specific groups related to each other, but also how each class lived. The element in 16th-century society that began to undermine social position was wealth.

OLD NOBLES AND NEW MERCHANTS

The 16th century was a time of great expansion and prosperity for the middle classes, and it also saw crisis and read-

Contemporary painting of *Market Place at Antwerp*. 16th century. The painting conveys something of the bustle of the scene. Note the distinction in dress between the middle classes, wearing sober black, and the more colorful costumes of the peasants who are selling their goods. The high, narrow buildings are characteristic of architecture in the Low Countries.

justment for the traditional noble landowning class. Despite their declining financial status, they continued to occupy the most important political posts and government offices. With the strengthening of the monarchy's power, the nobility retained their prestige while losing their old feudal authority over the peasant class.

In France and elsewhere, kings used their ability both to create new categories of nobles and to enlarge the existing ranks of aristocrats in order to enhance royal authority. The French monarchs, for example, limited the power of the old feudal families ("nobles of the sword") by elevating members of the middle class to the status of "nobles of the robe" to serve as bureaucrats in the state system (see Topic 44).

The rise in population and the growth of towns sharply affected the income of those who made their living by manufacturing, creating an ever-rising demand for their products. Moreover, the price revolution redistributed significant wealth to the manufacturing class of the towns by increasing profits. The commercial revolution made possible an equally rapid accumulation of wealth in the hands of a new middle class of merchants and traders. As a result, the definition of status relaxed, and position in the social hierarchy became more fluid.

The leading middle-class citizens were those involved in international trade, banking, and industry, who dominated civic affairs. These powerful families established social customs and patronized the arts. Beneath them were the urban shopkeepers and craftsmen, whose prosperity depended on local rather than international markets. Their economic and social status derived from their membership in guilds, the trade and craft organizations that controlled business and professional standards in the cities.

THE POOR IN TOWN AND COUNTRY

For all the increase in prosperity for the upper classes of society, most of the urban and rural population remained poor and often lived at the edge of subsistence. In the towns, the bulk of the population consisted of manual laborers who earned their daily wages by working on building sites, at ports, and as carters and carriers. Much of this work was seasonal, and in winter the laborers who crowded the towns in good weather often found themselves unemployed. Workers with some degree of specialized skill were employed in the small factories that produced textiles, metal and glass goods, and food products such as beer and bread.

Another principal source of employment in the towns was domestic labor. With the rise of middle-class prosperity, the demand for assistance in the home—maids, cooks, and personal servants—continued to grow. Domestic employment sometimes provided greater job security than casual

Marinus van Reymerswaele, *Bankers*. 15th century. The two men are engaged in counting the coins piled on the table and recording the transaction. The system of double-entry bookkeeping was invented earlier in the century by Florentine bankers and soon spread throughout Europe.

National Gallery, London

Sketch showing an episode from the Peasants' Revolt of 1524–1526. The scene depicts the destruction of a monastery. The main church is on the left, its doors about to be battered down, while other rebels are climbing steps to a large room on the upper floor of the main building, the monks' refectory, or dining-room.

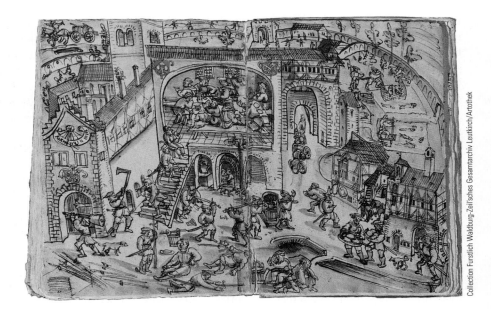

labor, although family servants depended on the goodwill of their employers. Whatever their occupation, workers in the towns played no part in the political affairs of their community and benefited only marginally from the better standard of living and enlarged horizons of the urban environment.

In the countryside, conditions were little better for the peasantry. Nature and the seasons determined the tempo of rural life, where almost all activities focused on farming and the raising of animals. Throughout much of Europe the most widespread and important agricultural product was grain (wheat, rye, barley, and oats), which was baked into bread, the principal item in the peasant diet. In the Mediterranean region, more specialized crops such as grapes and olives provided a more varied source of nutrition while also offering additional products and occupations. In England, the Netherlands, and Germany, the staple drink was beer, while in Italy, France, and Spain farmers used grapes to make wine.

Living conditions for the working classes in both town and country were grim. Urban laborers lived in crowded and unsanitary tenements in slum districts, while peasant housing generally consisted of small and unheated huts in which people dwelled alongside animals. For both groups, fire and disease were constant hazards and starvation a perpetual preoccupation.

EDUCATION, MARRIAGE, AND THE FAMILY

One of the effects of the Renaissance and Reformation was an increase in the importance of education for the nobility and middle classes. The poor and working classes of Europe, who comprised the overwhelming majority of the population, remained excluded from the rise in educational standards until the 19th century. In all classes of society, the family remained the basic social unit, although the period saw a transition from the traditional extended family to the more modern nuclear family.

EDUCATION IN RENAISSANCE AND REFORMATION

The humanists of the Renaissance believed that education should prepare citizens to assume their responsibilities to society as well as to shape individual character. Humanist education combined Classical precepts with Christian teaching to create a fully rounded personality.

In the 15th century, Vittorino da Feltre (1378–1446) translated these ideas into an actual curriculum, which he applied to the students who attended his famous secondary school at Mantua. Vittorino provided a core program of Latin, Greek, philosophy, mathematics, and music, as well as physical training. Vittorino's school attracted students from throughout Italy, and his model curriculum was widely adopted.

Many of the leading Protestant reformers adapted humanist principles to their religious concerns. Whereas Renaissance schools were designed principally to serve the needs of the upper classes, Reformation educators aimed at reaching a broader range of society. Some leaders, like Martin Luther, even encouraged the state to provide free public education for children of all classes. German Protestants introduced secondary school education, which added religious instruction to the traditional humanist curriculum of the liberal arts. Similarly, the newly founded Jesuit order established colleges whose students were taught the classics along with Catholic doctrine. For women, the Ursuline order, founded by St. Angela Merici, provided girls with training in religion and morals (see Topic 41).

MARRIAGE AND THE FAMILY

In all family arrangements, women were subservient to men. Although mothers were responsible for raising children, fathers had ultimate authority over them and arranged their marriages. Husbands also decided matters of family finances and managed their property. Once married, wives generally gave up their independence, including the right to own property in their own name.

Traditionally, European families had consisted of several generations and degrees of kinship living in the same household. A typical family unit might therefore contain father, mother, and children together with grandparents, uncles and aunts, and cousins. With the emphasis on the individual at the heart of both Renaissance and Reformation, this extended family arrangement tended to break up into smaller nuclear units made up of parents and their children. This pattern, typical of Western Europe, foreshadowed the family structure of the 19th and 20th centuries; in eastern Europe, the extended family remained the prevailing model. Despite the changing living arrangements, extended families continued to function as a unit in financial and political matters. This was as true for the old ruling families of the Italian city-states—the Medici and the Visconti, for example—as it was for the newer commercial dynasties of northern Europe.

Given the importance of family connections in business and politics, upper-class parents generally arranged their children's marriages. Such alliances involved the payment of large dowries by the parents of the bride to the husband. Even poor families were expected to provide a dowry for their daughters, making the raising of girls more of an economic strain. In some communities, private charities financed by the wealthy provided subsidies for the payment of dowries among needy families.

Protestants developed new attitudes toward the family. In theory, with the abolition of a celibate clergy, the relationship between husband and wife became the focus of family life, and marriage partners placed new emphasis on mutual love and respect. In practice, however, husbands continued to be the dominant force in most marriages. Martin Luther's example demonstrated the contradictions that often characterized Protestant views of marriage. Luther, a conservative in most social matters, encouraged his followers to maintain the authority of the husband: "The wife," he wrote, "is compelled to obey him by God's command." His own private life, however, seemed to reflect a different, more loving relationship. In 1525, Luther, who had been an Augustinian monk, married a former Cistercian nun, Katharine von Bora (1499–1552). For the 21 years of their marriage, she remained a constant companion and assistant to Luther, who wrote toward the end of his life, "Next to God's Word there is no more precious treasure than holy matrimony."

THE BURDENS OF GENDER: WOMEN IN A CHANGED WORLD

In the Renaissance period, women generally married while still in their teens, whereas men usually postponed marriage until their late thirties. This discrepancy in age was determined by the need for men to achieve financial independence; while the extended family had offered economic support for young families, nuclear families required that fathers had sufficient financial means to maintain their own wives and children. By the 17th century, as women increasingly entered the workplace, they too tended to marry at a later age.

In both courtship and marriage, women of all classes were expected to conform to different standards from men. Young women were kept under constant supervision in order to preserve their virginity before marriage. Newly wed husbands who found that their wives were not virgins had the right to break the marriage without being obliged to return the dowry. Men, on the other hand, were expected to be sexually experienced. For many single men in their twenties and thirties, professional prostitutes provided their services, often under state regulation. In reality, of course, both men and women engaged in sexual activity before marriage, and by the 18th century illegitimate births were commonplace.

EDUCATION, CULTURE, AND THE ECONOMY

The double standard was particularly striking among the aristocracy, who cultivated the courtly way of life. In the Renaissance, children of noble families received a higher level of education than their counterparts in the medieval period. Whereas the training of boys prepared them to participate in business and public affairs, the education of girls was mostly confined to the classics, painting, music, and the other fine arts. University students were almost entirely males, whereas women were educated at home by family or private tutors. As a result, women were unable to train for the professions, although printing made it easier for women to study.

Despite these obstacles, we know of several dozen women Renaissance humanists and a few prominent artists. Vittoria Colonna (1492–1547), for example, wrote love poems and religious sonnets that were widely admired and corresponded with Michelangelo. Generally, however, women found it extremely difficult to pursue intellectual careers, both because they were expected to marry and bear children and because men regarded intellectual pursuits as unwomanly. Among the well-known artists of the day was Sofonisba Anguissola of Cremona (c. 1535–1625), one of six sisters who painted. Anguissola, whose work was admired by Michelangelo, was court painter for Philip II of Spain and received the patronage of rulers and popes.

The medieval tradition of chivalry had required men to pay homage to and respect women. By contrast, Renaissance experts in life at court, such as Castiglione, expected women to serve primarily a purely decorative function in what was essentially a man's world of power and politics (see Topic 36). It was not uncommon for noblewomen in the feudal age to take charge of governments and manage estates in the absence of their husbands. In the leading families of the Renaissance period, however, aristocratic

Collection The Right Honorable Earl Spencer, Althorp House

Sofonisba Anguissola, *Self-Portrait*. 1561. Born in the northern Italian city of Cremona, Anguissola was influenced by Florence Mannerist artists such as Bronzino. Vasari wrote that she handled "design with greater study and better grace than any other woman of our times." By the time of this self-portrait, she had moved to Spain, to work for the Spanish court.

women were limited to performing traditional roles as wives, mothers, and daughters.

Women from the families of wealthy merchants had a greater range of responsibilities. While merchants traveled abroad, their wives ran the family business and were trained to keep records and balance the books. Contessina de' Medici, the wife of the Florentine banker Cosimo, employed a secretary to assist her with her correspondence, while the English diarist Samuel Pepys (1633–1703) taught his wife mathematics so that she could maintain the household accounts.

After the death of her husband, a widow was able to inherit his property and business. Many women used the capital thus acquired to enlarge existing businesses or start their own firms. In the 16th century, women in northern Europe engaged in international commerce and became members of overseas trading companies. In Ravensberg, Germany, in the same period, more than 10 percent of the members of the Merchant's Society were women.

For women of lower economic status, opportunities for social mobility and employment were also available in the towns. Most guilds restricted membership to men, but some allowed a widow to inherit her husband's membership, and a few even permitted women to become members in their

own right. One of the fields open to women was publishing. In Strasbourg in the 16th century and London in the 17th, widows ran publishing houses that they had inherited from their husbands. In the century following 1550, some 10 percent of all publishers in London were women.

In rural areas, women led equally complex but dependent lives. In farming households, wives and daughters were expected to perform multiple roles, including traditional domestic activities, feeding and caring for farm animals, and helping with labor in the fields. The wives of men who worked away from home often ran the farms on their own, including the heavy manual labor of plowing and harvesting. In many cases, women also engaged in cottage industries such as spinning, weaving, and basket making. If she became a widow, a country woman would generally seek to remarry in order to have a man to take charge of work on the farm.

Once they came of age, the daughters of rural families often migrated to the cities. There they looked for employment, generally in domestic work, which remained the chief form of urban women's work until modern times. Domestic labor involved long working hours and low pay, and young girls were often subjected to sexual violence by their employers. Women also found jobs in other fields, including manual labor in construction, mining, and retailing. In market towns, women ran most businesses involving the preparation, buying, and selling of food. In all occupations that they shared with men, women were paid significantly less. The overwhelming majority of townswomen were poor, and some of those who did not find employment or a husband supported themselves by prostitution.

The vast transformations that unfolded in the era of the Renaissance and Reformation brought widespread and generally beneficial changes to Europe. For women, however, they had mixed consequences. The overall pattern of European women's lives did not improve substantially until the 18th century, when the Industrial Revolution wrought a massive restructuring of European society.

FEAR OF WITCHES: SUPERSTITION AND PERSECUTION

Women were also seriously affected by one of the most striking aspects of the fanatical atmosphere that accompanied the religious upheavals of the 16th century—the growing fear of witches that seemed to grip society. When the papacy instituted the Inquisition against the Albigensians in the 13th century (see Topic 27), it also began to persecute witches as part of that same campaign. On the eve of the Reformation, the church renewed its interest in stamping out witchcraft. The campaign against witchcraft was not, however, limited to Catholic states, and the hysteria over witches appears to have swept Europe, affecting Germany, Switzerland, England and Scotland, and the English colonies in North America.

Witchcraft was an ancient form of worship that had long been widespread in Europe's villages and rural areas. In the Middle Ages, the church identified witches with worship of the devil and made witchcraft a heresy. The

Woodcut showing a witch being abducted by the Devil. 1555. The devil, painted in green, has horns and three-toed feet. The scale of the horse, rider, and captive contrasts with the peasants on the right, working in the fields outside the town nearby.

AKG London

Inquisition made witches a target of its activities, and during periods of social and economic crisis, witches often became targets of popular wrath. In 1484, the papacy condemned witches as having become instruments of Satan and the cause of a variety of evils. Two Dominican friars investigated witchcraft in Germany on behalf of the papacy and authored a handbook about the practices of witches and methods by which to identify them. Witches were said not only to have participated in nighttime ceremonies and sexual orgies but also to have cast spells on others.

At the time of the Reformation, the belief in witches seems to have become the source of popular hysteria, with people accusing each other indiscriminately and tens of thousands being prosecuted for witchcraft. The fear of witches in the 16th and early 17th centuries multiplied, and trials of accused persons were a daily occurrence in many parts of Europe. The victims of the witchcraft craze came from all walks of life, although people from the lower classes seem more likely to have been accused.

The frenzy over witchcraft had serious implications for the position of women; three out of four people charged with witchcraft were women, most of whom were widows. Most were from the lower classes, including peasants and domestic servants. The identification of women with witches further marginalized them in society, creating identifications in the popular mind with devil worship and sin. Some witch hunters thought women were evil by nature, an attitude supported both by the biblical tale of Eve's corruption of Adam and by medieval folk tales.

Certainly part of the cause of the witchcraft craze was the aroused passion of religious controversy during a time of heightened sensitivity to charges of heresy. The social turmoil of the period also seems to have contributed to the fear of unrest among the poorer classes. The great witchcraft fear declined in the second half of the 17th century, when the religious conflicts and the wars that accompanied them ended. As conditions began to settle down, the tensions and divisiveness that inspired the trials diminished, and by the early 18th century the superstitions that had fed the fear began to be dispelled.

The great contradiction of the witchcraft craze was, of course, that it occurred at the very time that reformers were seeking spiritual regeneration. Luther, Calvin, and other Protestant leaders condemned witches as savagely as they did the Catholic clergy, and its victims were burned at the stake by both churches.

OUTSIDERS IN CHRISTIAN EUROPE: JEWS, MUSLIMS, AND BLACKS

The 16th and 17th centuries saw much of European life dominated by religious conflict between Catholics and Protestants. On the fringes of European society, several non-Christian religious minorities had maintained a precarious existence for centuries. Jews and Muslims lived side by side in Spain and in Spanish possessions in Italy until 1492. Yet there were differences in the status of Muslims and Jews in Christian society. Muslims were tolerated partly because strong Muslim states with large Christian populations provided them with some degree of protection. In the Middle Ages, Jews were the only group to whom Christians granted the right of dissent. On the other hand, nowhere were Jews accorded the full rights of active citizenship.

The consolidation of the kingdom of Spain under Ferdinand and Isabella, together with the religious upheavals of the Reformation and Counter-Reformation, had a dramatic effect on the lives of the Jewish minority there. In the early 15th century, the largest concentrations of Jews in Europe were in Iberia, where perhaps 80,000 lived, as well as in Sicily, which had some 35,000. Another 35,000 Jews lived in Italy, while southern France and the German areas of the Holy Roman Empire had smaller numbers. As Jews were forced out of Spain, many moved to eastern Europe and others to the Ottoman Empire. In the 16th century, Jews were expelled from some Italian states, and by the end of that century, there were more than 100,000 Polish Jews (on Jewish life in Europe, see Topic 41).

As far back as the age of Classical Greece, artists portrayed black people on painted vases and in small figurines. The earliest Africans to live in ancient Europe were the slaves who were brought by traders toward the end of the Roman Republic at the time of the Punic Wars.

HISTORICAL PERSPECTIVES

THE FIRST AFRICANS IN EUROPE

TREVOR P. HALL   Bethune-Cookman College

The first Africans in Europe fell into three ca-tegories: (1) élite noblemen, clerics, and ambassadors; (2) freemen/women vendors, translators, sailors, artisans, and laborers; and (3) slaves. The major questions are, how many Africans lived in ancient Europe, what were they doing in Europe, where did they live, and when did they arrive?

Black Africans have lived in "Europe" since ancient times when North Africa and the Sahara Desert formed the southern frontier of the Roman Empire. Beginning in the 4th century A.D., German invaders sacked Rome and began settling in the Empire, and in the process disrupted long-distance trade with Africa and began the rapid political disintegration of the Empire in the West. Portugal and Spain were removed from Germanic control when Muslims from North Africa conquered the Iberian peninsula in A.D. 711 and linked it to Muslim states in Africa. From A.D. 711 to 1492, a few black Africans who were Muslims lived in Europe's southwest frontiers in Portugal and Spain. During this period, some Africans also lived in Genoa and Venice as Italian ships traded with North Africans from Morocco to Egypt.[1]

From time to time, African clerics from the Coptic Church of Christian Ethiopia visited Rome when benevolent Muslim leaders in Egypt permitted pilgrims to cross Islamic territories. One Portuguese tale has Prince Henry the Navigator of Portugal meeting an Ethiopian cleric in Portugal. The African convinced Prince Henry that the powerful Christian Kingdom of Ethiopia lay south of Muslim Egypt. According to the 15th-century Portuguese royal chronicler, Gomes Eannes de Azurara, one of the five reasons Prince Henry first sent ships to West Africa was to find the Christian king of Ethiopia whom the Portuguese called Prester John.[2] Prince Henry envisioned a military alliance with black Christians of Ethiopia that would destroy Islam by attacking its southern underbelly.

Searching for Ethiopia, Prince Henry the Navigator sent Portuguese mariners past Morocco to West Africa where in 1441, they kidnapped four black Muslim fishermen from the mouth of the Senegal River and brought them back to Europe. The Portuguese became the first to sail from Europe to West Africa. By the 1470s Spain sent ships to West Africa. Over the next four centuries, European ships would transport hundreds of thousands of West Africans to Europe.

The earliest European mariners in 15th-century West Africa were traders, not conquerors. These Portuguese established peaceful diplomatic relationships with several African kingdoms, especially states that had strategic Atlantic harbors. In 1488, four years before Christopher Columbus sailed to the Americas, a Muslim nobleman and Portuguese ally named Bemoim visited Portugal from his Wolof kingdom in modern-day Senegal. He sought Portuguese military assistance to regain his lost throne. The mission ended with Bemoim's death at the hands of his Portuguese patrons, but his visit marked the first of a long line of African nobles in Europe.[3]

From the 1480s through the 1700s, African nobles visited Portugal, Spain, and France. Most African nobles in early modern Europe lived in Portugal and came from the Congo. As early as the 1480s, a Congolese ambassador sailed to Portugal where he represented his nation.[4] In the 1490s, Congolese noble children lived in the Portuguese king's castle in Évora, Portugal. According to the modern historian Basil

[1] Jacques Heers, *Escravos E Servidão Doméstica Na Idade Média No Mundo Mediterranico* (Lisbon: Publicacões, 1983).

[2] Gomes Eannes de Azurara, *The Chronicle of the Discovery and Conquest of Guinea,* trans. and eds., Charles Raymond Beazley and Edgar Prestage (London: The Hakluyt Society, 1st wer., no. 100; reprint New York: Burt Franklin, 1899).

[3] José Goncalves and Paul Teyssier, "Textes Portugais sur les Wolofs au XV siècle—Batême du prince Bemoi (1488)" *Bulletin de'IFAN,* t. xxx, ser., B. no. 3 (Paris, 1968), 822–846.

[4] Antonio Brásio, *Hortórica Do Reino Do Congo* [Ms. 8080 da Biblioteca Nacional de Lisboa] (Lisboa: Centro De Estudos Historicos Ultramarinos, 1969).

Davidson, 20 young Congolese students were sent to Europe in 1516. A few years later, the son of the Congolese king visited the pope in Rome. One Congolese prince became a bishop in the Catholic Church and was then called Dom Henrique.[5] Other African ambassadors in early modern Portugal included representatives from Benin, Angola, and Ethiopia, as well as Serers from Senegal.

After Portuguese ships established direct maritime links with West Africans in 1441, other Africans migrated to Europe, where many retained their freedom. A few enslaved Africans in Europe regained their liberty and formed free African communities. In the centuries after 1441, most free Africans in Europe lived in the Portuguese capital Lisbon, or in the Spanish cities Seville and Valencia. After the 1520s, however, small groups of free blacks were found in England, France, and Holland after these nations started trading directly with West Africa.

European historians record isolated cases of Africans who were set free when they arrived in Europe aboard European ships. For example, in 1571 France, "a shipowner placed some blacks on sale in Bordeaux, but they were ordered released by the Parlement."[6] Holland had a similar case, in 1596, when 130 Africans whom Captain Pieter van der Haagen had brought to Middleburg were set free by the town council and ordered to find jobs as free workers.[7] The English romanticize about Africans who regained their freedom upon setting foot on English soil.[8]

Some free Africans discovered innovative ways to maintain their freedom. As early as March 17, 1490, the black man Pedro Alvares secured a letter from the king of England certifying him to be a free man before he migrated to Portugal.[9] One enslaved African regained his freedom from his Portuguese master, Joao de Coimbra, on March 23, 1498, when he jumped ship in East Africa during Vasco da Gama's maiden voyage to India. These cases were the exception; as a rule most free blacks in Europe worked, saved money, and purchased their freedom, or that of their families.

Some free blacks in Portugal worked as mariners and translators aboard European merchant ships that traded in West Africa and the Americas. Portuguese archival records indicate that some blacks who were granted their freedom in a deceased master's will were still kept in bondage. On March 20, 1518, King Manuel of Portugal acted on the request from a black fraternity in Lisbon to ensure that wills were honored.[10] Free blacks in Seville, Spain, also had a fraternity to protect their interests in the 16th century.[11] Once additional European nations joined Portugal and Spain in trading with Africa, free African communities appeared all over western Europe.

Most black Africans in early modern Europe lived in bondage. Most enslaved Africans lived in Lisbon, Portugal's capital city where the 9950 captives formed almost 10 percent of the population in 1551–1553.[12] Thousands of other enslaved Africans lived throughout Portugal, especially in the southern port towns in Algarve province. After Portugal, the greatest number of enslaved blacks lived in the Spanish cities of Seville and Valencia. From 1482 to 1516 some 5000 enslaved Africans arrived in Valencia from Portugal and its colonies.[13]

After the 1530s, France, England, and Holland sent ships to West Africa, and these European merchants transported captive Africans to Europe. By the early 1600s, England and France joined Spain and Portugal in establishing colonies in the West Indies and North America. Once European planters began exploiting enslaved African laborers in the Americas, plantation owners who returned to Europe transported captive Africans to Europe. Despite maritime trade from Africa to Europe, and planters bringing enslaved Africans from their Caribbean plantations, Europe never had more Africans than the 10 percent of 1551–1553 Lisbon.

[5] D. Charles-Martail De Witte, *Henri de Congo, Eveque titulaire d 'Utique* (Roma, 1968).

[6] William B. Cohen, *The French Encounter with Africans, White Response to Blacks, 1530–1880* (Bloomington: Indiana University Press, 1980), 5.

[7] Johannes Menne Posta, *The Dutch in the Atlantic Slave Trade, 1500–1815* (Cambridge: Cambridge University Press, 1990), 10.

[8] Folarin Shyllon, *Black People in Great Britain* (London: Oxford University Press, 1977).

[9] Arquivo Nacional da Torre do Tombo, "Chancelaria De. D. Joao II," livro 16, fol. 61. Printed in Azevedo "Os Escravos" *Archivo Historico Portuguez 1*, no. 9 (1903), 300.

[10] Arquivo Nacional da Torre de Tombo, "Chancelaria de D. Joao III," Liv. 22, fols. 100–100v, and Liv. 17, fol. 44v. Printed in Antonio Brásio, *Monumenta Missionaria Africana, Africa Ocidental*, 2d. ser. (1500–1569) (Lisboa: 1963), vol. 2, 151–152.

[11] Ruth Pike, *Aristocrats and Traders, Sevillian Society in the Sixteenth Century* (Ithaca: Cornell University Press, 1972).

[12] A. Saunders, *A Social History of Black Slaves and Freedmen in Portugal 1441–1555* (London: Cambridge University Press, 1982), 55.

[13] P. E. H. Hair, "Black African Slaves at Valencia, 1482–1516: An Onomastic Inquiry," *History in Africa* 7 (1980).

Detail of Benozzo Gozzoli, *The Journey of the Magi.* 1459. Length (entire work) 12 feet 4½ inches (3.77 m.). Although in theory the scene represents an episode from the Biblical story of the Nativity, in practice the riders and their attendants are recognizable as personalities from Early Renaissance Italy. The two seen here in front are Galeazzo Sforza of Milan and Sigismondo Malatesta of Rimini. Note the African attendant in the center.

During the Roman Empire, slave traders imported Africans as both domestic and farm laborers. After the fall of the Empire, Muslim and Christian traders continued to bring black African slaves into the Byzantine Empire and North Africa. Although medieval artists sometimes portrayed blacks in their works, the number of blacks in Europe remained small.

Blacks began to appear in Europe in larger numbers in the early 16th century, as a result of the Portuguese voyages of exploration. The increasing knowledge about remote regions of the world and their exotic inhabitants stimulated European curiosity about Africans. In addition to serving as domestic servants and manual laborers, blacks were prized as court entertainers and personal attendants for the ruling class. The early interest in Africa and its people would be replaced in later centuries by the horrors of the massive transatlantic slave trade.

Putting the Social Worlds of the Renaissance and Reformation in Perspective

Although European society during the Renaissance and Reformation underwent profound change, its effects were uneven. Among the most significant developments of the period were the growth of urban life and the rise of the merchant classes, which introduced an element of unprecedented social mobility. Other features of social change included the new importance attributed to education among urban dwellers, and the growing number of women of the poorer classes who found work and new lives in the towns. These changes greatly modified existing patterns of marriage and family arrangements. Rural life, on the other hand, retained its essentially medieval character of isolation and poverty as millions of peasants lived according to the cycle of nature.

Women were affected by the sweeping social changes in both favorable and unfavorable ways, depending on their status. The Renaissance, for example, saw the introduction of a double standard of sexual behavior for men and women. By contrast, poorer women who in earlier times had little opportunity to work outside the home now found new kinds of employment in the towns.

Still another new factor in society was the presence of a largely unknown minority—blacks from Africa—who, together with the Jews and Muslims, formed the only significant non-Christian elements in the population of Europe.

For all the inconsistency of these developments, the general impact was to intensify the slow but irrevocable breakdown of medieval patterns of European life. The broad structural forces that were transforming Europe—urbanization, the emergence of a global economy, and the development of new modes of production—led in the 18th century to revolutionary change.

Questions for Further Study

1. What were the principal barriers to class mobility? Was movement between classes at all possible?
2. What social and cultural constraints limited the role of women in European society? Does the witchcraft craze reveal anything about attitudes toward women?
3. How did Christian society treat "outsiders"?

Suggestions for Further Reading

Barstow, Anne L. *Witchcraze: A New History of European Witch Hunts*. San Francisco, 1994.

Bornstein, Daniel, and Roberto Rusconi, eds. *Women and Religion in Medieval and Renaissance Italy*. Chicago, 1996.

Clark, Stuart. *Thinking with Demons: The Idea of Witchcraft in Early Modern Europe*. New York, 1997.

Cohen, Elizabeth S., and Thomas V. Cohen. *Daily Life in Renaissance Italy*. Westport, CT, 2001.

Faur, Jose. *In the Shadow of History: Jews and Conversos at the Dawn of Modernity*. Albany, NY, 1992.

Hale, John. *The Civilization of Europe in the Renaissance*. New York, 1994.

Jardine, Lisa. *Worldly Goods: A New History of the Renaissance*. New York, 1996.

Kedar, Benjamin Z. *Crusade and Mission: European Approaches Towards the Muslim*. Princeton, NJ, 1984.

Levack, Brian P. *The Witch-Hunt in Early Modern Europe*. New York, 1987.

Ozment, Steven. *When Fathers Ruled: Family Life in Reformation Europe*. Cambridge, MA, 1983.

Rocke, Michael. *Forbidden Friendships: Homosexuality and Male Culture in Renaissance Florence*. New York, 1996.

Ruggiero, Guido. *The Boundaries of Eros: Sex, Crime and Sexuality in Renaissance Venice*. Oxford, 1985.

Stone, Lawrence. *The Family, Sex and Marriage in England, 1500–1800*. New York, 1979.

InfoTrac College Edition

Enter the search term *Renaissance* using the Subject Guide.

Enter the search term *Reformation* using the Subject Guide.

PART V

THE EARLY MODERN WORLD

The hundred and fifty years following the Reformation, with its conflicts and divisions, were marked by the intensification and culmination of many earlier trends. Europe began a period of consolidation, growth and expansion, and cultural innovation that established its global primacy.

In politics, the early modern period saw the successful concentration of power in the hands of absolutist monarchs in their long struggle with the nobles. In England, Henry VIII defied the papacy and established Protestantism in his realm, disciplined the nobility, and bent Parliament to his will. His daughter Elizabeth, avoiding direct confrontation, achieved an uneasy balance in her relationship with Parliament, but her successors,

James I and Charles I, again took up the struggle. The result was a far-reaching civil war that led to the triumph of Parliament and the temporary end of the monarchy. There followed a period of military dictatorship under Oliver Cromwell.

Elsewhere in Europe, royal power increased. In Spain, Philip II micromanaged not only his kingdom but also a vast overseas empire. In France in the 16th and 17th centuries, monarchs laid the foundations of absolutism, building up the royal administration, taming the nobility, and securing state authority over the appointment of bishops and other ecclesiastical officials.

The age was further marked by bitter religious conflicts that were in part the legacy of the Reformation and in part the result of politics.

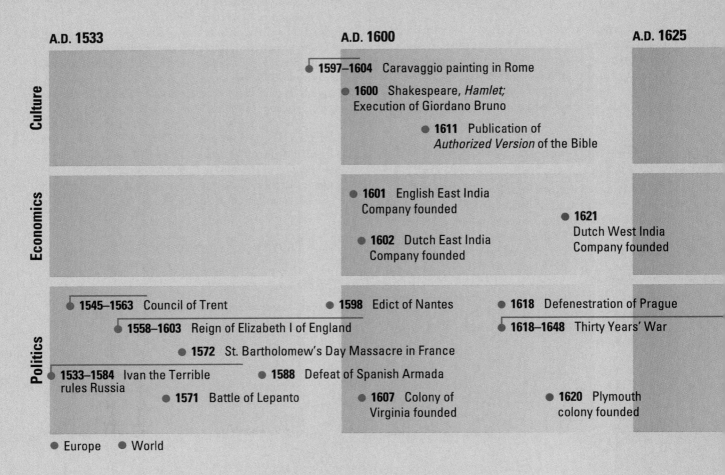

A.D. 1533　　　　　　　**A.D. 1600**　　　　　　　**A.D. 1625**

Culture

- **1597–1604** Caravaggio painting in Rome
- **1600** Shakespeare, *Hamlet;* Execution of Giordano Bruno
- **1611** Publication of *Authorized Version* of the Bible

Economics

- **1601** English East India Company founded
- **1602** Dutch East India Company founded
- **1621** Dutch West India Company founded

Politics

- **1545–1563** Council of Trent
- **1558–1603** Reign of Elizabeth I of England
- **1572** St. Bartholomew's Day Massacre in France
- **1533–1584** Ivan the Terrible rules Russia
- **1571** Battle of Lepanto
- **1598** Edict of Nantes
- **1588** Defeat of Spanish Armada
- **1607** Colony of Virginia founded
- **1618** Defenestration of Prague
- **1618–1648** Thirty Years' War
- **1620** Plymouth colony founded

● Europe　● World

Rijksmuseum, Amsterdam

Protestantism gave new urgency to Catholic pressure for spiritual and institutional reform. The Council of Trent produced a huge body of revised doctrine and settled several important disputes raging within the church. New religious orders such as the Jesuits were founded, and old institutions such as the Inquisition were revived.

Religion continued to dominate European politics. In the 16th and 17th centuries, religious wars devastated Germany, shaped much of the domestic history of France, and greatly influenced events in Spain and England. In eastern Europe the Catholic offensive against

A.D. 1650

A.D. 1700

● **1633** Galileo tried and condemned

● **1663** Bernini completes piazza and colonnades for St. Peter's, Rome

● **1642–1648** English Civil Wars

● **1643–1715** Reign of Louis XIV of France

● **1648** Peace of Westphalia

● **1660** English monarchy restored

Protestantism ensured that the region remained largely immune to Protestantism. From 1618 to 1648, most of Europe's great powers were drawn into a terrible religious and secular conflict, the Thirty Years' War.

Despite the rapid pace of political change, the social patterns of daily life evolved more slowly, gradually influencing the basic aspects of living, including the health and well-being of Europeans, diet and housing, and clothes. The period was one of economic growth, although not without its difficulties. The principal change after 1500 was the shift in trade patterns from the Mediterranean to the Atlantic and northern European coasts. The resulting commercial revolution was dominated at first by Spain and Portugal, but later by the English and the emergence of the Dutch Republic.

The cultural life of Europe in the early modern period was characterized by the emergence of a new style known as Baroque. In the Renaissance, artists sought ideal principles of beauty and harmony to express eternal values. Baroque artists, by contrast, tried to express the emotional states of individuals, whether in words, music, or painting. In doing so, they laid the ground for the arts in the modern era with their search for self-expression and the answers to personal questions.

CATHOLIC REFORM AND THE COUNTER-REFORMATION

The age of the Reformation was also a time of renewal and change within the Catholic Church. This Catholic reform movement resulted partly because the call for change inspired many devout Catholics to renew their religious faith and restore the purity of their church. After all, there had been Catholic reformers long before Luther and Calvin. On the other hand, the startling spread of Protestantism and the victories scored by the reformers and monarchs alike in breaking with Rome drove the papacy and the Catholic hierarchy to clean out their own house. As the Catholic Church began to be energized by its own reforms, the papacy struck back at the Protestants, declaring war against them everywhere and creating new institutions to combat the heresies of the day.

The Council of Trent that first met in 1545 began the process of both reaffirming the theological principles of the church and of launching the Counter-Reformation. Moreover, new religious orders dedicated to Catholic revival were founded by Angela Merici and Ignatius Loyola, while the papacy established the Inquisition to stamp out heretics. By the late 16th century, the offensive of the Catholic Church had not destroyed Protestantism but had at least halted its spread. Yet in international relations, the religious controversies of the age would continue to be fought out for almost another century.

SIGNIFICANT DATES

Catholic Reform and Counter-Reform

1425	Thomas à Kempis writes *The Imitation of Christ*
1478	Spanish Inquisition established
1492	Jews expelled from Spain
1452–1498	Life of Savonarola
1542	Papal Inquisition revived
1534–1549	Paul III reigns as pope
1545–1563	Council of Trent
1491–1556	Life of Ignatius Loyola
1515–1582	Life of Teresa of Avila
1600	Giordano Bruno burned at the stake

THE CATHOLIC CHURCH AND THE SPIRIT OF RENEWAL

Spiritual renewal and institutional reform were not new to the Catholic Church. Throughout the Middle Ages, movements had arisen within the faith to end corruption and rekindle popular belief, and some of these efforts were responses to broader problems in European society.

THE ROOTS OF CATHOLIC REFORM

The resulting growth in popular devotion was expressed by turning away from the formal religious practices of the church to mysticism and new forms of piety. Popular religious practices, like the payment of indulgences to escape the consequences of sin, were designed to generate divine grace and achieve salvation; they included pilgrimages, processions, and special masses for the dead. Many devout Christians joined special lay branches of the mendicant orders founded by St. Dominic and St. Francis.

The most significant expression of the new piety was mysticism. Mystics were convinced that believers experienced God not through theological discourse or institutional rituals but rather through love and emotional availability. Mystics sought to establish a sense of union with God through contemplation and spiritual meditation.

The focus of popular mysticism in the 14th century was the Rhine Valley of western Germany, where Meister Eckhart (1260–1327) developed a large following through his impassioned preaching. Eckhart denied the importance of traditional dogma, stressing instead the cultivation of a "divine spark" that would achieve oneness with God. Lay followers of the Dutch mystic Gerhard Groote (1340–1384) founded the Brethren of the Common Life for men and a similar organization known as the Sisters of the Common Life for women. Groote maintained that communion with God could best be achieved by imitating Christ and devoting oneself to good works. His followers founded schools and lived according to self-imposed rules of simplicity and humility.

Several localized efforts at church reform had been attempted in the late 15th and early 16th centuries. The Dominican friar Girolamo Savonarola (1452–1498) had tried to bring discipline and moral leadership to the people of Florence, where he held sway for two years before the church ordered his execution for heresy. Working within the church had been Cardinal Francisco Ximines (c. 1437–1517), confessor to Queen Isabella of Spain. He imposed stricter controls over the clergy and infused the Spanish Church with a spirit of discipline and fervor. New religious orders, such as the Capuchins, reached out to the common people in an ef-

Painting of *The Council of Trent*. 1586. The Council, which met sporadically from 1545 to 1563, redefined Catholic teachings and reaffirmed the dogmas of transubstantiation, the apostolic succession, and celibacy for the clergy—all of which had been challenged by Luther and his followers. The solemn grandeur of the scene was to be one of the effects sought for by Baroque artists.

© Fotoburg Marburg/Art Resource, NY

fort to help improve the lives of the poor and the sick. But leadership from Rome seemed to be needed if the church was to transform in a significant way.

POPE PAUL III

Soon after Luther launched the Protestant revolution against Rome, the Catholic Church had at its head a zealous and learned pope, Paul III (ruled 1534–1549). Paul had been a cardinal from the powerful Roman Farnese family and stood out among his fellow cardinals as an astute diplomat and genuine reformer. Paul's election to the papacy came at a crucial time because many people believed the church was on the edge of collapse. Paul gave vigorous leadership to the reforming party within the hierarchy, favoring the calling of a new council that would try to reconcile Protestants and Catholics and reform the church. Attacking the worldliness of the clergy, Paul appointed a special commission of ardent reformers to advise him. The commission recommended curbing the abuses in the sale of indulgences and reported to the pope on the corruption of high officials and cardinals. Paul appointed many new, reform-minded members of the College of Cardinals and approved the establishment of the Jesuit order.

THE COUNCIL OF TRENT

Paul's commission also aided in the detailed preparations for the Council of Trent, the great meeting of church reformers that he had proposed for 10 years. The more reactionary-minded clergy had steadily and bitterly opposed the idea of a council, which held its first session in the northern Italian city of Trento in 1545. Just as it began to get down to serious work, however, Paul died, so that the reform initiative was deprived of his leadership.

The council, which met on and off until 1563, devoted its energies to settling theological questions, reinforcing traditions within the church, and organizing a counterattack against the Protestants. Its sessions were often stormy and rife with dissension and division. Yet in the end, some important decisions were reached. The council condemned the selling of church offices and fake indulgences, limited the secular activities of the clergy, and demanded greater supervision of the clergy by bishops and cardinals. Bishops were now required to live in their dioceses, and priests and monks were exhorted to go among the people to preach and act as personal examples of spiritual uprightness. The council emphasized the importance of church tradition that went back centuries, an approach the Protestants countered with the argument that the church was a human institution.

In the theological sphere, the Council of Trent reaffirmed the basic doctrines that Luther and the Protestants had challenged. These included the seven sacraments, the idea of salvation both by good works and by faith, and the doctrine of transubstantiation that held that the bread and wine of the communion became by miracle the body and blood of Christ. The Latin translation of the Bible known as the Vulgate was proclaimed the official version of the Scriptures, the veneration of saints and relics was reasserted, and clergy were forbidden to marry.

EDUCATION AND CONVERSION: THE JESUITS AND THE URSULINES

The reforming spirit that Paul had inaugurated resulted in the creation of several new religious orders. The Capuchins, a Franciscan brotherhood, devoted themselves to preaching and working among the poor, while the Theatines focused on inspiring faith among the clergy. The most famous and important of the new organizations, however, was the Society of Jesus.

IGNATIUS LOYOLA AND THE JESUITS

The Jesuit order, as it is more commonly known, was founded by a Spanish soldier, later priest, named Ignatius Loyola (1491–1556). Loyola, descended from a noble family of the Basque country, had been a soldier in the army of Charles V. While convalescing from wounds he had received in 1521, Loyola began reading the lives of religious figures, including biographies of St. Francis and St. Dominic. As a result, he underwent a conversion and dedicated his life to doing God's work. Loyola engaged in meditation exercises and studied at universities in Spain and France, and in the process developed a small but dedicated following.

Loyola founded his society in 1524 at the University of Paris. His *Spiritual Exercises*, a work of powerful Christian

Engraving showing Ignatius Loyola. 16th century. Images such as this one, based on a portrait from life, were printed in large numbers and circulated widely. Both the Reformation and the Counter-Reformation movements used the new medium of printing to further their causes. Devotional images of popular saints, like this one, were intended to inspire the faithful.

inspiration and spiritual discipline, claimed that through critical self-study and the surrender of individual will, each person can achieve union with God. His teachings insisted on the importance of obedience and self-discipline rather than free choice. Ironically, Loyola came under suspicion by the Inquisition several times.

En route to Palestine to convert the Muslims, Loyola and his disciples, chief among them Francis Xavier, found themselves in Italy when they learned that unsettled conditions in the Holy Land made it impossible for them to continue their journey. They decided to remain in Italy and preach their message of devotion there. In 1537, he and his followers were ordained in Rome, and two years later he sent a draft of a constitution for a new order to the papacy for approval. In 1540 Pope Paul III endorsed it. The plan called for a centralized order governed along military lines by a "general" who reported directly to the pope. The Jesuits took the same kind of vows of poverty and chastity as members of other orders but were devoted to a militant spirit of defending and advancing the faith.

The Jesuits were trained to push back Protestantism by working among the Catholic masses as well as among their leaders. To the common people they preached the need for confession. They restructured secondary education so as to instill Catholic devotion in the young. In this spirit they launched a program to found a series of schools, later known as colleges, to provide Catholic education and discipline for tens of thousands of boys from among the poor as well as the upper classes. The Jesuit curriculum linked humanist education with Catholic religious teachings. Their schools became the training ground for generations of religious and secular leaders, many of whom found employment in the burgeoning state bureaucracies. In this way, the Jesuit order was able to influence government policies indirectly, while many Jesuits became private confessors to important nobles and rulers.

In the spirit of their new militancy, the Jesuits embarked on a worldwide program of missionary work aimed at converting "heathens" in Asia, Africa, and the Americas to the Catholic faith. By the end of the 16th century, Jesuit missions had been established in China, Japan, the Congo, Brazil, Mexico, and many other distant outposts of Catholic activity. Some of their missionaries, such as Francis Xavier, achieved widespread fame as zealous bearers of God's word to non-Christian civilizations around the world. Others spread knowledge of secular aspects of Western culture, particularly in China.

THE JESUITS IN CHINA

Not long after the Counter-Reformation, China fell under the rule of a new dynasty, the Qing, which lasted until 1911. The Qing invaded China from Manchuria to the south in 1644, at the collapse of the Ming dynasty, and were considered as foreigners by most Chinese. Unlike virtually all of their predecessors, they made serious efforts to establish contact with other peoples. One of the first Qing em-

Painting of St. Teresa of Avila, a devoted visionary, who founded the Carmelite order of nuns. 16th century. The dove of the Holy Spirit descends from the top left, as the words of the saint's prayer are legible in the ribbon above her head: "I shall sing for eternity of the mercies of the Lord."

Institut Amatller d'Art Hispanic, Barcelona

perors, Kang Hsi (1654–1722), signed a treaty with Peter the Great of Russia in 1689, in an attempt to establish recognized borders between the two empires.

Kang Hsi also encouraged the introduction, under careful control, of Western education and arts. Jesuit missionaries had already reached China; one of the first, Matteo Ricci (1552–1610), studied Chinese in order to teach Western astronomy, geography, and mathematics to Chinese scholars. Kang Hsi used other Jesuits as mapmakers and took Jesuit physicians with him on his travels. In some cases he appointed Jesuits to official positions at court. The Flemish missionary and astronomer Ferdinand Verbiest (1623–1688) became the director of the Imperial Astronomical Bureau in 1669 and played a part in negotiations to fix the Chinese–Russian border.

Encouraged by the Jesuit successes—and perhaps to keep an eye on future developments—the pope sent an ambassador to see if a permanent papal legation could be opened in Beijing. The emperor refused permission and required all Jesuits then resident in China to sign a statement declaring that they understood and accepted the imperial definition of Confucianism and ancestral rituals.

Thus the Jesuit order was to achieve significant influence in secular as well as religious affairs, especially through their educational programs and their private influence on individual monarchs. Yet the Jesuit experience was originally conceived as a weapon in the war for religious conviction that had been launched by the Protestant revolt. Loyola's "soldiers of Christ" were sometimes viewed too literally as religious warriors, but certainly Loyola was consumed with the passion for discipline and proselytizing. In 1622, the church made Loyola a saint.

THE URSULINES AND CATHOLIC WOMEN

Societies devoted to religious work by and among women had been founded before Luther's time. The Sisters of the Common Life, for example, had been inspired by the movement for popular religious devotion. St. Teresa of Avila (1515–1582) founded the Carmelite order of nuns, who devoted themselves to works of charity.

Most similar to the Jesuits, however, was the Ursuline order, founded by St. Angela Merici (1473–1540). The Ursulines were essentially an order of teaching nuns designed to educate girls in religious and moral affairs. Of Venetian background, the young Merici had been inspired by the good works of local nuns and religious orders and volunteered to work with the Franciscan monks. In 1516, she founded a girl's school for scriptural instruction. Although she never took official church vows, Merici devoted herself to helping the sick and the poor. In 1535, she founded the Company of St. Ursula, which was modeled on the Franciscan order. Because her followers—that is, women—chose to work among the people rather than remain in secluded cloisters, it was only some 30 years later that the papacy finally extended formal approval to the company.

THE WAR AGAINST THE HERETICS: THE SACRED CONGREGATION OF THE HOLY OFFICE

The reforms instituted from above by Pope Paul III were complemented by the devotion, discipline, and fervor of countless reformers such as Loyola and Merici. It was through the Inquisition, however, that the church fought its unremitting war against those who had left the Catholic fold. Its harsh and often brutal techniques, far from advancing the cause, often sparked the opposite effect, giving the Counter-Reformation a negative reputation.

THE INQUISITION

The movement known as the **Inquisition** had been suggested by Loyola with the support of Cardinal Giampietro Caraffa (ruled as Pope Paul IV 1555–1559), who became its head. Nevertheless, there had been precedents, including the formal papal Inquisition established in 1233 by Gregory IX, who had placed the war against the Albigensian heretics in the hands of the Dominicans.

The Inquisition, like its medieval predecessor, was a traveling tribunal that conducted inquiries in various locations. Persons accused of heresy were not given the names of their accusers, although they were often permitted to list their enemies as a way of checking against false accusations. Those who refused to confess were tried, often with the use of torture to extract confessions—and without confession, there could be no conviction. Because heresy was considered a civil as well as a religious crime, those found guilty were punished by the local rulers rather than by the church. Penance, fine, and imprisonment were the usual penalties, although burning at the stake was also used. The most notorious manifestation of the Inquisition was the so-called Spanish Inquisition, established in 1478 and headed by the infamous Tomas de Torquemada. Those responsible for the Inquisition in Spain often abused their authority and were fanatical in their efforts to uncover heretics and other nonconformists, including homosexuals and practitioners of magic.

In 1542, Pope Paul III revived the Inquisition and assigned it to the Sacred Congregation of the Holy Office under Cardinal Caraffa and six fellow cardinals. Known as the Roman Inquisition, its purpose was to combat Protestantism, but its effects were more widespread. It did succeed in eliminating most vestiges of Protestantism in the Italian states, although pockets of the older Waldensians still remained (see Topic 27).

The Inquisition demanded religious and intellectual conformity and terrorized university professors as well as students. The Roman Inquisition burned the Dominican philosopher Giordano Bruno (1548–1600) at the stake for his ideas about the nature of the physical universe, just as it tried Galileo, the Italian astronomer and mathematician, in 1633 for similar ideas. To prevent the spread of dangerous

THE SOCIAL LIFE OF EUROPEAN JEWRY

ELISHEVA CARLEBACH   Queens College, City University of New York

"It passes belief, all the strange things that can happen to us . . . " So wrote Glikl Hameln, a 17th-century Jewish woman, in her remarkable memoir. In it she promised to tell "everything that has happened to me from my youth upward," as a family remembrance and ethical guide for her 12 children. From her colorful descriptions we can glean some of the most important aspects of 17th-century western European Jewish life. Glikl belonged to a class of Jews who were able to prosper during times of turmoil as the medieval anti-Jewish barriers in western and central Europe began to break down. Her writing provides a marvelous look at the inner rhythms of Jewish life as well as the external forces that shaped it.

Glikl lived in Hamburg, a north German port city which contained two small but separate Jewish communities. The Ashkenazi community consisted of Jews of eastern and central European background; their language of daily discourse was Yiddish. One of Glikl's earliest memories was caring for Jewish refugees who fled westward from Poland's Cossack Rebellion of 1648. The Sephardi community, wealthier and more urbane, boasted a splendid synagogue. Its members were descendants of the Jews who had been expelled from Spain and Portugal at the end of the 15th century. Tens of thousands of exiles were left to seek new domiciles; many began to settle in western Europe in the 17th century. Many members of the Sephardi community had lived as marranos, secret Jews who passed down their Jewish identity for generations until they could escape the coercive pressures of the post-1492 Iberian world.

The Reformation shattered the absolute authority of the Roman Church throughout Europe and paved the way for Jews and members of other religious minorities

to be viewed in a more just and realistic way. Although some founders of Protestantism held to malevolent medieval images of Jews, the prolonged struggle over religious beliefs ultimately led to greater tolerance of different faiths. The chaos caused by the religious wars provided some Jews in central Europe entry into nascent economies. Glikl's family seems to have prospered as a result of the Thirty Years' War (1618–1648) when both sides of the conflict turned to Jewish financiers and suppliers. The new class of European Jews that emerged used their influence to become advocates for Jewish causes, founders of new communities, and patrons of Jewish scholarship.

Events such as the advance of the Ottoman Empire, the rupture in the church, and constant warfare appeared fearful and momentous to Europeans. These upheavals caused many Europeans, Christian and Jewish, to hope that the end of history was near. Several aspiring redeemers were announced; one 16th-century hopeful, David Reubeni, was greeted by the pope and the emperor. Glikl recalled the excitement of the appearance of Sabbatai Zevi in 1665, leader of a very widespread Jewish messianic movement.

While some kings and princes banned Jews from their territories, others pursued more lenient, or sometimes inconsistent policies. The reason for toleration of Jewish communities usually had less to do with the religious or cultural life of Jews than with the economic self-interest of the ruler. Because Jews had been excluded for centuries from land ownership as well as from crafts guilds, they developed acumen in the areas that were less restricted for them, finance and commerce. The exiled Spanish and Portuguese Jews and the marranos who followed them into Europe acquired a reputation for developing commerce on a grand scale. Retaining or readmitting Jews in western Europe came about as a result of a desire to develop national economies. When an Italian Jew, Simone Luzzatto, presented a plea for toleration to the Venetian authorities in the 17th century, or Menasseh ben Israel petitioned Oliver Cromwell to permit Jews to return to England, their arguments centered on the idea that a flourishing Jewish community aided the commercial and economic development of the cities and nations in which they lived. England and the Netherlands permitted Jews to settle for the purpose of developing their economies. The Jewish resettlement in western Europe reversed a centuries-long Medieval process of expulsion of Jews that had emptied the region of its Jewish communities.

Despite new economic and social opportunities, most European Jews in the 16th through 18th centuries still lived under great restrictions. In many cities, Jews were legally restricted to residing in quarters known as ghettos. The word *ghetto* may have orignated from the Italian word for *foundry*, the area of Venice that became the compulsory quarter for Jews in 1516. Jewish quarters existed throughout Europe, in Frankfurt, in Prague, in Rome, in some cases through the 19th century. Surrounded by walls, gates bolted at night, their purpose was to separate Jews from others in every socially significant way. The walled ghetto meant that Jews could not expand their quarters horizontally as their population grew by nature and immigration. Instead, they were forced to extend their living space by building vertically, erecting structures that were higher and closer together than in other areas of European cities. These conditions made the ghettos seem darker, more crowded, and with poorer sanitation than anywhere else in Europe. Ghetto populations were also more vulnerable to plagues and fires than other urban districts. When Christian masses were aroused by anti-Jewish agitation, the same conditions of the ghetto made it more dangerous. When Christian clerics wanted to use coercive measures, from compulsory sermons to burnings of Jewish books, as for example the Talmud in 1553, they knew just where to locate their targets.

Yet a closer look at life inside the ghetto walls, and the many ways these walls were breached, shows a more complex picture. During the Renaissance period, Jews and Christians mingled rather freely during the day. Jews left the ghetto to conduct every sort of business, including serving as physicians and teachers of Hebrew to Christians. Christians found many reasons, curiosity among them, to visit the crowded ghetto.

Jewish communities maintained a strong and distinctive social organization. Jews educated their own young, cared for their sick and poor, and buried their dead within the framework of an autonomous judicial and cultural structure, known as the *Kehillah*. In addition to serving the traditional functions of worship and study, synagogues also functioned as social centers where news and information circulated together with official announcements.

In addition to the formal communal structures, and essential to the fabric of daily life, were the overlapping networks of voluntary associations. Their goals were religious, educational, or social, such as study of holy texts, dowering poor brides, or occupational association. Rich and poor lived in proximity, creating a sense of mutual responsibility that expressed itself in every conceivable form of charitable endeavor.

These configurations of Jewish life, which combined medieval elements with recent European developments, endured through the late 18th century. The ideals of the Enlightenment began to change European thought, so that segregation on the basis of religion no longer remained acceptable policy for European states. When the French Revolution implemented the changes, Jews were granted legal and civic equality.

Map 41.1 The Two Major Divisions of European Jewry. Jews whose ancestors lived in medieval Germany are known as Ashkenazim; up to the beginning of the 20th century they spoke Yiddish. The Sephardic Jews of Spain fled the Inquisition of the late 15th century for North Africa, Holland (in particular Amsterdam), the Ottoman Empire (Istanbul and Salonika), and the Near East. Most American Jews are Ashkenazim.

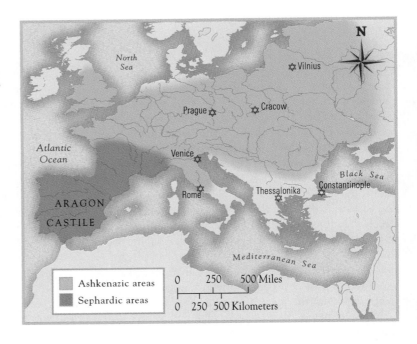

Engraving of an attack on Jews in the German city of Frankfurt. 1614. The religious fervor created by the campaigns for Reform and Counter-Reform created a general climate of intolerance, which often fastened on Europe's Jewish communities as victims. Scenes like this of mass beatings and the destruction of Jewish property were especially common in countries affected by the Reformation.

ideas, the Sacred Congregation instituted an *Index of Prohibited Books,* which established a master list of works that Catholics should not read.

THE JEWS IN THE AGE OF THE COUNTER-REFORMATION

The era of the Reformation and the Counter-Reformation created an atmosphere of repression and intolerance that also extended to non-Christians throughout society. The Spanish Inquisition had targeted those Jews who had converted to Christianity, known as the *conversos.* Many of these converted Jews continued to practice their own religion in secret. Over the next half century, more than 100,000 Jews emigrated, among them some of the most important merchants, physicians, and bankers.

The Jews were further victimized by the climate of religious zeal in the countries most affected by the Reformation. The German princes who followed Luther's teachings grew increasingly concerned about their Jewish populations when Luther found himself unable to convert them to his doctrines. As a result, many were expelled and their synagogues closed. In Italy, the formerly tolerant policies of the papacy were abandoned under the influence of the Inquisition. In the mid-16th century, the first *ghettos*—defined districts within which local Jews were forced to live behind walls and locked gates—were established in Venice and Rome. Nonetheless, Jewish communities throughout Europe managed to maintain a rich and vibrant social and cultural life.

Putting Catholic Reform and the Counter-Reformation in Perspective

Whether the movement for religious and spiritual renewal is called the Catholic Reformation, as Catholics describe it, or the Counter-Reformation, as Protestants refer to it, there is no doubt that significant change and renewal took place among Catholic believers as well as among leaders of the church. It is also clear that by the end of the 16th century the influence and power of the Roman Catholic Church had been greatly reduced in places where Protestants took over. Almost everywhere secular rulers had taken advantage of the church's weakness to assert their control over the religious lives of their subjects and the ecclesiastical institutions in their realms.

Although rulers everywhere assumed greater authority over the church, in countries that remained Catholic, such as Spain, the monarchs sometimes assisted the church in stamping out Protestantism. The centuries-long tradition of alliance between altar and throne had proven a useful tool of governance and was not easily or lightly broken. But despite the vigorous leadership provided to the church by Pope Paul III and the powerful reforming impulse generated by Loyola and others, few Catholic leaders of the late 16th century expected Protestantism to disappear. Moreover, the deep and often bitter religious disputes of the age would continue to affect secular affairs in profound ways. The century and a half following the start of Luther's movement was an age of religious wars. In Europe as a whole, the cultural and spiritual unity that had marked the Middle Ages had been irretrievably shattered.

Questions for Further Study

1. To what extent was the movement for change within the church a Catholic reform or a Catholic counter-reformation?
2. What methods did the Inquisition use against heretics? How did it justify such practices?
3. In the generally hostile environment that was Christian Europe, what forms did Jewish social and cultural life take and under what constraints did it thrive?

Suggestions for Further Reading

Birely, Robert. *The Refashioning of Catholicism, 1450-1700: A Reassessment of the Counter Reformation.* Washington, DC, 1999.

Cameron, E. *The European Reformation.* Oxford, 1991.

Caraman, Philip. *Ignatius Loyola.* San Francisco, 1990.

Jedin, Hubert. E. Graf, trans. *History of the Council of Trent,* 2 vols. London, 1957–1961.

Jensen, D. Lamar. *Reformation Europe: Age of Reform and Revolution.* Lexington, KY, 1981.

Jones, Martin D.W. *The Counter Reformation: Religion and Society in Early Modern Europe.* New York, 1995.

Lindberg, Carl. *The European Reformations.* New York, 1996.

Luebke, David Martin. *The Counter Reformation: The Essential Readings.* New York, 1999.

Meissner, William. *Ignatius Loyola: Psychology of a Saint.* New Haven, CT, 1994.

Mullett, Michael A. *The Catholic Reformation.* New York, 1999.

Po-Chia Hsia, R. *The World of Catholic Renewal, 1540-1770.* New York, 1998.

InfoTrac College Edition

Enter the search term *Counter-Reformation* using the Subject Guide.

CATHOLIC SPAIN AND THE STRUGGLE FOR SUPREMACY

For many decades following the beginning of the Protestant Reformation, religion continued to dominate European politics. Nowhere was the primacy of religion stronger than in the Spain of Philip II. A controversial figure whose historical image has been shaped largely by the religious question, Philip saw himself as the champion of Catholicism. Following in the tradition of his father, the Emperor Charles V, Philip undertook to free Spain of religious differences and remove all traces of dissent, moving in ruthless fashion against the Jews and Muslims of the kingdom. He very much acted the role of the "new monarch," building a highly centralized administration in the tradition of absolutism. He tried, too, to strengthen Spain's hold on its huge colonial possessions in the Americas and to extract from them the maximum profit.

Even under the "most Catholic monarch," the influence of religion on public policy was limited. Moreover, religious controversies prevented Philip from focusing on building and improving the government administration. In the Spanish Netherlands, where first the Anabaptists and then Lutheranism and Calvinism took hold, a bitter religious struggle for power led to a revolt of far-reaching consequences. Nor did Spain's foreign affairs escape the pernicious influence of religious struggle. After the diplomatic settlement with France in 1559, which recognized Spain's predominance in the Netherlands and in Italy, Philip became trapped in a monumental struggle for supremacy with Protestant England that ended in the ignominious defeat of the Spanish Armada.

SIGNIFICANT DATES

The Spanish Empire

1566	Revolt in the Netherlands erupts
1571	Ottomans defeated at Battle of Lepanto
1576	Pacification of Ghent
1579	Union of Arras
1588	Defeat of the Armada
1556–1598	Philip II reigns as king of Spain
1618	Thirty Years' War breaks out
1640	Portugal achieves independence
1648	United Provinces achieve independence

RELIGION AND MONARCHY: THE REIGN OF PHILIP II

Philip II (ruled 1556–1598) inherited the crown and the burdens of a far-flung empire from his father, the Emperor Charles V, who retired to a monastery in 1556 (see Topic 33). Philip's uncle Ferdinand, who became the new Holy Roman Emperor, received control of Austria, Bohemia, and Hungary. Philip became ruler of the Hapsburg domains in Italy—Milan, Naples, and Sicily—as well as of the Netherlands and Spain, and Spanish colonies outside of Europe.

At the time, Spain possessed the greatest military force and was one of the wealthiest states in the West, thanks largely to the silver and gold bullion supplied by the American colonies. Although a relatively large country, it was thinly populated and lacked significant resources of its own. When the king of Portugal died in 1580 without an heir, Philip occupied the country, laying claim to it because his mother was Isabella of Portugal and he had married Maria of Portugal (Portugal remained a Spanish possession until a revolt in 1640 secured its independence).

The legacy Philip inherited when he became king also included a fierce Catholicism, for the *reconquista* and the Spanish Inquisition had given Spain a reputation as the bastion of the Roman Catholic Church.

POLITICS AND RELIGION IN HAPSBURG SPAIN

Philip assumed the throne of Spain along with serious burdens, including the task of combating Protestantism in Europe and the Ottoman Turks in the Mediterranean. Moreover, the question of how to keep his widely spread possessions together concerned him deeply. Philip was an intensely serious and deeply religious man who seldom revealed his emotions. He married four times, but always for diplomatic reasons rather than for love, and he seldom spent time with his family. His father had imbued him with a deep distrust of official advisers, and especially of women, so that he tried to keep his own counsel as much as possible.

Painting of Philip II, king of Spain and Mary Tudor, daughter of Henry VIII who succeeded her father as queen of England. 16th century. After the Catholic couple married in 1554, Mary attempted to reconvert England to Catholicism. The two little dogs in the foreground of the painting symbolize fidelity.

Mary Evans Picture Library

Map 42.1 The European Empire of Philip II. The three chief regions are the Iberian peninsula (Spain, Navarre, and Portugal), the Kingdom of Naples and the Two Sicilys (Sicily and Sardinia), and parts of the Holy Roman Empire, notably the Netherlands. Because the Empire was regarded as a bastion of Catholicism, the Netherlands, where Protestantism was strong, threatened to be at risk.

Despite his religious faith, Philip was a shrewd and calculating ruler who used the church to further his domestic and foreign policies. He was not above employing the Inquisition to destroy resistance to his authority among the nobles and middle class, although, like other new monarchs, he worked to undermine the power of the church in his country. He insisted on his right to appoint clerical officials in Spain and objected to the pope's control over ecclesiastical courts in his realm. When the influence of the Jesuits grew too powerful, he resisted their policies and acted in defiance of several popes when they challenged his authority. Philip aided the church when it did not undermine his absolutism but insisted in return that it be a loyal ally of the government. The deep faith of his subjects enabled the king to use religion to arouse popular consensus behind the monarchy.

As a ruler, Philip was a micromanager who refused to allow his bureaucrats to make most of their decisions without his direct involvement. He spent much of his time in the seclusion of his private office in the Escorial palace outside of Madrid, working on official papers. Heeding his father's advice too well, he was unable to delegate any significant power. Nor did he broach any limitations on his authority. In each of the former kingdoms that constituted the Spanish crown, such as Castile, Aragon, and León, a *Cortes*, or medieval assembly representing the clergy, nobles, and commoners, often gave Philip considerable trouble. Only in Castile, where he concentrated his attention, was he able to use the *Cortes* to rubber stamp his decisions and legislated personally through the royal decrees. The rest of the kingdom was less effectively managed. In his other European possessions, as well as in the American empire, he used viceroys to represent and implement his will, but he

constantly fought the obstructionism of the powerful nobility. Moreover, the slowness of communications in the 16th century made colonial administration all the more difficult.

The administration of Philip's vast empire required tremendous resources, especially because he was almost constantly at war somewhere in the world. Nevertheless, only the more prosperous Castile and the American colonies provided much-needed revenue, whereas the bankers and nobles of the Low Countries felt that Spain was a drain on local resources. In Spain, the church owned half of the landed estates and the nobles owned most of the rest, yet both were essentially tax exempt. The old feudal nobility so ruthlessly impoverished the peasants, and their use of the most productive land for sheep grazing so depleted agricultural productivity, that Spain could not raise enough food for its own needs. Yet despite their poverty, the Spanish people were the most heavily taxed in Europe. To operate the government, Philip regularly resorted to borrowing and then just as regularly defaulted on the loans he had contracted.

Religious policies in Spain often hurt economic development, as with the campaigns against the Jews and Muslims. The Spanish Inquisition had been used initially against the *conversos*, the Jews who had converted to Christianity but who continued secretly to practice their own religion. Jews and *conversos* were among the most important merchants, physicians, and bankers, and many had achieved significant status in Spanish society. Large numbers of these economic leaders had left Spain to escape the repression and, in 1492, following the conquest of Granada, more than 100,000 Jews emigrated when the crown insisted that all Jews had either to convert or leave.

Similar policies affected the Muslims, who in 1502 were given the same choice as the Jews. Because most Muslims were modest farmers rather than merchants or professionals, and lacked the resources to emigrate, they opted to become Christians. Yet these *Moriscos*, like many of the *conversos*, were Christian in name only. Between 1568 and 1571, Philip brutally suppressed an uprising among the *Moriscos*, and in 1609 they were expelled from Spain. These policies seriously hurt the middle class, on whom most of the tax burden fell, and undermined a valuable source of economic prosperity.

SPAIN AND ITS OVERSEAS EMPIRE

The importance of the empire as a source of much-needed revenue explains why the Spanish crown held the colonies so tightly to the authority of Madrid. One result of this policy, however, was that when the supply of bullion from the Americas began to run dry, and other nations competed for a share of colonial trade, Spain began to suffer economic depression.

ECONOMIC POLICY AND THE COLONIES

After the brutal plundering of the ancient civilizations of the Americas had exhausted the easy supply of wealth, the Spanish introduced European mining techniques to the fabulously rich silver mines of Peru and Mexico. By the end of the 16th century, bullion still made up most of the value of imports from the Spanish possessions in the Americas. Even then, however, although the government directly secured almost half of all the bullion brought to Spain, it made up no more than 25 percent of all revenues. As the mines were gradually exhausted, other products from Asia and the New World began to take their place in Spain's overseas trade. By the end of the 17th century, new kinds of goods—particularly coffee, tea, cocoa, cotton, dyes, and tobacco—began to dominate imports to Europe.

Unlike the Portuguese, the Spanish began from the outset to settle their colonies and develop a local economy that mirrored the techniques and institutions found at home. They introduced European agricultural products into the Americas, including wheat and other grains, a wide variety of vegetables, and citrus fruit, while importing into Europe foodstuffs unknown there, such as the potato, the tomato, and corn.

The cultivation of sugar cane in the Western Hemisphere had a great impact on the economic and demographic patterns of the colonies, especially on the islands of the West Indies, where African slaves were brought in large numbers to work the plantations. Control of labor in the colonies was also managed under the *encomienda* system; this was similar to European manorialism, in which a grant of land gave the landholder the right to use the inhabitants of the land as forced workers. Local landholders and their overseers so widely abused the system, however, that it was eventually abandoned in the second half of the 16th century.

To control all trade, the government had established an agency known as the *Casa de Contratación*, which sought to make commerce a royal monopoly. Because the New World had been "discovered" by navigators in the employ of Queen Isabella of Castile, Castilian merchants were given a trade monopoly there. Trade with foreigners, including other Spanish merchants, was forbidden. This encouraged smuggling and the subterfuge of foreign merchants hiring Spanish ships to trade with the colonies. Direct commerce between the Americas and the Philippines, Spain's Pacific possession, was virtually prohibited.

A crucial shortcoming of Philip's reign was that such a potentially lucrative and important source of wealth as the American colonies was so thoroughly mismanaged. Several times in the course of the 16th century, Spain went into bankruptcy. Instead of making Spain a part of a developing and expanding overseas agricultural economy, Philip was content to allow the draining of its resources and the inhuman exploitation of its people. In doing so, he basked in the glow of the Hapsburg empire, little realizing that his policies had planted the seed of future crisis.

REBELLION IN THE NETHERLANDS: RELIGIOUS FREEDOM AND POLITICAL INDEPENDENCE

The Netherlands (sometimes called the Low Countries; their low elevation made them susceptible to flooding) had long been one of the most prosperous and strategically important areas of the Hapsburg domains, supplying Spain with large revenues. Throughout the Middle Ages, the Netherlands was the center of commerce and banking as well as a leading manufacturer of textiles. Amsterdam and Antwerp were important North Sea ports, and the country was densely populated and highly urbanized.

On the other hand, the 17 provinces that constituted the Netherlands had old traditions of self-government and feudal autonomy, and its inhabitants were deeply suspicious of Charles V when he inherited them, although he had been raised there. To complicate matters further, the southern provinces were primarily French- and Flemish-speaking, while the northern provinces were populated by people of German origin, whose language was Dutch. Charles annexed the provinces in 1548 and added them to the Hapsburg empire.

PHILIP II AND THE NETHERLANDS

To bring the two areas together, Charles had placed them under the regency of Philip, who lived there until he became king in 1556. Thereafter, Philip left the administration of the Netherlands in the hands of his sister, Margaret of Parma (1522–1586), who ruled with a group of Spanish advisers. Estrangement from Philip's absentee overlordship was made worse by the king's Catholic program. By the mid-16th century, Calvinism was spreading rapidly in the Netherlands and, like his father before him,

Philip encouraged local officials to use the Inquisition to stamp it and other heresies out. He also instructed his sister to enforce regulations against heresy. These policies enraged the local nobles, many of whom had become Calvinists and were already smarting under Philip's desire to centralize his control at the expense of their privileges. In 1566 Calvinists erupted in a fury that desecrated Catholic churches. Philip responded by sending 10,000 Spanish troops to the area under the command of the duke of Alva (1507–1582), who imposed an authoritarian military rule on the inhabitants.

Alva could not have alienated the people more if he had set out to do so deliberately. Not only did he levy new taxes, but he also established a special tribunal—popularly known as the Council of Blood—to root out heresy and crush the revolt. Alva was a brutal regent, responsible for thousands of deaths, including the execution of prominent Protestant nobles, and the expropriation of property. Tens of thousands of Protestants emigrated in the face of the terror that Alva unleashed. Outraged by his brutality, Margaret of Parma resigned the regency.

Alva's policies provoked full-scale rebellion as merchants and common people joined with the Protestant nobles against Spanish repression. Opposition to Philip centered on William of Nassau, Prince of Orange (ruled 1579–1584), who organized armed resistance in the north in 1568. Five years later Philip recalled Alva in a futile attempt to calm the population. William was an ideal leader of the rebellion. Born a Lutheran, he was raised as a Catholic. An experienced military leader, William raised a privateer army popularly called the "Sea Beggars." Although he had been an imperial official under Charles V and was not enthusiastic about leading a rebellion against Philip, under the pressures and heat of battle, he eventually became devoted to the Protestant cause.

THE REBELLION

For the first six years of the revolt, William and the rebel forces suffered one setback after another. William, who had used his own private wealth to help finance his army, was almost bankrupt, and his early military defeats spoiled his reputation. In 1572, however, the tide suddenly

Anthony Moro, *Portrait of William of Orange*, c. 1570. The painter was Dutch; he went to Spain to work for Charles V, who sent him to England to paint a portrait of Mary Tudor for her future husband, Philip II. Remaining there, he was knighted by Elizabeth, Mary's successor, as Sir Anthony More, and returned to his native land to paint this portrait of the leader of the Protestant revolt against Spanish rule.

© Erich Lessing/Art Resource, NY

changed when his soldiers captured the port of Brill, which inspired a series of uprisings throughout the northern provinces. To stop the advance of the imperial troops, William then opened the dikes and flooded the plains, a tactic that succeeded in cornering Philip's army and prompting the recall of Alva.

The war dragged on, and terrible atrocities and brutalities took place on both sides as religious passions inflamed the mutual hatreds. To terrorize the population, Alva had authorized his soldiers to pillage town after town and murder their inhabitants. In 1576, Antwerp was destroyed and thousands massacred. Three years later Spanish troops raped the women of Maestricht, who had helped defend the town against them, and then slaughtered much of the population.

The same year that Maestricht fell, Protestant and Catholic leaders of all 17 provinces joined together against Philip to form an alliance. The Catholic provinces of the South had been goaded into rebellion because of a special tax that Philip had imposed on them in order to fight the Protestants. The alliance suggested the possibility that national and political interests could be used in the Netherlands as the basis for forging a new state.

The united citizens of the Netherlands demanded that Philip withdraw his army and allow the provinces to be governed by their traditional assembly, the States General. But the unity that was achieved in adversity soon gave way to religious divisions between the Calvinist nobles of the North and the Catholic nobles of the South.

Philip's new military commander, Alexander Farnese, duke of Parma, skillfully manipulated these divisions by luring the Catholic aristocrats back into the Spanish fold after restoring their confiscated lands. After a series of victories, in 1579 Parma persuaded the southern provinces (which formed a Catholic alliance known as the Union of Arras) to make a separate peace with Philip. In the face of this abandonment, William brought together the Dutch leaders of the northern provinces into the Protestant Union of Utrecht, which announced that they would continue to resist the king.

In 1581, after trying unsuccessfully to become subjects first of the king of France and then of Queen Elizabeth of England, the northern provinces proclaimed their independence. After William was assassinated in 1584, the Dutch continued their struggle for self-government under his 17-

HAERLEM.

13· *Nachdem sich Harlem ergeben hatt*   *Da hangen vnd köpfen nam kein endt*   *Vom Hispanischen gesind dermaßen,*   *Gehangen seind mitt großer vnzucht*
ist angericht ein groß blut batt   *Die weiber auch wurden geschendt*   *Daß sie gar nacknd auf den straßen*   *Wider alle eher, vnd Gottes frucht*
                                            Anno   Dni. M. D. LXXIII am XIII. Julij.

Print showing Spanish atrocities committed against the Dutch rebellion, 1573. As the print indicates, the scene shown is outside the city of Haarlem (modern spelling), some 20 miles from Amsterdam. The inscriptions below describe the hangings and executions depicted in the engraving, which did much to reinforce Dutch resistance to Spanish rule.

year-old son Maurice. Philip never lived to see the end of the revolt of the Netherlands. In 1609, eleven years after his death, a truce was arranged at long last, but not before the Spanish had inflicted much additional brutality and terror on the Protestant population of the region. Spain recognized the Protestant Dutch Republic of the northern provinces in the treaty of Westphalia in 1648, while maintaining control of the southern Catholic provinces.

SPAIN VERSUS ENGLAND: THE ARMADA DISASTER

As if the Netherlands were not sufficient provocation to Philip's Catholic policies, another source of conflict lay in England, where Henry VIII had created and assumed control of the Anglican Church and severed ties with Rome. In 1554, before he assumed the throne, Philip had married the daughter of Henry and Catherine of Aragon, Mary Tudor. Although the marriage was extremely unpopular in England, Mary was hopelessly in love with Philip, who encouraged her efforts to restore Catholicism there (see Topic 39).

THE SPANISH-ENGLISH RIVALRY

Several factors operated to exacerbate English-Spanish hostility. When Mary died, Philip offered his hand to her sister, Elizabeth (ruled 1558–1603), the new English queen, but Elizabeth spurned the offer. However, the underlying reason for the longstanding hostility between Spain and England was economic rivalry. Elizabeth's ships and English pirates attacked Spanish galleons laden with bullion from the Americas. Moreover, the English, who were anxious to break into the Spanish monopoly imposed on their colonies, tried to force their way into the lucrative trade. Sir John Hawkins, an ambitious English merchant, violated Spanish policy and sold goods directly to the Spanish colonies. In the late 1570s, Hawkins' cousin Francis Drake seized a fortune in booty from Spanish ships along the Pacific coast of South America.

English and Spanish policy also clashed during the revolt in the Netherlands. Since the Middle Ages, England had close commercial contact with the Flemish cloth manufacturers, who purchased large quantities of English wool.

Then, too, the English supported the aspirations of the Dutch Protestants, and English privateers continued to harass Spanish shipping along the coast. For their part, Spanish envoys in England had even been implicated in plots to assassinate Elizabeth.

THE ARMADA AND THE ECLIPSE OF SPAIN

In 1587, Francis Drake, who was knighted by Elizabeth, destroyed a large Spanish fleet anchored in the harbor of Cadiz. In reaction to what he regarded as English perfidy and the wounding of his pride, Philip decided to attack England's power directly. He devoted significant resources and energy to building a huge fleet, known as the Invincible Armada, which was designed to seize control of the English Channel and permit a Spanish invasion of England. The invasion forces were to be commanded by the duke of Parma. It was an imaginative plan but one filled with danger because much of Philip's war against England rested on this effort.

The Armada consisted of 130 ships carrying some 27,000 men. Arrayed against it was a much weaker flotilla of English ships, which nevertheless were smaller and faster than the cumbersome Spanish vessels. Moreover, some of England's best naval officers, including Hawkins and Drake, were in command of the operations. When running battles between the two fleets drove the Spanish ships to take refuge off Calais, Hawkins sent fire ships into the harbor and caused the Spanish to panic. As the Armada moved north to try to return to Cadiz, the English attacked again, and ferocious storms destroyed more Spanish ships than did the enemy. When the battle was over, less than half of Philip's ships had survived, although most of Spain's firepower made it back home.

The outcome of the struggle between England and Spain had immediate significance for Spain and long-range meaning for Europe. Philip's prestige was damaged, and Spain's once-supreme military power had been compromised. Moreover, the English victory gave encouragement to the Protestant forces struggling against the Counter-Reformation. Had Philip's reign ended with the Battle of Lepanto in 1571, in which his forces defeated the Ottoman Turks, he would no doubt have been regarded as the greatest ruler of his age. Instead, it culminated in the Armada disaster. The moment of Spain's greatness had passed.

Putting Catholic Spain in Perspective

The abdication of Charles V in 1556 signaled the fact that even such an ambitious monarch realized the insurmountable challenges and difficulties of ruling the vast Hapsburg empire. The division of his empire confirmed that the day of universal empires was over. The ascension of Philip II to the throne of Spain, on the other hand, suggested that greatness might have still been possible on a more limited scale. But Philip was not up to the task, and circumstances seem to have conspired against him.

Philip was an intensely Catholic monarch in an age of religious divisiveness that had shattered a millennium of Catholic unity. Although his inheritance included a huge overseas empire stretching from the Atlantic to the Pacific, shortsighted administrative and economic policies rendered it less useful to Spain than it might have been. Even in Europe, however, Philip's empire was too diverse. Against the centralizing and heavy-handed absolutism of the Hapsburgs, local patriotism and religious faith joined forces to wrest the all-important Dutch provinces from Philip's orbit. The longstanding Hapsburg-Valois conflict had ended with the withdrawal of France, and in the end Spain's nemesis came unexpectedly from England. The Armada symbolized a new era in European history, one that marked the decline of Spain and ushered in the ascendancy of England.

Questions for Further Study

1. What were the chief concerns of Philip's domestic program?
2. What was the nature of the relationship between Spain and its colonies? How did Spain view its American possessions?
3. What were the major aims of Spanish foreign policy under Philip II?

Suggestions for Further Reading

Braudel, Fernand. S. Reynolds, trans. *The Mediterranean and the Mediterranean World in the Age of Philip II*, 2 vols, 2nd ed. Berkeley, CA, 1996.

Dunn, Richard S. *The Age of Religious Wars, 1559–1715*, 2nd ed. New York, 1979.

Elliott, John H. *The Revolt of the Catalans: A Study in the Decline of Spain, 1598–1640*. Cambridge, MA, 1963.

Kamen, Henry. *Philip of Spain*. New Haven, CT, 1997.

Maltby, William S. *Alba*. Berkeley, CA, 1983.

Martin, Colin, and Geoffrey Parker. *The Spanish Armada*. New York, 1999.

Parker, G. *The Grand Strategy of Philip II*. New Haven, CT, 1998.

Rodriguez-Salgado, Mia. *The Changing Face of Empire: Charles V, Philip II, and Habsburg Authority*. Cambridge, MA, 1988.

Stradling, Robert A. *Europe and the Decline of Spain: A Study of the Spanish System, 1580–1720*. London, 1981.

InfoTrac College Edition

Enter the search term *Philip II of Spain* using Key Terms.

CROWN AND PARLIAMENT IN TUDOR-STUART ENGLAND

The death of Henry VIII in the mid-16th century ended a tumultuous era in English history during which that ambitious monarch had established a powerful royal autocracy. Henry successfully defied the papacy and established Protestantism in his realm, disciplined the nobility, and bent Parliament to his will. The unanswered question was whether Henry's reign had set a precedent for further royal power at the expense of the social and economic elites represented in Parliament. Moreover, the religious controversy he stirred up continued to disturb English life for many years.

Contrary to his own expectations, Henry's daughter, Elizabeth I, proved to be one of the most important monarchs of English history. Brilliant and determined, she fought back the efforts at mastery of Philip II of Spain and strengthened England's hegemony on the seas, while presiding over an era of significant economic and cultural achievement. Moreover, shrewd tactician that she was, Elizabeth avoided direct confrontation and achieved an uneasy balance in her relationship with Parliament.

It was left to her successors, James I and Charles I, to take up the struggle between monarch and Parliament again. The result was a far-reaching civil war that ended with the triumph of Parliament and the temporary end of the monarchy, with the added complication of renewed religious struggle under the Puritans. In place of the monarchy there followed a difficult period of military dictatorship under Oliver Cromwell. Only then, after the English had experimented with alternative forms of government, did they return to the monarchy, but in a form that would share power increasingly with Parliament.

SIGNIFICANT DATES

Tudor–Stuart England

1558–1603	Elizabeth I rules as queen of England
1563	Thirty-Nine Articles adopted
1587	Mary Queen of Scots executed
1588	Defeat of Spanish Armada
1603–1625	James I rules as king of England
1611	King James Version of the Bible
1625–1649	Charles I rules as king of England
1628	Petition of Right
1642–1646, 1648	English Civil Wars
1649–1653	The Commonwealth
1658	Death of Oliver Cromwell
1660	Monarchy restored under Charles II

Portrait of Elizabeth I of England. 16th century. The queen is shown treading on the enemies of England. Her white dress and the figure of an ermine, which is shown on her ruffle to her left, both symbolize virginity. The painting is an official court portrait, intended to convey the queen's majesty rather than provide a literal description of her appearance.

By Courtesy of the National Portrait Gallery, London

ELIZABETH I AND THE POLITICS OF COMPROMISE

Following the brief reigns of Edward VI and Mary Tudor, Elizabeth I (ruled 1558–1603) became queen. The daughter of Henry VIII and Anne Boleyn, the young Elizabeth ascended the English throne at a crucial moment in history, when both domestic and foreign affairs were at a crossroads. The Elizabethan era achieved an extraordinary level of power and prosperity, which was rarely matched in English history. Furthermore, during her reign, English culture reached a peak that culminated in the creative genius of William Shakespeare (see Topic 47).

ELIZABETH THE QUEEN

Despite this aspect of real accomplishment, however, Elizabeth was a complex ruler. She believed genuinely in the advantages and legitimacy of absolute monarchy, yet she often compromised these principles for the sake of political expediency. Her personal sympathies in religion were, like those of her father, not predisposed toward Protestantism, although she restored the Protestant Church. Throughout her life she carefully cultivated suitors but never married, suppressing her personal inclinations for the sake of policy. She projected a strong, willful character in public, although in private she was often indecisive. In the end, it can be said that she embraced her country and its people as the inspiration for her life and work.

One of the first serious challenges she faced came from the north, in Scotland, where the Catholic Mary Stuart (ruled 1542–1567) ruled. After the death in 1560 of her husband, Francis II of France, Mary returned to Scotland. When her subjects, converted to Protestantism by John Knox, forced Mary into exile in 1568, she fled to England. Elizabeth treated her coolly and kept her under tight surveillance because as a direct descendant of Henry VII, Mary stood in the line of royal succession. Mary became the focus of several plots against Elizabeth hatched by Catholic dissidents. Finally, after Parliament demanded Mary's death and further plots were revealed, in 1587 Elizabeth had Mary executed.

THE RETURN TO PROTESTANTISM

From the religious point of view, the years from 1547 to 1558 were difficult ones for the average English citizen. Henry's break with the Roman Church had disconcerted many of his subjects, and the support of Edward VI for Protestantism had created further uncertainty. Mary Tudor had then added to the confusion of her subjects by attempting to bring England back into the Catholic faith, at first with moderation and then with brutality and bloodshed. Elizabeth, who had been brought up a Protestant, enjoyed a long reign in which she was able to bring a measure of clarity back to religious life: The secret of her success was pragmatism rather than religious fervor.

Mary Tudor's death heartened English Protestants, many of whom had left the country for exile abroad and now returned home, relishing the prospect of more radical reform. Elizabeth repealed Mary's Catholic legislation and restored the major laws setting up the Anglican Church passed by Henry VIII. Under Elizabeth, the Church of England simplified its structure and actually embraced the notion of predestination preached by the Calvinists, whose doctrines the exiles had absorbed abroad.

In 1563, the Thirty-Nine Articles adopted a position of compromise on many doctrinal issues but kept a good many long-established Catholic liturgical practices, although now translated into English. The kingdom continued to be home to many dissenters who wanted a purer church, as well as to Jesuits who worked secretly to reestablish Catholicism. The so-called nonconformists, who included Puritans and Presbyterians, kept the religious question unsettled for years to come. The **Puritans** spearheaded a religious reform movement that wanted to "purify" the Church of England of all remnants of Catholicism. They became noted for their spirit of moral and religious earnestness that drove them to want to reform the entire kingdom.

Elizabeth's reign also saw steady economic progress based on England's widening involvement in overseas trade and the reduction of the debt. Joint stock companies such as the East India Company competed with its Dutch and French counterparts for primacy in global trade (see Topic 46). Elizabeth positioned England against the expansionist policies of her would-be suitor, Philip II of Spain. In 1588, her sea captains, including Sir Francis Drake, destroyed the Spanish Armada, although Spain continued to be a major power for some time. Lasting peace between Spain and England came only after the death of Philip in 1598 and Elizabeth's death five years later.

TOWARD CONFRONTATION: JAMES I AND PARLIAMENT

During the last years of Elizabeth's reign, tensions with Parliament had risen as a result of the queen's demands for special financial grants to pay for her struggle with Spain. In response, Parliament had raised constitutional issues designed to further weaken the crown. The Stuart kings who followed her turned the relationship of the monarchy with Parliament into a major crisis.

COMPROMISE AND CONFRONTATION

Elizabeth was succeeded by James VI of Scotland, the son of Mary Stuart. He ascended the English throne as James I (ruled 1603–1625). Well educated and a fervent believer in the divine right of kings, James disliked the pretensions of Parliament. Before the authority of a monarch, he argued, no other authority could or should prevail. Having been raised in Scotland, he had little direct experience of issues involving English tradition and constitutional history.

Along with the crown, James inherited debt and hard times from the last years of Elizabeth's wars against Spain.

He made matters worse by spending lavishly on his court. In addition, the Puritans began pressing James, who had accepted Presbyterianism as the dominant form of Protestantism in Scotland, to move the Reformation forward. In this the radicals were disappointed. James was cautious in matters of faith, and his best-remembered contribution to religious life was the English translation of the Bible he commissioned, known as the King James Version, which appeared in 1611.

In politics James was as practical as Elizabeth in his thinking. Only a year after becoming king, he participated in a Protestant conference at Hampton Court, where radicals insisted that the episcopal system be abolished. James turned down their demands and took a hard line against the Calvinists, warning them that they would be banished if they continued waging religious war. On the other hand, after James issued an edict banishing Catholic priests, Protestant sympathies for him increased, especially when the so-called Gunpowder Plot was uncovered in 1605: A Catholic named Guy Fawkes (1578–1606) was caught placing 36 barrels of gunpowder under the houses of Parliament one day before the king was to appear before the assembly. Under torture, Fawkes revealed the names of fellow conspirators, who were tried and executed. November 5—when the explosion was to have occurred—is still celebrated in England as Guy Fawkes Day.

In the years following the plot against him, James experienced growing difficulties with Parliament. Twice—in 1611 and 1614—the king dissolved Parliament after it had turned down his proposed budgets and ruled by decree for several years. In 1621, when Parliament threatened to remove some of the king's powers, he went personally to the House of Commons to oppose the challenge. As his popularity began to suffer, James compounded his problems by arranging the marriage of his son Charles to a French princess, whose Catholic faith aroused resentment in England.

Although James angered members of Parliament with his high-handed behavior and his arguments in favor of divine right monarchy, about which he had written a treatise, the skillful monarch ended his reign with restored popularity when he went to war with Spain in 1624.

SOCIAL AND RELIGIOUS TRANSFORMATIONS

James's confrontations with Parliament had far-reaching implications, especially because membership in that body had begun to undergo important social change since the mid-16th century. In general, by the early 17th century England had a much larger group of entrepreneurs—virtually all of whom were not nobles—who had made money in trade, manufacturing, and in capitalist farming and sheep raising. The most significant development was the increase in the size of the gentry class—that is, either the younger, landless brothers of nobles or landowners who used their newfound wealth to purchase estates and country residences in order to achieve a higher social status. The rise of the gentry was accompanied by a decline in the importance of the old feudal nobility, whose role as military leaders had all but disappeared as the feudal armies were replaced by a royal army.

Although never a united group, the gentry were forming a majority in the House of Commons, the branch of Parliament that controlled government finances, and were beginning to insist on a larger share of political influence. By the time of the death of James I, the gentry formed perhaps three-quarters of the membership of the Commons. Finances were at the heart of the tension between the gentry and the monarchy. The monarchy required ever-larger income, and while the gentry bore an increasingly larger share of the tax burden, they demanded a voice in policy making and in how their tax money was to be spent. James I and his successors, however, correctly saw such pursuit of power as undermining royal absolutism.

Compounding these problems was the fact that the period of religious strife was by no means over in England, and religious issues were linked to the country's social transformation. The Calvinists and Puritans, both of which were gaining followers, continued to demand a more strenuous program of reform for the Church of England, which they wanted to see shorn of its remaining Catholic influences. The Puritan emphasis on the work ethic and high moral standards in everyday life reflected the values of some of the gentry and the merchant class that had come to dominate the House of Commons. The early settlements in the American colonies in Virginia, Massachusetts, Pennsylvania, and Rhode Island were organized by Puritans seeking communities of their own.

CHARLES I AND THE CIVIL WAR

The mounting political and religious trouble between Parliament and the monarchy reached the crisis point under Charles I (ruled 1625–1649). His marriage to Henrietta Maria, the sister of King Louis XIII of France, made him unpopular from the start. Matters worsened when Charles's requests for money were met with demands from Parliament for political reforms. He dismissed two Parliaments, but in 1628, he was forced to accept the Petition of Right, a constitutional document that asserted the legal rights and protections of the English people as they had evolved since Magna Carta—no taxation without Parliamentary consent, no billeting of troops in civilian homes, freedom from arbitrary arrest and imprisonment, and no martial law in peacetime.

THE CIVIL WAR

As soon as Charles had his money, however, he dissolved Parliament and refused to call another for more than 10 years. The gentry and Puritans of the Commons seethed with revolt, especially as Charles ran the government by imposing special levies that in the eyes of Parliament were improper and represented taxation without consent. The Puritans turned to Parliament for support, finding increasing common cause with sectors of the gentry.

The religious question provoked a crisis that forced Charles to call Parliament back into session. William Laud (1573–1645), archbishop of Canterbury, was a man of moderate persuasion but obstinate mind. Laud tried to bully the Puritans, prosecuting his Puritan critics in royal law courts, and in 1639 attempted to introduce a uniform *Anglican Book of*

Color engraving of the English king Charles I with his French wife, Henrietta Maria, c. 1630. The image is based on a painting by the Flemish artist Anthony van Dyck, who was knighted by the king in 1632 and became official court painter. Many of his works, like this one, are official portraits; he produced more than five hundred.

Alinari/Art Resource

Print of Quaker woman preaching. Mid-17th century. The Quakers were one of several radical Protestant groups to emerge during the English Civil Wars, several of which encouraged women to preach. This contemporary engraving makes fun of the practice. The preacher's audience is held gripped by her words, but at the window above the onlookers express astonishment and scorn.

Map 43.1 England in the Civil War. Note the site of Naseby, where King Charles I was captured at the battle fought there in 1645. The two major universities, the centers of intellectual life, split over the political division of the age: Cambridge sided with Parliament, while Oxford remained loyal to the king. The "bloodless revolution" had little military effect outside England.

Common Prayer in England as well as in Scotland. Riots against Laud's policies erupted in Scotland, where Presbyterianism was dominant, and Charles had to ask Parliament for the money to raise an army to put down the rebellion.

The so-called Long Parliament, which met from 1640 to 1660, had as its leader a Puritan opponent of the monarchy named John Pym. Under his guidance, the Commons passed a series of measures designed to limit the power of the king, including the abolition of royal courts such as the Star Chamber, which the king had used to try nobles, and an act requiring the king to call Parliament at least every three years. One member of the Commons, Oliver Cromwell (1599–1658), urged Parliament to abolish the *Book of Common Prayer* and bitterly attacked the institution of bishops in the Anglican Church. Archbishop Laud was impeached, and the following year the House of Commons issued the Grand Remonstrance: a restatement of Parliament's position and the measures it had passed.

All the while, Parliament had refused to grant Charles the money he needed for the army, preferring to deal directly with the Scots in the hope of forcing the king to give in to their wishes. Instead, Charles tried unsuccessfully to have the leaders of the Commons arrested. In June 1642, when the Commons put forward its last set of demands, including control of the church and the army and the right to appoint ministers, Charles fled London for the north of

England. There he condemned the Parliamentary leaders as traitors and took to the battlefields to reassert royal authority. Civil war had come.

The English Civil War, which lasted from 1642 to 1646, was a struggle in which both sides fought reluctantly. Neither Charles nor the leaders of Parliament had wanted matters to result in violence, but the issues were of great importance and fraught with decades of tension. Conflict between the freedoms and laws of England and the power of kings was exacerbated by religious passions that had been brewing since the time of Henry VIII.

Yet the underlying causes of the struggle, long debated by historians, do not appear to be quite so simple. The momentous decision to take up arms against the crown so divided the country, including the Puritans, that half of the members of the House of Commons sided with Charles. Marxist historians have argued that the more prosperous segments of the gentry, anxious to consolidate their power, led the fight for Parliament and the Puritans. On the other hand, another school of thought insists that the most prosperous group supported the king and that the less prosperous gentry, living off declining agricultural incomes, backed the Puritans and Parliament. Moreover, the southern and eastern areas of England, where merchants and businessmen were concentrated, opposed the king, whereas the more rural northern and western regions supported him. In the end, the Civil War is perhaps best seen as a complicated struggle that was fueled by religious conflict.

While Pym gave the rebels political direction, Cromwell provided military leadership. Cromwell designed what he called the New Model Army, whose soldiers were indoctrinated and impassioned by sermons and religious worship. In June 1645, after almost three years of fighting, the Civil War reached a turning point when the antiroyalists won a major victory at Naseby and took the king.

THE END OF THE MONARCHY

During the course of the Civil War, two broad factions emerged in the opposition to Charles: The Independents, whose leader in the Commons was Cromwell, wanted to replace the Anglican Church with a decentralized church in which each congregation chose the kind of worship it wanted; the Presbyterians, on the other hand, wanted a Calvinist church similar to the system in Scotland, where a central authority presided over local congregations. On the religious issue, Cromwell gave in to the majority, who were Presbyterians, and the victors proceeded to abolish the bishops and establish a Presbyterian church. To Cromwell, however, this was only a temporary compromise, and his determination to break the king's power only widened the divisions wrenching apart English society.

Charles's surrender made the struggle even more complicated because the question of what to do with the king revealed how deeply divided his foes were. When the Independents and the Presbyterians failed to agree on the fate of the king, the Civil War broke out again in 1647. This time, however, the Independents were pitted against the Presbyterians, while the Scots now supported the king. The Parliament's army added to the instability because it had gone unpaid for so long that it was threatening to rebel.

In fact, in June 1647 the army kidnapped Charles and demanded payment in return for his release. When the Presbyterians in London tried to stop the military, the soldiers occupied the capital, gaining the backing of the Independents and other radicals. The next year, Cromwell crushed the royalists completely, and his soldiers now insisted on the king's execution. In the House of Commons, the Presbyterian majority refused to support the army's demands, but their defiance prompted the army to purge the Parliament of all those who resisted.

The resulting Rump Parliament, consisting of fewer than 100 members, voted to try the king for crimes against his subjects. Charles was founded guilty and beheaded on January 30, 1649—he went to the block with great dignity, and his execution was by no means universally applauded. Cromwell declared England a republican "commonwealth" without a monarch and without a House of Lords.

THE PROTECTORATE: THE DICTATORSHIP OF OLIVER CROMWELL

The years from 1649 to 1660 are known in English history as the Interregnum, or the period between kings. For the first several years of that period, a council of state exercised executive authority, while the Rump Parliament served as the legislature. Unable to decide on a new constitutional system for the country, and increasingly frustrated by the hostility between religious factions, in 1653 Cromwell used the army to close down the Rump institution and replaced it with a new body of his own loyal supporters.

For the next five years, Cromwell ruled England as a military dictator, confusing even further the already debated question of sovereignty, or the source of political power. Under the monarchy, sovereignty had been explained as the divine right of kings; now, in times of upheaval, some claimed that sovereignty rested with the people. But what form of sovereignty did Cromwell exercise?

THE PROTECTORATE

Cromwell's hand-picked Parliament proved so destabilizing that a group of army officers took matters into their own hands. They drafted a constitutional document known as the Instrument of Government, which gave Cromwell the title of Lord Protector.

The new ruler of England was a man of the gentry class, a Puritan of the Independent persuasion who believed in parliamentary government. He said repeatedly that he wanted to bring genuine constitutional government and religious freedom to the country, but both goals eluded him. During his rule, he called three different Parliaments into session, but none was able to arrange a long-term constitutional settlement. Cromwell seemed to be inspired by high-minded ideals, but he was inflexible and unwilling to make the kind of realistic concessions required by the political process. In 1657, one Parliament offered him the crown, but he declined it. In the end, he believed the dictatorship to be the only way to bring peace to England.

Cromwell's tenure as Lord Protector of England was made difficult by the bitter factionalism within the Puritan ranks. The most radical group was known as the Diggers, who wanted to abolish private property, while the Levellers made quasi-democratic demands for parliamentary elections based on nearly universal male suffrage. Neither of these views found support among the landed gentry, from whose ranks Cromwell had come. A host of other ideologies surfaced during these years, and conspiracies against the Protectorate came from the defeated royalists as well as from the ranks of the Puritans.

The former king's son, the future Charles II, lived in France, where exiled nobles hatched countless plots to restore the monarchy. Caught between opposition to the monarchy and resistance to the Protectorate, Cromwell became reinforced in his conviction that only he had the objective interests of the country at heart.

Cromwell reorganized the country into 11 military and administrative districts, each in the hands of a major general who reported directly to him. The man who claimed to detest power could not, however, abide dissent. To control the opposition and those who would criticize the dictatorship, Cromwell created a system of domestic surveillance and prohibited all newspapers. He crushed a rebellion in Ireland with great brutality, convinced that the Catholicism of the Irish was a form of treason against the state. In religious

Print showing the royal court of Charles II. Late 17th century. The moment depicted is the entry of the king and his courtiers. The Restoration saw a return to the splendor and luxury that had disappeared under Oliver Cromwell; note the rich costumes of both men and women—the latter wearing full, heavy skirts.

Mansell/TimeLife Pictures/Getty Images

affairs, Cromwell's record was mixed. Among his Christian subjects, he allowed freedom of worship only for non-Anglican Protestants; on the other hand, he welcomed the return of Jews to England. In social matters, Cromwell tried to influence the tone of public life by banning plays, sports, and popular music, but these policies were never well received.

Cromwell's last days were spent in disillusionment and concern for the future of England. Before his death, he arranged for the Lord Protectorate to be given to his son, Richard (1626–1712), but his unseasoned successor lacked his father's energy and skill and could not maintain control. In truth, the English people were tired of military rule as well as of the drab tenor of life that Cromwell had imposed. In May 1660, General George Monck, who commanded the New Model Army in Scotland, seized control of the government and asked Charles II to return to England. After years of civil war and the execution of a king, of religious strife and a harsh dictatorship, the Stuart monarchy was restored.

Putting Tudor-Stuart England in Perspective

Despite the painful experiences of the mid-17th century, England did derive some positive long-term lessons about the balance of power between Parliament and the crown. The notion that there would be no taxation without the consent of Parliament was now a permanent part of the constitutional arrangement, as was the writ of habeas corpus and the prohibition against quartering soldiers among civilians.

The social transformation of the country that had produced the gentry class also reflected a permanent reality that guided domestic politics for the next two centuries. When, a generation after the restoration of the monarchy, Stuart rule proved unworkable, it was brought to an end peacefully, in what came to be called England's "bloodless revolution."

Questions for Further Study

1. How can Tudor religious policies best be characterized?
2. What were the origins of the civil wars in England?
3. Why was the monarchy restored after the end of the Protectorate?

Suggestions for Further Reading

Ashton, Robert. *The English Civil War: Conservatism and Revolution, 1603–1649.* London, 1978.

Aylmer, Gerald E. *Rebellion or Revolution? England, 1640–1660.* New York, 1986.

Brimacombe, Peter. *All the Queen's Men: The World of Elizabeth I.* New York, 2000.

Elton, Geoffrey R. *The Parliament of England, 1559–1581.* Cambridge, MA, 1986.

Guy, John. *The Tudors.* Oxford, 2000.

Kennedy, D.E. *The English Revolution, 1642-1649.* New York, 2000.

MacCaffrey, W.T. *Queen Elizabeth and the Making of Policy, 1572–1588.* Princeton, NJ, 1981.

Palliser, David M. *The Age of Elizabeth.* London, 1983.

Plowden, Alison. *Elizabeth Regina: The Age of Triumph, 1588-1603.* Stroud, 2000.

Russell, Conrad. *The Causes of the English Civil War.* New York, 1990.

Zagorin, Perez. *Rebels and Rulers, 1500–1660,* 2 vols. Cambridge, MA, 1982.

InfoTrac College Edition

Enter the search term *Elizabeth I* using Key Terms.

Enter the search term *Oliver Cromwell* using Key Terms.

RELIGIOUS WAR AND THE ASCENDANCY OF THE FRENCH MONARCHY

If in England the 16th and 17th centuries saw the conflict between constitutionalism and monarchy resolve itself in favor of Parliament, in France the same period witnessed the growing power of royal government and the foundations of French absolutism. After the conclusion of the Hundred Years' War in 1453, a succession of kings built up the royal administration, tamed the nobility, and secured state authority over the appointment of bishops and other ecclesiastical officials.

As in other states, the Reformation caused deep religious conflicts in France. These conflicts erupted into a series of wars of religion that took on the character of civil strife. The religious struggles, primarily those of the monarchy against the **Huguenots,** or French Calvinists, dominated events in the 16th century, temporarily ending the consolidation of the royal state. Nevertheless, the fact that the end of the strife came as a result of an edict of religious toleration by the king suggested the value that a strong monarchy could have in the country.

In the aftermath of the religious wars, the process of building the nation around the monarchy resumed. With the skillful and energetic leadership of two cardinals, Richelieu and Mazarin, who served as royal ministers, the French monarchs imposed ever-greater royal authority over the realm. The government these kings controlled reached into the lives of more subjects than ever before.

Religious strife was not, of course, confined to France. In the second decade of the 17th century, while Richelieu still presided as the king's chief minister, most of the great powers of Europe were plunged into a terrible religious and secular conflict known as the Thirty Years' War. The antagonism between Catholics and Protestants was certainly an important factor in bringing about the war, but not the only one: The conflict also involved a broader struggle for mastery between the Bourbon dynasty of France and the imperial aspirations of the Hapsburgs.

SIGNIFICANT DATES

France in the Age of Religious Conflict

1547–1559	Henry II rules as king of France
1572	St. Bartholomew's Day Massacre
1576	Holy League formed
1519–1589	Life of Catherine de' Medici
1574–1589	Henry III rules as king of France
1588–1589	War of Three Henries
1598	Edict of Nantes issued
1589–1610	Henry IV rules as king of France
1585–1642	Life of Cardinal Richelieu
1610–1643	Louis XIII rules as king of France
1618–1648	Thirty Years' War
1602–1661	Life of Giulio Mazarin
1643–1715	Louis XIV rules as king of France

RELIGIOUS CONFLICT: FROM THE ST. BARTHOLOMEW'S DAY MASSACRE TO THE EDICT OF NANTES

Nowhere did the spread of Protestantism, and especially of the militant Calvinist variety, inflame religious passions more than in France, where the bitter and bloody French Wars of Religion destroyed social tranquility and exasperated already existing economic and political tensions.

CATHERINE DE' MEDICI AND THE WARS OF RELIGION

The religious turmoil in France endured for a generation, from 1562 to 1598, but its roots went back further, to the reign of Henry II (ruled 1547–1559). Despite his energetic and robust appearance, Henry was a weak and pliable ruler who was influenced by his mistresses and his ambitious advisers. He continued the Valois-Hapsburg War against Emperor Charles V and then against Philip II, siding with the German Protestants in their struggles against the Hapsburg emperor, despite his own Catholic faith.

When peace came in 1559, Henry reversed himself, instituting severe restrictions against the Protestants in his own country. Later that year, when Henry was accidentally killed in a tournament, his Italian wife, Catherine de' Medici (1519–1589), daughter of Duke Lorenzo de' Medici of Urbino, became regent. Acting for her three sons, who succeeded each other as king over the following years, Catherine's religious policies ranged from toleration to persecution. During her regency, the religious question came to a head.

Calvinism had continued to spread despite persecutions by Henry II. During his reign, there were Huguenots among all social classes, from artisans to merchants, and half of the nobility had become Protestant. Because the

aristocracy had always challenged the king's efforts to create centralized government, the existence of so large a proportion of Huguenot nobles posed a special danger to the monarchy.

Beyond the nobility, the Huguenots formed a distinct minority of the French population, but they were zealous in their faith and determined to fight for their freedom to worship as they chose. The Huguenot Church was well organized, with a centralized administration that reached down to the provincial and congregational levels. By the time the Wars of Religion began, more than 2,000 Huguenot congregations existed throughout the country.

Catherine de' Medici tried unsuccessfully to diffuse the growing tensions by brokering religious compromise and fostering reforms in the French Church. The Catholic extremists, headed by the influential Guise family, demanded unremitting opposition to the Huguenots. The anti-Protestant campaign received support from the papacy and the Jesuits, as well as from Philip II of Spain.

The war broke out in 1562 when the private armies of the Guise slaughtered an entire congregation of Huguenots at the town of Vassy. The fighting spread, but both sides found themselves unable to win a clear victory. Catherine, who was concerned that the crusade against the Protestants might undermine the Valois monarchy, joined forces with the Catholic party led by the Guise family.

Map 44.1 Religious Conflict in France. The bitterness of France's religious wars was complicated by the extent of the geographical divisions. The Catholics were divided between the northern regions and Provence in the south, while central France was the scene of constant battles. The Edict of Nantes was proclaimed in a city that lay in the vicinity of disputed territory.

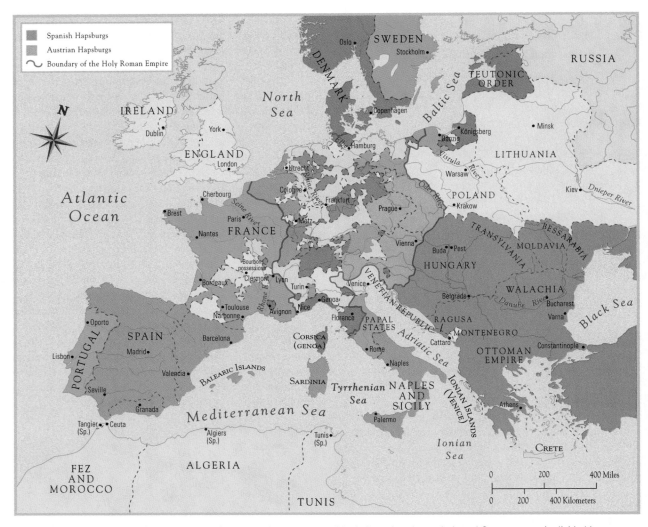

Map 44.2 Europe, c. 1560. While France and Spain have begun to resemble their modern forms, Italy and Germany remain divided into a series of smaller states. The Ottoman Empire is at its strongest, extending almost to the gates of Vienna. In Eastern Europe, only the island of Crete remained a Western possession, governed by Venice; it was taken by the Turks a century later.

In 1570, after the Huguenot military leader Gaspard de Coligny (1519–1572) defeated a royal army, Catherine decided to make peace. Reconciled with Catherine, de Coligny became an intimate adviser to her son, Charles IX (ruled 1560–1574), and urged him to support the Dutch Protestant rebellion against their Spanish rulers.

Fearing de Coligny's growing influence over her weak-minded son, Catherine conspired with the Guise to have de Coligny assassinated, but he escaped, although severely wounded. Coligny's survival led Catherine and the Guise to organize an even wider plot to eliminate the Huguenot leadership. Huguenot nobles had gathered in Paris for the marriage of Catherine's daughter Margaret to the Bourbon leader Henry of Navarre (the future Henry IV, he had wavered between Catholicism and Protestantism, but was now Huguenot). Catherine persuaded Charles to authorize what is known as the St. Bartholomew's Day Massacre (August 24, 1572). As the slaughter spread from Paris to

the countryside, thousands of Huguenots, including de Coligny, were killed.

HENRY IV AND THE EDICT OF NANTES

The brutal massacre, which destroyed much popular support for the Valois family, broke the tenuous truce, and the religious wars erupted again. In 1576, the Catholic party created the Holy League to wipe out the Protestants and to make Henry of Guise king of France in place of Catherine's son, Henry III (ruled 1574–1589), who had succeeded his brother Charles.

The subsequent War of the Three Henries (1588–1589) first saw Henry of Guise pitted against Henry III. The Catholic king, after having Guise murdered, now joined forces with the Protestant Henry of Navarre in defeating the Holy League. Following the defeat of the extreme Catholics, however, Henry III was assassinated, and Henry of Navarre now claimed the throne. As King Henry IV (ruled

Painting of the St. Bartholomew's Day Massacre of 1572. Late 16th century. As the scene shows, the killing of French Protestants involved residents of both town and countryside. Note that most of the attackers are wearing the dress of official government troops, while the victims are civilians.

1589–1610), he became the first Bourbon ruler of France. This action immediately drove the extreme Catholics into bitter opposition and provoked the intervention of Philip II of Spain. Henry IV countered this action by securing English support and converted again to Catholicism, thus undermining many of his critics.

Henry was determined to bring the devastating Wars of Religion to an end. With this goal in mind, in 1598 he issued the Edict of Nantes, a document that made Catholicism the official religion of the country but gave the Huguenots some guaranteed protections. Awarding them the right to control more than 100 fortified towns throughout France, the edict also granted them the right to free worship in certain localities and full political privileges. Henry's willingness to accept religious toleration was a pragmatic political decision based on his recognition that France was exhausted by the destructive wars and required strong, effective government. Henceforth, matters of state became paramount as France's rulers set about rebuilding both country and monarchy.

ROYAL GOVERNMENT AND ECONOMIC REVIVAL

The Wars of Religion had been deeply divisive of French society and had ruined the economy. The most pressing problem facing Henry IV was financial because the wars had drained the treasury, heaping enormous debt on the government. Only after putting the economy back on a firm footing could the king turn to rebuilding the power of the monarchy.

Henry and his Bourbon successors had the good fortune of being served by a succession of skillful and dedicated ministers. In reconstructing the economy, Henry had the assistance of a brilliant finance minister, Maximilien, duke of Sully (1560–1641). Like the king, Sully was earlier a Protestant but converted as a matter of policy. Beginning as a member of the king's finance commission, in 1598 he was made superintendent of finances.

Sully set out to increase royal revenues and reduce the debt. He established a new direct tax that was more easily calculated and collected. He raised the *gabelle*, a tax on salt, which virtually all citizens had to use as a preservative for keeping food. He reformed the tax-collecting mechanisms: Under earlier kings, the revenue agents took a portion of the revenues they collected for themselves, and Sully now forced them to accept a lower percentage. Sully also raised money by increasing the number of royal offices and, as previous kings had done, continued to sell them for cash to nobles of the robe, a new class of aristocrat created by the monarchy to hold the key bureaucratic positions. Sully induced the older, landowning nobility of feudal origins, the nobles of the sword, to retire to their rural estates with government pensions. At the same time, he required the payment of an annual fee from all those nobles of the robe who occupied government offices.

© Réunion des Musées Nationaux/Art Resource, NY

SuperStock

PUBLIC FIGURES AND PRIVATE LIVES

MARIE DE' MEDICI AND HENRY IV OF FRANCE

In 1600, Henry IV married Marie de' Medici (1573–1642), daughter of the grand duke of Tuscany, an alliance that solidified Henry's conversion to Catholicism. Marie was a strong-willed, self-possessed woman from one of Italy's most distinguished families. She thought of the French as culturally inferior and set about bringing some of the sophisticated tastes of her own background to the court at Paris. Henry, on the other hand, proved to be a popular sovereign who demonstrated a real concern for the welfare of even his most lowly subjects.

When Henry was assassinated in 1610, Marie became regent for their son, Louis XIII (ruled 1610–1643). She completely dominated her son, and when the nobles began to raise objections to her rule, she summoned the Estates General of the Realm in 1614 and declared Louis of age—the Estates General, which was without real power, was not called again for 175 years, on the eve of the French Revolution.

Although in theory the regency was now dissolved, Marie continued to exclude Louis from the affairs of state. Instead, she dismissed Sully and relied on the advice of the Florentine adventurer Concino Concini (d. 1617) and the French cleric, Cardinal Armand du Plessis de Richelieu (1585–1642). Concini set up an elaborate spy system among the nobility and became universally despised for his greed and duplicity. In 1617, the young Louis arranged to have Concini assassinated and forced his mother into exile. She returned, however, five years later and was reconciled with Louis, whom she persuaded to appoint Richelieu secretary of state.

After her husband's death, Marie had the Luxembourg Palace in Paris, a large and elaborate residence modeled in part on the Pitti Palace in Florence, built for herself. When Marie returned from exile in 1622, she commissioned the artist Peter Paul Rubens to paint a cycle of huge paintings dedicated to her and her marriage with Henry IV.

Marie's influence on French policy was considerable. She managed to keep the great nobles in check and established close relations with the Hapsburg Catholic powers, Spain and Austria. Her ambitions finally overstepped her talents when she tried to undermine Richelieu, whose growing influence over the king she began to resent. In 1631, Louis banished her again. She fled to the Netherlands, never returning to France.

While royal revenues were being increased, Sully had Henry cancel a portion of the public debt, so that he eventually was able to accumulate a surplus of funds. Sully negotiated trade treaties with the other powers and adopted the mercantilist policies that guided their trade programs. He used the new state income to invest in long-range economic development by building and improving roads, canals, and other infrastructure, a program that also had the immediate effect of putting people to work. Both Sully and the king were interested in increasing the general prosperity of all classes of French subjects, and Henry is reputed to have said, "There should be a chicken in every peasant's pot every Sunday."

THE CARDINALS AND THE STATE: THE ADMINISTRATIONS OF RICHELIEU AND MAZARIN

Between 1624 and 1661, the government of France was in the hands of two extraordinary ministers, Armand du Richelieu and Giulio Mazarin. Both were cardinals of the Catholic Church and proved to be two of the greatest statesmen in French history. The brilliant and crafty cardinals dedicated all of their energies toward making the French monarchy as absolute as possible and keeping themselves in power. They balanced and held in check the various forces working against royal authority: the nobility, the bureaucracy, and the Huguenots.

TOWARD ROYAL ABSOLUTISM

In light of the destructive force of the Wars of Religion, religious policy was perhaps the most sensitive issue confronting Richelieu. Under Marie de' Medici and her Italian advisers, the Huguenots had worried about renewed persecution. Incidents of local conflict with royal troops did erupt from time to time. In the 1620s, after one Huguenot stronghold had allied with the English against the monarchy, the government began to seize the fortified towns the Huguenots had been granted under the terms of the Edict of Nantes. Richelieu then secured the revocation of the edict and replaced it with the Peace of Alais, which granted the Huguenots only religious and political rights.

For years, the constant wars that disturbed French public life had required royal governments to raise monies for their armies, and this had proved to be a major impetus in the drive toward absolutism. Richelieu, needing revenues to finance his foreign and domestic policies, was no exception. He encouraged the sale of government offices, which continued to grow in number. By the 1630s, almost half of all government income came from this source. As a result, the efficient collection of taxes and control over local affairs assumed increasing importance.

Richelieu was never able to bring royal finances under control and had to resort to increasing taxes on ordinary citizens in order to meet the mounting national debt. The tax burden and the ever-growing power of the royal government sometimes sparked protests and uprisings in the countryside, especially among the peasantry and the nobility. Richelieu was able, however, to put them down with the royal troops.

CARDINAL MAZARIN AND THE FRONDE

Louis XIII died in 1643. Because his son, Louis XIV (ruled 1643–1715), was only five years old at the time, once again France came under the regency of the queen mother, this time Anne of Austria (1601–1666). Anne turned the gov-

Philippe de Champagne, *Triple Portrait of Cardinal Richelieu,* c. 1630. The painter, a Belgian, went to Paris in 1621 to help in the decoration of the Luxembourg Palace and remained as court painter to Louis XIII. This image conveys the many aspects of the cardinal's sharp intelligence and authority.

The National Gallery, London

ernment over to Giulio Mazarin (1602–1661), to whom she may have been secretly married (this suspicion has never been confirmed). Mazarin was an Italian-born soldier who had served in the papal diplomatic corps. Although never ordained as a priest, he was Richelieu's protégé, and Louis XIII had recommended that he be made a cardinal.

Mazarin continued the two policies of his predecessor: the centralization of power in the hands of the king, and increasing taxation to pay for the costs of royal government. These programs incurred the wrath of both the nobles and the members of the law court known as the Parlement of Paris, who in any case disliked Mazarin on principle because he was a foreigner. Mazarin further weakened his position by involvement in personal financial corruption. The nobles and the members of the Parlement joined forces against the monarchy when Mazarin tried to squeeze money out of them to meet the mounting costs of the French involvement in the Thirty Years' War (see following section). The result was an organized conspiracy against the government, known as the *Fronde*—a word that has come to mean violent political opposition from within the ruling class.

In 1648, the Parlement and nobles of the robe, who held many of the important bureaucratic offices, demanded that the king agree to levy no new taxes without consent. When Mazarin arrested the leaders of the Parlement, a popular revolt in Paris forced him and the royal family to flee the capital. The disturbances spread to other cities, and in several locations the protestors took over local governments and random acts of violence erupted. This first episode of the Fronde ended only after Mazarin pledged to concede the demands of the Parlement.

A second Fronde developed in 1650 around two nobles of the sword who held important military positions. This time, the ringleaders insisted that Mazarin be dismissed and that many of the traditional local powers of the old nobility be restored. The Spanish, with whom the French had continued to fight even after the end of the Thirty Years' War, sent aid to the Fronde. The effort failed, however, when the nobles began fighting among themselves. Mazarin shrewdly played one group off another and was able to use army elements loyal to the monarchy to crush the conspiracy. In 1652, Mazarin strengthened royal authority by having the

minority of Louis XIV declared at an end. Never again would the monarchy be seriously threatened by rebellious nobles. The failure of the Fronde had the opposite effect, strengthening the power of the state. After Mazarin's death in 1661, Louis XIV excluded his mother Anne from all participation in the affairs of state and assumed full powers over one of the most powerful forms of absolute monarchy in Western Europe.

A SCANDAL IN BOHEMIA: THE PROTESTANT REVOLT AND THE THIRTY YEARS' WAR

The last of the great wars of religion that shook Europe is known as the Thirty Years' War, a complex struggle that unfolded in four distinct phases between 1618 and 1648: the Bohemian Phase (1618–1625), the Danish Phase (1625–1629), the Swedish Phase (1630–1635), and the French-Swedish Phase (1635–1648). Much of the fighting took place in Germany, but the struggle dragged in most of the great states of Europe and many of the lesser powers as well. Three principal participants, Spain, Austria, and France, were at the center of the conflict.

The vast Hapsburg empire had been established when Charles V inherited the throne of Spain and three years later became Holy Roman Emperor. Eventually, he ruled over Austria, Bohemia, Hungary, and the Netherlands as well as Spain, the German lands of the Holy Roman Empire, and portions of Italy. When Charles retired in 1556, his holdings were divided. His son Philip II received Spain and its overseas colonies, the Netherlands, and Italy, while his brother Ferdinand took the imperial title along with Austria, Bohemia, and Hungary. From the time of Charles V, the French had felt encircled by the lands and ambitions of the Hapsburgs, and an ongoing struggle between first the Valois and then the Bourbon rulers of France and the Hapsburgs marked European politics for more than a century.

The religious wars engulfing the German states ended with the Peace of Augsburg in 1555. The two sides, however, continued to fight sporadically, eventually forming opposing military alliances: the Protestant Union, supported by France, England, and the Netherlands; and the Catholic League, supported by Spain and the Holy Roman Empire. Clearly, the war involved political and dynastic issues that had little to do with religion.

The war began in Bohemia, however, over religious issues. In 1609, the Holy Roman Emperor had pledged himself to a policy of religious toleration for Catholics and Protestants alike. He intended his promise to mollify the Calvinist nobles in Bohemia. When, however, Ferdinand II of Hapsburg (ruled as king of Bohemia 1617–1637, and as Holy Roman Emperor 1619–1637) became king of Bohemia in 1617, he began an effort to impose Catholicism and a rigid centralizing policy on the country.

SIGNIFICANT DATES

The Thirty Years' War

1608	Protestant Union formed
1609	Catholic League formed
1618	Defenestration of Prague
1618–1625	Bohemian Phase of war
1625–1629	Danish Phase of war
1630–1635	Swedish Phase of war
1635–1648	French-Swedish Phase of war
1648	Peace of Westphalia
1659	Peace of Pyrenees

Jacques Callot, etching from *The Miseries of War* series. 1632–1633. Callot, a French painter and engraver who worked for the Medici court in Florence, is best known for being the first artist to have made etching an independent art. This horrific image is one of a series showing the death and destruction visited on Germany by the Thirty Years' War.

THE CATHOLIC TRIUMPH

The result was a rebellion in 1618, begun when the nobles threw three imperial officials out of the window of the castle in Prague—the so-called defenestration of Prague. The Bohemians declared Ferdinand deposed and replaced him with Frederick II of the Palatinate, the leader of the Protestant Union and the most prominent Calvinist prince in the Holy Roman Empire. The war had begun.

The hostilities brought an invading army into Bohemia under Ferdinand, now Holy Roman Emperor, and his German ally, Duke Maximilian of Bavaria. In 1620, Catholic forces under the Flemish general Johann von Tilly won a crushing victory against the Calvinists at the Battle of the White Mountain. Ferdinand proceeded to end the autonomy of Bohemia and to declare Catholicism the official religion. The emperor also deprived the Calvinist nobles of their landed estates and forced tens of thousands of Protestants to leave the country.

Moreover, while Frederick was fighting in Bohemia, the Spanish intervened by invading and occupying the Palatinate, which was then divided between them and the Bavarians. The first phase of the Thirty Years' War ended triumphantly, with the Catholic forces in possession of Bohemia and the Palatinate and Spanish troops marching once again into the United Provinces in an effort to recapture the northern territories that Spain had lost in the Dutch revolt of the previous century.

In 1625, the Thirty Years' War was widened by intervention from an unexpected source. Christian IV (ruled 1588–1648), king of Denmark and Norway, invaded northern Germany. Ostensibly joining the struggle in order to assist the Protestant forces, Christian was really motivated by his own expansionist drives; he had already fought against Sweden for control of Lapland and now seemed bent on securing hegemony over the Baltic region around Denmark and Germany.

Christian's ambitions exceeded his abilities. Tilly defeated the Danish army in 1626, and the next year the commander of the imperial forces, Albrecht von Wallenstein, defeated Christian again. Wallenstein, a Bohemian nobleman who had raised an army on behalf of the emperor, had enriched himself on the lands taken from the Protestants.

Map 44.3 The Expansion of Sweden. Sweden's growth was created by its participation in the religious wars of the 17th century. Gustavus Adolphus used the assistance of the French to counter Hapsburg influence by pushing southward. The results, which were underwritten by the Treaty of Westphalia in 1648, saw the French victorious, with little permanent benefit for Sweden. Go to http://info.wadsworth.com/053461065X for an interactive version of this map.

His troops lived off the lands through which they moved, pillaging and destroying peasant villages and large estates with equal ferocity.

FROM THE SWEDISH VICTORY TO THE FRENCH INTERVENTION

By 1629, Christian was forced to withdraw from the war, and the Catholics occupied Denmark and the chief ports of northern Germany. Following these victories, the Emperor Ferdinand announced the Edict of Restitution, which gave back to the Catholic Church all lands taken from it since 1552. The edict also outlawed Calvinism, which had not been protected by the Peace of Augsburg in 1555, in all imperial territories. Yet the very extent of the Catholic victory proved its undoing. The German princes grew worried by the startling increase in imperial power and began to rebel against Ferdinand. At a meeting of the imperial diet in 1630, they demanded that he relieve Wallenstein of his command or see the end of Hapsburg control of the imperial crown.

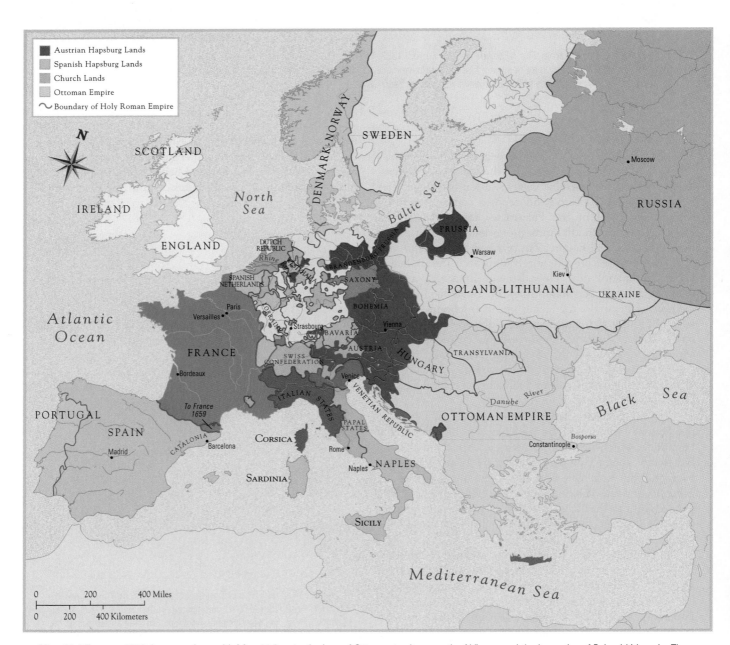

Map 44.4 Europe, 1648. In comparison with Map 44.2, note the loss of Ottoman territory south of Vienna and the huge size of Poland-Lithuania. The Holy Roman Empire continues to fragment, while France has consolidated its regions. A century or so before the founding of St. Petersburg, Moscow remains the only major city in Russia.

GUSTAVUS ADOLPHUS

Ferdinand gave in, and the price was high, because he was deprived of Wallenstein's military talents just as a major new phase of the war began. In 1630, King Gustavus Adolphus of Sweden (ruled 1611–1632) joined the Protestant cause. Gustavus Adolphus had proven to be a vigorous monarch who restructured the Swedish state, disciplined its nobles, and won major victories against the Russians and Poles in the Baltic. Yet he, too, was motivated by political as well as religious questions. Gustavus Adolphus aimed to make Sweden the predominant power in the Baltic and feared the spread of Hapsburg power along the coast of Germany.

Assisted financially by the French, the Swedish king organized a strong military force and moved rapidly and deeply into Germany, pushing the imperial armies before him. Gustavus Adolphus, who was a brilliant field commander, defeated Tilly at Breitenfeld in 1631 and Lech the next year. Recoiling from these blows, Ferdinand recalled Wallenstein to head the imperial forces. At Lutzen in 1632, the Swedes defeated Wallenstein's soldiers, but Gustavus Adolphus was mortally wounded and died shortly afterward.

The tide of battle soon turned against the Swedish army, which was still in Germany. In 1634, the imperial armies—although deprived once again of Wallenstein's command when the general was assassinated—won the Battle of Nordlingen and cleared southern Germany of Swedish troops. The following year, Ferdinand signed the Treaty of Prague with the German princes, bringing a settlement of the tensions between them and the Hapsburgs.

Although the war appeared to be over, in 1635 Cardinal Richelieu decided to involve Catholic France in the conflict, but on the side of the Lutheran Swedes against the Catholic Hapsburgs. Thus began the final phase of the war, in which political and dynastic issues were paramount.

For more than a decade, some of the most bitter and destructive fighting took place in Germany and the Netherlands. The international situation had become chaotic, and both sides realized that it was in the general interest to stop the carnage. Tentative peace talks started in 1641 but dragged on for seven more years.

THE PEACE OF WESTPHALIA

The French victories over the Spanish in 1643, followed by further victories in southern Germany, reactivated the negotiations. By 1648 all sides were ready to end the fighting (the struggle between Spain and France continued until peace was signed between them in 1659). The Peace of Westphalia was arranged as a result of a large meeting of representatives from all of the participants, including France, Spain, Denmark, Sweden, the United Provinces, and the Holy Roman Empire.

France, which dominated the fighting in the last years of the war, gained territories along its northeastern border, notably Alsace and Lorraine. Sweden, France's principal ally, secured control over lands in Germany. In a broad sense, the French finally won their longstanding struggle to tame the Hapsburg empire. The representatives agreed to the independence of the United Provinces and Switzerland, two areas that the Hapsburgs had claimed; at the same time, the German princes of the Holy Roman Empire pledged not to take up arms again against the emperor, who in turn acknowledged their autonomy.

Westphalia represented a major victory for Protestantism. The religious autonomy of the German princes was confirmed, both for Calvinists and Lutherans, and all Catholic properties seized before 1624 now became possessions of the Protestant states. Most far-reaching was the fact that the treaty finally ended the idea that the split between Catholic and Protestant could be healed.

Putting Religious War and the Ascendancy of the French Monarchy in Perspective

The end of the war signaled the final eclipse of Spain and the rise of France as the dominant power on the Continent. In addition, the religious passions that had been the cause of so much destruction and killing for a century began to subside. Henceforth, economic and political ambitions rather than dynastic and religious issues would determine relations among the states of Europe.

The Westphalia agreements established a peace that remained effective for more than a century. The Thirty Years' War had caused terrible destruction, including widespread economic havoc and millions of deaths; estimates suggest that the fighting had wiped out almost one-third of the people of Germany. Even though these figures may be exaggerated, European leaders recognized the extent of the carnage and concluded that diplomacy was a better solution than armed conflict.

Questions for Further Study

1. What was the relationship between politics and religion in France?
2. How did Richelieu and Mazarin strengthen the authority of the king?
3. What were the major issues involved in the Thirty Years' War?

Suggestions for Further Reading

Bergin, Joseph. *Cardinal Richelieu: Power and the Pursuit of Wealth*. New Haven, CT, 1985.

Diefendorf, Barbara. *Beneath the Cross: Catholics and Huguenots in Sixteenth-Century Paris*. New York, 1991.

Levi, Anthony H.T. *Cardinal Richelieu and the Making of France*. London, 2000.

Maltby, William S. *Alba*. Berkeley, CA, 1983.

Parker, Geoffrey, ed. *The Thirty Years War*. New York, 1997.

Parrot, David. *Richlieu's Army: War, Government and Society in France, 1624-1642*. New York, 2001.

Pennington, Donald H. *Seventeenth-Century Europe*, 2nd ed. London, 1989.

Salmon, John H.M. *French Government and Society in the Wars of Religion*. St. Louis, MO, 1976.

Sutherland, Nicola M. *The Massacre of St. Bartholomew and the European Conflict, 1559–1572*. New York, 1973.

InfoTrac College Edition

Enter the search term *Thirty Years' War* using Key Terms.

PATTERNS OF LIFE IN A TIME OF UPHEAVAL

The decades following the Reformation saw tumultuous political events and rapid cultural innovation. The social patterns of everyday life, however, changed slowly. This gradual evolution influenced the basic aspects of daily experience, including the health and well-being of all classes of Europeans, their diet and housing, and the way in which they dressed.

The two factors that affected health most acutely were the food supply and infectious disease, both of which remained largely beyond the control of humans until the Industrial Revolution of the 18th century. Life expectancy was low, and repeated cycles of disease continued to take their toll.

The rich and poor led vastly different lives in terms of diet and housing. For 200 years following the Black Death, food and nutrition improved for most Europeans. With the religious and political upheavals of the 16th and 17th centuries, however, general standards declined.

The same disparity marked the kind of housing available to rich and poor. More durable building materials, such as brick and stone, began to replace wood in public buildings and in the private residences of the wealthy. The houses of the nobility and the rich merchants of the cities used elaborate decorations and furnishings, reflecting a new level of domestic comfort and a growing concern for privacy. The urban poor, on the other hand, were increasingly crammed into densely populated and unsanitary tenement buildings, while the rural poor continued to live under much the same conditions as their ancestors had done.

One of the most visible manifestations of the social hierarchy was dress. For the poor and the peasantry, clothing style remained relatively unchanged for hundreds of years after the 14th century. For the rich, however, dress reflected the availability of new raw materials, including cotton and silk, and the development of new manufacturing processes.

Material aspects of life such as clothing and housing provide a way of understanding broad social and economic transformations. At the same time, they offer insight into the lives of average Europeans, who played no active part in the great political events of their times but who bring us into contact with the daily realities of human existence.

HEALTH AND MEDICINE

In the two centuries before the French Revolution, Europeans had achieved a rough balance between the rate of births and the rate of deaths. Infant mortality was high, with perhaps as many as one-third of all children in the 17th century dying before their first birthday. Among the chief factors keeping the death rate high were disease and starvation, and people lived to an average age of only 25. The wealthy tended to live somewhat longer than the poor, and childbirth made women especially vulnerable to illness and death.

THE CYCLE OF DISEASE

The great plague of the 14th century, the Black Death, was by no means unique. Throughout European history all segments of society, but especially the poor, were highly susceptible to disease. This was generally because of low resistance to illness caused either by diets lacking in nutritional value or by the famines that periodically struck the population—almost always, in fact, epidemics followed incidences of famine.

The plague recurred time and again from the 15th to the 17th centuries. In a 200-year period, the French town of Besançon experienced it 40 times, while Seville in southern Spain saw outbreaks during 11 of the years from 1507 to 1649. In Western Europe, the plague appeared for the last time in 1720 when it killed perhaps half the inhabitants of the French port city of Marseilles. In Eastern Europe, however, where health and sanitary conditions were even worse, the plague continued to ravage cities into the 19th century—thousands fell victim to it in Moscow in 1770 and in the Balkans as late as 1841.

Plague was merely one among a host of prevalent diseases, and often adverse conditions caused the spread of several different maladies at the same time: Smallpox, typhus, cholera, tuberculosis, influenza, grippe, whooping cough, diphtheria, and scarlet fever were some of the diseases that were an ever-present fear. At the time, diseases were often diagnosed incorrectly or confused with the plague, and contemporary descriptions of many illnesses make it difficult to identify them today.

Epidemics spread from one population group to another, usually following the movement of people along trade routes and other heavily traveled itineraries. The Black Death reached Europe on ships from the Crimea, and in the early 18th century cholera came to the Continent from India. Perhaps the best-known example of the movement of disease from one culture to another was the result of the so-called Columbian Exchange. Spanish explorers and soldiers brought diseases like smallpox to the Amerindians of the New World, where no resistance had been developed to these unknown illnesses. The result was the devastation of huge numbers of people.

The process also worked in the other direction. Syphilis, which had been rare in Europe, appears to have become widespread after 1492. One theory holds that members of Columbus's crew contracted it on their arrival in America following the first voyage. Syphilis became a real epidemic that spread rapidly around Europe, and by the end of the 16th century it had affected all classes of society, including many members of royal families.

MEDICAL CARE

The measures taken to deal with the plague in the 17th century were the same as those in the 14th. The rich fled the cities for more isolated homes in the country, while the poor remained in the crowded cities, often locked behind the town gates with the roads to and from the cities blocked. The sick were quarantined, dead bodies burned, and neighborhoods sometimes disinfected, although city officials often abandoned their duties until the danger was over. Medical treatment remained generally primitive until modern times. In the 16th century, some physicians believed they could treat syphilis by cauterizing sores with red-hot irons.

Madeleine de Boulogne, *Nuns Giving Care to Female Patients*, c. 1700. The (female) artist distinguishes clearly between the costumes of the nuns and the middle-class dresses of their patients. On the right-hand wall there hangs a painting of the crucified Christ; such images were commonly displayed in hospitals as a sign of divine suffering.

The Granger Collection, New York

Improved personal hygiene, the replacement of wood with stone or brick as building material for homes, and the elimination of animals from households all reduced fleas and help explain why the plague eventually disappeared. In the 18th century, however, smallpox, which replaced the plague as the most devastating disease, killed perhaps 60 million people. For many years, smallpox had been treated successfully by Muslim physicians, who developed the technique of inoculation. The practice was slowly adopted in the West during the 18th century. Moreover, some scholars suggest that the eventual elimination of particular diseases may be explained not only by such preventive measures, but also by the mutation of the bacteria or virus causing the disease.

Several important medical techniques—systematic observation and deductive reasoning, the use of dissection to study anatomy, and the discovery of the circulation of blood—led to a better understanding of the human body. Moreover, the number of doctors and their training increased greatly. Yet well into the 18th century, faith healing and peasant folk remedies based largely on superstition continued to be practiced widely. Sometimes herbs and drugs prescribed by apothecaries actually worked to cure a patient. Bloodletting and purging remained common and often harmful treatments. Surgery was performed without the use of anesthetic and under extremely unsanitary conditions, especially on battlefields and in hospital wards for the poor. Until the 19th century saw improved treatment of patients, medical knowledge had little practical impact on the health of most Europeans.

Despite the terrible toll on human life taken by the plague and other diseases, the cycle of European marriages and births generally compensated for the demographic losses. In 1451, for example, 21,000 inhabitants of Cologne died of plague, but within a few years 4,000 marriages had taken place in the same city. Similarly, after the plague had decimated the inhabitants of Verona, Italy, in 1637, many of the French soldiers occupying the town married the widows. In Germany as a whole, the devastating impact of the Thirty Years' War, which had claimed perhaps one-third of the population, soon eased as the population began to increase again. The overall demographic pattern in the West changed significantly in the course of the 18th century, when births finally began to gain over deaths, with the result that Europe experienced a far-reaching population explosion.

CHANGING TASTES: FOOD AND DIET

Ever since ancient times, the fundamental food source for Europeans was grain, supplemented by vegetables and only very occasionally by other kinds of food. Wealthier people ate meat, fish, and cheese, and were able to improve the taste and variety of their food with spices and sauces. Europe's diet changed significantly as a result of overseas exploration and the discovery of the Americas, and eventually the potato replaced grain as the staple ingredient for many poor people.

FARMING AND SCARCITY

In the Roman Empire and the Middle Ages, Europe's poor—the overwhelming majority of people—consumed the same monotonous, uninspiring diet, consisting largely of grains: The major crop was wheat. The problem with grain, and especially wheat, was that it required large amounts of land to produce relatively low yields. Wheat could not be grown two years in a row on the same land because the soil became rapidly depleted. Farmers therefore resorted to the two-field system, and later the three-field system, whereby some portion of the land was allowed to be restored by letting it lie fallow. Although effective, this method of growing made it impossible to use all the land at once. In addition, wheat cultivation also required the use of manure for fertilizer, which in turn meant that some of the land had to be reserved for the grazing of animals that produced the manure.

The supply of basic foods like grain was always precarious. Crop yields did increase slowly over time, especially between the 16th and 18th centuries, when the yield was almost twice that in the late Middle Ages. Nevertheless, most of Europe suffered from a condition of chronic scarcity.

THE EUROPEAN DIET

From wheat and other grains, peasants made two kinds of food: bread and gruel. Bread was the staple food item, and it has been estimated that in good times an adult peasant ate more than four pounds of bread per day. Peasant bread was generally made from wheat or rye, and often a combination of the two. Because the grain was ground into flour by rough stone wheels, the wheat germ and outer husk of bran remained as part of the flour. This flour produced a dark, rough-textured bread that was the principal—and often the only—food that peasants consumed. Gruel was a kind of thick porridge, like oatmeal, made by boiling grains in water. It was seldom if ever flavored with spices and rarely contained other ingredients.

Vegetables were also available except in winter and early spring. These most often included peas, beans, lentils, carrots, onions, and cabbages, and less fortunate rural dwellers cooked wild grasses and roots. Vegetables were boiled or mixed with grains to make soups. Only rarely, several times per year, did peasants eat meat or fish, which were usually the preserve of the nobles who owned the land and rivers. More prosperous peasants had a few animals from which they made cheese and butter, but these were eaten sparingly, and milk was reserved almost exclusively for the very young and the old.

An old European proverb, "Tell me what you eat and I will tell you who you are," reflects the social reality of how the diet of the poor differed significantly from that of the rich. The upper classes developed a passion for eating meat, whether it was beef, lamb, venison, or pork. For dinner parties, the nobility would often serve several courses of these

Jean Michelin, *The Baker's Cart*. 1656. The baking of bread, which involved both space and potentially dangerous hot ovens, generally took place on the outskirts of a town. The baker—or his employees—would then bring the bread into town by cart and travel around selling it. Note the heavy clothes and architecture of Northern Europe.

The Metropolitan Museum of Art, Fletcher Fund, 1927. (27.59) Photograph © 1983 The Metropolitan Museum of Art

meats, interspersed with fish and fowl of various kinds. They seldom ate vegetables, which they considered the loathsome diet of the poor. Not only would they prohibit peasants on their lands from hunting and fishing, but they devoted themselves to hunting as a favorite social pastime.

The meals of the ruling class were far more interesting and varied than those of the peasantry. Only they could afford the rare and costly spices that came from Asia, and their cooks used these and the juices of meats and fish to make sauces to flavor their food. They also could buy fruit, sugar, and honey, for making sweets and pastries. Moreover, the rich avoided the coarse dark bread eaten by the peasants, preferring finer grades of white bread made from sifted flour. Specialty breads contained brewer's yeast, milk, and sometimes eggs and sugar.

It is not surprising that the European diet was determined first and foremost by wealth and social status. The irony, however, is that the poorer classes seem to have consumed a more nutritious diet. Today we know that the common dark bread eaten by peasants was nutritiously bal-

anced, containing a mixture of carbohydrates, proteins, and minerals; when supplemented with vegetables, the vitamin and mineral content was even higher. During the winter and spring, however, the diet of the peasantry suffered because they did not have access to fresh vegetables, with the result that they often suffered from scurvy, brought on by a lack of vitamin C.

The rich, on the other hand, ate a much less healthy diet, heavy in protein but low in vitamins and minerals. This deficiency was compounded by the white bread they preferred, which lacked the minerals and vitamins of the peasant bread. Those with the most balanced, and therefore the healthiest, diets were probably the middle classes, who ate some meat and cheese but also consumed vegetables and often could not afford white bread.

NEW FOODS AND CONSUMPTION PATTERNS

The original purpose of the great European explorations that began in the 15th century had been to find a direct sea route to Asia in order to obtain prized spices and luxury products directly from their source. In the process, the explorers accomplished much more than this goal because the discovery of the Americas resulted in the importation of a host of new foods to Europe. Among these were the potato, tomatoes, squash, and Indian corn (maize). These new products changed the kinds of foods eaten in different cultures of the world, including several European countries. The chili pepper, which originally developed on the slopes of the Andes in Peru, is not related botanically to the pepper at all. Its piquant flavor led the early explorers to misname it, however, and it soon acquired worldwide popularity, transforming the cuisine of China and much of Asia as well as of Africa. In a similar fashion, the tomato became the rage in much of southern Italy, where it was first introduced into Naples by the Spanish in the 16th century. From there, its use spread to southern France, where Provençal cooking still uses it in great quantity. Sugar, which probably was native to India, was known in the West since ancient times and was as costly as any of the spices. In the 16th century, a Spanish merchant transported cane to Hispaniola, where it began to grow profusely and became the crop of many plantations.

The potato, which was native to South America, had a major impact on the European diet. Although it could not be used like wheat to make bread, it was rich in vitamins as well as in carbohydrates. It provided a solution to the lack of vitamins and minerals for the peasant diet during those months when vegetables were not available.

At first, most Europeans ridiculed the potato and felt it was unworthy of being consumed, but famines in the 18th century proved its importance. Soon, potatoes were being grown extensively in Ireland, Germany, and Eastern Europe, where they joined, and eventually replaced, wheat as the staple item in the peasant diet.

In the 15th and 16th centuries, the growing availability of once extremely rare foodstuffs enabled the wealthy of Europe to develop increasingly more sophisticated and luxurious eating habits. Elaborate formal dinners for the royal courts and official state occasions called for the training of expert chefs. Sauces, creams, and jellies were invented, and special dishes were named after monarchs. In Italy and France, multicourse meals were accompanied by rich table decorations, fanciful pastries, and elaborate eating rituals. Moreover, from Italy there spread to France and other countries the use of differently shaped plates, the fork, and serving utensils, often made from the gold and silver pouring into Europe from the Americas.

Once the price of pepper and chilies fell as their quantity grew, they ceased to be prestige items for the very wealthy. In their place, coffee, chocolate (or cocoa), tea, sugar, and tobacco rose in popularity among the privileged. In 1664 the British writer Samuel Pepys records in his diary that he went to a coffeehouse, still a novel establishment, "to drink jocolatte"; by the 18th century the use of habit-forming stimulants like coffee and tobacco became a virtual mania, and the popularity of coffeehouses among the middle classes had mushroomed.

Print showing the interior of a coffeehouse. Late 17th century. As the paintings on the wall show, the newly introduced coffeehouses were often luxuriously decorated. The scene captures the way in which they served as places for social encounters as much as for drinking the new beverage.

British Museum/Bridgeman Art Library

PERSPECTIVES FROM THE PAST

FOOD AND THE COLUMBIAN EXCHANGE

When Columbus set foot on the island of Hispaniola in October 1492, he began a complex process of interaction between the Old World and the New known as the Columbian Exchange. This process had a profound impact—both positive and negative—on both civilizations.

Among the many aspects of European and Amerindian life that each encountered was food. The Spanish introduced such vegetation as wheat, bananas, oranges and lemons, grapes, and sugar cane to the Western Hemisphere. The early European visitors also brought goats, sheep, horses, pigs, chickens, and cattle to the New World, with adverse ecological results, for as these animals roamed the ranges they destroyed the roots of plants and ate the leaves. On the other hand, as we have seen, the diet of much of the rest of the world was dramatically changed as vegetables and plants indigenous to the Americas were introduced to Europe, Africa, and Asia.

Food of the Amerindians

As the Spanish conquistadors ravaged Mexican and South American cultures, they were generally forced to live off the land and to become accustomed to eating local foods.

Hernán Cortés

The food they [the inhabitants of islands off the Yucatan] eat is maize and some chili peppers, as on the other islands, and *patata yuca,* just the same as is eaten in Cuba, and they eat it roast, for they do not make bread of it; and they both hunt and fish and breed many chickens [probably turkeys] such as those found on Tierra Firme, which are as big as peacocks.

From Hernán Cortés, *Letters from Mexico,* trans. and ed. A. R. Pagden Yale University Press, Copyright © 1971.

Bernal Díaz del Castillo

When we got on shore we found three Caciques, one of them the governor appointed by Montezuma, who had many of the Indians of his household with him. They brought many of the fowls of the country and maize bread such as they always eat, and fruits such as pineapples and zapotes, which in other parts are called mameies, and they were seated under the shade of the trees, and had spread mats on the ground, and they invited us to be seated, all by signs, for Julianillo the man from Cape Catoche, did not

understand their language, which is Mexican. Then they brought pottery braziers with live coals, and fumigated us with a sort of resin.

From Bernal Díaz del Castillo, *The Discovery and Conquest of Mexico, 1517–1521,* ed. Genaro Garcia and trans. A. P. Maudslay Farrar, Straus and Giroux, Copyright © 1956.

Food at the Royal Palace

The Amerindians ate several foods that the Europeans found strange and sometimes disquieting, including dogs and worms from the maguey plant. Columbus records that on first landing in the Americas he encountered "a serpent" about six feet long, no doubt an iguana, which his men killed—"The people here eat them and the meat is white and tastes like chicken." Díaz del Castillo tells that when his party met the Caciques, "they wished to kill us and eat our flesh, and had already prepared the pots with salt and peppers and tomatoes."

Montezuma's Banquet

Díaz del Castillo gives a detailed description of a great banquet.

For each meal, over thirty different dishes were prepared by his cooks according to their ways and usage, and they placed small pottery braziers beneath the dishes so that they should not get cold. They prepared more than three hundred plates of the food that Montezuma was going to eat, and more than a thousand for the guard. When he was going to eat, Montezuma would sometimes go out with his chiefs and stewards, and they would point out to him which dish was best, and of what birds and other things it was composed, and as they advised him, so he would eat, but it was not often that he would go out to see the food, and then merely as a pastime.

I have heard it said that they were wont to cook for him the flesh of young boys, but as he had such a variety of dishes, made of so many things, we could not succeed in seeing if they were of human flesh or of other things, for they daily cooked fowls, turkeys, pheasants, native partridges, quail, tame and wild ducks, venison, wild boar, reed birds, pigeons, hares and rabbits, and many sorts of birds and other things which are bred in this country, and they are so numerous that I cannot finish naming them in a hurry; so we had no insight into it, but I know for certan that after our Captain censured the sacrifice of human beings, and the eating of their flesh, he ordered that such food should not be prepared for him thenceforth.

Let us cease speaking of this and return to the way things were served to him at meal times. It was in this way: if it was cold they made up a large fire of live coals of a firewood made from the bark of trees which did not give off any smoke, and the scent of the bark from which the fire was made was very fragrant, and so that it should not give off more heat than he required, they placed in front of it a sort of screen adorned with figures of idols worked in gold. He was seated on a low stool, soft and richly worked, and the table, which was also low, was made in the same style as the seats, and on it they placed the table cloths of white cloth and some rather long napkins of the same material. Four very beautiful cleanly women brought water for his hands in a sort of deep basin which they call xicales [gourds], and they held others like plates below to catch the water, and they brought him towels. And two other women brought him tortilla bread, and as soon as he began to eat they placed before him a sort of wooden screen painted over with gold, so that no one should watch him

eating. Then the four women stood aside, and four great chieftains who were old men came and stood beside them, and with these Montezuma now and then conversed, and asked them questions, and as a great favor he would give to each of these elders a dish of what to him tasted best. . . .

They brought him fruit of all the different kinds that the land produced, but he ate very little of it. From time to time they brought him, in cup-shaped vessels of pure gold, a certain drink made from cacao, and the women served this drink to him with great reverence . . . .

Montezuma was fond of pleasure and song, and to these he ordered to be given what was left of the food and the jugs of cacao. . . .

As soon as the Great Montezuma had dined, all the men of the Guard had their meal and as many more of the other house servants, and it seems to me that they brought out over a thousand dishes of the food of which I have spoken, and then over two thousand jugs of cacao all frothed up, as they make it in Mexico, and a limitless quantity of fruit, so that with his women and female servants and break makers and cacao makers his expenses must have been very great. . . .

[W]hile Montezuma was at table eating, as I have described, there were waiting on him two other graceful women to bring him tortillas, kneaded with eggs and other sustaining ingredients, and these tortillas were very white, and they were brought on plates covered with clean napkins, and they also brought him another kind of bread, like long balls kneaded with other kinds of sustaining food, and pan pachol, for so they call it in this country, which is a sort of wafer. There were also placed on the table three tubes much painted and gilded, which held liquidambar mixed with certain herbs which they call tabaco, and when he had finished eating, after they had danced before him and sung and the table was removed, he inhaled the smoke from one of those tubes, but he took very little of it and with that he fell asleep.

From Bernal Díaz del Castillo, *The Discovery and Conquest of Mexico, 1517–1521*, ed. Genaro Garcia and trans. A. P. Maudslay Farrar, Straus and Giroux, Copyright © 1956.

Continued

Aztec Markets

The Aztecs had a highly sophisticated system of trade and barter, much of which was conducted in the central markets of large towns. Díaz del Castillo was much impressed by the market in Mexico at the Tlaltelolco square.

When we arrived at the great market place, called Tlaltelolco, we were astounded at the number of people and the quantity of merchandise that it contained, and at the good order and control that was maintained, for we had never seen such a thing before. The chieftains who accompanied us acted as guides. Each kind of merchandise was kept by itself and had its fixed place marked out. Let us begin with the dealers in gold, silver, and precious stones, feathers, mantles, and embroidered goods. Then there were other wares consisting of Indian slaves both men and women; and I say that they bring as many of them to that great market for sale as the Portuguese bring negroes from Guinea; and they brought them along tied to

THE SOCIAL PATTERN OF HOUSING

In the centuries before 1500, the housing of both the rich and the poor in Europe changed little and continued to use traditional materials, including straw thatching for roofs and wood. By the 16th century, however, urban housing began to use stone and brick. Moreover, the increasingly crowded cities made space a premium and building sites became smaller, so that houses took on a more vertical design.

BUILDING THE CITIES

Over time, the ever-present risk of fire, a constant preoccupation for medieval city dwellers, lessened because of the new construction materials. In Paris, large numbers of stone masons, plasterers, and tool makers began to transform public buildings and private houses by setting them on stone foundations. During the same period, builders in London abandoned wood and straw. After the great fire of London in 1666, which destroyed three of every four buildings, most of the new housing was made of brick. This transformation was visible as far east as Moscow, where a Western traveler observed the same change in the mid-17th century. On the Continent, municipal authorities now often prohibited the use of straw roofing and sometimes provided subsidies to encourage builders to make their roofs of tile or slate.

The wealthy nobility and merchants of the cities lived in massive and elaborately decorated palaces, generally designed by major architects. Many of the residences of the wealthy built after 1500 still stand today, most now used for public purposes. In Paris, for example, the National Archives of France was once the private house of the Guise family, while the Parisian site of the National Library is now located in a palace where Cardinal Mazarin lived. The palace of the Strozzi family in Florence today contains a library and is used for public exhibitions.

Middle-class housing was much less grand than the palaces of the nobility. Plans for several houses of the middle class in 16th-century Paris have survived. A typical residence was on three floors, with the rooms arranged around an open courtyard. A spiral staircase connected the levels. On the ground floor was the main reception room, together with the kitchen and larder, while the bedrooms were on the upper floors. Starting in Italy during the 17th century, ceilings—once only the underside of the flooring of the room above—began to be plastered, encased in wood, and painted. Wallpaper was first used in the 18th century.

Today we know much about housing through the painting of the period. In Amsterdam, the most common form of housing for the lower middle class was made up of two rooms, one at the front and one at the back. These houses, with their narrow façades, were later enlarged by the addition of rooms above and below, connected by a series of dangerously steep staircases or ladders. Even today, the house fronts along the canals of the city of Delft preserve the original appearance of the buildings in Vermeer's famous paintings of the period, which also illustrate the new vogue for glass window panes.

Poor city dwellers generally lived in rented lodgings in the least desirable quarters of the city. The cheapest and most wretched apartments were either in basements or attics. The poor lived alongside prostitutes and criminals in flea-ridden and unsanitary squalor, often subject to unannounced police searches. In the absence of running water and toilet facilities, chamber pots—emptied out of the window—were often kept side by side with cooking utensils.

COUNTRY LIVING

Peasant housing in Europe is much more difficult to document because of the perishability of the materials used in the countryside. Most houses were small huts built of wood,

long poles, with collars round their necks so that they could not escape, and others they left free. Next there were other traders who sold great pieces of cloth and cotton, and articles of twisted thread, and there were *cacahuateros* who sold cacao. In this way one could see every sort of merchandise that is to be found in the whole of New Spain. There were those who sold cloths of henequen and ropes and the sandals with which they are shod, which are made from the same plant, and sweet cooked roots, and other tubers which they get from this plant, all were kept in one part of the market in the place assigned to them. In another part there were skins of tigers and lions, of otters and jackals, deer and other animals and badgers and mountain cats, some tanned and others untanned, and other classes of merchandise.

From Bernal Díaz del Castillo, *The Discovery and Conquest of Mexico, 1517–1521*, ed. Genaro Garcia and trans. A. P. Maudslay Farrar, Straus and Giroux, Copyright © 1956.

Piet de Hooch, *The Linen Cupboard*. 1663. Painted by one of the most famous artists of the Delft school, the scene is of a quiet domestic interior in the house of a prosperous Dutch merchant. Note the inlaid furniture, the paneled wooden walls, and the rich costumes of the mistress and her maid. On the wall hang paintings, presumably by Piet's contemporaries.

Rijksmuseum, Amsterdam

straw, and mud. Farming people generally lived under the same roof as their animals, often sharing a single primitive room. These dwellings were generally unheated except for a small cooking stove, in front of which the inhabitants slept in cold weather.

Recent archeological excavations provide further data about how peasants lived. The sites of deserted villages throughout Europe reveal both the kinds of houses and other facilities—churches, cemeteries, wells, and streets—and the changing layout of the community. Nor were conditions always uniform. Some villages were more prosperous than others. In Burgundy, France, for example, one typical village consisted of around 25 dwellings on stone foundations, in which the living rooms had beaten earth floors and small slanting windows.

Many wealthy landowners lived in old and uncomfortable family manor houses dating back to the late medieval period. By the 16th century, it became fashionable for the new urban rich to invest their money in country residences. They commissioned elaborate stone villas containing works of art, surrounded by formal gardens. Most of the famous and elegant chateaux that dot the French countryside date from the period after 1600, when the French monarchy had created stable political and social conditions.

CLOTHING, FASHION, AND CLASS

Social distinctions were nowhere more striking than in the kind of clothing people wore. Among the peasants and the urban poor, the form of dress changed little over the centuries from about 1350 to 1600. The wealthy, on the other hand, were quick to adopt new styles and new materials for their clothing.

DRESS AND STYLE

As in the case of housing, paintings and engravings are also important sources of information about clothing. Even at a quick glance, the viewer can distinguish between peasants and the middle classes from their costumes. Some occupations involved their own uniforms or typical forms of dress. Soldiers, fishermen, shepherds, and blacksmiths each wore specific garments. Sometimes the color and design of clothing indicate a particular condition of life—widows, for example, traditionally dressed in plain black clothes, while butchers often wore red smocks.

Jean-Baptiste Chardin, *The Food Supplier.* 1739. Note the contrast between the costume of the peasant girl delivering food and the more elaborate one of the domestic servant in *The Linen Cupboard.* Chardin was famous for his scenes of daily life, filled with sharply observed detail.

Peasants owned simple garments of coarse, homespun fabric made of a mixture of hemp and wool and generally dyed black or some other dark color. The paintings of the 16th-century Flemish artist Pieter Bruegel the Elder and his sons Pieter the Younger and Jan record numerous scenes of peasants and tradesmen in villages and market towns, showing the details of their clothing. Until the Industrial Revolution of the 18th century, cotton was too expensive for all but the wealthiest people. Much of the cotton available in Europe was brought by Venetian galleys from Syria, sometimes in the form of raw cotton and sometimes already worked into cloth.

Poor peasants spent relatively little of their resources on clothing, which had to be practical, both for durability and for protection against the cold. When peasants acquired wealth, however, they generally spent lavishly on dress in order to demonstrate their new status and distance themselves from their origins. The standard form of dress for peasants was a loose shirt and tight-fitting pants that hugged the body. Most went barefoot, and wearing underwear became common only after 1300. The absence of undergarments caused the spread of ringworm, scabies, and other skin diseases. Both rich and poor generally did not wear nightclothes to bed.

For the nobility and the wealthy merchant class, clothing was an essential symbol of social status. At the beginning of the 17th century, the Venetian ambassador to the court of France observed that a man was considered rich only if he possessed some 30 suits of different kinds and styles, and changed them daily.

As style developed into fashion, clothing became associated with national origin. In the 15th century, the most common forms of dress were French, Italian, and English. At royal courts, the ladies of the nobility wore expensive dresses of cotton, silk, and velvet, embroidered and decorated with gold thread and jewels. By the 16th century, with the spread of the Hapsburg empire, the ruling classes of Europe adopted Spanish court dress, which was generally dark and severe, with padded stockings, high collars, and short capes. With the decline of Spain in the 17th century, however, the bright colors of French clothing became fashionable again.

Unlike today's world, in which styles change every season, in early modern Europe fashions remained in vogue for a century or so. The idea of constantly changing styles was introduced to the upper and middle classes of Europe only in the 18th century. The Industrial Revolution made inexpensive cotton readily available to most of the middle class, while the elaborate court etiquette of France established among the nobility a fetish for the new designs and the latest styles.

Along with the variations in clothing style, hygiene and other aspects of personal appearance also evolved. The ancient Romans had used soap for washing, and bathing was an important social activity for them. In pre–Black Death Europe, public bathhouses were common. As late as the 18th century, however, hardly anyone in Paris or London bathed, and those who did took only one or two baths per year. Instead, both men and women used perfumes to cover their body odor. While men grew facial hair, women deco-rated their faces with makeup. By the early 1600s, both sexes began to wear artificial hairpieces as a form of social distinction.

Putting Life in a Time of Upheaval in Perspective

The aspects of everyday life discussed in this topic—health, food, housing, and dress—are vital indicators of the condition of a society at a given moment in history. Differences in these factors among the various levels of European society underscore one constant point—the vast gulf separating the lifestyles of most ordinary people from those of the comfortable middle class and the wealthy nobility. Moreover, the fact that for hundreds of years the lifespan of Europeans remained short while the infant mortality rate stayed high, suggests a great deal about how people might have viewed issues of life, death, and faith. Similarly, the monotonous diet of most Europeans ex-plains much about the sense of excitement and the hunger for the strange and exotic generated by the overseas explorations of the 15th and 16th centuries.

Social behavior and custom also provide considerable insight about the workings of historical change. The relatively stable nature of these ordinary but fundamental aspects of life for centuries at a time reveals just how powerful the weight of tradi-tion was and how gradually the lives of most people were altered. Daily life as well as politics moved at a far slower pace, and popular attitudes toward change were much more cautious.

How people dressed and the kind of homes they lived in are important indices of social, and even psychological, attitudes. Fashion, as opposed to practical, everyday costume, is not only a sign of social distinction but also of the desire of wealthier classes to distance themselves from those below them and to ape those above. Standards of personal hygiene prevalent as late as the 18th century differed signifi-cantly from the generally accepted habits of the early 21st century in the West. That fact underscores the degree to which society has become more sophisticated, but it also tells us a great deal about the abysmally low level of material comfort to which millions of Europeans were accustomed.

The history of wars, religion, economics, and politics is of course fundamental to our ability to understand the past. It is often difficult, however, for us to grasp in an immediate sense how these events affected human lives. Social history, understood as the way in which real people lived, allows us to identify with people of earlier his-torical eras because we can compare our immediate daily experiences with theirs.

Questions for Further Study

1. What factors affected the health of Europeans? How would you judge the medical practices of the period?
2. In what ways were food and diet affected by the age of discovery?
3. How did class and social position affect such practices as housing and clothing?
4. Based on what you know about the lifespan of Europeans and infant mortality rates, what would you conclude were people's attitudes toward life, death, and faith?

Suggestions for Further Reading

Braudel, Fernand. *The Structures of Everyday Life*. London, 1981.

Fraser, Antonia. *The Weaker Vessel: Woman's Lot in Seventeenth-Century England*. London, 1984.

Goubert, Pierre. I. Patterson, trans. *The French Peasantry in the Seventeenth Century*. Cambridge, MA, 1986.

Grassby, Richard. *Kinship and Capitalism: Marriage, Family and Business in the English-Speaking World, 1580-1720*. New York, 2001.

Hanawalt, Barbara A., ed. *Women and Work in Preindustrial Europe*. Bloomington, IN, 1986.

Hardwick, Julie. *The Practice of Patriarchy: Gender and the Politics of Household Authority in Early Modern France*. University Park, PA, 1998.

Houston, Robert A. *Literacy in Early Modern Europe: Culture and Education, 1500–1800*. New York, 1988.

Kamen, Henry. *Early Modern European Society*. New York, 2000.

Ladurie, Le Roy. *The French Peasantry, 1450–1660*. Berkeley, CA, 1986.

Macfarlane, Alan. *Marriage and Love in England: Modes of Reproduction, 1300–1840*. New York, 1986.

Maynes, Mary J. *Schooling in Western Europe: A Social History*. New York, 1985.

Ozment, Steven. *Flesh and Spirit: Private Life in Early Modern Germany*. New York, 1999.

Schama, Simon. *An Embarrassment of Riches: An Interpretation of Dutch Culture in the Golden Age*. New York, 1987.

InfoTrac College Edition

Enter the search term *Black Death* using Key Terms.

The European Economy and Overseas Empire

From 1300 to 1650, while Europe underwent the cultural changes associated with the Renaissance as well as the religious upheavals of the Reformation, the Western economy was also transformed. The principal change after 1500 was the shift in trade patterns from the Mediterranean to the Atlantic and northern European coasts. The commercial revolution was dominated at first by Spain and Portugal, but the decline of their empires was accompanied by the emergence of new economic powers, especially the Dutch Republic.

Several other new features appeared in the economic expansion of the 16th and 17th centuries. For one thing, a new era emerged in banking and international finance as Italian banking firms like the Medici were overshadowed by the new international firm of the Fuggers of Germany. These bankers created networks of credit across the borders of the European states and engaged in high-level loans to monarchs and popes as well as to private business owners.

The new banking firms were overshadowed by the appearance of stock companies, which attracted investors in growing numbers. Besides the expansion of international finance, new industries and technologies evolved in this period, including growth in the printing business, luxury industries, and mining.

By the late 17th century, even the thriving Dutch commercial empire was beginning to decline as the English and French monarchies expanded their colonial holdings around the globe. Britain and France followed a rigidly conceived and highly centralized economic policy known as mercantilism, and the two powers increasingly competed for control of overseas markets and products. By the 18th century, the system of merchant capitalism that drove the commercial revolution was poised to provide the investment necessary to begin the new, industrial phase of capitalism.

SIGNIFICANT DATES

The European Economy

1367	Hanseatic League founded
Late 15th century	Collapse of Medici bank
1492	First voyage of Columbus
1459–1525	Life of Jacob Fugger II
c. 1575	Price revolution begins
1601	English East India Company founded
1602	Dutch East India Company founded
1609	Bank of Amsterdam founded
1620	Plymouth Colony founded
1621	Dutch West India Company founded
1651	Navigation Acts passed
1776	Adam Smith publishes *Wealth of Nations*

TRADE, FINANCE, AND PRICES

The three centuries following the discovery of the New World saw the development of an important economic phenomenon called commercial capitalism, in which merchants sought profits through buying, selling, and shipping goods. The profits derived from commerce were tremendous, and the unfolding of global trade patterns made life in Europe infinitely more interesting and colorful. Agriculture, however, remained the primary economic activity of most Europeans. In Eastern Europe, where the commercial revolution was less important, perhaps as much as 95 percent of the population lived off the land; even in Western Europe, where commerce was most intense, 60 or 70 percent of the inhabitants still farmed.

THE ATLANTIC AND NORTHERN COMMERCE

In the early 15th century, control of trade in the North Sea and the Baltic had moved into the hands of German cities, with the formation of the Hanseatic League. The league eventually included more than 80 cities and controlled a large fleet and impressive resources, giving it a virtual monopoly over trade in northern Europe. Although the league continued to exist for some 300 years, it began to decline by the end of the 15th century in the face of the growing commercial power of the Dutch.

Throughout the first half of the 16th century, Venice managed to control the trade in spices that came through Muslim hands from the eastern Mediterranean. Yet signs of change were clear as the Venetian galleys, which linked Italian ports with northern Europe, sailed at an alarmingly decreasing rate. As the Atlantic powers like Spain and Portugal developed direct sea routes around Africa to Asia and across the Atlantic to their new colonies in the Americas, the Italian commercial empires fell into serious decline.

By 1600, even the Iberian trading powers were being bypassed by the spectacular rise of Dutch, English, and French traders as commercial patterns shifted once again. The new and exotic products from overseas were flooding Europe's markets in ever-greater quantity and creating business opportunities that bypassed the rigid Spanish economic system. Moreover, in the waters off Newfoundland, a seemingly inexhaustible supply of codfish had been discovered that became the basis for a salted cod industry of major proportions, and the French and English eventually seized most of this business. Joint stock companies were formed to pool resources in order to take advantage of the increasing volume of trade.

Etching showing a European sugar mill worked by slave labor in the West Indies. 18th century. The vegetation is typical of the Caribbean Islands. Sugar cane, which is still the source of more than half the world's sugar, was originally native to East Asia. In the 18th century, colonists transplanted it to the warm, humid Caribbean region and cultivated large plantations.

By permission of the British Library. 145.c.4 Folio 122

THE GROWTH OF MANUFACTURING

The rising commercial activities were accompanied by the growth of manufacturing as new industries developed that became increasingly important in Europe's economy. Shipbuilding became a major and highly profitable industry. Metalworking, especially armor and cannon making, also grew enormously, while mining expanded as new technology allowed mine shafts to be sunk hundreds of feet below the surface. The new digging and draining methods opened up rich new mines in central Europe. The discovery of a way to extract silver from lead alloy led to a plentiful supply of silver for making coins, which in turn increased the money supply and economic growth.

One result of the rise in commerce was that merchants involved in the textile business turned increasingly to the domestic, or "putting out" system. Instead of supplying raw wool exclusively to the guild artisans, whose costs were relatively high, the merchants began to deliver the wool to individual workers in the villages. There they spun, wove, and dyed the cloth in their own homes, where they operated as family units and at a lower cost. The domestic system increased merchant profits and remained the basic method of finishing wool until the Industrial Revolution shifted production to factories.

FROM THE MEDICI TO THE FUGGERS

The depressed economic climate of the 14th century drove businesses to become more efficient. The invention of double-entry bookkeeping in mid-14th century Italy was accompanied by the introduction of insurance and book transfer procedures, and all of these procedures made business practices more sophisticated. Merchants from other regions of Europe learned most of the Italian techniques in business organization and began to establish their own firms. The most successful of these were the Fuggers, whose business centered in Augsburg in southern Germany. The earliest Fugger merchants had been weavers and small manufacturers of woolen textiles. Expanding the range of their commercial activity, they opened a branch in Venice, where they ran a wholesale warehouse in spices and silks, and by the 15th century were engaging in banking.

The Fugger dynasty achieved its first major success when it began lending money to the Holy Roman emperors. Jacob Fugger II (1459–1525) was the dominant figure in the rise of the dynasty. Jacob oversaw branches in major European cities such as Antwerp, Lisbon, and London. In addition to continuing operations in the spice trade, the Fuggers began to engage in a variety of banking operations, such as issuing credit, bills of exchange, and paying interest on deposits. They became major bankers to the kings of Spain and Portugal as well as to the popes. As a result of extending major loans to Emperor Charles V, Jacob eventually came to control the silver and copper mines of Austria and Hungary, enterprises that gave him a tremendous return on his investment. The house of Fugger collapsed in the late 16th century as the result of the Hapsburgs defaulting on their loans.

Illustration showing Jacob Fugger (right)—the greatest banker of his age—dictating to a secretary. 16th century. The file drawers behind the clerk's head, labeled with the names of the cities where the Fuggers did business, indicate the international scope of their affairs: The two lowest ones are for the Polish city of Cracow and Lisbon, the capital of Portugal.

Eventually, the private family banking firms that had dominated European finance for centuries gave way to large, stock-based banking companies regulated by the state. In the 17th century, England, France, and the Netherlands granted monopolies to companies engaged in overseas trade or for settling colonial areas. These establishments were better suited to the new era of commercial capitalism that was unfolding.

THE PRICE REVOLUTION

Throughout the 16th century, as Europe recovered from the devastating impact of the Black Death, population increased, perhaps by as much as one-third. By 1600, Europe may have had more than 100 million inhabitants, although the growth pattern was unevenly spread throughout the continent. The larger workforce meant an increase in the amount of food and in the demand for manufactured products; this expansion in turn stimulated economic activity in the towns as well as in the countryside.

One result of these demographic changes was that as the urban population of Europe increased significantly, a surplus labor force was created, driving down real wages. This setback was accompanied by a startling rise in prices in the later 16th century that had widespread repercussions. The causes and impact of this so-called price revolution have been seriously debated by historians, but a few factors seem obvious. The flow of gold and silver into Spain and Portugal in the early 16th century seems to have been the major cause of the inflationary cycle. The supply of bullion in Europe more than tripled, with some 16,000 tons of American silver flowing through the Spanish port of Seville alone by 1650.

Although Spain tried to regulate the bullion it collected by prohibiting its export, the wars it fought and the administrative costs of operating its far-flung government inevitably meant the circulation of silver throughout Europe. Other factors contributed to the inflation besides American bullion. The productivity of European silver mines increased as a result of the application of new mining techniques, and some monarchs sparked price increases by debasing their coinage. The increase in population may also have driven prices up. In any case, the inflation in commodity prices was immense—by the close of the 16th century, prices had risen to four times their level at the start of the century. Prices went up higher and faster in Western Europe than elsewhere on the continent, and the greatest impact was seen in basic necessities such as grains and bread.

Overall, the inflationary pattern increased prices no more than 3 percent per year, which by modern standards is not a significant jump. In the 16th century, however, the price revolution had the effect of redistributing income among social groups. Wages did not, however, rise accordingly, so that the standard of living for the poorer classes declined. Those living on fixed incomes, especially pensioners, were also hurt by the inflation. Similarly, people who rented out property at long-term rates suffered. On the other hand, merchants, farmers, and manufacturers benefited from the rise in prices, especially because the costs of production did not rise as quickly as prices.

The inflationary cycle, which was irregular but of long duration, had a negative impact on governments, whose expenses and deficits rose along with the prices. Cities felt the impact severely because they depended on the purchase of food, the cost of which rose steadily. The dislocation and social tensions created by the price revolution were felt for decades to come.

Merchant Capitalists and the State

The changes that were transforming the commercial revolution in the 16th and 17th centuries created a form of economic organization and activity known as *merchant capitalism*. Under this system, merchants with investment resources—venture capital—invested in overseas trade or in necessary support operations such as banking, insurance, and stock companies. The private ownership of shipping firms and banks entailed huge profits. Risks in commercial activity were high, but the general rise in prices made the profit potential even greater.

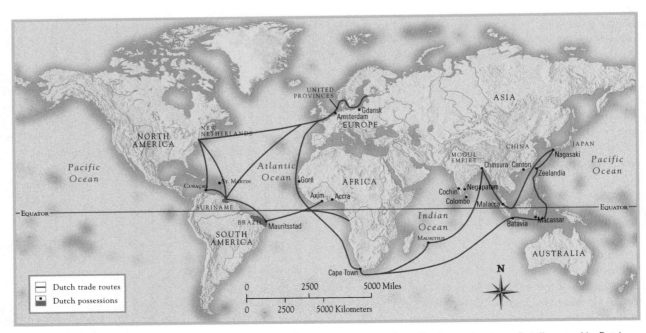

Map 46.1 The Dutch Sea Trade, c. 1650. Note the closeness of Dutch sea-routes to Australia; the continent was first discovered by Dutch sailors in the early 1600s but only claimed and occupied by the British almost two centuries later. The Dutch East India Company founded the city of Batavia in 1619 as the capital of their holdings in Indochina. It remained a Dutch colony until 1949, when, with the new name of Jakarta, it became the capital of the State of Indonesia.

Other developments encouraged commercial capitalism. Not all successful merchants had the cash to invest in risky ventures, but once the church had abandoned its prohibition against *usury*—charging interest on loans—credit was more readily available. The state was a major stimulus to capitalist development. In the increasingly competitive arena of a global economy, governments used their military power to protect national trade, while military contracts provided an incentive for investment in manufacturing.

THE MERCANTILIST SYSTEM

From the onset of the age of exploration, the state had undertaken to regulate the economic activity of its citizens through policies known as **mercantilism.** These policies were designed to increase national revenue and economic power at the expense of other states, as well as to enhance private business. Hence, at the very time that merchant capitalism was evolving, economic affairs were subjected to increasing state regulation. Mercantilism denied the right of businessmen to operate in a free market in order to ensure the primacy of the state's interests. Under the mercantilist system, the government imposed rigid controls on trade and manufacturing, including import tariffs and monopolies.

International trade was a particular object of mercantilist regulation because governments believed that a favorable trade balance was the only way to keep a sufficient quantity of bullion at home. Spain was the most vigorous advocate of this theory because precious metals were necessary to pay its massive military expenditures. On the other hand, the Dutch, whose wealth came from the fees its ships charged to carry the goods of other countries, sought to increase the overall volume of trade in which they were involved.

Tariffs were designed to protect domestic industries, whereas monopolies gave to a particular individual or company the sole right to trade, manufacture, or sell certain kinds of goods. Sometimes, as in the case of the Spanish empire, the purpose of controls was to block foreign competition or to prevent the all-important precious metals from going anywhere except to the home country.

In the later 18th century, the Scottish economist and philosopher Adam Smith (1723–1790), who advocated an unfettered free market system, attacked mercantilism because it obstructed the natural operation of economic laws. Smith insisted that the only real source of the "wealth of nations" was the flowering of rational self-interest. Depending on the circumstances, mercantilist policies helped or hurt national economies. In the Spanish case, controls hindered the development of domestic industries and retarded the economic welfare of the American colonies, while the monarchy's profligate spending made it impossible for the government to maintain bullion supplies at home. On the other hand, in the 17th century, French mercantilist controls under Louis XIV enabled the state to develop manufacturing, attract foreign artisans, and establish a solid economic base.

In all these ways, mercantilist regulations were part of the broader strategy through which the state attempted to centralize and impose its authority on all aspects of national—and in this case, international—life.

THE HEYDAY OF THE DUTCH REPUBLIC

Perhaps the European state with the most intelligent economic policy was the United Provinces of the Netherlands, which was ruled not by a king but by a class of wealthy urban merchants. The rise of the Dutch commercial empire is one of the most spectacular success stories of the age of the commercial revolution. More than any other nation, the Dutch Republic depended on international trade for its economic livelihood.

THE RISE OF THE NETHERLANDS

The foreign affairs of the seven northern provinces that constituted the Dutch Republic were governed by the legislative body known as the States General. Domestic issues, including economic policy, were determined by the provincial town councils, composed of oligarchies of merchants and landlords known as "regents."

The Dutch economy had several important strengths. Even during the long and bitter war of independence against Spain, the Dutch prospered on the seas, especially by attacking Spanish bullion ships. In addition, they wisely welcomed the Protestant immigrants who flocked to the northern provinces, a migration that included skilled artisans, bankers, and merchants. The regents managed to maintain a degree of religious freedom in the Netherlands that was unmatched anywhere, and this despite the Calvinist extremists who sometimes tried to work against the Catholics and Jews who lived there.

Because of excellent drainage and irrigation techniques and intensive farming methods, Dutch agriculture was the most productive in Europe. The herring fisheries were also important to the Dutch, who dried, salted, and smoked the catch and sold it throughout Europe. Finally, as their prosperity grew to depend more and more on commerce, the Dutch became master shipbuilders who designed and constructed the best ships of the day, many of which they sold to foreign merchants.

Like the Venetians, the Dutch were skilled at living and working on the water and at carrying their own products and those of other nations in their fleets. Their two chief cities, Antwerp (now in the modern state of Belgium) and Amsterdam, were at the trading crossroads of Europe and became two of the world's greatest commercial and business centers. These efficient and crowded cities were well positioned to take advantage of trade from the Mediterranean and the North Atlantic as well as from the Baltic and the North Sea. Antwerp, with 100,000 inhabitants in 1650, ranked second in size to Amsterdam but was a vital commercial hub: English wool and the spice trade of the 15th century both came through its port.

When the Spanish seized Antwerp during the revolt of the Netherlands, Amsterdam easily took its place as the principal Dutch port. Between 1600 and 1650, Amsterdam's population had grown from about 65,000 to 175,000, and its intricate network of docks and warehouses made it one of the most important *entrepôts* (trade intermediaries) in Europe. By building a series of canals, the Dutch were able to enlarge the size of the city to accommodate its growing population. Moreover, the Exchange Bank of Amsterdam, founded in 1609, soon became one of the principal banking institutions in Europe.

The Dutch ensured their economic prosperity by enlightened policies that deviated from the mercantilist norms of most other states. For example, they erected no tariffs either on imports or exports, and all their chief cities observed free trade policies. Because the trade in bullion was also free in the Netherlands—in contrast to policies in Spain and other states—Amsterdam became the chief center of the gold and silver trade.

The essence of Dutch prosperity was the "carrying trade." In 1600, Spanish and Portuguese ships carried a major portion of overseas trade, but by the mid-17th century, half of Europe's merchant ships were Dutch. Their chief strength lay in European commerce, where Dutch shipping made up perhaps three-quarters of all trade in the region. The Dutch Republic was the most prosperous example of merchant capitalism to emerge from the commercial revolution.

GLOBAL COMPETITION: THE INDIA COMPANIES

If the Dutch dominated the carrying trade in Europe, elsewhere in the world the English and French competed with them more effectively. In contrast to their policies of European free trade, the Dutch followed a more conventional mercantilist agenda outside of Europe. The overseas trade soon became a battleground of competing national companies struggling for dominance.

PRIVATE TRADING COMPANIES

In 1601, the English government of Queen Elizabeth I granted a charter to establish the English East India Company, which monopolized trade with India and operated until 1858. The English also attempted to develop a colonial enterprise along the Atlantic coast of North America, and in 1606 the crown extended charters to the Virginia Company, which tried unsuccessfully to establish a permanent settlement there. Farther north, the Plymouth Company was given the right to colonize anywhere from Virginia to Maine. In 1620, it founded the Plymouth Colony, which later merged with the Massachusetts Bay Colony. Nevertheless, these early experiments with permanent settlements did not generate large profits.

The States General of the Netherlands empowered private joint stock companies with almost complete economic and administrative authority to control its trade beyond Europe. In 1602, private merchants and investors of the Netherlands joined forces with the city government of Amsterdam to found the Dutch East India Company. The aim of the new company was to establish commercial primacy in the Indian Ocean and the Southeast Asia seas.

Unlike the Spanish and Portuguese, who made trade a state monopoly, the Dutch East India Company, controlled by the same class of wealthy business interests that dominated the town councils, was given extraordinary power to govern the entire Asian region. Company officials could conduct war on foreign shipping, appoint administrators for the colonies, and operate trading bases.

H.V. Schulylenberg, *Head Offices of the Dutch East India Company of Hugly in Bengal.* 1665. The Dutch flag flies in the lower left-hand corner. Note the attempt to impose European architectural order in an alien environment. The long, low building, with a central block and two side wings, houses the chief administrative offices.

Rijksmuseum, Amsterdam

Printed cloth from the Muslim city of Golconda, Hyderabad state, India. 17th century. The design provides a local view of the foreign (in this case, Dutch) traders in India. The two merchants seated at the table are notable for their costume and facial hair (and their pet dog); the servants waiting on them are natives, wearing local dress.

Although these and other firms assumed differing legal forms, most were joint stock companies in which individual investors pooled resources. This approach was especially useful in long-distance commerce, where the risks were considerable and required large investments. Although originally each voyage was considered a separate undertaking, later the companies established a permanent form of organization in which investors bought shares. In order to leave the company, investors had to sell their shares.

COMMERCIAL RIVALRY ON THE SEAS

The English and the Dutch were rivals in Asia, but both regarded the Portuguese as their principal enemy there. The Dutch East India Company succeeded in pushing the Portuguese out of East Asia and established direct commercial links with Japan and China. In the 18th century, the English company exercised administrative control of most of India, keeping that power until the English government took it from them.

The Dutch West India Company, set up in 1621, was given similar authority along the African coast and in the Americas. In North America, the company actually founded the Dutch settlement of New Netherlands along the Hudson River valley of the future New York. Regardless of how aggressive the Dutch traders were, however, they ultimately proved unable to seize and hold control of the Caribbean and the Atlantic seaboard, where the French and the English were operating. In the second half of the 17th century, the English took the New Netherlands from them, renaming it New York. Before long, the Dutch West India Company closed down. The French, who established their own East India companies in Asia, were less successful than the English and Dutch in the region. In North America, where they had greater success, they turned to a different system, governing Canada directly as a possession of the crown, rather than through a private company.

Most countries in the 17th century passed navigation laws designed to give their merchant marines monopolies over their international trade. In 1651, the English Parliament passed the Navigation Acts, which were designed to end the Dutch control over shipping and fishing in English waters. In response, the Netherlands declared war against England. In 1660, another law required that all commodities imported into England had to be carried on English ships (or on ships from the country of origin); moreover, in order to circumvent Amsterdam's primacy, the English government required all foreign goods to be brought

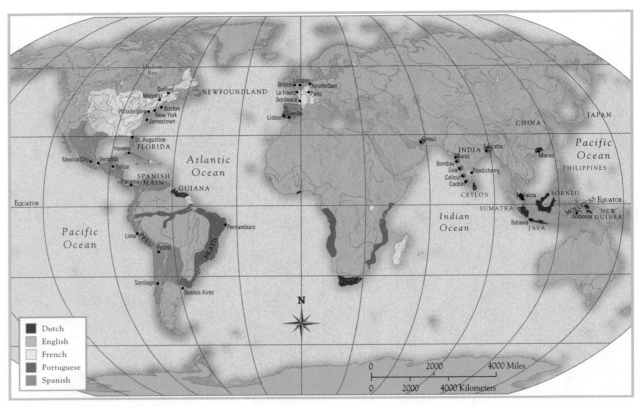

Map 46.2 European Possessions Overseas at the End of the 17th Century. Note the presence of the Dutch in the Far East and in the southern tip of Africa. Both Dutch and Portuguese colonies were to fall to the British over the following century. While North America is already the site of conflict between British and French, the scramble for Africa has not yet begun.

directly from the country of origin. Trade along Britain's coast and from its colonies in North America could be carried only on British ships.

These techniques of economic nationalism were applied in the spirit of mercantilism, but they had the effect of stim-ulating smuggling and were an important factor in driving the American colonies to break with England. In the 18th century, the competition among the commercial powers of Europe unfolded on a global scale and resulted in a continuing series of costly wars for dominance (see Topic 56).

Putting the European Economy and Overseas Empire in Perspective

By 1500, Europe had achieved a remarkable recovery from the disasters of the previous century. New products and better production techniques, combined with rationalized and diversified business organization, all contributed to building a reinvigorated and more prosperous economy. Finance and credit operations were already becoming international in scope when the age of exploration opened. The truly new aspect of the European economy was the commercial revolution that accompanied the encounter with the Western Hemisphere. The voyages of the Portuguese and Spanish seamen opened up an entirely new, unimagined world for the Europeans and set in motion economic forces that transformed the Old World. Moreover, out of the commercial concerns that developed among the great powers in the 17th and 18th centuries, there emerged a global economy and imperial interests that were to provide the basis for the Western dominance of the globe in the modern era.

Questions for Further Study

1. What was the price revolution and what were its causes?
2. In what ways did the state compete with merchants, and how did it support their interests?
3. What explains the economic prosperity of the Netherlands?

Suggestions for Further Reading

Braudel, Fernand. S. Reynolds, trans. *Civilization and Capitalism*, 3 vols. New York, 1979–1984.

Cameron, Rondo. *A Concise Economic History of the World.* New York, 1989.

Day, John. *Money and Finance in the Age of Merchant Capitalism.* Malden, MA, 1999.

Gauci, Perry. *The Politics of Trade: The Overseas Merchant in State and Society, 1660-1720.* Oxford, 2001.

Israel, Jonathan I., ed. *Dutch Primacy in World Trade, 1585–1740.* Oxford, 1989.

Kriedte, Peter. *Peasants, Landlords and Merchant Capitalists: Europe and the World Economy, 1500–1800.* Leamington, England, 1983.

McAlister, Lyle N. *Spain and Portugal in the New World, 1492–1700.* Minneapolis, 1984.

Musgrave, Peter. *The Early Modern European Economy.* New York, 1999.

Schama, Simon. *The Embarrassment of Riches: An Interpretation of Dutch Culture in the Golden Age.* New York, 1987.

Tracy, James E., ed. *The Rise of Merchant Empires.* Cambridge, MA, 1990.

InfoTrac College Edition

Enter the search term *mercantilism* using the Subject Guide.

THE BAROQUE ERA

By the early 17th century, in response to the enormous political and economic changes occurring throughout Europe, a new artistic style had developed: the **Baroque.** One of its features was the appearance of new forms and subjects, ranging from still life painting to the design of private townhouses to opera.

Despite the enormous range of the arts in the Baroque period, they shared certain characteristics in common. The expression of strong emotions, an interest in psychological states of mind, and the invention of elaborate technical display are all typical of 17th-century art.

In the fields of painting, sculpture, and architecture, the first major developments occurred in Rome. Caravaggio's dark, emotional style influenced countless painters in Italy and northern Europe. Bernini's contribution was a double one: As sculptor, he brought his extraordinary technique to subjects as different as religious ecstasy and portraits of his contemporaries. As architect and town planner, he left his mark on the most grandiose project of the times: St. Peter's, Rome.

In the North, many of the leading painters worked on secular themes: landscape, portraits, scenes from life. The only major northern religious painter was Rembrandt. Although Italy remained the center of religious painting, the years around 1600 saw the birth there of opera, a frankly popular form of entertainment aimed at a broad general public. In the North the situation was reversed. Few painters devoted their careers to sacred subjects, but in Germany, Bach composed some of the greatest religious music of all time.

The roots of the supreme writer in the English language, Shakespeare, were in the Renaissance. He wrote many of his masterpieces, however, in the first decade of the 17th century, and their extraordinary richness owes much to the new spirit of the age. The same is true of the greatest novel of the century, Cervantes' *Don Quixote.* In poetry, the works of Donne and others of the Metaphysical poets illustrate the Baroque interest in virtuosity and heightened states of emotion, with their special blend of the spiritual and the erotic.

EMOTION AND ILLUSIONISM: THE AFFIRMATION OF BAROQUE ART

By 1600, Italy was no longer at the center of European culture, and the chief powers in the North—England, France, and the Netherlands—began to develop their own independent schools of art. One factor in this shift was the Reformation, and the challenge to a single Universal Church. Another was the rise in northern Europe of the merchant class, which created a new public for the arts. A third factor was the spread of European culture in other parts of the world, as earlier exploration by the European powers became transformed into colonization, and England, France, the Netherlands, Spain, and Portugal established overseas territories in Africa, Asia, and the Americas.

One of the consequences of this diversification was the growth of new subjects for art. Instead of continuing to paint the same repertory of religious subjects, artists turned to genres like the portrait or scenes from daily life. Architects designed private houses or urban complexes as well as churches. New musical forms developed, including opera and purely instrumental works such as the *concerto grosso*. Writers aimed for a deeper sense of psychological understanding of human behavior.

Scala/Art Resource

Caravaggio, *The Calling of St. Matthew*, c. 1597–1601. 11 feet 1 inch by 11 feet 5 inches (3.38 by 3.48 m). The painter dramatizes the scene by directing a brilliant beam of light from the darkened figure of Jesus, half-hidden on the right. The glare illuminates the card-players around the tavern table and spotlights the future apostle, who points doubtfully at himself.

THE BAROQUE SPIRIT

Yet behind these different manifestations, certain common principles were in operation. The most striking was the expression of strong emotions. Far from seeking ideal statements of universal truth, as Renaissance artists had done, Baroque artists aimed to portray individual states of mind. The paintings of Rembrandt or the dramas of Shakespeare create specific characters with their own personal dramas. In doing so, the artists turned inward rather than outward to explore the depths of human feeling and not the calm heights of Classical perfection.

In order to express their new insights, artists forged a whole range of fresh techniques. Both painters and sculptors invented ways to convey complex illusions of light and shade. Musicians devised styles of increased virtuosity, which led to the growth of instrumental music, while the birth of opera added new dramatic possibilities. In literature, elaborate imagery and complicated grammatical structure made possible heightened emotional effects—the supreme example of the mid-17th century was Milton's *Paradise Lost*.

The subject of Milton's masterpiece is a reminder that attitudes toward religion continued to dominate European culture. Most artists working in northern Europe chose to work under the influence of Reformation ideas, while the leading figures in Italy dedicated themselves to the

Bernini, *St. Theresa in Ecstasy.* 1645–1652. Height of group 11 feet 6 inches (3.5 m). This famous work uses stone, gilded bronze, and natural light to bring the scene alive. Hidden from the viewer, a window above the saint sends sunlight to illuminate the gilded beams, as St. Theresa awaits the blow of the angel, about to pierce her to the heart with ecstatic love.

Canali Photobank, Italy

Counter-Reformation mission to restore the Catholic Church to its triumphant preeminence. At the same time, the 17th century saw the continued rise of science, which challenged both religious camps and laid the basis for the skepticism of the 18th-century Age of Reason.

THE MAKING OF BAROQUE ROME: CARAVAGGIO AND BERNINI

The spirit of the Counter-Reformation dominating Italian art in the 17th century aimed for effects of power and splendor to exalt the Catholic Church's triumphant resurgence. The most influential painter working there, however, Michelangelo Merisi (1573–1610), better known as Caravaggio, developed a personal style that had little to do with official propaganda.

THE CHIAROSCURO OF CARAVAGGIO

The dark drama of many of Caravaggio's paintings echoes the violence of his own life. Notorious for his stormy temper, the rebellious artist spent his last years in exile, after killing an opponent in a tennis match. His love of strong contrasts between light and dark—the Italian term is *chiaroscuro*—often dramatizes his scenes. In *The Calling of*

St. Matthew, Caravaggio's first important Roman commission, a beam of light follows the gesture of Jesus, who stands in the shadows and calls the future apostle. Matthew leans back into the darkness, as if trying to avoid the summons. The church disapproved of Caravaggio's directness, but both the public and his fellow artists fell under the spell of his dramatic realism and psychological perception.

THE PSYCHOLOGICAL REALISM OF BERNINI

The most important of all Italian artists of the Baroque was Gian Lorenzo Bernini (1598–1680). Throughout his long career he produced a bewilderingly varied range of sculptures, while his buildings and urban planning changed the face of Rome.

Bernini's marble and gilt bronze *St. Teresa in Ecstasy* is a masterpiece of dramatic expression. The saint, in the midst of her ecstatic vision, awaits the blow to the heart, which a smiling angel is poised to deliver. St. Teresa's billowing dress, the cloud on which she floats, and the golden beams of light pouring down on the scene are all brought to life with theatrical realism—an effect heightened by the figures to the sides of the chapel, who seem to be watching the action from stage boxes. The combination of heightened emotion, religious passion, and the sense of drama make for one of the supreme monuments of the Baroque style.

Aerial view of St. Peter's Basilica, Vatican City. The nave and façade were finished by Carlo Maderna between 1606 and 1612, and the colonnades around the piazza were built between 1656 and 1663 to the design of Bernini. The completion of the whole complex was one of the first great achievements of Baroque architecture.

Alinari/Art Resource, New York

Bernini poured his seemingly inexhaustible powers of invention into designing palaces, churches, and fountains. His most ambitious project was the *piazza* (square) in front of St. Peter's Basilica, where he created a huge space surrounded by an oval colonnade, with fountains and a central obelisk, which continues to provide the majestic setting for hundreds of thousands of pilgrims to the Vatican.

REMBRANDT AND HIS CONTEMPORARIES IN NORTHERN EUROPE

If the main architectural achievement of the Roman Baroque was religious in inspiration, the largest construction in northern Europe was Louis XIV's Royal Palace at Versailles (see Topic 50). The king intended the building to symbolize his secular power as Grand Monarch, the self-styled Sun King. On rising each morning, Louis made his way through the Hall of Mirrors, surrounded by his courtiers, and entered the main path of the garden, which ran on an east-west axis, following the path of the sun.

PAINTING IN FRANCE AND FLANDERS

For all the conscious splendor of Versailles, in general French and Flemish artists avoided the lavishness of the Italian Baroque. Nicholas Poussin (c. 1593–1665) claimed to detest the work of Caravaggio and intended his own lucid, restrained paintings as a deliberate criticism of the Italian painter's emotionalism. His famous *Et in Arcadia Ego* (*I Too Am in Arcadia*; the words of Death, present even in the tranquil countryside) conveys a still hush, its figures rapt in solemn thought.

Much of the art produced in northern Europe was specifically aimed at the new middle-class public. The most prolific of all northern artists, however, Peter Paul Rubens (1577–1640), produced works of just about every conceivable kind: portraits, landscapes, religious subjects, and mythological tales. In addition to his art, Rubens traveled widely as a diplomat, speaking six modern languages and reading Latin fluently.

Something of the restless energy of the man emerges in many of his vast paintings. Yet Rubens could also touch quieter, more intimate feelings. At the age of 53, after the death of his first wife, he married the 16-year-old Helene Fourment. His painting of Helene with two of their young children is a rare depiction of the quiet joys of married love, in contrast to the intensity of most Baroque art.

PAINTING IN THE NETHERLANDS: REMBRANDT

Unlike their colleagues elsewhere in Europe, artists in the Netherlands lacked the two chief sources of patronage: the church and the aristocracy. The Dutch Calvinist Church forbade the use of religious images, and the Netherlands never had the kind of wealthy and powerful nobility that existed in France or England. Dutch painters needed therefore to find middle-class customers to commission works.

One handy source of income was the portrait. The greatest painter of the age, Rembrandt van Rijn (1606–1669), began his career as a successful painter of middle-class patrons. One of his early masterpieces is a

Poussin, *Et Ego in Arcadia.* 1638–1639. 33½ inches by 47⅝ inches (85 by 121 cm). In an idealized landscape, four country dwellers decipher with difficulty the inscription on a gravestone, which reads: "I, too, am in Arcadia." The words are spoken by the spirit of Death, present even in this peaceful scene. The artist uses the calmly posed figures to recapture the lofty spirit of Classical Antiquity.

Copyright Réunion des Musées Nationaux/Art Resource, NY

Rubens, *Helene Fourment and her Children.* 1636–1637. 44½ inches by 32¼ inches (118 by 85 cm). After the death of his first wife, at the age of 53 Rubens married Helene Fourment, a girl of 16. The happiness of this marriage produced some of the great artist's most intimate and tender works. Here we see Helene with two of their children.

Copyright Réunion des Musées Nationaux/Art Resource, NY

group portrait, generally known as *The Night Watch*, although recent cleaning has revealed that the chief figures were originally bathed in light.

The complexity of the composition of *The Night Watch* illustrates the subtlety of Rembrandt's genius. As he began to produce more introspective and somber works, his clients gradually stopped commissioning him. They wanted cheerful portraits and colorful still lifes to decorate their houses, not deep spiritual meditations. By the end of his career, Rembrandt was producing religious paintings inspired by his lifelong meditation on the Scriptures. *Jacob Blessing the Sons of Joseph* conveys all the painful tenderness of the family's three generations, united lovingly at the old man's deathbed. The strong contrasts of light and darkness show the continuing influence of Caravaggio, but the sense of spiritual concentration is a far cry from the drama of Caravaggio and his followers.

MUSIC FOR A NEW PUBLIC: THE BIRTH OF OPERA AND THE WORKS OF BACH

As in the case of the visual arts, musical developments in Italy and northern Europe differed in their attitude toward religion. Italy saw the birth of musical forms that could satisfy the demand for popular secular entertainment, whereas in the North, Bach, Handel, and other composers produced some of the greatest sacred music ever written.

THE BIRTH OF OPERA

The inventors of opera, a group of Florentine intellectuals known as the "Camerata," intended it as a revival of ancient Greek tragedy. The first play set to music, *Dafne*, by Jacopo Peri (1561–1633), was staged in Florence in 1594. Within a

Staatliche Museen Kassel, Gemäldegalerie Alte Meister

Rembrandt, *Jacob Blessing the Sons of Joseph*. 1656. 5 feet 8¼ inches by 6 feet 9 inches (1.75 by 2.1 m). Painted toward the end of his life, in the year of his financial collapse, the scene—like that of Caravaggio's *Calling of St. Matthew*—uses light and shadow to deepen the emotions, as the old man, on the point of death, bids farewell to his family.

few years the new entertainment had spread throughout Europe. Opera houses sprang up in Austria and Germany and then in England, where by the late 17th century Italian singers could command astronomical fees. Under the encouragement of Louis XIV, French composers developed their own kind of operas, involving long sections of ballet.

Opera made a special appeal to Baroque tastes for three reasons. First, the combination of words and music could explore psychological states of mind more vividly and dramatically than either on its own. Even in later times, many operas contained a "mad scene" for one of the protagonists. Second, an operatic performance was a chance for virtuosity, both in the brilliance and flexibility of the singing and in the sumptuous stage settings and effects. Audiences loved to see magical transformation scenes or blazing fires that seemed to engulf the stage. Third, the design of the opera house, with its tiers of boxes and upper gallery, made it possible for all social classes to attend performances while maintaining them physically separate.

Claudio Monteverdi (1567–1643), the first great genius in the history of opera, proved the dramatic power of the medium as early as his first stage work, *Orfeo*. By skillful use of instrumentation and a vocal line that mirrored the character's emotions, Monteverdi breathed dramatic life into the familiar story. The composer spent the last 30 years of

his life at Venice, where 16 opera houses were built in the second half of the 17th century—an astonishing demonstration of the breadth of appeal of the new entertainment.

MUSIC IN GERMANY: BACH

Baroque composers in northern Europe generally did not write operas. The only important exception was Georg Frideric Handel (1685–1759), who composed a string of operatic masterpieces when he moved to England and became a naturalized citizen. London was one of the operatic centers of Europe, and Handel's operas written for performance there depict a wide range of characters and states of mind.

The greatest figure in Baroque music, Johann Sebastian Bach (1685–1750), wrote no operas and spent his life far from the glamour of London or the other musical capitals of Europe. His music was little known during his lifetime and virtually forgotten after his death. Rediscovered in the 19th century, Bach's music is now regarded as one of the supreme achievements of Western culture.

A devout Lutheran, Bach used music to glorify God and explore the deeper mysteries of the Christian faith. He composed masses, organ works, cantatas, and settings of sections of the Bible. His *Saint Matthew Passion* is a setting of the trial and Crucifixion of Jesus as recorded in the Gospel of St. Matthew. Bach proclaimed his Lutheranism by setting

PUBLIC FIGURES AND PRIVATE LIVES

ANNA MAGDALENA AND JOHANN SEBASTIAN BACH

Johann Sebastian Bach, "Klavierbuchlein fur Anna Magdalena Bach," 1725. Courtesy of Riemenschneider Bach Institute, Baldwin-Wallace College, Berea, OH.

AKG London

Bach came from a large family of musicians, and family life was important to him. His first wife died in 1720, after having given birth to seven children, of whom four died in infancy. Within a year the composer remarried a young singer, Anna Magdalena Wülken (1701–1760). He was 36 at the time, she 20. The prince of Cöthen, for whom Bach was then working, allowed the couple to save money by marrying in Bach's lodgings, and the composer used the money to buy Rhine wine at the city cellars.

Early in their marriage, Bach gave his wife a book of blank music paper, on which she wrote the title *"Clavier-Büchlein"* (Little Keyboard Book). He copied into it a series of short keyboard pieces, intended to help Anna Magdalena improve her playing. In 1725, he gave her a new book, in which he continued to write pieces. One of them is a song (perhaps by Bach, perhaps by G.H. Stölzel, a contemporary), *"Bist du bei mir."* The words are: "As long as you are with me, I could face my death and eternal rest with joy. How peaceful would my end be if your beautiful hands could close my faithful eyes." The illustration at left shows an excerpt from one of her notebooks—no portrait survives.

Throughout their life together, Anna Magdalena took part in performances of her husband's works and helped him to copy them out, as well as bearing him 13 children. Bach suffered from deteriorating eyesight, and in 1749 he underwent two disastrous operations that left him totally blind. A few months later he was dead. His modest estate was divided between his nine surviving children and his widow. His sons and daughters sold their share of his manuscripts, but Anna Magdalena kept hers, leaving them to the Music School of the Church of St. Thomas, Leipzig. She died in abject poverty 10 years after her husband.

The lives of both Johann Sebastian and Anna Magdalena were spent far from the tumultuous events of their times. The sheer amount of music Bach wrote and the couple copied out suggests that most of their time was dedicated to music and its performance. The products of their years together can now be seen as one of the summits of the Western musical tradition, and countless beginning pianists have learned to play with the aid of the pieces Bach wrote in the "Little Keyboard Book for Anna Magdalena."

the text in a German translation, rather than Latin, and he included several Lutheran *chorales*—a kind of hymn that Luther had popularized.

THE GOLDEN AGE OF LITERATURE: SHAKESPEARE AND CERVANTES

The leading writers of the early 17th century owe their formation to the Renaissance. The works of both Shakespeare and Cervantes represent the culmination of a tradition—in drama and the picaresque novel—that goes back to their predecessors of the preceding century. Yet both figures drew on the greater range of expressivity typical of Baroque art to create works that combined profundity with popular appeal. In the case of Shakespeare, moreover, the judgment of his contemporary and rival Ben Jonson (1572–1637) still holds true: "He was not of an age, but for all time!"

DRAMA IN ENGLAND: WILLIAM SHAKESPEARE

William Shakespeare (1564–1616) is universally acknowledged as the greatest writer in the English language, but

A C R O S S   C U L T U R E S

SHAKESPEARE AND POSTERITY

Few figures in the history of Western culture have had Shakespeare's broad and lasting appeal. Many of his plays, and even individual lines in them, have entered the Western imagination—and beyond: The great Japanese film director Akira Kurosawa (1910–1998) based his films *Throne of Blood* (1958) and *Ran* (1985) on

Courtesy of William Duiker

Macbeth and *King Lear*, respectively. Many people quote Shakespeare without realizing that they are doing so: "frailty, thy name is woman"; "to thine own self be true"; "not a mouse stirred"; and, from the same play as all the preceding—*Hamlet*—the most famous of all, "To be or not to be, that is the question."

Thus it comes as a surprise to discover that such universal admiration is, in fact, not so universal. The earliest reference to Shakespeare's London career comes in a tract by Robert Greene, a contemporary, published in 1592: "There is an upstart Crow, beautiful with our feathers, that with his 'Tyger's hart wrapt in a

little definite information is known of his life. Born at Stratford-upon-Avon, by 1592 he was active as an actor and playwright in London. His early plays, including *The Comedy of Errors*, imitated ancient Roman comedies with their complicated plots involving mistaken identities.

By 1595, with *Romeo and Juliet*, Shakespeare was deepening and enriching both the language and psychological understanding of his characters. In the four tragedies he wrote between 1600 and 1605 (the years in which Caravaggio was at work in Rome)—*Hamlet* (1600), *Othello* (1604), *King Lear* (1604), and *Macbeth* (1605)—he explored the great questions of human existence with a profundity and power of expression that have few if any

equals. In emotional depth and virtuosity of language, the plays remain among the peaks of Western culture and a constant challenge to performers and directors.

Toward the end of his career, Shakespeare explored the frontiers between tragedy and comedy in works written for the court of King James I. *The Tempest* (1611), his last play, creates a world of fantasy in which romantic love and low comedy combine to magical effect.

THE NOVEL: CERVANTES

Something of the same blend of farce and pathos characterizes the greatest novel of the 17th century, *Don Quixote* (1605–1615). Its author, Miguel de Cervantes (1547–1616), received a humanist education and served as a soldier at the

player's hyde' (a parody of a line in Henry VI, Part 3) supposes he is well able to bombast oute a blank verse as the best of you."

Several later writers also remained unimpressed. The 17th-century diarist Samuel Pepys thought A *Midsummer Night's Dream* "the most insipid, ridiculous play that I ever saw in my life." The great French Enlightenment figure Voltaire (see Topic 58) wrote "Shakespeare is a drunken savage with some imagination whose plays can please only in London and Canada."

Perhaps the most bizarre critic of the Bard, however, was a man whose name has entered the English language as a result of his attitude toward Shakespeare's plays: Thomas Bowdler (1754–1825). Bowdler trained as a doctor, but his inability to stand the sight of blood drove him to abandon his medical practice. After traveling widely in Europe, he retired to the Isle of Wight to prepare his ten-volume *Family Shakespeare*, which appeared in 1818. As he explains on the title page, "Nothing is added to the text; but those expressions are omitted which cannot with propriety be read aloud in a family," since he had cut out "whatever is unfit to be read by a gentleman in a company of ladies."

The *Family Shakespeare* became a best-seller, and encouraged by its success Bowdler turned his attention to another of the indisputably great works of English literature, Edward Gibbon's *History of the Decline and Fall of the Roman Empire*, from which he removed "all passages of an irreligious or immoral tendency." Ten years after his death, the verb "to bowdlerize" had already come to mean "to expurgate by omitting or modifying words or passages considered offensive or indelicate," and over time it acquired the sense of absurd and ridiculous censorship.

Meanwhile, the plays have continued to be edited, read, performed, and viewed on the widest of scales, with constant attempts to update or find modern equivalents for *Othello*, or *Hamlet,* or *Richard III*. Bowdler's attempt to "improve" the originals remains a fascinating example of an inability to communicate across cultures.

Battle of Lepanto. His most famous work was intended to poke fun at medieval tales of romance and chivalry. The book's principal character, Don Quixote, is an elderly and rather unworldly gentleman searching for the gallant world of the past in his own troubled times.

The conflict between Don Quixote's idealism and the brutal realities of the world forms Cervantes' main theme, as the novel wanders through an apparently random series of events. The hero is accompanied in his travels by his faithful squire Sancho Panza, who provides a measure of practical common sense to leaven his master's dreams. By the end of his journey, Don Quixote realizes that he cannot reconcile his ideal visions with the real world, and he dies with his illusions finally shattered.

Cervantes' hero has achieved the same archetypal fame in Western culture as Shakespeare's Hamlet or Lear. With its constant exploration of the interplay between illusion and reality, *Don Quixote* touches on many of the chief concerns of 17th-century art, while the Don himself has a depth of character and psychological truth worthy of the brush of a Rembrandt.

POETRY AND RELIGION

The English writers known as the Metaphysical poets combine religion and the erotic in a way typical of the age—Bernini's St. *Teresa in Ecstasy* is a counterpart in the visual arts to the poems of Richard Crashaw (1613–1649), with their blend of pain and religious fervor.

Mr. WILLIAM
SHAKESPEARES
COMEDIES,
HISTORIES, &
TRAGEDIES.

Publifhed according to the True Originall Copies.

LONDON
Printed by Ifaac Iaggard, and Ed. Blount. 1623.

Rare Books and Manuscript Division, New York Public Library, Astor, Lenox, and Tilden Foundations

Title page of the First Folio (first collected edition) of the works of Shakespeare, showing a portrait of the author. 1623. The edition was prepared by two of Shakespeare's fellow actors. So little is known of Shakespeare's life or appearance that it is difficult to judge the accuracy of this image. Certainly the text of the edition is badly flawed in places.

The leading poet of the group was John Donne (1572–1631), whose range and force of expression come close to rivaling those of Shakespeare. Donne's search to understand and expose the conflicting nature of human experience leads him to range from an analysis of sexual love to meditations on human mortality and the soul. The two chief themes of his writing are physical and religious passion, and the counterpoint he weaves between them leads to daring and memorable results.

The greatest of all 17th-century English poets was John Milton (1608–1674), whose artistic life became embroiled with the events of the English Civil War (see Topic 43). His active support for Cromwell and the Puritans brought him disgrace at the Restoration of Charles II in 1660. He spent the years of his enforced retirement in the composition of his major work, *Paradise Lost* (1667), the only successful epic poem in the English language.

The aim of *Paradise Lost* was to "justify the ways of God to men" by describing the fall of Adam and Eve. The poem's 12 books, written in blank verse, use imagery from the two great streams of Western culture—Classical Antiquity and Christianity—to reconcile humanist philosophical ideas with Christian doctrine. With the sure sense of drama of Bernini, Bach's spiritual convictions, and Rembrandt's understanding of the human heart, Milton's epic epitomizes the Age of the Baroque.

Putting the Baroque Era in Perspective

The arts served in the 17th century as weapons in the battle between Reformation and Counter-Reformation. In the process, they acquired new powers of expression and explored fresh areas of human experience. For all the apparent moral conflict between the Catholic Bernini and Puritan Milton, both drew on the advances of the Renaissance to produce works of dazzling insight.

There were times when the Baroque love of display and virtuosity crossed the line between extravagance and tastelessness, and for many at the beginning of the 21st century, Baroque art is less accessible than the more austere products of the Renaissance—the very word *Baroque* has come to mean "grotesque" or "exaggerated." The typical Baroque quest for illusionism can seem artificial and forced.

Yet many of the works created in the Baroque style retain much of the passion that their makers poured into them. Furthermore, in their struggle to represent the emotions and mental states of individuals, the greatest figures of the age—Bach, Rembrandt, and Shakespeare—created statements of universal truth.

Questions for Further Study

1. What common characteristics do all the arts share in the Baroque period? How do they vary in different parts of Europe?
2. How did Baroque artists deal with religious subjects? Did their approach differ from that of Renaissance artists?
3. What qualities have made Shakespeare's plays so widely admired and performed? Do the works still seem relevant, and, if so, why?

Suggestions for Further Reading

Adams, Laurie Schneider. *Key Monuments of the Baroque.* Denver, CO, 1999.

Boyd, M., ed. *Oxford Composer Companions: J. S. Bach.* Oxford, 1999.

Brown, Jonathan. *Kings and Connoisseurs: Collecting Art in Seventeenth-Century Europe.* Princeton, NJ, 1994.

Franits, Wayne. *Looking at Seventeenth-Century Dutch Art: Realism Reconsidered.* Cambridge, 1997.

Krautheimer, R. *The Rome of Alexander VII, 1655–1667.* Princeton, NJ, 1985.

Lagerlof, Margaretha R. *Ideal Landscape: Annibale Carracci, Nicholas Poussin and Claude Lorrain.* New Haven, CT, 1990.

Lavin, I. *Bernini and the Unity of the Visual Arts.* New York, 1980.

Levey, Michael. *Painting and Sculpture in France, 1700-1789.* New Haven, CT, 1993.

Millon, Henry A., ed. *The Triumph of the Baroque: Architecture in Europe, 1600-1750.* New York, 1999.

Muller, Sheila D., ed. *Dutch Art: An Encyclopedia.* New York, 1997.

North, Michael. *Art and Commerce in the Dutch Golden Age.* New Haven, CT, 1997.

Robb, Peter. M: *The Man Who Became Caravaggio.* New York, 2000.

Schama, Simon. *Rembrandt's Eyes.* New York, 1999.

Paliska, C.V. *Baroque Music.* Englewood Cliffs, NJ, 1981.

InfoTrac College Edition

Enter the search term *William Shakespeare* using Key Terms.

PART VI

THE OLD REGIME

The term *Old Regime* describes the political and social conditions that prevailed in Europe from about 1600 to the French Revolution in 1789. On the surface, life in Europe continued to follow patterns set in the Middle Ages. Most Europeans lived in farming communities. Although peasants in Western Europe were free, many still owed feudal obligations to landowners; in Eastern Europe most were still serfs.

Power remained in the hands of a hereditary aristocracy, and, to a lesser extent, of the reli-gious authorities. Whether in the Dutch republic, in England—a constitutional monarchy—or absolute monarchies such as France or Prussia, participation in government was limited to a tiny section of the population, who used their influence to protect their own interests. Moreover, in France as well as in Central and Eastern Europe, government evolved in the direction of royal absolutism.

Throughout Europe a legally recognized social hierarchy concentrated privilege and status

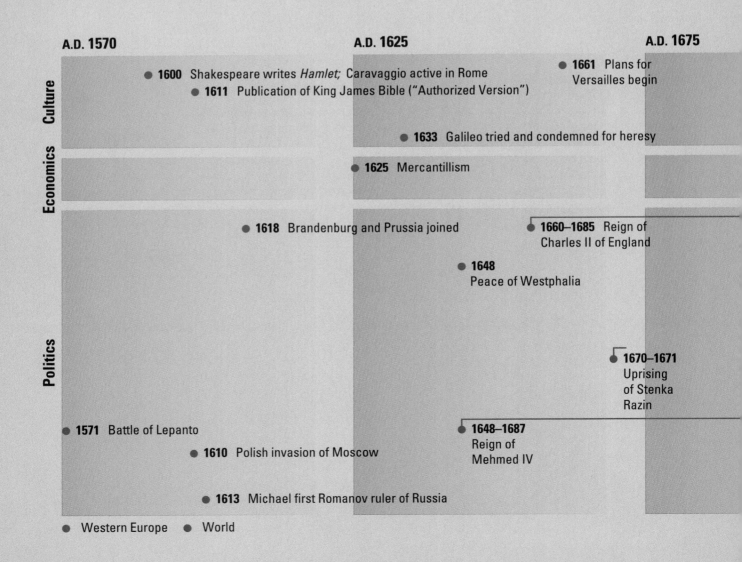

A.D. 1570   **A.D. 1625**   **A.D. 1675**

Culture

● **1600** Shakespeare writes *Hamlet;* Caravaggio active in Rome
● **1611** Publication of King James Bible ("Authorized Version")
● **1661** Plans for Versailles begin
● **1633** Galileo tried and condemned for heresy

Economics

● **1625** Mercantillism

Politics

● **1618** Brandenburg and Prussia joined
● **1660–1685** Reign of Charles II of England
● **1648** Peace of Westphalia
● **1670–1671** Uprising of Stenka Razin
● **1571** Battle of Lepanto
● **1610** Polish invasion of Moscow
● **1648–1687** Reign of Mehmed IV
● **1613** Michael first Romanov ruler of Russia

● Western Europe   ● World

Copyright © Frick Collection, New York

among traditional elites. The bulk of society—the peasantry, urban workers, and the middle classes—although excluded from government, bore the brunt of taxation. The trade in African slaves, and the institution of slavery itself, continued to be condoned and advanced by European states.

Yet behind the apparently permanent façade, there were signs of instability. The scientific revolution of the 17th century and the intellectual movement known as the Enlightenment of the

A.D. 1700

A.D. 1775

- **1748** Excavations begin at Pompeii
- **1751–1772** Diderot and others edit *Encyclopédie*
- **1685** Johann Sebastian Bach born
- **1759** Voltaire publishes *Candide*
- **c. 1715** Rococo style in art emerges in France
- **1720** South Sea Bubble
- **1776** Adam Smith's *Wealth of Nations*
- **1685** Edict of Nantes revoked
- **1734–1759** Charles III first Bourbon king of Naples
- **1683** Ottoman Turks besiege Vienna
- **1740–1786** Reign of Prussia's Friedrich the Great
- **1688** "Glorious Revolution" in England
- **1741–1764** Maria Theresa rules Austrian possessions
- **1689–1697** War of the League of Augsburg
- **1763** Treaty of Paris
- **1701–1714** War of Spanish Succession; Friedrich I king of Prussia
- **1707** Act of Union between England and Scotland
- **1713** Treaty of Utrecht
- **1714–1727** Reign of George I of England
- **1738–1746** War of Jenkins' Ear
- **1703** Hungarian uprising under Rákóczy
- **1700–1721** Great Northern War
- **1756–1763** Seven Years' War
- **1757** Battle of Plassey
- **1689–1725** Reign of Peter the Great in Russia
- **1759–1760** British take Quebec

18th century led slowly but inevitably to dissatisfaction with old ways and beliefs. Out of the English political experiment of the 17th century and the ideas of the Enlightenment there emerged theories of political sovereignty that recognized the right of ordinary citizens to resist oppression and overthrow despots. With the growth of cities, an increasing proportion of the population was within reach of education, and ideas began to spread far more rapidly. One of the major factors in the development of urban life was the Industrial Revolution, which began in the late 18th century.

In international affairs, the traditional rivalry between the two great powers of Europe, England and France, continued to dominate politics, while in the 18th century two new continental contenders began to emerge: the German state of Brandenburg-Prussia and Russia. Furthermore, with Europeans busily colonizing in Asia and the Americas, competition among the great powers resulted in military clashes on a global scale.

The buildup of a century and a half of pressure for change exploded in 1789 in the French Revolution. It was a sign of the new world that the revolutionary leaders hoped to create that they took inspiration from a revolution halfway across the globe: that of the Americans against their British colonial rulers.

THE SCIENTIFIC REVOLUTION AND WESTERN THOUGHT

During the Renaissance, as ancient scientific theories resurfaced, scholars throughout Europe began to speculate about issues that had been taken for granted in the medieval period: the nature of the physical universe, the relationship of Earth to the sun, the laws of mathematics. In order to put to the test beliefs based on tradition and Christian dogma, they started to try out theoretical ideas by means of practical experiments. In the 17th century, growing use of this **scientific method** produced a revolution in European intellectual attitudes, as scientists and thinkers such as Galileo, Descartes, and Newton laid the foundations of modern science. From then on, theologians and philosophers alike were faced with a new authority—scientific truth, objectively demonstrated.

Official church teaching, supported by the Bible, held that Earth formed the center of the universe, around which the sun, moon, and planets moved. The first to question this belief was the Polish astronomer Nicolaus Copernicus, who published his description of a universe centered around the sun in 1543. The German Johannes Kepler followed up the mathematical implications of Copernicus's revolutionary model and formulated three laws, describing the motions of the planets, which paved the way for Isaac Newton, the most prestigious mathematician and natural philosopher of early modern times, who produced a wide range of achievements. Among the most important were the theory of universal gravitation and his theories of light and motion. The astronomical observations of the Italian Galileo Galilei, using the newly invented telescope, further undermined official teaching.

The great Swiss physician Paracelsus also emphasized the importance of practical experiment. He based many of his theories on medieval alchemy, but his insistence on careful clinical observation and his use of a wide range of drugs helped lay the foundations of modern medicine. Other medical advances included the discovery of the circulation of the blood by the Englishman William Harvey.

The leading philosophical representative of the "new scientists" was the Englishman Francis Bacon, who urged the superiority of objective evidence over untested belief. Two French philosophers, René Descartes and Blaise Pascal, examined the implications of the rational method for theology and mathematics.

Thus, by the beginning of the 18th century there existed a scientific world view that challenged—implicitly, at least—centuries of accepted belief. The emphasis that scientists placed on reason, and their faith in the ability of the human mind to penetrate the mysteries of the universe, led in turn to the chief intellectual movement of the 18th century: the Enlightenment.

THE WEIGHT OF TRADITION: GOD, NATURE, AND THE WORLD

Throughout the thousand or so years that separated the fall of the Roman Empire from the Renaissance, scholars and theologians in Europe accepted a standard explanation of the nature of the physical universe. It was mainly derived from the writings of three ancient Greeks: Aristotle (384–322 B.C.) for physics, Galen (130–c. A.D. 200) for medicine, and Ptolemy (2nd century A.D.) for astronomy.

According to traditional Christian teaching, based on these authorities, the universe was finite. Earth, the most corrupt and degenerate—and therefore heaviest—part of the cosmos, was located at its center and was stationary. It was heavy, material, and subject to constant change. Around it there circled the planets, sun, stars, and heavens, moving outward from Earth in a widening series of spheres. The heavenly bodies were light, luminous disks, and in their superlunar realm, nothing ever changed. In the Renaissance, most scholars continued to accept these assumptions and tried to find complicated explanations for apparent inconsistencies rather than question the traditional explanations. When Galileo demonstrated that this distinction between Earth and the heavenly bodies was false, he created a storm of protest and bewilderment.

THE DAWN OF THE SCIENTIFIC REVOLUTION

Yet at the same time, the 15th and 16th centuries saw the first serious doubts about the accepted view of the nature of the universe. The Renaissance humanists discovered other Classical writers whose theories differed from those of Aristotle and Ptolemy. Among the most important was the physicist Archimedes (c. 287–212 B.C.), whose writings on dynamics proved highly influential.

Another reason for rethinking traditional views was a growing interest in various forms of magic, many of which were based on ancient precedents. Students of alchemy (a kind of medieval chemistry whose chief aim was to turn base metals into gold) believed that they could understand the nature of matter by using secret formulae to combine various ingredients. Others turned to the heavens and used astrology to interpret the movements of the planets. They hoped to read in them the meaning of the universe.

Various mystical schools of philosophy also flourished in the 16th century. The Hermetics were philosophers who believed that humans already possessed the key to an understanding of nature, locked up somewhere in existing texts (the term *hermetic*, taken from alchemy, refers to an airtight seal). They searched obscure writings, looking for hidden clues that would reveal the structure of the universe. Other thinkers turned to the Jewish mystical teachings of the *Kabbalah*, a Hebrew word, used to describe a body of esoteric Jewish mystical doctrines, which literally means "tradition."

More firmly based on Classical tradition were the Neoplatonists. The original school of **Neoplatonist** philos-ophy flourished from the 3rd to the 6th century A.D. It derived from the teachings of the 4th-century B.C. Greek philosopher Plato and described the universe as consisting of a systematized order, containing all levels and states of existence. Renaissance Neoplatonists revived the idea of seeking to escape from the bonds of earthly existence in order to rise upward toward union with God, or the One, from whose Divine Mind the World Soul proceeds.

Most of these scholars may now seem unlikely forerunners of the **scientific revolution,** but by rejecting traditional solutions to age-old problems, and by using chemical experiments and mathematical formulae, they created an increasingly open spirit of intellectual inquiry.

With the surge of technological expertise that developed in the Renaissance, practical engineers, navigators, and doctors began to apply the experimental approach to their own fields. The result was to create a new way of looking at the world. When writing of motion—and with an eye on Aristotle—the great medieval thinker St. Thomas Aquinas (1225–1274) provided the baffling explanation that "motion exists because things which are in a state of potentiality seek to actualize themselves." Aquinas seems to have theorized about how things move, rather than actually watching them in motion. At the end of the 16th century, Galileo watched workmen in the Arsenal at Venice moving great weights; he went on to form a theory of motion that disproved Aristotle, and demonstrated it by dropping weights from the top of the Leaning Tower of Pisa. The age of objective scientific proof had dawned.

REDEFINING THE UNIVERSE: FROM COPERNICUS TO GALILEO

In the early 17th century, Galileo's astronomical experiments produced a revolutionary break with church teaching. Half a century earlier, however, the cleric Nicolaus Copernicus (1473–1543) had already challenged traditional opinion.

THE COPERNICAN REVOLUTION

Born in Poland of a wealthy German family, Copernicus studied in Italy, at the University of Padua. He learned there of recently rediscovered Greek scientific texts and pursued his mathematical interests. Under the influence of Platonic thought, he sought to replace the highly complex astronomical system of Ptolemy with a simpler formulation. Convinced that the sun, and not Earth, lay at the center of the universe, he devised a system whereby Earth and the planets orbit the sun in a series of perfect divine circles.

Unlike his successor Galileo, Copernicus never really tested his ideas by practical experiment. He remained a theoretical philosopher. Nor did his work, based as it was on ancient teachings, represent a real break with the past. He did not even publish his ideas until 1543, the year of his death. Yet in two crucial ways Copernicus foreshadowed the "new science." In the first place his challenge to astronomical teachings based on the Bible was so serious that it drew the condemnation of first Protestant and then Catholic theologians.

Second, Copernicus's work revealed a new attitude. Before his time, scholars had always assumed that appearances were to be trusted. If the sun appeared to revolve around Earth, then it must be doing so. Questioning this assumption, Copernicus claimed that a system whereby Earth revolved around the sun was equally plausible. Scientific truth alone could be the basis of intellectual advance, even if it ran contrary to superficial observation. Indeed, the secrets of nature were often well concealed; in order to discover them it was often necessary to "twist the lion's tail," as Francis Bacon later observed.

The leading astronomer of the late 16th century, the Danish Tycho Brahe (1546–1601), collected important information about the planets and stars. In 1572 he discovered a new star, and three years later a comet, both of which disproved Aristotle's notions of fixed, unmoving heavenly bodies. Brahe refused to abandon his belief in the Ptolemaic system, but his remarkably accurate observations helped his successors to demonstrate that Earth revolved around the sun.

KEPLER AND HIS LAWS

Among Brahe's most brilliant pupils was the German astronomer Johannes Kepler (1571–1630). Kepler was convinced by Brahe's observations that the sun was the center of the universe. In trying to demonstrate this point, he formulated three laws, published in 1609 and 1619, to describe the motions of the planets in the solar system. According to the first law, each planet, including Earth, orbits the sun in an ellipse, of which the sun is at one focus. The second law claims that planets move faster when they are closer to the sun than when farther away. The third law describes the mathematical relationships between the planets' movements.

GALILEO GALILEI

The career of the Italian astronomer and physicist Galileo Galilei (1564–1642) demonstrated both the triumphs and the dangers of the scientific method. His experiments laid the foundations of modern physics, and he used his telescope to disprove Aristotle once and for all. He insisted that the Bible and the Aristotelian world it apparently supported should give way to modern science. As a result, he was tried and condemned by the Inquisition.

Galileo was born in Pisa in Italy to a talented aristocratic family. After beginning to study medicine at the University of Padua, Galileo changed to mathematics, and stayed on in Padua to teach there. The northern Italian city was already famous throughout Europe for its university, founded in 1222—the central building of the University of Padua today was begun in 1493, and is still in use. Research conducted by scholars at the university in the 16th century played a central role in the development of early modern

science. In addition to the Italians, foreign students such as William Harvey (see later section) studied there.

The telescope, a new astronomical tool, had been produced in Holland (its invention is generally credited to Hans Lippershey, a spectacle maker), and was used mainly for sighting ships. Driven by the curiosity that helped inspire the scientific revolution, Galileo designed and built his own model. Then he turned it toward the heavens to show a new vision: the mountains and craters of the moon, the phases of Venus, and sunspots. These observations proved that the universe is in a constant state of change. As early as 1597 he was convinced that Earth was in motion, and in 1610 he published his discovery of the satellites of Jupiter.

Galileo's attacks on traditional ideas, and his claims that he could demonstrate beyond doubt the essential truth of Copernicus's theories, created widespread controversy. One of his outraged colleagues, a Jesuit professor of philosophy at Padua, refused to look through a telescope for fear his traditional views might be shaken. More ominously, Galileo's Jesuit and Dominican opponents drew the attention of the Inquisition to his "heretical" ideas.

In 1616, after Galileo had defended his position in the presence of the pope, Paul V, the Inquisition censured him

Photograph of one of Galileo's telescopes. Date of telescope 1609. After Galileo's death in 1642, many of his instruments, including this one, were collected and preserved. They can now be seen in Florence's Museum of Science, one of the earliest examples in history of a museum dedicated to scientific rather than artistic works.

Scala/Art Resource

and prohibited him from spreading the doctrine that Earth moves, either by teaching or publication; the harsh reaction was in part because of the aggressive spirit of the Counter-Reformation, which sought to combat all traces of opposition to official views. After a period of tactful silence, Galileo returned to the attack when a former friend was elected pope as Urban VIII. In 1632 he published a *Dialogue Concerning the Two Chief World Systems*, in which he used imaginary characters to express his theories. The strategy failed to protect him. The Inquisition summoned him to Rome, imprisoned him, and in 1633 tried him for heresy. Despite his poor health and powerful friends, the tribunal forced him to undergo the humiliation of a public recantation, and sentenced him to house arrest for the remainder of his life. The case against him was reopened only in 1980, when Pope John Paul II—like Copernicus, a Pole—ordered that belated justice be done: In 1992, the church formally proclaimed its error.

Galileo spent the rest of his life under house arrest at his villa outside Florence, working on problems in physics. His last work, *Dialogues Concerning Two New Sciences* (1638), used observation and experiment to study a variety of phenomena, including motion. In trying to understand the practical character of natural events, rather than seeking to probe their cosmic purpose, he laid the foundation of modern physics.

MEDICINE AND THE HUMAN BODY

Throughout medieval Europe doctors remained largely dependent on more or less corrupted versions of the works of the Greek physician Galen of Pergamum (c. 130–c. 200). Galen catalogued illnesses, distinguished between anatomy and physiology, and described the course of various diseases. By contrast with the West, in the medieval Muslim world, significant medical and scientific research led to important medical discoveries, some of which gradually circulated in Europe.

PARACELSUS

The Renaissance, with its revival of interest in ancient texts, and its growing spirit of practical research, brought a wave of new interest. The figure who did most to change and improve methods of medical treatment was a Swiss alchemist and doctor called Theophrastus Bombast von Hohenheim; he proclaimed his superiority to ancient doctors by adopting the name by which he is best known, Paracelsus (1493–1541)—the name means "better than Celsus," who was an eminent Roman surgeon of the 1st century A.D.

Rejecting the authority of Aristotle and Galen, Paracelsus turned to his own careful observation in treating disease. After studying medicine at Ferrara in northern Italy, he taught at the University of Basle, Switzerland. He

was one of the earliest university teachers anywhere to lecture in German, his own language, rather than in Latin, and this in itself was a challenge to tradition. His unconventional approach, coupled with a legendary short temper, brought him into constant conflict with his colleagues, and he spent the last years of his life as a traveling physician. Constantly recording the various symptoms of illnesses, and their reaction to different drugs, Paracelsus was the first physician to emphasize the close relationship between chemistry and medicine.

THE CIRCULATION OF THE BLOOD

The first to make a breakthrough in understanding the system whereby blood circulates in the body was the Spanish theologian and physician Michael Servetus (1511–1553). In a theological treatise, *Christianity Restored* (1553), written while he was teaching in France, he described how blood is carried from the heart to the lungs to be purified, and then returns to the heart to be passed from there to the other parts of the body.

For all the importance of his work, Servetus failed to realize that the blood returns to the heart, circulating endlessly by means of the veins. This discovery was made by the English doctor William Harvey (1578–1657). As a young man, Harvey studied under Galileo at Padua and subsequently became personal physician to James I and Charles I. In a publication of 1628, Harvey described the blood circulation system and explained the function of heart valves and arterial pulse.

The increasing use of dissection improved knowledge of the human body and its organs. Surgeons thus became able to operate more effectively. More than half a century earlier, in 1543—the year in which Copernicus's revolutionary theory appeared—the Flemish biologist Andreas Vesalius (1514–1564) had published *On the Structure of the Human Body*. Vesalius based his anatomical treatise on his dissections of corpses. Church leaders who believed in the physical resurrection of the body on the Day of Judgment protested at his use of cadavers, however, and Vesalius abandoned his scientific studies to practice medicine at the Spanish court. By the following century, however, the wave of scientific progress had swept away such objections to the use of human cadavers.

THE ROYAL SOCIETY OF LONDON

The spectacular discoveries in anatomy, like those in astronomy and physics, inevitably aroused widespread interest. This led in turn to the establishment of organizations of scientists, to share research discoveries and promote their spread. The first such institution, the Lincean Academy, was founded in Rome in 1602. By far the most important, however, was the Royal Society of London for Improving Knowledge. The group began to meet informally at Oxford in the 1640s, during the Civil War. In 1660, 12 members formed an official organization, which received a royal charter two years later.

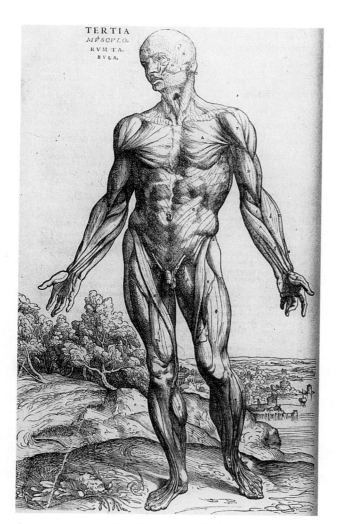

Andreas Vesalius, *Third Musculature Table,* from *De humani corporis fabrica.* 1543. The highly realistic drawing of the human muscular structure comes from a set of seven volumes dealing with human anatomy. The figure is set somewhat incongruously in a typical 16th-century landscape scene, which could almost come from an etching by Dürer (see Topic 36).

The declared aim of the Royal Society was to gather all knowledge about nature and encourage its use for the public good. The sheer quantity of information with which it was deluged soon forced the Society to function as a central clearinghouse for the circulation of ideas. In 1665 it began to publish on a regular basis *Philosophical Transactions,* the earliest scientific journal.

Similar organizations appeared in other parts of Europe. In France, Louis XIV encouraged the foundation of the Royal Academy of Sciences in 1666, and by the end of the century other academies existed in Berlin and Naples. The "new science," which had aroused so much official hostility a hundred years earlier, was now patronized by royalty and followed enthusiastically by an ever-widening group of nobles and educated middle-class men and women.

THE SCIENTIFIC METHOD: BACON, DESCARTES, AND PASCAL

Many founding members of the Royal Society believed in acquiring and evaluating information by the scientific method. They acknowledged Francis Bacon (1561–1626) as their inspiration. Bacon was a philosopher rather than a scientist, but his writings on the importance of science for human development led the way in stimulating scientific research.

A gifted and precocious young man, Bacon was a student at Cambridge by the age of 16. He distinguished himself there by attacking the works of Aristotle, which were regarded as the basis of all philosophical instruction. The character of Bacon's philosophy emerged as early as 1605, in *The Advancement of Learning.* He believed that the myths and fables of primitive peoples expressed true wisdom; Plato, Aristotle, and the other ancient philosophers had strayed from the truth by the arrogance that led them to invent their own intellectual systems. To find truth, it was necessary to study the world around us. Experiment was far more important than theorizing.

He returned to this conviction throughout his life. In *New Atlantis* he described an ideal society in which scientists would work for the state in gathering knowledge. In due course this would lead to establishing universal laws creating continuous improvements in human existence. Toward the end of his life, he tried to replace Aristotelianism with a new system of philosophy, described in *Novum Organum.* This appeared in Latin in 1620, but two years later Bacon broke with tradition and published an edition in English, the *New Organon.* This meant that a far wider audience read and thought about his challenge to Aristotle's views. In his last works, he poured his energies into what he believed to be his great mission: the exaltation of science as the savior of humanity. In the *New Atlantis* (1626), he even foreshadowed the formation of associations such as the Royal Society.

THE METHODOLOGY OF DESCARTES

If Bacon provided the philosophical underpinning to scientific research, the Frenchman René Descartes (1596–1650) set out the importance of the power of reasoning. After a period of travel, Descartes settled in Holland, where he created the branch of mathematics known as analytic geometry. His interest in mathematics led in turn to his most widely read book, *Discourse on Method* (1637).

In this work he aimed to unify all knowledge as the product of clear reasoning from verifiable evidence. The ideal of objective certitude that could be reached in mathematics should also exist, he claimed, in scientific and philosophical thought. To discover what kind of evidence could have such complete certitude, he adopted the method of universal doubt. Everything was open to question, even his own existence. In the famous phrase "*cogito, ergo sum*" ("I think, therefore I am"), he established his first certitude,

Frans Hals, *René Descartes*, c. 1640. Descartes lived in Holland from 1628 to 1649, and the great Dutch portraitist painted him there. Hals used his typically broad, dynamic brushstrokes to capture the wry, curious gaze of a man often called "the father of modern philosophy."

child, Pascal was a mathematical prodigy. At the age of 16 he completed an original treatise on conic sections, which helped lay the basis for integral calculus. He also made pioneering discoveries in fluid mechanics and hydrodynamics, and along with his countryman Pierre Fermat (1601–1665), originated the mathematical theory of probabilities.

Pascal's sister was a nun, and through her he came into contact with a new Catholic movement, Jansenism; the name was taken from that of a Dutch theologian, Cornelius Jansen (1585–1638). In opposition to the Jesuits' belief in free will, the Jansenists claimed that human destiny was in the hands of God, so that salvation could come only from unquestioning faith. The ultimate source of these teachings was St. Augustine. The hostility between Jansenists and Jesuits led in the 17th century to Louis XIV's persecution of the French Jansenists (on Louis XIV's efforts to stamp out Jansen's beliefs in France, see Topic 50).

The asceticism and piety of the Jansenists he met profoundly shook Pascal's confidence in the value of his scientific work. Late in 1654, at the age of 30, he underwent a mystical experience that led him to abandon science in favor of seeking salvation. In the *Reflections* (1670), the writings of his few remaining years, collected and published after his early death, Pascal urged the importance of spiritual values over dry logic and intellect. He claimed that "the heart has its reasons that the mind cannot know." A lone voice in the growing enthusiasm for scientific progress, he lamented the gulf between the material and the spiritual. The passion of his protests is an indication of the degree to which science had come to dominate 17th-century European intellectual life.

his existence, and following from there worked out his philosophical system.

Although the system, which became known as Cartesianism, is firmly based on reason, Descartes included in it a supreme being. His God, not necessarily to be identified with the God of the Old and New Testaments, created a world imbued with perfect mathematical principles.

As a practical scientist and physicist, Descartes produced mixed results. In his theoretical writings on physics, he was the first to make the important distinction between mass and weight. On the other hand, his attempt to locate that part of the human anatomy that contains the soul was a predictable failure. Descartes' profound influence on his contemporaries came less from the details of his theories than from his general intellectual stance. In particular, he taught the immense importance of never accepting a belief without thoroughly questioning it. After Descartes, it was never again safe to argue from tradition.

PASCAL AND FAITH

For all their temperamental differences, Bacon and Descartes shared an essential belief in the positive power of science. The all-too-brief career of the French mathematician and philosopher Blaise Pascal (1623–1662) shows a far more complex attitude toward scientific discovery. As a

NEWTON AND THE LAWS OF THE NATURAL UNIVERSE

Kepler's astronomy, Galileo's physics, and Descartes' idea of universal science reached a majestic synthesis in the work of the Englishman Isaac Newton (1642–1726), the most eminent mathematician and natural philosopher of early modern times. After attending Cambridge as a student, Newton later taught there. He became a fellow of the Royal Society and served as president from 1703 until his death. His whole life was devoted to ceaseless research—alchemy, optics, mathematics, chronology, chemistry, mechanics, theology, and the secrets of the Bible were only some of the fields to which he made significant contributions.

At the heart of Newton's work lay his belief that logic and reason were unsatisfactory tools for a scientist. It was necessary, he maintained, to prove everything by experiment or mathematics. Thus, his most widely read book, *The Mathematical Principles of Natural Philosophy* (1687), deliberately set out to refute Descartes' exaltation of rationalism. One of the last major scholarly works to be written in Latin, the book is generally referred to as the *Principia*, the first word of its Latin title.

Frans Hals, *René Descartes* (1596–1650), Statens Museum for Kunst, Copenhagen. Photography by Hans Peterson

By courtesy of the National Portrait Gallery, London

Portrait of the English physicist and mathematician, Sir Isaac Newton. 17th century. Newton's long hair (probably a wig) is characteristic of male dress after the Restoration in 1660. The great scientist served in several public positions, including as a Member of Parliament and as Master of the Royal Mint.

THE NEWTONIAN UNIVERSE

Even if the lay public could not always follow the details of Newton's reasoning, the implications of his discoveries had a growing effect on how people thought about the universe. If all motion, random though it might seem, was really the result of precise and unchanging forces, then the world was like a huge machine that functioned according to laws that could be mathematically expressed. God was like a watchmaker who put the machinery in motion. For Newton, in fact, the creation of the force of gravity was an act of God because he believed that bodies do not necessarily possess that quality. Like most of his fellow scientists in the 17th century, Newton remained profoundly religious and devoted much time in his later years to theology.

Yet many people increasingly saw the mechanistic view of the universe proposed by Newton as a welcome replacement for traditional theological disputes. After more than a century of bitter religious wars, the sheer levelheadedness and impartiality of scientific debate seemed a happy relief. Science was peaceful, verifiable, and, above all, useful. This is one reason why Newton received honors never before awarded to a scholar. He became a member of Parliament, served as director of the Royal Mint, and was the first scientist to be knighted for his work.

For a few thinkers, the Newtonian universe replaced the personal God of traditional belief with a natural order. The Dutch Jewish philosopher Baruch Spinoza (1632–1677) held that nature is a fixed and unchangeable order, which serves no particular purpose. God is neither Creator nor Redeemer, but simply natural law. Humans, as part of the universe, conform to the same laws. In his book, *Ethics* (1677), Spinoza writes: "I shall consider human activities and desires in exactly the same manner as if I were concerned with lines, planes, and solids." Few of his contemporaries, however, were as willing as Spinoza to break with tradition, and he was expelled from the Amsterdam Jewish community for his radical views.

For most thinkers in the 18th century, Isaac Newton's contribution stripped away the ignorance of the past and presented a new view of science and the universe. The newly optimistic spirit was neatly caught in Alexander Pope's ironic couplet, written in the early 1700s:

> Nature and nature's law lay hid in night.
> God said, "Let Newton be!" and all was light.

The most influential of his discoveries related to the problem of motion, which he defined in three laws. In formulating these laws, he arrived at concepts of mass, inertia, and force (a term in physics referring to the measurable influence that produces motion) in relation to velocity and acceleration, which dominated science down to the early 20th century and are still valid today. He extended his system to the entire universe, applying the same principles to the movements of the moon and planets. In order to explain the consistent nature of motion, he conceived the idea of the law of gravitation, whereby there exists a reciprocal force of attraction between every body in the universe.

Putting the Scientific Revolution in Perspective

During the 17th century, Western thought underwent wrenching change, and the foundations of the modern intellectual world were laid. The Aristotelian and medieval views of the world ended their 1,000-year-old monopoly, to be replaced by the Newtonian universe. Modern science had a generally accepted methodology, and physics, chemistry, mathematics, anatomy, and astronomy were already producing startling results.

Continued next page

Early researchers had been persecuted, imprisoned, and even executed, but by the early 18th century, scientists were honored members of society, supported by governments. The Counter-Reformation Catholic Church remained hostile to much of the new science, but its power was on the wane, at least in western Europe. Because leading figures such as Descartes and Newton saw no difficulty in reconciling their conclusions with a continuing religious faith, most Protestant communities accepted their work. During the Civil War in England, the Puritans had actually encouraged scientific research.

The scientific revolution did more than illuminate problems of astronomy or anatomy. By challenging centuries of tradition and ignorance, and by revealing the importance of questioning received wisdom, it paved the way for a vast rethinking of many of the basic assumptions underlying Western culture. The discovery of universal laws in nature led to a new belief in a "verifiable universe," in which it was possible to know and discover everything through the application of human logic. From the 17th-century scientific revolution was born the chief intellectual movement of the 18th century, the Enlightenment (see Topic 58). Furthermore, the demonstrated existence of "natural laws" in the universe inspired 18th-century thinkers and politicians to search for similar universal principles in government and devise new political constitutions. The eventual consequence at the end of the century was revolutionary social and political upheaval.

Questions for Further Study

1. What are the chief features of the scientific method? What new light did it shed on astronomy and medicine?
2. How did Descartes and Newton differ in their research methods? How did this affect their conclusions?
3. What were the long-term political consequences of the 17th-century scientific revolution?

Suggestions for Further Reading

Berlinski, David. *Newton's Gift: How Sir Isaac Newton Unlocked the System of the World*. New York, 2000.

Biagioli, Mario. *Galileo, Courtier*. Chicago, 1993.

Gingerich, Owen. *The Eye of Heaven: Ptolemy, Copernicus, Kepler*. New York, 1993.

Hall, A. Rupert. *The Revolution in Science 1500–1750*. London, 1983.

Jacob, Margaret C. *The Cultural Meaning of the Scientific Revolution*. New York, 1988.

Machamer, Peter, ed. *The Cambridge Companion to Galileo*. New York, 1998.

Rodis-Lewis, Genevieve. Jane Marie Todd, trans. *Descartes: His Life and Thought*. Ithaca, NY, 1998.

Sobel, Dava. *Galileo's Daughter*. New York, 1999.

Westfall, R.S. *Never at Rest: A Biography of Isaac Newton*. Cambridge, MA, 1980.

Willey, B. *The Seventeenth Century Background*. New York, 1982.

InfoTrac College Edition

Enter the search term *Copernicus* using Key Terms.

Enter the search term *Galileo* using Key Terms.

Enter the search term *Isaac Newton* using Key Terms.

Enter the search term *René Descartes* using Key Terms.

SOUTHERN EUROPE: SPAIN, ITALY, AND THE MEDITERRANEAN

For thousands of years the Mediterranean Sea had played a unique and vital role in the growth of civilization. The Mediterranean served as the meeting place of diverse and often hostile cultures and religions, and as the most important trade route of the entire region. Yet the 16th century saw the beginning of economic decline for the region, as the newly discovered sailing routes across the Atlantic and around Africa shifted the focus of trade from the Mediterranean to the Atlantic states.

What the Mediterranean lost in economic importance, Spain gained. In the mid-16th century, the resources of the vast Spanish empire enabled its monarchs to extend their political hegemony throughout Europe. Philip II ruled an empire that included not only Spain and huge tracts of the Americas, but also Milan, Naples, Sicily, Sardinia, and the Netherlands.

Within little more than a century after Philip's death, Spain—seething with domestic unrest and its economy devastated by a combination of virtually continuous warfare, agricultural deterioration, unchecked royal spending, and overtaxation—had lost most of its European possessions. In the diplomatic balance of power, Spain's predominance was overtaken by France.

By the 15th century, the Italian city-states had become centers of a vibrant economic revival and a brilliant cultural Renaissance. Despite Italy's achievements as the center of Western artistic and intellectual revival, however, the invasion of the peninsula by the French king Charles VIII in 1494 began a long period of foreign domination. In 1559, the destinies of Spain and Italy met when Philip II confirmed his hold over his Italian lands and ended a protracted struggle for mastery in Italy between Spain and France. Thereafter, Spain influenced Italian affairs until the early 18th century, when the Austrians became the predominant power in Italy.

SIGNIFICANT DATES

Spain

1492	Columbus's first voyage; beginning of shift in sea trade from Mediterranean to Atlantic
1532	Last Flanders galley
1453–1571	Mediterranean wars with the Turks
1571	First Holy League; Battle of Lepanto
1598–1621	Philip III rules as king of Spain
1621–1665	Philip IV rules as king of Spain
1683	Second Holy League
1700–1746	Philip V rules as first Bourbon king of Spain
1738–1746	War of Jenkins' Ear

THE ECLIPSE OF THE MEDITERRANEAN

In the 200 years between 1500 and 1700, the economic and political importance of the Mediterranean Sea diminished as the focus of power shifted to the Atlantic and northwestern Europe. One of the major reasons for this change was the new commercial sea route charted around Africa. Yet other factors, including the expansion of the Ottoman Empire, made the Mediterranean region the object of continuing European concern.

THE CHANGING DIMENSIONS OF TRADE

As the focus of European commerce, the Mediterranean had become something of an Italian lake by the 14th century because the carrying trade that sailed its waters was almost exclusively controlled by the Italian maritime states, especially Genoa and Venice.

By the 16th century, this profitable arrangement disappeared as Dutch and English ships began to take over the carrying trade, and the Portuguese began to use the new route around southern Africa, thereby cutting out the Muslim and Venetian middlemen. In 1521, the Venetian Republic, anxious to restore its declining trade position, offered to buy all the spices brought to Europe by Portugal, but the offer was refused. The last Flanders galley sailed from Venice in 1532, that to Alexandria in 1564, and the Beirut galley in 1570.

Mediterranean commerce did not, of course, come to an abrupt end. Rather, setbacks in the luxury trade were interspersed with sudden increases as it moved along its overall downward trajectory. A variety of circumstances accounted for this up and down movement, including interruptions of Portuguese and Dutch shipping caused by war in Europe and on the seas. In 1565, for example, as much pepper from India was passing through the Red Sea as arrived by the African route in Lisbon. The spice routes of the Levant remained active until well past the end of the century. In the 1600s, British trade with Italy increased greatly, and by the end of the century, Italian goods accounted for some 10 percent of all British imports. There is, in fact, some evidence that by the 18th century the volume of trade had begun to increase.

Nevertheless, the pattern and nature of the sea trade changed, and the Mediterranean became the location for a series of smaller, regional commercial economies, such as the Adriatic area, the eastern Mediterranean, and the Spanish-French coast. Locally produced items, such as finished woolens made in Florence, blown glass in Venice, and steel armor in Milan, were still sold throughout Europe, al-

Map 49.1 Southern Europe, c. 1700. Spanish rule in Central Europe and Northern and Southern Italy was to end the following century. Ottoman control of North Africa extended to Egypt (not visible on the map). Note the independent kingdom of Piedmont, in (modern) northwest Italy, which was to become the seed-bed of Italian unification in the next century.

though by the 17th century the French were offering serious competition in the manufacture of luxury goods.

THE MEDITERRANEAN WAR

In addition to the overseas discoveries of the great age of exploration, the Mediterranean economy experienced another change in the 15th century as a result of the capture of Constantinople by the Ottoman Turks in 1453. In 1565, the Turks unsuccessfully besieged the island fortress of Malta, ruled by the Knights of Saint John. By 1570, however, the Ottomans controlled some three-quarters of the Mediterranean coastline, a zone stretching east from the Istrian peninsula in the northern Adriatic, around Greece and the Balkans, across to Asia Minor and the Middle East, and thence westward across North Africa almost as far as Gibraltar. The Turkish expansion, coming on top of the new trade routes, seriously affected the economic well-being of the trading states, especially Venice.

In response to the Turkish threat, Venice, Spain, and the papacy joined forces in forming the Holy League in 1571, which marshaled a vast fleet of some 300 ships and 80,000 men. In October, this fleet met an equally strong Turkish force off the coast of Greece at Lepanto, an engagement that resulted in a major victory for the League. The Battle of Lepanto did not, however, profoundly alter the course of events. After Lepanto, in the western Mediterranean the Turks confined themselves mainly to the North African coast, although in the east they continued to secure strategic islands, including Crete in 1669.

Despite the frequent state of war between the Turks and the European powers, the economic unity of the Mediterranean did not end. The Ottomans were deeply interested in international trade. Muslim traders maintained representatives and branch offices in Venice and other western cities, while Turkish tax policy favored foreign merchants. The entire range of western commercial products, from coin, cloth, glass, and other manufactures to furs, lumber, and raw materials, found their way to the East, while Eastern commodities, including pepper, spices, oils, dyes, ivory, and slaves, continued to be supplied to Europeans. In this commercial sense, the Mediterranean Sea remained neutral in the European-Turkish wars.

On the other hand, if the Turkish military challenge did not stop Mediterranean commerce, merchants faced constant danger from the many pirates who roamed its waters, especially along the western shores of North Africa, where a series of "Barbary" states—named after the Berber tribes who inhabited the regions—had been established under Turkish rule. The Spanish and the Venetians led the struggle against these Muslim corsairs during the 17th century. After the Treaty of Utrecht in 1713–1714 (see below), the British controlled Gibraltar and Minorca and became the predominant naval force in the Mediterranean. Nevertheless, piracy persisted, and in the late 18th century the United States even had to pay tribute to protect its shipping. In 1801, however, the United States declared war against the pasha of Tripoli, and in 1815 against Algiers, thereby curtailing piracy.

FROM HAPSBURG TO BOURBON SPAIN

THE TWILIGHT OF SPANISH POWER

Philip III (ruled 1598–1621), the successor to his father Philip II (see Topic 42), took little interest in government. Devoting himself to religious ceremonies and the social life of the court, he left the direction of royal affairs to his favorite, the corrupt duke of Lerma (1552–1625). At home, he encouraged a new era of extravagant spending by his personal behavior, while abroad he was continually drawn into disputes that further drained the treasury. The economic plight of the realm worsened as population declined as a result of wars and emigration, a situation aggravated in 1609 to1610 when Lerma expelled the *Moriscos*—as the Muslims who had been forcibly converted to Christianity were called. The loss of the Moriscos, whose industry and business skills had enabled them to prosper, was a serious blow to the economy. Nor was Lerma's foreign policy any more successful, and in 1609 Spain was forced to end the revolt of the Netherlands by signing a truce that recognized the independence of the Protestant Dutch Republic, known as the United Provinces. Lerma was finally driven from power in 1618 by a conspiracy of young noblemen that included the count of Olivares (1587–1645).

Velazquez, *Portrait of the Count-Duke of Olivares,* c. 1640. The painting shows the Spanish politician and General at a critical point in his career, facing revolts in Flanders, Catalonia, and Portugal. The stormy weather and rearing horse convey a sense of tumult, as a city (Barcelona?) seems to be burning in the background to the left.

Philip IV (ruled 1621–1665), only 16 years old when he became king, proved an even weaker ruler than his father, but had in Olivares a tough and skillful minister. As the youngest son, Olivares had attended university and had prepared for a career in the church, but he succeeded unexpectedly to his father's title and wealth. Before Philip became king, Olivares had joined the prince's retinue and became a favorite courtier. Made a member of the highest noble rank, Olivares became Philip's chief minister in 1621. Although no less corrupt than Lerma, he quickly won the respect of the Spanish cortes by declaring an end to excessive spending at the court.

Olivares wanted to preserve Spain's status as a great power and to impose a rigidly centralized government on the nation. In foreign affairs, Olivares was determined to continue the war in Flanders, which soon became merely a minor aspect of two larger conflicts: the Thirty Years' War and the struggle between the Hapsburgs and the Bourbons.

Under Richelieu's leadership, France became the chief rival of Spain, which generally remained on the defensive both in Europe and the West Indies and steadily lost ground. The far-flung fighting required considerable money and large armies, and in order to meet both needs Olivares announced plans for a Union of Arms, according to which all parts of the empire would contribute men to a force of 140,000. The actual size of the army proved to be smaller, and some provinces refused to provide either men or money.

The crisis point was reached in 1640, when the French captured Arras and invaded Flanders, and separatist revolts broke out in Catalonia and Portugal. Catalonia represented a serious problem for Spanish unity because the fiercely independent Catalans had resisted all efforts by Olivares to undermine local privileges or to wrest increased taxes from the region. In 1640, as the war with France grew more precarious, Olivares sent troops to Catalonia, a move that sparked peasant uprisings against the soldiers and royal offi-

Velazquez, *Las Meninas (The Maids of Honor)*. 1656. 10 feet 5 inches by 9 feet (3.18 by 2.74 m). Velazquez has shown himself with paint palette in hand, wearing a red cross on his breast, symbol of the noble Order of St. James. He regarded this symbol as a sign of the recognition by the court that an artist was equal in social status to his patrons, even when they include Philip IV of Spain, who appears with his wife reflected in the rear mirror, watching work on a portrait of their daughter, the Infanta Margarita.

Derechos Reservados © Museo Nacional del Prado, Madrid

cials. Only after 12 years of savage fighting, during which Catalonia was overrun by Spanish and French armies, did Philip IV end the uprising.

Portugal, which had been seized by Philip II in 1580 but never formally incorporated into the Spanish realm, had been the object of Olivares' centralizing policies, including special taxation and a proposal to unite the cortes of Portugal and Castile. Governed by Philip's aunt, the viceroy Margaret of Savoy, Portugal seethed with discontent. After the outbreak of the Catalan revolt, the Portuguese rallied around the duke of Braganza, who led the break from Spain and was proclaimed King John IV (ruled 1640–1656) of an independent state.

In the wake of repeated setbacks, Olivares fell from power in 1643. Olivares, who objected to women "interfering" in political affairs, had alienated Philip IV's wife, Elizabeth (1602–1644), and the queen now insisted that Olivares be retired.

THE BOURBONS AND THE SPANISH SUCCESSION

On the death of Philip IV in 1665, Charles II (ruled 1665–1700) became king. Because he was only four years old at the time, the government was in the hands of his mother, Philip IV's second wife, Mariana of Austria (1634–1696). Moreover, Charles was not only mentally retarded but also handicapped by the famous "Hapsburg jaw," a physical deformity that afflicted family members in a more pronounced manner with each generation. The problem kept Charles from speaking or eating properly. After the end of the War of the League of Augsburg in 1697 (see Topic 50), Charles named Philip of Anjou, Louis XIV's grandson, as his heir. Less than a month later, the unfortunate Charles died.

Philip of Anjou ascended the throne of Spain as Philip V (ruled 1700–1746), the first Bourbon king of Spain. Philip's reign was thought by some to be the start of a new era of peace, but it began with the outbreak of the War of the Spanish Succession (see Topic 50) because the other powers feared the possible union of Spain and France. Philip was finally recognized as king of Spain by the Treaty of Utrecht (1713), in which he agreed that the crowns of the two nations would never be united.

From the outset, Philip had been influenced by Anne Marie, Princess Orsini (1635–1722), a handsome and intelligent woman who served as lady-in-waiting to the king's wife, Queen Maria Luisa (1688–1714), who ruled as regent while Philip was away during the war. Orsini supported French interests in Spain, and through her Louis XIV influenced Spanish policy. In 1708, however, Louis plotted with the British and Dutch to dismember the Spanish empire, and Orsini threw her support to Philip. When Maria Luisa died, Orsini's influence over Philip grew, together with that of the Italian Cardinal Giulio Alberoni (1664–1752).

For the remainder of Philip's reign, Spain was constantly embroiled in wars. In 1733, France and Spain concluded the Treaty of the Escorial, whereby the two states agreed to support each other in wars against the interests of

Sketch portrait of Charles III of Naples. 18th century. Charles ruled Naples from 1734 to 1759 and then succeeded to the Spanish throne on the death of his father, Philip V. A strongly absolutist monarch, Charles's attempts to expand Spanish holdings in South America met with defeat at the hands of the British.

Britain and Austria. In the War of the Polish Succession (1733–1735), in which each alliance supported a different claimant to the Polish throne, Spain occupied Naples and Sicily. Four years later, Spain and Britain began a prolonged trade war, known as the War of Jenkins' Ear, and this struggle was merged into the larger War of the Austrian Succession that erupted in 1740 (see Topic 56). Philip V died in 1746, before this conflict ended, leaving Spain weakened in power and reduced in status. By the time of Philip's death, the once-powerful Spanish empire had been seriously reduced in territory and prestige and overshadowed in international affairs by Britain and France.

EUROPE AND THE ITALIAN STATES

During the Renaissance and early modern period, while powerful, centralized monarchies emerged in France, England,

and Spain, Italy flourished as the land of culture but had no political identity. By the height of the Renaissance in the 15th century, the Italian peninsula consisted of about a dozen independent city-states, whose relations with each other were marked by economic competition and constant warfare. In response to the political anarchy of the period, Italy fell prey to foreign invasion and the larger struggle for power that consumed the great powers of Europe. For a century and a half, between 1559 and 1700, much of Italy came under the sway of the Spanish, whose policies greatly influenced social and economic conditions in the peninsula. After the War of the Spanish Succession, Spain's hegemony gave way to the influence of Austria, which dominated Italian affairs until national unification in the 19th century.

THE ITALIAN STATE SYSTEM

Five states dominated Italian affairs. In the north was the duchy of Milan, including the surrounding region of Lombardy. With the duchy of Savoy to its west, Venice to its east, and Genoa and Modena to the south, Milan was vulnerable to invasion. Because it lacked access to the sea, its economic life was more closely connected to Germany and Austria than to the rest of Italy. Venice, a republican oligarchy ruled by an elected doge and a hereditary senate, managed to maintain its maritime supremacy in the Mediterranean until the 16th century. Thereafter, its interest in the Venetian hinterland grew as its commercial empire shrank. South of Milan and Venice lay the city of Florence, which ruled the large region of Tuscany and had access to the Tyrrhenian Sea through the port of Leghorn (Livorno). South and east of Florence lay the Papal States, governed from Rome by the pope as an absolute monarch. Its territories spanned the peninsula from the Tyrrhenian to the Adriatic and included the virtually autonomous cities of Bologna and Ferrara. South of Rome and covering the remainder of the peninsula was the large Kingdom of Naples. The cities of Naples and Palermo were major commercial ports, while the large landed estates of

southern Italy and Sicily still provided much of the wheat for the Mediterranean world.

By the mid-16th century, a generation of war in the Italian peninsula left the independence and prosperity of these states in ruins. Peace came at last in 1559 with the Treaty of Cateau-Cambrésis, which left Milan, Naples, Sicily, and Sardinia directly in the hands of the Spanish Hapsburgs.

THE ERA OF SPANISH PREPONDERANCE

The century and a half of Spanish domination that followed Cateau-Cambrésis had an important impact on Italy. The period coincided with general economic difficulties for the peninsula, caused both by the changing sea routes and the fact that the position of the Italian bankers deteriorated as merchant and commercial capital began to develop in western and central Europe.

Spain attempted to centralize its administration in Italy, ruling its possessions through viceroys. In 1558, Philip II set up in Madrid a Council of Italy, whose members included two counselors from Milan and two from Sicily. One result of Spanish rule was that the political influence of the old aristocratic elites was seriously weakened, although they retained their legal and fiscal privileges on their huge estates. At the royal courts, however, a lavish and ornate social life developed among the aristocracy, and Spanish influence accelerated the aristocratic restructuring of Italian life. Campaigns were undertaken to counter periodic uprisings of the pro-French barons. The number of titles of nobility increased significantly, and Spanish nobles engaged in massive purchases of land. In addition, the close coordination between state and church that had marked Spanish history was now repeated in Spain's Italian possessions.

In Naples, Parliament, consisting of landowning nobles and members appointed by the crown, authorized the government to collect taxes, but after 1642 it was no longer summoned. Instead, the municipal government of the city of Naples became in effect the government for the entire realm. As Spain's need for money increased in the 17th century, the crown was forced to sell more of its land in the countryside, which was purchased by the quasi-feudal nobility. By the end of the century, some two-thirds of the kingdom's land consisted of noble estates. The middle class was small and without influence, so that the society of Spanish Italy proved to be inert and inflexible. Occasional popular outbreaks, most sparked by food shortages, plagued Spanish officials.

In Sicily, events took another course as a result of the island's different historical experience. The desire for independence remained strong in Sicily, but on the whole, Sicilians remained generally loyal to Spain. The island's society was rigidly feudal, with its agricultural land held by powerful barons in the form of massive estates that grew wheat and other cereals. In Sicily, however, the barons were pillars of the established order. The Parliament reflected a version of the hierarchical ordering of Old Regime society—three branches represented the barons, the church, and the crown.

SIGNIFICANT DATES

Italy

1454	Peace of Lodi
1494	French invasion of Italy
1527	Sack of Rome
1559	Treaty of Cateau-Cambrésis
1559–1700	Spanish preponderance in Italy
1713	Treaty of Utrecht grants Milan, Naples, and Sardinia to Austrians
1720	Duke of Piedmont becomes king of Sardinia
1734–1759	Charles III rules as first Bourbon king of Naples
1741–1790	Joseph II rules Austrian possessions

Milan was attached to Spain in 1540. Political power there was exercised by a royal governor, who ruled with a senate. Overall directives, of course, came from Madrid. In Milan, as in Naples, the aristocracy aped Spanish fashions and customs, especially in an ostentatious pomp called *spagnolismo* ("Spanishism").

With the other states of Italy, Spain's relations fell into two categories: Some states, such as the Duchy of Savoy, Genoa, and the Duchy of Tuscany, were satellite clients of Madrid, whereas the Papal States and Venice continued to operate as independent states.

THE AUSTRIAN HEGEMONY

Spanish preponderance in Italy came to an end at the close of the 17th century. With the death of Charles II, Philip IV's son, in 1700 Italy became once again the object of European attention. When Louis XIV's grandson secured the throne of Spain as Philip V, he laid claim to all of the former Hapsburg possessions. But the peace treaties that ended the War of the Spanish Succession stripped Spain of its Italian possessions: the Treaty of Utrecht (1713) granted Milan, Naples, and Sardinia to the Austrian Hapsburgs, while Sicily was given to the dukes of Savoy, whose realm was now elevated to a kingdom.

Austrian dominance brought Italy out of the political and social backwater of the Spanish period. Rule from Vienna not only proved more beneficial to the Italians but by the middle of the 18th century also brought to the peninsula the widespread reforms of enlightened despotism (see Topic 59). Under Joseph II (1741–1790), who became Holy Roman Emperor in 1765, Lombardy and the other Austrian possessions underwent even more far-reaching improvements.

In Naples, too, changes were significant. The nobility and urban upper classes demanded greater local autonomy and were governed by several effective administrators, including Wierich Lorenz, Count von Daun, who served as viceroy from 1713 to 1719. Lorenz not only improved the economy but also countered church influence in Naples and instituted university reforms.

In 1734, Elizabeth Farnese, wife of Philip V of Spain, succeeded in recapturing Sicily and Naples for her son, Don Carlos, who took the throne as Charles III (ruled Naples 1734–1759 and Spain 1759–1788), the first of the Neapolitan Bourbons. When Charles succeeded to the Spanish throne in 1759, he left the Kingdom of Naples to his son, Ferdinand (1751–1825), and an exceptionally able minister, Bernardo Tanucci (1698–1783), who ruled the realm until the young king came of age. Tanucci implemented reforms in the spirit of Enlightenment ideals, attempting to modernize the state administration.

Another key change in the Italian state system took place in 1737, when the last of the Medici rulers of Florence died. An international conference awarded the duchy to Francis of Lorraine (ruled 1738–1765), Maria Theresa's husband. Austrian authority in Italy was therefore extended further. Marked improvements in administration came along with a more liberal trade policy.

The one important counterpoint to Austrian hegemony in Italy was offered by the Savoyan rulers of the Kingdom of Sardinia. Savoy, the original homeland of the ambitious dynasty founded in 1026, lay at the strategically important location along the French Alps. In the 16th century, the Duchy of Savoy was occupied by the French, but the treaty of Cateau-Cambrésis restored its ruler, Emanuele Filiberto (ruled 1553–1580), to his realm. By skillful diplomacy he regained most of the territory that had been lost to the great powers and restored the capital at Turin.

Emanuele Filiberto's son, Carlo Emanuele (ruled 1580–1630), made the crucial decision to give portions of western Savoy to France in exchange for the tiny area of Saluzzo in 1601. The exchange marked the determination of the Savoyans to become an Italian power. In the years that followed, the dukes of Savoy gradually expanded their territory to include most of the northwestern region known as Piedmont, a program of expansion based on the skillful switching of sides in international disputes. The Savoyans developed a powerful military establishment to support their ambitions.

In 1713, Vittorio Amedeo II (ruled as duke 1675–1730, king of Sardinia 1713–1720, and king of Sardinia-Piedmont 1720–1730), who had played an important role in the War of the Spanish Succession along with his cousin Prince Eugene of Savoy (see Topic 50), was rewarded by his allies with the title of king of Sicily, which he then agreed to exchange for Sardinia in 1720. Thenceforth, the Kingdom of Piedmont-Sardinia was the only independent Italian state to play a vital role in international affairs. In the 19th century, its rulers would position themselves against the Austrian hegemony as they aspired to lead the movement to unite all of Italy under their rule.

Putting Southern Europe in Perspective

In 1500, the Mediterranean world was at the center of European civilization. While Italy represented the spectacular cultural achievements of the Renaissance, the empire of Charles V was the most powerful political and economic unit of the age. By the year 1600, the importance of the entire region had been eclipsed by the rise of

Continued next page

the states of northern and central Europe. A century later, Italy and Spain were minor players in the international arena. Spain, no longer the center of a transcontinental empire, had been reduced in territory and was economically depressed. Italy, occupied by foreign powers, underwent a long period of exploitation, only to reemerge again in the mid-18th century under the reforming impulse of the Austrian Hapsburgs.

Questions for Further Study

1. What changing conditions contributed to the decline of Spain and Italy?
2. Why did its American colonies not prevent the economic decline of Spain?
3. Why was Italy unable to achieve political centralization in the same way that France and England did?

Suggestions for Further Reading

Braudel, Fernand. *The Mediterranean and the Mediterranean World in the Age of Philip II*, 2 vols. New York, 1972–1973.

Carpanetto, Dino, and G. Ricuperati. C. Higgitt, trans. *Italy in the Age of Reason, 1685–1789*. New York, 1987.

Cochrane, Eric. J. Kirshner, ed. *Italy 1539–1630*. New York, 1988.

Darby, Graham. *Spain in the Seventeenth Century*. New York, 1994.

Elliott, John H. *The Count-Duke of Olivares: The Statesman in an Age of Decline*. New Haven, CT, 1986.

Frey, Linda, and M. Frey. *Societies in Upheaval: Insurrections in France, Hungary, and Spain in the Early Eighteenth Century*. New York, 1987.

Hanlon, Gregory. *Early Modern Italy, 1550-1800: Three Seasons of European History*. New York, 2000.

Kamen, Henry. *Philip V of Spain: The King Who Reigned Twice*. New Haven, CT, 2001.

Sella, Domenico. *Italy in the Seventeenth Century*. London, 1997.

InfoTrac College Edition

Enter the search term *Philip III of Spain* using Key Terms.

Enter the search term *Philip IV of Spain* using Key Terms.

ABSOLUTE MONARCHY: LOUIS XIV AND THE DIVINE RIGHT OF KINGS

In the 100 years after the mid-17th century, France stood at the center of European power. The sources of its strength included a population perhaps as large as 20 million by 1700, rich agricultural lands, and a strategic geographic location in western Europe, with its shores edging the English Channel and the North Sea, the Atlantic, and the Mediterranean. French preeminence was also the result of an efficient, centralized government, a powerful army, and a growing sense of national identity—all of which were characteristics of the new absolute monarchies then emerging. Much of the credit for these and other French achievements, both domestic and international, was the result of the policies of its ruler, King Louis XIV (ruled 1643–1715).

Louis advanced the centralization of the government and the building of a strong state bureaucracy, both of which had begun in the 16th century, by focusing supreme authority on his own person. The consolidation of royal power was achieved in part by further reducing the independence of an already weakened nobility and integrating its members into the structure of government. His long reign was also marked by prosperity in commerce and agriculture.

Louis would brook no domestic dissent and aimed to destroy any internal factors that threatened to weaken national unity, including religious differences. To a greater degree than any other king, he discovered the power of symbolism to mold opinion and create consensus among his subjects. His immense palace at Versailles was not only the most pronounced symbol of his grandeur, but also an important tool in bringing the nobility into the absolutist system. The resulting "absolute monarchy" that he forged became the model for many other European states and left a legacy of royal power that was destroyed only in the upheavals of the revolution of 1789.

Louis XIV espoused the beguiling ideology of power that identified reverence and obedience to his person with loyalty to and pride in France. With a thirst for military glory, he lavished huge sums on his army and undertook a series of foreign military campaigns that he hoped would round out the kingdom's borders and make it a powerful player in the international arena but that cost France dearly in resources and lives.

SIGNIFICANT DATES

The Age of Louis XIV

1648	Peace of Westphalia
1648–1653	Revolt of the Fronde against royal government
1602–1661	Life of Giulio Mazarin
1661	Plans for Palace of Versailles begin
1667–1668	War of Devolution
1672–1679	Dutch war
1619–1683	Life of Jean-Baptiste Colbert
1685	Edict of Nantes revoked
1689–1697	The War of the League of Augsburg
1701–1714	War of the Spanish Succession
1643–1715	Louis XIV rules as king of France

"I AM THE STATE": THE ABSOLUTIST GOVERNMENT

Contemporaries attributed to Louis XIV the phrase "I am the state." Whether he actually made this remark is unknown, but he certainly believed it. Louis did not, however, create centralized government or royal supremacy—these were the achievements of King Henry IV, and then of Louis XIII's chief minister, Cardinal Richelieu and his successor, Cardinal Mazarin (see Topic 44). Rather, Louis XIV reinforced the process and imbued **absolutism** with a theoretical framework and a brilliant practical example.

Louis was only a child of five years old when his father, Louis XIII, died in 1643. His Hapsburg mother, Anne of Austria, took up the reigns of power as regent and delegated extensive authority to Cardinal Mazarin. On the death of the Cardinal in 1661, Louis announced that he would be his own chief minister. The period from 1661 until his death in 1715 is known, therefore, as the "Age of Louis XIV," during which he ruled in his own right. His reign was the longest in European history.

Although he did not have a superior education, Louis XIV's appearance and personality were well suited to the role of king. His well-built body and heavy-featured face presented an impressive image. By today's standards he was short (about 5 feet 8 inches), but for his time he was of more than average height. Nevertheless, he wore platform shoes because he felt that the king should stand above his subjects. In public he dressed in the finest robes and furs and sported a long wig, cutting an elegant, if precious, figure. Serious by nature, he cultivated an imperious and dignified manner, yet he was always pleasant and courteous to his guests.

In 1660, Louis sought to solidify the Bourbon claim to the throne of Spain by marrying Princess Maria Theresa (1638–1683), daughter of the Spanish ruler Philip IV. Although they had six children—all of whom died before their father—Louis XIV had little romantic attachment to

Rigaud, *Louis XIV.* 1701. 9 feet by 6 feet 4 inches (2.77 by 1.94 m). Louis was 63 years old when this work was painted. The sagging face and stony gaze contrast with the gorgeous ermine-lined robes (decorated with the royal lily). The king's feet are arranged in a ballet pose, a reminder of the popularity of dancing at the French court.

© Réunion des Musées Nationaux/Art Resource, NY

his wife and kept several influential mistresses. He legitimized the six children he had with the Marquise de Montespan (1641–1707), but when he tired of her, she left the court. Her successor, Madame de Maintenon (1635–1719), actually married Louis on the death of Maria Theresa, but when Louis died, she too left Versailles.

DIVINE RIGHT MONARCHY AND THE STATE

Louis XIV sought unquestioned obedience from his subjects, regardless of their status or rank. He considered the royal will supreme over all political institutions. That he should wield such absolute authority was a claim based both on a political idea that had its roots in the Middle Ages and on a more recent concept. Medieval kings had been blessed with holy oil before assuming their thrones, thus, in effect, having been anointed by God. The concept of divine right implied that the monarch was God's earthly representative and that to oppose his will was a religious offense as well as political treason.

Although Louis XIV used such theories to justify his demand for far-reaching powers, he said that he used that

Painting of Madame de Maintenon, c. 1700. After the death of Louis XIV's wife, Maria Theresa, the king married his former mistress, who went to live with him at Versailles, part of which is visible at the back, through the window. The identity of the child is unknown; Louis had six children by his wife and six by an earlier mistress, the Marquise de Montespan.

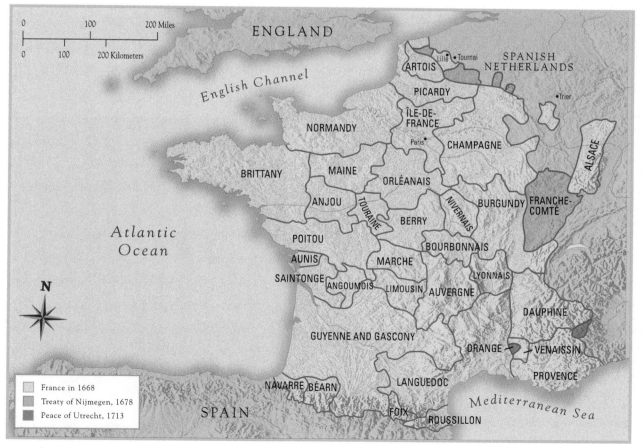

 Map 50.1 The France of Louis XIV. By 1713, with the Peace of Utrecht, France took on its modern appearance. Navarre split into two halves, the southern part going to Spain. The border with the modern state of Italy was to be modified the following century. Alsace remained contested by the new state of Germany from its creation in the 19th century, passing between France and Germany during the World Wars. In 1945, it was assigned to France. Go to http://info.wadsworth.com/053461065X for an interactive version of this map.

authority for the benefit of France. He wanted his subjects to think of the king as the embodiment of France and to see themselves as having a common destiny as subjects of a prosperous, well-ordered state. In order to generate a national consciousness, Louis tried to insert the state into more and more aspects of daily life, including the economy, religious affairs, and culture. In a kingdom in which regional loyalties were still strong and where the bulk of the inhabitants lacked a standard education or even a uniform language, the symbolism of the king was a powerful force around which to rally the masses.

Despite the theory of divine right, in actual practice age-old traditions of special rights and privileges enabled the nobility, the cities, the provinces, and the Catholic Church to limit royal authority. Louis XIV devoted considerable energy to undermining these limitations on his power, as his predecessors had done before him. His goal was for all individuals to owe loyalty to him rather than to corporations such as guilds, the church, or social class. His talents as ruler included the ability to choose intelligent and able ministers. Together with them, he reshaped the French government and its bureaucracy, reorganizing old and creating new administrative offices, and widening the powers of royal officials. As a reward for loyal service to the crown, the king sometimes gave high-ranking civil servants titles of nobility. Such bureaucratic "nobles of the pen" had little in common with the hereditary "nobles of the sword," whose estates and privileges were often of feudal origin and who worked incessantly to stave off royal encroachments on their rights.

Agents of the crown, from ministers to clerks, held office at the will of the monarch, and his ability to appoint and remove them made for a bureaucracy dependent on the king but free of other influences. The foundation of royal administration was the *intendants*, the king's chief representatives in the 30 provincial districts known as "generalities." As developed by Richelieu, the original duty of the *intendants* had been to collect taxes, but their responsibilities soon included conscripting soldiers, reporting on local economic conditions, taking part in lawsuits, and enforcing royal edicts. As the *intendants* intervened in more and more aspects of local affairs, they became the target of noble resentment, whose rights and privileges they deliberately undermined.

Two long-established administrative bodies, the estates and the parlements, continued to exercise independent authority, although their rights were also weakened. The estates were local legislative assemblies, composed of representatives of the clergy, the nobility, and the remaining population. Increasingly, however, their only purpose was to vote special sums of money to the king. The Estates General, France's national assembly, was last called in 1614 and would not meet again until 1789. The parlements, on the other hand, were provincial supreme courts of appeal that had the power to register the king's edicts. If they found just cause to do so, they could in effect veto royal action. In such instances, however, Louis XIV resorted to a royal prerogative that had been practiced by his predecessors in the 16th century: by invoking the *lit de justice*, he could appear personally before the parlement and declare his edict registered. The parlement of Paris, with jurisdiction over a vast area of central and northern France, was the only institution that presented serious resistance to Louis XIV's policies, but even here he usually had his way.

COLBERT AND THE PROSPERITY OF FRANCE

An important aspect of Louis' domestic policy was stimulation of trade and production to promote prosperity. As a result, government regulation of commerce and manufacturing increased under the policy known as mercantilism, which sought to make the kingdom as self-sufficient as possible in a government-regulated economy (on mercantilism, see Topic 46).

All economic affairs came under the direction of the Controller General Jean Colbert (1619–1683), a financial genius who had trained under Mazarin. Colbert's aims included full employment at home, a vigorous program of trade for a large French merchant marine, and lucrative overseas colonies. He negotiated favorable commercial agreements with other nations and built a powerful navy to protect the French merchant fleet. To promote colonial expansion, Colbert used government funds to found several overseas trading companies, including the East India Company and the West India Company.

Colbert did much to improve agricultural productivity and French forestry, although at first he increased the tax burden on the peasantry by raising the *taille*. Nevertheless, industry remained his major interest. He extended govern-

The Metropolitan Museum of Art, Gift of the Wildenstein Foundation, Inc. 1951. (51.34) Photograph © 1979 The Metropolitan Museum of Art

Portrait of Jean-Baptiste Colbert, finance minister to Louis XIV. Late 17th century. In addition to his reform of the taxation system and encouragement of industry, Colbert was also a patron of the arts. He helped organize the financing of the building program at Versailles, realizing its importance in both artistic and political terms.

ment loans to private manufacturers, organized companies, used tax policies to stimulate investment, and encouraged the immigration of skilled workers and artisans from abroad. Government regulations and inspectors ensured the high quality of French textiles, while Colbert fostered entirely new industries tied to colonization, such as sugar and tobacco refining. Roads were reconstructed and maintained, and a network of canals was built, including one that connected the Atlantic to the Mediterranean. Finally, Colbert restructured the French finances and reformed the tax policy to make the system more equitable: He lowered the *taille*, from which nobles were exempt, and raised taxes that were shared more equitably by all French subjects.

Colbert's policies were successful, and French industry and trade became preeminent in Europe. Nevertheless, the almost endless wars of Louis XIV set back prosperity and worsened living conditions at home for most of the population. Furthermore, while the economic programs sponsored by Colbert worked in the 17th century, by the mid-18th century France began to fall behind England, where new factory methods and machinery stimulated the Industrial Revolution.

NOBLES, JANSENISTS, AND HUGUENOTS: THE DOMESTIC OPPOSITION

In his desire to bring all elements in French society under the authority of his absolute government, Louis XIV sought to impose obedience and uniformity on the nobility and religious minorities. His methods in dealing with each group were different, but the aim was the same.

VERSAILLES: BUILDING A ROYAL COURT

Many aristocrats eventually accommodated themselves to Louis XIV's absolutism, realizing that government offices and royal favors represented a new avenue to status and influence. As the nobles were increasingly integrated into the state, they eschewed revolt and opposition in favor of cooperation and service to the king. Louis XIV intentionally made the royal court the center of social and political life for his "domesticated" nobility. The court, located originally in Paris, but eventually moved to Versailles, acted as a magnet for the entire range of nobles, from the wealthiest to the poorest. The location of the palace at Versailles kept the nobles out of Paris, where the bureaucracy was, and away from their own estates, making it difficult for them to amass regional power.

Louis XIV wanted to use the court as an instrument for molding the nobility into docile servants. In 1668, he ordered his architects to design a royal palace at Versailles, outside Paris, where his father had a hunting lodge. This 40-year project resulted in the most sumptuous royal residence in Europe, a tremendous complex consisting of an original central section designed by Louis Le Vau (1612–1670) and two later wings on each side. The northern wing was the work of the brilliant architect Jules Hardouin-Mansart (1646–1708), whose uncle François had introduced the sloping "mansard" roof. The palace was at the center of huge formal gardens, fountains, and walkways.

The great palace of Versailles, with its impressive façade and a luxurious interior resplendent with rich marbles, the golden glimmer of gilt, and mirrored hallways, proved to be an ideal stage for the court of the Sun King. To decorate the palace, Louis XIV hired a vast army of artists and craftsmen. Charles Le Brun (1619–1690), director of the famous Gobelins tapestry factories, labored for 18 years

Painting of an aerial view of the Palace of Versailles. 18th century. The painter leads the viewer's eye through the great entranceway, with its two semicircular structures back to the main palace itself, and then on to the sunlit formal garden at the rear. There are other gardens to left and right. The transformation of a simple hunting lodge into the most sumptuous royal residence in Europe took 40 years.

Chateau de Versailles, France/Peter Willi/Bridgeman Art Library

HISTORICAL PERSPECTIVES

LOUIS XIV: A BUREAUCRATIC KING

JOHN C. RULE   Ohio State University

Born on September 5, 1638, the infant prince Louis was dubbed "the God-given" by his delighted parents, Louis XIII and Anne of Austria, and by an ecstatic French people. The future Louis XIV's pedigree was impeccable. His mother's forebears were Hapsburgs of Spain, Burgundy, and Austria; his father sprang from a long line of Bourbon-Valois-Capetian kings of France; and his paternal grandmother descended from the Medici princes of Florence. Fortunately for France and for the Bourbon dynasty, Louis lived 77 years and ruled personally for 54.

In 1648 the kingdom was plunged into a bloody civil war, ironically named after a Parisian slingshot, the Fronde. Led by a band of prominent magistrates, great nobles, and princes of the blood, the revolt spread devastation to northern and eastern France. Ultimately the Frondeurs failed to wrest power from either Cardinal Mazarin or Queen Anne herself. Much credit for the preservation of the royal prerogative, and indeed for Louis XIV's own political and personal survival, was due to the dogged determination of his mother, the astute diplomacy of Cardinal Mazarin, and the dedicated service of a faithful group of secretaries of state and their clerks. The Fronde offered the young king practical lessons in statecraft: a fear of overmighty subjects and ambitious princes, like his cousin, the Prince of Condé; and a trust of an inner group of "new men" in politics, career diplomats and enterprising provincial magistrates.

Cardinal Mazarin, Louis' faithful guide and tutor, died early in 1661. His enemies accused the cardinal of ruling through fear, favor, and fraud. But whatever his faults, Mazarin instilled in his tutee the desire and courage to rule by himself, without a principal minister. When his courtiers asked him to whom they would now address their petitions, Louis replied: "To me." Even his mother was heard to chuckle, but the last laugh was on the king's foes from the Fronde era. Louis excluded from the High Council relatives, churchmen, great nobles, and feudal functionaries like the chancellor of France. This realignment of the High Council and subsequent growth of government departments is termed the Ministerial Revolution of the 1660s.

One of the most significant accomplishments of Louis XIV's reign, of which the Ministerial Revolution represented but a part, was the king's choice to rule his kingdom through a patrimonial bureaucratic government. That is a government of civilian ministers, who through councils and bureaus, formally governed France by executive decrees drafted in the king's name. Informally, these ministers governed through factions of cousins, clients, and "creatures" of the crown, experts and clerks in the various ministries.

Louis XIV promoted two families of Mazarin's "faithful" secretaries to lead the patrimonial bureaucratic government: the Colberts and the Le Telliers. Both families had risen from the financial-legal elite; both had recently been ennobled. These new ministers drew their support in large measure from the urban elites clustered in the provincial capitals, port cities, industrial towns, army strongholds, and from Paris itself. Both families, and their allies among the administrators, sought to influence local politics by extending to urban elites and factions at court, among other rewards, offices in the government, clerical preferment, careers in the armed forces, inexpensive leases of royal

on paintings and murals showing the glories of the king. Cabinetmakers produced the finest examples of furniture in rare woods and gilt mountings, while glassworkers made glittering chandeliers and embroiderers decorated cushions, bedspreads, and linens. Overall, the architecture of Versailles and its interiors reflect the "grand style" of the Age of Louis XIV, an elegant, Classically inspired backdrop for the daily rituals of court life.

For Louis XIV, Versailles was a system of government and social control as well as a residence. He deliberately encouraged practices in which courtiers competed with each other to carry out minor acts of service that symbolized their status, from awakening the king to lighting his way at night by bearing candles. Maintaining the kind of lifestyle required at Versailles strained the financial resources of many nobles, which in turn made them increas-

lands, long-term loans, contracts for public works, advantageous marriages for their children, noble titles, and even the "honor" of being presented at court. It was government by faction, patronage, and gesture.

The rise of royal patrimonial government witnessed the rapid centralization and increase in bureaucracy. The department of finances, headed by Controller General Colbert, quintupled in size, as did the ministries of the marine, headed by Colbert's son, and war, headed by the Le Telliers. The ministry of foreign affairs followed a similar pattern of expansion under the guidance of Colbert's brother, Croissy, and his nephew, Torcy, two of France's ablest diplomats.

Colbert and Michel-François Le Tellier vied with one another to satisfy the king's passion for the arts and architecture and, above all, for collecting. Perhaps the king felt deprived as a young man of what he considered to be a regal prerogative: the privilege of surrounding himself with objects of beauty and magnificence. Cardinal Mazarin had amassed a far greater collection of such objects than had Louis XIV. Thus Colbert and the Le Telliers dispatched agents across Europe to purchase paintings, prints, drawings, sculpture, jewels, precious plate, furniture, and rare books. These treasures were housed in the Louvre palace, rebuilt as an art gallery, a library, and home for scholars and artists. These privileged artists and men of letters trumpeted Louis as an Apollo of the Arts, a Mars in War, a New Alexander, Louis the Great.

And it was as Louis the Great that the king sought to satisfy his *gloire*, or desire for reputation, by building one of the greatest royal residences and sets of government in the West—the palace of Versailles. Versailles represented the king's vision of a new capital, a city of marble, set in a garden spot, built entirely at his orders; and though only 12 miles from Paris, it was a world apart, remote from overmighty magistrates, street mobs, and the stink of Seine River refuse.

In the mid-1660s Louis instructed Colbert to find money for the construction of his new capital at the site of his father's hunting lodge at Versailles.

Completing the work far outstretched Colbert's life and that of the marquis of Louvois. Satellite palaces at the Trianon and Marly were added, as were the extensions of the gardens. "Such wonders rival ancient Rome," exclaimed a visiting noble. "The palace," said an official, "spreads and sustains the glory of His Majesty." Other observers were not so kind. The gossipy duke of Saint-Simon thought of Versailles as a "cold, dark, damp and malodorous pile." And the English poet Matthew Prior remarked that Louis XIV's "house is . . . the foolishest in the world; he is strutting in every panel and galloping over one's head in every ceiling, and if he turns to spit he must see himself in person or his Viceregent the Sun."[1] By the end of the century Versailles had, however, become not only a shrine to kingship and the seat of government but one of the greatest tourist attractions in all Europe.

Louis was a man of enormous pride of family and dynasty. His quest for *gloire* in the field of military conquest and religious conformity has been bitterly criticized by Frenchmen and foreigners alike. But his actions at the time were popular, especially among the new urban elite, the financiers, and men of commerce, the solid Catholic middle class, patriotic churchmen, the "new men" in politics, the army and navy, and the arts. After the disturbances of the Fronde and the earlier religious wars, these groups sought a prince who would bring a measure of domestic order and external security to the kingdom. Both of these goals were to a certain extent realized: militarily, with the addition of provinces in the northeast of France and domestically with the extension of royal government, public works, town planning, and encouragement of the arts.

Louis XIV died in September 1715, fearing that he had loved war too much but certain that, though "I am dying the State lives on."

[1]John C. Rule, ed., *Louis XIV and the Craft of Kingship* (Columbus, Ohio: Ohio State University Press, 1970), 42.

ingly dependent on royal patronage. Perhaps as many as 10,000 people, including a vast retinue of cooks and servants, crowded into Versailles, where unheated rooms and a lack of toilet facilities created as much stench as glamour. Because anyone who served at Versailles was exempt from taxes, many of the service personnel were stand-ins for middle-class Parisians who had purchased their positions at court.

RELIGIOUS DISSENT AND ITS SUPPRESSION

Ever since the 15th century, French kings had enjoyed a high degree of control over the French Catholic Church. The Jesuits controlled education for most of the nobility and served as confessors to the 17th-century kings, including Louis XIV. Over the years, a working alliance between the crown and the French clergy evolved, and in

The Salon de la Guerre (War Chamber) at Versailles. Begun 1676. The stucco medallion showing a victorious Louis XIV on horseback is Classical in style, as are some of the decorative motifs. The whole effect, though, is one of Baroque magnificence, with plentiful use of inlaid stone and gilding.

1682, a French ecclesiastical assembly adopted the Declaration of Gallican (after Gaul, the ancient Roman name for France) Liberties, which proclaimed a degree of independence from papal authority.

Yet two religious groups—the Huguenots (Calvinists) and the Catholic Jansenists—disturbed the religious uniformity that was expressed in the formula adopted by Louis, "One king, one law, one faith." During the civil-religious wars of the 16th century, many of the old nobles of the sword had converted to Protestantism largely as an act of defiance against the monarchy, and by the reign of Louis XIV there were still some 1.5 million Huguenots.

From the start of his personal rule, Louis worked systematically to undermine the Edict of Nantes (1598) (see Topic 44), which had granted the Huguenots a measure of toleration and civil liberties and had made France an anomaly among continental monarchies. He drove them out of public office and certain professions, taxed them heavily, and quartered troops in their towns. In 1685 Louis XIV revoked the Edict entirely, leaving French Protestants little choice but conversion to Catholicism. Some went underground or did convert, but perhaps as many as 200,000 left for the Dutch Republic, Prussia, England, and the New World, depriving France of valuable skills and experience.

Although the Jansenists were smaller in number than the Huguenots, they had many prominent followers, including the philosopher Blaise Pascal (see Topic 48) and many of the magistrates in the Paris parlement. The Jansenists formed a closely knit group whose theological beliefs about predestination were close to those of Calvinism. They asserted the central importance of God's grace in achieving salvation, questioned the authority of all human beings, including kings and popes, and openly opposed the Jesuits. In 1660, Louis XIV persuaded the papacy to ban Jansenism and then destroyed its headquarters at Port-Royal.

The attacks against the Huguenots and the Jansenists earned Louis a reputation as a religious bigot and persecutor, but Louis saw both issues as a matter of religious unity and in terms of the maintenance of his authority as an absolute ruler.

WAR, DIPLOMACY, AND THE QUEST FOR FRENCH HEGEMONY

Louis XIV was a man obsessed by the quest for glory—for France, certainly, but above all for himself. He believed that his achievements would reflect on the French people, and to that end he embarked on a succession of foreign wars that some authorities believe was aimed at achieving what he called France's "natural boundaries"—the Rhine, the Pyrenees, the Alps, and the sea. In the process, Louis created the image of an aggressive, warlike France, and made himself an object of hatred throughout Europe.

MILITARY REFORM

In planning and executing his wars, as in pursuing his other policies, Louis XIV had the help of able advisers. From his vantage point as head of economic planning, Colbert had become an advocate of French sea power, having expended huge sums on building a strong navy and a merchant marine. Colbert believed that the chief obstacle to French commercial predominance was the Dutch Republic, the most prosperous trading state, in whose ships much of Europe's trade goods were carried.

In contrast to Colbert's naval strategy, the argument for a powerful land army was made by François Le Tellier, the marquis de Louvois (1641–1691). Louvois, who succeeded his father as war minister in 1666, encouraged Louis XIV in his search for military glory. He completely reorganized the army, introducing the idea of promotion on the basis of merit, providing his troops with standard uniforms, and standardizing enlistment and drafting procedures. Colonel Jean Martinet (?–1672) introduced such vigorous drill regulations that his name became a synonym for a strict disciplinarian. Gradually, Louvois increased the size of the army from about 20,000 to 400,000. He also created the first real "standing army," a permanent military force always ready for deployment, which took the place of both the mercenary private armies and the old fighting groups raised for specific purposes and commanded by feudal nobles. Such a regular army created the need for much greater government revenue. Furthermore, Louvois set up an elaborate supply system, replete with supply depots, and greatly increasing the production of munitions and gunpowder. Working alongside Louvois was Marshal Sébastien de Vauban (1633–1707), the greatest military engineer of the age. He designed and built a ring of fortresses and fortified towns to protect the frontiers, an approach to defense that the French followed for the next 300 years. He also planned brilliant siege operations against enemy installations.

THE WAR OF DEVOLUTION AND THE DUTCH CAMPAIGN

Louis' first foreign adventure was the War of Devolution (1667–1668), waged against Spain on the basis of a claim to the Spanish Netherlands through his wife, the daughter of Philip IV's first marriage. The immediate point of the claim was that Louis had never received the large dowry that Philip had promised to pay.

When the Spanish king died and left all of his property to a son by a second marriage, Louis protested and called on an old Flemish tradition whereby property devolved to the children of a first marriage. Louis launched an attack against the fortified cities of Flanders and Franche-Comté

(Burgundy). Victory seemed in his grasp, but England, Sweden, and the United Provinces joined in an alliance and forced Louis to the peace table. By the treaty of Aix-la-Chapelle (1668), Spain ceded to France strategic sections of the Belgian Netherlands, including fortified cities. The first of his wars ended, therefore, with a minor victory for Louis, intensifying his thirst for glory.

Louis blamed the Dutch for having organized the alliance against him and believed that the Dutch would make an easy target because their country was on the edge of civil war. The republican, middle-class government there, which Louis despised, was led by Jan De Witt (1625–1672), whose party was supported by middle-class town dwellers, the wealthiest business leaders, aristocrats, and religious liberals. The head of the opposition was the prince of Orange, William III (*stadholder* of the United Provinces 1672–1702, king of England 1689–1702), whose family had held the title of *stadholder* for generations and had the backing of the Calvinist clergy and nobles.

Louis declared war against the Dutch Republic in 1672, and De Witt assumed command of the Dutch forces. The French marched rapidly into Lorraine, and from there down the Rhine into the Dutch Republic. The Dutch murdered De Witt and his brother, whom they blamed for their setbacks, and William III took command. Acting boldly, William organized a determined Dutch resistance and ordered the dikes opened, thereby flooding the northern areas of the Dutch Republic and halting the French advance. But when Louis refused the generous peace terms offered by William, he aroused the fears of Prussia, the Holy Roman Empire, and Spain into joining a coalition against him. When Parliament forced Charles II of England to join the anti-French alliance, Louis agreed to make peace. The Dutch, who promised henceforth to remain neutral, lost nothing. Instead, in the treaties of Nijmegen (1678 and 1679), Spain agreed to surrender to France the province of Franche-Comté and several fortified sections of Flanders, the latter areas being contiguous to those obtained in the War of Devolution.

THE WAR OF THE LEAGUE OF AUGSBURG

The prestige of Louis XIV and the international stature of France were at a new high, although this had been achieved at a great cost. Louis had succeeded in extending French frontiers, but he nevertheless aspired to win greater glory on the battlefield. The precise extent of his ambitions remains unclear, but to his foreign contemporaries his goal appeared to be nothing less than the establishment of French hegemony over the West. Within a few years after the last Nijmegen treaty in 1679, Louis began pushing along his northern and eastern borders, where a medley of tiny estates, towns, and fiefs coexisted without clear jurisdiction. His most important gain in this process was Strasbourg, the principal city of Alsace, which he absorbed in 1681. Alarmed by this thrust into Germany, Emperor Leopold I (ruled 1658–1705) of the Holy Roman Empire formed the League of Augsburg in 1686, eventually bringing German states such as Saxony, Bavaria, and the Palatinate together with England, Spain, Sweden, and the United Provinces. It was this League against which the ever bolder Louis XIV fought his third war.

The conflict had its immediate origins in the fall of 1688, when Louis sent an army into the Palatinate, a territory located west of the Rhine. This War of the League of Augsburg assumed an international character as a result of the fighting between France and England in North America, the West Indies, and India, where it was known as "King William's War." In the two earlier wars, Louis had enjoyed the neutrality of England, but the Glorious Revolution that unseated the English monarch now put William III of Orange, Louis' staunch enemy, on the English throne (see Topic 51). William set as his goal the defeat of France. The war began in 1689 and lasted almost a decade. For the first several years, the French armies won one important victory after another in Europe, while the war at sea went in favor of the allies. The Peace of Ryswick (1697) followed a long and ruinous struggle that drained French economic strength and manpower. By its terms, Louis was forced to give back all the territories that his "chambers of reunion" had declared to be his, with the exception of Strasbourg. In addition, the borders of the Spanish Netherlands were henceforth to be protected by Dutch soldiers, and Louis promised to reduce the high import tariffs against Dutch goods that Colbert had introduced. Perhaps most humiliating of all, Louis had to recognize William III as the legitimate king of England.

THE WAR OF THE SPANISH SUCCESSION

The fourth and last war of Louis XIV brought the Sun King full circle. Louis had been induced to conclude a peace agreement in 1697 because he saw a grand opportunity to achieve Bourbon dominance over Spain. Although greatly weakened, the Spanish crown still controlled a vast empire in America as well as a portion of the Netherlands and the southern half of Italy. The hapless King Charles II (ruled 1665–1700), the son born from Philip IV's second marriage, proved to be the last Hapsburg king of Spain. Because Charles had no direct heirs, Louis hoped to gain the Spanish throne for one of his own children, since the dowry of his Spanish wife had never been paid. The major stumbling block was the fact that the Emperor Leopold I, a Hapsburg, was the nearest male relative of Charles II and therefore claimed the Spanish throne for himself.

The War of the Spanish Succession (1701–1714) brought together the Grand Alliance of England, the Holy Roman Empire, the United Provinces, Hanover, and several German princes, all determined that Louis XIV would not get his way. For his part, Louis had joined forces with Savoy and Bavaria, although England later persuaded the duke of Savoy to change sides in return for the title of king. The brilliant John Churchill, duke of Marlborough (1650–1722), drove the French from Germany at the Battle of Blenheim in 1704, while Prince Eugene of Savoy (1663–1736) pushed them out of Italy. A bloody engagement at Malplaquet in 1709 secured the Spanish Netherlands for the allies at the cost of an unprecedented 40,000 casualties. As one defeat followed another for the French, Louis XIV rallied his subjects with a patriotic appeal and called up his last recruits, melting gold ornaments from Versailles to raise the necessary funds to fight the war.

By 1712, an exhausted France and a weakened Grand Alliance agreed to a negotiated settlement. William III had died at the beginning of the war, but his successor, Queen Anne (ruled 1702–1714), pursued the conflict relentlessly in the colonies and on the seas, where it was known as "Queen Anne's War." When the Tories came to power, however, they pushed for peace. Moreover, Leopold's son became emperor as Charles VI (ruled 1711–1740), raising the specter of a Hapsburg ruling Spain, Austria, and the Holy Roman Empire. The Treaty of Utrecht (1713) recognized Louis' grandson as King Philip V (ruled 1713–1746) of Spain, with the stipulation that the thrones of Spain and France would never be united. As compensation, the Hapsburgs of Austria obtained the Spanish Netherlands, Naples, Milan, and Sardinia. Britain's reward was in the form of overseas possessions, gaining Newfoundland, Nova Scotia, and Hudson's Bay from France, and Gibraltar, along with the *Asiento* (a monopoly of the slave trade going to Spanish America) from Spain. The Dutch got back their frontier fortifications, while the Hohenzollern ruler of Brandenburg was recognized as king of Prussia.

As a result of the War of the Spanish Succession, France lost colonies but none of its European territory and had the satisfaction of seeing a Bourbon on the throne of Spain. Louis' daring bid for hegemony had failed, although it had taken the combined weight of Europe's great powers to defeat him. France was burdened with a devastated economy, marked by inflation, a huge debt, ever-higher taxes, and a serious decline in its overseas trade. Crop failures and famine made the conditions caused by war even worse.

Putting Louis XIV in Perspective

The long reign of Louis XIV was fraught with contradictions: Versailles stands not only as the timeless symbol of royal grandeur, but also as an expression of the ambition of one man. As a result of the succession of costly wars that he fought, Louis succeeded in acquiring more territory than any French monarch since the Middle Ages, but the wars also weakened the absolutist state that he had worked so tirelessly to create. He did not succeed in stamping out Protestantism in France, and the prosperity built by Colbert dissipated. Even the immense authority that he accumulated could not be passed on intact to his successors. In the end, the historical memory of glittering mirrors and elegant palaces remains as the vivid legacy of Louis XIV. Yet perhaps only a grand monarch of his stature could have acknowledged his own limitations—on his deathbed in 1715, the Sun King lectured his heir, the Dauphin Louis, to avoid the excesses of state spending and war that he had pursued so relentlessly.

Questions for Further Study

1. How would you describe the goals and methods of the absolutist state?
2. What was the nature of the relationship between Louis XIV and the French nobility? What role did Versailles play in that relationship?
3. Were Louis XIV's foreign policies a failure or a success?

Suggestions for Further Reading

Beik, William. *Absolutism and Society in Seventeenth-Century France.* New York, 1985.

Briggs, Robin. *Early Modern France, 1560–1715.* New York, 1977.

Burke, Peter. *The Fabrication of Louis XIV.* New Haven, CT, 1992.

Dunlap, Ian. *Louis XIV.* New York, 2000.

Goubert, Pierre. *Louis XIV and Twenty Million Frenchmen.* New York, 1972.

Hattan, R.M., ed. *Louis XIV and Absolutism.* Columbus, OH, 1977.

Kettering, Sharon. *French Society, 1589-1715.* Harlow, 2001.

Le Roy Ladurie, Emmanuel, with the collaboration of Jean-Francois Fitou. Arthur Goldhammer, trans. *Saint-Simon and the Court of Louis XIV.* Chicago, 2001.

Mettam, Roger. *Power and Faction in Louis XIV's France.* Oxford, 1988.

Rule, John, ed. *Louis XIV and the Craft of Kingship.* Columbus, OH, 1970.

InfoTrac College Edition

Enter the search term *Louis XIV* using Key Terms.

ENGLAND AND THE RISE OF CONSTITUTIONAL MONARCHY

The general trend toward absolute monarchy in the 17th century, exemplified by the reign of Louis XIV in France, revealed several exceptions: Poland, the United Provinces, and principally England. In the latter, despite the centralizing efforts of the Tudor rulers, especially Elizabeth I, a different tradition of government developed. A special set of religious, economic, and social conditions, combined with the peculiar personalities of Elizabeth's successors, led to the taming of royal authority.

Restrictions on royal power had been evolving in England since the Middle Ages. Feudal nobles, resisting encroachments on their rights by the kings, had enacted a series of charters that sought to protect basic liberties against royal tyranny. Parliament, consisting of the House of Lords and the House of Commons, had acquired increasing control over legislation and taxation. Finally, much of English common law, made up of legal customs and precedents compiled by judges over the centuries, had the effect of reinforcing individual rights. So strong had the force of common law become that some legal scholars argued that even the king was bound by it.

In the first half of the 17th century, the English had directly assaulted the principle of absolute monarchy. The confrontation between Parliament and the Stuart kings led to the dictatorial rule of Oliver Cromwell. Cromwell's death created a general sense of relief but left the country without an effective government. The restoration of the Stuart family to the throne in 1660 was therefore a widely popular move. Nevertheless, it seemed that the Stuarts were incapable of learning any lessons from the bloody fate of their predecessor, Charles I. In 1688, three years after the accession of James II, England experienced the "Glorious" Revolution, in which William III of the United Provinces and his wife Mary, daughter of James II, were put on the throne. In accepting the partnership of Parliament, the new monarchs eliminated any further danger of absolute monarchy in England.

Parliamentary rule continued to evolve during the course of the 18th century, as a new form of government began to develop in which day-to-day executive power was exercised by a cabinet of ministers that was responsible to the House of Commons. The members of the elected house came increasingly from two political parties: the Whigs and the Tories.

SIGNIFICANT DATES

Constitutional Monarchy in England

1662	Act of Uniformity
1670	Treaty of Dover
1660–1685	Charles II reigns as king of England
1685–1688	James II rules as king of England
1688	Glorious Revolution
1688	John Locke's *Two Treatises on Civil Government*
1689	Bill of Rights
1707	Act of Union
1702–1714	Anne rules as queen of England
1714–1727	George I rules as king of England
1676–1745	Life of Robert Walpole
1721–1760	George II rules as king of England

By Courtesy of the National Portrait Gallery, London

Portrait of Charles II of England. Late 17th century. Seen here in an uncharacteristically serious mood, Charles was known as the "Merry Monarch." The restoration of the monarchy in England, which he ushered in, saw a revival of the arts and scientific studies. Restoration drama, in particular comedy, marked one of the high points in the history of the theater in England.

THE STUART RESTORATION

Cromwell's experiment with republicanism convinced a majority of the English people that monarchy—albeit a chastised monarchy with severely limited powers—was a better system of government. The tumultuous experiences of the past 50 years made it clear not only that Parliament must share power with the monarch, but also that moderate Protestantism was firmly entrenched in England. Surprisingly, neither Charles II nor James II proved capable of absorbing these lessons.

CHARLES II

Known as the "Merry Monarch," Charles II (ruled 1660–1685) was a man who combined refined taste and polished manners with lustful appetites. The Puritans, scandalized by his private life, accused him of indulging in "fornication, drunkenness, and adultery." He was an avid patron of the theater, and among his numerous mistresses was the actress Nell Gwyn (1650–1687), who bore him two sons. Cromwell's rigid Calvinist policies, including the banning of plays, sports, and popular music, had never been well received, and Charles now presided over a reinvigorated court life and a new moral laxity among the nobility. Gambling was the rage, and the king led the way in hunting, dancing, and riding. Restoration drama was particularly known for bawdy scenes and dialogue that Puritans found shocking. A monarch without principles, Charles was a shrewd tactician, always willing to compromise or retreat. With the memory of his father's beheading always vivid, he trusted no one; the king, wrote one of his advisers, "lived with his ministers as he did with his mistresses; he used them but he was not in love with them."

At first, there was little evidence to suggest that a strong monarchy would be restored with the Stuarts, and the notion of "divine right" did not resurface. No effort was made to reestablish either the special law courts used against the enemies of the crown or the king's old feudal privileges. The return of the Stuarts brought with it the restoration of Anglicanism as the state church in England and Ireland. In Scotland, where it had never been established, Charles encountered serious opposition in his efforts to impose Anglicanism. Those Protestants who refused to accept the Church of England were called dissenters, groups that were especially numerous among artisans and merchants. Legal restrictions were imposed on dissenters, including the Corporation Act (1661), which excluded them from town offices. The next year, Charles issued the Declaration of Indulgence, designed to grant tolerance to Catholics and dissenters. In response, the strongly Anglican Parliament passed the Act of Uniformity (1662), which required clergymen to accept the *Anglican Book of Common Prayer* and deprived more than 1,000 Calvinist ministers of their parishes.

Charles II remained uncomfortable with the Church of England because at heart he and his brother James were Catholics—both had been influenced by their mother and the strongly Catholic atmosphere of the French court, where they had spent their exile. This problem ultimately caused the final undoing of the Stuarts. In 1670, Charles concluded the secret Treaty of Dover with Louis XIV, whereby he secured a financial subsidy in return for supporting the French war against the United Provinces and swearing to convert to Catholicism. But in view of the strong anti-Catholic sentiment in the realm, Charles was careful to keep his sentiments to himself. In 1673 he was forced to withdraw the Declaration of Indulgence in place of the Test Act, which drove Catholics from office. Anti-Catholic sentiment reached a new pitch in 1678, when rumors of a "Popish Plot," deliberately manufactured by a rogue named Titus Oates (1649–1705), caused people to believe that Catholics intended to assassinate the king, burn London, and massacre Protestants. In Oxford, a crowd surrounded the royal coach in the mistaken belief that it contained the king's Catholic mistress. Nell Gwyn, who was in fact inside, pleaded with the mob, "Pray good people, be civil; I am the *Protestant* whore." Only when near death in 1685 did Charles formally convert to Catholicism.

JAMES II AND THE CRISIS OF THE RESTORATION

Because Charles II had no legitimate children, the crown was due to pass to his brother James, the duke of York (ruled as king, 1685–1688). Less tactful than Charles, James had declared his conversion in 1672. In the aftermath of the Popish Plot, however, Parliament tried several times to enact an Exclusion Bill that would have kept James or any other Catholic from the royal succession. The issue of whether Parliament had the right to change the succession to the crown was of great importance. The bill failed to pass, but from the debates that it engendered there eventually emerged two distinct factions, or "parties." The Whig party, which supported the bill, gained the backing of a variety of people, from liberal Anglicans and landowners who wanted to

strengthen Parliament against the king to dissenters and the business class. The Tory group, which opposed the Exclusion Bill, favored a strong hereditary monarchy and sought to avoid another destructive civil war. (The words *Whig* and *Tory* were originally labels used by one side to slander the other: *Whig* was the term for a Scottish horse thief, while *Tory* was the term for an Irish cattle rustler.) Because the Whigs were divided among themselves, however, Charles was able to fend off their efforts. Nor were the Whigs the only opponents of the king; a widespread radical underground had opposed royal authority since the start of the Restoration.

When James succeeded to the throne in 1685, he took the place of a king who had actually succeeded in strengthening the monarchy and in ruling for the last four years without Parliament. But James lacked his brother's political skills, and within several years dramatic changes took place in England's political order. His Catholic beliefs, together with his increasing emphasis on royal authority, aroused widespread fear and opposition. Trouble erupted from the moment James became king; uprisings in Scotland and England greeted his accession, although he put them down easily.

Like Charles, James promised to uphold the constitutional system and the Anglican Church, but he soon gave evidence to the contrary. He created a professional standing army run by Catholic officers, which he stationed near London, a move that shocked even his Tory supporters. In open violation of the Test Act of 1673, he used a Declaration of Indulgence to appoint Catholics and others to posts in local and royal government, as well as in Oxford and Cambridge Universities, arguing in self-defense that he was not subject to previous parliamentary acts. In 1688, he issued a second Declaration of Indulgence, and when seven Anglican bishops—including the archbishop of Canterbury—refused to read it from their pulpits, he had them arrested, although they were later acquitted.

James II pushed royal authority to the limits, but the event that brought his reign to the crisis point was the birth of a son. Until then, his heirs had been two daughters by a first marriage—Mary (1662–1694), who had married her cousin William III of the United Provinces (see Topic 50), and Anne (1665–1714), who married a Danish prince. These daughters and their husbands were all Protestants, so that the prospect of one of them inheriting the throne had not caused alarm among the English. But in June 1688, a son was born to James and his second wife, the Catholic Mary Beatrice (1658–1718). Because this son took precedence over his half-sisters in the royal succession, this meant that England would one day have a Catholic king, a prospect that the nobles and gentry found intolerable.

Map 51.1 England and the Netherlands, c. 1688. Note the break between the Austrian Netherlands, under Hapsburg rule, and the United Provinces of Holland. The period saw the growth of Amsterdam from a medieval fishing village to one of the leading commercial centers of Europe. Although The Hague is the seat of government in Holland, Amsterdam remains its economic heart.

THE GLORIOUS REVOLUTION

The events in England that followed the birth of James II's son in 1688 have been dubbed the "Glorious" Revolution—an upheaval that forced James from the throne and inaugurated the era of constitutional monarchy with the reign of William and Mary.

WILLIAM AND MARY

English leaders, both Whig and Tory alike, quickly joined forces to oust James. They made proposals to William III of Orange, *stadholder* of the Dutch Republic, to assume the crown with his English wife Mary, James II's daughter. Risking his fleet and the independence of his own country, William landed an invasion force of 14,000 men at Torbay on the southwest coast of England in early November. James quickly discovered that most of his soldiers had deserted him. In December, after having been once captured, he escaped and fled to France, where he joined his young son, who was known as the "Old Pretender," and recognized by Louis XIV as the legitimate English sovereign. Although the fighting in England was minor, in Ireland a popular Catholic uprising in support of James erupted. William crushed the Irish revolt only in July 1690 at the Battle of the Boyne, in which his 35,000 troops defeated some 21,000 Catholic soldiers. In the process, William executed priests and political leaders and devastated much of the land.

THE TRIUMPH OF PARLIAMENT

This unspectacular but tradition-breaking revolution was a decisive turning point in the development of representative government. Early in 1689, Parliament drafted the Declaration of Rights, the fundamental document on which the Revolutionary Settlement of 1689 rested. This Bill of Rights (as it became known once enacted into law) stipulated that all sovereigns were to be Anglican. More important, it provided that the sovereign could not suspend laws or interfere with free speech, elections, or parliamentary discussion. Furthermore, Parliament was to meet regularly, and the monarch could neither maintain an army nor levy taxes without its consent, whereas the people had the right to petition the ruler. The bill also safeguarded individual rights, making it illegal for an English citizen to be arrested without a warrant or denied just bail. In addition, Parliament approved the Toleration Act, which barred non-Anglicans from public office and imposed severe restrictions on Catholics, but which granted all Protestants full freedom of worship. The triumph of Parliament as set forth in these reforms fundamentally altered the nature of government in England.

William and Mary were asked to accept the Declaration of Rights before being offered the crown. They agreed to rule jointly because William would not tolerate serving merely as Queen Mary's consort, and Mary refused to rule by herself. Only 15 years old when they had married, Mary made herself subservient to her husband and was constantly humiliated by William's mistress, who lived in the

Engraving showing William and Mary being presented with the crown of England. Late 17th century. The representatives of the church stand to the left, while the presentation is accompanied by a proclamation of the Declaration of Rights, read by the Lord Chief Justice. William and Mary could not be crowned until they had accepted the conditions set out in this document.

PERSPECTIVES FROM THE PAST

RESISTANCE AND REVOLUTION

As the power and authority of centralized states expanded in the 15th and 16th centuries, some political philosophers and active opponents of the absolute monarchs developed theoretical arguments sustaining the right of resistance. Religious reformers like Luther and Calvin, no matter how conservative their political and social views, contributed to the theory of resistance by allowing that magistrates could oppose superior authority in order to uphold divine law. During the wars of religion in France, Huguenots claimed that royal tyrants were not ruling with God's will and that because the king's role was to defend justice, magistrates could legitimately oppose those who failed to do so. This was the theme of an influential work by Philippe Duplessis-Mornay, *A Defense of Liberty Against Tyrants* (1579). The argument was broadened significantly some years later by the Catholic philosopher Juan de Mariana, whose essay on *The King and the Education of the King* (1598) extended the right of resistance to ordinary citizens in cases where kings deliberately violated their own laws and the well-being of their subjects. During the 17th century, other writers expanded on the theory of resistance, especially under the influence of Enlightenment thought.

The English Bill of Rights

In 1689, after the Glorious Revolution, Parliament passed the Bill of Rights, which guaranteed basic civil rights and consolidated the gains of the revolution.

Whereas the said late King James II having abdicated the government, and the throne being thereby vacant, his Highness the prince of Orange (whom it hath pleased Almighty God to make the glorious instrument of delivering this kingdom from popery and arbitrary power) did (by the device of the lords spiritual and temporal, and diverse principal persons of the Commons) cause letters to be written to the lords spiritual and temporal, being Protestants, and other letters to the several counties, cities, universities, boroughs, and Cinque Ports [five port towns on the English Channel, having special privileges], for the choosing of such persons to represent them, as were of right to be sent to parliament, to meet and sit at Westminster upon the two and twentieth day of January, in this year 1689, in order to such an establishment as that their religion, laws, and liberties might not again be in danger of being subverted; upon which letters elections have been accordingly made.

And thereupon the said lords spiritual and temporal and Commons, pursuant to their respective letters and elections, being now assembled in a full and free representation of this nation, taking into their most serious consideration the best means for attaining the ends aforesaid, do in the first place (as their ancestors in like case have usually done), for the vindication and assertion of their ancient rights and liberties, declare:

1. That the pretended power of suspending laws, or the execution of laws, by regal authority, without consent of parliament is illegal.
2. That the pretended power of dispensing with the laws, or the execution of law by regal authority, as it hath been assumed and exercised of late, is illegal.
3. That the commission for erecting the late court of commissioners for ecclesiastical causes, and all other commissions and courts of like nature, are illegal and pernicious.
4. That levying money for or to the use of the crown by pretense of prerogative, without grant of parliament, for longer time or in other manner than the same is or shall be granted, is illegal.
5. That it is the right of the subjects to petition the king, and all commitments and prosecutions for such petitioning are illegal.

6. That the raising or keeping a standing army within the kingdom in time of peace, unless it be with consent of parliament, is against law.

7. That the subjects which are Protestants may have arms for their defense suitable to their conditions, and as allowed by law.

8. That election of members of parliament ought to be free.

9. That the freedom of speech, and debates or proceedings in parliament, ought not to be impeached or questioned in any court or place out of parliament.

10. That excessive bail ought not to be required, nor excessive fines imposed, nor cruel and unusual punishments inflicted.

11. That jurors ought to be duly impaneled and returned, and jurors which pass upon men in trials for high treason ought to be freeholders.

12. That all grants and promises of fines and forfeitures of particular persons before conviction are illegal and void.

13. And that for redress of all grievances, and for the amending, strengthening, and preserving of the laws, parliament ought to be held frequently.

From *The Statutes,* Eyre and Spotiswoode, Copyright © 1871.

Locke's Second Treatise on Government

John Locke, one of the most influential thinkers of the Enlightenment, wrote the Second Treatise *between 1681 and 1683, before the Glorious Revolution. The essay proposed government as the guarantor of life, liberty, and property, the three essential points of Enlightenment political ideals, and influenced colonial leaders during the American Revolution.*

When any one, or more, shall take upon them to make laws, whom the people have not appointed so to do, they make laws without authority, which the people are not therefore bound to obey; by which means they come again to be out of subjection, and may constitute to themselves a new legislative, as they think best, being in full liberty to resist the force of those,

who without authority would impose any thing upon them. Every one is at the disposure of his own will, when those who had, by the delegation of the society, the declaring of the public will, are excluded from it, and others usurp the place, who have no such authority or delegation. . . .

In these and the like cases, *when the government is dissolved,* the people are at liberty to provide for themselves, by erecting a new legislative, differing from the other, by the change of persons, or form, or both, as they shall find it most for their safety and good. For the *society* can never, by the fault of another, lose the native and original right it has to preserve itself; which can only be done by a settled legislative, and a fair and impartial execution of the laws made by it. But the state of mankind is not so miserable that they are not capable of using this remedy, till it be too late to look for any. To tell *people* they *may provide for themselves,* by erecting a new legislative, when by oppression, artifice, or being delivered over to a foreign power, their old one is gone, is only to tell them, they may expect relief when it is too late, and the evil is past cure. This is in effect no more, than to bid them first be slaves, and then to take care of their liberty; and when their chains are on, tell them, they may act like freemen. This, if barely so, is rather mockery than relief; and men can never be secure from tyranny, if there be no means to escape it, till they are perfectly under it: And therefore it is, that they have not only a right to get out of it, but to prevent it. . . .

From David Wootton, ed., *Modern Political Thought: Readings from Machiavelli to Nietzsche,* Hackett Publishing Co., copyright © 1996.

Rousseau on the Social Contract

In 1771 Rousseau wrote An Inquiry into the Nature of the Social Contract *in which he added to theories of the social contract the notion of the General Will, a universal moral law through which humans recognized their interdependence and advocated the idea that the people have the right to dissolve the contract.*

What, then, is the government? An intermediate body established between the subjects

Continued

and the sovereign for their mutual correspondence, charged with the execution of the laws and with the maintenance of liberty both civil and political. [Book III, Chapter 1.]

So soon as the people are lawfully assembled as a sovereign body, the whole jurisdiction of the government ceases, the executive power is suspended, and the person of the meanest citizen is as sacred and inviolable as that of the first magistrate, because where the represented are, there is no longer any representative. [Book III, Chapter 14.]

These assemblies, which have as their object the maintenance of the social treaty, ought always to be opened with two propositions, which no one should be able to suppress, and which should pass separately by vote. The first: "Whether it pleases the sovereign to maintain the present form of government." The second: "Whether it pleases the people to leave the administration to those at present entrusted with it."

I presuppose here what I believe I have proved, viz., that there is in the State no fundamental law which cannot be revoked, not even this social compact; for if all the citizens assembled in order to break the compact by a solemn agreement, no one can doubt that it could be quite legitimately broken. [Book III, Chapter 18.]

From Lynn Hunt, Thomas R. Martin, Barbara H. Rosenwein, R. Po-chia Hsia, Bonnie G. Smith, eds., *Connecting with the Past,* Vol. I, D.C. Heath, Copyright © 1995.

The Declaration of Independence

When Thomas Jefferson drafted the Declaration of Independence in 1776, he had in mind the writings of Locke and other European philosophers.

When in the course of human events, it becomes necessary for one people to dissolve the political bands which have connected them

royal palace. Nevertheless, because William was frequently out of the country conducting military campaigns, Mary ruled alone for much of the time, a task she carried out with intelligence and vigor. Outwardly, William treated her with bad-tempered indifference, but when she died of smallpox in 1694, he grieved deeply.

The forces that controlled Parliament and had brought about these settlements were by no means democratic. The House of Lords, whose members were appointed by the monarch, was composed of landed nobility and could veto legislation passed by the Commons. The system of election for the House of Commons enabled the nobles and landed gentry to control the countryside, but the wealthy members of the middle class who exercised influence in the cities were hardly represented in the House. For a century and a half after the Glorious Revolution, England was ruled by an essentially aristocratic Parliament that chiefly represented the interests of the landlords.

After the Glorious Revolution, the temporary alliance that had bound Tories and Whigs together in common opposition to James II fell apart. Real socioeconomic differences separated the Whig and the Tory parties: the Tories, who had supported the revolution reluctantly, were landed gentry whose interests centered on rural life and who wanted England to keep aloof from continental affairs; the Whigs, by contrast, were active in commerce and overseas trade and had seen the revolution as a chance to secure the supremacy of Parliament over the king.

Taxation was now under the control of Parliament, and with state finances on a stable footing as a result of parliamentary supervision, private bankers were more willing to lend money to the government. Unable to raise taxes, William therefore borrowed more than one million pounds to fight the War of the League of Augsburg. In this way, the concept of a permanent national debt, as opposed to private royal debts, came into being. In 1694, with the approval of Parliament, he took the extraordinary step of granting a royal charter to the Bank of England, a private institution that managed the national debt by holding government deposits, sending funds abroad, and advancing credits. England also reformed its monetary system and issued new coinage in consultation with Sir Isaac Newton, master of the Mint. In addition, regular procedures were established for issuing insurance and trading stocks, thus creating an environment in which commerce and manufacturing could prosper.

THE LEGITIMACY OF REVOLUTION

Together with the mid-century Civil War, the Glorious Revolution of 1688–1689 broke the pattern of absolutist government that had entrenched itself elsewhere in Europe. The principal theorist of the Glorious Revolution was John Locke (1632–1704), whose ideas had circulated before 1688, especially among the Whigs. In *Two Treatises on Civil Government* (1690), Locke sought to justify the events of 1688 (on Locke as an Enlightenment figure, see Topic 58).

with another, and to assume among the powers of the earth, the separate and equal station to which the laws of nature and of nature's God entitle them, a decent respect to the opinions of mankind requires that they should declare the causes which impel them to the separation.— We hold these truths to be self-evident, that all men are created equal, that they are endowed by their Creator with certain unalienable rights, that among these are life, liberty, and the pursuit of happiness—That to secure these rights, governments are instituted among men, deriving their just powers from the consent of the governed,—That whenever any form of government becomes destructive of these ends, it is the right of the people to alter or to abolish it, and to institute new government, laying its foundation on such principles and organizing its powers in such form, as to them shall seem most likely to effect their safety and happiness. Prudence, indeed, will dictate that governments long established should not be changed for light and transient causes; and accordingly all experience hath shewn, that mankind are more disposed to suffer, while evils are sufferable, than to right themselves by abolishing the forms to which they are accustomed. But when a long train of abuses and usurpations, pursuing invariably the same object evinces a design to reduce them under absolute despotism, it is their right, it is their duty, to throw off such government, and to provide new guards for their future security.—Such has been the patient sufferance of these colonies; and such is now the necessity which constrains them to alter their former systems of government. The history of the present king of Great Britain is a history of repeated injuries and usurpations, all having in direct object the establishment of an absolute tyranny over these states. To prove this, let facts be submitted to a candid world.

Portrait of John Locke, c. 1700. His writings played a major role in the Glorious Revolution, and he also became one of the founders of the European Enlightenment. He published the theoretical arguments on which the Declaration of Rights was based, *Two Treatises of Civil Government,* in 1690, the year after William and Mary's accession.

By Courtesy of the National Portrait Gallery, London

Locke believed that in order to escape the brutalities of their original "state of nature," people established government and set up rulers, whose principal role was to defend the natural rights of individuals in society. In establishing a "social contract" with their ruler, subjects gave up part of their natural rights, but they retained the fundamental rights to life, liberty, and the pursuit of property. If the sovereign interfered with these rights, or failed to protect them, then the people were free to remove him. Other revolutionaries, in America and in France, would later use Locke's "right to revolution."

THE CABINET SYSTEM AND THE HOUSE OF COMMONS

In the years following the Glorious Revolution, England not only developed the fundamental institutions of constitutional monarchy but also evolved the principles and practice of ministerial government. As a result, by the mid-18th century Parliament had extended its reach beyond its legislative functions and into the executive branch of government.

With the backing of the Whig party, William III spent much of his energy and considerable resources on war and diplomacy, for the Glorious Revolution had taken place in the midst of the wars of Louis XIV. Because of his interest in foreign affairs, William tended to leave the administration of domestic matters to his ministers. By day-to-day practice rather than by design, the king soon discovered that the government ran more smoothly, and policy matters were settled more easily, if all of his ministers were from the same party that controlled the House of Commons. Thus he began to appoint Whig ministers when the Whigs held a majority in the Commons and Tories when they were in the preponderance. In this way, the ability of a cabinet—as the body of ministers came to be called—to remain in office depended increasingly on its ability to command the confidence of a majority in Parliament. To this day, this principle of "ministerial responsibility" prevails, and government ministers must appear before the House of Commons to answer the questions of its members.

Because the Glorious Revolution was, in an immediate sense, a struggle to determine the royal succession, Parliament continued to assert its authority in this vital area. When Queen Mary died, William ruled by himself, but thereafter the succession was in doubt because William and Mary were childless. In 1701, Parliament passed the Act of Settlement, which excluded the son of James II and all other Catholics. Instead, the crown was to pass to Mary's sister, Anne. If Anne did not have children, the crown would then go at her death to Sophia (1630–1714), the granddaughter of James I and the wife of the elector of the German state of Hanover.

GOOD QUEEN ANNE

On William's death in 1702, Anne (ruled 1702–1714) became queen of England. A rather dull woman, she was fat and so crippled with gout that she had to be carried in a chair during her coronation. But she drew a deliberate contrast between William, who was Dutch by birth and sentiment, and her own "English heart," and won the sympathy of the British people, who called her "Good Queen Anne." In a less worshipful mood, a popular ballad of the day alluded to "Brandy-faced Nan," in view of the fact that she was a heavy drinker.

Unlike her predecessor, Anne's reign was marked by tensions between royal authority and Parliament. She disagreed often with Parliament and was one of the last English rulers to veto its acts and to preside regularly over cabinet meetings. Near the end of her life, she also broke with what was fast becoming established tradition when she appointed a Tory cabinet despite a Whig majority in the House of Commons. Yet Anne was careful to avoid any real crisis because she realized that her half-brother—the son of James II—still had many supporters.

In order to make sure that the thrones of both England and Scotland would pass to the Protestant descendants of Sophia of Hanover, in 1707 the parliaments of the two realms enacted the Act of Union, which created a single state known as the United Kingdom of Great Britain. The English Parliament was transformed into the Parliament of the United Kingdom, which now included Scottish lords and commoners. The union was achieved in part by force and pressure, but many Scots saw the advantages of dissolv-ing the trade barriers between the two territories. The Scots kept their own court system but lost their own parliament and their capital. In Ireland, on the other hand, where William had returned to a harsh policy of restrictions against the Catholics, peace still proved elusive.

As a sovereign, Anne was surrounded constantly with male politicians, but in private she preferred the company and the advice of Sarah Churchill (1660–1744), the wife of the brilliant military commander John Churchill. Sarah Churchill had become Anne's trusted friend before the Glorious Revolution and had helped the princess escape during the upheaval in 1688. When Anne ascended the throne, she appointed her friend to lady of the queen's bedchamber, a position in which Sarah gained significant political influence. A Whig in politics, she dispensed patronage, controlled the cabinet, and helped herself to a large pension. Eventually, Sarah's increasingly haughty attitude alienated Anne, and she fell from royal favor.

THE BRITISH CONSTITUTION IN THE AGE OF WALPOLE

Queen Anne, who died in 1714, was the last Stuart monarch. Although she had 17 pregnancies, only five babies were born alive, and none of her children lived past the

Portrait of George I of England. Early 18th century. In 1714, George became the first Hanoverian ruler of England. Originally ruler of the German state of Hanover, he appears here in the robes of the English monarchy. He was never very popular with his subjects, perhaps because he made no serious effort to learn English.

By Courtesy of the National Portrait Gallery, London

age of eleven. She was succeeded by the first Hanoverian king, George I (ruled 1714–1727). George, a German who never learned English and had little interest in British affairs, was not terribly popular with his new subjects. He was not interested in the details of government, and at first he even tried to conduct cabinet meetings in broken Latin, but quickly gave that up and stopped attending them. Instead, the king left politics and the administration of the kingdom in the hands of his ministers.

During this period, the office of prime minister became increasingly important. By 1722, Sir Robert Walpole (1676–1745) had emerged as Great Britain's most prominent political leader. Walpole, the third son of a well-to-do member of the gentry, rose to power in Whig politics. He served for more than half his life in Parliament. A skillful administrator, Walpole was made secretary of war in 1708, during the reign of Queen Anne. In 1712, his enemies impeached him on charges of corruption and expelled him from Parliament, but he was restored to favor by George I, whose confidence he had won. Walpole was especially intent on guarding against efforts by supporters of the Stuart pretender, known as Jacobites (from the Latin for James), to unseat the Hanoverians. In 1715, "James III," the Old Pretender, supported by some Tories, actually landed in Scotland but was easily defeated and forced to flee once again.

In 1721 Walpole became chancellor of the exchequer, and he eventually emerged as the king's "prime," or chief, minister. In that position, he nominated the other ministers who served in his cabinet and wielded enormous patronage in the form of jobs, pensions, contracts, and honors, which he used to remain in power for more than 20 years. Although George II (ruled 1727–1760) did not share his father's enthusiasm for Walpole, Queen Caroline (1683–1737) helped keep him in office. Walpole kept the support of Parliament through bribery, eloquence, and political skill.

Despite Walpole's extraordinary power, his immediate successors did not imbue the position of prime minister with the authority that he had wielded. The monarch remained the head of state and the ruler of the kingdom, in whose name all laws were enacted and treaties negotiated. In addition, the British monarch still commanded enormous prestige and exercised considerable informal authority. Nevertheless, by the mid-18th century, the sovereign needed Parliament to make laws, levy taxes, control the judiciary, or maintain an army. He had delegated most of his executive functions to the prime minister and his cabinet, where the real affairs of state were conducted.

Among the great powers of Europe, Great Britain could boast a unique form of government by the mid-18th century. The country was governed by an "unwritten constitution" consisting of traditions, laws, and charters that stretched back to the Middle Ages. As it evolved between 1688 and the death of Walpole in 1745, that system was one in which the aristocracy and a landowning elite divided political power between them in cooperation with the monarchy. In this arrangement, the role of Parliament was crucial because it was the body that made laws, imposed taxes, and appropriated the revenues needed for the government to function.

Putting England and the Rise of Constitutional Monarchy in Perspective

The fact that the English revolutions took place while Louis XIV sat on the throne of France reflects the range of political systems that unfolded in 17th-century Europe: At one extreme stood the *Grand Monarque,* who perfected the instruments of absolutist power at Versailles, while at the other extreme Cromwell experimented with a republican dictatorship built on the ruins of a decapitated monarchy. The governments of most European states were closer to the French than to the English model.

The English had not been entirely spared from experience with absolute monarchy: The Tudor sovereigns came close to realizing such status in the 16th century, but the Civil War and the Puritan Revolution had stopped the growth of royal power. The restored Stuart kings tried to see how far they could go in reviving royal authority, but when they pushed too far, the forces that controlled Parliament staged the Glorious Revolution. Parliament won the struggle for power, and over the next half-century it extended its authority indirectly as a result of the evolution of the cabinet system of government. Limited, constitutional monarchy became the counterpoint to absolute monarchy based on the divine right of kings.

In retrospect, of course, the British system proved more stable and long-lived than the French form of government. England had its revolution in the 17th century, whereas France experienced a more serious turmoil 100 years later. The events that took place in England between 1640 and 1688 constituted a political rather than a social revolution, but the revolution nonetheless confirmed an important social fact, namely, that the landed gentry and merchant class had emerged as the country's uncontested ruling elite. Moreover, unlike the aristocracy on the Continent, in England nobles were not exempt from taxation, and therefore had a greater stake in the success of Parliament. If Great Britain avoided having its own Sun King, it owed its good fortune to a combination of factors, especially the existence of this elite and the strong tradition of individual rights embedded in the common law. Yet, regardless of the differences between the French and British experiences, one essential pattern remained common to both nations: the increasing centralization of power in the modern state.

Questions for Further Study

1. In what ways were the issues that led to the Glorious Revolution different from those behind the earlier civil wars?
2. What general principles of popular sovereignty emerged from the revolution?
3. What are the origins of the cabinet system of government?

Suggestions for Further Reading

Black, Jeremy, ed. *Britain in the Age of Walpole*. New York, 1984.

Earle, Peter. *The Making of the English Middle Class*. London, 1989.

Harris, Tim. *Politics Under the Later Stuarts*. London and New York, 1993.

Hill, Christopher. *The World Turned Upside Down: Radical Ideas During the English Revolution*. New York, 1972.

Hutton, Richard. *Charles the Second*. Oxford, 1990.

Jones, J.R. *The Revolution of 1688 in England*. London, 1972.

InfoTrac College Edition

Enter the search term *Stuart Restoration* using Key Terms.

Enter the search term *Charles II of England* using Key Terms.

Enter the search term *James II of England* using Key Terms.

Enter the search term *Queen Anne of England* using Key Terms.

CENTRAL EUROPE AND THE SHIFTING BALANCE OF POWER

By the 17th century, most Western European countries had a strong central government. The nobility had been tamed or incorporated into the state, the urban merchant classes were growing in prominence, and most agricultural populations had been largely freed from the restrictions of feudalism. In Central and Eastern Europe, by contrast, the growth of absolute monarchy left the nobility with considerable power and status, the middle classes were weak, and the peasants continued to live as serfs.

The chief political organization of central Europe was the Holy Roman Empire, nominally ruled by the Hapsburgs. In practice, however, the Empire consisted of a welter of separate states, each with its own ruler and political system. Many of these states used war or marriage to increase their power. In the early 17th century, Hapsburg attempts to revive the Empire led to their defeat in the Thirty Years' War. In midcentury, the Emperor Leopold I tried a different approach by seeking to unify Austria, Bohemia, and Hungary under centralized rule.

The Hohenzollerns, who had become the rulers of Brandenburg in 1415, emerged as the monarchs of a major new power during the 17th century. Early in the century, the Hohenzollerns added to their holdings by inheriting the territory of Prussia to the northeast and some scattered lands on the Rhine. Poor and undefended by natural frontiers, Brandenburg-Prussia suffered badly in the Thirty Years' War. In the midst of the destruction of many villages and a fall in population, in 1653 the young Elector Friedrich Wilhelm was able to increase his power at the expense of the regional assemblies.

Friedrich Wilhelm, later known as the Great Elector, welded together his scattered principalities into a single state. He created a powerful standing army second only to the military force of Austria. In order to pay for his army, he forcibly introduced permanent taxation over the protests of the Estates. The Prussian landowning nobles, known as Junkers, tried unsuccessfully to resist, but in return he allowed them to retain control over the serfs on their estates. By the time of the Great Elector's death in 1688, his tough programs at home and shrewd foreign policy had produced a powerful unified state with formidable military forces.

THE FICTION OF THE HOLY ROMAN EMPIRE

By contrast with the growing prosperity of Western Europe in the 16th and 17th centuries, economic conditions in Central and Eastern Europe were poor. Most of the wealth was concentrated in the hands of the landowning nobility, the middle classes remained small and politically weak, and most peasants were forced to work as unpaid serfs. The establishment of absolute monarchies in Austria, Prussia, and Russia did little to relieve these conditions (for a discussion of Russia and Poland, see Topic 53).

One of the most important factors making it possible for rulers to assert their domination was the climate of uncertainty created by decades of wars. As the states of Central and Eastern Europe fought against one another and against outside invaders, even the most independent nobles realized the necessity for a strong central authority. By seizing their opportunity, rulers such as Prussia's Friedrich Wilhelm (ruled 1640–1688) were able to control three vital sources of power: the imposition of taxes, control of a standing army, and conduct of foreign affairs. In return, they allowed their nobles to continue to maintain their estates and legal rights over their peasants.

The largest political confederation in central Europe was the Holy Roman Empire. Founded by Charlemagne, it was effectively established in 962 as an organization of some 300 German states and included the Low Countries, eastern France, northern and central Italy, and western Bohemia. According to procedures set up in 1356 (see Topic 29), its emperor, usually the dominant German sovereign, was elected by the seven "elector" princes and, until the end of the 15th century, crowned by the pope. The Hapsburg dynasty, which had ruled Austria since 1278, became rulers of the Holy Roman Empire in 1436, and they continued to serve as emperors, at least in theory, until Napoleon finally dismantled the Empire in 1806.

THE HOLY ROMAN EMPIRE AFTER THE THIRTY YEARS' WAR

The tendency for the individual member-states of the Holy Roman Empire to go their separate ways, already notable in the 15th century, increased during the Reformation, which set the Catholic Hapsburg emperor against the Protestant princes, most of whom ruled the northern states. One of the reasons the emperor Ferdinand II (ruled 1619–1637) became embroiled in the disastrous Thirty Years' War was to enforce the Counter-Reformation and impose Catholicism on Protestants in Bohemia and Hungary. Educated by Jesuits, Ferdinand fervently supported the propagation of Catholic dogma by authoritarian means (on the Thirty Years' War, see Topic 44).

Far from strengthening the Empire, the negotiations that finally brought the war to an end effectively destroyed any chance of the emperor's reestablishing central authority. The Peace of Westphalia (1648) established the separation of politics and religion and ended the emperor's attempt to turn Germany into an absolute monarchy. The treaty made it instead into a collection of absolute monarchies and confirmed the sovereignty of each member-state. In addition, it further reduced Hapsburg power over the Empire by allowing outsiders, France and Sweden, to participate in the deliberations of the Imperial Diet, the Holy Roman Empire's assembly to which the various member-states sent representatives.

By the mid-17th century the ancient organization existed in name only. The Diet continued to meet, but for all practical purposes the Empire was a political fiction. The "rulers" of its various member-states included some 2,000 imperial knights, 80 princes (50 ecclesiastical and 30 secular), more than 100 counts, around 70 prelates, and 66 city governments. Their territories ranged in size from three or four acres to the entire kingdom of Bohemia. All of the individual rulers were theoretically subordinate to the emperor, but in practice remained politically independent. The Empire had no central administration or taxation system, no common law or customs union, and not even a common calendar.

THE HAPSBURGS TURN EAST: THE TURKISH DEFEAT

Traditional Hapsburg territory in Central Europe consisted of three distinct regions: the hereditary lands of Austria, the Kingdom of Bohemia, and the Kingdom of Hungary. The Thirty Years' War put an end to Hapsburg expansion westward by legitimizing the independence of the other German states. In consequence, the emperor Leopold I (ruled 1658–1705) decided to create a larger and more powerful centralized state, the equal of those in Western Europe, by unifying these three regions and making Bohemia and Hungary subordinate to Austria.

Control over Austria was assured by the emperor's traditional ascendancy over the local feudal nobility. The Kingdom of Bohemia was still suffering the effects of the Thirty Years' War. In 1620, Ferdinand II crushed a revolt led by Bohemia's Protestant Czech nobility, killed his opponents, and confiscated their estates. He replaced them with a new upper class. For the most part, these newcomers were aristocratic mercenaries from all over Europe. Having no allegiance to Bohemia, they owed their position, and thus their loyalty, to the emperor.

With the help of this new ruling class, the Hapsburgs established direct control over Bohemia. The Bohemian peasants were required to work a minimum of three days a week without pay for their new masters, and about one-quarter of them worked every day except Sundays and religious holidays. These serfs were also responsible for paying taxes, thereby lifting the burden from the aristocracy.

HUNGARY AND THE OTTOMAN EMPIRE

The real difficulty in Leopold's scheme lay farther east, in Hungary. The Hapsburgs were the elected rulers of the kingdom. In practice, however, since the early 16th century most of Hungary was in Turkish hands, as part of the

Ottoman Empire. Many central and eastern European peasants, accustomed to exploitation at the hands of their Christian masters, found Turkish rule less oppressive than that of the Hapsburgs, especially because the Turks did not require them to become Muslims. In Hungary, moreover, the Protestant nobility tended to side with the Turks against the hated Catholic Austrians.

In the reign of Mehmed IV (ruled 1648–1687), Turkish power, which had suffered a serious setback at the Battle of Lepanto in 1571, temporarily revived—the restoration of strong central government was largely the result of energetic and effective grand viziers. The Turks once again moved westward against Austria, encouraged by Louis XIV of France, who wanted to use the Turks against his old enemies the Hapsburgs. After two unsuccessful campaigns in 1663 and 1664, an Ottoman army of more than 100,000 poured up the Danube Valley and besieged Vienna in July 1683. The Austrian forces were too weak to resist, and the emperor Leopold fled up the river to Passau, to try to put together a coalition of troops to oppose the Turks.

For the next two months, as the rest of Europe waited with horrified fascination to see if the easternmost bastion of Catholicism would fall, the Turkish encampment outside Vienna provided a vision of luxury never before seen in the West. The Turks had brought with them supplies for a long wait: oxen, camels, and mules; a flock of 10,000 sheep; corn, coffee, sugar, and honey. The quarters of the commander, Kara Mustapha, included bathrooms with perfumed waters, opulent beds, priceless carpets, and glittering chandeliers. Elsewhere were gardens with fountains and a menagerie with rare birds and animals.

After a tense summer of negotiating, Leopold succeeded in putting together an international relief force. In September, combined troops including Poles, Bavarians, and Saxons, with the blessing of Pope Innocent XI (ruled 1676–1689), came to the rescue. French troops were conspicuous by their absence from the coalition of Christians against Muslims. Louis XIV placed national political interests above religion, and in any case he was also involved in a bitter quarrel with the pope.

Among the heroes of the relief of Vienna was the Polish king, John Sobieski (ruled 1674–1696), who personally led the charge of his country's cavalry. The combined armies came crashing down on the Turks from the heights of the Kahlenberg, overlooking the city, and drove them into a hurried retreat toward Hungary. The Turkish commander stayed only long enough to prevent his two favorite possessions from falling alive into Christian hands: he decapitated a particularly beautiful wife and his ostrich.

EUGENE OF SAVOY

Over the following decade, Leopold's forces pursued the Turks down the Danube and drove them out of Hungary. Among the emperor's potent weapons was the most brilliant general of the age, Eugene, prince of Savoy (1663–1736). French by birth, Eugene had clashed with the domineering Louis XIV, and renounced his country. Renowned for his qualities of leadership and strategic insights, Eugene was also a notable

patron of the arts, and for his Viennese home he commissioned the superb palace and park known as the Belvedere.

In a series of campaigns, the Austrians conquered all of Hungary and added Transylvania (now part of Romania). The final decisive battle took place at Zenta in 1697, where forces under Eugene wiped out a Turkish army triple their size. By the Peace of Carlowitz, of January 1699, the Turks recognized Hapsburg rule over Hungary. Once in possession, Leopold was quick to impose Catholicism and clamp on Hungary the fetters of Austrian rule. The country became an Austrian colony. Many Hungarian Protestants were executed for treason. The remaining landowning nobles kept their holdings along with the serfs who worked on them, in return for their recognition of the ultimate authority of Vienna.

THE UPRISING OF RÁKÓCZY

Yet Hapsburg attempts to integrate Hungary into a single state, along with Austria and Bohemia, were immediately challenged by a series of uprisings. Hungarian resistance to Austria proved stronger than that of the Bohemians. The Hungarian nobles, although weakened, had not been completely eliminated, as had the Protestant nobility of Bohemia. In addition, both aristocracy and peasants were beginning to develop a shared sense of national identity that was to reach its fulfillment in the 19th century.

In 1703, the young Francis Rákóczy (ruled 1704–1711), a member of a noble Hungarian and Transylvanian family, led a patriotic uprising against the Hapsburg empire. Because the Austrians were at the time involved in the War of the Spanish Succession (see Topic 50), Rákóczy's forces were unexpectedly successful, and in 1704 the nobles elected him prince.

Hungarian independence lasted only a few years. The Austrians rallied to inflict a series of crushing defeats, and in 1711 Rákóczy fled into exile. Nevertheless, the Hapsburg emperor was forced to accept the traditional status of the Hungarian aristocracy, in return for their acceptance of Austrian rule. Leopold's aim of creating a single powerful state

---

SIGNIFICANT DATES

Central Europe in the 17th Century

1618	Brandenburg and Prussia joined
1620	Ferdinand II of Austria crushes Protestant Czech uprising
1640–1688	Reign of Friedrich Wilhelm, the Great Elector
1648	Peace of Westphalia
1660	Friedrich founds Prussian Army
1683	Ottoman siege of Vienna
1697	Eugene of Savoy defeats Ottoman forces at Zenta
1701	Friedrich I crowned king of Prussia
1703	Rákóczy leads Hungarian uprising

was thus only partly fulfilled. Austria, Bohemia, and Hungary shared a centralized administration, but the framework under which it operated was loose. The unhappy consequences of Leopold's actions would emerge a century and a half later.

THE RISE OF THE HOHENZOLLERNS

One of the chief landowning families of northeastern Germany in the 16th century was the Hohenzollerns. The decline of the traditional aristocracy had permitted wealthy landowners like the Hohenzollerns to rise to political power. The senior branch of the family became Electors of Brandenburg, a small territory around Berlin, and the junior line acquired the rule of Prussia, a province on the Baltic Sea that technically formed part of the Kingdom of Poland. The two possessions joined together in 1618, when in the absence of a direct heir Prussia passed to Brandenburg by inheritance.

The provinces had few advantages. They shared no common interests or loyalties and lacked natural frontiers.

They were poor, thinly populated, and unproductive, and Brandenburg's bleak and arid lands had won it the nickname of "the sandbox of Europe." Furthermore, centralized administration of the territories was made difficult by their individual governments. The overall power of the Elector was limited by the existence of provincial assemblies known as Estates. Controlled by the great noble landowners called Junkers, these Estates passed laws, authorized, collected, and spent taxes, and raised troops. The Junker-dominated provincial administrations ran their provinces on a day-to-day basis, reserving the Elector as the court of final appeal.

The lack of defendable borders meant that Brandenburg-Prussia lay vulnerable to the ravages of the Thirty Years' War. Brandenburg, in particular, became the battleground for the rival armies of Sweden and the Hapsburgs. By 1648, the population had actually declined and, in the course of the war, Berlin lost half its inhabitants, and many villages were abandoned.

Paradoxically, by the end of the 17th century the state of Prussia (the name by which the joint territories became known) was on its way to becoming one of the leading po-

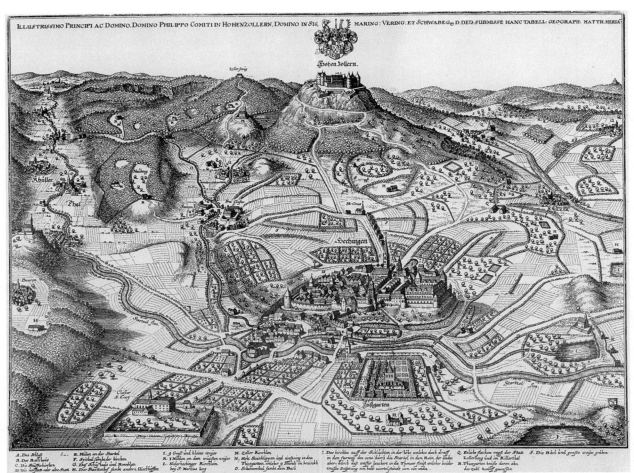

Matthew Meria, engraving of the castle and estates of the Hohenzollern. 17th century. The inscription at the top dedicates the work to the Hohenzollern Count Philip; the family crest appears just below. In the foreground are farms and gardens forming part of the estate; the walled garden just right of center at the bottom is labeled "Garden for Walking."

AKG London

litical and military powers in Europe. In part this was made possible because the state of almost total collapse underlined the need for wholesale reconstruction; however, Prussia's rise to greatness was largely the result of the policies of its remarkable ruler, Friedrich Wilhelm, whose achievements won him the title of the Great Elector.

THE GREAT ELECTOR: JUNKERS AND ARMY IN PRUSSIA

The Elector of Brandenburg for most of the Thirty Years' War was Friedrich Wilhelm's father, Georg Wilhelm (ruled 1619–1640). Weak and vacillating, Georg Wilhelm was described by one of his descendants as "utterly unfit to rule."

Famous for his piety and gluttony, he spent most of the war switching from one side to the other. By 1638, with his revenues fallen by seven-eighths, he retired to East Prussia and died there.

At the age of 14, in the middle of the war, Friedrich Wilhelm had been packed off to the Netherlands. He studied at the University of Leiden, becoming acquainted with new developments in science and technology, while in his spare time he caught up with the latest techniques of warfare and politics. He also became a dedicated Calvinist. By the time he succeeded his father in 1640, at the age of 20, his subjects were exhausted and terrorized by the horrors of a war in which they were only marginally involved.

Tall and powerfully built, with piercing blue eyes, Friedrich Wilhelm used cunning diplomacy allied with ruthless force to achieve his objectives. His first aim was to

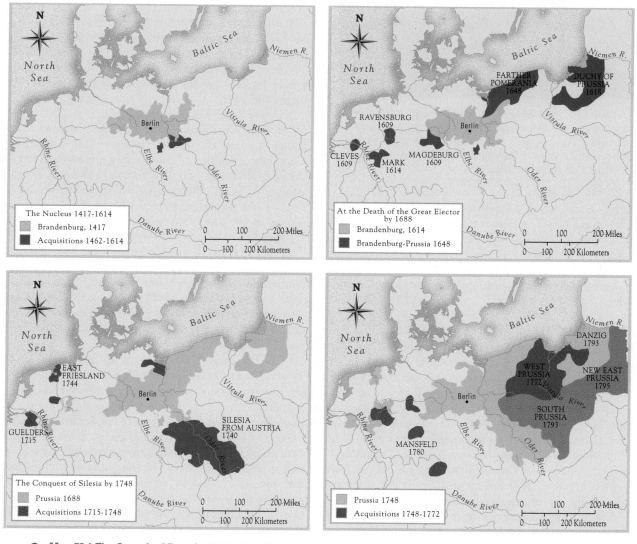

Map 52.1 The Growth of Prussia, 1417–1795. The maps illustrate successive stages in the growth of what was to become the modern state of Germany. Note the position of Berlin, between two of the great rivers of Central Europe, the Elbe and the Oder. By the time of the latest of these maps, the southern part of modern Germany is still part of the Holy Roman Empire. Go to http://info.wadsworth.com/053461065X for an interactive version of this map.

AKG London

Portrait of Friedrich Wilhelm I, king of Prussia. Late 17th century. The king, who is best known for his reforms of the Prussian army, has chosen to pose for his portrait in military armor, rather than the robes of state. In his right hand he holds the baton of command of a Prussia Field Marshal.

extricate himself from the fighting and to clear his territory of foreign soldiers. The Peace of Westphalia in 1648, which finally brought the war to an inconclusive end, awarded Brandenburg-Prussia some new territory. More important, Friedrich Wilhelm successfully defended the Calvinists in the negotiations, winning acknowledgment as the leader of German Protestant interests.

CONFLICT WITH THE ESTATES

The bitter events of the previous generation made it clear that a state without an effective standing army was at the mercy of foreign invaders. Thus the creation of a military force became the new Elector's priority. Yet building a single army to defend all of the provinces was an expensive proposition, requiring a considerable increase in tax revenues. Because each of the provincial Estates insisted on maintaining control over the collection and spending of taxes, and refused to grant funds except for its own province, Friedrich Wilhelm spent the next few years in a series of political struggles for financial control.

The first breakthrough came in Brandenburg, where in 1653 the Elector and the Estates reached an apparent compromise. The agreement guaranteed the Junkers' social and economic privileges and allowed them to turn more peasants into serfs. Furthermore, Friedrich Wilhelm promised to consult the Estates over future policy and appointments. In return the Junkers voted the Elector a large sum of money, to be paid over the next six years.

THE PRUSSIAN ARMY

In 1660 Friedrich Wilhelm founded his permanent standing army. Once in command of his force, he used it to collect more taxes, without the consent of the Estates. In East Prussia the Estates struggled to preserve their rights, even enlisting the support of Poland. Friedrich Wilhelm used the army to occupy the province and eliminated those Junkers who continued to defy him by imprisoning and hanging them. By the 1670s, Prussia was an absolute monarchy, in which the Elector controlled the finances and the army.

The Elector's troops not only served as a fighting force, but they also helped shape and even direct the growth of the state, thereby making Prussia unique among European nations. Soldiers functioned as tax collectors and policemen, developing thereby into a rapidly expanding state bureaucracy. Other divisions in the army also worked on public building projects, digging canals and settling underpopulated areas. As prosperity grew, Friedrich Wilhelm became increasingly successful in persuading his former Junker opponents to head his government departments and above all to become army officers.

By 1688, the Prussian army stood at 30,000 and could be expanded in wartime to 40,000. Well trained and well equipped, it was the second strongest military power in the Germanies, after that of Austria. So professional a force was the envy of Europe, and the European powers vied with one another to hire it. Friedrich Wilhelm adroitly used his army to earn ever-increasing foreign subsidies by timely changes of side, as war continued to rack both Eastern and Western Europe. When the Swedes invaded Poland in 1656 (see Topic 53), he fought first for Sweden and then for Poland. In the Dutch War of 1672–1679, he supported first the Netherlands, then France, and then the Netherlands again. This was no reflection of the indecisiveness of his father. Between 1660 and 1688 he collected handsome payments from a wide range of European powers, without having to do much fighting.

By the time of Friedrich Wilhelm's death in 1688, Prussia was a formidable centralized state, with absolute rule imposed from above. The Elector had won the grudging support of the nobles by allowing them to exploit the peasants; social reform was not part of Friedrich Wilhelm's program. The Prussian economy prospered, thanks to improved agriculture and a revival of commerce—both made possible by a generation of peace. The state became a haven for immigrants who could be of use to the state and religious refugees: Lutherans, Calvinists, Jews, and, after the revocation of the Edict of Nantes in 1685 (see Topic 50), French Huguenots. The only religious minority to whom Friedrich Wilhelm would not grant entry was the Jesuits, whom he thought too intolerant. Many of the newcomers brought skills that helped in the development of agriculture and industry. A large number of the Huguenots joined the army.

Print showing a recruiting drive for soldiers to serve in the Prussian army. 18th century. New recruits, having signed up at the table in the center, are welcomed with a drink of ale. In the foreground, some celebrate by practicing their sword-fighting technique, while to the left others seem happy to escape.

THE FIRST KINGS OF PRUSSIA

It says much for Friedrich Wilhelm's creation that Prussia survived his less dynamic immediate successor, and the eccentricity of the state's next ruler, to increase its international prestige. The Great Elector's son, Friedrich III (ruled 1688–1713 as Elector of Brandenburg and 1701–1713 as king of Prussia), was distinguished more for his ostentatious cultural programs than for his attention to the affairs of state. His principal achievement was to persuade the Hapsburg Holy Roman Emperor to grant him the title of king of Prussia. At the end of 1700, on the eve of the War of the Spanish Succession (see Topic 50), Friedrich promised the Hapsburg ruler diplomatic support and a contingent of soldiers in any eventual conflict. In return, Leopold I allowed the Elector to crown himself king; after his coronation in January 1701, Friedrich became the only German king, ruling as Friedrich I.

Friedrich's son and successor, Friedrich Wilhelm I (ruled 1713–1740), was known to his enemies, as well as to his few friends, as the Sergeant Major. Tightfisted and prudish, he was notorious for bouts of uncontrollable temper, in which he would attack generals and bureaucrats alike with his stick. Crude and violent in his tastes, he was tormented by boils, gout and colic, and religious anxieties. His obses-sive concern for punctuality, obedience, and hard work, all of which he ruthlessly imposed on his hapless subjects, had much to do with creating the image of Prussian character.

His top priority was the army, which had doubled to 80,000 by the time of his death to become the third or fourth strongest in Europe. He formed a special battalion of grenadiers, all of gigantic height, whom his agents recruited throughout Europe. The force became known as the "Battalion of Giants." He is said to have told the French ambassador: "I am utterly indifferent to the most beautiful girl or woman on earth; tall soldiers are my weakness."

Despite his personal oddities, Prussia prospered under his rule. Rigorous state planning and centralized industrial development doubled revenues by 1740. For all Friedrich Wilhelm's obsessive militarism, his army did little actual fighting. His two reasons for avoiding military action were his belief that "God forbids unjust wars" and his reluctance to risk the lives of his precious troops. On the other hand, social rigidity increased, and the peasants and serfs continued to bear the brunt of the entire state system.

The Great Elector had inherited three small provinces, which were disunited, impoverished, and torn by war. By the time Friedrich Wilhelm I died, Prussia was on the verge of becoming one of the great powers of Europe.

Putting Central Europe and the Shifting Balance of Power in Perspective

Beginning in the mid-17th century, the states of Austria and Prussia began to dominate central Europe. The Hapsburg rulers of the combined territory of Austria, Bohemia, and Hungary were from one of the oldest of Europe's aristocratic families and titular monarchs of the Holy Roman Empire. The Hohenzollerns rose from governing insignificant provinces to presiding over an awesome military machine. Both dynasties established absolutist rule, with the monarch in complete control of financial, military, and foreign policy. The power of the local legislative assemblies was broken.

The relapse into authoritarian government was accompanied by a reinforcement of the social order. The Hungarian nobles extracted some concessions from a reluctant emperor, and the Prussian Junkers obtained a share of the growing prosperity by accepting state and military positions. In both countries, however, the middle classes never had a chance to expand: In Friedrich Wilhelm I's Prussia, private enterprise was rigorously discouraged. As for the peasants and serfs, they continued to work for the nobles, pay taxes to the state, and serve in the armies.

Of the two powers, the unity of the larger and more diverse Hapsburg empire was less secure, and the centralized administration less effective. The Great Elector started with the advantage of building his state virtually from scratch, whereas Leopold and his successors had to weld together peoples with established national and religious differences. In future struggles for power in central Europe, Prussia was victorious; it went on in the 19th century to unify the German states and create the German empire.

Questions for Further Study

1. How did the rulers of Brandenburg-Prussia create one of the most powerful European states?
2. What role did the Ottoman Turks play in European affairs in the century from the Battle of Lepanto to the siege of Vienna?
3. How did the Hapsburgs prevent the growth of Czech and Hungarian independence? What were the later consequences of their repression?
4. What were the chief differences between the lives of Central European peasant farmers and those in Western Europe?

Suggestions for Further Reading

Carsten, F.L. *The Origins of Prussia*. Westport, CT, 1982.

Dwyer, Philip G. *The Rise of Prussia, 1700-1830*. Harlow, 2000.

Ingrao, Charles W. *The Habsburg Monarchy, 1618-1815*. New York, 2000.

Macartney, Carlile A. *The Hapsburg and Hohenzollern Dynasties in the Seventeenth and Eighteenth Centuries*. New York, 1970.

McKay, Derek *The Great Elector: Frederick William of Brandenburg-Prussia*. Harlow, 2001.

Parvev, Ivan. *Hapsburgs and Ottomans between Vienna and Belgrade (1683-1739)*. New York, 1995.

Wangermann, E. *The Austrian Achievement*. New York, 1973.

Wheatcroft, Andrew. *The Hapsburgs, Embodying Empire*. New York, 1995.

InfoTrac College Edition

Enter the search term *Holy Roman Empire* using Key Terms.

THE BALTIC AND EASTERN EUROPE IN TRANSITION

By the early 16th century, virtually all the lands of the Eastern Slavs were subject to the ruler of the Principality of Moscow, the "Tsar of all the Russias." In midcentury, Ivan the Terrible (Ivan IV) drove out the few remaining Mongols from Russian territory and concentrated yet more power in his hands by purging the old Muscovite nobles. The 20 years of chaos and violence that followed his turbulent reign were justifiably named the Time of Troubles.

With the election of Michael Romanov as hereditary tsar in 1613, some degree of temporary order was restored. But while the monarch regained autocratic rule and the nobles received concessions, peasant hardships, which were already considerable, increased. The resulting popular unrest, coupled with the religious controversy of the Old Believers, produced more uprisings.

The reign of Peter the Great came as a turning point in Russian history. Following a policy of westernization, he introduced sweeping reforms in civil administration and the military. The tsar retained absolute power, but the creation of a bureaucracy along Western lines and the modernization of the army led eventually to Russia taking its place alongside the great powers of Western Europe. After victory in a long conflict with Sweden known as the Great Northern War (1700–1721), Peter founded the city of St. Petersburg on the Baltic as his new capital.

In the second half of the 17th century, Sweden had conquered most of the territory around the Baltic Sea, but rule of this new Swedish empire dangerously overextended the home country's resources. Despite the efforts of Charles XII, Sweden's king and military hero, the Great Northern War brought a series of defeats.

By contrast with the autocratic monarchies of Russia and Sweden, the nobles in Poland retained considerable power, including the right to elect their king. By the late 17th century, Poland was virtually governed by the Diet, an aristocratic national assembly. Notoriously argumentative and inefficient, the Diet could not even enforce its decisions on the rare occasions it succeeded in making them. In consequence, internal weakness combined with the scheming of Poland's neighbors to create the conditions for complete collapse: In 1794 Poland ceased to exist as an independent country and was partitioned among Austria, Prussia, and Russia.

THE EMERGENCE OF RUSSIA

The transformation of the Principality of Moscow into the capital of the territory of all the Eastern Slavs was finally accomplished in the reign of Ivan III (ruled 1462–1505), called Ivan the Great. With the Turkish capture of Constantinople, capital of the old Byzantine Empire, in 1453, Ivan claimed the title of "tsar"—the Russian equivalent of "Caesar," or "emperor"—and proclaimed himself the heir of the Roman and Byzantine empires, adopting the double-headed eagle of Byzantium as the imperial crest.

IVAN THE TERRIBLE

The Russian state became even more autocratic during the reign of Ivan IV (ruled 1533–1584)—known as Ivan the Terrible, although his nickname in Russian, Ivan Groznyi, is really better translated as Ivan the Awe Inspiring.

Ivan became grand prince of Moscow at the age of three. His youth was warped by fear and neglect and blighted by the sudden death of his mother, perhaps as the result of poisoning. After a period of bloody misrule by the *boyars* (the Russian nobles) during his early years, Ivan was crowned tsar and grand prince of all Russia in 1547; he was the first to bear this title officially. Married seven times, Ivan

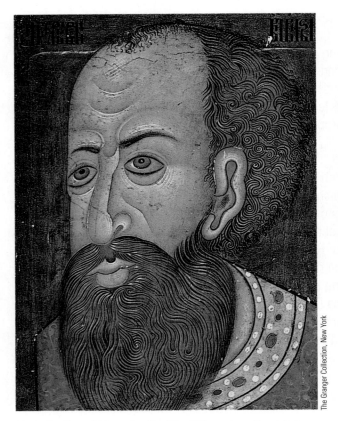

Portrait of Ivan IV, Ivan the Terrible. 16th century. The style is that of Byzantine icons: Note the artificial treatment of the hair and beard. For all his justified reputation for cruelty, Ivan was the first Russian ruler to make a serious attempt to establish trading and diplomatic relations with the states of Western Europe.

The Granger Collection, New York

oscillated between states of tender affection and savage cruelty, combining drunken abandon and religious obsession.

On assuming full power, the tsar continued the policy of his predecessors in strengthening the position of the monarchy by reducing the influence of the traditionally independent princes and boyars. Under Ivan, these perpetually feuding nobles lost power to a new rising nobility, the *dvoranye*, who were granted land directly by the tsar in return for their services to him, and thus were bound in allegiance to him. Ivan revised the legal code, strengthening the hold of masters over peasants. A special army unit, the *streltsy* (shooters), was formed and garrisoned in towns throughout Russia to enforce state policy. Agriculture and industrial production improved, and the Russian economy became increasingly internationalized, as foreign exports (mainly raw materials) and imports increased.

The tsar continued the "gathering of Russia" by driving out the remaining Mongols and gaining control of most of southeastern Russia. He initiated a long and eventually unsuccessful attempt to win territory on the Baltic, losing in the end to an alliance of Poland and Lithuania. Later in Ivan's reign, Russian forces had greater success in the east, where they began the conquest of Siberia that was completed half a century later.

The last 20 years of Ivan's rule were marked by a growing reign of terror. In 1565 he assumed despotic powers, surrounding himself with a special elite guard known as the *oprichniky*. Its 6,000 members dressed in black and rode black horses. In order to provide them with estates—the land they ruled occupied half the kingdom—Ivan uprooted some 12,000 boyars and confiscated their holdings. When Philip, the saintly metropolitan archbishop of Moscow, reproached the oprichniky for their terrorist behavior, Ivan had him strangled.

The climax of his violence came in 1570. Suspicious that the city of Novgorod was planning to join his enemies the Lithuanians, Ivan razed it and had some 60,000 of its inhabitants killed. A few years later he began to disband the oprichniky, merging them by 1575 with the army. In 1581, in a sudden fit of anger with his son, Ivan struck him in the face. Within four days, his heir was dead. When Ivan died three years later, leaving no adequate successor, his country was on the brink of anarchy.

THE TIME OF TROUBLES

The years following Ivan's death are generally called the Time of Troubles (1584–1613), during which life in Russia was marked by civil war, economic crisis, and foreign invasions. The discontent of the peasants led to a series of uprisings, encouraged by the wandering armies of cossacks, who were originally bands of outlawed warrior peasants. Even the powerful boyar Boris Godunov (ruled 1598–1605), who ruled first as regent and then as tsar, failed to maintain control. Best known as the self-titled protagonist of Pushkin's drama (1831) and Mussorgsky's powerful opera (1874), Boris was overthrown by the pretender False Dimitri I, a former monk.

Only a Polish invasion in 1610, during which Polish forces briefly occupied Moscow, finally persuaded the rival boyars of the necessity of restoring some semblance of order. In 1613 they elected as tsar Michael Romanov (ruled 1613–1645), a distant relative of Ivan the Terrible's first wife. The young ruler was in poor health and thus the least threatening of the various candidates. All subsequent Russian tsars, until 1917, came from the Romanov family.

The reigns of Michael and his successor, Alexis (ruled 1645–1676), saw the restoration of imperial power and the simultaneous granting of concessions to the nobles, including the reduction of their military service. Once again the peasants paid the price because in 1649 Alexis introduced a law code that legalized serfdom.

THE OLD BELIEVERS

The peasants' resentment of their ever-worsening conditions deepened as the result of a bitter religious controversy in the latter part of the 17th century. Nikon (1605–1681), the powerful and formidable patriarch of Russia from 1652 to 1666, introduced a long list of changes to traditional services and rituals. His innovations, based on the liturgy of the Greek rather than the Russian Orthodox Church, deeply shocked the mass of old-fashioned believers. The peasants, in particular, crushed by financial and military obligations, reacted with bitterness to the loss of the traditional liturgy, their one remaining comfort.

The changes were in many cases symbolic rather than substantial (for example, three fingers were to be used instead of two for making the sign of the cross) but the result was a schism that split the Russian Church. The traditionalists, who called themselves the Old Believers, resisted the changes by political and social protests. When government forces tried to impose reform, groups of Old Believers gathered inside the wooden churches they had constructed and committed suicide by setting fire to the buildings. The religious controversy underlined the degree to which the church was really a state agency, and the resulting disillusionment of the lower classes with ecclesiastical authority lasted into the 20th century.

As chaos in Russia mounted, the cossacks once again seized their opportunity. Along with a great band of runaway serfs, religious dissidents, and other malcontents, a cossack army led by Stenka Razin (died 1671) swarmed up the Volga in 1670–1671, killing landlords and tsarist officials and proclaiming freedom. Government troops easily defeated the disorderly force. Razin, who was captured and executed in Red Square, torn limb from limb, later became one of Russian folklore's great heroes.

The revolt led to increased repression. Frightened by the violence of the rebels, the nobles redoubled the bonds of serfdom, while rallying around the autocratic rule of the tsar. Finally, with the restoration of central authority, the Romanovs began to improve the imperial administration and rebuild the economy. To achieve this goal, they encouraged contact with Western traders and manufacturers, thus preparing the way for the reforming, if autocratic, rule of Peter the Great.

Woodcut showing Cossack warrior on horseback. 17th century. These Slavic warrior peasants lived in the steppe land of modern Ukraine and were famous for their riding skills. They never accepted outside authority but served as irregular troops under their own leaders. A Cossack mounted regiment fought for the Soviet Union as late as World War II.

PETER THE GREAT AND THE ALLURE OF THE WEST

Under Peter the Great (ruled 1682–1725), Russia became transformed into a modern and aggressive European state. Without relaxing his autocratic rule, Peter improved government at both the central and provincial levels. He encouraged expansion in industry and commerce, rebuilt the army, and created a navy, using Western models for many of these reforms. Peter's chief purpose was to increase Russian military power. By raising Russia's fighting forces, he aimed to make his country the equal of the other great European nations. Many of his successors, both Russian and later Soviet, followed the same policy. By the end of his reign, Russia had replaced Sweden as the leading state in northern Europe, with a permanent place in European power politics.

Peter's early life was overshadowed by violence and marked by a series of palace coups and Moscow riots. He ascended to the throne in 1682 at the age of 10, and seven years later he overthrew the regency of his sister Sofia, making himself sole ruler. Nearly seven feet tall, he was a figure of almost demoniacal energy, ruthless and impetuous. He staggered his contemporaries by his massive consumption of food and drink, and by his incessant activity; he moved without stopping from carpentry to drilling troops to personally decapitating his opponents.

THE ARMY AND THE CHURCH

The central task in Peter's reform program was to increase Russia's military might. In place of the old amateur militias and various professional bands (such as the streltsy), he created a single standing army. From 1699 onward, all its members were recruited, dressed, trained, and armed alike. He introduced conscription of nobles and serfs for lifelong service. At the same time he built a navy whose vessels were manned by foreign officers and Russian conscripts. By the end of his reign the army contained around 130,000 men, and the fleet was made up of 48 ships and almost 800 galleys.

Building the armed forces and paying for their wars consumed some 85 percent of the royal exchequer's revenues. New taxes were necessary to pay for these extraordinary expenses, and Peter replaced the old tax on households with a "soul" tax levied on all individual males, with the important exceptions of nobles and clergy. The Old Believers had to pay double, and the neighbors of any man who fled to avoid the tax were required to pay for him. This latter provision was meant to deter peasants from escaping from their villages, and thus reinforced serfdom. Peter and his advisers also introduced indirect taxes, levied on items as varied as beehives and horse collars, and established state monopolies on tobacco, salt, dice, and rhubarb.

The church, with its vast wealth and estates, lost its independence and became subordinated to the state. When the old patriarch died in 1700 he was not replaced, and a government department took over control of church prop-

erty and received monastic revenues. The state paid the monks and clergy a salary and laid down detailed regulations for their daily lives. The aim was to discipline them along military lines and to make them submit to the government.

THE INFLUENCE OF THE WEST

A further blow to ecclesiastical authority was the establishment of secular institutes of education along Western lines. As a young man, Peter had made friends in the Foreign Quarter of Moscow. Early in his reign he took a trip to Western Europe—his journey is known as the "Great Embassy" of 1697–1698—to see for himself the conditions there. On his return he set up several schools. The School of Navigation and Mathematics was founded in 1701, run initially by English and Scottish teachers. Other institutes included those for languages (1701), medicine (1707), and engineering (1712). As a further contribution to general education, Peter began Russia's first newspaper in 1703.

After his inspection of Western manufacturing methods and economic systems, the tsar tried to apply Western mercantilism to Russian agriculture and industry. The aim was to improve the Russian economy, and thus increase the taxable income of its citizens. Although the economy did begin a long period of growth, the overwhelming predominance of the state prevented the development of a middle class; private enterprise had little scope in a system dominated by government controls. Without the incentive of profits, few manufacturers introduced expensive new equipment, and agricultural methods remained generally medieval.

Not content with changing public policies, Peter also tried to Westernize the private lives and attitudes of his

Colored engraving of the Muscovite cavalry. 18th century. In contrast to the previous illustration of a Cossack horseman, these conventional Russian cavalry officers wear small leather helmets and traditional metal armor. They carry short bows, used to fire iron-tipped arrows.

© bpk, Berlin, Kulturbesitz, Berlin

Contemporary caricature showing Peter the Great cutting off the beard of a boyar (Russian noble). 18th century. Eliminating his subjects' traditional long beards was one of Peter's ways of making them more Western. Those men who insisted on retaining their beards had to pay a tax on them. Note the difference in dress between the boyar (high boots, old-fashioned tunic, and cloak) and Peter's more Westernized attire.

Archiv fur Kunst und Geschichte

Map 53.1 Russian Expansion into Europe, 1589–1796. The crucial event in Russia's move to the West was the foundation of St. Petersburg, where work began in 1709. With the breakup of the Soviet Union in the last decade of the 20th century, some of the gains shown here became independent, notably the Ukraine. The Crimea, taken by Catherine the Great, proved to be the site of fierce fighting in the mid-19th century Crimean War, the Russian Revolution, and World War II. It was still the object of contention in the early years of the 21st century. Go to http://info.wadsworth.com/053461065X for an interactive version of this map.

subjects. He introduced decrees ordering Russian men to shave off their beards (those who refused had to pay a special tax), wear Western clothes, and bring Russian women out of seclusion. In this last respect he set an example. After a brief early marriage, he took as his mistress and drinking companion Catherine Skovorotsky (ruled 1725–1727), a tough, illiterate peasant from Lithuania. Peter married Catherine in 1712, and she ruled as empress on his death.

THE GREAT NORTHERN WAR AND THE FOUNDING OF ST. PETERSBURG

Like his predecessors, Peter devoted most of his energies to enlarging and securing Russia's territories. Among his conquests were parts of Persia, including coastal regions of the Caspian Sea, and further holdings in Siberia. In addition, he was determined to obtain easier access to Europe by sea, either through the Baltic, which was then under Swedish control, or the Black Sea, which was held by the Ottoman Turks. His campaigns against the Turks were inconclusive, and in 1700 he signed the Treaty of Constantinople with them, winning a few concessions, in order to concentrate on the struggle with Sweden.

THE GREAT NORTHERN WAR (1700–1721)

The war against Sweden occupied most of the rest of Peter's reign. His principal opponent was the Swedish king, Charles XII (see separate section), whose prowess as a military commander led to a series of early defeats for the Russian forces. As Peter's domestic reforms began to produce results, however, his troops recovered. At the decisive Battle of Poltava in 1709 he destroyed the Swedish army and advanced into Finland. By 1714, the new Russian fleet was able to defeat the Swedes and threaten the mainland of Sweden. By the Treaty of Nystad (1721), which ended the war, Russia kept Lithuania, Poland, and Estonia, all former Swedish conquests, and gave Finland back to Sweden.

THE GROWTH OF ST. PETERSBURG

Russia's new openness toward the West was symbolized by the creation of the city of St. Petersburg (Petrograd), which

ACROSS CULTURES

CATHERINE WILMOT IN RUSSIA

Travelers often keep diaries of their experiences in remote (to them) places, and these informal accounts sometimes reveal aspects of a culture that more formal writings omit. The young Irishwoman Catherine Wilmot first visited the continent of Europe in 1801, accompanying an Irish nobleman and his wife. Three years later, in 1804, she visited Russia, and her diary describing her experiences sheds interesting and unusual light on the world of the minor Russian aristocracy. It was edited for publication by the Marchioness of

Courtesy of William Duiker

Londonderry and H.M. Hyde in *The Russian Journals of Martha and Catherine Wilmot, 1803-1808* (Macmillan, 1934).

In St. Petersburg, she entertained herself on the "Mountain of Ice," an ice slide more than

SIGNIFICANT DATES

Russia from Ivan the Great to Peter the Great

1462–1505	Reign of Ivan the Great
1547–1584	Reign of Ivan the Terrible
1584–1613	Time of Troubles
1610	Polish invasion of Moscow
1649	Alexis legalizes serfdom
1671	Uprising led by Stenka Razin
1689–1725	Reign of Peter the Great
1700–1721	Great Northern War
1709	Work begins on building St. Petersburg

was built to replace Moscow as capital. In 1702, in the early skirmishes of the Great Northern War, Peter's forces seized a small Swedish fortress, which stood where the River Neva flows into the Baltic Sea. The land, gloomy and unprepos-

sessing, marshy and largely uninhabited, was nonetheless to provide the setting for Peter's new city.

Serious building began in 1709, after the Russian victory at Poltava. The city's organizers laid down a strict plan. The streets were to be broad and straight, with buildings set uniformly along them. The chief architects were Western, many of them Dutch, because Peter intended his new capital to resemble a Dutch port city. Separate parts of the city were set aside for each social class: a district for the nobility, another one for the artisans, and so on. The plan included provisions for public welfare, including street lighting, drainage canals, and parks.

To carry out this highly organized scheme, Peter made full use of his autocratic powers. He ordered the nobles and merchants to build elaborate palaces and villas and to move to the new city from Moscow when the buildings were complete. Once again, however, the peasants paid the heaviest price. Each summer, peasant workers were drafted to labor on the construction sites, while their families had to cover the costs of their upkeep. Most villages preferred to keep the

80 feet long. "It was perfectly smooth for Water had been thrown on it which froze instantly." Climbing the stairs to the top, "we sit down in an Arm Chair with one companion. The Chair has Skates instead of feet. A man who is behind you pushes you. He is provided with Skates. He directs the chair, and there you are without the least possibility of stopping till you arrive at the end of your journey. I should think the sensation must resemble the flight of a Bird."

Her picture of life on a country estate—she stayed at Troitskoe with the Princess Dashkaw—underlines the role played by servants. "It is really astonishing, but the number of servants is dreadful. Think of two, three or even four hundred to attend a small family. A Russian Lady scorns to use her own feet to go up stairs, and I do not Romance when I assure you that two powdered footmen support her lily white elbows and nearly lift her from the ground, while a couple more follow with all manner of Shawls, Pelises, etc., etc., etc. There is not a Bell in Russia except to the Churches, but if a fair one gently calls four or five footmen are ready in an antechamber to obey her summons. We have a little theatre here, and our labourers, our Cooks, our footmen, and chamber maids turn into Princes, Princesses, Shepherds and Shepherdesses, etc., etc., and perform with a degree of spirit that is astonishing."

Other pastimes include rides through the forest on sledges drawn by three horses: "The Solitude of this Forest, which in the night is broken sometimes by the marauding of the wolves, is seldom interrupted in our course, excepting by Wood cutters who look like Satyrs rather than human beings and whose endless beards, clogged in snow and lengthened by icicles, crackle in responsive measure to their hatchets' strokes. The appearance of the Ladies of the Castle however—like magic—suspends all labour, and till the Traineau is out of sight a circle of these Shaggy Satyrs clothed in the skins of Beasts with Fur nightcaps in their paws assemble to shew their devotion and reverence by bowing repeatedly their bearheads to the ground."

stronger men at home on their farms and sent young boys or the elderly. In consequence, many workers died from the heat of summer or from accidents, and the swampy nature of the ground created a constant danger of collapse.

For all of the difficulties, the grandiose project began to take shape. At Peter's death, more than 6,000 government buildings and private residences stood on the former marshy river mouth. Less than 60 years later, in 1782, the population of St. Petersburg was almost 300,000, one of the largest in the world. During the reign of Peter's youngest daughter, Elizabeth (ruled 1741–1761), the Italian architect Bartolomeo Rastrelli (1700–1771) Europeanized Russian architecture with his Baroque and rococo palaces. One of them, the Winter Palace (Hermitage), housed the royal court and now contains the Hermitage Museum, today among the world's great art collections.

For all the undoubted achievements of Peter's reign, the price was high and the results mixed. Government remained inefficient and corrupt. Moreover, the tsar could issue orders on high, but day-to-day administration was in the hands of local bureaucrats, who maintained their arbitrary tyranny over the helpless lower classes. The condition of the serfs became even more hopeless than under Ivan the Terrible. Religious opposition to the process of Westernization came from Old Believers and reformed Orthodox Christians alike. Many conservative nobles, who were opposed to the tsar's reforms, looked to Peter's son Alexis to restore former conditions. Peter, knowing his son to be pious and old-fashioned, had him and his followers eliminated in a purge in 1718. He claimed the right to nominate his own successor, but died before doing so, thus leaving the way open for the palace revolutions that marked 18th-century Russian political life.

Yet if Peter's reforms of government and the economy were only partially successful, his creation of a formidable military machine and aggressive foreign policy changed the course of European history. By winning the Baltic provinces, Russia replaced Sweden as the leading power in northern Europe. Newly Westernized in outlook, Russia was now ready to assume its role as a major actor on the stage of European power politics.

THE COLLAPSE OF THE SWEDISH EMPIRE

The years of Russia's increasing influence saw the decline of the two other leading northern European powers, Sweden and Poland. Poland's deterioration had been on course for more than a century, but Sweden had only recently acquired an empire. In the early 17th century the charismatic Swedish king, Gustavus Adolphus (ruled 1611–1632), raised his country from a state of insecurity and weakness to dominance in the Baltic. By the time of his death in one of the battles of the Thirty Years' War, Sweden was one of the leading military powers in Europe.

CHARLES XI AND THE STRUGGLE WITH THE NOBLES

Charles XI (ruled 1660–1697) was less concerned with foreign affairs than with weakening the hold of Sweden's high nobility. Charles came to the throne at the age of five, and during the early years of his reign a group of nobles led by his uncle took control of government. Incompetent and rapacious, they plundered crown lands and oscillated in their foreign policy between support of Louis XIV and his enemies. At home they emulated Louis' opulent Versailles lifestyle.

When Charles finally assumed full control, he set about concentrating power in his own hands. Shy and pious, he conscientiously constructed an absolute monarchy whereby the ruler took full control. With the support of the lower nobility, the middle classes, clergy, and peasants, he compelled the high nobility to hand back the royal properties they had taken. By the end of his reign, the crown's holdings of land had risen from 1 percent of the total country to 30 percent.

With the increase in state income, Charles was free to avoid foreign campaigns, with their highly uncertain rewards, and to concentrate on domestic matters. He reformed the army by recruiting conscript citizens and paid them for their service by giving them farms, or the income from farms, regained from the nobles. The army's excellent training, and the speed with which it could mobilize, were of great help to Charles's successor. His reform of the bureaucracy saw merit rather than birth rewarded by promotion.

The king's power remained supreme. In 1693, Sweden's Diet—its name had been changed from Council of State to King's Council—declared the monarch to be "by God, Nature, and the Crown's high, hereditary right . . . an absolute sovereign king." So disciplined and orderly and popular an absolute ruler offered the promise of great possibilities for his country, but Charles died of stomach cancer at the early age of 41.

CHARLES XII AND THE GREAT NORTHERN WAR

Charles XII (ruled 1697–1718), the son and successor of Charles XI, was trained from childhood to serve as king. He was well educated in science, philosophy, and the arts, especially music and theater, and accompanied his father on official business. He was tall and fair and so drawn by dreams of military glory that he remained a bachelor, claiming that he was "married to the army." He used hard exercise and self-denial to toughen himself, and made a point of personally leading his troops into battle.

A century earlier, a favorable combination of circumstances enabled Sweden to acquire a Baltic empire. Defending these holdings, however, became increasingly difficult for a country with a small population and modest resources. When Peter the Great became ruler of Russia, Sweden's chief rival, the days of the Swedish empire were numbered. The brief life of Charles XII was dedicated to an increasingly hopeless attempt to hold on to Sweden's empire, in the face of Russian, Polish, Prussian, and Danish opposition. Ironically enough, Sweden's warrior king, one of the military geniuses of the age, presided over the end of Sweden as an imperial power.

The Great Northern War began with a series of Swedish successes, including an invasion of Denmark and a victory over the Russians at Narva (1700). The momentum seemed irresistible, and Charles led his forces deep into Russian territory. In the winter of 1708–1709, one of the harshest on record, the Swedish Army traveled into the interior of Russia. By the time Charles made an assault on the Russian camp at Poltava the following June, his troops were demoralized and underequipped. To make matters worse, Charles was confined to a stretcher because he had been shot in the foot in an earlier fight. The result was a disaster for the invaders. Most of the Swedish Army surrendered to the Russians, Charles fled to the Ottoman court in Turkey, and Peter the Great emerged as the leader of a new major European power.

For the next few years Charles remained in Turkey. In 1714 he galloped home in a mere 14 days and nights to rebuild his forces and reconquer lost territory. By 1718 he had put together an army of 60,000. Late in the year he invaded Norway, only to be killed by a stray bullet at the siege of Fredricksheld, a shot perhaps fired by one of his own soldiers.

During Charles's long absences abroad, his father's efficient bureaucracy continued to govern Sweden. On his death, the bureaucracy introduced parliamentary government, inaugurating Sweden's Age of Liberty. At the same time, it made peace with all of Sweden's enemies. The empire was divided among Hanover, Denmark, Prussia, and Russia, with the last of these receiving the Baltic provinces. Sweden's imperial age was over.

POLAND: THE TRIUMPH OF THE NOBILITY

In the late Middle Ages, the union of Poland and Lithuania (1386) produced one of Europe's leading powers, second in size only to Russia. Many of the commercial routes for trade between the Black Sea and the Baltic passed through Poland, bringing prosperity with them. By the 16th century, however, commerce had shifted westward. The Renaissance and Counter-Reformation brought some renewal to Catholic Poland, but on the whole the country began a period of growing decline, which led inexorably to its extinction in the late 18th century.

THE KING AND THE MAGNATES

In complete contrast to the absolutist Sweden of Charles XI, 17th-century Poland was dominated by the nobility, known as the *magnates*. These powerful aristocrats retained the power to elect the king, and saw to it that the ruler they chose was too weak to have any control over them. As a result, the Polish throne offered little more than the prestige of a royal title, appealing mainly to petty German princes. The Polish magnates governed their country through the Diet, or parliament. The Diet, fearful of a rising bourgeoisie, had actually introduced legislation to restrict trade, and with the decline of commerce the middle class all but disappeared. As for the peasants, the great majority of the population, they were enserfed under conditions as grim as any in Europe.

THE DELUGE

By the reign of John II (ruled 1648–1668), Poland was so beset by problems that the period is known in Polish tradition as the Deluge. The magnates were sending the grain, timber, and other raw materials produced on their estates for sale in Western Europe, thereby lining their own pockets but impoverishing Poland. The population was falling, the currency was debased, what little city life existed was in decline, and serfdom was spreading.

At a time when only strong centralized government could have counteracted these tendencies, the Diet introduced a device that further restricted the possibility of concerted action. In 1652 the *liberum veto* (free veto) was used for the first time. This meant that a single member of the Diet could veto a decision by his negative vote. Even more dangerously, every member could use the liberum veto to dissolve the Diet and annul previous decisions.

Already notorious for its indecisiveness and inefficiency, the Diet now became paralyzed. In the century following the introduction of the liberum veto, no fewer than 57 Diets were convened. Administration, which was already disorganized, degenerated into chaos. The king could only watch helplessly, as the magnates took charge, with their vast labor force of serfs, their private armies, and their control over provincial assemblies.

Poland's neighbors seized their opportunity. First the Russians and then the Swedes invaded; pious Polish Catholics saw the devastating Swedish invasion of 1655–1660 as God's punishment on their country for having harbored Protestants. In 1655 the Swedes captured Warsaw, the Polish capital, and many of the magnates hastened to declare allegiance to the Swedish monarch as a means of saving their own skins. Only the death of the Swedish king five years later brought the war to an end.

After further losses to Russia, and with the threat of a massive Turkish onslaught, John could take no more. In 1668 he abdicated and went to France, where he became the titular abbot of Saint-Germain-des-Prés.

His successors fared little better. John III Sobieski (ruled 1674–1696) helped restore Polish prestige by his heroic actions at the relief of the Turkish siege of Vienna in 1683 (see Topic 52). The last years of his reign, however, saw a return to conspiracies and rebellions. A string of powerless puppet kings followed him, as the country degenerated into a collection of feudal territories ruled over by local magnates.

Only in 1772, when Russia, Prussia, and Austria began to plot the carving up of Poland among themselves, was the country driven to act. The government enacted reforms, strengthening the power of the king and improving the conditions of the peasants. The Polish patriot Thaddeus Kosciusko (1746–1817) returned from America, where he was in the American Revolutionary army and had been in charge of construction at West Point, to serve as major general in the Polish Army.

The changes were too late, and in any case the ill-equipped Polish troops were no match for Europe's three most formidable professional armies. In 1793, Prussian and Russian forces occupied parts of the country. Kosciusko led a rebellion against them, but he was captured by the Russians, later returning to America and then to France, from where he continued to campaign for Polish liberty. By 1795 the dismemberment of Poland was complete.

Putting the Baltic and Eastern Europe in Perspective

The most important political development in Eastern Europe in the 17th century was the emergence of Russia as a leading European power. Sweden's brief period as the ruler of an empire was never likely to last for long. The willful destruction of Poland by its own nobility continued, and Poland ceased for some time to have significant political or economic influence. Russia's appearance in international affairs, however, marked a significant break with the past.

Continued next page

Unlike Western Europe, the countries of Eastern Europe showed no sign of introducing social reform. In Russia, successive tsars maintained authoritarian rule, while Poland's magnates continued their domination. In Sweden, bureaucratic absolutism was replaced for a while in the early 18th century by parliamentary government, but by the end of the century absolute rule was back. In both Poland and Russia peasant conditions remained dismal.

Russia's success was chiefly the result of its military prowess. Even Peter the Great had failed to do much to improve his country's administrative system, and the Russian economy remained backward, inhibited by the massive state bureaucracy. The deficiencies of central state planning were to hamper Russia's economic progress for centuries. As for Peter's attempts at Westernization, they led in the 19th century to a bitter polarization of Russian intellectuals into pro-Westerners and pro-Slavs (for a discussion of the controversy see Topic 68).

Yet once awakened, the mighty country was quick to assume its new position. Throughout the 18th century its chief rivals, Prussia and Austria, had little choice but to acknowledge as an equal a state that only 100 years earlier had seemed far from the mainstream of European life.

Questions for Further Study

1. What role did the Orthodox Church play in Russian affairs? How did this differ from the function of organized religion in the West?
2. What means did Peter the Great use to Westernize Russia? What was the effect of his reforms on Russian society?
3. Which were the chief factors leading to the dismemberment of Poland?
4. How did the Great Northern War affect political developments in northern Europe?

Suggestions for Further Reading

Anderson, M.S. *Peter the Great*. London, 1978.

Bain, Robert N. *Charles the Twelfth and the Collapse of the Swedish Empire, 1682-1719*. New York, 1995.

Bushkovitch, Paul. *Peter the Great: The Struggle for Power, 1671-1725*. New York, 2001.

Duffey, C. *Russia's Military Way to the West*. London, 1982.

Dukes, P. *The Making of Russian Absolutism 1613–1801*. London, 1982.

Dunning, Chester, S.L. *Russia's First Civil War: The Time of Troubles and the Founding of the Romanov Dynasty*. University Park, PA, 2001.

Frost, Robert I. *The Northern Wars: War, State and Society in Northeastern Europe, 1558-1721*. New York, 2000.

Lincoln, W. Bruce. *Sunlight at Midnight: St. Petersburg and the Rise of Modern Russia*. New York, 2001.

Lukowski, Jerzy. *The Partition of Poland, 1772, 1792, 1795*. New York, 1999.

Massie, Robert K. *Peter the Great: His Life and Work*. New York, 1992.

InfoTrac College Edition

Enter the search term *Peter the Great* using Key Terms.

THE CULTURE OF THE OLD REGIME

The 18th century marks a period of transition in the arts. When it dawned, Louis XIV still ruled as absolute monarch, and the works produced for his court were intended to satisfy the royal taste. By the end of the century, artists throughout Europe were creating for a much wider audience.

One of the highest achievements of art in the Old Regime was reached in drama at the French court. In the latter part of the 17th century, the three greatest names in the history of the French theater were all active at the same time, working under the patronage of Louis XIV. Pierre Corneille and Jean Racine wrote tragedies generally based on Classical themes, while Molière virtually created the form of French comedy.

In the decades following the death of Louis XIV, the audience for arts and ideas began to broaden. New institutions appeared that satisfied the growing demand for cultural and intellectual exchange. Among them were learned academies and salons, informal gatherings for discussion, which permitted women to play an increasingly important cultural role.

With the number of readers rapidly increasing, and writers less dependent on aristocratic patronage, literary ideas were spread in new forms. By the mid-18th century, the popular press was firmly established, and newspapers and periodicals circulated widely. The publications dispensed facts, literature, and opinion. The same period saw the rise of the popular novel, which reflected a middle-class rather than aristocratic morality.

In the visual arts, the heavy magnificence of the Baroque Era gave way to the more delicate charm of the rococo. Painters like the French Jean-Honoré Fragonard depicted elegant and romantic encounters.

Eighteenth-century musicians also tried to develop increased expressivity. Within a few years a new musical style appeared, the Classical, which made possible greater emotional variety. The first great master of the Classical style was Haydn, whose symphonies virtually created a new musical form. Even more versatile was Wolfgang Amadeus Mozart, whose music combined beauty with learning.

By the end of the Old Regime, artists, writers, and intellectuals were already foreshadowing the coming revolutionary changes and the Romantic movement of the 19th century.

THE ARTS IN TRANSITION

The 18th century produced a remarkably varied range of artistic styles. The elevated grandeur of Corneille's and Racine's tragedies, the charmingly erotic scenes depicted in Watteau's canvasses, the social intrigues of Mozart's operas: all of these varied forms seem to have little in common. Yet they, and the visions of other artists of the same period, share the characteristic of being addressed to an increasingly widening public.

Hitherto, most artists had served a patron, generally the church, the monarchy, or the aristocracy. Works of art, whether for the public domain or for private entertainment, conformed to the requirements of their commissioners. Ever since the 16th century, sections of the European aristocracy had cultivated the arts, playing music, patronizing artists, and engaging in amateur artistic pursuits. Toward the end of the 17th century, however, economic expansion, urbanization, and the spread of literacy produced a new public, as the middle classes began to develop an interest in the arts. Corneille's plays represent, in fact, one of the earliest attempts to address a middle-class audience.

With the change in audience came a change in the status of the artist. Although still dependent on some form of patronage—the artist as fiery, free-thinking creator did not appear until the 19th century—writers, painters, and musicians acquired a new social status. Friedrich II of Prussia entertained at his court the leading composers of the day, wrote music and played the flute, and boasted of his intimate friendship with the great French writer Voltaire. The relationship was a fiery one. When Friedrich had "squeezed all the juice from the rind," he dropped Voltaire, who in turn made sure that his own version of the break circulated as widely as possible.

When in his later years the Austrian composer Haydn traveled throughout Europe, he was feted and honored as one of the most famous figures of his times. Haydn's own career, in fact, was symbolic of the new status of the creative artist. He spent his early years as an employee at the court of one of the leading aristocratic families, the Esterhazys, as director of the prince's music; when he wanted to write music for another patron, he was obliged to ask permission. With the growth of his fame, he was able to negotiate a revised contract under which the Esterhazys no longer had exclusive rights to his work. By the time he reached his sixties, he was free to live in Vienna and travel abroad, although he still continued to compose for the Esterhazys.

The new social position that artists occupied, together with the broad changes in society that made it possible, was inevitably reflected in their works. Although the artistic styles of the 18th century were far more varied than those of the Baroque Era, many of the age's most important achievements reflect a new preoccupation: a conscious engagement with social issues. Racine and Mozart, along with Richardson and many others, used their art to explore ways of advancing and reforming society. By the mid-18th century, the intellectual movement known as the Enlightenment (see Topic 58) provided an underpinning for these concerns.

TRAGEDY AND COMEDY AT THE COURT OF LOUIS XIV

For Louis XIV, the arts served as a means of projecting his vision of himself as Grand Monarch. The court at Versailles provided an appreciative audience for the theater, and in the latter part of the 17th century three great playwrights dominated French drama. All of them concentrated on depicting universal human types and emotions, rather than reflecting the world of the court.

THE COMEDIES OF MOLIÈRE

Molière was the stage name of Jean-Baptiste Poquelin (1622–1673). He was the son of a court furnisher, but rather than follow his father's profession, at the age of 21 he joined a group of actors to form a theatrical company. The actors soon went bankrupt, and Molière spent some time in prison for debt. Undeterred, he left Paris for the provinces to learn the craft of acting and playwriting. When he returned to the capital 13 years later with his own troupe, he performed before the king. In 1665 Louis became patron of his company, and Molière wrote romances and comedies for the royal courts at Saint-Germain and Versailles. He also poured out a stream of plays for a wider public, often acting in them. He died on stage in the middle of a performance of his last play, *Le Malade imaginaire (The Hypochondriac)*—of overwork, it was said.

Ironically for one favored by Louis XIV, Molière's source of comedy was the deflation of pomposity and arrogance. Taking a human weakness or delusion, such as hypochondria, miserliness, or misanthropy, he carries it to an absurd and often explosive conclusion. Yet revelation comes through laughter, not ridicule, and the characters remain believable. Tartuffe, the oily hypocrite in the play of the same name (1664–1669), or Jourdain, the amiable social climber of *Le Bourgeois gentilhomme* (1670), are not merely symbols but living personalities.

Only in one play, *L'Avare (The Miser;* 1668), does a human foible seem cruel and deluded. The miserliness of its chief character, Harpagon, is revealed as a perverse mania, reducing its victim to a childishness that provides the comic element. On the whole the message of Molière's works is to underline the humanity of even the most absurd of his characters and to advocate reason and balance—the Classical middle way.

THE CLASSICAL TRAGEDIES OF CORNEILLE AND RACINE

The two leading tragedians of the age were Pierre Corneille (1606–1684) and Jean Racine (1639–1699). Both used as their starting point themes from Classical mythology or history, but their approaches were very different.

Corneille was already writing when Louis XIV came to the throne, creating a new kind of play—the Classical verse tragedy—for a middle-class audience. His dramas are serious in tone, often dealing with conflicts of principles that call into question established morality. They thus appealed to a middle-class public that was questioning traditional ideas. *Horace* (1640) is based on incidents recorded by the ancient Roman historian Livy, and tells of a patriot who saves the state, but at the cost of the life of his pacifist sister. *Polyeucte* (1643) presents the dilemma of a martyr, whose wish for a glorious death is tempered by duty to his faithful wife. Corneille's plays are self-consciously artificial. They make no attempt to represent literal time, place, or action. Instead, they provide abstract intellectual conflict in the cut and thrust of rhetorical debate.

Racine's first tragedy was produced by Molière's company in 1664, and he went on to write works for the leading Paris theaters. Using the Classical verse tragedy form perfected by Corneille, he brought to it a new understanding of human emotions. In plays such as *Phèdre* (1677), he explored the psychological state of mind of his characters. His dominating theme is the human tendency toward self-destruction through ambition, jealousy, passion, and other forms of what his contemporary La Rochfoucauld (1613–1680) called self-love. His characters realize the tragedy of the human condition, while their understanding of their own helplessness reinforces their suffering and our pity for them. In his last play, *Athalie* (1691), the queen whose name gives the play its title expresses this sense of abandonment in a hostile world: "Pitiless God, Thou hast willed it all!"

ACADEMIES AND SALONS IN THE REPUBLIC OF LETTERS

The growing popularity of science in the 17th century led to the formation of learned societies, or academies, for the discussion and spread of new ideas and discoveries. Among the most famous was the Royal Society of London, which received its royal charter in 1660. By the 18th century, the taste for semipublic discussion of ideas of all sorts spurred the creation of many more or less formal groups. Many of these groups sprang up in provincial cities in various parts of Europe, often in relatively small centers. As a result, knowledge of new ideas and values became more widespread than before.

In some cases these organizations sponsored the arts. London's Royal Academy of Arts was founded in 1768 by George III to encourage painting and still maintains an art school and holds open exhibitions annually. The Royal Academy's first president, Sir Joshua Reynolds (1723–1792), also sponsored the Literary Club for the discussion of literary topics. Among its members were Samuel Johnson (1709–1784), perhaps the most brilliant if idiosyncratic writer and critic of his time, the statesman and philosopher Edmund Burke (1729–1797), and the writer Oliver Goldsmith (c. 1730–1774).

Some organizations had specific goals. Catherine the Great entrusted the Imperial Russian Academy with preparing a standard Russian grammar and the first Russian dictionary, in addition to giving it the general task of providing translations of scientific and philosophical works into Russian.

By midcentury the creation of academies swelled to a flood. In Florence alone, there flourished the Accademia delle Belle Arti for painting and drawing, the Accademia della Crusca (*crusca* literally means bran; the academy was formed to preserve the purity of the Italian language by "separating the wheat from the chaff"), the Accademia dei Georgofili (literally "farming-lovers"; its members discussed scientific and economic aspects of farming), the Accademia

Painting of the young Mozart entertaining a Paris salon. 1766. Leopold Mozart, the composer's father, took the young genius on a European tour when he was seven years old, in 1763. Paris was one of the last stops, where Mozart played for the French royal court, published his compositions for the first time, and composed his first symphonies.

The Granger Collection, New York

PUBLIC FIGURES AND PRIVATE LIVES

ELIZABETH ROBINSON MONTAGU AND EDWARD MONTAGU

Picture Library, National Portrait Gallery, London

Picture Library, National Portrait Gallery, London

The first salon may have been established by a French noblewoman, the Marquise de Rambouillet (1588–1665). Suffering from an illness that required her to remain in bed wrapped in blankets and furs, she entertained guests from a bedroom alcove in her Parisian home. The salon eventually became an established institution in Paris, where women brought the talented and the powerful into their homes. By the middle of the following century, when the influence of the salon was at its height, the practice had spread to other European cities.

In Great Britain, the salon was the creation of Elizabeth Montagu (1720–1800). Elizabeth developed a serious interest in literature at an early age and read widely. High-spirited and outgoing, she married Edward Montagu (d. 1775), grandson of the first earl of Sandwich, in 1742. Edward was a wealthy and serious-minded man who owned coal mines and estates, liked agriculture and mathematics, and served in Parliament for more than 30 years.

The couple lived in the country, where Elizabeth earned a reputation as an accomplished hostess. Their one child, a son, died after only a year, and thereafter the couple led increasingly separate lives. Soon she moved the household to London, where the social season offered more distractions, and she made the Montagu home in Mayfair a gathering place for the most important intellectuals of the city—to a friend she explained, "I never invite idiots to my house."

At first Elizabeth entertained at literary breakfasts, but she soon added more elaborate evening assemblies, which became known as "conversation parties." She refused to allow card playing, encouraging her guests instead to discuss literary subjects. On occasion, a well-known actor would recite. For 50 years, Elizabeth presided over the intellectual society of London, and writers, artists, and politicians vied with one another for invitations to the Montagu salon, where wit counted more than high birth.

The term "Bluestockings" was first applied to the women intellectuals who attended Montagu's salon. The origin of the name is disputed, but one version of the story recounts that because Elizabeth allowed her guests to dress casually, one of her poorer friends always wore blue wool stockings instead of those made of more elegant black silk. Soon the word became a collective term for the women who attended and hosted such receptions, although it later came to be used derogatively to mean a woman who was pedantic, plain, and unfeminine.

In 1775, Edward Montagu died and left Elizabeth a large income and many estates. She went to Paris the next year, where she became familiar with the works of Voltaire. She also built a large and sumptuous house in London, which became the new center for her salon. To demonstrate her social consciousness, each May she invited the chimney sweeps of London to eat roast beef and plum pudding on the lawn of her home. By 1798, when she was almost blind and very feeble, her entertaining had all but ceased. She died two years later.

The salon not only permitted women to lead and take an active part in cultural debate alongside men, but it also provided a forum that brought together aristocrats and middle-class intellectuals, helping both groups to get to know one another's ways. Furthermore, the salons of Berlin and Vienna, by their inclusion of Jews, encouraged a greater official tolerance toward Jewish minorities; many of Berlin's leading salons, in fact, were run by Jewish women. The most successful *salonières*, or hostesses, achieved considerable power behind the scenes, promoting their pet writers' work or advancing the political careers of their favorites. As one of them boasted, "It is possible to obtain through women what one wants from men."

del Cimento (Academy for Scientific Testing), and the portentously named Accademia Toscana di Scienze e Lettere "La Colombaria" (Tuscan Academy for Science and Letters "The Dovecote," so-called because of the small size of the room in which its members met).

Although some of the academies encouraged women to become members, most retained quotas. One of Italy's most admired 18th-century poets was Maria Maddalena Morelli (1727–1800), better known as Corilla. In 1776, the Roman Academy crowned her on the steps of the capitol for her abilities in declamation and improvisation. But most educated, serious women who were interested in participating in the literary and intellectual debates of the day had to do so informally. As a result of this constraint, women developed a new kind of cultural institution known as the **salon:** gatherings in private homes for the purpose of intellectual discussion (the term *salon* comes from the French word for sitting room).

THE POPULAR PRESS, NOVELS, AND THE CIRCULATION OF IDEAS

With the rapid growth of a middle-class reading public, literary culture began to spread in new ways. Just as conversation became the chief activity of the salons, so reading aloud came to occupy many middle-class families in their own homes. Because women were on their own territory in front of the family hearth, their tastes in literature became increasingly important.

THE GROWTH OF THE PRESS
The appearance of the popular press provided a potential challenge to governments, which were accustomed to controlling the spread of information. In 1662, the British Parliament passed the Licensing Act, limiting the number of licensed printers to 20, "to prevent abuses in printing seditious, treasonable, and unlicensed books and pamphlets." Yet the pressure for new sources of information was too great to resist: In 1695, Parliament decided not to renew the Licensing Act, and the next two decades saw the birth of scores of journals. The first London daily paper, the *Courant*, appeared in 1702, to be followed by a string of competitors. Even the imposition of state taxes on publications and their advertisements failed to discourage their proliferation.

Much of the contents of the dailies was practical: news of markets and shipping, prices of stocks and exchange rates, and "Names and Descriptions of Persons becoming Bankrupt." Details of births, marriages, deaths, and inquests began to appear. The largest number of pages was devoted to small commercial advertisements. The weekly magazines tended to include articles on more general topics, including politics, reviews of books and plays, and fashion.

In addition, the leading periodicals exercised a more general cultural impact. *The Spectator*, founded in 1711 by the English essayist and statesman Joseph Addison

(1672–1719), helped form the taste of the age and shaped the values and behavior of its educated middle-class subscribers. Addison's impact was acknowledged by influential London figures, such as Dr. Johnson, but it also had a wider effect as his publication reached provincial and foreign readers. Among many others, David Hume in Edinburgh and Benjamin Franklin in Philadelphia both admired Addison's style, and used it as a model.

The rise in circulation of both daily and weekly publications was rapid and consistent. The total annual sale in Great Britain rose from 2,250,000 in 1711 to 7,000,000 in 1753 and to 12,230,000 in 1776 (the figures are available because of the tax paid on each copy sold). Because many papers were bought by clubs and coffeehouses, the total readership was far larger than the number of copies in circulation. With its growth, the popular press acquired considerable power. The opponents of the British prime minister Sir Robert Walpole accused him of paying out more than £50,000 in bribes to newspapers in the last 10 years of his administration, and the freedom of the press became a major political issue.

WOMEN'S MAGAZINES
Many of the new publications were specifically addressed to women, who constituted an important and growing class of readership. In the Netherlands and Germany, women contributed many of the articles, and one of the leading Dutch papers, *The Quintessence of News*, was founded by a woman, Madame du Noyer. The most important French periodical for women, the *Journal des Dames*, first appeared in 1759, when its male publishers announced it as a "delicious nothing" for society ladies. Its women editors soon changed its character, however, publishing articles and reviews dealing with the question of women's rights and making thinly veiled attacks on the government.

By the latter part of the 18th century, middle-class families throughout Europe were exposed to a bewildering range of dailies, weeklies, and periodicals, many of which circulated outside their country of origin. One enterprising publisher even found a way to help readers who were spoiled for choice. The *Grand Magazine of Magazines, or Universal Register* contained "all that is curious, useful, or entertaining in the magazines, reviews, or chronicles, at home or abroad."

THE RISE OF THE POPULAR NOVEL
Popular novels had appeared in France as early as the reign of Louis XIV, many of them written by women. From the early 18th century on, popular writers in Europe made a deliberate appeal to middle-class ideals and values. The social background and accepted attitudes of the books reflected a world dominated by class consciousness and economic status. The rise or fall of individuals, often because of marriage, is paralleled by critical developments in fortune and character.

The first significant popular writer in English was Samuel Richardson (1689–1761). His novel *Pamela* (1740), written in the form of a series of letters, describes the triumph of a servant girl, who marries her master after successfully fighting off his attempts at seduction. Produced in only two months, *Pamela* proved a bestseller throughout Europe, especially in France. A later novel, *Clarissa* (1748), also deals with seduction, but its moral vision is more complex. Its two chief characters, the virtuous Clarissa and the cunning and immoral (and aristocratic) Lovelace, are both victims of a sexuality that is at the same time obsessive and destructive.

THE ART OF THE ROCOCO

With the death of Louis XIV in 1715, the French aristocracy abandoned the Baroque extravagance of Versailles for the elegant domestic comfort of Paris, and a new artistic style developed to provide an appropriate setting. The **rococo**—the word derives from the French *rocaille*, or grotto decoration—was intended as a contrast to the Baroque. Rarely weighty or serious, it aims for charm and lightness and replaces Baroque drama with grace and harmony. The interior decoration of buildings such as the Hotel de Soubise in Paris was appropriate for an age that put a new emphasis on civilized conversation. Rococo art, with its frank desire to please, also ap-

Fragonard, *Love Letters*. 1773. 10 feet 5 inches by 7 feet 1 inch (3.17 by 2.17 m). Both in subject—an amorous encounter—and style, this is typical of later rococo painting. The jungle of trees and bushes seems to impart a heady, humid air to what at first glance seems an innocent meeting. Rococo artists often aimed to emphasize the erotic nature of their scenes.

pealed to middle-class clients, who were in search of works that were appropriate to an intimate domestic setting, rather than intended for grandiose palaces.

Many rococo artists explored the theme of romantic dalliance. The last great French rococo painter, Jean-Honoré Fragonard (1732–1806), achieved an erotic effect with great subtlety. His superb lightness of touch and sense of color often emerge in the scenery surrounding his figures. The sense of warmth in the air in paintings such as *Love Letters* (1773) adds a touch of danger to the apparently innocent couple in the foreground.

RELIGIOUS ART AND THE ROCOCO

The lightness of the rococo style did not lend itself naturally to religious subjects in painting but inspired some remarkable architecture. Some of the finest of all rococo buildings can be seen in southern Germany and Austria, where the bitter wars of the 17th century had discouraged the building of new churches. With the more stable conditions of the first part of the 18th century, construction started again, producing a series of rococo masterpieces.

Germain Boffrand, Salon de la Princesse, Hotel Soubise, Paris, c. 1737–1740. Oval 33 feet by 26 feet (10.06 by 7.92 m). The architecture and decoration (painting and sculptures) all combine to create a characteristic rococo effect. The paintings flowing from ceiling to walls break down the distinction between horizontal and vertical elements, and the reflections in the large mirrors further confuse the viewer's sense of space.

Balthasar Neumann, Nave and High Altar of Vierzehnheiligen Pilgrim Church, near Bamberg, Germany. 1743–1772. The oval shape of the altar, typical of pilgrimage churches, is echoed in the oval ceiling paintings. The architect has rejected the soaring lines of the Gothic style and the balance of Renaissance symmetry for an intricate interweaving of surfaces, volumes, and space.

The German architect Balthasar Neumann (1687–1753), an engineer by profession, designed several churches and episcopal palaces. Perhaps his most elaborate and intricate work is the interior of the Vierzehnheiligen (Fourteen Saints) Pilgrimage Church (1743–1772) near Bamberg, in southern Germany. The decoration flows down from the ceiling, encrusting walls and columns, in a deliberate rejection of Renaissance notions of balance and symmetry. For those accustomed to the austerity of much religious architecture, the sheer lightness and exuberance of Neumann's creation may seem out of place, but it succeeds in producing a sense of joy that is not inappropriate.

THE CLASSICAL STYLE IN MUSIC: MOZART AND HAYDN

As music, like literature, began to find an ever-widening audience, composers tried to express more complex and varied emotions. By the mid-18th century, composers had developed a style to meet the requirement of unity through variety: the Classical style. Its first great master was the Austrian Franz Joseph Haydn (1732–1809), whose more

than 100 symphonies won him the name of "Father of the Symphony."

WOLFGANG AMADEUS MOZART

The life of the Austrian Wolfgang Amadeus Mozart (1756–1791) illustrates that not all artists were as fortunate as Haydn. When Haydn met the young Mozart in 1781, he observed to the young man's father, "Before God and as an honest man, your son is the greatest composer known to me either in person or by name." Posterity has seen no reason to doubt Haydn's judgment, yet Mozart's career was dogged by a constant alternation of successes and setbacks. A child prodigy, he traveled throughout Europe with his father, composing and performing to the acclaim of his aristocratic audiences.

Mozart was less fortunate in his patron than Haydn. After serving the archbishop of Salzburg, where he was born, Mozart tried to follow his great contemporary's example and obtain some measure of independence. When he asked for his freedom, the reigning archbishop, Hieronymous Colloredo, had him literally kicked out of the palace. Haydn managed to win his independence through the cooperation of his employer, and remained tied to some degree to noble patronage. Mozart's break was complete and violent.

Mozart spent the last 10 years of his life in Vienna, struggling to find a permanent position and pouring out works to earn a living—symphonies and concertos for orchestral concerts, piano sonatas and string quartets, religious music for

Joseph Lange, *Mozart at the Pianoforte*. 1789. 13½ inches by 11½ inches (35 by 30 cm). This unfinished portrait shows the composer for once without the white wig customarily worn in the 18th century. Mozart must have liked the painting, because he had a copy made and sent to his father.

church performance, even music for Masonic ceremonies (Mozart was a Freemason). The Viennese public acclaimed many of his works. With no fixed income, however, Mozart lived on the brink of financial disaster, partly because of his habit of spending money on gambling and entertainment as fast as he earned it. In 1791, he died at the age of 35 and was buried in a pauper's grave.

Mozart's music reflects little of the outward turbulence of his daily life. Perhaps more than any other musician, in his finest works he combined pure grace with profound learning to create an ideal beauty. Yet his music does not lack in drama or seriousness. Mozart's operas provide perhaps the easiest, and most enjoyable, access to his work. *The Marriage of Figaro* (1786) was based on a play of the same name by the French dramatist Pierre-Augustin Beaumarchais (1732–1799), which attacked the immorality of the aristocracy. It showed its hero, Figaro, outwitting the attempts of his noble employer to seduce Figaro's wife-to-be. Mozart's opera adds to the social protest of the original a sense of humanity, rather than personal resentment. Figaro expresses the frustration of centuries of men and women who had suffered from the injustices of class discrimination.

Putting the Culture of the Old Regime in Perspective

By the end of Mozart's life, the French Revolution had broken out and the Old Regime was swept away. Some of the art of the 18th century may have distracted its aristocratic public from the changing times and attitudes. Yet the elegant world of rococo art was to be cut short by the guillotine as the result of a revolution at least partly because of other cultural developments in the 18th century.

The social criticisms of Mozart's operas and Richardson's novels were directed at the injustice and immorality of the ruling classes. Discussion of the issues of social and political reform began to circulate increasingly widely through popular literary forms. Academies and salons made it possible for the upper and middle classes to actually meet on equal social terms and raised the question of whether high birth was really superior to inherent ability.

The lowering of social and cultural barriers was limited. Most Europeans—the lower classes—continued to live as they had for centuries. An 18th-century Italian peasant, Russian serf, or Welsh shepherd was equally deprived educationally and economically dependent. It would take the Industrial Revolution, with its cities and factories, to draw attention to the hardships of the working classes and the poor, and to give them the chance to fight to improve their lot.

Yet with the spread of culture in the 18th century, the foundation was laid for future struggles. The forerunners of artists and writers of more recent times who campaigned for political causes were those who in the 18th century used their newly gained freedom to deal with the problems of their societies.

Questions for Further Study

1. What role did social criticism play in the arts in the 18th century?
2. What are the main features of the rococo style? How do they differ from the style of Baroque art?
3. What changes, if any, were there in the status of women in middle-class 18th-century society?
4. In what ways was the public for the arts a broader one than in the Renaissance or the 17th century? What were the causes?

Suggestions for Further Reading

Conisbee, P. *Painting in Eighteenth-Century France.* Ithaca, NY, 1981.

Darnton, R. *The Literary Underground of the Old Regime.* Cambridge, MA, 1982.

Ferguson, M., ed. *First Feminists: British Women Writers 1578–1799.* Bloomington, IN, 1984.

Kalnein, W., and M. Levey. *Art and Architecture of the 18th Century in France.* Baltimore, MD, 1972.

Levey, M. *Painting and Sculpture in France, 1700-1789*. New Haven, CT, 1993.

Minor, Vernon Hyde. *Baroque and Rococo: Art and Culture*. New York, 1999.

Osborne, Charles. *The Complete Operas of Mozart*. London, 1992.

Robbins Landon, H.C. *Essays on the Viennese Classical Style*. New York, 1970.

Roston, M. *Changing Perspectives in Literature and the Visual Arts, 1650-1820*. Princeton, NJ, 1990.

Varriano, J. *Italian Baroque and Rococo Architecture*. New York, 1986.

InfoTrac College Edition

Enter the search term *Old Regime culture* using Key Terms.

Enter the search term *Louis XIV and arts* using the Subject Guide.

Enter the search term *Corneille* using Key Terms.

Enter the search term *Racine* using Key Terms.

Enter the search term *Mozart* using Key Terms.

Europe and the World Economy

The overseas discoveries made during the age of exploration in the 16th century had important repercussions for Europe and its economic life. The most dramatic impact came from the flow of huge amounts of gold and silver bullion to Europe from the New World, which produced an inflationary cycle that drove prices upward and created economic hardships for many millions of people. In addition, new patterns of trade emerged, particularly the shift of the center of gravity from the Mediterranean to the Atlantic, and new sources of wealth developed. The resulting "commercial revolution" saw a sharp rise in trade, both within Europe and on an international scale, and involved important new products from abroad and the increasing exportation of European-made goods. By the 18th century, a world market had come into being, with Western Europe at its center.

One feature that both reflected and affected Western values was the growth and spread of the slave trade, as well as efforts to combat it. Similarly, the allure of large and quickly made profits sparked by the prosperity often resulted in risky schemes for financial speculation that caused serious setbacks for European investors. As the profits and opportunities in commerce grew, the centralization and strict state regulation that marked the old economic doctrine of mercantilism began to give way. By the 18th century, private commercial and financial interests had become closely linked with state policy. Finally, the colonial expansion beyond Europe's borders that was a prelude to or came along with the growth in trade had adverse consequences not only on non-European peoples and their cultures, but also on the peace and prosperity of the West.

TOWARD A WORLD ECONOMY

In the aftermath of the great age of discovery, the nature of international trade, and of Europe's position in it, underwent a major transformation, as what had been essentially a series of regional economies blended and merged into an integrated world marketplace. As a byproduct of these changes, the new trade patterns had a profound impact on the material and social life of Europe.

CHANGING TRADE PATTERNS

Before the commercial revolution, a series of distinct regional trade patterns and isolated markets had characterized world commerce. Trade within Europe, consisting of long-established local complexes such as those in the eastern Mediterranean, along the southern coast of France, or between Great Britain and Flanders, represented by far the bulk of European trade. Moreover, as central governments consolidated their control over national territories in Great Britain and France, domestic markets loomed increasingly more important. Europe's commercial relations with the rest of the world were also limited largely to two distinct but crucial patterns: the shipment of bullion from colonies in the Americas to mother countries in Europe and the importation of spices from Asia.

By the 18th century, all continents were linked in an integrated, worldwide marketplace. New markets, such as that in the Baltic region, had expanded the volume of trade within Europe, while the old mercantilist monopolies that had once restricted trade between colonies and their mother country had been dissolved. Colonial items, in the form of raw materials and finished products, were increasingly being processed in Europe and then reexported to other parts of the world; the English, for example, reexported Virginia tobacco and the French sugar from the West Indies. One of the most successful innovations of the commercial revolution was the development of triangular trade. In the typical example, English manufactured goods, such as printed fabrics, were traded to Africa for slaves. The slaves were in turn exchanged in the West Indies for sugar, which was then sold and consumed in Great Britain. Triangular trade flourished in the 18th century, when the British obtained the *asiento,* or the exclusive right to trade slaves in the Spanish colonies, a right that gave them access to Spanish-American markets for illegal goods.

As the volume of domestic and international trade increased, European merchants adjusted and refined their business practices, including marine insurance, credit banking facilities, stock exchanges, and uniform weights and measures. Tremendous fortunes were made in trade among the merchant class in the 18th century, especially in Great Britain and France, which had overtaken not only Spain and Portugal but also the Dutch Republic in the carrying trade. Commercial profits, along with the rising demand for European manufactured goods, acted as a stimulus to the Industrial Revolution (see Topic 60).

One result of Europe's central role in the growth of global trade was that the West became infinitely more wealthy than any other region of the world. Europe's prosperity was, of course, the product of many factors, not the least of which were the natural resources of the Americas and the forced labor of millions of African slaves. Profits led to the accumulation of significant amounts of capital by European merchants. In addition, the general standard of living throughout western Europe increased, especially among the intermediate levels of society, although most Europeans, consisting of manual laborers and peasants, still lived close to the margin of subsistence.

NEW WORLD COMMODITIES AND OLD WORLD TASTES

In the mid-1600s, however, trade patterns began to undergo important changes. Eastern spices and Western bullion were still the most important commodities from overseas, but new products were beginning to increase in significance. The imports of bullion began to fall steadily after 1620, while the European spice market became saturated. Large amounts of New World bullion—including as much as one-third of all silver—were sent to Asia, while spices and a variety of other luxury goods came back. In the years after 1640, such products as sugar, coffee, tea, tobacco, raw cotton and cotton fabrics, dyes, and furs assumed an increasing role in world trade. These new goods had a dual impact: They accounted for the continual expansion of the volume of trade and altered patterns of consumption and diet in Europe. The 18th century saw a tremendous increase in the new kind of trade; between 1698 and 1775, Great Britain experienced a growth of some 500 percent in exports and almost as much in imports, most of the increase in colonial trade. French trade also expanded significantly in the 18th century.

Tobacco was the first new product from the Americas to be used widely by Europeans. Most of the American tobacco was grown in Virginia and Maryland and then shipped to Europe, where it was blended and sold for smoking, chewing, or to be used as snuff. As tobacco became immensely popular, governments throughout Europe imposed import duties and excise taxes on the product to raise revenues. In many nations, including France, Austria, Spain, and the Italian and German states, tobacco became a profitable state monopoly.

Of increasing importance was the importation of textiles, and especially of cotton fabrics. Cotton had been known in Europe for centuries, but had not been widely used. In the 17th century, however, imports of raw cotton from India and America began to increase substantially. Moreover, one of the most popular goods imported from abroad was the brightly colored Indian cotton of exceptionally light weight known as calico (so-called after the Indian city of Calicut). These printed fabrics were of fine quality, and the large-scale Indian textile industry produced inexpensive products because they were made by low-cost hand labor. The demand for calicoes grew rapidly because they could be used for a variety of purposes, including dresses, underclothing, stockings, and upholstery. By 1680, the

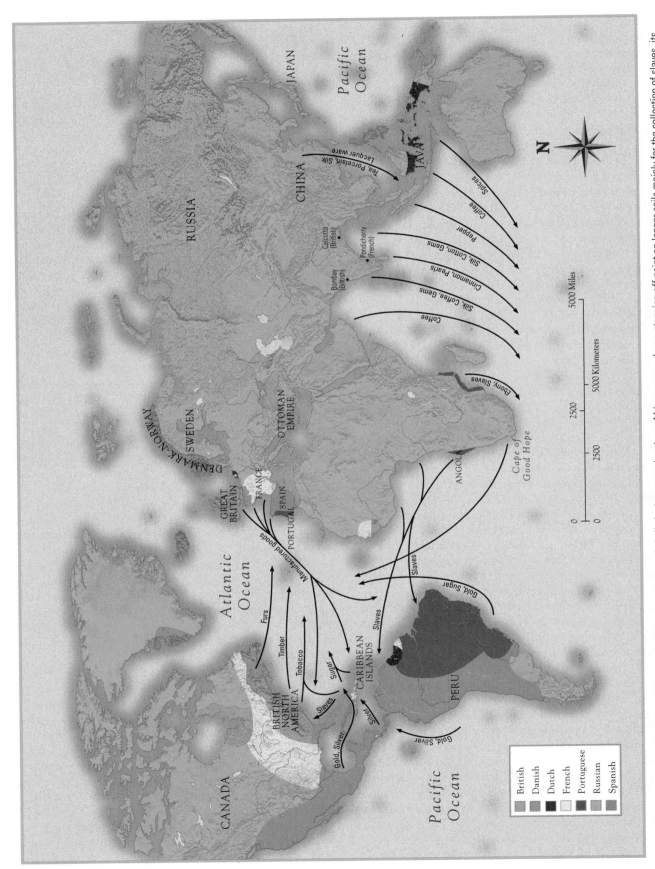

Map 55.1 European Sea Trade, c. 1750. Apart from the Americas, trade is limited to coastal regions. Africa was used as a stopping-off point on longer sails mainly for the collection of slaves, its interior yet unexplored. Australia, which was still untouched by the Europeans, was to be claimed by the British at the end of the century.

English East India Company's textile imports were more important than its spice imports.

So much in demand were calicoes by the early 18th century that Great Britain and France both imposed limitations on their importation in order to protect domestic clothing makers. In 1700, the British Parliament passed an act forbidding the importation of all printed calicoes, although it allowed white calicoes to be brought in to encourage the English dye and printer factories (printed calicoes could, however, be imported for reexport). The Calico Act of 1720 prohibited the use or wearing of calico prints in Great Britain, but such restrictions only increased the demand for the fabric and stimulated the growth of the domestic cotton industry. The act was repealed in 1774, by which time the English textile industry had so developed that it could supply the home market with enough cotton fabrics.

Three beverages—coffee, tea, and cocoa—had far-reaching effect on European tastes. The trade in coffee, which had been introduced into Europe from the Middle East and Asia in the early 17th century, was largely in the hands of the English and the Dutch, the latter eventually growing their own supply in Java. By the end of the century, coffee had become a popular drink in Great Britain, often replacing beer. Coffeehouses and cafés became meeting places for social and intellectual discourse.

Even more popular was tea, long a staple drink in China and India. In 1664, the English East India Company, which enjoyed a monopoly on the China tea trade, presented King Charles II with the rare gift of two pounds of tea; by 1790, the company was selling millions of pounds of tea per year to the home market. Throughout the century, coffee remained the drink of the privileged classes, while tea became a staple used by all social classes in Great Britain.

Together with tea, sugar imported from the West Indies had an important effect on nutrition and worked both a commercial and a social revolution in Europe. Grown originally in southern Spain and Sicily, sugar was taken to the Canaries shortly after 1500 and then to Brazil and to the British and French West Indies, where the sugar cane thrived in the heat and humidity. By 1650, it had become another staple item in the European diet, its demand fueled by the growing use of tea, coffee, and cocoa. Sugar refineries in France numbered 18 by 1683 and processed some 18 million pounds of raw sugar each year. As the quantity of sugar produced increased steadily in the 18th century, its price fell and it ceased to be a luxury item as more people could afford it. At this point, American trade, which was based largely on sugar, became more valuable than Asian trade. Sugar also yielded two subsidiary products, molasses and rum. Molasses became a cheap and sweet addition to the European diet and was the raw material from which rum was produced.

THE SLAVE TRADE

One essential aspect of the craze for American products such as cotton, tobacco, and sugar was their relationship to the slave trade. These and other products, but principally sugar, were grown in the New World on large "plan-

Engraving showing slaves picking and processing cotton in the West Indies. 18th century. The slaves are Africans, transported to the West Indies to work, in this case, on French cotton plantations. The engraving illustrates the entire process from the picking of the cotton on the right to the loaded bales in the left foreground.

The Granger Collection

HISTORICAL PERSPECTIVES

THE SLAVE TRADE AND THE EUROPEAN ECONOMY

CHARLES L. KILLINGER   Valencia Community College

European trade in African slaves and the commercial products they produced and consumed affected the economic development of modern Europe in many important ways; however, economic historians have questioned the scale of the profits from the slave trade and the nature of their impact on European industrialization. They have also studied the influence of the slave trade on the African and American colonial economies. In the context of the European economy, the primary questions facing students of the slave trade are these: How profitable was the slave trade? In what ways did the slave trade contribute to the growth of the European economy?

Although Europeans had been trading in African slaves since the middle of the 15th century, it was not until 300 years later that the trade increased most dramatically and its profits peaked. By 1700, Portuguese and Spanish slave trade had dwindled with the decline of their imperial power, and the British had surpassed the Dutch through a series of maritime victories. In the Treaty of Utrecht of 1713 (see Topic 49), the British gained the treasured *asiento (el pacto del asiento de negros)*, the exclusive contract for supplying slaves to Spanish America; although vessels of many nations continued to participate, the British now dominated the shipping of African slaves to the New World. During the 18th century, slavers transported nearly 6 million Africans to the Americas, almost two-thirds of those imported over the entire duration of the trade.

As a result of the massive importation of free labor into the Western Hemisphere, the plantation economy expanded greatly. Plantations in the Americas produced agricultural commodities for export, including tobacco, ginger, indigo, cotton, and sugar. Because all of these products were extremely labor-intensive, the use of free labor guaranteed low production costs. The primary beneficiaries were the British and French, and the most lucrative part of that triangular trade was the importation of slave-grown sugar from Caribbean islands.

In the 18th century, primarily on the strength of sugar production, the British West Indies surpassed India, China, and North America as sources of imported British goods, and the French colony of St. Domingue (Haiti) outstripped every British possession in annual sugar production. By the end of the century, 200,000 slaves in the British colony of Jamaica were producing 50,000 tons of sugar annually; a half-million slaves on St. Domingue were producing 100,000 tons each year. By 1700, Brazil was still importing huge numbers of slaves despite the decline of the sugar industry there, while in the second half of the century Spanish imports increased as sugar production in Cuba grew.

The success of the West Indian plantations satisfied the demands of mercantilism (see Topic 46), the dominant European economic practice of the day. The major European nations competed for markets and sources of raw materials for industrial production in order to achieve a favorable balance of trade and thereby gain an advantage over their adversaries. Slave labor ensured a competitive advantage to the West Indian plantation colonies; in turn, the colonies not only enriched their owners, but also contributed to the national strength, especially of the British and French empires.

In an effort to impose mercantilist regulation of the trade, European nations competed for exclusive rights to slave markets and granted national monopolies to slave-trading companies. In 1672, for example, Britain granted such a monopoly to the Royal African Company, a joint-stock company, to compete with the Dutch for general control of international commerce. Soon it was exporting £100,000 worth of goods annually to Africa in order to meet the West Indian demand for slaves. London and Bristol merchants and shippers, envious of the trade, succeeded in breaking the company's monopoly in 1698. Thus both government and private merchants of the day clearly regarded the slave trade as profitable and potentially quite lucrative; however, Parliament dissolved the company a half-century later because of continuing financial difficulties.

The complexity of the triangular trade and the versatility of European merchants illustrate one problem in measuring slave profits with any accuracy: They are extremely difficult to isolate from general commercial profits. For example, in the early 18th century, the London financial house of Perry, Lane and Company shipped slaves to Virginia in exchange for tobacco and other commodities. Because of this overlap in its activities, its records do not clearly discriminate between profits from slaves and profits from tobacco, which were only partly grown by slave labor.

The more significant and controversial question involves broader considerations that tie together the history of the Old and New Worlds. Although there is no consensus about the specific relationship between international trade and the industrialization of Europe, strong evidence links the two in some fundamental way. In particular, the role of the Caribbean islands as both sources of raw materials and as markets has led historians to consider the slave trade a contributing factor to the development of European industry.

Controversy has focused on several issues. Some have argued that the Caribbean and African colonies provided only weak markets with a minimal capacity to consume European exports. Because the major Caribbean product, sugar, was simply consumed by Europeans and not converted into an industrial product, some scholars have argued that the impact of such imports was also insignificant. These historians contend that profits from the slave trade and related European exports made up such a small percentage of gross domestic product as to be negligible.

Other economic historians, analyzing the same statistics, have disagreed. They have shown, for example, that gross revenues of Jamaican sugar planters increased proportionally to imported slaves and that the Caribbean share of total imports into Britain rose substantially in the second half of the 18th century. Although variables other than the slave trade—such as population growth—may have contributed, gross revenues from sugar shipped to Britain increased significantly over the 18th century.

Such a debate, regardless of its outcome, tends to ignore the broader economic impact of the slave trade. It is more useful to study the slave trade not as an iso-lated issue, but as an integral part of Atlantic commercial expansion. The development of the British economy after 1750 provides a good context. English iron foundries produced tools for colonial plantations and chains for the slave trade. Manufacturers produced pottery, furniture, firearms, and ammunition for sale to the slave-worked plantations. English mills produced cotton fabrics exclusively for export to Caribbean and African markets. In fact, the expansion of the British textile industry (see Topic 60), often considered the essence of the Industrial Revolution, was intricately joined to the expansion of the slave trade. Accordingly, the cumulative impact of these new markets appears substantial.

There is another point to consider: Enormous quantities of sugar and other slave-grown commodities provided significant profits that produced a "multiplier effect" on the economy. The most convincing example is the mid-18th-century growth in British demand for colonial staples such as sugar. Increased demand for colonial imports created an opportunity for British exports to Africa and the Caribbean. British industries increased production to supply the thriving colonial markets, expanding employment and spinning off profits. These profits generally enriched the middle class, spurring consumer spending and creating great individual fortunes in the process. Profits also stimulated the related sugar-refining and shipbuilding industries, generated activity in banking and insurance, provided capital for developing factories, mines, and railroads, and led governments to expand their navies in order to protect their growing merchant fleets.

An important byproduct of the slave trade was its impact on European cities. Population and economic activity exploded in such slave ports as Liverpool and Bristol in Great Britain and Bordeaux in France. The development of Liverpool greatly increased the demand for exports, which fueled the further development of the fabric mills and factories of Manchester. Consequently it may be argued that the slave trade contributed to another modern trend, the urbanization of the continent.

Despite the inability of historians to agree either on the level of profits of the slave trade or its precise impact on Europe, the weight of evidence suggests that profits were high and that they contributed significantly to European economic development. When considered in the broadest sense, the economic consequences of the slave trade were momentous.

Watercolor of the interior of a transatlantic slave ship. 18th century. The horrendously overcrowded conditions and lack of any sanitation meant that the average shipload arrived with one in five of its "passengers" dead—which, of course, served the purposes of the slave traders. Images such as this helped arouse public opinion against the slave trade.

© National Maritime Museum, London

tation" economies by slave labor. The slave trade had flourished since ancient times, when whites and Africans had been taken into captivity by the Roman Empire and Muslim traders. The Ottoman seizure of Constantinople in 1453, however, cut off Europe's supply of white slaves, who had been taken principally from the Black Sea region and the Balkans. In the second half of the 15th century, increasingly larger numbers of African slaves were imported into Europe.

With the discovery of the New World, Europeans began to ship African slaves across the Atlantic to the sugar plantations of Brazil and the West Indies. The massive African slave trade, fueled by the wholesale deaths of Amerindians, began in 1518, when the Emperor Charles V ended Indian slavery and agreed to substitute Africans as the source of plantation labor. By the end of the 18th cen-

tury, perhaps 9 million African slaves had been brought to the Americas, half of whom went to the West Indies. Despite a 20 percent fatality rate on the transatlantic voyage, profits in slavery were high. At first, the Portuguese were the most active slavers, but by the 16th century the Dutch and French had begun to participate. In 1562, Sir John Hawkins (1532–1595) captained the first English slaving voyage, breaking the Spanish West Indies monopoly. The English eventually dominated the slave trade, both as a carrying trade and in order to supply its colonies in Jamaica and Barbados as well as the tobacco regions of Virginia and Maryland. Once in the New World, however, disease, forced labor under appalling conditions, and unspeakable living conditions continually decimated the slave population, so that new waves of slaves had to be imported regularly.

Engraving of a slave auction in the American South. Early 19th century. Taken from an antislavery tract, this image shows the cruelty whereby families were torn apart and sold to different owners. Note the evident prosperity of the purchasers and the flogging of a newly bought slave in the background.

The Granger Collection

THE SPECULATION CRAZE: STOCK BOOMS AND CRASHES

The expansion of commercial capitalism in the 17th and 18th centuries was made difficult by a persistent shortage of money, which in turn was caused by the decline in the supply of gold and silver bullion. The money shortage affected governments as well as private investors because after the costly wars of Louis XIV ended with the peace treaties of 1713–1714, France and Great Britain found themselves deeply in debt. To meet the need for capital, Western states developed modern financial institutions such as stock companies, stock exchanges, and state-run banks, all of which expanded credit.

These developments, together with the return of peace after 1714, encouraged renewed economic confidence and led to unprecedented investment in commercial undertakings. This atmosphere of unrestrained financial speculation, fueled by the fiscal plight of Britain and France, led to the first stock crashes in modern times, which people at the time called "bubbles"—schemes designed to cheat or swindle the public.

JOHN LAW AND THE MISSISSIPPI BUBBLE

Britain and France found it increasingly difficult to deal with the huge debts accumulated during the wars, and both countries faced the possibility of bankruptcy if they could not pay the annual interest on their obligations. In each case, the government believed it could solve the problem by allowing private stock companies to manage the public debt for them. The idea was that trading and financial concessions given to these companies would create profits large enough to pay off the interest owed by government and still give investors a huge return.

In France, the experiment was organized by a strange character named John Law (1671–1729), a Scottish financier with a bent for mathematics. Law had led a wild life as a youth, having been imprisoned for killing a man in a duel. Later, while traveling on the Continent, he learned much about gambling as well as the banking business. In Paris after the death of Louis XIV in 1715, Law became a friend of the regent, the duke of Orleans, and devised a plan for solving the problem of French finances. Law believed that paper money, backed by the government's wealth in trade and land, could take the place of gold and silver coin. He therefore set up a bank in 1716 as a private joint-stock company, authorized by government charter. The bank issued notes, accepted deposits, and dealt in bills of exchange and promissory notes. The idea, which was modeled after the Bank of Amsterdam, was sound and proved so successful that in 1718 the regent bought out the bank's stockholders and made it a royal institution. Branches were established in

Museum Boymans van Beuningen, Rotterdam

Painting of the Amsterdam Stock Exchange. 17th century. The painting shows the open courtyard, off which were the offices. The earliest example of a building for the purchase and sale of stocks (it was built in 1608), the Amsterdam Exchange was a center for unrestrained and reckless transactions, which were limited to its restricted opening hours: Dealing could only take place between noon and 2 P.M.

principal cities, and many of its notes, made legal tender in 1719, were used to pay off the government debt.

The problem with Law's scheme was that he was too ambitious and extended his operations to unchecked financial speculation. In 1717, he organized the Mississippi Company (officially known as the Company of the West), which received a monopoly of the trade with the French colony of Louisiana. The company took over the government debt and purchased the government's tobacco monopoly. Within another year, the company—now called the Company of the Indies—bought out the East India Company and several other trading firms, and then took over the collection of taxes. Law therefore came to control government finances through his bank as well as most of the country's overseas trade.

Each expansion that Law undertook was financed by the issuance of more and more stock, the purchase of which was made easy by the fact that the bank rapidly increased the quantity of its notes. By the spring of 1720 the face value of notes in circulation had gone from about 150 million to almost 2.7 billion livres. The result was an inflation that pushed prices up by 88 percent. In addition, Law's bank actually lent money for the purchase of company stock. This crazed specu-

lation and expansion were sustained by the fact that the shares in Law's enterprise were constantly increasing in value, to the point where the price bore no relation to actual earnings. So amazing seemed the prosperity engineered by Law that in January 1720 the king made him finance minister. The next month, the bank and the company were joined together.

The bubble in Mississippi shares finally burst that spring, when the price of shares became so high that some speculators decided to sell their holdings in order to protect their investments. As the selling turned into a panic, Law's empire collapsed because the banknotes that investors received for their stocks were then turned in for gold and silver, and the bank's reserves of specie was exhausted. In December, Law fled into exile.

THE SOUTH SEA BUBBLE

The Mississippi Bubble had a serious impact. It undermined French public confidence in stock companies as well as in banks and paper money, yet the inflation had enabled the government to pay off part of the public debt. Moreover, Law's fiasco had international reverberations because at almost the same time another bubble—the South Sea Bubble—burst in London.

Copyright Guildhall Library Corporation of London

Engraving depicting the "bursting" of the South Sea Bubble. 1721. The Wheel of Fortune, labeled "Company of Traders," rides over a series of books with the titles "Journal," "Ledger," and "Cash Book," while the goddess of Fortune rises to the sky, scattering stock certificates as she goes. The division between the stricken investors, on the left, and those seated on the right, contemplating their misery, is reminiscent of Biblical scenes of the damned and the blessed.

The Bank of England, organized in 1694 by William of Orange, managed the public debt for the government and, like Law's bank, issued notes. In 1710, however, a charter was issued for a joint-stock company known popularly as the South Seas Company (officially the "Governor and Company of Merchants of Great Britain Trading to the South Seas and Other Parts of America and for the Encouragement of Fishing"), which took over part of the government's debt. Under the terms of a special agreement, holders of government bonds were to turn them in to the company in exchange for company stock. The interest paid by the government on its bonds would be passed on as dividends to the stockholders. In addition, the company was granted a monopoly on all British trade with Spanish America. The South Sea Company was further strengthened when England obtained the *asiento*, which permitted it to send some 4,800 slaves and one merchant ship per year to South America.

As company profits grew, speculative fever mounted, especially as news of Law's operations reached English investors in 1719. The company eventually offered to take over the entire government debt and pay the government a bonus for the privilege. By June 1720, the price for South Sea Company stock had increased 10 times to more than £1000 per share. The thirst for speculation became a craze as innumerable companies—almost 200 in a single year—were created, many of dubious legitimacy, and sold stock to the public with only a minimum downpayment. The South Sea Company, concerned over the increased competition, persuaded Parliament to pass the Bubble Act, which prevented any company from selling stock without a royal charter. With the crash in Paris already underway, prices began to tumble on the London exchange, and by December the South Sea stock had collapsed to £120.

The British crash exposed a widespread scandal of government corruption as it was discovered that ministers and parliamentary officials had taken bribes from some of the companies. In an effort to clean up this scandal, Sir Robert Walpole was appointed as the king's chief minister (see Topic 51). The South Sea Company actually survived on a much reduced scale as a holding company for government securities, and the Bank of England reemerged as the principal financial institution of the nation.

The effects of the bubbles on both sides of the channel were eventually overcome as governments and private investors learned caution from the dangers of speculation. These episodes were, however, symptomatic both of the end of the old mercantilist principle—which held that government protection and monopolies were needed to protect national economic prosperity—and the rise of the new capitalist doctrine, developed first by Adam Smith and then by the later Manchester School (see Topic 58), that accompanied the commercial expansion and the Industrial Revolution.

Putting Europe and the World Economy in Perspective

A global economy had begun to emerge in the 18th century as a result of the expansion of trade. At the center of that commercial economy was an increasingly prosperous Europe, which reaped huge profits from the growing interdependence in production and markets that characterized the world of commerce. European states took tremendous resources from the Americas, first in the form of gold and silver bullion and then in agricultural products.

This economic transformation drastically altered the lives of millions of Europeans, whose hunger for the new products—coffee, tea, sugar, tobacco, and others—resulted in important changes in diet, nutrition, and customs. As the market in such goods as sugar, tobacco, and cotton grew, Europeans began to raid the African continent to obtain the labor its New World enterprises required, creating a slave trade that persisted with unrelenting horror for three and a half centuries. The European exploitation of the rest of the world that began with the overseas discoveries came to a head as a result of the commercial revolution, to be superseded only in the next century as Western imperialism carved up the continents. As the 18th century opened, the expansion of commerce was closely tied to the evolution of banking systems and public finance, a relationship that led to a series of financial schemes that ended in crisis. By the end of the century, however, these scandals had been set behind as Europe moved into the age of industrial capitalism.

Questions for Further Study

1. What were the principal elements in the emerging world economy?
2. In what ways was the slave trade tied to the European economy? Was it profitable?
3. What were the new forms of investment that emerged? What were the principal causes of the speculation crashes?

Suggestions for Further Reading

Braudel, Fernand. S. Reynolds, trans. *Civilization and Capitalism*, 3 vols. New York, 1979–1984.

Cameron, Rondo. *A Concise Economic History of the World*. New York, 1989.

Carswell, John. *The South Sea Bubble*. New York, 2002.

Day, John. *Money and Finance in the Age of Merchant Capitalism*. Oxford, 1999.

Eltis, David. *The Rise of African Slavery in the Americas*. New York, 2000.

Epstein, S.R. *Freedom and Growth: The Rise of States and Markets in Europe, 1300-1750*. New York, 2000.

Frank, A.G. *World Accumulation, 1492–1789*. New York, 1978.

Klein, Herbert S. *The Atlantic Slave Trade*. New York, 1999.

Kriedte, Peter. *Peasants, Landlords and Merchant Capitalists: Europe and the World Economy, 1500–1800*. Leamington, England, 1983.

Northrop, David, ed. *The Atlantic Slave Trade (Problems in World History)*. Lexington, MA, 2001.

Phillips, Caryl. *The Atlantic Sound*. New York, 2000.

Thomas, Hugh. *The Slave Trade: The Story of the Atlantic Slave Trade, 1440-1870*. New York, 1997.

Van Zaanden, J.L. *The Rise and Decline of Holland's Economy: Merchant Capitalism and the Labour Market*. Manchester, 1993.

InfoTrac College Edition

Enter the search term *slavery* using the Subject Guide.

THE GLOBAL CONFLICT: WARS FOR EMPIRE

With the spread of European colonization, wars among the leading European powers tended to extend to their colonial possessions. Virtually every major European conflict in the 18th century involved the colonies and ended with the redistribution of territory outside Europe.

At the end of the War of the Spanish Succession in 1713 (see Topic 50), Spain was forced to make important concessions to British traders in the Spanish-American colonies. Ill feeling between Spain and Britain continued to smolder, and the War of Jenkins' Ear broke out in 1739—the first important confrontation to involve two European countries fighting over a colonial dispute.

There followed the War of the Austrian Succession (1740–1748), a complex series of interlocking power struggles, which brought France and Spain together to contend with Britain for supremacy in America. In 1744 France declared war on Britain, and in return the British seized the French settlement of Louisbourg in Canada. Both countries, however, were too committed to European campaigns to do more than skirmish overseas. Clearly, however, a definitive struggle for control of North America was at hand. In the meantime, the French continued to build a chain of forts down the Ohio River, to block British expansion west of the Appalachians and keep them restricted to the Atlantic seaboard. The British prepared for war by dispatching two regiments to America—the first British regular soldiers to serve there.

In 1755, in fighting near the French stronghold of Fort Duquesne, the British forces were routed and their general killed. The following year saw a fresh outbreak of general hostilities in the Seven Years' War (1756–1763), which set Britain and Prussia together against France, Austria, and Russia. The British provided financial subsidies to the Prussians and attacked the French fleet and coast to reduce France's pressure on Prussia. In return, the Prussians pinned down French troops and thereby restricted French efforts in North America.

After early setbacks, Britain increased its American war effort at the insistence of the prime minister, William Pitt. Massive forces crossed the Atlantic, defeated the French at Louisbourg, and then took Quebec and Montreal. By the end of the war, Britain had acquired its first empire.

Meanwhile, in Europe, Friedrich II's Prussian forces were engaged in a tenacious but increasingly desperate attempt to keep their enemies at bay. In 1762, however, the unexpected withdrawal of Russia broke up the quadruple alliance. Prussia kept Silesia and emerged from the war firmly established as one of Europe's leading military powers.

BRITAIN VERSUS SPAIN IN THE WEST INDIES

As the leading European colonial powers continued to expand their holdings in Asia, Africa, and the Americas, rivalries hitherto fought out on European soil began to spread to the colonies abroad. In the context of the commercial expansion of the 18th century, the domestic economic benefits of overseas territories—access to raw materials, new markets for the sale of manufactured goods—encouraged the colonizers to defend and add to them.

At the same time, the three strongest colonial powers, Britain, France, and Spain, tried equally hard to prevent the growth of each other's overseas holdings. As a result, the incessant wars fought out by the major European nations throughout the 18th century almost invariably involved them in conflicts both in Europe and elsewhere. Most of the conflicts of the 18th century in Europe involved colonial powers like Britain and Spain that were also simultaneously fighting outside Europe. In addition, the peace negotiations that ended the European wars served to pursue colonial competition outside Europe because treaties generally reassigned colonial holdings, and thus inextricably linked them with European power politics.

The first major redistribution of colonies occurred at the end of the War of the Spanish Succession, from which the British emerged the principal victors. By the Treaty of Utrecht (1713), the French gave up Newfoundland, Nova Scotia, and the Hudson Bay territory to the British, retaining New France (Quebec). Spain held on to its American possessions, but was forced in return to award Britain trading privileges there.

THE WAR OF JENKINS' EAR

British expansion only exacerbated the ill feelings between the rising imperial power and a declining Spain, which was embittered by the concessions it had been forced to grant. The focus of tension was the Caribbean, where British undercover traders and Spanish coast guards—often private operators hired by the government—were in constant friction. Most of the illicit ships operated out of Jamaica, a British possession in the middle of Spanish territory. When British vessels fell into the hands of the Spanish *guarda-costas*, who were patrolling in search of booty as much as enforcing the law, their crews generally received rough handling.

As reports of the Spanish ill-treatment spread back to Great Britain, public indignation over the behavior of their traditional enemies began to rise. In 1738, an English sailor, Robert Jenkins (active 1731–1738), brought to the House of Commons a jar containing his ear; he claimed it had been ripped off by a Spanish coast guard. The prime minister, Sir Robert Walpole (see Topic 51), already under pressure, was accused by his opponents of weak-kneed indifference to Spanish aggression. After trying unsuccessfully to cool tempers, Walpole gave way and declared war on Spain—the War of Jenkins' Ear—in 1739.

The immediate cause of hostilities was allegedly national honor, but deeper considerations prompted the clash. In the first place, Spain, one of the first great imperialist powers, was beginning to decline just at the moment that British fortunes were rising. Furthermore, the real issue at stake was not the theoretical right of smugglers to ply their trade in peace, but the practical ability of one colonial power to deny access to a rival. The War of Jenkins' Ear was in itself trivial enough, and in any case the hostilities between Britain and Spain soon became subsumed in the far more involved War of the Austrian Succession, but it set an important precedent. For the first time two European powers went to war over questions of trade outside Europe.

Anti-Spanish cartoon published at the time of the War of Jenkins' Ear. 1738. On the left Sir Robert Walpole, the Prime Minister, sits back, trying to decide whether to sign the Declaration of War against Spain, while Captain Robert Jenkins thrusts his ear, in his left hand, toward Walpole. The crouching dog in the bottom left-hand corner, with its features distorted in a grimace, presumably symbolizes Spain.

DYNASTY AND POWER POLITICS: THE WAR OF THE AUSTRIAN SUCCESSION

In the years from 1740 to 1763, the chief European nations fought out a complex series of interrelated power struggles. The War of the Austrian Succession (1740–1748) was followed by a brief period of uneasy peace dominated by feverish diplomatic activity. In 1756 hostilities broke out again, in the form of the Seven Years' War (1756–1763). By its close, there were two main victors: Britain, which had won its first empire, and Prussia, which had confirmed its status as a great power.

The initial cause of the War of the Austrian Succession was the death of the Emperor Charles VI (ruled 1711–1740). In 1713, Charles had decided that the Hapsburg empire would be regarded as indivisible and named his young and inexperienced daughter, Maria Theresa (ruled 1740–1780), as his successor. Most of the powers of Europe, including Prussia, agreed to abide by this pronouncement. The Prussian king Friedrich II (ruled 1740–1786) subsequently contested Maria Theresa's right to inherit her father's possessions and invaded the resource-rich province of Silesia (on Friedrich's career, see Topic 59). Despite her youth and inexperience, Maria Theresa ultimately proved to be one of the most capable rulers in the long line of Hapsburg monarchs. Years later, Friedrich admiringly described the tenacious young empress as "the only man among my opponents."

Britain came to Maria Theresa's aid. The British foreign secretary, Sir John Carteret (1690–1763), was an enthusiastic player of diplomatic games who claimed that his favorite pastime was "knocking the heads of the kings of Europe together, and jumbling something out of it that may be of service to this country." In 1743, Carteret put together an alliance of Austria, Britain, and Piedmont-Sardinia, but his achievement only succeeded in driving the former rivals France and Spain to form a counteralliance.

KING GEORGE'S WAR

Meanwhile, the hostilities between Britain and Spain, the latter now joined by France, continued in America, where the struggle was generally known as King George's War, after the reigning King George II (ruled 1727–1760). George was the last British king to personally command in battle, fighting in the European phase of the War of the Austrian Succession. Events in Europe were fluctuating too violently for any country to risk committing substantial forces to the American front. The British made disorganized raids on Spanish territories on the mainland and in the Caribbean, but were beaten back, as much by tropical disease as by the Spanish. The only notable reversal in King George's War occurred in 1745, when New England colonial forces captured the French-held Cape Breton Isle and its fortress of Louisbourg, which commanded the St. Lawrence estuary.

British and French troops continued to skirmish elsewhere. In India, the French took the British town of Madras in 1746. The next year, the British Navy defeated two French fleets off the Atlantic coast, and thereby prevented them from carrying reinforcements to overseas French territories.

By 1748, amid general frustration and exhaustion, peace negotiations at Aix-la-Chapelle (Aachen) brought about an end to the war and a restoration of conquered territory. Britain handed back Louisbourg and regained Madras in return. The only real winners were Prussia, which held on to Silesia, and Maria Theresa, whose right to succeed her father was generally recognized. Eight years of conflict had revealed that British superiority at sea was counterbalanced by French supremacy on land. The resulting stalemate left virtually all the disputes between the European powers unresolved, not the least of them the battle for control of North America.

THE DIPLOMATIC REVOLUTION

The period from 1749 to 1756 saw intense negotiation and counternegotiation, as the leading participants prepared for the inevitability of renewed conflict. By the time war broke out again in 1756, the alliances of the War of the Austrian Succession were reversed in a series of changes known as the Diplomatic Revolution. When the Seven Years' War broke out, the chief enemies were the same: Prussia versus Austria, and Britain versus France. Britain, however, now supported Prussia instead of Austria, and France was allied with Austria rather than Prussia.

The break between Britain and Austria was caused by Britain's refusal to support Maria Theresa's demands for the return of Silesia. The British had backed the Austrians in the earlier war mainly because they were the enemies of France, but they had no interest in becoming embroiled in Austria's territorial disputes. Early in 1756, Britain and Prussia signed the Convention of Westminster, and the French—who were furious with Friedrich for allying Prussia with the hated British—hastened to negotiate a defensive alliance with Austria.

At this point, a new player appeared on the scene. The empress of Russia, Elizabeth (ruled 1741–1762), was deeply mistrustful of the British and Prussian agreement. She tried to persuade the French and Austrians to join Russia in an offensive triple alliance to crush Prussia's growing power. With hostilities between the British and French in North America becoming increasingly serious, the French hesitated, unwilling to encourage a European war that would overstretch French resources.

While they tried to decide, Friedrich of Prussia suspected that a coalition of powers was planning to attack him. With characteristic boldness he struck first, taking military action on the principle that "negotiations without arms produce as little impression as musical scores without instruments." In August 1756 the Prussians invaded Saxony, thereby provoking the French into action and bringing into being the alliance that Friedrich wrongly suspected already existed. The Seven Years' War was under way.

Like the earlier War of the Austrian Succession, the Seven Years' War involved action both in Europe and America. On the European front, the Prussians battled their various enemies and struggled to hold on to Silesia. Across the Atlantic, the British and French fought the decisive struggle for control of North America. Both Prussia and Britain emerged victors.

The two wars were interdependent. Britain provided Prussia with an annual subsidy, maintained the so-called Army of Observation in Germany to protect Prussia against a French attack, and made periodic assaults on the French fleet and coast. The purpose of these moves was to reduce French pressure on Prussia. In return, the Prussians' military activities pinned down French troops in Europe and prevented them from throwing all their effort into the North American campaign.

THE STRUGGLE FOR NORTH AMERICA: THE ASCENDANCY OF BRITAIN

Although the British and French were officially at peace until the declaration of war in 1756, fighting between them had continued ever since the end of the War of the Austrian Succession. In India, the British and French East India companies struggled for commercial dominance, as the Moghul empire (the Muslim empire ruling most of north and central India in the 16th and 17th centuries) continued to break up. The British soldier and administrator, Robert Clive (1725–1774), defeated the French in 1751 and captured a string of French strongholds; he subsequently overcame the local ruler of Bengal at the Battle of Plassey (1757), to establish the British East India Company's control over all Bengal and neighboring provinces. The British victory at Plassey thus played a key role in establishing British control in India and laid the foundation for their eventual Indian empire.

BRITISH AND FRENCH COLONISTS IN NORTH AMERICA

The most important stage for Anglo-French rivalries, however, was North America, where the culminating struggle—the American side of the Seven Years' War—is often called the French and Indian War.

The attitude of the two nations toward their American colonies was very different. The 13 British colonies in North America grew rapidly, as immigrants from the home country arrived in increasing numbers. By the time war officially broke out, the colonial population numbered around a million and a half. Some of the communities were already the size of a small European city. In 1760, for example, Philadelphia had some 23,000 inhabitants and a well-

Miniature illustration of an employee of the British East India Company. Mid-18th century. Miniature painting was a popular art in Moghul India. This example, by a local artist, shows the Englishman, in a cloudless landscape, impeccably dressed in the style of his London contemporaries. Like many Company employees, however, he has to some degree, "gone native"—he sits cross-legged on the ground, smoking a water pipe.

Victoria & Albert Museum, London/Art Resource

developed commercial life; by 1776, it was the third or fourth largest city in the British Empire.

By contrast, the French were much less enthusiastic about emigrating to Canada or Louisiana, areas that presented formidable environmental challenges to 18th-century immigrants. Unlike the bustling British settlements, the French colonies consisted of large empty spaces with only a scattering of inhabitants. Although smaller, the French com-

SIGNIFICANT DATES

War in the Colonies

1713	Treaty of Utrecht
1739	War of Jenkins' Ear
1740–1748	War of the Austrian Succession
1746	French take Madras from British
1756–1763	Seven Years' War
1757	British victorious at Battle of Plassey
1758	French lose Guadeloupe to British
1759–1760	British take Quebec and Montreal
1763	Treaty of Paris

munities were efficiently run and on occasion more profitable than the British. Without the distractions of urban life, the new settlers concentrated on sugar planting, fur trading, and other commercial operations.

These differences significantly affected French and British relations with the Native American populations. In order to establish settlements and encourage further immigration from the homeland, the British set up large land investment schemes, making land available by driving native residents from their traditional hunting grounds. The French, by contrast, were interested in trading rather than building settlements. As a result, they were more likely to find native residents cooperative.

THE FRENCH AND INDIAN WAR

This cooperation became of considerable importance when French forces began to seal off the Ohio Valley, to block the British on the Atlantic seaboard and prevent them from moving westward. In the years before the official outbreak of war, the French built a north-south chain of forts along the Ohio and Mississippi valleys, to connect their settlements in Louisiana with those in Canada. The Iroquois and other local tribes supported the French attempts to keep out the British.

In 1754, in an encounter near Fort Duquesne (site of the future city of Pittsburgh), French and Indian fighters combined to defeat a force of Virginian levies under the command of the young George Washington (see Topic 59). The colonial troops had been dispatched by the Ohio Company of Virginia, a land investment company. The following year, the British government sent regular British soldiers to America for the first time. Once again the French and Indian combined forces proved more effective. Ambushing the British troops nine miles from Fort Duquesne, they killed the expedition's general and captured his men. The French maintained the initiative. In 1757 the distinguished French commander, Louis Joseph de Montcalm (1712–1759), took Fort William Henry, and a year later defeated a British expedition at Ticonderoga.

Yet by the time of the British defeat at Ticonderoga, the French were losing their superiority. The autocratic British politician William Pitt (1708–1778), despite George II's implacable hostility toward him, took charge as secretary of state in 1756. The king dismissed him in 1757, but the disastrous news from America forced his reappointment, and Pitt took full and determined control over foreign and military affairs.

THE BATTLE FOR CANADA

When Pitt came to power, his strategy was to concentrate on driving the French from Canada. British forces attacked from three different directions: up the St. Lawrence via Louisbourg, into the Ohio Valley against Fort Duquesne, and from the Hudson Valley via Ticonderoga. The last of these attacks was frustrated by Montcalm's victory, but the other two succeeded. By 1758, the British were in control of Louisbourg and Fort Duquesne; the latter was renamed Fort Pitt, in honor of the prime minister.

The British continued to advance. In 1759, the young general James Wolfe (1727–1759) led his troops up the St. Lawrence to Quebec, which was defended by a force under Montcalm. On the night of September 12, advancing soldiers silently climbed the cliffs west of the city, to the Plains of Abraham. After a short, bloody battle, in which Montcalm and Wolfe were both fatally wounded, the French fled. The following year, the British besieged Montreal, while back in Europe the British fleet decimated that of France. With France unable to send reinforcements, Montreal fell, and with it all of Canada.

WAR IN THE CARIBBEAN

With the accession of George III (ruled 1760–1820) in 1760, a triumphant but war-weary Britain began to move toward peace negotiations with France. Peace talks actually began, but in 1761 the new Spanish king, Charles III (ruled

Painting showing British troops storming Quebec on the Plains of Abraham. Late 18th century. The British are visible on the left, disembarking and climbing up, as dawn breaks, to take the city from the west. Their victory in the ensuing battle, in which the commanders on both sides were killed, saw the French lose control over Canada.

The Granger Collection

1759–1788), talked the French into renewing their old alliance and opposing British colonial expansion in the Caribbean. Early the following year, Britain declared war on Spain, and the colonial war entered its final phase.

The French had already lost Guadeloupe to Britain in 1758. Now the British added the important French islands of Martinique and Grenada, and the neutral St. Lucia and St. Vincent, to their Caribbean holdings. Spain lost Havana, Cuba, while the Spanish position in the Pacific was badly shaken by the capture of Manila in the Philippines by a British expedition sent from India.

THE TREATY OF PARIS

Between February and August of 1763, the negotiations of the Treaty of Paris among Britain, France, and Spain formalized the new distribution of territory. In America, France ceded to Britain the territories of Canada, Cape Breton Island, and all of Louisiana east of the Mississippi (except for New Orleans). In return, the French received two small islands, St. Pierre and Miquelon, which are still French territory and became an overseas department in 1976.

In Asia, Spain regained Manila. As for India, both Britain and France agreed to restore their mutual conquests, returning to the positions they had occupied in 1749. French influence in India was effectively ended, however, because the terms of the treaty prohibited them from rebuilding their fortifications.

In 1759, with the war at its height and with news pouring in of British victories, Pitt observed that "peace will be as hard to make as war." His successor as prime minister, the Earl of Bute (served 1762–1763), feared that if Britain assumed too dominant a position, the rest of Europe would band together against her in resentment. The terms of the Treaty of Paris reflected the British concern to provide at least some satisfaction to France and Spain.

The greatest loss of all to France had been Canada; perhaps French authorities took some comfort in Voltaire's description of the former French possession as a "wretched country, covered with snow and ice eight months out of twelve, and inhabited by savages, bears, and beavers." France had lost its North American empire, but French commercial power remained formidable.

THE SEVEN YEARS' WAR AND THE SUCCESS OF PRUSSIA

Friedrich's gamble in invading Saxony in 1756 and launching a preventive war seemed at first to pay off. He followed one of his favorite maxims, "If you must go to war, fall on your enemy like thunder and lightning." After capturing Dresden, he advanced on the Hapsburg territory of Bohemia. By bringing about the very alliance of Austria,

Engraving of British Government offices in Calcutta. Late 18th century. Calcutta was founded by the British East India Company in 1690; Fort William, the nucleus of the magnificent buildings seen here across the river, was begun in 1696. The contrast between the colonial palaces and the squalor of the lives of the locals seen in the foreground is perhaps unconsciously ironic.

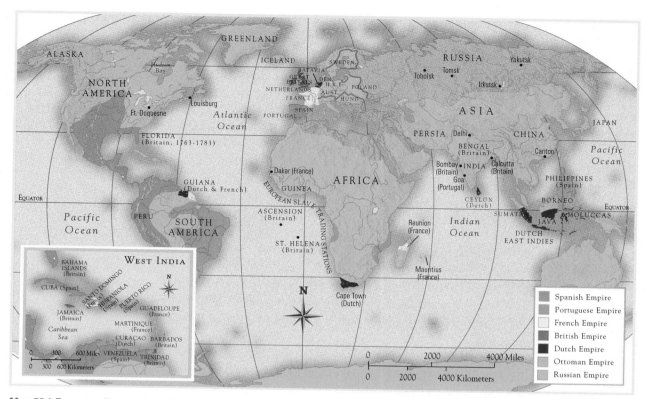

Map 56.1 European Possessions Overseas, c. 1780. India was divided between the British, Portuguese, and Dutch; South America between the Spanish and Portuguese. Note the large Spanish holdings in North America. The Ottoman Empire now controlled most of the Middle East and North Africa. The dismemberment of most of these holdings after the end of World War I and the collapse of the Ottoman Empire continued to bring instability to the region (and the world) in the early 21st century.

France, and Russia that he had moved to prevent, however, he undid the benefits of his surprise attack. In 1757 an Austrian army drove the Prussians out of Bohemia. Thereafter the fighting followed the same pattern. Friedrich kept his troops moving, beating back repeated attacks by the allies, and winning impressive tactical victories, but he never managed to break the strategic stalemate. Prussia's long-term prospects seemed doomed. Either the fighting would continue indecisively, with the Prussians gradually losing territory, or the allies would make a breakthrough and crush their enemy.

THE END OF THE SEVEN YEARS' WAR

At the beginning of 1762, with Prussian resources stretched to the breaking point and on the verge of collapse, rescue arrived from the most unexpected of directions. Friedrich's old enemy, the Russian Empress Elizabeth, whose suspicion of Prussia had helped create the anti-Prussian alliance, died at St. Petersburg. Her nephew and liberal successor, Peter III (ruled December 1761–June 1762), had long admired Friedrich's enlightened domestic policies. On his accession he ordered the immediate suspension of Russian attacks on the Prussians, and in May 1762 the Prussians and Russians signed a peace treaty whereby all conquests were returned. Friedrich's luck was all the greater in that six weeks after signing the treaty Peter was deposed by his ambitious wife,

Catherine II (see Topic 59)—while under arrest, Peter was assassinated by a group of guardsmen under mysterious circumstances.

With Russia out of the action and France fully occupied in dealing with Britain, the alliance collapsed, leaving Maria Theresa no choice but to accept the loss of Silesia. The Treaty of Hubertusburg (1763) between Prussia, Austria, and Saxony restored the prewar situation, with the Austrians recognizing Prussian possession of Silesia. Saxony regained its independence, but Friedrich paid no compensation for the damage Prussia had inflicted.

Unlike the War of the Austrian Succession, the Seven Years' War significantly changed the balance of power in Europe by reinforcing Prussia's status; at the same time, it underlined the growing importance of colonial strength. Even though the Treaty of Paris sealed Britain's victory on terms that were not excessively vindictive, Britain clearly emerged from the colonial wars as the indisputable imperial leader in Europe.

The triumph did not last long. Within 10 years of the Peace of Paris, Britain's 13 North American colonies were beginning their successful attempt to break away. Their loyalty to Britain had been assured by the threatening presence of France on American soil. With the French driven out and the British asserting their control with ever more unpopular taxes, conditions were right for the Revolutionary

War—in which, ironically enough, the colonists received assistance from France (on the American Revolution, see Topic 59).

Prussia was the other main victor, but its emergence as a major power was bought at considerable cost. Friedrich spent the first half of his reign (23 years) in virtually continuous war, devoting much energy during the second half to keeping the peace by skillful, if ruthless, diplomacy.

Furthermore, the Prussian Army's invincibility did not long survive Friedrich's death. It fell behind in training and equipment and was decisively crushed by Napoleon's French troops at Jena (1806). Yet the Prussian successes of the mid-18th century proved its right to be taken seriously as an important power and foreshadowed events a century later, when Prussia, against the will of a declining Hapsburg Austria, succeeded in uniting Germany.

Putting Wars for Empire in Perspective

At a casual glance, the history of the 18th century seems as filled with conflict as the bloody 16th century. There are important differences, however, between the destructive wars of the earlier period, often fueled by religious hatreds, and the 18th century's careful search for a stable balance of power. European countries fought one another for specific political and economic goals, and not to wipe out whole groups or classes.

When it became clear that the war aims would—or, as the case might be, would not—be achieved, the combatants stopped fighting and made peace. The various treaties of the century sought not so much to reward the winners and punish the losers, as to recreate and maintain the balance. The prudence of 18th-century European statesmen was, of course, dictated by realism rather than charity. In so fluctuating a world, yesterday's enemy might well become tomorrow's most important ally.

The 18th century's other distinction was that of spreading both war and diplomacy beyond the boundaries of Europe to a global context. Battles fought in the Philippines or along the Mississippi affected the political and economic developments of countless European citizens. The wider horizons required new resources: Britain's success in the conflicts outside Europe was largely the result of the strength and efficiency of its navy, an indispensable force in empire building.

The careful diplomatic balance achieved at Paris and Hubertusburg was destined to be of short duration. Along with the growth of international trade and revolutionary developments in industry, the revolutionary political movements of the late 18th century wrought vast changes in European political life. One factor remained constant, however. Starting with the 18th-century wars for empire, European political and economic life was permanently linked to that of the rest of the world.

Questions for Further Study

1. How did the European powers use the wars in the colonies to continue their struggle for domination in Europe?
2. What role did the British Navy play in Britain's success in the colonial wars?
3. What have been the lasting effects of the 18th-century colonial wars in Africa, Asia, and the Americas?
4. How did war and diplomacy interconnect in settling the colonial disputes of the 18th century? Was the process different from the relationship between war and diplomacy in earlier periods?

Suggestions for Further Reading

Anderson, Fred. *Crucible of War: The Seven Years War and the Fate of Empire in British North America.* New York, 2000.

Anderson, M.S. *The War of the Austrian Succession 1740-1748.* New York, 1995.

Bearce, George D. *British Attitudes Toward India.* Westport, CT, 1982.

Brewer, John. *The Sinews of Power.* New York, 1989.

Browning, Reed. *The War of the Austrian Succession.* New York, 1995.

Davis, L., and R. Hittenback. *Mammon and the Pursuit of Empire: The Political Economy of British Imperialism.* Cambridge, MA, 1987.

Ehrman, John. *The Younger Pitt : The Consuming Struggle.* Stanford, CA, 1996.

Evans, Eric J. *William Pitt the Younger.* London, 1999.

Mommsen, W. P.S. Falla, trans. *Theories of Imperialism.* Chicago, 1982.

Mori, Jennifer. *William Pitt and the French Revolution 1785-1795.* London, 1997.

Peters, Marie. *The Elder Pitt (Profiles in Power).* London, 1998.

Raudzens, George. *Empires: Europe and Globalization, 1492-1788.* Sutton, 1999.

Sen, Sudipta. *Empire of Free Trade: The East India Company and the Making of the Colonial Marketplace.* Philadelphia, 1998.

InfoTrac College Edition

Enter the search term *American Revolution* using Key Terms.

EUROPEAN SOCIETY IN THE EIGHTEENTH CENTURY

In 1789, European society was struck by the great upheaval known as the French Revolution. The leaders of that tumultuous event, who used language as an essential aspect of politics, believed that they were building a new, radically different social order. For this reason, they called the world that had existed before the revolution the *Ancien Régime*—the "Old Regime." Historians still use the term to describe the way of life and the institutions that characterized Europe before 1789.

Although the society of the Old Regime was based on traditional notions of hierarchy and privilege, what appeared on the surface to be a stable social order was being undermined by powerful forces. European economic life and population were both expanding rapidly. Major innovations were introduced in agriculture and manufacturing that would bring revolutionary transformations. The social structure, which for centuries had seemed to be ordained by God, adjusted to new conditions, especially as the nobility was forced to make concessions to a middle class that was growing in wealth and insisted on sharing power and status. These social realities were rationalized and justified by the intellectual climate of the times, which questioned the principles on which the social structure of the Old Regime rested.

Royal absolutism, itself based on the idea of a stable society, also underwent change. Many of the rulers cloaked their power in the trappings of "enlightened" monarchy while seeking to increase government efficiency and control. To sustain the increasing centralization of government and pay for the frequent colonial and European wars of the period, rulers constantly squeezed more and more taxes from their subjects, taxes that eventually sparked rebellion in the New World against Britain and threw the Old Regime in France into crisis. The great revolutionary upheaval that erupted in 1789 was the climax of a process that had been underway for decades.

SOCIETY AND THE OLD REGIME

The Old Regime was an intricate network of political, economic, and social relationships. Its political character was defined by the system of absolute monarchy, with its divine right theory and increasingly centralized state bureaucracy. The economic life of Europe was overwhelmingly rural and agrarian, burdened by isolation and chronic food shortages, and while evolving financial practices often produced instability, restrictive mercantilist policies still constrained commerce. The social patterns of the 18th century had their roots in the Middle Ages.

THE NATURE OF THE OLD REGIME

Unlike modern society, in which status is defined largely by wealth and economic function, in most countries during the Old Regime a person's position was fixed by birth and heredity within one of three "estates": (1) the clergy, either of the Roman Catholic or the Protestant churches, the upper levels of which were often linked by family ties to the nobility; (2) the noble elites, who possessed an array of legal powers and privileges; and (3) the overwhelming bulk of society, consisting of the rural peasantry and several groups that lived in the towns—the artisans who were members of highly restrictive guilds, manual laborers, and a small but growing commercial middle class, whose ranks would be swelled in the course of the Industrial Revolution.

The social system of the Old Regime was deliberately based on the notion of inequality and difference, and during the 18th century the hierarchical structure of society actually grew more rigid. In some parts of Europe, so-called sumptuary laws, which regulated extravagance in food or dress, were designed to make social distinctions visible by prohibiting people in one order from wearing clothes worn by those in a higher order. In other countries, members of the middle class were forbidden to marry into noble families, while nobles generally could not be members of guilds or engage in commerce.

Such laws were, however, largely unnecessary, because the social hierarchy was maintained by the constraints of the community of which one was a member. Most 18th-century Europeans had access to special privileges and bore certain responsibilities only in so far as they were members of a given group or community—the nobility or the clergy, a town, a village, or a guild. The nobles, for example, were exempt from direct taxation and could expect certain services from the peasants who worked their land, while the church collected an annual offering known as the *tithe*. In a similar fashion, members of artisan guilds enjoyed the exclusive right to engage in their craft, while inhabitants of a particular village might have access to certain grazing lands or forests. Tradition was the moral basis of 18th-century society. Most people, guided by a belief in a divinely sanctioned order and the experience of their ancestors, did not want or expect change. If people—whether nobles or peasants—expressed grievances against the existing order, it was usually because their traditional rights had been undermined by the ever-expanding power of the central government.

Despite these rigid patterns of thought and behavior, the society of the Old Regime was neither uniform nor static. It was distinguished by the startling contrast—sharper perhaps than in modern industrial societies—between the lives of people in each of the social orders. The highest ranks of society displayed refined tastes and manners, lived on magnificent estates, and enjoyed a luxurious standard of living; the less fortunate peasants and the urban destitute lived in extreme poverty. Sharp differences also existed within the orders as well as from region to region. Although some nobles were very wealthy, others were hardly distinguishable from the wealthier peasants in their communities. Within the church, the economic and social differences between a bishop and a village priest were sharp. Similarly, whereas most peasants in Western Europe lived well above the subsistence level and enjoyed some legal status, those in Eastern Europe generally tended to be serfs or existed in dire economic straits. In countries with strong commercial economies, such as Britain and the Netherlands, the middle classes were growing rapidly in wealth and status, whereas they hardly existed in the Holy Roman Empire or Russia.

THE GROWTH IN POPULATION

One of the most powerful sources of change in the 18th century stemmed from shifting demographic patterns. Europe's population had experienced periods of growth throughout its history, although disease or warfare had at times depopulated parts of the Continent. About midcentury, however, the population began to increase at a startling rate. Population figures for this period can only be estimates rather than exact numbers because most countries did not conduct census surveys until the 19th century, and accurate figures were available only much later. Nevertheless, it is clear that between 1700 and 1800, the number of inhabitants in Europe almost doubled, from slightly more than 100 million to about 190 million, and by 1850 the population had increased to more than 265 million. The demographic growth pattern, which continued well into the 19th century at rates varying from 40 to 60 percent, was more rapid in Western and Central Europe but occurred almost everywhere, in rural as well as urban areas.

In England (including Wales), the population increased from 5.5 million to more than 9 million in the century after 1700, and reached 14 million by 1831. France, the most populous western European country at the beginning of the 18th century, grew from 16 to 17 million to more than 24 million by the time of the Revolution of 1789. Even in 18th-century Russia, the demographic pattern repeated itself, with the population growing from 18 to 30 million.

The causes of this dramatic explosion in population are much debated. One theory holds that in traditional agricultural societies the birthrate tends to remain relatively high, so that declining mortality rates explain population growth. Yet although the annual death rate generally declined from the 18th century onward, in many areas of Southern and Eastern Europe, as well as in large cities, the rate of deaths did not fall below that of births until after 1850. Similarly,

Map 57.1 Growth of European Population, c. 1800–1850. The map shows the impact of the First Industrial Revolution. The greatest increase is in areas convenient for shipping (northwest and southern France, the Low Countries, and Scandinavia), rich in natural resources (Poland, northern Italy), or both of these (the Baltic states and, preeminently, England and Wales). Southern Europe was to remain underpopulated until after 1945.

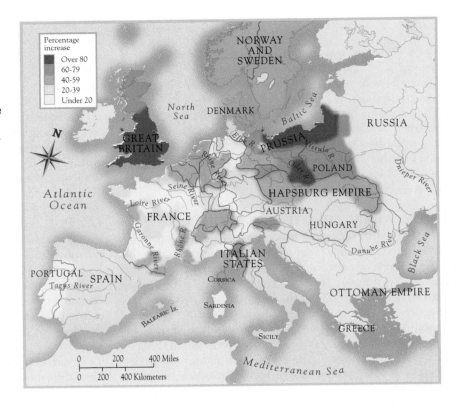

strong population growth occurred before the most important advances in medicine could have affected infant mortality and adult health. Nor did the Industrial Revolution cause the demographic explosion because the upward movement of population began before industrialization.

Food supply appears to have been the most significant factor in the growth of population. Until the 18th century, English demographic growth reflected a relationship between marriage patterns and the availability of food. In periods of population growth, when the demand for food was greater, prices for basic staples rose. Because even in good times the poorer classes lived close to the edge of subsistence, higher food prices—which meant, in effect, a reduction in real wages—tended to discourage marriage in order to avoid the financial burden of maintaining a family. On the other hand, population decline lowered the demand for food and deflated prices, which in turn made marriage and children more feasible.

Over the course of the 18th century, fundamental changes transformed the society of the Old Regime. The depressed economic conditions prevalent in the 17th century slowly improved. Along with the demographic growth, rapid commercial and financial expansion took place. Most significant of all, Europe was about to experience two far-reaching revolutions, one in agriculture and one in industry (see Topic 60).

MARRIAGE AND THE FAMILY

The family remained the basic unit of European social life. The traditional family was a patriarchy, with the husband wielding authority over wife and children. In upper- and middle-class families, the interests of the family as a whole were generally regarded as taking precedence over those of its individual members, and marriages were usually arranged according to considerations of finance and status.

Throughout Europe, the nuclear family, consisting of parents and children, had been the rule among the upper classes since the 16th century. When finances permitted, married couples set up independent households separate from parents, but young people generally delayed marriage until at least their mid-twenties in order to accumulate sufficient savings. Among noble families, the first-born son usually married at a younger age because his inheritance rights imposed the responsibility to father future heirs.

In Western Europe, where most lower-class couples married in their mid-twenties, the illegitimacy rate was surprisingly low. In mid-century, however, the number of illegitimate children began to increase. In Central Europe, for example, the illegitimacy rate appears to have increased fivefold between 1700 and 1800. The increase in illegitimacy may have been the result of the breakdown of village communities and the weakening role of churches in everyday life.

In any case, the average married couple had five children, and more of them survived infancy and childhood than in earlier times. Several factors, however, acted as a break on the birthrate: About half of all women between the ages of 15 and 44 remained unmarried. Moreover, birth control—achieved by such devices as sheepskin condoms, the vinegar douche, and sponges, and by the application of

Jan Steen, *The Village School,* c. 1665. One of the pupils, whose written exercise lies crumpled on the ground, is about to be punished by having his hand struck with a wooden spoon. Steen's many paintings of "childish" errors often have a moralistic or satirical tone, whereby the children's behavior seems to be symbolic of adult foolishness.

Reproduction of *The Village School* by Jan Steen. Courtesy of the National Gallery of Ireland

herbal potions—was increasingly practiced by the upper classes. Members of noble families generally married younger, but after 1650 declining revenues and the need to keep estates intact contributed to a decline in the average number of children from six to two.

Along with the other developments that began to transform Western society, attitudes toward children began to change. Rousseau, for example, believed that childhood was a stage in human development, and that childhood experiences often proved crucial to adult behavior. Parental kindness and love did not begin in the Old Regime, but a new spirit of humanism and compassion increasingly led parents to treat their offspring as children rather than as small adults in their dress, in matters of discipline, and in recreation.

Economically, children were viewed both as a burden and as an opportunity, especially among the lower classes. In peasant families, they were expected to work in the fields or in cottage industries at an early age, and in the towns teenage males were apprenticed in shops. Nevertheless, large numbers of children represented an expense, and in hard times could be a serious burden on poor families. As a result, many parents resorted to infanticide or placed unwanted children in foundling homes, which were supported by private charities. In some large cities, perhaps 30 percent or more of all children were given up by their parents or by unwed mothers. If

such unfortunate children survived—mortality rates were shockingly high in these institutions—they were usually sent to workhouses or otherwise exploited.

AGRICULTURE AND THE WORLD OF THE PEASANTRY

European society in the 18th century was still overwhelmingly rural, and the peasantry represented the largest portion of the population—between 80 and 85 percent. Peasant life was harsh and often unrewarding. Few rural dwellers, except those in military service or on religious pilgrimage, ever traveled much beyond the village where they were born. They ate more or less the same kind of foods that their ancestors had eaten hundreds of years earlier. The staple item in peasant diets was black bread, which provided considerable nourishment. This was supplemented by soups made of grains and vegetables, especially beans, peas, and turnips, and by rice and pasta. By the 18th century, potatoes and tomatoes introduced from the Americas had become important ingredients in the peasant diet. Meat and fish were rarities, especially on the Continent.

Peasants and tenant farmers were constantly dependent on nature because the productivity of the grain harvest was the crucial fact of life. If the harvest failed, the result could be severe hardship if not starvation. Ironically, in such circumstances rural dwellers found it more difficult to obtain food than did people in towns, where municipalities generally kept reserve supplies. The yield ratio—that is, the relationship between the quantity of seed planted and the quantity of the crop harvested—generally went up in Europe in the 18th century.

The village and the immediate countryside around it represented the universe within which the peasants lived and died. Sons learned their father's trade, families intermarried, and loyalty was concentrated in the extended family. The church was the center of civic and religious life, and the priest was often the only local person who had a minimum of literacy. For the peasant, the village community functioned as the real government because it was responsible for public order, charities, maintaining roads, and enforcing access to common pasture lands and forests. In Western Europe, where rural society was organized around the villages, the owners of small plots would often decide communally what crops to plant. In Eastern Europe, where the land was held in the form of huge estates, the noble landowners made such decisions.

FREE PEASANTS AND SERFS

Conditions among the peasantry varied widely from one part of Europe to another. In Western and Central Europe—Britain, France, the Low Countries, Spain, northern Italy, and portions of Germany—most rural dwellers were legally free peasants. In places such as Portugal, southern Italy, Sardinia, and Sicily, their lives were overshadowed by stark

Le Nain, *Family of Country People*, c. 1640. 3 feet 8 inches by 5 feet 2 inches (1.14 by 1.56 m). The painting shows the hardships of peasant life during the Thirty Years' War; the family here is eating simple black bread and soup. The fact that the figures shown here—and in other paintings by the same artist—seem to exhibit a calm, stoic dignity and piety has led some scholars to speculate that these works were intended to reassure wealthy patrons.

Copyright Réunion des Musées Nationaux/Art Resource, NY

poverty and the exactions of absentee landowners. In France, slightly more than half of the free peasants owned their own land, and these were generally small and inefficient plots. The rest of the free peasants were tenant farmers or day laborers. On the eve of the French Revolution, free peasants still owed nobles tithes as well as special fees—known as *banalités*—for the use of the lord's mill, wine press, and baking oven. Such obligations were bitterly resented.

Moreover, in addition to these feudal obligations, the peasantry also bore the burden of taxation.

The farther east they lived, the greater the degree of authority landowners exercised over peasants. In Eastern Europe, serfs rather than free peasants predominated. These legally unfree peasants lived and worked on huge estates owned by powerful nobles. At a time when serfdom was being eliminated in most western regions of the Continent, in

Map 57.2 Grain Production in the 18th Century. England's commercial supremacy derived from the fact that while it became a center for manufacturing and commerce (see previous map), its agriculture continued to flourish. Other notable farming lands—Sicily, southern Spain, southern Greece—lacked political stability and a thriving population to exploit their natural resources,

the 16th and 17th centuries, it became the widespread practice in Eastern Europe. As in the Middle Ages, peasants in Eastern Germany were bound to their lord's estates and could neither marry nor move without their master's consent. By contrast, Russian serfs were bound personally to the landlord, much as slaves, and could be transferred from one estate to another. Russian monarchs from Peter the Great to Alexander I rewarded loyal nobles with huge tracts of state land and the serfs who lived on them. Throughout Eastern Europe the oppressed peasantry and serfs often rose in rebellion against their landlords.

ARISTOCRATS, URBAN CLASSES, AND THE POOR

In sharp contrast to the precarious and harsh existence of the peasantry stood the aristocracy, the social elite that controlled most of the wealth and status in society. The nobles, who were by far the smallest class in terms of numbers, were long established in their legally sanctioned privileges and their estates. The middle class, on the other hand, although larger than the nobility, was not yet socially pervasive or powerful. In the larger cities of Europe, such as Paris or Rome, most of the population was poor, a social fact that presented unexpected challenges to governments and represented a new political element as the Old Regime drew to a close.

THE ARISTOCRACY

Aristocrats were by birth at the top of the social hierarchy. Although they represented only a small portion of the overall population—ranging from less than 2 percent to perhaps as much as 5 percent, depending on the country—the nobles dominated society. Among the legal privileges they enjoyed were immunity from certain forms of punishment, exemption from direct taxation, and judgment by their peers.

Since the Middle Ages, the European aristocracy had performed vital military and governmental functions. Feudal lords first received their estates from the king in return for serving as military officers and providing a specified number of soldiers. As the power of the monarchs

The National Gallery, London

Gainsborough, *Husband and Wife in a Landscape*. Mid-18th century. This example is typical of "Grand Manner portraiture," of which Gainsborough was a master. The couple seems to be on a hunting excursion—the husband has his gun and hunting dog—but the elegant way in which both are dressed is hardly appropriate. As always, Gainsborough appears to be more interested in the landscape and the weather than in his apparent subjects.

grew and centralized states developed, nobles continued to hold a virtual monopoly on the highest ranks of the officer caste in most countries. Similarly, nobles had once served as advisers to medieval kings, and in the modern state system they controlled the upper levels of the royal administration. In the late 17th and early 18th centuries, some sovereigns, such as Louis XIV of France and Friedrich Wilhelm I of Prussia, flooded their bureaucracies with commoners in a deliberate effort to weaken the hold of the nobility on the state, although the policy was reversed after 1750.

The major source of noble wealth was revenue derived from their landed estates. Sometimes they obtained money, which was always in short supply, through inheritance, marriage, or a royal pension. Most nobles were unwilling to earn income from such business activities as trade or finance, and in some countries they were prohibited from doing so. But as some nobles found their revenues from agriculture diminishing by the end of the century, they were more willing to take advantage of the nonagricultural resources available on their lands and set up mining operations, foundries, and other commercial activities.

Like the peasantry, the aristocracy was not a compact or uniform social group. In England, many landowners rented their land to tenant farmers. In Prussia, on the other hand, the Junkers managed their estates directly with a labor force still consisting of serfs, as in Russia. Yet because the number of noble landowners was declining in Prussia—by 1789 some two-thirds of the Junkers no longer possessed estates—the legal code of 1794 prohibited non-nobles from owning land; in Russia, on the other hand, increasing numbers of nobles were being given large estates by the monarchy.

The nobility, especially those of ancient lineage, jealously guarded their privileges and status, but financial difficulties or state policy often led to new blood entering the ranks. Some noble titles, for instance, were inseparable from the ownership of particular estates, so that commoners who were able to buy that property were also buying noble status. In France, about 3,700 offices were held by royal appointment, which automatically gave noble status to their holders. During the course of the 18th century, the king ennobled between 6,500 and 10,000 people.

For the most prestigious noble families, the center of life was at the royal court, where proximity to the sovereign

Painting of *The Oyster Luncheon.* 1731. The luxury and abandon of this scene, as the waiter brings yet another tray of oysters to an already sated group of diners, makes an obvious contrast to the peasant family in the picture on p. 590. The statue of Venus and Cupid in the niche on the right refers to the fact that oysters were considered an aphrodisiac.

Giraudon/Art Resource

was an exclusive privilege. Those nobles who lived at Louis XIV's palace at Versailles enjoyed special honors, although their lives were constantly guided by the will, and sometimes the whim, of the king.

In country houses, where an extended noble family could live in relative privacy, the interior layout was designed for several particular purposes. Hosts would greet their guests in a grand entrance hall on the ground floor, while common spaces—a drawing room, a dining room, a library or study, and perhaps a conservatory—were designed for entertaining. A large staircase off the entrance led to the upstairs quarters, including the bedrooms and rooms reserved for family activities and other private circumstances. Servants were housed in their own wing of rooms, while gardeners usually lived in separate cottages on the estate.

CITIES AND THE MIDDLE CLASS

In the 18th century, urban dwellers were a minority of the population in most countries, with the exception of states with longstanding commercial experience such as England and the Dutch Republic. London was the largest European city, with a population of about 1 million, while Paris was only half that size. Some 20 cities, including Rome, Amsterdam, St. Petersburg, and Vienna, had more than 100,000 inhabitants. The rapid growth of Europe's cities came in the 19th century, when industrialization drew large numbers of rural dwellers to urban centers.

The social and economic differences between Eastern and Western Europe also affected the role and importance of cities in each region. In Eastern Europe, cities tended to be smaller in size, less cosmopolitan, and subject to more direct government control. In the West, they had larger populations and more diverse ones and often enjoyed a greater degree of municipal self-government. In commercial cities, such as Amsterdam, Venice, and Frankfurt, elite oligarchies of nobles and merchants still dominated city councils.

Although rural dwellers greatly outnumbered those who lived in cities, urban centers exerted considerable influence on European society. In addition to serving as the seats of national and regional governments, large cities were centers of education and culture, of foreign ideas and influences, and of economic activity. Peasants in the hinterland often resented the towns as parasites exploiting the countryside by draining food and other resources while serving as dangerous sources of immorality for village youth.

THE URBAN POOR

Poverty was a serious problem in 18th-century society, especially in the cities, where streets were sometimes lined with beggars. For the poor, urban living conditions were often worse than in the country, and the death rate remained high throughout the 18th century. This was particularly true of children, who were more susceptible to disease caused by overcrowding, bad water, and the almost universal lack of sewers. By the end of the century, perhaps 10 percent of the entire populations of Britain and France lived on charity or begging. Some cities, such as Venice, where as much as 20 percent of the city's population was without employment,

Hogarth, *Gin Lane*. 1750. Hogarth's engravings convey a grim picture of contemporary London life. Here the path to destruction, caused by excessive alcohol, leads downward. On the left, a couple pawns their last possessions (the pawnshop is indicated by the three balls hanging outside and by the inscription over the door: "Gripe, Pawnbroker"). Below, on the top step, a mother under the influence of her Gin cheerfully neglects her child, while below at the bottom right we see the results: beggary.

Metropolitan Museum of Art (Harris Brisbane Dick Fund, 1932)

granted municipal licenses to the poor to beg and live off the largesse of the many well-to-do tourists who flocked to the city each year. Despite a tradition of Christian teaching that the poor were God's blessed children, changing social mores made the attitude among the middle classes more harsh. Some political economists, for example, insisted that charity only induced the poor to lead useless lives and encouraged crime. The role of the state in dealing with the problem was still affected by such prejudice, as witnessed by the fact that in the mid-1700s in France beggars and vagrants were still subject to arrest and imprisonment, although their only crime was unemployment. Private charitable groups, particularly religious orders, provided much needed assistance, but poverty remained an ugly and pervasive reality of life in 18th-century Europe.

WOMEN AND THE OLD REGIME

Women were subordinate to men in every society of the Old Regime and had few legal rights of their own. In many societies, women could not own property directly or sue on their own in courts of law. In such cases, fathers, husbands, or other male relatives would manage estates or represent women. In Britain, a husband exercised total control over his wife's property, unless marriage contracts stipulated otherwise. In most cases husbands could file for separation but wives could not, although courts in France and England began to offer some measure of protection for women whose spouses mismanaged their estates. Some women, of course, exercised power as rulers, while the authority of others varied within a particular family setting. But for most women, their role was limited to family responsibilities, reproduction, and the rearing of children, along with work that could be performed in the home. By the end of the 18th century, however, some aspects of the lives of women had begun to change. In aristocratic and upper-middle-class circles, women played an increasingly important role in intellectual life, while among the working classes the Industrial Revolution began to bring many women out of the home and into the factory.

Childbirth and its attendant risks remained a constant issue for most young women of all classes. Because the church maintained the view that sexual activity between husband and wife was legitimate only for the purpose of having children, it condemned all forms of contraception except abstinence. Nevertheless, the increasing use of birth control, especially among the upper classes, enabled some women to limit or escape the burdens of childrearing. Although abortion was similarly prohibited by the church, it too was widely practiced.

WOMEN AND WORK

In the countryside, wives and daughters generally worked in the fields alongside male family members, particularly to harvest crops, and were central to the so-called **cottage industry,** where families worked in the home to produce textiles and

some finished goods (see Topic 60). While husbands planted and tended cereal crops, women often raised vegetables for family consumption, made cheese and butter, cared for livestock, and sold excess eggs and milk in village markets.

In cities, women from the laboring class worked as household servants for the wealthy—40 percent of all British working women fell into this category—or worked as seamstresses and laundresses. Some women also sold vegetables, fish, and other foodstuffs in city markets, where such women were important elements in the urban economy. Among the lower rungs of the middle classes, wives and daughters served as salesclerks in family shops or helped their artisan husbands informally in craft workshops. Much female work of this kind was undertaken as part of a family business, usually within or near the home: Women's labor was regarded as a nonessential contribution to the labor of males. In reality, however, among the poor and laboring classes, women's labor often made the difference between survival and destitution.

UPPER-CLASS WOMEN

Among the upper-middle and noble classes, the role of women was far different. In both groups, family wealth freed them from having to earn an income. In middle-class and gentry families, women managed household establishments, while aristocratic women, who had large retinues of staff, enjoyed considerable leisure, which was used either for personal improvement such as music and reading or for social visits.

Wealthy women played an increasingly large role in the organization and functioning of their homes in the late 18th century. Interior decor became more comfortable and "feminine" in appearance, while wives would often entertain female friends in the afternoons over tea or cards. In the evenings, after formal dinner parties, the men usually remained in the dining room or retired to the library for tobacco and brandy, while the women retired to the drawing room for conversation and sweets. During the 18th century, however, some aristocratic women presided over a mixed company of men and women in their own salons, where intellectual discussions took place (on the salon, see Topic 54).

In the royal courts of Europe, women played still other roles and encountered different opportunities. There, in the extravagant world of luxury, high politics, and intrigue, wives of noblemen were expected to be accomplished in the social graces, not only in order to preside at elaborate dinners and balls, but also to flatter and influence men of influence. Yet despite the privilege that aristocratic women enjoyed, they shared with their lower-class sisters a series of proscriptions and burdens that were mapped out by convention, by their parents, and by the cultural constructs of gender. Not least of the difficulties they faced were the repeated dangers of pregnancy and childbirth.

The position of courtesan held a particular fascination with the opportunities it offered to those women, regardless of the status into which they were born, who were willing to bear the degradation of having sex with their patrons. Prostitution had, of course, always existed in European society, and courtesans obtained rewards by their physical attraction. An en-

PUBLIC FIGURES AND PRIVATE LIVES

JEANNE BÉCU DU BARRY AND LOUIS XV

Giraudon/Art Resource

© Chateau de Versailles, France/Giraudon/Superstock

One of the most successful courtesans in 18th-century Europe was Marie Jeanne Bécu, the Comtesse du Barry (1743–1793), mistress to the French sovereign, Louis XV. Her life was a case study in the limits and constraints of women in the Old Regime.

She was born Jeanne Bécu, the illegitimate daughter of a young woman from the village of Vaucouleurs. In 1748, her family moved to Paris, where the mother worked as a cook in the home of a wealthy businessman. Jeanne was taken into a convent at the age of seven, where she learned the rudiments of reading and writing, and left when she was 16. Beautiful and quick-witted, she worked as a clerk in a millinery shop and had several affairs with married men. In 1763, she met in a gambling house the self-styled Count Jean du Barry, an adventurer who moved both in the Paris underworld and in aristocratic circles. Du Barry ran a profitable business as a procurer of young women for his noble friends. Jeanne served as hostess in his home, where she befriended many important aristocrats.

In 1768 she married Jean's brother, the real Count du Barry, in order to appear at the court, where she met the 58-year-old king privately at Versailles. Louis was particularly lonely at the time because his wife had died a month earlier, and he was without an official mistress. Madame de Pompadour (1721–1764), the immensely influential royal mistress for 20 years, had died some years earlier. Louis was captivated.

Jeanne could not become the new royal mistress until she was officially "presented" at court, a move blocked by a conspiracy between the foreign minister the Duke de Choiseul—who hoped his own sister would become the royal mistress—and the Austrian ambassador, who was trying to persuade Louis to marry an Austrian princess. The anti–du Barry party did everything it could to prevent the presentation, but to no avail—in April 1769, she entered the royal chamber, resplendent in formal dress and diamonds. She was given her own apartment in the palace and a retinue of servants, and over the years Louis bestowed sumptuous gifts on her, including a chateau.

Jeanne du Barry chose not to exercise her influence in political matters, preferring instead to be a patron of the arts. As a result, she remained immensely unpopular at a court that was increasingly bent on extravagance and intrigue. On the death of Louis in 1774, she was banished to a nunnery, where she remained for two years, and then was allowed to move to her private estate. She lived there with a lover, the Duke de Brissac, until the outbreak of revolution in 1789, traveling to London in order to aid the noble émigrés living in exile. By the time she had returned to France, she had lost much of her famed beauty. In December 1793, during the Reign of Terror, she was condemned as a counter-revolutionary and guillotined.

terprising young woman could become the lover and companion of a wealthy aristocrat or a royal patron, perhaps even of the king himself. Yet courtesans had to cultivate many other talents, including the art of flirtation; literary, musical, and conversational skills; and highly polished social charms.

Regardless of religious proscriptions or secular laws against illicit sex, courtesans were institutionalized by the 18th century in the courts and in society at large. Sexual in-fidelity had become more commonplace in aristocratic circles, and married couples—men and women alike—felt free to have affairs. In some cities, courtesans were highly paid professionals who had agents and paid special taxes. In the royal courts, talented young women were actually taken under wing and trained by aristocratic male mentors, who could then present their ward to a royal patron in return for any future influence she might have.

Putting European Society in the Eighteenth Century in Perspective

As the 18th century opened, the Old Regime appeared to be safely and permanently entrenched, much as it had been for centuries—a world of privilege, tradition, and hierarchy. Yet before the century was out, that well-ordered society and many of its values had been turned upside down by a revolutionary upheaval that shook all of Europe.

In retrospect, the period was rent with the forces of change. The commercial and financial life of Europe was expanding rapidly, while the population was growing at an unprecedented rate. Both in agriculture and manufacturing, revolutionary transformations were taking place that would have far-reaching repercussions. Even the social structure, which had appeared fixed by divine sanction, was undergoing important adjustments as the old aristocracy was forced to make room for an increasingly aggressive middle class that wanted a share of power and privilege. Throughout Europe, a new intellectual ferment was questioning many of the fundamental premises that underlay the social structure of the Old Regime.

Absolutist government, which rested on the notion of secure social foundations, was undergoing change. Some rulers sought to justify their authority by appearing to be "enlightened" and disinterested sovereigns, and all of them struggled to improve the efficiency of their bureaucracies and the power of their arms. To support the growth of central government and the luxury of the royal court, to fight the all-too-frequent wars that marked the century, rulers made more incessant demands for taxes, demands that ultimately produced a rebellion in the New World against the Old, and the political crisis of the Old Regime in France.

Questions for Further Study

1. In what ways was privilege built into the social system of the Old Regime?
2. How was society changing in the 18th century?
3. What differences existed between the aristocrats and the upper reaches of the middle classes?
4. What does the life of Jeanne Bécu du Barry reveal about the lives of women in the Old Regime?

Suggestions for Further Reading

Earle, Peter. *The Making of the English Middle Class: Business, Society, and the Family in London, 1660–1730.* Berkeley, CA, 1989.

Epstein, S.R., ed. *Town and Country in Europe, 1300-1800.* New York, 2001.

Houston, Robert A. *Literacy in Early Modern Europe: Culture and Education, 1500–1800.* New York, 1988.

Macfarlane, Alan. *Marriage and Love in England: Modes of Reproduction, 1300–1840.* New York, 1986.

Martin, A. Lynn. *Alcohol, Sex, and Gender in Late Medieval and Early Modern Europe.* New York, 2001.

O'Brian, Patrick, ed. *Urban Achievement in Early Modern Europe: Golden Ages in Antwerp, Amsterdam and London.* New York, 2001.

Pollock, Linda A. *Forgotten Children: Parent-Child Relations from 1500 to 1900.* Cambridge, MA, 1984.

Roche, Daniel. M. Evans, trans. *The People of Paris: An Essay in Popular Culture in the Eighteenth Century.* Berkeley, CA, 1987.

Rogers, Katherine. *Feminism in Eighteenth-Century England.* Urbana, IL, 1982.

Stone, Lawrence. *The Family, Sex and Marriage in England, 1500–1800.* New York, 1977.

Traer, James F. *Marriage and the Family in Eighteenth-Century France.* Ithaca, NY, 1980.

InfoTrac College Edition

Enter the search term *Old Regime society* using Key Terms.

THE AGE OF REASON

Toward the end of the 17th century, scientists and intellectuals began to circulate to a wider public the ideas and principles behind 17th-century science. During the 18th century, philosophers applied the same scientific attitudes to broader questions of human behavior. The school of thought that developed was called the Enlightenment, and the period during which it flourished—1740 to 1790—is often known as the Age of Reason.

The center of Enlightenment thinking was France, where a group of intellectuals known as the *philosophes* developed a consistent view of the world. The highest power, they believed, was reason used critically because only by its means could true knowledge be gained. Reason, in turn, reflected the rational essence of Nature, which is ordered, operating according to logical and unchanging laws.

At the same time, Enlightenment thinkers were believers in practical information and experiment. The chief expression of this conviction was the *Encyclopédie,* a vast multiauthored work describing the contemporary state of science, technology, and philosophy. Despite government interference, the 17 volumes of the *Encyclopédie* appeared between 1747 and 1771, and its sales throughout Europe helped spread the ideas behind the Enlightenment.

The leader in the Enlightenment battle against organized religion was Voltaire. Poet, novelist, and historian, Voltaire also wrote on science and philosophy. The most famous intellectual of his time, in the last 25 years of his life Voltaire constantly attacked organized religion—he called it "the infamous thing"—which he believed caused so much bigotry and fanaticism.

Other thinkers dealt with scientific and social issues. Georges Buffon was the first modern classifier of the animal world, while Marie-Jean Condorcet used his work as a mathematician to reinforce his belief that the human race was capable of systematic progress. In Italy, Cesare Beccaria studied new approaches to criminals and their punishment. The Scottish economist Adam Smith, in writing *The Wealth of Nations* (1776), founded economics as a social science.

Although he was one of the contributors to the *Encyclopédie,* Jean-Jacques Rousseau strongly contested the *philosophes'* notion that civilization would lead to an improved society. On the contrary, he held that humans were good but civilization was evil. The way to happiness, therefore, lay in a return to a simple, natural life. An advocate of free love and unrestrained emotion, Rousseau devised a social contract that proposed a new kind of relationship between individuals and their government.

THE SEEDS OF THE ENLIGHTENMENT

The intellectual movement known as the **Enlightenment,** which reached its peak in the latter part of the 18th century, represented the fusion of several currents of thought from the late 17th century. The scientific revolution had led the way in seeking to understand how the world works, revealing in the process that many of the teachings of traditional Christianity about natural science and astronomy were simply wrong (see Topic 48).

THE PHILOSOPHY OF JOHN LOCKE

One of the fathers of the Enlightenment was the English philosopher John Locke (1632–1704). In *An Essay Concerning Human Understanding* (1690), Locke discussed the origin and nature of knowledge. At birth, he argued, the human mind was a blank tablet—a *tabula rasa*—that was filled up by sense impressions gained through direct experience. As a result, all human beings were born as equals, whereas status and privilege usually determined the kind of experiences that each person underwent. Education was, therefore, of prime importance in creating a just and equitable society.

In a truly revolutionary move, Locke rejected the traditional Christian teaching of original sin and the traditional political system of monarchy. Instead, he believed in the essential goodness of humanity and argued that political power should have a broad popular base. In his *Two Treatises on Civil Government* (1690), written in the wake of the English Revolution, Locke posited the contract theory of government, according to which individuals living in a state of nature entered freely into a political compact in order to protect the essential individual rights of life, liberty, and property. Citizens would act loyally toward government, but if government broke its part of the contract by undermining these liberties, then the people had the right to change it.

As the scientific revolution had demonstrated, it was possible for humans to make progress in understanding the workings of nature by using reason. Similar beneficial change could be created in society by following the same positive course. Although many of the rationalists who followed Locke abandoned the traditional beliefs of Christianity, and some rejected the very notion of God, Locke was not an atheist and strongly advocated a degree of religious freedom—although not for Catholics, Jews, or atheists.

By the early part of the 18th century, these ideas had begun to crystallize. Thinkers increasingly rejected the past and looked forward to social and political reform. Custom and tradition, far from being valuable, were the shackles that bound the human race and prevented progress. Hope for humanity lay not in contemplating the rewards of the next life—the existence of which in any case could not be objectively demonstrated—but in concentrating on improvements in the real world. With this optimistic attitude, civilization could reach new heights and redress many of the existing injustices.

THE *PHILOSOPHES:* THE BATTLE AGAINST SUPERSTITION

The center of Enlightenment thought was France, where its representatives fought a constant battle against the weakening absolutism of Louis XV and the power of the Catholic Church. Important Enlightenment movements developed in Germany and Italy, and Enlightenment ideas also circulated in North America, especially toward the end of the century, where they influenced the first pronouncements of the founding fathers. Eastern Europe was relatively little affected, its rulers being fully aware of the subversive character of Enlightenment doctrines. Furthermore, most Eastern European countries had a low level of literacy and only a small middle class to be affected by intellectual developments.

In France, the movement's leaders were the **philosophes.** Literally translated, the word means "philosophers" in French, but the *philosophes* were not so much original thinkers as popularizers and propagandizers, who circulated

Engraving of the *Philosophes* at supper. The figure wearing an elaborate hat, with his left arm raised, is Voltaire. He is flanked by Diderot and Condorcet. The leading French representatives of the Enlightenment were aware that their strength lay in presenting a united front in the face of the authorities, and group discussions— sometimes open to the public—were a way to show solidarity.

The Granger Collection

the ideas of others in the form of pamphlets, plays, novels, or works of history.

Few Enlightenment thinkers completely ruled out the possibility of the existence of a divine force in the universe; even the highly skeptical Edinburgh philosopher David Hume (1711–1776) argued only against the provability of such a power. Most of them, however, attacked the power of the clergy and all traditional superstition. In place of the Christian God stood nature—or Nature—whose laws benevolently governed the universe. The same order that existed in astronomy and physics could be found in morality, or politics, or even economics. Only by seeking to understand these natural laws and following them could humans achieve happiness. By emphasizing happiness, rather than salvation, the *philosophes* rejected the traditional Christian view that misery in this life would receive compensation in the next.

The concern with general well-being led to protests at the ill-treatment of prisoners and the insane, and condemnation of slavery. Most Enlightenment thinkers were pacifists and internationalists, who saw patriotism—along with religion—as the cause of most wars. Above all, they believed in freedom. The France of Louis XV, although less repressive than that of his predecessor, still maintained restrictions on freedom of speech, religion, trade, and work. For all their fervor, however, the *philosophes* were not revolutionaries. They advocated not immediate democracy, but a gradual transition by means of rulers who were "enlightened despots" such as Friedrich II of Prussia (see Topic 59). They did not aim at radical change, even though many of their ideas inspired the leaders of the French Revolution. Furthermore, Enlightenment thought circulated chiefly among the urban aristocracy and educated middle classes.

In addition, few of the *philosophes* had much time for women's rights, even though some of them reached their audience by means of the salons of the more advanced women of the day. By contrast with centuries of earlier thinkers, they acknowledged women's ability to reason, and encouraged female education, but on the whole they accepted the conventional notion of women as inferior to men. The only real attempt to argue for fundamental change, Mary Wollstonecraft's *Vindication of the Rights of Women* (1792), found few sympathizers.

DIDEROT AND THE *ENCYCLOPÉDIE*

One of the leading French *philosophes*, Denis Diderot (1713–1784), sought to provide an organized basis for Enlightenment thought by preparing an immense encyclopedia. He intended the work to describe the contemporary state of science, technology, and philosophy, and at the same time to establish a classification system for human knowledge. Working with the physicist and mathematician Jean Le Rond d'Alembert (1717–1783) as his co-editor, Diderot began work on the project in 1747; the last of its 17 volumes of text and 11 of engravings appeared in 1771. The *Encyclopédie*, with its articles by various contributors, provided a wealth of information on a bewildering range of subjects, from metallurgy to political economy to the raising of asparagus.

Implicit in this philosophy was the idea that no political or religious system should try to limit or control the minds of individuals. The authors of the *Encyclopédie* opposed all corporate privilege, in fact, and believed that no group—the guilds, for example—had exclusive rights to any area of knowledge. As the leading German philosopher of the Enlightenment, Immanuel Kant (1724–1804), pointed out, the very essence of the Enlightenment was to "dare to know." If this meant rejecting established wisdom or resisting authority, then the *philosophes* were prepared to do so. Voltaire had to leave France, Hume was threatened with excommunication (and thus ostracism), and Diderot spent time in jail. Church and government authorities both tried to stop publication of the *Encyclopédie*, or at least censor it, but Diderot succeeded in completing his project.

The *Encyclopédie* sold not only in Europe's great cities, but also in small provincial towns. It helped an entire generation to see their lives in an entirely fresh way and led them to challenge hitherto unquestioned assumptions. Its

Illustration from the *Encyclopedie.* Mid-18th century. The scene shows a scientific laboratory, in which various experiments are being conducted. In the foreground a kneeling figure seems to be performing a dissection, while at the table behind others are mixing liquids. The various vessels on the shelf above are numbered and named in the accompanying text.

tone of optimism, and its conviction that humans had their destiny in their own hands, powerfully influenced the Declaration of Independence of the new American nation.

CHARLES-LOUIS MONTESQUIEU

A more specific influence on the political growth of America was the political philosophy of one of the contributors to the *Encyclopédie,* Charles-Louis Montesquieu (1689–1755). Aristocratic by birth, Montesquieu argued against the abolition of monarchy. His ideal system of government was based on a division of powers among king, lords, and commons. This separation of powers would, he believed, create a series of "checks and balances" capable of safeguarding personal liberty. The framers of the American Constitution adapted the principle, transforming Montesquieu's three divisions into the executive, judicial, and legislative branches of government.

Montesquieu's other important contribution to the study of politics was his book *The Spirit of the Laws* (1748). In it he claimed that different forms of government were appropriate to different geographic conditions. Small states such as Venice or 5th-century B.C. Athens were best suited by a republican government, whereas vast countries like Russia required an absolute monarchy. Pioneering in its aims, Montesquieu's work was the first serious attempt to examine the relationship between politics and environment.

"THE INFAMOUS THING": VOLTAIRE AND NATURAL MORALITY

Perhaps the most versatile genius produced by the Enlightenment—if less original than Diderot—was François-Marie Arouet (1694–1778), best known to us as Voltaire, his pen name. As a writer, Voltaire moved with ease from drama to satire to history. His studies included science and politics. He was an honored guest at the courts of Louis XV and Friedrich II, but also spent time in prison. Above all, Voltaire was fully committed to the great issues and battles of his times. An enemy of all forms of tyranny, he spent most of his life in exile.

His early satirical writings pilloried French aristocratic society and won him a jail sentence in the Bastille (1717–1718). Undeterred, he continued with an epic poem on Henry IV of France, which he published in 1723. After he spent another few months in prison in 1726, the authorities released him on the condition that he left France.

Voltaire chose to spend his exile in England, where the system of government seemed to him far more just and liberal than in France. Returning home in 1729, he wrote his *Letters on the English* (first published in English in 1733; in French in 1734), extolling English social and political liberalism and religious toleration, and praising the ideas of Newton and Locke. In advocating the experimental approach to science, he held that doubt is the beginning of wisdom and the basis of tolerance.

His contemporaries were enraged by the book's attack on French society and political institutions, and the uproar it

created drove him out of Paris into the country. He spent most of the next 15 years living in isolation with his mistress, Madame du Châtelet (1706–1749). A woman of considerable learning, and a prolific writer on scientific subjects—among her works was a translation of Newton's *Principia*—she exercised an important intellectual influence on Voltaire. The two of them returned briefly to Versailles in 1744, but life at the court of Louis XV was sterile and frustrating, and they soon withdrew.

The death of Madame du Châtelet in 1749 came as a bitter blow, and the following year Voltaire accepted an invitation to visit the court of Friedrich II at Potsdam. At first he established a close friendship with the king and worked on a history of the age of Louis XIV, his most important historical work. Two such powerful temperaments were probably bound to clash before long, however. The king made it clear that royal friendship had its limits: When Voltaire dared to criticize his patron's verse, the king abruptly dismissed him. In 1753, Voltaire left Prussia in disillusionment and circulated throughout Europe his own version of the falling-out.

The last 20 years of his life were spent in the village of Ferney, near Geneva, where he set up his own court. A pro-

Pigalle, *Voltaire*. 1770–1776. Height 4 feet 9½ inches (1.47 m). The head, modeled from life, shows the venerable philosopher at the age of 76. The position of the statue is based on an ancient Roman statue. The contrast between the thoughtful face and the active movement of the rest of the body perhaps symbolizes Voltaire's intellectual vigor.

cession of the leading figures in European political and intellectual life came to visit him, to discuss, and above all to listen to the sage of Ferney. Voltaire returned to Paris only in 1778, but the hero's welcome he received proved too much for his poor health, and the excitement probably hastened his death.

"THE INFAMOUS THING"

Voltaire's writings touched on all of the great questions raised by Enlightenment thinkers, but the most frequently recurring theme is the importance of freedom of thought. From the beginning of his career he castigated bigotry and intolerance, and to the end of his life he poured out a stream of pamphlets condemning prejudice and fanaticism: "The superstitious man is ruled by fanatics and he becomes one himself." Many of the letters in his vast correspondence ended with the phrase he made famous: "Crush the infamous thing!" The "thing" in question is organized religion, together with the intolerance bred of superstition.

The chief agents of prejudice, he believed, were the Christians, both Catholic and Protestant. Voltaire ridiculed the notion of the Bible as the inspired word of God. Rather, he saw it as a collection of anecdotes and contradictions that had no relevance to the modern world. Furthermore, it had provided the basis for centuries of disputes and persecutions that were as violent as they were pointless. The results, he said, were self-interested priests and false traditions.

Voltaire's attacks on organized religion were particularly bitter. His book *Candide* contains a famous scene based on an actual historical event; after the earthquake that destroyed most of Lisbon in 1755, killing more than 30,000 people, some of the victims who managed to survive the devastation were solemnly burned alive by the "wise men," the priests and monks, in a superstitious attempt to avert further disaster. Yet his position was fully in line with the Enlightenment's chief aims and goals, and most Enlightenment thinkers actively campaigned against the outward manifestations of organized religion.

Yet Voltaire was no atheist. The God in whom he believed created the world but could not be tied down to any single religion. Like many of the *philosophes*, the sage of Ferney held that only natural morality—the true religion common to all humans—could cure the ignorance and arrogance that plagued the world: "The only book that needs to be read is the great book of Nature."

SCIENCE AND SOCIETY: SOCIAL AND ECONOMIC THOUGHT

Many of the *philosophes*, including Voltaire, took an active interest in science and mathematics. Marie-Jean Condorcet (1743–1794), who helped in the preparation of the *Encyclopédie*, was a mathematician with a special interest in probability theory. Believing as he did in the inevitability of human progress, Condorcet looked forward to a time when even human biology might improve. Condorcet's optimism

was tested by his experience. He played an important role in the French Revolution but incurred the hostility of the extremists for his moderate opinions. After two years in hiding, he was arrested and thrown into prison, where he committed suicide.

The naturalist Georges-Louis Buffon (1707–1788) also believed in the possibility of physical progress. He ran a series of experiments to try to extend the human lifespan to 120 years or more. Buffon is best known for his work on the classification of the animal kingdom, and he also directed the royal gardens in Paris (the present *Jardin des Plantes*). The 44-volume *Natural History* (1749–1804), whose production he led, was one of the major scientific achievements of the 18th century.

CESARE BECCARIA AND PRISON REFORM

The center of the Enlightenment in Italy was Milan, where the brothers Alessandro (1741–1816) and Pietro (1728–1797) Verri headed a group of liberal intellectuals and published the influential journal *Il Caffè* (*The Cafe*). Among the younger members of the group was the economist and criminologist Cesare Beccaria (1738–1794), who derived an interest in political and social issues from his reading of Montesquieu.

In 1764, at the age of 26, Beccaria published *On Crimes and Punishments*, the first systematic treatment of rational criminal punishment. The work was an instant success and was translated into a variety of languages. Eventually its ideas led the way to criminal reform in many European countries, including Russia, and helped shape the U.S. system of criminal justice. Beccaria's main thesis was that his contemporaries' attitude toward criminals was unreasonable and inefficient. The harsh system of punishments, with long prison terms or death sentences for relatively minor crimes, was based on the belief that criminals were hopelessly evil. Because they were believed incapable of repentance, they deserved no mercy. Furthermore, the penalties were applied inconsistently.

As a child of the Enlightenment, Beccaria believed that all humans were capable of improvement. Prisons should thus be places for rehabilitation, whose occupants were adequately housed and fed and given the chance to work, rather than centers of futile and vindictive punishment. His book argued passionately against the death penalty and torture, pointing out that such savage penalties do not stop crime; in any case, torture was uncivilized, and capital punishment was an abuse of the natural rights of humans.

ADAM SMITH AND FREE TRADE

In his economic lectures, Beccaria anticipated the ideas of the leading economist of the 18th century, the Scot, Adam Smith (1723–1790). While traveling in Europe, Smith met and was influenced by members of a French school of economists known as the *physiocrats*. Their most famous principle was **laissez faire**—"let it be": the natural laws of economics require only noninterference to be successful. Smith also visited Voltaire at Ferney.

On returning home, Smith retired to his native town of Kirkcaldy, near Edinburgh. He spent the next 10 years

Perspectives from the Past

The Age of Reason

The Enlightenment was known as the Age of Reason because the *philosophes* argued that superstition, faith, and tradition should be replaced by logic, scientific inquiry, and a secular spirit of the quest for knowledge of the natural laws that governed the universe. These principles informed the works of all the major writers of the era.

On Method

René Descartes (1596–1650) was one of the leading figures of the scientific revolution. Perhaps his greatest contribution to the Enlightenment is the set of principles he enunciated in 1637 on the proper method to be followed in pursuing "scientific" truth.

I believed that the four [principles] following would prove perfectly sufficient for me, provided I took the firm and unwavering resolution never in a single instance to fail in observing them.

The *first* was never to accept anything for true which I did not clearly know to be such; that is to say, carefully to avoid precipitancy and prejudice, and to comprise nothing more in my judgment than what was presented to my mind so clearly and distinctly as to exclude all ground of doubt.

The *second*, to divide each of the difficulties under examination into as many parts as possible, and as might be necessary for its adequate solution.

The *third*, to conduct my thoughts in such order that, by commencing with objects the simplest and easiest to know, I might ascend by little and little, and, as it were, step by step, to the knowledge of the more complex; assigning in thought a certain order even to those objects which in their own nature do not stand in a relation of antecedence and sequence.

And the *last*, in every case to make enumerations so complete, and reviews so general, that I might be assured that nothing was omitted.

The long chains of simple and easy reasonings by means of which geometers are accustomed to reach the conclusions of their most difficult demonstrations, had led me to imagine that all things, to the knowledge of which man is competent, are mutually connected in the same way, and that there is nothing so far removed from us as to be beyond our reach, or so hidden that we cannot discover it, provided only we abstain from accepting the false for the true, and always preserve in our thoughts the order necessary for the deduction of one truth from another. . . .

From Brian Tierney, Donald Kagan, and L. Pearce Williams, eds., *Great Issues in Western Civilization*, 4th ed., Vol. II. McGraw-Hill, Copyright © 1992.

Natural Law

Most of the philosophes believed that the universe and the human condition were based on natural law, and that a discovery of truth could be achieved by understanding those laws. The following extract is from an article by Denis Diderot written for his Encyclopédie.

In its broadest sense the term [natural law] is taken to designate certain principles which nature alone inspires and which all animals as well as all men have in common. On this law are based the union of male and female, the begetting of children as well as their education, love of liberty, self-preservation, concern for self-defense.

It is improper to call the behavior of animals natural law, for, not being endowed with reason, they can know neither law nor justice.

More commonly we understand by natural law certain laws of justice and equity which only natural reason has established among men, or better, which God has engraved in our hearts.

The fundamental principles of law and all justice are: to live honestly, not to give offense to anyone, and to render unto each whatever is his. From these general principles derive a great many particular rules which nature alone, that is, reason and equity, suggest to mankind. . . .

Man, by nature a dependent being, must take law as the rule of his action, for law is nothing other than a rule set down by the sovereign. The true foundations of sovereignty are power, wisdom, and goodness combined. The goal of laws is not to impede liberty but to direct properly all man's actions.

From *Encyclopedia*: Selections by Denis Diderot, D'Alembert.

The Principles of Morals

David Hume (1711–1776), perhaps the most important English philosopher of the 18th century, sought to understand the world beyond the senses. In this essay from 1751 on the nature of morals, he revealed his belief that morality was capable of scientific, rational analysis.

There has been a controversy started of late, much better worth examination, concerning the general foundation of MORALS; whether they be derived from REASON or from SENTIMENT; whether we attain the knowledge of them by a chain of argument and induction, or by an immediate feeling and finer internal sense; whether, like all sound judgment of truth and falsehood, they should be the same to every rational intelligent being; or whether, like the perception of beauty and deformity, they be founded entirely on the particular fabric and constitution of the human species. . . .

It must be acknowledged, that both sides of the question are susceptible of specious arguments. Moral distinctions, it may be said, are discernible by pure *reason*: else, whence the many disputes that reign in common life, as well as in philosophy, with regard to this subject; the long chain of proofs often produced on both sides, the example cited, the authorities appealed to, the analogies employed, the fallacies detected, the inferences drawn, and the several conclusions adjusted to their proper principles? Truth is disputable; not taste: what exists in the nature of things is the standard of our judgment: what each man feels within himself is the standard of sentiment. Propositions in geometry may be proved, systems in physics may be controverted; but the harmony of verse, the tenderness of passion, the brilliancy of wit, must give immediate pleasure. No man reasons concerning another's beauty; but frequently concerning the justice or injustice of his actions. . . .

David Hume, *An Inquiry Concerning the Principles of Morals,* Section I.

A Call for Toleration

Voltaire used his brilliant style and sense of irony to debunk many aspects of the Old Regime and its dependence on superstition. In the following essay, he tried to point out that a major step toward toleration was often just a matter of putting oneself in the other person's place.

One does not need great art and skilful eloquence to prove that Christians ought to tolerate each other—nay, even to regard all men as brothers. Why, you say, is the Turk, the Chinese, or the Jew my brother? Assuredly; are we not all children of the same father, creatures of the same God?

But these people despise us and treat us as idolaters. Very well; I will tell them that they are quite wrong. It seems to me that I might astonish, at least, the stubborn pride of a Mohammedan or a Buddhist priest if I spoke to them somewhat as follows:

This little globe, which is but a point, travels in space like many other globes; we are lost in the immensity. Man, about five feet high, is certainly a small thing in the universe. One of these imperceptible beings says to some of his neighbours, in Arabia or South Africa: "Listen to me, for the God of all these worlds has enlightened me. There are nine hundred million little ants like us on the earth, but my ant-hole alone is dear to God. All the others are eternally reprobated by him. Mine alone will be happy."

They would then interrupt me, and ask who was the fool that talked all this nonsense. I should be obliged to tell them that it was themselves. I would then try to appease them, which would be difficult. . . .

From Lynn Hunt, Thomas R. Martin, Barbara H. Rosenwein, R. Po-chia Hsia, Bonnie G. Smith, eds., *Connecting with the Past,* Vol. I. D.C. Heath, Copyright © 1995.

working on his most famous publication, *The Wealth of Nations* (1776), while involving himself on an almost daily basis in Edinburgh's intellectual and cultural life. In *The Wealth of Nations* he worked out his theory of the division of labor, money, prices, wages, and distribution; the classic system of economics he described laid the foundations of the science of political economy.

Smith argued that if market forces were allowed to operate without state intervention, an "invisible hand" would guide self-interest for the benefit of all. This was another example of Enlightenment optimism. He was in favor of open competition and strongly opposed to price rings (the predecessors of the modern cartels), observing: "People of the same trade seldom meet together even for merriment or diversion, but that the conversation ends in some conspiracy against the public, or in some contrivance to raise prices."

THE OUTSIDER: ROUSSEAU AND THE SOCIAL CONTRACT

Enlightenment belief in the blessings of civilization found one eloquent dissenter: Jean-Jacques Rousseau (1712–1778). Tormented and quarrelsome, Rousseau's unstable temperament shaped most of his life. He lost his mother at birth and was separated from his father at the age of 10. After a brief period as an engraver's apprentice, he met and fell in love with a French noblewoman, Madame de Warens (1700–1762). The two settled down in the country for almost 10 years (1732–1741), a period Rousseau later recalled in his autobiographical *Confessions* (1765–1770) as idyllic.

In 1741 he set out for Paris, where he devoted himself to music. In the 1750s, Diderot commissioned him to produce some articles on music for the *Encyclopédie,* and his short opera *The Village Soothsayer* (1752) was an instant success. In 1745 he began an affair with an illiterate servant girl, Thérèse Levasseur.

The first of his major philosophical works, *Discourse on the Sciences and the Arts,* appeared in 1750. It laid out one of his basic principles: the savage, "natural" condition is superior to civilization. Rousseau was convinced that the growth of society had corrupted the natural goodness of the human race and destroyed the freedom of the individual. Humans, in short, were good; society was bad.

THE SOCIAL CONTRACT

Rousseau soon became identified with the notion of the "noble savage," but he never advocated a return to some form of primitive existence. Instead he urged the creation of a new social order. In 1762 he published *The Social Contract,* one of the most radical political works of the 18th century, and one that proved immensely influential on modern political theory.

Rousseau's ideal was a society in which there was no hereditary, privileged aristocracy. All members should have joined freely, surrendering their individual rights to the group. The "rulers" would be the servants of the community, answerable to the people's will, and instantly removable if the people so decided. Unlike his contemporaries, Rousseau claimed that if the people really governed themselves, there would be no need for checks and balances, separation of powers, or protection of rights.

Clearly such a system could operate only in a small society. In any case, Rousseau did not intend *The Social Contract* to be taken as a practical program, although in the bloodiest days of the French Revolution, the extremist Robespierre claimed to be following Rousseau's recommendations in unleashing the Reign of Terror. Its purpose was to set out the basic theory of democratic government. For conservatives, Rousseau was a dangerous emotionalist and an anarchist, whereas for liberals and democrats, a forerunner of totalitarian dictatorship. Few political thinkers have inspired more controversy.

ROUSSEAU AND THE ROLE OF WOMEN

For all the importance of *The Social Contract,* most of Rousseau's readers were more interested in the social ideas expressed in his novels than in his political philosophy. His two most popular books, *The New Heloise* (1761) and *Émile* (1762), were bestsellers throughout Europe. These works reveal Rousseau's ideas about education, society, and the role of women. The first of them owed much of its popularity to its praise of the open display of emotion, while the other dealt with education, recommending that children be protected from the harmful effects of civilization and exposed instead to the moral influence of nature.

In both books, women are assigned specific social roles as nurturers and educators. Julie, the heroine of *The New Heloise,* inspires her children with a sense of right and wrong—law enforcer rather than lawmaker. In *Émile,* the two children who are the tale's principal characters are both given unconventional educations, but their training is not the same. Émile, the boy, learns knowledge and self-control so that he can become confident and in charge of his own destiny in the wider world. Sophie, his future partner, is educated for the domestic sphere, where she will serve as Émile's faithful and obedient companion. For all Rousseau's revolutionary political thinking, he was quite prepared to institutionalize the traditional "separate spheres" for women and men. Women, he believed, far from receiving a natural education, should be kept away from nature lest they became disruptive.

Putting the Age of Reason in Perspective

For many Enlightenment thinkers, their movement marked humanity's coming of age. The power of pragmatism and critical reason, they believed, had replaced what they regarded as the childish superstitions of the Middle Ages. Their strenuous opposition to the Old Regime and all of its works was to help bring it crashing down, and by undermining respect for established authority they laid the foundations for the increasing intellectual freedom of the 19th century. Some of their ideas, such as Rousseau's praise of open emotional expression, were taken up by the romantics.

On the other hand, most of the *philosophes* fully realized that further human progress would be neither smooth nor painless. Many of them were concerned about the desperate state in which most of Europe's population lived. Smith and Hume both wrote about the conditions of the rural and urban poor, and the French physiocrat Jacques Turgot tried to redistribute taxes more fairly and abolish compulsory labor. Hume even argued on his deathbed that "man will never be enlightened." Most Enlightenment thinkers, in fact, aimed to bring about progress on a limited scale, through their local societies and academies, in the hope that someday the total accumulation of their efforts might produce significant change.

The upheavals of the French Revolution and the subsequent Napoleonic era seemed to bear out Hume's skeptical conclusion. Yet in the long run the Enlightenment proved decisive in changing basic attitudes in Western culture. Never again did traditional religion occupy the position it held before the 18th century. From the end of the 18th century, democracy became an increasingly admired political ideal, even if it could not be attained in practice. Science and technology maintained their role as catalysts of social change, while the *Encyclopédie* illustrated the immense value of knowledge and practical information.

Condorcet once described the intellectuals of his time as a "class of men less concerned with discovering the truth than with propagating it." For all the immensity of the task, the leaders of the Enlightenment led the way to the social and political revolutions of the 19th century.

Questions for Further Study

1. What were the main goals of the Enlightenment? How did its philosophers set about achieving their aims, and how successful were they?
2. What effect did Enlightenment thinking have on European economic development?
3. How did the ideas of Voltaire and Rousseau differ? Which of the two was closer to the ideals of the Enlightenment?
4. How far did Beccaria's attitude toward prison reform anticipate or inspire modern approaches?

Suggestions for Further Reading

Behrens, C. *Society, Government, and the Enlightenment: The Experiences of Eighteenth-Century France and Prussia.* New York, 1986.

Chartier, R. *The Cultural Origins of the French Revolution.* Durham, NC, 1991.

Hampson, N. *The Enlightenment.* London, 1982.

Munck, Thomas. *The Enlightenment: A Comparative Social History 1721-1794.* New York, 2000.

O'Hagan, Timothy. *Rousseau.* New York, 1999.

Rendall, J. *The Origins of Modern Feminism: Women in Britain, France and the United States.* New York, 1984.

Roche, Daniel. Arthur Goldhammer, trans. *France in the Enlightenment.* Cambridge, MA, 1998.

Sklar, J. *Montesquieu.* Oxford, 1987.

Scott, H.M. *Enlightened Absolutism.* Ann Arbor, MI, 1990.

Spencer, S. *French Women and the Age of Enlightenment.* Bloomington, IN, 1984.

InfoTrac College Edition

Enter the search term *Enlightenment* using the Subject Guide.

Enter the search term *Voltaire* using Key Terms.

Enter the search term *Diderot* using Key Terms.

Enter the search term *Rousseau* using Key Terms.

GLOSSARY

absolutism Form of government in which rule rested in the hands of a king who claimed to rule by divine right and was responsible only to God.

abstract expressionism Painting style of the mid-20th century that made no reference to recognizable subjects—they were abstract—and sought to express interior states of feeling.

Anabaptist Sixteenth-century sect that made concern over the idea of baptism a central aspect of its doctrine. Rejecting the idea of predestination, the Anabaptists based their doctrine on the belief that adults alone, not children, were able to choose to enter a religious faith.

anarchists Those espousing a political theory that advocated the overthrow of all forms of authority, especially governments.

Australopithecus Species of hominid dating to about 4 million years ago. Between four and five feet tall, they had broad thumbs and could use their hands to grip, and also walked upright.

Babylonian Captivity The removal of the papacy for 75 years to Avignon, France, in the last quarter of the 14th century.

Baroque Seventeenth-century artistic style featuring the appearance of new forms and subjects, ranging from still life painting to the design of private townhouses to opera. The expression of strong emotions, an interest in psychological states of mind, and the invention of elaborate technical display were key features of the Baroque style.

Bauhaus The 20th century's most influential school of architecture and design. The innovations of Gropius and his colleagues derived from a new attitude toward the nature and function of a building, based on the possibilities of advanced construction techniques.

benefice In medieval society, a special grant of land to a vassal in return for cavalry service. Vassals could use the benefice to defray the expenses incurred in providing their horses, armor, and weapons.

Black Death A pandemic of plague (pneumonic and bubonic) in 1347–1348, which swept across Europe, wiping out perhaps 35 million people—one-third of the population.

Blitzkrieg Literally, "lightning war." A combination of rapid-moving, heavily armed armored tanks, supported by aircraft and motorized infantry units, applied by the Germans during World War II.

Bolsheviks Radical Marxists, led by Lenin and dedicated to violent revolution; seized power in Russia in 1917 and subsequently were renamed the Communists.

bourgeoisie Originally medieval merchant-artisans, city dwellers who represented a new culture opposed to the ideals and values of the feudal system and became influential allies of the kings in their struggles to resist the power of the traditional lords. The middle classes.

caliph A term meaning "deputy of the Prophet," used for the supreme head of all Muslims in the medieval world.

chansons de geste Vernacular literature in the Middle Ages, heroic epics in the tradition of minstrels' recounting heroic deeds.

Chartists Group of mid-19th-century radical reformers in Britain who called for wholesale parliamentary reform; among the provisions were universal adult male suffrage, a secret ballot, and the abolition of property qualifications for members of Parliament.

chivalry Late medieval code of behavior whereby knights were bound by the ideals of loyalty, honor, and pride.

collectivization Stalinist program in the Soviet Union that required all peasants to turn their land and livestock over to the state, keeping only their houses and personal property. Every collective received production quotas. Peasants shared the work as well as the profits or losses the cooperative earned.

communes Self-governing centers in late medieval Europe, particularly in northern and central Italy, founded by townspeople who either rebelled against their overlords or purchased charters from them. The communes developed distinctive forms of self-government that stimulated patriotism and civic pride and controlled all aspects of economic activity.

conceptual artists Artists of the 1970s who aimed to create "objects" or experiences that were not intended to be bought or sold, or put in a museum. Their works, often consisting of unlikely materials such as cornflakes or ice, were installed and then dismantled.

consuls The two chief magistrates of the Roman Senate, who were elected annually. Each consul had his own army, to prevent the other one from seizing power.

cottage industry System in which families worked in the home to produce textiles and some finished goods.

Cubism Artistic style of the 20th century whose adherents abandoned traditional perspective, and in a series of experimental canvasses, tried to find new ways of seeing their subjects geometrically.

cuneiform The earliest known form of writing, invented by the Sumerians around 3000 B.C., from two Latin words, *cuneus* ("wedge") and *forma* ("shape"). The wedge-shaped symbols were drawn or impressed on soft clay tablets.

Dadaist movement Artistic movement of the early 20th century that was born out of anger, frustration, and despair. Its response was to reject the past and all its works, and to create meaningless nonsense.

demesne Part of the arable land of a medieval manor, reserved for the lord's use and farmed for him by the peasants.

diaspora The gradual spread of Jews throughout many parts of the ancient world. The term is sometimes still used for Jews living outside Israel. Today used to describe the dispersal of peoples around the globe.

dictator In the Roman republic, leader who would, in time of national crisis, serve as supreme commander for a maximum term of six months.

Enlightenment The 18th-century intellectual movement, fusing several currents of thought from the late 17th century, in which philosophers applied the same attitudes of the scientific revolution to broader questions of human behavior.

Epicureanism Greek philosophy, popular in Roman times, based on the teachings and writings of Epicurus (341–271 B.C.), whose aim was to free humans from the threat of divine retribution or the fear of the unknown. It held that we are free to live our lives according to principles of moderation and prudence in the pursuit of pleasure.

Expressionists Artists of the early 20th century, mainly German, who used their art to express strong emotions.

Fascism Political program, originating in Italy, that combined left-wing and right-wing elements and took advantage of the postwar atmosphere of nationalist frustration and fear of Bolshevik revolution that pervaded Italian political life. Benito Mussolini created the Fascist regime in Italy in 1922.

feudalism A set of contractual arrangements between free men in the Middle Ages; it was, however, restricted to noble landowners. Feudal relationships involved two elements: vassalage, a personal bond established between two men based on military service, and a relationship between the king and powerful magnates.

Futurists Artists of the early 20th century, mainly Italian, who boldly rejected all traditional forms of culture and turned instead to the cult of the machine and the technological future.

Gothic Medieval architectural style that took Romanesque barrel vaults and stone supporting ribs and combined them to form high, pointed rib vaults. The results were lofty, light, and airy structures, with the spaces between the vaults cut away and filled with stained-glass windows. To ensure that the buildings were stable, architects added outside supports called "flying buttresses" that shored up the walls.

Great Schism The existence of two popes in the late medieval church (one in Rome and one in Avignon). *See also* Babylonian Captivity.

guilds Cooperative associations in medieval Europe, which maintained a monopoly of crafts and trade in a region, settled disputes, insisted on quality control, and established fair weights and measures.

Hellenistic Term used to refer to the history and culture of the peoples "Hellenized"—that is, brought under Greek influence—by Alexander's conquests.

helots Serfs acquired from Spartan conquests, not bought and sold as slaves of individual Spartiates, but belonging to the state, who mostly worked the land.

heresy Holding of religious beliefs different from the church's official doctrines.

hominids The forerunners of modern humans.

Homo erectus Hominid species that appeared around a million years ago and is far closer to our own species than previous hominid varieties.

Homo neanderthalis Another variant of *Homo sapiens*, the earliest found in Europe in the Neander Valley of the river Rhine. Neanderthal people flourished from about 40,000 to 80,000 years ago.

Homo sapiens Hominid species from which our own subspecies, *Homo sapiens sapiens*, developed.

Homo sapiens sapiens Modern humans; sometimes called Cro-Magnon.

Huguenots French Calvinists (Protestants).

humanism A late medieval spirit conditioned by a rebirth of interest in Classical culture and its values, and a new emphasis on human beings as the center of the world.

iconoclastic controversy Byzantine movement of the 8th century, condemning the use of icons (images of sacred figures).

imperialism *See* New Imperialism.

Impressionists Artists of the 19th century who sought to give a literal impression of light and color. Avoiding any kind of organized form, and hoping to paint without interpreting their subject, they tried to reproduce the overall visual impact of what they saw.

Inquisition A traveling tribunal during the 16th century that conducted inquiries into heresy in various locations. Those who refused to confess were tried, often with the use of torture to extract confessions—and without confession, there could be no conviction. Because heresy was considered a civil as well as a religious crime, those found guilty were punished by the local rulers rather than by the church. The most active tribunal was that in Spain.

jihad In Islam, a holy war to convert unbelievers, in which those who die fighting for the cause win salvation.

laissez faire Literally translated as "let it be," the 18th-century belief, espoused by Adam Smith, that the natural laws of economics require only noninterference to be successful.

latifundia Large landed estates in early Roman times, most of which were in southern Italy and Sicily.

lay investiture The medieval practice in which laymen began investing bishops not only with symbols of their fiefs but with spiritual symbols as well.

liberalism Ideology that held that people should be free. Political liberalism held that a representative system was the wisest form of government because it allowed for stability, the participation of the middle classes, and the protection of basic freedoms such as equality before the law and freedom of speech. Liberal economic theory, which argued that prosperity would result from economic forces that were allowed to operate freely without government intervention, lay at the core of political liberalism.

Mannerism Sixteenth-century artistic style in which the figures were deliberately distorted and exaggerated, replacing the calm, Classical balance of Renaissance art with sophisticated elegance and intricate fantasy.

manors Estates owned by a lord and worked by peasants in exchange for protection.

Marxism The theories of Karl Marx, including the belief that historical change depends not only on economic factors, but also on an inherent and inevitable class struggle, ending in a "dictatorship of the proletariat," which would abolish existing political systems, make all production public, and bring about a classless society in which the state would "wither away."

mercantilism Eighteenth-century economic theory and policies designed to increase national revenue (based on the supply of gold and silver) and economic power at the expense of other states, as well as to enhance private business and international trade.

Mesopotamia The land between the rivers Tigris and Euphrates, where urban life first developed; a flat region of the Middle East stretching from eastern Asia Minor to the Persian Gulf.

Modernism Revolutionary new artistic and literary styles that emerged in the years before 1914.

monasticism The general concept of monasticism is common to many religions, in which the followers of many faiths have sought to withdraw from the ordinary world and the corruption of society in order to devote themselves completely to worship and prayer.

mystery religions Greco-Roman religions that offered secret initiation ceremonies, individual salvation, and intense emotions. They emphasized that the lives of their members had an essential meaning and purpose.

nationalism An awareness of cultural and territorial identity—the identity of people who share a common language, history, and traditions in a given region.

Nazism Nazi ideology, especially the policies of state-controlled economy, racist nationalism, and national expansion. Also called "National Socialism," after the National Socialist German Workers' Party, founded in Germany in 1919 and brought into power in 1933 under Adolf Hitler.

Neoclassicism An 18th-century European revival of the art of ancient Greece and Rome.

Neolithic (New Stone) Age Period between 7000 and 4000 B.C. when settled and stable human communities were cultivating crops and domesticating animals, but had not discovered metals and still used stone tools and weapons.

Neoplatonist Adherent to a philosophy that flourished from the 3rd to the 6th century A.D., deriving from the teachings of the 4th-century B.C. Greek philosopher Plato and describing the universe as consisting of a systematized order, containing all levels and states of existence. Renaissance Neoplatonists revived the idea of seeking to escape from the bonds of earthly existence in order to rise upward toward union with God.

New Imperialism An increasingly frenzied drive on the part of many European powers during the latter half of the 19th century for territorial conquest beyond Europe. This surge of aggression resulted in the domination of virtually all of Asia and Africa by a handful of Western powers.

nominalists Adherents to a medieval school of thought based on method and solid fact, which claimed that knowledge should rest on direct experience and not on abstract reason.

Old Regime The transition in European history that led up to the French Revolution of 1789.

Paleolithic (Old Stone) Age Period some 10 thousand years ago, from the first use of stone implements around 2.5 million years ago to the introduction of farming around 8000 B.C. The latter stages are sometimes called the Mesolithic, or Middle, Stone Age.

patricians The kings and ruling class of early Rome, who formed a kind of self-perpetuating aristocracy based on a closed group of families who intermarried among themselves.

perioikoi Spartan "dwellers around," consisting of conquered neighboring peoples who vastly outnumbered the Spartiates and had no political rights.

phalanx A new infantry formation of the Greek Archaic era, consisting of rows of eight men, each heavily armed.

philosophes Literally translated from the French, "philosophers." The 18th-century *philosophes* were not so much original thinkers as popularizers and propagandizers who circulated the ideas of others in the form of pamphlets, plays, novels, or works of history.

plebeians The majority of early Romans, who were without privileges of birth or rank.

plainsong Medieval form of music, consisting of a single or "monophonic" musical line to which one voice (either a solo or a group in unison) chants the words of a religious text, generally without any form of accompaniment.

polis A Greek word generally translated as "city-state," the chief form of social and political organization from the beginnings of Greek culture.

Puritans English religious group that spearheaded a reform movement that sought to "purify" the Church of England of all remnants of Catholicism.

Ramapithecus The earliest species of hominid, dating to about 8 to 4 million years ago.

Reformation A movement of spiritual and institutional reform in the early 16th century that became a genuinely revolutionary wave breaking the thousand-year religious unity of western and central Europe by creating a series of new Protestant churches that rejected the authority of Rome.

Renaissance The period between 1300 and 1550 that saw a flowering of artistic and literary genius, beginning in Italy. It was accompanied by the rise of a new world view that placed a concern for the human condition at the center of intellectual life.

revolutionary syndicalism A unique current of radical thought in the 1870s, which evolved when elements of the anarchist tradition merged with an aspect of trade union strategy. Its principal theorist, Fernand Pelloutier, propounded the view that the seed of the future stateless society lay in the concept of the union. Syndicalists proposed direct action by the working class to bring about the revolution, with the general strike as their principal weapon.

rococo Artistic style of the mid-18th-century that was intended as a contrast to the Baroque. Rarely weighty or serious, it aimed for charm and lightness, and replaced Baroque drama with grace and harmony.

Romanesque Medieval architectural style whose characteristics are partly the result of the need for large buildings capable of containing crowds of people. Heavy stone walls could support Roman-style stone arches and barrel-vaulted stone roofs, providing a structure that, unlike the early Christian basilicas, was fireproof.

Romanticism Artistic style of the late 18th and early 19th centuries. Romantic artists, writers, and composers explored the irrational, probing the world of emotion. Two aspects of life had a special appeal: nature, with its mysterious unpredictability, and the exotic, in the form of remote times and faraway places.

salon Cultural institution of the 18th century, involving gatherings in private homes for intellectual discussion.

scholasticism The medieval attempt to reconcile the sacred teachings of the church with the knowledge acquired by human reason and experience. Its practitioners sought to apply Greek philosophical ideas—principally those of Aristotle—to Christian doctrine. They believed that reason, although always subordinate to faith, served to increase the faithfuls' understanding of their beliefs.

scientific method The method of testing theoretical ideas by means of practical experiments.

scientific revolution Seventeenth-century movement away from the medieval world view to a more rational, scientific perspective.

serfs Peasants attached by heredity to the land, who could not leave the manor without the lord's permission. Serfs owed certain services and dues to the lord, such as obligatory labor on the demesne for two or three days each week and the payment of a yearly tax known as the *taille*.

Social Darwinism Social Darwinists asserted, based on Charles Darwin's idea of survival of the fittest, that those in society who were emerging at the top were evidently the fittest and thus qualified to "survive." The bitter strife of competitive industry, they claimed, would lead slowly but inevitably to the upward movement of civilization.

socialism Ideology that called for a community in which the products of common labor are divided among all, according to their needs; for economic equality that should be accompanied by similar political and social reform.

Sophists Itinerant teachers in ancient Greece, who debated the skills of rhetoric and the qualities needed for success in political life.

Stoicism Philosophy founded by Zeno (335–263 B.C.), who taught that the force governing the world was Reason. Through the power of Reason it was possible to learn virtue, which was the supreme good. Those who lived virtuously were under the protection of Divine Providence, which would never allow them to suffer evil.

subinfeudation Feudal system whereby the same individual could be both a lord to one man and a vassal to another. Moreover, a noble could become the vassal to more than one lord.

Surrealism Artistic movement of the early 20th century that set out to discover the deeper meanings that lie beneath the surface of the conscious mind.

Symbolists Writers of the 19th century who aimed to use poetry as a means of escaping from reality.

syndicalism *See* revolutionary syndicalism.

totalitarianism Political theory in which governments are dominated by one political party and the most basic civil liberties are suspended. Such governments normally control the educational systems, economic policy, and mass media, and create an array of social institutions to indoctrinate and mobilize the population.

tyrant The popular leaders of ancient Greece who rode to power on the wave of revolt, rather than rising to power in a constitutional way.

utopians The earliest socialist thinkers, whose ideas were derided by their more militant successors as being naive and impractical.

vassal A soldier who served a man of greater authority during the Middle Ages.

CREDITS

This page constitutes an extension of the copyright page. We have made every effort to trace the ownership of all copyrighted material and to secure permission from copyright holders. In the event of any question arising as to the use of any material, we will be pleased to make the necessary corrections in future printings. Thanks are due to the following authors, publishers, and agents for permission to use the material indicated.

Part 1: © bpk, Berlin, Aegyptisches Museum/bpk. Photo: Margarete Buesing **5:** © Culver Pictures **6:** © C. M. Dixon **8:** Colorphoto Hans Hinz, Allschwil/Bâsel **9:** Hirmer Fotoarchiv **10 bottom:** Pubbli Aer Foto **10 top:** The Ancient Art & Architecture Collection Ltd. **16:** The University of Pennsylvania Museum (neg. # T4-1000) **17 center:** Hirmer Fotoarchiv **17 bottom:** Hirmer Fotoarchiv **17 top:** Hirmer Fotoarchiv **18:** The Metropolitan Museum of Art, Harris Brisbane Dick Fund, 1959 (59.2), photograph © 1984 The Metropolitan Museum of Art **20:** © The British Museum **25:** Hirmer Fotoarchiv **26:** Courtesy of William Duiker **27:** © AP/Wide World Photos **29 left:** © Baldwin H. Ward and Kathryn C. Ward/CORBIS **29 right:** The Metropolitan Museum of Art, Harris Brisbane Dick Fund, 1959 (59.2), photograph © 1984 The Metropolitan Museum of Art **30:** © bpk, Berlin, Aegyptisches Museum/bpk. Photo: Margarete Buesing **31:** John P. Stevens/The Ancient Art & Architecture Collection Ltd. **35:** Hirmer Fotoarchiv **38:** © Erwin Böhm **40:** © Bettmann/CORBIS **44 left:** Hirmer Fotoarchiv **44 right:** © C. M. Dixon **46:** Hirmer Fotoarchiv **47 top:** The Oriental Institute, University of Chicago **47 bottom:** © The British Museum **54:** Copyright Réunion des Musées Nationaux/Art Resource, NY **55:** © The Barnes Foundation, Merion Station, Pennsylvania/CORBIS **58 top:** The Metropolitan Museum of Art, Fletcher Fund, 1957. (57.80.10) **58 bottom:** © Werner Forman Archive/Art Resource, NY **61 left:** Neg. No. 319376, Photo Edward Bailey. Courtesy Department of Library Services, American Museum of Natural History **61 right:** Neg. No. 319377, Photo Edward Bailey. Courtesy Department of Library Services, American Museum of Natural History **62:** The Ancient Art & Architecture Collection Ltd.

Part 2. 65: © Scala/Art Resource, NY **68:** © The British Museum **69:** Robert Harding Picture Library, London **70:** Leonard Von Matt **71:** © Erich Lessing/Art Resource, NY **74:** Hirmer Fotoarchiv **75:** Colorphoto Hans Hinz, Allschwil/Bâsel **76:** The Metropolitan Museum of Art, Fletcher Fund, 1932 (32.11.1) **79:** The Ancient Art & Architecture Collection Ltd. **80:** © The British Museum **85:** © Alinari/Art Resource, NY **86:** Hirmer Fotoarchiv **90 left:** The Ancient Art & Architecture Collection Ltd. **90 right:** © Scala/Art Resource, NY **94:** © Giraudon/Art Resource, NY **95:** The Art Archive/Museo Capitolino Rome/Dagli Orti (A) **98:** © Rhoda Sidney/PhotoEdit **99:** © Scala/Art Resource, NY **100:** Courtesy of William Duiker **102 top:** Hirmer Fotoarchiv **102 bottom:** Capitoline Museums, Rome/Barbara Malter **104:** © D. Lada/H. Armstrong Roberts **111 left:** © Margot Granitsas/Photo Researchers **111 right:** © Erich Lessing/Art Resource, NY **112:** © The British Museum **113:** © Vanni/Art Resource, NY **117:** The Art Archive/Museo Nazionale Reggio Calabria/Dagli Orti (A) **120:** Hirmer Fotoarchiv **124:** © Scala/Art Resource, NY **125:** © bpk, Berlin, Photo Christa Begall Staatliche Museen zu Berlin **126:** Art & Architecture Collection, Miriam and Ira D. Wallach Division of Art, Prints and Photographs, The New York Public Library, Astor, Lenox and Tilden Foundations **130:** © Scala/Art Resource, NY **131:** Hirmer Fotoarchiv **132 top:** © Scala/Art Resource, NY **132 bottom:** © Richard Nowitz/Photo Researchers **135:** German Archaeological Institute, Rome **138:** © Alinari/Art Resource, NY **139:** © Scala/Art Resource, NY **141:** © Nimatallah/Art Resource **142:** © Scala/Art Resource, NY **144:** © Scala/Art Resource, NY **148:** © C. M. Dixon **151:** The Art Archive/Archaeological Museum Venice/Dagli Orti (A) **152:** © Scala/Art Resource, NY **154 left:** The Granger Collection, New York **154 right:** Louvre, Paris, France/Peter Willi/Bridgeman Art Library **158:** © Scala/Art Resource, NY **164:** © The Image Bank/Guido Rossi/Getty Images **166:** © Werner Forman Archive/Art Resource, NY **170:** © Scala/Art Resource, NY **171:** © Scala/Art Resource, NY **173 bottom:** © Superstock **173 top:** Pubbli Aer Foto **179:** R. Sheridan/The Ancient Art & Architecture Collection Ltd. **180:** © Scala/Art Resource, NY **182:** © Alinari/Art Resource, NY **183:** © C. M. Dixon **184:** The Ancient Art & Architecture Collection Ltd. **187:** © Alinari/Art Resource, NY **190:** © Scala/Art Resource, NY **192:** Ernst Herzfeld Papers, Freer Gallery of Art and Arthur M. Sackler Gallery Archives. Smithsonian Institution, Washington, D.C.: Gift of Ernst Herzfeld, 1946. Photographer: Ernst Herzfeld, photo file 8, vol. 1, image 71, negative # 1781 **194:** © Scala/Art Resource, NY

Part 3. 199: © Giraudon/Art Resource, NY **203:** Michael Holford **206:** © Cliché Bibliothéque National de France, Paris **207:** The Board of Trinity College, Dublin **208:** Kunsthistorisches Museum, Wien oder KHM, Wien **212:** Staatsbibliothek, Bamberg **214:** British Library. Y. T. 26 Folio 2 **216:** INDEX, Firenze **217:** Archbishop of Canterbury and Trustees of Lambeth Palace Library **220:** © Erich Lessing/Art Resource, NY **221:** © Alan Oddie/PhotoEdit **224:** © John Lamb/Getty Images **225:** Canali Photobank, Italy **226:** Courtesy of William Duiker **228:** Ara Güler, Istanbul **231:** © Mehmet Biber/Photo Researchers **232:** © bpk, Berlin, Photo: Georg Niedermeiser **234:** © Roger Wood/CORBIS **235:** Institut Amatller d'Art Hispánic–Arxiu Mas. **237:** Yoram Lehmann, Jerusalem **240:** Copyright Réunion des Musées Nationaux/Art Resource, NY **244:** © Alinari/Art Resource, NY **245:** © Cliché Bibliothéque National de France, Paris **246:** AKG London **254:** Masters and Fellows of Trinity College, Cambridge **255:** Oesterreichische Nationalbibliothek, Vienna **259:** The Art Archive/British Library **260:** © Cliché Bibliothéque National de France, Paris **264:** The Granger Collection, New York **265:** Roger Viollet/Getty Images **265 left:** Roger Viollet/Getty Images **266 right:** © Giraudon/Art Resource, NY **270:** Burgerbibliothek Bern, cod. 120.II,f. 101r **274:** © Superstock **275:** Ullstein Bilderdienst **278:** © Cliché Bibliothéque National de France, Paris **281:** © Scala/Art Resource, NY **284:** © Scala/Art Resource, NY **288:** © bpk, Berlin, Kupferstichkabinett/bpk. Photo: Joerg P. Anders **290:** © Scala/Art Resource, NY **291:** © Jean Dieuzaide **293:** © Réunion des Musées Nationaux/Art Resource, NY **296:** © Scala/Art Resource, NY **297:** © The British Museum **300:** British Library, London, UK/Bridgeman Art Library **301:** INDEX/Firenze **307:** Colorphoto Hans Hinz, Allschwil/Bâsel **308:** Aerofilms.com **309:** © Sonia Halliday **310:** © Giraudon/Art Resource, NY **311:** © Scala/Art Resource, NY **312:** Cameraphoto Arte, Venice/Art Resource, NY **317:** Ms. 13076-77, f. 12v, Bibliotheque Royale Albert 1er, Brussells **320:** The Walters Art Museum, Baltimore **321 top:** © Cliché Bibliothéque National de France, Paris **321 bottom:** British Library, London, UK/Bridgeman Art Library **323:** © Giraudon/Art Resource, NY **328:** © Scala/Art Resource, NY **329:** © Cliché Bibliothéque National de France, Paris

Part 4. 337: By courtesy of the Trustees of the National Gallery, London **341 left:** © Cliché Bibliothéque National de France, Paris **341 right:** © Giraudon/Art Resource, NY **342:** © Giraudon/Art Resource, NY **343 right:** By courtesy of the National Portrait Gallery, London **343 left:** Hulton Getty Collection **346:** Kunsthistorisches Museum, Wien oder

KHM, Wien **350 bottom:** © Scala/Art Resource, NY **350 top:** © Christie's Images Incorporated (2003) **353 left:** © Erich Lessing/Art Resource, NY **353 right:** INDEX/Tosi **355:** © Scala/Art Resource, NY **358:** Summerfield Press, Ltd. **359:** © Canali **361 top:** INDEX/Tosi **361 bottom:** Summerfield Press Ltd. **362:** © Scala/Art Resource, NY **363:** © Erich Lessing/Art Resource, NY **364:** © Erich Lessing/Art Resource, NY **365:** © Erich Lessing/Art Resource, NY **370 top:** © Scala/Art Resource, NY **370 bottom:** Canali Photobank, Italy **374:** Rare Books Division, The New York Public Library, Astor, Lenox and Tilden Foundations **375:** 375, The Metropolitan Museum of Art, Fletcher Fund, 1919 (19.73.120) **376:** Copyright Réunion des Musées Nationaux/Art Resource, NY **377:** By courtesy of the Trustees of the National Gallery, London **378:** Derechos Reservaados © Museo Nacional del Prado, Madrid **379:** Photograph © 2003 Museum of Fine Arts, Boston. Albrecht Dürer, German, 1471–1528. *The Fall of Man (Adam and Eve)*, 1504 Engraving. Catalogue Raisonné: BARTSCH (Intaglio). 001:Meder, 1, II, a. Platemark: 25 x 19.4 cm (9 15/16 x 7 5/8 in.). Museum of Fine Arts, Boston. Centennial gift of Landon T. Clay: 68.187 **385:** Ara Güler, Istanbul **386:** © National Maritime Museum, London **390:** © Novosti **393:** Bibliotheque Nationale, Paris, France/Bridgeman Art Library **397:** © Newberry Library, Chicago/SuperStock **400:** The Metropolitan Museum of Art, Gift of J. Pierpont Morgan , 1900. (00.18.2) Photograph © 1979 The Metropolitan Museum of Art **401:** The Granger Collection, New York **403:** The Ancient Art & Architecture Collection Ltd. **407:** The Toledo Museum of Art, Toledo, Ohio (Purchased with funds from the Libbey Endowment, Gift of Edward Drummond Libbey) **409:** © Mary Evans Picture Library **410:** © Snark/Art Resource, NY **411:** The Ancient Art & Architecture Collection Ltd. **416:** Musees Royaux des Beaux-Arts de Belgique/A.C.L. **417:** National Gallery, London **418:** Collection Furstlich Waldburg-Zeil'sches Gesamtarchiv Leutkirch/Artothek **420:** Collection The Right Honorable Earl Spencer, Althorp House **421:** AKG London **424:** Palazzo Medici-Riccardi, Florence, Italy/Bridgeman Art Library

Part 5. 427: Rijksmuseum, Amsterdam **430:** © Fotoburg Marburg/Art Resource, NY **431:** AKG London **432:** Institut Amatller d'Art Hispánic–Arxiu Mas. **436:** © Foto Marburg/Art Resource, NY **439:** © Mary Evans Picture Library **442:** © Erich Lessing/Art Resource, NY **443:** © CORBIS/Bettmann **447:** By courtesy of the National Portrait Gallery, London **449:** © Alinari/Art Resource, NY **450:** © Mary Evans Picture Library **452:** Mansell/TimeLife Pictures/Getty Images **457:** AKG London **458 left:** © Réunion des Musées Nationaux/Art Resource, NY **458 right:** © Superstock **459:** The National Gallery, London **461:** © CORBIS/Bettmann **466:** The Granger Collection, New York **468:** The Metropolitan Museum of Art, Fletcher Fund, 1927. (27.59) Photograph © 1983 The Metropolitan Museum of Art **469:** British Museum, London, UK/Bridgeman Art Library **473:** Rijksmuseum, Amsterdam **474:** © Giraudon/Art Resource, NY **478:** By permission of the British Library. 145. C.4 Folio 122 **479:** Herzog Anton Ulrich Museums Braunschweig Kunstmuseum des Landes Niedersachsen **482:** Rijksmuseum, Amsterdam **483:** © Victoria & Albert Museum, London/Art Resource, NY **487:** © Scala/Art Resource, NY **488:** Canali Photobank, Italy **489:** © Alinari/Art Resource, NY **490:** Copyright Réunion des Musées Nationaux/Art Resource, NY **491:** Copyright Réunion des Musées Nationaux/Art Resource, NY **492:** Staatliche Museen Kassel, Gemäldegalerie Alte Meister **493 left:** Johann Sebastian Bach, "Klavierbuchlein fur Anna Magdalena Bach," 1725. Courtesy of Riemenschneider Bach Institute, Baldwin-Wallace College, Berea, OH. **493 right:** AKG London **494:** Courtesy of William Duiker **496:** Rare Books Division, The New York Public Library, Astor, Lenox and Tilden Foundations

Part 6. 499: © Frick Collection, New York **503:** © Scala/ Art Resource, NY **505:** National Library of Medicine, Bethesda, MD **506:** Frans Hals, René Cartes (1596–1650), Statens Museum for Kunst, Copenhagen. Photography by Hans Peterson **507:** By courtesy of the National Portrait Gallery, London **511:** © Scala/Art Resource, NY **512:** Derechos Reservaados © Museo Nacional del Prado, Madrid **513:** © CORBIS/Bettmann **518:** © Réunion des Musées Nationaux/Art Resource, NY **519:** © Art Resource, NY **520:** The Metropolitan Museum of Art, Gift of the Wildenstein Foundation, Inc. 1951. (51.34) Photograph © 1979 The Metropolitan Museum of Art **521:** Chateau de Versailles, France/Peter Willi/Bridgeman Art Library **524:** © Giraudon/Art Resource, NY **529:** By courtesy of the National Portrait Gallery, London **531:** © CORBIS/Bettmann **535:** By courtesy of the National Portrait Gallery, London **536:** By courtesy of the National Portrait Gallery, London **542:** AKG London **544:** AKG London **545:** © Foto Marburg/Art Resource, NY **548:** The Granger Collection, New York **549:** The Granger Collection, New York **550:** © bpk, Berlin, Kulturbesitz, Berlin **551:** AKG London **552:** Courtesy of William Duiker **559:** The Granger Collection, New York **560 right:** Picture Library, National Portrait Gallery, London **560 left:** Picture Library, National Portrait Gallery, London **562 bottom:** © Scala/Art Resource, NY **562 top:** © Frick Collection, New York **563 top:** Anthony Kersting **563 bottom:** © Internationale Stiftung Mozarteum (ISM) **569:** The Granger Collection, New York **572 top:** © National Maritime Museum, London **572 bottom:** The Granger Collection, New York **573:** Museum Boymans van Beuningen, Rotterdam **574:** Copyright Guildhall Library Corporation of London **578:** © CORBIS/Bettmann **580:** © Victoria & Albert Museum, London/Art Resource, NY **581:** The Granger Collection, New York **582:** © CORBIS/Bettmann **589:** Reproduction of *The Village School* by Jan Steen. Courtesy of the National Gallery of Ireland **590:** Copyright Réunion des Musées Nationaux/Art Resource, NY **591:** The National Gallery, London **592:** © Giraudon/Art Resource, NY **593:** The Metropolitan Museum of Art, Harris Brisbane Dick Fund, 1932 [32.35 (124)] **595 left:** © Giraudon/Art Resource, NY **595 right:** © Chateau de Versailles, France/Giraudon/ Superstock **598:** The Granger Collection, New York **599:** © CORBIS/Bettmann **600:** © Giraudon/Art Resource, NY

Index

Note: Page references in *italics* indicate map or figure.

Abbasid dynasty, 233, 234
Abelard, Peter (1079–1142), 289–290
Abortion, 114
  in Roman Empire, 181
Absolutism, 459, 517, 518
  in France, under Louis XIV, 517–527
  in Prussia, 544
Abu-Bakr, 232
Abu-Nuwas (762–815), 236
Academies, 17th and 18th century Europe, 559–561
Academy, Athens, 107, 123
Accademia delle Belle Arti, Florence, 559
Acquitaine, 266
Acropolis, 89, 97, *102*, 103
Act of Settlement (1701), England, 536
Act of Supremacy (1534), England, 412
Act of Uniformity (1662), England, 529
Act of Union (1707), Great Britain, 536
Addison, Joseph (1672–1719), 561
Aeneid (Vergil), 169–170
Aeschylus (525–456 B.C.), 91, 98
Africa
  prehistoric people in, 8
Africans, first to visit in Europe, 422–423
Age of Reason. *See* Enlightenment
Agesander, *124*
Agriculture
  in ancient Greece, 110, 111
  in ancient Mesopotamia and Egypt, 57–58
  Byzantium, 226–227
  in Carolingian Empire (manorialism), 246–247
  development of ancient civilizations and role of, 14–15
  in Europe, 17th century, 467
  in Europe, 18th century, 589–591
  grain production in England, 18th century, *590*
  in medieval Europe, 253–254, 327–328
  Neolithic, 8
  plantation system in Americas, 441, *478, 569*
  Roman, 139–140, 159, 177
  in Spanish-American colonies, 441
Agrippina (mother of emperor Nero), 163, 182
Ahmose (c. 1570–1546 B.C.), Egypt, 28
Aigospotamoi, Battle of (405 B.C.), 93

Akhenaton (c. 1340–c. 1334 B.C.), Egypt, 23, 30
Akkadian civilization, 13–14, 27
  conquest of Sumeria by, 17–18
  culture of Sumeria and, 18
  fall of, 18
  literature, 50
Alaja Huyuk, relief carving from, *35*
Alaric (ruled A.D. 395–410), Visigoth, 195
Alberti, Leone Battista (1404–1472), 359
Albigensian movement, 284, 285, 433
Alcibiades (c. 450–404 B.C.), Greece, 91, 92, 93, 94
Alcuin of York (c. 732–804), 245
Alembert, Jean Le Rond d (1717–1783), 599
Alexander I (the Great, d. 323 B.C.), Macedon, 66, 88, 95, 119
  Asian empire and successor kingdoms of, 120, *121*, 122
Alexander VI (ruled 1492–1503), pope, 351, 400
Alexandria, Egypt, 223
  Hellenistic era, 121, 122, 125, *126*
Alexius (ruled 1081–1118), Byzantium, 228
Alexius Comnenus I (ruled 1081–1118), Byzantium, 277, 383
Alfred the Great (871–899), England, 250, 264
al-Ghazali (1059–1111), 236
Alhambra Palace, Granada, Spain, *235*
Ali, Shiite Muslims and, 232–233
Alighieri, Dante (1265–1321), 297, 305, 306–307
Alimentary institution, Rome, 165, 181
Altar of Peace (Ara Pacis), Rome, *141, 170*
Amarna style, Egyptian art, 30
Ambassadorships, 354, *355*
Ambrose of Milan, St. (c. 339–397), 211–212
Amenhotep II (c. 1453–1419 B.C.), Egypt, 28
Amenhotep III (c. 1386–1350 B.C.), Egypt, 28
Amenhotep IV (Akhenaton) (c. 1340–c. 1334 B.C.), Egypt, 30

American colonies, British, 449. *See also* United States
  European wars for empire in, 577, 580–581
  revolution of 1776 in, 583
  trading companies in, 482
Americas
  European explorations in, *402*
  food exchanges between Europe and, 468–473
  maps of, *397*
  Spanish Empire in, 401–403, 441
Amorites, 18, 19. *See also* Babylonian civilization
Amphitheater, Roman, 172, 183–184
Amsterdam, 481
Anabaptists, 411–412
Ancient world
  artists and artistic production in, 46–50
  commerce in, 53, 59–61
  economic life of, 57–59
  Egypt. *See* Egypt, ancient
  environment, first life forms, and early hominids, 3, 4–6
  first people, 3, 6–7
  Hebrews, 33, 38–40
  Hittites, 33, 34–36
  literature, 48–49, 50–51
  Mesopotamia. *See* Mesopotamia
  Near East. *See* Near East, ancient
  Neolithic Age (New Stone Age), 3, 8–10
  Paleolithic Age (Stone Age), 3, 7
  Persian empire, 33, 37–38
  Phoenicians, 33, 36–37
  religion, political organization, and art in, 43–46
  slavery, human rights, and law in, 53, 61–62
  social system of, 53, 54
  women in, 53, 54–57
Angles, 195, 202
Anglican Church. *See* Church of England (Anglicans)
Anglo-Saxons, 201, 206–208
  Christianity and, 207–208
Anguissola, Sofonisba, 419, *420*
Anjou, 266
Annals (Tacitus), 175
Anne (ruled 1702–1714), England, 526, 536

613

The Annunciation (Duccio), *311*

Anthony (c. 250–355), monk, 215

Antigonus Gonatas (ruled 276–239 B.C.), Macedonia, 120, 122

Antiochus (ruled 280–261 B.C.), Seleucid Syria, 122

Antiochus IV (ruled 175–164 B.C.), 123

Antonine emperors, Rome, 166

Antoninus Pius, Roman emperor (A.D. 138–161), 166, 187

Antony, Mark, 147, 155
   relationship with wife Fulvia, 154–155

Antwerp, 481

Apollonius (c. 262–190 B.C.), 125

Aquinas, Thomas (c. 1225–1274), 287, 291, 296, 297, 406, 502
   successors to, 305, 306

Aquitaine, 268–269

Arabia, 231

The Arabian Nights, 236

Ara Pacis (Altar of Peace), Rome, *141, 170*

Archimedes (c. 287–212 B.C.), 125–126, 502

Architecture
   ancient Egypt, 25, 26, *27*, 46–47, 50
   ancient Greece, 76, 89, 97, *102, 103–104*
   Baroque, *489, 521, 522–523*
   Byzantine, *221, 222, 224–225*
   Carolingian, *246*
   Hellenistic, *125, 126*
   Islamic, *231, 234, 235, 237*
   medieval Europe, Gothic, *307–309*
   medieval Europe, Romanesque, 287, *291, 293–294*
   Persia, *38*
   Renaissance, Italian, 358
   Rococo, *562, 563*
   Roman, *132, 168, 171–175, 187*
   Russian, *224*

Arianism, 202, 206, 213

Aristarchus of Samos (active c. 270 B.C.), 125

Aristocracy
   ancient Egypt and Mesopotamia, 54
   ancient Greece, Athens, 79
   ancient Greece, Sparta, 82, 83
   J.-J. Rousseau on elimination of, 604
   medieval Europe, 252, 255–256, 261, 262
   Old Regime, 18th century, 587, 591–593
   Roman Empire, 182–183
   Roman Republic, 131

Aristophanes (c. 450–385 B.C.), 99

Aristotle (384–322 B.C.), 37, 97, 108, 114, 236, 502
   scholasticism and, 289, 291

Art. *See also* Architecture; Illuminated manuscripts; Literature; Mosaics; Music; Painting and drawing; Pottery; Sculpture; Theater
   ancient Greek, 75–76, 98–102, 143
   Baroque, in early modern Europe, 486–497
   Byzantine, 224–225
   Carolingian, *240, 244, 245, 246*
   Egyptian Amarna style, 30
   Etruscan, *130, 131*
   Europe, 18th century, 557–565
   Islamic, *231, 234, 235, 236–237*
   medieval Europe, Gothic age, 305–313
   Minoan, 69, *70*
   Mycenaean, 70, *71*
   Paleolithic (Stone Age), 7, 8
   Renaissance. *See* Art, Renaissance
   Rococo, 18th century, 557, 562–563
   Roman, 168, 169–176

Art, Renaissance, 357–372. *See also* Literature, Renaissance
   about artists of, 366–369
   harmony and color in Venetian painting, 364–371
   harmony and design in High Renaissance, 362–364
   modern style in, 358–359
   in Northern Europe, 377–379
   tradition and experimentation in later Quattrocento, 359–362

Arthur, king of Britain, 207, 255

Artist(s)
   of ancient Near East, 46–50, 59–60
   Renaissance, in their own words, 366–369

Art of ancient Near East 42–52
   artists and artistic production, 46–50
   literature, 48–51
   perspectives on, 51
   religion, political organization, and, 45–46
   religion and, 43–45

Aryan people, 70

Ashurbanipal (c. 669–630 B.C.), Assyria, 20

Ashurnasirpal II, relief sculpture from palace of, *47*

Asian philosophy, 6th century B.C., 105

Asiento slave contract, 570, 575

Aspasia (c. 465–?), 117
   relationship with Pericles, 90

Assyrian civilization, 14, 19–21
   culture and art, 20, *47*, 50
   end of empire, 20–21
   military, 19–20
   religion and political organization in, 45–46

Astronomy, 125, 502–504

Ataulf (d. 415), Visigoth, 205

Athenodorus, *124*

Athens, ancient, 65–66, 78
   classical culture in, 97–108
   democracy in, 80–82
   empire of, 88, 89–91
   English poet Lord Byron in, 100–101
   in Hellenistic empire, 123–124
   marriage in classical, 114–115
   Peloponnesian War, 88, 91–93
   Persian Wars, 83–86
   Sicilian Expedition, 88, 91–93
   social structure, 79

Atlantic trade and commerce, 478

Attalus III of Pergamum (ruled 138–133 B.C.), 136

Attila (c. 406–453), Hun, 203, 214

Augustine, St. (A.D. 354–430), 195, 212–213, 506
   City of God, 195, 213, 296
   Confessions, 212–213

Augustine of Canterbury (d.c. 605), 207

Augustulus, Romulus, last Roman Emperor, 204

Augustus, Roman Emperor (27 B.C.–14 A.D.), 155, 157, 158–162, 182
   arts program of, 169, 170
   economics of peace and, 158–159
   family legislation under, 181
   law, agriculture, and image of, 159, 162
   new order established by, 158

Aurelian (ruled A.D. 270–275), Rome, 193

Aurelius, Marcus, 161, 166, 195

Australopithecine, 6, 7

Australopithecus, 5

Austrasia, Carolingian Empire, 240, *241*

Austria, 241, 439, 540
   Bismarcks alliance system and annexation of Bosnia by, 84–86
   hegemony of, over Italian city-states, 515
   war of succession to throne of, 513, 577, 578, 579–580

Avars, 223, 241

Averroes (1126–1198), 236

Avicenna (980–1037), 236

Avignon, France, popes at, 322, *323*

Babylonian Captivity, 322–323

Babylonian civilization, 14, 19, 21, 33, 42

Bach, Johann Sebastian (1685–1750), 492
   relationship with wife Anna Magdalena, 493

Bacon, Francis (1561–1626), 501, 505

Balboa, Vasco de, 401

Balkans, 219. *See also specific individual countries*
   map, c. 1450–1500, 387

Bankers (Van Reymerswaele), *417*

Banking and finance
European, 14th–17th centuries, 478–480
Fugger dynasty, 479
Jewish money lending, 259
medieval Europe, 257, 259, 327–328
Roman Republic, 140–141, 179
Bank of England, 534, 575
Barbary states, 511
Barbosa, Duarte, 399
Baroque arts, 486–497
emotion and illusionism in visual,
487–489
literature, 493–496
music, 491–493
Northern European visual, 490–491
Roman visual, 489–490
Bary, Jeanne Bécu, Comtesse du
(1743–1793), 595
Basil (329–379), 215
Basil II (ruled 976–1025), Byzantium, 224
Baths, public, in ancient Rome, 172
Bayeaux Tapestry, *264*
Beaumarchais, Pierre-Augustin
(1732–1799), 564
Beccaria, Cesare (1738–1794), 601
Becket, Thomas (c. 1118–1170), murder
of, 266–267
Bede, Venerable (c. 673–735), 207, 208
Bedouins, 188
Bela III (ruled 1173–1196), Hungary, 386
Belgium
Franks in, 201. *See also* Carolingian
Empire
Benedictine rule, 215, *216*, 274
Benedict of Nursia (c. 480–c. 543), 215, *216*
Benefice, 253
Bernard of Clairvaux (1090–1153), 276,
279
Bernini, Gian Lorenzo (1598–1680), 488,
489–490
Bible, 14, 51, *55*. *See also* New Testament;
Old Testament
Dead Sea Scrolls, 188–189
English translation of, 324
Gutenberg, *374*
King James version, 374, 448
Septugint translation, 122–123
Vulgate translation, 212, 431
Bill of Rights
English, 531, 532
Birth control
methods of, 18th century Europe,
588–589
in Roman Empire, 181
The Birth of Venus (Botticelli), *361, 362*
Bishops, Christian church, 192, 207, 214.
See also Papacy
medieval election of, 261
Bitel, Lisa M.

on Christianity and Churches
ambivalence toward women, 330–331
Black Death, 313, 315–317
Boccaccios description of, 318
European society before and after,
328–332
map of European regions affected by, *316*
medical advice from year 1348 about,
318–319
in Near East, 319
reoccurring of, 15th through 17th
centuries, 466
social upheaval caused by, 317–322
Blacks
as outsiders in 16th and 17th century
Europe, 421–424
Blenheim, Battle of (1704), 526
Boccaccio, Giovanni (1313–1375), 307,
315, 318
Boffrand, Germain, *562*
Bohemia, 325, 439, 540
J. Hus and kingdom of, 388
Thirty Years' War in, 460, 461
Bohemian phase of Thirty Years' War,
460–461
Boleslav I (ruled 992–1025), 388
Bonaiuto, Andrea de, *290*
Boniface VIII, pope, *300, 301,* 322, 333
Book of Kells, 207
Book of the Dead, Egypt, 50
Book of Vices, 259
Borgia, Cesare (1476–1507), 377
Borgia, Lucrezia (1480–1519), 377
Bosch, Hieronymus (c. 1450–1516), 378
Botticelli, Sandro (c. 1480–1485), *307,
357, 359, 361, 362*
Boule council, Greece, 81, 82
Boulogne, Madeleine de, *466*
Bourbon dynasty
France, 457, 517–527
Spain, 513
Bourgeoisie, defined, 258. *See also* Middle
class
Bouvines, Battle of (1214), 297
Bowdler, Thomas, 495
Boyars, 548, *551*
Boyne, Battle of (1690), 531
Bracciolini, Poggio (1380–1459), 352
Brahe, Tycho (1546–1601), 503
Brandenburg, 539
Brandenburg-Prussia, 539. *See also* Prussia
Braudel, Fernand, 63
Brazil, Portuguese claims on, 400–401
Brethren of the Common Life, 324, 430
Britain. *See also* England; Great Britain
Celtic, 201, 207
Germanic tribes invade, 195, 206–208
Roman excursions into, 162, 163, 195
Bronze Age peoples, 64, 67, 68–71

Brueghel, Pieter (1525–1569), 378, 474
Brunelleschi, Filippo (1377–1446), 357,
358
Bruni, Leonardo (1370–1444), 352
Bruno, Giordano (1548–1600), 433
Buddhism, 105
Buffon, Georges-Louis (1707–1788), 601
Bulgars, 223
invasions of, into Europe, 9th century,
249
Bureaucracy. *See also* Civil service
Carolingian, 244
France, in age of Louis XIV, 520, 522–523
Burgundians, 202, 204
Burgundy, 204
as part of Carolingian Empire, 240, *241*
Burials, prehistoric, 6
Burke, Edmund (1729–1797), 559
Byron, George Gordon, Lord (1788–1824)
in Athens, 100–101
Byzantium, 186, 219–229
arts of, 223–225
collapse of, 383–384
Constantine and, 186, 188, 191–192,
194, 219
Crusades and decline of, 279–281
economy, society, and government of,
226–228
emergence of state of, 220–221
iconoclastic controversy in, 223
Justinian, rule of, 221–222
map of empire, *222*
military threats to, 222–223,
277–278
Mongol invasions into, 384
in northern Europe (Slav civilization),
223–224
Ottoman empire and, *383,* 384–386
Slav expansionism and, *384*

Cabot, John (Giovanni Caboto), 400
Cabral, Pedro Alvares, 397
Cada Mosto, Alvise, 398
Caesar, Gaius Julius (c. 100–44 B.C.), 133,
152
reforms, dictatorship, and assassination
of, 153–155
Calico Act (1720), England, 569
Caligula, Roman emperor (ruled A.D.
37–41), 162
Caliphs, 232
Calixtus II, pope, 276
Callicrates, Greece, 103
The Calling of St. Matthew (Caravaggio),
487
Calvin, John (1509–1564). *See also*
Calvinism
Protestant Reformation and role of, *410,*
411

Calvinism, 410–411
defeat of, in Thirty Years' War, 460–462
in England, 449
French. *See* Huguenots
social vision of, 411
spread of, in Europe, 441–442
Cambyses (c. 530–522 B.C.), Persia, 31, 37
Canaanites, 33, 36
Canada, British and French conflict over, 581
Canterbury Cathedral, 267
Canterbury Tales (Chaucer), 307
Canute (ruled 1016–1035), Denmark, 264
Capet, Hugh (ruled 987–996), 267–268
Capetian monarchy, France, 267–269, 298–301
Capitalism
Adam Smith on economics and, 575, 601–604
commercial, 18th century, 566–576
commercial, 14th–17th centuries, 478–480
emergence of, in Italian city-states, 257–258
merchant, 16th and 17th centuries, 480–481
Capitularies, Carolingian Empire, 242, 244
Caracalla (ruled A.D. 211–217), Rome, 182, 187
Caravaggio (Michelangelo Merisi, 1573–1610), 486, 487, 489
Cardinals, Catholic Church, 274
in French government, 458–460
Carenuova, Battle of (1237), 302
Caribbean, wars for empire in, 578, 581–582
Carlebach, Elisheva, on social life of European Jews, 16th–18th centuries, 434–435
Carmelite Order, 432, 433
Caroline (1683–1737), England, 537
Carolingian Empire, 239–251
Charlemagne as ruler of, 240–244
disintegration of, 248–250
government of, 242–243, 244
manoralism and economy of, 246–248
maps of, 222, 241, 248
perspective on, 250
Renaissance and classical civilization in, 244–246
Carpaccio, 355
Carteret, John (1690–1763), 579
Carthage, 36–37, 66, 128
Punic Wars between Rome and, 134–135
Cartoons
T. Nast, on evolution, 5
War of Jenkin's Ear (1738), 578
Caryatids statues, 103, 104
Casa de Contratacin, 441

Casimir III (the Great, ruled 1333–1370), Poland, 388
Cassian, John (360–435), 215
Cassiodorus (c. 485–c. 585), 215, 245
Castiglione, Baldassare (1478–1529), 373, 376
Çatal Hüyük, 9
Cateau-Cambrésis, Treaty of (1559), 514
Cathedrals
medieval Gothic, 307–309
medieval Romanesque, 291, 293–294
Cathedral schools, 287, 288
Catherine deMedici (1519–1589), as French regent, 455–456
Catherine II (the Great, ruled 1762–1796), Russia, 583
Catholic Church. *See also* Catholics; Christian church; Christianity
Augustine and, 210, 212–213
classical heritage and, 211–212
corruption and abuse in medieval, 261, 406
Crusades of, 256, 259, 278–281
development of monastic orders, 210, 215–216, 217–218
development of papacy, 210, 213–215. *See also* Papacy
discontent in, and emergence of Reformation, 406–407
dogma, 281
foundation in Rome, 190
Inquisition, 283–285, 433–436
Investiture Controversy in, 269, 275–277
Jansenism in, 506, 524
mysticism in, 430–441
papal government under Innocent III, 281–285
political organization of, 207
popular forms of religion in 14th century and, 324
reform and renewal in medieval, 274
reform in 16th century. *See* Counter-Reformation
relations with states. *See* Church-state relations
rise of popular devotion, 285
schism between eastern and western church, 277–278, 322, 323–324. *See also* Orthodox Church
schism in, and Babylonian captivity, 322–325
theology. *See* Theology, Christian
women in medieval, 216–218, 332–333
Catholic League, 460
Catholics
ambivalent attitudes of medieval, toward women, 261, 330–331
in England, under Charles II, 529–530
Thirty Years' War and, 460–463

Catullus (c. 84–c. 54 B.C.), 145
Caudine Forks, Battle of (321 B.C.), 133
Cave paintings, Paleolithic, 7, 8
Caxton, William (c. 1422–1491), 374
Cellini, Benvenuto (1500–1571), 367–368
Celts, 207
Central Europe. *See also* Austria; Germany; Holy Roman Empire
balance of power in 17th century, 540–542
Carolingian Empire in, 239–251
Prussia and rise of Hohenzollerns in, 542–546. *See also* Prussia
in twelfth century, 268
Cerularius, Michael, 277
Cervantes, Miguel de (1547–1616), 494–495
Chaeronea, Battle of (338 B.C.), 95
Chaldean tribes, 21
Champagne, Philippe de, 459
Chansons de geste (song of deeds), 292
Chardin, Jean-Baptiste, 474
Charlemagne (Frankish king, ruled 771–814, Holy Roman emperor, 800–814), 240–244, 292
crowned Holy Roman Emperor, 244
death of, and disintegration of empire, 248–250
government of, 242–244
military conquests of, 241
Charles, Kingdom of, 248–249
Charles I (ruled 1625–1649), England, civil war and, 449–451
Charles II (ruled 1660–1685), England, 451, 452, 529, 530
Charles II (ruled 1665–1700), Spain, 513, 515, 526
Charles III (1734–1759), Naples and Spain, 513, 515, 581–582
Charles IV (1347–1378), Bohemia and Holy Roman Empire, 303, 388
Charles Robert of Anjou (1308–1342), Hungary, 387
Charles the Bald (ruled 843–877), Carolingian Empire, 248–249
Charles V (1516–1556), Holy Roman Emperor, 346, 401, 408, 410, 413
Charles VI (ruled 1711–1740), Holy Roman Emperor, 526, 572, 579
Charles VII (ruled 1422–1461), France, 341, 342
Charles VIII (ruled 1483–1498), France, 342–343, 354
Charles X (ruled 1660–1697), Sweden, 554
Charles XII (ruled 1697–1718), Sweden, 554
Chartres Cathedral, France, 308
Chaucer, Geoffrey (1340–1400), 307
Chauvet, France, cave paintings, 7

Children
  alimentary institution, Rome, 165, 181
  care of, following Black Death Years',
    331
  changing ideas about, 589
  in classical Athens, 114
  education of. *See* Education
  in Old Regime, 18th century, 588–589
Childrens Crusade (212), 280
China
  Jesuits in, 432–433
  M. Polos travels to, 393, *394, 395*
  philosophy in, 105
  Portuguese description of (1521),
    399–400
  prehistoric people in, 5, 6, 8
  trade with, 180, 393
Chivalry, medieval, 255–256, 261
Christian Church, 210–218. *See also*
    Catholic Church; Orthodox Church;
    Protestant Church
  Augustine and, 210, 212–213
  classical heritage and, 211–212
  Crusades, 256, 259, 278–281
  development of monastic orders, 210,
    215–216, 217–218
  development of papacy, 210, 213–215.
    See also Papacy
  Investiture Controversy in, 275–277
  organization of early, 192
  papal government under Innocent III,
    281–285
  reform and renewal in medieval, 273,
    274
  Reformation. *See* Reformation
  schism between east and west in, 220,
    277–278, *322,* 323–324
  women in medieval, 216–218
Christianity, 123, 186
  in Byzantium, 219–229
  classical learning and, in Renaissance
    humanism, 375–376
  conversion of Russia to, 224
  dogma of, 192
  early medieval, 219–218
  heresies from. *See* Heresies, Christian
  Jews and emergence of, 188–189
  map, c. A.D. 600, *211*
  map, spread of in Roman empire,
    191
  origins and rise of, 189–192
  Orthodox, 206, 213, 220
  reconquest of Spain by, *271*
  relationship of, with Jews, 258
  theology of, 108, 289–291, 306
  views of women within, 216–217,
    330–331
Christian IV (ruled 1588–1648)
  Denmark and Norway, 461, 462
Churchill, Sarah (1660–1744), 536

Church of England (Anglicans), 449
  Charles II and, 529–530
  foundation of, 412
  reestablishment of, under Elizabeth I,
    447–448
Church of St. Basil, Moscow, *224*
Church-state relations, 295
  papal supremacy and, 282–283
  political theory and, in High Middle
    Ages, 296–297
Cicero, Marcus Tullius, 137, *138,* 139, 142,
    145, 352
Cimabue (1240?–1302?), 311
Cimbri tribe, 150
Ciompi worker uprising, Florence, 321
Cistercian order, 276
Cities
  ancient Near East, 9, 13, 15, 61, 63
  housing in 17th century European, 472
  medieval European, 252, 257–258
  social upheaval and changes in, due to
    Black Death, 321–322, 329
  women in, post-Black Death cities,
    332–333
Citizenship, Roman, 153, 178, 187
City life
  in ancient Near East, 61
  in Hellenistic world, 122–123
  Old Regime, 18th century, 587, 593–594
The City of God (Augustine), 195, 213,
    296
City-states
  ancient Greece *(polis),* 67, 71–73
  ancient Near East, 13
  Hellenistic, 122
  Italian, 256, 257–258
Civilization, term, 11
Civil service
  Byzantine, 228
  Carolingian, 244
  Roman, 178–179
Civil war
  English, 17th century, 449, *450,* 451
  English War of the Roses, 344
  Roman, 152–153, 194
Class
  in ancient Near East, 54
  diet and, 467–468
  gentry, in 17th century England,
    448–449
  middle. *See* Middle class
  poor. *See* Poverty and poor classes
  ruling. *See* Aristocracy; Nobility; Ruling
    class
Classical civilization, 64–66
  Carolingian Empire and, 245–246
  Dantes *Divine Comedy* and, 306–307
  in Greece, 97–109. *See also* Greece,
    Classical era (480–323 B.C.)
  Hellenistic Age and, 119–127

  influence of, on Byzantium, 220
  influence of, on Christianity and
    medieval Europe, 211–212
  Muslims and Greek philosophy, 236
  rebirth of interest in 14th–16th
    centuries. *See* Renaissance
  Roman. *See* Rome, ancient; Rome,
    imperial; Rome, republic
  Romanesque architecture and, 293–294
  scholasticism and Aristotle, 289–291
Claudius, Roman emperor (ruled A.D.
    41–54), 157, 163
Cleisthenes, ancient Greece, 78, 81–82
Clemens, Samuel Langhorne (Mark
    Twain), 174
Clement V (ruled 1305–1314), pope, 322,
    324
Clement VII (ruled 1523–1534), pope, 410
Cleopatra (ruled 51–30 B.C.), Egypt, 121,
    147, 152, 153, 154–155
Clergy, 216, 252, 261. *See also* Monastic
    orders; Papacy; Religious orders
  attitudes of medieval, toward women,
    261
  exemption of, from courts, 214
  medieval Europe, 261, 274–277
  of Old Regime of 18th century, 587
Clive, Robert (1725–1774), 580
Clothing
  social class and style of, in 16th and
    17th century, 465
Clovis (ruled 481–511), Franks, 205, 206
Cluny, Abbey of, 274
Coffee, *469,* 569
Cohn-Haft, Louis, on marriage in classical
    Athens, 114–115
Coinage, metal, 75, 247, 257
Colbert, Jean (1619–1683), 47, 257, 520
Coligny, Gaspard de (1519–1572), 456
Colonies
  ancient Greek, 72–73, 75
  British, in Americas. *See* American
    colonies
  Columbian Exchange between Europe
    and American, 466
  European global, c. 1780, *583*
  Phoenician, 36–37. *See also* Carthage
  Roman, 155
  Spanish, in Americas, 401–403, 441
Colonna, Vittoria (1492–1547), 419
Colosseum, Roman, 163, *164,* 172
Columba, monk (521–597), 207
Columbian Exchange
  disease, 466
  new foods from, 470–473
Columbus, Christopher, 392, *400,* 401
Commerce. *See also* Banking and finance;
    Manufacturing; Trade and trade routes
  ancient Greece, 75, 110
  ancient Near East, 9, 53, 59–61

Commerce. *See also* Banking and finance;
   Manufacturing; Trade and trade routes
   (*continued*)
   Europe, 18th century, 566–572
   Europe, 14th through 17th centuries,
      478–480
   Rome, 140–141, 159
Commercial products
   imported from European colonies, 18th
      century, 567–559
   medieval European, 256, *257*
Commodities. *See* Commercial products
Commodus, Roman emperor (ruled A.D.
   180–192), 166
Communes
   Italian city-state, 349
   medieval, 258
Comnena, Ann (1083–c. 1153), 228
Concordat of Worms (1122), 276–277
Concrete, Roman use of, 172
Condorcet, Marie-Jean (1743–1794), 601
Conegliano, Cima da, 369
Confessions of Augustine, 212–213
Confraternities, 324
Confucius (c. 551–479 B.C.), 105
Constantine (ruled A.D. 306–337), 186,
   213
   foundation of Constantinople by, 194,
      219
   legalization of Christianity by (A.D.
      313), 188, 191–192, 211
   successors to, 220–221
Constantinople, 186, 233
   as center of Orthodox Church, 222
   Crusaders in, 280
   fall of, to Ottoman Turks, 368, 385
   founding of, 194, 219
   visit of western bishop Liutprand of
      Cremona to, 226–227
Constantinople, Treaty of (1700), 551
Constantius II, emperor (ruled 337–361),
   Byzantium, 220
Constitution
   ancient Greece, 81
   British, 531, 536
   United States, 600
Constitutionalism in England and Great
   Britain, 295, 298
Constitution of Melfi (1231), 302
Consuls, Roman Republic, 131
Contraception. *See* Birth control
Copernicus (1473–1543), Nicolaus, 501,
   502–503
Cordova, Spain, 235
Corilla (Maria Maddalena Morelli
   1727–1800), 561
Corinth, 91, 95, 135–136
Corinthian order, Greek architecture, *103*
Corneille, Pierre (1606–1684), 557,
   558–559

Cornelius Nepos (c. 99–c. 24 B.C.), Rome,
   142
Cortés, Hernn, 402
Cossacks, *549*
Cottage industry, 594
Cotton and textile industry, 567, 569
Council of Chalcedon (451), 213
Council of Constance (1414), 324, 325
Council of Elders, Sparta, 83
Council of Ephesus (431), 213
Council of Four Hundred, Athens, 93
Council of Lyons, (1245), 302
Council of Nicea (A.D. 325), 192, 213, 220
Council of the Best Men (Areopagus),
   Athens, 81
Council of Trent (1545–1563), 427, 429,
   430, 431
Counter-Reformation, 429–437
   education and conversion, role of Jesuits
      and Ursulines, 431–433
   Inquisition and war against heretics,
      433–436
   Jews in age of, 434–435, 436
   spirit of renewal in Catholic Church
      and, 430–431
Country living
   Europe, 17th century, 472–474
   Europe, 18th century, 592, *593*
Court(s)
   English, 266, 298
   French, 300
   papal *curia,* 275
   Roman, 150, 178
Courtesans
   European, 18th century, 594, *595*
   Greek *hetaira,* 90, 117
The Courtier (Castiglione), 373, 376
Cranach, Lucas (the Younger), *407*
Cranmer, Thomas (1489–1556), 412, 413
Crashaw, Richard (1613–1649), 495
Crassus (c. 112–53 B.C.), Rome, 151, 152
The Creation of Adam (Michelangelo), *370*
Crécy, Battle of (1346), 341
Crete, 68
Crime
   in medieval cities, 329
Criminal justice and prison reform, 601
Cro-Magnon people (*Homo sapiens
   sapiens*), 6–7
Cromwell, Oliver (1599–1658), 450,
   451–452
Cromwell, Thomas (1485–1540), 412
Crusades, 200, 256, 259, 278–281
   crusader states, 279, *280*
   decline of Byzantium and subsequent,
      279–281
   First, 278–279
   Peasants, *278*
   routes followed by crusaders, *279*
Cuneiform writing, 16, *17*

Cunningham, Lawrence, on Francis of
   Assisi, 282–283
Curia (papal courts), 275
Cyclades, 68
Cynics, 124
Cyril (827–869), 219, 224
Cyrus the Great (559–530 B.C.), Persia, 21,
   37, 39, 83, 93
Czechs, Jan Hus and, 388

Daily life
   ancient Greece, 116–117
   Europe, in 16th and 17th centuries,
      465–476
   peasant, in medieval Europe, 254–255
   in Roman world, 177–185
Dante Alighieri (1265–1321), 297, 305,
   306, *307,* 314
Darius (521–486 B.C.), Persia, 37–38, 78
   defeat of, at Marathon, 83–84
Dark Ages. *See* Europe, medieval
   (300–1300)
Darwin, Charles (1809–1882)
   theory of evolution and, 4–5
David (c. 1000–c. 971 B.C.), Hebrews, 39
David (Michelangelo), *365*
Dead Sea Scrolls, 188–189
The Decameron (Boccaccio), 307, 315, 318
Declaration of Independence, United
   States, 534–535, 600
Declaration of Indulgence, England,
   529–530
Declaration of Rights (1689), England, 531
Deities, 42
   ancient Greek, 73–74, 116
   Egyptian, 25, 27, 43
   Hebrew, 39
   Hellenistic mystery religions, 123
   Islam, 232
   Mesopotamian, 43–44
   Roman, 143
Delian League, 89
Deluge period in Polish history, 555
Demesne, 247
Democracy(ies)
   in ancient Greece at Athens, 80–82
Democritus (active c. 460 B.C.), Greece,
   105
Demosthenes (384–322 B.C.), Greece, 95,
   115, 137
Denmark
   invasions of England by Viking Danes,
      250, 264
   Thirty Years' War in, 461
Descartes, René (1596–1650), 501, 505,
   506, 602
D'Este, Isabella (1474–1539)
   relationship with Francesco Gonzaga,
      353
De Witt, Jan (1625–1672), 525

Dias, Bartholomeu, 392, 397
Dickens, Charles (1812–1870)
  on Renaissance Italy, 360
Dictator, Roman Republic, 131
Diderot, Denis (1713–1784), 599–600
  on natural law, 602–603
Diet. *See* Food and diet
Dimitri (ruled 1359–1389), Russia, 390
Dinosaurs, 4
Diocletian (ruled A.D. 284–305), Rome,
  reforms of, 192–194
Diogenes (c. 400–c. 325 B.C.), Greece, 124
Dionysius of Halicarnassus (fl. 30–8 B.C.),
  Greek, 106–107
Dionysus, dramatic festivals of, 98
Diplomacy
  emergence of, in Italian Renaissance,
    336, 354–355
Disease
  smallpox, 467
  in 16th and 17th centuries, 465, 466, 467
  14th century plague. *See* Black Death
Dispensations, Church, 323
Divination, Mesopotamian, 44–45
Divine Comedy (Dante Alighieri), 305,
  306–307, 314
Divine right to rule, concept of, 518–519
Divorce. *See* Marriage and divorce
Doctors of the Church, 211
Dome of the Rock Mosque, Jerusalem, *237*
Domesday Book, 266
Dominican Order, 284, 285
Domitian, Roman emperor, 157, 165
Domna, Julia (A.D. ?167–217), 182
Donatello (1386?–1466), 357, *358*
Donation of Pepin, 240
Donne, John (1572–1631), 496
Don Quixote (Cervantes), 494–495
Doric order, Greek architecture, *103*
Dover, Treat of (1670), 529
Draco, ancient Greek, 80
Drake, Francis, 444
Dress. *See* Clothing
Duccio (1255/1256–1318/1319), *311*
Duns Scotus, John, 306
Dürer, Albrecht (1471–1528), *346, 373,*
  375, 378, 379
Dushan, Stephen (ruled 1331–1355),
  Serbia, 384
Dutch East India Company, 482–483, *483*
Dutch Republic, 441–444, 481–482, 511,
  525. *See also* Netherlands
Dutch West India Company, 483

Earth
  earliest life forms and evolution of life
    on, 4
  human evolution, 4–7
Eastern Europe, 382–391, 547. *See also*
  specific individual countries

collapse of Byzantium and, 383–384
emergence of Russia in 18th century,
  548–554
Great Northern War (1700–1721), 547,
  551, 554
Hungary, Bohemia, and Poland, state
  formation in, 386–388
influence of Byzantium throughout, 219
Jewish communities in, *258*
map, Years' c. 1450–1500, *387*
Moscow, growth of principality of,
  388–390, 547
Ottoman expansion into, 384–386
Poland, 18th century, 554–555
Russia, 548–553
serfs in, 590–591
Sweden, collapse of empire, 554
East India Company, English, 482, 569, *580*
Ebla, Syria, 18
Ecclesiastical History of the English Nation
  (Bede), 208
Eck, Johann, 408
Eckhart, Meister (1260–1327), 324
Eclogues (Bucolics) of Vergil, 169
Economy
  A. Smith on *laissez faire* principle
    applied to, 601–604
  ancient Greece, 75, 110, 111–113
  ancient Mesopotamia and Egypt, 23,
    57–59
  Byzantium, 227–228
  Carolingian Empire, 246–248
  effects of Black Death on, 317
  Europe in 18th century, 566–576
  in France, 16th–17th centuries, 457,
    520–521
  Germanic tribes, 203
  Hellenistic world, 123
  of medieval Europe, 253, 256–258, 259
  of medieval Jewish life, 259
  of medieval monasteries, 216
  Roman, 139–141, 158–159, 179–180
  slave trade, impact of, 570–571
  Spanish empire and impact on,
    401–404, 441
  trade and. *See* Trade and trade routes
  transformations in European, Years'
    1300–1650, 477–485
  world. *See* World economy
Edict of Milan (A.D. 313), 191–192
Edict of Nantes (1598), 456–447, 524, 544
Edict of Restitution (1629), 462
Edict of Worms, 408
Education
  ancient Greece, 107, 108, 123
  ancient Near East civilizations, 16
  Carolingian Empire and liberal arts,
    245–246
  Catholic Jesuit and Ursuline orders and,
    431–433

medieval European universities, 287,
  288–289
in Muslim world, 234
Northern European humanism and,
  375–376
Renaissance and Reformation, 352–354,
  418
Rome, 142, 175, 178
of women, 142, 376
Education of an Orator (Quintilian), 175
Edward the Confessor (ruled 1042–1066),
  England, 264
Edward I (1272–1307), England, 260, 298
Edward III (ruled 1327–1377), England,
  340, 341
Edward VI (ruled 1547–1553), England,
  412–413
Egypt
  Ptolemaic, 120, 121
  Roman rule, 128, 135
Egypt, ancient, 2, 23–32
  agriculture and economy of, 23
  architecture and pyramids, 25, 26, *27*
  art, *25, 27, 30, 31*
  class and social structure of, 54
  decline of, 30–31
  early dynastic period, 25
  Hebrews in, 39
  Herodotus in, 26
  hieroglyphic writing from, *17*
  Hyksos invasion of, 23
  literature of, 48, 50
  map, *24, 34*
  Middle Kingdom, 23, 27–28
  mummification of dead in, 25, 26
  New Kingdom, 23, 28–30, 55
  Nile River and valley environment, 23,
    24, 32
  Old Kingdom, 23, 27
  perspectives on, 31–32
  pharaohs of, 23, 29
  reign of Akhenaton, 30
  religion, 25, 30, 42, 43
  unification of, 24–25
  womens status in, 55
Einhard, 240, 244
Elagabalus (ruled A.D. 218–222), Rome,
  182–183
El Cid, Rodrigo Daz de Vivar (d. 1099),
  271
Eleanor of Aquitaine (1122?–1204), *266,*
  268–269, 299, 340
Electors, Holy Roman Empire, 269, 540
Eleusinian Mysteries, 123
Elizabeth (ruled 1741–1762), Russia, 579,
  583
Elizabeth I (ruled 1558–1603), England,
  412, 443, 444, 447–448, 482
Empedocles (active c. 495 B.C.), 105
Empires. *See* Imperialism

Encomienda system, 441

Encyclopédie (Diderot), 599–600, 601, 602–603

England. *See also* Great Britain
    Act of Union (1707), 536
    in age of Henry II, 267
    Anglican Church. *See* Church of England (Anglicans)
    Anglo-Saxons in, 201, 206–208
    Baroque literature in (Shakespeare), 493–495
    Charles I and civil war in, 449, 450, 451
    Charles II and restoration of monarchy in, 452
    constitutionalism and representative government in, 295, 298, 528, 531, 534
    development of common law in, 266
    Elizabeth I, reign of, 447–448
    expulsion of Jews from, 260
    Glorious Revolution in, 530, 534
    grain production, 18th century, *590*
    Great Rebellion of 1381 in, 320–321
    Hanoverian dynasty in, 536–537
    Henry VIII, 412
    Hundred Years' War with France, 315, 340–342
    James I, relationship with Parliament, 448–449
    king-vassal relationship and Magna Carta, 297–298
    monarchies in medieval, 263, 264–267, 297–298
    Neolithic megalith Stonehenge, *10*
    Norman conquest of, 264–266
    Parliament, evolution of, 298. *See also* Parliament, British
    political philosophy of resistance and revolution in, 532–535
    Protectorate of Oliver Cromwell, 451–452
    Reformation in, 412–413
    Stuart dynasty in, 448–453, 529–536
    Tudor dynasty in, 344–345, 412, 447–448
    Viking invasions in, 250
    War of the Roses, 344
    war with Spain, 16th century, 444

Enlightened despotism, 586, 599

Enlightenment, 597–605
    despots and. *See* Enlightened despotism
    French *philosophes* and, 598–600
    J. Locke and development of, 598
    selections of writings from, 602–603
    social and economic thought in, 601–604
    Voltaire and natural morality, 600–601

Ennius (239–169 B.C.), 144

Environment
    ancient Egypt, 23, 24–25, 32

of ancient Near East, 13, 14–15
    Earths, and evolution of life, 3, 4–6

Epic of Gilgamesh (poem), 2, 42, 50

Epicureanism, 124, 143

Epicurus (341–271 B.C.), Greece, 124

Epidaurus, theater at, 98

Epidemics
    Europe in 14th century, 315–319
    Greece, 91
    Rome, 195

Epirus, kingdom of, 134

Equites class, Rome, 141, 148–149, 150, 177

Erasmus, Desiderius (1466–1536), 373, 374, *375–76*, 406

Eratosthenes (275–194 B.C.), 125

Erechtheum temple, 103–104

Erikson, Leif, 250

Erik the Red, Viking, 250

Escorial, Treaty of (1733), 513

Eshnunna, figures from temple of, *47*

Essenes, 189

Estates General, France, 301, 342

Estates of Old Regime, 18th century, 587

Et Ego in Arcadia (Poussin), 490

Etruscans, 113, 128, 129–131, 133
    art, *130, 131*
    foundation of Rome and, 130–131
    society, 129–130

Eugene (1663–1736), prince of Savoy, 541

Euripides (c. 484–406 B.C.), 99

Europe. *See also* Central Europe; Eastern Europe; Northern Europe; Southern Europe; Western Europe
    Black Death in, 315, *316*, 317
    emergence of unique civilization in, 199, 208–209, 239–251
    expansionism of. *See* European Reconnaissance
    invasions and migrations of Germanic tribes in, 186, 194–195, *202*
    invasions of Muslims, Bulgars, and Magyars into, 9th century, 249
    Islam and, 199, 230–238
    in Paleolithic Age (Stone Age), 7
    religious divisions, c. 1500, *408*
    Rome. *See* Rome, ancient; Rome, imperial; Rome, republic of

Europe, early modern period (1540–1700), 426–428
    Baroque era in arts, 486–497
    Catholic Counter-Reformation, 429–437
    clothing, fashion, and class in, 474–475
    economy, trade, and commerce in, 478–480
    England in, 446–453
    food and diet in, 467–472
    France in, 454–464
    health and medicine in, 466–467
    map, in c. 1560, *456*

map, in year 1648, *462*
    merchant capitalists in, 480–481
    Netherlands, United Provinces of, 481–482
    private trading companies and colonies in, 482–485
    social patterns of housing in, 472–474
    Spain in, 438–445

Europe, medieval (300–1300), 198–200
    Byzantium and, 219–229
    Catholic Church reform, and papacy in, 273–286
    centralization of monarchial governments in, 295–304
    Charlemagne, and Carolingian empire, 239–251
    Christianity in early, 210–218
    economy and society in late, and transition to Renaissance, 326–335
    famine, plague, and political and social upheavals of 14th century, 314–325
    feudal monarchies of early, 263–272
    feudal social order of, 252–262
    Germanic kingdoms in, 201–209
    in High Middle Ages, *303*
    Jewish life in, 258–260
    music, literature, and architecture of, 287, 291–294, 305, 306–309
    painting and sculpture in, 305, 309–312
    philosophy and theology of, 289–291, 305, 306
    scholarship and education in, 287, 288–289
    trade routes in, 256, *257*

Europe, Old Regime (1570–1775), 498–500
    absolutism in France, age of Louis XIV, 517–527
    constitutional monarchy in England, 528–538
    culture and arts of, 557–565
    economy in, 566–576
    Enlightenment and Age of Reason in, 597–605
    in Russia, 547, 548–553
    scientific method and new thought in, 501–508
    shifting balance of power in Central Europe, 539–546
    society and social structure in, 586–596
    in Spain, Italian states, and Austria, 509–516
    in Sweden and Poland, 554–555
    wars for empire in, 577–585

Europe, Renaissance and Reformation era (1450–1550), 336–338
    arts and letters of Renaissance Europe, 373–381
    Eastern European nations, 382–391
    England, 344–345, 412–413

explorations in age of European Reconnaissance, 392–404
France, Valois kings, 342–344
Hundred Years' War and, 339, 340–342
Italian city-states and emergence of Renaissance, 348–356
Italian Renaissance visual arts, 357–372
Reformation and advance of Protestantism, 405–414
social worlds of, 415–425
Spain, 345–464
European expansionism
European exploration and. *See* European Reconnaissance
global European possessions at end of 17th century, *484*
Spanish colonies in Americas, 401–403, 441
European Reconnaissance, 338
early European travelers, 393–395
global European possessions at end of 17th century, *484*
knowledge and wealth as motives for, 395
medieval Crusades as, 200
Portuguese as initiators of, 397, 398–400
role of maps and technology in, 395–396
Spain in Americas, economic impact, 400–404
Evolution of life on earth, 4–5
Expulsion of Adam and Eve from Eden (Masaccio), *359*

Factories
Roman, 180
The Fall of Man (Dürer), *379*
Families and family life
ancient Greece, 113–116
Germanic tribes, 202–204
medieval Europe, 260
medieval Europe, late period, 329–332
Mesopotamian and ancient Egyptian, 54
in Muslim world, 234
Old Regime in Europe, 18th century, 588–589
prehistoric, 6
Roman, 137, 141–143, 177, 180–181
Family of Country People (Le Nain), *590*
Famine, 466
Europe, 14th century, 315
Fawkes, Guy (1578–1606), 448
Ferdinand (ruled 1479–1516), Aragon, Sicily, 345
Ferdinand II (ruled 1619–1637), Holy Roman Empire, 460, 461, 462, 540, 541
Feudalism, 200, 252–262
clergy and secular society under, 261
defined, 253
Jewish life and, 258–260

monarchies in age of, 263–272
peasants and aristocrats in rural Europe, 253–256
perspectives on, 261
practices and institutions of, 253
rise of cities in age of, 257–258
three estates of (clergy, nobility, peasants), 262
trade expansion in age of, 256–257
women and, 260–261
Ficino, Marsilio, 349, 352
First Settlement, Rome, 158, 160
First Triumvirate, Rome, 152
Flanders, 340
Baroque painting in, 490
Flemish school of Renaissance art in, 373, 377–378
medieval textile industry in, 256
Flavian emperors, Rome, 164, 165
Florence, Italian city-state, 349, *350*, 351
Ciompi worker uprising in, 321–322
Food and diet
in ancient Greece, 111–112
in ancient Mesopotamia and Egypt, 58–59
European, in 16th and 17th centuries, 465, 467–472
medieval European peasant, 254–255
new foods introduced by European explorations, 468–473, 567–569
The Food Supplier (Chardin), *474*
Fossil record, 5
Fourth Lateran Council (1179), 260, 281
Fragonard, Jean-Honoré (1732–1806), 557, 562
France
administration of Cardinals Richelieu and Mazarin in, 458–460, 518
in age of Henry II, *267*
Baroque painting in, 490
competition with Britain for North American empire, 580–581
Estates General of (nobles, clergy, bourgeoisie), 300–301, 342
expulsion of Jews from, 260
Franks in, 201, 239. *See also* Carolingian Empire
Henry IV and Edict of Nantes, 456–458
Hundred Years' War between England and, 315, 340–342
Louis XIV, reign of, 517–527
map, Years' 1668–1713, *519*
medieval, consolidation of monarchy in, 298, *299*, 300–301
medieval, feudal monarchies in, 263, 267–269
Old Regime in. *See* Europe, Old Regime (1570–1775)
peasant revolts in 13th century, 318–321

revolution of 1789. *See* French Revolution of 1789
royal absolutism in, 459
social structure of 18th century, 591–594
troubadours of medieval, 292
Valois dynasty and consolidation of monarchy in, 342–344
war between Holy Roman Empire and, 410
wars of religion in, 16th century, *455*, 456
Franciscan Order, 282–283
Francis I (ruled 1515–1547), France, 343, 410
Francis of Assisi, 282–283, *284*, 285
Franks, 195, 201, 203. *See also* Carolingian Empire
conversion of, to Christianity, 205–206
Frederick I Hohenstaufen (Barbarossa 1152–1190), Holy Roman Empire, 263, 270, 280, 295, 388
Frederick II, Elector of Saxony, 408–409
Frederick II Hohenstaufen (ruled 1212–1250), Holy Roman Empire, 235, 270, 296, 301
Hohenstaufen Empire under, *302*
Free trade, Adam Smith on, 601–604
French and Indian War, 580–581
French Revolution of 1789
influence of J.-J. Rousseau on, 604
Friedrich II (the Great ruled 1740–1786), Prussia, 558, 577, 579
as enlightened despot, 599
War of Austrian Succession, Seven Years' War, and, 579–580, 582–584
Friedrich Wilhelm (Elector), Prussia, 539, 540, 543, *544*
army of, 544, *545*
conflict between Junkers noble class and, 544
Friedrich Wilhelm I (ruled 1713–1740), Prussia, 545
Froissart, Jean (c. 1337–1410?), 333
Fronde, French conspiracy in 17th century, 460
Fugger, Jacob II (1459–1525), 479
Fulvia, relationship with husband Mark Antony, 154–155

Gabrieli, Andrea (c. 1520–1586), 379
Gabrieli, Giovanni (c. 1556–1612), 379
Gainsborough, Thomas, *591*
Galen of Pergamum (A.D. 130–c. 200), 502, 504
Galileo Galilei (1564–1642), 433, 501, 503–504
Gallienus (ruled A.D. 253–268), Rome, 193
The Garden of Earthly Delights (Bosch), *378*

Gaul, 153
  invasion of Rome by, in 390 B.C., 133,
    134
  revolts against Roman rule in, 152
  Visigoth kingdom in, 205
Gentry class, English, 448–449
Geography, maps and, in age of European
    Reconnaissance, 395, 397
George I (ruled 1714–1717), Great Britain,
    536, 537
George II (ruled 1727–1760), Great
    Britain, 537, 579
Georgics (Vergil), 159, 169
Germanic kingdoms, 201–209
  Anglo-Saxon England, 206–208
  combined traditions of Rome and,
    208–209
  Franks, and conversation to Christianity,
    205–206
  invasion of Europe and Rome by, 186,
    194–195
  migrations to Western Europe, 202
  perspective on, 209
  society of, 202–204
  Visigoths, Ostogoths, and Lombards,
    204–205
Germany
  Baroque music in, 492–493
  Franks in, 201. *See also* Carolingian
    Empire
  Holy Roman Empire and, 301–303. *See
    also* Holy Roman Empire
  Investiture Controversy in, 275
  medieval, feudal monarchies in, 263,
    269–270
  Prussia. *See* Prussia
  in 12th century, 268
Ghetto, European Jewish, 435
Ghiberti, Lorenzo (1378–1455), 358
Ghirlandaio, Domenico (1449–1492), 359
Gin Lane (Hogarth), 593
Giotto di Bondone (c. 1266–1337), 310,
    311, 312, 313
Giovanni Arnolfini and His Bride (Van
    Eyck), 377
Gladiators, Rome, 177, 183–184
Global economy. *See* World economy
Glorious Revolution, England, 526,
    530–534
Golden Age of Roman arts, 168, 169–170
Goldsmith, Oliver (c. 1730–1774), 559
Gonzaga, Francesco, (ruled 1484–1519),
    Mantua
  relationship with Isabella Deste, 353
Gothic architecture, 305, 307, 308, 309
Goths, 202, 203
Government. *See also* Political
    organization
  ancient Greece, 72–73
  bureaucratic. *See* Bureaucracy

Byzantium, 220, 228
  Carolingian, 242–243, 244
  emergence of representative, in England,
    528–538
  papal, Innocent III and, 281–282
  Roman, 131–132, 138–139, 148–149,
    178–179
  in Spanish and Portuguese colonies,
    403–404
Gozzoli, Benozzo, 424
Gracchus, Gaius (153–121 B.C.), Rome,
    147, 148–149, 150
Gracchus, Tiberius (163–133 B.C.), Rome,
    147, 157
Grand jury, 266
Great Britain. *See also* England
  building empire in North America,
    580–582
  formation of (1707), 536
  grain production in England, 18th
    century, 590
  King Georges War, 579
  Old Regime in. *See* Europe, Old Regime
    (1570–1775)
  Seven Years' War and, 579–580
  social structure of 18th century, 591–594
Great Mosque, Qayrawan, Tunisia, 234
Great Northern War (1700–1721), 547,
    551, 554
Great Rebellion (1381), 320
Great Schism, 323–324
Greece, ancient, 64–77
  Archaic era. *See* Greece, Archaic era
  Bronze Age cultures preceding, 68–71
  city-state (polis) political organization in
    emerging, 67, 71–73
  Classical era. *See* Greece, Classical era
    (480–323 B.C.)
  colonies and markets of early, 72,
    74–75
  ideas and art of early, 75–76
  influence of Mesopotamians on, 21
  maps, 72, 84
  religion, myth, and Homeric epics,
    73–74, 143
Greece, Archaic era (600 B.C.–480 B.C.),
    78–87
  Athens, democratic experiment in early,
    80–82
  city-states and rise of tyrants during,
    79–80
  Persian Wars, 83–86, 113
  social structure in, 79
  Sparta, conservatism and militarism in,
    82–83
Greece, Classical era (480–323 B.C.),
    88–118
  architecture of, 102, 103–104
  Athens, defeat of, in Peloponnesian
    War, 93–94

Athens, dominance of, following Persian
    Wars, 88, 89–91
  freedom and slavery in, 117–118
  Hellenistic kingdoms influenced by. *See*
    Hellenistic Age
  history and philosophy in, 104–108
  land, farming, and food in, 110, 111–112
  manufacturing, trade, and mining in
    classical, 112–113
  marriage, family life, and sexual
    behavior in, 56, 113–116
  painting and sculpture, 99–102
  Peloponnesian War, 88, 89, 91–93
  Philip of Macedon and end of
    independence, 95
  theater in, 98–99
  women in, 90, 99, 110, 116–117
Greenhouse effect, 4
Gregory VII (ruled 1073–1085), pope, 269,
    275–276, 296
Gregory IX (ruled 1227–1241), pope, 285
Gregory XI (ruled 1370–1378), pope, 323
Gregory of Tours (538–594), 208, 259
Gregory the Great (ruled 590–604), pope,
    205, 207, 214, 292
Groote, Gerhard (1340–1384), 324, 430
Gudea (c. 2144–2124 B.C.), Sumeria, 18
Guicciardini, Francesco, 353
Guido of Arezzo, 287, 293
Guilds, medieval, 258
Guiscard, Robert, 269, 277
Gunpower Plot (1605), 448
Gupta Empire in India, fall of, 195
Gustavus Adolphus (ruled 1611–1632),
    Sweden, 463, 554
Gutenberg, Johann (c. 1397–1491), 374
Guzmán, Dominic de, 284

Hadrian, Roman emperor (ruled A.D.
    117–138), 165, 166, 171, 178, 187
  architecture, sculpture, and, 168,
    171–172
  inauguration of reign by, 161
Hagia Sophia Church, Constantinople,
    221, 222, 224–225, 385
Hall, Trevor P., on first Africans in Europe,
    422–423
Hals, Frans, 506
Hammurabi (c. 1792–1750 B.C.), Babylon,
    14, 19, 42, 49, 54
Handel, Georg Frideric (1685–1759), 492
Hannibal (247–183/182 B.C.), Carthage,
    128, 134–135, 139
Hanseatic League, 326, 478
Hapsburgs. *See also* Holy Roman Empire
  in Austria. *See* Austria
  in Spain and, 345–346, 439–441
  Thirty Years' War and, 460–462, 512
  war between French Valois kings and,
    410

Hardouin-Mansart, Jules (1646–1708), 521

Harvey, William (1578–1657), 501, 504

Hastings, Battle of (1066), 264

Hatshepsut (c. 1498–1483 B.C.), Egypt, 47, 50, 55

    relationship with Thutmose III, 29

Hauteville, Tancred de, 269

Hautville, Roger de (1031–1101), 235

Hawkins, John (1532–1595), 444, 572

Haydn, Franz Joseph (1732–1809), 557, 558, 563

Head Offices of the Dutch East Indian Company of Hugly in Bengal (Schulylenberg), *482*

Health. *See* Disease; Medicine

Hebrews, 2, 33, 38–40, 42. *See also* Jews

    ban on religious imagery, 43

    migrations and kingdoms of, 39

    religion of, 39–40

    slavery and law, 62

    women's status among, 55–57

Hecataeus (fl.c. 500 B.C.), Greece, 106

Heisenberg, Werner, 105

Helene Fourment and her Children (Rubens), *491*

Hellenistic Age, 119–127

    Alexander the Great and his empire, 120

    map, *121*

    religion and philosophy in, 123–124

    science, medicine, and technology in, 125–126

    society and economy in, 122–123

    successor states to Alexander, 120–122

Héloïse (c. 1098–1164), 290

Helot class, Sparta, 82

Henry (the Navigator, 1394–1460), Portugal, 397

Henry I (the Fowler, ruled 919–936), German states, 269

Henry II (1154–1189), England, 266, *267*, 299

Henry II (ruled 1547–1559), France, 340, 455

Henry III (1039–1056), 274

Henry III (ruled 1216–1272), England, 298

Henry III (ruled 1517–1589), France, 456

Henry IV, Germany, 269, 274–275

Henry IV (of Navarre, ruled 1589–1610), France, 456–457

    relationship with Marie deMedici, 458

Henry V, emperor, 276

Henry VI (ruled 1191–1197), Holy Roman Empire, 270, 301

Henry VI (ruled 1422–1471), England

    relationship with Margaret of Anjou, 343

Henry VII (ruled 1485–1509), England, 345, 412

Henry VIII (ruled 1509–1547), England, 412

Heraclius emperor (ruled 610–621), Byzantium, 222, 223

Heresies, Christian, 192, 324–325

    Albigensian (Catharism), 284, 285, 433

    Arianism, 202, 206, 213

    Inquisition and war against, 283–285, 433–436

    J. Hus, 325

    J. Wycliffe, 324

    Lollards, 324–325

    Monophysites, 213, 222

    Nestorianism, 213

    Waldensian, 284

Hermetics, 352, 502

Hermit, 215

Herodotus (484–420 B.C.), 37, 89, 91, 97, 129

    account of his trip to Egypt, 26

    history of Persian Wars, 85, 104

    on reasons for writing history, 107

Herophilus (c. 335–c. 280 B.C.), 125

Hetaira, 90, 117

Hieroglyphic writing, Egyptian, *17*

Hilda of Whitby (614–680), *217*

Hildegard of Bingen, 332

Hinduism, 105

Histories (Tacitus), 175

Historiography

    ancient Greek, 89, 91, 94, 97, 104–105

    Byzantine, 221

    classical Greek attitudes on, 106–107

    Renaissance, 353

    Roman, 168, 169, 175–176

History of Rome (Livy), 169

History of the Peloponnesian War (Thucydides), 91, 104–105

History of the Persian Wars (Herodotus), 26, 89, 104

A History of the Wars of Justinian (Procopius), 221

Hittite kingdom, 19, 33, 34–36, 50, 58

    art, *35*, *44*

    old kingdom and empire of, 35–36

    religion, 44

    womens status in, 55

Hogarth, William, 593

Hohenzollerns, rule of Prussia by, 539, 542–543

Holland, Franks in, 201. *See also* Carolingian Empire

Holy League, 456, 511

Holy Roman Empire, 200, 295, 439, 515. *See also* Germany

    Charlemagne crowned emperor of, 244

    church-state relations and, 296–297

    electors, 269, 540

    fiction of, in 17th century, 539, 540

    Hapsburgs and, 345–346

    Imperial Diet of, 540

    Otto I and, 269

Thirty Years' War and, 460–61, 539, 540

    war between France and, 16th century, 410

Homer, 70, 73–74, 77, 169

Hominids, 3, 5

Homo erectus, 3, 6

Homo neanderthalis, 5–6, 7

Homo sapiens sapiens, 3, 5, 6–7

Homosexuality

    ancient Greece, 115–116

Honorius III (ruled 1216–1227), pope, 302

Hooch, Piet de, *473*

Horace (65–8 B.C.), 168, 170

Housing

    Europe, in 16th and 17th centuries, 465, 472–473

    Roman private, 173, 174

Hubertusburg, Treaty of (1763), 583

Huguenots, 454

    French monarchy and wars against, 455–456, *457*

    Louis XIV and, 524

Human evolution, 4–7

Humanism

    classical culture, Italian Renaissance, and, 326, 333, 352–354, 373

    in late Middle Ages, 333

    in Northern Europe, 375–376, 406

Human rights

    in ancient Near East, 61–62

Hume, David (1711–1776), 561, 599

    on principles of morals, 603

Hundred Years' War, 315, 333, 340–342

    early phase of, 341

    Joan of Arc and end of, 341–342

    maps of territorial changes in, *340*

    origins of, 340

Hungary, 439

    kingdom of, 386–387, 540

    Ottoman Empire and, 385–386, 540–541

    uprising of Rákczy (1703), 541–542

Huns, 195, 203–204

Hunting, art and, 7

Hus, Jan (1373–1415), 325, 406

Husband and Wife in a Landscape (Gainsborough), *591*

Hyksos kingdom, 28, 39

Ibn Khaldun, on Black Plague, 319

Iconoclasic controversy in Byzantium, 223

Icons, art of, *225*

Ictinus, Greece, 103

Iliad (Homer), 70, 73–74, 77

Illuminated manuscripts, *212*, *216*

    Benedicts Rule, *216*

    Bible, *55*, *245*

    Black Death and burning of Jews, *317*

    Book of Kells, *207*

    Book of Vices, *259*

Illuminated manuscripts (*continued*)
    in Carolingian Empire, *245, 246*
    Drapers Market, Bologna, *328*
    Europeans mistreatment of American
      indigenous people, *403*
    Frederick II, Holy Roman Empire, *301*
    Investiture Controversy, *275*
    Italian bankers, *328*
    Ivan III, *390*
    Lecture of Henricus de Alemania, 288
    Marco Polos travels, *393*
    of medieval farming, *254, 255*
    Palermo imperial court, *270*
    Salzburg *Astronomical Notices, 255*
    Scholastic History, Peter the Eater, *260*
    Très Riches Heures du Duc de Berry, 310,
      311
    of Wat Tyler, *321*
Imhotep (c. 2630 B.C.), Egypt, 25
The Imitation of Christ (Thomas Kempis),
    324
Imperialism, 15th century-17th century
    Portugal, 397
    Spain, 401–403
Incest taboo, 6
Index of Prohibited Books, 377, 436
India
    British imperialism in, 580, 582
    European competition for empire in,
      579, 580
    European trade with, 483
    fall of Gupta empire in, 195
    M. Polos travels to, 393, *394, 395*
    miniature painting in, *580*
    Portuguese explorations in, 397, 399
    Roman trade with, 179
Indo-Europeans, 33, 34–35
Indulgences, church, 323, 406
Indus Valley civilization, 70
Infanticide, 82
Innocent III (ruled 1198–1216), pope, 280,
    281–285, 296
    church-state relations and papal
      supremacy, 282–283, 297, 302
    heresy and Inquisition, 283–285
    papal government and, 281–282
Innocent IV (ruled 1243–1254), 302
Inquisition, 283–285, 433–436
    death of Joan of Arc and, 341–342
    persecution of Galileo by, 503–504
    in Spain, 345, 433, 436, 440
    witch hunts and, 420–421
Intellectuals
    ambivalent attitudes toward women by
      medieval, 330–331, 332
    of Enlightenment, 18th century,
      597–605
    in Renaissance Italian city-states, 348,
      352–354
    salons of 18th century and, 560, 594

International style
    medieval Gothic, 310
Interregnum, 451–452
Investiture Controversy, 269, *274,*
    275–277
Ionian Greeks, revolt of, 83–84
Ionic order, Greek architecture, *103,* 104
Iran, Muslim rule in, 233. *See also* Persia
Ireland, 250, 413
    Christianity introduced into, 207–208
    revolts in, 451–452, 531
Iron Age, 67, 71–73
Isabel (ruled 1474–1504), Castille, Spain,
    345, 400
Isis, worship of, 178
Islam, 199, 230–238. *See also* Muslims
    Arabian peninsula and people, 231
    doctrines of, 232
    expansion of, into Mediterranean
      region, 233–234
    influence of science, arts, and culture of,
      in Europe, 236, 237, 238
    invasions, into Europe in 9th century,
      249
    map of empire, *222, 233*
    Muhammad and founding of, 230,
      231–233
    relationship of, with Jews, 258–259
    in Spain and Sicily, 234–235
    threat of, to Byzantium, 223
Israel, kingdom of, 33, 39
    womens status in, 55–57
Italian city-states, 513–515
    Austrian domination of, 515
    C. Dickens on travels to, 360
    changing trade patterns and, 510–511
    domination of medieval trade by, 256
    emergence of capitalism in, 257–258
    emergence of diplomacy in, 354–355
    patronage and statecraft, 354
    political and social institutions of, 349
    of Renaissance era, 349–352
    Spanish domination of, 514–515
    system of, during Old Regime, 514
Italy
    Baroque art in, *488,* 489–490
    Enlightenment in, 601
    Etruscans and foundation of Rome in,
      129–131
    French invasion of, 15th century, 354
    German imperial intrusion into
      medieval, 269–270, 302–303
    Greek trade with, 113
    Hapsburg domains in, 439
    humanist spirit in, 326, 333, 352
    Investiture Controversy in, *275*
    Lombards in, 205
    map of, c. 1450, *351*
    medieval literature, 306–307
    natural environment, 140

    Ostrogoths in, 201, 205, 221
    Renaissance in. *See* Art, Renaissance
    Romanization of, 133
    Rome. *See* Rome, imperial; Rome,
      republic of
Ivan I (ruled 1328–1341), Russia, 390
Ivan III (ruled 1462–1505), Russia, 548
Ivory carving
    Byzantine, *220*
    medieval European, *214, 220*
    Phoenician, *50, 58*

Jacob Blessing the Sons of Joseph
    (Rembrandt), *492*
Jacobites, Great Britain, 537
Jacquerie revolt, 318–320, *321*
Jadwiga (ruled 1384–1399), Poland, 388
James I (ruled 1603–1625), England,
    confrontations with Parliament,
    448–449
James II (ruled 1685–1688), England,
    Glorious Revolution against rule of,
    530–535
James V (ruled 1528–1542) Scotland, 413
Janequin, Clément, (c. 1485–c. 1560),
    379–380
Jansenism, 506, 524
Jefferson, Thomas (1743–1826), 534–535
Jenkins, Robert (active 1731–1738), 578
Jericho, Palestine, *9, 10*
Jerome, St. (c. 347–420), 212
Jerusalem, 21, 33, 39, 40
    Dome of the Rock in, *237*
Jesuits, religious order of, 431–433, 506,
    523
Jesus (c. 6 B.C.–c. A.D. 30), 189–190
Jews, 21, 38. *See also* Hebrews
    in age of Counter-Reformation, 436
    Ashkenazi, 260, 434, 436
    coming of Christianity and, 188–189
    diaspora of, 39, 258
    life of, in medieval Europe, 258–260
    Marranos, in Spain, 345
    as outsiders in 16th and 17th century
      Europe, 421
    in Roman world, 187–189
    Sephardic, 260, 434, *436*
    social life of 16th–17th century,
      434–435
    in Spain, 440
Jews, persecution of, 122
    in early modern Europe, *436*
    in medieval Europe, 259–260, 317
    in Roman Empire, 187, 188
Joan of Arc, 341–342
John (1199–1126) England, 282, 296
John II (ruled 1481–1495), Portugal, 397,
    400
John II (ruled 1648–1668), Poland,
    555

John II Sobieski (ruled 1674–1696), Poland, 555

John IV (ruled 1640–1656), Portugal, 513

John of Luxembourg (ruled 1310–1346), Czech lands, 388

John Paul II, pope, 504

John Sobieski (ruled 1674–1696), Poland, 541

Johnson, Ben (1572–1637), 493

John XXIII, pope, 324

Joint stock companies, 478, 482–483

Joseph II (1741–1790), Holy Roman emperor, 515

The Journey of the Magi (Gozzoli), *424*

Judaea, Roman province of, 187

Judah, kingdom of, 21, 33, 39
women's status in, 55

Judaism, 39–40. *See also* Hebrews; Jews

Judeo-Christian tradition, women and, 217

Julian, emperor (361–363), Byzantium, 220

Julio-Claudian emperors, Rome, 162–163, 177

Julius II (ruled 1503–1513), 352

Junkers, 539, 542–546, 592

Justinian the Great, emperor (527–565), Byzantium, 205
church architecture and, *221, 222*
wars of, 221–222

Jutes, 195

Juvenal (A.D. ?60–?130), 175, 187

Kang Hsi (1654–1772), 433

Kant, Immanuel (1724–1804), 599

Kassites, 14, 19

Kempis, Thomas, 324

Kepler, Johannes (1571–1630), 501, 503

Khafre (c. 2530–2494 B.C.), Egypt, *27, 46*

Khan, Genghis (c. 1162–1227), 384, 393

Khayyam, Omar (d. ?1122), 236

Khufu (c. 2551–2228 B.C.), Egypt, *27*

Kiev, state of, 224, 225
decline of, 389

Killinger, Charles L., 570–571

King Georges War, 579

Kings Peace (387 B.C.), 94

King Williams War, 526

Kish, earliest writing samples from, *17*

Knights, medieval, 255–256

Knights of St. John of Jerusalem (Hospitalers), 279

Knights of the Temple (Templars), 279

Knossos, palace of, 68, 69

Knox, John (c. 1505–1572), 413

Koran, 230, 232, 234

Kosciusko, Thaddeus (1746–1817), Poland, 555

Kosovo, Battle of (1389), 385

Krum (ruled 802–814), Bulgaria, 223

Kurosawa, Akira, 494

Labor. *See also* Worker(s)
Europe, early modern period, 480

Ladislas I (ruled 1077–1095), Hungary, 386

Lagash, 15, 18

Laissez faire economics principle, Adam Smith and, 601–604

La Madeleine, abbey church of, tympanum, *293*

Lamentation over the Dead Christ (Giotto), *312*

Land ownership. *See* Land tenure

Land tenure
in ancient Greece, 110, 111
aristocrats, 18th century Old Regime, 592, 593
Byzantium, 226–227
Carolingian Empire and manor system, 246–248
feudalism and, 253
latifundia in Roman Republic, 137, 139–140, 180, 246
manorialism in Carolingian Empire, 246
reform, in Roman Republic, 148

Lange, Joseph, *563*

Langton, Stephen, 282, 297

Languages
Arabic, 230
Aramaic, 20, 186
Indo-European, 33, 34, 201
Latin, 169–170, 175–176, 178, 288, 352
printing technology and vernacular, 374–375
Sanscrit, 70

Laocoon and His Sons (Agesander, Athenodorus, Polydorus), *124*

Lao-tzu (active c. 570 B.C.), 105

La Sainte Chapelle, Paris, 309

Lascaux, France, cave paintings, 7, 8

Las Meninas (The Maids of Honor) (Velazquez), *512*

The Last Supper (Leonardo da Vinci), *362*

Lateran Councils, 260, 281

Latifundia, 137, 139–140, 180, 246

Latin League, 133

Laud, William (1573–1645), 449–450

Lauritsen, Frederick M., on Dead Sea Scrolls, 188–189

Law. *See also* Human rights
ancient Greece, 80
ancient Near East, 14, 18, 19, 39–40, 54, 61–62
Byzantine, 221–222
English common, 266, 298
Germany kingdoms, 208–209
Hammurabis code of, 14, 19, 54
Hebrew (Judaism), 39–40
regulation of sexual behavior, 114–115
Roman, 132–133, 177, 178, 181
rule of, 19

slavery and, in ancient Near East, 62
Spain, 271

Law, John (1671–1729), 573–574

Lay investiture, 261, 275, 296

League of Augsburg (1697), 513, 525–526

League of Corinth, 88

Lebanon, 18

Lechfeld, Battle of (955), 269

Legnano, Battle of (1176), 270

Leo I (ruled 440–461), pope, 203, 213, 214

Leo III, Emperor, Byzantium, 223

Leo III (795–816), pope, 244

Leo IV, pope, 249

Leo IX (ruled 1049–1054), pope, 274

Leonardo da Vinci (1452–1519), 357, *362*

Leopold I (ruled 1658–1705), Holy Roman emperor, 525–526, 540

Leo X, pope, 407

Lepanto, Battle of (1571), *368, 386, 444,* 511, 541

Lerma, Duke of (1552–1625), Duke of, 511

Letter to Posterity (Petrarch), 333

Leuctra, Battle of (372 B.C.), 94

Le Vau, Louis (1612–1670), 521

Libraries
Alexandria, Egypt, 121, 125
Ashurbanipals, Assyria, 20

Licensing Act (1662), British, 561

Liege homage, 263

Life, earliest forms of, on Earth, 4

Lincean Academy, Rome, 504

The Linen Cupboard (Piet de Hooch), *473*

Lion Gate, Mycenae, *71*

Literacy rates, European, 288

Literary salon. *See* Salons

Literature. *See also* Religious literature
ancient Greek, 73–74, 98–99
of ancient Near East, 48–51
Baroque, 488, 493–496
emergence of vernacular, 291–292
Islamic, 236–237
medieval European, 241, 287, 291–292, 306–307
Mesopotamian, 48–49, 50–51
Roman, 137, 144–145, 168
of theater. *See* Theater

Literature, Renaissance, 373–381
northern humanists and emphasis on education, 375–376
political strategy in Castiglione and Machiavelli, 376–377
printing revolution and, 373, 374–375

Liutprand of Cremona (920–972), visit to Constantinople, 226–227

Livia, 182

Livy (59 B.C.–A.D. 17), 169

Locke, John (1632–1689), 534, *535,* 598
from *Second Treatise on Government,* 533

Lollards, 324–325

Lombard League, 270, 302

Lombards, 202, 205
Lombardy, 270, 349
Lorraine, France, 248
Lothair, Kingdom of, 248–249
Lothair (ruled 840–877), Carolingian
    Empire, 248–249
Louis, Kingdom of, 248–249
Louisiana Colony and Mississippi Bubble,
    573–574
Louis the German (ruled 843–877),
    Carolingian Empire, 248–249
Louis the Pious (ruled 814–840),
    Carolingian Empire, 248
Louis VI (the Fat, ruled 1108–1137),
    France, 268–269
Louis VII (ruled 1137–1180), France, 268,
    299
Louis VIII (ruled 1223–1226), France, 300
Louis XI (the Spider, ruled 1461–1483),
    France, 298, 342
Louis XIV (ruled 1643–1715), France, 460,
    505, 506, 517–527
    bureaucratic government of, 522–523
    concept of divine right and, 518–520
    economic affairs directed by J. Colbert,
        520–521
    France in age of, *519*
    religious dissent in kingdom of, 523–524
    theater at court of, 558–559
    Versailles royal court, *521*, 522–523, *524*
    wars of, and quest for hegemony,
        524–526
Louis XV, France, relationship with Jeanne
    Bécu du Bary, 595
Love Letters (Fragonard), *562*
Loyola, Ignatius (1491–1556), 431–433
Lucretius (c. 95–c. 55 B.C.), 143
Lucullus (c. 117–55 B.C.), 151
Luther, Martin (1483–1546), 405, 407–409
    establishment of Lutheran Church,
        408–409
    on marriage, 419
    Ninety-Five Theses of, 407–408
Lutheranism
    establishment of Lutheran Church,
        408–409
    social strife and spread of, 409–410
Lyceum, Greece, 108, 123
Lycurgus, ancient Greece, 82
Lydian empire, 83
Lysippus (mid-4th century), 102
Lysistrata (Aristophanes), 99

Maccabaeus, Judas (d. 160 B.C.), 187
Macedon, kingdom and empire, 95, 120
    after Alexander, 122
    Roman rule, 135
Machiavelli, Niccol (1469–1527), 373,
    376–377
Madonna of the Meadows (Raphael), *364*

Madrigals, 379–380
Maecenas (c. 70–8 B.C.), 169
Maesa, Julia (? A.D. 226), 182–183
Magazines, womens, 561
Magellan, Ferdinand, 401
Magic, 45, 502
Magna Carta, signed 1215, 295, 297–298
Magyars, 269
    invasions of Europe by, in 9th century,
        249
    Kingdom of Hungary and, 386–387
Maintenon, Madame de (1635–1707), 518,
    519
Mammals, evolution of, 4
Mannerism, 357, 371
Manor, 246, *247*
Manorialism, 200
    in Carolingian Empire, 246–247
Mantegna, 357
Mantinea, Battle of (362 B.C.), 94
Mantua, Italian city-state, 353
Manufacturing
    in ancient Greece, 112–113
    in Europe, medieval period, 256–257,
        328
    in Europe, 14th–17th centuries, 479
    Roman empire, 140–141, 158, 180
Manuscripts. *See* Illuminated manuscripts
Manzikert, Battle of (1071), 277
Maps and geography, in age of European
    Reconnaissance, 395, *397*
Marathon, Battle of (490 B.C.), 78, 84, 99
Marcus Aurelilus, Roman emperor (ruled
    A.D. 161–180), 161, 166, 195
Margaret of Anjou, relationship with
    Henry VI of England, 343
Maria Theresa (ruled 1740–1780), Austria,
    579
    Seven Years' War and, 583–584
Marius, Gaius (157–86 B.C.), Rome, 147,
    149–150
Market Place at Antwerp, 416
Marriage and divorce
    age of, late medieval period, 330
    in ancient Greece, 56, 113–114
    disease cycles and, 467
    exogamy, 6
    in late medieval Europe, 329–332
    in Mesopotamia, 56–57
    in Old Regime, 18th century Europe,
        588–589
    in Renaissance and Reformation,
        418–419
    in Roman Republic, 142
Marsilio of Padua, 297
Martel, Charles (c. 688–741), 235, 240
Martin Luther and the Wittenberg Reformers
    (Lucas Cranach the Younger), *407*
Martin V (ruled 1417–1431), pope, 324
Mary (1662–1694), England, 530, 531, 534

Mary Stuart (ruled 1542–1567), Scotland,
    413, 447
Mary Tudor (ruled 1553–1558), England,
    413, *439*, 447
Masaccio (1401–1428), 357, 359
Matilda of Flanders, relationship with
    William the Conqueror (Duke of
    Normandy) of England, 265
Mattias Corvinus (ruled 1458–1490),
    Hungary, 387
Maximilian (ruled 1493–1519), Holy
    Roman emperor, *346*
Mazarin, Giulio (1602–1661), Cardinal,
    458, 459–450, 518
Mecca, Sanctuary at, *231*
Medes, 33
Medici, Catherine de (1519–1589), as
    French regent, 455–456
Medici, Cosimo de (ruled 1434–1464),
    349, 352
Medici, Lorenzo de (ruled 1469–1492),
    349
Medici, Marie de (1573–1642), relationship
    with Henry IV of France, 458
Medici family, Italian city-states, 328, 349,
    352, 357, 515
Medicine
    Enlightenment and advances in,
        504–505
    European, 17th century, 466–467
    in Hellenistic kingdoms, 125
    in Islamic world, 236
Medieval commonwealth, 199–200
Mediterranean Sea region, diminished
    importance of, between 1500 and
    1700, 509, 510–511
Megaliths, Neolithic, 10
Mehmed II (ruled 1451–1481), portrait of,
    385
Mehmed IV (ruled 1648–1687), 591
Melanchthon, Philip (1497–1560), 409
Memphis, Egypt, 25
Menes (ruled c. 3100 B.C.), Egypt, 25
Menetho (c. 280 B.C.), Egypt, 25
Menkaure (c. 2494–2472 B.C.), Egypt, 27
Mentuhotep (c. 2061–2010 B.C.), Egypt,
    27
Mercantilism, 481, 566, 570, 575
    economic nationalism and, 482–484
    in France, 520–521
Mercator, Gerardus (1512–1594), 395
Merchant(s). *See also* Commerce; Trade
    and Trade routes
    Carolingian, 247–248
    changing trade patterns in 18th century
        and growth of, 567
    emerging class of, in 16th century,
        416–417
    medieval guilds operated by, 258
    in Roman Republic, 137, 141

Merchant capitalism, 16th and 17th centuries, 481. *See also* Mercantilism
Meria, Matthew, *542*
Merici, Angela (1473–1540), 433
Merovingian dynasty, 206, 296
Mesopotamia, 2, 13–22
  Akkadian civilization, 17–18
  Assyrian civilization and empire building in, 19–21
  Babylonian civilization and legal code, 19
  birth of civilization at Tigris and Euphrates Rivers, 14–15
  class and social structure in, 54
  influence of, on Greek civilization, 21
  perspectives on, 21
  role of agriculture in development of civilization in, 14–15
  significant dates, 18
  Sumerian civilization, and rise of cities, 15–17
  women's status in, 54, 56
Messina, Antonello da (c. 1430–1479), 368, 377
Metalworking
  Hittite iron smelting, 61
  Neolithic, 8
Methodius (825–884), 219
Metopes, Parthenon, 101, *102*
Mexico, 441
  Aztec banquet and markets, 470–473
  Spanish conquest of, 402
Michael VIII Paleologus, 280, 383
Michelangel Buonarroti (1475–1564), 357, 363–364, *365*, 370
Middle Ages. *See* Europe, medieval (300–1300)
Middle class
  ancient Greece, 79
  emerging interest in arts by, 18th century Europe, 558
  medieval Europe, 252, 260
  Old Regime, 18th century, 587, 593
  Renaissance, in Italian city-states, 349
Middle East, 13. *See also* Near East
  as geographical term, 14
Mieszko I (ruled 960–992), Poland, 388
Migrations
  of Germanic tribes into Roman empire, 186, 194–195, *202*
Milan, Italian city-state, 349, 354, 515
Military
  ancient Greek, 79
  Assyrian, 19–20
  Louis XIV's reform of, France, 525
  medieval feudalism and, 253, 255–256
  O. Cromwell's New Model Army, England, 450–451, 452
  Prussian, 544, *545*
  Roman, 149, 162, 163–165, 178, 179
  Russian, 548, *549*, *550*

Milton, John (1608–1674), 488, 496
Milvian Bridge, Battle of (A.D. 312), 191, 194
Mining in ancient Greece, 113
Minnesinger poets, 237
Minoan culture, 65, 67, 68–70
Missi dominici, Carolingian Empire, 243, 244
Mississippi Bubble, 573–574
Mithraism, 178
Modern Devotion, 324
Molire, Jean-Baptiste Poquelin (1662–1673), 557, 558
Monarchies, 9th and 10th century medieval European (feudal), 263–272
  England, 264–267
  France, 267–269
  Germany and Italy (Holy Romany Empire), 269–270
  Spain and Reconquista, 270–271
Monarchies, 11th and 12th centuries, 295–304
  emergence of centralized authority in, 295
  in England, 297–298
  in France, 298–301
  in Holy Roman Empire (Germany, Italy), 301–303
  political theory and church-state relations, 296–297
Monarchies, 14th through 18th centuries
  Byzantium, collapse of, 383–386
  emergence of new, 14th and 15th centuries, 339–347
  England, 344–345, 412, 447–453
  France, 342–344, 454–460, 462–463, 517–527
  Holy Roman Empire, 460–462
  Hundred Years' War and, 340–342
  Hungary, Bohemia, and Poland, 386–388
  Moscow principality, 388–390, 547
  Poland, 554–555
  Portugal, 397–400, 513
  Russia, 547–553
  Spain, 345–346, 400–404, 438–445
  Sweden, *461*, 463, 554
  Thirty Years' War and, 460–463
Monasticism, 215
Monastic orders, 210. *See also* Religious orders
  Benedictine, 215–216
  Cistercian, 276–277
  for women, 217–218
Mongols, invasions into Eastern Europe by, 384, 387, 389
Monophysites, 213, 222
Montagu, Edward (d. 1775), 560
Montagu, Elizabeth Robinson (1720–1800), 560

Montcalm, Louis Joseph de (1712–1759), 581
Montesquieu, Charles-Louis (1689–1755), 600
Monteverdi, Claudio (1567–1643), 492
Moravia (Czechs), 224, 388
More, Thomas (1478–1535), 373, 375, 412
Moriscos, 345, 513
Moro, Anthony, *442*
Mosaics
  Byzantine, *190*, 224, *225*
  medieval European, *244*
  Roman, *184*
  Vandal, *203*
Moscow, 547, 548. *See also* Russia
  growth of principality of, in 14th through 16th centuries, 388, 389
  origins of, 390
Moses, 39
Mozart, Wolfgang Amadeus (1756–1791), 557, 558, *559*, *563–564*
Muhammad, 230, 231–233. *See also* Islam; Muslims
Music
  Baroque, 487, 491–493
  Classical style, 18th century, 563–564
  medieval European, Gothic, 309
  medieval European, polyphonic, 287, 292–293
  opera, 491–492
  Renaissance, 379–380
Muslims. *See also* Islam
  as Moriscos, in Spain, 345, 513
  as outsiders in 16th–17th century Europe, 421
  rule in, Sicily, 230, 235
  rule of, in Spain, 230, 234, 235
  Shiite, 232–233
  society and social structure, 233–234
  in Spain, early modern period, 440–441, 511
  Sunnite, 233
  Women's status as, 234
Mycenaean culture, 64, 67, 70–71
My Secret (Petrarch), 333
Mystery religions in Hellenistic kingdoms, 123
Mysticism
  Counter-Reformation, 430–431
  medieval, 324

Naples, Kingdom of, 349, 352, 514, 515
Nasrid Dynasty, Spain, 235
Nast, Thomas, 5
Nationalism
  economic, linked to mercantilism, 482–484
Natural History (Pliny), 168, 175
Navigation, 15th century advances in, 396
Navigation Acts (1651), English, 483

Neanderthal people, 3, 5–6, 7
Near East, ancient, 33–41
    art. *See* Art of ancient Near East
    Egypt. *See* Egypt, ancient
    Hebrews, 33, 38–40
    Hittites, 33, 34–36
    map, *15, 34*
    Mesopotamian civilizations of. *See*
        Mesopotamia
    Persian empire, 33, 37–38
    Phoenicians, 33, 36–37
    trade routes in, 9
Nebuchadnezzar (c. 605–562 B.C.),
    Babylon, 21, 30
Neo-Babylonian empire, 21
Neolithic Age (New Stone Age), 3
    agriculture in, 8–9
    society, 9–10
NeoPlatonists, 352, 502
Nero, Roman emperor (ruled A.D. 54–68),
    157, 163, 175
Nerva, Roman emperor (ruled A.D. 96–98),
    165, 181
Nestorianism, 213
Netherlands
    Baroque art in, 490–491
    Dutch sea trade, 17th century, 478, 480,
        481
    revolt of, against Spain, 441–444, 511
    rise of, as commercial empire in 17th
        century, 481–482
    War of Devolution and, 525
Neumann, Balthasar (1687–1753), 563
Neustria, Carolingian Empire, 240, *241*
Nevsky, Alexander (c. 1220–1263), Russia,
    389, 390
New Model Army, 450–451, 452
New Testament, 190, 207
Newton, Isaac (1642–1726), 501, 506, 507
New York Kouros, 76
Nicene Creed, 213
Nicholas II, pope, 269
Nicias (c. 470–413 B.C.), Greece, 91, 92
Nijmegen, Treaties of (1678–1679), 525
Nikon (1605–1681), patriarch, Russia, 549
Nile River, 23, 24, 32
Nimrud, Assyria, 20, *47*
Ninety-Five Theses, Martin Luther's,
    407–408
Nineveh, Assyria, 14, 20–21, 33
Nobility. *See also* Aristocracy
    Louis XIV's attempt to control French,
        521–523
    medieval Europe, 255–256, 262
    old, in 16th century, 416–417
    Old Regime, 18th century, 587,
        591–593, 595–595
    Prussian (Junkers), 539, 542–546
Nominalists, 306
Normandy, 264, 266

North America. *See also* United States
    European struggle for empire in,
        580–582
    revolution in, 583
Northern Europe
    Baroque art in, 490–491
    late Gothic art in, 310–311
    Renaissance art in, 377–379
    Renaissance humanists in, 375–376
    Renaissance music in, 379–380
    trade and commerce in, 14th–17th
        centuries, 478
Norway
    Thirty Years' War and, 461
    Vikings, 250
Novel (fiction), 494–495
    rise of, in 18th century Europe, 561–562
Nubia, 28, 31
Numidia kingdom, 149
Nuns Giving Care to Female Patients
    (Boulogne), 466
Nystad, Treaty of (1721), 551

Oates, Titus, (1649–1705), 530
Obsidian, ancient trade in, 9
Ockham's razor, 306
Octavian, 147, 155, 157. *See also* Augustus,
    Roman Emperor
Odyssey (Homer), 73–74, 77
Oedipus the King (Sophocles), 98
Old Believers, Russia, revolt of, 549
Old Regime. *See* Europe, Old Regime
    (1570–1775)
Old Testament, 20, 21, 38–39, 43
    Dead Sea Scrolls, 188–189
    moral and ethical code of, 51
    women in, 55–57
Olivares (1587–1645), Count-Duke of,
    Spain, *511,* 512–513
Olympic games, 75
On Midwifery and the Disease of Women
    (Soranus), 181
Opera, birth of, 491–492
Oracle at Delphi, 81, 85
Oratory, 95, 115, 137, 143
Oresteia (Aeschylus), 99
Origen (c. 185–254), 211
Orthodox Church, 192, 222, 249, 384
    in Russia, 224, 549
    schism with western church and
        independence of, 277–278, *322,*
        323–324
Ostrogoths, 195, 201, 203, 205, 221
Otto I (936–973), Germany, 249, 269
Ottokar II (ruled 1253–1278), Czech
    lands, 388
Ottoman Empire, 383, 385
    collapse of Byzantium and role of, *383,*
        384, 385
    expansionism of, and conflict with

Europeans and, 385–386, 511,
        540–541
The Oyster Luncheon, 592

Pachominus (c. 290–346), 215
Painting and drawing
    ancient Egyptian, *25*
    ancient Greek, 102
    Baroque, 487, 489, 490, 491, 492
    Byzantium, *228*
    medieval European, *206, 217, 228, 281,
        284, 290, 296,* 309–312
    miniature, in India, 580
    Paleolithic, 7, 8
    Renaissance, Italian, 359–362
    Rococo, 557, 562
    Roman, *139, 142, 144, 180*
Pakistan, 70
Palace schools, 246
Paleologus dynasty, restoration in
    Byzantium, 383–384
Palestine, 9, 33, 39
    Roman rule of, 187
Palestrina, Giovanni Pierlugi da
    (1525–1594), 379
Pantheon, Roman, 172, *173*
Papacy, 200, 210, 213–215. *See also specific
    popes*
    Babylonian Captivity of, 322–323
    church schism and, 220, *322,* 324–325
    church-state relations in High Middle
        Ages and, 296–297
    courts (*curia*), 275
    donation of Papal States land to, 240
    from Leo to Gregory, 214–215
    primacy of Rome and, 213–214
    search for doctrinal unity by, 213
Papal Court, Renaissance music at, 379
Papal States, 240, 269, 302, 349, 351–352
Paracelsus (Theophrastus Bombast von
    Hohenheim 1493–1541), 501, 504
Paradise Lost (Milton), 488, 496
Paris, Treaty of (1763), 582
Parlement of Paris, 300, 460
Parliament, British
    Bill of Rights, 531
    cabinet system and, 535–537
    confrontations between James I and,
        448–449
    development of representative
        government and, 531, 534
    evolution of, 298
    House of Commons, 449, 535–537
    Long (1640–1660), 450
Parthenon, 89, 103
    sculptures of, 100–102
Pascal, Blaise (1623–1662), 501, 506, 524
Patriarch of Constantinople, church
    schism and, 220, 277–278
Patricians, Roman Republic, 131, 141

Patrick, St. (c. 390–461), 207
Patronage, 343
    Italian Renaissance, 354
Paul III (ruled 1534–1549), pope, 431, 433
Paul IV (ruled 1555–1559), pope, 433, 503
Paul of Tarsus (the Apostle, died c. A.D. 65), 190, 216
Pazzi Conspiracy, 350, 351
Peace of Augsburg (1555), 410, 460
Peace of Carlowitz (1699), 541
Peace of Constance (1183), 270
Peace of Lodi (1454), 354
Peace of Nicias (421 B.C.), 91, 103
Peace of Ryswick (1697), 526
Peace of Westphalia (1659), 463, 540
Peasants
    ancient Greek, 79
    diet, 16th and 17th centuries, 467–468
    housing, 17th century, 472–473
    medieval European, 247, 252, 253, 254–255, 262
    in Old Regime of 18th century, 587, 589–591
    revolts of, Reformation and, 409–410
    revolts of, 14th century, 318–321
    Roman, 140
Peasants Crusade, *278*
Peasant War (1524), 409–410, *418*
Peloponnesian War (431–404 B.C.), 88, 89, 91, *92*, 93
Peoples of the Sea, 30, 33, 36
Pepin III (ruled 751–768), Merovingian, 240, 296
Pepin of Landen (d.c. 639), 240
Pergamum, kingdom of, *125*, 135, 136
Peri, Jacopo (1561–1633), 491
Pericles (c. 495–429 B.C.), Greece, 89–91, 97
    relationship with Aspasia, 90
Perioikoi social class, Sparta, 82
Persia, 33, *192*. See also Iran
    threat of, to Byzantium, 223
Persian empire, 14, 21, 31, 33, 37–38, 65
    under Cyrus and Darius, 37–38, 83–84
    invasions and war with ancient Greece, 78, 83–86
Persian Wars, 37, 83–86, 113
Peru, 403, 441
Peter (the Great, ruled 1682–1725), Russia, 549–553
    attempts by, to westernize Russia, 550–551
    creation of St. Petersburg, 551–553
    military campaigns, *551*
Peter III (December 1761–June 1762), 583
Petrarch (1304–1374), 322, 352
    humanism and, 333
Petronius (?–A.D. 66), 175
Phalanx, 79
Phalaris (570–554 B.C.), 80

Pharos (lighthouse) at Alexandria, *126*
Phidias (c. 500–c. 430 B.C.), 89, 100
Philip Augustus (ruled 1180–1223), France, 260, 280, 283, 297, 298–300
Philip II (ruled 1556–1598), Spain, 413, 426, 438–441, 509, 514
Philip III (ruled 1598–1621), Spaion, 511
Philip IV (ruled 1621–1665), Spain, 512, 513
Philip IV (the Fair, ruled 1285–1314), France, 300–301, 322
Philip V (ruled 1700–1746), Spain, 513, 515, 526
Philip V (ruled 221–179 B.C.), Macedon, 135
Philip VI (ruled 1328–1350), France, 340
Philip of Macedon (ruled 359–336 B.C.), 66, 88, 95
Philippics (Demosthenes), 95
Philosophes, French Enlightenment, 597, 598–604
Philosophy
    ancient Greece, 91, 97, 105–108, 236
    Asian, 6th century B.C., 105
    of Enlightenment, 18th century, 597–604
    Hellenistic, 123–124, 143–144
    Islamic, 236
    Neoplatonists, 352, 502
    Newtonian universe and, 507
    nominalists, 306
    political. *See* Political theory and philosophy
    Roman, 143–144
    Scholasticism, 289–291, 305, 306
Phoenicians, 2, 33, 36–37
    Carthage colony of, 134. *See also* Carthage
    ivory carving by, 50
    trade conducted by, 36–37
Physics, 506–507
Pico della Mirandola (1463–1494), 352
Pictures from Italy (Dickens), 360
Piedmont-Sardinia, Kingdom of, 515
Piero della Francesca (c. 1420–1492), 359, *361*
Piombo, Sebastiano del, *400*
Pisistratus (605–?527 B.C.), 81
Pitt, William (1708–1778), 577, 581, 582
Pizarro, Francisco, 402–403
Plague. *See* Black Death; Epidemics
Plainsong, 292
Plassey (1757), Battle of, 580
Plataea, Battle of (479 B.C.), 86
Platagenet (Angevin) dynasty, England, 266
Plato (c. 469–399 B.C.), 91, 94, 97, 105–108
    Neoplatonists in Renaissance and, 352
    Theory of Forms, 108, 363

Plautus (c. 254–184 B.C.), 137, 144
Plebians, Roman Republic, 131–132, 141
Pliny the Elder (A.D. 23–79), 113, 168, 175
Plutarch, 36, 82, 154
Poetry
    Baroque, 495
    Roman love, 144–145
    Vergil, 169–170
Poitiers, Battle of (1356), 341
Poland
    domination of nobility in 17th century, and dismemberment of, 554–555
    emergence of state of, 388
    Jewish communities in medieval, *258*
Polis (Greek city-state), 67, 71–73, 122
Political organization. *See also* Government
    ancient Egypt, 45
    ancient Greece, Athens, 80–82, 93
    ancient Greece, city-states, 67, 71–73
    ancient Greece, Sparta, 82–83
    of Christian and Catholic church, 192, 207, 274
    Hellenistic kingdoms, 122
    medieval England, 264, 266
    medieval Spain, 271
    Mesopotamia (Sumeria, Assyria), 15–16, 45–46
    Roman Republic, 131–132, 138–139, 148–152, 178
Political propaganda
    Roman empire, 160–161
Political theory and philosophy
    B. Castiglione, 376
    N. Machiavelli, 348, 376–377
    political, on legitimacy of revolution, 532–535
Polo, Marco (c. 1254–c. 1324), travels of, 393, 394, 395
Poltava, Battle of (1709), 551
Polybius (c. 203–120 B.C.), Greece, 123, 132
Polyclitus (mid-5th century B.C.), *99–100*
Polydorus, *124*
Polyphonic style, music, 292–293
Pompeii, Roman Republic, 173–175
    aerial view of, *173*
    art from, *142*, *180*
    travels of Mark Twain in, 174
    women in, 181–182
Pompey (Gnaeus Pompeius, 106–48 B.C.), Rome, 147, 151–153, 187
Popes. *See* Papacy
Popish Plot, England, 530
Population, European
    Black Death and. *See* Black Death
    excessive, and famine in 14th century, 315
    growth of, after decimation of Black Death, 329, 479–480

Population, European (*continued*)
  growth of, between Years' 1000 and
    1300, 253
  growth of, in 16th century, 416
  growth of, in 18th century, 587, 588
Portrait of Baldassare Castiglione (Raphael),
  376
Portrait of Erasmus of Rotterdam (Drer), 375
Portugal, 439
  declaration of independence from Spain,
    513
  exploratory voyages of, 396, 398–400
  imperialism of, 397
  role of Prince Henry the Navigator, 397
  shipbuilding and navigational advances
    of, 396
Pothos (Scopas), 102
Pottery
  ancient Greek, *74, 75, 76, 80, 111, 112*
  Roman, 180
Poussin, Nicholas (c. 1593–1665), *490*
Poverty and poor classes
  Old Regime, 18th century, 587
  urban and rural, in 16th century,
    417–418
Praxiteles (active c. 370–330 B.C.), 102
Prés, Josquin des, 379
Presbyterian Church, 413
Presocratic philosophers, 105
Press, growth of popular, in 17th and 18th
    century Europe, 557, 561
Prices
  inflationary, 479–480
Priesthood
  Christian, 217. *See also* Clergy; Papacy
  Egyptian, 42, 45
  Sumerian, 16
Primogeniture, 261
The Prince (Machiavelli), 373, 376–377
Principia (Newton), 506
Printing, 373, 374–375. *See also* Publishing
  implications of Renaissance, 374
  Licensing Act (1662), British, 561
  vernacular languages promoted by,
    374–375
Prison reform, 601
Procopius (B.C. 500), 221
Prophets
  Hebrew, 40
  Muhammad, 231–233
Prostitution
  ancient Greece, 90, 115, 117
  Europe, 15th and 17th centuries, 419
  Europe, 18th century, 594–595
  medieval Europe, 329
Protectorate, Oliver Cromwell and
    English, 451–452
Protestant church
  advance of, in continental Europe,
    410–412

in England. *See* Church of England
  (Anglicans)
  establishment of Lutheran Church,
    408–409
  Lutheran movement and social conflict,
    409–410
  M. Luther and, 407–408
Protestants
  Calvinists. *See* Calvinism
  Puritans, in England, 448, 449, 451
  suppression of, in France, 455–457
  Thirty Years' War and, 460–463
Protestant Union, 460
Provinces, Roman Republic, *153*
  administration of, 138–139
Provisions of Oxford, 298
Prussia, 539, 540
  army of, 544
  first kings of, 545
  growth of, *543*
  Old Regime in. *See* Europe, Old Regime
    (1570–1775)
  rise of Hohenzollerns in, 542–543
  rule of Friedrich II in, 582–584
  rule of Friedrich Wilhelm and, 543–544
  Seven Years' War and, 579–580,
    582–584
Ptolemaic Egypt, 121
Ptolemy (323–285 B.C.), Egypt, 120, 395,
    502
Ptolemy II, Egypt, 123
Ptolemy XIII, Egypt, 153
Publishing
  popular, 17th and 18th century Europe,
    561–562
  Renaissance, 374
  in vernacular languages, 374–375
Punic Wars, 128, 134–135, 139
Puritans, 448, 449, 451
Pyramids, Egyptian, 25, 26, *27*
Pyrrhus (ruled 306–302, 297–272 B.C.),
    134
Pythagoras (active c. 550 B.C.), Greece,
    105

Qing dynasty, China, 432–433
Quakers, *450*
Queen Annes War, 526
Quintilian (c. A.D. 35–c. 95), 168, 175

Race
  Hellenistic kingdoms, 122
Racine, Jean (1639–1699), 557, 558–559
Ramses I (1307–1306 B.C.), Egypt, 47
Ramses II (1304–1237 B.C.), Egypt, 24, 30,
    31, 39, 47
Raphael (1483–1520), 357, 362, *363, 364,*
    376
Razi (Rhazes, c. 865–930), 236
Razin, Stenka (d. 1671), 549

Recared (ruled 586–601), Visigoth, 205
Reconnaissance. *See* European
  Reconnaissance
Reformation, 336–337, 405–414
  advance of Protestantism in Europe,
    410–412
  defined, 405
  England, and Anglican Church,
    412–413
  Hapsburg-Valois wars and, 410
  Lutheranism, 409–410
  M. Luther and, in Germany, 407–409
  peasant rebellions and, 409–410
  roots of, 406–407
  social world of, 415–425
Religion. *See also* Christianity; Deities
  ancient Egypt, 25, 30, 43, 45
  ancient Greece, 73–74, 116
  in ancient world, 15–16, 19, 38, 42–46
  Hebrew (Judaism), 39–40
  Hellenistic kingdoms, 123–124
  Hittite, 44
  Islam, 231–233
  Mesopotamian (Sumerian, Assyrian),
    43–44, 45–46
  Roman, 143, 178
Religious literature, 42
  Hebrew. *See* Bible; New Testament; Old
    Testament
  Mesopotamian, 42, *48–49,* 50–51
Religious orders
  Benedictine, 215–216
  Carmelites, *432,* 433
  Dominican, 284, 285
  Franciscan, 282–283
  Jesuits, 431–433
  Ursuline, 433
  for women, 217–218, 433
Rembrandt van Rijn (1606–1669),
    490–491, *492*
Renaissance, 336, 348–356
  art in transition from medieval to,
    309–312, 313
  art of. *See* Art, Renaissance
  diplomacy and politics in, 354–355
  humanism and, 348, 352, 373, 375–376
  intellectual world of early, 352–354
  Italian city-states and emergence of,
    349–352
  music of, 379–380
  social world of, 415–425
The Republic (Plato), 107
The Resurrection (Piero della Francesca),
    361
Revolts and revolutions
  in Gaul, against Romans, 152
  Hungarian Rkczy uprising (1703),
    541–542
  Ionian Greeks, 83–84
  in Ireland, 451–452, 531

of Netherlands, against Spain, 441–444,
511
Old Believers, Russia, 549
peasant, in 14th century, 318–321
Sicilian Vespers, 302
worker, 321–322
writings on legitimacy of, 532–535
Revolutionary Settlement of 1689,
England, 531
Reynolds, Joshua (1723–1792), 559
Rhodes, 123, 124, 135
Ricci, Matteo (1552–1610), 433
Richard I (Lion-Hearted, ruled
1189–1199), England, 280, 297
Richard II (ruled 1377–1399), England,
321
Richard III (ruled 1483–1485), England,
344–345
Richardson, Samuel (1689–1761),
561–562
Richeliu, Armand du, Cardinal, 458, *459*
Rkczy, Francis (ruled 1704–1711),
Hungary, 541–542
Robespierre, Maximilien de (1758–1794),
604
Rococo art, 557, 562–563
Roland, Carolingian military leader, 241,
292
Roman Catholic Church. *See* Catholic
Church
Romanesque architecture, 287, *291*,
293–294
Romanov, Michael (ruled 1613–1645),
Russia, 549
Rome (city), 168, 171, 172, 173
Baroque art, 17th century, 489–490
Jewish community in, 187–188
Rome, ancient, 66
annexation of eastern Mediterranean by,
135–136
empire. *See* Rome, imperial
Etruscans and foundation of, 66, 128,
129–131
map, *129*
perspectives on history of, 136, 145, 156,
166, 176, 184–185
Punic Wars between Carthage and,
134–135
Romanization of Italy, 133–134
Roman Republic. *See* Rome, republic of
social class in early, 131
Rome, eastern empire. *See* Byzantium
Rome, imperial, 66, 157–197
agriculture in, 177
architecture in, 171–175
art, 169–170, *171*
Augustan revolution in, 158–162
bureaucracy of, 178–179
Christianity, rise of, 66, 189–192

citizenship in, 153, 178, 187
debate on decline of, 195–196
economy, commerce, and trade in,
179–180
family life and sexuality in, 177,
180–181
five good emperors of, 165–166
Flavian emperors, 163–165
foundation of Constantinople and
decline of, 194–195
Jews as religious minority in, 187–189
Julio-Claudians and problem of
succession, 162–163
law in, 178
legal and administrative systems, 177,
178–179
literature of, 169–170, 175–176
maps, *159*, *172*, *193*
military and emperors, 163–165
model of, *148*
political propaganda in, 160–161
reforms of Diocletian in late, 192–194
slaves, criminals, and gladiators in,
183–184
women and, 177, 181–183
Rome, republic of, 66, 131–133, 137–156
civil war, 147, 151–153, 194
dictatorship, assassination of Julius
Caesar, 153–155
economy, land, trade, and class in,
139–141
Gracchus brothers failed reforms in, 147,
148–149
influence of Greek civilization in, 137,
143–144
literature of, 144–145
map, *140*
Octavian and death of, 155
provincial administration in, 138–139,
153
religion and philosophy in, 143–144
struggle for power in, 149–151
women and family life in, 141–143,
154–155
Rousseau, Jean Jacques (1712–1778), 589,
604
on role of women, 604
Social Contract, 533–534, 604
Royal Academy of Arts, England, 559
Royal Academy of Sciences, France, 505
Royal Africa Company, 570
Royal Society of London, England,
504–505, 559
Rubaiyat (Khayyam), 236
Rubens, Peter Paul (1577–1640), 490, *491*
Rule, John C., on bureaucratic government
of Louis XIV, 522–523
Ruling class. *See also* Aristocracy
diet of 17th century, 467–468

Gallo-Roman, 206
Old Regime, 18th century, 587, 591–593
Roman Republic, 131, 143
Rurik (d.c. 879), Russia, 224
Russia, 547–553
boyars, 548, *551*
C. Wilmot diary of 1801 trip to,
552–553
Christian conversion of, 224
Cossack warriors, *549*
expansion of, into Europe, *551*
Ivan the Terrible, rule of, 548
Moscow principality and, 388–390, 547,
548
Old Believers revolt, 549
Peter the Great, rule of, 549–553
serfs, 590–591
Time of Troubles (1584–1613), 548–549
veneration of icons in, 225

Sacrificial rituals, Mesopotamian, 44–45
Saint-Senin, Toulouse, France, *291*
Saladin (1137?–1193), 279–280
Salian dynasty, 269
Salic Law, 340
Salisbury Oath, 266
Salons
conducted by Elizabeth Robinson
Montague, 560
Europe, 17th and 18th centuries,
559–561
Rome, 142, 182
Samnites, conflict with Rome, 133–134
Sappho, 145
Sardinia, Kingdom of, 515
Sargon (c. 2371–2316 B.C.), Akkadia, 13,
17, 18
Satyricon (Petronius), 175
Saul (c. 1025–c. 1000 B.C.), Hebrew, 39
Savonarola, Girolomo (1452–1498), 350,
430
Saxons, 195, 202
Otto I, king of, 269
Schmalkaldic League, 410
Scholastic History manuscript, Peter the
Eater, *260*
Scholasticism, 287, 289–291
successors to Aquinas, 305, 306
system of, 289–290
T. Aquinas and, 291, 297
The School of Athens (Raphael), *363*
Schulylenberg, H. V., 482
Science
ancient Greece, 108
Enlightenment of 18th century and,
601–604
Hellenistic kingdoms, 125–126
Islamic culture, 236
Scientific method, 501, 505–506

Scientific Revolution, 17th and 18th
    centuries, 501–508, 602
  in astronomy and physics, 502–504
  dawn of, 502
  in medicine and anatomy, 504–505
  Newton and laws of natural universe,
    506–507
  scientific method and, 505–506
Scipio (236–184 B.C.), Rome, 135
Scotland, 298
Sculpture
  ancient Greek, *76, 79, 85, 94, 95,
    99–102, 113, 117, 120*
  Baroque, *488, 489*
  Byzantine, *220*
  Carolingian, *240*
  Cyclades, 68
  Egyptian, *27, 30, 31, 46, 54*
  Etruscan, *130, 131*
  Hellenistic, *124*
  medieval European, *214, 220, 240, 266,
    293, 309–312*
  Mesopotamian, *18, 20, 35, 44, 47, 58,
    62*
  Neolithic, *10*
  Paleolithic, *7, 9*
  Phoenician, *50, 58*
  Renaissance Italian, *358*
  Roman, *132, 135, 138, 141, 151, 152,
    158, 166, 168, 170, 171, 179, 182,
    183*
Scurlock, Joann, on status of women in
    ancient Mesopotamia, 56–57
Second Triumvirate, 155
Seleucids, kingdom of, 121–122
Seleucus (306–281 B.C.), Seleucid Syria,
    120, 122
Selim I (the Grim, ruled 1512–1520), 385
Seljuk Turks, 277
Semitic peoples, 13, 38
Senate, Roman, 131, 163
Seneca (4 B.C.?–A.D. 65), 163
Senwosret III (c. 1878–1844 B.C.), Egypt,
    28
Serfs, 247
  ancient Greece, Sparta, 82, 117
  Byzantium, 227
  medieval European, 247, 254, 258, 327
Servetus, Michael (1511–1553), 504
Seven Years' War (1756–1763), 577,
    579–580
  success of Prussia and, 582–584
Severus, Alexander (ruled A.D.222–235),
    183, 192
Severus, Septimius (ruled A.D. 193–211),
    Rome, 182
Sexual behavior
  ancient Greece, 114–116
  expectations about womens, 419

Roman, 180–181
  18th century, 594–595
Sforza, Franceso (ruled 1450–1466), 349,
    354
Sforza, Lodovico, 343
Shakespeare, William (1564–1616),
    493–494, 496
  subsequent generations' evaluation of,
    494–495
Shebaka (712–698 B.C.), Egypt, 31
Shelley, Percy Bysshe (1792–1822), 174
Shiite Muslims, 232–233
Shipbuilding, advances in, and European
    Reconnaissance, 396
Sicilian Expedition, 91–93, 99, 105
Sicilian Vespers revolt, 302
Sicily, 37, 113
  Athenian war with city-states of, 88,
    91–93, 99
  Kingdom of, 270, 301–303
  Muslim rule in, 230, 235
  Roman rule of, 134
  Spanish domination of, 16th century,
    514–515
Siete Partidas legal code, Spain, 271
Signorie, Italian city-states, 349
Silesia, 583
Silver Age of Roman arts, 168, 175–176
Simony (sale of church offices), 261, 406
Sisters of the Common Life, 430, 433
Sixtus IV (ruled 1471–1484), pope, 351
Slavery
  in American colonies, 403
  ancient Greece, 110, 117–118
  ancient Near East societies, 61–62
  in medieval Europe, 254, 259
  Portuguese description of African,
    398–399
  Roman Republic and Empire, 139, 177,
    183
  slave trade, 18th century, 569–572
  in United States, *572*
Slavs, 223, 249
  expansionism of, and fall of Byzantium,
    384
  influence of Byzantium on, 223–224
Smith, Adam (1723–1790), 481, 575,
    601–604
Snake Goddess (Minoan), 69, *70*
Soaemias, Julia (?–A.D. 235), 183
Social reform
  Enlightenment thinkers and, 601–604
Social unrest. *See also* Revolts and
    revolutions
  Europe, in 14th century, 317–322
Social War (91–88 B.C.), Rome, 150
Society and social structure. *See also* Class
  ancient Egypt, 54
  ancient Greece, Athens, 79

ancient Greece, Sparta, 82
Byzantium, 227–228
Carolingian Empire, 246–247
effects of Black Death on, 317–322,
    328–332
England, 17th century, 448–449
Etruscans, 129–130
European Old Regime, 18th century,
    586–596
Hellenistic world, 122–123
in medieval Europe, 252–262, 328–332
Mesopotamia, 54
Muslim, 233–234
Neolithic Near East, 9–10
reform. *See* Social reform
in Renaissance and Reformation
    (15th–16th century), 415–425
Roman republic, 131, 141
Socrates (c. 469–399 B.C.), 91, 94, 97, 118,
    123
  death of, 93–94
  Plato and teachings of, 105–108
Solomon (c. 971–931 B.C.), Hebrews, 39
  temple of, in Jerusalem, 40, 187
Solon (c. 630–560 B.C.), Greece, 78
  political reforms of, 80–81
Song of El Cid, 271, 292
The Song of Roland, 241, 255, 287, 292
The Song of Solomon, 42
Song of the Nibelungs, 292
Sophist philosophers, 105
Sophocles (496–406 B.C.), 89, 98–99
Soranus (active 2nd century A.D.), 181
Southern Europe. *See also* Italian city-
    states; Italy; Spain
  eclipse of Mediterranean in (Years'
    1500–1700), 509, 510–511
  map, c. 1700, *510*
South Sea Bubble, 574–575
Spain
  Baroque literature in, 494–495
  Bourbons and succession to throne, 18th
    century, 513
  Charlemagnes invasion of, 241
  creation of kingdom of, from Aragon
    and Castile, 345
  decline of, and Old Regime, 511–513
  economic policies and imperial colonies
    of, 441
  European empire of, 16th century, *440*
  Hapsburg rule of, 345–346, 439–441,
    511–513
  Inquisition in, 345, 433, 436, 440
  King George's War with Britain, 579
  medieval kingdoms of, 270–271
  Muslim rule of, 230, 234, 235
  Philip II, reign of, 439–444
  rebellion of Netherlands against,
    441–444

Reconquista of, from Muslims, *271*
Roman empire and, 151, 165
Visigoths in, 201, 205
war between England and, 16th century, 444
war of Spanish succession, 526
Spanish Armada, defeat of, 444
Sparta, 65, 66, 78, 81, 82–83
military system and training in, 82
Peloponnesian War and, 91–93
Persian Wars and, 83–86
political organization, 82–83
power struggle with Thebes, 94
Spartacus, slave rebellion led by, 151
The Spearbearer (Polyclitus), 99, *100*
Spinoza, Baruch (1632–1677), 507
St. Bartholomew's Day Massacre, 456, *457*
St. George (Donatello), *358*
St. Petersburg, Russia, construction of, 551–553
St. Theresa in Ecstasy (Bernini), *488*, 489
Stained glass, Gothic cathedrals, 308, *309*
State
concept of territorial, Akkadians and, 17
divine right to rule, 518–520
Roman versus Germanic concepts of, 208
Steen, Jan, *589*
Stephen (ruled 977–1038), Hungary, 386
Stephen II (ruled 752–757), pope, 240
Stocks, booms, crashes, and speculation in 18th century, 573–575
Stoicism, 123–124, 143
Stonehenge, England, *10*
Strabo (64 or 63 B.C.–after A.D. 21), 123
Straits of Gibraltar, 235
Strasbourg Oaths, 248
Stuart dynasty, England, 448–453, 529–530
Student life, medieval universities, 289
Stylites, Simeon (c. 390–459), 215
Subinfeudation, 253
Suger, Abbot (1081–1151), 268, 308
Suleiman I (the Magnificent, ruled 1520–1566), 385, 386, 387
Sulla, Lucius (138–78 B.C.), Rome, 150–151
Sully, Maximilien, duke of (1560–1641), 457–458
Sumerian civilization, 13, 15–17
agriculture and food in, 58
Akkadian conquest of, 17–18
art, *16*, *18*, *44*, *58*, *62*
culture and renaissance after fall of Akkadians, 18
invention of writing in, 16, *17*
political organization and religion in, 15–16
religion, 42, 43–44, 45
renaissance, following Akkadian fall, 18
technology and trade in, 16

Summa Theologica (*Summary of Theology*), 291, 306
Sunnite Muslims, 233
Suppiluliumas (1375–1335 B.C.), Hittites, 33, 35, 55
Sweden
collapse of empire, 18th century, 554
invasion of Poland by, 544
Thirty Years' War and expansionism of, *461*, 462–463
Vikings, 250
Switzerland
Calvinism in, 410–411
Synod, 207, 275
Synod of Whitby (664), 207, 217
Syracuse, 91, 92
Syria, 33
Muslim rule of, 233
Roman rule and, 128, 135, 136
Seleucid rule of, 121–122

Tacitus (A.D. c. 56–120), 163
comparison of Germans and Romans by, 160–161, 202, 208
histories of, 175–176
Tallis, Thomas (c. 1505–1585), 380
Tamerlane (c. 1336–1405), 385
Taoism, 105
Taxation
in medieval England, 298
in Roman Republic, 138, *179*
Tea, 569
Technology. *See also* Tools
advances in medieval agriculture, 253–254
European Reconnaissance and advances in, 395–396
Hellenistic era, 125–126
Islamic empire, 236
of prehistoric people, 6–7
printing, 374–375
Sumerian, 16
Temples
ancient Egyptian, 46–47
of Solomon, Hebrew, *40*, *187*
Terence (c. 195–159 B.C.), 137, 144
Teresa of Avila (1515–1582), *432*, *433*
Terrorism
Gunpowder Plot, England (1605), 448
Tertullian (c. 160–225), 211
Test Act of 1673, England, 530
Teutonic Knights, 302
Teutoni tribe, 150
Textile industry
cotton and, 567, 569
Flanders, 256
Thales of Miletus (active c. 585 B.C.), Greece, 105
Theater
ancient Greece, 89, 98–99

Baroque, 493–495
at court of Louis XIV, 17th century, 557, 558–559
Roman, 172
Thebes, 47, 88, 93, 120
power struggle with Sparta, 94
Themistocles (c. 525–460 B.C.), Greece, 85–86
Theodoric the Great (493–526), Ostrogoth, 205
Theodosius the Great, emperor (ruled 379–395), Byzantium, 75, 220
Theodosius III, emperor (ruled 715–717), Byzantium, 223
Theology, Christian, 108
Augustine, 213
heirs to Aquinas, 305, 306
T. Aquinas and scholasticism, 287, 291, 294, 297
The Thirty Tyrants, Athens, 93
Third Lateran Council (1179), 260, 281
Thirty Years' War (1618–48), 460–463
Holy Roman Empire after, 539, 540
Thucydides (c. 460–c. 399 B.C.), 91, 97, 104–105
on historical method, 107
Thutmose III (c. 1504–1450 B.C.), Egypt, 23
relationship with Queen Hatshepsut, 29
Tiberius, Roman emperor (ruled A.D. 14–37), 162
Tiglath-Pileser I (c. 1115–1077), Assyria, 19
Tiglath-Pileser III (c. 744–727 B.C.), Assyria, 20
Time of Troubles (1584–1613), Russia, 548–549
Tintoretto (1518–1594), 369
Titian (c. 1490–1576), 357, 369, *370*, *371*
Titus, Roman emperor (ruled A.D. 79–81), 157, 164, 165, *187*
Tobacco, 567
Toleration Act, England, 531
Tombs
ancient Egyptian, 47, 50
Tools. *See also* Technology
navigational, 396
plough, 253, *254*
of prehistoric people, 6–7
telescope, 503
Tordesillas, Treaty of (1494), 401
Torquemada, Tomas de, 345, 433
Toulouse, Kingdom of, 205
Tours, Battle of (732), 235, 240
Trade and trade routes. *See also* Commerce
A. Smith on free, 601–604
ancient Greece, 112–113
ancient Near East, 9, 59, 60
changing patterns of, in 15th–16th centuries, 510–511

Trade and trade routes. *See also* Commerce (*continued*)
global, in 16th and 17th centuries, 393–395, 478, 480, 481, 482–484
global, in 18th century, 567, 568
Hanseatic League and, *327*
in luxury goods in 13th–14th centuries, 393–395
medieval Europe, 256, *257*, *259*, 327–328
Phoenician, 36–37
Roman, 140–141, 159, 179–180
slave trade, 18th century, 569–572
Sumerian, 16
Trading companies, private
stock speculation, 18th century, 573–575
in 17th century, 478, 482–483
Trajan, Roman emperor (A.D. 98–117), 165
Très Riches Heures du Duc de Berry (Limbourg brothers), *310*, 311
Triangular trade, 18th century, 567, 571
Troubadours, 292
Tudor dynasty, England, 344–345, 412
Tutankhamen (c. 1334–1325 B.C.), Egypt, 30
Twain, Mark (Samuel Langhorne Clemens, 1835–1910), 174
Twelve Tables (Roman law), 132–133
Tyler, Wat, 321
Tyrants in ancient Greece, 65, 78, 79–80

Ugarit, 36
Ulfilas (c. 311–383), 202
Umar (d. 644), 232
Umayyad Dynasty, 233
Union of Arras, 443
United Kingdom. *See* Great Britain
United States
slavery in, *572*
Universities, 107
medieval, 287, 288–289
University of Paris, 289, 290
Ur, Sumeria, 13, 15, 18
street life and architecture of, *61*
Urban design and planning
Roman, 168, 171, 172, 173
Urban II (ruled 1088–1099), pope, 277, 278
Urban life. *See* City life
Urban proletariat. *See also* Worker(s)
Roman, 140, 183
Urban VI (ruled 1378–1389), pope, 323, 324
Ur-Nammu (c. 2112–2095 B.C.), neo-Sumeria, 18
Uruk, Sumeria, 13, 15
Utica, 36
Utrecht, Treaty of (1713), 511, 513, 515, 526, 570, 578

Valerian (ruled A.D. 253–260), Rome, 193
Valla, Lorenzo (1407–1457), 352
Valois dynasty, France, 342–344
war between Hapsburgs and, 410
Vandals, 197, 202, 203, 204, 221
Van Dyck, Anthony, *449*
Van Eyck, Jan (before 1395–1441), 373, *377*, 378
Van Reymerswaele, Marinus, *417*
Varangians, 250
Vasari, Giorgio (1511–1574), 311, 366–367
Vasco da Gama, 392
Vassal, 253
Vatican Council, 4th (1215), 284
Velazquez, Diego, *511*, *512*
Venice, Italian city-state, 349, 350, 354
changing trade patterns in 15th and 16th centuries, 510
domination of medieval trade by, 256, 327, 478
harmony and color of Renaissance painting in, 364–371
music at St. Mark's Cathedral, 379
Venus of Urbino (Titian), *370*
Venus of Willendorf, 7, 9
Verbiest, Ferdinand (1623–1688), 433
Vercingetorix, Gaul, 152
Verdun, Treaty of (843), 248
Vergil (70–19 B.C.), 139, 159, 168, 306
poetry of, 169–170
Verri, Alessandro (1741–1816) and Pietro (1728–1797), 601
Versailles Palace, France, 490, *521*, *522*, 523, *524*
Vesalius, Andreas (1514–1564), 504, *505*
Vespasian, Roman emperor (ruled A.D. 69–79), 157, 163, 164–165
Vespucci, Amerigo, 400
Vieira, Cristavao, 399
Vikings, 224, 494
invasions of, into Europe in 9th century, 249–250
The Village School (Steen), *589*
Visconti, Gian Galeazzo (ruled 1395–1402), 349
Visigoths, 195, 201, 203, 209
kingdom of, 205
Vladimir (ruled 980–1015), Kiev, Russia, 389
Voltaire (François-Marie Arouet) (1694–1778), 558, 599, 600–601
call for toleration, 603
on organized, religion, 601
sculpture of, by Pigalle, *600*
Voltolina, Laurencius de, *288*

Wages
in late medieval period, 327
Waldensians, 284, 433

Walpole, Robert (1676–1745), 537, 575, 578
Warfare. *See also specific wars*
importance of, to Germanic tribal societies, 202–204
weapons used in. *See* Weapons
War of Devolution (1667–1668), 525
War of Jenkins' Ear (1739), 513, 577, 578
War of the Austrian Succession (1740–1748), 513, 577, 578, 579–580
War of the League of Augsburg (1697), 513, 525–526, 534
War of the Polish Succession (1733–1735), 513
War of the Roses, 344
War of the Spanish Succession (1701–1714), 513, 515, 526, 577, 578
War of the Three Henries (1588–1589), 456
Washington, George, 581
The Wealth of Nations (A. Smith), 604
Weapons
English longbow, 341
Welfare programs
in medieval cities, 329
Roman, 165
Western Europe. *See also* France; Great Britain; Italy; Portugal; Spain
Carolingian Empire in, 239–251
West Indies
British-Spanish conflict over, 578
Columbus discovers, 400
Spanish empire and, 401
Westphalia, Treaty of (1648), 444
White Mountain, Battle of (1620), 461
Willaert, Adrian (c. 1490–1562), 379
William (ruled 1066–1087), England, 264–266
relationship with Matilda of Flanders, 265
William III (of Orange 1689–1702), England, 525, 575
Glorious Revolution and, 531, 534, 535–536
revolt of Netherlands against Spanish rule and, *442–444*
William of Ockham (c. 1285–1349), 306
Wilmot, Catherine, travel diary of trip to Russia (1801), 552–553
Witches and witch hunts, 331, 420–421
Wlken, Anna Magdalena (1701–1760), relationship with husband Johann Sebastian Bach, 493
Wolfe, James (1727–1759), 581
Women
aristocratic, 18th century, 594–595
contraceptive use. *See* Abortion; Birth control
J.-J. Rousseau on role of, 604
marriage of. *See* Marriage and divorce

military leaders, 341–342
prehistoric, 6
ratio of men to, in Rome Empire, 181
salons conducted by. *See* Salons
status of. *See* Women, status of
work and. *See* Women and work
Women, education of
    Renaissance and, 376
    in Rome, 142
Women, status of
    ancient Egypt, 29, 55
    ancient Greece, 90, 99, 116–117
    Christianity and, 216–217
    Enlightenment *philosophes* and, 599, 604
    Etruscan, Italy, 130
    in medieval Europe, 260–261
    in medieval Europe, late, 329,
      330–333
    Mesopotamia, 55, 56–57
    in Muslim world, 234
    in Old Regime, 18th century Europe,
      594–595
    in Renaissance and Reformation,
      419–421
    Rome, 141–143, 154–155, 177, 181–183
    witch hunts and, 331, 420–421

Women and work
    cottage industry, 18th century, 594
    prostitution. *See* Courtesans;
      Prostitution
    in 16th and 17th centuries, 420
Worker(s)
    cottage industry, 18th century Europe,
      594
    in late medieval Europe, 327
Worker revolts
    Black Death and medieval, 321–322
World economy
    European exploration, Spanish empire,
      and, 403–404
    slave trade and, 569–572
    trade and, 16th and 17th centuries, 478,
      480
    trade and, 18th century, 567, 568
Writing and alphabets
    Arabic calligraphy, *232*
    cuneiform, Sumerian, 16, *17*
    Cyrillic, 224
    earliest examples of, *17*
    Etruscan alphabet, 131
    Greek, 69, 75
    hieroglyphics, Egyptian, *17*

    Hittites, 35
    Minoan, 69
    Phoenician alphabet, 33, 75
Wycliffe, John (c. 1330–1384), 324, 388,
    406

Xanophanes of Colophon (c. 570–c. 460
    B.C.), Greece, 105
Xavier, Francis, 432
Xenophon (c. 430–c. 354 B.C.), Greek, 94
Xerxes (ruled 486–465 B.C.), invasion of
    Greece by Persian, 84–86
Ximines, Francisco (c. 1437–1517), 430

Yaroslav (the Wise, ruled 1015–1054),
    Kiev, Russia, 389

Zacharias (ruled 741–752), pope, 240
Zama, Battle of (202 B.C.), 135
Zeno (335–263 B.C.), Greece, 124
Zenobia (ruled 267–272), Palmyra, 231
Zenta, battle of (1697), 541
Zoroastrianism, 38
Zoser (c. 2668–2649 B.C.), Egypt, 25
Zwingli, Huldrych (1484–1531), 410–411